THE OXFORD HISTORY OF INDIA

From the Earliest Times to the end of 1911

THE OXFORD HISTORY OF INDIA

From the Earliest Times to the end of 1911

BY

VINCENT A. SMITH, C.I.E.

M.A. (Dubl. & Oxon), Hon. Litt.D. (Dublin), Indian Civil Service Retired, M.R.A.S.
Gold Medallist of the Royal Asiatic Society;
Author of *Asoka, The Early History of India, A History of Fine Art in India and Ceylon, Akbar the Great Mogul, &c.*

SECOND EDITION
Revised and continued to 1921

BY

S. M. EDWARDES, C.S.I., C.V.O.

Late of the Indian Civil Service

GYAN

Published by

Gyan Publishing House
5, Ansari Road
Daryaganj, New Delhi-110002
Phone: 011-47034999, 9811692060
E-mail: books@gyanbooks.com

Distribution Network
gyanbooks.com
India, USA, Canada, UK, Australia, France

ISBN : 978-81-212-2872-5 (HB)
First Published, 1923

2nd Impression 2021

Printed at: Gyan Press, Delhi.

The Oxford History of India
Author: Vincent A. Smith

THE OXFORD HISTORY OF INDIA

From the Earliest Times to the end of 1911

BY

VINCENT A. SMITH, C.I.E.

M.A. (Dubl. & Oxon), Hon. Litt.D. (Dublin), Indian Civil Service Retired, M.R.A.S.
Gold Medallist of the Royal Asiatic Society;
Author of *Asoka*, *The Early History of India*, *A History of Fine Art in India and Ceylon*, *Akbar the Great Mogul*, &c.

SECOND EDITION

Revised and continued to 1921

By S. M. EDWARDES, C.S.I., C.V.O.
Late of the Indian Civil Service

OXFORD
AT THE CLARENDON PRESS
1923

PREFACE

THE purpose of this book is to provide in one volume of moderate bulk and price a compendious up-to-date History of India as a whole, based on the results of modern research and extending from the earliest times to the end of 1911. It has been designed with the desire to preserve due proportion throughout in the Ancient, Hindu, Muhammadan, and British Periods alike, the space being carefully allotted so as to give prominence to the more significant sections. The author has sought to attain scrupulous accuracy of statement and impartiality of judgement, so far as may be. The subject has engaged his attention for nearly half a century.

While foot-notes have been confined within narrow bounds, the authorities used are indicated with considerable fullness. The lists of authorities are not intended to be bibliographies. They merely mention the publications actually consulted. Chronological tables, maps, and other aids for the special benefit of professed students have been provided, but it is hoped that the volume may prove readable by and useful to all persons who desire to possess some knowledge of Indian history and do not find a mere school-book sufficient. No book on lines at all similar is in existence. The older works of Meadows Taylor, Marshman, and other authors are necessarily useless for the Hindu Period, which was treated consecutively and critically for the first time in the *Early History of India*, published originally in 1904, and revised in subsequent editions. The accounts of the Muhammadan Period in the writings of Elphinstone and in other books now current are inadequate and out of date, being far behind the present state of knowledge in every section. In the present work much unfamiliar material concerning that period has been utilized, as explained in the second section of the Introduction. The British Period, the subject of innumerable books, offers less opportunity for novelty or originality of treatment.

Notwithstanding the obvious truism that no man can be master in equal degrees of all the parts of India's long story, it is desirable in my opinion that a general history should be the work of a single author. Composite histories, built up of chapters by specialists, suffer from the lack of literary unity and from the absence of one controlling mind so severely that their gain in erudition is apt to be outweighed by their dullness.

The memorable visit of Their Majesties the King-Emperor and his consort at the close of 1911 seems to be the best stopping-place for the narrative. The years since that event have been passed for the most part under the shadow of the Great War, with which history cannot yet dare to meddle. A bare list of some of the happenings during those terrible years is appended.

The spelling of Asiatic words and names follows the principle observed in my work on Akbar, with, perhaps, a slight further indulgence in popular literary forms. The only diacritical mark used as a general rule is that placed over long vowels, and intended as a guide to the approximate pronunciation. Consonants are to be pronounced as in English. Vowels usually have the Italian sounds, so that *Mīr* is to be read as 'Meer' and *Mūl-* as 'Mool-'. Short *a* with stress is pronounced like *u* in 'but', and when without stress as an indistinct vowel like the *A* in 'America'. The name *Akbar* consequently is pronounced 'Ukbur' or 'Ukber'. No simpler system is practicable, for we cannot revert to the barbarisms of the old books.

Much research and care have been devoted to the collection and reproduction of the numerous illustrations.

My acknowledgements are due to the Secretary of State for India for general liberty to use illustrations in official publications; to B. Lewis Rice, Esq., C.I.E., for the use of two illustrations from *Mysore and Coorg from the Inscriptions*; and to K. Panikkar, Esq., for the loan of an engraving of Māhādajī Sindia. A few coins have been copied from the *Journal and Proceedings of the Asiatic Society of Bengal*, by permission.

Copyright extracts are reproduced by permission of Messrs. Kegan Paul, Trench, Trübner & Co. (from Gover); Mr. William Heinemann (from Professor Macdonell); Robert Sewell, Esq., I.C.S. Retired (Vijayanagar); and the India Society (from version of Kabīr).

The kind attention of readers is invited to the list of Additions and Corrections.

NOTE.—As the book probably will be used in colleges, it seems well to say that the two sections of the Introduction are not intended for junior students, who may leave them unread.

CONTENTS

INTRODUCTION

BOOK I. ANCIENT INDIA

BOOK II. HINDU INDIA FROM THE BEGINNING OF THE MAURYA DYNASTY IN 322 B.C. TO THE SEVENTH CENTURY A.C.

BOOK III. THE MEDIAEVAL HINDU KINGDOMS FROM THE DEATH OF HARSHA IN A.D. 647 TO THE MUHAMMADAN CONQUEST

CONTENTS

CONTENTS

BOOK VII. THE RULE OF THE EAST INDIA COMPANY TO 1818

BOOK VIII. THE RULE OF THE EAST INDIA COMPANY FROM 1819 TO 1858

CONTENTS

BOOK IX. INDIA UNDER THE CROWN; THE VICEROYS FROM 1858 TO 1911

APPENDIXES

LIST OF ILLUSTRATIONS

LIST OF ILLUSTRATIONS

MAPS AND PLANS

ABBREVIATIONS

A. C.—After Christ.
A. D.—Anno Domini.
A. H.—Anno Hijrae (Hegirae).[1]
Āīn.—*Āīn-i Akbarī*, by Abu-l Fazl, transl. Blochmann and Jarrett.
A. S.—Archaeological Survey.
A. S. B.—Asiatic Society of Bengal.
As. Res.—*Asiatic Researches.*
A. S. W. I.—Archaeological Survey of Western India.
A. V.—*Atharvaveda.*
B. C.—Before Christ.
B. M.—British Museum.
E. & D.—*The History of India as told by its own Historians*, by Sir H. M. Elliot and Professor John Dowson, 8 vols., 1867–77.
E. H. I.—*The Early History of India*, by Vincent A. Smith, 3rd ed. (Oxford, Clarendon Press, 1914).
E. I. Co.—East India Company.
Ep. Ind.—*Epigraphia Indica*, Calcutta, in progress.
Gaz.—*Gazetteer.*
H. F. A.—*A History of Fine Art in India and Ceylon*, by Vincent A. Smith (Oxford, Clarendon Press, 1911).
I. G.—*Imperial Gazetteer of India* (Oxford, Clarendon Press, 1907, 1908).
Ind. Ant.—*Indian Antiquary*, Bombay, 1872 to date.
I. O.—India Office, London.
J. A. O. S.—*Journal of the American Oriental Society.*
J. & Proc. A. S. B.—*Journal and Proceedings of the Asiatic Society of Bengal*, Calcutta.
J. As.—*Journal Asiatique*, Paris.
J. A. S. B.—*Journal of the Asiatic Society of Bengal*, Calcutta.
J. Bom. Br. R. A. S.—*Journal of the Bombay Branch of the Royal Asiatic Society.*
J. B. O. (or *J. B. & O.*) *Res. Soc.*—*Journal of the Bihar and Orissa Research Society.*
J. P. H. S.—*Journal of the Panjab Historical Society.*
J. R. A. S.—*Journal of the Royal Asiatic Society*, London.
J. U. P. H. S.—*Journal of the United Provinces Historical Society.*
MM.—Mahāmahopādhyāya, a title.
N. S.—New style.
N. W. P.—North-Western Provinces.
O. S.—Old style.
Prog. (Progr.) Rep.—*Progress Report.*
R. A. S.—Royal Asiatic Society.
R. I.—Rulers of India Series.
R. V.—*Rigveda.*
S. B. E.—*Sacred Books of the East.*
U. P.—United Provinces of Agra and Oudh.

NOTE.—An index number above the title of a book indicates the edition; e. g., *Annals of Rural Bengal*[7] means the 7th edition of that work.

[1] The word *hijra* is rendered by 'withdrawal' more precisely than by 'flight', the equivalent usually given.

ADDITIONS AND CORRECTIONS

PAGE 34, l. 1. Messrs. F. E. Pargiter and K. P. Jayaswal attach to the Puranic genealogies a value higher than I have been disposed to allow. Jayaswal ventures to assign 1727 B. C. for the beginning of the Brihadratha dynasty. Such an attempt to give an approximately precise date for events so remote necessarily involves many assumptions (*J. B. O. Res. Soc.*, vol. iv (1918), p. 33). I take this opportunity of emphasizing the high value of Mr. Pargiter's book, *The Purāṇa Text of the Dynasties of the Kali Age*, the outcome of much patient labour, and indispensable to the student of primary authorities.

PAGES 48, 58 *n.*, 70. Messrs. BANERJI and JAYASWAL have published a satisfactory edition of the Khāravela inscription with adequate facsimiles in *J. B. O. Res. Soc.*, vol. iii (Dec. 1917), pp. 425–507. Although the interpretation is open to doubt on certain minor points, the main chronological results as stated on p. 58 *n.* are established. Exact dates depend on the year assumed for the accession of Chandragupta, which may be as early as 325. The King of Rājagṛiha (Magadha) defeated by Khāravela and forced to retire on Mathurā was Pushyamitra, the first of the Śunga dynasty. He was called also Bṛihaspati (Bahapati in the inscription, Bahasati of coins and certain short inscriptions). The two alternative names are substantially synonymous, Bṛihaspati being the regent of the *nakshatra* or zodiacal asterism Pushya, also named Tishya, in the constellation Cancer or the Crab. Many other facts and inferences of importance are recorded in or deducible from the Khāravela record. See my short article in *J. R. A. S.*, July 1918. Now (August 1918) I am disposed to agree with K. P. Jayaswal and Harit Krishna Deb (*J. B. O. Res. Soc.*, iv. 91–5) that the term *Navanandāḥ* should be interpreted as meaning the 'New' or 'Later' Nandas, not the 'Nine'. On that supposition they are to be distinguished from Kshemendra's *Pūrvanandāḥ*, the 'Early' Nandas, namely Nanda (or Nandi-) vardhana and Mahānanda (or -nandin). Harit Krishna Deb gives good reasons for believing that Chandragupta Maurya was a kinsman of the respectable Early Nandas, and not a Śūdra or low-caste man, like the Later Nandas of ill-repute. The Khāravela inscription proves that Nandavardhana was reckoned as a Nanda.

PAGE 65. Balōchistan is correct, not Balūchistan as in *I. G.* (M. Longworth Dames, *J. R. A. S.*, 1914, p. 457).

PAGE 71, l. 42. Add after 'text', 'A still later work is *An Epitome of Jainism, a Critical Study*, &c., by PURAN CHAND NAHAR and KRISHNACHANDRA GHOSH, VEDANTACHINTAMONI, Calcutta, Gulab Kumar Library, 46 Indian Mirror Street. The book, which seems to be based on full knowledge, is badly produced and disfigured by careless proof-reading. The authors controvert Mrs. Stevenson on various matters.

PAGE 157. The illustration of the Lauriya-Nandangaṛh Asoka pillar was accidentally misplaced.

PAGE 171, end. Insert 'Mr. PANNA LALL, I.C.S., in 'The Dates of Skandagupta and his Successors' (*Hindustan Review*, Jan. 1918), argues that the reign of Skandagupta ended about A. D. 467; that Hiuen Tsang erroneously attributed the defeat of Mihiragula to Bālāditya; that there were only two emperors or kings named Kumāragupta; and that Fleet erred in his interpretation of the Mandasōr inscription. My review (*J. R. A. S.*, Oct. 1918) accepts the essayist's conclusions'.

PAGES 174, 175. From 'Srong-tsan Gampo' to 'India'. The text follows the opinions of A. H. Francke and Hoernle, now proved to be erroneous by Berthold Laufer (*J. A. O. S.*, vol. 38 (1918), pp. 31–46). The chronology of the Chinese and Mongolian authors should be followed. King Srong-tsan Gampo was born in A. D. 617, and ascended the throne in A. D. 629, when in his thirteenth year. The date of his marriages, A. D. 641, as stated on p. 180, is correct. He died in A. D. 650, not 698. The Tibetan alphabet came, not from Khotan, but from India. Relations between Tibet and Khotan began in A. D. 670 when the Tibetans conquered the 'Four Garrisons' (Khotan, Kucha, Tokmak, Kashgar). See Waddell in *J. R. A. S.*, 1909, pp. 945–8 ; and I. J. Schmidt's translation of the history by Sanañ Setsen (Ssanang Ssetsen) *Geschichte der Ost-Mongolen*, &c. (St. Petersburg and Leipzig, 1829), pp. 29, &c. A copy of Schmidt's rare book is in the Malan Library, Indian Institute, Oxford.

PAGE 191, l. 29. An error of Kielhorn led me to confound Visala deva with the much latter Vigraha-rāja. The statements assuming their identity in *E. H. I.*[3], pp. 386, 387, require correction.

PAGE 216. Add, after 'Probsthain, 1916' (l. 38): 'vol. ii, with 8 plates, 32 pp. ; Pondicherry, sold by the translator, 32 Perumal Covil Street, 1918. The volume has been reduced to a few pages because the author was called up to serve in the army.'

PAGE 261. A new and excellent translation of Kabīr's poems made directly from the Hindī has been published at Hamīrpur, U.P., in 1917 by Mr. AHMAD SHAH, who edited the text in 1911 (Cawnpore). The Tagore and Underhill version is from the Bengālī. Mr. Ahmad Shah's works are favourably reviewed at length by GRIERSON in *J. R. A. S.*, 1918, pp. 151–60.

PAGE 262. Another version of Ibn Batuta's travels in India, China, &c., will be found in the Hakluyt Society's edition of *Cathay and the Way Thither* by Yule and Cordier, 1916, vol. iv, pp. 1–166, including Introductory Notice, pp. 1–79. The notes are not up to date.

PAGE 339, l. 47. Aungier's grave is no longer 'nameless'. It has been identified with certainty sufficient to justify the insertion of a new marble tablet in one of the inner walls of the tomb believed to be that of Aungier. The tablet was put up in 1916. Aungier died on June 30, 1677 (*Prog. Rep. A. S. W. I.*, 1916–17, p. 42).

PAGES 396, 397. Another full account of the siege of Hooghly (Hūglī or Bandel), written in 1633 by Father John Cabral, S.J., who was present, has been translated by the Rev. L. Besse, S.J., and published in the *Catholic Herald of India* (Jan. 30–April 10, 1918) by the Rev. H. Hosten, S.J., who has kindly sent me a reprint. The narrative is of great interest. The Mogul attack was invited by a traitor, Martin Afonso de Mello.

PAGE 439. Sarkar's improved version of the famous letter is printed in *The Modern Review* (Allahabad) for Sept. 1908, p. 21. The text of the document has been settled by collation of the London manuscript with another belonging to the A. S. B. Its date is said to be 'evidently the close of A. D. 1679'. It purports to have been composed by Nil Prabhu Munshī.

PAGE 483 *n*. Sirāju-d daula was older than twenty-five, having been born in A. H. 1140 (=Aug. 1727–July 1728). He succeeded his grandfather in A. H. 1169 (=Oct. 1755–Sept. 1756). He was, therefore, twenty-nine or thirty years of age at his death (*Bengal Past and Present*, xii. 244 ; citing Persian authorities).

PAGE 492, note 2. But see Forrest.

PAGE 509. Sir G. Forrest's *Life of Clive* was published in Sept. 1918.

PAGE 510, l. 1. For an account of the strange career of Willem Bolts, who was a Dutchman, see *Ind. Ant.*, 1917, pp. 277 foll.

INTRODUCTION

SECTION 1

The geographical foundation; diversity in unity and unity in diversity; the scenes and periods of the story; sea-power; forms of government; the history of thought.

The geographical unit. The India of this book is almost exclusively the geographical unit called by that name on the ordinary maps, bounded on the north, north-west, and north-east by mountain ranges, and elsewhere by the sea. The extensive Burmese territories, although now governed as part of the Indian empire, cannot be described as being part of India. Burma has a separate history, rarely touching on that of India prior to the nineteenth century. Similarly, Ceylon, although geologically a fragment detached from the peninsula in relatively recent times, always has had a distinct political existence, requiring separate historical treatment. The island is not now included in the Indian empire, and its affairs will not be discussed in this work, except incidentally. Certain portions of Balōchistan now administered or controlled by the Indian Government lie beyond the limits of the geographical unit called India. Aden and sundry other outlying dependencies of the Indian empire obviously are not parts of India, and the happenings in those places rarely demand notice.

Vast extent of area. Formal, technical descriptions of the geographical and physical features of India may be found in many easily accessible books, and need not be reproduced here. But certain geographical facts with a direct bearing on the history require brief comment, because, as Richard Hakluyt truly observed long ago, 'Geographie and Chronologie are the Sunne and the Moone, the right eye and the left eye of all history.' The large extent of the area of India, which may be correctly designated as a sub-continent, is a material geographical fact. The history of a region so vast, bounded by a coast-line of about 3,400 miles, more or less, and a mountain barrier on the north some 1,600 miles in length, and inhabited by a population numbering nearly 300 millions, necessarily must be long and intricate. The detailed treatment suitable to the story of a small country cannot be applied in a general history of India. The author of such a book must be content to sketch his picture in outlines boldly drawn, and to leave out multitudes of recorded particulars.

Continental and peninsular regions. Another geographical fact, namely, that India comprises both a large continental, subtropical area, and an approximately equal peninsular, tropical area, has had immense influence upon the history.

Three territorial compartments. Geographical conditions

divided Indian history, until the nineteenth century, into three well-marked territorial compartments, not to mention minor distinct areas, such as the Konkan, the Himalayan region, and others. The three are: (1) the northern plains forming the basins of the

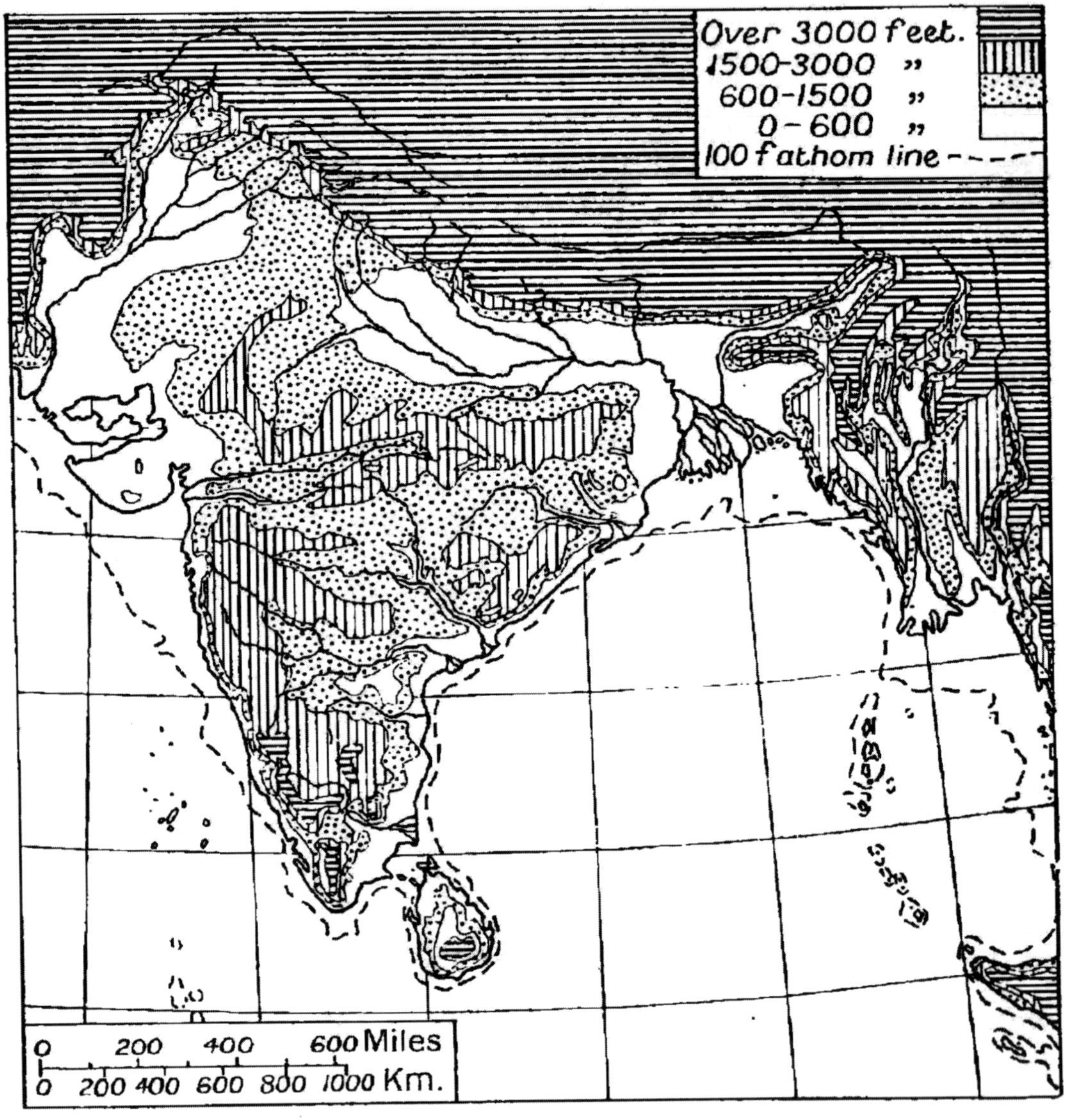

INDIA PHYSICAL.

Indus and Ganges; (2) the Deccan plateau lying to the south of the Narbadā, and to the north of the Krishnā and Tungabhadrā rivers; and (3) the far south, beyond those rivers, comprising the group of Tamil states. Ordinarily, each of those three geographical compartments has had a distinct, highly complex story of its own. The points of contact between the three histories are not very numerous.

Dominance of the north. The northern plains, the Āryāvarta of the old books, and the Hindostan of more recent times, always have been the seat of the principal empires and the scene of the events most interesting to the outer world. The wide waterways of the great snow-fed rivers and the fertile level plains are natural advantages which have inevitably attracted a teeming population from time immemorial. The open nature of the country, easily accessible to martial invaders from the north-west, has given frequent occasion for the formation of powerful kingdoms ruled by vigorous foreigners. The peninsular, tropical section of India, isolated from the rest of the world by its position, and in contact with other countries only by sea-borne commerce, has pursued its own course, little noticed by and caring little for foreigners. The historian of India is bound by the nature of things to direct his attention primarily to the north, and is able to give only a secondary place to the story of the Deccan plateau and the far south.

No southern power ever could attempt to master the north, but the more ambitious rulers of Āryāvarta or Hindostan often have extended their sway far beyond the dividing line of the Narbadā. When Dupleix in the eighteenth century dreamed of a Franco-Indian empire with its base in the peninsula he was bound to fail. The success of the English was dependent on their acquisition of rich Bengal and their command of the Gangetic waterway. In a later stage of the British advance the conquest of the Panjāb was conditioned by the control of the Indus navigation, previously secured by the rather unscrupulous proceedings of Lords Auckland and Ellenborough. The rivers of the peninsula do not offer similar facilities for penetration of the interior.

Changes in rivers. The foregoing general observations indicate broadly the ways in which the geographical position and configuration of India have affected the course of her history. But the subject will bear a little more elaboration and the discussion of certain less conspicuous illustrations of the bearing of geography upon history. Let us consider for a moment the changes in the great rivers of India, which, when seen in full flood, suggest thoughts of the ocean rather than of inland streams. Unless one has battled in an open ferry-boat with one of those mighty masses of surging water in the height of the rains, it is difficult to realize their demoniac power. They cut and carve the soft alluvial plains at their will, recking of nothing. Old beds of the Sutlaj can be traced across a space eighty-five miles wide. The Indus, the Ganges, the Kosi, the Brahmaputra, and scores of other rivers behave, each according to its ability, in the same way, despising all barriers, natural or artificial. Who can tell where the Indus flowed in the days of Alexander the Great? Yet books, professedly learned, are not afraid to trace his course minutely through the Panjāb and Sind by the help of some modern map, and to offer pretended identifications of sites upon the banks of rivers which certainly were somewhere else twenty-two centuries ago. We know that they must have been somewhere else, but where they were no man can tell. So with the Vedic rivers, several of which bear the ancient names. The rivers of the Rishis were not the rivers of to-day. The descriptions prove that in the old, old days their character often differed completely from what it now is, and experience teaches that their courses must have been widely divergent. Commentators in their arm-chairs with the latest edition of the Indian *Atlas* opened out before them are not always willing to be bothered with such inconvenient facts. Ever since the early Muhammadan invasions the changes in the rivers have been enormous, and the contemporary histories of the foreign conquerors cannot be understood unless the reality and extent of those changes be borne constantly in mind. One huge river-system, based on the extinct Hakrā or Wahindah river, which once flowed down from the mountains through Bahāwalpur, has wholly disappeared, the final stages having been deferred until the eighteenth century. Scores of mounds, silent witnesses to the existence of numberless forgotten and often nameless towns, bear testimony to the desolation wrought when the waters of life desert their channels. A large and fascinating volume might be devoted to the study and description of the freaks of Indian rivers.

Position of cities. In connexion with that topic another point may be mentioned. The founders of the more important old cities almost invariably built, if possible, on the bank of a river, and not only that, but between two rivers in the triangle above the confluence. Dozens of examples might be cited, but one must suffice. The ancient imperial capital, Pātaliputra, represented by the modern Patna, occupied such a secure position between the guarding waters of the Sōn and the Ganges. The existing city, twelve miles or so below the confluence, has lost the strategical advantages of its predecessor. Historians who forget the position of Pātaliputra in relation to the rivers go hopelessly wrong in their comments on the texts of the ancient Indian and foreign authors.

Changes of the land. Changes in the coast-line and the level of the land have greatly modified the course of history, and must be remembered by the historian who desires to avoid ludicrous blunders. The story of the voyage of Nearchos, for instance, cannot be properly appreciated by any student who fails to compare the descriptions recorded by the Greeks with the surveys of modern geographers. When the changes in the coast-line are understood, statements of the old authors which looked erroneous at first sight are found to be correct. The utter destruction of the once wealthy commercial cities of Korkai and Kāyal on the Tinnevelly coast, now miles from the sea and buried under sand dunes, ceases to be a mystery when we know, as we do, that the coast level has risen. In other localities, some not very distant from the places named, the converse has happened, and the sea has advanced, or, in other words, the land has sunk. The careful investigator of ancient history needs to be continually on his guard against the insidious deceptions of the modern map. Many learned professors, German and others, have tumbled headlong into the pit. The subject being a hobby of mine I must not ride the steed too far.

The scenes of Indian history. Emphasis has been laid on the fact that most of the notable events of Indian history occurred in one or other of the three great regions separated from each other by natural barriers. Hindostan, the Deccan, and the far

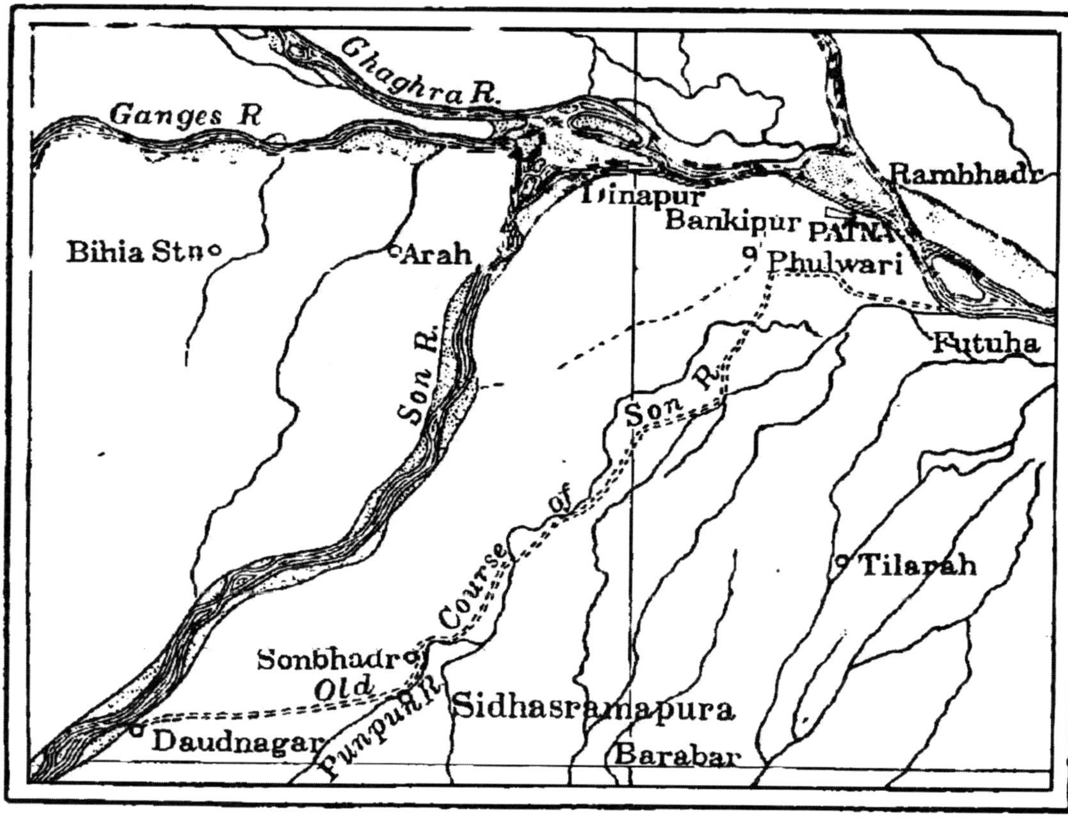

CHANGED COURSE OF SŌN.

south continued to be thus kept apart until the rapid progress of scientific discovery during the nineteenth century overthrew the boundaries set by nature. The mighty Indus and Ganges are now spanned by railway bridges as securely as a petty water-course is crossed by a six-foot culvert. The No Man's Land of Gondwāna—the wild country along the banks of the Narbadā and among the neighbouring hills—no longer hides any secrets. Roads and railways climb the steepest passes of the Western Ghāts, which more than once tried the nerves of our soldiers in the old wars. The magnificent natural haven of Bombay always was as good as it is now, but it was of no use to anybody as long as it was cut off from the interior of India by creeks, swamps, and mountains. The changes in modern conditions, which it would be tedious to enumerate, have made Bombay the premier city of India. Royal command may decree that the official head-quarters of the Government of India should shift from Calcutta to Delhi, but no proclamations can make the inland city of the Moguls the real capital of India, so long as the Indian empire is ruled by the masters of the sea. The claim to the first place may be disputed

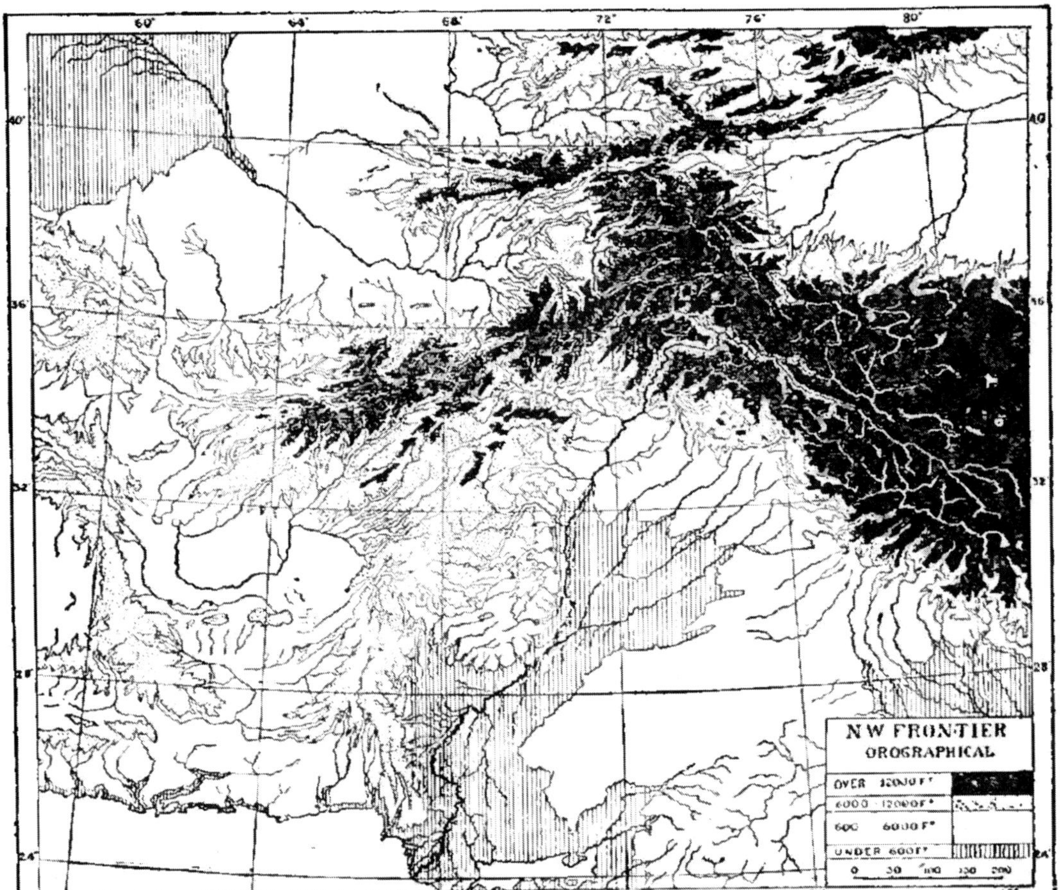

NORTH-WESTERN PHYSICAL FEATURES.

between Calcutta and Bombay. No rival can share in the competition.

Fortresses. The progress of modern science has not only destroyed the political and strategical value of the natural barriers offered by mountains, rivers, and forests. It has also rendered useless the ancient fortresses, which used to be considered impregnable, and were more often won by bribery than by assault. Asīrgarh in Khāndēsh, which in the sixteenth and seventeenth centuries was reckoned to be one of the wonders of the world, so that it was 'impossible to conceive a stronger fortress', defied the arms of Akbar, yielding only to his gold. Now it stands desolate, without a single soldier to guard it. When Lord Dufferin decided to pay Sindia the compliment of restoring Gwālior Fort to his keeping, the transfer could be effected without the slightest danger to the safety of the Empire. The numberless strongholds on the tops of the hills of the Deccan before which Aurangzēb wasted so

NORTH-WESTERN PASSES AND COUNTRIES.

many years are now open to any sightseer. The strategical points which dominated the military action of the Hindu and Muhammadan sovereigns are for the most part of no account in these days. The sieges of fortresses which occupy so large a space in the earlier history will never occur again. Modern generals think much more of a railway junction than of the most inaccessible castle.

The northern record. One reason why the historian must devote most of his space to the narrative of events occurring in northern India has been mentioned. Another is that the northern record is far less imperfect than that of the peninsula. Very little is known definitely concerning the southern kingdoms before A. D. 600, whereas the history of Hindostan may be carried back twelve centuries earlier. The extreme deficiency of really ancient records concerning the peninsula leaves an immense gap in the history of India which cannot be filled.

Sea-power. The arrival of Vasco da Gama's three little ships at Calicut in 1498 revolutionized Indian history by opening up the country to bold adventurers coming by sea. The earlier maritime visitors to the coasts had come solely for purposes of commerce without any thought of occupation or conquest. It is needless here to recall how the Portuguese pointed out to their successors, Dutch, French, and English, the path of conquest, and so made possible the British empire of India. The country now is at the mercy of the power which commands the sea, and could not possibly be held by any power unable to control the sea routes. The strategical importance of the north-western passes has declined as that of Bombay and Karāchī has risen.

Endless diversity. The endlesss diversity in the Indian subcontinent is apparent and has been the subject of many trite remarks. From the physical point of view we find every extreme of altitude, temperature, rainfall, and all the elements of climate. The variety of the flora and fauna, largely dependent upon climatic conditions, is equally obvious. From the human point of view India has been often described as an ethnological museum, in which numberless races of mankind may be studied, ranging from savages of low degree to polished philosophers. That variety of races, languages, manners and customs is largely the cause of the innumerable political subdivisions which characterize Indian history before the unification effected by the British supremacy. Megasthenes in the fourth century B.C. heard of 118 kingdoms, and the actual number may well have been more. Even now the Native or Protected States, small and great, may be reckoned as about 700. In all ages the crowd of principalities and powers has been almost past counting. From time to time a strong paramount power has arisen and succeeded for a few years in introducing a certain amount of political unity, but such occasions were rare. When no such power existed, the states, hundreds in number, might be likened to a swarm of free, mutually repellent molecules in a state of incessant movement, now flying apart, and again coalescing.

Unity in diversity. How then, in the face of such bewildering diversity, can a history of India be written and compressed into a single volume of moderate bulk? The difficulties arising from the manifold diversities summarily indicated above are real, and present serious obstacles both to the writer and to the reader of Indian history. A chronicle of all the kingdoms for thousands of years is manifestly impracticable. The answer to the query is found in the fact that India offers unity in diversity. The underlying unity being less obvious than the superficial diversity, its nature and limitations merit exposition. The mere fact that the name India conveniently designates a sub-continental area does not help to unify history any more than the existence of the name Asia could make a history of that continent feasible. The unity sought must be of a nature more fundamental than that implied in the currency of a geographical term.

Political union. Political union attained by the subjection of all India to one monarch or paramount authority would, of course, be sufficient to make smooth the path of the historian. Such political union never was enjoyed by all India until the full establishment of the British sovereignty, which may be dated in one sense so recently as 1877, when Queen Victoria became Empress of India; in another sense from 1858, when Her Majesty assumed the direct government of British India; and in a third sense from 1818, when the Marquess of Hastings shattered the Marāthā power, and openly proclaimed the fact that the East India Company had become the paramount authority throughout the whole country. Very few rulers, Hindu or Muhammadan, attained sovereignty even as extensive as that claimed by the Marquess of Hastings. The Mauryas, who after the defeat of Seleukos Nikator held the country now called Afghanistan as far as the Hindu Kush, exercised authority more or less direct over all India Proper down to the northern parts of Mysore. But even Asoka did not attempt to bring the Tamil kingdoms under his dominion. The empires of the Kushāns and Guptas were confined to the north. In the fourteenth century Muhammad bin Tughlak for a few years exercised imperfect sovereign powers over very nearly the whole of India. Akbar and his historians never mention the Tamil states, and so far as appears never heard of the powerful Hindu empire of Vijayanagar, which broke up in 1565. But the Great Mogul cherished a passionate desire to subdue the kingdoms of the Deccan plateau. His success, however, was incomplete, and did not extend beyond Ahmadnagar in the latitude of Bombay. His descendants pursued his policy, and at the close of the eighteenth century Aurangzēb's officers levied tribute two or three times from Tanjore and Trichinopoly. Thus Aurangzēb might be regarded as being in a very loose sense the suzerain of almost all India. The Kābul territory continued to be part of the empire until 1739. The periods of partial political unification thus summarily indicated afford welcome footholds to the historian, and are far easier to deal with than the much longer intervals when no power with any serious claim to paramountcy existed.

The political unity of all India, although never attained perfectly in fact, always was the ideal of the people throughout the centuries. The conception of the universal sovereign as the Chakravartin Rājā runs through Sanskrit literature and is emphasized in scores of inscriptions. The story of the gathering of the nations to the battle of Kurukshetra, as told in the *Mahābhārata*, implies the belief that all the Indian peoples, including those of the extreme south, were united by real bonds and concerned in interests common to all. European writers, as a rule, have been more conscious of the diversity than of the unity of India. Joseph Cunningham, an author of unusually independent spirit, is an exception. When describing the Sikh fears of British aggression in 1845, he recorded the acute and true observation that 'Hindostan, moreover, from Caubul to the valley of Assam, and the island of Ceylon, is regarded as one country, and dominion in it is associated in the minds of the people with the predominance of one monarch or one race '.[1] India therefore possesses, and always has possessed for considerably more than two thousand years, ideal political unity, in spite of the fact that actual complete union under one sovereign, universally acknowledged by all other princes and potentates, dates only from 1877. The immemorial persistence of that ideal goes a long way to explain the acquiescence of India in British rule, and was at the bottom of the passionate outburst of loyal devotion to their King-Emperor so touchingly expressed in many ways by princes and people in 1911.

Fundamental unity of Hinduism. The most essentially fundamental Indian unity rests upon the fact that the diverse peoples of India have developed a peculiar type of culture or civilization utterly different from any other type in the world. That civilization may be summed up in the term Hinduism. India primarily is a Hindu country, the land of the Brahmans, who have succeeded by means of peaceful penetration, not by the sword, in carrying their ideas into every corner of India. Caste, the characteristic Brahman institution, utterly unknown in Burma, Tibet, and other border lands, dominates the whole of Hindu India, and exercises no small influence over the powerful Muhammadan minority. Nearly all Hindus reverence Brahmans,[2] and all may be said to venerate the cow. Few deny the authority of the Vedas and the other ancient scriptures. Sanskrit everywhere is the sacred language. The great gods, Vishnu and Siva, are recognized and more or less worshipped in all parts of India. The pious pilgrim, when going the round of the holy places, is equally at home among the snows of Badrīnāth or on the burning sands of Rāma's Bridge. The seven sacred cities include places in the far south as well as in Hindostan. Similarly, the cult of rivers is common to all Hindus, and all alike share in the affection felt for the tales of the *Mahābhārata* and *Rāmāyana*.

India beyond all doubt possesses a deep underlying fundamental unity, far more profound than that produced either by geographical isolation or by political suzerainty. That unity transcends the innumerable diversities of blood, colour, language, dress, manners, and sect.

Limitations of unity. But the limitations are many. Caste, which, looked at broadly, unites all Hindus by differentiating them from the rest of mankind, disintegrates them by breaking

[1] *History of the Sikhs*[2] (1853), p. 283.

[2] The Lingāyats of the Kanarese country are the principal exception, but others exist.

them up into thousands of mutually exclusive and often hostile sections. It renders combined political or social action difficult, and in many cases impossible; while it shuts off all Hindus in large measure from sympathy with the numerous non-Hindu population. The Muhammadans, by far the largest part of that population, are not concerned with most of the reasons which make all Hindus one in a sense. An Indian Muslim may be, and often is, far more in sympathy with an Arab or Persian fellow-believer than he is with his Hindu neighbour. The smaller communities, Christians, Jews, Parsees, and others, are still more distant from the Hindu point of view.

Nevertheless, when all allowances are made for the limitations, the fundamental unity of Hindu culture alone makes a general history of India feasible.

Dravidian culture. The Brahmanical ideas and institutions, although universally diffused in every province, have not been wholly victorious. Prehistoric forms of worship and many utterly un-Aryan social practices survive, especially in the peninsula among the peoples speaking Dravidian languages. We see there the strange spectacle of an exaggerated regard for caste coexisting with all sorts of weird notions and customs alien to Brahman tradition. While it is not improbable that the Dravidian civilization may be as old as or even older than the Indo-Aryan Brahmanical culture of the north, which was long regarded in the south as an unwelcome intruder to be resisted strenuously, the materials available for the study of early Dravidian institutions are too scanty and imperfectly explored to permit of history being based upon them. The historian's attention necessarily must be directed chiefly to the Indo-Aryan institutions of the north, which are much more fully recorded than those of the south. An enthusiastic southern scholar has expressed the opinion that 'the scientific historian of India . . . ought to begin his study with the basin of the Krishnā, of the Cauvery, of the Vaigai [in Madura and the Pāndya country] rather than with the Gangetic plain, as it has been now long, too long, the fashion'. That advice, however sound it may be in principle, cannot be followed in practice at present; and, so far as I can see, it is not likely that even in a distant future it will be practicable to begin writing Indian history in the manner suggested.

Lack of political evolution. The interest attaching to the gradual evolution of political institutions is lacking in Indian history. The early tribal constitutions of a republican, or at any rate, oligarchical character, which are known to have existed among the Mālavas, Kshudrakas, and other nations in the time of Alexander the Great, as well as among the Lichchhavis and Yaudhēyas at much later dates, all perished without leaving a trace. Autocracy is substantially the only form of government with which the historian of India is concerned. Despotism does not admit of development. Individual monarchs vary infinitely in ability and character, but the nature of a despotic government remains much the same at all times and in all places, whether the ruler be a saint or a tyrant.

Extinction of tribal constitutions. The reason for the extinction of the tribal constitutions appears to be that they were a Mongolian institution, the term Mongolian being used to mean tribes racially allied to the Tibetans, Gūrkhas, and other Himalayan nations. The Mongolian element in the population of northern India before and after the Christian era was, I believe, much larger than is usually admitted. When the Mongolian people and ideas were overborne in course of time by the strangers who followed the Indo-Aryan or Brahmanical cult and customs, the tribal constitutions disappeared along with many other non-Aryan institutions. The Brahmanical people always were content with autocracy.[1] I use the term 'autocracy' or the equivalent 'despotism' without qualification intentionally, because I do not believe in the theory advocated by several modern Hindu authors that the ancient Indian king was a 'limited' or constitutional monarch. Those authors have been misled by taking too seriously the admonitions of the text-book writers that the ideal king should be endowed with all the virtues and should follow the advice of sage counsellors. In reality every Indian despot who was strong enough did exactly what he pleased. If any limitations on his authority were operative, they took effect only because he was weak. A strong sovereign like Chandragupta Maurya was not to be bound by the cobwebs of texts. Long afterwards, Akbar, notwithstanding his taste for sententious moral aphorisms, was equally self-willed.

Village and municipal institutions. Much sentimental nonsense with little relation to the actual facts has been written about the supposed indestructible constitution of the Indo-Aryan village in the north. The student of highly developed village institutions, involving real local self-government administered on an elaborately organized system, should turn to the south and examine the constitution of the villages in the Chola kingdom as recorded for the period from the tenth to the twelfth centuries of the Christian era, and no doubt of extremely ancient origin.[2] Those institutions, like the tribal constitutions of the north, perished long ago, being killed by rulers who had no respect for the old indigenous modes of administration. The development of municipal institutions, which furnishes material for so many interesting chapters in European history, is a blank page in the history of India.

History of Indian thought. The defects in the subject-matter of Indian history pointed out in the foregoing observa-

[1] On this obscure subject see the author's papers entitled 'Tibetan Affinities of the Lichchhavis' (*Ind. Ant.*, vol. xxxii (1903), pp. 238 foll.; and 'Tibetan Illustration of the Yaudhēya Tribal Organization' (ibid., vol. xxxv (1906)), p. 290); and K. P. Jayaswal, 'Republics in the Mahābhārata' (*J. O. & B. Res. Soc.*, vol. i, pp. 173–8). A well-executed treatise on the subject would be welcome.

[2] *E. H. I.*[3] (1914), pp. 459, 464, with references.

tions undoubtedly tend to make the political history of the country rather dry reading. The more attractive story of the development of Indian thought as expressed in religion and philosophy, literature, art, and science cannot be written intelligibly unless it is built on the solid foundation of dynastic history, which alone can furnish the indispensable chronological basis. Readers who may be disposed to turn away with weariness from the endless procession of kingdoms and despots may console themselves by the reflection that a working acquaintance with the political history of India is absolutely essential as a preliminary for the satisfactory treatment of the story of the development of her ideas.

I have tried to give in this work, so far as unavoidable limitations permit, an outline of the evolution of Indian thought in various fields. Students who desire further information must consult special treatises when such exist.

Divisions of the history. The main divisions of a book on Indian history hardly admit of variation. I have drawn the line between the Ancient Period and the Hindu Period at the beginning of the Maurya dynasty as a matter of convenience. In the Hindu Period the death of Harsha in A. D. 647 marks a suitable place for beginning a fresh section. The subdivisions of the Muhammadan Period, occupying Books IV, V, VI, and including the Hindu empire of Vijayanagar, are almost equally self-evident. Three books, VII, VIII, and IX, are devoted to the British Period. The dividing line between Books VII and VIII should be drawn in my opinion at the year 1818, and not at the close of the administration of the Marquess of Hastings. The significance of the events of 1858, when the series of Viceroys begins, cannot be mistaken.

AUTHORITIES

The subject-matter of this section has been treated previously by the author in several publications, namely, in *E. H. I.*[3] (1914), Introduction ; *Oxford Student's History of India*, latest ed., chap. i ; and the *Oxford Survey of the British Empire* (1914), chap. vii. A good formal geographical book is the *Geography of India* by G. PATTERSON (*Christian Literature Soc. for India*, London, 1909). See also *I. G.* (Indian Empire), 1907, vol. i, and the Atlas of the same work (1909). The little book entitled *The Fundamental Unity of India* (Longmans, 1914), by Prof. RADHAKUMUD MOOKERJI is well written, learned, and accurate, notwithstanding its avowed political purpose. The influence of sea-power upon Indian history is expounded by Sir A. LYALL in *The Rise and Expansion of the British Dominion in India* (Murray, 1910).

SECTION 2

The Sources, or the Original Authorities.

Undated history before 650 B.C. A body of history strictly so-called must be built upon a skeleton of chronology, that is to say, on a series of dates more or less precise. In India, as in Greece, such a series begins about the middle or close of the seventh century before Christ.[1] Nothing approaching exact chronology being attainable for earlier times, the account which the historian can offer of those times necessarily is wanting in definiteness and precision. It is often difficult to determine even the sequence or successive order of events. Nevertheless, no historian of India and the Indians can escape from the obligation of offering some sort of picture of the life of undated ancient India, in its political, social, religious, literary, and artistic aspects, previous to the dawn of exact history. The early literature, composed chiefly in the Sanskrit, Pāli, and Tamil languages, supplies abundant material, much of which is accessible in one or other European tongue. The thorough exploration of the gigantic mass of literature, especially that of the southern books, is a task so vast that it cannot ever be completed. Large fields of study have been hardly investigated at all. But a great deal of good work has been accomplished, and the labours of innumerable scholars, European, American, and Indian have won results sufficiently certain to warrant the drawing of an outline sketch of the beginnings of Indian life and history. Although the lines of the sketch are somewhat wanting in clearness, especially with reference to the Vedic age and the early Dravidian civilization, we moderns can form a tolerably distinct mental picture of several stages of Indian history prior to the earliest date ascertained with even approximate accuracy. Such an outline sketch or picture will be presented in the second chapter of Book I.

Chronological puzzles. Definite chronological history begins about 650 B.C. for Northern India. No positive historical statement can be made concerning the peninsula until a date much later. Even in the north all approximate dates before the invasion of Alexander in 326 B.C. are obtained only by reasoning back from the known to the unknown. The earliest absolutely certain precise date is that just named, 326 B.C.

The student may be glad to have in this place a brief exposition of the special difficulties which lie in the way of ascertaining precise

[1] 'The first exact date we have bearing on the history of Greece' is April 6, 648 B.C., when an eclipse of the sun occurred which was witnessed and noted by the poet Archilochus (Bury, *Hist. of Greece*, ed. 1904, p. 119). But the earliest really historical date known with any approach to accuracy seems to be that of Cylon's conspiracy at Athens, which is placed *about* 632 B.C. The archonship of Solon is put in either 594–593 or 592–591 B.C. (ibid., pp. 178, 182).

dates for the events of early Hindu history. Numerous dates are recorded in one fashion or another, but the various authorities are often contradictory, and usually open to more than one interpretation. Dates expressed only in regnal years, such as 'in the 8th year after the coronation of King A. B.', are not of much use unless we can find out by other means the time when King A. B. lived. Very often the year is given as simply 'the year 215', or the like, without mention of the era used, which to the writer needed no specification. In the same way when modern Europeans speak of the 'year 1914', everybody understands that to mean 'after Christ', A. D. or A. C. In other cases an era may be named, but it is not certain from what date the era is to be reckoned. For example, many dates recorded in the Gupta era were known long before historians could make confident use of them. When Fleet was able to prove that Gupta Era, year 1 = A. D. 319–20, the whole Gupta dynasty dropped at once into its proper historical setting. The fixation of that one date brought order into several centuries of early Indian history. Dated inscriptions of the Indo-Scythian or Kushān kings are even more abundant, but up to the present time we do not know to which era a record of theirs dated, say, 'in the year 98' should be referred; and in consequence an important section of Indian history continues to be the sport of conjecture, so that it is impossible to write with assurance a narrative of the events connected with one of the most interesting dynasties. That chronological uncertainty spoils the history of religion, art, and literature, as well as the purely political chronicle, for the first two centuries of the Christian era.

More than thirty different eras have been used in Indian annals from time to time.[1] Difficulties of various kinds, astronomical and other, are involved in the attempt to determine the dates on which the various eras begin. Although those difficulties have been surmounted to a large extent many obscurities remain.

Synchronisms; old and new styles. Several puzzles have been solved by the use of 'synchronisms', that is to say, by the use of stray bits of information showing that King A. of unknown date was contemporary with King B. of known date. The standard example is that of Chandragupta Maurya, the contemporary of Alexander the Great for some years. The approximate date of King Meghavarna of Ceylon in the fourth century A. C. is similarly indicated by the 'synchronism' with the Indian King Samudragupta; many other cases might be cited.

The testimony of foreign authors is specially useful in this connexion, because they often give dates the meaning of which is known with certainty. Indian historians obtain much help in that way from the chronicles of Greece, China, and Ceylon, all of which have well-known systems of chronology. The subject might be further illustrated at great length, but what has been said may suffice to give the student a notion of the difficulties of

[1] Cunningham's *Book of Indian Eras* (1883) discusses 27, and many more are mentioned in records.

Hindu chronology, and some of the ways in which many of them have been cleared away.

In the Muhammadan period chronological puzzles are mostly due to the innumerable contradictions of the authorities, but trouble is often experienced in converting Muslim Hijrī dates exactly into the terms of the Christian era. Akbar's fanciful Ilāhī, or Divine Era, and Tippoo Sultan's still more whimsical chronology present special conundrums. In the British period nearly all dates are ascertained with ease and certainty, subject to occasional conflict of evidence or confusion between the old and new styles, which differ by ten days in the seventeenth and by eleven days in the eighteenth century.[1]

Six classes of sources of Hindu history. The nature of the sources of or original authorities for Hindu history from 650 B. C. will now be considered briefly. The native or indigenous sources may be classified under five heads, namely: (1) inscriptions, or epigraphic evidence; (2) coins, or numismatic evidence; (3) monuments, buildings, and works of art, or archaeological evidence; (4) tradition, as recorded in literature; and (5) ancient historical writings, sometimes contemporary with the events narrated. The sixth source, foreign testimony, is mostly supplied either by the works of travellers of various nations, or by regular historians, especially the Cingalese, Greek, and Chinese. The value of each class of evidence will now be explained.

Inscriptions. Inscriptions have been given the first place in the list because they are, on the whole, the most important and trustworthy source of our knowledge. Unfortunately, they do not at present go further back than the third century B.C. with certainty, although it is not unlikely that records considerably earlier may be discovered, and it is possible that a very few known documents may go back beyond the reign of Asoka. Indian inscriptions, which usually are incised on either stone or metal, may be either official documents set forth by kings or other authorities, or records made by private persons for various purposes. Most of the inscriptions on stone either commemorate particular events or record the dedication of buildings or images. The commemorative documents range from the simple signature of a pilgrim to long and elaborate Sanskrit poems detailing the achievements of victorious kings. Such poems are called *prasasti*. The inscriptions on metal are for the most part grants of land inscribed on plates of

[1] Pope Gregory XIII undertook to reform the Roman calendar by correcting the error which had gradually grown to inconvenient dimensions in the course of centuries. Accordingly he decreed in 1582 that October 5 by the old calendar of that year should be called October 15. The reform was adopted either immediately or soon by Portugal, France, and several other nations; but in Great Britain and Ireland the change was not effected until 1752, when Parliament passed an Act enacting that September 2 of that year should be deemed to be September 14, new style; eleven days being dropped out of the reckoning. Russia still adhered to the old style until 1917 and was then nearly 13 days in error.

copper. They are sometimes extremely long, especially in the south, and usually include information about the reigning king and his ancestors. Exact knowledge of the dates of events in early Hindu history, so far as it has been attained, rests chiefly on the testimony of inscriptions.

Records of an exceptional kind occur occasionally. The most remarkable of such documents are the edicts of Asoka, which in the main are sermons on *dharma*, the Law of Piety or Duty. At Ajmēr in Rājputāna and at Dhār in Central India fragments of plays have been found inscribed on stone tablets. Part of a treatise on architecture is incised on one of the towers at Chitōr, and a score of music for the *vīnā*, or Indian lute, has been found in the Pudukottai State, Madras. A few of the metal inscriptions are dedications, and one very ancient document on copper, the Sohgaura plate from the Gorakhpur District, is concerned with Government storehouses.

The inscriptions which have been catalogued and published more or less fully aggregate many thousands. The numbers in the peninsula especially are enormous.

Coins. The legends on coins really are a class of inscriptions on metal, but it is more convenient to treat them separately. The science of numismatics, or the study of ancient coins, requires special expert knowledge. Coins, including those without any legends, can be made to yield much information concerning the condition of the country in the distant past. The dates frequently recorded on them afford invaluable evidence for fixing chronology. Even when the outline of the history is well known from books, as is the case for most of the Muhammadan period, the numismatic testimony helps greatly in settling doubtful dates, and in illustrating details of many kinds. Our scanty knowledge of the Bactrian, Indo-Greek, and Indo-Parthian dynasties rests chiefly on inferences drawn from the study of coins.

Archaeological evidence. The archaeological evidence, regarded as distinct from that of inscriptions and coins, is obtained by the systematic skilled examination of buildings, monuments, and works of art. Careful registration of the stratification of the ruins on ancient sites, that is to say, of the exact order in which the remains of one period follow those of another, often gives valuable proof of date. The excavations on the site of Taxila, for instance, have done much to clear up the puzzle of the Kushān or Indo-Scythian chronology already mentioned. The scientific description of buildings erected for religious or civil purposes, such as temples, *stūpas*, palaces, and private houses, throws welcome light on the conditions prevailing in ancient times. The study of works of art, including images, frescoes, and other objects, enables us to draw in outline the history of Indian art, and often affords a most illuminating commentary on the statements in books. The history of Indian religions cannot be properly understood by students who confine their attention to literary evidence. The testimony of the monuments and works of art is equally important, and, in fact, those remains tell much which is not to be learned from books. Intelligent appreciation of the material works wrought by the ancients is necessary for the formation of a true mental picture of the past. Such observations apply equally to the Hindu and the Muhammadan periods.

Tradition almost the sole source of undated history. The knowledge, necessarily extremely imperfect, which we possess concerning ancient India between 650 and 326 B.C. is almost wholly derived from tradition as recorded in literature of various kinds, chiefly composed in the Sanskrit, Pāli, and Tamil languages. Most of the early literature is of a religious kind, and the strictly historical facts have to be collected laboriously, bit by bit, from works which were not intended to serve as histories. Some valuable scraps of historical tradition have been picked out of the writings of grammarians ; and several plays, based on historical facts, yield important testimony. Tradition continues to be a rich source of historical information long after 326 B.C.

Absence of Hindu historical literature explained. The trite observation that Indian literature, prior to the Muhammadan period, does not include formal histories, although true in a sense, does not present the whole truth. Most of the Sanskrit books were composed by Brahmans, who certainly had not a taste for writing histories, their interest being engaged in other pursuits. But the Rājās were eager to preserve annals of their own doings, and took much pains to secure ample and permanent record of their achievements. They are not to blame for the melancholy fact that their efforts have had little success. The records laboriously prepared and regularly maintained have perished almost completely in consequence of the climate, including insect pests in that term, and of the innumerable political revolutions from which India has suffered. Every court in the old Hindu kingdoms maintained official bards and chroniclers whose duty it was to record and keep up the annals of the state. Some portion of such chronicles has been preserved and published by Colonel Tod, the author of the famous book, *Annals and Antiquities of Rajasthan*, first published in 1829, but that work stands almost alone. The great mass of the Rājās' annals has perished beyond recall.[1] Some fragments of the early chronicles clearly are preserved in the royal genealogies and connected historical observations recorded in the more ancient Purānas ; and numerous extracts from local records are given in the prefaces to many inscriptions. Thus it appears that the Hindus were not indifferent to history, although the Brahmans, the principal literary class, cared little for historical composition as a form of literature, except in the form of *prasastis*, some of which are poems of considerable literary merit. Such Sanskrit histories as exist usually were produced in the border countries, the best being the metrical chronicle of Kashmīr, called the *Rāja-taranginī*, composed in the twelfth century. Even that

[1] The survey of Rājputāna literature now in progress will disclose many more historical works.

work does not attain exactly to the European ideal of a formal history. Several Brahman authors, notably Bāna in the seventh century, wrote interesting works, half history and half romance, which contain a good deal of authentic historical matter. Our exceptionally full knowledge of the story of Harsha vardhana, King of Thānēsar and Kanauj, is derived largely from the work of Bāna entitled 'The Deeds of Harsha'.

Historical or semi-historical compositions are numerous in the languages of the south. The Mackenzie collection of manuscripts catalogued by H. H. Wilson contains a large number of texts which may be regarded as histories in some degree.

Foreign evidence. The indigenous or native sources enumerated above, which must necessarily be the basis of early Hindu history, are supplemented to a most important extent by the writings of foreigners. Hearsay notes recorded by the Greek authors Herodotus and Ktesias in the fifth century B. C. record some scraps of information, but Europe was almost ignorant of India until the veil was lifted by the operations of Alexander (326 to 323 B. C.) and the reports of his officers. Those reports, lost as a whole, survive in considerable extracts quoted in the writings of later authors, Greek and Roman. The expedition of Alexander the Great is not mentioned distinctly by any Hindu author, and the references to the subject by Muhammadan authors are of little value. Megasthenes, the ambassador of Seleukos Nikator to Chandragupta Maurya in the closing years of the fourth century, wrote a highly valuable account of India, much of which has been preserved in fragments.

Formal Chinese histories from about 120 B. C. have something to tell us, but by far the most important and interesting of all the foreign witnesses are the numerous Chinese pilgrims who visited the Holy Land of Buddhism, between A. D. 400 and 700. Fa-hien, the earliest of them (A. D. 399–414), gives life to the bald chronicle of Chandragupta Vikramāditya, as constructed from inscriptions and coins. The learned Hiuen Tsang, or Yuan Chwang, in the seventh century, does the same for Harsha vardhana, and also records innumerable matters of interest concerning every part of India. I-tsing and more than sixty other pilgrims have left valuable notes of their travels. A book on the early history of Hindu India would be a very meagre and dry record but for the narratives of the pilgrims, which are full of vivid detail.

Alberūnī. Alberūnī, justly entitled the Master, a profoundly learned mathematician and astronomer, who entered India in the train of Mahmūd of Ghaznī early in the eleventh century, applied his powerful intellect to the thorough study of the whole life of the Indians. He mastered the difficult Sanskrit language, and produced a truly scientific treatise, entitled 'An Enquiry into India' (*Tahkīk-i Hind*), which is a marvel of well-digested erudition. More than five centuries later that great book served as a model to Abu-l Fazl, whose 'Institutes of Akbar' (*Āīn-i Akbarī*) plainly betray the unacknowledged debt due to Alberūnī.

Muhammadan histories. Muhammadans, unlike the Brahmans, always have shown a liking and aptitude for the writing of professed histories, so that every Muslim dynasty in Asia has found its chronicler. The authors who deal with Indian history wrote, as a rule, in the Persian language. Most of the books are general histories of the Muslim world, in which Indian affairs occupy a comparatively small space, but a few works are confined to Indian subjects. The most celebrated is the excellent and conscientious compilation composed by Firishta (Ferishta) in the reigns of Akbar and Jahāngīr, which forms the basis of Elphinstone's *History of India* and of most modern works on the subject.

A comprehensive general view of the Indian histories in Persian is to be obtained from the translations and summaries in the eight volumes of *The History of India as told by its own Historians* (London, 1867–77) by Sir Henry Elliot and Professor John Dowson. Sir Edward Bayley's incomplete work entitled the *History of Gujarāt* is a supplement to Elliot and Dowson's collection. The English translations of the *Tabakāt-i Nāsirī* by Raverty; of the *Āīn-i Akbarī* by Blochmann and Jarrett; of the *Akbarnāma* and the *Memoirs of Jahāngīr* by H. Beveridge; of Badāonī's book by Ranking and Lowe; and Prof. Jadunāth Sarkar's learned account of Aurangzēb's reign may be specially mentioned. Many other important books exist. The author of this volume has published a detailed biography of Akbar.

The modern historian of India, therefore, when he comes to the Muhammadan period, finds plenty of history books ready made from which he can draw most of his material. He is not reduced to the necessity of piecing together his story by combining fragments of information laboriously collected from inscriptions, coins, traditions, and passing literary references, as he is compelled to do when treating of the Hindu period. His principal difficulties arise from the contradictions of his authorities, the defects of their mode of composition, and endless minor chronological puzzles.

The epigraphic, numismatic, and monumental testimony is needed only for the completion and correction of details.

The histories written in Persian have many faults when judged by European standards, but, whatever may be the opinion held concerning those defects, it is impossible to write the history of Muhammadan India without using the Persian chronicles as its foundation.

Foreign evidence for the Muhammadan period. Foreign testimony is as valuable for the Muhammadan period as it is for the Hindu. From the ninth century onwards Muslim merchants and other travellers throw light upon the history of mediaeval India. Some scanty notes recorded by European observers in the fifteenth century have been preserved; and from the sixteenth century numerous works by European travellers present a mass of authentic information supplementary to that recorded by the Muslim historians, who looked at things from a different point of view, and omitted mention of many matters interesting to foreign observers and modern readers. The reports of the Jesuit missionaries for the Mogul period possess special value, having been written by men highly educated, specially trained, and endowed with powers of keen observation. Large use is made in this volume of those reports which have been too often neglected by modern writers. References to the works of the leading Jesuits and the other foreign travellers will be given in due course.

Authorities for Indo-European history and British Period. State papers and private original documents of many kinds dating as far back as a thousand years ago are fairly abundant in most countries of Europe, and supply a vast quarry of material for the historian. In India they are wholly wanting for both the Hindu and the pre-Mogul Muhammadan periods, except in so far as their place is supplied by inscriptions on stone and metal. A few documents from the reigns of Akbar and his successors survive, but most of what we know about the Moguls is derived from the secondary evidence of historians, as supplemented by the testimony of the foreign travellers, inscriptions, and coins. The case changes with the appearance of Europeans on the scene. The records of the East India Company go back to the beginning of the seventeenth century, and the Portuguese archives contain numerous documents of the sixteenth century.

From the middle of the eighteenth century, the commencement of the British period, the mass of contemporary papers, public and private, is almost infinite. Considerable portions of the records have been either printed at length or catalogued, and much of the printed material has been worked up by writers on special sections of the history, but an enormous quantity remains unused. In the composition of this work I have not attempted to explore manuscript collections, and have necessarily been obliged to content myself with printed matter only so far as I could manage to read and digest it. No person can read it all, or nearly all. The leading authorities consulted will be noted at the end of each chapter.

Present state of Indian historical studies. A brief survey of the present state of Indian historical studies will not be out of place in connexion with the foregoing review of the original authorities.

No general history of the Hindu period was in existence before the publication in 1904 of the first edition of the *Early History of India.* The more condensed treatment of the subject in this volume is based on the third edition of that work, published in 1914, but much new material has been used ; and the subject has been treated from a point of view to some extent changed. Many sections of the story need further elucidation, and it is certain that research will add greatly to our knowledge of the period in the near future. Numerous eager inquirers are now at work, who contribute something of value almost every month.

The Muhammadan period. The publication in 1841 of Elphinstone's justly famous *History of India* made possible for the first time systematic study of the Indo-Muhammadan history of Hindostan or Northern India down to the battle of Pānīpat in 1761. Although Elphinstone's book, mainly based on the compilations of Firishta and Khāfī Khān, is of permanent value, it is no disparagement of its high merit to say that in these changed times it is no longer adequate for the needs of either the close student or the general reader. Since Elphinstone wrote many authorities unknown to him have become accessible, archaeological discoveries have been numerous, and corrections of various kinds have become necessary. Moreover, the attitude of readers has been modified. They now ask for something more than is to be found in the austere pages of Elphinstone, who modelled his work on the lines adopted by Muslim chroniclers.

The history of the Sultans of Delhi is in an unsatisfactory state. Much preliminary dry research is required for the accurate ascertainment of the chronology and other facts. The subject is not attractive to a large number of students, and many years may elapse before a thoroughly sound account of the Sultanate of Delhi can be written. A foundation of specialized detailed studies is always needed before a concise narrative can be composed with confidence and accuracy. I have not attempted in this volume to probe deeply among the difficulties connected with the histories of the Sultanate, but venture to hope that I may have succeeded in presenting the subject with a certain amount of freshness, especially in dealing with the reign of Muhammad bin Tughlak. Although considerable advance has been made in the study of the history of the Bahmanī empire and other Muslim kingdoms which became independent of Delhi in the fourteenth century, there is plenty of room for further investigation. The chapters on the subject in this volume are based on the examination of various and sometimes conflicting authorities. The story of the extensive Hindu empire of Vijayanagar (1336–1565) has been largely elucidated by the labours of Mr. Sewell, whose excellent work has been continued and in certain matters corrected by several authors of Indian birth. In these days some of the best historical research is done by Indian scholars, a fact which has resulted in a profound change in the presentation of the history of their land. The public addressed by a modern historian differs essentially in composition and character from that addressed by Elphinstone or Mill.

The true history of the Mogul dynasty is only beginning to be known. The story of Bābur, Humāyūn, and Akbar has been illuminated by the researches of Mr. and Mrs. Henry Beveridge, and the study of Akbar's life by the author of this volume includes much novel matter. The interesting reign of Jahāngīr has been badly handled in the current books, Elphinstone's included. The publication of a good version of that emperor's authentic *Memoirs*, and the use of the forgotten third volume of Du Jarric's great work, not to speak of minor advantages, have enabled me to give an abbreviated account of Jahāngīr's reign, which, so far as it goes, may fairly claim to be nearer to the truth than any narrative yet printed.

The reign of Shāhjahān, prior to the war of succession, still awaits critical study, based on the original authorities; but my treatment of the material available will be found to present a certain amount of novelty. The long and difficult reign of Aurangzēb is being discussed by Professor Jadunāth Sarkār with adequate care and learning. His work, so far as it has been published, is an indispensable authority. The dreary history of the later Moguls has been considerably elucidated in the monographs by Irvine and other works by specialists.

The British Period. James Mill's famous work, the *History of British India,* published between 1806 and 1818, brought together for the first time, to use the author's words, 'a history of that part of the British transactions, which have had an immediate relation to India'. Mill's book, notwithstanding its well-known faults, will always be valuable for reference. But it is a hundred years old, and much has happened since it was written. A history of the British period, whether long or short, must now be planned on somewhat different lines, and must include at least the whole of the nineteenth century.

No really satisfactory work on the period exists. The reason perhaps is that the material is too vast to be handled properly. The absence of any first class work on a large scale renders impossible at present the preparation of a condensed history capable of satisfying the ideals of an author or the requirements of skilled critics. The composition of a sound, large work on the subject would be more than sufficient occupation for a long life. A writer who aims only at producing a readable, reasonably accurate, and up-to-date general history of India within the limits of a single volume, must be content to do his best with so much of the over-abundant material as he has leisure to master.

Changed methods. It will be apparent from the foregoing summary review of the present condition of Indian historical studies, that the writer of a comparatively short history, while enjoying various advantages denied to his predecessors even a few years ago, is not at present in a position to supply a uniformly authentic and digested narrative in all the sections of his work. In some fields the ground has been thoroughly, or at any rate, laboriously cultivated, whereas in others, it has been but lightly scratched by the plough of investigation.

The value and interest of history depend largely on the degree in which the present is illuminated by the past. Our existing conditions differ so radically from those which prevailed in the times of our grandfathers and great-grandfathers, and our positive knowledge of the facts of the past has increased so enormously that a new book on Indian history—even though avowedly compressed—must be composed in a new spirit, as it is addressed to a new audience. Certain it is that the history of India does not begin with the battle of Plassey, as some people think it ought to begin, and that a sound, even if not profound knowledge of the older history will always be a valuable aid in the attempt to solve the numerous problems of modern India.

Authorities

The references here given for pre-Muhammadan history are merely supplementary to those in *E. H. I.*[3] (1914). The easiest book on systems of chronology, suitable for the use of ordinary people, is the *Book of Indian Eras*, by Sir Alexander Cunningham (Calcutta, Thacker, Spink, and Co., 1883). Chronological lists of events are given in *The Chronology of India from the Earliest Times to the Beginning of the Sixteenth Century*, by C. Mabel Duff (Mrs. W. R. Rickmers), Constable, Westminster, 1899; a good book, no longer quite up to date; and in *The Chronology of Modern India for four hundred years from the close of the fifteenth century* (A.D. 1494–1894), by J. Burgess (Grant, Edinburgh, 1913).

For the ancient musical score inscription, of about seventh century A.C. on a rock at Kudimiya-malai in the Pudukottai State, see *Ep. Ind.*, xii, 226.

The extremely ancient Sohgaura copper-plate, perhaps about half a century prior to Asoka, was edited and described by Bühler (*Vienna Or. J.*, vol. x (1896), p. 138; and also in *Proc. A. S. B.*, 1894); but the document needs further elucidation.

The excavations at Taxila, which are likely to continue for many years, have been described in preliminary reports, e.g., in *J. R. A. S.*, 1915, p. 116. See also *J. P. H. S.*, the *Archaeol. S. Reports*, and *A Guide to Taxila* (1918).

For historical allusions in Tamil literature the student may consult M. Srinivasa Aiyangar, *Tamil Studies* (Madras, 1914); and Prof. S. Krishnaswami Aiyangar, *Ancient India* (London, Luzac, 1911; and Madras, S.P.C.K. Depository).

Tod may be read most conveniently in the Popular Edition (2 vols., Routledge, 1914). An annotated edition, prepared by Mr. William Crooke, is ready, but held up by war conditions. The *Mackenzie MSS.* were catalogued by H. H. Wilson (1828; and Madras reprint, 1882). Probably the best small book on the British Period to the Mutiny is *India, History to the End of the E. I. Co.*, by P. E. Roberts (Clarendon Press, 1916), in which India Office MS. records have been utilized.

BOOK I

ANCIENT INDIA

CHAPTER 1

Prehistoric India ; the elements of the population.

Antiquity of man. Man has existed on the earth for a time beyond the possibility of computation, but certainly to be estimated in hundreds of thousands rather than in thousands of years. By far the greater part of the long story of the 'ascent of man' is and always must remain unknown. The extreme limit of human tradition as preserved in Egypt may be placed roughly at 5000 B.C. or 7,000 years from the present day. Beyond that limit nothing can be clearly discerned, nor is any trustworthy estimate of date practicable. Indian tradition does not go back so far as that of Egypt and Babylonia. Evidence, however, exists that certain parts of India were occupied by human beings at a time immensely remote, when the hippopotamus and other strange beasts of which no memory remains dwelt in Indian forests and waters.

Palaeolithic or 'quartzite' men. The pleasant belief of poets that primitive man enjoyed in an earthly paradise a golden age free from sin, sorrow, want, and death finds no support from the researches of sober, matter-of-fact science. On the contrary, abundant and conclusive evidence proves that the earliest men, whether in India, Europe, or elsewhere, were rude savages, cowering for shelter under rocks or trees, or roughly housed in caves and huts. They lived by the chase or on jungle produce, and may not have known how to make a fire. They were certainly unable to make pottery and were ignorant of any metal. They were dependent for tools or weapons of all kinds on sticks, stones, and bones. The sticks, of course, have perished, and in India bone implements are rarely found, probably by reason of the white ants. Stone tools, which are imperishable, may be said to constitute the sole memorial of the most ancient Indian men, whose skulls and bones have vanished. They did not construct tombs of any sort. The stone implements, laboriously shaped by chipping into forms suitable for hammering, cutting, boring, and scraping, are found in large numbers in many parts of India, more especially in the districts along the eastern coast. The Madras or Chingleput District presents the 'most numerous and important traces of palaeolithic man known in Southern India'. The chipped stones, which had to serve all purposes of peace or war, are usually pieces of a hard rock called quartzite, but when quartzite was not available other hard minerals were used. The 'quartzite men', as Logan calls them, may possibly have been of the same race as the 'river-drift' men of Europe, who made similar tools; and it is also possible that they may have been preceded in India by some earlier people of whom no trace remains. So far as our positive knowledge extends, or is likely to extend, the 'quartzite men' rank as the oldest inhabitants of India. That stage in the long story of mankind which is marked by the exclusive use of merely chipped stone implements is called technically Palaeolithic, from Greek words meaning 'old stone'.

Neolithic men. In the next stage of human advance men were for a long time still ignorant of metals, except gold, and were consequently obliged to continue using stone tools. They did not altogether give up the use of tools merely chipped, but most of their implements, after the chipping had been completed, were ground, grooved, and polished, and thus converted into highly finished objects of various forms, adapted to divers purposes. That further stage of advance is called Neolithic, from Greek words meaning 'new stone'. The remains of Indian neolithic man are far more abundant than those of his palaeolithic forerunner, and have been noted in most provinces. They can be studied to special advantage in the Bellary District, Madras, where Foote discovered the site of an ancient factory, with tools in every stage of manufacture. The neolithic people used pottery, at first hand-made, and later, turned on the potter's wheel. They kept domestic animals, cultivated the land, and were in a state of civilization far above that of palaeolithic man. Several authors suppose that the neolithic folk were not descended from the palaeolithic, and that the two periods were separated by a gap of many centuries or millenniums. That theory, although supported by certain observed facts, is improbable, because gaps rarely occur in nature, and there is little reason to suppose that 'a break in the chain of humanity' ever occurred. The seeming gap probably is to be explained by the imperfection of the record and our consequent ignorance. The neolithic people certainly were the ancestors of the users of metal tools and thus of a large proportion of the existing Indian population. Ample proof exists that the transition from stone to metal was ordinarily gradual, and that both materials often were used side by side. The early metal forms are close copies of the stone forms.

Burial and cremation. While the 'quartzite men' presumably were content to leave their dead to be devoured by the beasts, the neolithic people buried theirs and constructed tombs. In Europe sepulchres of neolithic age are extremely numerous, and commonly of the 'megalithic' kind, that is to say, built with huge blocks and slabs of stone arranged so as to form a chamber for the deceased. In India graves of the neolithic period seem to be surprisingly rare, perhaps because they have not been sought. In fact, the only clearly recorded examples appear to be those found by Cockburn in the Mirzāpur District, U.P., where the bodies interred in deep graves lay extended north and south on stone slabs. The tombs were surrounded by stone circles. The Indian megalithic tombs, of which hundreds have been noted in the peninsula, usually contain iron objects and may be assigned to the Early Iron Age. Similar tombs containing stone implements only do not seem to be recorded. Many prehistoric cemeteries exist in the Tinnevelly District along the course of the Tāmraparni river, the most ancient seat of the pearl and chank or conch-shell fishery. The largest covers an area of 114 acres, a fact which implies the former existence of a dense population. The bodies were interred in great earthenware jars. The peculiarities of the Tinnevelly interments suggest many problems as yet unsolved.

Burial urn, Tinnevelly.

Burial preceded cremation or burning of the dead in most countries, and India appears to conform to that general rule. The Hindu preference for cremation, which has been established for many centuries, seems to be a result of Indo-Aryan Brahmanical influence.

Mining and trade. The connexion between the early settlements on the Tāmraparni river and the pearl fishery is not an isolated fact. The position of the neolithic and early iron age settlements of both Europe and Asia was largely determined by the facilities offered for mining and for trade in articles specially valued. Professor Elliot Smith rightly affirms that the coincidence in the distribution of the megalithic monuments of Europe and Asia with that of mining centres is

> 'far too exact to be due to mere chance. Ancient miners in search of metals or precious stones, or in other cases pearl-fishers, had in every case established camps to exploit these varied sources of wealth; and the megalithic monuments represent their tombs and temples.' [1]

The extraordinary graves in Tinnevelly may be those of foreign colonists who settled there for trading purposes, and continued to reside for centuries. Gold-mining was equally attractive to the ancient men, who knew the use of gold long before they acquired a knowledge of copper or iron for the purpose of making tools. A late neolithic settlement, for instance, existed at Maski in the Nizam's Dominions, where the old gold-miners' shafts are the deepest in the world. The mines probably were still worked in the days of Asoka (240 B. C.), who recorded one of his edicts on a rock at Maski.[2] Similar connexions between other Indian

[1] *Manchester Memoirs*, vol. 60, part 1, 1915, p. 29 of reprint.

[2] *The Foote Collection of Indian Prehistoric and Protohistoric Antiquities*, Madras, 1916, vol. ii, pp. 29, 125. The inscription has been published in a separate memoir (1915) by the Hyderabad Archaeological Survey.

prehistoric settlements and mines or fisheries will be detected when attention is directed to the subject. The investigation of the prehistoric remains of India has not gone far as yet.

Iron age ; copper age. In southern India stone tools were superseded directly by iron, without any intermediate step. The time when iron became the ordinary material of tools and weapons is called the Iron or Early Iron Age. In northern India the case is different. There the metal first used for tools, harpoons, swords, and spear-heads was copper, practically pure. Copper implements and weapons, often of peculiar forms, but sometimes closely resembling those found in Ireland, have been discovered in large numbers in the Central Provinces, Chutiā Nāgpur, old beds of the Ganges near Cawnpore, and elsewhere. Silver objects are associated with them, but no iron.[1] Probably copper tools were in use when the *Rigveda* hymns were composed, but commentators differ. Iron certainly was known to the authors of the *Atharvaveda*, a very ancient book, and was in common use in 500 B.C. We may safely assume that the metal was utilized in northern India from at least 1000 B.C. It may have been introduced very much earlier, and from Babylonia. The earliest of the copper tools may well be as old as 2000 B.C. In southern India the discovery or introduction of iron may have occurred much later and quite independently.

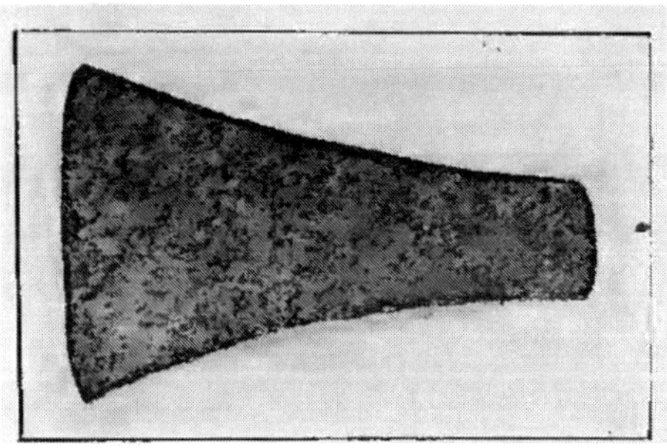

Copper axe (celt).

No bronze age in India. In several extensive regions of Europe a Bronze Age intervened between the Neolithic and the Early Iron Periods. Bronze is an alloy of copper and tin, usually made with about nine parts of copper to one of tin. It is much harder than pure copper and consequently better adapted for the manufacture of tools and weapons. No bronze age can be traced in India. The few Indian implements made of bronze, only five or six in number, which are of early date, vary much in the percentage of tin which they contain, and may have been either imported or made as experiments. It is certain that tools or arms made of bronze never came into general use. The numerous bronze objects found in the megalithic tombs of southern India and in the Tinnevelly urns are either ornamental or articles of domestic use, such as bowls. They are never implements or weapons. Many of the bronze objects seem to have been imported. In modern India alloys of copper and zinc are more commonly used than the alloys made with tin.

Earliest inhabitants of India. In prehistoric times communication between the north and south must have been difficult and rare. The people of either region presumably knew little or nothing of those in the other, and the two populations probably were

[1] The ancients knew methods of hardening copper, hammering being one, and an admixture of iron another.

totally different in blood. Even now they are very distinct in their ideas and customs, although physical characters have become blended. Peninsular India, built up of the most ancient rocks, has been permanent land for uncounted millions of years. The plains of northern India, on the contrary, were formed ages later by the gradual filling up of a sea with material brought down from the highlands of Asia. Although the sea had been filled up long before the appearance of man on the earth, the surface of the regions now forming the basins of the Indus and Ganges must have taken thousands of years to become fit for human habitation.

COPPER HARPOON.

It is highly probable that the earliest inhabitants of India, whoever they may have been, settled on the ancient high and dry land of the peninsula, and not in the plains of the north. 'Quartzite man', as we have seen, is to be traced for the most part to the south of the Narbadā. Numbers of queer tribes with extraordinary customs, hidden away in different parts of the peninsular area, look like the descendants of the true 'aborigines' or earliest people. Northern India presents fewer such specimens, but certain parts of that region, especially the Āravallis and the Salt Range, are composed of primaeval rocks like the peninsula, and undoubtedly were dry land in a very early stage of the earth's history. In those parts certain tribes now in being may be the descendants of 'aborigines' as ancient, or almost as ancient, as those of the peninsula.

North and South. It is desirable to understand and remember that the distinction between the peoples of the north and those of the south goes back far beyond the dawn of history. The peninsula was isolated by reason of its position and ordinarily could not receive either new inhabitants or novel institutions except by sea. The unceasing immigration of strangers by land into northern India, which has made the population there the mixture which it is, did not affect the south, which was shut off by the wide and almost impenetrable barrier of hill and forest, represented by the Narbadā, the Vindhya, and the Sātpura ranges. It is worth while to dwell upon the natural separation of the north from the south even in the most remote ages, because the roots of the present go down deep into the past to a depth far beyond measurement. The incomplete unity of India discussed in the first section of the Introduction depends mainly on the diffusion through the reluctant south of the Hindu ideas of the north, a process which probably had not begun earlier than 1000 B.C. Its slow and gradual progress forms no small element in the real inner history of India, that history which never has been and hardly can be reduced to writing. The conflict between the Dravidian ideas of the south and the Indo-Aryan ideas of the north, which has lasted for three thousand years more or less, still continues, although on the surface the victory of the north seems to be complete.

The modern population mixed. In my judgement it is absolutely impossible to decide who were the earliest inhabitants of India, either in the north or south, or to ascertain whence they came. Nor can we say what their bodily type was. The modern population of India almost everywhere is far too mixed to admit of the disentangling of distinct races each of a well-marked physical type. In the United Provinces of Agra and Oudh, where I served, the low-caste Chamār or leather-dresser and even the sweeper (Bhangī, &c.) often is handsome, and better looking than many Brahmans. I do not believe that anything worth knowing is to be learned by measuring the skulls or otherwise noting the physical characters of individuals in a population of such mixed origin. So in England it often happens that in one family, one member will be long-headed (dolicho-cephalic) and another short-headed (brachy-cephalic). The absurdity of classing two brothers as belonging to distinct races because their heads differ in shape is obvious. The inferences drawn by anthropologists in India often have been quite as absurd. The mixture of races on Indian soil was going on for countless ages before any history was recorded, and it is hopeless now to unravel the different lines of descent.

Two main types: the fair type. When India as a whole is looked at broadly, without theorizing, anybody can see that the population comprises two main physical types. The tall, fair-skinned, long-nosed, and often handsome type is chiefly found in northern India among the upper Hindu castes and the Muhammadans. It is well exemplified by the Brahmans of Kashmīr, who may be of tolerably pure Indo-Aryan descent. The type occurs in southern India among the Nambudri Brahmans of Malabar, whose ancestors came from the north. The ancestry of the tall, fair people in fact is known to a large extent. They are mostly, or perhaps wholly, descended, with more or less intermixture of other strains, from some or other of the innumerable strangers from the north-west who are known to have poured into the basins of the Indus and Ganges during the last four thousand years. Where such immigration has not taken place the type does not occur. Its appearance occasionally among low-caste and outcaste people probably is due to irregular unions.

The short, dark type. The second type, short in stature, often ugly in face, snub-nosed, and dark-skinned, is found in almost all the jungle tribes occupying the regions built of primaeval rocks, and to a very large extent among the low-caste population of the plains. We may feel assured that the people of that type represent and in great measure are actually descended from the neolithic peoples, or perhaps even from the palaeolithic. Some of the isolated jungle tribes may have preserved their descent comparatively pure, with little admixture of outside blood. The people of the peninsula originally may have been and probably were, as previously said, originally quite distinct from those of the north, but it seems to be impossible to draw any definite line of physical, that is to say, bodily distinction between the bulk of the inhabitants of the two regions at the present time.

The modified Mongolian type. A third and less prominent element of the population is now found chiefly in the Himalayan region. The Tibetans may be taken as the type. The Burmese and Gūrkhas are more or less similar to them in appearance. All those nations and several other communities exhibit modified forms of the yellow-tinted Mongolian type of the Chinese, and usually are beardless. The evidence of ancient sculptures, as seen at Barhut (Bharhut) and Sānchī, combined with that of certain institutions, indicates clearly that eighteen hundred or two thousand years ago the Tibetan type was much more prominent in the plains of northern India than it is at the present day. In the *Mahābhārata*, for instance, we find Draupadī married to five brothers at once. That kind of marriage, technically called polyandry, still is a Tibetan and Himalayan custom, and is absolutely opposed to Aryan principles.[1] The famous Lichchhavis of Vaisāli in Tirhūt administered criminal justice on Tibetan lines. Many other proofs might be adduced to show that the Himalayan type was and is a considerable factor in the formation of the mixed population of northern India, especially in Bengal and Bihār.

Many arrivals of the fair type. The tall, fair people, as has been said, clearly are descended from immigrants from the north-west, belonging to diverse races, who resembled more or less the Afghans of the border, the Persians, and the Turks of Central Asia. No man can tell when such people began to pour into the tempting plains of India, but the process certainly was going on several thousand years ago and continued with intervals on a large scale until the reign of Bābur in the sixteenth century. Since that time the inflow of strangers from the north-west has been small.

The Indo-Aryans. The earliest invaders or settlers about whom anything at all definite is known were the people of the *Rigveda* hymns, who called themselves Aryans, and are conveniently designated as Indo-Aryans in order to distinguish them from their brethren who remained at the other side of the passes. They separated themselves sharply from the non-Aryan dark-skinned early inhabitants of India, and were no doubt tall and fair. They

[1] The term 'phratrogamy' might be coined to denote the form of polyandry which requires all the husbands to be brethren. Polyandry, both in the 'phratrogamic' and the unrestricted form, was prevalent in the highlands of Ceylon until checked by legislation in 1859. The practice may still exist in a quiet way (*Papers on the Custom of Polyandry as practised in Ceylon*, Colombo, Government Printer, 1899).

were akin to the Iranians or Persians, who also called themselves Aryans. It is certain that they slowly worked their way across the Panjāb and down the courses of the Indus and Ganges. Probably they advanced as far as Prayāg (Allahabad) at a tolerably early date, but Bihār and Bengal long continued to be reckoned as non-Aryan countries. The peninsula was not affected at all by the early Indo-Aryan movements. The people there went on their own way and developed a distinct Dravidian form of civilization. The later conversion of southern India to Hinduism was the result of 'peaceful penetration' by missionaries or small colonies, and was not a consequence of the southward march of Indo-Aryan tribes. The amount of Aryan blood in the people to the south of the Narbadā is extremely small, in fact, negligible.

Lasting effect of Indo-Aryan movements. The Indo-Aryan movement must have continued for a long time. The guesses of some of the best European scholars place it somewhere between 2400 and 1500 B.C., but they are only guesses, and no near approach to accuracy is possible. Perhaps 2000 B.C. may be taken as a mean date.[1] It is a strange fact that the Vedic Indo-Aryans, the earliest known swarm of immigrants, have stamped an indelible mark on the whole country from the Himālaya to Cape Comōrin. Modern Hinduism, however much it may differ from the creed and social usages of the ancient Rishis, undoubtedly has its roots in the institutions and literature of the Vedic Indo-Aryans. Plenty of other strangers have come in since, but none of them, not even the Muslims, have produced effects comparable in magnitude with those resulting from the Indo-Aryan settlements made three or four thousand years ago.

The Greeks and the Sakas. Nothing positive is known concerning any influx of foreigners which may have taken place during many centuries after the close of the Indo-Aryan movement, except the comparatively small settlements of Greek origin in

[1] Professor Macdonell inclines to later dates and suggests 1500 B.C. as the earliest limit for the Vedic literature. The estimates which assume considerably earlier dates seem to me more probable. B. G. Tilak goes further than other scholars of reputation, and on astronomical grounds argues temperately that the *Aditi*, or pre-Orion period, the earliest in the Aryan civilization, may be roughly placed between 6000 and 4000 B.C.; that the Orion period, from about 4000 to 2500 B.C., was the most important in the history of Aryan civilization, the separation of the Parsees having taken place between 3000 and 2500 B.C.; that the *Taittirīya Samhitā* and several of the *Brāhmanas* should be assigned to the third period, from 2500 to 1400 B.C., during which the hymns had already become antiquated and unintelligible; that the fourth and last period of the old Sanskrit literature extended from 1400 to 500 B.C., and saw the composition of the *Sūtras* and the evolution of the philosophical literature. I do not possess the knowledge of either astronomy or Vedic texts which would qualify me to pass judgement on Mr. Tilak's startling propositions as expounded in *Orion, or Researches into the Antiquity of the Vedas*, Ashtekar & Co., Poona, 1916. So far as I understand the matter his dates are carried back too far.

the Panjāb and north-western frontier consequent on Alexander's invasion in 326 B.C. and the existence of the Bactrian kingdom and its offshoots between 246 B.C. and A.D. 50. The next extensive immigration of which any definite knowledge has survived is that of the Sakas, which began in the second century B.C. The term Saka was used by the Indians in a vague way to denote all foreigners from the other side of the passes, without nice distinctions of race or tribe. It may have included both ugly, narrow-eyed Mongols, and handsome races like the Turks, who resemble the Aryans in physique. The Sakas formed kingdoms in the Panjāb, at Mathurā, and in the Kāthiāwār peninsula.

The Yueh-chi. In the first century after Christ another nomad tribe from Central Asia called the Yueh-chi descended upon the plains of northern India. Their leading clan, the Kushāns, founded a great empire which extended southwards apparently as far as the Narbadā. The Kushāns appear to have been big fair-complexioned men, probably of Turkī race, and possibly akin to the Iranian or Persian Aryans. The Saka and Yueh-chi conquests must have introduced a large element of foreign blood into the Indian population. Obscure indications exist of Iranian invasions in the third century of the Christian era, but nothing definite has been ascertained about them, if they really occurred.

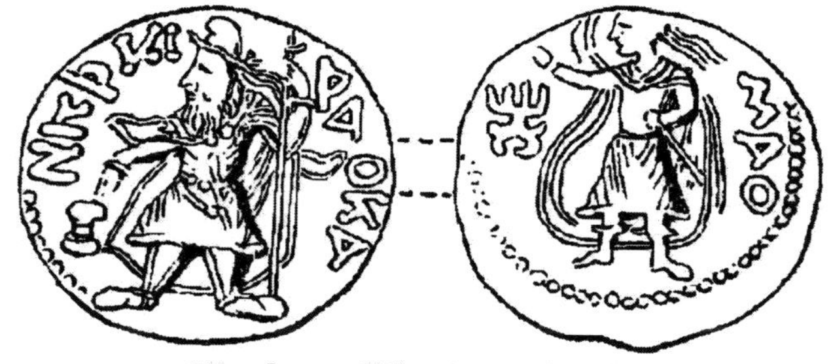

Kushān (Kanishka) coin.

The Hūnas or Huns. There is no doubt that during the fifth and sixth centuries great multitudes of fierce folk from the Central Asian steppes swooped down on both Persia and India. Those invaders are called by the Indians Hūnas, or in English Huns, a term used in a general sense like the earlier term Sakas, to cover a mass of various tribes.[1] Other Huns who invaded Europe are known to have been hideous creatures of the Mongolian kind; but the assailants of India are distinguished as Ephthalites or White Huns, a name which may imply that they were fair people like the Turks. Many of the Rājpūt castes or clans, as well as the Jāts, Gūjars, and certain other existing communities, are descended either from the Hūnas or from allied hordes which arrived about the same time. The appearance of the existing castes so descended indicates that their foreign ancestors must have been mostly of the tall, fair, good-looking type. The population of the Panjāb and the United Provinces is free from Mongolian features except in the sub-Himalayan and Himalayan regions.

The Hun irruptions mark a distinct epoch in the history of northern India, the significance of which will be explained later.

[1] A Brahman author, writing about A.D. 1600, applied the term to the Portuguese.

They are mentioned prominently in this place because they contributed some of the best elements to the population.

Type of Muhammadan settlers. The last movement which introduced a large new class of recruits to the Indian population was that of the Muhammadans, beginning with the inroads of the Arabs at the commencement of the eighth century and ending with the establishment of the Mogul dynasty in the sixteenth century. Subsequent Musalmān immigration has been on a small scale. The Muslim invaders and settlers, other than the Arab conquerors of Sind, belonged to various Asiatic races, including a certain number of narrow-eyed, yellow-tinted, beardless Mongols. But the majority were collected from nations or tribes of better appearance, and were tall, good-looking, fair-complexioned, bearded men. They comprised Iranian Persians akin to the Indo-Aryans, Turks, Afghans of many varieties, and sundry peoples of mixed descent. The admixture of Mongol blood having been overborne by the other elements has left little trace in the features of modern Indian Muslims. The effect of the immigration on the whole has been to increase materially the proportion of tall, fair-complexioned people in the country. The physical type of the Muhammadan immigrants was far more like that of the Indo-Aryan Brahmans than it was to the dark 'aboriginal' type indigenous in India.

Rapid spread of Islām. The rapidity of the spread of Islām, the religion of Muhammad, and the dramatic suddenness with which the adherents of his creed rose to a position of dominant sovereignty constitute one of the marvels, or it might be said the miracles of history. No cut-and-dry explanation that can be offered is felt to account adequately for the astounding facts. But history records not a few other unexplained marvels, and we must be content to acknowledge that many things in the past, as in the present, pass man's understanding.

The prophet Muhammad, a native of Mecca, was more than fifty years of age before he attained any considerable success. He believed himself to be the divinely appointed messenger of a revelation destined to supersede the Jewish and Christian religions, as well as the rude paganism of his countrymen. His fellow citizens at Mecca were so hostile that in A.D. 622 he was obliged to quit his birthplace and take refuge at Medina. That event, renowned as the Flight, or Hijra, is the epoch of the Muhammadan Hijrī Era, vulgarly called the Hegira.[1] The remaining ten years of his life sufficed to make him substantially the sovereign of Arabia and the accepted Prophet of the Arabs. Soon after his death in A.D. 632 his successors, the early Khalīfs ('Caliphs'), found themselves in conflict with the mighty Persian and Byzantine empires. Nothing could withstand the furious enthusiasm of the

[1] Muhammadan dates are usually designated as A.H. (*anno hegirae*). For example, A.H. 1335=A.D. 1916–17, from October to October. The Hijrī year is lunar, of about 354 days, and so is 11 days shorter than the solar year.

Arabs from the desert, beneath whose attack ancient thrones tottered and fell.

Within the brief space of eighty years from the Prophet's death his Arab followers had become the masters, not only of Arabia, but of Persia, Syria, western Turkistan, Sind, Egypt, and southern Spain. They carried their new religion with them, and either imposed it on their opponents at the point of the sword, or compelled them to ransom their lives by heavy payments.

Islām in the borderlands. The Indian borderlands soon attracted the attention of the Khalīfs. The Arabs reached the coast of Makrān as early as A.D. 643. The conquest of Sind was effected by Muhammad bin Kāsim in A.D. 712, and thenceforward for centuries that country remained under Arab rule. Kābul was subdued or made tributary at a later date. From the beginning of the eighth century many Arabs and Muslims of other nations must have settled in Sind and the neighbouring countries, effecting a marked change in the character of the population. But India proper remained substantially unaffected, although Arab traders occasionally visited the western kingdoms for business purposes. The Indian Rājās rarely troubled themselves about events taking place to the west of the Hakrā river, then the boundary between Sind and Hind.[1]

Islām in India proper. The annexation of the Panjāb to the Ghaznī kingdom about A. D. 1020 by Sultan Mahmūd necessarily involved extensive settlement of Muslim strangers in that province, although the rest of India continued to be free from their presence. From the closing years of the twelfth century, when Muhammad of Ghōr began the systematic conquest of the country, a constant stream of Muslim immigrants continued to flow in; and during the period of the growth of the Sultanate of Delhi newcomers arrived without ceasing. During the decline of the Sultanate from 1340 to 1526 the immigration must have diminished, but in the latter year it received a fresh impetus from the victories of Bābur. During the next two centuries a certain number of Muhammadans from beyond the border effected a lodgement, although the total was not very great. The older colonies, however, multiplied, crowds of converts from Hinduism were made, and intermarriages between the old and new Muslims took place. The tendency of the Muslim population is to increase, its fertility being superior to that of the Hindus. The immigrant Muhammadans, although thoroughly naturalized, retain their distinctness and never become merged in the Hindu majority, as their predecessors the Sakas, Hūnas, and the rest were absorbed. The reason is to be found in the definite character of the Muslim creed resting on scriptures of known date, and consisting essentially of only two doctrines, the unity of God and the divine mission of Muhammad. That simple creed inspires intense devotion and

[1] The Hakrā, which finally dried up in the eighteenth century, used to flow through the Bahāwalpur State and the region which is now the Sind desert.

offers unbroken resistance to the seductions of Hinduism, although Indo-Muhammadan social practice is affected considerably by its surroundings. The looser beliefs of the early immigrants from Central Asia were not strong enough to withstand the subtle influence of the Brahmanical environment. The Shamanism of the nomad invaders, like the demon-worship of the Dravidians, yielded before the attractive force of the Hindu system, so that each successive wave of pre-Muhammadan foreigners quickly melted away in the ocean of caste.

Smaller foreign communities. Since the fifteenth century a considerable population of mixed Indo-European blood, originating from unions of Portuguese, English, and other Europeans with Indian women, has grown up, which forms an important element in the population of the great cities, the Bombay Konkan, and the settlements on the lower Himalayan ranges.

The Jews, Parsees, Armenians, and certain other small foreign communities maintain their isolation so strictly that they hardly affect the racial character of the general population.

Language no proof of race. Sanskrit, with its derivative vernaculars; the old Persian, or Zend language; Greek, Latin, German, English, and many other European tongues, form a well-defined group or family of languages which is designated either as Indo-Germanic or as Aryan. Many authors have shown a tendency to assume that the various peoples who speak Aryan tongues must be of Aryan race, connected one with the other more or less closely by ties of blood. That assumption is wholly unwarranted. Community of language is no proof of community of blood. The population of India, as we have seen, comprises extremely various elements, descended from all sorts of people who formerly spoke all sorts of languages. In the north, for instance, no trace remains of the Central Asian tongues spoken by the diverse tribes comprised under the terms Saka, Hūna, or Yueh-chi. The descendants of those people now speak Hindī and other languages closely related to Sanskrit. Similar cases may be observed all over the world. Languages become extinct and are replaced by others spoken by races whose position gives them an advantage. Thus, in Great Britain, the Cornish language is absolutely extinct, and the Cornish people, who are of different race from the English, now speak nothing but English.

Aryan ideas and institutions have shown marvellous power and vitality in all parts of India, but the proportion of Aryan blood in the veins of the population, which is small almost everywhere, is non-existent in some provinces.

Languages. The most important family of Indian languages, the Aryan, comprises all the principal languages of northern and western India, Hindī, Bengālī, Marāthī, Gujarātī, and many others, descended from ancient vernaculars or Prākrits, closely akin both to the Vedic and to the later literary forms of Sanskrit.

The family or group of tongues second in importance is the Dravidian in the peninsula, comprising Tamil, Telugu, Malayālam,

Kanarese, and Tulu, besides some minor tongues. Both Tamil and Telugu have rich literatures. The Tamil is the principal and perhaps the oldest language of the group. The grammar and structure of the Dravidian speech differ wholly from the Aryan type. The most ancient Tamil literature, dating from the early centuries of the Christian era, or even earlier, was composed on Dravidian lines and independent of Sanskrit models. The later literature in all the languages has been largely influenced by Brahmanical ideas and diction. The linguistic family is called Dravidian because Dravida was the ancient name of the Tamil country in the far south. In fact, Tamil is really the same word as the adjective Drāvida. Three other families of languages, namely, the Munda, the Mon-Khmēr, and the Tibeto-Chinese, are represented on Indian soil, but as they possess little or no literature, and are mostly spoken by rude, savage, or half-civilized tribes, it is unnecessary to discuss their peculiarities. The speakers of those tongues have had small influence on the course of history.

The Indo-Aryan movement. The Indo-Aryans, after they had entered the Panjāb—the 'land of the five rivers', or 'of the seven rivers' according to an ancient reckoning—travelled generally in a south-easterly direction. They consequently called the south *dakshina*, or 'right-hand', a word familiar in its English corruption as 'the Deccan'. The larger part of the tribes crossed the Panjāb and then moved along the courses of the Ganges and Jumna, but some sections at an early period had advanced a considerable distance down the Indus, while others, at a later date, apparently marched eastward along the base of the mountains into Mithilā or Tirhūt. While resident in the Panjāb the strangers had not yet become Hindus, but were only Hindus in the making. The distinctive Brahmanical system appears to have been evolved, after the Sutlaj had been passed, in the country to the north of Delhi. The apparently small tract between the rivers Sarasvatī and Drishadvatī, which it is difficult to identify with precision, is specially honoured by Manu as Brahmāvarta, 'the land of the gods'; the less-exalted title of Brahmarshi-desa, 'the land of divine sages', being given to the larger region comprising Brahmāvarta or Kurukshetra, roughly equivalent to the tract about Thānēsar, with the addition of Matsya or eastern Rājputāna, Panchāla, or the Doāb between the Ganges and Jumna, and Surasena, or the Mathurā district.[1]

[1] The difficulty in precise identification of the Sarasvatī and Drishadvatī is due to the extensive changes in the course of the rivers of northern India which are known to have occurred. Modern maps are utterly misleading, and it is impossible to construct maps of the ancient river system for any time preceding the Muhammadan invasions. The following passage may be commended to the attention of careful students: 'It is, however, a reasonable conjecture that within the period of history the Sutlej united with the Sarasvatī and Ghaggar to form the great river [*scil.* Hakrā] which once flowed into the Indus through Bahāwalpur, and that then Brahmāvarta was a Doāb [space between rivers] which

When the legal treatise ascribed to Manu had assumed its present shape, perhaps about A.D. 200 or earlier, the whole space between the Himālaya and the Vindhyas from sea to sea was recognized as Āryāvarta, or 'Aryan territory'. The advance thus indicated evidently was a slow business and occupied a long time. The dark-skinned inhabitants of the country subdued by the invaders were called Dasyus and by other names. They are now represented generally by the lower castes in the plains and by certain tribes in hilly regions.

Aryan penetration of the south. Although there is no reason to believe that any large Indo-Aryan tribal body ever marched into the peninsula, which was well protected by the broad belt of hills and forests marked by the Narbadā river and the Sātpura and Vindhya ranges, the peaceful penetration of the Deccan by Indo-Aryan emissaries began many centuries before the Christian era. Tradition credits the Vedic Rishi Agastya, or a namesake of his, with the introduction of Aryan ideas and institutions into the Dravidian south. Probably the chief line of communication was along the eastern coast, and certainly the propagation of the new ideas was effected by Brahmans. The obscure story of the gradual advance of the caste system and other Indo-Aryan institutions in India to the south of the Narbadā has not yet been thoroughly investigated, and it is impossible to discuss the subject in these pages.

Distinct Dravidian civilization. When the Brahmans succeeded in making their way into the kingdoms of the peninsula, including the realms of the Āndhras, Cheras, Cholas, and Pāndyas, they found a civilized society, not merely a collection of rude barbarian tribes. The Dravidian religion and social customs differed widely from those of northern India. Caste was unknown, as it now is in Burma, and the religion is described as demon-worship. The original demons have since been adopted by the Brahmans, given new names, and identified with orthodox Hindu gods and goddesses. The Hindu theory that mankind is divided into four *varnas*, or groups of castes—Brahman, Kshatriya, Vaisya, and Sūdra—was wholly foreign to the southerners. To this day Kshatriyas and Vaisyas do not exist among them.[1] The laws of marriage and inheritance also differed completely from those of the Brahmans. Even now, when Hinduism, with its strict caste rules and its recognized system of law, has gained the mastery, the old and quite different Dravidian ideas may be traced in a thousand directions. The ancient Dravidian alphabet called Vatteluttu, of Semitic origin, is wholly distinct from any of the northern alphabets. Tradition as recorded in the ancient Tamil literature indicates that from very remote times wealthy cities existed in the south and that many of the refinements and luxuries

might be compared with that of the Ganges and Jumna' (C. Pearson, 'Alexander, Porus, and the Panjāb', in *Ind. Ant.*, vol. xxxiv, 1905, p. 254).

[1] The fact is not affected by the ludicrous efforts of certain castes to obtain recognition as Kshatriyas.

of life were in common use. The good fortune of Tamil Land (*Tamilakam*) in possessing such eagerly desired commodities as gold, pearls, conch-shells, pepper, beryls, and choice cotton goods attracted foreign traders from the earliest ages.[1] Commerce supplied the wealth required for life on civilized lines, and the Dravidians were not afraid to cross the seas. Some day, perhaps, the history of Dravidian civilization may be written by a competent scholar skilled in all the lore and languages required for the study of the subject, but at present the literature concerned with it is too fragmentary, defective, and controversial to permit of condensation. Early Indian history, as a whole, cannot be viewed in true perspective until the non-Aryan institutions of the south receive adequate treatment. Hitherto most historians of ancient India have written as if the south did not exist.

AUTHORITIES

Prehistoric India. V. A. SMITH, 'Prehistoric Antiquities,' chap. iv, vol. ii, *I. G.*, 1908, with a large number of selected references; the first general outline of the subject. R. B. FOOTE, (1) *Catalogue of Prehistoric Antiquities in the Madras Museum*, Madras, 1901; (2) *Indian Prehistoric and Protohistoric Antiquities, Foote Collection*, Madras, 1916, 2 vols.; (3) several articles in *A. S. India, Annual Rep.*, for 1902–3 and 1903–4, and in the *Progress Reports, A. S., Southern Circle*. A. C. LOGAN, *Old Chipped Stones of India*, Calcutta, Thacker, Spink, 1906. The investigation is being continued by the BIHAR AND ORISSA RESEARCH SOCIETY, as well as by the ARCHAEOLOGICAL SOCIETY and the ARCHAEOLOGICAL SURVEY OF HYDERABAD. Occasional articles appear elsewhere, but no general work on Prehistoric India exists. Ample material is available, and a good book on the subject is badly wanted.

Languages. Sir G. GRIERSON, (1) chap. vii in vol. i, *I. G.*, 1907, with ample list of references; (2) *The Languages of India*, Calcutta, 1903, reprinted from *Census Report, India*, 1901; (3) *Linguistic Survey of India*, not yet completed. The work is on a vast scale, and eleven large quarto volumes or parts have appeared. Several more volumes are yet to come.

Dravidian religion. WHITEHEAD, *The Village Gods of South India*, Oxford University Press, 1916; ELMORE, *Dravidian Gods in Modern Hinduism*, Hamilton, N.Y., 1915 (reprinted from University Studies of the University of Nebraska, 1915).

[1] The Tamil Land of early ages was much more extensive than the area in which Tamil is now spoken. It included the Kanarese, Malayālam, and Tulu-speaking countries. Ceylon, too, was in close relations with the Tamil-speaking peoples of the mainland. The jewels and spices of the island may therefore be reckoned among the attractions of Tamil Land. The Telugu-speaking country possessed cotton manufactures and diamond mines.

CHAPTER 2

Literature and Civilization of the Vedic and Epic Periods; the *Purānas*; caste.

Isolation of the oldest literature. The Vedic Indo-Aryans, whose progress has been sketched in bare outline, are known to us through their literature only, which is all, or almost all, so ancient that it cannot be illustrated either by contemporary books or from monuments. No literature in any Indo-European or Aryan language is nearly as old as the hymns of the *Rigveda*, which 'stands quite by itself, high up on an isolated peak of remote antiquity'; and even if some literary fragments from Egypt or Babylonia in languages of different families be as old, they do not help us to understand the Vedic scriptures. No buildings of anything like Vedic age survive in India, nor are there any contemporary material remains, except the copper tools and weapons of the north already mentioned, which may be reasonably assigned to an early stage of the Vedic period. The oldest Indo-Aryan literature, as a rule, must be interpreted by means of itself, and we must be content to learn from it alone what we can discover about the Indo-Aryans whose Rishis composed that literature. External sources of information are almost wholly wanting, but the *Zend-Avesta*, the scriptures of the ancient Iranians or Persians, although not so old as the Veda, contributes illustrative matter of value.

The Veda; faith and science. The oldest literature of the Indo-Aryans is known collectively as Veda, which means 'knowledge'—the best of all knowledge in Hindu eyes. It is also designated in the plural as 'the Vedas', 'the three Vedas', or 'the four Vedas'. Most Hindus accept the whole Veda, forming in itself an enormous literature, as inspired revelation (*sruti*) in opposition to later venerable books classed as traditional learning (*smriti*). But the adherents of the Ārya Samāj, and possibly those of some other sects, allow the rank of revealed matter to the hymns alone, while denying it to the rest of the Veda. The belief that the Vedas were revealed complete as they stand without any process of development seems to be widely held,[1] and means for reconciling such belief with the results of scientific investigation of the documents may not be beyond the powers of human ingenuity. In these pages theories of inspiration will not be further noticed, and the Vedic literature will be treated merely as what it professes to be, the production of individual men, who composed their works at times widely separated and with varying degrees of literary power.

The Veda, regarded as literature, demands from students of humanity the most respectful attention on account of its remote antiquity, its unique character, and the light which it sheds upon

[1] Hopkins (p. 3) quotes the verse:
Na hi chhandānsi kriyante, nityāni chhandānsi;
'Vedic verses are not made, they are eternal.'

the evolution of mankind, especially in India. The *Rigveda*, as Whitney observes, contains 'the germs of the whole after-development of Indian religion and polity'.

Definition of the Veda. Opinions have varied concerning the definition of the Veda. Kautilya, in the *Arthasāstra* ascribed to the fourth century B.C., states that

> 'the three Vêdas, Sāma, Rik, and Yajus, constitute the triple Vedas. These together with Atharvaveda and the Itihāsaveda are known as the Vedas. . . . Purāna, Itivritta (history), Ākhyāyika (tales), Udāharana (illustrative stories), Dharmasāstra, and Arthasāstra are (known by the name) Itihāsa.'[1]

Kautilya's definition is wider than that ordinarily accepted, which excludes the later, although ancient literature comprised by him under the comprehensive term *Itihāsa*. Common usage recognizes four and only four Vedas, namely (1) the *Rigveda*,[2] (2) the *Sāmaveda*, (3) the *Yajurveda*, and (4) the *Atharvaveda*.

The claim of the last named to be included in the canon has not always been recognized, and not long ago it could be said that 'the most influential Brahmans of southern India still refuse to accept the authority of the fourth Veda, and deny its genuineness'.

But for most people the Vedas are four, and must be described as such.

Contents of the Veda. The essential fundamental part of each of the four Vedas is a *samhitā*, or collection of metrical hymns, prayers, spells, or charms, mixed in some cases with prose passages. But certain supplementary writings are also considered by general consent to be actually part of the Vedas, and are regarded by many Hindus as inspired revelation like the *samhitās*. Those supplements written in prose are the *Brāhmanas* and the *Upanishads*. The *Brāhmanas* are theological and ritual treatises designed as manuals of worship and explanations of the *samhitās*. They are of considerably later date than the verses but still very ancient, and in some cases preserve the written accent, which was disused very early. They are the oldest examples of Indo-European or Aryan continuous prose composition. The *Brāhmanas* include certain mystic treatises called *Āranyakas*, or 'Forest-books', supposed to be 'imparted or studied in the solitude of the forest'. The *Upanishads*, exceeding a hundred in number, are philosophical tracts or books, 'which belong to the latest stage of Brāhmana

[1] *Arthasāstra,* revised translation by R. Shama Sastri (Bangalore Government Press, 1915), Book I, chaps. 3, 5, pp. 7, 11. Kautilya, it will be observed, places the *Sāmaveda* first.

[2] The name *Rigveda* is a compound of the words *rich* and *veda*, *ch* becoming *g* by the rules of *sandhi*. *Rich* signifies 'any prayer or hymn in which a deity is praised. As these are mostly in verse, the term becomes also applicable to such passages of any *Veda* as are reducible to measure according to the rules of prosody. The first *Veda*, in Vyāsa's compilation, comprehending most of these texts, is called the *Rigveda*; or as expressed in the Commentary on the Index, "because it abounds in such texts (*rich*)"' (Colebrooke).

literature'. Certain of the *Upanishads* are the parts of the Veda best known to Hindu readers in modern days, as being the foundation of the later and more systematic Vedānta philosophy.

The Sūtras. The *Sūtras*, 'compendious treatises dealing with Vedic ritual on the one hand, and with customary law on the other', are admitted by all to rank only as traditional learning (*smriti*), but they are usually regarded as included in the Veda. They are written in a laboriously compressed style, sometimes approaching the structure of algebraic formulas, unintelligible without the help of authoritative commentaries. Such exaggerated value used to be attached to mere brevity of expression that a *sūtra* writer was supposed to derive as much pleasure from the saving of a short vowel as from the birth of a son. The *Sūtras* comprise the *Srauta*, dealing with the ritual of the greater sacrifices; the *Grihya*, explaining the ceremonial of household worship; and *Dharma*, treating of social and legal usage. The third section is that which mainly concerns the historian, being the foundation of the *Dharmasāstras*, such as the well-known *Laws of Manu*, so called.

Sāma- and Yajurvedas. Having enumerated the principal classes of works usually included in the Veda, we return to the metrical *samhitās* which are the real Veda. Only two need be noticed particularly, because the Sāma- and Yajurvedas are comparatively unimportant. The former is a hymn-book, 'practically of no independent value, for it consists entirely of stanzas (excepting only 75) taken from the *Rigveda* and arranged solely with reference to their place in the Soma sacrifice'. The *Yajurveda*, which also borrows much matter from the *Rigveda* and exists in several forms, is a book of sacrificial prayers, and includes some prose formulas.

The Rigveda samhitā. The *Rigveda* unquestionably is the oldest part of the literature and the most important of the Vedas from the literary point of view. The *samhitā* contains 1,017 (or by another reckoning 1,028) hymns, arranged in ten books, of which the tenth certainly is the latest. The collection about equals in bulk the *Iliad* and *Odyssey* together. Books II-VII, known as the 'family books', because they are attributed to the members of certain families, form 'the nucleus of the *Rigveda*, to which the remaining books were successively added'.

Difficulties of the Vedic hymns. The Vedic hymns present innumerable difficulties to the student. The language and grammar, which differ widely from those of the 'classical' Sanskrit, require profound expert investigation before the verses can be compelled to yield sense so as to permit the text to be construed. Even when a literal version in more or less grammatical English has been produced, the meaning behind the words often eludes the translator. The ideas of the Rishis are so remote from those of the modern world that the most learned Sanskritist, whether Indian or foreign, may fail to grasp them. Interpretations consequently differ to an enormous extent, and after all possible has been said and done much remains obscure. Subject to such inherent difficulties and to necessary limitations of space, I will try to give the reader some slight notion of the contents of the *Rigveda* and *Atharvaveda* hymnals, to indicate the nature of the poets' religion, and to draw a faint sketch of the social condition of the Indo-Aryans.

The poetry of the Veda. Professor Macdonell observes that

'by far the greater part of the poetry of the *Rigveda* consists of religious lyrics, only the tenth [and latest] book containing some secular poems. . . . The *Rigveda* is not a collection of primitive popular poetry. . . . It is rather a body of skilfully composed hymns produced by a sacerdotal class,'

for use in a ritual which was not so simple as has been sometimes supposed. The metres and arrangement are the highly artificial work of persons who may be justly called learned, although probably ignorant of the art of writing. The same competent critic holds that, although the poetry is often marred for our taste by obvious blemishes, the diction is generally simple and unaffected, the thought direct, and the imagery frequently beautiful or even noble. The poems naturally vary much in literary merit, having been composed by many diverse authors at different times. The best may be fairly called sublime, while the worst are mechanical and commonplace.

Subject-matter. Most of the hymns are invocations addressed to the gods, conceived as the powers of nature personified. Agni, or Fire, and Indra, primarily the god of thunder, and secondarily the god of battle, are the favourite deities. Indeed the religion may be regarded as being based upon fire-worship. The gods are represented as great and powerful, disposed to do good to their worshippers, and engaged in unceasing conflict with the powers of evil. The poets usually beg for material favours and seek to win the deity's good will by means of prayers and sacrifices. Nothing indicates that images were used as aids to worship. The Heaven or Sky, personified as Varuṇa, is the subject of striking poems, and the Sun is addressed as Sūrya, or by other names in several compositions of much merit.

Two specimens of *Rigveda* poetry may help readers to form some estimate of the poetic skill of the Rishis and to appreciate their religious aspirations.

Hymn to the Dawn. The first is part of a hymn to the Dawn (*Ushas*), who is styled by Professor Macdonell ' this fairest creation of Vedic poetry '. The rendering is his.

To the Dawn

(*R. V.*, i, 113 ; *Hist. of Sanskrit Liter.* (1900), p. 83.)

There Heaven's Daughter has appeared before us,
The maiden flushing in her brilliant garments.
Thou sovran lady of all earthly treasure,
Auspicious Dawn, flush here to-day upon us.

In the sky's framework she has shone with splendour ;
The goddess has cast off the robe of darkness.
Wakening up the world with ruddy horses,
Upon her well-yoked chariot Dawn is coming.

Bringing upon it many bounteous blessings,
Brightly shining, she spreads her brilliant lustre.
Last of the countless morns that have gone by,
First of bright morns to come has Dawn arisen.

Arise! the breath, the life, again has reached us:
Darkness has gone away and light is coming.
She leaves a pathway for the sun to travel:
We have arrived where men prolong existence.

The tenth book. Commentators have different views concerning the exact meaning of the Rigvedic mythology, some denying that the gods addressed severally were really regarded as separate beings. However that may be, the latest book, the tenth, exhibits a somewhat advanced aspect of religious thought which prepares the way for the speculations of the Upani hads and the Vedānta. From among the many versions of the celebrated Creation Hymn, 'the earliest specimen of Aryan philosophic thought', I choose the metrical rendering by Max Müller, who wrote it with the aid of a friend.

CREATION HYMN

(*R. V.*, x, 129; *Chips from a German Workshop* (1869), vol. i, p. 78).

Nor Aught nor Nought existed; yon bright sky
Was not, nor heaven's broad woof outstretched above.
What covered all? what sheltered? what concealed?
Was it the water's fathomless abyss?
There was not death—yet was there nought immortal,
There was no confine betwixt day and night;
The only One breathed breathless by itself,
Other than It there nothing since has been.
Darkness there was, and all at first was veiled
In gloom profound—an ocean without light—
The germ that still lay covered in the husk
Burst forth, one nature, from the fervent heat.
Then first came love upon it, the new spring
Of mind [1]—yea, poets in their hearts discerned,
Pondering, this bond between created things
And uncreated. Comes this spark from earth
Piercing and all-pervading, or from heaven?
Then seeds were sown, and mighty powers arose—
Nature below, and power and will above—
Who knows the secret? who proclaimed it here,
Whence, whence this manifold creation sprang?
The Gods themselves came later into being—
Who knows from whence this great creation sprang?
He from whom all this great creation came,
Whether his will created or was mute,
The Most High Seer that is in highest heaven,
He knows it—or perchance even He knows not.

The Atharvaveda. The *Atharvaveda* or *Atharvana* is described as being on the whole 'a heterogeneous collection of spells . . .

[1] Macdonell translates better:
Desire then at the first arose within it,
Desire, which was the earliest seed of spirit.

a collection of the most popular spells current among the masses', and consequently breathing the spirit of a prehistoric age. Some of its formulas may go back to the most remote ages prior even to the separation of the Indo-Aryans from the Iranians. The fact that the book preserves so much old-world lore makes it rather more interesting and important for the history of civilization than the *Rigveda* itself. But it is far inferior as literature. The *Atharvaveda* may now be read at small cost in the literal annotated version by Whitney as revised by Lanman. Although every line has been Englished word for word, much remains unintelligible as it stands in the translation.

A specimen spell. A specimen, selected chiefly because it is short, will illustrate the character of the spells, and the extreme obscurity of the subject-matter.

AGAINST THE POISON OF SNAKES

(*A. V.*, vi, 12, Whitney and Lanman, vol. i, p. 289.)

'1. I have gone about the race of snakes, as the sun about the sky, as night about living creatures other than the swan; thereby do I ward off thy poison.

2. What was known of old by priests, what by seers, what by gods; what is to be, that has a mouth—therewith do I ward off thy poison.

3. With honey I mix the streams; the rugged mountains are honey; honey is the Pārushnī [a river], the Sipālā; weal be to thy mouth, weal to thy heart.'

Such sentences read very like nonsense at first sight. They must, of course, have had a definite meaning for the author, which may be discoverable, but it is not easy to make sense of them. The spell quoted is a perfectly fair sample of the collection and the translation.

A notable poem. Fortunately, the *Atharvaveda* includes some compositions of a higher order, although, as Lanman observes, they are 'few indeed'. The best known of such passages, that expressing the omniscience of the heavens personified as Varuna, deserves quotation. The sentiments and diction find many echoes in the Hebrew poetry of the Old Testament.

THE OMNISCIENCE OF VARUNA

(*A. V.*, iv, 16, 1–5; after Muir, in Kaegi, p. 65.)

As guardian, the Lord of worlds
Sees all things as if near at hand.
In secret what 'tis thought to do
That to the gods is all displayed.

Whoever moves or stands, who glides in secret,
Who seeks a hiding-place, or hastens from it,
What thing two men may plan in secret council,
A third, King Varuna, perceives it also.

And all this earth King Varuna possesses,
His the remotest ends of yon broad heaven;
And both the seas in Varuna lie hidden,[1]
But yet the smallest water-drop contains him.

[1] 'Also the two oceans are Varuna's paunches' (Lanman); 'The loins of Varuna are these two oceans' (Macdonell).

Although I elimbed the furthest heaven, fleeing,
I should not there eseape the monareh's power;
From heaven his spies descending hasten hither,
With all their thousand eyes the world surveying.

Whate'er exists between the earth and heaven,
Or both beyond, to Varuna lies open.
The winkings of eaeh mortal eye he numbers,
He wields the universe, as diee a player.

The Indo-Aryan tribes. The Indo-Aryan invasion or immigration evidently was a prolonged movement of a eonsiderable number of tribes, five or more, apparently related one to the other, who ealled themselves eolleetively Āryas, as the Iranians did.[1] The term *Ārya*, whieh seems originally to have meant merely 'kinsman', was understood in later times to imply nobility or respeetability of birth, as eontrasted with *Anārya*, 'ignoble'. The habits of the tribes, while dwelling to the west of the Indus, were those of an agrieultural and pastoral people, who reekoned their wealth in terms of eows. The deseription of the Indo-Aryans by some writers of authority as 'nomads' is opposed to the evidence of the hymns. Many passages of the *Rigveda*, both in the earliest and the latest books, testify to the habitual eultivation of *yava*, whieh primarily means 'barley', but may inelude wheat, whieh is not mentioned separately.[2]

The tribes as they settled down in interior India naturally would have beeome more agrieultural and less pastoral, like the Gūjars and Āhīrs of later ages. Some of the tribal names, as, for example, Pūru and Chedi,[3] survived into the Epie period, while many died out. Eaeh tribe was a group of families, and in eaeh family the father was master. The whole tribe was governed by a Rājā, whose power was eheeked to an undefined extent by a tribal eouneil. The tribes dwelt in fortified villages, but there were no towns. The details reeorded suggest that the life of the people was not unlike that of many tribes of Afghanistan in modern times before the introduetion of fire-arms.[4]

Arts of peace and war. The bow and arrow were the prineipal weapons, but spears and battle-axes were not unknown. Chariots, eaeh earrying a driver and a fighting man, were employed in battle,

[1] Compare the story of the gradual Hellenization of the land of Greeee (Bury, ehap. i, see. 4).

[2] e.g. *R. V.*, x, 134, 2 'As men whose fields are full of barley reap the ripe eorn removing it in order'; and vii, 67, 10 'barley eut or gathered up' (Griffith). Barley is grown all over north-western India, in Afghanistan and in the Himalayan valleys up to a height of 14,000 feet. Riee, unknown to the *Rigveda*, is often mentioned in the *Atharvaveda*, e.g. iv, 34, 35. But the theory that the Indians originally were nomads is supported by Megasthenes, who was told that 'the Indians were in old times nomads like those Seythians who do not plough but wander about in their waggons, &e.' (Arrian, *Indika*, chap. 7).

[3] Pūru seems to be the Pōros of Greek authors.

[4] Diseussion eoneerning the original seat or home of the Aryans is omitted purposely, beeause no hypothesis on the subjeet seems to be established.

a fact which implies considerable advance in the mechanical arts. Armour was worn. The Rigvedic Indo-Aryans were also acquainted with the processes of weaving, tanning, and metallurgy, although their knowledge of iron is doubtful. We have seen that the copper implements of the Gangetic basin may reasonably be referred to Rigvedic times. Bronze tools and weapons were not ordinarily used. Gold was familiar and was made into jewellery. The tribes fought with each other when so disposed, but all united in hostility to the dark-skinned Indians, whom they despised, and whose lands they annexed.

Diet. The Indo-Aryans, while sharing the ancient Iranian veneration for the cow, felt no scruple about sacrificing both bulls and cows at weddings or on other important occasions. The persons who took part in the sacrifice ate the flesh of the victim, whether bull, cow, or horse. But meat was eaten only as an exception. Milk was an important article of food, and was supplemented by cakes of barley or wheat (*yava*), vegetables, and fruit.

Strong drinks. The people freely indulged in two kinds of intoxicating liquor, called *soma* and *surā*. The Parsees of Yezd and Kirmān in Persia, as well as those of the Deccan and Bombay in India, who still occasionally offer *soma* sacrifices, identify the plant with one or other species of *Asclepias* or *Sarcostemma*. The plants of that genus have a milky juice which can be transformed into a rather unpleasant drink. But the real *soma* plant may have been different, and has not yet been clearly identified.[1] *Surā* probably was a kind of beer. *Soma* juice was considered to be particularly acceptable to the gods, and was offered with elaborate ceremonial. The *Sāmaveda* provides the chants appropriate for the ceremonies.

Amusements. Amusements included dancing, music, chariot-racing, and dicing. Gambling with dice is mentioned so frequently in both the *Rigveda* and the later documents that the prevalence of the practice is beyond doubt. One stanza from the well-known 'Gambler's Lament' (*R. V.*, x, 34, in Kaegi, p. 84) may be quoted:

> My wife rejects me and her mother hates me;
> The gamester finds no pity for his troubles.
> No better use can I see for a gambler,
> Than for a costly horse worn out and aged.

Dimness of the picture. When all possible care has been bestowed on the drawing of the outline, it must be confessed that the picture of the Indo-Aryans in the Rigvedic period remains indistinct and shadowy. The impossibility of fixing the age of the poems or of the life which they illustrate within limits defined even approximately leaves the Indo-Aryans suspended in the air, so to speak, and unconnected with any ascertained historical realities. The difficulties of the language of the poems, the strange modes of expression, and the remoteness of the ideas hinder

[1] Kautilya prescribes that 'Brāhmans shall be provided with forests for *soma* plantation' (*Arthasāstra*, Book II, chap. 2). See also *Jātakas*, Nos. 525 and 537.

a vivid realization of the people by whom and for whom the literature was produced. The matter of the greater part of the *Atharvaveda*, as already observed, produces an impression of prehistoric antiquity even deeper than that produced by the *Rigveda*, although it is certain that the book, as a book, is later in date.

Vedic Aryans and Hinduism. However dim may be the picture of the life of the Vedic Indo-Aryans, it is plain that their religion and habits differed materially from those of Hindus in modern or even in early historical times. The detestation of cow-slaughter and the loathing for beef, which are to-day the most prominent outward marks of Hinduism, have been so for many centuries, perhaps for something like two thousand years. The Indo-Aryans had not those marks. It is quite certain that they freely sacrificed bulls and cows and ate both beef and horse flesh on ceremonial occasions. Nevertheless, it is true that the roots of Hinduism go down into the Rigvedic age. The pantheon, that is to say, the gods viewed collectively, although widely different from that of Hinduism, contains the germs of later Hindu developments. Even now the Vedic deities are not wholly without honour, and in southern India the Nambudri Brahmans[1] of Malabar devote their lives to keeping up Vedic ritual as they understand it. The predominance of the Brahman had already begun when the *Rigveda* was composed, and the foundations of the caste system had thus been laid. The *Yajurveda* helps to bridge the gap between the *Rigveda* and Hinduism. It refers to the country between the Sutlaj and the Jumna, not to the Indus basin. The god Siva is introduced under that name, while Vishnu is more prominent than in the earlier work. The old nature worship has dropped into the background, and a much more mechanical form of religion, depending on elaborate ceremonies and highly skilled priests, is described.

Vedic political history. The hymns of the *Rigveda* contain abundant material for political history in the shape of names of kings, kingdoms, and tribes. They even describe battles and other incidents. The references occur in a manner so natural and incidental that in all probability they record a genuine tradition and are concerned with real events. But the utter impossibility of determining an even approximate chronology for either the hymns or the events mentioned in them renders the information almost valueless for historical purposes. The attempts made to connect the Vedic names with Hindu history by means of the long genealogies preserved in the Purānas and other works have failed to yield tangible results. Bharata, Sudās, Janamejaya, and other kings named in the hymns, although they may be accepted as real persons, cannot be invested with much interest from the historian's point of view.

Historical geography. The study of the geographical data in the hymns is more fruitful, and throws a certain amount of light on the course of the Indo-Aryan migration and the origins of

[1] The name is also written Nambutiri or Nāmburi.

Hinduism. In fact, the accepted belief in the Indo-Aryan immigration from Central Asia depends largely on the interpretation of the geographical allusions in the *Rigveda* and *Yajurveda*. Direct testimony to the assumed fact is lacking, and no tradition of an early home beyond the frontier survives in India. The amount of geographical knowledge implied in the literature is considerable. Such knowledge in those ancient days could have been acquired only by actual travelling. The hymn 'In Praise of the Rivers (*Nadī-stuti*)' in the tenth book (x. 75) is specially interesting as a display of geographical information. The author, while devoting his skill chiefly to the praises of the Sindhu or Indus, enumerates at least nineteen rivers, including the Ganges.

The fifth stanza, which gives a list of ten streams, small and great, in order from east to west, is remarkable :

> Attend to this my song of praise, O Gangā,
> Yamunā, Sarasvatī, Sutudrī, Parushnī ;
> Together with Asiknī, O Marudvridhā, and with
> Vitastā, O Ārjīkīyā, listen with Sushomā.

The names of the Ganges, Jumna, and Sarasvatī remain unchanged. The Sutudrī is the modern Sutlaj, although its course has been greatly altered. The Parushnī is supposed to be the Rāvi. The Asiknī and Vitastā undoubtedly mean respectively the Akesines or Chināb, and the Vyath or Jhelum. The Marudvridhā is the Maruwārdwan, which flows from north to south through the Maru valley of the Kashmīr-Jamū State, and joins the Chināb on its northern bank at Kashtwār. The Sushomā is the Sohān in the Rāwalpindi District, and the Ārjīkīyā probably is the Kanshi in the same district.

The mention of the Marudvridhā is surprising, and it is difficult to understand how a stream of so little importance, hidden away among high mountains in an almost inaccessible valley, can have come to the knowledge of the author. The list suggests matter for curious speculation.[1]

River changes. It is of much importance, as already observed, that careful students of early Indian history and interpreters of the Vedas or other ancient records should bear in mind the fact that the snow-fed rivers of northern India have undergone immense changes even within historical times. The entire Indus system has been subject to tremendous transformations both in the mountains and in the plains. Earthquakes, elevations, subsidences, and landslips have affected the upper courses of the rivers, while the changes in the soft alluvium of the plains have occurred frequently on a gigantic scale and are still in progress. Some rivers, notably the Hakrā or Wahindah, which once formed the boundary between Sind and Hind, have ceased to exist. Others, like the Kurram in the west and the Sarasvatī in the east, which

[1] See Max Müller, *India, What can it Teach us* (1883), pp. 163–75 ; Stein in *J. R. A. S.*, 1917, p. 91 ; and the translations by Griffith and others. I think the Ārjīkīyā must be the Kanshi, and not as Stein suggests.

once were violent and impetuous, have dwindled into feeble, inconsiderable streams. The positions of the confluences in both the Indus and the Gangetic systems have shifted many miles. The existing delta of the Indus has been formed since the time of Alexander the Great. The whole group of rivers connected with or related to the Sutlaj has been completely transformed more than once. The Sutlaj itself has wandered over a bed eighty-five miles in width. Illustrations of the subject might be adduced in endless detail. What has been said may suffice to inspire caution in the interpretation of ancient texts and in attempts to identify places mentioned in those texts.[1]

Vedāngas and Upavedas. Two supplementary sections of the vast Vedic literature which are known as Vedāngas ('members of the Veda') and Upavedas ('subsidiary Vedas') may be briefly mentioned.

The Vedāngas comprise six groups of treatises written in the *sūtra* style on subjects more or less closely connected with ritual or the preservation of the Vedic texts. The subjects are: (1) phonetics or pronunciation (*sikshā*); (2) metre (*chhandas*); (3) grammar (*vyākarana*); (4) etymology (*nirukti* or *nirukta*); (5) religious practice (*kalpa*); and (6) astronomy, or rather astrology (*jyotisha*).

The Upavedas treat of more distinctly secular subjects, namely: (1) medicine (*Āyurveda*); (2) war, or literally 'archery' (*Dhanurveda*); (3) music (*Gandharvaveda*); and (4) architecture and art (*Arthasāstra*).[2]

Vedānta. The term Vedānta ('end of the Veda') is now commonly applied to the philosophy taught in most of the Upanishads. So used it is interpreted to mean the 'final goal of the Veda'. In practice many people when speaking of the Vedas mean the Upanishads, and by them the Vedānta is regarded as 'the ultimate bound of knowledge'. In a more literal sense the term means the treatises, namely, the Upanishads, appended to the end of the Brāhmanas. The concise phrase *tat tvam asi*, 'that art thou', is accepted as summing up the ontology of the Vedānta.

The epics. When passing from the Vedic lyrics to the Sanskrit epics we enter a new world. Not only are the grammar, vocabulary,

[1] Students who desire to appreciate the force of the remarks in the text should read, mark, and digest Raverty's difficult memoir entitled 'The Mihrān of Sind and its Tributaries; a Geographical and Historical Study' in *J. A. S. B.*, vol. lxi, part 1, 1892. Unfortunately the copious matter is ill arranged, so that the treatise is exceptionally hard reading. It deals chiefly with the Indus, pp. 297–317; Hydaspes or Vitastā, pp. 318–36; Chināb, pp. 336–52; Rāvī, pp. 352–71; Biās, pp. 372–90; Sutlaj, pp. 391–418; Hakrā, pp. 418–22 and 454–66. Discussion of results occupies pp. 469–508. I have learned much by repeated reading of the disquisition. For extensive changes in the rivers of the far south see *The Tamils Eighteen Hundred Years Ago*, 1904, p. 236.

[2] Weber, *History of Indian Literature* (Trübner, 1882), pp. 271, 273. The term *Arthasāstra* has another meaning in Kautilya's work on statecraft.

metres, and style different, but the religion has been transformed and social conditions have been profoundly modified. Before those changes can be further considered it is necessary to explain briefly the character of the epics regarded as books.

Two huge poems or masses of verses, the *Rāmāyana* and the *Mahābhārata*, are commonly described as epics.

The Rāmāyana. The *Rāmāyana* deserves the name of epic because it is essentially a single long narrative poem composed by one author named Vālmīki, and is devoted to the celebration of the deeds of the hero Rāma with due regard to the rules of poesy. The work is in fact the first example of the Sanskrit *Kāvya* or artificially designed narrative poem. The simple, easily intelligible style, while free from the ingenuities and verbal gymnastics favoured by later authors, is by no means devoid of ornament. Five out of the seven books seem to constitute the epic as conceived by Vālmīki. Critics regard the first and last books as later additions. Episodes unconnected with the story are few. The grammar and language, which are remote from those of the Veda, closely approximate to those of 'classical' Sanskrit. The poem is known in three different recensions, the variations being due to the liberties taken by professional reciters. It is not possible to determine which form represents the original composed by Vālmīki, but the Bombay recension on the whole seems to preserve the oldest text. The text of narrative poems not being regarded as sacred like that of the Vedas, no obligation to preserve its purity was recognized. The seven books contain about 24,000 *slokas*, or 48,000 lines.

Theme of the Rāmāyana. The main theme is the story of Prince Rāma, the son of King Dasaratha of Ayodhyā by Queen Kausalyā. The jealousy of Kaikeyī, the second queen, drove Rāma into exile and secured possession of the throne for her son, Bharata. Lakshmana, the third prince, voluntarily shared the exile of Rāma and Sītā his beloved wife. The adventures of the banished prince, the abduction of Sītā by Rāvana, the giant king of Lankā, the aid given to the prince by Hanumān, king of the monkeys, the vindication of Sītā from unjust aspersions on her chastity, and a thousand other incidents are even more familiar to Hindus in every part of India than the Bible stories are to the average European Christian. The story ends happily, and Rāma shares the kingdom with Bharata.

The heroic legend thus indicated has been edited by Brahmans so as to transform the poem into a book of devotion consecrated to the service of God in the form of Vishnu. Rāma, who is pictured as an incarnation of the deity, has thus become the man-god and saviour of mankind in the eyes of millions of devout worshippers, who have his name in the ejaculation, 'Rām, Rām', continually on their lips. He is venerated as the ideal man, while his wife, Sītā, is reverenced as the model of womanhood. Hindus unacquainted with Sanskrit bathe in 'the lake of the deeds of Rām' by the help of vernacular translations or imitations, among which the most celebrated is the noble poem entitled the *Rām-charit mānas*, composed by Tulsī Dās in the days of Akbar. The moral teaching of the *Rāmāyana* in all its forms tends to edification, and the influence of Tulsī Dās in particular may be truly described as wholly on the side of goodness.

The Mahābhārata. The *Mahābhārata*, as we possess it in two recensions, a northern and a southern, cannot be designated correctly as an epic poem. It is a gigantic mass of compositions by diverse authors of various dates extending over many centuries, arranged in eighteen books or *parvans*, with a supplement called the *Harivamsa*, which may be reckoned as the nineteenth book. The number of *slokas* exceeds 100,000, and the lines consequently are more than 200,000. The *Harivamsa* contains over 16,000 *slokas*. The episodes, connected by the slightest possible bonds with the original narrative nucleus, constitute about four-fifths of the whole complex mass, which has the character of an 'encyclopaedia of moral teaching' as conceived by the Brahman mind.

The epic portion. The subject of the truly epic portion of the *Mahābhārata* is the Great War between the Kauravas, the hundred sons of Dhritarāshtra, led by Duryodhana, and the Pāndavas, the five sons of Pāndu, brother of Dhritarāshtra, led by Yudhishthira. The poet relates all the circumstances leading up to the war, and then narrates the tale of the fierce conflict which raged for eighteen days on the plain of Kurukshetra near Thānēsar, to the north of modern Delhi and the ancient Indraprastha.[1] All the nations and tribes of India from the Himālaya to the farthest south are represented as taking part in this combat of giants. The Pāndava host comprised the armies of the states situated in the countries equivalent to the United Provinces of Agra and Oudh, Western Bihār, and Eastern Rājputāna, with contingents from Gujarāt in the west and from the Dravidian kingdoms of the extreme south. The Kaurava cause was upheld by the forces of Eastern Bihār, Bengal, the Himālaya, and the Panjāb. The battles ended in the utter destruction of nearly all the combatants on both sides, excepting Dhritarāshtra and the Pāndavas. But a reconciliation was effected between the few survivors, and Yudhishthira Pāndava was recognized as king of Hastināpur on the Ganges. Ultimately, the five sons of Pāndu, accompanied by Draupadī, the beloved wife of them all, and attended by a faithful dog, quitted their royal state, and journeying to Mount Meru were admitted into Indra's heaven.

The epic narrative, thus inadequately summarized, now occupies about 20,000 *slokas*, but in its earliest form comprised only 8,800. That fact, which is clearly recorded, proves beyond doubt the unlimited rehandling which the *Mahābhārata* has undergone at the hands of professional reciters, poets of different ages, and Brahman editors. The mediaeval Hindī epic, the *Chand-Rāisā*, has been subjected to similar treatment and expanded from

[1] See map on p. 29. The caution that the rivers have changed immensely must be remembered. The map shows only the courses as in recent times.

5,000 to 125,000 verses. The original form of that poem is said to be still in existence.

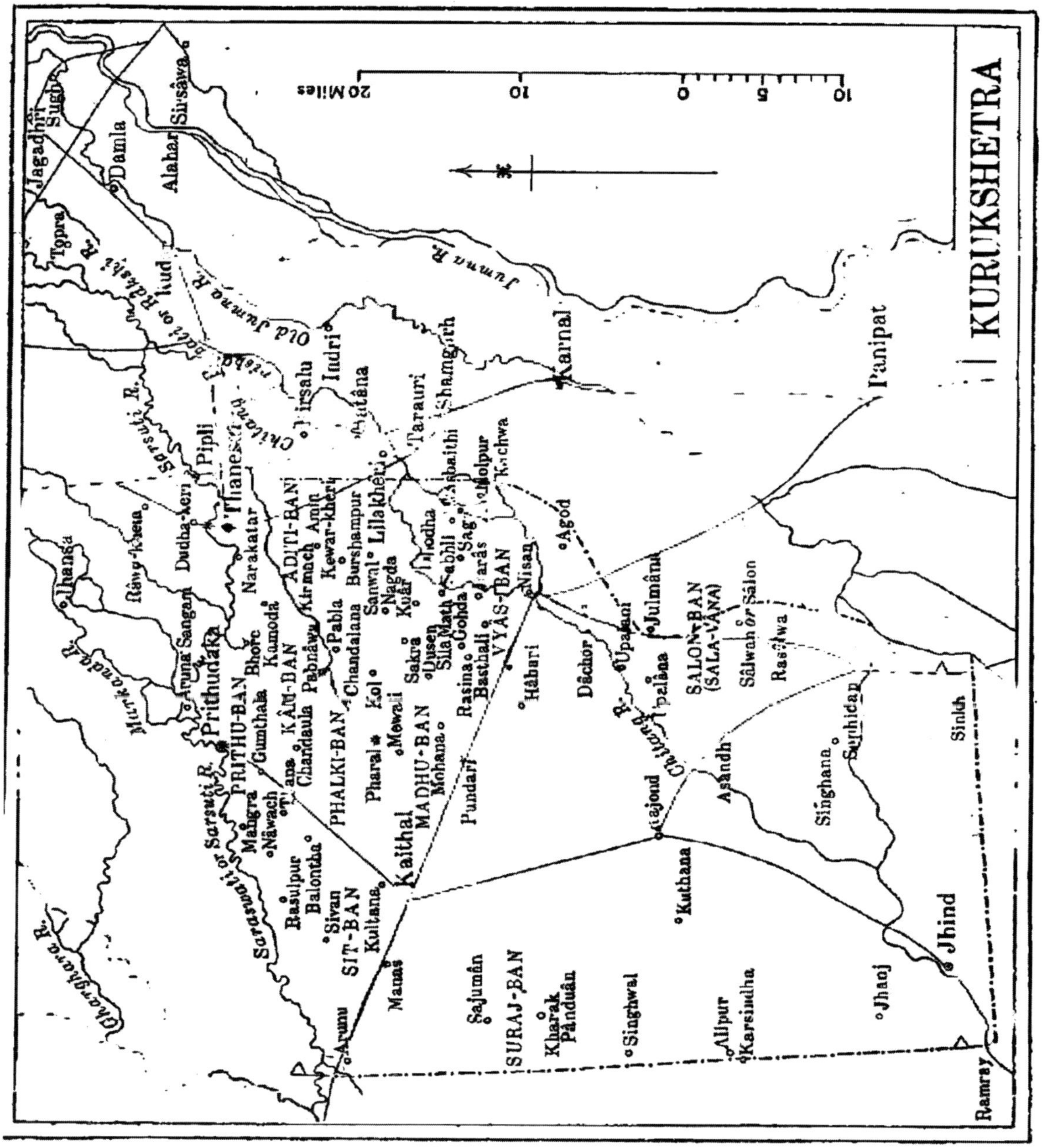

The Bhagavad-Gītā, &c. The profound philosophical poem called the *Bhagavad-Gītā*, which may be Englished as 'the Lord's Song', or in Edwin Arnold's phrase as 'the Song Celestial', divided into eighteen chapters or discourses, has been thrust into the sixth book of the *Mahābhārata*.

Other notable episodes, or inserted poems, are the charming tale of Nala and Damayantī, accessible in Milman's elegant English version; the story of Sakuntalā, forming the groundwork of Kālidāsa's play; and the legend of Sāvitrī, the Hindu Alcestis.

Age of the epics. The separate heroic and legendary tales imbedded in both the *Rāmāyana* and the *Mahābhārata* may in some cases go back to the most remote antiquity, but both of the epics in their existing form are far later than any of the Vedic hymns, and probably posterior to all the *Brāhmanas*. The two epics, as Hopkins has proved in detail, are intimately related and include a large number of substantially identical verses. The language of both belongs essentially to the same period in the development of Sanskrit. Probably the greater part of the existing text of the *Mahābhārata* was complete by A.D. 200, but the work as a whole cannot be said to belong to any one era. The original work of Vālmīki, that is to say, Books II—VI of the *Rāmāyana*, is believed by Professor Macdonell to have been completed before the epic kernel of the *Mahābhārata* had assumed definite shape.

The Rāmāyana not historical. Most Hindus regard the epic narratives as statements of absolute historical facts, and would not be disturbed by sceptical criticism more than the ordinary unlearned Christian is by the so-called 'higher criticism' of the Gospels.[1] Foreign scholars, and even trained Indian scholars to a large extent, naturally look upon the poets' tales in a different light. Professors Jacobi and Macdonell, for instance, regard the *Rāmāyana* as being neither historical nor allegorical, but a poetic creation based on mythology. That interpretation sees in Sītā ('the furrow') an earth-goddess, and in Rāma an equivalent of Indra. Such speculations may or may not be accepted, but I feel fairly certain that the *Rāmāyana* does not hand down much genuine historical tradition of real events, either at Ayodhyā or in the peninsula. The poem seems to me to be essentially a work of imagination, probably founded on vague traditions of the kingdom of Kosala and its capital Ayodhyā. Dasaratha, Rāma, and the rest may or may not be the names of real kings of Kosala, as recorded in the long genealogy of the solar line given in the *Purānas*. But the investigation of the genealogies, on which a distinguished scholar has lavished infinite pains, is inconclusive, and the story of the epic is so interwoven with mythological fiction that it is impossible to disentangle the authentic history. The attempts to fix an approximately definite date for the adventures of Rāma rest on a series of guesses and are altogether unconvincing to my mind.

The Great War. The traditional belief that the Great War of the Mahābhārata actually was fought in the year 3102 B.C., the era of Yudhishthira, is strongly held. Although that date will hardly bear criticism, most people seem to be agreed that the poet of the original epic based his tale on the genuine tradition

[1] 'According to the Hindu notion the stories which are called mythology by Europeans are nothing short of history' (Ketkar, ii. 477).

of a real Great War, just as the author of the *Iliad* had his imagination guided by dim recollections of an actual siege of Troy. The story, however, has been so much edited and moralized by different hands at times widely apart that little genuine tradition can be left. Persistent local memory undoubtedly has always recognized the sites of Hastināpura on the Ganges, the original Kaurava capital, and of Indraprastha on the Jumna, the newer town founded by the Pāndavas. But nothing visible exists at either site to confirm the popular belief. Hastināpura is supposed to be marked by a small hamlet of the same name on the high bank of the Ganges in the Meerut District, and the absence of remains is explained by the theory that the ancient town has been washed away by the Ganges. Every tourist is familiar with the fact that the walled village of Indarpat, situated near the bank of the Jumna between Shāhjahān's Delhi and Humāyūn's tomb, is pointed out as occupying part of the site of Indraprastha. The Nigambōdh Ghāt, or river stairs, and the Nīlīchatrī temple farther north, near Salīmgarh, are believed to have been included in the ancient city, the northern limit of which is supposed to have extended to 'the north-eastern end of the street called Darība—almost in the heart of the modern city '.[1] As at Hastināpur, no ancient remains of any sort have been found to support the identification of the site. The traditions fixing the positions of the two towns, however, may be accepted, and we may believe that a famous local war between the chiefs of Indraprastha and Hastināpura, supported severally by many tribes of northern India, occurred at a very remote date. Beyond that it is difficult to go. The reasons for believing that the Pāndavas were, as Hopkins suggests, 'a new people from without the pale', and for discrediting the alleged relationship between them and the Kauravas, are strong and cut at the root of the whole story. If the Pāndavas were non-Aryan hill-men, which in my judgement is probable, the poets and editors have transformed the story of their doings to such an extent that nothing truly historical is left.

The allegation that the chiefs of all India, including even the Pāndyas from the extreme south of the peninsula, took part in the fray is absolutely incredible.[2] Whether the date of the battle be placed about 3000 B.C., as some people argue, or two thousand years later, as others prefer, it is impossible that at either period distant powers like the Pāndyas or the King of Assam (Prāgjyotisha) should have been interested in the local quarrels between the Kauravas and Pāndavas, which directly concerned only a small area in the neighbourhood of the city now called Delhi. The entire framework of the story is essentially incredible and

[1] Carr Stephen, *Archaeology and Monumental Remains of Delhi*, Lūdiāna and Calcutta, 1876, p. 5.

[2] Compare the 'catalogue of ships' interpolated in the *Iliad*. As all Greece desired to be credited with a share in the Trojan war after it had been made famous by Homer, so all India claimed places in the Great War of the *Mahābhārata*.

unhistorical. It may be that the royal genealogies for ages before and after the Great War, as recorded in the *Purānas* at length and in the epics less fully, are not wholly fictitious. But even if it be admitted that the lists often give the names in the proper order with approximate correctness, and indicate the existence of certain real relations friendly or hostile between the princes of certain dynasties, we are still a long way from finding intelligible history. The attempt to construct a rationalized narrative out of the materials available rests on a series of assumptions and guesses which can never lead to conclusions of much value. I confess my inability to extract anything deserving the name of political history from the epic tales of either the *Rāmāyana* or the *Mahābhārata*.

Social conditions. Both poems describe much the same state of society; but that proposition is subject to the qualification that certain parts of the *Mahābhārata* retain distinct traces of early practices, such as cow-killing and human sacrifice, which were regarded with horror when the later parts of the work were composed.[1] Other features are clearly non-Aryan, notably the polyandry of the Pāndavas, who all shared the one wife, Draupadī, after the manner of the Tibetans and certain other Himalayan tribes in the present day. The name Pāndava means 'pale-face', and the conjecture seems to be legitimate that the sons of Pāndu may have been the representatives of a yellow-tinted, Himalayan, non-Aryan tribe, which practised polyandry. That hypothesis involves the further inference (which may be supported for other reasons) that the alleged relationship between the Pāndavas and the Kauravas was an invention of the Brahman editors who undertook to moralize the old tales and bring them all into the Aryan fold. The subject is too speculative for further discussion in this place.

When the epics were finally recast in their present shape, be the date A. D. 200 or another, the doctrine of *ahimsā*, or non-injury to living creatures, had gained the upper hand. It is taught emphatically in many passages, although others, as observed above, retain memories of older practices.

The Vedic nature-worship had been mostly superseded by the cult of Brahmā, Vishnu, and Siva. New gods and goddesses unknown to the Veda, such as Ganēsa and Pārvatī, had arisen; and the Vedic deities had been reduced to a subordinate position, except Indra, who still retained high rank as the king of the heaven which warriors hoped to attain. The doctrine of rebirth, often loosely called transmigration of souls, had become generally accepted, and the belief in the incarnations of Vishnu had been formulated. The *Bhagavad-Gītā*, of which the date is quite uncertain, presents the Supreme Deity incarnate in the guise of the charioteer Krishna, who expounds the religion of duty, subject to the limitations of the four orders or *varnas*, in 'plain but noble language'. The tribal organization of the State is much less

[1] For details and references see Vidya, p. 118, and Hopkins, p. 378.

prominent than it was in the Vedic period, and territorial kingdoms had arisen. The life of the court of Ayodhyā as depicted in the *Rāmāyana* is much the same as that of any old-fashioned Hindu state in recent times. Caste was already an ancient institution, and it may be said with confidence that the atmosphere of the epic world is that of familiar Hinduism, with certain exceptions indicated above, which occur chiefly in the *Mahābhārata*. The kingdoms mentioned were numerous and comparatively small. No hint seems to be given that a great paramount power existed. But it is not safe to affirm that the political and social conditions depicted in the epics are those of any one definite age. Both works as literary compositions may be roughly placed between 400 B.C. and A.D. 200. The *Rāmāyana* in its original form may have been composed by Vālmīki in the earlier half of the six centuries thus indicated, and it seems probable that the redaction of the *Mahābhārata* to something like its present shape took place in the later half of the same period. But determination of the dates of composition of the poems, if it could be effected, would not throw any light on the historical place of Rāma, Arjuna, and the other epic heroes. They are, I think, the creatures of imagination, guided more or less by dim traditions of half-forgotten stirring events which happened 'once upon a time', but cannot be treated as ascertained facts which came into existence at any particular period. The Indian epic heroes, in short, seem to me to occupy a position like that of the Knights of the Round Table in British legend, and it is as futile to attempt the distillation of matter-of-fact history, whether political or social, from the *Mahābhārata* and *Rāmāyana* as it would be to reconstruct the early history of Britain from the *Morte d'Arthur* or from its modern version, the *Idylls of the King*.

The Purānas. The nature of the works called *Purānas* which have been referred to demands brief explanation. The *Purānas* commonly recognized in the north of India are eighteen in number. Others, about which little is known to European scholars, are used in the south. A *Purāna*, according to the Indian definition, best exemplified by the *Vishnu Purāna*, should treat of five subjects, namely, primary creation, secondary creation, genealogies of gods and patriarchs, reigns of various Manus, and the history of ancient dynasties. The treatises consequently are bulky and crowded with legendary matter of various kinds. They have been well described by Bühler as 'popular sectarian compilations of mythology, philosophy, history, and the sacred law; intended, as they are now used, for the instruction of the unlettered classes, including the upper divisions of the Sūdra *varna*'.[1] Much of the contents comes down from remote antiquity, as the name *Purāna*, meaning 'old', testifies, but the books as they stand are of various dates. The *Vāyu Purāna*, one of the oldest, finally edited perhaps in the fourth century after Christ, is closely connected with the supplement to the *Mahābhārata* entitled the *Harivamsa*, already

[1] *Laws of Manu, S.B.E.*, xxv, p. xci.

mentioned. The Puranic genealogies of kings in prehistoric times, as intimated above, seem to be of little value, but those of the historical period or Kali Age, from about 600 B.C., are records of high importance and extremely helpful in the laborious task of reconstructing the early political history of India. Each of the *Purānas* is more or less specially consecrated to the service of a particular form of the godhead.

Caste. The existing institution of caste is peculiar to India, is at least three thousand years old, is 'the most vital principle of Hinduism', dominating Indian social life, manners, morals, and thought; and is founded on the intellectual and moral superiority of the Brahmans, which dates from Rigvedic times. It consists essentially in the division of Hindu mankind into about three thousand hereditary groups, each internally bound together by rules of ceremonial purity, and externally separated by the same rules from all other groups. Those propositions describing the institution of caste as it exists to-day in general terms are as accurate as any brief abstract description of an institution so complex can be.

Definition of a caste. A caste may be defined as a group of families internally united by peculiar rules for the observance of ceremonial purity, especially in the matters of diet and marriage. The same rules serve to fence it off from all the other groups, each of which has its own set of rules. Admission to an established caste in long settled territory can be obtained nowadays by birth only, and transitions from one caste to another, which used to be feasible in ancient times, are no longer possible, except in frontier regions like Manipur. The families composing a caste may or may not have traditions of descent from a common ancestor, and, as a matter of fact, may or may not belong to one stock. Race, that is to say, descent by blood, has little concern with caste, in northern India, at all events, whatever may be the case in the south. The individual members of a caste may or may not be restricted to any particular occupation or occupations. The members may believe or disbelieve any creed or doctrine, religious or philosophical, without affecting their caste position. That can be forfeited only by breach of the caste regulations concerning the *dharma*, or practical duty of members belonging to the group. Each caste has its own *dharma*, in addition to the common rules of morality as accepted by Hindus generally, and considered to be the *dharma* of mankind. The general Hindu *dharma* exacts among other things reverence to Brahmans, respect for the sanctity of animal life in varying degrees, and especially veneration for horned cattle, pre-eminently the cow. Every caste man is expected to observe accurately the rules of his own group, and to refrain from doing violence to the feelings of other groups concerning their rules. The essential duty of the member of a caste is to follow the custom of his group, more particularly in relation to diet or marriage.[1]

[1] 'Caste means a social exclusiveness with reference to diet and marriage. . . . Birth and rituals are secondary' (Shama Sastri, *The Evolution of Caste*, p. 13).

Violation of the rules on those subjects, if detected, usually involves unpleasant and costly social expiation and may result in expulsion from the caste, which means social ruin and grave inconvenience.

The Hindus have not any name for the caste institution, which seems to them part of the order of nature. It is almost impossible for a Hindu to regard himself otherwise than as a member of some particular caste, or species of Hindu mankind. Everybody else who disregards Hindu *dharma* is an 'outer barbarian' (*mlēchchha*) no matter how exalted his worldly rank or how vast his wealth may be. The proper Sanskrit and vernacular term for 'a caste' is *jāti* (*jāt*), 'species', although, as noted above, the members of a *jāti* are not necessarily descended from a common ancestor. Indeed, as a matter of fact, they are rarely, if ever, so descended. Their special caste rules make their community in effect a distinct species, whoever their ancestors may have been.

The fiction of four original castes. The common notion that there were four original castes, Brahman, Kshatriya or Rājanya, Vaisya, and Sūdra, is false. The ancient Hindu writers classified mankind under four *varnas* or 'orders', with reference to their occupations, namely: (1) the learned, literate, and priestly order, or Brahmans; (2) the fighting and governing classes, who were grouped together as Rājanyas or Kshatriyas, irrespective of race, meaning by that term ancestry; (3) the trading and agricultural people, or Vaisyas; and (4) common, humble folk, day labourers, and so forth, whose business it was to serve their betters. Every family and caste (*jāti*) observing Hindu *dharma* necessarily fell under one or other of those four heads. Various half-wild tribes, and also communities like sweepers, whose occupations are obviously unclean, were regarded as standing outside the four orders or *varnas*. Such unclean communities have usually imitated the Hindu caste organization and developed an elaborate system of castes of their own, which may be described by the paradoxical term 'outcaste castes'.

Nobody can understand the caste system until he has freed himself from the mistaken notion based on the current interpretation of the so-called *Institutes of Manu*, that there were 'four original castes'. No four original castes ever existed at any time or place, and at the present moment the terms Kshatriya, Vaisya, and Sūdra have no exact meaning as a classification of existing castes. In northern India the names Vaisya and Sūdra are not used except in books or disputes about questions of caste precedence. In the south all Hindus who are not Brahmans fall under the denomination of Sūdra, while the designations Kshatriya and Vaisya are practically unknown.[1]

The Purusha-sukta hymn. The famous *Purusha-sukta*

[1] According to the Census of 1901 for the Madras Presidency the figures are: Brahman, 3·4 per cent.; Sūdra, 94·3 = 97·7 per cent. The small residuum is made up of a few Telingas and Kanarese who called themselves Kshatriyas or Vaisyas (Richards, *The Dravidian Problem*, p. 31).

hymn included in the latest book of the *Rigveda* (x, 90), and commonly supposed to be 'the only passage in the Veda which enumerates the four castes', has nothing to do with caste. The hymn has for its subject a cosmogony or theory of creation. The poet tries to picture creation as the result of immolating and cutting up Purusha, that is to say 'embodied spirit, or Man personified and regarded as the soul and original source of the universe, the personal and life-giving principle in all animated beings'. The Vedas, horses, cattle, goats, and sheep, the creatures of the air, and animals both wild and tame are depicted as being products of that 'great general sacrifice'. The poet proceeds next to expound the creation of the human race, and finally, of the sun, moon, and elements. I quote Colebrooke's version because it is free from the effect of the prepossession of other translators, who, under the influence of Manu and his followers, have assumed the reality of a reference to the supposed 'four original castes'.

'10. Into how many portions did they divide this being whom they immolated? what did his mouth become? what are his arms, his thighs, and his feet now called?

11. His mouth became a priest [*Brāhmana*]; his arm was made a soldier [*Rājanya*]; his thigh was transformed into a husbandman [*Vaisya*]; from his feet sprang the servile man (*Sūdra*].

12. The moon was produced from his mind; the sun sprung from his eye; air and breath proceeded from his ear; and fire rose from his mouth.

13. The subtile element was produced from his navel; the sky from his head; the earth from his feet; and space from his ear; thus did he frame worlds.' [1]

The general drift of the whole passage is plain enough. The verses give a highly figurative, imaginative theory of creation. Both the Brahman and fire come from Purusha's mouth, just as the servile man or Sūdra and earth both proceed from his feet. No suggestion of the existence of caste groups is made. Mankind is simply and roughly classified under four heads according to occupation, the more honourable professions being naturally assigned the more honourable symbolical origin. It is absurd to treat the symbolical language of the poem as a narrative of supposed facts.

Distinctions between varna and jāti. Most of the misunderstanding on the subject has arisen from the persistent mistranslation of Manu's term *varna* as 'caste', whereas it should be rendered 'class' or 'order', or by some equivalent term.[2]

[1] Colebrooke, *Miscellaneous Essays*, 1873, vol. i, p. 184.

[2] 'The words Brahmans, Kshatriyas, Vaisyas, and Sudras were names of classes rather than of castes during the pre-Buddhistic period' (Shama Sastri, p. 13). '*Varna*, once a common name of all classes, perhaps taken from the colour of the garments that differed with different classes, as for example, white for the Brāhmans, red for the Kshatriyas, yellow for the Vaisyas, and black for the Sūdras, came to mean a caste in post-Buddhistic literature' (ibid., p. 44).

The compiler of the *Institutes of Manu* was well aware of the distinction between *varna* and *jāti*. While he mentions about fifty different castes, he lays much stress on the fact that there were only four *varnas*. The two terms are carelessly confused in one passage (x, 31), but in that only. Separate castes existed from an early date. Their relations to one another remain unaffected whether they are grouped theoretically under four occupational headings or not.

Enormous number of existing castes. My statement that three thousand distinct castes, more or less, exist at the present day is made on the authority of an estimate by Ketkar. Whether the number be taken as 2,000, 3,000, or 4,000 is immaterial, because the figure certainly is of that order. Many reasons, which it would be tedious to specify, forbid the preparation of an exact list of castes. One of those reasons is that new castes have been and still are formed from time to time. But the intricacies of the caste system in its actual working must be studied in the numerous special treatises devoted to the subject, which it is impossible to discuss in this work.

Antiquity of the institution. The assertion made on an earlier page that the institution in some of its essential features is at least three thousand years old probably errs on the side of caution. We know that caste existed before 300 B.C., because the most obvious features of the institution are noticed by the Greek authors of ascertained date; and it is reasonable to believe that castes, separated from one another by rules of ceremonial purity, as they now are, were in existence at least six or seven centuries earlier. I do not find any indication of the existence of caste in Rigvedic times. But the pre-eminence of the 'Brahman sacrificers', which was well assured even in that remote age, is the foundation of the later caste system. The people of the *Ṛigveda* had not yet become Hindus.

The learned, priestly, and intellectually superior class of the Indo-Aryans who were called Brahmans gradually framed extremely strict rules to guard their own ceremonial purity against defilement through unholy food or undesirable marriages. The enforcement of such rules on themselves by the most respected members of the Indo-Aryan community naturally attracted the admiration of the more worldly classes of society, who sought to emulate and imitate the virtuous self-restraint of the Brahmans. It being clearly impossible that ordinary soldiers, business men, peasants, and servants could afford to be as scrupulous as saintly, or at least professedly religious Brahmans, a separate standard of *dharma* for each section of society necessarily grew up by degrees. Kings, for instance, might properly and must do things which subjects could not do without sin, and so on. The long-continued conflict with the aboriginal Indians, who held quite different ideals of conduct, made both the Brahmans and their imitators more and more eager to assert their superiority and exclusiveness by ever-increasing scrupulosity concerning both diet and marriage.

The evolution of caste. The geographical isolation of interior India favoured the evolution of a distinct and peculiar social system. A student of the *Rigveda* texts, without knowledge of historical facts, might reasonably presume that the Indus basin where the immigrants first settled would have become the Holy Land of Hinduism. The Rishis never tire of singing the praises of the mighty Indus with its tributary streams. But the strange fact is that the basin of the Indus, and even the Panjāb beyond the Sutlaj, came to be regarded as impure lands by the Brahmans of interior India at quite an early date.[1] Orthodox Hindus are still unwilling to cross the Indus, and the whole Panjāb between that river and the Sutlaj is condemned as unholy ground, unfitted for the residence of strict votaries of *dharma*. The reason apparently is that the north-western territories continued to be overrun by successive swarms of foreigners from Central Asia, who disregarded Brahmans and followed their own customs. The inroads of those foreigners blotted out the memory of the Indo-Aryan immigration from the north-west, which is not traceable either in the popular Puranic literature or in the oral traditions of the people. To the east of the Sarasvatī and Sutlaj the Indo-Aryans were usually safe from foreign invasion and free to work out their own rule of life undisturbed. They proceeded to do so and thus to create Hinduism with its inseparable institution of caste. Internally the Indian territory was broken up into a multitude of small units, each of which had a tendency towards an exclusive, detached way of living.

Effect of ahimsā on caste. The sentiment in favour of respecting animal life, technically called the *ahimsā* doctrine, had a large share in fixing on the necks of the people burdensome rules of conduct. That sentiment, which is known to have been actively encouraged by Jain and Buddhist teachers from about 500 B.C., probably originated at a much earlier date. The propagation of *ahimsā* necessarily produced a sharp conflict of ideas and principles of conduct between the adherents of the doctrine and the old-fashioned people who clung to bloody sacrifices, cow-killing, and meat eating. Communities which had renounced the old practices and condemned them as revolting impieties naturally separated themselves from their more easy-going and self-indulgent neighbours, and formed castes bound strictly to maintain the novel code of ethics.[2] The *Mahābhārata*, as already noted, contains many

[1] The combined testimony of the *Jātakas* and the Greek authors proves that in the fourth century B.C. Taxila in the north-western Panjāb still was a centre of Vedic learning. The change may have been due to the Indo-Scythian rule in the first two centuries A.C.

[2] Mr. Shama Sastri, who believes the existing caste system to be of comparatively modern post-Buddhistic origin, expresses his view of the effect of Jain and Buddhist teaching in language stronger than I am disposed to use :

'It is easy to perceive that if the Brahmans of the Gupta period ceased to continue to observe the long-established custom of marrying wives

inconsistent passages which indicate the transition from the ancient ideas to the new. The same conflict of ideals and practice still goes on, and may be observed in many localities of both southern and northern India. The first Rock Edict of Asoka, published about 256 B.C., enables us to fix one date in the long story and to mark an early instance of the change of attitude produced by Buddhist teaching.

'Formerly, in the kitchen of His Sacred and Gracious Majesty the King each day many [hundred] thousands of living creatures were slaughtered to make curries. But now, when this pious edict is being written, only three living creatures are slaughtered daily for curry, to wit, two peacocks and one antelope—the antelope, however, not invariably. Even those three living creatures henceforth shall not be slaughtered.'

Any person acquainted with modern India does not need to be told how the habit of flesh or fish eating separates certain castes from their vegetarian brethren.

Effect of the Muhammadan conquest. It is impossible to pursue the subject, which branches off into endless ramifications. One more observation may be recorded to the effect that the process of the Muhammadan conquest, from the time of Mahmūd of Ghaznī, tended to tighten the bonds of caste. The Hindus, unable on the whole to resist the Muslims in the field, defended themselves passively by the increased rigidity of caste association. The system of close caste brotherhoods undoubtedly protected Hindus and Hinduism during many centuries of Muslim rule. Modern Hinduism is incapable of accepting the old legal fiction that foreign outsiders should be regarded as fallen Kshatriyas. When the compiler of the *Laws of Manu* was writing it seemed quite natural to treat Persians, Dards, and certain other foreign nations as Kshatriyas who had sunk to the condition of Sūdras by reason of their neglect

from the three lower classes, it was not from any intention to preserve the purity of their blood, for it was already tainted and saturated with that of the other classes. It appears to be mainly an act of self-preservation against the charge of sexual intemperance brought by the Jaina and Buddhist monks. It is also easy to perceive that if they discontinued the immemorial custom of eating flesh and drinking liquor along with the employment of flesh-eating people as cooks in their households, it was not from any love of vegetarianism, but mainly from a determined effort to avoid the charges of intemperance and cruelty to animals brought against them by the Buddhists. Thus the passing of the Brāhmans from class life into caste life was . . . brought about against the will of the Brāhmans themselves; for it demands a good deal of self-denial to give up the pleasures of the bed and the table.

As a compensation for this self-denial, the reformed or reforming Brāhmans apparently perceived a decided advantage accruing to themselves; for that reform moved a death-blow to the existenee of Buddhism itself. . . . Thus, with the introduction of flesh and liquor as articles of diet not condemned for the common people, the Vaisyas and Sūdras seem to have formed themselves into separate castes, following the Brāhmans' (p. 11). Those propositions seem to me to be only slightly exaggerated expressions of important truths.

of sacred rites and their failure to consult Brahmans (x, 44). The change in the Hindu attitude towards foreigners seems to be mainly due to the Muhammadan conquest. We may take it that from the eleventh and twelfth centuries of the Christian era the caste institution has subsisted in substantially its modern form. That proposition is subject to the qualification that minor local and superficial modifications are taking place continually. But the institution as a whole remains unchanged and unshaken.

Demerits of caste. The demerits of the peculiar Hindu institution are obvious. Anybody can perceive that it shuts off Indians from free association with foreigners, thus making it difficult for the Indian to understand the foreigner, and for the stranger to understand the Indian. It is easier for the English administrator to attain full sympathy with the casteless Burman than it is for him to draw aside the veil which hides the inmost thoughts of the Chitpāwan or Nambudri Brahman. No small part of the mystery which ordinarily confines interest in Indian subjects to a narrow circle of experts is due ultimately to caste. It is not pleasant for an Englishman or Frenchman to know that, however distinguished he may be personally, the touch of his hand is regarded as a pollution by his high-caste acquaintance. Yet that is the disagreeable fact. Within India caste breaks up society into thousands of separate units, frequently hostile one to the other, and always jealous. The institution necessarily tends to hinder active hearty co-operation for any purpose, religious, political, or social. All reformers are conscious of the difficulties thus placed in their path. Each individual finds his personal liberty of action checked in hundreds of ways unknown to the dwellers in other lands. The restrictions of caste rules collide continually with the conditions of modern life, and are the source of endless inconveniences. The institution is a relic of the ancient past and does not readily adapt itself to the requirements of the twentieth century. Although necessity compels even the strictest Brahmans to make some concessions to practical convenience, as, for instance, in the matters of railway travelling and drinking pipe water, the modifications thus introduced are merely superficial. The innate antique sentiment of caste exclusiveness survives in full strength and is not weakened materially even by considerable laxity of practice. The conflict between caste regulations and modern civilization is incessant, but caste survives. Further, the institution fosters intense class pride, fatal to a feeling of brotherhood between man and man. The Malabar Brahman who considers himself defiled if an outcaste stands within twenty paces of him cannot possibly be interested in a creature so despised. The sentiment pervades all classes of Hindu society in varying degrees of intensity. Such objections to the caste institution, with many others which might be advanced, go far to justify, or at any rate explain, the vigorous denunciations of the system found abundantly in Indian literature as well as in the writings of foreigners. Four stanzas by Vemana, the Telugu poet, may serve as a summary of the numerous Indian diatribes on the subject.

CASTE

If we look through all the earth,
Men, we see, have equal birth,
Made in one great brotherhood,
Equal in the sight of God.

Food or caste or place of birth
Cannot alter human worth.
Why let caste be so supreme?
'Tis but folly's passing stream. . . .

Empty is a caste-dispute:
All the castes have but one root.
Who on earth can e'er decide
Whom to praise and whom deride?

Why should we the Pariah scorn,
When his flesh and blood were born
Like to ours? What caste is He
Who doth dwell in all we see? [1]

The dictum of Sir Henry Maine, the eminent jurist, that caste is 'the most disastrous and blighting of human institutions' may suffice as a sample of adverse opinions expressed by European writers.

The merits of caste. The hostile critics have not got hold of the whole truth. Much may be said on the other side, which needs to be presented. An institution which has lasted for thousands of years, and has forced its passage down through the peninsula all the way to Cape Comōrin in the face of the strongest opposition, must have merits to justify its existence and universal prevalence within the limits of India.[2] The most ardent defenders of caste, of course, must admit its unsuitability for other lands. 'Thinking men', as Sir Madhava Row observed, 'must beware lest the vast and elaborate social structure which has arisen in the course of thousands of years of valuable experience should be injured or destroyed without anything to substitute, or with a far worse structure to replace it.' The institution of caste cannot be treated properly as a thing by itself. It is an integral part of Hinduism, that is to say, of the Hindu social and economic system. It is, as Ketkar justly observes, intimately associated with the Hindu philosophical ideas of *karma*, rebirth, and the theory of the three *gunas*. But such abstract ideas cannot be discussed in this place. More writers than one have observed that the chief attribute of the caste

[1] Gover, *The Folk-songs of Southern India*, London, Trübner, 1872, p. 275; a charming and instructive book.

[2] 'The hatred which existed between the early Dravidians and the Aryans is best preserved in the Kuricchans' (a hill tribe in Malabar, corresponding to the Kuravas of the Tamil country) custom of plastering their huts with cow-dung to remove the pollution caused by the entrance of a Brahman' (*Tamil Studies*, p. 90). The Kuravas in Travancore rank very low and bury their dead (*The Travancore State Manual*, ii. 402).

system regarded historically is its stability. The Hindu mind clings to custom, and caste rules are solidified custom. That stability, although not absolute, has been the main agent in preserving Hindu ideas of religion, morals, art, and craftsmanship. The Abbé Dubois was much impressed by the services which the institution renders to social order. Monier Williams concisely observes that 'caste has been useful in promoting self-sacrifice, in securing subordination of the individual to an organized body, in restraining vice, [and] in preventing pauperism'. Similar quotations might be largely multiplied.[1]

The future of caste. With reference to the future, the practical conclusion is that talk about the abolition or even the automatic extinction of caste is futile. Caste within India cannot be either abolished or extinguished within a measurable time. The system grew up of itself in remote antiquity because it suited India, and will last for untold centuries because it still suits India on the whole, in spite of its many inconveniences. Hindu society without caste is inconceivable. Reformers must be content to make the best of a system which cannot be destroyed. The absolutely indispensable compromises with modern conditions will arrange themselves from time to time, while the huge mass of the Indian agricultural population will continue to walk in the ancestral ways. The deep waters of Hinduism are not easily stirred. Ripples on the surface leave the depths unmoved.

The 'Laws of Manu'. In connexion with the subject of the evolution of caste, the famous law-book commonly called the 'Laws', or 'Code', or 'Institutes of Manu' (*Mānava-dharma-sāstra* in Sanskrit) demands notice. The treatise, written in lucid Sanskrit verse of the 'classical' type, comprises 2,684 couplets (*sloka*) arranged in twelve chapters; and is the earliest of the metrical law-books. It professes to be the composition of a sage named Bhrigu, who used the works of predecessors. The date of composition may lie between 200 B.C. and A.D. 200. About one-tenth of the verses is found in the *Mahābhārata*.

The *Laws of Manu* form the foundation of the queer medley of inconsistent systems of jurisprudence administered by the Privy Council and the High Courts of India under the name of Hindu Law. The prevalent error concerning the supposed 'four original castes' rests partly, as proved above, on erroneous interpretation of the text, and partly on fictitious explanations of the facts of caste offered by the author. The early Sanskritists unduly exalted the authority of the *Laws of Manu*, which they regarded as veritable laws instead of the mere rulings of a text-book writer, which they actually are. The fuller knowledge of the present day sees the book in truer perspective, but the old errors still exert a baneful influence in many directions.

[1] Some of the quotations are taken from Aiya, *The Travancore State Manual*, 1906, vol. ii, pp. 229 foll.

The books named are merely those which the author has found most useful.

The first place is due to Prof. A. A. MACDONELL, *A History of Sanskrit Literature* (Heinemann, 1900), a masterly summary of an enormous subject. KAEGI, *The Rigveda*, transl. by ARROWSMITH (Boston, 1886), is a good small book. The metrical version of *The Hymns of the Rigveda* by GRIFFITH (2 vols., 2nd ed., Benares, 1887) is an unpretentious work of sound scholarship. The literal translation of the *Atharva Veda* by WHITNEY AND LANMAN (2 vols., Harvard Or. Series, 1905) is indispensable, but difficult to understand. *The History of Sanskrit Literature* by WEBER (transl., 2nd ed., Trübner, 1882) is highly technical. MAX MÜLLER'S *Chips from a German Workshop* (vol. 1868), and *India, What can it Teach us ?* (1883) are still of service. I have also derived benefit from COLEBROOKE, *Miscellaneous Essays* (collected ed. in 2 vols., Trübner, 1873); MANNING, *Ancient and Mediaeval India* (2 vols., 1869) ; and R. W. FRAZER, *A Literary History of India* (1898). RAJENDRALAL MITRA'S essays on 'Beef in Ancient India' and cognate topics, reprinted in *Indo-Aryans* (London and Calcutta, 1881), are sound and important. Mr. B. G. TILAK temperately expounds an extreme theory in *Orion, or Researches into the Antiquity of the Vedas* (Poona, 1916).

For the Epic period, HOPKINS, *The Great Epic of India* (New York and London, 1901), is of high authority. *Epic India* by C. V. VAIDYA (Bombay, 1907), although a rather fanciful book, has some good points. Mr. F. E. PARGITER'S papers on early Indian history in the *J. R. A. S.* from 1908 present novel views.

The most illuminating book on caste which I have met with is *The History of Caste in India* by SHRIDAR V. KETKAR (vol. i, Ithaca, N.Y., 1909 ; vol. ii, 'An Essay on Hinduism', Luzac, London, 1911). The book apparently is not known as well as it deserves to be. *The Evolution of Caste*, a pamphlet by R. SHAMA SASTRI (44 pp., S. P. C. K. Press, Madras, 1916), is a suggestive paper. A short essay entitled 'Caste in India' was published by me in *East and West* (Bombay, June 1913). 'Influence of the Indian King upon the growth of Caste' by H. J. MAYNARD (*J. P. H. S.*, vol. vi, pp. 88–100) is a novel and important essay.

Certain other writers are quoted in the notes, and a very long list of books might be given.

CHAPTER 3

The pre-Maurya states ; the rise of Jainism and Buddhism ; the invasion of Alexander the Great ; India in the fourth century B.C.

Continuity of Indian civilization. China excepted, no region of the world can boast of an ancient civilization so continuous and unbroken as that of India. Civilized life may have begun earlier in Egypt and Babylonia, but in those countries the chain connecting the distant past with the present was rudely snapped long ago. No living memory of the Chaldees and Pharaohs or of their institutions survives. In India the ideas of the Vedic period still are a vital force, and even the ritual of the Rishis is not wholly disused. The lack of ancient records inscribed on imperishable material, such as abound in Egypt and Babylonia, forbids the writing of early Indian history in a manner at all comparable with that feasible in the countries named. The historian of India has nothing but tradition to guide him until quite a late period, and his handling of really ancient times is necessarily devoid of any chronological framework, being vague and sketchy.

Dated history begins in seventh century B.C. No attempt at Indian history dated even in the roughest fashion can be made before the seventh century B.C. The first exact date known, as already mentioned, is 326 B.C., the year of Alexander's invasion. By reckoning back from that fixed point, or from certain closely approximate Maurya dates slightly later, and by making use of the historical traditions recorded in literature, a little information can be gleaned concerning a few kingdoms of northern India in the seventh century. No definite affirmation of any kind can be made about specific events in either the peninsula or Bengal before 300 B.C. The scanty record of events in the northern kingdoms has to be mostly picked out of books written primarily to serve religious purposes. Those books, Jain, Buddhist, and Brahmanical, naturally deal chiefly with the countries in which religious movements were most active. The traditionary accounts are deeply tinged by the sectarian prejudices of the writers, and often hopelessly discordant.

India in the seventh century B.C. Recent excavations give reason for believing that a capital city occupied part of the site of Taxila in the Panjāb at a remote period, but at present it is not possible to say anything more definite about the history of that region. Other cities, too, both in the north and the south of India, seem to have been in existence from immemorial antiquity. In the seventh century B.C. we may be assured that although vast territories in most parts of India were still covered by forest, the home of wild beasts and scanty tribes of savage men, extensive civilized settlements of long standing existed in the plains of the Indus and Ganges basins.

Ujjain in Sindhia's dominions, still a considerable town retaining its ancient name unchanged, ranks as one of the seven sacred cities of India, and rivals Benares in its claims on Hindu veneration.[1] In the seventh century it was the capital of the kingdom of Avanti, known later as Mālwā, which evidently was one of the leading Indian powers for a considerable time until the supremacy passed into the hands of Magadha. Kosala, or Northern Oudh, of which the capital was Srāvastī on the Rāptī, probably represented by Sahet-Mahet, was another important state which competed with Magadha for the headship of Āryāvarta.

Magadha. Magadha, or South Bihār, the seat of the Magadha tribe, rose to unquestioned pre-eminence in the fourth century B.C., and at a much earlier date had been intimately associated with the development of historical Jainism and Buddhism. The literary traditions of northern India consequently are mostly

[1] The seven sacred cities are Benares (Kāsī), Hardwār (Māyā), Kānchī (Conjeeveram), Ayodhyā (Oudh), Dvāravatī (Dvārikā), Mathurā, and Ujjain or Avantikā.

devoted to the affairs of Magadha, and the history of that state has to do duty as the history of India, because hardly anything is known about the annals of less prominent kingdoms.

King Bimbisāra. The regular story of Magadha begins with the Saisunāga Dynasty, established before 600 B.C., perhaps in 642 B.C., by a chieftain of Benares named Sisunāga (or Sisunāka), who fixed his capital at Girivraja or old Rājagriha, among the hills of the Gayā District.[1]

The first monarch about whom anything substantial has been recorded is the fifth king, Bimbisāra or Srēnika, who extended his paternal dominions by the conquest of Anga, the modern Bhāgalpur and Mungir Districts. He built the town of New Rājagriha (Rājgir), and may be regarded as the founder of the greatness of Magadha. He appears to have been a Jain in religion, and sometimes is coupled by Jain tradition with Asoka's grandson, Samprati, as a notable patron of the creed of Mahāvīra. His reign of twenty-eight years may be dated approximately from 582 to 554 B.C., according to the amended reckoning.

Persian occupation of Indus valley. During the period of his rule, according to one theory, or that of Darsaka, according to another, at a date subsequent to 516 B.C., Darius, son of Hystaspes, the capable autocrat of Persia (521–485 B.C.), dispatched an expedition commanded by Skylax of Karyanda in Karia with orders to prove the feasibility of a sea passage from the mouths of the Indus to Persia. Skylax equipped a fleet on the upper waters of the Panjāb rivers in the Gandhāra country, made his way down to the coast, and in the thirteenth month reached the sea. Darius was thus enabled to annex the Indus valley and to send his fleet into the Indian Ocean. The archers from India supplied a contingent to the army of Xerxes, the son of Darius, and shared the defeat of Mardonius at Plataea in Greece in 479 B.C.

The province on the Indus annexed by Darius was formed into the twentieth satrapy, which was considered to be the richest and most populous province of the Persian empire. It paid a tribute of 360 Euboic talents of gold-dust, equivalent to at least a million sterling, and constituting about one-third of the total bullion revenue of the Asiatic provinces. The Indian satrapy, which was distinct from Arīa (Herat), Arachosia (Kandahār), and Gandharia (Taxila and the north-western frontier), must have extended from the Salt Range to the sea, and probably included part of the Panjāb to the east of the Indus. The courses of the rivers in those days were quite different from what they now are, and there is reason for believing that extensive tracts now desert were then rich and populous. The high tribute paid is thus explained.

No distinct evidence exists to show that there was any communication in the fifth century B.C. between the Persian province on the Indus and the growing kingdom of Magadha. But it would

[1] See Jackson, 'Notes on Old Rājagriha' (*Ann. Rep. A. S., India*, for 1913–14 (1917), pp. 265–71, Pl. lxxi.

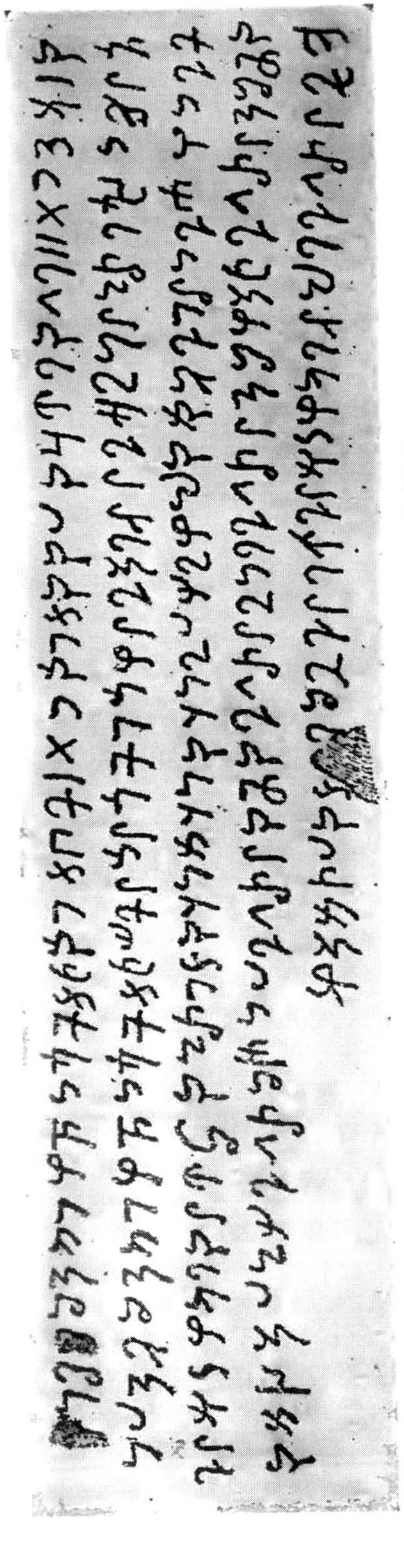

KHAROSHTHI SCRIPT ON SILVER SCROLL.

be extremely rash to affirm that no such communication existed. It is not known at what date Persia ceased to exercise effective control over the twentieth satrapy. At the time of Alexander's invasion the Indus was still recognized as the official boundary between the Persian empire and India, but the authorities do not mention the presence of Persian officials along the course of the river, the banks of which were occupied by sundry small states with rulers of their own, and seemingly independent.

The Kharoshthī alphabet, derived from the Aramaic script, and written from right to left, which continued to be used on the north-western frontier until about the fourth century of the Christian era, appears to have been introduced by Persian officials and may be regarded as a memorial of the days when the Indus valley was part of the Achaemenian empire.

King Ajātasatru. Bimbisāra was succeeded in or about 554 B.C. by his son Ajātasatru or Kūnika, whose reign may be taken as having lasted for twenty-seven years. He built the fortress of Pātali on the Sōn, which afterwards developed into the imperial city of Pātaliputra. His mother was a lady of the famous Lichchhavi tribe, and he was married to a princess of Kosala. He waged successful wars against both the Lichchhavis and his consort's kingdom. Kosala disappears from history as an independent kingdom, and evidently was absorbed by Magadha.

The Lichchhavis. The Lichchhavi nation, tribe, or clan, which played a prominent part in Indian legend and history for more than a thousand years, claims a few words of notice.[1] The Lichchhavis dwelt in the land of the Vrijjis, the region now called the Muzaffarpur District of Bihār to the north of the Ganges. Their capital was Vaisāli, a noble city ten or twelve miles in circuit, represented by the villages and ruins at

[1] The spelling of the name varies.

or near Basārh, twenty miles to the north of Hājīpur, and on the southern side of the river about twenty-seven miles distant in a direct line from Pātaliputra (Patna). The Lichchhavis were governed by an assembly of notables, presided over by an elected chief (*nāyaka*). Good reason exists for believing that they were hill-men of the Mongolian type akin to the Tibetans. They certainly followed the unpleasant Tibetan custom of exposing the bodies of the dead, which were sometimes hung upon trees, and their judicial procedure in criminal cases was exactly the same as the Tibetan. The first Tibetan king is said to have belonged to the family of Sākya the Lichchhavi, a kinsman of Gautama, the sage of another branch of the Sākyas. The more I consider the evidence of such traditions and the unmistakable testimony of the early sculptures as at Barhut and Sanchī, dating from about 200 B.C., the more I am convinced that the Mongolian or hill-man element formed a large percentage in the population of northern India during the centuries immediately preceding and following the Christian era. I think it highly probable that Gautama Buddha, the sage of the Sākyas, and the founder of historical Buddhism, was a Mongolian by birth, that is to say, a hill-man like a Gūrkha with Mongolian features, and akin to the Tibetans. Similar views were expressed long ago by Beal and Fergusson, who used the terms Scythic or Turanian in the sense in which I use Mongolian.

The Lichchhavis retained an influential position for many centuries. The marriage of Chandragupta I with a Lichchhavi princess at the close of the third century A. C. laid the foundation of the greatness of the Imperial Gupta dynasty, and the tribe supplied a line of rulers in the Nepāl valley up to the seventh century.

In early times the Mallas of Pāwā and Kusinagara, who are often mentioned in Buddhist legends, probably were akin to the Lichchhavis.

Mahāvīra, the founder of historical Jainism, likewise may have been a Mongolian hill-man. The Brahman writers regarded the Lichchhavis as degraded Kshatriyas, a purely fictitious mode of expression.

Kings Darsaka and Udaya. Ajātasatru was succeeded in or about 527 B. C. by his son Darsaka, who is mentioned in a play by the early dramatist Bhāsa, which came to light in 1910. He was followed about 503 by his son Udaya, who built the city of Kusumapura on the Ganges, a few miles from Pātaliputra on the Sōn. The two names are sometimes used as synonyms. The position of the confluence of the Sōn with the Ganges and the courses of both rivers in the neighbourhood of Pātaliputra have undergone extensive changes since the days of Udaya.

Parricide story. Buddhist tradition from various sources is unanimous in affirming that Ajātasatru, weary of awaiting the course of nature, murdered his father, and the crime is said to have been instigated by Devadatta, the heretical cousin of the Buddha. I used to accept the story of the parricide as historically true, but am now disposed to reject it as being the outcome of *odium theologicum*, or sectarian rancour, which has done so much to falsify the history of ancient India. The Jains, representing Ajātasatru as a devout follower of their religion who 'ruled the country for eighty years according to the laws of his father', ignore and implicitly deny the accusation of parricide. The truth seems to be that Ajātasatru, like many later Indian sovereigns, did not confine his royal favour to any one sect. At different times he bestowed his bounty on the followers of the 'former Buddhas' led by Devadatta, on the adherents of Gautama's reformed Buddhism, and on the Jains. Both Buddhists and Jains claimed him as one of themselves. The Jain claim appears to be well founded. When the Buddhists had secured pre-eminence in northern India in consequence of Asoka's patronage, leanings towards Jainism became criminal in the eyes of ecclesiastical chroniclers, who were ready to invent the most scandalous stories in order to blacken the memory of persons deemed heretical. The legends told by orthodox Buddhists about Gautama's cousin Devadatta seem to have no other foundation. It will be shown presently that the history of the Nandas has been falsified in a similar fashion. For those reasons I now reject the Buddhist tale of Ajātasatru's murder of his father. According to the traditions of the Jains, their ancient temples in Magadha were destroyed by the Buddhists when they attained power.

Kings and prophets. The main interest of the reigns of Bimbisāra and his son lies in the close association of both kings with the lives of Gautama Buddha and Vardhamāna Mahāvīra Tirthankara, who are usually described respectively as the founders of Buddhism and Jainism. The traditions concerning the intercourse of the kings with the prophets are discrepant in many particulars which need not be discussed, but it seems to be fairly certain that King Bimbisāra was related to Mahāvīra, and was contemporary for some years with both him and Gautama Buddha.

Credible evidence affirms that Ajātasatru visited both of those teachers, and that during his reign Gautama Buddha died. In the third edition of *The Early History of India* (1914) I assumed that Gautama died in 487 B.C., in the reign of Ajātasatru, which began about 502 B.C. I refrained from defining the date of Mahāvīra's death. But, if the revised reading of the Khāravela inscription is correctly interpreted (*post*, p. 58 *n.*), all the Saisunāga dates must be moved back more than fifty years. The tentative chronology in the table on page 70 *post* has been revised accordingly. If it is at all correct, it supports the Ceylon date, 544 or 543 B.C., for the death of Gautama Buddha. But no hypothesis can reconcile all the conflicting testimonies and traditions.

Religion in sixth century B.C. The sixth century B.C. was a time when men's minds in several widely separated parts of the world were deeply stirred by the problems of religion and salvation. The Indian movement was specially active in Magadha and the neighbouring regions where the Hinduizing of the population was incomplete and distinctions of race were clearly marked. Intelligent members of the governing classes, who were regarded as Kshatriyas by the Brahmans from the west, were inclined to consider themselves better men than their spiritual guides, whose arrogant class-pride aroused warm opposition. It seems to me almost certain, as already indicated, that the Saisunāgas, Lichchhavis, and several other ruling families or clans in or near Magadha were not Indo-Aryan by blood. They were, I think, hill-men of the Mongolian type, resembling the Tibetans, Gūrkhas, Bhūtias, and other Himalayan tribes of the present day. The racial distinction between the Brahmans and their pupils necessarily evoked and encouraged the growth of independent views on philosophy and religion. The educated men of the upper classes, called Kshatriyas by the Brahmans, rebelled against the claim of the strangers to the exclusive possession of superior knowledge and the key of the door to salvation.

Many sects arose advocating the most diverse opinions concerning the nature of God and the soul, the relation between God and man, and the best way of attaining salvation. Most Indian thinkers contemplate salvation or deliverance (*moksha*) as meaning the release of the soul from all liability to future rebirths. At that time the religion favoured by the Brahmans, as depicted in the treatises called *Brāhmanas*, was of a mechanical, lifeless character, overlaid with cumbrous ceremonial. The formalities of the irksome ritual galled many persons, while the cruelty of the numerous bloody sacrifices was repugnant to others. People sought eagerly for some better path to the goal of salvation desired by all. Some, who hoped to win their object by means of transcendental knowledge, sounded the depths of novel systems of philosophy. Others sought to subdue the body and free the soul by inflicting on themselves the most austere mortifications and cruel self-tortures.

Jainism and Buddhism. All the numerous schools and sects which then sprang up or flourished died out in the course of time save two. The doctrines of the two surviving sects now known as Jainism and Buddhism have brought into existence two powerful churches or religious organizations which still affect profoundly the thoughts of mankind.

Buddhism, although almost extinct in the land of its birth, is at this day one of the greatest spiritual forces in the world, dominating, as it does in various forms, Ceylon, Burma, Siam, Tibet, Mongolia, China, and Japan. Jainism, which never aspired to such wide conquests, now claims but a comparatively small number of adherents, resident chiefly in Rājputāna and western India. The influence of the religion, however, even now is much greater than that indicated by the census returns. In former times it pervaded almost every province of India and enjoyed the patronage of mighty kings.

Both Jainism and Buddhism as historical religions originated in Magadha or the territories adjoining that kingdom in the reigns of Bimbisāra and his son Ajātasatru. Those two faiths, it need hardly be said, did not come into being independently of previous conditions. The teaching of Mahāvīra the Jain and of Gautama the Buddha was based on the doctrine of earlier prophets. Mahāvīra started his religious life as a reformer of an ancient ascetic order said to have been founded by Pārsvanāth two centuries and a half earlier. Gautama's preaching was related to the cult of the 'former Buddhas', whose prophet was Devadatta, Gautama's cousin. But we need not trouble about the obscure precursors of Jainism and Buddhism, who may be left to the research of antiquarians. The history of India is concerned seriously only with those historical religions as started respectively by Mahāvīra and Gautama. Although the stories of the lives of both prophets are obscured by a veil of legend and mythology, certain facts seem to be established with sufficient certainty. We will take first Jainism, the minor and probably the older religion of the two.

MAHĀVĪRA VARDHAMĀNA.

Career of Mahāvīra. Vardhamāna, better known by his title in religion of Mahāvīra, was the son of a Lichchhavi noble of Vaisāli. He gave up his honourable rank and joined the ascetic order of Pārsvanāth, in which he remained for some years. Becoming dissatisfied with the rules of that order, he started on his own account as a religious leader when about forty years of age. During the remainder of his life, which lasted more than thirty years, he travelled as a preacher through Magadha or South Bihār; Videha, otherwise called Mithilā or Tirhūt; and Anga or Bhāgalpur. In the course of his ministry he organized a new religious order consisting of professed friars and nuns, lay brethren and lay sisters. When he died at Pāwā in the Patna District his adherents are said to have exceeded 14,000 in number. Being related through his mother to the reigning kings of Videha, Magadha, and Anga, he was in a position to gain official patronage for his teaching, and is recorded to have been in personal touch with both Bimbisāra and Ajātasatru, who seem to have followed his doctrine. The traditional dates for his death vary so much that it is impossible to obtain certainty in the matter. The date most commonly accepted, 527 B.C., is difficult to reconcile with the well-attested fact of his interview with Ajātasatru and with the Khāravela inscription. Professor Jacobi advocates 477 B.C. as the approximate year of the decease of Mahāvīra.

GAUTAMA BUDDHA.
(Sārnāth, fifth century.)

Career of Buddha. The career of Gautama, the sage of the Sākyas (Sākyamuni), known generally as Buddha or the Buddha, because he claimed to have attained supreme knowledge of things spiritual (*bodhi*), was very similar to that of Mahāvīra. Gautama, like his rival prophet, was the son of a noble Sākya, the Rājā of Kapilavastu in the Nepalese Tarāi, a dependency of Kosala, and was classed by the Brahmans as a Kshatriya. The legends relate in endless imaginative detail the story of the young prince's disgust for the luxurious life of a palace, and of his resolve to effect the Great Renunciation. Leaving his home, he went to Gayā and there sought salvation by subjecting his body to the severest penances. But while sitting under the holy tree he made the discovery that mere asceticism was futile, and decided to spend the rest of his life in preaching the truth as he saw it. He proceeded to the Deer Park at Sārnāth near Benares, where five disciples joined him. From that small beginning arose the great Buddhist *Sangha* or Order. Gautama continued his preaching for forty-five years and died aged eighty at Kusinagara, which probably was situated in Nepalese territory at the junction of the Little Rāptī with the Gandak near Bhavēsar Ghāt. The well-known remains near Kasiā in the Gorakhpur District appear to be those of the monastic establishment of Vēthadīpa, subordinate to the head monastery at Kusinagara. Both were called *Parinirvāna* monasteries as being connected with the death of Buddha.[1] The date of his decease, like that of Mahāvīra, cannot be determined with accuracy. I formerly accepted 487 or 486 B.C. as the best attested date, but the new reading of the Khāravela record pushes back all the early dates. It appears that both Mahāvīra and Buddha were contemporary with kings Bimbisāra and Ajātasatru, both dying in the reign of the latter.

Jainism and Buddhism contrasted. The close parallelism of the careers of the two prophets, combined with certain superficial resemblances between the doctrines of the sects which they founded, induced some of the older scholars to regard Jainism as a sect of Buddhism. That opinion is now recognized to be erroneous. The two systems, whether regarded as philosophies or religions, are essentially different. The word 'sects' as applied above to the Jain and Buddhist churches is correctly used. because both Mahāvīra and Buddha may be justly regarded as having been originally Hindu reformers. Neither prophet endeavoured directly to overthrow the caste framework of Hindu society so far as it had been established in their time, although both rejected the authority of the Vedas and opposed the practice of animal sacrifice. Followers of either Mahāvīra or Gautama were not asked to give up their belief in the Hindu gods, which always have received veneration from both Jains and Buddhists. Indra, Brahmā, and other gods play a prominent part in Buddhist legend and belief. In Ceylon even the great gods Siva and Vishnu are worshipped as satellites of Buddha. The Jains of the present day continue, as their forefathers always did, to employ Brahmans as their domestic chaplains for the performance of birth or death ceremonies, and even sometimes, it is said, for temple worship. Jainism has never cut itself away from its roots in Hinduism. Many Jains consider themselves to be Hindus, and describe their religion accordingly in census returns. That continuous close connexion between Brahmanical Hinduism and Jainism probably is the principal reason why the latter faith made no conquests outside of India.

Buddhism developed a much more independent existence. Both as a philosophy and a religion it so adapted itself to the needs of foreigners that in the course of time it nearly died out in India while acquiring new life in foreign lands. The Jains give the laity a prominent place, while the Buddhists rely mainly on their organized *Sangha*—the Community or Order of ordained friars. That organized Order has been the main instrument of Buddhist missionary expansion. No avowed Buddhist in any country would dream of describing himself as a Hindu by religion.[2] Readers

[1] See the author's article 'Kusinagara' in Hastings, *Encycl. of Religion and Ethics*. Kasiā cannot represent Kusinagara, because that site was and long had been deserted in the time of the Chinese pilgrims, whereas building was continuous at Kasiā all through the Gupta period and afterwards.

[2] For unavowed, veiled, or crypto-Indian Buddhists see Nagendra Nāth Vasu, *The Modern Buddhism and its Followers in Orissa* (Hare Press,

who desire to understand thoroughly the philosophical, ethical, and theological tenets of Jainism and Buddhism, the points of agreement or divergence in the two systems, and the church regulations must study some or other of the many excellent books now available. Only a few points can be noted here.

Jain doctrines. Jain teaching lays stress upon the doctrine that man's personality is dual, comprising both material and spiritual natures. It rejects the Vedantist doctrine of the universal soul. Jains believe that not only men and animals, but also plants, minerals capable of growth, air, wind, and fire possess souls (*jīva*) endowed with various degrees of consciousness.[1] They hold that it is possible to inflict pain on a stone, or even on air or water. The belief in a supreme Deity, the creator of the universe, is emphatically denied. God is defined as being 'only the highest, the noblest, and the fullest manifestation of all the powers which lie latent in the soul of man'. From that point of view Jainism may be said to anticipate Comte's 'religion of humanity'.

In ethics or practical morality 'the first principle is *ahimsā*, non-hurting of any kind of life, howsoever low may be the stage of its evolution'. The strange doctrine affirming the existence of *jīvas* in objects commonly called inanimate extends the Jain idea of *ahimsā* far beyond the Brahmanical or Buddhist notions.

The reader of Indian history is sometimes perplexed by the apparent contradiction of principles involved when a king orders the execution of a convict, guilty perhaps only of the killing of an animal. The following authoritative ruling on the subject helps to make intelligible the position taken up by Kumārapāla, king of Gujarāt in the twelfth century, who ruthlessly inflicted the capital penalty on all persons who in any way offended against the *ahimsā* doctrine:

> 'A true Jaina will do nothing to hurt the feelings of another person, man, woman, or child; nor will he violate the principles of Jainism. Jaina ethics are meant for men of all positions—for kings, warriors, traders, artisans, agriculturists, and indeed for men and women in every walk of life. . . . "Do your duty. Do it as humanely as you can." This, in brief, is the primary principle of Jainism. Non-killing cannot interfere with one's duties. The king, or the judge, has to hang a murderer. The murderer's act is the negation of a right of the murdered. The king's, or the judge's, order is the negation of this negation, and is enjoined by Jainism as a duty. Similarly, the soldier's killing on the battle-field.'

Calcutta, 1911), with the extremely learned Introduction by M. M. H. P. Sāstri.

[1] Compare Wordsworth, *Prelude* (ed. 2, 1851), Book III, p. 49:

> To every natural form, rock, fruit, or flower,
> Even the loose stones that cover the high-way,
> I gave a moral life: I saw them feel,
> Or linked them to some feeling: the great mass
> Lay bedded in a quickening soul, and all
> That I beheld respired with inward meaning.

The poet felt those sentiments while he was an undergraduate at Cambridge.

Jainism is an austere religion, demanding severe self-control in diverse ways, and imposing many inconvenient restraints. The teaching theoretically condemns caste, but in practice 'the modern Jaina is as fast bound as his Hindu brother in the iron fetters of caste'.

The Jains are divided into two main sects, the Svetāmbara, or 'white-robed', and the Digambara, or 'sky-clad', that is to say nude, which separated about the beginning of the second century A.C. Each sect has its own scriptures. A modern offshoot of the Svetāmbaras, called Sthānaka-vāsī, rejects the use of idols in worship.

Jains highly approve of suicide by slow starvation. The practice, abhorred by Buddhists, seems to outsiders inconsistent with the *ahimsā* doctrine, but Jain philosophy has an explanation, which will be found expounded in Mrs. Stevenson's book.

The teaching of Buddha. Gautama Buddha, like Mahāvīra and almost all prophets in his country, took over from the common stock of Indian ideas the theories of rebirth and *karma*, accepted generally by Indian thinkers as truths needing no proof. The *karma* doctrine means that the merits and demerits of a being in past existences determine his condition in the present life. Buddha held that to be born is an evil, that the highest good is deliverance from rebirth, that good *karma* will effect such deliverance, and that the acquisition of good *karma* requires a strictly moral life. His disciples were admonished to aim at purity in deed, word, and thought; observing ten commandments, namely, not to kill, steal, or commit adultery; not to lie, invent evil reports about other people, indulge in fault-finding or profane language; to abstain from covetousness and hatred, and to avoid ignorance. Special stress was laid on the virtues of truthfulness, reverence to superiors, and respect for animal life.

He held that men should follow what he called the 'Noble Eightfold Path', practising right belief, right thought, right speech, right action, right means of livelihood, right exertion, right remembrance, and right meditation. That path was also described as the Middle Path, lying midway between sensuality and asceticism. Men and women of the laity could attain much success in travelling the way of holiness, but full satisfaction could be obtained only by joining the *Sangha* or Order of ordained monks, or rather friars. Women were permitted to become nuns, but nuns never occupied an important place in Buddhism. The *Sangha* of monks developed into a highly organized, wealthy, and powerful fraternity, which became the efficient instrument for the wide diffusion of Buddhism in Asia.

Popular Buddhism. Buddha can hardly be said to have intended to found a new religion. He taught an abstruse doctrine of metaphysics, which he used chiefly as the rational basis of his practical moral code. He was unwilling to discuss questions concerning the nature of God or the soul, the infinity of the universe, and so forth, holding that such discussions are unprofitable.

Without formally denying the existence of Almighty God, the Creator, he ignored Him. Buddha, although he denied the authority of the Vedas, did not seek to interfere with the current beliefs in the Hindu gods or with familiar superstitions ; and, as a matter of fact, popular Buddhism from the very earliest times has always differed much from the austere religion of the books. Modern Burma, where everybody worships the Nats or spirits, while accepting without question the orthodox teaching of the monks, offers the best illustration of the state of things in ancient Buddhist India, as vividly represented in the sculptures. Buddhism in practice was a cheerful religion in India long ago, as it is in Burma now. The change to Puranic Hinduism has made India a sadder land.

Transformation of Buddhism. The person of Buddha inspired in his disciples such ardent affection and devotion that very soon after his death he was regarded as being something more than a man. By the beginning of the Christian era, if not earlier, he had become a god to whom prayer might be offered. The primitive Buddhism which ignored the Divine was known in later times as the Hīna-yāna, or Lesser Vehicle of salvation, while the modified religion which recognized the value of prayer and acknowledged Buddha as the Saviour of mankind was called the Mahā-yāna, or the Greater Vehicle.

While the original official Buddhism was a dry, highly moralized philosophy much resembling in its practical operation the Stoic schools of Greece and Rome, the later emotional Buddhism approached closely to Christian doctrines in substance, although not in name. In another direction it became almost indistinguishable from Hinduism.

No Buddhist period. It must be clearly understood that Brahmanical Hinduism continued to exist and to claim innumerable adherents throughout the ages. It may well be doubted if Buddhism can be correctly described as having been the prevailing religion in India as a whole at any time. The phrase 'Buddhist period', to be found in many books, is false and misleading. Neither a Buddhist nor a Jain period ever existed. From time to time either Buddhism or Jainism obtained exceptional success and an unusually large percentage of adherents in the population of one kingdom or another, but neither heresy ever superseded Brahmanical Hinduism. Mahāvīra, as has been mentioned, had about 14,000 disciples when he died, a mere drop in the ocean of India's millions. Subsequent royal patronage largely extended his following, and at times Jainism became the state religion of certain kingdoms, in the sense that it was adopted and encouraged by certain kings, who carried with them many of their subjects. Instances of kings changing their creed are numerous. Buddhism probably continued to be an obscure local sect, confined to Magadha and the neighbouring regions, until Asoka gave it his powerful patronage more than two centuries after the death of Buddha. The fortune of Buddhism was made by Asoka, but even he never attempted to force all his subjects to enter the Buddhist fold. While he insisted on certain rules of conduct concerning diet and other matters being observed by everybody in accordance with the orders of government, he did not interfere with anybody's faith. Akbar pursued the same policy in the sixteenth century. Even in Asoka's age it is likely that the majority of the people in many, if not in most, provinces followed the guidance of the Brahmans. The relative proportions of orthodox Hindus and Buddhist dissenters varied enormously according to locality. Many details on the subject can be extracted from the narratives of the Chinese pilgrims in the fifth and seventh centuries after Christ, and there can be no doubt that similar relations between the various Indian sects or religions must have existed in earlier times.

The Hinduism of the Brahmans did not remain unchanged. The attacks delivered by Mahāvīra, Buddha, and other less celebrated prophets on the elaborate ritual and bloody sacrifices favoured by the Brahmans of the sixth century B.C. resulted, not only in the development of Jainism and Buddhism as distinct sects or religions, but in profound modification in the ideas of those Hindus who still professed obedience to the Vedas and to Brahman gurus. The *ahimsā* principle of non-injury to animal life gained many adherents, so that the more shocking elements in the old Hindu ritual tended to fall into disrepute. The change of feeling, as already noted, can be traced in many passages of the *Mahābhārata*. Bloody sacrifices still retain the approval of considerable sections of the population, but the general tendency during the last two thousand years has been to discredit them. The movement of sentiment on the subject continues to this day, and may be observed on a large scale in the peninsula. The slaughter of victims in appalling numbers is still practised in the Telugu country. For instance, at Ellore in the Kistna (Krishnā) District, a thousand victims may be slain on one day at a certain festival, so that the blood flows down from the place of sacrifice 'in a regular flood'. But in the Tamil country 'there is a widespread idea that animal sacrifices are distasteful to good and respectable deities', with the result that such offerings are going out of fashion.[1] The reader will not fail to take note of the proof that two thousand years are not nearly enough for the completion of a single change in religious sentiment throughout India. Perhaps the zeal of ardent reformers may be chilled by the thought.

Brahmanical cults. The reaction against the atheistic tendency of both Jainism and Buddhism on the one hand and against the formalism of a religion of ritual on the other resulted in the evolution among Brahmanical Hindus of the religion of *bhakti*, or lively loving faith in a personal, fatherly God. Although it is impossible to fix dates, Bhandarkar has shown that such devotion to the Deity under the name of Vāsudeva may be traced

[1] Whitehead, *The Village Gods of Southern India* (1916), pp. 66, 94.

back as far as Pānini's time, whatever that was.[1] Other facts indicate the existence of the worship of Vāsudeva in the two centuries immediately preceding the Christian era. The noble *Bhagavadgītā*, the date of which cannot be determined, offers the earliest formal exposition of the *bhakti* doctrine, the Deity being represented under the name and person of Krishna.

The Bhakti religion, which still has numerous adherents in the western parts of Hindostan and many other provinces of India, seems to have arisen in the Brahmarshi region in the neighbourhood of Mathurā and Delhi. Vāsudeva and Krishna both became identified with Vishnu, whose cult has a long history. Simultaneously the cults of Siva and other forms of the Deity were developed, especially in the south. It is impossible to trace the details of religious evolution in a general history, but it is important to remember that much was happening inside the fold of Brahmanical Hinduism while Buddhism and Jainism were being founded and started on their more conspicuous adventures outside.

The 'Nine Nandas'. The dynastic lists of the older Purānas, which are the best authority on the subject, state that the Saisunāga dynasty comprised ten kings, of whom the last two were named Nandivardhana and Mahānandin. Their reigns are said to have covered eighty-three years. They were followed by the Nine Nandas, namely, King Mahāpadma and his eight sons, whose rule altogether is said to have lasted a century. It is clear that the history has been falsified in some way and that the chronology cannot be right. The traditions about the Nandas as recorded in the Purānas, sundry Jain and Buddhist books, the *Mudrā Rākshasa* drama, perhaps composed in the fourth or fifth century A. C., and by the Greek writers, are hopelessly discrepant in many respects, but it is certain that the king deposed and slain by Chandragupta Maurya with the aid of his Brahman minister Chānakya, alias Kautilya or Vishnugupta, was a Nanda, that he was of low caste, that he was a heretic hostile to the Brahmans and Kshatriyas, and that he was a rich, powerful sovereign, believed by the Greeks to control an army of 20,000 horse, 200,000 foot, 2,000 chariots, and 3,000 or 4,000 elephants. Many unsuccessful attempts have been made to harmonize the conflicting traditions and to evolve a reasonable scheme of chronology. I cannot pretend to solve the puzzle, but would suggest that the existence in the twelfth century of a form of the Vikrama era called A-nanda or 'without Nanda' may possibly give the clue. It has been proved that the Hindī poet Chand used the A-nanda mode of computation, leaving out the period of 91 (or 90) years belonging to the dynasty of the Nine Nandas, who were considered to be unholy persons unworthy of inclusion in orthodox Hindu annals. That fact suggests that the dynasty of the Nine Nandas may have begun 91 years before the accession of Chandragupta Maurya, which took place about 322 B.C. If that hypothesis should prove

[1] Most probably the seventh century B. C. in my opinion, for which good authority might be cited.

correct, the beginning of the dynasty of the Nine Nandas must be placed in about 413 B.C. The last two Saisunāga kings of the Puranic lists, namely, *Nandi*-vardhana and Mahā-*nandin*, must be reckoned also as Nandas as their names would seem to indicate. It is unquestionable that the Nanda king dethroned by Chandragupta Maurya was a heretic in Hindu eyes, because the concluding verse of Kautilya's *Arthasāstra* states that 'this *Śāstra* (scripture) has been made by him who from intolerance (of misrule) quickly rescued the scriptures (*śāstram*) and the science of weapons (*sastram*) and the earth which had passed to the Nanda king.' The necessary inference seems to be that the hated Nanda king was either a Jain or a Buddhist, whom orthodox writers did not care to acknowledge as a lawful sovereign. The supposition that the last Nanda was a follower of either Mahāvīra or Gautama is confirmed by the fact that one form of the local tradition attributed to him the erection of the Pānch Pahārī at Patna, a group of ancient *stūpas* which might be either Jain or Buddhist.[1]

Invasion of Alexander the Great. The invasion of India by Alexander the Great of Macedon in 326 B.C., which occurred during the rule of the Nandas in Magadha and is more interesting than any other episode of early Indian history to most European readers, made so little impression on the minds of the inhabitants of the country that no distinct reference to it is to be found in any branch of ancient Indian literature. Our detailed knowledge of his proceedings is derived solely from Greek authors.[2] The name of Sikandar or Alexander is often on the lips of the people in the Panjāb, but it is doubtful how far a genuine tradition of the Macedonian invader survives in that country. Spurious traditions are apt to be generated from confused recollections of the investigations and talk of modern archaeologists. There is also reason to believe that the popular memory sometimes confounds Sikandar of Macedon with his namesakes, the Lodī Sultan of Delhi (1489–1517) and the image-breaking Sultan of Kashmīr (1394–1420). A genuine tradition of Philip's son undoubtedly has been preserved in the families of no less than eight chieftains in the neighbourhood of the Indus and Oxus, all of whom claim the honour of descent from Alexander. The claims may be well founded to some extent, because the historians record that Kleophis, Queen of the Assakēnoi,

[1] The rendering of the *Arthasāstra* text is that of Shāma Sastri. The text of the Khāravela inscription has been settled in 1917 by R. D. Banerji and K. P. Jayaswal as far as possible. Khāravela's 13th year=the year 165 or 164 of the era of 'Rājā Muriya', *scil.* Chandragupta, which began about 322 B.C., and so=about 157 or 158 B.C. A Nanda king, probably Nandivardhana, had made a canal about 300 years before the fifth year of Khāravela (165 B.C.), and so in about 465 B.C. Full publication of the record is awaited. For the Patna *stūpas* see Beal, *Records*, ii. 94. Some people ascribed them to Asoka.

[2] Archaeological evidence, chiefly numismatic, corroborates the Greek historians in certain details.

was reputed to have borne a son to Alexander.[1] The Tungani soldiers who formed the garrison of Yarkand in 1835 also alleged that Macedonian soldier colonists left behind by the conqueror were their ancestors.

Alexander, after completing the conquest of Bactria to the south of the Oxus, resolved to execute his cherished purpose of surpassing the mythical exploits of Herakles his reputed ancestor, Semiramis the fabled Assyrian queen, Cyrus, king of Persia, and the divine Dionysos, by effecting the subjugation of India. When he undertook the task very little accurate information about the scene of the proposed conquests was at his disposal. The sacred soil of India had never been violated by any earlier European invader, nor had the country been visited by travellers from the west, so far as is known. Wild tales concerning the marvels to be seen beyond the Indus were current, but nothing authentic seems to have been on record, and the bold adventurer was obliged to collect the necessary intelligence as he advanced.

Alexander, however, although adventurous, was not imprudent. He never moved without taking adequate precautions to maintain communication with his distant base in Macedon thousands of miles away, and to protect his flanks from hostile attack. His intelligence department seems to have provided him with information accurate enough to ensure the success of each operation.

Campaign in the hills. He crossed the Hindu Kush mountains in May, 327 B.C., and after garrisoning either Kābul itself or a stronghold in the neighbourhood, spent the remainder of the year in subduing the fierce tribes which then as now inhabited the valleys of Suwāt (Swat) and Bājaur. He gave them a lesson such as they have never received since from Afghans, Moguls, or English, and penetrated into secluded fastnesses which no European has ever seen again. His ruthless operations effected their purpose so thoroughly that his communications were never harassed by the tribes.

The Indus crossed. In February, 326 B.C., at the beginning of spring, he crossed the Indus, then regarded as the frontier of the Persian empire, by a bridge of boats built at Und or Ohind above Attock. Thence he advanced to Takkasila or Taxila, 'a great and flourishing city', the capital of Āmbhi, ruler of the region between the Indus and the Hydaspes or Jihlam (Jhelum) river. Āmbhi, who was at feud with the chiefs of neighbouring principalities, welcomed the invader and received him hospitably at his capital. The rich presents offered by the Indian king were requited tenfold by his generous and politic guest. It is worthy of note that the supplies tendered by Āmbhi comprised '3,000 oxen fatted for the shambles' besides 10,000 or more sheep.

[1] The chieftains referred to are: (1) the former Mīrs of Badakhshān, dispossessed about 1822; (2–5) the chiefs of Darwāz, Kulāb, Shighnān, and Wakhan; and (6–8) the chiefs of Chitrāl, Gilgit, and Iskardo (Burnes, *Travels into Bokhara*, &c., 2nd ed., 1835, vol. iii, pp. 186–90).

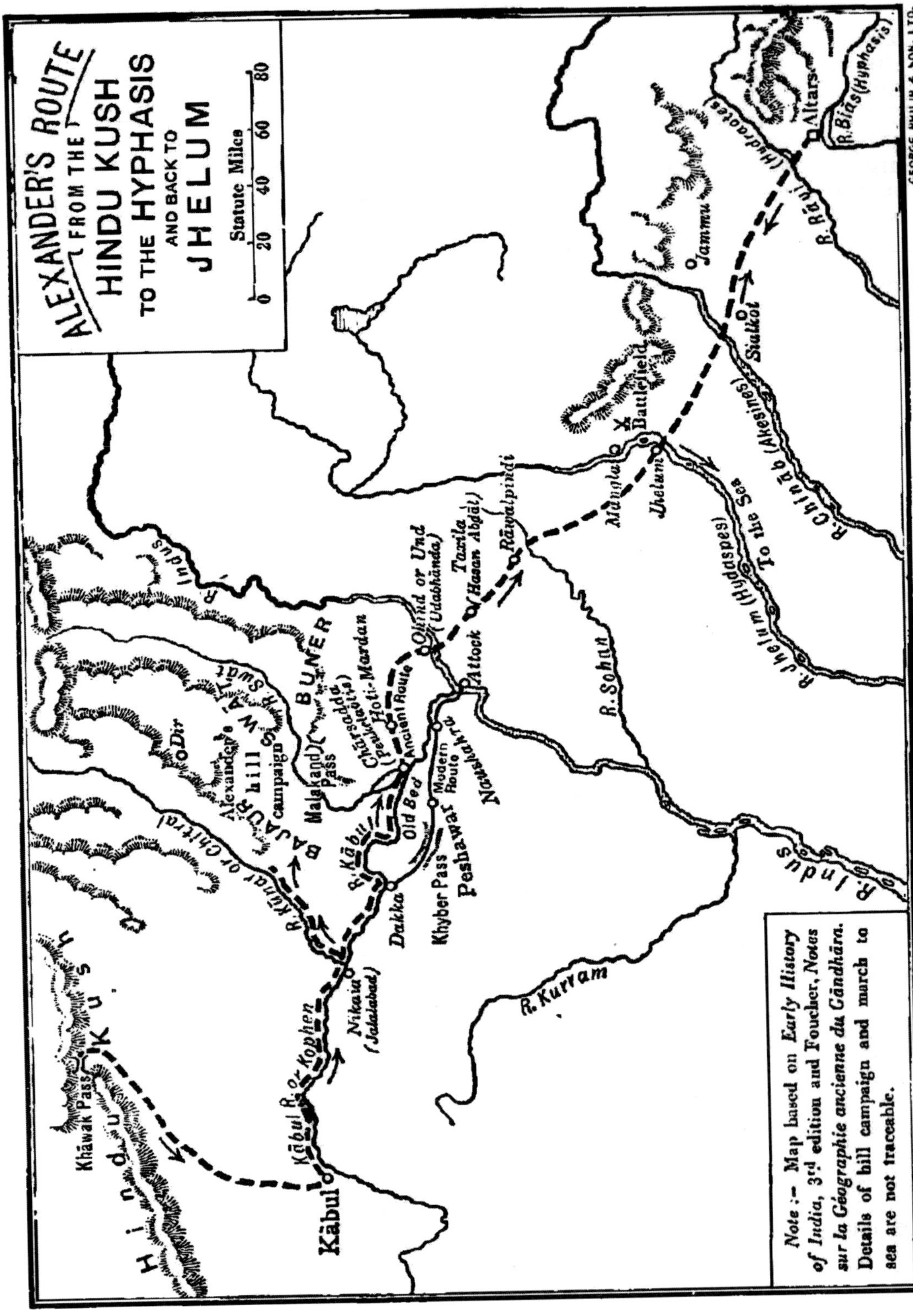
ALEXANDER'S ROUTE
FROM THE
HINDU KUSH
TO THE HYPHASIS
AND BACK TO
JHELUM
Statute Miles
0 20 40 60 80
Note :– Map based on Early History of India, 3rd edition and Foucher, Notes sur la Géographie ancienne du Gāndhāra. Details of hill campaign and march to sea are not traceable.
Hindu Kush
Khāwak Pass
Kābul
Kābul R. or Kophen
Nikaia (Jalalabad)
Dakka
Khyber Pass
Peshawar
R. Kurram
R. Kunar or Chitral
BAJAUR
Alexander's hill campaign
Dir
SWAT
R. Swat
BUNER
Malakand Pass
Chārsadda (Peukelaotis)
Hoti-Mardan
Ancient Route
Modern Route
Old Bed
R. Kābul
Naushahra
Ohind or Und (Udabhānda)
Attock
R. Indus
Taxila (Hasan Abdāl)
Rāwalpindi
R. Sohan
Mangla
Jhelum
Battlefield
R. Jhelum (Hydaspes)
To the Sea
R. Chināb (Akesines)
Sialkot
Jammu
R. Rāvi (Hydraotes)
Altars
R. Biās (Hyphasis)
GEORGE PHILIP & SON. LTD.
WAXTYPE

That statement, made incidentally, is good evidence that in 326 B.C. the people of Taxila were still willing to fatten cattle for slaughter and the feeding of honoured guests, in Vedic fashion.

Taxila. The situation of Taxila in a pleasant valley, amply supplied with water, well adapted for defence, and lying on the highroad from Central Asia to the interior of India, was admirably suited for the site of a great city. The occupation of the site began at a period so remote that when the excavations now in progress under skilled guidance shall be further advanced we may hope to find traces of the most ancient known urban settlement in India. The brilliantly successful operations conducted by the Director-General of Archaeology have as yet barely touched the Bir mound in the southern part of the ruins of Taxila, which represents the city where Alexander halted.[1] The remains of the ancient capital, or rather series of successive capitals, gradually shifted from south to north, cover a space of at least twelve square miles at Hasan Abdāl and several other villages situated about twenty miles to the north-west of Rāwalpindi, which is the strategical representative of Taxila. The cantonment of Rāwalpindi is the most important military station in India. The line of the ancient highway has been followed by the Grand Trunk Road and the North-Western Railway.

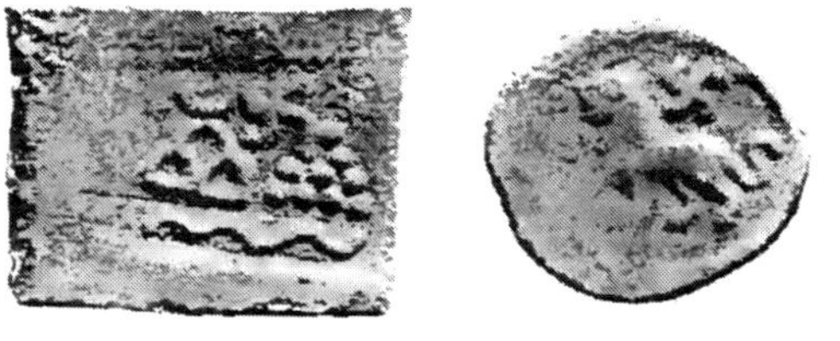

Coins of Taxila.

In the time of Alexander the Panjāb was divided among a large number of small states, Taxila being the capital only of the tract between the Indus and the Hydaspes. Its military importance, therefore, was less than that of its modern representative. The invader having been received by the local king as a friend, no fighting took place in the neighbourhood of Taxila, and no information concerning its defences is recorded. Āmbhi supplied a contingent of five thousand men to help Alexander.

The testimony of the Buddhist *Jātaka* or Birth stories, which, although undated, may be applied fairly to the age of Alexander, proves by a multitude of incidental allusions that Taxila was then the leading seat of Hindu learning, where crowds of pupils from all quarters were taught the 'three Vedas and the eighteen accomplishments'. It was the fashion to send princes and the sons of well-to-do Brahmans on attaining the age of sixteen to complete their education at Taxila, which may be properly described as a university town. The medical school there enjoyed a special reputation, but all arts and sciences could be studied under the most eminent professors.

Strange Taxilan customs. The willing offering of 3,000 oxen to be converted into beef has been noted as a remarkable feature in the social usage of the Taxilans. They had also several

[1] The remark refers to 1917.

peculiar customs, which struck the Greek observers as 'strange and unusual'. The practices described are so startling that it is well to quote the exact words of Strabo, who copied Aristoboulos, a companion of Alexander, and an author deserving of the fullest credit.

'He makes mention of some strange and unusual customs which existed. Those who are unable from poverty to bestow their daughters in marriage expose them for sale in the market-place in the flower of their age, a crowd being assembled by sound of the [conch] shells and drums, which are also used for sounding the war-note. When any person steps forward, first the back of the girl as far as the shoulders is uncovered for his examination and then the parts in front, and if she pleases him and allows herself at the same time to be persuaded, they cohabit on such terms as may be agreed upon. The dead are thrown out to be devoured by vultures. The custom of having many wives prevails here and is common among other races. He says that he had heard from some persons of wives burning themselves along with their deceased husbands and doing so gladly; and that those women who refused to burn themselves were held in disgrace. The same things have been stated by other writers.'[1]

The marriage market obviously suggests comparison with the similar institution in the territory of Babylon, fully described with approval by Herodotus (1. 196), who observes that the sales took place once a year in every village. He heard that the Venetians of Illyria had a like custom. The casting out of the dead to be devoured by vultures was a practice of the Zoroastrian Iranians, and also of the Tibetans. The definite proof of the usage of widow-burning or suttee at such an early certain date is interesting. Among the Kathaioi of the eastern Panjāb also 'the custom prevailed that widows should be burned with their husbands'. The scanty evidence as to Taxilan institutions taken as a whole suggests that the civilization of the people was compounded of various elements, Babylonian, Iranian, Scythian, and Vedic. Suttee probably was a Scythian rite introduced from Central Asia.

Religion and civilization. When the fact is remembered that in later times the Panjāb came to be regarded as an unholy, non-Aryan country, it is worthy of note that the *Jātakas* represent Taxila as the seat of study of the three Vedas and all the other branches of Hindu learning. The population of the Panjāb in Alexander's time probably included many divers races. Strabo (Book XV, chap. i, secs. 61, 63–8) gives an interesting account of the Brahman ascetics of Taxila, chiefly derived from the works of Aristoboulos and Onesikritos. It is clear that the Brahmanical religion was firmly established, notwithstanding the survival of strange customs, and in all likelihood the co-existence of Zoroastrian or Magian fire-worship and other foreign cults. It is manifest that a high degree of material civilization had been attained, and that all the arts and crafts incident to the life of a wealthy,

[1] Strabo, Book XV, chap. i, sec. 62; transl. McCrindle in *Ancient India as described in Classical Literature* (Constable, 1901), p. 69. In sec. 28 Strabo observes that Taxila was governed by 'good laws'.

cultured city were familiar. The notices accorded by Alexander's officers permit no doubt that in the fourth century B. C. the history of Indian civilization was already a long one. Their statements have a material bearing upon discussions concerning the date of the introduction of writing and the chronology of Vedic literature.

Advance against Pōros. Alexander, after allowing his army a pleasant rest at hospitable Taxila, advanced eastward, to attack Pōros, or Pūru, the king of the country between the Hydaspes (Jihlam) and Akesines (Chināb), who felt himself strong enough to defy the invader. The Greeks, who were much impressed by the high stature of the men in the Panjāb, acknowledged that 'in the art of war they were far superior to the other nations by which Asia was at that time inhabited'. The resolute opposition of Pōros consequently was not to be despised. Alexander experienced much difficulty in crossing the Hydaspes river, then, at

POROS MEDAL.

the end of June or the beginning of July, in full flood and guarded by a superior force. His horses would not face the elephants on the opposite bank. After a delay of several weeks he succeeded in stealing a passage at a sharp bend in the river some sixteen miles above his camp and getting across with the help of a convenient island. The hostile armies met in the Karri Plain marked by the villages Sirwāl and Pakral.

Battle of the Hydaspes. The army of Pōros, consisting of 30,000 infantry, four thousand cavalry, three hundred chariots, and two hundred mighty war elephants, was defeated after a hard fight, and annihilated. All the elephants were captured or killed, the chariots were destroyed, twelve thousand men were slain, and nine thousand taken prisoners. The total Macedonian casualties did not exceed a thousand. The primary cause of the Greek victory was the consummate leadership of Alexander, the greatest general in the history of the world. Pōros, a giant six and a half feet in height, fought to the last, and received nine wounds before he was taken prisoner. The victor, who willingly responded to his captive's proud request that he might be treated as a king, secured the alliance of the Indian monarch by prudent generosity.

The elephants on which Pōros had relied proved unmanageable in the battle and did more harm to their friends than to their foes. The archers in the chariots were not a match for the mounted bowmen of Alexander; and the slippery state of the ground hindered the Indian infantry from making full use of their formidable bows, which they were accustomed to draw after resting one end upon the earth, and pressing it with the left foot. The Indian infantry man also carried a heavy two-handled sword slung from the left shoulder, a buckler of undressed ox-hide, and sometimes javelins in place of a bow.

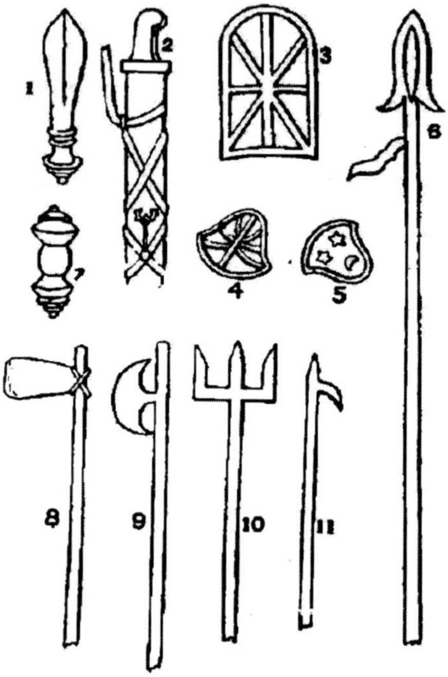

Ancient Indian Arms.[1]

Advance to the Hyphasis. In due course Alexander advanced eastwards, regardless of the rain, defeated the Glausai or Glaukanikoi, crossed both the Akesines (Chināb) and the Hydraotes or Rāvi, stormed Sangala, the stronghold of the Kathaioi, and threatened the Kshudrakas (Oxydrakai), who dwelt on the farther bank of the Rāvi. The king then advanced as far as the Hyphasis or Biās, where he was stopped by his soldiers, who refused firmly to plunge farther into unknown lands occupied by formidable kingdoms. The limits of the Greek advance were marked by the erection of twelve altars of cut stone on the northern bank of the Biās, at a point where it flows from east to west between Indaura in the Kāngrā and Mirthal in the Gurdāspur District, close to the foot of the hills. The cutting back of the northern bank, which has extended for about five miles, has swept away all traces of the massive buildings.[2]

Retreat and river voyage. Alexander, intensely disappointed, was forced to return along the way by which he had come. He appointed Pōros to act as his viceroy over seven nations which shared the territory between the Hyphasis and Hydaspes, while he himself made preparations for executing the astonishingly bold project of taking his army down the course of the Panjāb rivers to the sea. A fleet, numbering perhaps two thousand vessels of all sizes, had been built by his officers on the upper waters of the Hydaspes. When all was ready in October, 326 B. C., the

[1] (1) Dagger; (2) sword, hung from shoulder; (3) infantry shield; (4), (5) cavalry shields; (6) pike or javelin; (7) *vajra*, carried in king's hand; (8), (9) axes; (10) trident; (11) elephant goad.

[2] Addenda to *E. H. I.*, 3rd ed. (1914), p. 511, as confirmed by later communications from Mr. Shuttleworth.

voyage began, the ships being escorted by an army of 120,000 men marching along the banks. The extensive changes in the courses of the rivers of the Panjāb and Sind, as mentioned more than once, forbid the tracing of Alexander's progress in detail, but he certainly passed through the Sibi country, now in the Jhang District, and then inhabited by rude folk clad in skins and armed with clubs, who submitted and were spared. Seven centuries later, when Sibī had become more civilized, its capital was Sivipura or Shōrkōt[1] A neighbouring tribe, called Agalassoi by the Greeks, who dared to resist the invader, met with a terrible fate. The inhabitants of one town to the number of 20,000 set fire to their dwellings and cast themselves with their wives and children into the flames—an early and appalling instance of the practice of *jauhar* so often recorded in Muhammadan times.

The most formidable opposition to the Greek invaders was offered by a confederacy of the Mālavas (Malloi), Kshudrakas (Oxydrakai), and other tribes dwelling along the Rāvi and Biās. The confederate forces, said to have numbered 80,000 or 90,000 well-equipped infantry, 10,000 cavalry, and 700 or 800 chariots, should have sufficed to destroy the Macedonian army, but the superior generalship of Alexander as usual gave him decisive victory. The survivors of the Mālavas submitted. The Kshudrakas, luckily for themselves, had been late for the fighting and so escaped the ruthless slaughter which befell their allies.

Wealth of the Mālavas. The presents offered by the envoys of the Mālavas and their allies indicate the wealth of the community and the advanced state of their material civilization. The gifts comprised 1,030 (or according to another account 500) four-horsed chariots; 1,000 bucklers; a great quantity of cotton cloth; 100 talents of 'white iron', probably meaning steel; the skins of crocodiles ('very large lizards'); a quantity of tortoise shell; and some tame lions and tigers of extraordinary size.

Patala. Several nations in Upper Sind having been subdued, Alexander reached Patala at the apex of the delta as it then existed. The town was not far from Bahmanābād, the ancient city subsequently superseded by Mansūriya. It is impossible to fix localities with accuracy for the reason already stated. Alexander made arrangements for establishing a strong naval station at Patala.

Movements of Alexander and Nearchos. He sent Krateros with elephants and heavy troops into Persia through the Mulla Pass and across Balōchistan, while he himself advanced to the mouths of the Indus, then in a position very different from that which they now occupy. In those days the Runn of Cutch was a gulf of the sea and one arm of the Indus emptied itself into it. Most of the existing delta has been formed since Alexander's time.

Early in October, 325 B.C., Alexander, having spent about ten months on the voyage down the rivers, quitted the neighbourhood of the modern Karāchī with his remaining troops, crossed the

[1] The name Sibipura occurs in a Buddhist inscription from Shōrkōt dated 83 [G. E.]=A. D. 402–3 (Vogel in *J. P. H. S.*, vol. i, p. 174).

Arabis or Habb river forming the boundary between India and Gedrosia,[1] and started to march for Persia through absolutely unknown country. The troops suffered terribly from heat and thirst, which destroyed multitudes of the camp followers, but in February the remnant of the soldiers emerged in Karmania, having got into touch with the fleet which had started late in October and sailed round the coast under Admiral Nearchos. The story of the adventures of both Alexander and Nearchos is of surpassing interest, but unfortunately far too long for insertion. Its interest depends on the details. In May, 324 B.C., Alexander arrived safely at Sūsa in Persia. His Indian expedition had lasted just three years. He died at Babylon, near the modern Baghdad, in June, 323 B.C., in the thirty-third year of his age. 'Into thirteen years he had compressed the energies of many lifetimes.'

ALEXANDER THE GREAT.

Disappearance of Greek authority. Alexander undoubtedly had intended to annex permanently the Indian provinces in the basin of the Indus and to include them in his vast empire extending across Asia into Greece. The arrangements which he made to carry out his intention were suitable and adequate, but his premature death rendered his plans fruitless. When the second partition of the empire was effected at Triparadeisos in 321 B.C., Antipater appointed Pōros and Āmbhi as a matter of form to the charge of the Indus valley and the Panjāb. The conditions, however, did not permit them to fulfil their commission, and by 317 at latest all trace of Macedonian authority in India had vanished.

Effect on India of the invasion. Although the direct effects of Alexander's expedition on India appear to have been small, his proceedings had an appreciable influence on the history of the country. They broke down the wall of separation between west and east, and opened up four distinct lines of communication, three by land and one by sea. The land routes which he proved

[1] See Addenda, *E. H. I.*, ed. 3 (1914), p. 511. I am now convinced that Tomaschek is right. The Arabis certainly means the Habb (Hab of *I. G.*) and not the Purāli.

to be practicable were those through Kābul, the Mulla Pass in Balōchistan, and Gedrosia. Nearchos demonstrated that the sea voyage round the coast of Makrān offered few difficulties to sailors, onee the necessary loeal information had been gained, whieh he laeked. The immediate formation of Greek kingdoms in Western Asia ensured from the first a certain amount of exehange of ideas between India and Europe. The establishment of the Graeco-Baetrian monarchy in the middle of the third century B.C. brought about the aetual subjugation of certain Indian districts by Greek kings. The Hellenistic influence on Indian art, which is most plainly manifested in the Gandhāra seulptures dating from the early centuries of the Christian era, may be traced less conspieuously in other directions. There is good reason to believe that Buddhist teaehing was considerably modified by contact with the Greek gods, and that the use of images in particular as an essential element in the Buddhist cult was mainly due to Greek example. Whatever Hellenistie elements in Indian eivilization can be deteeted were all indirect consequences of Alexander's invasion. The Greek influenee never penetrated deeply. Indian polity and the structure of society resting on the caste basis remained substantially unchanged, and even in military science Indians showed no disposition to learn the lessons taught by the sharp sword of Alexander. The kings of Hind preferred to go on in the old way, trusting to their elephants and chariots, supported by enormous hosts of inferior infantry. They never mastered the shock tacties of Alexander's cavalry, which were repeated by Bābur in the sixteenth century with equal suecess.

Indian influence on Europe. On the other hand, the West learned something from India in consequence of the communications opened up by Alexander's adventure. Our knowledge of the faets is so scanty and fragmentary that it is diffieult to make any positive assertions with confidenee, but it is safe to say that the influence of Buddhist ideas on Christian doetrine may be traeed in the Gnostic forms of Christianity, if not elsewhere. The notions of Indian philosophy and religion whieh filtered into the Roman empire flowed through channels opened by Alexander.

The information about India collected by Alexander's officers under his intelligent direetion reeeived no material additions until the closing years of the fifteenth century, when Vaseo da Gama finally rent the veil whieh had so long hidden India from Europe and Europe from India.

India in the fourth century B.C. Although it is impossible to write the history of any Indian state in the fourth century B.C., exeept that of Magadha to a eertain extent, we are not altogether ignorant of the eonditions, political, social, eeonomieal, and religious which prevailed in that age. It is clear that no paramount imperial power existed. In the Panjāb and Sind, the two provinees actually visited by Alexander, the separate states were numerous and independent. The country between the Hydaspes and the Hyphasis alone was occupied by seven distinct nations or tribes. Some of the states, like Taxila and the realm of Pōros, were ruled by Rājās. Others, like the territories of the Mālavas and Kshudrakas (Malloi and Oxydrakai), were governed as republics, apparently by aristocratic oligarchies. The Kshudrakas, who sent a hundred and fifty of their most eminent men to negotiate terms, pleaded their special attachment to freedom and self-government from the most ancient times. Unfortunately the nature of the government in the numerous republican states of ancient India is imperfectly recorded. The existence of such states is noticed in the *Arthasāstra*, and their characteristics are the subject of a special section of the *Mahābhārata*.[1]

The statement made by Megasthenes twenty years or so after Alexander's invasion that 118 distinct nations or tribes were said to exist in the whole of India proves that the large number of distinct governments in the Panjāb and Sind was in no way exceptional. Such states were engaged in unceasing wars among themselves, with endless changes of rank and frontiers. Alexander profited by the dissensions of the Panjāb Rājās, and the *Arthasāstra* frankly lays down the principles :

> 'Whoever is superior in power shall wage war. Whoever is rising in power may break the agreement of peace.
>
> The king who is situated anywhere on the circumference of the conqueror's territory is termed the enemy.'

Such maxims, German in their unscrupulousness, could not but result in chronic warfare. The treatise quoted is in my opinion a faithful mirror of Indian political conditions in the days of Alexander. The administrative system described in it will be noticed more conveniently in connexion with the account of the Maurya government.

Extensive commerce. The numerous details recorded both by the Greeks and by Kautilya prove beyond doubt that the Indians of the fourth century B.C. were advanced in material civilization, that they conducted extensive commerce internal and foreign, and were amply supplied with the luxuries of life. Incidental observations show that the countries of the extreme south were well known in the north, and that active intercourse for business purposes bound together all parts of India. A few details will establish the accuracy of that proposition.

We learn that the best elephants came from the eastern realms; Anga (Bhāgalpur and Mungir), Kalinga (Orissa), and Karusa (Shāhābād) being specially named. The worst animals came from Saurāshtra (Kāthiāwār), and Panchajana (probably the Pānch Mahāls in Gujarāt). Those of medium quality were obtained along the Dasān river of Bundēlkhand and farther west.

Kautilya was of opinion that the commerce with the south was

[1] *Sānti Parva*, 107; transcribed and translated by K. P. Jayaswal, 'Republics in the *Mahābhārata*' (*J. B. O. Res. Soc.*, vol. i (1915), p. 173). An interesting monograph on the ancient Indian republics and their disappearance might be written, and, if well done, would be a valuable contribution to Indian history.

of greater importance than that with the north, because the more precious commodities came from the peninsula, while the northern regions supplied only blankets, skins, and horses. Gold, diamonds, pearls, other gems, and conch shells are specified as products of the south. The Tāmraparni river in Tinnevelly, the Pāndya country of Madura, and Ceylon are named. We hear of textile fabrics from Benares, Madura, the Konkan, and even from China. Commerce by land and sea with foreign countries was regulated by many ordinances, and passports were required by all persons entering or leaving India.[1] The coinage was of a primitive character. The coins most commonly used were of the kind called 'punch-marked', because their surface is stamped with separate marks

PUNCH-MARKED COINS.

made at different times by different punches. Such coins in base silver are found all over India. Specimens in copper occur, but are rare. The greater number are roughly square or oblong bits of metal cut out of a strip. The circular pieces are scarce. Roughly cast coins of early date are common in some localities.

Religion. Certain matters concerning the history of religions have been discussed in connexion with Taxila. A few other miscellaneous observations will not be out of place. The deities specifically mentioned include Zeus Ombrios—the rain-god—which term must be intended to denote Indra; the Indian Herakles worshipped by the Surasenas of Mathurā, who may be identified with Krishna's brother Balarāma; and the river Ganges.[2] The dated references to the Krishna cult and the veneration of the Ganges are worth noting.

The authority of the Brahmans was secure and fully recognized. They occupied a town in the Mālava territory, which probably was an *agrahāra* or proprietary grant, and everywhere they were

[1] *Arthasāstra*, Book II, chaps. 2, 11, 16, 28, 34; Book VII, chap. 12.
[2] Strabo, Book XV, chap. i, secs. 59, 69; Arrian, *Indika*, chap. 8.

the councillors of the Rājās. In Sind they used their influence to induce the local chiefs to resist the invader, and paid with their lives for their advice.[1]

Quintus Curtius notes the cult of trees, and asserts that violation of sacred trees was a capital offence. Brahmans are said to have been accustomed to eat flesh, but not that of animals which assist man in his labours. That remark seems to imply the sacredness of horned cattle in the eyes of Brahmans, although other people might still eat beef.

TENTATIVE CHRONOLOGY OF THE SAISUNĀGA AND NANDA DYNASTIES

Serial No.	*King, as in Matsya Purāna*	*Probable date of accession B.C.*	*Remarks.*
	Saisunāgas.		
1	Sisunāga	642	Originally Rājā of Kāsī or Benares. No events recorded; 60 years allowed for four reigns.
2	Kākavarna		
3	Kshemadharman		
4	Kshemajit or Kshatraujas		
5	Bimbisāra or Srenika	582	Built New Rājagriha; conquered Anga; contemporary with Mahāvīra and Buddha; reputed to be a Jain.
6	Ajātasatru or Kūnika	554	Built fort of Pātaliputra; defeated rulers of Vaisāli and Kosala; death of Buddha; death of Mahāvīra.
7	Darsaka	527	Mentioned in *Svapna-Vāsavadattā* of Bhāsa.
8	Udāsin or Udaya	503	Built city of Kusumapura on the Ganges near Pātaliputra on the Sōn.
9	Nandivardhana	470	Few events recorded; may be considered to be Nandas, as indicated by the names. (Khāravela inscription.)
10	Mahānandin		
	The Nine Nandas.		
11, 12	Mahāpadma and 8 sons, 2 generations	413 (91 years before Chandragupta)	Low caste heretics, hostile to Brahmans and Kshatriyas; destroyed by Chandragupta and Kautilya.
	Mauryas.		
13	Chandragupta	322 (? 325)	Date approximately correct.

[1] Arrian, *Anab.*, Book VI, chaps. 7, 17.

CHRONOLOGY OF ALEXANDER THE GREAT

(Dates accurate)

B. C.
334. A. started on campaign against Persia; battle of the Granicus (Thargelion).
333. Battle of Issus.
332. Conquest of Egypt.
331. Foundation of Alexandria in Egypt; battle of Gaugamela (Arbela).
330. A. in Persia; death of Darius.
328–7. A. in Baetria.

Indian Expedition (leading dates only)

327. May. Crossing of Hindu Kush range.
327. June to December. Campaign in the hills of Bājaur and Suwāt (Swat).
326. February. Crossing of the Indus.
326. Beginning of July. Battle of Hydaspes.
326. September. Arrival at the Hyphasis; erection of altars; forced return.
326. End of October. Beginning of voyage down the rivers.
325. January. Defeat of the Mālavas (Malloi).
325. October, beginning of. A. started on march through Gedrosia.
325. October, end of. Nearchos started on voyage along the coast to Persian Gulf.
324. February. A. and the remains of his army in Karmania.
324. May. A. at Sūsa in Persia.
323. June. Death of Alexander at Babylon.

AUTHORITIES

The references given here are merely supplementary to those in *E. H. I.*[3] (1914), and in the foot-notes to this chapter.

Sir J. H. MARSHALL has issued preliminary reports of his excavations at Taxila in the *Annual Reports of the Archaeol. Survey of India*; *J. P. H. S.*, vol. iii (1914, 1915); and *J. R. A. S.* for 1914 and 1916.

The articles by S. V. VENKATESVARA on 'The Ancient History of Magadha' (*Ind. Ant.*, 1916, pp. 16, 28) are useful and suggestive, even when not convincing.

SHAMASASTRY (SHAMA SASTRI) published his revised version of KAUTILYA's *Arthaśāstra* in an 8vo volume at Bangalore, 1916.

The difficult and hitherto obscure subject of Jainism has been made fairly intelligible by two authoritative books, namely, Mrs. SINCLAIR STEVENSON, M.A., Sc.D., *The Heart of Jainism*, Oxford University Press, 1915; and JAGMANDERLAL JAINI, M.A., *Outlines of Jainism*, Cambridge University Press, 1916. Both have been quoted in the text.

Sir R. G. BHANDARKAR's treatise on Vaishnavism, &c., in the *Grundriss* (Strassburg, 1913) is important.

The story of Alexander's reign prior to the Indian expedition may be read best in BURY, *A History of Greece* (Macmillan, 1904). The fullest account of the Indian campaign is that in *E. H. I.*[3]

The dates of the dynastics have been arranged to suit the new readings of the Khāravela inscription, *ante*, p. 58 *n*.

BOOK II

HINDU INDIA FROM THE BEGINNING OF THE MAURYA DYNASTY IN 322 B.C. TO THE SEVENTH CENTURY A.C.

CHAPTER 1

Chandragupta Maurya, the first historical emperor of India, and his institutions; Bindusāra.

From darkness to light. The advent of the Maurya dynasty marks the passage from darkness to light for the historian. Chronology suddenly becomes definite, almost precise; a huge empire springs into existence, unifying the innumerable fragments of distracted India; the kings, who may be described with justice as emperors, are men of renown, outstanding personalities whose qualities can be discerned, albeit dimly, through the mists of time; gigantic world-wide religious movements are initiated, of which the effects are still felt; and the affairs of secluded Hind are brought into close touch with those of the outer world.

The manners of the court, the constitution of the government, the methods of administration, the principles of law, and the course of commerce under the Maurya sovereigns for nearly a hundred years in the fourth and third centuries B.C. are known to us in the twentieth century A.C. far more intimately than are the doings and institutions of any other Indian monarch until the days of Akbar, the contemporary of Queen Elizabeth.

Authorities for the Maurya age. We are indebted for this extraordinary wealth of knowledge concerning a section of the remote past mainly to three sources, namely, the treatise on statecraft composed by Chandragupta Maurya's able minister, the Brahman variously known as Vishnugupta, Kautilya (Kautalya), or Chānakya; the testimony of the Greeks who visited India either with Alexander or a generation later; and the imperishable records of Asoka inscribed on rocks and pillars. Indian tradition recorded in various forms, combined with critical study of the monuments which have defied the ravenous tooth of time, enables the historian to fill in the outline of his picture with certain additional details. When all sources of information have been exhausted the result is a picture of astonishing completeness. The external political facts, although on record to a considerable extent, are known far less perfectly than the particulars of the internal government and administration.

The revolution in Magadha. The exact course of the events which led to the overthrow of the Nandas and the establishment of the Mauryas in their royal seat is not fully ascertained. Many alleged incidents of the revolution in Magadha are depicted vividly in the ancient political drama entitled the 'Signet of Rākshasa' (*Mudrā-Rākshasa*), written, perhaps, in the fifth century after Christ. But it would be obviously unsafe to rely for a matter-of-fact historical narrative on a work of imagination composed some seven centuries after the events dramatized. The information gleaned from other authorities is scanty, and in some respects discrepant. It appears, however, to be certain that Chandra or Chandragupta, who when quite young had met Alexander in 326 or 325 B.C., was a scion of the Nanda stock. According to some accounts he was a son of the last Nanda king by a low-born woman. Acting under the guidance of his astute Brahman preceptor, Vishnugupta, better known by his patronymic Chānakya, or his surname Kautilya or Kautalya, Chandragupta, who had been exiled from Magadha, attacked the Macedonian officers in command of the garrisons in the Indus basin after Alexander's death, and destroyed them, with the aid of the northern nations. About the same time the youthful adventurer and his wily counsellor effected a revolution at Pātaliputra (Patna), the capital of the Magadhan monarchy, and exterminated the Nanda family. It is not clear whether the Magadhan revolution preceded or followed the attack on the Macedonian garrisons. However that may have been, Chandragupta undoubtedly succeeded to the throne of Pātaliputra, secured his position against all enemies, and established a gigantic empire. He is the first strictly historical person who can be properly described as emperor of India.

Chronology. Alexander having died at Babylon in June, 323 B.C., the news of his passing must have reached the Panjāb a month or two later. It may be assumed with safety that the campaign against the foreign garrisons began in the following cold season of 323 to 322, and we cannot be far wrong if we date Chandragupta's accession in 322 B.C. The Magadhan revolution seems to have occupied at least a year from beginning to end.[1] If it had been completed before Alexander's death, which is possible, the change of dynasty might be antedated to 325 B.C. The true date certainly lies between 325 and 320 inclusive, which is sufficiently precise for most purposes.

War and peace with Seleukos. Alexander not having left an heir capable of wielding his sceptre, his dominions were divided among his generals. The supreme power in Asia was disputed by Antigonos and Seleukos. After a long struggle the latter recovered Babylon in 312, and assumed the style of king six years later. He is known in history as Seleukos Nikator, the Conqueror, and is called King of Syria, but would be more accurately described as the King of Western Asia. Hoping to recover Alexander's

[1] Malayaketu, son of the king of the mountains, says:
Nine months have o'er us passed since that sad day
My father perished. (*Mudrā-Rākshasa*, Act IV.)

Indian provinces, he crossed the Indus to attack the reigning Indian sovereign, Chandragupta Maurya. The invader was defeated, probably somewhere in the Panjāb, and compelled to retire beyond the frontier. The terms of peace involved the cession by Seleukos to Chandragupta of the provinces of the Paropanisadai, Aria, and Arachosia, the capitals of which were respectively Kābul, Herāt, and Kandahār, and also Gedrosia, the modern Balōchistan. The Indian king gave in exchange a comparatively small equivalent in the shape of five hundred elephants, which Seleukos needed for the wars with his western enemies. A matrimonial alliance also was arranged, which may be interpreted as meaning that a daughter of Seleukos was married to Chandragupta.

Megasthenes. The peace so concluded between Syria and India remained inviolate, and Seleukos, in or about the year 302 B.C., sent as his envoy to the court of Pātaliputra an officer named Megasthenes, who had served in Arachosia (Kandahār). The ambassador employed his leisure in compiling an excellent account of the geography, products, and institutions of India, which continued to be the principal authority on the subject until modern times. Unfortunately his book is no longer extant as a whole, but a great part of it has been preserved in the form of extracts made by other authors. Megasthenes is a thoroughly trustworthy witness concerning matters which came under his own observation. His work has been sometimes discredited unfairly because he permitted himself to embellish his text by the insertion of certain incredible marvels on hearsay testimony.

Chandragupta's empire. Little more than what has been stated is known concerning the political events of Chandragupta's reign, which lasted for twenty-four years. His dominions certainly included the country now called Afghanistan, the ancient Ariana, as far as the Hindu Kush range ; the Panjāb ; the territories now known as the United Provinces of Agra and Oudh, Bihār, and the peninsula of Kāthiāwār in the far west. Probably they also comprised Bengal. It is safe to affirm that Chandragupta, when his reign terminated about 298 B.C., was master of all India north of the Narbadā, as well as of Afghanistan. At present there is no good evidence that his conquests extended into the Deccan, but it is possible that he may have carried his victorious arms across the Narbadā. Late traditions in Mysore go so far as to assert the extension of the Nanda dominion to that country.

Chandragupta's severity. The Roman historian Justin, who affirms that Chandragupta was the author of India's liberty after Alexander's death, adds the comment that 'when he had gained the victory and ascended the throne, he transformed nominal liberty into slavery, inasmuch as he oppressed with servitude the people whom he had rescued from foreign rule'.

The known facts concerning his administration prove that he was a stern despot, who lived in daily fear of his life, and enforced strict order by a highly organized autocracy supported by punishments of ruthless severity. All tradition agrees that the ship of state was steered with exceptional ability by his Brahman minister, whose writings show that his statecraft was not hampered by any moral scruples. The date or manner of the minister's disappearance from the scene is not recorded. According to the confused traditions collected in the seventeenth century by the Tibetan author Tāranāth, Chānakya continued to guide the counsels of Chandragupta's successor, Bindusāra. The statement may be well founded.[1]

The fate of Chandragupta. The only direct evidence throwing light on the manner in which the eventful reign of Chandragupta Maurya came to an end is that of Jain tradition. The Jains always treat the great emperor as having been a Jain like Bimbisāra, and no adequate reason seems to exist for discrediting their belief. The Jain religion undoubtedly was extremely influential in Magadha during the time of the later Saisunāgas, the Nandas, and the Mauryas. The fact that Chandragupta won the throne by the contrivance of a learned Brahman is not inconsistent with the supposition that Jainism was the royal faith. Jains habitually employ Brahmans for their domestic ceremonies, and in the drama cited above a Jain ascetic is mentioned as being a special friend of the minister Rākshasa, who served first the Nanda and then the new sovereign.

Once the fact that Chandragupta was or became a Jain is admitted, the tradition that he abdicated and committed suicide by slow starvation in the approved Jain manner becomes readily credible. The story is to the effect that when the Jain saint Bhadrabāhu predicted a famine in northern India which would last for twelve years, and the prophecy began to be fulfilled, the saint led twelve thousand Jains to the south in search of more favoured lands. King Chandragupta abdicated and accompanied the emigrants, who made their way to Sravana Belgola ('the white Jain tank') in Mysore, where Bhadrabāhu soon died. The ex-emperor Chandragupta, having survived him for twelve years, starved himself to death. The tradition is supported by the names of the buildings at Sravana Belgola, inscriptions from the seventh century after Christ, and a literary work of the tenth century. The evidence cannot be described as conclusive, but after much consideration I am disposed to accept the main facts as affirmed by tradition. It being certain that Chandragupta was quite young and inexperienced when he ascended the throne in or about 322 B. C., he must have been under fifty when his reign terminated twenty-four years later. His abdication is an adequate explanation of his disappearance at such an early age. Similar renunciations

[1] Wilford printed a story that the 'wicked minister' repented and retired to 'Shookul Teerth, near Broach, on the banks of the Nerbudda', where he died. Chandragupta is said to have accompanied Chānakya (*As. Res.*, ix. 96). One version of the story is said to be based on the *Agni Purāna*, and another on alleged traditions related by Wilford's Pundit. See *Rāsmālā*, i. 69 *n*.

of royal dignity are on record, and the twelve years' famine is not incredible. In short, the Jain tradition holds the field, and no alternative account exists.

King Bindusāra. Chandragupta was succeeded by his son Bindusāra, whose title Amitraghāta, 'slayer of enemies', suggests a martial career. Unfortunately nothing definite is recorded concerning him except a trivial anecdote showing that he maintained friendly correspondence with Antiochos Soter, whose ambassador, Deïmachos, replaced Megasthenes. An envoy named Dionysios sent by Ptolemy Philadelphos of Egypt (285–247 B.C.) to the court of Pātaliputra must have presented his credentials to either Bindusāra or his son Asoka. A tradition recorded by Tāranāth represents Bindusāra as having conquered the country between the eastern and the western seas. The tradition may well be founded on fact, because the immense extent of Asoka's empire is known, and he himself made no conquests except that of Kalinga. Asoka's dominion in the peninsula extended over the northern districts of Mysore, and it seems likely that the conquest of the Deccan was effected by Bindusāra. But, as already remarked, it is possible that the southern extension of the empire may have been the work of Chandragupta, who certainly held the remote province of Kāthiāwār or Surāshtra in the west.

Maurya organization. The narrative of political events will now be interrupted to permit of a survey of the institutions of the Maurya empire according to the authorities above mentioned. Most of the arrangements adopted by Chandragupta remained in force during the reigns of his son and grandson. The modifications introduced by Asoka will be noticed in due course. The reader should understand that the Nanda kingdom of Magadha was strong, rich, extensive, protected by a numerous army, and no doubt administered on the system described in the *Arthasāstra*. The enlargement of the kingdom into an empire did not necessarily involve radical changes in the administrative machinery, although it is reasonable to credit Chandragupta and his prime minister with effecting improvements and increasing the efficiency of the mechanism of government. The Maurya state was organized elaborately with a full supply of departments and carefully graded officials with well-defined duties. The accounts leave on my mind the impression that it was much better organized than was the Mogul empire under Akbar, as described in Abu-l Fazl's survey. Akbar's officials, except certain judicial functionaries, all ranked as military officers. Even the underlings in the imperial kitchen were rated and paid as foot soldiers. The bulk of the army was composed of irregular contingents supplied by either subordinate ruling chiefs or by high officials with territorial jurisdiction, and the standing army was quite small. The Mauryas, on the contrary, had a regular civil administration and maintained a huge standing army paid directly by the Crown—an instrument of power infinitely more efficient than Akbar's militia, which failed miserably when confronted with small Portuguese forces, whereas the Maurya was more than a match for Seleukos. The control of the Maurya central government over distant provinces and subordinate officials appears to have been far more stringent than that exercised by Akbar, who did not possess the terrible secret service of his early predecessor. That service was worked very much on the lines followed by the modern German government and with an equal absence of scruple. The Maurya government, in short, was a highly organized and thoroughly efficient autocracy, capable of controlling an empire more extensive than that of Akbar as long as the sovereigns possessed the necessary personal ability. They were equal to the task for three generations. Although the figure of Bindusāra is shadowy, and absolutely nothing definite is known about his acts, he must have been a competent ruler. Otherwise he could not have reigned for a quarter of a century and transmitted to his son Asoka the gigantic empire created by and inherited from his father Chandragupta.

Pātaliputra, the capital. Pātaliputra, Chandragupta's capital, was a great and noble city extending along the northern bank of the Sōn for about nine miles, with a depth of less than two miles. Much of the area is now covered by Patna, Bankipore, and sundry neighbouring villages. Kusumapura, the more ancient site, stood on the Ganges, and evidently became merged in Pātaliputra, for the two names are often used as synonyms. The Maurya city was built in the tongue of land formed by the junction of the Sōn with the Ganges, a defensible position recommended by the writers of text-books and frequently adopted by the ancient Indians in actual practice. Modern Patna no longer enjoys the strategical security of its predecessor, the confluence being now at the cantonment of Dinapore, about twelve miles above Patna. The old river beds and even the ancient embankments or quays may still be traced. The city was defended by a massive timber palisade, of which the remains have been found at several places. The gates were sixty-four, and the towers five hundred and seventy in number. The palisade was protected by a deep moat filled with water from the Sōn.

The palace. The imperial palace, which probably stood close to the modern village of Kumrahār, was chiefly constructed of timber, like the splendid regal edifices of Mandalay in Burma. Its gilded pillars were adorned with golden vines and silver birds, and a fine ornamental park studded with fish-ponds and well furnished with trees and shrubs served as setting for the edifices. Reasons exist for believing that the buildings were designed in imitation of the Persian palace at Persepolis, but the resemblance is not yet definitely established.

According to a Greek author the abode of Chandragupta excelled the palaces of Susa and Ekbatana in splendour, and there is no reason to doubt the truth of the statement. The court was maintained and served with barbaric ostentation. Gold vessels measuring six feet across are said to have been used. The king, when he appeared in public, was either carried in a golden palanquin or mounted on an elephant with gorgeous trappings. He was clothed in fine muslin embroidered with purple and gold. The luxuries of all parts of Asia, including China, were at his disposal. Within the spacious precincts of the palace the sovereign relied for protection chiefly on his Amazonian bodyguard of armed women. It was considered lucky that when he got up in the morning he should be received by his female archers. The harem or women's quarters were on an extensive scale and carefully guarded. No commodities were allowed to pass in or out except under seal.

Royal amusements. Although the early Brahman writers repeatedly condemned hunting as a grave form of vice, and solemnly debated whether it or gambling should be considered the worse, the ancient kings indulged freely in the pleasures of the chase. Large game preserves were enclosed for the exclusive royal use, and the slightest interference with the sport of kings entailed instant capital punishment. The tradition of the sanctity of the imperial hunting-ground long survived. Jahāngīr in the seventeenth century did not hesitate to kill or mutilate some unlucky men who had accidentally spoiled his shot at a blue bull. In England the Norman kings were equally tenacious of their sporting privileges. Asoka kept up the practice of hunting for many years, but abandoned it, as will be narrated presently, when he adopted Buddhist ideas. Chandragupta, who still followed the chase when Megasthenes was at his court late in his reign, is alleged to have been a Jain. It is not easy to understand how a Jain, even a king, could possibly hunt at any time. It may be that Chandragupta was a Brahmanical worshipper of Siva, or possibly, as Dr. Spooner thinks, a Magian, for the greater part of his reign, and that he was not converted to Jainism by Bhadrabāhu until almost the end.[1] Gladiatorial combats, such as even Akbar enjoyed watching, and the fights between animals, which may still be witnessed in the Native States, were included in the list of royal amusements. The races run with chariots, to each of which a mixed team of horses and oxen was harnessed, with horses in the centre and an ox at each side, were a curious kind of diversion. Such races are not to be seen nowadays in India, so far as I know, although good trotting oxen are still to be found. The course measured about 6,000 yards and the races were made the subject of keen betting.[2]

[1] *Arthasāstra* (Book II, chap. 4) prescribes that in the centre of the capital city shrines should be provided for Aparājita, Apratihata, Jayanta, Vaijayanta, Siva, Vaisravana (i. e. Kuvera), and the Asvins. The first four are Jain deities.

[2] Dr. Coomaraswamy informs me that 'bull-racing' is a 'very common pastime in Ceylon, and creates immense excitement. The bulls are harnessed to the light cars called "hackeries"'. In 1679, when Dr. Fryer was at Surat, ox-races were still in favour. He describes them in his customary quaint fashion: 'The Coaches . . . Those for Journeying are something stronger than those for the Merchants to ride about the City or to take the Air on: which with their nimble Oxen they will, when they meet in

Courtesan attendants. Aecomplished courtesans of the daneing-girl elass enjoyed a privileged position at eourt, an evil praetiee eontinued by most Indian princes up to reeent times, and perhaps, in some eases, to the present day. Sueh women were employed as housemaids, shampooers, and garland makers. They were entitled to present the king with water, perfumes, dress, and garlands. They held the royal umbrella, fan, and golden piteher, and attended the sovereign when he was seated on his throne, or riding in a litter or ehariot. They were subjeet to striet offieial control, and those who practised their profession paid lieenee fees to the treasury. Similar customs at Vijayanagar in the south are recorded in the sixteenth century. The seeret serviee of the Maurya government did not disdain to make use of intelligenee collected by the public women.

Iranian influence. Up to the time of Alexander's invasion the Indus was regarded as the traditional frontier of the Persian empire, although at that date the Great King does not seem to have aetually asserted his authority over the Indian satrapy conquered in the time of Darius the son of Hystaspes. The proximity of the Panjāb to territory whieh was a Persian provinee for a century or more, and the constant although unreeorded intercourse which must have existed between the Aehaemenian monarchy and the Indian kingdoms, cannot have failed to make Persian institutions familiar to the people of Hind. At a somewhat later date the eontinuance of strong Persian influenee upon India is indicated by the prevalenee of the Kharoshthī seript, a varicty of Aramaie, in the provinces near the frontier ; by the long continued use of the Persian title of Satrap ; by the form of the Asoka inscriptions ; and by the arehitecture. Some small partieulars whieh happen to be recorded are suffieient to show that in the time of the first Maurya emperor the court was affected by Iranian practices. The *Arthasāstra* rule that the king, when eonsulting physieians and ascetics, should be seated 'in the room where the sacred fire has been kept' seems to be an indieation that Magian ritual was honoured at the Maurya court. We are told also that the eeremonial washing of the king's hair was made the oecasion of a splendid festival when the eourtiers vied one with the other in offering rieh presents to the king. That observance appears to be an obvious imitation of the Persian hair-washing eeremony on the sovereign's birthday, as described by Herodotus. Researches

the fields, run races on, and contend for the Garland as much as for an Olympiak Prize : which is a Diversion *To see a Cow gallop*, as we say in scorn ; but these not only pluck up their Heels apace, but are taught to amble, they often riding on them' (Fryer, *A New Account*, &c., ed. Crooke, Hakluyt Soe., 1915, vol. iii, pp. 157, 158). I have not found anywhere a notice of mixed teams of horses and oxen. The *Arthasāstra* (Book IV, chap. 20) provides official rules for gambling. Superintendents of gambling and betting collected the licence fee, and 5 per cent. of the winnings, as well as the charges for hire of the accessories and for water-supply and accommodation in gaming houses.

now in progress promise to reveal the existence of Magian influence on Indian religions and other institutions to a degree previously unsuspected, but I abstain from the discussion of doubtful hypotheses. The facts so far as disclosed suggest that the influence was Magian rather than Zoroastrian in the strict sense. The undoubted close relationship between Vedic religion and that of Irān must be borne in mind. Legendary accounts of the early connexion of Persia with India may be read in Firishta and other authors. Whatever may be the fate of the various hypotheses debated by scholars, there can be no doubt that ancient India was largely indebted to Iranian ideas and practices.[1]

Autocracy. The normal government of an Indian kingdom appears to have been always untempered autocracy or despotism.[2] The royal will was not controlled by any law, and the customary respect shown to Brahmans was an ineffective check upon a sovereign resolved to have his own way. According to the *Arthasāstra* a Brahman convicted of ordinary heinous crime, murder included, was exempt from torture, and should be either banished or sentenced to the mines for life. But the author expressly authorizes the execution by drowning of a Brahman guilty of high treason, whereas other traitors were to be burnt alive. A strong, tyrannous man like Chandragupta would not have allowed himself to be hampered by nice regard for Brahman privileges. The sovereign was not bound to consult anybody, but in practice the most self-willed despot is obliged to depend largely upon his ministers. 'Sovereignty is possible only with assistance. A single wheel can never move. Hence he [the king] shall employ ministers and hear their opinion.'[3] The Maurya monarch, according to the ruling of Chānakya, was not constrained to limit his Privy Council to any particular number of ministers. The Council should 'consist of as many members as the needs of his dominion require'. The sovereign was recommended to be content with the advice of not more than four ministers on any given matter. In any case the decision rested with him alone. Akbar in the sixteenth century, although it is unlikely that he had ever heard of Chānakya or his treatise, acted on the principles laid down in that work so far as his relations with his ministers were concerned.

The only real check. The only real check upon the arbitrary royal authority was the ever-present fear of revolution and assassination. A king who trampled on custom and overstrained his power was apt to come to an untimely end. Chandragupta, who had won the throne by rebellion and the extermination of his prede-

[1] The Ionic Jandiāla temple in the Sir Kap section of Taxila appears to have been a fire-temple (*J. P. H. S.*, iii. 77 ; *Ann. Rep. A. S., India*, 1912–13, p. 35, pl. xxxiv, *b*). It dates from about the beginning of the Christian era.

[2] The text refers only to monarchical governments ; and not to the tribal republics or oligarchies, such as those of the Mālavas, Kshudrakas, Lichchhavis, and Yaudhēyas.

[3] *Arthasāstra*, Book I, chap. 7.

cessor's family, naturally led an uneasy life, and was obliged to take unceasing precautions against conspiracies. He dared not incur the risk either of sleeping in the day-time or occupying the same bedroom two nights in succession. A king of Burma at the beginning of the nineteenth century is recorded to have taken similar precautions. The dramatist already cited, who tells the traditional story of the revolution which overthrew the Nandas, gives a vivid account of the varied expedients by which the adherents of the old dynasty sought to destroy the young usurper, and how all failed, so that the disappointed ex-minister exclaims :

> 'Tis ever thus.—Fortune in all befriends
> The cruel Chandragupta. When I send
> A messenger of certain death to slay him,
> She wields the instrument against his rival,
> Who should have spoiled him of one-half his kingdom ;
> And arms, and drugs, and stratagems are turned
> In his behalf against my friends and servants ;
> So that whate'er I plot against his power
> Serves but to yield him unexpected profit.

The usurper's powerful military force, which will be now described, secured him in possession of his dangerous throne.

The normal Indian army. An Indian army, in accordance with immemorial tradition, comprised four 'arms'—namely elephants, chariots, cavalry, and infantry. The war-elephants were regarded as the most important because

> 'the victory of Kings depends mainly upon elephants; for elephants, being of large bodily frame, are able not only to destroy the arrayed army of an enemy, his fortifications, and encampments, but also to undertake works that are dangerous to life'.

The high value thus set upon elephants, justified by the conditions and experience of purely Indian warfare, was discredited when a bold European general like Alexander confounded the traditional Indian tactics by novel methods of attack.

Chariots, which had been in use in Rigvedic times, played an important part in ancient Indian warfare for many centuries. It is not known with certainty when or why they went out of fashion. The Chinese pilgrim, Hiuen Tsang, writing in the middle of the seventh century, when giving a general description of India, states that the army was composed of the four divisions or 'arms' above mentioned, and remarks that officers used to ride in chariots.

> 'The army is composed of Foot, Horse, Chariot, and Elephant soldiers. The war-elephant is covered with coat-of-mail, and his tusks are provided with sharp barbs. On him rides the Commander-in-Chief, who has a soldier on each side to manage the elephant. The chariot in which an officer sits is drawn by four horses, whilst infantry guard it on both sides.'[1]

Apparently at that time chariots were used by officers only.

The same author, when describing the army organized by his

[1] Watters, *On Yuan Chwang*, vol. i, p. 171. The translation by Beal (*Records*, i. 83) differs materially and appears to be erroneous.

contemporary, Harsha of Kanauj, credits that powerful king with possessing originally 5,000 elephants, 20,000 cavalry, and 50,000 foot. After some years he is said to have increased his war elephants to 60,000, and his cavalry to 100,000.[1] No mention of chariots is made. It is legitimate to infer that the use of chariots was obsolescent in the pilgrim's time, and did not survive the seventh century. I do not know of any subsequent mention of their employment in warfare.

Four-horsed chariot of sun.

The Rājpūt horsemen in later ages were renowned for their courage and the undisciplined fury of their charges. The only authentic record we possess of action by cavalry in ancient times is in the Greek narratives of the battle of the Hydaspes. The mounted troops of Pōros on that occasion did their best, but could not resist effectively the Macedonian cavalry. The Indians were almost all destroyed. It was customary in India to employ enormous hosts of foot soldiers, but the line between soldiers and followers not being strictly drawn, the military value of the infantry often was very small.

The Maurya army. Chandragupta maintained the traditional 'four-fold' army. His military organization does not betray any trace of Greek ideas. The force at the command of the last Nanda was formidable, being estimated at 80,000 horse, 200,000 foot, 8,000 chariots, and 6,000 fighting elephants. The Maurya raised the numbers of the infantry to 600,000, and of the elephants to 9,000. But his cavalry is said to have mustered only 30,000. The number of his chariots is not recorded. Assuming that he maintained them as in the time of his predecessor, that each chariot required at least three, and that each elephant carried at least four men, his total force must have amounted to not less than 690,000, or in round numbers 700,000 men. Megasthenes expressly states that the soldiers were paid and equipped by the state. They were not a mere militia of contingents. It is not surprising that an army so strong was able both to 'overrun and subdue all India', as Plutarch asserts, and also to defeat the invasion of Seleukos, whose force must have been far inferior in numbers. According to the *Arthasāstra* an Indian army was organized in

[1] Watters summarizes the passage, omitting details. Beal (i. 213) accidentally gives 2,000 as being Harsha's original cavalry force. Julien clearly is right in stating 20,000 as the number.

squads of ten men, companies of a hundred, and battalions of a thousand eaeh. Chandragupta probably followed the same practice. The author of the treatise, who eontemplated India as being divided in the normal manner into a multitude of small states, does not deseribe the constitution of the empire whieh he did so much to establish. He therefore treats the Rājā as the Commander-in-Chief of the army, and betrays no knowledge of any professional head-quarters organization. But Megasthenes informs us that Chandragupta's host was controlled and administered under the direction of a War Office elaborately constituted. A commission of thirty members was divided into six Boards (*panchāyats*), each with five members, and severally charged with the administration of the following departments, namely: Board No. I (in conjunction with the admiral), Admiralty; Board No. II, Transport, Commissariat, and Army Service; Board No. III, Infantry; Board No. IV, Cavalry; Board No. V, War-chariots; and Board No. VI, Elephants.

BOYS ARMED AS SOLDIERS.

No similar organization is recorded elsewhere, and the credit of devising such efficient maehinery must be divided between Chandragupta and his exceptionally able minister.

Equipment. The equipment of the army was effective and adequate. A fighting elephant carried at least three arehers besides the driver. The ehariots usually were four-horsed, but two-horsed cars also were in use. Each chariot had at least two fighting men in addition to the driver. Six men formed the complement of each of the four-horsed chariots employed by Pōros at the battle of the Hydaspes. Each horseman was armed with two lances resembling the Greek *saunia*, and was protected by a buckler. The principal weapon of the infantry was a straight broadsword suspended by a belt from the shoulder.[1] Javelins and

[1] Col. Hendley noted that many Rājpūts in recent times earried the sword in the same way (*J. I. A.*, No. 130, 1915, p. 8).

bows and arrows were additional arms. The arrow was discharged with the aid of pressure from the left foot on the extremity of the bow resting on the ground, and with such force that neither shield nor breastplate could withstand it. At the Hydaspes the Indian archers were rendered ineffective by the greasy condition of the ground which prevented the soldier from securing a firm rest for the end of his bow.[1]

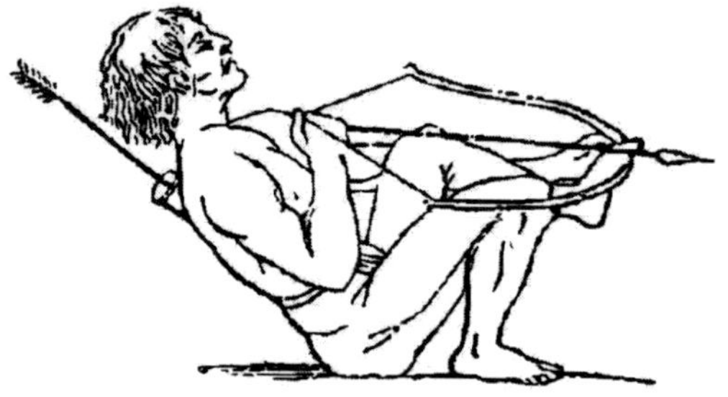

Veddah bow.

Defensive armour was supplied to men, elephants, and horses.

The transport animals included horses, mules, and oxen.

According to Chānakya, an ambulance service was provided in the rear during an action consisting of surgeons supplied with instruments, medicines, and dressings, and of women with prepared food and beverages (Book X, chap. 3).

It is clear, therefore, that the army, as improved by Chandragupta, was extremely formidable.

Diplomacy and force. But the Maurya did not rely solely on his armed strength. Indian statesmen have always shown a leaning towards the employment of diplomacy in preference to force. The dictum of Chānakya that 'intrigue, spies, winning over the enemy's people, siege, and assault are the five means to capture a fort,' is characteristic, and indicates the nature of the subsidiary means employed to create the Maurya empire. Long afterwards, Akbar was content to secure by bribery the fortress of Asīrgarh, which his arms were unable to reduce, and Aurangzēb gained possession of Marāthā forts usually by the same ignoble means. The writers of text-books debated the relative value of force and diplomacy. The author of the *Arthasāstra* had no hesitation in deciding that 'skill in intrigue (or "diplomacy") is better', because the crafty intriguer can always overthrow kings who are superior in warlike spirit and power (Book IX, chap. 1).

Similarly, Machiavelli was prepared to prove by many examples that the prince who 'best personated the fox had the better success'.[2] The theory of politics expounded in the *Arthasāstra* is substantially identical with that of *The Prince*.

Bāna's criticism of Kautilya or Chānakya. It is right to add that the cynical principles of the *Arthasāstra*, worked out 'on ground cleared of the hindrances of private justice', did not meet with universal acceptance. King Harsha's friend Bāna in the seventh century regarded them with horror :

[1] Compare the Veddah method as illustrated from Tennent, *Ceylon*[2], vol. i, p. 499.

[2] *The Prince*, transl. in Universal Library ed., Routledge, 1893, p. 110.

'Is there anything', he exclaims, 'that is righteous for those for whom the science of Kautilya, merciless in its precepts, rich in cruelty, is an authority; whose teachers are priests habitually hard-hearted with practice of witchcraft; to whom ministers, always inclined to deceive others, are councillors; whose desire is always for the goddess of wealth that has been cast away by thousands of kings; who are devoted to the application of destructive sciences; and to whom brothers, affectionate with natural cordial love, are fit victims to be murdered?'

The treatise criticized having been written avowedly 'for the benefit of the Maurya', we may feel assured that Bāna's scruples were not shared by Chandragupta, who evidently acted, as Justin indicates, in accordance with the principles of his preceptor. The late conversion of the first Maurya emperor to the merciful creed of Jainism, if it be a fact, as I think it was, may be ascribed to a revulsion of conscience from the hateful teaching of the Atharvan Brahman.[1]

Severity of the government. Whatever we may think about the principles of Chandragupta, his masterful government was effective. The text-books define the art of governing as *dandanīti*, 'the science of punishment'. The details preserved show clearly that that definition was accepted heartily by Chandragupta, who acted on it without hesitation. Whether we consult the *Arthasāstra* or the Greek authorities we receive the same impression of ruthless severity in the enforcement of fiscal regulations for the benefit of the treasury, and of stern repression of crime. Megasthenes noted that while he resided in the imperial camp with a population of 400,000 people the daily thefts reported did not exceed 200 drachmae in value, equivalent to about eight pounds sterling. Such security of property was attained by the application of a terribly severe code, based, as Chānakya observes, on the precepts laid down 'in the scriptures of great sages'. When we come to the history of the purely Hindu empire of Vijayanagar in the sixteenth century we shall find that property in that realm was protected by the most appalling penalties for even petty thefts.

Torture. A person in the Maurya dominion accused of theft and arrested within three days after the commission of the crime was ordinarily (with certain exceptions) subjected to torture in order to elicit a confession, unless he could prove either an alibi or enmity on the part of the complainant. Although the author of the *Arthasāstra* was fully aware of the danger of eliciting false confessions by torture and insists on the necessity for the production of conclusive evidence, it seems clear that the police must have relied chiefly on the use of torture. The general principle is

[1] Many passages in the *Arthasāstra* prove that the author was a follower of the *Atharva*, the Veda of magic and spells. Book XIV, entitled 'Secret Means', treats of weird sorceries supposed to compass the destruction of an enemy.

laid down that 'those whose guilt is believed to be true shall be subjected to torture'. In the face of such a comprehensive rule exceptions would have had little practical effect. All experienced magistrates, among whom the author of this book may be included, know how deeply the tradition of torturing a prisoner in order to extort a confession, true or false, is engrained in the mind of every Indian policeman and how difficult it is to check the practice even under modern conditions. The author of the *Arthaśāstra* gives a horrible list of eighteen kinds of torture, remarking calmly that 'each day a fresh kind of the torture may be employed', and that in certain aggravated cases, by special order, the prisoner might be 'subjected once or many times to one or all of the above kinds of torture'.

When the prisoner had been convicted, the modes of punishment were many, including fines, mutilation, and death in various forms, with or without torment.

Mutilation could sometimes be compounded for by a fine. The caste and rank of the offender were taken into consideration. A Brahman could not be tortured, but might be branded, exiled, or sent to the mines for life. The authorities were instructed to take notice of 'equitable distinctions among offenders, whether belonging to the royal family or to the common people'.

Theft to the value of 40 or 50 silver *panas* (probably nearly equivalent to shillings) was punishable with death.

Among other capital offences were homicide, housebreaking, breaching the dam of a tank, and damage to royal property, with many more. Megasthenes notes that death was the penalty for injury to an artisan in the royal employment, and that even evasion of the municipal tithe on goods sold was punished in the same drastic fashion.

There is no reason to suppose that the severity of the criminal code was seriously modified under the Buddhist government of Asoka. His Censors were specially charged to deal with cases of unjust imprisonment or corporal punishment, and prisoners lying under sentence of death are mentioned.

The *Arthaśāstra* prescribes the modest fine of only 48 *panas* on the superintendent of a jail for inflicting unjust torture; and even if he beat a prisoner to death he was merely to be fined 1,000 *panas*. Asoka's institution of Censors may, perhaps, have rendered the redress of such wrongs somewhat easier than it can have been in the time of his grandfather; but it is always difficult to detect or punish the misdoings of officials.

Town prefect and census. The author of the *Arthaśāstra* contemplated the division of a normal small kingdom into four provinces, each administered by a governor. He applied the same principle to the administration of the capital city, and presumably to that of other large towns. The capital was divided into four quarters or wards, each in charge of a sub-prefect (*sthānika*), who was assisted by subordinates (*gopa*), each responsible for from ten to forty households. The whole city was administered by a prefect (*nāgaraka*), whose duties resembled those of the *kotwāl* in later times.

The town authorities were expected to know everything about everybody within their jurisdiction, and to keep a sharp watch upon all comings and goings. The official activities included the maintenance of a permanent census, the *gopa* being required to 'know not only the caste, *gotra* [caste sub-division], the name, and occupation of both men and women in the households of his block, but also to ascertain their income and expenditure'. Such inquisitorial registration enormously enhanced the power of the central government for taxation and all purposes.

Precautions against fire and simple sanitary regulations were enforced. A person who intentionally set fire to a house was to be thrown into the same fire.

Maurya municipal commission. Chandragupta's municipal organization for his huge imperial capital was more complex. He provided a commission of thirty members, divided like that for the War Office, into six Boards or Committees. The Commissioners in their collective capacity had charge, in addition to their special departments, of all matters concerning the public welfare, including the repairs of public works, the maintenanee of markets, harbours, and temples, and the regulation of prices. The departmental functions of the six Boards or Committees were as follows: (1) industrial arts; (2) care of foreigners; (3) registration of births and deaths; (4) retail trade and barter, with supervision of weights and measures, and the due stamping of produce sold; (5) supervision of manufactures and sale of the same duly stamped; and (6) collection of the tithe on the price of goods sold.

The perfection of the arrangements thus indicated is astonishing, even when exhibited in outline. Examination of the departmental details increases our wonder that such an organization could have been planned and efficiently operated in India in 300 B.C. Akbar had nothing like it, and it may be doubted if any of the ancient Greek cities were better organized.

Board No. 1; arts. Artisans were regarded as being devoted in a special manner to the royal service, and capital punishment was inflicted on any person who impaired the efficiency of a craftsman by causing the loss of a hand or eye. Board No. 1 no doubt regulated wages, enforced the use of pure and sound materials, and exacted a full tale of work in exchange for the proper wage. The subject might be illustrated at length from the rules of the *Arthasāstra* concerning the duties of departmental officers as described in that work, and from the practice of later ages, but it is impossible here to follow out the details.

Board No. 2; foreigners. Board No. 2 performed duties which in modern times are entrusted to consuls and in ancient Greece were carried out by the officers called *proxenoi* (πρόξενοι). The members of the Board were required to find lodgings for foreigners, to keep them under observation, to escort them out of the country; and in case of sickness or death to provide for the treatment or burial of the stranger, whose property they were obliged to protect and account for. The existence of such officials and regulations affords conclusive proof that the Maurya empire was in constant intercourse with foreign states and that many strangers visited the capital on business.

Board No. 3; births and deaths. The registration of births and deaths was expressly designed both to facilitate taxation, probably a poll-tax of so much per head, and for the information of the government. It was a development and necessary consequence of the register or permanent census described in the *Arthasāstra*. It may be assumed that the exceptionally efficient government of Chandragupta introduced improvements on the arrangements of his predecessors.

Boards 4–6; trade and tolls. It has always been the practice of Indian rulers to exercise strict supervision over private trade and to levy duties on sales, the goods being stamped officially to guarantee payment. Manufactures were treated on the same principles. Procedure in such matters varied so little in India from age to age that the best comment on the statement of Megasthenes is afforded by an extract from the travels of Tavernier, the French jeweller who journeyed through India on business in the seventeenth century. He states that at Benares there were

> 'two galleries where they sell cottons, silken stuffs, and other kinds of merchandise. The majority of those who vend the goods are the workers who have made the pieces, and in this manner foreigners obtain them at first hand. These workers, before exposing anything for sale, have to go to him who holds the contract [*scil.* for collecting the tax on sales], in order to get the king's stamp impressed on the pieces of calico or silk, otherwise they are fined and flogged.'

The stamp usually was impressed in vermilion. It is called 'identity-stamp' (*abhijnāna-mudrā*) by Chānakya, and is the *σύσσημον* of the Greek accounts.[1] False statements made by importers or vendors were punishable as theft, that is to say, by fine, mutilation, or even death. Evasion of the municipal tithe collected by the sixth Board was specially made a capital offence, as already noted.

Full particulars of the methods of collection of duties on sales and manufactures will be found in the *Arthasāstra*, and some indication of the nature of Indian trade in the fourth century B.C. has been given in the account of the Nanda dynasty.

Viceroys. We have seen that according to the *Arthasāstra* the normal small kingdom described in that book should be divided into four provinces, each under a governor (*sthānika*). We do not know positively how many viceroys were required for Chandragupta's immense empire extending from the Hindu Kush to at least as far as the Narbadā, but it is noticeable that four viceroys seem to have sufficed for the still larger empire of Asoka. They will be mentioned more particularly in the history of his reign.

[1] McCrindle repeatedly mistranslated the words *ἀπὸ συσσήμου* as meaning 'by public notice'.

Departments. The *Arthasdstra* deseribes in mueh detail the duties of the heads of the numerous departments in the administration of a properly regulated Hindu state. The book refers to about thirty sueh departments. The Greek aeeounts prove that the departmental organization was maintained by Chandragupta. We hear speeifieally of offieers in eharge of markets, rivers, eanal irrigation, publie works, and sundry branehes of fiseal business, besides the superintendents of hunters, wood-eutters, blaeksmiths, earpenters, and miners. Innumerable details might be filled in from the *Arthasāstra*, but limitations of spaee permit notiee of only a few seleeted topies.

Official corruption. In spite of the drastie penal eode and the enhaneed severities visited upon offending offieials the publie serviee suffered from eorruption. The experieneed minister reeords his opinion that

'just as it is impossible not to taste the honey or the poison that finds itself at the tip of the tongue, so it is impossible for a government servant not to eat up, at least, a bit of the King's revenue. Just as with fish moving under water it eannot possibly be discerned whether they are drinking water or not, so it is impossible to deteet government servants employed on official duties when helping themselves to money. It is possible to mark the movements of birds flying high up in the sky; but it is not possible to aseertain the seeret movements of government servants.'

'There are', the same authority observes, 'about forty ways of embezzlement; what is realized earlier is entered later on; what is realized later is entered earlier; what ought to be realized is not realized;' and so on through the whole list.

Rewards were promised to informers who diselosed eases of defaleation; but, on the other hand, the informer who failed to prove his eharges was liable to severe punishment, whieh might be eapital.

Secret service. The seeret service to whieh referenee has been made may be deseribed as the mainstay of the government, next to the army. The king employed hosts of spies or deteetives, masquerading in disguises of all kinds, who were eontrolled by an espionage bureau, as in modern Germany. Cipher writing was used and the serviees of earrier pigeons were enlisted. The doetrine of the neeessity for eonstant espionage in every braneh of the administration pervades the whole of the *Arthasāstra*, whieh treats every form of villany as legitimate when employed in the business of the state. The evidenee of Chānakya's treatise is eorroborated by the Greek testimony. News writers at the head-quarters of provineial administrations supplied seeret reports to the government, and the information obtained from eourtesans was not despised. We are told that the king, having set up spies over his ministers, 'shall proceed to espy both eitizens and eountry people'. The drama already eited more than onee exhibits the system at work.

Property in land. The question whether or not private property in land existed in aneient India has been often debated, but without any satisfactory result, by reason of the ambiguity lurking in the term property. The disputants who affirm the existence of private property in land use the term in one sense and their opponents in another. The clearest example of absolute private property in land, apparently closely resembling the English freehold, is to be found in Malabar, the home of the Nāyars (Nairs), Coorgs, and Tulus, whom Dubois regarded as the three aboriginal tribes of the western coast. He expressed the opinion that Malabar 'is the only province in India where proprietary right has been preserved intact until the present day. Everywhere else the soil belongs to the ruler, and the cultivator is merely his tenant.'

The Abbé then proceeds to explain at considerable length exactly what he means.[1]

The proposition enunciated by Dubois that 'everywhere else the soil belongs to the ruler' has been generally accepted in northern and western India, and is now, as Baden-Powell testifies, the doctrine current in the Native States.

The commentator on the *Arthaśāstra* (Book II, chap. 24) had no doubt on the subject. He declares that 'those who are well versed in the scriptures admit that the King is the owner of both land and water, and that the people can exercise their right of ownership over all other things excepting these two'. The author of the treatise, as a whole, seems to accept that view. The rules in chapter 1 of Book II, for instance, instruct the king that 'lands prepared for cultivation shall be given to tax-payers (*karada*) only for life (*ekapurushikāni*)'; and that 'lands may be confiscated from those who do not cultivate them, and given to others'. The author evidently held that land of all kinds was at the disposal of the government. Most native Indian governments, including those of the Muhammadan dynasties, have taken in the shape of land revenue and cesses so large a proportion of the produce that the actual cultivator was left at most a bare subsistence. The government share, it is true, was always limited theoretically, but in practice the state usually took all it could extort. In those circumstances no room was left for economic rent, or for a landlord class receiving rent. Nothing intervened between the poverty-stricken peasant and the state. Ordinarily the peasant's customary right to retain his land as long as he paid all official demands was respected, but his ill-defined right of occupancy, which was not protected by positive law, differed widely from ownership. In the Bombay Presidency, where the State still deals directly with the cultivating peasant or 'ryot', the ownership of the government is expressly recognized by law.

In Bengal and the Upper Provinces the British authorities have gone out of their way to develop, or even to create a class of rent-receiving landlords, whose rights are often described as amounting

[1] *Hindu Manners*, &c., ed. Beauchamp, 3rd ed. (1906), p. 56. See *The Travancore State Manual*, Trivandrum, 1906, for the theory and details of the Malabar 'birth-right' tenure.

to full ownership. But in the background there is always the lien of the State on the soil to enforce the punctual payment of the land revenue, that is to say, the cash commutation for the share of the produce to which every Indian government is entitled by immemorial tradition. The so-called 'ownership' was in former times and still is also subject to the customary rights of subordinate tenure-holders and of the cultivating peasants; those rights being substantial, although undefined by law and inadequately secured before the middle of the nineteenth century.

Land revenue. The land revenue, or State share of the produce, which always has been the mainstay of Indian finance, may be regarded as rent rather than as taxation on the assumption that the ultimate property in land is vested in the State. The normal share of the produce admitted to be claimable by the government was one-fourth. But Akbar took one-third, and the Sultans of Kashmīr claimed one-half. The nominal percentage of land revenue to the produce did not much matter, because the government usually made up for any deficiency by exacting a multitude of extra periodical cesses, not to speak of occasional forced contributions. The ordinary result was that the peasant might consider himself lucky if he was left enough to fill tolerably the stomachs of himself and family and to provide seed. Nothing was available for the payment of rent to a private landlord.

In Anglo-Indian official phraseology the term 'settlement', a translation of the Persian word *bandobast*, is applied to the whole process by which the amount of the land revenue or crown-rent is assessed, and the officer who carries out the operations is called a 'settlement officer'. The authorities do not explain the nature of the 'settlements' made in Maurya times, and we do not know whether the assessment was varied yearly or fixed for longer periods.

Irrigation. Irrigation, which is essential in most parts of India for the security of the crops and consequently of the revenue, received close attention, and was under the supervision of departmental officers. A system of canals with sluices was maintained, and water-rates of varying amounts were levied as they are now.

Roads. The main roads were kept in order by the proper department, and pillars marking the distances, equivalent to our milestones and the Mogul *kōs mīnārs*, were set up at intervals of ten *stadia*, or about 2,022½ English yards, half a *kōs* by Indian reckoning. The Mogul emperors were content with a pillar for each *kōs*. A great highway, now represented by Lord Dalhousie's Grand Trunk Road, connected Taxila and the north-western frontier with Pātaliputra, the capital. The *Arthasāstra* mentions the construction of roads as one of the duties of a king. Rules were laid down concerning the correct width of each class of road.

Liquor. The drinking of and traffic in liquor were recognized officially and encouraged as a source of revenue. The whole business was under the control of a Superintendent, who was responsible for the necessary police and licensing arrangements, as well as for the collection of the government dues. Public-houses or drinking-shops were not to be close together, and the consumption, whether on or off the premises, was duly regulated. The shops were to be made attractive by the provision of seats, couches, scents, garlands, water, and other comforts suitable to the varying seasons. Chānakya mentions six principal kinds of liquor. Special licences for manufacture were granted for a term of four days on the occasions of festivals, fairs, and pilgrimages.

General observations. It is impossible to reproduce in a reasonable space nearly all the information on record concerning the institutions of Chandragupta Maurya and his immediate predecessors. The particulars recounted in the foregoing pages may suffice to give the modern student a fairly accurate and vivid notion of the nature of the civilization of northern India at the close of the fourth century B.C. Many readers probably will be surprised to learn of the existence at such an early date of a government so thoroughly organized, which anticipated in many respects the institutions of modern times. The dark spots on the picture are the appalling wickedness of the statecraft taught in the *Arthasāstra* and the hateful espionage which tainted the whole administration and was inspired by the wicked statecraft of the books. The policy inculcated by Kautilya or Chānakya was not the invention of that unscrupulous minister. The book attributed to him on substantial grounds is avowedly founded upon many earlier treatises no longer extant, all of which seem to have advocated the same principles. The author of the *Arthasāstra*, while frequently disagreeing with his predecessors concerning details, clearly was in general agreement with them concerning the policy to be pursued. Attention has been drawn to the emphatic repudiation of the *Arthasāstra* doctrines by Bāna in the seventh century after Christ. He does not stand quite alone, although it might be difficult to cite any passage exactly similar from other authors. The spirit of the *Dharmasāstras* is far more humane than that of Chānakya's ruthless treatise, and the story of Rāma, whether told in Sanskrit or Hindī, is that of a noble prince. Kāmandaka, on the other hand, describes the author of the *Arthasāstra* as 'wise and Brahma (god)-like'; and Dandi calls him 'a revered teacher'.

How did the atrocious policy taught in the books of the *Arthasāstra* class originate and gain wide acceptance? The minister professes to write in accordance with the 'customs of the Āryas', and to revere the 'triple Veda', but his practical advice, so far as it has a Vedic foundation, is based on the fourth Veda, the *Atharva*, a storehouse of sorcery and spells. The question which I have asked suggests curious speculations.[1]

[1] The 'triple Veda' (*trayī*) is defined as comprising the '*Sāma*, *Rik*, and *Yajus*'. The order of enumeration is noteworthy. The author, when specifying the 'four sciences', places first *Anvīkshakī* or philosophy (comprising *Sānkhya*, *Yoga*, and *Lokāyata*); and assigns the 'triple Veda' to the second place. The third science called *Vārta* deals with the practical affairs of common life, namely, agriculture, cattle-breeding,

Authorities

Most of the necessary references will be found in *E. H. I.*[3] Oxford, 1914. The revised version of the *Arthasāstra* by R. Shamasastry (Shama Sastri) is now conveniently available in an octavo volume published at Bangalore Government Press in 1915. A considerable literature of books and essays is growing up round the text of the *Arthasāstra*, which came to light in 1905. The most important treatise subsequent to the publication of *E. H. I.*[3] is *Public Administration in Ancient India* by Pramathanatha Banerjea (Macmillan, 1916); a learned and accurate work, although the author's notion that the Maurya monarchy was 'limited' (p. 50) or 'constitutional' (p. 51) is not tenable. *Studies in Ancient Hindu Polity*, vol. i, by Narendra Nath Law, with a good introduction by Professor Radhakumud Mookerji, is also useful (Longmans, 1914). The *Positive Background of Hindu Sociology*, Book I, by Professor Benoy Kumār Sarkār (Pānini Office, Allahabad, 1914), may be consulted with advantage on certain matters, notwithstanding its cumbrous title.

Many parts of the *Arthasāstra* still remain obscure, and the treatise must become the subject of much more discussion from various points of view.

CHAPTER 2

Asoka Maurya and his institutions ; diffusion of Buddhism ; end of the Maurya dynasty ; the successors of the Mauryas.

Accession of Asoka. When the reign of Bindusāra terminated in 273 B.C. he was succeeded by one of his sons named Asoka-vardhana, commonly called Asoka, who seems to have been selected by his father as heir apparent, and possibly may have enjoyed for some time the rank of sub-king or *uparāja*. According to tradition he had served as Viceroy, first at Taxila in the north-west, and subsequently at Ujjain in Mālwā. The fact that his formal consecration or coronation (*abhisheka*) was delayed for some four years until 269 B.C. confirms the tradition that his succession was contested, and it may be true that his rival was an elder brother named Susīma, as affirmed by one of the many wild legends which have gathered round Asoka's name. The story told by the monks of Ceylon that he slaughtered 98 or 99 brothers in order to clear his way to the throne is absurd and false ; the fact being, as the inscriptions prove, that Asoka took good care of his brothers and sisters long after his succession. The grotesque tales about Asoka's alleged abnormal wickedness prior to his conversion to Buddhism, which were current in the north as well as the south, are equally baseless and obviously concocted for purposes of edification.

and trade ; the fourth, styled alternatively *Arthasāstra* or *Dandanīti*, is the subject of his treatise. 'This *Arthasāstra*', he says in his opening sentence, 'is made as a compendium of almost all the *Arthasāstras*, which, in view of acquisition and maintenance of the earth, have been composed by ancient teachers.' See Book I, chaps. 1–4, and the concluding chapter of the work.

Authorities. The monkish legends, whether of Ceylon or other countries, do not afford a safe basis for a matter-of-fact history of the great Buddhist emperor, although some of the Ceylon dates seem to be correct, while others are erroneous. The only sound foundation for his history is to be found in his numerous and wonderful inscriptions, which may be fairly considered the most remarkable set of inscriptions in the world. Their testimony is supplemented by that of a few other epigraphs, by literary tradition in many forms and languages, and by inferences deduced from study of the extant monuments and their distribution. The coins of Asoka's age, which do not bear his name or titles, are of little use to the historian. The *Arthasāstra* and certain other books in various languages provide materials for illustrative comment on the narrative.

Little political activity. Asoka having been a man of peace for the greater part of his long reign, the recorded political events during it are few, and nothing is known about his military force. The interest of the story is centred on the movement initiated by him which transformed Buddhism from a local sect into one of the world-religions and on the gradual development of the emperor's personal character and policy. His imperishable records constitute in large measure his autobiography written in terms manifestly dictated by himself.

Asoka waged only one war of aggression, that directed to the acquisition of Kalinga on the coast of the Bay of Bengal. His gigantic empire, which extended from the Hindu Kush to the northern districts of Mysore, consequently must have been inherited, with the exception of Kalinga, from his father, and must have been acquired either by Bindusāra or by Chandragupta, or by both.

Chronology. His inscriptions date the events of the reign by regnal years reckoned from the time of his consecration or coronation in 269 B.C. The month in which that ceremony took place not being known, it is impossible to equate accurately the regnal with the calendar years. Nor is it practicable to define the dates B.C. with absolute precision for various reasons. Two of the chief of those reasons are that the exact year of Chandragupta's accession is not ascertainable, and that the length of Bindusāra's reign is variously stated as either twenty-five or twenty-eight years. For convenience dates will be given in this chapter as if they were precise, but the reader is invited to bear in mind that they are subject to slight correction for possible error, probably not exceeding two years. Asoka's reign, as counted from his father's death, extended to forty or forty-one years; or, as counted from his consecration, to thirty-six or thirty seven years. The dated inscriptions begin in the ninth and come down to the twenty-eighth regnal year, equivalent approximately to the period including 261 and 242 B.C. The reign is taken as extending from 273 to 242 B.C.

Asoka's early years. No definite political event can be assigned to the early years of Asoka's government. His personal reminiscences prove that he then lived the life of his predecessors, consuming flesh food freely, enjoying the pleasures of the chase, and encouraging festive assemblies accompanied by dancing and drinking. No sound reason exists for believing that his conduct was particularly sinful or vicious. The nature of his diet and amusements in those days affords conclusive evidence that he cannot have been a follower of the Jain religion. It may be presumed that he was a Brahmanical Hindu, and most likely a worshipper of Siva. His religious cult or ceremonial possibly may have been affected by Magian practices of Iranian origin, but it is not probable that he was a professed Zoroastrian. The sudden change in his beliefs and habits was produced by the remorse which he felt for the unmerited sorrows inflicted upon the people of the kingdom of Kalinga in the east by his attack on and annexation of that country in 261 B.C.

The Kalinga war. The Kalinga war, which was the turning point in Asoka's career, thus became one of the decisive events in the history of the world. The miseries of the campaign, the sufferings of the prisoners, and the wailings for the dead were soon forgotten by the vanquished, as they have been forgotten by other conquered nations after thousands of wars; but the effect which they produced upon the conscience of the victor is still traceable in the world of the twentieth century.

Asoka himself tells us in the striking language of his longest Rock Edict (No. XIII) how he was haunted by remorse for the calamities caused by his ambition, and was driven to take refuge in the Law of Piety or Duty, which he identifies elsewhere with the doctrine of the Buddha.

'Kalinga was conquered by His Sacred and Gracious Majesty when he had been consecrated eight years [261 B.C.]. 150,000 persons were thence carried away captive, 100,000 were there slain, and many times that number perished.

Directly after the annexation of the Kalingas began His Sacred Majesty's zealous protection of the Law of Duty, his love of that Law, and his giving instruction in that Law (*dharma*). Thus arose His Sacred Majesty's remorse for having conquered the Kalingas, because the conquest of a country previously unconquered involves the slaughter, death, and carrying away captive of the people. That is a matter of profound sorrow and regret to His Sacred Majesty.'

The royal author proceeds to develop in detail the sentiment above expressed in general terms, and continues:

'Thus, of all the people who were then slain, done to death, or carried away captive in the Kalingas, if the hundredth or the thousandth part were to suffer the same fate, it would now be matter of regret to His Sacred Majesty. Moreover, should any one do him wrong, that too must be borne with by His Sacred Majesty, if it can be possibly borne with. Even upon the forest folk in his dominions His Sacred Majesty looks kindly and he seeks their conversion, for, if he did not, repentance would come upon His Sacred Majesty. They are bidden to turn from evil ways that they be not chastised. For His Sacred Majesty desires that all animate beings should have security, self-control, peace of mind, and joyousness.'

True conquest. Asoka goes on to explain that true conquest consists in the conquest of men's hearts by the Law of Duty or Piety,[1] and to relate that he had already won such real victories, not only in his own dominions, but in kingdoms six hundred leagues away, including the realm of the Greek king Antiochos, and the dominions of the four kings severally named Ptolemy, Antigonos, Magas, and Alexander, who dwell beyond (or 'to the north of') 'that Antiochos'; and likewise to the south, in the kingdoms of the Cholas and the Pāndyas, as far as the Tāmraparni river; and also in the king's dominions among the various tribes or nations called Yonas, Kāmbojas, Nabhapamtis of Nābhaka, Bhojas, and Pitinikas, as well as among the Āndhras and Pulindas [2]—in fact, 'everywhere', he says, 'men hearing His Sacred Majesty's ordinance based on the Law of Duty and his instruction in that Law, practise and will practise that Law'.

The royal preacher then extols the true conquest wrought by the Law as being full, not only of transitory delight, but of precious fruit which remains sound in the next world. He concludes by exhorting his sons and grandsons to pursue the path of true conquest; and, if perchance they should become involved in a conquest by force of arms (or 'from self-will', as Hultzsch), to take their pleasure in patience and gentleness, so that they may by effort attain that joy of spirit which avails for both this world and the next.

Special Kalinga edicts. The subject is continued in the two special edicts which the victor composed a little later for the benefit of the conquered provinces, one being addressed to the high officers of a town named Samāpā, and the other to those of a second town called Tosali. A postscript enjoins the viceroys of Taxila and Ujjain, the governments which Asoka himself had held as Prince, to apply the principles enunciated, and to take effectual steps by means of periodical tours and public proclamations on certain holidays to see that the imperial commands were translated into practice.

The emperor starts by affirming that 'all men are my children', echoing a saying attributed to Buddha. He then seeks to win the confidence of the unsubdued border tribes, and announces that specially trained officers will be sent to look after their interests. He laments that some servants of the state, failing to realize his

[1] Milton offers a surprisingly exact parallel passage:

> They err, who count it glorious to subdue
> By conquest far and wide, to overrun
> Large countries, and in fields great battles win,
> Great cities by assault . . .
> But if there be in glory aught of good,
> It may by means far different be attained
> Without ambition, war, or violence;
> By deeds of peace, by wisdom eminent,
> By patience, temperance (*Paradise Regained*, iii. 71–92).

[2] Rock Edict V adds the Rāshtrikas of the Marāthā country, and the Gāndhāras of the north-western frontier.

paternal sentiments, had at times gone so far as to inflict unjust imprisonment or torture. He warns his officers that they must beware of yielding to the vices of 'envy, lack of perseverance, harshness, impatience, want of application, laziness, and indolence', threatening them with his displeasure if they should fail in their duty.

Those admirable instructions, which could not be bettered to-day, show how Asoka's remorse for the horrors of his one aggressive war bore fruit in the practical administration of his frontier provinces.

Contemporary powers. The references in the edict first quoted to other potentates, nations, and tribes obviously have much historical importance. When duly interpreted they prove that Asoka was contemporary with Antiochos Theos, grandson of Seleukos Nikator, the foe and afterwards the ally of Asoka's grandfather; with Ptolemy Philadelphos of Egypt;[1] with Magas, the ruler of Cyrene to the west of Egypt; and with an Alexander, probably King of Epirus. Chronologists show that the last year in which those four princes were alive together appears to have been 258 B.C., and that the edict consequently cannot be much later in date. It is actually dated in either the thirteenth or fourteenth regnal year, equivalent to 257 or 256 B.C. The document further proves that the emperor of India enjoyed the privilege of friendly intercourse with the Hellenistic kings named, that he was at liberty to conduct Buddhist propaganda in their dominions, and that he succeeded in gaining attention to his teaching. We also learn that the Tamil kingdoms of the Cholas and Pāndyas were then in existence, the Maurya emissaries penetrating as far as the Tāmraparni river in Tinnevelly, the seat of the pearl and the conch-shell trade, chiefly conducted at the now vanished port of Korkai. Another edict mentions two more Tamil kingdoms, namely that of Keralaputra, or the Malabar coast, and that of Satiyaputra, probably equivalent to the Satyamangalam province of the later kingdom of Madura. That province skirted the borders of Mysore, Malabar, Coimbatore, and Madura, along the line of the western Ghāts. We thus obtain a welcome glimpse of the history of the Far South at a definite date; the first, and for a long time the only chronological foothold in the story of the Tamil kingdoms.

Coin of Ptolemy Philadelphos.

We are further informed concerning the names of sundry

[1] Ptolemy was a king with great power and wealth, and a liberal patron of literature and science. Euclid lived at Alexandria in his time. Ptolemy founded colonies on the Red Sea coast.

considerable tribes or nations who were included more or less completely in Asoka's dominions or had been brought under his influence.

The accuracy of the Greek accounts concerning the relations between Seleukos Nikator and Chandragupta is confirmed by the edicts, which disclose the friendship of the grandson of Seleukos with the grandson of Chandragupta.[1]

Foreign Buddhist missions. The surprising intimation that Buddhist missions were dispatched in the middle of the third century B.C. to distant Hellenistic kingdoms in Asia and Africa, and perhaps in Europe, opens up a wide field for reflection and speculation.

While the primary authority for the history of Asoka must always be his inscriptions, much valuable supplementary information is obtained from other sources. One of those sources is to be found in the chronicles of Ceylon called the *Mahāvamsa* and *Dīpavamsa*. The latter, the older of the two, seems to have been composed in the fourth or fifth century A. C. The statements of the edicts concerning the imperial Buddhist propaganda are amplified by the Ceylonese chroniclers, who describe nine distinct missions, which embraced seven Indian countries lying between the Himalayas and Peshāwar in the north and a region called Mahishamandala in the south, usually identified with the southern portion of the Mysore state. Two other missions are said to have been dispatched to countries outside India proper, namely, Suvarnabhūmi, or Lower Burma, and Lankā, or Ceylon. The chronicler gives the names of the missionaries employed in each case, and some of those names are also recorded in inscriptions from the Bhīlsā topes. The list may be accepted as correct, subject to the remark that the propaganda in Lower Burma seems to have had little effect. The earliest form of Buddhism in that country, so far as definite evidence goes, was of the Mahāyānā kind,

[1] The versions of the edicts are extracted from those in *Asoka*[2], Oxford, 1909, with corrections. The name of the conquered province is written in the edict both in the singular and the plural. It was sometimes known as the 'Three Kalingas'.

The name Tāmraparni refers to the river in the Tinnevelly District, and not to Ceylon, as wrongly stated in *Asoka*[2], pp. 156, 174. The intercourse of Asoka with the island did not begin until after the accession of Devānampiya Tissa, several years subsequent to the date in the thirteenth and partly in the fourteenth regnal year, equivalent to about 257 and 256 B. C. Tissa's accession may be dated about 251 B. C. Exact dates in the early history of Ceylon cannot be determined with complete certainty. The Satiyaputra kingdom should be identified as in the text, and not with the Tulu country, as in *E. H. I.*[3], Oxford, 1914, pp. 163, 185, 446, 459. See *Ind. Ant.*, vol. xli (1912), p. 231 ; vol. xlv (1916), p. 200.

For the meaning of *Devānampiya* and *Piyadasi* used as royal titles see *Asoka*[2], p. 22. Mr. Yazdani interprets *Piyadasi* as meaning 'the well-wisher (of all)'. However the titles may be analysed etymologically they were used merely as formal royal style or *protocole*, and are best translated by approximate equivalents.

different from the Buddhism of Asoka, and apparently imported from northern India.

Mission to Ceylon. The mission to Ceylon was a complete success, although the conversion of the island was not suddenly effected by a series of astounding miracles as related in the monkish stories. It was, no doubt, a gradual, although tolerably rapid process, aided materially by powerful royal encouragement.[1] The mission came in 251 or 250 B.C. on the initiative of King Tissa, who ascended the throne about that time, and reigned, like his

THE BO-TREE AT ANARAJAPOORA.

friend Asoka, for forty years. During his rule he expended most of his energy in measures for the propagation of the Buddhist religion, and in erecting splendid buildings for its service. The leading missionary was Mahendra or Mahinda, Asoka's younger brother, who settled down in the island and died there about 204 B.C. His memory is perpetuated by monuments which bear his name. He was aided by his sister, who is remembered by her title Sanghamitrā, 'Friend of the Church', or 'Order', and was as successful among the women as Mahendra was among the men. The Indian tradition which represents Mahendra as the younger brother of Asoka is of greater authority than the island legends which describe him as a son of the emperor.

Buddhism won a decisive victory in Ceylon during the long reign of Tissa, and has never lost its hold on the island, where its influence,

[1] I believe that the missionaries came from Mahendra's monastery at Madura in Pāndya territory.

on the whole, has been for good. A well-informed and sympathetic writer observes that:

'The missions of King Asoka are amongst the greatest civilizing influences in the world's history; for they entered countries for the most part barbarous and full of superstition, and amongst these animistic peoples Buddhism spread as a wholesome leaven.

The history of Ceylon and Burma, as of Siam, Japan, and Tibet, may be said to begin with the entrance into them of Buddhism; and in these lands it spread far more rapidly and made a far deeper impression than in China with its already ancient civilization.

As to-day Christianity spreads very rapidly amongst the animistic peoples of Africa, India, and the South Sea islands, exerting a strong influence and replacing superstition and chaos by a reasonable belief in One God and an orderly universe, so Buddhism in these eastern lands has exerted a beneficent influence by putting Karma, the law of cause and effect, in the place of the caprice of demons and tribal gods, and a lofty system of morals in the place of tribal custom and *taboo*.

The Buddhist missionaries, moreover, brought with them much of the culture of their own land. It seems clear, for instance, that it was Mahinda who brought into Ceylon the arts of stone carving and of irrigation which his father had so successfully practised in India; and the Ceylon Buddhist of to-day thinks of his religion as the force to which his country owes the greatness of her past history. . . . Not far from the ruined city of Anurādhapura a lovely rocky hill rises out of a dense sea of jungle, and here is the rock-hewn 'study' and the tomb of the great and gentle prince Mahinda, who about 250 B.C. brought Buddhism to Ceylon.

From that day to this Buddhism has been the dominant religion of the island. Its king, Tissa, entered into alliance with Asoka, and did all he could to foster the religion of Gautama; and he and all his successors built the great Sacred City of Anurādhapura, in which vast hill-like dāgobas, higher than St. Paul's Cathedral and covering many acres of ground, rear their mighty domes above the trees of a royal park and royal baths and palaces given to the Sangha. . . . The 7,774 Bhikkhus [monks or friars] who to-day keep alive the religion are thus descendants in an unbroken succession of the great Mahinda himself, and in Ceylon monasticism has had a unique chance of proving its worth.'[1]

Anurādhapura or Anurājapura, the Buddhist Rome, may serve as the measure and symbol of Asoka's influence on the world.

Council of Pātaliputra. But the monkish authors of Ceylon, whom many European writers on Buddhism have been too ready to accept as primary authorities, give none of the credit to the emperor. According to them, the conversion of the island and other lands was the work of the saint or *thera* named Tissa, who convoked a church council at Pātaliputra and then sent out his emissaries. The Ceylonese stories, written many centuries after the events described, have no just claim to be regarded as authorities superior to the words of Asoka, who never mentions either the saint or the

[1] K. J. Saunders, *The Story of Buddhism*, Oxford University Press, 1916, pp. 76–9. 'Rome of to-day is a mean thing, the Forum a mean jostle of littleness, compared with the extended enormous ruin of the Sacred City—vast, resigned, silent, leisurely, with full consciousness of an eternity of desolation to face' (Farrer, *In Old Ceylon*, 1908, p. 346).

Council, while emphatically presenting all the measures taken for the furtherance of religion as having been initiated by himself. I believe Asoka's word. The Council of Pātaliputra may be accepted as a fact, because it is vouched for by Indian as well as Ceylonese tradition. But, in my opinion, the monks have dated it wrongly. The probability is that it was convoked towards the close of the reign of Asoka, after the publication of his principal sets of inscriptions, the Fourteen Rock Edicts, and the Seven Pillar Edicts. It may have been the occasion for the promulgation of his latest known records, the Minor-Pillar Edicts, which deal specially with the deadly sin of schism, although those documents do not refer expressly to the Council.

Upagupta and Thera Tissa. Northern tradition, which was much more likely to be well founded than the tales composed by the Ceylon monks and distorted by theological bias, testifies that the instructor of Asoka in Buddhism was Upagupta of Mathurā, son of Gupta the perfumer of Benares. A monastery bearing his name still existed in the seventh century A.C. at Mathurā. No doubt is possible that Upagupta was a real historical person, the fourth patriarch of the Buddhist church. The incidents of his story have been transferred by the Ceylon chroniclers to the Thera Tissa, the son of Moggali. The proof that the two names refer to the same person is absolutely conclusive.

Asoka a monk. The admonitions of Upagupta produced many effects besides the dispatch of missionaries. He took his imperial pupil in 249 B.C. on a tour round the principal holy places of the faith,[1] beginning with the Lumbini Garden, the modern Rummindēī in the Nepalese Tarai, where the perfect inscription on a pillar still standing commemorates the emperor's visit. Asoka also gave up hunting and the practice of eating meat, in which he had previously indulged. All slaughter of animals for the royal kitchen was prohibited. Asoka at least once temporarily assumed the garb of a monk. Long afterwards the Chinese pilgrim I-tsing saw a statue representing him as so robed. Buddhist 'orders' not being irrevocable, it is open to any layman to become a monk for a short time and then to return to the world. In fact, every male Burmese at the present day is expected to make a stay, long or short, in a monastery.

Imperial review of policy. In 242 B.C., Asoka, who was then growing old, and had been on the throne for over thirty years, undertook to review the measures taken during his reign for the promotion of religion, the teaching of moral duty, and the welfare of his subjects. That review was embodied in a series of edicts inscribed on pillars, and hence called the Seven Pillar Edicts, which must be read as an appendix or supplement to the earlier

[1] M. Foucher has proved that a sculpture on the eastern gate at Sānchi must represent the solemn visit of Asoka to the sacred tree at Bodh Gayā (*La Porte orientale du Stūpa de Sānchī*, Paris, 1910, pp. 30, 75).

proclamations engraved on rocks. The foreign missions are not mentioned; I do not know why.

Ahimsā. The fifth Pillar Edict expresses the emperor's matured views on the subject of *ahimsā*, or abstention from injury to or slaughter of animals. He indicates his disapproval of the practice

FACSIMILE

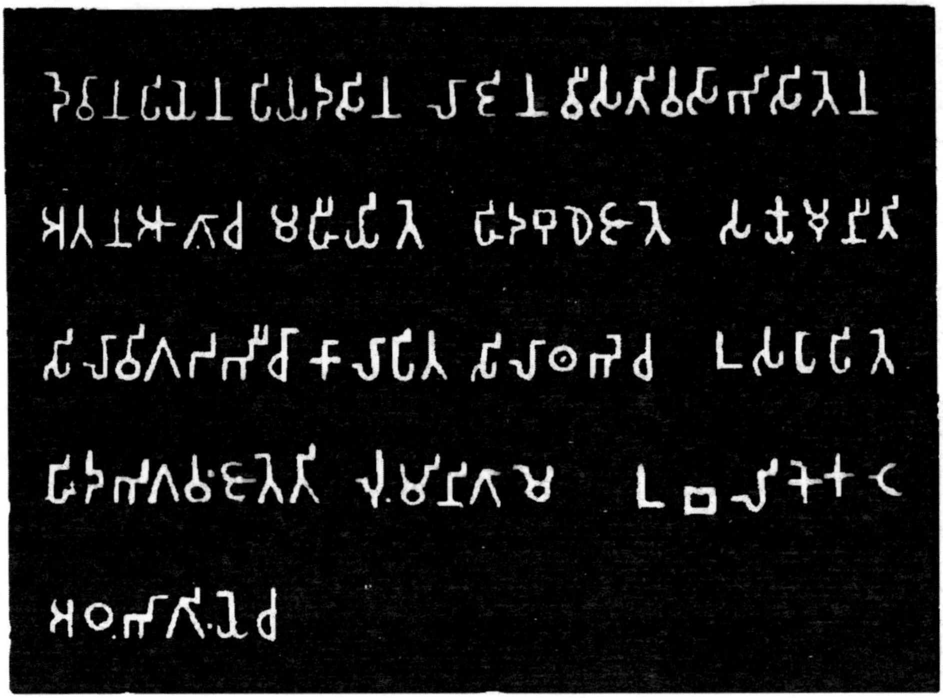

TRANSLITERATION

1 Devānapiyena piyadasina lājina vīsativasābhisitena
2. atana āgācha mahīyite hida budhe jāte sakyamuniti
3. silā vigadabhīchā kālāpita silāthabhecha usapāpite
4. hida bhagavam jāteti lumminigāme ubalikekate
5. athabhāgiyecha

ASOKA'S INSCRIPTION ON THE RUMMINDEĪ PILLAR.

of castration or caponing, and publishes many rules for the protection of living creatures. It is a surprising fact that horned cattle are not included in the list of animals the slaughter of which was forbidden; whereas the *Arthasāstra* (Book II, chap. 26) contains the clause:

'Cattle such as a calf, a bull, or a milch cow shall not be slaughtered.'

We have seen that the government of Taxila had felt no scruple in presenting Alexander with thousands of cattle fatted for slaughter. That Taxilan sentiment probably explains Asoka's abstention from forbidding a practice which his old subjects in the north-west would not readily abandon. It is unlikely that the feelings of the public of Taxila had changed materially during the seventy-four years which had elapsed since the Macedonian visit to their city. The facts thus noted throw light on the obscure problem of the development of the passionate feeling in favour of the sanctity of the cow, which is now the most conspicuous and universal outward mark of Hinduism. It is clear that the feeling in anything like its present vehemence was not fully developed in the days of either Alexander or Asoka.

The prohibitions against animal slaughter in Pillar Edict V coincide to a considerable extent with those recorded in the *Arthasāstra*. Both documents, for instance, forbid the killing of parrots, starlings, and 'Brạhminy' ducks.

Asoka's last years. The publication of the Seven Pillar Edicts in 242 B.C. is the last event in Asoka's reign which can be precisely dated. The Council of Pātaliputra may be placed, as already observed, a little later, somewhere about 240 B.C., and I would assign the same date approximately to the Minor Pillar Edicts which denounce the sin of schism. The Council is said to have been convoked in order to repress heresy, and the publication of the special edicts directed against divisions in the church may be reasonably regarded as a result of the deliberations of the Council. Some traditions represent Asoka as having become in his old age a doting devotee, who wasted the resources of the empire in indiscriminate charity to monks and monasteries. It has also been asserted that he abdicated. His authentic records give no support to such legends or notions. They exhibit him to the last as a masterful autocrat ruling Church and State alike with a strong hand, as Charlemagne did in Europe more than a thousand years later. It is possible, of course, that Asoka may have descended from the throne towards the close of his life and devoted the short remainder of his days to religious exercises, but there is no good evidence that he actually did so.

Classes of inscriptions. It will be convenient at this point to explain briefly the nature and distribution of the remarkable inscriptions so often cited. They fall naturally into two main classes, those inscribed on rocks *in situ* or on detached boulders, and those inscribed on highly finished monolithic columns or pillars. The rock edicts, which are the earlier in date, occur mostly in the more distant and out-of-the-way localities. The columns or pillars are found in the home provinces, where the fine sandstone needed for their construction was procurable.

The records, of which many are substantially and some absolutely perfect, may be arranged in eight groups in chronological order as follows:

(i) The Minor Rock Edicts; two documents dating from about 258 or 257 B.C. No. 1 is found in variant recensions at seven localities; but No. 2 is known at one only.

(ii) The Bhābrū Edict, on a detached boulder, now in Calcutta.

The purport of the record is unique. The date probably is the same as that of the Minor Rock Edicts.

(iii) The Fourteen Rock Edicts, in seven more or less complete recensions, varying considerably, and dating from 257 and 256 B.C.

(iv) The Kalinga Edicts, in two recensions, referring only to the conquered province, and substituted for certain of the Fourteen Rock Edicts ; they may be dated in 256 B.C.

(v) The Cave Inscriptions, being records of dedications inscribed on the walls of three caves hewn in the rock of the Barābar hills near Gayā, in 257 and 250 B.C.

(vi) The Tarāi Pillar Inscriptions, being two commemorative records on columns in the Nepalese Tarāi, erected in 249 B.C.

(vii) The Seven Pillar Edicts in six recensions (excepting Edict 7, which is found at one place only), dating from 243 and 242 B.C.

(viii) The Minor Pillar Edicts, four in number, dating between 242 and 232 B.C. Two documents, one at Sārnāth, and the other at Sānchī, are inscribed on separate columns ; the others are postscripts to the Pillar Edicts at Allahabad.

Distribution of inscriptions. The distribution of the inscriptions is indicated on the map of Asoka's empire. The Rock Edicts, including the Minor Rock Edicts, the Bhābrū Edict, and the Cave Inscriptions, are widely distributed from the extreme north-western corner of the Panjāb to the northern districts of Mysore. They are found on the coasts of both the Bay of Bengal and the Arabian Sea, so that they may be said to cover an area extending from 34° 20′ to 14° 49′ N. lat., and from about 72° 15′ to 85° 50′ E. long., that is to say, twenty degrees of latitude and thirteen of longitude. Additions to the list probably will be discovered when Afghanistan and certain other frontier regions shall be open to research. The Maski inscription in the Nizam's Dominions was not noticed until 1915. It is particularly precious because it is the only record which specifies the emperor's personal name Asoka.[1] All the other documents describe him by his titles only. It is not unlikely that more records may be found within the limits of India. Although some of the sites of the Rock Edicts are now in the wilderness, every one of the localities in Asoka's time was frequented either as a place of pilgrimage or for other good reason.

The positions of more than thirty monolithic columns or pillars of Asoka are recorded. Ten of those now visible are inscribed. The area of their distribution is not so large as that of the rock inscriptions, probably owing to the difficulty of obtaining suitable blocks of stone. One, which formerly stood at a village in the Ambāla (Umballa) District, Panjāb, is now at Delhi. Others still exist at Sānchī in the Bhopāl State, Central India. Those two localities are the most remote from Pātaliputra the capital.

Extent of the empire. The extent of Asoka's empire is known with sufficient precision from the details of the distribution of

[1] It begins with the words *Devānampiyasa Asokasa*.

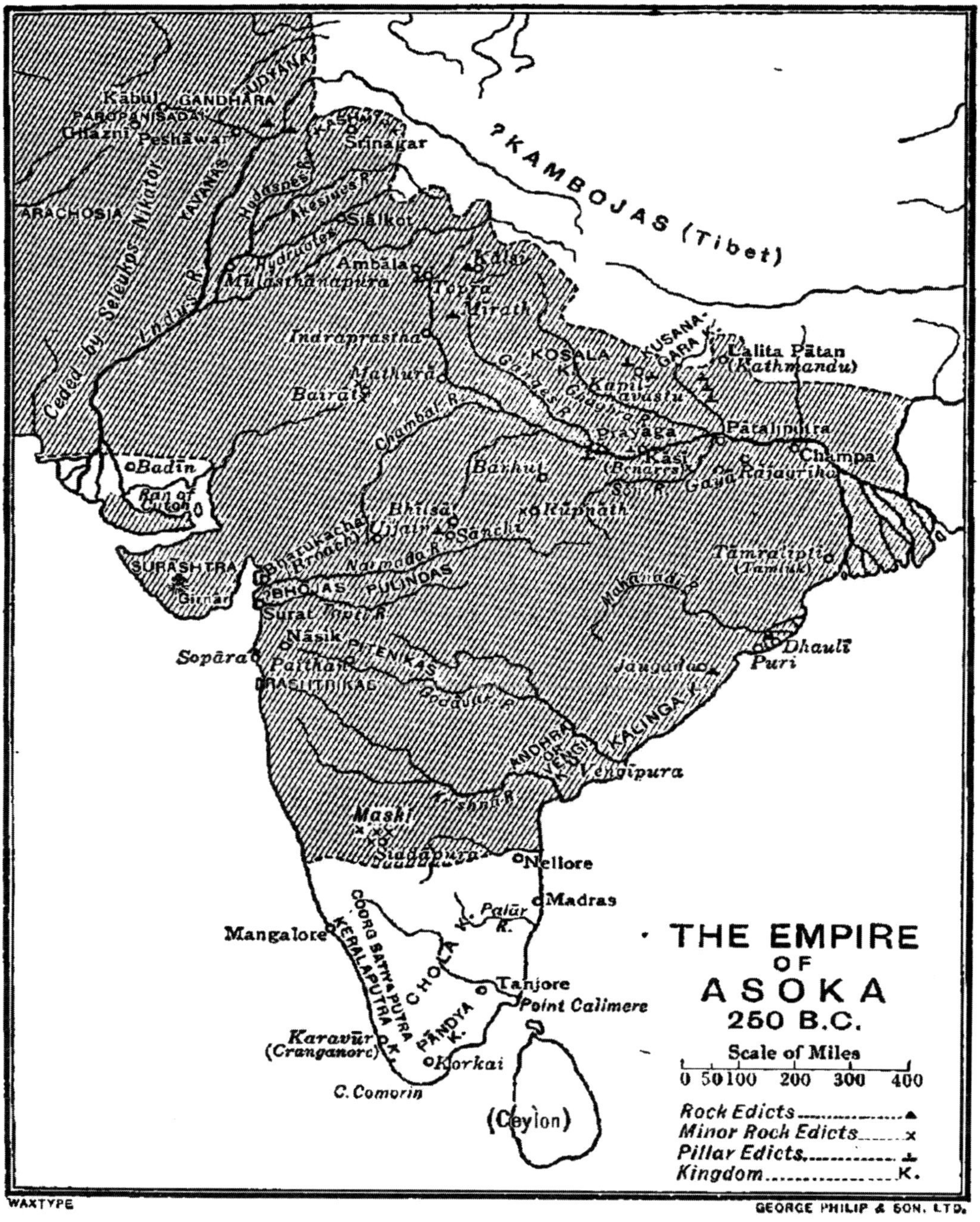

WAXTYPE

GEORGE PHILIP & SON, LTD.

E 3

his monuments, from the internal testimony of his inscriptions, and from various forms of literary historical tradition.

The empire comprised the countries now known as Afghanistan, as far as the Hindu Kush; Balōchistan and Makrān, Sind, Cutch (Kachchh); the Swāt (Suwāt) Valley, with adjoining tribal territories, Kashmīr, Nepāl, and the whole of India proper, excepting Assam, as far south as the northern districts of Mysore. The Tamil states of the extreme south were independent. It is possible, but not clearly proved, or perhaps probable, that the emperor also exercised jurisdiction in Khotan, now in Chinese Turkistan.

The reader, of course, will understand that the empire thus defined was not all under the direct imperial rule. It necessarily comprehended numerous autonomous states, owing more or less obedience or paying some sort of homage to the sovereign power. It also included many wild or half-wild tribes in the hills and forests who cared little for any government, and ordinarily lived their own life in their own way.

Viceroys. But the area actually governed by imperial officers was enormous. We hear of four Viceroys, who seem to have been usually, if not always, princes of the imperial family.

The viceroy of the north-west, whose capital was Taxila, controlled the Panjāb, and his jurisdiction may have extended over Sind, Balōchistan, Makrān, and Afghanistan, to use modern names.

An eastern viceroy resided at a town called Tosali, probably in Kalinga. The western provinces were administered from Ujjain; and the capital of the Deccan was Suvarnagiri ('Golden hill'), probably situated somewhere in one of the ancient goldfields.[1] It is possible that there may have been other viceroys, but only four happen to be mentioned. The reader may remember that the *Arthasāstra* recommends that a kingdom should be divided into four provinces.

Censors. Asoka inherited from his predecessors a good bureaucratic organization. The higher officials or ministers were called *mahāmātras*, as in the *Arthasāstra*, and a regular gradation of official ranks existed. About the time of the promulgation of the Fourteen Rock Edicts the emperor created a new class of ministers called *Dharma-mahāmātras*, whose title may be rendered by the term Censors. They received instructions to enforce the Law of Duty or Piety (*dharma*) among people of all religions and ranks, including even members of the royal family. Similar officials have been appointed in several Hindu states in modern times.[2]

The moral principles and rules of conduct enjoined in the Edicts, although expressly associated with Buddhist doctrine in some of

[1] Maski, where the Asoka inscription was discovered in 1915, is situated in country which 'abounds in numerous ancient gold workings'. The shaft at Hutti is 'the deepest in the world' (*Hyderabad Archaeol. Series*, No. 1, 1915). Maski was an important settlement even in the late neolithic period (*Foote Coll. Indian Prehistoric*, vol. of notes, pp. 31, 125, 126).

[2] The *muhtasibs* appointed by Aurangzēb to enforce Islamic law had similar duties.

the documents, were suitable to a large extent for the adherents of any denomination. The stringency of the regulations prohibiting the slaughter or mutilation of animals, increasing with Asoka's years, no doubt pressed hardly on many classes. The imperial legislation, which directly affected the Brahmanical custom of bloody sacrifices, hampered the activities of hunters, fishermen, and many other poor people. It is likely that the discontent which must have been caused by the strict enforcement may have had much to do with the break up of the empire which ensued on Asoka's decease. It was the business of the Censors to see that the imperial commands were obeyed. It is easy to imagine the many openings which were offered for vexatious interference with private life, for malicious accusations, and for bribery to secure immunity from penalties. If we may judge from the history of later Hindu and Jain kings who pursued the same ideals and issued similar regulations, it may be assumed that offenders were liable even to capital punishment.

Summary of moral code. Asoka's moral code is most concisely formulated in the second Minor Rock Edict recorded on a rock in the north of the Mysore state and there only.

'Thus saith His Majesty:

"Father and mother must be obeyed; similarly respect for living creatures must be enforced; truth must be spoken. These are the virtues of the Law of Duty (or 'Piety', *dharma*) which must be practised. Similarly, the teacher must be reverenced by the pupil, and proper courtesy must be shown to relations.

This is the ancient standard of duty (or 'piety')—leads to length of days, and according to this men must act."'[1]

The three obligations—of showing reverence, respecting animal life, and telling the truth—are inculcated over and over again in the edicts. In the summary quoted above reverence is placed first, but the general tenor of the teaching is to lay stress primarily on the respect for animal life.

Sundry virtues taught. The imperial moralist did not limit his catalogue of indispensable virtues to the three named in the summary. He took much pains to inculcate the duties of compassion to all, kind treatment of slaves and hired servants, almsgiving, and toleration for the creeds of other people. Moreover, he displayed anxious solicitude for the bodily well-being of his subjects. Special attention was paid to the comfort of travellers by the provision of wells, rest-houses, and trees planted along the roads to supply both shade and fruit. Arrangements for the healing of man and beast alike were made, not only within the limits of the empire, but also in the territories of friendly independent kingdoms.

Extracts from the edicts. A few brief extracts from the edicts serve better than any paraphrase to enable the student to appreciate their spirit.

[1] Mr. Yazdani compares the style of this document with that of the *Sikshāvallī* section of the *Taittirīya Upanishad*, transl. in *S. B. E.*, xv, part ii. There is some resemblance.

'Everywhere in my dominions the subordinate officials, and the Commissioner and the District Officers every five years must proceed on circuit, as well for their other business as for this special purpose, namely, to give instruction in the Law of Duty (or "Piety") to wit—"A meritorious ('excellent') thing is the hearkening to father and mother; a meritorious thing is liberality to friends, acquaintances, relations, Brahmans, and ascetics; a meritorious thing is abstention from the slaughter of living creatures; a meritorious thing is small expense and small accumulation"' (*Rock Edict III*).

'There is no such almsgiving as the almsgiving of the Law of Duty (or "Piety")—friendship in duty, liberality in duty, association in duty. Herein does it consist—in proper treatment of slaves and servants, hearkening to father and mother, &c.' (*Rock Edict XI*).

'A man must not do reverence to his own sect or disparage that of another man without reason. Depreciation should be for specific reasons only, because the sects of other people all deserve reverence for one reason or another.

By thus acting, a man exalts his own sect, and at the same time does service to the sects of other people. By acting contrariwise, a man hurts his own sect, and does disservice to the sects of other people' (*Rock Edict XII*).[1]

'Both this world and the next are difficult to secure save by intense love of the Law of Duty (or "Piety"), intense self-examination, intense obedience, intense dread, intense effort' (*Pillar Edict I*).

'"The Law of Duty is excellent."

But wherein consists the Law of Duty? In these things, to wit—little impiety, many good deeds, compassion, liberality, truthfulness, and purity' (*Pillar Edict II*).

'With various blessings has mankind been blessed by former kings, as by me also; by me, however, with the intent that men may conform to the Law of Duty (or "Piety"), has it been done even as I thought' (*Pillar Edict VII*).

It would be easy to illustrate in detail every one of Asoka's precepts from Buddhist books, as well as from the existing practice in countries where Buddhism now prevails. Jain and Brahmanical writings also might be quoted to show that the morality inculcated was, on the whole, common to all the Indian religions. The Jains, however, go even farther than the Buddhists in applying the principle of *ahimsā*, or non-injury to living creatures, while those Brahmanical Hindus who considered bloody sacrifices indispensable necessarily were unable to give complete assent to the imperial doctrine. The gradual growth of a feeling of distaste for animal sacrifices discussed in an earlier chapter of this work undoubtedly was stimulated by the action of Asoka continued for many years and supported by all the power of an efficient imperial organization. The Buddhist teaching was superior to that of the rival religions in the prominence it gave to the 'happiness of all creatures' as the main object of morality. Buddhism, in spite of its agnostic,

[1] 'Every sect favourably regards him who is faithful to its precepts, and in truth he is to be commended' (Akbar's 'Happy Sayings', *Āīn*, vol. iii, tr. Jarrett, p. 391).

pessimistic philosophy, is in practice a creed which tends to cheerfulness; a fact apparent to all observers in Burma.

Asoka an ardent Buddhist. Asoka, although tolerant of competing creeds, and even willing to pursue the policy of concurrent endowment, as proved by his costly gifts to the Ājīvika ascetics, an order closely akin to the Digambara or nude Jains, was personally an ardent Buddhist. His zeal for the teaching of Gautama Buddha is expressed emphatically in the unique Bhābrū Edict of early date, inscribed on a boulder in Eastern Rājputāna and addressed to the Church.

'You know, Reverend Sirs, how far extend my respect for and faith in the Buddha, the Sacred Law, and the Church.

Whatsoever, Reverend Sirs, has been said by the Venerable Buddha, all that has been well said.'

He then proceeds to enumerate seven passages or texts from the Sacred Law, which he commends to the study of monks and nuns, as well as of the laity, male and female. All of those passages have been identified in the Canon. They begin with the well-known First Sermon, and end with the remarkable admonition by Buddha to his son Rahula on the necessity of speaking the exact truth.[1]

Three of the Minor Pillar Edicts (Sārnāth, Sānchī, and Kausāmbī), which prescribe the penalty of excommunication for schism, and the two Tarāi Pillar Edicts are equally Buddhist.

Asoka's hard work. Asoka worked hard, very hard; carrying out conscientiously the instructions of his grandfather's preceptor.

'If a king is energetic', says the author of the *Arthasāstra*, 'his subjects will be equally energetic . . . when in court, he shall never cause his petitioners to wait at the door. . . . He shall, therefore, personally attend to the business of gods, of heretics, of Brahmans learned in the Vedas, of earth, of sacred places, of minors, the aged, the afflicted, and the helpless, and of women; all this in order, or according to the urgency or pressure of such kinds of business.

All urgent calls he shall hear at once, and never put off; for when postponed they will prove too hard or even impossible to accomplish. . . . Of a king the religious vow is his readiness for action; satisfactory discharge of duties in his performance of sacrifice; equal attention to all is as the offer of fees and ablution towards consecration.

In the happiness of his subjects lies his happiness; in their welfare his welfare; whatever pleases himself he shall consider as not good, but whatever pleases his subjects he shall consider as good.

Hence the king shall ever be active and discharge his duties; the root of wealth is activity, and of evil its reverse.'

Asiatic idea of kingship. The Asiatic idea of kingship has ordinarily required that the monarch should hear personally as many causes and complaints as possible, should dispose of them on

[1] The Chinese version of the admonition to Rahula has been translated into French by M. Sylvain Lévi (*J. As.*, 1896, Mai-Juin), and into English by Beal (*Texts from the Buddhist Canon commonly known as Dhammapada*; Kegan Paul, 1902). Rockhill gives a summary abstract of the Tibetan version in *Udānavarga* (Kegan Paul, 1892).

the spot by final orders untrammelled by legal formalities, and that he should be easily accessible to the meanest of his subjects, even at the cost of much personal inconvenience. Long after Asoka's time the Timūrid emperors of India acted on those principles, and made the daily public audiences an essential feature of their policy. Even Jahāngīr, who sometimes failed in the higher duties of his station, was extremely particular to do justice as he conceived it in person, and to appear in public three times a day.

A saying of Akbar that 'divine worship in monarchs consists in their justice and good administration' reproduces one of the sentiments quoted above from Kautilya.

Asoka on himself. Asoka expressed similar ideas with all possible emphasis :

'For a long time past it has not happened that business has been dispatched and that reports have been received at all hours.

Now by me this arrangement has been made that at all hours and in all places—whether I am dining, or in the ladies' apartments, or in my private room, at the gymnasium, or on the parade ground, or in the palace gardens—the official Reporters should report to me on the people's business ; and I am ready to do the people's business in all places. . . . I have commanded that immediate report must be made to me at any hour and in any place, because I never feel full satisfaction in my efforts and dispatch of business. For the welfare of all folk is what I must work for—and the root of that, again, is in effort and the dispatch of business. And whatsoever exertions I make are for the end that I may discharge my debt to animate beings, and that while I make some happy here, they may in the next world gain heaven' (*Rock Edict VI*, amended version).

It is easy to criticize such regulations from the point of view of an official in Europe and to prove that the orderly dispatch of business would be hindered and obstructed by constant interruptions. The criticism would be sound whether in Europe or Asia, but the extreme importance attached by the eastern nations to the personal intervention and the accessibility of their rulers wins so much popularity for a sovereign who satisfies the sentiment of his people that a king may find it worth his while to submit to the inconveniences which necessarily result from regulations such as those laid down by Asoka.

Maurya art. When writing on another occasion about the art of the Gupta period, I recorded an observation which is equally applicable to the Maurya age, especially to the reign of Asoka, and may be repeated here, as I cannot express my meaning better.

'In India the establishment of a vigorous dynasty ruling over wide dominions has invariably resulted in the application of a strong stimulus to the development of man's intellectual and artistic powers. Such a dynasty, exercising its administrative duties effectively, fostering commerce, maintaining active intercourse, commercial and diplomatic, with foreign states, and displaying the pomp of a magnificent court, both encourages the desire to do great things, and provides the material patronage without which authors and artists cannot live.' [1]

[1] *Ostasiatische Zeitschrift*, April-Juni, 1914, p. 1.

The reign of Asoka presents in perfection all the conditions enumerated in that extract as being favourable to the development of notable schools of art and literature. It may be that art had flourished almost in equal measure under the rule of his father Bindusāra and his grandfather Chandragupta. In fact, there are substantial grounds for believing that buildings of exceptional magnificence were erected in the time of the first Maurya emperor. Splendid architecture necessarily involves the successful cultivation of sculpture, painting, and all the decorative arts. Greek testimony, as already mentioned, declares that the palace of Chandragupta surpassed the royal abodes of Persia, and records some details of the rich ornament of the building. But the whole has vanished, and there is little reason to expect or hope that the excavations at Taxila and Pātaliputra begun in 1913 will reveal much art work of the time of the early Maurya kings preserved well enough to furnish material for satisfactory aesthetic criticism. The principal reason is that, so far as our present knowledge extends, the great edifices built by Asoka's predecessors were constructed mainly of perishable wood, just as the magnificent structures at Mandalay were constructed by the latest Burmese sovereigns. In the time of Chandragupta Maurya and his son brick and stone seem to have been used chiefly for the foundations and plinths of timber superstructures. Wooden architecture implies the execution of most of the decorative features in material equally perishable. Unless the progress of exploration should disclose an unexpected treasure of early Maurya sculpture in stone or terra-cotta, materials for the history of art during the reigns of Chandragupta and Bindusāra must continue to be scanty. The general use of stone in northern India for building, sculpture, and decoration certainly dates from the reign of Asoka, who was influenced by Persian and Greek example. I do not either assert or believe that prior to the days of Asoka the art of building in stone was absolutely unknown in India, or that all artistic work was executed in perishable material; but the ascertained facts indicate that previous to his reign permanent materials were used rarely and sparingly either for architecture or for ornament. When Megasthenes was at Pātaliputra the city was defended by a wooden palisade. The walls, the stone palace within the city, and many sacred edifices are ascribed to Asoka.[1]

The definite history of Indian art, therefore, still begins with Asoka. At present it is impossible to write any earlier chapter.

Asokan sculpture. No building of Asoka's age is standing, unless some of the *stūpas* near Bhīlsā may have been built by him. An early *stūpa*, being merely a domical mound of masonry, does

[1] The text refers only to Asoka's empire, and more especially to northern India. In the Tamil countries, during the early centuries of the Christian era, Hindu temples were built of wood or brick. Stone structures did not come into fashion until late in the sixth century, in the Pallava kingdom (Jouveau-Dubreuil, *Pallava Antiquities*, Probsthain, London, 1916, p. 74).

not offer much scope for architectural design. We can judge of Asokan art better from sculpture than from architecture. The noble sculpture of Asoka's age exhibits a mature form of art, the evolution of which through earlier attempts is hidden from our eyes for the reasons explained above. Many details indicate that the artist in stone closely followed the example set by his fellow craftsmen in wood and ivory. Indeed, ordinary Indian usage seems to have favoured the exercise of his skill by a carver in any material that came to his hand. If Asoka insisted, as he did, on his statuary and reliefs being executed in enduring stone, he was able to utilize the services of skilled Indian workmen accustomed to work in more perishable materials, who were clever enough to adapt their technique to the permanent medium. The art of his time, although obviously affected by Persian and Hellenistic influences, is mainly Indian in both spirit and execution. Take, for instance, the celebrated Sārnāth capital. Much of the design was suggested by Persia. But even the lions in the round are wholly different from and far superior to their Persian prototypes in pose and style, while the bas-reliefs of the guardian animals of the four quarters on the sides of the abacus are purely Indian. It is improbable that they could have been executed by any sculptor who had not been soaked in ancient Indian tradition, although his previous practical experience might have been gained by working in wood or ivory.

Capital, Sārnāth.

Perfect execution. The perfection of the execution of the best examples of Asokan sculpture is astonishing. Sir John Marshall, who has had wide experience of Greek art, praises the Sārnāth capital in the following terms :

'Lying near the column were the broken portions of the upper part of the shaft and a magnificent capital of the well-known Persepolitan bell-shaped type with four lines above, supporting in their midst a stone wheel or *dharmachakra*, the symbol of the law first promulgated at Sārnāth. Both bell and lions are in an excellent state of preservation and masterpieces in point of both style and technique—the finest carvings, indeed, that India has yet produced, and unsurpassed, I venture to think, by anything of their kind in the ancient world.'

The same expert critic elsewhere comments on 'the extraordinary precision and accuracy which characterizes all Maurya work, and which has never, we venture to say, been surpassed even by the finest workmanship on Athenian buildings'.

The skill of the stone-cutters of the age could not be surpassed.

GREAT STŪPA, SĀNCHĪ (restored).

The monolithic columns of fine-grained sandstone, some of which exceed forty feet in height, exclusive of the separate capital, are marvels of technical execution.[1] The art of polishing hard stone was carried to such perfection that it is said to have become a lost art beyond modern powers. The sides of the Barābar caves excavated in most refractory gneiss rock are polished like glass mirrors. The burnishing of Fīrōz Shāh's *Lāt*, the column from Topra, now at Delhi, is so exquisite that several observers have believed the column to be metallic. Quaint Tom Coryate in the seventeenth century described the monument as 'a brazen pillar'; and even Bishop Heber, early in the nineteenth century, received the impression that it was 'a high black pillar of cast metal'. The stonework of Asoka's time is equally well finished in all other respects. Most of the inscriptions are incised with extreme

[1] See illustration of Lauriya-Nandangarh pillar on p. 157.

accuracy in beautifully cut letters. Dr. Spooner notes similar 'absolute perfection' in the carpentry of the mysterious wooden platforms at Kumrahār, probably dating from the reign of Chandragupta.

Skill in all arts. The engineering ability displayed in the handling and transport of huge monolithic columns conveyed over immense distances is remarkable. When the excavations in progress at Taxila and Pātaliputra shall be more advanced, additional evidence of the skill of the Maurya engineers may be expected. Some has been disclosed already. The combined testimony of books, material remains, and pictorial relief sculpture proves that in the fourth and third centuries B. C. the command of the Maurya monarchs over luxuries of all kinds and skilled craftsmanship in all the manual arts was not inferior to that enjoyed by the Mogul emperors eighteen centuries later. Some fine jewellery, dating from 250 B. C. and associated with a gold coin of Diodotos and debased silver punch-marked coins, has been found in the Bir mound, the oldest part of the Taxila site.[1] The relief sculptures at Bharhut (Barhut) and Sānchī, some of which are little if at all later than the time of Asoka, and may be regarded as pictures executed in stone, exhibit most vividly all the details of the life of the age. It was a bustling, cheerful life, full of wholesome activity and movement. The artists delighted in representing it with frank realism, and in decorating their panels with ornaments of charming design treated with good taste.

Education. Asoka's decision to publish his views on Buddhist doctrine and the moral code deemed suitable for 'all sorts and conditions of men' in documents composed in vernacular dialects and inscribed in two distinct scripts implies a comparatively wide diffusion of education in his empire. The sites of all the inscriptions were carefully chosen at places where crowds of people either passed or congregated for one reason or another. The heavy cost of publication in such an enduring form would have been wasted if people could not read the edicts. Probably the numerous Buddhist monasteries served the purpose of schools, as they do now in Burma, and so produced a higher general percentage of literacy among the population than that existing at present. Most of the records are incised in the Brāhmī script, the ancient form of the modern characters used in writing Sanskrit and the allied languages of northern and western India; but two sets of the Fourteen Rock Edicts placed near the north-western frontier were engraved in the Kharoshthī script, a form of Aramaic writing used in that region. The language of the records exhibits several dialectic varieties, suitable for the different provinces.

Literature. The style of the Asoka inscriptions is not wanting in force and dignity. It recalls in some cases that of certain Upanishads. The most interesting of the documents present unmistakable internal evidence of being essentially the composition of the emperor himself. The edicts undoubtedly are closely

[1] *J. P. H. S.*, iii. 9; *Ann. Rep. A. S., India*, 1912–13, p. 41, pl. xxxix.

related as literature to the *Arthasāstra* of Kautilya or Chānakya, who devotes a chapter to the subject of the drafting of royal orders and correspondence. A famous collection of moral aphorisms (*Chānakya Çataka*) attributed to Chandragupta's minister has been printed and may have been arranged by him. The chronology of ancient Indian literature is so ill defined that it would be difficult to name any other literary works as dating from the Maurya age. Professor Rhys Davids's belief that the *Kathāvatthu*, an important Buddhist treatise in Pāli, was actually composed in the time of Asoka is not shared by all scholars. But it is certain that the reigns of three emperors covering ninety years, during which magnificent courts were maintained and every form of art and luxury was cultivated with success, cannot have been unadorned by the works of eminent authors. It is clear that in the fourth century B.C. Indian literature could look back on a long past extending over many generations. Its history cannot have been interrupted in the third century at a time when the Indian empire had attained its widest extent and was in close touch with the civilizations of western Asia and northern Africa.

Asoka and Akbar. Few if any students of Indian history will be disposed to dispute the proposition that the most conspicuous and interesting names in the long roll of Indian monarchs are those of Asoka and Akbar. It so happens, as already observed, that both are better known to us than any others. Although it is impossible to draw a portrait of Asoka, he has disclosed so much of his character in his edicts that he seems to me at all events, after many years of special study, a very real and familiar figure. His remorse for the sufferings caused by the Kalinga war would have amused Akbar, who was one of the most ambitious of men and eager for the fame of a successful warrior, *gloriae percupidus*, as the Jesuit says. Akbar never was disturbed because his numerous aggressive wars caused infinite suffering. In that respect he resembled most ambitious kings. The attitude of Asoka was peculiar and obviously sincere. He has his reward in the vast diffusion of Buddhism, which constitutes his special work in the world, and may be counted to his credit as that 'true conquest' which was his ideal.

Asoka, although devout and zealous in the cause of his religion, was equally energetic in performing his kingly duties. There is no occasion for doubting that he did his best to live up to the admirable principles which he took so much pains to inculcate. Nothing could be better than the instructions addressed to his officers in the newly conquered province of Kalinga, which have been quoted.

A proclamation issued by Mr. Robert Cust to the Sikhs in the year 1848, between the first and the second Sikh wars, under instructions from John Lawrence, is strangely similar in both sentiment and expression :

'If any of your relations have joined the rebels, write to them to come back before blood is shed ; if they do so, their fault will be forgiven . . . what is your injury I consider mine: what is gain to you I consider my gain. . . . Consider what I have said and talk it over with your relations . . . and tell those who have joined in the rebellion to return to me, as children who have committed a fault return to their fathers, and their faults will be forgiven them. . . . In two days I shall be in the midst of you with a force which you will be unable to resist.' [1]

I think that Asoka, who was a capable man of affairs, as well as a pious devotee, always kept an iron hand within the velvet glove, like John Lawrence, who was equally pious and equally practical.

The excellence of the art of Asoka's reign indicates that the Maurya emperor resembled Akbar in being a man of good taste. He spared no cost or pains, and knew how to employ people who used sound materials and did honest work. The administration of the Mauryas strikes me as having been singularly efficient all round in peace and war. The 'extraordinary precision and accuracy' noted by Sir John Marshall as characteristic of Maurya work in stone are the outward expression of similar accuracy and precision in the working of the government machine. Living under the eyes of the innumerable spies employed by the Maurya kings must have been dangerous and unpleasant for individuals at times; but the espionage system, worked as Chānakya describes it, was an instrument of extraordinary power in the hands of a strong, capable sovereign. If Asoka had not been capable he could not have ruled his huge empire with success for forty years, and left behind a name which is still fresh in the memory of men after the lapse of more than two millenniums.

Asoka's sons. We do not know how or where Asoka passed away from the scene of his strenuous labours. A Tibetan tradition is said to affirm that he died at Taxila, and if that should be true it is possible that the researches in progress at that site so full of surprises may throw some light on the last days of the great Buddhist emperor. The names of several of his sons are on record. One, named Tīvara, is mentioned in an inscription. Another, called Kunāla and by other names, is the centre of a cycle of wild legends of the folklore type. A third, named Jalauka, the subject of a long passage in the Kashmīr chronicle, clearly was a real personage, although certain fabulous stories are attached to his name. Several localities still identifiable are associated with his memory. He did not share his father's devotion to Buddhism, but on the contrary was an ardent worshipper of Siva, as was his consort Isānadēvī. He is also credited with the expulsion from the valley of certain unnamed non-Hindu foreigners (*mlēchchhas*). He may have been the viceroy of his father and become independent after the death of Asoka. The chronicler includes both Asoka and Jalauka in the list of the kings of Kashmīr.

Asoka's grandsons. Asoka seems to have been succeeded

[1] Issued under direction of John Lawrence to the headmen of the Hoshyārpur District (Aitchison, *Lord Lawrence* (Rulers of India), 1905, p. 45 *n.*).

directly by two grandsons, Dasaratha in the eastern, and Śamprati, son of Kunāla, in the western provinces. The real existence of the former is vouched for by brief dedicatory inscriptions in caves granted to the Ājīvika ascetics, and not far from the similar caves bestowed on the same order by Asoka. The inscriptions, which were recorded immediately after the accession of Dasaratha, are conclusive evidence of that prinee's rule in Magadha.

The existence of the other grandson named Samprati has not yet been verified by any early inscription. But there is no reason to doubt that he actually ruled the western provinces after his grandfather's death. Aeeording to Jain authorities Ujjain was his capital. His name has been handed down by numerous local

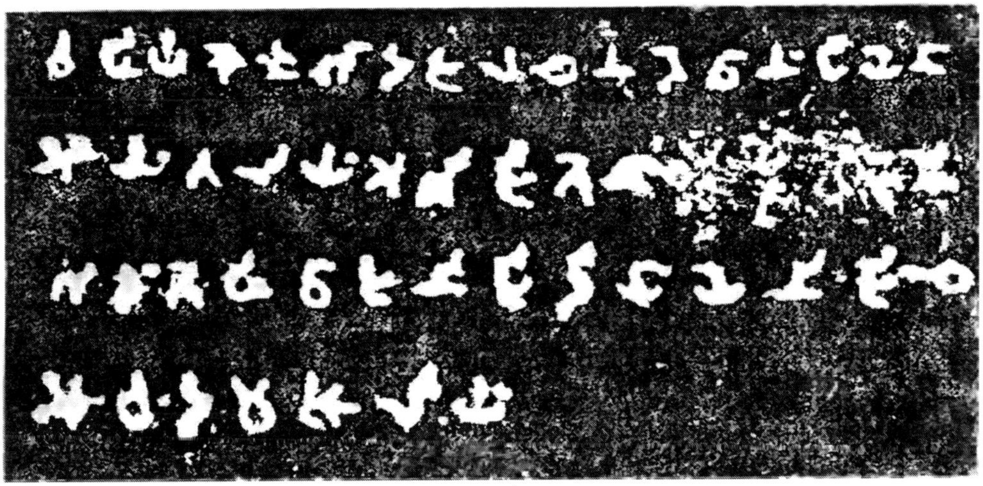

INSCRIPTION OF DASARATHA.

traditions extending from Ajmēr in Rājputāna to Satrunjaya in Kāthiawār, where the most ancient of the erowd of Jain temples is said to have been founded by him. He is also credited with the erection of a temple at Nādlai in Jodhpur, now represented by a more modern building on the site ; and with the foundation of the fortress of Jahāzpur, which guarded the pass leading from Mewār to Bundi. He is reputed to have been as zealous in promoting the cause of Jainism as Asoka had been in propagating the religion of Gautama.[1]

It seems reasonable to assume that Asoka's empire was divided in the first instanee between his two grandsons ; but no decisive proof of the supposed fact has been discovered, and nothing is known about the further history of either Dasaratha or Samprati.

The last Maurya. The Purānas record the names of several others successors of Asoka, with various readings, which need not

[1] Tod, *Annals of Mewār*, chap. iv (pop. ed., i, 201 *n.*) ; Forbes, *Rāsmālā* (1856), i, p. 7 ; *Rājputāna Gaz.* (Simla, 1880), iii, 52 ; *Bombay Gaz.* (1896), vol. i, part 1, p. 15.

be recited, as nothing material is known about the princes named. It is impossible to determine the extent of the dominions ruled by those later Mauryas. Brihadratha, the last prince of the dynasty, was slain about 185 B.C. by his commander-in-chief, Pushyamitra (or Pushpamitra) Sunga.

The Sunga dynasty. The usurper established a new dynasty known as that of the Sungas, which is said to have lasted for 112 years until 73 B.C. Their dominions apparently included Magadha and certain neighbouring provinces, extending southwards as far as the Narbadā. The names of the founder of the dynasty and some of his descendants ending in *mitra* have suggested the hypothesis that Pushyamitra may have been an Iranian, a worshipper of the sun (Mithra). He celebrated the *asvamedha* or horse sacrifice, a rite certainly associated with sun-worship. It marked the successful assertion by the prince performing it of a claim to have vanquished all his neighbours.

Menander's invasion. Pushyamitra successfully repelled the invasion of a Greek frontier king, apparently Menander, the Milinda of Buddhist tradition, who was king of Kābul and the Panjāb. He advanced (about 155 B.C.) with a strong force into the interior of India; annexed the Indus delta, with the peninsula of Surāshtra (Kāthiāwār), and some other territories on the western coast; occupied Mathurā on the Jumna; besieged Madhyamikā, now Nagarī near Chitōr in Rājputāna; invested Sākētam in southern Oudh; and threatened, or perhaps took Pātaliputra, the Sunga capital.

Madhyamikā, then the chief town of a branch of the Sibi people, who seems to have emigrated from the Panjāb, was in those days a place of much importance, which an invader could not safely pass by. Although the ruins have supplied much material for the building of Chitōr, traces of a Maurya edifice can still be discerned, and two inscriptions of the Sunga period have been found, which record the performance of *asvamedha* and *vājapeya* sacrifices.

Brahmanical reaction. Pushyamitra, whatever his origin may have been, was reckoned to be a Hindu. Sun-worship is consistent with Hinduism, and even at this day sects of Sauras or sun-worshippers exist. Good reasons warrant the belief that in ancient times the cult of the sun in north-western India, Surāshtra, and Rājputāna, was much more prominent than it is now. Tradition represents the first Sunga king as a fierce enemy of Buddhism and relates that he burnt a multitude of monasteries, carrying his ravages as far north as Jālandhar. The reign of Pushyamitra appears to mark a violent Brahmanical reaction against Buddhism, which had enjoyed so much favour in the time of Asoka. It is possible that the Hinduism of the Sungas may have been coloured by Magian practices. They were followers of the sacrificial Sāmaveda.[1]

The celebrated grammarian Patanjali was a contemporary of Pushyamitra, whose story is partly told in 'Mālavikā and Agni-

[1] M. M. Haraparshād Sāstri, in *J. & Proc. A. S. B.*, 1912, p. 287.

mitra' (*Mālavikāgnimitra*), a play by Kālidāsa, composed probably in the fifth century A. C.

The Kanva dynasty. Devabhūti, or Devabhūmi, the last of the Sungas, a man of licentious habits, lost his life while engaged in a scandalous intrigue. His death was contrived by his Brahman minister, Vasudeva, who seated himself on the vacant throne, and so founded a short-lived dynasty of four kings, whose reigns collectively occupied only forty-five years. The brevity of the rule of each indicates a period of disturbance. Nothing is known about the doings of the Brahman kings, whose dynasty is called Kānva or Kānvāyana. The last of them was killed, about 28 B. C., by an Āndhra king whose identity is doubtful.

The Āndhras. It will be convenient to give in this place a brief notice of the Āndhra dynasty comprising thirty kings, whose rule endured for the exceptionally long period of four centuries and a half in round numbers. The details of their history are too obscure and controverted for discussion in this work. The original kingdom of the Āndhras, the Telugu speaking people of the country afterwards called Telingāna, was situated in the deltas of the Godāvarī and Krishna. It was reckoned powerful even in the time of Megasthenes, but nothing is known about its rulers at that date. The historical dynasty seems to have been established about the time of Asoka's death. His inscriptions mention the Āndhras in terms which apparently imply that their Rājā was in some measure subordinate to the emperor. It may be assumed that his decease enabled the Āndhras, like many other people, to assert their complete independence. After a short interval we find the kings exercising authority in the region of the western Ghāts, so that their dominion stretched right across the Deccan from sea to sea. They engaged in wars with both the dynasties of western Satraps, namely, the early Kshaharāta line which had its capital in the western Ghāts, and the somewhat later family which ruled at Ujjain. Both of the Satrap dynasties were of foreign origin, and associated with the Sakas. The Āndhra kings assumed the position of protectors of Hinduism and the caste institution. The most powerful of the later Āndhras was Gautamīputra Yajna Srī, who reigned for twenty-nine years, from about A. D. 173 to 202, or possibly a little earlier. The story of the decline and fall of the dynasty has not been fully recovered. The end of it may be placed somewhere about A. D. 225. Although the Āndhras may at some time or other have controlled Magadha and the ancient imperial capital, Pātaliputra, clear evidence that they did so has not yet come to light.

Āndhra coin.

CHRONOLOGY

(Dates nearly correct, but the Indian ones not guaranteed exact)

Maurya Dynasty

B.C.	*Event.*
326 or 325.	Chandragupta Maurya in his youth met Alexander.
323, June.	Death of Alexander at Babylon.
323–322.	Expulsion of Macedonian garrisons.
322.	Accession of **Chandragupta Maurya.** [Date possibly earlier.]
312.	Seleukos Nikator recovered Babylon and established Seleukidan era.
306.	Seleukos assumed title of king.
305.	Seleukos invaded India unsuccessfully.
302.	Megasthenes sent to Pātaliputra as ambassador.
298.	Accession of **Bindusāra Amitraghāta.** Deïmachos succeeded Megasthenes as ambassador.
285.	Ptolemy Philadelphos, king of Egypt, acc.
280.	Seleukos Nikator died; Antiochos Soter acc.
278 or 277.	Antigonos Gonatas, king of Macedonia, acc.
273.	**Asoka**[-vardhana] acc.
272.	Alexander, king of Epirus, acc.
269.	Consecration or coronation (*abhisheka*) of Asoka. [218 A. B. (*anno Buddhae*) in chronology of Ceylon].
261.	Antiochos Theos, king of Syria, acc.; the Kalinga war.
259.	Asoka abolished the imperial hunt, and dispatched missionaries.
258.	Magas, king of Cyrene died; ? Alexander, king of Epirus, died.
257, 256.	The Fourteen Rock Edicts, the Kalinga Edicts, and appointment of Censors.
254.	Asoka enlarged for the second time the *stūpa* of Konagamana.
251.	Tissa, king of Ceylon, acc.
251 or 250.	Mission of Mahendra (Mahinda) to Ceylon. [236 A. B.]
249.	Asoka's pilgrimage to the holy places.
? 248.	Independence of Bactria and Parthia.
247.	Ptolemy Philadelphos, king of Egypt, died.
247 or 246.	Antiochos Theos, king of Syria, died.
246.	She-hwang-ti became ruler of T'sin in China.
242.	Publication of the Seven Pillar Edicts.
242 or 239.	Antigonos Gonatas, king of Macedonia, died.
240–232.	Council of Pātaliputra; Minor Pillar Edicts condemning schism.
232.	Asoka died; his grandson **Dasaratha** acc. in eastern provinces; and probably **Samprati,** another grandson, acc. in western provinces.
221.	She-hwang-ti became emperor of China.
211.	Tissa, king of Ceylon, died; Uttiya acc.
204.	Mahendra (Mahinda) died in Ceylon.
203.	Sanghamitrā, sister of Mahendra, died in Ceylon.
185.	**Bridhadratha,** the last Maurya king, killed.

Sunga Dynasty

185. **Pushyamitra (Pushpamitra)** acc. Brahmanical reaction ; Patanjali.
155. Invasion of Menander.
73. **Devabhūti (-bhūmi)**, the last Sunga king, killed.

73–28. *Kānva* or *Kānvāyana Dynasty.*

Āndhra Dynasty

about 230 Beginning of dynasty.
30 kings for about 4½ centuries.

A. D.
173–202. **Yajna Srī**, king. [Possibly 7 or 8 years earlier.]
about 225. End of dynasty.

AUTHORITIES

The following references are additional to those in the foot-notes and in *E. H. I.*[3] (1914) and *Asoka*[2] (1909).

Professor HULTZSCH's edition of the Asoka inscriptions, of which a large part is in print, cannot be completed while the war lasts. The new Maski inscription has been well edited in *Hyderabad Archaeological Series*, No. 1 (Baptist Mission Press, Calcutta, 1915 ; price one rupee).

For the Ājīvikas see HOERNLE's exhaustive article in HASTINGS, *Encycl. of Religion and Ethics*, vol. i (1908). D. R. BHANDARKAR describes remains at Nagarī or Madhyamikā in *Progr. Rep. A. S., Western Circle*, 1915–16, p. 52.

Ancient India, by Prof. RAPSON (Cambridge University Press, 1914), is a good sketch.

Sundry papers in *J. R. A. S.* and other periodicals throw some fresh light on the period.

CHAPTER 3

The Indo-Greek and other foreign dynasties of north-western India ; the Kushāns or Indo-Scythians ; Greek influence ; foreign commerce ; beginning of Chola history.

Revolt of Bactria and Parthia. About the middle of the third century, within a year or two of 250 B.C., while Asoka was at the height of his power, two important provinces, Bactria and Parthia, broke away from the Seleukidan empire, and set up almost simultaneously as independent kingdoms, with results which subsequently had considerable effect upon India.

Parthia. The movement in Parthia, the territory lying to the south-east of the Caspian Sea and inhabited by hardy horsemen with habits similar to those of the modern Turkomans, was of a national character, and seems to have lasted for several years. The independence of the kingdom may be dated approximately in 248 B.C. The chief named Arsakes, who had led his countrymen in their fight for liberty, founded the Arsakidan dynasty of Persia which lasted for nearly five centuries until it was superseded by the Sassanians in A.D. 226. The Parthian power gradually extended eastwards until it comprised most of the dominions once ruled by the Achaemenian dynasty of Persia; but its influence on India did not make itself felt until more than a century after the foundation of the kingdom.

MAP OF BACTRIA, ETC.

Bactria. The revolution in Bactria, the rich and civilized region between the Hindu Kush and the Oxus, which was reputed to contain a thousand towns and had been regarded as the premier province of the empire in Achaemenian times, was effected in the ordinary Asiatic manner by the rebellion of a governor named Diodotos.

Inasmuch as the newly formed kingdom adjoined Asoka's Kābul or Paropanisadai province, echoes of the revolution must have been heard at the court of Pātaliputra, although Indian documents are silent on the subject. While Asoka lived his strong arm and his friendly relations with the Hellenistic princes protected India against the ambition of Alexander's successors. When he had vanished from the scene and his empire had crumbled to pieces, many years did not elapse until the provinces beyond the Indus became the object of Greek aggression.

Coin of Diodotos II.

Syrian raid on Kābul. Euthydemos, the third king of Bactria, had become involved in a quarrel with Antiochos the Great of Syria, which was ended about 208 B.C. by the formal recognition of Bactrian independence. Shortly afterwards Antiochos crossed the Hindu Kush, and attacked an Indian prince named Subhāgasena (Sophagasenas), ruler of the Kābul valley. The invader, having extorted a large cash indemnity and many elephants, went home through Arachosia (Kandahār) and Drangiana. That raid had no permanent effect.

Coin of Euthydemos.

Demetrios, King of the Indians. But Demetrios, the fourth king of Bactria, and son of Euthydemos, became so powerful that he was able to subdue all Ariana or Afghanistan, and even to annex considerable territories in the Panjāb and western India. Hence he was known as 'King of the Indians'. The nearly contemporary square coins of Pantaleon and Agathokles present Indian features derived from the native coinage of Taxila and prove that Greek principalities, connected in some way with the conquests made by Demetrios, were established on the north-western frontier late in the second century B.C. A rival named Eukratides deprived Demetrios of Bactria about 175 B.C. and founded a new line of frontier princes. The names of about forty such rulers are known from coins. It is impossible to ascertain the exact relationship between the princes or to specify their respective territories with precision.

Coin of Demetrios.

Menander. The most remarkable king was Menander, who reigned in Kābul from about 160 to 140 B.C. His invasion of India has been already described. He acquired a widespread reputation, and it is said that when he died various cities contended for the honour of giving sepulture to his ashes. His fine coinage is abundant in many interesting types. Specimens have been found in India even to the south of the Jumna.

Antialkidas. We obtain an unexpected and startling glimpse of a slightly later king named Antialkidas, who ruled at Taxila, from an inscription at Besnagar near Bhīlsā in Central India, which may be dated between 140 and 130 B.C. The record was incised by direction of Dion's son, Heliodoros of Taxila, who was sent as envoy to the ruler of Besnagar by King Antialkidas. Heliodoros dedicated a monolithic column to the honour of Vāsudeva, a form of Vishnu, whose worshipper he professed himself to be. The document is of value in the history of Indian religions as giving an early date for the *bhakti* cult of Vāsudeva, and as proving that people with Greek names and in the service of Greek kings had become the followers of Hindu gods.

Heliodoros Column.

End of Bactrian monarchy. In the interval between 140 and 120 B.C. a swarm of nomad tribes from the interior of Asia, consisting of Sakas and others, attacked both Parthia and Bactria.[1] Two Parthian kings were killed, and Greek rule in Bactria was extinguished. The last Graeco-Bactrian king was Heliokles, a member of the family of Eukratides. The end of the Bactrian monarchy, which had lasted little more than a century, may be placed somewhere between 140 and 130 B.C. Precise dates are not ascertainable.

Parthia and India. Mithridates I of Parthia (*c.* 171 to 136 B.C.) had annexed the country between the Indus and the Hydaspes, that is to say, the kingdom of Taxila, towards the close of his reign, about 138 B.C. The kings of Parthia were not able to retain effective control of the territory thus annexed, but the connexion established between the Parthian or Persian kingdom and India was sufficiently close to bring about the adoption of the Persian title of Satrap or Great Satrap by many Indian rulers of foreign origin. The use of that title continued for several hundred years. The last ruler to use it was the Saka Satrap of Surā-

[1] Indians used the term Saka (Śaka, Shaka) vaguely to denote foreigners from beyond the passes. In later times the name was often applied to Muhammadans, as in the *Ektinga Mahātmya*.

shtra who was conquered and dethroned by the Gupta emperor towards the close of the fourth century A.C.

Indo-Greek and Indo-Parthian princes. Although Heliokles, the last Greek king of Bactria, probably had disappeared before

Coin of Eukratides.

130 B.C., numerous princes with Greek names continued to govern principalities in the Kābul country and along the north-western frontier of India much longer. The last of them was named

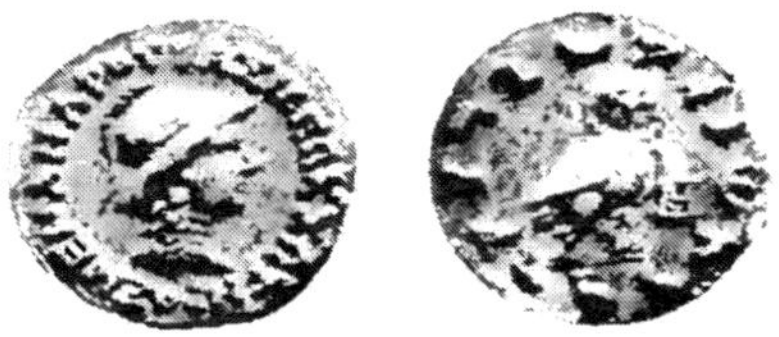

Coin of Menander.

Coin of Antialkidas.

Hermaios, who shared his power with a barbarian chief named Kujula-Kara-Kadphises, a member of the Great Yueh-chi horde, in the first century after Christ.

Coin of Heliokles.

During the interval sundry ruling families of foreigners appear in the frontier provinces, some of the princes having distinctly Parthian names. The details are too obscure and doubtful for discussion in this work.

Gondophernes and St. Thomas. The most interesting personage among those princes is Gondophernes, whose name is clearly Persian or Parthian. His reign may be placed between A.D. 20 and 48. He ruled an extensive realm which included Arachosia or the Kandahār country, Kābul, and the kingdom of Taxila. The name of Gondophernes or Gondophares has become more or less familiar to European readers because early ecclesiastical legends, going back to the third century A.C., affirm that the apostle St. Thomas preached Christianity in his dominions and was there martyred. Another group of traditions alleges that the same apostle was martyred at Mailāpur (Mylapore) near Madras. Both stories obviously cannot be true; even an apostle can die but once. My personal impression, formed after much examination of the evidence, is that the story of the martyrdom in southern India is the better supported of the two versions of the saint's death. But it is by no means certain that St. Thomas was martyred at all. An early writer, Heracleon the Gnostic, asserts that he ended his days in peace. The tale of his visit to the kingdom of Gondophares may have originated as an explanation of the early presence in that region of 'Christians of St. Thomas', disciples who followed the practices associated with the name of the apostle. Some writers try to reconcile the two stories in some measure by guessing that St. Thomas may have first visited the kingdom of Gondophernes and then gone on to the peninsula. But that guess is no real explanation. The subject has been discussed by many authors from every possible point of view, and immense learning has been invoked in the hope of establishing one or other hypothesis, without reaching any conclusion approaching certainty. There is no reason to expect that additional evidence will be discovered.

Coin of Hermaios.

Coin of Gondophernes.

The puzzle of Kushān dates. The principal puzzle of Indian history still awaiting solution is that concerning the chronology of the powerful foreign kings of Kābul and north-western India who belonged to the Kushān clan or sept of the Yueh-chi horde of nomads. The most famous of those kings being Kanishka, the problem is often stated as being 'the question of the date of Kanishka'. Until it is solved, the history of northern India for three centuries or so must remain in an unsatisfactory condition. But definite progress towards a conclusive solution of the problem based upon solid facts has been made. It may now be affirmed with confidence that the order of the five leading Kushān kings is finally settled,[1] and that the uncertainty as to the chronology has been reduced to a period of forty years in round numbers. Or to state it otherwise, the question is, 'Did Kanishka come to the throne in A. D. 78, or about forty years later?'

When the third edition of the *Early History of India* was published in 1914, my narrative was based upon the working hypothesis that Kanishka's accession took place in A. D. 78; although it was admitted to be possible that the true date might be later. Further consideration of the evidence from Taxila now available leads me to follow Sir John Marshall and Professor Sten Konow in dating the beginning of Kanishka's reign approximately in A. D. 120, a date which I had advocated many years ago on different grounds. In the following narrative the correctness of that hypothesis will be assumed without any examination of the intricate archaeological evidence, which cannot be presented advantageously in a brief summary.

Ancient cross, Kottayam.

The Yueh-chi migration. The horde of nomads called the Great Yueh-chi, who were driven out of Western China between 174 and 160 B. C., migrated westwards along the road to the north of the Taklamakān (Gobi) desert. In the course of their long wanderings they encountered another nomad nation, the Sakai or Sakas (Se or Sai of the Chinese), who dwelt to the north of the Jaxartes or Syr Daryā river. The Sakai, being defeated by the Yueh-chi, were constrained to yield their pasture-grounds to the victors, and themselves to seek new quarters in the borderlands of India.

The victorious Yueh-chi, in their turn, were vanquished by a third horde named Wu-sun and driven from the lands which had been wrested from the Sakas. The Yueh-chi then settled in the valley of the Oxus, with their head-quarters to the north of the river,

[1] The five referred to are Kadphises I, Kadphises II, Kanishka, Huvishka, and Vāsudeva I. The word Englished as Kushān appears in various forms in diverse scripts and languages. The long vowel in the second syllable is correct. The name of the sept in Khotanese may have been really Kuṣi or Kushi (nom. from stem *Kuṣa*); the word represented by 'Kushān' being a genitive plural. It would, perhaps, be more correct to speak of the Kushi (Kuṣi) sept, but I retain Kushān as being familiar and in accordance with the views of some scholars.

but probably exercising more or less authority over Bactria to the south.

Kadphises I. In the course of time, which cannot be defined precisely, the Great Yueh-chi horde lost their nomad habits and occupied the Bactrian lands, becoming divided into five principalities, at a date which cannot be determined with any approach to exactness. More than a century later, the Kushān section or sept of the Yueh-chi attained a predominant position over the other sections of the horde, under the leadership of a chieftain named Kujula-Kara-Kadphises, who is conveniently designated by modern historians as Kadphises I. He may be regarded as having become king of the Kushāns or Yueh-chi from somewhere about A. D. 40.[1]

Kadphises I was soon impelled to attack the rich territories to the south of the Hindu Kush, presumably finding the limits of Bactria too narrow for the growing population of his dominions.

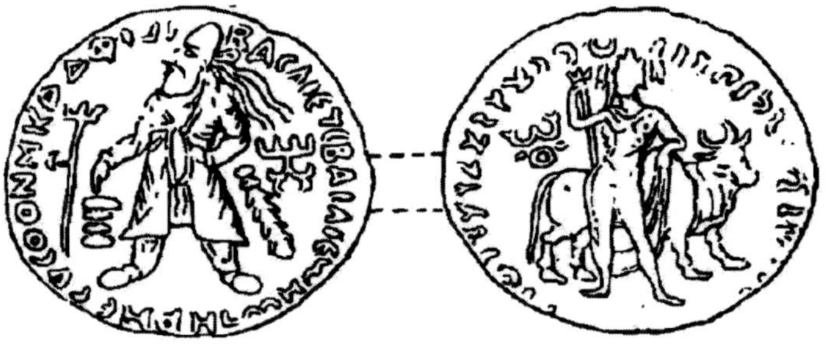

Coin of Kadphises II.

He enjoyed a long life and prosperous reign, in the course of which he consolidated his strength in Bactria, and conquered the Kābul region south of the mountains. He annexed Ki-pin, which may be interpreted with good reason as meaning Gandhāra, including the kingdom of Taxila to the east of the Indus, where he seems to have succeeded Gondophernes in A. D. 48. He also attacked the Parthians.

The operations indicated must have occupied many years, during which the Kushān or Indo-Scythian rule gradually replaced that of the Indo-Greek, Saka, and Indo-Parthian princes in the Indian borderlands. Kadphises I attained the age of eighty, and may be assumed to have died about A. D. 77 or 78.

Kadphises II. He was succeeded by his son Wima Kadphises, whose personal name is transliterated as Wēmo (Ooēmo) in his Greek coin legends, and is given as Yen-kao-ching by Chinese historians. It is convenient to designate him as Kadphises II. He set himself to accomplish the conquest of northern India, and effected his purpose. It is reasonable to believe, although strict proof is lacking, that the Saka era of A. D. 78 dates from the beginning of his reign, either from his actual accession or from his formal enthronement a little later. That hypothesis seems now to present less difficulties than any other. The evidence for the extent of the Indian conquests of Kadphises II is meagre and rests largely on the distribution of his extremely numerous coins.

[1] Between A. D. 25 and 81, but nearer to the earlier year, according to Franke, pp. 72, 73.

The abundance of his coinage certainly implies a long reign. He seems to have secured the supremacy in the Gangetic valley at least as far down as Benares, and also of the Indus basin. It may be that his power extended southwards as far as the Narbadā. The Saka satraps in Mālwā and western India appear to have owned him as their overlord.

Collision with China. The course of his conquests brought him into collision with the Chinese, who had first entered into relations with western Asia in the reign of the Emperor Wu-ti (140 to 86 B. C.), when an embassy under Chang-kien was dispatched from the Middle Kingdom to the powers on the Oxus. Chang-kien returned home about 120 B. C., the exact date being stated variously by different authorities. For some reason or other Chinese intercourse with the western regions ceased in A. D. 8; and when the first Han dynasty came to an end in A. D. 23, Chinese influence in those countries had been reduced to nothing.

Fifty years later Chinese ambition reasserted itself, and General Pan-chao, in the time from A. D. 73 to 102, advanced victoriously through Khotan and the other districts now called Chinese Turkistan and across Persia, until he carried his country's flag right into Parthia and to the shores of the Caspian Sea.

The advance through Khotan opened up the road to the south of the Taklamakān (Gobi) desert. The route to the north of that desert was cleared in A. D. 94 by the reduction of Kucha and Karāshahr.

Chinese victory. The progress of Chinese arms alarmed the Kushān monarch, namely Kadphises II, according to the chronology adopted in this chapter. In A. D. 90 he boldly asserted his equality with the Son of Heaven by demanding in marriage the hand of a Chinese princess. The proposal being resented as an insult, General Pan-chao arrested the Kushān envoy and sent him home. Kadphises II then prepared a formidable force of 70,000 cavalry under the command of his viceroy Si, which was dispatched across the Tsung-ling range or Tāghdumbāsh Pāmīr. The appalling difficulties of the route, involving the crossing of the Tāshkurghān Pass, 14,000 feet high, so shattered the Kushān host that when it emerged in the plain of either Kāshgar or Yarkand it was easily defeated. Kadphises II was compelled to pay tribute to China, and the Chinese annals note that in the reign of the Emperor Ho-ti (A. D. 89–105) the Indians often sent missions to China bearing presents which were regarded as tribute.

Interval between Kadphises II and Kanishka. The extensive issues of coin by Kadphises II prove, as already observed, that he enjoyed a reign of considerable length. But, inasmuch as his father, according to Chinese authority, had died at the age of eighty, it is unlikely that Kadphises II can have reigned for much more than thirty years. The close of his life and rule may be placed somewhere about A. D. 110. It is recorded that he appointed military governors to rule the Indian provinces, and it is possible that those officers controlled India for some years after his decease.

They may have issued the anonymous coins of the so-called Nameless King, who used the title of Sotēr Megas or Great Saviour, and certainly was closely associated with Kadphises II. Kanishka, the next king, was not a son of Kadphises II, his father's name being Vajheshka ; and there is some reason for believing that he was a member of the Little Yueh-chi section of the horde, who seem to have settled in the Khotan region, whereas his predecessor was a Great Yueh-chi from Bactria. On the whole, it seems to be probable that an appreciable space of time intervened between the death of Kadphises II, which may be dated in or about A. D. 110, and the accession of Kanishka, which may be assigned to A. D. 120 approximately. Nothing is on record to show how the sceptre was transferred from the hands of Kadphises II to those of Kanishka.

Era of Kanishka. A new era running from the accession of Kanishka, or perhaps from his formal enthronement a little later, came into use in northern India, including Kābul. The regnal reckoning thus started either by Kanishka himself, or by his subjects, continued to be used by people in the reigns of his successors. Private inscriptions certainly so dated extend from the year 3 to the year 99. Consequently, if the date of Kanishka's accession was known, the chronology of the period would exhibit few difficulties.

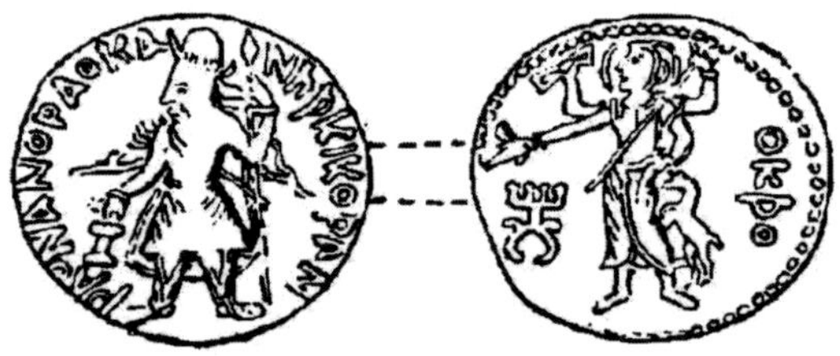
Coin of Kanishka.

Kanishka's dominions. Kanishka is described as having been king of Gandhāra. The capital of his Indian dominions, and apparently the seat of his central government, was Purushapura or Peshāwar, where he erected remarkable Buddhist buildings. Portions of those edifices have been disclosed by the researches of the Archaeological Department. Kanishka in his earlier years annexed the valley of Kashmīr, consolidated his government in the basins of the Indus and Ganges, and warred with the Parthians. At a later date he avenged his predecessor's defeat in Chinese Turkistan. There seems to be no doubt that he succeeded in accomplishing the supremely difficult feat of conveying an effective army across the Pāmīrs and subduing the chiefs or petty kings in the Khotan, Yarkand, and Kāshgar regions who had been tributary to China. He exacted from one of those princes hostages who were assigned residences in the Panjāb and the Kābul province. Tradition affirms that Kanishka, who must have been then an old man, was smothered while on his last northern campaign by officers who had grown weary of exile beyond the passes. Kanishka spent most of his life in waging successful wars. While absent on his distant expeditions he left the government of the Indian province in the hands, first of Vāsishka, apparently his elder, and then of Huvishka, apparently his younger son. Those princes, while acting as their father's colleagues, were allowed to assume full regal titles. Vāsishka evidently predeceased Kanishka, but Huvishka lived to ascend the imperial throne, which he occupied for at least twelve, and perhaps for twenty, years. No coins bearing the name of Vāsishka are known. The extensive and varied coinage of Huvishka may have been issued only after Kanishka's death, but it is possible that part of it was minted while Huvishka occupied the position of his father's colleague.[1]

The Chinese admissions that their information concerning the Western Countries was interrupted by the death in A. D. 124 of Pan-yang, the historian, who had succeeded his father Pan-chao as governor of Turkistan, and that Khotan was lost to the empire in A. D. 152 as the result of a local revolution in the course of which Governor Wang-king was killed, are in agreement with the belief that Kanishka established his suzerainty over the chiefs or petty kings of Chinese Turkistan between the years 125 and 160. The silence of Chinese annalists, as distinguished from Buddhist story-tellers, concerning Kanishka is explained by the well-known unwillingness of the historians of the Middle Kingdom to dwell on events discreditable to the imperial court.

Kanishka's religion. Modern research has disclosed the existence of a large number of inscriptions incised in the reigns of Kanishka and his successors, which give some indications of the extent of his dominions and other particulars concerning him. But his fame rests mainly on the fact that in the latter part of his career he became an active and liberal patron of the Buddhist church. Buddhist authors, writing for purposes of edification, consequently treat him as having been a second Asoka. We do not know what reasons induced Kanishka to show favour to the Buddhist church. The explanations given in the books look like an adaptation of the stories about the conversion of Asoka. Kanishka, as his coins prove, honoured a curiously mixed assortment of Zoroastrian, Greek, and Mithraic gods, to which Indian deities were added. We find the Sun and Moon with their Greek names, Hēlios and Selēnē (spelt 'Salēnē'), as well as Herakles. The moon again appears as an Iranian deity under the name of Māo. Other strangely named gods, obviously Iranian or Persian, are Athro, or Fire, Miiro, or the Sun, Nāna, Oaninda, Lrooaspo, &c. The Indian Siva, who had already appeared in a two-armed form on the coins of the Parthian Gondophernes and the Great Yueh-chi,

[1] The theory stated in the text, first suggested by R. D. Banerji, is the only one adequate to explain the facts. The known dates include :

Kanishka—year 3 (Sārnāth) ; 18 (Mānikyāla) ; and 41 (Āra) :

Vāsishka—with full titles, year 24 in words and figures (Īsāpur, Mathurā) ; year ? 28 (Sānchī, probable) ; year 29 (Mathurā, possible) :

Huvishka—year 33 (Mathurā) ; 51 (Wardak, W. of Kābul) ; and 60 (Mathurā) :

Vāsudeva—74 (Mathurā) ; 80, 83, 87, 98 (same place).

All the dated inscriptions were recorded by private persons ; none are official.

Kadphises II, is seen on Kanishka's coins in both the two-armed and four-armed forms. Buddha (Boddo) is figured standing and clad in Greek costume; and also seated in the Indian manner. The queer assembly of deities offers an unlimited field for speculation. Perhaps it may be safely said that Kanishka followed the practice of his Parthian predecessors in adopting a loose form of Zoroastrianism which freely admitted the deities of other creeds. We know that Indian monarchs, as for example, Harsha of Kanauj in the seventh century, often felt themselves at liberty to mix Buddhism with other cults; and it is probable that Kanishka, even after his alleged 'conversion', continued to honour his old gods. His successor, Huvishka, certainly did so. It is obvious that the character of Buddhism in north-western India and the neighbouring countries must have been profoundly modified by the lax practices to which the coinage of Kanishka and Huvishka bears witness.

Buddha coin of Kanishka.

Kanishka's Council. Kanishka followed the example set by Asoka in convening a Council of theologians to settle disputed questions of Buddhist faith and practice. The decrees of the Council took the form of authorized commentaries on the canon, which were engraved on sheets of copper, enclosed in a stone coffer, and placed for safety in a *stūpa* erected for the purpose at the capital of Kashmīr where the Council met. It is just possible that the documents may be still in existence and may be disclosed by some lucky excavation. The Buddhist sect which alone sent delegates to Kanishka's Council was formally classed as belonging to the *Hīna-yāna*, or Lesser Vehicle, the more primitive form of Buddhism. But the cult actually practised more extensively in Kanishka's time was that usually associated with the *Mahā-yāna*, or Great Vehicle, as is clearly proved by the numerous sculptures of the age.

Images of Buddha. The early Buddhists, whose doctrines are expressed in the stone pictures of Sānchī and Barhut (Bharhut), did not dare to form an image of their dead teacher. When they wished to indicate his presence in a scene, they merely suggested it by a symbol, an empty seat, a pair of footprints, and so forth.

The Buddhists of the Kushān age had no such scruples. They loved to picture Gautama, as the Sage of the Śākyas, the Bodhisattva, and the Buddha, in every incident of his last life as well as of his previous births. His image in endless forms and replicas became the principal element in Buddhist sculpture. The change obviously was the result of foreign influence, chiefly Greek (or more accurately, Hellenistic), and Persian or Iranian.

Transformation of Buddhism. The transformation of Buddhism which was effected for the most part during the first two or three centuries of the Christian era is an event of such significance in the history of India and of the world that it deserves exposition at some length. The observations following, which were printed many years ago, still express my opinion and are, I think, in accordance with the facts. Although they are rather long, it seems worth while to reprint them without material modification.

Buddhism had been introduced into the countries on the north-western frontier of India as early as the reign of Asoka in the third century B.C.; and in 2 B.C. an unnamed Yueh-chi chieftain was interested in the religion of Gautama so far as to communicate Buddhist scriptures to a Chinese envoy. Buddhist sculpture of some sort must have been known in those regions for centuries before the time of Kanishka, but it was not the product of an organized school under liberal and powerful royal patronage, so that remains of such early Buddhist art are rare. Probably the ancient works were executed chiefly in wood.

When the great monarch Kanishka actively espoused the cause of Buddhism and essayed to play the part of a second Asoka, the devotion of the adherents of the favoured creed received an impulse which speedily resulted in the copious production of artistic creations of no small merit.

The religious system which found its best artistic exponents in the sculptors of Kanishka's court must have been of foreign origin to a large extent. Primitive Buddhism, as expounded in the *Dialogues*, so well translated by Professor Rhys Davids, was an Indian product based on the Indian ideas of rebirth, of the survival and transmission of *karma*, or the net result of human action, and of the blessedness of escape from the pains of being.

Primitive Buddhism added to those theories, which were the common possession of nearly all schools of Indian thought, an excellent practical system of ethics inculcating a Stoic devotion to duty for its own sake, combined with a tender regard for the feelings of all living creatures, human or animal; and so brought about a combination of intellect with emotion, deserving the name of a religion, even though it had no god.

But when the conversion of Asoka made the fortune of Buddhism it sowed at the same time the seeds of decay. The missionaries of the imperial preacher and their successors carried the doctrines of Gautama from the banks of the Ganges to the snows of the Himalaya, the deserts of Central Asia, and the bazaars of Alexandria.

The teaching which was exactly attuned to the inmost feelings of a congregation in Benares needed fundamental change before it could move the heart of the sturdy mountaineer, the nomad horseman, or the Hellenized Alexandrian. The moment Indian Buddhism began its foreign travels it was bound to change. We can see the transformation which was effected, although most of the steps of the evolution are hidden from us.

Influence of the Roman empire. Undoubtedly one of the principal agencies engaged in effecting the momentous change was the unification of the civilized world, excepting India and China, under the sway of the Caesars.[1] The general peace of the Roman empire was not seriously impaired by frontier wars, palace revolutions, or the freaks of half-mad emperors. During that long-continued peace nascent Christianity met full-grown Buddhism in the academies and markets of Asia and Egypt, while both religions were exposed to the influences of surrounding paganism in many forms and of the countless works of art which gave expression to the ideas of polytheism. The ancient religion of Persia contributed to the ferment of human thought, excited by improved facilities for international communication and by the incessant clash of rival civilizations.

Novel ideals. In such environment Buddhism was transmuted from its old Indian self into a practically new religion. The specially Indian ideas upon which it had been founded sank into comparative obscurity, while novel ideals came to the front. The quietist teacher of an order of begging friars, who had counted as a glorious victory the recognition of the truth, as he deemed it, that 'after this present life there would be no beyond'; and that 'on the dissolution of the body, beyond the end of his life, neither gods nor men shall see him', was gradually replaced by a divinity ever present to the hearts of the faithful, with his ears open to their prayers, and served by a hierarchy of Bodhisattvas and other beings, acting as mediators between him and sinful men.

In a word, the veneration for a dead Teacher passed into the worship of a living Saviour. That, so far as I understand the matter, is the essential difference between the old Indian Buddhism, the so-called Hīna-yāna, and the newer Buddhism or Mahā-yāna. Although the delegates to Kanishka's Council were classed officially as Hīnayānists, the popular cult of the time unquestionably was the expression of Mahāyānist ideas, which were formulated and propagated by Nāgārjuna, who was to some extent the contemporary of Kanishka.

The age from A. D. 105 to 273, during which Palmyra flourished as the chief emporium for the commerce between East and West, and the Kushān kings ruled in north-western India, may be taken as marking the time when the Mahāyāna system was developed and the art forming its outward expression attained its highest achievement. It is hardly necessary to add that the movements of the human mind never fit themselves into accurately demarcated chronological compartments, and that all evolutions, such as that of the newer Buddhism, have had their beginnings long before

[1] I agree with Lüders that in the Āra inscription Kanishka took the title of 'Caesar' (*Kaïsarasa*); but, as it is possible to dispute the reading, it is better not to lay stress upon it. Kanishka's accumulated titles imply a claim to the sovereignty of the four quarters of the world (*Sitzungsber. d. königl. Preuss. Akad. der Wissenschaften*, 1912, p. 829).

the proeess of ehange beeomes elearly visible. The rigorous doetrine of the earliest form of Buddhism was too ehilly to retain a hold upon the hearts of men unless when warmed and quiekened by human emotion. The Buddhism of the people in every eountry always has been different from that of the Canon, although the authority of the seriptures is nowhere formally disputed. When it is said that the development of the Mahāyāna was mainly the result of foreign influenee, I must not be understood as denying that the germs of the transformed religion may have existed in India from a very early stage in the history of the Buddhist ehureh.

A KUSHĀN KING, MĀT.

Literature and art. In literature the memory of Kanishka is assoeiated with the names of the eminent Buddhist writers Nāgārjuna, Asvaghosha, and Vasumitra. Asvaghosha is deseribed as having been a poet, musieian, seholar, religious eontroversialist, and zealous Buddhist monk, orthodox in ereed, and a striet observer of diseipline. Charaka, the most eelebrated of the early Indian authors treating of medieal seienee, is reputed to have been the eourt physician of Kanishka.

Arehiteeture, with its subsidiary art of seulpture, enjoyed the liberal patronage of Kanishka, who was, like Asoka, a great builder. The tower at Peshāwar, built over the relies of Buddha, and ehiefly eonstrueted of timber, stood four hundred feet high. The Sir Sukh seetion of Taxila hides the ruins of the eity built by Kanishka, as yet almost unexplored. A town in Kashmīr, still represented by a village, bore the king's name ; and Mathurā (Muttra) on the Jumna was adorned by numerous fine buildings and artistie seulptures during the reigns of Kanishka and his suecessors. A remarkable portrait statue of Kanishka, unluekily lacking the head, has been found near Mathurā, with similar statues of other prinees of his line. Those works do not betray any marks of Greek influenee.

The Gandhāra school. Mueh of the Buddhist seulpture of

the time of Kanishka and his successors is executed in the style of Gandhāra, the province on the frontier which included both Peshāwar and Taxila. That style is often and properly called Gracco-Buddhist because the forms of Greek art were applied to Buddhist subjects, with considerable artistic success in many cases. Images of Buddha appear in the likeness of Apollo, the Yaksha Kuvera is posed in the fashion of the Phidian Zeus, and so on. The drapery follows Hellenistic models. The style was transmitted to the Far East through Chinese Turkistan, and the figures of Buddha now made in China and Japan exhibit distinct traces of the Hellenistic modes in vogue at the court of Kanishka. The explorations of Sir M. A. Stein and other archaeologists have proved that the Khotan region in Chinese Turkistan was the meeting place of four civilizations—Greek, Indian, Iranian, and Chinese—during the early centuries of the Christian era, including the reign of Kanishka. The eastward advance of the Roman frontier in the days of Trajan and Hadrian (A. D. 98–138) was favourable to the spread of Hellenistic ideas and artistic forms in India and other Asiatic countries. The Indo-Greek artists found their inspiration in the schools of Pergamon, Ephesus, and other places in Asia Minor rather than in the works of the earlier artists of Greece. In other words, the Gandhāra style is Graeco-Roman, based on the cosmopolitan art of Asia Minor and the Roman empire as practised in the first three centuries of the Christian era. Much of the best work in that style was executed during the second century A. C. in the reigns of Kanishka and Huvishka.

Head of Bodhisattva.

Other sculpture. Although the Gandhāra school of sculpture was the most prolific, the art of other centres in the age of Kanishka and Huvishka was not negligible in either quantity or quality. Sārnāth near Benares, Mathurā on the Jumna, and Amarāvatī on the Krishnā (Kistna) river in the Guntūr District, Madras, offer many examples of excellent sculpture. Each of the three localities named had a distinctive style. The best known works are the elaborate bas-reliefs from Amarāvatī, more or less familiar to all visitors to the British Museum from the exhibition of a series of specimens on the grand staircase of that institution. Tradition connects the buildings at Amarāvatī with Nāgārjuna. The work there extended over many years, but most of it probably was executed in Huvishka's reign.

Huvishka. Huvishka or Hushka, presumably Kanishka's son, who had governed the Indian provinces for many years on behalf of his father, while he was engaged in distant wars, succeeded to the imperial throne about A. D. 162. Little is known about the events of his reign. His coinage, which exhibits considerable artistic merit, is even more varied than that of Kanishka, and presents recognizable portraits of the king as a burly, middle-aged or elderly man with a large nose. The Yueh-chi princes had no resemblance to the 'narrow-eyed' Mongolians. They were big pink-faced men, built on a large scale, and may possibly have been related to the Turks. They dressed in long-skirted coats, wore soft leather boots, and sat on chairs in European fashion. Their language was an Iranian form of speech; and their religion, as we have seen, was a modified Zoroastrianism. The name of Huvishka was associated with a town in Kashmīr and with a Buddhist monastery at Mathurā. His coin types exhibit the strange medley of Greek, Indian, and Iranian deities seen on the coinage of Kanishka, but no distinctively Buddhist coins have been found. So far as appears, he retained possession of the extensive territories ruled by Kanishka. His death may be dated somewhere about A. D. 180 or 185. He must have been an old or elderly man, because his inscriptions, which overlap those of his predecessor, range from the year 33 to the year 60 of Kanishka's regnal era.

BODHISATTVA.

End of the Kushān empire. Huvishka's successor was Vāsudeva I, in whose time the empire began to break up. The manner in which the Kushān power in India came to an end has not been clearly ascertained, but there is no doubt that Huvishka was the last monarch to maintain an extensive empire until his death. Such indications as exist concerning the decay of the empire are chiefly

GANDHĀRA FRIEZE.

derived from the study of coins, and the inferences drawn from material so scanty are necessarily dubious. But it is certain that the coinage of the successors of Vāsudeva, some of whom bore the same name, became gradually Persianized, and the suggestion seems to be reasonable that the dissolution of the Kushān empire in India was connected in some way with the rise of the Sassanian power in A.D. 226, and the subsequent conquests of Ardashīr Bābegān, the first Sassanian king, and his successors, which are alleged to have extended to the Indus, but without sufficient evidence. Strong Kushān dynasties continued to exist in Kābul and the neighbouring countries until the Hun invasions of the fifth century; and some principalities survived even until the Arab conquest of Persia in the seventh century.

The name of Vāsudeva proves the rapidity with which the Kushāns had been changed into Hindus. Its form suggests the worship of Vishnu as Vāsudeva, but the coins bear the images of Siva and his bull, which had already appeared on the coins of Kadphises II. The history of the third century, whether religious or political, is too obscure and uncertain for further discussion in these pages.

Greek influence. The question as to the extent of Greek, or more accurately, Hellenistic influence upon Indian civilization is of interest, and always has been warmly debated by European scholars, who naturally desire to find links connecting the unfamiliar doings of isolated India with the familiar Greek ideas and institutions to which Europe owes so much. It will be well, therefore, to devote a few pages to the consideration of the facts bearing on the question. The trade relations between the Hellenistic world and India which existed for centuries, and will be noticed presently, are not relevant in this connexion. Such relations had little effect on the ideas or institutions of either India or Europe. The business people, then, as they usually do in all ages, confined themselves to their trade affairs without troubling about anything else. They left no records, and, so far as appears, did not communicate much information to scholarly persons like Pliny and Strabo. If modern Europe had to depend upon Bombay and Calcutta merchants for its knowledge of India it would not know much.

Effects of Alexander's campaign. Alexander's fierce campaign produced no direct effects upon either the ideas or the institutions of India. During his brief stay in the basin of the Indus he was occupied almost solely with fighting. Presumably he was remembered by the ordinary natives of the regions which

MEDALLION, AMARĀVATĪ.

he harried merely as a demon-like outer barbarian who hanged Brahmans without scruple and won battles by impious methods in defiance of the scriptures. The Indians felt no desire to learn from such a person. They declined to learn from him even the art of war, in which he was a master ; preferring to go on in their own traditional way, trusting to a 'four-fold' army and hosts of elephants. When Chandragupta Maurya swept the Macedonian garrisons out of the Panjāb, that was the end of Hellenism on Indian soil for the time. The failure of the invasion by Seleukos Nikator a few years later secured India from all further Greek aggression.

Maurya civilization. Then followed seventy or eighty years of peaceful, friendly intercourse between the Maurya court and the Hellenistic princes of Asia and Africa, to which we are indebted for the valuable account of the Maurya empire compiled by Megasthenes. His book does not indicate any trace of Hellenic influence upon the political or social institutions of India. On the contrary, the close agreement of the testimony recorded by the Greek ambassador with the statements of the Sanskrit books proves clearly that the Maurya government managed its affairs after its own fashion in general accordance with Hindu tradition, borrowing something from Persia but nothing from Greece. Even the Maurya coinage continued to be purely Indian, or at any rate Asiatic, in character. Asoka did not care to imitate the beautiful Bactrian issues, or to follow Greek example by putting his image and superscription on his coins. He was content to use the primitive punch-marked, cast, or rudely struck coins which had formed the currency of India before his time.

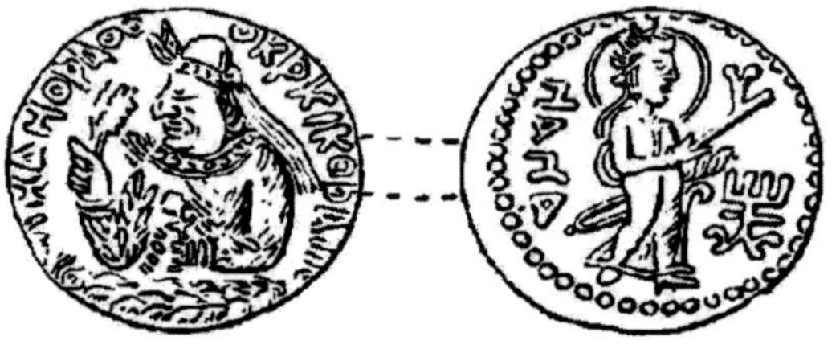

Coin of Huvishka.

In the domain of the fine arts some indications of the operation of Greek example and good taste may be discerned. The high quality of Maurya sculpture clearly was due to the happy blending of Indian, Iranian, and Hellenic factors.

It is reasonable also to connect Asoka's preference for the use of stone in building and sculpture with the opportunities which he enjoyed for studying the Hellenistic practice of working in permanent material.

Coin of Vāsudeva.

The design of Indian buildings, so far as is known, rarely owed anything to Greek principles, but the excavations at Taxila suggest, or perhaps prove, that in some cases Greek models may have been imitated in that region. Columns of the Ionic order undoubtedly were inserted in Taxilan buildings. Taxila, however, was half-foreign and only half-Indian, so that practices considered legitimate there would not have been approved in the interior provinces.

Demetrios and others. Direct contact between the Hellenistic states and the Panjāb was brought about early in the second century B.C., forty or fifty years after Asoka's death, by the conquests of the Bactrian sovereign Demetrios, 'King of the Indians'. The elephant's head on his coins is a record of his Indian connexions. A little later we find a king with the Greek name of Pantaleon striking coins in the square Indian shape, copied from the indigenous coinage of Taxila. About the same time Agathokles also adopted bilingual legends, first employed by Demetrios, giving his regal style in both Greek and a kind of Prakrit. The Indian tongue is inscribed in Brahmī, an old form of the script now called Nāgarī or Devanāgarī. Bilingual legends continued to be used by many kings.

Coin types. Antialkidas (*c.* 140–130 B.C.), the king of Taxila who sent Heliodoros as envoy to the Rājā of Besnagar, adopted the Indian standard of weight for his coins. The idea of striking coins with two dies, obverse and reverse, one side bearing the effigy and titles of the king, was foreign to India, and was gradually adopted by Indian princes in imitation of the issues minted by dynasties of foreign origin—Sakas, Parthians, Yueh-chi, and the rest. Indian artists, who attained brilliant success in other fields, never cared greatly about die-cutting, and consequently never produced a really fine coin. The best Indian coins, being a few gold pieces struck by the Gupta kings before and after A.D. 400 under the influence of western models, although good, are not first-rate, and do not bear comparison with the magnificent dies of the earlier Bactrian kings, not to speak of Syracusan masterpieces.

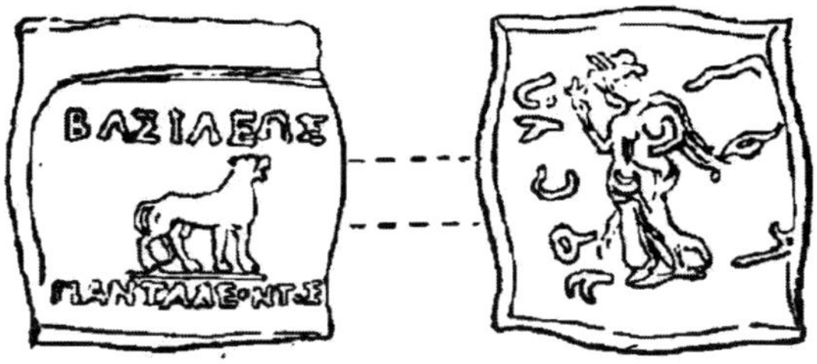

Coin of Pantaleon.

Indo-Roman gold coinage. The Yueh-chi, Indo-Scythian, or Kushān kings of the first and second centuries A.C. evidently maintained active trade communications with the Roman empire, then far extended eastwards. Hence we find an unmistakable copy of the head of either Augustus or Tiberius on certain coins of Kadphises I, who seems to have made an alliance with Hermaios, the last Greek king of Kābul. Kadphises II carried much farther his imitation of Roman usage by striking an abundant and excellent issue of gold coins agreeing closely with the Caesarian *aurei* in weight and not much inferior in fineness. Imported Roman coins have been often found in the Panjāb, Kābul, and neighbouring territories, but the bulk of the considerable inflow into India of Roman gold, as testified to by Pliny in A.D. 77, seems, so far as the northern kingdom was concerned, to have been melted down and reissued as orientalized *aurei*, first by Kadphises II, and afterwards by Kanishka, Huvishka, and Vāsudeva. In peninsular India the Roman *aureus* circulated as currency, just as the British sovereign now passes current in

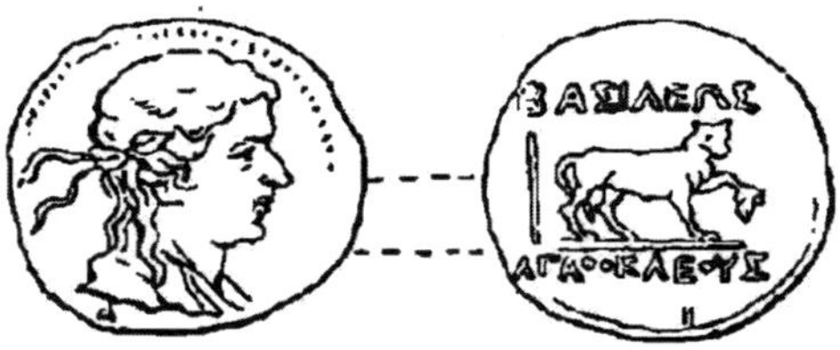

Coin of Agathokles.

Coin of Nero.

many lands. The gold indigenous currency of the south, introduced apparently at a later date, has never had any connexion with European models.

Greek script and gods. Kanishka, Huvishka, and Vāsudeva used for their coin legends the Khotanese language, a near relative of the Saka tongue, but engraved it in a form of Greek characters only. For some reason or other they did not use any Asiatic script. The strange mixture of deities found in the coin types of Kanishka and Huvishka and the peculiarities of the Graeco-Buddhist school of sculpture have been sufficiently discussed above. The presumed influence of Hellenistic polytheism on the development of the later Buddhism has also been examined. The evidence of all kinds shows that, while foreigners like Heliodoros were ready to adopt Indian gods, the Indians were slow to worship Greek deities. The few Greek deities named on the Kanishka and Huvishka coins belonged also to the Persian pantheon and were taken over from the Parthians. The tendency certainly was for Indo-Greek princes and people to become Hinduized, rather than for the Indian Rājās and their subjects to become Hellenized. The Brahmans were well able to take care of themselves and to keep at arm's length any foreign notions which they did not wish to assimilate.

Scanty traces of Greek rule. The visible traces of the long-continued Greek rule on the north-western frontier of India are surprisingly scanty, if the coin legends be excluded from consideration. No inscription in the Greek language or script has yet (1917) been found, and the Greek names occurring in inscriptions are few, perhaps half a dozen. Two records, one of which comes from Taxila, mention the District Officer serving under some Indo-Greek king by the designation of 'meridarch' (μεριδάρχης), a detail which indicates the use of Greek for official purposes to a certain extent. Greek must have been spoken at the courts of the Indo-Greek kings, but the language does not seem to have spread among any Indian nation. The exclusive use of a Greek script to express Khotanese legends on the coins of Kanishka and his successors may be due, as has been suggested, to Khotanese having been first reduced to writing in the Greek character. The Greek lettering on the coins does not imply a popular knowledge of the Greek alphabet. Only a small proportion of the Indian population has ever been able to read coin legends, whatever the language or script might be. The coins of the ruling power for the time being are accepted as currency without the slightest regard to the inscriptions on them.

Summary. To sum up, it may be said that Greek or Hellenistic influence upon India was slight and superficial, much less in amount than I believed it to be when the subject first attracted me thirty years ago. If any considerable modification of the Indian religions was effected by contact with Hellenism, Buddhism alone was concerned, Jainism and Brahmanical Hinduism remaining untouched. The remarkable local school of Graeco-Buddhist sculpture in the Gandhāra frontier province, which was imitated to some extent in the interior, permanently determined the type of Chinese and Japanese Buddhist images. Some details of Hellenistic ornament became widely diffused throughout India. An undefinable but, I think, real element of Greek feeling may be discerned in the excellent sculpture of Asoka's age. If any buildings on a Greek plan were erected they were apparently confined to Gandhāra. Indian artists never produced fine coin-dies. Any at all good were copied from or suggested by Graeco-Roman models. The Greek language never obtained wide currency in India, but must have been used to some extent at the courts of the border princes with Greek names. Many of those princes must have been of mixed blood. 'The Indo-Bactrian Greeks', it has been said, 'were the Goanese of antiquity.' The early medical knowledge as expounded by Charaka, Kanishka's physician, has been supposed to betray some acquaintance with the works of Hippocrates, but the proof does not seem to be convincing.

Long after the period treated in this chapter, western influence again made itself felt in Indian art, literature, and science during the rule of the Gupta emperors. That subject will be noticed in due course.

Commerce by land. Some reference has been made to the commerce between India and the Roman empire during the rule of the Kushān kings. The overland commerce of India with western Asia dated from remote times and was conducted by several routes across Persia, Mesopotamia, and Asia Minor. Between A.D. 105 and 273 the principal dépôt of the trade was Palmyra or Tadmor in Syria. The Chinese silk trade followed the same roads.

Commerce by sea. The sea-borne trade of the peninsula with Europe through Egypt does not seem to have been considerable before the time of Claudius, when the course of the monsoons is said to have become known to the Roman merchants. But a certain amount of commerce with Egypt must have existed from much earlier days. In 20 B.C. we hear of a mission to Augustus from 'King Pandion', the Pāndya king of Madura in the far south. During the first and second centuries of the Christian era the trade between southern India and the Roman empire was extensive. Merchants could sail from an Arabian port to Muziris or Cranganore on the Malabar coast in forty days during July and August and return in December or January after transacting their business. There is reason to believe that Roman subjects lived at Muziris and other towns. The trade was checked, and perhaps temporarily stopped, by Caracalla's massacre of the people of Alexandria in A.D. 215. Payment for the Indian goods was made in *aurei*, of which large hoards have been found.

Goods and ports. The goods most sought by the foreign visitors were pearls from the fisheries of the Tāmraparni river in Tinnevelly; beryls from several mines in Mysore and Coimbatore; corundum from the same region; gems of various kinds from

Ceylon; and pepper with other spices from the Malabar coast. The list is not exhaustive. The two principal ports on the Malabar coast were Muziris or Cranganore, and Bakarai or Vaikkarai, the haven of Kottayam, now in the Travancore State. Korkai on the Tāmraparni river was the principal seat of the pearl trade. Puhār, also called Pukār or Kāvērīpaddinam, then at the mouth of the Kāvērī (Cauvery) river, was for some time a rich and prosperous port. It, with the other ancient ports in that region, is now desolate, a gradual elevation of the land having changed the coast-line.

The Tamil states. The Tamil states of the far south became wealthy and prosperous in virtue of their valuable foreign trade, and attained a high degree of material civilization at an early period. Megasthenes heard of the power of the Pāndya kingdom, and the names of the states are mentioned in Asoka's edicts. Boundaries varied much from age to age, but three principal powers, the Pāndya, Chera or Kerala, and Chola, were always recognized. Asoka named a fourth minor kingdom, the Keralaputra, absorbed subsequently in the Pāndya realm, which was reputed the most ancient of the states, and may be described roughly as embracing the Madura and Tinnevelly Districts. The Kerala or Chera kingdom included the Malabar District with the modern Cochin and Travancore States, and sometimes extended eastwards. The Chola kingdom occupied the Coromandel or Madras coast. Cotton cloth formed an important item in the commerce of the Cholas, who maintained an active fleet, which was not afraid to sail as far as the mouths of the Irawaddy and Ganges, or even to the islands of the Malay Archipelago.

Tamil literature. During the early centuries of the Christian era Tamil was the language of all the kingdoms named, Malayālam not having then come into being. A rich literature grew up, of which the golden age may be assigned to the first three centuries A.C. Madura may be called the literary capital. The period indicated produced three works of special merit, the 'Kural' (Cural), the 'Epic of the Anklet', and the 'Jewel-belt'. The 'Kural' is described as being 'the most venerated and popular book south of the Godāvarī . . . the literary treasure, the poetic mouthpiece, the highest type of verbal and moral excellence among the Tamil people'. The author taught ethical doctrine of singular purity and beauty, which cannot, so far as I know, be equalled in the Sanskrit literature of the north. A few stanzas from Gover's excellent versions may be quoted:

LOVE

Loveless natures, cold and hard,
  Live for self alone.
Hearts where love abides regard
  Self as scarce their own. . . .

Where the body hath a soul,
Love hath gone before.
Where no love infils the whole,
Dust it is—no more.

PATIENCE

How good are they who bear with scorn
And think not to return it !
They're like the earth that giveth corn
To those who dig and burn it. . . .

Though men should injure you, their pain
Should lead thee to compassion.
Do nought but good to them again,
Else look to thy transgression.

Dynastic history. No continuous narrative of political events in the Tamil kingdoms can be constructed for the period dealt with in this chapter, or, indeed, until centuries later. But the literature gives a few glimpses of dynastic history. Karikkāl or Karikāla, the earliest known Chola king, whose mean date may be taken as A.D. 100, contemporary with Kadphises II, is credited with the foundation of Puhār or Pukār, and with the construction of a hundred miles of embankment along the Kāvērī river (Cauvery), built by the labour of captives from Ceylon. Almost continual war with the island princes is a leading feature in the story of the Tamil kingdoms for many centuries. It need hardly be added that the kings fought among themselves still more continuously. The first historical Pāndya king was contemporary more or less exactly with Karikāla Chola's grandson, with a certain powerful Chera monarch, and with Gajabāhu, king of Ceylon, who reigned in the last quarter of the second century, and gives the clue to the chronology.. After that time no more dynastic history is possible until the Pallavas make their appearance in the fourth century.

SYNCHRONISTIC TABLE OF THE FOREIGN DYNASTIES AND THEIR CONTEMPORARIES

(All Indian dates of events are merely approximate)

B. C.	
c. 250–248.	Revolts of Bactria and Parthia.
c. 232.	Death of Asoka.
c. 208.	Recognition of Bactrian independence.
c 200–190.	Demetrios, 'King of the Indians'.
c. 190–180.	Pantaleon and Agathokles, kings of Taxila.
c. 174–160.	Western migration of the Great Yueh-chi from China.
c. 160–140.	Menander (Milinda), king of Kābul.
c. 140–130.	Antialkidas, king of Taxila; Heliokles, last Greek king of Bactria; invasions of Sakas, &c.
c. 138.	Conquest of kingdom of Taxila by Mithridates I, king of Parthia.

B. C.	
c. 122–120.	Return of Chang-K'ien to China.
c. 95.	Maues, Saka or Indo-Parthian king of Arachosia and Panjāb, acc.
c. 58.	Azes I acc. in same regions; 58–57, epoch of Vikrama era.
30.	Roman conquest of Egypt.
A. D.	
14.	Augustus Caesar died; Tiberius, Roman emperor, acc.
c. 20–48.	Gondophernes (Gondophares, &c.); king of Taxila, &c.; probably succeeded Azes II.
23.	End of First Han dynasty of China.
c. 40.	Kadphises I (Kujula Kara Kadphises, &c.), Kushān, became king of all the Great Yueh-chi.
41.	Claudius, Roman emperor, acc.
c. 48.	Kadphises I succeeded Gondophernes at Taxila.
c. 77 or 78.	Death of Kadphises I.
78.	? Kadphises II acc.; epoch of the Saka era.
89–105.	Ho-ti, Chinese emperor.
c. 90.	Defeat of Kadphises II by Pan-chao, Chinese general.
98.	Trajan, Roman emperor, acc.
105.	Rise of Palmyra to importance.
c. 110.	Death of Kadphises II.
c. 110–20.	? The 'Nameless King' in N.W. India.
116.	Conquest of Mesopotamia by Trajan.
117.	Hadrian, Roman emperor, acc.; retrocession of Mesopotamia.
c. 120.	Kanishka Kushān (? Little Yueh-chi) acc.; year 1 of his regnal era.
c. 123.	Sārnāth inscription of Kanishka (year 3).
c. 138.	Mānikyāla inscription of Kanishka (year 18); Antoninus Pius, Roman emperor, acc.
c. 144–50.	Vāsishka, (?) son and viceregal colleague of Kanishka in India (year 24 to (?) 30).
c. 150–62.	Huvishka, (?) son and viceregal colleague of Kanishka in India (years 30–42).
c. 161.	Āra inscription of Kanishka (year 41); Marcus Aurelius, Roman emperor, acc.
c. 162.	Huvishka succeeded Kanishka as Kushān emperor.
c. 182.	Vāsudeva I acc.
193.	Septimius Severus, Roman emperor, acc.
c. 194–218.	Inscriptions of Vāsudeva I (years 74–98).
c. 220.	Death of Vāsudeva I.
226.	Establishment of Sassanian dynasty of Persia by Ardashīr or Artaxerxes I.
240.	Shāpur (Sapor) I acc. in Persia.
273.	Destruction of Palmyra by Aurelian.

Authorities

References in addition to those in *E. H. I.*[3] (1914) might be given to numerous papers in the *J. R. A. S.* and other periodicals, which it would be tedious to specify. Special attention may be directed to Sir John Marshall's articles on Taxila in *J. P. H. S.*, vol. iii, and *Ann. Rep. A. S., India, for* 1912–13. The exploration of the site will continue for years.

Another notable contribution is Professor Sten Konow's paper

'Indoskythische Beiträge' in *Sitzungsber. d. königl. Preuss. Akad. der Wissenschaften*, 1916, a copy of which I was fortunate enough to receive through an official channel. The Besnagar pillar is discussed in *Ann. Rep. A. S., India, for* 1908–9, in *Progr. Rep. A. S., Western Circle, for* 1914–15, and *Ann. Rep. A. S., India, for* 1913–14.

Buddhist China, a good book by R. F. JOHNSTON (Murray, 1913), contains valuable observations on the development of Mahāyāna doctrines in India at an early date from Hīnayāna discussions and disputes. Professor POUSSIN discourses exhaustively on Bodhisattvas in Hastings, *Encycl. Rel. and Ethics, s. v.*

CHAPTER 4

The Gupta period; a golden age; literature, art, and science; Hindu renaissance; the Huns; King Harsha; the Chalukyas; disorder in northern India.

Definite chronology from A. D. 320. The transition from the unsettled and hotly disputed history of the foreign dynasties to the comparatively serene atmosphere of the Gupta period is no less agreeable to the historian than the similar passage from the uncertainties of the Nandas to the ascertained verities of the Mauryas. In both cases the experience is like that of a man in an open boat suddenly gliding from the misery of a choppy sea outside into the calm water of a harbour.

The chronology of the Gupta period, taking that period in a wide sense as extending from A. D. 320, or in round numbers from A. D. 300, to A. D. 647, or the middle of the seventh century, is not only certain in all its main outlines, but also precise in detail to a large extent, except for the latter half of the sixth century.

It is possible, therefore, to construct a continuous narrative of the history of northern and western India for the greater part of three centuries and a half, without the embarrassment which clogs all attempts at narrative when the necessary chronological framework is insecure.

Rise of the Gupta dynasty. The exact course of events which brought about the collapse of the Indo-Scythian or Kushān empire in India at some time in the third century is not known. The disturbed state of the country seems to be the explanation of the lack of contemporary inscriptions or other memorials of the time, and of the hopeless confusion of tradition as recorded in books. Many independent states must have been formed when the control of a paramount authority was withdrawn. The Lichchhavis of Vaisāli, last heard of in the days of Buddha, now emerge again after eight hundred years of silence. It would seem that the clan or nation must have obtained possession of Pātaliputra, the ancient imperial capital, and have ruled there as tributaries or feudatories of the Kushāns, whose head-quarters were at Peshāwar. Early in the fourth century a Lichchhavi princess gave her hand to a Rājā in Magadha who bore the historic name of Chandragupta. The matrimonial alliance with the Lichchhavis so enhanced his power that he was able to extend his dominion over Oudh as well as Magadha, and along the Ganges as far as Prayāg or Allahabad. Chandragupta recognized his dependence on his wife's people by striking his gold coins in the joint names of himself, his queen (Kumāra Dēvī), and the Lichchhavi nation.[1] He felt himself sufficiently important to be justified in establishing a new era, the Gupta, of which the year 1 ran from February 26, 320, presumably the date of his enthronement or coronation, to March 13, 321. The era continued in use in parts of India for several centuries. The reign of Chandragupta I was short, and may be assumed to have ended about A. D. 330. His son and successor was always careful to describe himself as being 'the son of the daughter of the Lichchhavi', a formula implying the acknowledgement that his royal authority was derived from his mother.

Coin of Chandragupta I.

Samudragupta. Samudragupta, the second Gupta monarch,[2] who reigned for forty or fifty years, was one of the most remarkable and accomplished kings recorded in Indian history. He undertook and succeeded in accomplishing the formidable task of making himself the paramount power in India. He spent some years first in thoroughly subduing such princes in the Gangetic plain as declined to acknowledge his authority. He then brought the wild forest tribes under control, and finally executed a military progress through the Deccan, advancing so far into the peninsula that he came into conflict with the Pallava ruler of Kānchī (Conjeeveram) near Madras. He then turned westward and came home through Khāndēsh, no doubt using the road which passed Asīrgarh. That wonderful expedition must have lasted at least two or three years. Samudragupta did not attempt to retain permanently his conquests to the south of the Narbadā, being content to receive homage from the vanquished princes and to bring back to his capital a vast golden treasure. He celebrated the *asvamedha* or horse sacrifice, which had been long

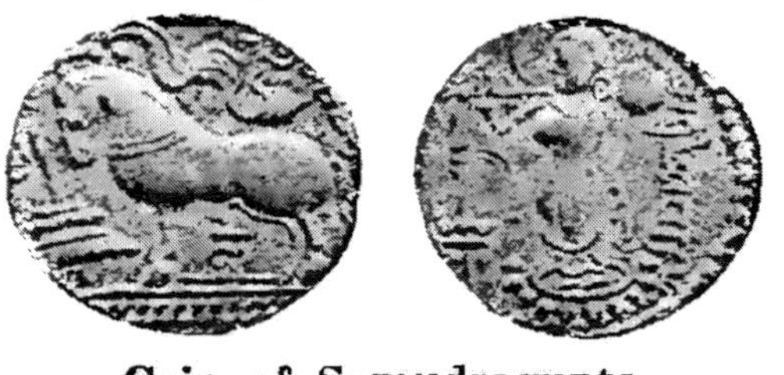

Coin of Samudragupta.
Horse-sacrifice type.

[1] That seems to me the natural interpretation of the coin legends. Mr. Allan, of the British Museum, regards the coins as having been struck by Samudragupta in honour of his parents, a view which I cannot accept.

[2] Kācha (Kacha), who struck a few gold coins, may have intervened for a few months, if he was distinct from Samudragupta; but the best opinion is that they were identical.

in abeyance, in order to mark the successful assertion of his claim to imperial rank, and struck interesting gold medals in commemoration of the event.

Samudragupta's empire. At the close of Samudragupta's triumphal career his empire—the greatest in India since the days of Asoka—extended on the north to the base of the mountains, but did not include Kashmīr. The eastern limit probably was the Brahmaputra. The Narbadā may be regarded as the frontier on the south. The Jumna and Chambal rivers marked the western limit of the territories directly under the imperial government, but various tribal states in the Panjāb and Mālwā, occupied by the Yaudhēyas, Mālavas, and other nations, enjoyed autonomy under the protection of the paramount power.

Tribute was paid and homage rendered by the rulers of five frontier kingdoms, namely Samatata, or the delta of the Brahmaputra; Davāka, perhaps Eastern Bengal; Kāmarūpa, roughly equivalent to Assam; Kartripura, probably represented by Kumaon and Garhwāl; and Nepāl.

Relations with foreign powers. Samudragupta further claims that he received respectful service from the foreign Kushān princes of the north-west, whom he grouped together as 'Saka chiefs', and even from the Sinhalese.[1] It is clear, therefore, that his name was known and honoured over the whole of India proper. He did not attempt to carry his arms across the Sutlaj or to dispute the authority of the Kushān kings who continued to rule in and beyond the Indus basin. The fact of the existence of friendly relations with Ceylon about A. D. 360 is confirmed by a Chinese historian who relates that King Meghavarman of Ceylon (*c.* 352–79) sent an embassy with gifts to Samudragupta and obtained his permission to erect a splendid monastery to the north of the holy tree at Bōdh Gayā for the use of pilgrims from the island. The extensive mound which marks the site of the building has not yet been excavated.

Personal gifts. Samudragupta was a man of exceptional personal capacity and unusually varied gifts. His skill in music and song is commemorated by certain rare gold coins or medals which depict the king seated on a couch playing the Indian lute (*vīnā*). He was equally proficient in the allied art of poetry, and

[1] The great inscription, which records in line 23 the rendering of 'acts of respectful service' by 'Daivaputra-Shāhi-Shāhānushāhi-Saka-murundas, Sinhalese, and others', must be interpreted in the light of modern research as meaning that the civilities were tendered by Meghavarman, king of Ceylon, and by sundry Kushān princes of the north-west, described collectively as 'Saka-murundas', or 'Saka chiefs', who used the styles of Daivaputra (=Chinese 'Son of Heaven'), Shāhi, or 'king'; and Shāhānushāhi or 'King of Kings'. *Shāhānu* is a genitive plural. See Konow's paper as cited in chap. 3. The Purānas treat the Murundas as distinct from the Sakas, but originally the word meant simply 'chief'= Chinese *wang*. In practice the name Murunda was employed to denote a section of the Sakas.

The Conquests of SAMUDRAGUPTA, 340 A.D. and the GUPTA EMPIRE, 400 A.D. (Travels of Fa-hien)

is said to have composed numerous works worthy of the reputation of a professional author. He took much delight in the society of the learned, whose services he engaged in the defence of the sacred scriptures. Although himself a Brahmanical Hindu with a special devotion to Vishnu, like the other members of his house, that fact did not prevent him from showing favour in his youth to Vasubandhu, the celebrated Buddhist author.

Coin of Samudragupta. Lyrist type.

The exact date of Samudragupta's death is not known; but he certainly lived to an advanced age, and when he passed away had enjoyed a reign of apparently uninterrupted prosperity for nearly half a century.

Chandragupta II. About A.D. 375 he was succeeded by a son specially selected as the most worthy of the crown, who assumed his grandfather's name and is therefore known to history as Chandragupta II. Later in life he took the additional title of Vikramāditya ('Sun of power'), which was associated by tradition with the Rājā of Ujjain who is believed to have defeated the Sakas and established the Vikrama era in 58–57 B.C. It is possible that such a Rājā may really have existed, although the tradition has not yet been verified by the discovery of inscriptions, coins, or monuments. The popular legends concerning 'Rājā Bikram' probably have been coloured by indistinct memories of Chandragupta II, whose principal military achievement was the conquest of Mālwā, Gujarāt, and Surāshtra or Kāthiāwār, countries which had been ruled for several centuries by foreign Saka chiefs. Those chiefs, who had been tributary to the Kushāns, called themselves Satraps or Great Satraps. The conquest was effected between the years A.D. 388 and 401. 395 may be taken as the mean date of the operations, which must have lasted for several years. The advance of the imperial arms involved the subjugation of the Mālavas and certain other tribes which had remained outside the frontier of Samudragupta, although enjoying his protection. Rudrasimha, the last of the Satraps, was killed. A scandalous tradition, recorded by an author of the seventh century, affirmed that the king of the Sakas, 'while courting another man's wife, was butchered by Chandragupta, concealed in his mistress's dress'. The reader is at liberty to believe or disbelieve the tale as he pleases.

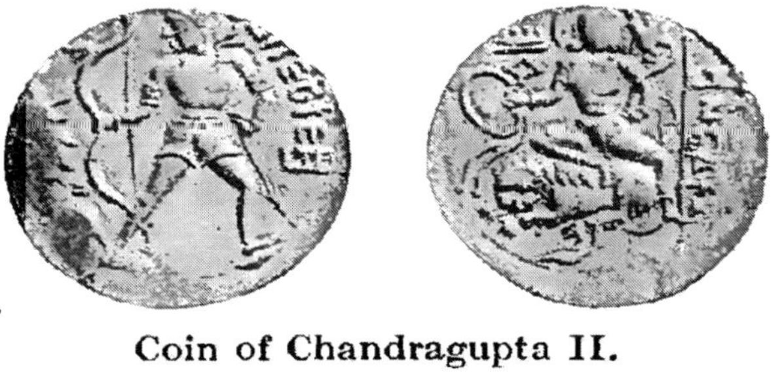

Coin of Chandragupta II.

Trade with west; Ujjain. The annexation of the Satraps' territories added provinces of exceptional wealth and fertility to the northern empire, which had become an extremely rich and powerful state at the beginning of the fifth century. The income from the customs duties collected at the numerous ports on the western coast which were now brought under Gupta rule must have been a valuable financial resource. From time immemorial Bharōch (Broach), Sopāra, Cambay, and a multitude of other ports had carried on an active sea-borne trade with the countries of the west. Ujjain appears to have been the inland centre upon which most of the trade routes converged. The city, dating from immemorial antiquity, which still retains its ancient name unchanged and exists as a prosperous town in Sindia's Dominions, has been always reckoned as one of the seven sacred Hindu cities, little inferior to Benares in sanctity. Longitudes were reckoned from its meridian in ancient times. The favourable position of the city for trade evidently was the foundation both of its material prosperity and of the sanctity attaching to a site which enjoyed the favour of successive ruling powers by whom religious establishments of all kinds were founded from time to time.

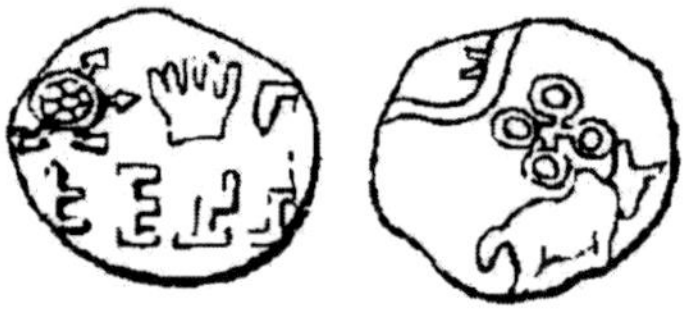

Coin of Ujjain.

The Great Satraps of Mahārāshtra. Two distinct dynasties of foreign Saka princes using the style of Great Satrap ruled in western India, and should not be confounded by being lumped together under a single designation as the 'Western Satraps'.

The earlier dynasty ruled in Mahārāshtra or the region of the western Ghāts, its capital apparently being at or near Nāsik. The date of its establishment is not known, and so far the names of only two princes, Bhūmaka and Nahapāna, have been recovered, but others may have existed. About A.D. 117, during the assumed interval between the death of Kadphises II and the accession of Kanishka, an Āndhra king called Gautamīputra extirpated the line of Nahapāna and annexed the dominions of the dynasty, restriking their coins.

The Great Satraps of Ujjain. At nearly the same time, or probably a few years earlier, a chieftain named Chashtana became Great Satrap of Mālwā, with his capital at Ujjain. He must have been a subordinate of Kadphises II. His reign was not long, and his son did not come to the throne. Possibly both father and son may have been killed in battle, for the times were troubled. Chashtana's grandson, named Rudradāman, in or about A.D. 128, and certainly before A.D. 130, won afresh for himself the position of Great Satrap, presumably under the suzerainty of Kanishka, and became the ruler of western India, including the provinces which the Āndhra had wrested from the Satrap of Mahārāshtra a few years previously. Chashtana's successors must have continued to be tributaries of Huvishka. When the Kushān empire broke up, the rulers of the west, who continued to style themselves Great Satraps, became independent, and preserved their authority until the twenty-first Great Satrap was killed by Chandragupta II at the close of the fourth century, when his country was incorporated in the Gupta empire, as already mentioned. The names and dates of the Great Satraps of Ujjain have been well ascertained, chiefly from coins, but little is known about the details of their history.[1]

Character of Chandragupta II. The principal Gupta kings, except the founder of the dynasty, all enjoyed long reigns, like Akbar and his successors in a later age. Chandragupta Vikramāditya occupied the throne for nearly forty years until A. D. 413. The ascertained facts of his career prove that he was a strong and vigorous ruler, well qualified to govern and augment an extensive empire. He loved sounding titles which proclaimed his martial prowess, and was fond of depicting himself on his coins as engaged in the sport of kings, personal combat with a lion. Lions were numerous in the northern parts of the United Provinces as late as the time of Bishop Heber in 1824, but are now found only in Kāthiāwār. The last specimen recorded in northern India was killed in the Gwālior State in 1872.

Fa-hien, Chinese pilgrim. The indispensable chronological skeleton of Gupta history constructed from the testimony of numerous dated inscriptions and coins is clothed with flesh chiefly by the help of foreign travellers, the pilgrims from China who crowded into India as the Holy Land of Buddhism from the beginning of the fifth century. Fa-hien or Fa-hsien, the earliest of those pilgrims, was on his travels from A. D. 399 to 414. His laborious journey was undertaken in order to procure authentic texts of the *Vinaya-pitaka*, or Buddhist books on monastic discipline. The daring traveller after leaving western China followed the route to the south of the Taklamakān (Gobi) Desert, through Sha-chow and Lop-nor to Khotan, where the population was wholly Buddhist, and chiefly devoted to the Mahāyāna doctrine.[2] He then crossed the Pāmīrs with infinite difficulty and made his way into Udyāna or Suwāt (Swat), and so on to Taxila and Purushapura or Peshāwar. He spent three years at Pātaliputra and two at Tāmralipti, now represented by Tamlūk in the Midnapore District of Bengal. In those days Tāmralipti was an important port. Its modern successor is a small town at least sixty miles distant from the sea. Fa-hien sailed from Tāmralipti on his return journey, going home by sea, and visiting Ceylon and Java on the way. His stay in India proper, extending from A. D. 401 to 410, thus fell wholly within the limits of the reign of Chandragupta II. About six years were spent in the dominions of that monarch.

The enthusiastic pilgrim was so absorbed in the religious task to which his life was devoted that he never even mentions the

[1] Much difference of opinion has been expressed concerning the date of Nahapāna, and the question has not been settled.

[2] The details of the pilgrim's route from Lop-nor to Khotan have not been worked out properly by any of the translators and are obscure; but he certainly passed Lop-nor.

name of any reigning sovereign. His references to the facts of ordinary life are made in a casual, accidental fashion, which guarantees the trustworthiness of his observations. Although we moderns should be better pleased if the pious traveller had paid more attention to worldly affairs, we may be thankful for his brief notes, which give a pleasing and fairly vivid picture of the condition of the Gangetic provinces in the reign of Chandragupta II. He calls the Gangetic plain Mid-India or the Middle Kingdom, which may be taken as equivalent roughly to the modern Bihār, the United Provinces of Agra and Oudh, Mālwā, and part of Rājputāna. The whole of Mid-India was under the rule of the Gupta emperor.

State of the country. The towns of Magadha or South Bihār were large; the people were rich and prosperous; charitable institutions were numerous; rest-houses for travellers were provided on the highways, and the capital possessed an excellent free hospital endowed by benevolent and educated citizens. Pātaliputra was still a flourishing city, specially interesting to Fa-hien because it possessed two monasteries—one of the Little, and one of the Great Vehicle, where six or seven hundred monks resided, who were so famous for their learning that students from all quarters attended their lectures. Fa-hien spent three happy years at the ancient imperial capital in the study of the Sanskrit language and Buddhist scriptures. He was deeply impressed by the palace and halls erected by Asoka in the middle of the city, and still standing in the time of the pilgrim. The massive stone work, richly adorned with sculpture and decorative carving, seemed to him to be the work of spirits, beyond the capacity of merely human craftsmen. The site of that palace, somewhere in the heart of the modern city, has not yet been fully identified.

Pātaliputra probably continued to be the principal royal residence in the reign of Samudragupta, but there are indications that in the time of his successor Ajodhyā was found to be more convenient as the head-quarters of the government.

In the course of a journey of some 500 miles from the Indus to Mathurā on the Jumna the traveller passed a succession of Buddhist monasteries tenanted by thousands of monks. Mathurā alone had twenty such institutions with three thousand residents. Fa-hien noted that Buddhism was particularly flourishing along the course of the Jumna.

Administration. He liked the climate and was pleased with the mildness of the administration. He notes that people were free to come or go as they thought fit without the necessity of being registered or obtaining passes; that offences were ordinarily punished by fine only; the capital penalty not being inflicted, and mutilation being confined to the case of obstinate rebellion, meaning probably professional brigandage. Persons guilty of that crime were liable to suffer amputation of the right hand. The revenue was derived mainly from the rent of the crown lands, 'land revenue' in modern language. The royal guards and officers were paid regular salaries.

Habits of the people. The Buddhist rule of life was generally observed.

'Throughout the country', we are told, 'no one kills any living thing, or drinks wine, or eats onions or garlic . . . they do not keep pigs or fowls; there are no dealings in cattle, no butchers' shops or distilleries in their market-places.'

The Chandālas or outcastes, who did not observe the rules of purity, were obliged to live apart, and were required when entering a town or bazaar to strike a piece of wood as a warning of their approach, in order that other folk might not be polluted by contact with them.

Those observations prove that a great change had occurred in the manners of the people and the attitude of the government since the time of the Mauryas. The people of Taxila had had no scruple in supplying Alexander with herds of fat beasts fit for the butcher; even Asoka did not definitely forbid the slaughter of kine; while the *Arthasāstra* not only treated the liquor trade as a legitimate source of revenue, but directed that public-houses should be made attractive to customers. Fa-hien's statements may be, and probably are, expressed in terms too comprehensive, and without the necessary qualifications. Sacrifice, for instance, must have been practised by many Brahmanical Hindus. It is hardly credible that in A. D. 400, 'throughout the whole country', nobody except the lowest outcastes would kill any living thing, drink strong liquor, or eat onions or garlic.[1] But Fa-hien's testimony may be accepted as proving that the *ahimsā* sentiment was extraordinarily strong in 'Mid-India' when he resided there. Evidently it was far more generally accepted than it is at the present day, when Buddhism has been long extinct. The pilgrim's statements, no doubt, apply primarily to the Buddhists, who seem to have been then the majority. The traveller's account of the precautions enforced on Chandāla outcastes in order to protect caste people from defilement may be illustrated by modern descriptions of the customs prevalent either now or not long ago in the extreme south of the peninsula; but it is not applicable to northern India in recent times; nor, so far as I know, can similar evidence for that region be quoted from any other author for any age. That remark does not imply disbelief of Fa-hien's positive statement on the subject. It merely means that the extreme rigour of caste rules directed against the possibility of personal pollution as described by the pilgrim has ceased to be observed in northern India for many centuries.

Good government. Fa-hien's incidental observations taken as a whole indicate that the Gupta empire at the beginning of the fifth century was well governed. The government let the people

[1] The assertion in the same chap. xvi that 'in buying and selling they use cowries' must not be pressed to mean that coins were unknown. Chandragupta II coined freely in gold, and more sparingly in silver and copper.

live their own lives without needless interference; was temperate in the repression of crime, and tolerant in matters of religion. The foreign pilgrim was able to pursue his studies in peace wherever he chose to reside, and could travel all over India without molestation. He makes no mention of any adventures with robbers, and when he ultimately returned home he carried to his native land his collections of manuscripts, images, and paintings. Many other Chinese pilgrims followed his example, the most illustrious being Hiuen Tsang or Yuan Chwang in the seventh century.

Kumāragupta I. In A.D. 413 Chandragupta II was succeeded by a son named Kumāragupta who ruled the empire for more than forty years. Details of the events of his reign are not on record, but it is probable that he added to his inherited dominions, because he is known to have celebrated the horse-sacrifice, which he would not have ventured to do unless he had gained military successes.

Coin of Kumāragupta I.

Skandagupta, the last great Gupta. He died early in A.D. 455, when the sceptre passed into the hands of his son Skandagupta. In the latter part of Kumāragupta's reign the empire had been attacked by a tribe or nation called Pushyamitra, perhaps Iranians, who were repulsed. Soon after the accession of Skandagupta a horde of Hūnas, or Huns, fierce nomads from Central Asia, made a more formidable inroad, which, too, was successfully repelled. But fresh waves of invaders arrived and shattered the fabric of the Gupta empire. The dynasty was not destroyed. It continued to rule diminished dominions with reduced power for several generations. Skandagupta, however, was the last of the great imperial Guptas, as Aurangzēb Ālamgīr was the last of the Great Moguls.

The Gupta golden age. Before we deal more closely with the Hun invasions and their consequences we shall offer a summary review of the golden age of the Guptas, which may be reckoned as extending from A.D. 320 to 480, comprising the reigns of Chandragupta I; Samudragupta; Chandragupta II, Vikramāditya; Kumāragupta I; and Skandagupta, who followed his grandfather's example in taking the title Vikramāditya.

A learned European scholar declares that 'the Gupta period is in the annals of classical India almost what the Periclean age is in the history of Greece'. An Indian author regards the time as that of 'the Hindu Renaissance'. Both phrases are justified. The age of the great Gupta kings presents a more agreeable and satisfactory picture than any other period in the history of Hindu India. Fa-hien's testimony above quoted proves that the government was free from cruelty and was not debased by the horrible system of espionage advocated by Kautilya and actually practised by the Mauryas. Literature, art, and science flourished in a degree beyond the ordinary, and gradual changes in religion were effected without persecution. Those propositions will now be developed in some detail.

Hindu renaissance. The energetic and long continued zeal of Asoka probably succeeded in making Buddhism the religion of the majority of the people in northern India, during the latter part of his reign. But neither Brahmanical Hinduism or Jainism ever died out. The relative prevalence of each of the three religions varied immensely from time to time and from province to province. The Buddhist convictions of the Kushān kings, Kanishka and Huvishka, do not seem to have been deep. In fact, the personal faith of those monarchs apparently was a corrupt Zoroastrianism or Magism more than anything else. Their predecessor, Kadphises II, placed the image of Siva and his bull on his coins, a practice renewed by Huvishka's successor, Vāsudeva I. The Satraps of Ujjain, although tolerant of Buddhism, were themselves Brahmanical Hindus. The Gupta kings, while showing as a family preference for devotion to the Deity under the name of Vishnu or Bhagavata, allowed Buddhists and Jains perfect freedom of worship and full liberty to endow their sacred places. Although we moderns can discern from our distant point of view that the Hindu renaissance or reaction had begun the conquest of Buddhism in the fifth century,

LAURIYA-NANDANGARH PILLAR.

or even from an earlier date, Fa-hien was not conscious of the movement. India was simply the Buddhist Holy Land in his eyes, and the country in which the precepts of his religion were best observed.

Sanskrit. The growing power of the Brahmans, as compared with the gradually waning influence of the Jain and Buddhist churches, was closely associated with the increased use of Sanskrit, the sacred language of the Brahmans. Asoka never used Sanskrit officially. All his proclamations were composed and published in easily intelligible varieties of the vernacular tongue, and so were accessible to anybody who knew how to read. The Āndhra kings too used Prakrit. The earliest known inscriptions written in grammatical standard Sanskrit date from the time of Kanishka,

MONKEYS, AJANTĀ.

when we find a short record at Mathurā dated in the year 24 (= about A. D. 144), and a long literary composition at Girnār in Surāshtra, recorded about A. D. 152, which recites the conquests of the Great Satrap Rudradāman.

Literature ; Kālidāsa. The increasing use of Sanskrit is further marked by the legends of the Gupta coins, which are in that language, and by the development of Sanskrit literature of the highest quality. Critics are agreed that Kālidāsa surpasses all rivals writing in Sanskrit whether as dramatist or as poet. Something like general assent has been won to the proposition that the literary work of the most renowned of Indian poets was accomplished in the fifth century under the patronage of the Gupta kings. Good reason has been shown for believing that Kālidāsa was a native of Mandasōr in Mālwā (now in Sindia's dominions), or of some place in the immediate neighbourhood of that once famous town. He was thus brought up in close touch with the court of Ujjain, and the active commercial and intellectual life which centred in that capital of western India. His early descriptive poems, the *Ritusamhāra* and the *Meghadūta*, may be assigned to the reign of Chandragupta II, Vikramāditya, the conqueror of Ujjain, and his dramas to that of Kumāragupta I (A.D. 413–55); but it is probable that his true dates may be slightly later. *Sakuntalā,* the most famous of his plays, secured enthusiastic admiration from European critics the moment it was brought to their notice, and the poet's pre-eminence has never been questioned in either East or West.[1]

WOMAN AND CHILD, AJANTĀ.

Other literature. Good authorities are now disposed to assign the political drama entitled the 'Signet of the Minister' (*Mudrā Rākshasa*) to the reign of Chandragupta II, Vikramāditya; and the interesting play called 'The Little Clay Cart' (*Mrichchhaka-tikā*) may be a little earlier. The *Vāyu Purāna*, one of the most ancient of the existing Purānas, may be assigned to the first half of the fourth century in its present form. All the Purānas contain matter of various ages, some parts being extremely ancient; any date assigned to such a composition refers only to the final literary form of the work.

[1] For Kālidāsa's birthplace see M. M. Haraparshad Shastri in *J. B. & O. R. Soc.*, vol. i, pp. 197–212. I accept the continuous tradition that the *Ritusamhāra* is an early work of Kālidāsa.

COLUMN, GUPTA PERIOD.

The eminent Buddhist author, Vasubandhu, lived in the reigns of Chandragupta I and Samudragupta, dying in the third quarter of the fourth century. Samudragupta, while prince and passing under the name of Chandraprakāsa, was intimate with Vasubandhu, who attended his father's court.

Science. The sciences of mathematics and astronomy, including astrology, were cultivated with much success during the Gupta period. The most famous writers on those subjects are Āryabhata, born in A.D. 476, who taught the system studied at Pātaliputra, and including Greek elements; Varāhamihira (A.D. 505–87), who was deeply learned in Greek science and used many Greek technical terms; and, at the close of the period, Brahmagupta, who was born in A.D. 598.

Fine arts. The skill of Samudragupta in music has been recorded. We may be assured that the professors of that art, as the recipients of liberal royal patronage, were numerous and prosperous. The three closely allied arts of architecture, sculpture, and painting attained an extraordinarily high point of achievement. The accident that the Gupta empire consisted for the most part of the provinces permanently occupied at an early date by the Muhammadans, who systematically destroyed Hindu buildings for several centuries, obscures the history of Gupta architecture. No large building of the period has survived, and the smaller edifices which escaped destruction are hidden in remote localities away from the track of the Muslim armies, chiefly in Central India and the Central Provinces. They closely resemble rock-cut temples.

The most important and interesting extant stone temple of Gupta age is one of moderate dimensions at Dēogarh in the Lalitpur subdivision of the Jhānsi District, U.P., which may be assigned to the first half of the sixth, or perhaps to the fifth, century. The panels of the walls contain some of the finest specimens of Indian sculpture. The larger brick temple at Bhītargāon in the Cawnpore District, U.P., may be ascribed to the reign of Chandragupta II. It is remarkable for vigorous and well-designed sculpture in terra-cotta. Fragments, including some beautiful sculptures, indicate that magnificent stone temples of Gupta age stood at Sārnāth near Benares and elsewhere. Sārnāth has proved to be a treasure-house of Gupta figures and reliefs, among which are many of high quality dating from the time of Samudragupta and his successors. The Gupta artists and craftsmen were no less capable in working metals. The pillar at Delhi, made of wrought iron in the time of Samudragupta, is a marvel of metallurgical skill. The art of casting copper statues on a large scale by the *cire perdue* process was practised with conspicuous success. A copper image of Buddha about 80 feet high was erected at Nālandā in Bihār at the close of the sixth century ; and the fine Sultānganj Buddha, 7½ feet high, is still to be seen in the Museum at Birmingham. It dates from the reign of Chandragupta II. The highest development of the arts may be assigned to the fifth century, the age of Kālidāsa, in the reigns of Chandragupta II and his son. Two of the finest caves at Ajantā, Nos. XVI and XVII, were excavated in the same century of brilliant achievement.[1] It is needless to dwell upon the high merits of the paintings in the Ajantā caves, which are now freely recognized. A Danish artist, who has published a valuable professional criticism, declares that 'they represent the climax to which genuine Indian art has attained'; and that 'everything in these pictures from the composition as a whole to the smallest pearl

HIPPOGRYPH, GUPTA.

[1] *J. R. A. S.*, 1914, p. 335.

or flower testifies to depth of insight coupled with the greatest technical skill '.[1]

The closely related frescoes at Sīgiriya in Ceylon were executed between A.D. 479 and 497, just after the close of the reign of Skandagupta.

Hindu art at its best. The facts thus indicated in outline permit no doubt that the fine arts of music, architecture, sculpture, and painting attained a high level of excellence during the Gupta period, and more especially in the fifth century, which in my judgement was the time when Hindu art was at its best. The Gupta sculpture exhibits pleasing characteristics which usually enable a student familiar with standard examples to decide with confidence whether or not a given work is of Gupta age. The physical beauty of the figures, the gracious dignity of their attitude, and the refined restraint of the treatment are qualities not to be found elsewhere in Indian sculpture in the same degree. Certain more obvious technical marks are equally distinctive. Such are the plain robes showing the body as if they were transparent, the elaborate haloes, and the curious wigs. Others might be enumerated. Many of the sculptures are dated.

Exchange of ideas. The extraordinary intellectual vitality of the Gupta period undoubtedly was largely due to the constant and lively exchange of ideas with foreign lands in both East and West. Between A.D. 357 and 571 we read of ten embassies or missions, some probably only of a commercial character, which were sent to China from one part of India or the other. The stream of Buddhist pilgrims from the Celestial Empire, set in motion by Fa-hien, continued to flow, while, in return, another stream of Indian sages flowed to China. One of the earliest of such travellers was Kumārajīva in A.D. 383. Active communication between the Indian coasts and the islands of the Archipelago was maintained. The Chinese say that the conversion of the Javanese to Buddhism was effected by Gunavarman, Crown Prince of Kashmīr, who died at Nanking in China in A.D. 431. The Ajantā frescoes record intercourse between western India and Persia early in the seventh century. Three missions to Roman emperors in A.D. 336, 361, and 530 are mentioned. The coinage bears unmistakable testimony to the reality of Roman influence, and the word *dīnār*, the Latin *denarius*, was commonly used to mean a gold coin.

The conquest of western India by Chandragupta II at the close of the fourth century brought the Gangetic provinces into direct communication with the western ports, and so with Alexandria and Europe. Trade also followed the land routes through Persia. The effect of easy communication with Europe is plainly visible in the astronomy of Āryabhata and Varāhamihira, who must have known Greek. The belief of Windisch that the many striking resemblances in form between the classical Indian dramas and the plays of the school of Menander are not accidental rests on sub-

[1] *Ann. Rep. Archaeol. Dept. Nizam's Dom.*, for 1914–15, App. H, by Axel Jarl.

stantial arguments. The influence of Greek taste on the sculpture of the Gupta age, although necessarily less obvious, is not less certain. The works are truly Indian. They are not copies or even imitations of Greek originals, and yet manifest the Greek spirit, forming a charming combination of East and West, such as we see on a vast scale in the inimitable Tāj many centuries later. When the intercourse with Europe died away in the seventh century India developed new schools of sculpture in which no trace of foreign example can be detected. Some expert critics maintain that the works of the eighth century mark the highest achievement of Indian art; but those of the fifth century commend themselves, as already observed, to my taste, and appear to me to be on the whole superior to those of any other age.

The Huns. The meagre annals of the Gupta monarchs subsequent to Skandagupta present little matter of interest, and may be passed by with a mere allusion. But the nature of the foreign inroads which broke down the stately fabric of the Gupta empire demands explanation. The work of destruction was effected by hordes of nomads from Central Asia who swarmed across the north-western passes, as the Sakas and Yueh-chi had done in previous ages. The Indians generally spoke of all the later barbarians as Hūnas or Huns, but the Huns proper were accompanied by Gurjaras and other tribes. The section which encamped in the Oxus valley in the fifth century was distinguished as the White Huns or Ephthalites. They gradually occupied both Persia and Kābul, killing the Sassanian king Fīrōz in A.D. 484. Their first attack on the Gupta empire about A.D. 455 was repulsed, but the collapse of Persian resistance opened the flood-gates and allowed irresistible numbers to pour into India. Their leader, Toramāna, who was established in Mālwā in A.D. 499 or 500, was succeeded about A.D. 502 by his son Mihiragula ('Sun-flower'), whose Indian capital appears to have been Sākala or Siālkōt in the Panjāb.

Coin of Toramāna.

India at that time was only one province of the Hun empire which extended from Persia on the west to Khotan on the east, comprising forty provinces. The head-quarters of the horde were at Bāmyin near Herat, and the ancient city of Balkh served as a secondary capital. The power of Mihiragula in India was broken about A.D. 528 by Yasodharman, king of Mālwā, helped perhaps by the Gupta king of Magadha. Mihiragula retired to Kashmīr, where he seized the throne, and died. His history is obscured by fanciful legends.

Soon after the middle of the sixth century the Hun kingdom on the Oxus was overthrown by the Turks, who became masters of the greater part of the short-lived Hun empire.

A turning-point in history. The barbarian invasions of the fifth and sixth centuries, although slurred over by the Indian authorities, constitute a turning-point in the history of northern and western India, both political and social. The political system of the Gupta period was completely broken up, and new kingdoms were formed. No authentic family or clan traditions go back beyond the Hun invasions. All genuine tradition of the earlier dynasties has been absolutely lost. The history of the Mauryas, Kushāns, and Guptas, so far as it is known, has been recovered laboriously by the researches of scholars, without material help from living tradition.[1] The process by which the foreigners became Hinduized and the Rājpūt clans were formed will be discussed in the next chapter.

Valabhī and other kingdoms. When the Gupta power became restricted at the close of the fifth century western India gradually passed under the control of rulers belonging to a foreign tribe called Maitraka, possibly Iranian in origin. The Maitrakas established a dynasty with its capital at Valabhī (Walā, or Vala of *I. G.*, Wullubheepoor of the *Rās Mālā*), in the Surāshtra peninsula, which lasted until about 770, when it seems to have been overthrown by the Arabs. The names and dates of the long line of the kings of Valabhī, who used the Gupta era, are known with sufficient accuracy. The kingdom attained considerable wealth and importance. In the sixth century the capital was the residence of renowned Buddhist teachers, and in the seventh it rivalled Nālandā in Bihār as a centre of Buddhist learning. The modern town is insignificant and shows few signs of its ancient greatness.

After the overthrow of Valabhī its place as the chief city of western India was taken by Anhilwāra (Nahrwālah, &c., or Pātan), which in its turn was superseded in the fifteenth century by Ahmadābād.

The Gurjaras, who have been mentioned as associated with the Huns, founded kingdoms at Bharōch (Broach) and at Bhinmāl in southern Rājputāna.

The history of India during the sixth century is exceedingly obscure. The times evidently were much disturbed.

About the middle of that century a chief belonging to the Chalukya clan, which probably was connected with the Gurjaras and had emigrated from Rājputāna, founded a principality at Vātāpi, the modern Bādāmi in the Bījāpur District, Bombay, which developed into an important kingdom in the early years of the seventh century, and became for a time the leading power in the Deccan, which will be noticed more particularly in a later chapter.

Nothing definite of moment can be stated about the Tamil kingdoms of the Far South during the period dealt with in this chapter.

Ample material for seventh century. The embarrassing

[1] The Jain traditions of Samprati constitute a small exception to the statement in the text.

lack of material for the history of the latter half of the sixth century is no longer felt when the story of the seventh has to be told. The invaluable description of India recorded by Hiuen Tsang or Yuan Chwang, the eminent Chinese pilgrim; his biography written by his friends; the official Chinese historical works; and an historical romance composed by Bāna, a learned Brahman who enjoyed the friendship of King Harsha, when combined with a considerable amount of information derived from inscriptions, coins, and other sources, supply us with knowledge surpassing in fullness and precision that available for any other period of early Hindu history, except that of the Mauryas. Harsha of Kanauj, the able monarch who reduced anarchy to order in northern India, and reigned for forty-one years, as Asoka had done, is not merely a name in a genealogy. His personal characteristics and the details of his administration, as recorded by men who knew him intimately, enable us to realize him as a living person who achieved greatness by his capacity and energy.

King Harsha, A. D. 606–47. Harsha, or Harsha-vardhana, was the younger son of Prabhākara-vardhana, Rājā of Thānēsar, the famous holy town to the north of Delhi, who had won considerable military successes over his neighbours—the Gurjaras, Mālavas, and others, in the latter part of the sixth century. His unexpected death in A. D. 604 was quickly followed by that of his elder son, who was treacherously assassinated by Sasānka, king of Gaura, or Central Bengal. His younger son, Harsha, then only sixteen or seventeen years of age, was constrained by his nobles to accept the vacant throne, and to undertake the difficult task of bringing northern India into subjection and tolerable order. The young sovereign, who reluctantly accepted the trust imposed upon him in October 606, was obliged to spend five years and a half in constant fighting. The Chinese pilgrim who came to India a few years later tells us that during that strenuous time Harsha 'went from east to west subduing all who were not obedient; the elephants were not unharnessed, nor the soldiers unhelmeted'. His conquests were achieved with a force of 5,000 elephants, 20,000 cavalry, and 50,000 infantry. He seems to have discarded chariots. When he had finished his task the cavalry had increased to 100,000, and the elephants are said to have numbered 60,000, a figure hardly credible, and probably erroneous. Harsha's subjugation of upper India, excluding the Panjāb, but including Bihār and at least the greater part of Bengal, was completed in 612, when he appears to have been solemnly enthroned. But the new era established by him, which attained wide currency, was reckoned from the beginning of his reign in October 606. His last recorded campaign in 643 was directed against Ganjām on the coast of the Bay of Bengal. A few years earlier he had waged a successful war with Valabhī, which resulted in the recognition of Harsha's suzerainty by the western powers. In the east his name was so feared that even the king of distant Assam was obliged to obey his imperious commands and to attend his court.

WAXTYPE

GEORGE PHILIP & SON, LTD.

MAP OF INDIA, A. D. 640.

War with the Chalukyas. The Chalukya kingdom in the Deccan, founded, as has been mentioned, in the middle of the sixth century, was raised to a paramount position by its king, Pulakesin II, the contemporary of Harsha. The northern monarch, impatient of a rival, attacked Pulakesin about A. D. 620, but was defeated, and obliged to accept the Nārbadā as his southern frontier. So far as is known that defeat was Harsha's only failure. During the greater part of his reign, although his armies may have been given occupation from time to time, he was free to devote his exceptional powers to the work of administration and to consecrate an extraordinarily large share of his time to religious exercises and discussions.

Kanauj the capital. The ancient town of Kanauj (Kanyākubja) on the Ganges, which was selected by Harsha as his capital, was converted into a magnificent, wealthy, and well-fortified city, nearly four miles long and a mile broad, furnished with numerous lofty buildings, and adorned with many tanks and gardens. The Buddhist monasteries, of which only two had existed in the fifth century, numbered more than a hundred in Harsha's time, when Brahmanical temples existed in even larger numbers. The inhabitants were more or less equally divided in their allegiance to Hinduism and Buddhism. The city, after enduring many vicissitudes, was finally destroyed by Shēr Shāh in the sixteenth century. It is now represented by a petty Muhammadan country town and miles of shapeless mounds which serve as a quarry for railway ballast. No building erected in Harsha's reign can be identified either at Kanauj or elsewhere.

Administration ; literature. Harsha, who was only forty-seven or forty-eight years of age when he died late in A. D. 646 or early in 647, was in the prime of life throughout his long reign. We hear nothing of the elaborate bureaucratic system of the Mauryas, although an organized civil service must have existed. The king seems to have trusted chiefly to incessant personal supervision of his extensive empire, which he effected by constantly moving about, except in the rainy season when the roads were impassable. He marched in state to the music of golden drums, and was accommodated, like the Burmese kings of modern times, in temporary structures built of wood and bamboos, which were burnt on his departure. Many provinces were governed in detail by tributary Rājās. The Chinese pilgrim thought well of the royal administration, although it was less mild than that of the Guptas in the fifth century. The penalty of imprisonment, inflicted after the cruel Tibetan fashion, which left the prisoner to live or die, was freely awarded, and mutilation was often adjudged. The roads, apparently, were not as safe as they had been in the days of Vikramāditya. Official records of all events were kept up in each province by special officers. Education was widely diffused, and the great Buddhist monasteries at Nalāndā in Magadha and other places were centres of learning and the arts. The king himself was an accomplished scholar. He is credited with the composition of a grammatical work, sundry poems, and three extant Sanskrit plays, one of which, the *Nāgānanda*, with an edifying Buddhist legend for its subject, is highly esteemed and has been translated into English. A Brahman named Bāna, who was an intimate friend of the king, wrote an account of part of his master's reign in the form of an historical romance, which gives much accurate and valuable information wrapped up in tedious, affected rhetoric, as tiresome as that of Abu-l Fazl in the *Akbarnāma*.

Religion. Harsha, who was extremely devout, assigned many hours of each day to devotional exercises. Primarily a worshipper of Siva, he permitted himself also to honour the Sun and Buddha. In the latter part of his reign he became more and more Buddhist in sentiment, and apparently set himself the task of emulating Asoka. He 'sought to plant the tree of religious merit to such an extent that he forgot to sleep or eat'; and forbade the slaughter of any living thing or the use of flesh as food throughout the 'Five Indies', under pain of death without hope of pardon.

SIGNATURE OF HARSHA.

The details of his proceedings make interesting reading; indeed, the historical material is so abundant that it would be easy to write a large volume devoted solely to his reign. Hiuen Tsang or Yuan Chwang, the most renowned of the Chinese pilgrims, being our leading authority, it is desirable to give a brief account of his memorable career.

Hiuen Tsang or Yuan Chwang. He was the fourth son of a learned Chinese gentleman of honourable lineage, and from childhood was a grave and ardent student of things sacred. When he started on his travels at the age of twenty-nine (A.D. 629) he was already famous as a Buddhist sage. His intense desire to obtain access to the authentic scriptures in the Holy Land of India nerved him to defy the imperial prohibition of travelling westward, and sustained him through all the perils of his dangerous journey, which exceeded three thousand miles in length, as reckoned from his starting place in western China to Kābul, at the gates of India. The narrative of his adventures, which we possess in detail, is as interesting as a romance. The dauntless pilgrim travelled by the northern route, and after passing Lake Issik Kul, Tashkend, Samarkand, and Kunduz arrived in the kingdom of Gandhāra about the beginning of October 630. Between that date and the close of 643 he visited almost every province in India, recording numberless exact observations on the country, monuments, people, and religion, which entitle him to be called 'the Indian Pausanias'.[1]

He returned by the southern route, crossing the Pāmīrs, and passing Kāshgar, Yarkand, Khotan, and Lop-nor—a truly wonderful journey. Eight years, 635 to 643, had been mostly spent in Harsha's dominions. Early in 645 he reached his native land, bringing with him a large and valuable collection of manuscripts, images, and relics. He occupied the remainder of his life in working up the results of his expedition with the aid of a staff of scholars, and died in 664 at the age of sixty-four or sixty-five. His high character, undaunted courage, and profound learning deservedly won the respect and affection of the Chinese emperor and all his people. The memory of the Master of the Law, the title bestowed upon him by universal consent, is still as fresh in Buddhist lands as it was twelve hundred years ago.

It is impossible to overestimate the debt which the history of India owes to Hiuen Tsang.

Assemblies at Kanauj and Prayāg. King Harsha, who was in camp in Bengal when he first met the Master, organized in his honour a splendid assembly at Kanauj the capital, which was attended by twenty tributary Rājās, including the King of Assam from the extreme east, and the King of Valabhī from the extreme west. After the close of the proceedings at Kanauj, Harsha carried his honoured guest with him to Prayāg (Allahabad), where another crowded assembly was held, and the royal treasures were distributed to thousands of the holy men of all the Indian religions, Brahmanical, Jain, and Buddhist. On the first day the image of Buddha received honours of the highest class, the effigies of the Sun and Siva being worshipped respectively on the second and third days with reduced ceremonial. The assembly at Prayāg in 643 was the sixth of its kind, it being Harsha's custom to distribute his accumulated riches at intervals of five years. He did not live to see another celebration. The pilgrim was dismissed with all honour and presented with lavish gifts.

Death of Harsha; results. Either late in 646 or early in 647 the king died, leaving no heir. The withdrawal of his strong arm threw the whole country into disorder, which was aggravated by famine.

Then a strange incident happened. A Chinese envoy named Wang-hiuen-tse was at Harsha's court, attended by an escort of thirty men. A minister who had usurped the vacant throne attacked the envoy, plundered his goods, and killed or captured

[1] See map prepared by the author at the end of vol. ii of Watters, *On Yuan Chwang's Travels in India* (1905). For the benefit of readers unfamiliar with Greek history it may be mentioned that Pausanias travelled through Greece in the second century A.C. and recorded his detailed observations in the form of an *Itinerary* divided into ten books. The Chinese pilgrim's *Travels* or *Records of Western Lands* comprise 12 books (*chuan*); but the last three books, equivalent to chaps. xvi–xviii of Watters, seem to be interpolated and are of inferior authority (Watters, ii, 233).

the men of his escort. Wang-hiuen-tse succeeded in escaping to Nepāl, which was then tributary to Tibet. The Tibetan king, the famous Srong-tsan Gampo, who was married to a Chinese princess, assembled a force of Tibetans and Nepalese, who descended into the plains, stormed the chief city of Tirhūt, defeated the Indian army with great slaughter, and captured the usurper with his whole family. The captive was sent to China, where he died. Tirhūt remained subject to Tibet until A.D. 703.

The death of Harsha having loosened the bonds which had held his empire together, the experiences of the third and sixth centuries were repeated, and a rearrangement of kingdoms was begun, of which the record is obscure. It is impossible to say exactly what happened in most of the provinces for a considerable time after his disappearance from the scene.

His rival, Pulakesin II, Chalukya, who had successfully defended the Deccan against aggression from the north, had met his fate five years before Harsha's death. He was utterly defeated and presumably killed in 642 by Narasimha-varman, the Pallava king of Kānchī or Conjeeveram in the far south, who thus became the paramount sovereign of the peninsula. The story will be told from the southern point of view in a later chapter.

Unity of history lost. The partial unity of Indian history vanishes with Harsha and is not restored in any considerable measure until the closing years of the twelfth century, when the extensive conquests effected by and for Muhammad of Ghōr brought the most important provinces under the sway of the Sultans of Delhi. The story of Hindu India from the middle of the seventh century until the Muhammadan conquest, which may be dated approximately in A. D. 1200 for the north and A. D. 1300 for the south, cannot be presented in the form of a single continuous narrative. The subject will be treated in Book III.

CHRONOLOGY

A.D.	
320.	Chandragupta I, acc.; epoch of the Gupta era.
c. 330.	Samudragupta, acc.
c. 360.	Embassy from Meghavarna, king of Ceylon.
c. 375.	Chandragupta II, acc.
c. 395.	Conquest of western India.
405–11.	Travels of Fa-hien in Gupta empire.
413.	Kumāragupta I, acc.
448.	Establishment of Huns in Oxus basin, and epoch of Hun era.
455.	Skandagupta, acc.; first Hun war.
476.	Āryabhata, astronomer, born.
c. 480–90.	Partial break up of Gupta empire.
484.	Fīrōz, king of Persia, killed by the Huns.
c. 490–770.	Dynasty of Valabhī.
499.	Latest date of Budhagupta.
500.	Accession of Toramāna in Mālwā (coins dated 52, *scil.* of Hun era).

A. D.
502. Accession of Mihiragula in Mālwā.
505. Varāhamihira, astronomer, born.
c. 528. Defeat of Mihiragula, the Hun, by Indian powers.
542. Death of Mihiragula.
578. Brahmagupta, astronomer, born.
606. Harsha-vardhana, acc.; epoch of Harsha era.
606–12. Conquest of northern India by Harsha.
c. 620. Defeat of Harsha by Pulakesin II, Chalukya.
622. Flight of Muhammad to Medina; epoch of Hijrī era.
629–45. Travels of Hiuen Tsang (Yuan Chwang).
641. Arab conquest of Persia.
642. Defeat of Pulakesin II, Chalukya, by the Pallavas.
643. Harsha's assemblies at Kanauj and Prayāg.
645. Hiuen Tsang arrived in China.
647. Death of Harsha; usurpation by minister
664. Death of Hiuen Tsang.

AUTHORITIES

Most of the necessary references will be found in *E. H. I.*[3] (1914). A few others are given in the notes to the text. Gupta art has been dealt with by the author in a well-illustrated paper entitled 'Indian Sculpture of the Gupta Period, A. D. 300–650', published in *Ostasiatische Zeitung*, April–June, 1914, just before the war. The same subject is treated in the *Catalogue of the Museum of Archaeology at Sārnāth* by DAYA RAM SAHNI and J. PH. VOGEL (Calcutta, 1914); and in the *Reports* of the Archaeological Survey.

The B. M. *Catalogue* of the Coins of the Gupta Dynasties, &c., by JOHN ALLAN (London, 1914) supersedes earlier publications to a large extent.

The most important publication on the Ajantā paintings since *H. F. A.* (1911) is the atlas of plates entitled *Ajantā Frescoes*, with introductory essays, issued by the India Society (Oxford University Press, 1915).

Two important essays appear in the *Bhandarkar Commemoration Volume*, Poona, 1917. D. R. Bhandarkar in 'Vikrama Era' rejects the hypothesis (*ante*, p. 151) that the era was founded by Vikramāditya. It seems to have been called *Krita* originally.

Prof. K. B. Pathak in 'New Light on Gupta Era and Mihirakula' justifies his title. He shows sound reasons for believing that the establishment of the Hūnas in the Oxus basin (*ante*, p. 163) took place in A. D. 488, the epoch of the Hun era; that Toramāna became king of Mālwā in A. D. 500 (or late in A. D. 499); that he was succeeded in A. D. 502 by his son Mihiragula, who was born in A. D. 472 and died in A. D. 542, at the age of seventy. Those dates, which seem to be correct, have been inserted in the table. They rest mainly upon the evidence of Jain chronicles supported by certain inscriptions and coins. Pathak dates the *Meghadūta* of Kālidāsa (*ante*, p. 159) in the reign of Skandagupta. Mr. K. P. Jayaswal expounds other and less convincing theories in *Ind. Ant.*, 1917, pp. 145–53.

BOOK III

THE MEDIAEVAL HINDU KINGDOMS FROM THE DEATH OF HARSHA IN A.D. 647 TO THE MUHAMMADAN CONQUEST

CHAPTER 1

The transitional period ; Rājpūts ; the Himalayan kingdoms and their relations with Tibet and China.

A period of transition. The disorder following upon Harsha's death, in which the attack on the Chinese envoy with the consequent subjugation of Tirhūt by the Tibetans was an episode, lasted for a considerable number of years concerning which little is known. That time of confusion may be regarded conveniently for purposes of systematic study as forming the transition from Early to Mediaeval India, during which the hordes of foreign invaders were absorbed into the Hindu body politic and a new grouping of states was gradually evolved. The transitional period was marked by the development of the Rājpūt clans, never heard of in earlier times, which begin from the eighth century to play a conspicuous part in the history of northern and western India. They become so prominent that the centuries from the death of Harsha to the Muhammadan conquest of Hindostan, extending in round numbers from the middle of the seventh to the close of the twelfth century, might be called with propriety the Rājpūt Period. Nearly all the kingdoms were governed by families or clans which for ages past have been called collectively Rājpūts. That term, the most generally used, is sometimes replaced by Chhattrī, the vernacular equivalent of the Sanskrit Kshatriya, or by Thākur.

Origin of the Rājpūts. The term Rājpūt, as applied to a social group, has no concern with race, meaning descent or relationship by blood. It merely denotes a tribe, clan, sept, or caste of warlike habits, the members of which claimed aristocratic rank, and were treated by the Brahmans as representing the Kshatriyas of the old books. The huge group of Rājpūt clan-castes includes people of the most diverse descent. Many of the clans are descended from the foreigners who entered India during the fifth and sixth centuries, while many others are descended from indigenous tribes now represented, so far as the majority of their members is concerned, either by semi-Hinduized peoples or by inferior castes.

Probably it would be safe to affirm that all the most distinguished clan-castes of Rājputāna or Rājasthān are descended mainly from foreigners, the ' Scythians ' of Tod. The upper ranks of the invading hordes of Hūnas, Gurjaras, Maitrakas, and the rest became Rājpūt clans, while the lower developed into Hindu castes of less honourable social status, such as Gūjars, Āhīrs, Jāts, and others.

Such clan-castes of foreign descent are the proud and chivalrous Sīsōdias or Guhilōts of Mewār, the Parihārs (Pratihāras), the Chauhāns (Chāhumānas), the Pawārs (Pramāras), and the Solankis, otherwise called Chaulukyas or Chalukyas.[1]

The Rāshtrakūtas of the Deccan; the Rāthors of Rājputāna, whose name is only a vernacular form of the same designation; the Chandēls and the Bundēlas of Bundēlkhand, are examples of ennobled indigenous peoples. The Chandēls evidently originated from among the Gonds, who again were closely associated with the Bhars. It is impossible to pursue further the subject, which admits of endless illustration.

Brahmans and Kshatriyas. In ancient times the line of demarcation between the Brahmans and the Kshatriyas, that is to say, between the learned and the warrior groups of castes, was not sharply defined. It was often crossed, sometimes by change of occupation, and at other times by intermarriage. Ordinarily, the position of the leading Brahman at court was that of minister, but sometimes the Brahman preferred to rule directly, and himself seized the throne. Thus in early times the Sunga and Kānva royal families were Brahman. Similar cases of Brahman dynasties occur later. In the seventh century Hiuen Tsang noted the existence of several Brahman Rājās, as at Ujjain and in Jijhoti or Bundēlkhand. Usurpations by Brahman ministers also continued to happen. When a Brahman succeeded in founding a dynasty, and so definitely taking up Kshatriya work, his descendants were recognized as Kshatriyas, and allowed to intermarry freely with established Kshatriya families. It must be remembered that the Brahmans themselves are of very diverse origin, and that many of them, as for instance the Nāgar Brahmans, are descended from the learned or priestly class of the foreign hordes. The Maga Brahmans were originally Iranian Magi. During the transitional stage, while a Brahman family was passing into the Kshatriya group of castes, it was often known by the composite designation of Brahma-kshatri. Several cases of the application of that term to royal families are recorded, the most prominent being those of the Sīsōdias of Mewār and the Sēnas of Bengal.

Rājpūts not a race. The Rājpūts, as already stated, are not to be regarded as a people originally of one race, bound together by ties of blood descent from a common ancestor. Even within

[1] Pandit Mohanlāl Vishnulāl Pandia admits that Bāpa, the Guhilōt ancestor, was brought up as a concealed or reputed Brahman (*J. & Proc. A. S. B.*, 1912, pp. 62–99), and has not succeeded in refuting the reasoning of D. R. Bhandarkar concerning the origin of the Rānās of Mewār. If the frank statement of facts as revealed by modern research should give offence in any quarter that result is to be regretted. But, as Asoka observed long ago, 'truth must be spoken'.

the limits of Rājputāna the clans were originally descended from many distinct racial stocks. Such common features as they presented depended on the similarity of their warlike occupations and social habits. Now, of course, the operation of complicated caste rules concerning intermarriage during many centuries has produced an extensive network of blood-relationship between the clans, which have become castes.

Those condensed observations may help the student to understand in some measure why the Rājpūt clans begin to play so prominent a part in Indian history from the eighth century. The Hun invasions and their consequences, as observed in the chapter preceding, broke the chain of historical tradition. Living clan traditions rarely, if ever, go back beyond the eighth century, and few go back as far. The existing clan-castes only began to be formed in the sixth century. The Brahmans found their advantage in treating the new aristocracy, whatever its racial origin, as representing the ancient Kshatriya class of the scriptures, and the novel term Rāja-putra or Rājpūt, meaning 'king's son', or member of a ruling family or clan, came into use as an equivalent of Kshatriya.

Before entering upon a summary review of outstanding features in the history of the leading Rājpūt kingdoms of the plains, we must bestow a passing glance on the Himalayan States—Nepāl, Kashmīr, and Assam—and on their relations with Tibet and China.

China and the Indian border. The short-lived Hun empire was broken up by the Western Turks, who in their turn succumbed to the Chinese. For a few years, from 661 to 665, China enjoyed unparalleled prestige. Kāfiristān (Kapisa or Ki-pin) was a province of the empire, and the ambassadors in attendance at the imperial court included envoys from the Suwāt valley and from all the countries extending from Persia to Korea. Such glory did not last long. In 670 the Tibetans occupied Kashgaria, and a little later the Turks regained power. In the first half of the eighth century an ambitious emperor, Hiuen-tsung, succeeded in once more establishing Chinese rule over the western countries. Even kings of Kashmīr then received investiture from China. The advance of the Arabs in the middle of the eighth century put an end to Chinese claims to sovereignty over the mountains of Kashmīr, and since that time no state of the Indian borderland, except Nepāl, has had political relations with China.

Tibet; Srong-tsan Gampo. In the seventh and eighth centuries Tibet was a powerful state, in close touch with India as well as with China. The routes from China through Lhāsa and Nepāl into India now closed were then open and frequently used by pilgrims and other travellers. Srong-tsan Gampo, the most renowned of Tibetan kings, whose long reign is placed by the best authorities between A.D. 630 and 698, annexed Nepāl, defeated the usurper who had dared to occupy the throne vacated by Harsha, occupied Tirhūt, and strengthened his position by marrying a Chinese princess as well as a Nepalese one. Acting under the influence of his Buddhist consorts he introduced their religion into his kingdom, and gave his people the means of acquiring knowledge by borrowing the Khotanese alphabet, originally imported from India. He founded Lhāsa, for which, according to tradition, he prepared the site by filling up a lake with stones.

In the first half of the eleventh century Atīsa and other eminent monks from the seats of learning in Magadha came to Tibet on the invitation of the reigning king and effected extensive reforms or changes in the Buddhist church, which became the foundation of modern Lamaism.

'The object of all these reformations was not, as is often supposed, to go back to the early Buddhism as it was preached by Gautama, but to build up a church which represented the doctrines of the Mahāyāna school of Buddhism in a pure form. The doctrines of Nāgārjuna were propounded by all the great teachers of Tibet. But the Kāla-chakra philosophy with its monotheistic tendencies was also favoured by them.'[1]

Nepāl. The kingdom of Nepāl as at present constituted is an extensive territory lying along the northern frontier of British India for about five hundred miles from Kumaon on the west to Sikkim on the east. The Nepāl of ancient Indian history means the restricted valley about twenty miles long and fifteen broad, in which the capital, Kāthmandu, and other towns are situated. Some of the adjoining country may have been included at times in the kingdom, but the bulk of the territory now comprised in the Nepāl state, whether in the hills or the strip of plain at their base, used to be occupied by independent tribes and principalities.

Gūrkha Coin.

The valley certainly formed part of Asoka's empire, but the Kushāns do not seem to have meddled with it. In the fourth century A.C. Nepāl acknowledged in some degree the sovereignty of Samudragupta. In the seventh century the influence of Tibet was paramount, and after Harsha's death the country became actually subject to Tibet for half a century.[2] Harsha apparently

[1] A. H. Francke, *Antiquities of Indian Tibet* (Calcutta, 1914), p. 52. For the Kāla-chakra and other late corrupt forms of Buddhism see the excellent little book by Nagendra Nath Vasu and M. M. H. P. Sastri, entitled *Modern Buddhism and its Followers in Orissa* (Calcutta, 1911).

[2] In A. D. 703 both Nepāl and India [*scil.* Tirhūt] threw off the Tibetan sovereignty. The king of Tibet was killed while attempting to reassert his authority (Parker, 'China, Nepaul, &c.' in *J. Manchester Oriental Soc.*, 1911, pp. 129–52). That date, recorded in the histories of the T'ang dynasty, was not known to earlier European writers.

had exercised some authority in Nepāl, as his era became current there. The Gūrkhas who now rule Nepāl conquered the country in 1768. The foreign policy of the state is controlled by the government of India, although China from time to time has asserted claims to tribute. The long and blood-stained story of the mediaeval dynasties is not of general interest, and may be left to students specially concerned with the local history.

Modern students of Nepalese affairs have been chiefly interested in the silent conflict of religions which has gone on for centuries and still may be watched in progress. A corrupt form of Buddhism, which allows even the strange institution of married monks, may be seen slowly decaying and yielding to the constant pressure of Brahmanical Hinduism, which is the religion of the government. The Nepalese libraries contain a rich store of Buddhist manuscripts, first made known by the labours of Brian Hodgson between 1820 and 1858, which have supplied much material for the study of the various forms of Buddhist religion and philosophy.

The general current of Indian history has not been affected by the transactions in Nepāl, which usually has remained isolated. The existing government discourages foreign visitors, and guards the passes so strictly that very little is known about the greater part of the area of the state.

Art. The art of Nepāl is closely related to that of Tibet. The craftsmen of both countries excel in metal-work, and the Tibetan artists have been eminently successful in producing realistic portrait statuettes of Buddhist saints and similar images of deities belonging to the populous pantheon of later Buddhism. Some of the Tibetan painting has considerable merit. The architecture of Nepāl in modern times is usually copied from Chinese models.

Kashmīr. The history of Hindu Kashmīr, from the seventh century after Christ, when the trustworthy annals begin, is recorded in ample detail in the metrical chronicle called the *Rājataranginī*, written in the twelfth century by a learned Brahman named Kalhana or Kalyāna, which has been admirably edited and translated by Sir M. A. Stein. The story, although of much interest in itself, has little concern with the general history of India; the reason being that the mountain barriers which enclose the vale of Kashmīr have usually sufficed to protect the country against foreign invasion and to preserve its isolated independence. Nevertheless, both the Mauryas and the Kushāns exercised effective authority over the valley. The Guptas did not concern themselves with it, and Harsha, while in a position to bring pressure to bear upon the Rājā, did not attempt to annex the country.

The narrative of the doings of the mediaeval Hindu rulers teems with horrors. Harsha, a half-insane tyrant who reigned in the latter part of the eleventh century, has been justly described as the 'Nero of Kashmīr'. Few regions in the world can have had worse luck than Kashmīr in the matter of government, a fate due partly to the cowardly character of the population, which invited oppression. The avowed policy of the Hindu rulers throughout the ages was to fleece the peasantry to the utmost and to leave them at best a bare subsistence. The majority of the people was forced to accept Islām in the fourteenth century, and dynasties of Muhammadan Sultans ruled until Akbar annexed the kingdom in 1587 with little difficulty. The lot of the common

TIBETAN BRONZE.

people continued to be hard, whether the government was in the hands of Hindus or Musalmans. In modern times the Kashmīrīs were oppressed successively by the Afghans and the Sikhs, and never enjoyed the advantages of decently good administration until late in the nineteenth century.

But, although Kashmīr has ordinarily occupied a position politically isolated from India, the influence of the country on the religion and civilization of its neighbours has been considerable. The valley has been the abode of Sanskrit learning at least from the time of Asoka, and has played an important part as being the intermediate stage through which Indian civilization and art reached Khotan and the adjoining territories of Chinese Turkistan, and so passed into the Far East. The valley includes many sacred sites both Buddhist and Brahmanical. Jainism does not seem to have entered it. An interesting local style of architecture was

MĀRTAND TEMPLE.

developed in the eighth and ninth centuries. The Mārtand temple dedicated to the Sun-god in the reign of Lalitāditya (A.D. 724–60) is the best-known example, but many others exist.

Assam. Assam, roughly equivalent to the ancient Kāmarūpa, resembled Kashmīr in being protected by natural fortifications, and thus enabled, as a rule, to preserve its independence. The country does not seem to have been included in either the Maurya or the Kushān empire, but in the fourth century, its ruler, who belonged to an ancient Hindu dynasty, acknowledged in some degree the overlordship of Samudragupta. Buddhism never succeeded in establishing itself. Nevertheless, the ruling king in the seventh century insisted on receiving a visit from Hiuen

Tsang, the Chinese Buddhist pilgrim, who was hospitably entertained. The king, although not directly subject to Harsha, was constrained to obey his imperious commands and to attend humbly in his train when summoned. Certain Muhammadan leaders who invaded the country on several occasions between 1205 and 1662 always met with disaster more or less complete. The Muslim historian who describes the latest venture, that made by Aurangzēb's general Mīr Jumla in the seventeenth century, expresses the horror with which the country and people were regarded by outsiders in striking phrases which deserve quotation.

'Assam', he observes, 'is a wild and dreadful country abounding in danger. . . . Its roads are frightful like the path leading to the nook of Death ;

Fatal to life is its expanse like the unpeopled city of Destruction. . . .

The air and water of the hills are like the destructive Simoom and deadly poison to natives and strangers alike.'

The inhabitants 'resemble men in nothing beyond this, that they walk

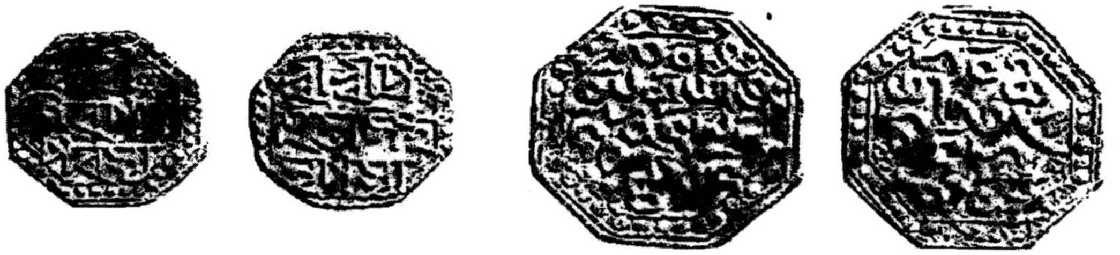

Āhōm Coins.

erect on two feet'. They were reputed to be expert magicians. 'In short, every army that entered the limits of this country made its exit from the realm of Life ; every caravan that set foot on this land deposited its baggage of residence in the halting-place of Death.'[1]

Early in the thirteenth century Assam was invaded by the Āhōms, a Shan tribe from Upper Burma, who gradually acquired the sovereignty of the country, which they retained until it was occupied by the Burmese in 1816 and by the British in 1825. The Āhōms brought with them a tribal religion of their own, which they abandoned in favour of Hinduism about the beginning of the eighteenth century. Their language, too, is almost, if not completely, extinct. The Āhōms have become merged in the Hindu population, and speak Assamese, an Aryan language akin to Sanskrit and Bengali. When in power they had an efficient, although severe or even cruel, system of administration. They produced a considerable historical literature, and carried the art of carving wood to a high degree of excellence. The Muslim writer quoted expresses unbounded admiration of the decorations of the palace at Garhgāon. No trace of them remains.

[1] Talish, as transl. by Prof. Jadunath Sarkar in *J. B. & O. Res. Soc.*, vol. i, pp. 179–95.

Assam is a province of much interest to the student of Indian religion as being the meeting ground of Mongolian and Indian ideas. The contact has resulted in the evolution of a peculiar Tantric form of Hinduism, which offers special honour to female forms of the deity called Saktis. The temple of Kāmākhyā near Gauhātī is recognized as one of the most important shrines of the cult. All the processes by means of which the members of rude animistic tribes become fanatical Hindus, and strange tribal gods are converted into respectable Brahmanical deities, may be illustrated in Assam.

CHRONOLOGY

(Miscellaneous Dates)

A. D.	
630.	Srong-tsan Gampo, king of Tibet, acc.
639.	Srong-tsan Gampo founded Lhāsa.
641.	Srong-tsan Gampo married Chinese and Nepalese princesses.
643.	Hiuen Tsang visited Kāmarūpa.
647.	Death of Harsha of Kanauj.
661–5.	Chinese supremacy over Kapisa.
670.	Tibetans wrested Kashgaria or Chinese Turkistan from China.
703.	Nepāl and Tirhūt became independent of Tibet.
713.	Hiuen-tsung, Chinese emperor, acc.
720, 733.	Kings of Kashmīr received investiture from China.
751.	Chinese defeated by the Arabs.
1038.	Mission of Atīsa to Tibet (Waddell, *Lhāsa*[3], p. 320).
1089–1111.	Harsha, king of Kashmīr.
1339.	Muhammadan dynasty established in Kashmīr.
1587.	Annexation of Kashmīr by Akbar.
1768.	Gūrkha conquest of Nepāl.

Authorities

The authorities are indicated sufficiently in the foot-notes and in *E. H. I.*[3] (1914). The learned and beautiful book entitled *The Gods of Northern Buddhism*, by Alice Getty and J. Deniker (Clarendon Press, 1914), is a treasury of Tibetan art and mythology.

CHAPTER 2

The northern and western kingdoms of the plains.

Countless kingdoms. During the five and a half centuries intervening between the death of Harsha and the Muhammadan conquest, in which no permanent foreign occupation was effected, except in the Panjāb, the greater part of India was indifferent to the Muhammadan power and knew nothing about it. The countless Hindu states, which took shape from time to time, varying continually in number, extent, and in their relations one with the other, seldom were at peace. It would, however, be a mistake to suppose that their rulers and people thought of nothing else than war and rapine. Royal courts of no small magnificence were maintained, and the arts of peace were cultivated with success.

Stately works of architecture, enriched lavishly with sculptures often of high merit, were erected in almost every kingdom; and learned men, writing for the most part in the Sanskrit language, enjoyed liberal and intelligent patronage from princes who not unfrequently wielded the pen as well as the sword. Hindī, Bengālī, Gujarātī, and the other languages now spoken gradually attained the dignity of recognized existence, and the foundations of vernacular literatures were laid.

In a general history it is impossible to narrate in detail the stories of the several states, which are recorded in many cases with so much fullness that they would suffice to fill several volumes each as large as this work.

The effects of the great foreign invasions in the fifth and sixth centuries lasted for hundreds of years. The Gurjaras, with their kinsmen and allies bearing other names, had been converted, as has been shown, into ruling Rājpūt clans, and had acquired a dominant position in Rājputāna, which served as the basis of more extended dominion. In the ninth and tenth centuries the Gurjara-Pratihāras (Parihārs) became the leading power in north-western India. Bengal came under the sway of the Pālas, apparently an indigenous dynasty, for more than four centuries; while Mālwā, Gujarāt, and several other kingdoms obtained a large share of wealth and power.

The course of history. The history of northern India ordinarily pursued its own course, regardless of the events happening in the peninsular kingdoms. But occasionally the rulers of the Deccan made inroads into the rich plains of Āryāvarta or Hindostan, which resulted in the temporary extension of their power to the banks of the Ganges. No northern prince attempted to conquer the Deccan. The Tamil realms of the Far South formed a world of their own, its isolation being complete, save for frequent wars with the kings of the Deccan and Ceylon and for extensive foreign trade.

The ancient states of the Pāndyas, Cholas, and Cheras were overshadowed for a long time, especially in the seventh century, by the Pallava dynasty of uncertain origin, which had its capital at Kānchī (Conjeeveram). In the eleventh century the Chola kingdom became paramount in the south, and probably was the most powerful state in India.

Changes so extensive, disconnected, and incessant as those indicated cannot be described in a single continuous narrative arranged in strict chronological order. The political revolutions were accompanied by silent local modifications in religion, manners, and art equally incapable of comprehensive narration.

The never-ending dynastic wars and revolutions did not bring about any development of political institutions. No republics were formed, no free towns were established. All the states continued to be governed in the old-fashioned way by despotic Rājās, each of whom could do what he pleased, so long as his power lasted, unless he suffered his will to be controlled by Brahman or other religious guides.

Lack of unity. It will be convenient to deal in this chapter only with certain outstanding features in the history of some of the more prominent northern and western kingdoms of the plains. The fortune of the peninsular states will similarly form the subject of the chapter following; the few points of contact between the two being duly noted.

The lack of unity in the subject-matter involves the same defect in its treatment by the historian. The facts which make India one in a certain sense, as explained in the Introduction to this work, are not capable by themselves of securing the political unity of all the Indian diverse races and creeds under one government. The confused picture drawn in outline in these chapters is a faithful representation of the normal condition of India when left to her own devices. Even now, in the twentieth century, she would relapse quickly into that condition, if the firm, although mild control exercised by the paramount power should be withdrawn.

Gurjara-Pratihāra kingdom. The Gurjaras, aided by the allied or kindred tribes bearing other names who entered India in the early years of the sixth century, established kingdoms or principalities in various places. The state among those so founded that was most closely associated with the general history of India was the Gurjara kingdom of southern Rājputāna, the capital of which was Bhinmāl or Bhilmāl to the north-west of Mount Ābū, the site of the fire-pit from which the Parihārs and several other Rājpūt clans originated according to the legend. When Hiuen Tsang visited that Gurjara kingdom in the first half of the seventh century the king, although undoubtedly of foreign descent, was already recognized as a Kshatriya.

About A. D. 725 a new local dynasty was founded by a chief named Nāgabhata, who belonged to the Parihār (Pratihāra) section or sept of the Gurjaras. Nearly a century later, in or about A. D. 816, his descendant, another Nāgabhata, invaded the Gangetic region, captured Kanauj, deposed the reigning king, and presumably transferred the seat of his own government from Bhilmāl to the imperial city of Harsha, where his descendants certainly ruled for many generations. The Parihārs remained in possession for two centuries until 1018–19 when Sultān Mahmūd of Ghaznī occupied Kanauj and forced the Rājā to retire to Bārī.

Kanauj. Kanauj must have suffered much during the long-continued troubles which ensued on the decease of Harsha. Nothing definite is known about it until 731 when its king, Yasovarman by name, sent an embassy to China, probably to invoke the assistance of the emperor against the Rājā's powerful enemies. No help came. In or about 740 Yasovarman was defeated and slain by Lalitāditya, the most renowned of the kings of Kashmīr, the builder of the Mārtand temple. Yasovarman's successor similarly was overthrown by Lalitāditya's son. Again, about 810, Dharmapāla, king of Bengal, deposed the reigning king of Kanauj, replacing him by a nominee of his own. That nominee in his turn was expelled, as related above, by Nāgabhata Parihār of Bhinmāl. Thus, within a space of about seventy-six years (c. A. D. 740–816), four kings of Kanauj were violently deposed by hostile powers. The fact illustrates vividly the disturbed condition of northern India in that age.

The Gurjara empire of Bhoja. King Mihira Parihār of Kanauj, commonly known by his cognomen of Bhoja, reigned with great power and might for half a century (c. A. D. 840–90). His successors being known to have held both Saurāshtra and Oudh, those countries may be assumed to have formed part of Bhoja's dominions,

A TIBETAN BRONZE; KUVERA AND SAKTI.

which were extensive enough to be described as an empire without exaggeration. Its limits may be defined as, on the north, the foot of the mountains; on the north-west, the Sutlaj; on the west, the Hakrā, or 'lost river', forming the boundary of Sind, and then the Mihrān to the Arabian Sea; on the south, the Jumna, forming the frontier of Jejāka-bhukti; on the south-west, the lower course of the Narbadā; and on the east, the frontier of the Pāla kingdom of Magadha. His son, Mahendra-pāla (c. A. D. 890–908), seems to have retained possession of all the dominions of his father. An inscription of his which mentions the province and district of Srāvastī suggests that that famous city was still inhabited in the tenth century. Magadha or South Bihār seems to have been tributary for a short time.

Hardly anything is known about the internal condition of the transitory Gurjara or Parihār empire of Kanauj. An Arab traveller tells us that in the middle of the ninth century the king, namely Bhoja, commanded a powerful army, including the best cavalry in India and a large force of camels. The territories in Rājputāna have always been famous for their breed of camels, which is still maintained. The Mahārājā of Bīkanēr's camel-corps has played an honourable part in the Great War. The extreme mobility of Bhoja's cavalry and camelry must have given him an immense advantage over the less active armies of the ordinary Hindu state. The king was extremely rich, and 'no country in India was more safe from robbers', a brief remark which implies the existence of efficient internal administration.

Bhoja was a Hindu specially devoted to the worship of Vishnu in the boar incarnation and of the goddess Bhagavatī or Lakshmī. He placed on his coins, which are very common, the words *Ādi Varāha*, meaning 'primaeval boar' or Vishnu. The coins, like the other issues of the White Hun and Gurjara princes, are degenerate imitations of Sassanian pieces, with reminiscences of the Greek drachma, the name of which survived in the word *dramma* applied to the Gurjara coins. The foreign invaders of India in those times never took the trouble to devise coin types of their own and were content to use barbarous and degraded derivatives of the Persian coinage.

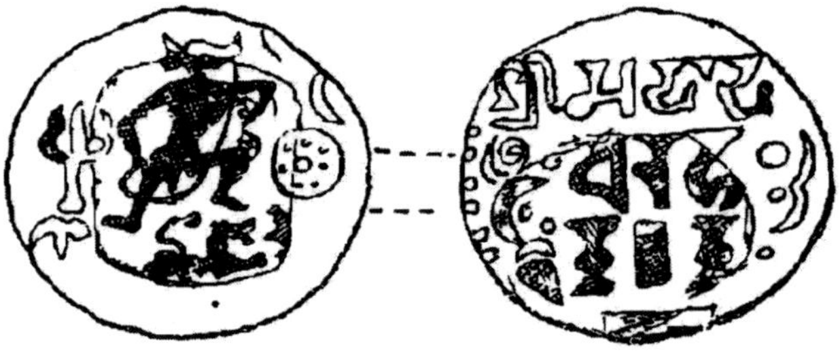

Coin of Ādi Varāha (Bhoja).

Rājasekhara. Mahendrapāla, the son and successor of Bhoja, was the pupil of Rājasekhara, a poet from the Deccan who attended his court and was the author of four extant plays. One of those, entitled *Karpūra-manjarī* from the name of the heroine, is a curious and interesting work, written wholly in Prākrit. Professor Lanman has published a clever English translation of it. The dramatist also composed a work on the art of poetry, which has been edited in the Gaikwār's *Oriental Series*.

Before we proceed to describe the decline and fall of the Gurjara empire and the capture of Kanauj by Sultan Mahmūd of Ghaznī in 1018–19, it will be convenient to give a brief account of the Pāla dynasty of Bengal and the Chandēl rulers of Jijhoti or Bundēlkhand, the two leading kingdoms of northern India which were contemporary with the Gurjara kingdom or empire of Kanauj; adding a slight notice of other states.

Bengal; Ādisūra. The history of Bengal and Bihār after the decease of Harsha is obscure. The rulers of part of Magadha or

South Bihār in the latter part of the seventh century were members of the imperial Gupta family, who had as neighbours in another section of the province Rājās belonging to a clan called Maukhari.

Bengal tradition has much to say about a king named Ādisūra, who ruled at Gaur or Lakshmanāvatī, and sought to revive the Brahmanical religion which had suffered from Buddhist predominance. He is believed to have imported five Brahmans from Kanauj, who taught orthodox Hinduism and became the ancestors of the Rādhiya and Vārendra Brahmans. His date may be placed in or after A. D. 700.

The Pāla dynasty; Dharmapāla. Then Bengal suffered from prolonged anarchy which became so intolerable that the people (*c.* A. D. 750) elected as their king one Gopāla, of the 'race of the sea', in order to introduce settled government. We do not know the details of the events thus indicated. Gopāla's son, Dharmapāla, who enjoyed an unusually long reign, was the real founder of the greatness of his dynasty, which is conveniently known as that of the 'Pāla Kings' of Bengal, because the names of the sovereigns ended in the word *-pāla*. Dharmapāla succeeded in carrying his arms far beyond the limits of Bengal and Bihār. He made himself master of most of northern India, and, as already mentioned, was strong enough to depose one Rājā of Kanauj and substitute another in his place. He is said to have effected the revolution with the assent of nine northern kings, whose designations indicate that the influence of the Bengal monarch extended even to Gandhāra on the north-western frontier. Those events must have happened about or soon after A. D. 810.

SCULPTURE, PĀLA PERIOD.

Dharmapāla, like all the members of his house, was a zealous Buddhist. He founded the famous monastery and college of Vikramasīlā, which probably stood at Pattharghāta in the Bhāgalpur District. The Buddhism of the Pālas was very different from the religion or philosophy taught by Gautama, and was a corrupt form of Mahāyāna doctrine.

Devapāla. Dharmapāla's son Devapāla, who is reckoned by Bengal tradition to have been the most powerful of the Pālas, also enjoyed a long reign. His rule and that of his father together covered something like a hundred years, and may be taken as having extended through almost the whole of the ninth century. Devapāla's general, Lāusena or Lavasena, is said to have annexed both Assam and Kalinga. No buildings of Pāla age seem to have survived, but the remembrance of the kings is preserved by many great tanks or artificial lakes excavated under their orders, especially in the Dinājpur District. Sculpture in both stone and metal was practised with remarkable success. The names of two eminent artists, Dhīmān and Bitpālo or Vītapāla, are recorded, and it is possible that some of the numerous extant works may be attributed rightly to them.

Mahīpāla, &c.; the Sēnas. The popular memory has attached itself to Mahīpāla, the ninth king of the dynasty (c. A.D. 978–1030), more than to any other. He reigned for about half a century and underwent the strange experience of being attacked about A.D. 1023 by Rājendra Chola, the Tamil king of the Far South, who prided himself on having advanced as far as the bank of the Ganges. The mission of Atīsa to Tibet, as already mentioned, was dispatched in A.D. 1038, in the reign of Nayapāla, the successor of Mahīpāla.

The dynasty, which underwent various ups and downs of fortune, lasted until the Muhammadan conquest of Bihār in 1199. Part of Bengal came under the sway of a new dynasty, that of the Senas, early in the eleventh century. Vallāla-sena or Ballāl Sen, who seems to have reigned from about 1158 to 1170, is credited by Bengal tradition with having reorganized the caste system, and introduced the practice of 'Kulinism' among Brahmans, Baidyas, and Kāyasths. The Senas originally were Brahmans from the Deccan, and their rise seems to have been a result of the Chola invasion in 1023. The details of their chronology and history are obscure.

Among the more important Indian ruling families the Pālas and the Āndhras alone attained the distinction of enduring each for four and a half centuries.

Chandēl dynasty. But the Chandēl dynasty of Jijhoti or Bundēlkhand, although it never attained a position as exalted as that of the greatest Āndhra and Pāla kings, had a still longer history, and played a considerable part on the Indian political stage for about three centuries. The early Chandēl Rājās appear to have been petty Gond chiefs in the territory now called the Chhatarpur State in the Central India Agency. In the ninth century they overthrew neighbouring Parihār (Pratihāra) chieftains of foreign origin, who must have been connected with the Bhinmāl–Kanauj dynasty, and advanced their frontier towards the north in the region now called Bundēlkhand, until they approached the Jumna. The principal towns in the kingdom, which was called Jejāka-bhukti or Jijhoti, were Khajurāho in Chhatarpur, Mahoba in the Hamīrpur District, and Kālanjar in the Bāndā District, U.P. The military power of the king-

TEMPLE, KHAJURĀHO.

dom depended largely on the possession of the strong fortress of Kālanjar.

The Chandēl Rājās, who probably had been tributary to Bhoja of Kanauj, became fully independent in the tenth century. King Dhanga, whose reign covered the second half of that century, was the most notable prince of his family. He joined the Hindu confederacy formed to resist Amīr Sabuktigīn, the earliest Muslim invader, and shared the disastrous defeat suffered by the allies on the Afghan frontier. Ganda, a later Rājā, took part in the opposition to Sultan Mahmūd, which will be noticed presently more particularly. In the second half of the eleventh century Rājā Kīrtivarman restored the glories of his house, defeated Karnadeva, the aggressive king of Chedi, the ancient Mahākosala, equivalent in large measure to the modern Central Provinces, and widely extended the frontiers of his dominions. Kīrtivarman is memorable in literary history as the patron of the curious allegorical play, entitled the *Prabodha chandrodaya*, or 'Rise of the Moon of Intellect', which was performed at his court about A.D. 1065, and gives in dramatic form a clever exposition of the Vedānta system of philosophy. The Rājā's memory is also preserved by the name of the Kīrat Sāgar, a lake situated among the hills near Mahoba.

The last Chandēl Rājā to enjoy the position of an independent king of importance was Paramardi or Parmāl, who was defeated by Prithīraj Chauhān in 1182, and by Ḳutbu-d dīn Ībak in 1203. After that date the Chandēl Rājās sank into obscurity, but long continued to reign as local princes in the jungles of Bundēlkhand. Durgāvatī, the noble Queen of Gondwāna, who so gallantly resisted the unprovoked aggression of Akbar's general, Āsaf Khān, in 1564, was a Chandēl princess. She was married to a Gond Rājā, thus renewing the ancient relation between the tribesmen of the forest and their ennobled Rājpūt kinsmen of the plain. The dynasty even now has a representative in the Rājā of Gidhaur in the Monghyr (Mungir) District of Bihār, whose ancestor emigrated from Bundēlkhand in the thirteenth century.

Chandēl architecture. One of the beautiful lakes which Chandēl princes formed by damming up valleys among the low forest-clad hills of Bundēlkhand has been mentioned. Many others exist, on the banks of which I often pitched my tents in my youth. The embankments are gigantic structures faced with stone and sometimes crowned by magnificent temples of granite, or rather gneiss. A large group of such temples still standing at Khajurāho is familiar to all students of Indian architecture. Some of the best examples were erected by King Dhanga in the second half of the tenth century. The Jain religion had numerous adherents in the Chandēl dominions during the eleventh and twelfth centuries, although it is now nearly extinct in that region. Ancient Jain temples and dated images may still be seen in many villages. Buddhism had but a slight hold on the country, and Buddhist images, although not unknown, are rare.

Rājā Bhoja of Dhār. The Pawārs or Paramāras, one of the clans of foreign origin supposed to have been born from the fire-pit of Mount Ābū, founded a dynasty in Mālwā, which took its share in the wars of the period and attained considerable distinction. The most renowned prince of the dynasty was Rājā Bhoja, who reigned for more than forty years, from about 1018 to 1060.[1] He was an accomplished scholar and a liberal patron of Sanskrit learning. His name in consequence has become proverbial as that of the ideal Hindu prince. The defeat of Bhoja in or about 1060 by the allied armies of Gujarāt and Chedi reduced the Rājā of Mālwā to a position of little political importance. Dhār or Dhārā, now the head-quarters of a petty state, was the capital of Bhoja, who adorned the town with handsome edifices, of which some vestiges remain in spite of the long-continued Muslim occupation. The immense Bhojpur lake formed by damming the Betwa river and a smaller stream, and covering an area exceeding 250 square miles, was constructed by Rājā Bhoja. Early in the fifteenth century the dam was cut by Hoshang Shāh, Sultan of Mālwā, with the result that a large area of valuable land was reclaimed for cultivation. The Indian Midland Railway now traverses the dry bed of the lake.

Gujarāt. A passing reference to the Solanki or Chaulukya dynasty of Gujarāt established by Mūlarāja in the tenth century must suffice, although stories about Mūlarāja occupy a prominent place in the semi-historical legends of the province. If tradition may be believed, Mūlarāja was a son of the king of Kanauj, apparently Mahīpāla, who probably had appointed his son to be viceroy in the west. Mūlarāja seems to have seized an opportunity to rebel and set up as an independent sovereign.

We now return to the north and resume the thread of the story of Kanauj with that of other northern kingdoms.

Mahīpāla of Kanauj. The Parihār empire began to break up in the reign of Mahīpāla (*c.* A. D. 910–40), who was a grandson of Bhoja. His power suffered a severe shock in A.D. 916 when Indra III, the Rāshtrakūta king of the Deccan, captured Kanauj. Although the southern monarch did not attempt to secure a permanent dominion on the banks of the Ganges, his successful raid necessarily weakened the authority of Mahīpāla, who could no longer hold the western provinces. The Chandēl king helped Mahīpāla to recover his capital. Some years later Gwālior became independent, but the Kanauj kingdom still continued to be one of the leading states.

Rājā Jaipāl of Bathindah. The rule of the Parihārs had never extended across the Sutlaj, and the history of the Panjāb between the seventh and tenth centuries is extremely obscure. At some

[1] Care should be taken not to confound him with Bhoja or Mihira Parihār of Kanauj who reigned from about A. D. 840 to 890, and has been forgotten by Indian tradition. Names like Mahīpāla, Mahendrāpala, and many others occur in distinct dynastic lists, and it is easy to confound the bearers of the names.

time not recorded a powerful kingdom had been formed, which extended from the mountains beyond the Indus, eastwards as far as the Hakrā or 'lost river', so that it comprised a large part of the Panjāb, as well as probably northern Sind. The capital was Bathindah (Bhatinda), the Tabarhind of Muhammadan histories, now in the Patiāla State, and for many centuries an important fortress on the military road connecting Mūltān with India proper through Delhi. At that time Delhi, if in existence, was a place of little consideration. In the latter part of the tenth century the Rājā of Bathindah was Jaipāl, probably a Jat or Jāt.

Freedom of the Hindu states. Until almost the end of the tenth century the Indian Rājās were at liberty to do what they pleased, enjoying exemption from foreign invasion and freedom from the control of any paramount authority. Their position was gravely disturbed when an aggressive Muhammadan power, alien in religion, social customs, ideas, and methods of warfare, appeared on the scene and introduced an absolutely novel element into the interior politics of India, which had not been seriously affected either by the Arab conquest of Sind at the beginning of the eighth century or by the later Muslim occupation of Kābul.

Coin of Sabuktigīn.

Amīr Sabuktigīn. An ambitious Muhammadan chief named Sabuktigīn, Amīr of Ghaznī, effected a sudden change. In A.D. 986–7 (A.H. 376) he made his first raid into Indian territory, and came into conflict with Rājā Jaipāl of Bathindah. Two years later the Hindu prince retaliated by an invasion of the Amīr's territory, but being defeated was compelled to sign a treaty binding him to pay a large indemnity and to surrender four forts to the west of the Indus besides many elephants. Jaipāl broke the treaty and was punished for his breach of faith by the devastation of his border-lands and the loss of the Lamghān or Jalālābād District. After a short interval, in or about A.D. 991, Jaipāl made a vigorous effort to ward off the growing Muslim menace by organizing a confederacy of Hindu kings, including among others Rājyapāla, the Parihār king of Kanauj, and Dhanga, the ruler of the distant Chandēl kingdom to the south of the Jumna. The allies were defeated disastrously somewhere in or near the Kurram (Kurmah) valley, and Peshāwar passed under Muhammadan rule.

Sultan Mahmūd. In A.D. 997 the crown of Ghaznī descended after a short interval to Sabuktigīn's son Mahmūd, who assumed the title of Sultan, the royal style preferred by the Muhammadan kings in India for several centuries. Mahmūd was a zealous Musalman of the ferocious type then prevalent, who felt it to be a duty as well as a pleasure to slay idolaters. He was also greedy of treasure and took good care to derive a handsome profit from his holy wars. Historians are not clear concerning either the exact number or the dates of his raids. The computation of Sir Henry Elliot that Mahmūd made seventeen expeditions may be accepted. Whenever possible he made one each year. Hindu authorities never mention distinctly his proceedings, which are known only from the testimony of Muhammadan authors, who do not always agree.

It was the custom of the Sultan to quit his capital early in October and utilize the cold weather for his operations. Three months of steady marching brought him into the heart of the rich Gangetic provinces ; and by the time he had slain his tens of thousands and collected millions of treasure he was ready at the beginning of the hot season to go home and enjoy himself. He carried off crowds of prisoners as slaves, including no doubt skilled masons and other artisans whom he employed to beautify his capital ; as his successors did in later times. It would be tedious to relate in full the story of all his murderous expeditions. Their character will appear sufficiently from a brief notice of the more notable raids.

Early raids. In November 1001, not long after his accession, in the course of his second expedition, he inflicted a severe defeat near Peshāwar on Jaipāl, who was taken prisoner with his family. The captive, who was released on terms after a time, refused to survive his disgrace. He committed suicide by fire and was succeeded by his son Ānandpāl, who continued the struggle with the foreigners, but without success. . He followed his father's example and organized a league of Hindu Rājās, including the rulers of Ujjain, Gwālior, Kanauj, Delhi, and Ajmēr, who took the field with a host which was larger than that opposed to Sabuktigīn, and was under the supreme command of Vīsala-deva, the Chauhān Rājā of Ajmēr. The hostile forces watched each other on the plain of Peshāwar for forty days, during which the Hindus received reinforcements from the powerful Khokhar tribe of the Panjāb, while the Sultan was compelled to form an entrenched camp. The camp was stormed by a rush in force of the new allies, who slew three or four thousand Musalmans in a few minutes. Victory seemed to be within the grasp of the Hindus when it was snatched from their hands by one of those unlucky accidents which have so often determined the fate of Indian battles. The elephant carrying either Ānandpāl himself or his son Brahmanpāl, for accounts differ as usual, turned and fled. The Indians, on seeing this, broke in disorder. The Muhammadan cavalry pursued them for two days and nights, killing eight thousand and capturing enormous booty. Loosely organized confederacies of Hindu contingents each under its own independent chief almost always proved incapable of withstanding the attack of fierce foreign cavalry obeying one will.

Kāngrā. The decisive victory thus gained enabled the Sultan to attack with success the strong fortress of Kāngrā or Bhīmnagar, with its temple rich in treasure accumulated by the devotion of generations of Hindus (A. D. 1009). Vast quantities of coined money and gold and silver bullion were carried off. The treasure included

'a house of white silver, like to the houses of rich men, the length of which was thirty yards and the breadth fifteen. It could be taken to pieces and put together again. And there was a canopy, made of the fine linen of Rūm, forty yards long and twenty broad, supported on two golden and two silver poles, which had been cast in moulds'.

The Sultan returned to Ghaznī with his booty and astonished the ambassadors from foreign powers by the display of

'jewels and unbored pearls and rubies, shining like sparks, or like wine congealed with ice, and emeralds like fresh sprigs of myrtle, and diamonds in size and weight like pomegranates'.

The fortress was held by a Muslim garrison for thirty-five years, after which it was recovered by the Hindus. It did not pass finally under Muhammadan rule until 1620, when it was captured by an officer of Jahāngīr. The buildings were ruined to a great extent by the earthquake of 1905.

Mathurā and Kanauj. The expedition reckoned as the twelfth was directed specially against Kanauj, the imperial city of northern India, then under the rule of Rājyapāla Parihār. The Sultan, sweeping away all opposition, crossed the Jumna on December 2, 1018, and was preparing to attack Baran or Bulandshahr when the Rājā, by name Hardatt, tendered his submission and with ten thousand of his men accepted the religion of Islām.

Mathurā, the holy city of Krishna, was the next victim. 'In the middle of the city there was a temple larger and finer than the rest, which can neither be described nor painted.' The Sultan was of opinion that two hundred years would have been required to build it. The idols included 'five of red gold, each five yards high', with eyes formed of priceless jewels. 'The Sultan gave orders that all the temples should be burnt with naphtha and fire, and levelled with the ground.' Thus perished works of art which must have been among the noblest monuments of ancient India.

Rājyapāla, not daring to attempt the serious defence of his capital, fled across the Ganges. The seven forts which guarded Kanauj were all taken in one day, in January 1019, and the Sultan's troops were let loose to plunder and make captives. It was reported that the city contained nearly ten thousand temples, but it is not said distinctly that they were destroyed. The Sultan, after making an excursion into the Fatehpur District and to the borders of Jijhoti (Bundēlkhand), retired to Ghaznī with his prisoners and plunder.

Collapse of Ganda Chandēl. The cowardly flight of the Kanauj Rājā angered his fellow Rājās who, under the command of a Chandēl prince, combined against Rājyapāla, slew him, and replaced him by Trilochanapāla.

Mahmūd, who regarded the slain Rājā as his vassal, resolved to punish the chiefs who had dared to defy his might. He marched again in the autumn of A.D. 1019, forced the passage of the Jumna, and entered the territory of Ganda Chandēl, who had assembled a host so vast that the Sultan was frightened. But Ganda, a faint-hearted creature, stole away in the night, and allowed the enemy to carry off to Ghaznī 580 elephants and much other booty. When Mahmūd came back again in 1021–2 Ganda once more refused to fight, and was content to buy off the invader.

Somnāth. The most celebrated and interesting of Mahmūd's expeditions was the sixteenth, undertaken with the object of sacking the temple of Somnāth or Prabhāsa Pattana on the coast of Surāshtra or Kāthiāwar, which was known to be stored with incalculable riches. The authorities differ concerning the chronology of the operations, probably because some of them ignore the fact that Mahmūd spent about a year in Gujarāt.[1] He seems to have quitted Ghaznī in December, A.D. 1023 (A.H. 414), with a force of 30,000 horsemen besides volunteers. He advanced by Multān and from Ajmēr through the Rājputāna desert to Anhilwāra or Pātan in Gujarāt. The march through a country lacking in both food and water required extensive commissariat arrangements and a considerable expenditure of time. The Sultan consequently did not appear before Somnāth until the middle of the eleventh month of A.H. 414, or about March, A.D. 1024, or, according to other authorities, 1025. A fiercely contested fight gave the invaders possession of the fortified temple and of an enormous mass of treasure. The number of the slain exceeded fifty thousand.

The object of worship was a huge stone *lingam* enshrined in the sanctum of a temple constructed mainly of timber. The principal hall had fifty-six columns of wood covered with lead.

The Sultan returned through Sind by a route more westerly than that he had used in coming. His army suffered severely from want of water. He arrived at Ghaznī about April 1026, loaded with plunder.

The Somnāth expedition was the last important military operation of Mahmūd. His final Indian expedition in A.D. 1027 was directed against the Jats in the neighbourhood of Multān. The remainder of his life was occupied by domestic troubles, and he died in April, A.D. 1030 (A.H. 421), at the age of sixty-two.

Results of the raids. The Panjāb, or a large part of it, was annexed to the Ghaznī Sultanate. That annexation constitutes the sole claim of Mahmūd to be counted as an Indian sovereign. While Muhammadan historians regard him as one of the glories of Islām, a less partial judgement finds in his proceedings little deserving of admiration. His ruling passion seems to have been avarice. He spent large sums in beautifying his capital and in endowing Muhammadan institutions in it. Like several other ferocious Asiatic conquerors he had a taste for Persian literature, and gained a reputation as a patron of poets and theologians. Firdausī, the author of the immense Persian epic, the *Shāhnāma*,

[1] For the year's stay see Forbes, *Rāsmālā*, i, 79, and Elphinstone. The *I. G.* (1908), *s. v.* Somnāth, correctly dates the operations in 1024–6.

considering himself to have been treated with insufficient generosity, composed a bitter satire upon the Sultan which is extant. Such matters, which occupy a prominent place in the writings of Elphinstone and other authors, really have no relevance to the history of India and need not be noticed further. So far as India was concerned Mahmūd was simply a bandit operating on a large scale, who was too strong for the Hindu Rājās, and was in consequence able to inflict much irreparable damage. He did not attempt to effect any permanent conquest except in the Panjāb, and his raids had no lasting results in the interior beyond the destruction of life, property, and priceless monuments.

Alberūnī. The most distinguished ornament of Sultan Mahmūd's reign was the profound scholar commonly called Alberūnī,[1] who had little reason to feel gratitude to the raiding Sultan, although patronized intelligently by his son Masaūd. Alberūnī, who was born in A. D. 973 and died in A. D. 1048, was a native of the Khwārizm or Khiva territory, and was brought to Ghaznī either as a prisoner or as a hostage. When the Sultan succeeded in occupying the Panjāb, Alberūnī took up his residence for a time in the newly acquired province, and used the opportunity to make a thorough survey of Hindu philosophy and other branches of Indian science. He mastered the Sanskrit language, and was not too proud to read even the Purānas. He noted carefully and recorded accurately numerous observations on the history, character, manners, and customs of the Hindus, and was thus able to compose the wonderful book conveniently known as 'Alberūnī's India', which is unique in Muslim literature, except in so far as it was imitated without acknowledgement more than five centuries later by Abu-l Fazl in the *Āīn-i Akbarī*. The author, while fully alive to the defects of Hindu literary methods, was fascinated by the Indian philosophy, especially as expounded in the *Bhagavad-Gītā*. He was consumed with a desire to discover truth for its own sake, and laboured conscientiously to that end with a noble disregard of ordinary Muhammadan prejudices. As his learned translator observes:

His book on India is 'like a magic island of quiet impartial research in the midst of a world of clashing swords, burning towns, and plundered temples'.

His special subjects were 'astronomy, mathematics, chronology, mathematical geography, physics, chemistry, and mineralogy', all treated with such consummate learning that few modern scholars are capable of translating his treatises, and the versions, when accomplished, are often beyond the comprehension of even well-educated readers. Alberūnī undoubtedly was one of the most gifted scientific men known to history. Some of his writings have been lost, and others remain in manuscript. The translation by Sachau of his *Chronology of Ancient Nations*, published in

[1] His full designation was Abū-Rihān (Raihān) Muhammad, son of Ahmad. He became familiarly known as Bū-Rihān, Ustād ('Master'), Al-Berūnī ('the foreigner'). The spellings Al-Bīrūnī and Al-Bērūnī are both legitimate.

1879, is a valuable work of reference, but very difficult to understand.

The Gaharwārs of Kanauj. The Parihār dynasty of Kanauj came to an end in some manner unknown prior to A.D. 1090 and was succeeded by Rājās belonging to the Gaharwār (Gahadavāla) clan, who were connected with the Chandēls and were of indigenous origin. Govindachandra, grandson of the founder of the new dynasty, enjoyed a long reign lasting for more than half a century (*c.* A.D. 1100 to 1160), and succeeded in restoring the glory of the Kanauj kingdom to a considerable extent. Numerous inscriptions of his reign are extant.

Coin of Govindachandra.

Rājā Jaichand. His grandson, renowned in popular legend as Rājā Jaichand (Jayachchandra), was reputed by the Muhammadan writers to be the greatest king in India and was known to them as King of Benares, which seems to have been his principal residence. The incident of the abduction of his not unwilling daughter by the gallant Rāi Pithorā or Prithīrāj Chauhān of Ajmīr is a famous theme of bardic lays.

When Jaichand essayed to stem the torrent of Muslim invasion in 1194, Muhammad of Ghōr (Shihābu-d dīn, or Muizzu-d dīn, the son of Sām) defeated the huge Hindu host with immense slaughter at Chandrāwar in the Etawah District near the Jumna. The Rājā was among the slain, and his capital, Benares, was plundered so thoroughly that 1,400 camels were needed to carry away the booty. That battle put an end to the independent kingdom of Kanauj, but local Rājās more or less subordinate to the ruling power of the day long continued to rule in the ancient city. The Gaharwār Rājās were succeeded by Chandēls. Innumerable migrations of Rājpūt clans caused by the early Muhammadan invasions are recorded in village traditions and rude metrical chronicles kept by court bards.

The Chauhāns ; Prithīrāj. The Chauhān chiefs of Sāmbhar and Ajmēr in Rājputāna fill a large place in Hindu tradition and in the story of the Muhammadan conquest of Hindostan. One of them named Vigraharāja (IV) may be mentioned as a noted patron of Sanskrit literature, who was credited with the composition of a drama, fragments of which are preserved on stone tablets at Ajmēr. His brother's son was Rāi Pithorā or Prithīrāj, already mentioned, who carried off Jaichand's daughter about A.D. 1175, and defeated the Chandēls in 1182. He led the resistance to Muhammad of Ghōr ten years later, was defeated at the second battle of Tarāin, captured, and executed. His city of Ajmēr was sacked, and the inhabitants were either massacred or enslaved.

He is the most popular hero of northern India to this day, and his exploits are the subject of bards' songs and vernacular epics.

The Chand Rāisā. The most celebrated of such epics is the *Chand Rāisā* composed by Prithīrāj's court poet Chand Bardāī. The poem, written in archaic Hindī, has been constantly enlarged by reciters, as no doubt the Homeric poems were, and is believed to comprise about 125,000 verses. But the original composition, of only 5,000 verses, is said to be still in existence and in the custody of the poet's descendant, who resides in the Jodhpur State, and still enjoys the grant of lands made to his illustrious ancestor. It is much to be desired that the precious original manuscript should be copied and printed. The supposed error in Chand Bardāī's dates does not exist. He used a special form of the Vikrama era, ninety or ninety-one years later than that usually current. Many other compositions of a similar character are to be found in Rājputāna.

History of Delhi. Delhi, meaning by that term the old town near the Kutb Mīnār, was founded, according to an authority cited by Raverty, in A. D. 933–4.[1] It was held in the eleventh century by Rājās of the Tomara clan, who erected numerous temples, which were destroyed by the Muhammadans, who used the materials for their buildings. In the twelfth century the city was included in the dominions of Prithīrāj. The wonderful iron pillar, originally erected somewhere else, perhaps at Mathurā in the fourth century, seems to have been moved and set up in its present position by the Tomara chief in the middle of the eleventh century. It is a mass of wrought iron nearly 24 feet in length and estimated to weigh more than six tons. The metal is perfectly welded and its manipulation is a triumph of skill in the handling of a refractory material. It is not the only proof that the ancient Indians possessed exceptional mastery over difficult problems of working in iron and other metals.

The current belief that Delhi is a city of immemorial antiquity rests upon the tradition that the existing village of Indarpat marks the site of part of the Indraprastha of the *Mahābhārata* at a very remote age. The tradition may be correct, but there is not a vestige of any prehistoric town now traceable. The first of the many historical cities, known collectively as Delhi, was founded near the close of the tenth century after Christ, and did not attain importance until the time of Ānanga Pāla Tomara in the middle of the eleventh century. Most people probably have a vague impression that Delhi always was the capital of India. If they have, their belief is erroneous. Delhi never figured largely in Hindu history. It was ordinarily the head-quarters of the Sultans of Hindostan from 1206 to 1526, but did not become the established Mogul capital until Shāhjahān moved his court from Agra in 1648. It continued to be the usual residence of his successors until 1858 when their dynasty was extinguished. Since 1912 a new Delhi has been declared the official capital of the Government of India. The decision then taken is open to criticism from many points of view.

[1] But other dates also are recorded.

A. D.
647. Death of Harsha.
c. 700. Ādisūra in Bengal.
712. Arab conquest of Sind.
731. Embassy to China of Yasovarman, king of Kanauj.
c. 740. Yasovarman defeated by Lalitāditya, king of Kashmīr (A. D. 733–69).
c. 750. Pāla dynasty of Bengal founded by Gopāla.
c. 810. Dharmapāla, king of Bengal, deposed a king of Kanauj and appointed another.
c. 816. Parihār capital transferred from Bhinmāl to Kanauj.
c. 840–90. Bhoja, or Mihira, the powerful Parihār king of Kanauj.
933–4. Probable date of foundation of Delhi.
c. 942–97. Mūlarāja, king of Gujarāt.
c. 950–99. Dhanga, the most powerful of the Chandēl kings.
973–1048. Alberūnī, scientific author.
997. Sultan Mahmūd of Ghaznī, aee.
1001. Sultan Mahmūd defeated Jaipāl.
1008–19. The Sultan defeated Ānandpāl and took Kāngrā.
1018–19. The Sultan took Kanauj.
c. 1018–60. Bhoja Pawār, king of Mālwā.
c. 1023. Incursion of Rājendra Chola into Bengal.
Dec. 1023—April 1026. Somnāth expedition of Sultan Mahmūd.
1030. Death of Sultan Mahmūd.
1038. Atīsa sent on Buddhist mission to Tibet by Nayapāla, king of Bengal.
c. 1049–1100. Kīrtivarman, Chandēl king.
c. 1100–60. Govindachandra, Gaharwār, king of Kanauj.
c. 1158–70. Ballāl Sen (Vallāla Sena), king of part of Bengal.
1182. Parmāl Chandēl defeated by Rājā Prithīrāj Chauhān.
1192. Defeat and death of Prithīrāj.

Authorities

Full references are given in *E. H. I.*[3] A few supplementary ones are in the foot-notes to this chapter.

CHAPTER 3

THE KINGDOMS OF THE PENINSULA

Section 1. The Deccan Proper and Mysore.

Groups of states. The mediaeval history of the peninsula concerns itself chiefly with those of two groups of states, namely, the kingdoms of the Deccan plateau lying between the Narbadā on the north and the Krishnā and Tungabhadrā on the south, and those beyond those rivers. Mysore, which belongs geographically to the Far South, having been generally more elosely eonnected with the Deccan kingdoms than with the Tamil states, may be treated as an annexe of the Deeean proper. The history of the Tamil group of kingdoms—Pāndya, Chera, Chola, and Pallava—forms a distinct subject. The Deccan proper, Mysore or the Kanarese country, and Tamilakam or Tamil Land were constantly in close touch one with the other, but the points of contact between the peninsular powers and those of northern India were few.

Difficulties of the subject. Although modern research has had much success in piecing together the skeleton of peninsular history, it is not often possible to clothe the dry bones with the flesh of narrative. The greater part of the results of painstaking, praiseworthy, and necessary archaeological study must always remain unattractive to the ordinary reader of history and extremely difficult to remember. The names of the sovereigns and other notables of southern India present peculiar obstacles in the path of the student of history. They are often terribly long, and each king commonly is mentioned by several alternative cumbrous names or titles which are extremely confusing.[1] Names, too, frequently recur in the lists and are liable to be misunderstood. The kingdoms, moreover, were so completely isolated from the outer world that their history in detail can never possess more than local interest. For those reasons, to which others might be added, the story of the mediaeval southern kingdoms is even less manageable than that of the northern realms, which is sufficiently perplexing. In this chapter no attempt will be made to narrate consecutively the history of any of the dynasties, the treatment being confined to summary notices of a few leading powers and personages, coupled with observations on the changes which occurred in religion, literature, and art in the course of the centuries. Notwithstanding the political isolation of the South, religious and philosophical movements originated in that region which profoundly affected the thought of the North. The influence exercised by Rāmānuja and other southern sages on the whole country from Cape Comorin to the recesses of the Snowy Mountains is the best evidence of that inner unity of Hindu India which survives the powerful disintegrating forces set in motion by diversity in blood, language, manners, customs, and political allegiance.

Early mediaeval history. The history of the Deccan for a considerable time subsequent to the disappearance of the Āndhra power early in the third century A. C. is extremely obscure. Our information concerning Mysore or the Kanarese country is somewhat fuller than that available for the Deccan proper, and two dynasties which fill a large space in the publications of the archaeologists may receive passing notice.

Kadambas. A clan or family called Kadamba enjoyed independent power in the districts now called North and South Kanara and in western Mysore from the third to the sixth century. Their capital Banawāsi, also known as Jayanti or Vaijayanti, was so ancient that it is mentioned in the edicts of Asoka. The Kadambas

[1] e. g., an inscription mentions a man called Mēdini Mīsara Gandakattāri, Trinetra-Sāluva Narasana Nāyaka; and the King Pulakēsin Chalukya I appears also as Satyāsraya, Ranavikrama, and Vallabha. No author who meddles largely with such names can expect to be read.

resembled several other royal families of distinction in being of Brahman descent, although recognized as Kshatriyas by reason of their occupation as rulers. Kadamba chiefs in subordinate positions may be traced as late as the beginning of the fourteenth century, and the powerful Rāyas of Vijayanagar, who founded a great kingdom early in that century, are supposed by some authorities to have had Kadamba connexions.

Gangas. A still more distinguished dynasty was that of the Gangas, who ruled over the greater part of Mysore from the second to the eleventh century, and played an important part in the incessant mediaeval wars. The Gangas of the tenth century were

FACE OF GOMATA, SRAVANA BELGOLA.

zealous patrons of Jainism, which had a long history in the peninsula from the fourth century B. C. The colossal statue of Gomata, 56½ feet in height, wrought out of a block of gneiss on the top of an eminence at Sravana Belgola, and justly described as being unrivalled in India for daring conception and gigantic dimensions, was executed in about A. D. 983 to the order of Chāmunda Rāya, the minister of a Ganga king.[1]

A branch of the Gangas ruled in Orissa for about a thousand years from the sixth to the sixteenth century.

Early Chalukyas. The most prominent of the early mediaeval dynasties in the Deccan was that of the Chalukyas, founded in the middle of the sixth century by Pulakesin I, who established himself as lord of Vātāpi or Bādāmi, now in the Bījāpur District of the Bombay Presidency.[2] His grandson, Pulakesin II (608–42),

[1] Two similar but smaller colossi of much later date exist at Kārakala or Kārkala and Yenūr in South Kanara. For the former see *H. F. A.*, pl. liii.

[2] The Chalukyas adopted the figure of a boar as their emblem, which was borrowed later by the Rāyas of Vijayanagar and other dynasties.

was almost exactly the contemporary of Harsha of Kanauj (606–47), and in the Deccan occupied a paramount position similar to that enjoyed in northern India by his rival. When Harsha, about A.D. 620, sought to bring the Deccan under his dominion, Pulakesin was too strong for him and repelled his attack, maintaining the Narbadā as the frontier between the two empires. The court of the sovereign of the Deccan was visited in A.D. 641 by Hiuen Tsang, the Chinese pilgrim, who was much impressed by the power of Pulakesin, and the loyalty of his warlike vassals. The capital probably was at or near Nāsik, and the traveller experienced much difficulty in penetrating the robber-infested jungles of the Western Ghāts. Even then the country was known as Mahārāshtra, as it is now. The Buddhist monasteries in the kingdom numbered more than a hundred with a population of monks exceeding five thousand. A large proportion of the inhabitants of the realm did not follow the Buddhist religion. Hiuen Tsang gives a brief and indistinct account of the Ajantā caves, which he seems to have visited. Most of the excellent sculptures and paintings in the caves had then been completed.

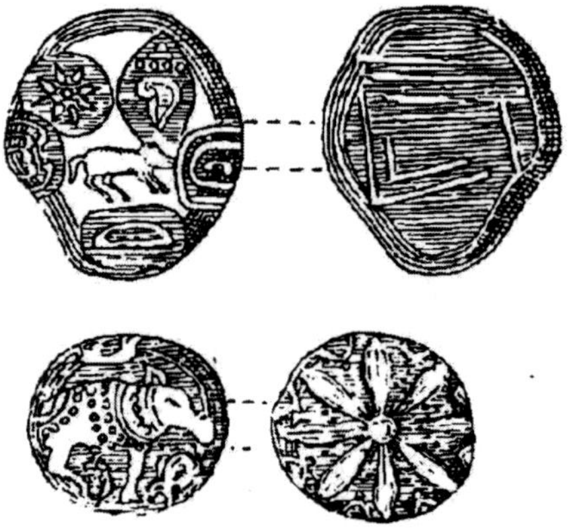

Punch-marked coin.
Early Chalukya coin.

The fame of Pulakesin extended even to distant Persia, whose king exchanged embassies with him. The intercourse with Persia is commemorated in the cave frescoes.

The loyal valour of the chieftains of the Deccan did not avail to save their lord from ruin. Only a year after Hiuen Tsang's visit the Chalukya king was utterly defeated and presumably slain by the Pallava king of Kānchī (642), named Narasimhavarman, who thus became the paramount power in the peninsula. The acts of the conqueror will be noticed more particularly as part of the story of the Pallavas.

Thirteen years later (655) a son of Pulakesin revenged his father's death and captured Kānchī. The conflict between the Pallavas and the Chalukyas continued for many years, with varying fortune, until the middle of the eighth century (753), when a Rāshtrakūta or Ratta chieftain overthrew the reigning Chalukya. The sovereignty of the Deccan, which had been held by the Chalukyas for some two hundred years, thus passed to the Rāshtrakūtas in whose hands it remained for nearly two centuries and a quarter.

Chalukyas and Rāshtrakūtas. The Chalukya or Solanki princes, although provided by obsequious Brahmans with a first-class Hindu pedigree going back to the hero Rāma of Ajodhya, really were of foreign origin, and belonged to the Hūna-Gurjara group of invading tribes. The Rāshtrakūtas or Rattas seem to have been indigenous, and naturally were hostile to the foreigners.

Usually, although not always, the Rājpūt clans of foreign descent were opposed to the clans formed from indigenous tribes.

Religion. The early Chalukya kings, while tolerant of all religions, like most Indian rulers, were themselves Brahmanical Hindus. In their time Buddhism slowly declined, while the sacrificial form of Hinduism grew in favour, and became the subject of numerous treatises. Handsome temples were erected in many places, and the practice of excavating cave-temples was borrowed by orthodox Hindus from their Jain and Buddhist rivals. The sixth-century Brahmanical caves at Bādāmī contain excellent sculptures in good preservation. The Jain creed had many followers in the Southern Marāthā country.

A COPPER-PLATE GRANT.

It is needless to detail the wars of the Rāshtrakūtas. The reign of Krishna I (acc. *c.* A.D. 760) is memorable for the rock-cut temple called Kailāsa at Ellora, now in the Nizam's Dominions, which is one of the most marvellous works of human labour. The whole temple, hewn out of the side of a hill and enriched with endless ornament, stands clear as if built in the ordinary way.

Amoghavarsha. King Amoghavarsha (*c.* 815–77) enjoyed one of the longest reigns recorded in history. Sulaimān, the Arab merchant who travelled in western India in the middle of the ninth century, knew the Rāshtrakūta sovereign by his title of Ballharā, a corruption of Vallabha Rāi, and states that he was acknowledged not only as the most eminent of the princes of India, but also as the fourth of the great monarchs of the world, the other three being the Khalīf (Caliph) of Baghdad, the emperor of China, and the emperor of Rūm or Constantinople. The Rāshtrakūta kings kept on the best of terms with the Arabs of Sind, and enriched their subjects by encouraging commerce. Amoghavarsha possessed multitudes of horses and elephants, with immense wealth, and maintained a standing army regularly paid. His capital was Mānyakheta, now Mālkhēd in the Nizam's Dominions. He adopted the Jain religion and showed marked favour to learned Jains of the Digambara or nude sect. The rapid progress of Jainism in the Deccan during the ninth and tenth centuries involved a decline in the position of Buddhism.

Chalukyas of Kalyāni. In A.D. 973 the second Chalukya dynasty, with its capital at Kalyāni, was founded by Taila or Tailapa II, who dethroned the last of the Rāshtrakūtas. The kings of the new dynasty fought numerous wars with their neighbours. At the beginning of the eleventh century the Chalukya country was cruelly ravaged by Rājarāja the Great, the Chola king, who threw into it a vast host of hundreds of thousands of merciless soldiers, by whom even Brahmans, women, and children were not spared.

In A.D. 1052 or 1053 Somesvara Chalukya defeated and slew Rājādhirāja, the then reigning Chola king, in a famous battle fought at Koppam on the Krishnā.[1]

Vikramānka. Vikramānka or Vikramāditya, who reigned from A.D. 1076 to 1126, was the most conspicuous member of his dynasty. He secured his throne by a war with one brother, and later in life had to fight another brother who rebelled. He continued the perennial wars with the southern powers, the Cholas in that age having taken the place of the Pallavas and become the lords of Kānchī, which Vikramānka is said to have occupied more than once. His success in war with his neighbours was so marked that he ventured to found an era bearing his name, which never came into general use. His exploits in war, the chase, and love are recorded at great length in an historical poem composed by Bilhana, his chief pundit, a native of Kashmīr. The poem, which recalls Bāna's work on the deeds of Harsha, was discovered by Bühler in a Jain library, and well edited and analysed by him. It is interesting to note that Vikramānka was chosen by one of his consorts as her husband at a public *swayamvara* in the ancient epic fashion.

The celebrated lawyer, Vijnānesvara, author of the *Mitāksharā*, the leading authority on Hindu law outside of Bengal, lived at Kalyāni in the reign of Vikramānka, whose rule appears to have been prosperous and efficient.

Bijjala Kalachurya. During the twelfth century the Chalukya power declined, and after 1190 the Rājās sank into the position of petty chiefs, most of their possessions passing into the hands of new dynasties, the Yādavas of Devagiri and the Hoysalas of Dorasamudra.

A rebel named Bijjala Kalachurya and his sons held the Chalukya throne for some years. Bijjala abdicated in 1167.

The Lingāyat sect. His brief tenure of power was marked by

[1] Fleet (*Ep. Ind.* xii, 298), correcting an earlier identification of the battle-field, as in *E. H. I.*[3], p. 431.

the rise of the Lingāyat or Vīra Saiva sect, which is still powerful in the Kanarese country, especially among the trading classes. The members of the sect worship Siva in his phallic (*lingam*) form, reject the authority of the Vedas, disbelieve in the doctrine of rebirth, object to child-marriage, approve of the remarriage of widows, and cherish an intense aversion to Brahmans, notwithstanding that the prophet of their creed was Basava, alleged to have been a Brahman minister of Bijjala, and said by some to have been originally a Jain. The sect when established displayed bitter hostility to Jainism.

Vishnuvardhana Hoysala. The Hoysala or Poysala kings of the Mysore territory were descended from a petty chieftain in the Western Ghāts, and first rose to importance in the time of Bittideva or Bittiga, better known by his later name of Vishnuvardhana, who died in A.D. 1141,[1] after a reign of more than thirty years, more or less in subordination to the Chalukya power. The Hoysalas did not become fully independent until about A.D. 1190. Bittiga engaged in wars of the usual character, which need not be specified, and so extended his dominions; but his substantial claim to remembrance rests on the important part played by him in the religious life of the peninsula and on the wonderful development of architecture and sculpture associated with his name and the names of his successors. Bittiga in his early days was a zealous Jain and encouraged his minister Gangarāja to restore the Jain temples which had been destroyed by Chola invaders of the Saiva persuasion. In those days, although many, perhaps most, Rājās practised the normal Hindu tolerance, political wars were sometimes embittered by sectarian passion, and serious persecution was not unknown. The destruction of Jain temples by the Cholas was an act of fierce intolerance. About the close of the eleventh or the beginning of the twelfth century Bittiga came under the teaching of the famous sage Rāmānuja, who converted him to faith in Vishnu. The king then adopted the name of Vishnuvardhana and devoted himself to the honouring of his new creed by the erection of temples of unsurpassed magnificence. The current Vaishnava story that Vishnuvardhana ground the Jain theologians in oil-mills certainly is not true. The statement seems to be merely a picturesque version of the defeat of the Jain disputants in argument. Good evidence proves that the converted king continued to show toleration for various forms of religion. One of his wives and one of his daughters professed the Jain creed.

Hoysala style of art. The style of the temples built by Vishnuvardhana and his successors in the twelfth and thirteenth century, which was used alike by Jains and Brahmanical Hindus, should be termed Hoysala, not Chalukyan as in Fergusson's book. It is characterized by a richly carved base or plinth, supporting the temple, which is polygonal, star-shaped in plan, and roofed by a low pyramidal tower, often surmounted by a vase-shaped

[1] Lewis Rice in *J. R. A. S.*, 1915, p. 529.

ornament. In many cases there are several towers, so that the temple may be described as double, triple, or quadruple. The whole of a Hoysala building is generally treated as the background for an extraordinary mass of complicated sculpture, sometimes occurring in great sheets of bas-reliefs, and generally comprising many statues or statuettes, almost or wholly detached. The temple at Halebīd or Dorasamudra, described by Fergusson, is the best known, but many others equally notable exist. Much of the sculpture is of high quality. It was the work of a large school of artists, scores of whom, contrary to the usual Indian practice, have recorded their names on their creations. Artistic skill is not yet dead in Mysore.[1]

Rāmānuja. Rāmānuja, the celebrated Vaishnava philosopher and teacher, who converted the Hoysala king, was educated at Kānchī, and resided at Srīrangam near Trichinopoly in the reign of Adhirājendra Chola ; but owing to the hostility of that king, who professed the Saiva faith, was obliged to withdraw into Mysore, where he resided until the decease of Adhirājendra freed him from anxiety. He then returned to Srīrangam, where he remained until his death. The exact chronology of his long life is not easy to determine. His death may be placed about the middle of the twelfth century. His system of metaphysics or ontology based on his interpretation of the Upanishads is too abstruse for discussion or analysis in these pages. He is regarded as the leading opponent of the views of Sankarāchārya.[2]

The later Hoysalas. Vīra Ballāla, grandson of Vishnuvardhana, extended the dominions of his house, especially in a northerly direction, where he encountered the Yādavas of Devagiri (A.D. 1191–2). His conquests made the Hoysalas the most powerful dynasty in the Deccan at the close of the twelfth century. Their short-lived dominion was shattered in 1310 by the attack of Malik Kāfūr and Khwāja Hājī, the generals of Alāu-d dīn Khiljī, who ravaged the kingdom and sacked the capital, Dorasamudra or Halebīd, which was finally destroyed by a Muhammadan force a few years later, in 1326 or 1327. After that date the Hoysalas survived for a while as merely local Rājās.

Yādavas of Devagiri. The Yādavas of Devagiri or Deogiri, known in later ages as Aurangābād, were descendants of feudatory nobles of the Chalukya kingdom. In the closing years of the twelfth century, as mentioned above, they were the rivals of the Hoysalas. The most influential member of the dynasty was Singhana early in the thirteenth century, who invaded Gujarāt and other regions, establishing a considerable dominion which lasted only for a few years. In 1294 the reigning Rājā was attacked by Alāu-d din Khiljī, who carried off an enormous amount of treasure. In 1309 Rāmachandra, the last independent sovereign of the Deccan, submitted to Malik Kāfūr. His son-in-law,

[1] *Ind. Ant.*, 1915, pp. 89 foll.

[2] For an abstract of the doctrine see *Srī Rāmānujāchārya*, part ii, by T. Rajagopala Chariar, Madras, Natesan & Co., n.d.

Harapāla, having ventured to revolt against the foreigner, paid the penalty by being flayed alive at the order of his barbarous conqueror (1318). That tragedy was the end of the Yādavas.

The story of the Hindu kingdom of Vijayanagar, which was founded about 1336, and developed into an extensive empire to the south of the Krishnā, will be related with considerable detail in a later chapter in connexion with the southern Muhammadan dynasties.

SECTION 2. THE TAMIL POWERS OF THE FAR SOUTH.

Origin of the Pallavas. At the close of chapter 3 of Book II we took a passing glance at the early history of the Tamil kingdoms during the first and second centuries of the Christian era. It is impossible to construct anything like a continuous narrative until a date much later.

After the time of Karikāla Chola and Gajabāhu of Ceylon the power which appears first on the stage of history is that of the Pallavas. In the middle of the fourth century Samudragupta encountered a Pallava king of Kānchī or Conjeeveram, and it is not unlikely that the dynasty may have originated in the third century after the disappearance of the Āndhras.

The Pallavas constitute one of the mysteries of Indian history. The conjecture that they were Pahlavas, that is to say Parthians or Persians from the north-west, was suggested solely by a superficial verbal similarity and may be summarily dismissed as baseless. Everything known about them indicates that they were a peninsular race, tribe, or clan, probably either identical or closely connected with the Kurumbas, an originally pastoral people, who play a prominent part in early Tamil tradition. The Pallavas are sometimes described as the 'foresters', and seem to have been of the same blood as the Kallars, who were reckoned as belonging to the formidable predatory classes, and were credited up to quite recent times with 'bold, indomitable, and martial habits'. The present Rājā of Pudukottai, the small Native State lying between the Trichinopoly, Tanjore, and Madura Districts, is a Kallar and claims the honour of descent from the Pallava princes. He has abandoned the habits of his forefathers and is a respectable ruler of the modern type, guided by the counsels of the Collector of Trichinopoly.[1]

[1] According to Srinivasa Aiyangar, who writes with ample local knowledge, the Pallavas belonged to the ancient Nāga people, who included a primitive Negrito element of Australasian origin and a later mixed race. Their early habitat was the Tondai mandalam, the group of districts round Madras; Tanjore and Trichinopoly being later conquests. The Pallava army was recruited from the martial tribe of Pallis or Kurumbas. The Pallava chiefs were the hereditary enemies of the three Tamil kings, and were regarded as intruders in the southern districts. Hence the term Pallava in Tamil has come to mean 'a rogue', while a section of the Pallava subjects who settled in the Chola and Pāndya countries became known

The history of the Pallavas, although alluded to in some vernacular writings, had been almost wholly forgotten by everybody, and was absolutely unknown to Europeans before 1840, when inscriptions of the dynasty began to come to light. Since that date the patient labours of many investigators have recovered much of the outline of Pallava history and have restored the dynasty to its rightful place in Indian history, a place by no means insignificant.

Limits of the Tamil states. The normal limits of the territories of the three ancient ruling races of the Tamil country were defined by immemorial tradition and well recognized, although the actual frontiers of the kingdoms varied continually and enormously from time to time.

The Pāndya kingdom, as defined by tradition, extended from the Southern Vellāru river (Pudukottai) on the north to Cape Comorin, and from the Coromandel (*Chola-mandala*) coast on the east to the 'great highway', the Achchhankōvil Pass leading into Southern Kērala, or Travancore. It comprised the existing Districts of Madura and Tinnevelly with parts of the Travancore State.

The Chola country, according to the most generally received tradition, extended along the Coromandel coast from Nellore to Pudukottai, where it abutted on the Pāndya territory. On the west it reached the borders of Coorg. The limits thus defined include Madras with several adjoining Districts, and a large part of the Mysore State. But the ancient literature does not carry the Tamil Land farther north than Pulicat and the Venkata or Tirupathi Hill, about 100 miles to the north-west of Madras. In the middle of the seventh century, when Hiuen Tsang, the Chinese pilgrim, travelled, the Pallavas held most of the Chola traditional territory, and the special Chola principality was restricted to a small and unhealthy area, nearly coincident with the Cuddapah District.

The Chera or Kērala territory consisted in the main of the rugged region of the Western Ghāts to the south of the Chandragiri river, which falls into the sea not far from Mangalore, and forms the boundary between the peoples who severally speak Tulu and Malayālam.

No such traditional limits are attributed to the dominions of the Pallavas, although their early habitat, the Tondainādu, comprising the districts near Madras, was well known. They held as much territory as they could grasp, and Kānchī or Conjeeveram, their capital, was in the heart of *Chola-mandalam*. The facts indicate that they overlay the ancient ruling powers, and must have acquired their superior position by means of violence and blackmail, as the Marāthā freebooters did in the eighteenth century.

as Kallar or 'thieves'. All these people doubtless belonged to the Nāga race. Those statements support the view expressed in the text, as formulated many years ago. See Jouveau-Dubreuil, *The Pallavas*, Pondicherry, 1917.

Outline of Pallava history. For about two hundred years from the middle of the sixth to the middle of the eighth century the Pallavas were the dominant power in the Far South. All the princes of the ancient royal families seem to have been more or less subordinate to them in that period. Simhavishnu Pallava, in the last quarter of the sixth century, recorded a boast that he had vanquished the Pāndya, Chola, and Chera kings, as well as the ruler of Ceylon.

? Pallava coin.

In the time of their glory the home territories of the Pallavas comprised the modern Districts of North Arcot, South Arcot, Chingleput or Madras, Trichinopoly, and Tanjore; while their sovereignty extended from the Narbadā and Orissan frontier on the north to the Ponnaiyār or Southern Pennār river on the south, and from the Bay of Bengal on the east to a line drawn through Salem, Bangalore, and Berar on the west.[1]

Although the Pallavas had to cede the Vengī province between the Krishnā and the Godāvarī to the Chalukyas early in the seventh century, and never recovered it, that century was the time in which they attained their highest point of fame and during which they raised the imperishable monuments which constitute their best claim to remembrance. At the close of the ninth century the sceptre passed definitely from the hands of the Pallavas into those of the Cholas.

Having thus outlined the general course of Pallava history, we proceed to more definite chronicling and to a brief account of Pallava achievements.

Mahendra-varman. Mahendra-varman I (*c.* A.D. 600–25), son and successor of the victorious King Simhavishnu mentioned above, is memorable for his public works, which include rock-cut temples and caves, the ruined town of Mahendravādi between Arcot and Arconam, and a great reservoir near the same. About A.D. 610 he was defeated by Pulakesin II Chalukya, who wrested from him the province of Vengī, where a branch Chalukya dynasty was established which endured for centuries.

Narasimha-varman. Mahendra's successor, Narasimha-varman (*c.* A.D. 625–45), was the most successful and distinguished member of his able dynasty. In A.D. 642 he took Vatāpi (Bādāmi), the Chalukya capital, and presumably killed Pulakesin II, thus putting an end to the rule of the Early Chalukyas, and making the Pallavas the dominant power not only in Tamil Land, but also in the Deccan for a short time.

Hiuen Tsang at Kānchī. Two years before that victory Hiuen Tsang, the Chinese pilgrim, had visited Kānchī, which seems to have been the southern terminus of his travels. Civil war in Ceylon prevented him from crossing over to that country.

[1] *I. G.* (1908), *s. v.* Chingleput District. Trichinopoly and Tanjore were not included in the Tondai nādu.

His observations on the island and on the Pāndya territory were based on information collected at Kānchī. The pilgrim does not mention the king's name, nor does he use the term Pallava. To him the kingdom of Kānchī was simply Dravida or the Tamil country. He notes that the soil was fertile and well cultivated, and credits the inhabitants with the virtues of courage, trustworthiness, public spirit, and love of learning. The language, whether spoken or written, differed from that of the north. It was Tamil then as now. The capital of Malakūta, or the Pāndya

GANESA RATHA.

country, presumably Madura, was a city five or six miles in circumference. A modern observer much admired the plan of Kānchī:

> 'Here', Professor Geddes writes, 'is not simply a city made monumental by great temples and rich and varied innumerable minor ones; what rejoices me is to find the realization of an exceptionally well-grouped and comprehensive town plan, and this upon a scale of spacious dignity, combined with individual and artistic freedom to which I cannot name any equally surviving parallel whether in India or elsewhere.' [1]

That testimony to the good taste of the architect of Pallava times is supported by the excellence of the buildings and sculpture. The kingdom contained more than a hundred

[1] *Town Planning of Ancient Dekhan*, p. 78, by C. P. Venkatarama Aiyar, Madras, 1916.

Buddhist monasteries occupied by over ten thousand monks of the Sthavira school, while non-Buddhist temples, chiefly those of the nude Jain sect, were nearly as numerous. Certain buildings were ascribed to Asoka. The Buddhist edifices seem to have been taken over and modified or reconstructed by the Hindus, and so have mostly escaped notice.

In 1915 Mr. T. A. Gopinātha Rao, after a few hours' search, discovered five large images of Buddha in Conjeeveram, two being in the Hindu temple of Kāmākshī.[1] Further investigation will assuredly disclose many traces of Buddhism in the Pallava country.

MUKTESVARA TEMPLE, KĀNCHI.

Pallava art. Narasimha founded the town of Māmallapuram or Mahābalipuram and caused the execution of the wonderful Rathas, or 'Seven Pagodas' at that place, each of which is cut out from a great rock boulder. His artists also wrought the remarkable relief sculptures in the rocks at the same place. The most notable of those works is the celebrated composition which, as commonly stated, depicts the Penance of Arjuna. The alternative explanation, although plausible, seems to be erroneous.[2]

[1] *Ind. Ant.*, 1915, p. 127.

[2] *Pallava Antiquities*, i, 75. In *H. F. A* (1911), p. 222, pl. xlvi, I followed the older interpretation, which appears to be correct (*Ind. Ant.*, 1917, pp. 54–7).

The sculptures were continued by Narasimha's successor, but had to be abandoned incomplete about A.D. 670 in consequence of the Chalukya attacks.

The splendid and numerous structural temples at Kānchī and other places are slightly later in date, and were mostly erected in the reign of Rājasimha in the early years of the eighth century.

It thus appears that the history of Indian architecture and sculpture in the south begins at the close of the sixth century under Pallava rule. Earlier works, which were executed in impermanent materials, necessarily have perished. It is impossible here to go further into details, but it may be said that the Pallava school of architecture and sculpture is one of the most important and interesting of the Indian schools. The transition from wood to stone effected for northern India under Asoka in the third century B.C. was delayed for nearly a thousand years in the Far South. That fact is a good illustration of the immense length of the course of Indian history and of the extreme slowness with which changes have been effected so as ultimately to cover the whole country.

End of the Pallavas. A severe defeat inflicted in A.D. 740 on the reigning Pallava king by the Chalukya may be regarded as the beginning of the end of the Pallava supremacy. The heirs of the Pallavas, however, were not the Chalukyas, who had to make way for the Rāshtrakūtas in A.D. 753, but the Cholas, who, in alliance with the Pāndyas, inflicted a decisive defeat on the Pallavas at the close of the ninth century. Pallava chiefs continued to exist as local rulers down to the thirteenth century, and nobles bearing the name may be traced even later. But after the seventeenth century all trace of the Pallavas as a distinct race or clan disappears, and their blood is now merged in that of the Kallar, Palli, and Vellāla castes.

There is every reason to believe that future historians will be able to give a fairly complete narrative of the doings of the Pallava kings, and that the mystery which surrounds their origin and affinities may be elucidated in large measure. The brief notice of the subject in this place may be concluded by a few words on the history of religion during the Pallava rule.

Religion. The earliest king who can be precisely dated, and who ruled in the fifth century, certainly was a Buddhist. The later kings were mostly Brahmanical Hindus, some being specially devoted to the cult of Vishnu, and others to that of Siva. Mahendra, who originally was a Jain, was converted to the faith of Siva by a famous Tamil saint, and, with the proverbial zeal of a convert, destroyed the large Jain monastery in South Arcot, which bore the name of Pātaliputtiram, transferred at an early date from the ancient capital of India. The testimony of Hiuen Tsang proves that in the seventh century the nude or Digambara sect of Jains was numerous and influential, and his language implies that the various sects lived together peaceably as a rule, although exceptions may have occurred. The prevailing form of religion throughout the Pallava country in modern times is Saiva.

Parāntaka I Chola. The Chola chronology is known with

accuracy from A.D. 907, the date of the accession of Parāntaka I, son and successor of Āditya, the conqueror of the Pallavas. Parāntaka, who reigned for forty-two years, was an ambitious warrior king, and among other achievements drove the Pāndya king into exile, captured Madura his capital, and invaded Ceylon. Wars between the Tamil sovereigns and the rulers of Ceylon were almost incessant. The events are recorded in a multitude of Indian inscriptions as well as in the chronicles of the island.

Rājarāja the Great. The most prominent of the Chola monarchs were Rājarāja-deva the Great, who came to the throne in A.D. 985, and his son Rājendra Choladeva I, whose reign ended in A.D. 1035. The interval of fifty years covers the period of the most decisive Chola supremacy over the other Tamil powers. The Pāndyas, who never admitted willingly the pretensions of their rivals, which they long resisted, were forced to submit more or less completely to their overlordship.

Coin of Rājarāja.

The exploits of both Rājarāja and his at least equally aggressive son are celebrated in innumerable inscriptions beginning from the eighth year of Rājarāja, whose earliest conquest was that of the Chera kingdom.[1]

His conquests on the mainland up to his fourteenth year comprised the Eastern Chalukya kingdom of Vengī, which had been wrested from the Pallavas at the beginning of the seventh century, Coorg, the Pāndya country, and large areas in the table-land of the Deccan. During subsequent years he subdued Quilon or Kollam on the Malabar coast, Kalinga, and Ceylon. About A.D. 1005 he sheathed the sword and spent the rest of his days in peace. During his declining years he associated the Crown Prince with him in the government, according to the current practice of the southern dynasties.[2] Rājarāja possessed a powerful navy and annexed a large number of islands, probably including the Laccadives and Maldives. When he passed away, he left to his son substantially the whole of the modern Madras Presidency, except Madura and Tinnevelly.

Rājendra Choladeva I. Rājendra Choladeva I carried his arms even further than his father had done. He sent a fleet across the Bay of Bengal, and thus effected the temporary occupation of Pegu, as well as of the Andaman and Nicobar islands. He even ventured on an expedition to the north, about A.D. 1023, and defeated Mahīpāla, the Pāla king of Bihār and Bengal. In commemoration of that exploit he assumed the title of Gangaikonda, and built in the Trichinopoly District a new capital city

[1] Not of the Chera fleet, as in *E. H. I.*[3], p. 465. The correction is due to T. A. Gopinātha Rao in *Travancore Archaeol. Ser.*, vol. ii, pp. 3–5.

[2] That practice accounts for sundry discrepancies in the accession dates.

called Gangaikonda-Cholapuram, adorned by a magnificent palace, a gigantic temple, and a vast artificial lake. The ruins, which have never been properly described or illustrated, have been much damaged by spoliation for building material.

The later Cholas. The death of Rājendra's son, Rājādhirāja, on the battle-field of Koppam in A. D. 1052 or 1053, when fighting the Chalukya, has been already mentioned. Ten years later the Chalukyas were defeated in their turn in another hard-fought contest.

King Adhirājendra, who was assassinated in A. D. 1074, has been named as having been the enemy of the sage Rāmānuja. Rājendra Kulottunga I, the successor, but not the son of Adhirājendra, was the most conspicuous of the later Cholas, who are known as Chalukya-Cholas, because of their relationship with the Eastern Chalukyas of Vengī. Rājendra, who reigned for forty-nine years, effected extensive conquests, and also directed an elaborate revision of the revenue survey of his dominions in A. D. 1086, the year of the survey for the Anglo-Norman Domesday Book.

During the thirteenth century the Chola power gradually declined, and later in that century the Pāndya kings reasserted themselves and shook off the Chola yoke.

The Muhammadan inroad in 1310 and the subsequent rise of the Hindu empire of Vijayanagar extinguished the ancient Chola dynasty with its institutions.

Chola administration. The administration of the Chola kingdom was highly systematized and evidently had been organized in very ancient times. Our definite knowledge of the details rests chiefly upon inscriptions dated between A. D. 800 and 1300. Certain records of Parāntaka I supply particularly full information about the actual working of the village assemblies during the first half of the tenth century. The whole fabric of the administration rested upon the basis of the village, or rather of unions of villages. It was usually found more convenient to deal with a group or union of villages (*kūrram*) rather than with a single village as the administrative unit. Each *kūrram* or union managed its local affairs through the agency of an assembly (*mahāsabhā*), which possessed and exercised extensive powers subject to the control of the royal officers (*adhikārin*). The assembly was elected by an elaborate machinery for casting lots, and the members held office for one year. Each union had its own local treasury, and enjoyed full control over the village lands, being empowered even to sell them in certain contingencies. Committees were appointed to look after tanks, gardens, justice, and other departments.

A certain number of *kūrrams* or unions constituted a District (*nādu*), a group of Districts formed a *kōttam* or Division, and several Divisions formed a province. The kingdom was divided into six provinces. That specially designated as *Chola-mandalam* was roughly equivalent to the Tanjore and Trichinopoly Districts.

The theoretical share of the gross produce claimed by the state as land revenue was one-sixth, but petty imposts in great variety were levied, and the total demand has been estimated as fourfifteenths. It may well have been often much more. Payment could be made either in kind or in gold. The currency unit was the gold *kāsu*, weighing about 28 grains Troy. Silver coin was not ordinarily used in the south in ancient times. The lands were regularly surveyed, and a standard measure was recorded.

Details concerning the military organization are lacking. A strong fleet was maintained. Irrigation works were constructed on a vast scale and of good design. The embankment of the artificial lake at Gangaikonda-Cholapuram, for instance, was sixteen miles in length, and the art of throwing great dams or 'anicuts' across the Kāverī (Cauvery) and other large rivers was thoroughly understood. Various public works of imposing dimensions were designed and erected. The single block of stone forming the summit of the steeple of the Tanjore temple is 25½ feet square, and is estimated to weigh 80 tons. According to tradition it was brought into position by being moved up an incline four miles long. It seems that forced labour was employed on such works. The principal roads were carefully maintained. The particulars thus briefly summarized give an impression that the administrative system was well thought out and reasonably efficient. The important place given to the village assemblies assured the central government of considerable popular support, and individuals probably submitted readily to the orders of their fellow villagers who had the force of public opinion behind them. The system appears to have died out along with the Chola dynasty early in the fourteenth century, and ever since that distant time has been quite extinct. While it is obvious that a dead institution of such antiquity cannot be revived in its old form, it is permissible to regret that modern conditions present so many difficulties in the way of utilizing village assemblies.

Chola art. The story of South Indian art, meaning by that term architecture and sculpture, because no paintings to signify have survived,[1] is of special interest, inasmuch as the art appears to be wholly of native growth, untouched by foreign influence, and to have moved slowly through a long course of natural evolution. The early works of art, executed in impermanent materials, have perished utterly and cannot be described. But beyond all doubt they existed in large numbers and were the foundation of more enduring works. The artists who designed the Pallava temples and wrought the sculptures on the rocks of Māmallapuram were not novices. They had served their apprenticeship, and when the call came to them to express their ideas in imperishable forms of stone they brought to bear on the new problem the skill acquired by generations of practice. The art of the Chola period is the continuation of that of Pallava times. No violent break separates the two stages. The changes which occurred took place gradually by a process of spontaneous development.

The earliest Chola temple described hitherto is that at Dādā-

[1] M. Jouveau-Dubreuil has noted some faint traces of Pallava frescoes. A fine series of paintings executed in the fourth century exists at Sīgiriya in Ceylon (*H. F. A.*, plates lviii–lx).

puram in the South Arcot District dating from the tenth century. The best known examples of Chola architecture, the huge temples of Tanjore and Gangaikonda-Cholapuram, are slightly later in date. Their design pleases the eye because the lofty tower over the shrine dominates the whole composition. In later Chola art the central shrine was reduced to insignificance, while endless labour was lavished on mighty *gopurams* or gateways to the temple enclosure, as at Chidambaram. The result, although imposing, is unsatisfying.

The Hindu temples of Ceylon seem to belong to the school of the earlier Cholas, as exemplified in comparatively small buildings.

The figure sculpture in the panels of the Gangaikonda-Cholapuram temple is of high quality and recalls the best work in Java. Similar sculptures are to be seen elsewhere.

Religion. The Chola kings, apparently without exception, were votaries of the god Siva, but as a rule were tolerant of the other sects in the normal Indian manner. Sometimes, however, they violated the good custom, as when a Chola army destroyed the Jain temples in the Hoysala country, and a Chola king drove Rāmānuja into exile.

Pāndya coin.

The dynasty is said to have patronized Tamil literature.

The Pāndya kingdom. The remaining Tamil powers—the Pāndya and Chera—require little notice. In the seventh century, Hiuen Tsang, who did not personally visit the Pāndya country, gives no information about the character of the government, nor does he name the capital, which must have been Madura. The Pāndya Rājā at that time presumably was tributary to the Pallavas of Kānchī. Buddhism was almost extinct, the ancient monasteries being mostly in ruins. He was informed that near the east side of the capital the remains of the monastery and *stūpa* built by Asoka's brother, Mahendra, were still visible.[1] It is to be feared that search for the site is not now likely to be successful. No attempt has been made so far to trace Buddhist monuments in the Pāndya kingdom. Hindu temples were then numerous, and the nude Jain sect had multitudes of adherents.

Persecution of the Jains. Very soon after Hiuen Tsang's stay in the south, the Jains of the Pāndya kingdom suffered a terrible persecution at the hands of the king variously called Kūna, Sundara, or Nedumāran Pāndya, who originally had been a Jain and was converted to faith in Siva by a Chola queen. He signalized his change of creed by atrocious outrages on the Jains who refused to follow his example. Tradition avers that eight thousand of them were impaled. Memory of the fact has been preserved in various ways, and to this day the Hindus of Madura, where the

[1] I think it probable that Mahendra undertook the conversion of Ceylon from his base at Madura, and not at all in the manner described in the Buddhist ecclesiastical legends.

tragedy took place, celebrate the anniversary of 'the impalement of the Jains' as a festival (*utsava*).[1]

The later Pāndyas. The Pāndya chiefs fought the Pallavas without ceasing, and at the close of the ninth century joined the Cholas in inflicting on their hereditary enemies a decisive defeat. The Pāndyas also engaged frequently in war with Ceylon. In the eleventh and twelfth centuries they were obliged unwillingly to submit to the Chola suzerainty, but in the thirteenth century they regained a better position, and might be considered the leading Tamil power when the Muhammadan attacks began in 1310. After that time they gradually sank into the position of mere local chiefs.

Marco Polo's visit. A glimpse of the Pāndya kingdom in the days of its revival is obtained from the pages of the Venetian traveller, Marco Polo, who visited Kāyal on the Tāmraparni twice, in 1288 and 1293. That town was then a busy and wealthy port, frequented by crowds of ships from the Arabian coast and China, in one of which the Venetian arrived. He describes Kāyal (Cael) as 'a great and noble city', where much business was done. The king possessed vast treasures and wore upon his person the most costly jewels. He maintained splendid state, showed favour to merchants and foreigners so that they were glad to visit his city, and administered his realm with equity.

In consequence of the gradual elevation of the land, Old Kāyal is now two or three miles from the sea. Traces of ancient habitations may be discerned for miles, but the site is occupied only by a few miserable fishermen's huts.[2] It would be difficult to find a more striking example of the vicissitudes of fortune. Many ruined buildings must be hidden beneath the sands, but no serious attempt to excavate the locality has been made. Several Jain statues have been noticed both at Kāyal and at the still more ancient neighbouring site of Korkai.

Chera coin.

The Chera kingdom. Little is known about the details of the mediaeval history of the Chera kingdom, which was subject to the more powerful members of the Chola dynasty. The conquest was the first military operation on a large scale undertaken in the reign of Rājarāja Chola, about A.D. 990. The kingdom ordinarily included the greater part of the modern Travancore State. Village assemblies exercised extensive powers, as in the Chola territory. The Kollam or Malabar era of A.D. 824–5, as commonly used in inscriptions, seems to mark the date of the foundation of Kollam or Quilon.

[1] T. A. Gopinātha Rao, *Elements of Hindu Iconography*, vol. i, Introd., p. 55; Madras, 1914.

[2] *Ind. Ant.*, vi, 80–3, 215.

SELECTED DATES

A.D.	
c. 600–25.	Mahendra-varman Pallava (cave-temples, &c.).
608–42.	Pulakesin II Chalukya.
c. 610.	Eastern Chalukya dynasty of Vengī founded.
c. 620.	Defeat of Harsha of Kanauj by Pulakesin.
c. 625–45.	Narasimha-varman Pallava (*rathas*, reliefs, &c.). Kūna (alias Sundara or Nedumāran) Pāndya, who impaled the Jains, was contemporary.
640.	Hiuen Tsang at Kānchī.
641.	Hiuen Tsang at the court of Pulakesin.
642.	Defeat and deposition of Pulakesin by Narasimha-varman Pallava.
740.	Defeat of Pallavas by Chalukyas.
753.	Overthrow of Early Chalukyas by the Rāshtrakūtas or Rattas.
c. 760.	Krishna I Rāshtrakūta, acc.; Kailāsa temple at Ellora.
c. 815–77.	Amoghavarsha Rāshtrakūta.
907.	Parāntaka I Chola, acc.
973.	Taila founded Second Chalukya Dynasty of Kalyāni.
c. 983.	Colossal Jain statue at Sravana Belgola.
985.	Rājarāja Chola, acc.
c. 1023.	Expedition of Rājendra Choladeva to Bengal.
1052 or 1053.	Battle of Koppam; Cholas defeated by Chalukyas.
1076–1126.	Vikramānka or Vikramāditya Chalukya.
c. 1110–41.	Bittiga or Vishnu-vardhana Hoysala; Rāmānuja.
c. 1160–7.	Bijjala usurper; Lingāyat sect founded.
1288, 1293.	Marco Polo visited Kāyal.
1310.	Invasion by Malik Kāfūr.
1318.	Harapāla Yādava flayed alive.
1326–7.	Destruction of Dorasamudra and the Hoysala power.
1336.	Foundation of Vijayanagar.

AUTHORITIES

Most of the necessary references are given in the foot-notes and in *E. H. I.*[3] (1914); but the recent publications of Prof. G. JOUVEAU-DUBREUIL, of the College, Pondicherry, which are not well known, deserve prominent notice :

1. *Archéologie du Sud de l'Inde*; Tomes I et II; Paris, Geuthner, 1914;
2. *Pallava Antiquities* (in English); vol. i; London, Probsthain, 1916;
3. *Dravidian Architecture* (in English); Madras, S.P.C.K. Press, 1917;
4. *The Pallavas* (in English), 87 pp.; Pondicherry; sold by the author, 1917. An important work.

The learned Professor's studies are characterized by penetrating insight, scientific method, and convincing logic.

Another valuable treatise is *Tamil Studies* by M. SRINIVASA AIYANGAR; Madras, Guardian Press, 1914. Many of the author's views are disputable, and the quotations in Tamil character are somewhat excessive, but much may be learned from the book. The *Travancore Archaeological Series* in progress since 1910 contains a great mass of useful facts. One of the latest disquisitions is a short paper, 'The Early Cholas', by H. KRISHNA SASTRI in *Ann. Rep. A. S., India*, for 1913–14 (Calcutta, 1917).

BOOK IV

CHAPTER 1

The Rise of the Muhammadan Power in India and the Sultanate of Delhi, A.D. 1175–1290.

Rise and decline of Muhammadan power. The Muhammadan conquest of India did not begin until the last quarter of the twelfth century, if the frontier provinces of Kābul, the Panjāb, and Sind be excluded from consideration. It may be reckoned to have continued until 1340, when the empire of Sultan Muhammad bin Tughlak attained its maximum extent, comprising twenty-four provinces more or less effectively under the control of the Sultan of Delhi.[1] The provinces included a large portion of the Deccan, and even a section of the Ma'abar or Coromandel coast.

After 1340 the frontiers of the Sultanate of Delhi rapidly contracted, many new kingdoms, both Musalmān and Hindu, being formed. The quick growth of the Hindu empire of Vijayanagar checked the southern progress of Islām and recovered some territory which had passed under Muslim rule. Elsewhere, too, Hindu chiefs asserted themselves, and it may be affirmed with truth that for more than two centuries, from 1340 to the accession of Akbar in 1556, Islām lost ground on the whole.

Under Akbar and his successors the Muslim frontier was extended from time to time until 1691, when the officers of Aurangzēb were able for a moment to levy tribute from Tanjore and Trichinopoly in the Far South. After the date named the Marāthās enlarged the borders of Hindu dominion until 1818, when their power was broken and they were forced to acknowledge British supremacy, as based on the conquest of Bengal and Bihār between 1757 and 1765. That, in brief, is the outline of the rise, decline, and fall of Muhammadan sovereign rule in India. From 1818 to 1858 the empire of Delhi was merely titular.

This chapter and the next will be devoted to a summary account of the progress of the Muhammadan conquest from A.D. 1175 to 1340. Most of the conquests, after the earliest, were made by or for the Sultans of Delhi, whose line began in 1206.

The dynasty of Ghōr (Ghōrī). The first attack was made by a chieftain of the obscure principality of Ghōr, hidden away among the mountains of Afghanistan to the south-east of Herat. Little is known about the country, which has never been visited by any European. Even the position of the ancient town of Ghōr, believed to be now in ruins, has not been ascertained with precision. The fortune of the Ghōr chiefs was made by means of a quarrel

[1] The list is in Thomas, *Chronicles*, p. 203.

with the successors of Sultan Mahmūd of Ghaznī. One of those successors named Bahrām having executed two princes of Ghōr, the blood-feud thus started prompted Alāu-d dīn Husain to take vengeance by sacking Ghaznī in A. D. 1150 (=A. H. 544). The unhappy city was given to the flames for seven days and nights, during which

> 'plunder, devastation, and slaughter were continuous. Every man that was found was slain, and all the women and children were made prisoners. All the palaces and edifices of the Mahmūdi kings which had no equals in the world'

were destroyed, save only the tombs of Sultan Mahmūd and two of his relatives. Shortly afterwards Khusrū Shāh, the representative of Mahmūd, was obliged to leave Ghaznī and retire to Lahore (1160). But Ghaznī was not incorporated in the dominions of Ghōr until twelve or thirteen years later (1173), when it was annexed by Sultan Ghiyāsu-d dīn of Ghōr, who made over the conquered territory with its dependencies. including Kābul, to the government as Sultan of his brother Muhammad, the son of Sām, who is also known by his titles of Shihābu-d dīn and Muizzu-d dīn (r-daulat). It is most convenient to designate him as Muhammad Ghōrī, or 'of Ghōr', Sultan of Ghaznī, and conqueror of Hindostan.

Early operations of Muhammad Ghōrī. He began his Indian operations by a successful attack on Multān (1175–6), which he followed up by the occupation of Ūchh, obtained through the treachery of a Rānī. Three years later he moved southwards and attempted the conquest of rich Gujarāt. But Mūlarāja of Anhilwāra was too strong for the invader, who was defeated and repulsed with heavy loss (1178). The victory protected Gujarāt, as a whole, from any serious Muhammadan attack for more than a century, although intermediate raids occurred, and Anhilwāra was occupied two years later. Such checks to the progress of Islām as Mūlarāja inflicted were rare.

In 1187 Muhammad Ghōrī deposed Khusrū Malik, the last prince of the line of Sabuktigīn and Mahmūd, and himself occupied the Panjāb. Having already secured Sind he was thus in possession of the basin of the Indus, and in a position to make further advances into the fertile plains of India, teeming with tempting riches, and inhabited by idolaters, fit only to be 'sent to hell' according to the simple creed of the invaders.

First battle of Tarāin. The Sultan organized a powerful expedition as soon as possible, and in 1191 (A. H. 587) advanced into India. The magnitude of the danger induced the various Hindu kings to lay aside their quarrels for a moment and to form a great confederacy against the invader, as their ancestors had done against Amīr Sabuktigīn and Sultan Mahmūd. All the leading powers of northern India sent contingents, the whole being under the command of Rāi Pithorā or Prithīrāj, the Chauhān ruler of Ajmēr and Delhi. The Hindu host met the army of Islām at Tarāin or Talāwarī, between Karnāl and Thānēsar, and distant fourteen miles from the latter place. That region, the modern Karnāl District, is marked out by nature as the battle-field in

MINARET AT GHAZNĪ.

which the invader from the north-west must meet the defenders of Delhi and the basin of the Ganges. The legendary ground of Kurukshetra, where the heroes of the *Mahābhārata* had fought before the dawn of history was not far distant, and Pānīpat, where three decisive battles were lost and won in later ages, is about thirty miles farther south. The Sultan, who met the brother of Prithīrāj in single combat, was severely wounded, and as a consequence of that accident his army was 'irretrievably routed'. The Hindus did not pursue, but permitted the defeated foe to retire and gather strength for a fresh inroad.

Second battle of Tarāin. In the following year the Sultan returned, met the Hindu confederates on the same ground, and in his turn defeated them utterly (1192, A. H. 588). Rāi Prithīrāj, when his cumbrous host had been broken by the onset of ten thousand mounted archers, fled from the field, but was captured and killed. His brother fell in the battle. Rajā Jaichand of Kanauj fell in another fight. Ajmēr, with much other territory, was occupied at once by the victors. In fact, the second battle of Tarāin in 1192 may be regarded as the decisive contest which ensured the ultimate success of the Muhammadan attack on Hindostan. All the numerous subsequent victories were merely consequences of the overwhelming defeat of the Hindu league on the historic plain to the north of Delhi. No Hindu general in any age was willing to profit by experience and learn the lesson taught by Alexander's operations long ago. Time after time enormous hosts, formed of the contingents supplied by innumerable Rājās, and supported by the delusive strength of elephants, were easily routed by quite small bodies of vigorous western soldiers, fighting under one undivided command, and trusting chiefly to well-armed mobile cavalry. Alexander, Muhammad of Ghōr, Bābur, Ahmad Shāh Durrānī, and other capable commanders, all used essentially the same tactics by which they secured decisive victories against Hindu armies of almost incredible numbers. The ancient Hindu military system, based on the formal rules of old-world scriptures, was good enough for use as between one Indian nation and another, but almost invariably broke down when pitted against the onslaughts of hardy casteless horsemen from the west, who cared nothing for the *shāstras*. The Hindu defenders of their country, although fully equal to their assailants in courage and contempt of death, were distinctly inferior in the art of war, and for that reason lost their independence. The Indian caste system is unfavourable to military efficiency as against foreign foes.

Kutbu-d dīn Aibak. After the victory of Tarāin the Sultan returned to Khurāsān, leaving the conduct of the Indian campaign in the hands of Kutbu-d dīn Aibak or Ībak, a native of Turkestan, who had been bought as a slave, and was still technically in a servile condition while conquering Hindostan. In 1193 (A. H. 589) Kutbu-d dīn occupied Delhi, and advanced towards Benares. Kanauj does not appear to have been molested, but must have come under the control of the invaders. Soon afterward Gwālior fell, and in 1197 Anhilwāra, the capital of Gujarāt, was occupied, although the province was not subdued.

Conquest of Bihār. The subjugation of the eastern kingdoms was effected with astounding facility by Kutbu-d dīn's general, Muhammad Khiljī, the son of Bakhtyār. The Muslim general, acting independently, after completing several successful plundering expeditions, seized the fort of Bihār, probably in 1197, by an audacious move, and thus mastered the capital of the province of that name. The capture of the fort was effected by a party of two hundred horsemen. The prevailing religion of Bihār at that time was a corrupt form of Buddhism, which had received liberal patronage from the kings of the Pāla dynasty for more than three centuries. The Muhammadan historian, indifferent to distinctions among idolaters, states that the majority of the inhabitants were 'shaven-headed Brahmans', who were all put to the sword. He evidently means Buddhist monks, as he was informed that the whole city and fortress were considered to be a college, which the name Bihār signifies. A great library was scattered. When the victors desired to know what the books might be no man capable of explaining their contents had been left alive. No doubt everything was then burnt. The multitude of images used in mediaeval Buddhist worship always inflamed the fanaticism of Muslim warriors to such fury that no quarter was given to the idolaters. The ashes of the Buddhist sanctuaries at Sārnāth near Benares still bear witness to the rage of the image-breakers. Many noble monuments of the ancient civilization of India were irretrievably wrecked in the course of the early Muhammadan invasions. Those invasions were fatal to the existence of Buddhism as an organized religion in northern India, where its strength resided chiefly in Bihār and certain adjoining territories. The monks who escaped massacre fled, and were scattered over Nepāl, Tibet, and the south. After A.D. 1200 the traces of Buddhism in upper India are faint and obscure.

Conquest of Bengal. Bengal, then under the rule of Lakshmana Sēna, an aged and venerated Brahmanical prince, succumbed even more easily a little later, probably at the close of 1199. Muhammad Khiljī, son of Bakhtyār, riding in advance of the main body of his troops, suddenly appeared before the capital city of Nūdīah (Nuddea) with a party of eighteen troopers, who were supposed by the people to be horse dealers. Thus slenderly escorted he rode up to the Rājā's palace and boldly attacked the doorkeepers. The raider's audacity succeeded. The Rājā, who was at his dinner, slipped away by a back door and retired to the neighbourhood of Dacca, where his descendants continued to rule as local chiefs for several generations. The Muslim general destroyed Nūdīah, and transferred the seat of government to Lakshmanāvatī or Gaur, an ancient Hindu city. Muhammad secured the approval of his master, Kutbu-d dīn, by giving him plenty of plunder, and proceeded to organize a purely Muhammadan provincial administration, in practical independence. Mosques and other Muslim edifices were erected all over the kingdom. The conquest so easily effected was final. Bengal never escaped from the rule of Muhammadans for any considerable time until they were superseded in the eighteenth century by the British, whose victory at Plassey was gained nearly as cheaply as that of Muhammad Khiljī.

Conquest of Bundēlkhand. The strong Chandēl fortress of Kālanjar in Bundēlkhand was surrendered by the minister of Rājā Parmāl (Paramarrdi), in 1203, to Kutbu-d dīn.

Coin of Paramarrdi.

The gratified historian of the conqueror's exploits states that

'the temples were converted into mosques and abodes of goodness, and the ejaculations of the bead-counters [worshippers using rosaries] and the voices of the summoners to prayer ascended to the highest heaven, and the very name of idolatry was annihilated. . . . Fifty thousand men came under the collar of slavery, and the plain became black as pitch with Hindus.'

The victor passed on and occupied Mahoba, the seat of the Chandēl civil government.

Death of Muhammad of Ghōr. In the same year Ghiyāsu-d dīn, the Sultan of Ghōr, died and was succeeded by his brother Muhammad, who thus united in his person all the dominions of the family. Muhammad had returned to Ghaznī after the capture of Kālanjar. Two years later, in 1205, he was recalled to the Panjāb in order to suppress a revolt of the powerful Khokhar tribe. The Sultan treated the foe in the drastic manner of the times. He 'sent that refractory race to hell, and carried on a holy war as prescribed by the canons of Islām, and set a river of the blood of those people flowing'. But fate overtook him. As he was on the march towards Ghaznī in March 1206 (A. H. 602) he was stabbed by a sectarian fanatic at Dhamiāk, a camping-ground now in the Jihlam (Jhelum) District.

The first Sultan of Delhi. Kutbu-d dīn, who had been dignified with the title of Sultan by Muhammad Ghōrī's brother's son, Ghiyāsu-d dīn Mahmūd, succeeded Muhammad Ghōrī as sovereign of the new Indian conquests, and from 1206 may be reckoned as the first Sultan of Delhi. But his enthronement took place at Lahore. The new sovereign sought to strengthen his position by marriage alliances with influential rival chiefs. He himself married the daughter of Tāju-d dīn Yalduz (Eldoz), and he gave his sister to Nāsiru-d dīn Kubācha, who became the ruler of Sind. Īltutmish (Altamsh), governor of Bihār, married Kutbu-d dīn's daughter.

The three persons named, Yalduz, Kubācha, and Īltutmish, had been slaves like Kutbu-d dīn himself. The dynasty founded by Kutbu-d dīn and continued by other princes of servile origin is consequently known to history as the Slave Dynasty.

Kutbu-d dīn died in 1210 from the effects of an accident on the polo-ground, having ruled as Sultan for a little more than four years.

Ferocity of the early invaders. He was a typical specimen of the ferocious Central Asian warriors of the time, merciless and fanatical. His valour and profuse liberality to his comrades endeared him to the bloodthirsty historian of his age, who praises him as having been a 'beneficent and victorious monarch. . . . His gifts', we are told, 'were bestowed by hundreds of thousands, and his slaughters likewise were by hundreds of thousands.' All the leaders in the Muslim conquest of Hindostan similarly rejoiced in committing wholesale massacres of Hindu idolaters, armed or unarmed. Their rapid success was largely due to their pitiless 'frightfulness', which made resistance terribly dangerous, and could not always be evaded by humble submission. The author of the *Tabakāt-i Nāsirī* quoted above thoroughly approved of the ferocity of his heroes, and centuries later we find much the same temper shown in the writings of Firishta and Badāonī.

The modern reader of the panegyrics recorded by Muslim authors in praise of 'beneficent' monarchs who slaughtered their hundreds of thousands with delight often longs for an account of their character as it appeared to the friends and countrymen of the victims. But no voice has come from the grave, and the story of the Muhammadan conquest as seen from the Hindu point of view was never written, except to some extent in Rājputāna. The current notions of Indian mediaeval history, based chiefly on the narrative of Elphinstone, who worked entirely on materials supplied by Muslim authors, seem to me to be largely erroneous and often to reflect the prejudices of the historians who wrote in Persian.

Architecture of the early Sultans. The prevailing favourable or at least lenient judgement on the merits of the earlier and appallingly bloodthirsty Sultans in India is due in no small measure to the admiration deservedly felt for their architectural works. The 'Kutb' group of buildings at Old Delhi, although named after the saint from Ūsh who lies buried there, rather than after the first Sultan, undoubtedly is in part the work of Kutbu-d dīn Aibak, who built the noble screen of arches. The question whether the famous Mīnār was begun by him and completed by Īltutmish, or was wholly built by the later sovereign, has given rise to differences of opinion depending on the interpretation of certain inscriptions.

Indo-Muhammadan architecture, which derives its peculiar character from the fact that Indian craftsmen necessarily were employed on the edifices of the foreign faith, dates from the short reign of Kutbu-d dīn Aibak. The masterpieces of the novel form of art cost a heavy price by reason of the destruction of multitudes of equally meritorious ancient buildings and sculptures in other styles. The materials of no less than twenty-seven Hindu temples were used in the erection of the 'Kutb' mosque.

The end of Muhammad, son of Bakhtyār. The ludicrous facility with which Bihār and Bengal had been overrun and annexed tempted Muhammad bin Bakhtyār to a more adventurous enterprise.

'The ambition of seizing the country of Turkestan and Tibbat [Tibet] began to torment his brain; and he had an army got ready, and about 10,000 horse were organized.'

Unfortunately, the information available is not sufficient to determine exactly either the line of his march or the farthest point of his advance. He seems to have moved through the region now known as the Bogra and Jalpaiguri Districts, and to have

GREAT ARCH, KUTB MOSQUE.

crossed a great river supposed to be the Karatōya by a stone bridge of twenty arches, the site of which has not been identified. The rivers have completely changed their courses. The Tīsta, for instance, now a tributary of the Brahmaputra, formerly joined the Karatōya. He is said to have reached 'the open country of Tibbat', but what that phrase may mean it is not easy to say. Beyond a certain point, perhaps to the north of Darjeeling, he was unable to proceed, and was obliged to retreat. His starving force, finding the bridge broken, attempted to ford the river. All were drowned, except about a hundred including the leader, who struggled across somehow. Muhammad, overcome by shame and remorse, took to his bed and died, or, according to another account, was assassinated.[1] His death occurred in the Hijrī year 602, equivalent to A.D. 1205–6. Early in the reign of Aurangzēb Mīr Jumla attempted to invade Assam and failed nearly as disastrously as his predecessor had done. The mountains to the north of Bengal were never reduced to obedience by any Muhammadan sovereign.

Sultan Īltutmish. Ārām, the son of Kutbu-d dīn, who succeeded to the throne, did not inherit his father's abilities, and was quickly displaced (1211) in favour of his sister's husband, Īltutmish, corruptly called Altamsh, who assumed the title of Shamsu-d dīn, 'the sun of religion'. Much of his time was spent in successful fighting with his rival slave chieftains, Yalduz and Kubācha. Before he died in 1236 he had reduced the greater part of Hindostan to subjection, more or less complete.

Coin of Īltutmish.

The Kutb Mīnār was built in large part, if not wholly, under his direction about A.D. 1232. He made other important additions to the Kutb group of buildings, and is buried there in a beautiful tomb, 'one of the richest examples of Hindu art applied to Muhammadan purposes that Old Delhi affords'. Īltutmish is also responsible for a magnificent mosque at Ajmēr, built like that at Delhi from the materials of Hindu temples.

Chingiz Khān. In his days India narrowly escaped the most terrible of all possible calamities, a visit from Chingiz Khān, the dreaded Great Khān or Khākān of the Mongols.[2] He actually advanced as far as the Indus, in pursuit of Jalālu-d dīn Mankbarnī, the fugitive Sultan of Khwārizm or Khiva, who took refuge at the court of Delhi, after surprising adventures. The western Panjāb was plundered by the Mongol troopers, but no organized invasion of India took place. Chingiz Khān had some thoughts of going home to Mongolia through India and Tibet, and is said to have asked permission to pass through the territories of Īltutmish; but happily he changed his mind and retired from Peshāwar.

[1] See Blochmann in *J. A. S. B.*, part i for 1875, p. 282.

[2] The spelling of the name varies much. Howorth gives Chinghiz as the most correct form. Raverty uses both Chingiz and Chingīz. The coin of a governor of Multān with the same name has حىكر without dots or vowel marks. The *Encycl. Brit.* has the form Jenghiz, while Chambers gives Genghis. Chingiz seems to be the simplest and safest spelling. Mongol (Monggol) is the same word as Mughal (Mogul, &c.), but it is convenient to confine the term Mongol to the heathen followers of Chingiz, who were mostly 'narrow-eyed' people, reserving the term Mogul in its various spellings for the more civilized tribes, largely of Turkī blood, who became Muhammadans in the fourteenth century, and from whom sprang the Chagatāi or Jagatāi section of Turks to which Bābur and his successors in India belonged. The Turkī races ordinarily resemble Europeans in features, and have not the Mongolian 'narrow eyes' strongly marked, but Turks and Mongols intermarried freely, and the Mongol blood often asserted itself. It shows in the portraits of Akbar.

Chingiz Khān was the official title of the Mongol chieftain Temujin or Tamūrchi, born in 1162, who acquired ascendancy early in life over the tribes of Mongolia. About the beginning of the thirteenth century they elected him to be the head of their confederacy and he then adopted the style of Chingiz Khān, probably a corruption of a Chinese title. In the course of a few years he conquered a large portion of China and all the famous kingdoms of Central Asia. Balkh, Bokhāra, Samarkand, Herāt, Ghaznī, and many other cities of renown fell under his merciless hand and were reduced to ruins. The vanquished inhabitants, men, women, and children, were slain literally in millions. Those countries even to this day have not recovered from the effects of his devastations. He carried his victorious hordes far into Russia to the bank of the Dnieper, and when he died in 1227 ruled a gigantic empire extending from the Pacific to the Black Sea.

The author of the *Tabakāt-i Nāsirī*, who admired a Muslim, but abhorred a heathen slayer of men, has drawn a vivid sketch of the conqueror, which is worth quoting :

> ' Trustworthy persons have related that the Chingiz Khān, at the time when he came into Khurāsān, was sixty-five [lunar] years old, a man of tall stature, of vigorous build, robust in body, the hair on his face scanty and turned white, with cat's eyes, possessed of great energy, discernment, genius, and understanding, awe-striking, a butcher, just, resolute, an overthrower of enemies, intrepid, sanguinary, cruel.'

The author goes on to say that the Khān was an adept in magic, and befriended by devils. He would sometimes fall into a trance and then utter oracles dictated by the devils who possessed him. Perhaps, like Akbar, Peter the Great, and several other mighty men of old, he may have been an epileptic.

Sultan Raziyyatu-d dīn. Sultan Īltutmish, knowing the incapacity of his surviving sons, had nominated his daughter Raziyya or Raziyyatu-d dīn ('accepted by religion') as his successor.[1] But the nobles thought that they knew better and placed on the throne Prince Ruknu-d dīn, a worthless debauchee. After a scandalous reign of a few months he was put out of the way and replaced by his sister, who assumed the title of Sultan and did her best to play the part of a man. She took an active part in the wars with Hindus and rebel Muslim chiefs, riding an elephant in the sight of all men. But her sex was against her. She tried to compromise by marrying a chief who had opposed her in rebellion. Even that expedient did not save her. Both she and her husband were killed by certain Hindus. She had a troubled reign of more than three years. The author of the *Tabakāt-i Nāsirī*, the only contemporary authority for the period, gives Sultan Raziyyatu-d dīn a high character from his Muslim point of view. She was, he declares,

Coin of Raziyya

[1] She also bore the title of Jalālu-d dīn (Thomas, *Chronicles*, p. 138). Ibn Batuta gives her name simply as Raziyyat—his words are *wa bintari tasmī Razīyyat* (Defrémery, iii. 166).

'a great sovereign, and sagacious, just, beneficent, the patron of the learned, a dispenser of justice, the cherisher of her subjects, and of warlike talent, and was endowed with all the admirable attributes and qualifications necessary for kings; but as she did not attain the destiny in her creation of being computed among men, of what advantage were all these excellent qualifications unto her?'

Sultan Nāsiru-d dīn. A son and grandson of Sultan Iltutmish were then successively enthroned. Both proved to be failures and were removed in favour of Nāsiru-d dīn, a younger son of Iltutmish (1246), who managed to retain his life and office for twenty years. The historian, Minhāj-i Sirāj, who has been quoted more than once, held high office under Nāsiru-d dīn and called his book by his sovereign's name. His judgement of a liberal patron necessarily is biased, but no other contemporary authority exists, and we must be content with his version of the facts. So far as appears, the Sultan lived the life of a fanatical devotee, leaving the conduct of affairs in the hands of Ulugh Khān Balban, his father-in-law and minister. 'At this time', the historian observes, 'many holy expeditions, as by creed enjoined, were undertaken, and much wealth came in from all parts.'

Mongol raids. The Mongols whom Chingiz Khān had left behind, or who crossed the frontier after his retirement, gave constant trouble during the reign. They had occupied and ruined Lahore in 1241–2 and continued to make many inroads on Sind, including Multān. Nāsiru-d dīn, who had no family, nominated Ulugh Khān Balban as his successor.[1]

The nature of the warfare of the period is illustrated by the description of the campaign in Sirmūr, a hill state of the Panjāb, to the south of Simla.

'Ulugh Khān Azam, by stroke of sword, turned that mountain tract upside down, and pushed on through passes and defiles to Sirmūr, and devastated the hill-tract, and waged holy war as by the faith enjoined; over which tract no sovereign had acquired power, and which no Musalmān army had ever before reached, and caused such a number of villainous Hindu rebels to be slain as cannot be defined or numbered, nor be contained in record nor in narration.'

Sultan Balban. Balban, as Elphinstone observes, 'being already in possession of all the powers of king, found no difficulty in assuming the title'. He had been one of the 'Forty Slaves' attached to Sultan Iltutmish, most of whom attained to high positions. Balban's first care was to execute the survivors of the forty, in order to relieve himself of the dangers of rivalry. He had no regard for human life, and no scruples about shedding blood. He was, indeed, a 'ruthless king'. 'Fear and awe of him took possession of all men's hearts,' and he maintained such pomp and dignity at his court that all beholders were impressed with respect for his person. He never laughed. His justice, executed

[1] Elphinstone's account of the reigns intervening between Iltutmish and Balban is incorrect in several particulars. Ibn Batuta alleges that Balban murdered Nāsiru-d dīn.

without respect of persons, was stern and bloody. He secured his authority in the provinces by an organized system of espionage, and spies who failed to report incidents of importance were hanged. He refused to employ Hindu officials. Before his accession he had put down the Mewātī brigands who infested the neighbourhood of Delhi with such severity that the country was quieted for sixty years.

The disgusting details must be quoted in order to show the character of the Sultan and the age. After the army had successfully traversed the haunts of the robbers for twenty days, it returned to the capital with the prisoners in January 1260.

'By royal command many of the rebels were cast under the feet of elephants, and the fierce Turks cut the bodies of the Hindus in two. About a hundred met their death at the hands of the flayers, being skinned from head to foot; their skins were all stuffed with straw, and some of them were hung over every gate of the city. The plain of Hauz-Rānī and the gates of Delhi remembered no punishment like this, nor had one ever heard such a tale of horror.'

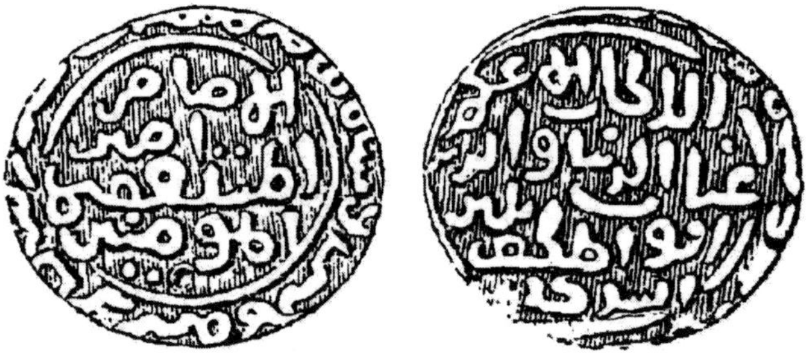

Coin of Balban.

Even after those cruelties the Mewātīs broke out again. Six months after the executions Ulugh Khān (Balban) once more invaded the hills by forced marches so as to surprise the inhabitants (July 1260).

'He fell upon the insurgents unawares, and captured them all, to the number of twelve thousand—men, women, and children—whom he put to the sword. All their valleys and strongholds were overrun and cleared, and great booty captured. Thanks be to God for this victory of Islām!'

When quite an old man he spent three years in suppressing the rebellion in Bengal of a Turkī noble named Tughril who had dared to assume royal state. The rebel's family was exterminated, including the women and the little children. The country-side was terrified at the sight of the rows of gibbets set up in the streets of the provincial capital. The governorship of Bengal continued to be held by members of Balban's family until 1338, when the revolt occurred which resulted in the definite independence of the province. However horrible the cruelty of Balban may appear, it served its purpose and maintained a certain degree of order in rough times. When he died 'all security of life and property was lost, and no one had any confidence in the stability of the kingdom'.

Refugee princes. Balban's magnificent court was honoured by the presence of fifteen kings and princes who had fled to Delhi for refuge from the horrors of the Mongol devastations. No other Muhammadan court remained open to them. Many eminent literary men, the most notable being Amīr Khusrū the poet, were associated with the refugee princes. The Sultan's main anxiety was caused by the fear of a Mongol invasion on a large scale, which prevented him from undertaking conquests of new territory. His eldest and best loved son was killed in a fight with the heathens. That sorrow shook the strong constitution of Balban, the 'wary old wolf, who had held possession of Delhi for sixty years'. He died in 1286 at an advanced age.

Sultan Kaikobād. Balban left no heir fit to succeed him. In those days no definite rule of succession existed and the nobles were accustomed to select whom they pleased by a rough election. Kaikobād, a grandson of Balban, aged about eighteen years, who was placed on the throne, although his father was living in Bengal, as governor of that province, disgraced himself by scandalous debauchery, and was removed after a short reign.

End of the Slave Kings. Balban's hopes of establishing a dynasty were thus frustrated, and the stormy rule of the Slave Kings came to an end. They were either fierce fanatics or worthless debauchees. The fanatics possessed the merits of courage and activity in warfare, with a rough sense of justice when dealing with Muslims. Hindu idolaters and Mongol devil-worshippers had no rights in their eyes and deserved no fate better than to be 'sent to hell'. The Sultan took no count of anybody except the small minority of Muhammadan followers on whose swords the existence of the dynasty depended. 'The army', says the historian, 'is the source and means of government.' Naturally such rulers made no attempt to solve the problems of civil government. Politically, they acquired a tolerably firm hold on the regions now called the Panjāb, the United Provinces of Agra and Oudh, with Bihār, Gwālior, Sind, and some parts of Rājputāna and Central India. Their control of the Panjāb was disputed by the Mongols, from the time of Chingiz Khān (1221). Bengal was practically independent, although Balban's severities enforced formal submission to the suzerainty of Delhi and the occasional payment of tribute. Mālwā, Gujarāt, and all the rest of India continued to be governed by numerous Hindu monarchs of widely varying importance to whom the tragedies of the Sultanate were matters of indifference.

CHRONOLOGY

	A.D.
Sultan MUHAMMAD OF GHŌR (Ghōrī, with titles of Shihābu-d dīn and Muizzu-d dīn, son of Sām)	
Occupied Multān and Uchh	1175–6
Defeated by Rājā of Gujarāt	1178
Deposed Khusrū Malik of Lahore	1187
First battle of Tarāin	1191
Second battle of Tarāin	1192
Reduction of Delhi, Benares, Bihār, &c.	1193–7
Conquest of Bengal	1199–1200
Capture of Kālanjar	1203
Death of the Sultan	1206

Sultans of Delhi; the Slave Kings	A.D.
Kutbu-d dīn Aibak or Ībak	1206
Ārām Shāh	1210
Īltutmish (Altamsh)	1211
Mongol invasion	1221, 1222
Death of Chingiz Khān	1227
Ruknu-d dīn and Raziyyatu-d dīn (Raziyya)	1236
Bahrām, &c.	1240
Nāsiru-d dīn Mahmūd	1246
Ghiyāsu-d dīn Balban	1266
Muizzu-d dīn Kaikobād	1286
Murder of Kaikobād; end of dynasty	1290

Authorities

The leading contemporary authority, and to a large extent the only one, is the *Tabakāt-i Nāsirī*, translated in full by Raverty (London, 1881), with learned but diffuse annotation. Part of the work is translated in *E. & D.*, vol. ii. Other Persian authorities are given in that volume and vol. iii. Firishta mostly copies from the *Tabakāt-i Nāsirī* through the *Tabakāt-i Akbarī*. Elphinstone's account requires correction in some particulars, as he relied chiefly on Firishta. Raverty's *Notes on Afghanistan* (London, 1888), a valuable, though an ill-arranged and bulky book, has been serviceable to me.

CHAPTER 2

The Sultanate of Delhi continued; A.D. 1290 to 1340; the Khiljī and Tughlak dynasties.

Sultan Jalālu-d dīn Khiljī. Kaikobād having been brutally killed, a high official named Fīrōz Shāh, of the Khalj or Khiljī tribe, who was placed on the throne by a section of the nobles, assumed the title of Jalālu-d dīn. Although the Khalj or Khiljī tribe is reckoned by Raverty among the Turks, the contemporary author Ziāu-d dīn Baranī, who must have known the facts, states that Jalālu-d dīn 'came of a race different from the Turks', and that by the death of Sultan Kaikobād 'the Turks lost the empire'. Jalālu-d dīn was an aged man of about seventy when elected. His election was so unpopular that he did not venture to reside in Delhi, and was obliged to build himself a palace at the village of Kilūghari or Kilūkheri, a short distance outside, which became known as Naushahr or 'Newtown'. The year after his accession a famine occurred so severe that many Hindus drowned themselves in the Jumna. The administration of the Sultan is criticized as having been too lenient, and it seems probable that he was too old for his work. On one occasion he is recorded to have lost his temper and to have cruelly executed an unorthodox holy man named Sīdī Maulā. That irregular execution or murder was believed to have been the cause of the Sultan's evil fate. A Mongol invasion made in strong force in the year 1292 was stopped by negotiation, and probably by the payment of heavy blackmail. The historian's account seems to lack candour. Many of the Mongols elected to stay in India, becoming nominally Musalmāns. They were spoken of as New Muslims, and settled down at Kilūghari and other villages near Delhi.

Murder of Jalālu-d dīn. In 1294 Alāu-d dīn, son of the Sultan's brother, and also son-in-law of Jalālu-d dīn, obtained permission for an expedition into Mālwā. But he went much farther, plunging into the heart of the Deccan, and keeping his movements concealed from the court. He marched through Berar and Khāndēsh, and compelled Rāmachandra, the Yādava king of Dēogiri and the western Deccan, to surrender Ellichpur (Ilichpur). Alāu-d dīn collected treasure to an amount unheard of, and showed no disposition to share it with his sovereign. In fact, his treasonable intentions were patent to everybody except his doting old uncle and father-in-law, who closed his ears against all warnings and behaved like a person infatuated. Ultimately, Jalālu-d dīn was persuaded to place himself in his nephew's power at Karā in the Allahabad District. When the Sultan grasped the traitor's hand the signal was given. He was thrown down and decapitated. His head was stuck on a spear and carried round the camp. Lavish distribution of gold secured the adhesion of the army to the usurper, and Alāu-d dīn became Sultan (July 1296).

Thuggee. Jalālu-d dīn, although he did not deserve his cruel fate, was wholly unfit to rule. We are told that often thieves brought before him would be released on taking an oath to sin no more. One of his actions was particularly silly. At some time during his reign about a thousand thugs (*thags*) were arrested in Delhi. The Sultan would not allow one of them to be executed. He adopted the imbecile plan of putting them into boats and transporting them to Lakhnauti (Gaur), the capital of Bengal. That piece of folly probably is the origin of the river thuggee in Bengal, a serious form of crime still prevalent in modern times, and possibly not extinct even now. The story, told by Ziāu-d dīn Baranī, is of special interest as being the earliest known historical notice of thuggee. It is evident that the crime must have been well established in the time of Jalālu-d dīn. The organization broken up by Sleeman presumably dated from remote antiquity.[1]

Sultan Alāu-d dīn Khiljī. The African traveller Ibn Batuta in the fourteenth century expressed the opinion that Alāu-d dīn deserved to be considered 'one of the best sultans'.[2] That some-

[1] By an unlucky slip, when editing Sleeman, I attributed Jalālu-d dīn's folly to Fīrōz Shāh Tughlak (1351–88), a more sensible monarch. My eye was caught by the page-heading (*E. & D.*, iii. 141), '*Tārīkh-i Fīrōz-Shāhī*' (*Rambles and Recollections*, ed. 1915, p. 652).

[2] *wa kāna min khaiyār alsalātīn*, 'il fut au nombre des meilleurs sultans' (Defrémery, iii. 184). The obvious rashness of Ibn Batuta's expression of opinion may serve as a warning when similar praise of other bloodthirsty monarchs is found in the pages of divers authors, and contradiction is not so easy as it is in the case of Alāu-d dīn.

what surprising verdict is not justified either by the manner in which Alāu-d dīn attained power or by the history of his acts as Sultan. Ziāu-d dīn Baranī, the excellent historian who gives the fullest account of his reign, justly dwells on his 'crafty cruelty', and on his addiction to disgusting vice. 'He shed', we are told, 'more innocent blood than ever Pharaoh was guilty of', and he 'did not escape retribution for the blood of his patron'. He ruthlessly killed off everybody who could be supposed to endanger his ill-gotten throne, cutting up root and branch all the nobles who had served under his uncle, save three only. Even innocent women and children were not spared, a new horror. 'Up to this time no hand had ever been laid upon wives and children on account of men's misdeeds.' The evil precedent set by 'one of the best sultans' was often followed in later times. Elphinstone's judgement of Alāu-d dīn's character is too lenient. The facts do not warrant the assertions that he exhibited a 'just exercise of his power', and that his reign was 'glorious'. In reality he was a particularly savage tyrant, with very little regard for justice, and his reign, although marked by the conquest of Gujarāt, many successful predatory raids, and the storming of two great fortresses, was exceedingly disgraceful in many respects.[1]

Coin of Alāu-d dīn Khiljī.

Political events. The political events of Alāu-d dīn's reign comprised numerous plots and revolts, savagely suppressed; five or six invasions of the Mongols; the conquest of Gujarāt; repeated raids on the Deccan, and the capture of two strong Rājpūt fortresses, Ranthambhōr and Chitōr, the former of which is now in the Jaipur, and the latter in the Udaipur State. The Mongol invasions seem to have begun in A.D. 1297 and to have continued until about 1305, but the exact chronology of the reign has not been settled. The conspiracies and revolts may be passed over without further notice. The most serious Mongol invasion is assigned to 1303, when a vast host of the fierce foreigners invested Delhi for two months and then retired. The histories suggest a supernatural reason for their unexplained withdrawal, but it may be suspected that they were simply bought off by a huge ransom. Their final attack on Multān is dated in 1305. It is certain that during the remaining years of Alāu-d dīn's reign Hindostan enjoyed a respite from their ravages.

[1] The reign of Alāu-d dīn requires critical study in a separate monograph. Many points are obscure, and the chronology is far from settled. I cannot attempt to clear up the difficulties in this work. Badāonī, writing in the sixteenth century, was equally puzzled, and plaintively remarks: 'Historians have paid little attention to the due order of events, but God knows the truth.'

Massacre of Mongols. Early in the reign, apparently in 1297 or 1298, an attempted rising of the recently converted Mongols settled in the villages near Delhi induced Alāu-d dīn to perpetrate a fearful massacre, in the course of which all the male settlers, estimated to number from 15,000 to 30,000, were slaughtered in one day.

Expeditions to the south. The expeditions into the Deccan conducted by the eunuch Malik Kāfūr, the infamous favourite of the Sultan, were ended in 1311, when the victorious general returned to Delhi with an almost incredible amount of spoil collected from the accumulated treasures of the south. The Hindu kingdoms of the Yādava dynasty of Dēogiri (Daulatābād), the Hoysala dynasty of Mysore, with its capital at Dōra Samudra; and of the Ma'abar or Coromandel coast were overrrun, plundered, and to a certain extent subjugated. Musalmān governors were established even at Madura, the ancient capital of the Pāndyas. The invaders practised dreadful cruelties.

Ranthambhōr and Chitōr. The first attack on Ranthambhōr in the year 1300 failed, but in the year following the fortress fell after a long siege.

The romantic legends recorded by the Rājpūt bards concerning the sack of Chitōr in 1303 may be read in Tod's pages. They cannot be regarded as sober history and are far too lengthy to be repeated here. But there can be no doubt that the defenders sacrificed their lives in a desperate final fight after the traditional Rājpūt manner, and that their death was preceded by

> 'that horrible rite, the *jauhar*, where the females are immolated to preserve them from pollution or captivity. The funeral pyre was lighted within the "great subterranean retreat", in chambers impervious to the light of day, and the defenders of Chitōr beheld in procession the queens, their own wives and daughters to the number of several thousands. . . . They were conveyed to the cavern, and the opening closed upon them, leaving them to find security from dishonour in the devouring element.'

Tod inspected the closed entrance, but did not attempt to penetrate the sacred recesses.

Follies of the Sultan. Alāu-d dīn was intoxicated by the successes of his arms. 'In his exaltation, ignorance, and folly he quite lost his head, forming the most impossible schemes, and nourishing the most extravagant desires.' He caused himself to be dubbed the 'second Alexander' in the *khutba* or 'bidding prayer' and in the legends of his extensive coinage, dreaming dreams of universal conquest. He persuaded himself that he had the power to establish 'a new religion and creed', with himself as prophet, but had sense enough to listen patiently to the bold remonstrances of the historian's uncle, the *kotwāl* or magistrate of Delhi, and to recognize the fact that 'the prophetic office has never appertained to kings, and never will, so long as the world lasts, though some prophets have discharged the functions of royalty'. In that matter Alāu-d dīn showed himself wiser than

Akbar, who persisted in a similar project and so made himself ridiculous.

Policy towards Hindus. 'Alāu-d dīn's policy in relation to the Hindus, the bulk of his subjects, was not peculiar to himself, being practised by many of the earlier Muslim rulers. But it was defined by him with unusual precision, without any regard to the rules laid down by ecclesiastical lawyers. Ziāu-d dīn states the Sultan's principles in the clearest possible language.

He required his advisers to draw up 'rules and regulations for grinding down the Hindus, and for depriving them of that wealth and property which fosters disaffection and rebellion'. The cultivated land was directed to be all measured, and the Government took half of the gross produce instead of one-sixth as provided by immemorial rule. Akbar ventured to claim one-third, which was exorbitant, but Alāu-d dīn's demand of one-half was monstrous.

> 'No Hindu could hold up his head, and in their houses no sign of gold or silver . . . or of any superfluity was to be seen. These things, which nourish insubordination and rebellion, were no longer to be found. . . . Blows, confinement in the stocks, imprisonment and chains, were all employed to enforce payment.'

Replying to a learned lawyer whom he had consulted, the Sultan said:

> 'Oh, doctor, thou art a learned man, but thou hast had no experience; I am an unlettered man, but I have seen a great deal; be assured then that the Hindus will never become submissive and obedient till they are reduced to poverty. I have, therefore, given orders that just sufficient shall be left to them from year to year, of corn, milk, and curds, but that they shall not be allowed to accumulate hoards and property.'

Tyranny. His tyranny was enforced by an organized system of espionage and ferocious punishments. Prices were regulated by order, and state granaries on a large scale were constructed. His measures succeeded in preserving artificial cheapness in the markets of the capital even during years of drought, but at the cost of infinite oppression. All his fantastic regulations died with him.

Buildings and literature. Alāu-d dīn loved building and executed many magnificent works. He built a new Delhi called Sīrī on the site now marked by the village of Shāhpur, but his edifices there were pulled down by Shēr Shāh and have wholly disappeared. He made extensive additions to the 'Kutb' group of sacred structures, and began a gigantic *mīnār* which was intended to far surpass the noble Kutb Mīnār. The unfinished stump still stands. When building Sīrī he remembered that 'it is a condition that in a new building blood should be sprinkled; he therefore sacrificed some thousands of goat-bearded Mughals for the purpose'.

In early life he was illiterate, but after his accession acquired the art of reading Persian to some extent. In spite of his personal indifference to learning several eminent literary men attended his court, of whom the most famous is Amīr Khusrū, a voluminous and much admired author in both verse and prose.

Death of Alāu-d dīn. The tyrant suffered justly from many troubles in his latter days, and 'success no longer attended him'. His naturally violent temper became uncontrollable, and he allowed his guilty infatuation for Malik Kāfūr to influence all his actions. His health failed, dropsy developed, and in January 1316 he died. 'Some say that the infamous Malik Kāfūr helped his disease to a fatal termination.'

Malik Kāfūr placed an infant son of the Sultan on the throne, reserving all power to himself. He imprisoned, blinded, or killed most of the other members of the royal family, but his criminal rule lasted only thirty-five days. After the lapse of that time he and his companions were beheaded by their slave guards.

Sultan Kutbu-d dīn Mubārak. Kutbu-d dīn or Mubārak Khān, a son of Alāu-d dīn, who had escaped destruction, was taken out of confinement and enthroned. The young sovereign was wholly evil, the slave of filthy vice, and no good for anything. He was infatuated with a youth named Hasan, originally an outcast *parwārī*, the lowest of the low, whom he ennobled under the style of Khusrū Khān. 'During his reign of four years and four months, the Sultan attended to nothing but drinking, listening to music, debauchery, and pleasure, scattering gifts, and gratifying his lusts.' By good luck the Mongols did not attack. If they had done so there was no one to oppose them. Kutbu-d dīn Mubārak attained two military successes. His officers tightened the hold of his government on Gujarāt, and he in person led an army into the Deccan against Dēogiri, where the Rājā, Harpāl Dēo, had revolted. The Hindu prince failed to offer substantial resistance and was barbarously flayed alive (1318). After his triumphant return from the Deccan the Sultan became still worse than before.

> 'He gave way to wrath and obscenity, to severity, revenge, and heartlessness. He dipped his hands in innocent blood, and he allowed his tongue to utter disgusting and abusive words to his companions and attendants. . . . He cast aside all regard for decency, and presented himself decked out in the trinkets and apparel of a female before his assembled company;'

and did many other evil deeds.

Ultimately the degraded creature was killed by his minion, Khusrū Khān, aided by his outcast brethren, 'and the basis of the dynasty of Alāu-d dīn was utterly razed'.

The vile wretches who thus attained momentary power abused it to the utmost. Khusrū even ventured to marry his late sovereign's chief consort, who had been a Hindu princess. The usurper favoured Hindus as against Muslims, and it was said that 'Delhi had once more come under Hindu rule'. The orgy of low-born triumph did not last long. After a few months the usurper was defeated and beheaded by Ghāzī Malik, a Karaunia Turk noble, governor of Debālpur in the Panjāb. Everything was in confusion and no male scion of the royal stock had been left in existence.

Ghiyāsu-d dīn Tughlak Shāh. The nobles having thus a free hand, and recognizing the fact that the disordered State required a master, elected Ghāzī Malik to fill the vacant throne. He assumed the style of Ghiyāsu-d dīn Tughlak, and is often called Tughlak Shāh (A. D. 1321). His father, a Turk, had been a slave of Balban ; his mother, a Jat woman, was Indian born. His conduct justified the confidence bestowed on him by his colleagues. He restored a reasonable amount of order to the internal administration and took measures to guard against the ever pressing danger from Mongol inroads.

He sent his son Jūnā Khān into the Deccan, where the countries conquered by Alāu-d dīn had refused obedience. The prince reached Warangal or Orangal, now in the eastern part of the Nizam's dominions, and undertook the siege of the fort. The strong walls of mud resisted his efforts, pestilence broke out, his men deserted, and he was forced to return to Delhi with only 3,000 horse, a mere remnant of his force. But a second expedition was more successful, resulting in the capture of both Bīdar and Warangal. At that time Warangal had recovered its independence, and was under the rule of a Hindu rājā. The Sultan meantime, having been invited to intervene in a disputed succession, had marched across Bengal as far as Sunārgāon near Dacca, and on his way home had annexed Tirhūt. He left Bengal practically independent, although he brought to Delhi as a prisoner one of the claimants to the provincial throne.

Coin of Tughlak Shāh.

Murder of Tughlak Shāh. His son Jūnā, or Muhammad, who had returned from the south, was then in charge of the capital. His proceedings had given his father reason to suspect his loyalty. The Sultan desired his son to build for him a temporary reception pavilion or pleasure-house on the bank of the Jumna. Jūnā Khān entrusted the work to Ahmad, afterwards known as Khwāja Jahān, who was head of the public works department and in his confidence. The prince asked and obtained permission to parade the elephants fully accoutred before his father, who took up his station in the new building for afternoon prayers. The confederates arranged that the elephants when passing should collide with the timber structure, which accordingly fell on the Sultan and his favourite younger son, Mahmūd, who accompanied him. Jūnā Khan made a pretence of sending for picks and shovels to dig out his father and brother, but purposely hindered action being taken until it was too late. The Sultan was found bending over the boy's body, and if he still breathed, as some people assert that he did, he was finished off (A. D. 1325). After nightfall his body was removed and interred in the massive sepulchre which he had prepared for himself in Tughlakābād, the mighty fortress which he had built near Delhi.[1]

Accession of Muhammad bin Tughlak, February 1325. The parricide gathered the fruits of his crime, as Alāu-d dīn Khiljī had done, and seated himself on the throne without opposition.[2] He occupied it for twenty-six years of tyranny as atrocious as any on record in the sad annals of human devilry and then died in his bed. Like Alāu-d dīn he secured favour by lavish largess, scattering without stint the golden treasure stored by his father

TOMB OF TUGHLAK SHĀH.

within the grim walls of Tughlakābād. It was reported that Tughlak Shāh had constructed a reservoir filled with molten gold in a solid mass.

Ibn Batuta; character of the Sultan. Our knowledge of the second sovereign of the Tughlak dynasty, who appears in history as Muhammad bin (son of) Tughlak, is extraordinarily detailed and accurate, because, in addition to the narrative of an unusually

[1] The facts as recorded by Ibn Batuta (vol. iii, p. 213) are certain, having been related to the traveller by Shaikh Ruknu-d dīn, the saint, who was present when the carefully arranged 'accident' occurred. No reason whatever exists for giving Jūnā Khān the 'benefit of the doubt'.

[2] 'Lorsque le sultan Toghlok fut mort, son fils Mohammed s'empara du royaume, sans rencontrer d'adversaire ni de rebelle.'

good Indian historian (Ziāu-d dīn Baranī), we possess the observations of the African traveller, Ibn Batuta, who spent several years at the court and in the service of the Sultan until April 1347, when he succeeded in retiring from his dangerous employment. He was then sent away honourably as ambassador to the emperor of China. But the ships on which the members of the embassy embarked were wrecked off Calicut and the mission was broken up. Ibn Batuta escaped with his life, and ultimately made his way safely to Fez in northern Africa, in November 1349, after twenty-five years of travel and astounding adventures. He experienced the usual fate of men who come home with strange traveller's tales, and was deemed to be a daring liar. But he was no liar, so far as his book deals with India. His account of his Indian experiences, with which alone we are concerned, bears the stamp of truth on every page. Most of his statements concerning Muhammad bin Tughlak are based on direct personal knowledge.[1] Ziāu-d din of Baran (Bulandshahr) also was a contemporary official and wrote in the reign of Muhammad bin Tughlak's cousin and successor, Fīrōz Shāh. Although he naturally does not exhibit the impartial detachment of the foreign observer, his narrative is full of vivid detail. If space permitted the materials would suffice for a long story, but in a short history room can be found only for a brief selection of the doings of one of the most astonishing kings mentioned in the records of the world.

Notwithstanding that Muhammad bin Tughlak was guilty of acts which the pen shrinks from recording, and that he wrought untold misery in the course of his long reign, he was not wholly evil. He was 'a mixture of opposites', as Jahāngīr was in a later age.

He established hospitals and almshouses, and his generosity to learned Muslims was unprecedented. It was even possible to describe him with truth both as 'the humblest of men' and also as an intense egotist. Elphinstone's just summary of his enigmatic character deserves quotation :

'It is admitted, on all hands, that he was the most eloquent and accomplished prince of his age. His letters, both in Arabic and Persian, were admired for their elegance long after he had ceased to reign. His memory was extraordinary ; and, besides a thorough knowledge of logic and the philosophy of the Greeks, he was much attached to mathematics and to physical science ; and used himself to attend sick persons for the purpose of watching the symptoms of any extraordinary disease. He was regular in his devotions, abstained from wine, and conformed in his private life to all the moral precepts of his religion. In war he was distinguished for his gallantry and personal activity, so that his contemporaries were justified in esteeming him as one of the wonders of the age.

Yet the whole of these splendid talents and accomplishments were given to him in vain ; they were accompanied by a perversion of judgement, which, after every allowance for the intoxication of absolute power, leaves us in doubt whether he was not affected by some degree of insanity.

[1] 'Quant aux aventures de ce roi-ci, la plupart sont au nombre de ce que j'ai vu durant mon séjour dans ses États' (vol. iii, p. 216).

His whole life was spent in pursuing visionary schemes, by means equally irrational, and with a total disregard of the sufferings which they occasioned to his subjects; and its results were more calamitous than those of any other Indian reign.'

To that discriminating passage the remark may be added that the Sultan, like Jahāngīr afterwards, believed himself to be a just man, and was persuaded that all his atrocities were in accordance with the principles of justice and Muslim law. There is no reason to suppose that his conscience troubled him. On the contrary, he deliberately defended his conduct against criticism and avowed his resolve to continue his course to the end.

'I punish', he said, 'the most trifling act of contumacy with death. This I will do until I die, or until the people act honestly, and give up rebellion and contumacy. I have no such minister (*wazīr*) as will make rules to obviate my shedding blood. I punish the people because they have all at once become my enemies and opponents. I have dispensed great wealth among them, but they have not become friendly and loyal. Their temper is well known to me, and I see that they are disaffected and inimical to me.'

Thus, he went on, unmoved from his fell purpose, although sometimes permitting himself to be influenced by mere rage and the lust of vengeance. His inhuman tyranny was the direct cause of the break up of the empire of Delhi.

Premising that the authorities are discrepant concerning the order of events, and that the chronology of the reign is consequently uncertain to some extent, the leading events of the Sultan's rule will be now narrated.[1]

Evacuation of Delhi. In the year A.D. 1326–7 (A.H. 727) the Sultan, having taken offence at the inhabitants of Delhi because they threw into his audience-hall abusive papers criticizing his policy, decided to destroy their city. He marched to Dēogiri in the Deccan, where he constructed the strong fort to which he gave the name of Daulatābād, and resolved to make his capital there, in a situation more central than Delhi.[2] Ibn Batuta, who was in the Sultan's service from about 1341 or 1342 to 1347, gives the following account:

'He decided to ruin Delhi, so he purchased all the houses and inns from the inhabitants, paid them the price, and then ordered them to remove to Daulatābād. At first they were unwilling to obey, but the crier of the monarch proclaimed that no one must be found in Delhi after three days.

The greater part of the inhabitants departed, but some hid themselves in the houses. The Sultan ordered a rigorous search to be made for any that remained. His slaves found two men in the streets; one was paralyzed, and the other blind. They were brought before the sovereign, who ordered the paralytic to be shot away from a manjanik [catapult], and the blind

[1] My narrative is based on the table constructed by Defrémery and Sanguinetti, chiefly on the authority of Khondamir (*Voyages d'Ibn Batuta* (1858), vol. iii, pp. xx-xxiv), as checked by the coin dates. But the subject requires special investigation in a separate essay. Obscurities in detail remain.

[2] A gold coin was struck at Dēogiri in A.H. 727 (Thomas, No. 174, p. 209).

man to be dragged from Delhi to Daulatābād, a journey of forty days' distance. The poor wretch fell in pieces during the journey, and only one of his legs reached Daulatābād. All the inhabitants of Delhi left; they abandoned their baggage and their merchandize, and the city remained a perfect desert.

A person in whom I felt confidence assured me that the Sultan mounted one evening upon the roof of his palace, and, casting his eyes over the city of Delhi, in which there was no fire, smoke nor light, said: "Now my heart is satisfied, and my feelings are appeased."

Some time after he wrote to the inhabitants of different provinces, commanding them to go to Delhi and repeople it. They ruined their own countries, but they did not populate Delhi, so vast and immense is that city. In fact, it is one of the greatest cities in the universe. When we entered this capital we found it in the state which has been described. It was empty, abandoned, and had but a small population.'

Ziāu-d dīn confirms the traveller's account, saying:

'The city, with its *sarāis*, and its suburbs and villages, spread over four or five *kōs* [about 7 to 10 miles]. All was destroyed. So complete was the ruin, that not a cat or a dog was left among the buildings of the city, in its palaces or in its suburbs.'

According to Firishta the population of Delhi was removed to Daulatābād for the second time in 1340 (A. H. 741).

The Mongols bought off. The numerous revolts which characterized the reign began as early as 1327, when the governor of Multān rebelled. About the same time Tarmashirīn, Khān of the Jagatāi or Chagatāi section (*ulūs*) of the Mongols, advanced with a large force to the gates of Delhi, and had to be bought off by a heavy payment of blackmail. The Sultan was then obliged to remain for three years at Delhi in order to guard against a repetition of the invasion.[1]

Attack on Persia. Early in the reign an abortive attempt to conquer the Persian province of Khurāsān with a gigantic cavalry force ended in the dispersal of the army and widespread ruin.

Forced currency. The Sultan's extravagances naturally disordered his finances. Casting about for relief he bethought himself of the paper currency of China, and argued that if the Chinese emperor could use paper money with success he could pass copper or brass as if it were silver in virtue of his royal command. Accordingly he issued orders to that effect and struck vast quantities of copper money, inscribed with legends denoting their value as if the pieces were silver. The official issues were supplemented by an immense unauthorized coinage.

'The promulgation of this edict turned the house of every Hindu into a mint, and the Hindus of the various provinces coined millions and hundreds of thousands (*karōrs*, *lākhs*) of copper coins. With these they paid their tribute, and with these they purchased horses, arms, and fine things of all kinds. . . . Every goldsmith struck copper coins in his workshop and the treasury was filled with these copper coins.'

[1] Ziāu-d dīn accuses the Sultan of 'patronizing and favouring the Mughals' (*E. & D.*, iii. 251). He used the savages as instruments of his cruelty.

But the smash soon came, and the Sultan was obliged to repeal his edict, 'till at last copper became copper, and silver, silver'. The discarded coins were piled up in mountainous heaps at Tughlakabad, and 'had no more value than stones'.[1]

Attack on China. Another disastrous project was that of the conquest of China, to be effected through Nepāl, and by crossing the Himalayan ranges. A force of 100,000 cavalry under the command of Khusrū Malik, son of the Sultan's sister, was despatched on that crazy enterprise in 1337–8 (A. H. 738). Naturally, the horsemen came to grief among the mountains, and when they encountered the Chinese were defeated.

The few men, about ten, who survived to return to Delhi were massacred by their bloodthirsty master.

Fate of Bahāu-d dīn. Another sister's son of the Sultan named Bahāu-d dīn rebelled at a date not specified. He failed and was betrayed. His appalling fate is thus related by Ibn Batuta :

'They bound his legs and tied his arms to his neck, and so conducted him to the Sultan. He ordered the prisoner to be taken to the women his relations, and these insulted and spat upon him. Then he ordered him to be skinned alive, and, as his skin was torn off, his flesh was cooked with rice. Some was sent to his children and his wife, and the remainder was put into a great dish and given to the elephants to eat, but they would not touch it. The Sultan ordered his skin to be stuffed with straw, and to be placed along with the remains of Bahādur Būra,[2] and to be exhibited throughout the country.'

When Kishlū Khān, governor of Sind, received the loathsome objects he ordered them to be buried. His action infuriated the Sultan, who pursued the governor to death, and flayed alive a Kāzī who had supported him.

Even after the lapse of so many centuries it is painful to copy the accounts of such horrors, but it is necessary to tell the truth about a man like Muhammad bin Tughlak, and not to permit him to escape condemnation because he was attentive to the ritual of his religion, decent in private life, and extravagantly liberal to persons who attracted his capricious favour.

Many pages might be filled with stories of the crimes committed by the murderous tyrant, but I forbear.

Ruin of the country. The internal administration of the country went to ruin. The taxes were enhanced to a degree unbearable, and collected so rigorously that the peasantry were reduced to beggary, and people who possessed anything felt that they had no resource but rebellion. The Sultan came to hate his subjects and to take pleasure in their wholesale destruction. At one time he

'led forth his army to ravage Hindostan. He laid the country waste from

[1] The forced currency bears the dates A. H. 730, 731, and 732 = A. D. 1329–32.

[2] A relative of Balban and claimant to the viceregal throne of Bengal.

Kanauj to Dalmau [on the Ganges, in the Rāi Barēli District, Oudh], and every person that fell into his hands he slew. Many of the inhabitants fled and took refuge in the jungles, but the Sultan had the jungles surrounded, and every individual that was captured was killed.'

The victims, of course, were all or nearly all Hindus, a fact which added to the pleasure of the chase.

The short-lived empire. Muhammad bin Tughlak, in the early part of his reign, controlled more or less fully an empire far larger than that under the rule of any of his Muhammadan predecessors. It was divided into twenty-four provinces, comprising, in modern terms, the Panjāb, the United Provinces of Agra and Oudh, Bihār, Tirhūt, Bengal, Sind, Mālwā, Gujarāt, and a large portion of the Deccan, including part of Mysore and the Coromandel coast or Ma'abar.[1] The degree of subjection of the various provinces varied much, but in a large part of the enormous area indicated the Sultan's authority, when he chose to assert it, was absolute.

The earlier revolts, which were many, were suppressed in the ruthless manner of which some examples have been cited. Later, the Sultan's tyranny became so intolerable, and the resources at his command so much reduced, that he was unable to resist rebellion with success or to prevent the break up of his empire.

The turning-point was reached in 1338–9 = A. H. 739, when both Bengal and Ma'abar or Coromandel revolted and escaped from the Delhi tyranny.

The decline and fall of the Sultanate, which may be dated from that year, or from 1340 in round numbers, will form the subject of the next chapter.[2]

CHAPTER 3

The Decline and Fall of the Sultanate of Delhi, A.D. 1340–1526; the Tughlak dynasty concluded; Tīmūr; the Sayyids; the Lodī dynasty; Islām in Indian life.

Revolt of Bengal. Bengal had been ruled since the close of the twelfth century by governors who were expected to recognize the suzerainty of Delhi and to send tribute more or less regularly to court. We have seen how Balban suppressed with merciless ferocity Tughril Khān's attempt to attain formal independence. After the extermination of Tughril Khān and his followers, the

[1] The list (from Sirāju-d dīn) is in Thomas, *Chronicles*, p. 203. By a slip the text mentions 23 provinces, while the list specifies 24. The name Ma'abar, given correctly in Arabic characters (معبر), is misprinted Malabar in the English transliteration. No Sultan of Delhi had any concern with Malabar on the western coast. Briggs, the translator of Firishta, confounded Ma'abar with Malabar, and other people have made the same mistake.

[2] The chronology and authorities will be given at the end of chapter 3.

governorship was held by Balban's second son, the father of Sultan Kaikobād, and after him by other members of Balban's family. A contest between two brothers for the viceregal throne resulted, as already mentioned, in the interference of Tughlak Shāh, who marched across Bengal and carried off to Delhi Bahādur Shāh, the claimant whose pretensions had been disallowed. The captive was pardoned and sent back to Bengal by Muhammad bin Tughlak, but rebelled unsuccessfully. He was killed and his stuffed skin was hawked about the empire along with that of the Sultan's nephew, until both were buried by Kishlū Khān, with tragic results, as already stated.

In 1338–9 (A.H. 739) Fakhru-d dīn or Fakhra started a rebellion in Eastern Bengal, which eventually involved the whole province and brought about its complete separation from the Sultanate of Delhi. Muhammad bin Tughlak was too much occupied elsewhere to be able to assert his sovereignty over Bengal. He let the province go, and it continued to retain its independence until reconquered by Akbar. Occasional ceremonial admissions of the superior rank of the Sultan or Pādshāh of Delhi did not impair the substantial independence of the kings of Bengal.

Bengal coin of Fakhru-d dīn.

Rebellions in the south. About the same time, approximately 1340, Saiyid Hasan, the governor of Ma'abar or Coromandel, revolted, and slew the Sultan's officers.

In 1341–2 (A.H. 742) Muhammad bin Tughlak marched southwards, intent on restoring his authority in the peninsula and inflicting condign punishment on the rebel. But when he arrived at Warangal, and was still distant three months' march from his goal, an epidemic of cholera broke out in the camp, which killed many and endangered the life of the sovereign, who was attacked by the disease. He was forced to retire to Daulatābād, and thence to Delhi, having given permission that any persons who desired to do so might return to their old homes in the capital. The Warangal or Telingāna territory was lost to the empire.

Famine. Thousands of people made the attempt to return, but few survived the journey, because an awful famine then raged throughout Mālwā, and was particularly severe at Delhi. All cultivation had ceased, failure of the rains combining with misrule and anarchy to make agriculture impossible. The famine lasted for several years. The Sultan made some feeble efforts to restore tillage by offering loans from the treasury, but the cattle had perished and the people were too exhausted to make use of money.

Vijayanagar and Bahmanī kingdoms. A few years earlier the southern expansion of the Muslim power had been checked, and territory had been lost to the Hindus by the rapid rise of the kingdom of the Rāyas of Vijayanagar to the south of the Krishnā. The traditional date for the foundation of the city is 1336. Ten years later the new kingdom had become an important power.

In 1347 the rebellion of Hasan or Zafar Khān, an officer of the Sultan, and either an Afghan or a Turk, laid the foundation of the great Bahmanī kingdom, with its capital at Kulbargā or Ahsanābād.

The history of both the Bahmanī and Vijayanagar kingdoms or empires will be narrated with considerable fullness in Book V and need not be pursued farther in this place.

Submission to the Egyptian Khalīf. At this time of general insurrection the crazy Sultan took it into his head to fancy that his sovereignty required the sanction of the Khalīf (Caliph), the head of Islām. He took much pains to satisfy himself as to the identity of the prince entitled to the rank of Khalīf, and at length was convinced that the Sultan of Egypt possessed the power to grant the desired investiture. An embassy was sent to Egypt, and the ambassador dispatched from that country with a favourable reply was received with extravagant veneration. Muhammad bin Tughlak professed himself to be merely the vicegerent of the Khalīf, removed his own name from the coinage, and replaced it by that of the supreme ruler of Islām. The coins struck on that principle were issued during about three years, from 1340 to 1343 (A. H. 741–3). Fīrōz Shāh, the successor of Muhammad bin Tughlak, also secured investiture from the Egyptian Khalīf, and was as proud of the honour as his cousin had been.

Khālīf coin of Muhammad bin Tughlak.

Death of the Sultan. The historians give ample details of the endless revolts which marked the latter years of Muhammad bin Tughlak's disastrous reign, and of his attempts at suppression, in some measure successful. 'The people were never tired of rebelling, nor the king of punishing.'

It is needless to follow the wearisome story through all its horrors. The Sultan, after ineffectual efforts to recover the Deccan, where he retained nothing except Daulatābād, moved into Gujarāt in order to suppress the disorders of that province, where he spent three rainy seasons. He quitted Gujarāt late in 1350 to pursue a rebel, and crossed the Indus into Sind, although his health had failed. While he was still on the bank of the river and a considerable distance from Thatha (Tattah), the capital of Lower Sind, his illness increased and developed into a violent fever which killed him in March 1351. Thus 'the Sultan was freed from his people, and the people from their Sultan'. It is astonishing that such a monster should have retained power for twenty-six years, and then have died in his bed. The misery caused by his savage misrule is incalculable. Politically, he destroyed the hardly-won supremacy of the Delhi Sultanate.

Court of the Sultan. The arrangements and ceremonial of the court of Sultan Muhammad bin Tughlak differed widely from those, mainly based upon the Persian model, which were observed by Akbar and his successors, as described in detail by Abu-l Fazl and numerous European travellers. At the Sultan's court the proceedings were dominated by the forms of religion, each ceremony being preceded by the ejaculation 'In the name of God', and precedence being given to theologians. The Mogul ceremonial, on the contrary, was purely secular, precedence being given first to members of the royal family and then to officials according to rank.

Executions. The interior of the Sultan's palace was approached by three gates in succession. Outside the first gate were platforms on which the executioners sat. The persons condemned were executed outside the gate, where their bodies lay exposed for three days. The remains were then collected and thrown into a pit near the huts of the executioners. The relatives were not allowed to give the victims decent burial, but sometimes managed to do so by means of bribery. The approaches to the palace were commonly blocked by mangled corpses.[1]

Audience-halls. The second gate opened on a spacious audience-hall for the general public.

The 'scribes of the gate' sat at the third portal, which could not be passed without the authorization of the Sultan, who gave his formal audiences inside in the 'Hall of a Thousand Columns'. The columns were of varnished wood, and the ceiling was of planks, admirably painted. The formal audience usually was given after prayers in the afternoon, but sometimes at daybreak.

Order of precedence. The order of precedence for placing and presentations was (1) the Chief Kāzī, or judge of Muslim law; (2) the Chief Preacher; (3) the other Kāzīs; (4) leading lawyers; (5) principal descendants of the Prophet (Sayyids); (6) Shaikhs, or holy men; (7) brothers and brothers-in-law of the Sultan, who had no son; (8) principal nobles; (9) foreign notables; (10) generals.

Ceremonial at the 'Īds. Special ceremonial was observed on the occasions of the two great Īd festivals (*'Idu-l fitr* and *'Idu-l kurbān*). One peculiar incident may be mentioned. On those occasions there was set up a great perfume-holder (*cassolette*) made of pure gold in sections, each of which required several men to carry it. Inside were three niches or compartments occupied by men whose business it was to diffuse incense from the burning of two kinds of aloe-wood, with ambergris, and benzoin. The whole audience-hall was filled with the vapour. Boys carrying gold and silver barrels of rose-water and orange-water sprinkled the contents freely over all present.

[1] Badāonī says: 'Moreover there was constantly in front of his royal pavilion and his civil Court a mound of dead bodies and a heap of corpses, while the sweepers and executioners were wearied out with their work of dragging (the wretched victims) and putting them to death in crowds' (transl. Ranking, i. 317).

Daughters of Hindu kings made captive during the year were compelled to dance and sing, and then distributed to persons of distinction.

Ceremonial when the Sultan returned. When the Sultan returned from a progress a large leather reservoir was provided, filled with essence of roses and syrup dissolved in water, which everybody was free to drink.

The Sultan, on several occasions when entering the capital, caused small catapults to be mounted on elephants from which were discharged gold and silver coins to be scrambled for by the populace. In that proceeding he followed the precedent set by Alāu-d dīn Khiljī immediately after his usurpation, when he sought to win popular acquiescence by scattering in the same way 'golden stars', the half- and quarter-*fanams* forming part of the immense booty brought from the Deccan.

Meals in public. The Mogul sovereign always dined alone in the private apartments of the palace. Muhammad bin Tughlak used to dine in the audience-hall and share his meal with about twenty persons of eminence.

He also provided a public banquet twice a day, once before noon and again in the afternoon. The order of precedence was the same as that observed at levées, the judges and theologians being served first. The menu included loaves like cakes; other loaves split and filled with sweet paste; rice, roast meats, fowls, and mince.[1]

Accession of Fīrōz Shāh, 1351. The death of the Sultan left his army camped on the bank of the Indus masterless and helpless. The fighting force, as usual in India, was hampered by a crowd of women, children, and camp followers. When it attempted to start on its long homeward march it was assailed by Sind rebels and Mongol banditti. Much baggage was lost, and the women and children perished. Fīrōz Shah, the first cousin of the deceased sovereign and governor of one-fourth of the kingdom, was then in the camp, but was unwilling to assert himself and occupy the seat of his terrible relative. The army endured utter misery for three days by reason of the want of guidance. Then all the chief men, Muslims and Hindus alike, decided that the only person who could deliver the expeditionary force from destruction was Fīrōz Shāh. Although he professed unwillingness to accept the responsibility of government, and probably was sincere in his reluctance, he was forced to ascend the throne and assume command. He was enthroned in the camp on March 23, 1351. The existence of a leader soon effected an improvement, and the new Sultan ultimately succeeded in bringing back the survivors of the army to Delhi through Multān and Dēbālpur.

[1] Ibn Batuta, transl. Defrémery and Sanguinetti, tome iii, pp. 217–42. The whole account, which is well worth reading, has not been translated at all in *E. & D.*; but some details from another and less authoritative author are given in vol. iii, pp. 575 foll. For Alāu-d dīn see Ziāu-d dīn Baranī in *E. & D.*, iii. 158.

A pretender. Meanwhile, Khwāja Jahān, the aged governor of Delhi, misled by an untrue report of Fīrōz Shāh's death, had set up as Sultan a child falsely alleged to be the son of Muhammad bin Tughlak. When Fīrōz Shāh approached the capital, Khwāja Jahān, finding resistance hopeless, surrendered. The Sultan wished to spare him, but his advisers insisted that high treason must meet its just punishment. The old man, accordingly, was executed. The late Sultan, as a matter of fact, had left no son, so that the enthronement of a supposititious child could not be justified.

Wars with Bengal. In 1353–4 (A.H. 754) Fīrōz Shāh engaged in a war with the king of Bengal which lasted for eleven months. The Bengal monarch was defeated in a battle, the locality of which is not clearly indicated. Fīrōz Shāh offered a silver *tanka* for each enemy head. If the historian may be believed the heads counted and paid for exceeded 180,000. The campaign had no result except the wanton slaughter thus evidenced. No territory was annexed and the practical independence of the eastern province continued unimpaired. Some years later the war with Bengal was renewed. After some fighting terms of peace were arranged, and from that time, about 1360 (A.H. 761), the independence of Bengal was uncontested. The Sultan was entangled on his return in the wild country of Chutiā Nāgpur and was not heard of for six months. Fīrōz Shāh made no attempt to recover his late cousin's dominions in the Deccan. On the contrary, he tacitly acknowledged the autonomy of the Bahmanī king by receiving an embassy from him, and he likewise received envoys from the ruler of Ma'abar.

Attacks on Sind. The Sultan sought to avenge his predecessor by making two attempts to subdue Thathah in Sind. On the first occasion, about 1361, he assembled 90,000 cavalry and 480 elephants. The result was disastrous. Supplies failed and all the horses perished. Under pressure of dire necessity retreat to Gujarāt was ordered. The army, misled, it was alleged, by treacherous guides, suffered unutterable misery in crossing the Runn of Cutch. For six months no news from it reached Delhi, and everybody believed that the Sultan had perished. Order was maintained by Khān Jahān, the resourceful minister in charge of the capital, and in due course the Sultan with the remnant of his army emerged in Gujarāt.

After receiving reinforcements and equipping a fresh force Fīrōz Shāh again advanced into Sind from Gujarāt. On this occasion the invaders secured the crops in time, with the result that the people of the country in their turn suffered from famine. When Thathah appeared to be seriously threatened the Jām with another chief surrendered, and accompanied Fīrōz Shāh to Delhi, where they took up their residence, apparently as hostages. A relative of theirs continued to rule at Thathah, so that the government of Delhi failed to secure any substantial benefit from two costly campaigns and a final nominal success.

Personal tastes of Fīrōz Shāh. It seems to be plain that Fīrōz Shāh possessed no military capacity. His early campaigns both in the east and the west were absolutely futile, and during the greater part of his long reign he abstained from war. His personal tastes were wholly inconsistent with the pursuit of glory in the field. He was extremely devout, although he allowed himself the kingly privilege of drinking wine, and spent much time in hunting. He was fond of the study of history, and his master-passion was a love for building.

He followed the example of his predecessors, by building a new Delhi called Fīrōzābād, which included the site of Indarpat or Indraprastha, famous in epic legend. The two inscribed Asoka columns now standing near Delhi were brought there by order of Fīrōz Shāh, the one from Toprā in the Ambāla District, and the other from Meerut. The contemporary historian describes in interesting detail the ingenious devices used to ensure the safe transport and erection of the huge monoliths.

The Sultan also founded the cities of Hisār Fīrōza (Hissar, to NW. of Delhi), and of Jaunpur (to the NW. of Benares), making use in each case of earlier Hindu towns and buildings. He has left on record under his own hand a list of the principal works executed during his reign of thirty-seven years, comprising towns, forts, mosques, colleges, and many other buildings, besides embankments and canals. The canal constructed to supply Hisār Fīrōza with water was repaired in the reign of Shāhjahān and has been utilized in the alinement of the Western Jumna Canal. His chief architect was Malik Ghāzī Shahna, whose deputy was Abdu-l Hakk, also known as Jāhir Sundhār. Asiatic kings, as a rule, show no interest in buildings erected by their predecessors, which usually are allowed to decay uncared for. Fīrōz Shāh was peculiar in devoting much attention to the repair and rebuilding of 'the structures of former kings and ancient nobles . . . giving the restoration of those buildings the priority' over his own new constructions.

Internal administration. The internal administration of the country, as distinct from the Sultan's personal hobbies, was in the hands of Khān Jahān, the minister, a converted Hindu from Telingāna. When he died in 1370–1 (A. H. 772) his place was taken by his son, who assumed the same title of Khān Jahān, and conducted the government to the end of the reign. Sultan Alāu-d dīn, who had been in the habit of paying cash salaries to his officers, had disapproved of the system of payment by *jāgīrs*, or the assignment of lands and of the revenue which otherwise would be paid to the state, believing that that system tended to produce insubordination and rebellion. But Fīrōz Shāh and his advisers made the grant of *jāgīrs* the rule. Akbar reverted to cash payments from the treasury and direct official administration so far as was practicable.

Alleged prosperity. The statements of Ziāu-d dīn Baranī in praise of Fīrōz Shāh cannot be accepted without reserve. It is no doubt true that the Sultan 'made the laws of the Prophet his guide', and desired to check oppression. But when we are told that

'the peasants grew rich and were satisfied . . . Their houses were replete with grain, property, horses, and furniture; every one had plenty of gold and silver; no woman was without her ornaments, and no house was wanting in excellent beds and couches. Wealth abounded and comforts were general. The whole realm of Delhi was blessed with the bounties of the Almighty':

the exaggeration of courtly flattery is obvious. The historian states that it had been the practice of previous Sultans to leave the peasant only one cow and take away all the rest. The milder rule of Fīrōz Shāh, although it certainly diminished the tyranny practised, cannot have produced a paradise.

Slave raiding. We are informed by the same author that

'the Sultan was very diligent in providing slaves, and he carried his care so far as to command his great fief-holders and officers to capture slaves whenever they were at war, and to pick out and send the best for the service of the court. . . . Those chiefs who brought many slaves received the highest favour. . . . About 12,000 slaves became artisans of various kinds. Forty thousand were every day in readiness to attend as guards in the Sultan's equipage or at the palace. Altogether, in the city and in the various fiefs, there were 180,000 slaves, for whose maintenance and comfort the Sultan took especial care. The institution took root in the very centre of the land, and the Sultan looked upon its due regulation as one of his incumbent duties.'

Such wholesale slave raiding clearly must have been the cause of much suffering, even though it be admitted that the slaves after capture were well treated. Sir Henry Elliot absurdly called Fīrōz Shāh 'this Akbar of his time', forgetting that Akbar at a very early date in his reign forbade the enslavement of prisoners of war. The slaves, of course, all became Musalmāns, and the proselytism thus effected probably was the chief reason why the Sultan favoured the system. After his death most of his slaves were killed by his successors. During his lifetime they must have been a strong bulwark of the throne.

Abolition of torture. We have the good fortune to possess a tract written by Fīrōz Shāh himself which enumerates his good deeds as he understood them to be. One reform, the abolition of mutilation and torture, deserves unqualified commendation, and the orders must have been acted on to a considerable extent during his lifetime. The enumeration of the 'many varieties of torture' employed under former kings is horrible:

'amputation of hands and feet, ears and noses; tearing out the eyes, pouring molten lead into the throat, crushing the bones of the hands and feet with mallets, burning the body with fire, driving iron nails into the hands, feet, and bosom, cutting the sinews, sawing men asunder; these and many similar tortures were practised.

The great and merciful God made me, His servant, hope and seek for His mercy by devoting myself to prevent the unlawful killing of Musalmāns and the infliction of any kind of torture upon them or upon any men.'

Intolerance. But Fīrōz Shāh could be fierce when his religious fanaticism was roused. He records the following facts:

'The sect of Shīas, also called *Rawāfiz*, had endeavoured to make proselytes. . . . I seized them all and I convicted them of their errors and perversions. On the most zealous I inflicted capital punishment (*siyāsat*), and the rest I visited with censure (*tāzīr*), and threats of public punishment. Their books I burnt in public and by the grace of God the influence of this sect was entirely suppressed.'

An immoral sect, which followed obscene practices, resembling those of certain Hindu Sāktas, was dealt with in a drastic fashion, which had more justification than his treatment of the Shīas.

'I cut off the heads of the elders of this sect, and imprisoned and banished the rest, so that their abominable practices were put an end to.'

He caused the 'doctors learned in the holy Law' to slay a man who claimed to be the Mahdī, 'and for this good action', he wrote, 'I hope to receive future reward'.

He was much shocked on hearing of the erection of certain new Hindu temples.

'Under divine guidance I destroyed these edifices, and I killed those leaders of infidelity who seduced others into error, and the lower orders I subjected to stripes and chastisement, until this abuse was entirely abolished.'

He went in person to a certain village named Malūh, apparently near Delhi, where a religious fair was being held, which was attended even by 'some graceless Muṣalmāns'.

'I ordered that the leaders of these people and the promoters of this abomination should be put to death. I forbade the infliction of any severe punishment on the Hindus in general, but I destroyed their idol temples and instead thereof raised mosques.'

He caused certain Hindus of Kohāna who had built a new temple to be executed before the gate of the palace, 'as a warning that no *zimmī* [*scil.* non-Muslim paying the *jizya* as the price of his life] could follow such wicked practices in a Musalmān country'.

The historian witnessed the burning alive of a Brahman who had practised his rites in public.

Those unquestionable facts prove that Fīrōz Shāh carried on the savage tradition of the early invaders, and believed that he served God by treating as a capital crime the public practice of their religion by the vast majority of his subjects. He was far indeed from sharing the views held by Akbar in middle and later life, although that sovereign in the early years of his reign had followed to some extent the precedent set by Fīrōz Shāh.

Bought conversions. The Sultan continues:

'I encouraged my infidel subjects to embrace the religion of the prophet, and I proclaimed that every one who repeated the creed and became a Musalmān should be exempt from the *jizya* or poll-tax. Information of this came to the ears of the people at large, and great numbers of Hindus presented themselves, and were admitted to the honour of Islām. Thus they came forward day by day from every quarter, and, adopting the faith, were exonerated from the *jizya*, and were favoured with presents and honours.'

Such was the origin of a large part of the existing Muhammadan population. Several other sovereigns continued the process of conversion by bribery.

The jizya. The *jizya* in Delhi was assessed in three grades; namely, 1st class, 40 *tankas*; 2nd class, 20 *tankas*; 3rd class, 10 *tankas*. In former reigns Brahmans had been excused. Fīrōz Shāh, after consultation with his learned lawyers, resolved to include them. The Brahmans assembled, and fasted near his new palace on the Ridge for several days until they were at the point of death. The difficulty thus threatened was compromised by the assessment of a reduced all-round rate on Brahmans of 10 *tankas* and 50 *jaitals*. The silver *tankah* of 175 grains was worth a little less than the later rupee of 180 grains.[1]

A *jaital*.

Credit due to the Sultan. Fīrōz Shāh, when due allowance is made for his surroundings and education, could not have escaped from the theory and practice of bigoted intolerance. It was not possible for him in his age to rise, as Akbar did, to the conception that the ruler of Hindostan should cherish all his subjects alike, whether Musalmān and Hindu, and allow every man absolute freedom, not only of conscience, but of public worship. The Muslims of the fourteenth century were still dominated by the ideas current in the early days of Islām, and were convinced that the tolerance of idolatry was a sin. Fīrōz Shāh, whatever may have been his defects or weaknesses, deserves much credit for having mitigated in some respects the horrible practice of his predecessors, and for having introduced some tincture of humane feeling into the administration. He was naturally a kind charitable man, and his good deeds included the foundation of a hospital.

Death of Fīrōz Shāh in 1388. Anarchy. Fīrōz Shāh, who had been forty-two years of age when called to the throne, lost capacity for affairs as the infirmities of advancing years increased. Experiments made in the way of associating his sons with himself in the government were not successful, and his minister, the younger Khān Jahān, was tempted to engage in treasonable practices. In September 1388 the old Sultan died, aged about eighty. The government fell into utter confusion. A series of puppet sultans, all equally wanting in personal merit, pass rapidly across the stage. The kingdom, in fact, ceased to exist, and the governor of every province assumed practical independence. For

Coin of Fīrōz Shāh.

[1] Thomas, *Chronicles*, pp. 218 *n*., 219 *n*., 232, 281 *n*. 64 *jaitals* made one *tankah* in the fourteenth century. A Brahman, consequently, paid about ten rupees a year. The coin No. 207 of Thomas shows that the word جیتل should be vocalized as *jaital*.

about three years, from 1394 to 1397, two rival Sultans had to find room within the precincts of the Delhi group of cities. Sultan Mahmūd, a boy grandson of Fīrōz Shāh, was recognized as king in Old Delhi, while his relative Nusrat Shāh claimed similar rank in Fīrōzābād a few miles distant.

'Day by day, battles were fought between these two kings, who were like the two kings in the game of chess.'

It is not worth while to either remember or record the unmeaning struggles between the many rival claimants to a dishonoured throne.

Mahmūd and his competitor, Nusrat Shāh, were the last of the series of nominal Sultans who filled up the interval between the death of Fīroz Shāh in 1388 and the invasion of Tīmūr ten years later.

Invasion of Tīmūr, 1398. Amīr Tīmūr (Tīmūr-i-lang, the Tamerlane or Tamburlaine of English literature) was a Barlās Turk, whose father was one of the earliest converts to Islām. Born in 1336 Tīmūr attained the throne of Samarkand in 1369, and then entered on a career of distant conquests, rivalling those of Chingiz Khān, whom he equalled in ferocity and cruelty, although he was a Musalmān and equipped with considerable knowledge of Muslim lore. He died in 1405, when meditating the conquest of China and looking forward with eager anticipation to the slaughter of millions of unbelievers. He needed no formal pretext for his attack on India. The feebleness of the government, the reputed wealth of the country, and the fact that most of the inhabitants were idolaters offered more than sufficient inducement to undertake the conquest.

Early in 1398 one of his grandsons, commanding an advanced guard, laid siege to Multān, and captured it after six months. In the autumn Tīmūr himself crossed the Indus, with a large cavalry force, said to number 90,000; sacked Tulamba, to the north-east of Multān, massacring or enslaving the inhabitants. Near Pānīpat, where Mahmūd Tughlak essayed to oppose him, the invader won an easy victory. He then occupied Delhi and was proclaimed king. Some resistance by the inhabitants provoked a general massacre. Previously nearly 100,000 prisoners had been slain in cold blood. The city was thoroughly plundered for five days, all the accumulated wealth of generations being carried off to Samarkand, along with a multitude of women and other captives. Tīmūr was careful to bring away all the skilled artisans he could find to be employed on the buildings at his capital.

He had no intention of staying in India. He returned through Meerut, storming that city, and slaying everybody. He then visited Hardwār, and marching along the foot of the mountains, where it was easy to cross the rivers, quitted India as he had come by the way of the Panjāb, 'leaving anarchy, famine, and pestilence behind him'.

The so-called Sayyids. The appalling atrocities of Tīmūr's raid, which have been barely indicated in the preceding paragraphs, destroyed all semblance of government in Upper India. The rest of the country, of course, remained wholly unaffected by it, and it is probable that many kingdoms hardly knew that the invasion had occurred. No regular Sultan's government was established at Delhi until more than half a century after Tīmūr's departure. From 1414 to 1450 the affairs of the city and a very small territory adjoining were administered, first by Khizr Khān, who had been governor of the Panjāb, and then by three of his successors. Those princes, who never assumed the royal style or struck coins in their own names, professed to regard themselves as Tīmūr's deputies.[1] They pretended to be Sayyids, and consequently are described in the history text-books as the Sayyid dynasty. Their insignificant doings do not merit further notice. The last of the line, named Alāu-d dīn, was allowed to retire to Budāon, where he lived in peace for many years.

Sultan Bahlōl Lodī. Bahlōl Khān, an Afghan of the Lodī tribe, who had become governor of the Panjāb and independent of Delhi, seized the throne in 1450, and was proclaimed Sultan. He engaged in a war with the king of Jaunpur in the east, that kingdom having thrown off its allegiance during the anarchy following on Tīmūr's invasion; and when he died had succeeded in dispossessing Husain Shāh, the king of Jaunpur, and in replacing him by his own son Bārbak Shāh as viceroy. He may be said to have recovered a certain amount of control over territory extending from the foot of the mountains to Benares, and as far south as the borders of Bundēlkhand.

Pathān Kings of Delhi. Many authors, including some who should have known better, erroneously call all the Sultans of Delhi from 1206 to 1450 Pathāns or Afghans. In reality Bahlōl Lodī was the first Pathān or Afghan Sultan. The only other Afghan rulers in Delhi were the Sūr family of Shēr Shāh, who disputed the kingdom with Humāyūn and Akbar. All historical errors are hard to kill. I do not know any error which has shown more vitality than the false designation 'Pathān Kings of Delhi' applied to Turks and people of all sorts.

Sikandar Lodī. The nobles promptly chose Nizām Khān, a son of Bahlōl, as his father's successor. He assumed the royal style of Sultan Sikandar Ghāzī (1489). The principal political event of his reign was the expulsion of his brother Bārbak Shāh from Jaunpur, and the definite annexation of that kingdom. The Sultan also annexed Bihār and levied tribute from Tirhūt. The reader must understand that in those days 'annexation' meant no more than an extremely lax control over the Afghan military chiefs of districts, who were compelled by superior force to yield temporary and imperfect obedience to the Sultan of Delhi.

Muhammadan authors speak well of Sultan Sikandar, who was a furious bigot. He entirely ruined the shrines of Mathurā, converting the buildings to Muslim uses, and generally was extremely

[1] E. Thomas proved that Firishta was mistaken in asserting that the so-called Sayyids struck coin in the name of Tīmūr. The coins they issued bore the names of the regular Sultans of Delhi who preceded them.

hostile to Hinduism. He strictly followed Koranic law, and was a careful, scrupulous ruler, within the limits of his excessive bigotry. He took a special interest in medical lore. His reign was remarkable for the prevalence of exceptionally low prices for both food and other things, so that 'small means enabled their possessor to live comfortably'.

Agra, which had been ruined by Sultan Mahmūd of Ghaznī, and had sunk into insignificance, was improved by Sultan Sikandar, who generally resided there. Sikandara, where Akbar's tomb stands, is named after the Lodī monarch.

A terrible earthquake, extending to Persia, occurred in 1505, and did much damage in northern India. But the historians, as usual, fail to give any particulars, confining their efforts at description to piling up adjectives.

Sikandar died a natural death at the close of 1517.

The kingdom of Jaunpur. It will be convenient to notice briefly in this place the history of the short-lived kingdom of Jaunpur, the relations of which with the Lodī Sultans supplied the most important political events of their reigns. The foundation of the Muhammadan city of Jaunpur by Fīrōz Shāh Tughlak has been mentioned. In 1394 Mahmūd Tughlak appointed a powerful eunuch noble entitled Khwāja Jahān to be 'Lord of the East' (*Maliku-sh shark*) with his head-quarters at Jaunpur. In those days the control exercised by Delhi was so feeble that every provincial governor was practically independent. After the violence of Tīmūr had shattered the Delhi government in 1398, Khwāja Jahān's adopted son seized the opportunity and set up as an independent king with the style of Mubārak Shāh Sharkī (*scil.* Eastern), in 1399.

Coin of Ibrāhīm of Jaunpur.

The newly made king was quickly succeeded in 1400 by his younger brother Ibrāhīm, who reigned prosperously for forty years. Like Sikandar Lodī he was a bigoted Musalmān, and 'a steady, if not bloody persecutor'. He won the approval of the historians who shared his religious sentiments, but, as usual, the other side of the case is not on record. Ibrāhīm's son Mahmūd also is spoken of as a successful ruler. Husain Shāh, the last independent king, was overcome by Bahlōl Lodi in or about 1476, and driven to take refuge with his namesake of Bengal.

The expedient attempted at the beginning of Sikandar Lodī's reign of leaving Jaunpur to his elder brother Bārbak Shāh in full sovereignty was a failure, and led to war, in which Delhi was successful.

The experiment, when repeated at the time of Ibrāhīm Lodī's accession, again failed. Jalāl Khān, Ibrāhīm's brother, who had been set up as king of Jaunpur, was defeated and killed. From that time the 'Kingdom of the East' no longer pretended to an independent existence. It may be considered to have come to an end in or about 1476, when Bahlōl Lodī expelled his brother Bārbak Shāh.

All the members of the Jaunpur dynasty were patrons of Persian and Arabic literature. Their principal memorial is the group of

ATĀLA DEVĪ MOSQUE, JAUNPUR.

noble mosques at Jaunpur, designed in a peculiar style, including many Hindu features. The buildings are unusually massive, have no minarets, and are characterized by stately gateways with sloping walls. The mosques date from the reigns of Ibrāhīm, Mahmūd, and Husain Shāh.

Ibrāhīm Lodī. The new Sultan, Ibrāhīm, who succeeded his father Sikandar, could not succeed in keeping on good terms with his Afghan nobles, and his reign was mostly occupied by conflicts with them. When he was victorious he took cruel vengeance.

Ultimately the discontent of the Afghan chiefs resulted in an invitation being sent by Daulat Khān Lodī to Bābur, the King or Pādshāh of Kābul. Bābur, after several indecisive incursions, started on his final invasion in November 1525; and on April 21, 1526, inflicted on Sultan Ibrāhīm a crushing defeat at Pānīpat, which cost him his throne and life. The battle will be described in connexion with the reign of the victor.

Low prices. The reign of Ibrāhīm was even more remarkable than that of his father for the extreme lowness of prices, due partly to copious rain followed by abundant harvests, and largely to the want of metallic currency. We are told that 'gold and silver were only procurable with the greatest difficulty', and that sellers were ready to offer most extravagant quantities of produce for cash. 'If a traveller wished to proceed from Delhi to Agra, one *bahlōlī* would suffice for the expenses of himself, his horse, and four attendants.'[1]

The coin referred to appears to be the piece weighing about 140 grains, composed of billon or mixed copper and silver in varying proportions. The most valuable pieces cannot have been worth more than two or three pence each. Tīmūr's invasion, apparently, must have produced tremendous economic effects, which have been very imperfectly recorded. Gold and silver seem to have been still abundant in the time of Fīrōz Shāh Tughlak, before Tīmūr's operations.

A *bahlōlī*.

The Sultanate of Delhi. The bloodstained annals of the Sultanate of Delhi, extending over nearly three centuries and a quarter (1206–1526), are not pleasant reading. They do not repay minute study in detail, except for special purposes. The episodes of Chingiz Khān and Tīmūr are filled with sickening horrors, and the reigns of several Sultans offer little but scenes of bloodshed, tyranny, and treachery. All the Sultans without exception were fierce bigots. Even Fīrōz Shāh Tughlak, who exhibited a certain amount of kindly humanity, and felt some desire to do good to his people, was by no means free from the savage intolerance of his contemporaries.

Many of the Sultans, including the most ferocious, had nice taste in the refinements of Arabic and Persian literature. They liked to be surrounded by men learned in the peculiar lore of Islām, and were liberal patrons of the accomplishments which interested them.

They introduced into India several new styles of architecture, based primarily on the model of buildings at Mecca, Damascus, and other cities of the Muslim world, but profoundly modified by Hindu influences. The innumerable Hindu buildings overthrown supplied materials for the new mosques and colleges, for the construction of which the conquerors were compelled to utilize

[1] Thomas, *Chronicles*, p. 360; *E. & D.*, iv. 476.

the services of Indian craftsmen. The buildings of the Sultanate consequently display characteristics which distinguish them readily from the Muslim edifices in other parts of the world. Numerous authors group all the styles of architecture during the period of the Sultanate under the term 'Pathān', a most inappropriate and misleading designation. Bahlōl Lodī, who came to the throne in the middle of the fifteenth century, was the first Pathān ruler of Delhi, and his dynasty consisting of three members (1451–1526) was the only Pathān line of Sultans. The Sūr family of Shēr Shāh, who enjoyed a certain amount of contested and precarious power as rulers of Hindostan from 1542 to 1556, also were Pathāns or Afghans, but they cannot be reckoned properly in the succession of Sultans. No such thing as a Pathān style of architecture ever existed. Several distinct styles current in different localities and at various times during the period of the Sultanate may be distinguished, but the subject is too technical for further notice in this place.

Causes of Muslim success. The Muhammadan invaders undoubtedly were superior to their Hindu opponents in fighting power and so long as they remained uncorrupted by wealth and luxury were practically invincible. The explanation of their success, already briefly discussed in relation to the earliest campaigns, is not far to seek. The men came from a cool climate in hilly regions, and were for the most part heavier and physically stronger than their opponents. Their flesh diet as compared with the vegetarian habits prevalent in India, combined with their freedom from the restrictions of caste rules concerning food, tended to develop the kind of energy required by an invading force. Their fierce fanaticism, which regarded the destruction of millions of non-Muslims as a service eminently pleasing to God, made them absolutely pitiless, and consequently far more terrifying than the ordinary enemies met in India. While they employed every kind of frightfulness to terrify the Indians, they were themselves ordinarily saved from fear by their deep conviction that a Ghāzī—a slayer of an infidel—if he should happen to be killed himself, went straight to all the joys of an easily intelligible paradise, winning at the same time undying fame as a martyr. The courage of the invaders was further stimulated by the consciousness that no retreat was open to them. They must either subdue utterly by sheer force the millions confronting their thousands or be completely destroyed. No middle course was available. The enormous wealth in gold, silver, and jewels, not to mention more commonplace valuables, accumulated in the temples, palaces, and towns of India fired their imagination and offered the most splendid conceivable rewards for valour. The Hindu strategy and tactics were old-fashioned, based on ancient text-books, which took no account of foreign methods; and the unity of command on the Indian side was always more or less hampered by tribal, sectarian, and caste divisions. Each horde of the foreigners, on the contrary, obeyed a single leader in the field, and the commanders knew how to make use of shock tactics, that is to say, well-directed cavalry charges, which rarely failed to scatter the Hindu hosts. Elephants, on which Hindu tradition placed excessive reliance, proved to be useless, or worse than useless, when pitted against well-equipped, active cavalry. The Hindu cavalry does not seem to have attained a high standard of efficiency in most parts of the country.

Thus it happened that the Muslims, although insignificant in numbers when compared with the vast Indian population, usually secured easy victories, and were able to keep in subjection for centuries enormous multitudes of Hindus.

Nature of the Sultans' government. Bengal, after it had been overrun by a few parties of horsemen at the close of the twelfth century, remained for ages under the heel of foreign chiefs who were sometimes Afghans, and the province never escaped from Musalmān rule until it passed under British control. The wars with Bengal of which we read during the period of the Sultanate were concerned only with the claim preferred by Delhi to receive homage and tribute from the Muslim rulers of Bengal. Those rulers, in their turn, often seem to have left Hindu Rājās undisturbed in their principalitics, subject to the payment of tribute with greater or less regularity. Indeed the same practice necessarily prevailed over a large part of the Muslim dominions. Some sort of civil government had to be carried on, and the strangers had not either the numbers or the capacity for civil administration except in a limited area. The Sultans left no fruitful ideas or valuable institutions behind them. Alāu-d dīn Khiljī, an unlettered savage, issued, it is true, many regulations, but they were ill-founded and died with him.

The government both at head-quarters and in the provinces was an arbitrary despotism, practically unchecked except by rebellion and assassination. A strong autocrat, like Alāu-d dīn, never allowed legal scruples to hamper his will, and Muhammad bin Tughlak, who professed reverence for the sacred law, was the worst tyrant of them all. The succession to the throne usually was effected by means of an irregular election conducted by military chiefs, and the person chosen to be Sultan was not necessarily a relative of his predecessor.

Islām in Indian life. The permanent establishment of Muhammadan governments at Delhi and many other cities, combined with the steady growth of a settled resident Muslim population forming a ruling class in the midst of a vastly more numerous Hindu population, necessarily produced immense changes in India. The Muhammadan element increased continually in three ways, namely, by immigration from beyond the northwestern frontier, by conversions, whether forcible or purchased, and by birth. In modern times statistics prove that Muhammadans in India tend to multiply more rapidly than Hindus, and the same ratio probably held good in the days of the Sultanate. We do not possess any statisties concerning the growth of the Muhammadan population in any of the three ways mentioned, but we know that it occurred in all the ways. It was impossible that the presence of a strange element so large should not bring about important modifications of Indian life.

Strength of Muhammadan religion. The Muhammadans were not absorbed into the Indian caste system of Hinduism as their foreign predecessors, the Sakas, Huns, and others, had been absorbed in the course of a generation or two. The definiteness of the religion of Islām, founded on a written revelation of known date, preserved its votaries from the fate which befell the adherents of Shamanism and the other vague religions of Central Asia. When the Sakas, Huns, and the rest of the early immigrants settled in India and married Hindu women they merged in the Hindu caste system with extraordinary rapidity, chiefly because they possessed no religion sufficiently definite to protect them against the power of the Brahmans. The Muslim with his Korān and his Prophet was in a different position. He believed in his intelligible religion with all his heart, maintained against all comers the noble doctrine of the unity of God, and heartily despised the worshippers of many gods, with their idols and ceremonies. The Muhammadan settlers consequently regarded themselves, whether rich or poor, as a superior race, and ordinarily kept apart so far as possible from social contact with the idolaters. But, in course of time, the barrier was partially broken down. One cause which promoted a certain degree of intercourse was the necessity of continuing the employment of unconverted Hindus in clerkships and a host of minor official posts which the Musalmāns could not fill themselves. Another was the large number of conversions effected either by fear of the sword or by purchase. The Hindus thus nominally converted retained most of their old habits and connexions. Even now their descendants are often half-Hindu in their mode of life.

Evolution of Urdū. The various necessities which forced the Muhammadans and Hindus to meet each other involved the evolution of a common language. Some Muhammadans learned Hindī and even wrote in it, as Malik Muhammad of Jāis did in the time of Humāyūn. Multitudes of Hindus must have acquired some knowledge of Persian. A convenient compromise between the two languages resulted in the formation of Urdū, the camp language, the name being derived from the Turkī word *urdū*, 'camp', the original form of the English word 'horde'. Urdū is a Persianized form of Western Hindī, as spoken especially in the neighbourhood of Delhi. Its grammar and structure continue to be Hindī in the main, while the words are largely Persian. The language of Persia after the Muhammadan conquest became filled with Arabic words, which, consequently, are numerous in Urdū. No definite date can be assigned to the beginnings of Urdū, which shades off into Hindī by insensible gradations, but it is certain that during the Sultanate period the evolution of a language intelligible to both the conquerors and the conquered went on unceasingly. Urdū gradually became the vernacular of

Indian Muhammadans and developed a literature. Many Hindī words occur in the writings of Amīr or Mīr Khusrū, who died in 1325, and is sometimes reckoned as a writer of Urdū.

Modification of Hindu religion. The introduction of the religion of the Prophet as a permanent factor in the life of India could not but modify the notions of Hindu thinkers. Although it is hardly necessary to observe that the idea of the unity of God always has been and still is familiar to even uneducated Hindus, it seems to be true that the prominence given to that doctrine by Muslim teaching encouraged the rise of religious schools which sought for a creed capable of expressing Muhammadan and Hindu devotion alike.

Rāmānand and Kabīr. The most famous teacher whose doctrine was the basis of such schools was Rāmānand, who lived in the fourteenth century, and came from the south. He preached in Hindī and admitted people of all castes, or of no caste, to his order. He had twelve apostles or chief disciples, who included a Rājpūt, a currier, a barber, and a Muhammadan weaver, namely, Kabīr. The verses of Kabīr, which are still familiar in northern India, show clear traces of Muhammadan influence. He condemned the worship of idols and the institution of caste. Both Musalmāns and Hindus are included among his followers, who are known as Kabīrpanthīs, or 'travellers on the way of Kabīr', who claimed to be 'at once the child of Allāh and of Rām'.

A few stanzas may be quoted to prove how Hinduism and Islām reacted one upon the other in the days of the Lodī Sultans :

I

O Servant, where dost thou seek Me ? Lo ! I am beside thee.
I am neither in temple nor in mosque ; I am neither in Kaaba nor in Kailash :
Neither am I in rites and ceremonies, nor in Yoga and renunciation.
If thou art a true seeker, thou shalt at once see Me : thou shalt meet Me in a moment of time.
Kabīr says, 'O Sadhu ! God is the breath of all breath.'

II

It is needless to ask of a saint the caste to which he belongs;
For the priest, the warrior, the tradesman, and all the thirty-six castes, alike are seeking for God.
It is but folly to ask what the caste of a saint may be ;
The barber has sought God, the washer-woman, and the carpenter—
Even Raidas was a seeker after God.
The Rishi Swapacha was a tanner by caste.
Hindus and Moslems alike have achieved that End, where remains no mark of distinction.

XLII

There is nothing but water at the holy bathing places ; and I know that they are useless, for I have bathed in them.
The images are all lifeless, they cannot speak ; I know, for I have cried aloud to them.

The Purana and the Koran are mere words; lifting up the curtain, I have seen.
Kabīr gives utterance to the words of experience; and he knows very well that all other things are untrue.[1]

Such teaching is closely akin to that of the Persian mystics, Jalālu-d dīn Rūmī, Hāfiz, and the rest, whose doctrine was embraced in the sixteenth century by Abu-l Fazl and Akbar. Kabīr is the spiritual ancestor of Nānak, the founder of the Sikh sect.

Dr. Farquhar truly observes that

'it is a most extraordinary fact that the theology of Kabīr was meant to unite Hindus and Muhammadans in the worship of the one God; yet the most implacable hatred arose between the Sikhs and the Muhammadans; and from that hatred came the Khālsā, the Sikh military order, which created the fiercest enemies the Mughal emperors had. It is also most noteworthy that caste has found its way back into every Hindu sect that has disowned it.'[2]

Seclusion of women. Although ancient Indian literature, such as the *Arthasāstra* of Kautilya, alludes occasionally to the practice of the seclusion of women, many records indicate that the seclusion, even among the wealthy and leisured classes, although practised, was less strict than it is now in most parts of India. The example of the dominant Muslims, combined with the desire of the Hindus to give the female members of their families every possible protection against the foreigners, has made the practice of living 'behind the curtain' both more fashionable and more widely prevalent than it used to be in ancient times.

CHRONOLOGY OF THE SULTANATE, 1290–1526

The Khiljī (Khalj) Dynasty

JALĀLU-D DĪN (FĪRŌZ SHĀH)	acc. 1290
Famine	1291
Mongol inroad	1292
Annexation of Ellichpur (Īlichpur)	1294
ALĀU-D DĪN, acc.; murder of Jalālu-d dīn	1296
Conquest of Gujarāt	1297–8
Mongol invasions	1297–1305
Massacre of Mongols at Delhi	? 1298
Southern campaigns of Malik Kāfūr	1302–11
Sack of Chitōr	1303
KUTBU-D DĪN MUBĀRAK	acc. Jan. 1315
Destruction of Harpāl Dēo Yādava	1318
[Khusrū Khān, usurper, &c.]	1318–20

[1] *One Hundred Poems of Kabir.* Translated by Rabindranath Tagore, assisted by Evelyn Underhill. Published by the India Society, London, at the Chiswick Press, 1914. Miss Underhill dates Kabīr from about 1440 to 1518. He used to be placed between 1380 and 1420.

[2] *Primer of Hinduism,* 2nd ed., Oxford University Press, 1912, p. 138.

The Tughlak Dynasty

GHIYĀSU-D DĪN TUGHLAK SHĀH (Ghāzī Malik)	acc. 1321
Wars in Bengal and Deccan	about 1321–4
MUHAMMAD ĀDIL BIN TUGHLAK (Fakhru-d dīn Jūnā, also styled Ulugh Khān)	Feb. 1325
Evacuation of Delhi; foundation of Daulatābād	1326–7
Forced currency of brass and copper for silver	1329–32
Expedition against China	1337–8
Revolt of Bengal and Ma'abar	1338–9
General break-up of empire began about	1340
Prolonged famine for several years began	1342
Vijayanagar a powerful kingdom	1346
Bahmanī kingdom of the Deccan founded	1347
The Sultan in Gujarāt and Sind	1347–51
FĪRŌZ SHĀH TUGHLAK	acc. 1351
War in Bengal	1353–4
Attacks on Sind	about 1360–2
Death of Fīrōz Shāh	Sept. 1388

Break up of the Sultanate

Sundry insignificant princes, MAHMUD TUGHLAK, &c.	1388–98
Invasion of TĪMŪR	1398
Independence of Jaunpur	1399
Anarchy	1399–1414
The so-called SAYYIDS at Delhi and neighbourhood	1414–50

The Lodī Dynasty

SULTAN BAHLŌL LODĪ	acc. 1450
Recovery of Jaunpur	about 1476
SULTAN SIKANDAR LODĪ	acc. 1489
Earthquake in Hindostan and Persia	1505
SULTAN IBRĀHĪM LODĪ	acc. 1517
First battle of Pānīpat, defeat and death of Ibrāhīm; end of the Sultanate	1526

AUTHORITIES

The leading authority for the Khiljī and Tughlak dynasties is the *Tārīkh-i Fīrōz Shāhī* by Ziāu-d dīn Baranī in *E. & D.*, iii. For the reign of Muhammad bin Tughlak I have made large use of Ibn Batuta's travels, translated into French by Defrémery and Sanguinetti (with Arabic text), Paris, 1853–8. Part of that work has been rendered into English in *E. & D.*, vol. iv, App. The English translation of the *Travels* by Lee (Or. Trans. Fund, 1829) is not much good, having been made from an imperfect manuscript. Other authors will be found in *E. & D.*, iv; and, of course, Firishta, Badāonī, &c., give abstracts. The history of Tīmūr's invasion, from his own *Memoirs* and other sources, is in *E. & D.*, iv, and the Lodī history in vol. v. I have also found E. Thomas, *Chronicles of the Pathan Kings of Delhi*, useful, but the whole period needs critical examination in detail. The exact dates often are uncertain.

CHAPTER 4

The Muhammadan kingdoms of Bengal, Mālwā, Gujarāt, and Kashmīr.

Scope of this chapter. Although it is impossible in the course of a general survey of Indian history to delineate in detail the story of each outlying kingdom, it is necessary for the completion of the picture to draw a sketch of the prominent events which happened in the more important of such kingdoms. The history of the Muhammadan Bahmanī kingdom or empire of the Deccan, founded in 1347, which possesses features of special interest; the complicated affairs of the five kingdoms erected on the ruins of the Bahmanī empire; and the history of the Hindu empire of Vijayanagar will be narrated in Book V. The short-lived kingdom of Jaunpur has been already dealt with. This chapter will be devoted to a summary notice of the more interesting passages in the histories of the Muhammadan kingdoms of Bengal, Mālwā, Gujarāt, and Kashmīr, during the period of the Delhi Sultanate. No attempt will be made to write a series of consecutive narratives.

Bengal

The independence of Bengal, that is to say, the definite separation of the Muhammadan provincial government from the Sultanate of Delhi, may be dated from 1340, as the result of Fakhru-d dīn's rebellion against the tyranny of Muhammad bin Tughlak. A few years later Fīrōz Shāh Tughlak practically renounced all claim to the suzerainty of Delhi over the revolted province, which continued under a separate government until 1576, when Akbar's generals defeated and killed Dāūd Shāh, the last of the Afghan kings. The vicissitudes of the various dynasties which ruled Bengal between 1340 and 1526, when the Sultanate of Delhi came to an end, present few events of intrinsic importance, or such as the memory readily retains. The wars, rebellions, and assassinations which usually fill so large a space in the histories of Muslim dynasties become almost unreadable when the drama is presented on a purely provincial stage isolated from the doings of the larger world. The story of the independent Muhammadan kings of Bengal seldom offers any points of contact with that world, even within the limits of India. The province ordinarily went its own way, apparently disregarding and disregarded by all other kingdoms, except for certain wars on its frontiers. Very little is known at present concerning the condition of the huge Hindu population during the period in question, that population being almost wholly ignored by the historians writing in Persian. Bengālī scholars are, it is understood, engaged on researches which may throw some light on the inner history of the province during the Sultanate, but the results of their labours are not yet easily accessible.

Husain Shāh. The best and most famous of the Muhammadan Kings of Bengal was Husain Shāh (Alāu-d dīn Husain Shāh,

A. D. 1493–1518), a Sayyid of Arab descent who had held the office of vizier or prime minister under a tyrant named Shamsu-d dīn Muzaffar Shāh. When the tyrant was deposed and killed the chiefs unanimously elected Husain Shāh to be their sovereign. He justified their choice. His name is still familiar throughout Bengal; and no insurrection or rebellion occurred during his reign, which lasted for twenty-four years. He died at Gaur, having 'enjoyed a peaceable and happy reign, beloved by his subjects, and respected by his neighbours'.

He hospitably received his namesake the fugitive king of Jaunpur.

Nusrat Shāh. Husain Shāh left eighteen sons, the eldest of whom, Nusrat Shāh, was elected by the chiefs as his successor. Nusrat Shāh departed from the usual custom of Asia in regard to his brothers, whom he treated with affection and liberality. He occupied Tirhūt, and arranged with Bābur honourable terms of peace. He is said to have become a cruel tyrant during his latter years.

Buildings. The mosques of Gaur and the other old cities of Bengal were constructed almost entirely of brick and in a peculiar style. At Gaur the tomb of Husain Shāh and the Lesser Golden Mosque built in his reign, with the Great Golden Mosque and the Kadam Rasūl built by Nusrat Shāh may be mentioned as being specially noteworthy. The huge Ādīna mosque at Pandua, twenty miles from Gaur, built by Sikandar Shāh in 1368, has about four hundred small domes, and is considered to be the most remarkable building in Bengal. The vast ruins of Gaur are estimated to occupy from twenty to thirty square miles.

Hindu literature. The learned historian of Bengālī literature states that the most popular book in Bengal is the translation of the Sanskrit *Rāmāyana* made by Krittivāsa, who was born in A. D. 1346. It may be called the Bible of Bengal, where it occupies a position like that held in the upper provinces by the later work of Tulsī Dās. Some of the Muhammadan kings were not indifferent to the merits of Hindu literature. A Bengālī version of the *Mahābhārata* was prepared to the order of Nusrat Shāh, who thus anticipated the similar action of Akbar. An earlier version of the same poem is believed to date from the fourteenth century, and another was composed in the time of Husain Shāh, by command of his general, Parāgal Khān. 'Frequent references are found in old Bengali literature indicating the esteem and trust in which the Emperor Husen Sāhā was held by the Hindus.' In fact, it seems to be true that 'the patronage and favour of the Muhammadan emperors and chiefs gave the first start towards the recognition of Bengālī in the courts of the Hindu Rājās', who, under the guidance of their Brahman teachers, were more inclined to encourage Sanskrit.[1]

[1] Dinesh Chandra Sen, *History of the Bengali Language and Literature*, Calcutta University, 1911, pp. 12, 14, 170, 184, 201, 203.

Mālwā

Mālwā (Mālava), the extensive region now included for the most part in the Central India Agency, and lying between the Narbadā on the south, the Chambal on the north, Gujarāt on the west, and Bundēlkhand on the east, had been the seat of famous kingdoms in the Hindu period. Īltutmish raided the country early in the thirteenth century. In 1310 it was brought more or less into subjection by an officer of Alāu-d dīn Khiljī, and thereafter continued to be ruled by Muslim governors until the break-up of the Sultanate of Delhi.

The Ghōrī Dynasty. Shortly after Tīmūr's invasion in 1398 the governor, a descendant of the great Sultan, Shihābu-d dīn Muhammad of Ghōr, set up as king on his own account under the style of Sultan Shihābu-d dīn Ghōrī (1401). He had enjoyed his new rank for only four years, when he died suddenly, probably having been poisoned by his eldest son. The independent kingdom thus founded lasted for a hundred and thirty years from 1401 until 1531, when it was annexed by Gujarāt. Four years later Humāyūn brought the country temporarily under the dominion of Delhi, but it did not become finally part of the Mogul empire until the early years of Akbar's reign (1561–4). The political annals of the Muhammadan kingdom present few features of permanent interest, and the Sultans are now remembered chiefly for their magnificent buildings at Māndū.

The first capital of the new kingdom was Dhār, where Rājā Bhoja had once reigned, but the second Sultan, who assumed the title of Hoshang Shāh, moved his court to Māndū, where he erected many remarkable edifices. He was defeated in a war with Gujarāt, and was a prisoner for a year, but was restored to his throne, and retained his ill-gotten power until 1432, when he was succeeded by his son, Sultan Mahmūd, the third and last king of the Ghōrī dynasty, a worthless drunken creature.

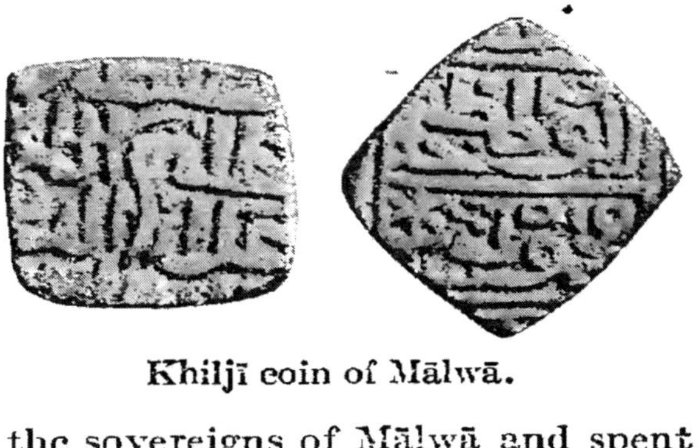

Khiljī coin of Mālwā.

The Khiljī Dynasty. Sultan Mahmūd Ghōrī was poisoned in 1436[1] by his minister, Mahmūd Khān, a Khiljī or Khalj Turk, who seized the throne and founded the Khiljī dynasty, which lasted almost a century. He was by far the most eminent of the sovereigns of Mālwā and spent a busy life fighting his neighbours, including the Sultan of Gujarāt, various Rājās of Rājasthān, and Nizām Shāh Bahmanī. Firishta, ignoring the irregularity of the methods by which he won his crown, specially extols his justice and gives him a good general character.

[1] A. H. 840—A. D. July 16, 1436–July 4, 1437, as proved by coin No. 15 in Wright's *Catalogue*. The books give the date as 1435.

'Sultan Mahmūd', we are told, 'was polite, brave, just, and learned; and during his reign, his subjects, Muhammadans as well as Hindus, were happy, and maintained a friendly intercourse with each other. Scarcely a year passed that he did not take the field, so that his tent became his home, and his resting-place the field of battle. His leisure hours were devoted to hearing the histories and memoirs of the courts of different kings of the earth read.'

It is pleasant to learn that in his time the Hindus were treated with consideration. Husain Shāh, later in the century, pursued the same intelligent policy in Bengal, as already mentioned. The fight with the Rānā of Chitōr apparently must have been indecisive, because the Rānā commemorated his alleged victory by the erection of a noble Tower of Victory, which still stands at Chitōr; while the Sultan, making a similar claim for himself, built a remarkable seven-storied tower at Māndū. That monument unfortunately has collapsed and fallen to ruin so completely that the Archaeological Department experienced considerable difficulty in determining its site.

Sultan Nāsiru-d dīn parricide. The next Sultan, Ghiyāsu-d dīn (1469–1501), was poisoned by his son Nāsiru-d dīn. When Jahāngīr was staying at Māndū in 1617 he liked the place greatly, and was so much impressed by the old buildings, which at that time had not fallen into irretrievable ruin, that he spent three lākhs of rupees in repairing them and adapting the most suitable to his own use. He lodged in the palace built by Bahādur the last king of Gujarāt. He tells the story of the parricide Sultan in a lively passage, which deserves quotation. Having mentioned some of the principal edifices, Jahāngīr goes on to say:

'After this I went to the building containing the tombs of the Khaljī rulers. The grave of Nāsiru-d dīn, son of Sultan Ghiyāsu-d dīn, whose face is blackened for ever, was also there. It is well known that that wretch advanced himself by the murder of his own father, Ghiyāsu-d dīn, who was in his 80th year. Twice he gave him poison, and he [the father] twice expelled it by means of a poison antidote amulet (*zahr-muhra*) he had on his arm. The third time he [the son] mixed poison in a cup of sherbet and gave it to his father with his own hand, saying he must drink it. As his father understood what efforts he was making in this matter, he loosened the *zahr-muhra* from his arm and threw it before him, and then turning his face in humility and supplication towards the throne of the Creator, who requires no supplication, said:

"O Lord, my age has arrived at 80 years, and I have passed this time in prosperity and happiness such as has been attained to by no king. Now as this is my last time, I hope that thou wilt not seize Nāsir for my murder, and that reckoning my death as a thing decreed, thou wilt not avenge it."

After he had spoken these words, he drank off that poisoned cup of sherbet at a gulp and delivered his soul to the Creator. . . .

It is reported that when Shīr Khān, the Afghan [Shēr Shāh], in the time of his rule, came to the tomb of Nāsiru-d dīn, he, in spite of his brutish nature, on account of Nāsiru-d dīn's shameful conduct, ordered the head of the tomb to be beaten with sticks. Also when I went to his tomb I gave it several kicks, and ordered the servants in attendance on me to kick the tomb. Not satisfied with this, I ordered the tomb to be broken open, and his impure remains to be cast into the fire. Then it occurred to me that since fire is Light, it was a pity for the Light of Allah to be polluted by burning his filthy body; also, lest there should be any diminution of torture for him in another state from being thus burnt, I ordered them to throw his crumbled bones, together with his decayed limbs, into the Narbada.'[1]

Nāsiru-d dīn proved to be a cruel brute when in power. He died of fever in 1512, and was succeeded by his son, Mahmūd II, the last king of his race, who was defeated by Bahādur Shāh of Gujarāt, and executed. The other male members of the royal family were exterminated, with the exception of one who was at Humāyūn's court, and the kingdom was annexed to Gujarāt (A.H. 937=A.D. 1531).

Buildings. The fortified city of Māndū, now in ruins, stood on the extensive summit of a commanding hill, protected by walls about twenty-five miles or more in total length. The massive buildings still recognizable are numerous, and of much architectural merit. They include a splendid Jāmi Masjid, or chief mosque, the Hindōlā Mahall, the Jahāz Mahall, the tomb of Hoshang Shāh, and the palaces of Bahādur and Rūpmatī, besides many other remarkable edifices built of sandstone and marble, which have been repaired and conserved to a considerable extent by the officers of the Archaeological Department and the authorities of the Dhār State. The hill, which was dangerously infested by tigers and other wild beasts for more than two centuries, can now be visited and explored in the utmost comfort.

Gujarāt

The country. The name Gujarāt is of wide and indefinite signification. It may be taken in its most extended sense to mean all the territory in which the Gujarātī language is spoken, and so to include the peninsula of Cutch (Kachchh), which is not usually reckoned as part of Gujarāt.[2] In the ordinary use of the term, Cutch being excluded, Gujarāt comprises a considerable region on the mainland and also the peninsula now known as Kāthiāwār, which used to be called Saurāshtra by the ancient Hindus and Sorath by the Muhammadans. The definition of the mainland region has varied from time to time. Some people fix the southern boundary at the Narbadā, while others extend it to Damān. Certainly, in Muhammadan times, Surat at the mouth of the Tāptī and Damān farther south always were considered as belonging

[1] *Memoirs of Jahāngīr*, transl. Rogers and Beveridge, R. As. Soc., 1909, vol. i, pp. 365–7. Firishta expresses disbelief in the accusations of parricide preferred against Hoshang Shāh and Nāsiru-d dīn Shāh, but, so far as I can judge, the charges seem to be true in both cases. As regards the latter, it is highly improbable that both Shēr Shāh and Jahāngīr should have been misinformed. Cases of parricide among the Muhammadan Sultans are numerous.

[2] Gujarātī is the official and literary language of Cutch, but the spoken vernacular is a special dialect of that tongue.

to Gujarāt. The Gujarāt on the mainland of the Muhammadan period may be taken as extending north and south from the neighbourhood of Sirohi and Bhinmāl in Rājputāna to Damān, and east and west from the frontier of Mālwā to the sea, and the Runn of Cutch. The region so defined comprises in modern terms six Districts of the Bombay Presidency, namely, Ahmadābād, Kaira, Pānch Mahāls, Broach (Bharōch), Surat, and part of the Thāna District, with the Baroda State or Dominions of the Gaikwār, and many smaller native states. The peninsula of Kāthiāwār, which is shared by a great multitude of such states, is now and was in the Muhammadan period reckoned as part of Gujarāt.

The province, especially the mainland section, enjoys exceptional natural advantages, being fertile, well supplied with manufactures, and possessed of numerous ports where profitable overseas commerce has been practised since the most remote times. A country so desirable necessarily has attracted the attention of all the races which have effected conquests in northern and western India. Sultan Mahmūd of Ghaznī's famous raid in A. D. 1024 effected the destruction of the temple at Somnāth and provided his army with much booty, but no attempt at permanent conquest was then made. The Muslim invasions in the latter part of the twelfth century also failed to produce any permanent result, and the country continued to be ruled by Hindu dynasties. In 1297 an officer of Alāu-d dīn Khiljī annexed it to the Sultanate of Delhi. Muslim governors continued to be appointed from the capital after that date as long as the Sultanate lasted.

Independence. Zafar Khān, the last governor, who was appointed in 1391, and had been practically independent, formally withdrew his allegiance in 1401,[1] and placed his son Tātār Khān on the provincial throne as Sultan, with the title of Nāsiru-d dīn Muhammad Shāh. The new Sultan seems to have been poisoned by his father in 1407. But four years later the old man, who had become Sultan Muzaffar Shāh, was poisoned in his turn by his grandson, Alp Khān, who assumed the style of Ahmad Shāh.

Ahmad Shāh. Ahmad Shāh, who reigned for thirty years from 1411 to 1441, may be regarded as the real founder of the independent kingdom of Gujarāt. His father and grandfather during their few years of power had controlled only a comparatively small territory in the neighbourhood of Ahmadābād, then called Asāwal. Ahmad Shāh devoted his energy and considerable ability to extending his territories, spreading the religion of the Prophet, and improving the administration of his own dominions. Throughout his reign he never suffered a defeat, and his armies invariably prevailed over those of the Sultanate of Mālwā, the chiefs of Asīrgarh, Rājputāna, and other neighbouring countries. Sultan Ahmad was a close friend of Sultan Fīrōz Bahmanī, and, like him, was zealous in fighting the infidels and destroying their temples. He built the noble city of Ahmadābād adjoining the old Hindu

[1] Wright gives A. H. 806 = A. D. 1403–4; following a paper by G. P. Taylor in *J. Bom. Br. R. A. S.*, for 1902.

town of Asāwal. 'Travellers', the local historian avers, 'are agreed that they have found no city in the whole earth so beautiful, charming, and splendid.'

Sultan Mahmūd Bīgarhā. Sultan Mahmūd Begarā or Bīgarhā, a grandson of Ahmad Shāh, ascended the throne at the age of thirteen in (A.H. 863) 1459 and reigned prosperously for fifty-two years until (A.H. 917) 1511. He was by far the most eminent sovereign of his dynasty. His achievements and personal peculiarities were so remarkable that travellers carried his fame in a legendary form to Europe. Although a mere boy at the time of his accession he seems to have assumed a man's part from the first and to have been able to dispense with a Protector, such as was imposed on Akbar at the same age.

'He added glory and lustre to the kingdom of Gujarāt, and was the best of all the Gujarāt kings, including all who preceded and all who succeeded him; and whether for abounding justice and generosity, for success in religious war, and for the diffusion of the laws of Islām and of Musalmāns; for soundness of judgement, alike in boyhood, in manhood, and in old age; for power, for valour, and victory—he was a pattern of excellence.'

Coin of Mahmūd Bīgarhā.

That vigorous eulogy by the leading Muslim historian of his country seems to be justified by the facts as seen from his point of view. We must, however, be content to accept the old Sultans as they were, and to admit that most of them were fierce, intolerant fanatics, whatever their other merits might be. The more fanatical they were the better the historians liked them.

Mahmūd was eminently successful in war. He made himself master of the strong fortresses of Champānēr to the north-east of Baroda, and of Jūnāgarh in Kāthiāwār; overran Cutch and gained victories over the Sultan of Ahmadnagar and other potentates.

Towards the end of his reign he came into conflict with the Portuguese and allied himself with the Sultan of Turkey against them, thus entering the field of European politics. In 1507 an officer of his secured the aid of some Turkish troops and ten ships for an attack on the Portuguese, whom the Ottoman Government was most anxious to expel from the Indian seas. On that occasion the Muhammadan assailants were successful and sank a great ship with a valuable cargo, near Chaul, to the south of Bombay. But two years later, in 1509, the Musalmān fleet was annihilated in a battle fought off Diu in Kāthiāwār, then included in the Gujarāt kingdom. The foreigners, who finally secured Goa from Bījāpur in 1510, were thenceforward always able to maintain their possessions against the Indian powers, but did not obtain a fort at Diu until 1535. Even victorious Akbar was unable to disturb them seriously, although no project was nearer to his heart than the expulsion of the hated intruders from the soil of his richest province.

The personal peculiarities of Mahmūd made a deep impression on his contemporaries, and became known in Europe, as told in fantastic tales chiefly conveyed through the agency of the Italian traveller, Ludovico di Varthema. The Sultan's moustaches were so long that he used to tie them over his head and his beard reached to his girdle. His appetite, like that of Akbar's secretary, Abu-l Fazl, was so abnormal that he was credited with eating more than twenty pounds' weight of food daily. He was believed to have been dosed with poison from childhood and thus to have become immune against its effects, while his body was so saturated with venom that if a fly settled on his hand it would drop dead. The legend has found its way into English literature through Samuel Butler's reference to it :

> The Prince of Cambay's daily food
> Is asp, and basilisk, and toad.[1]

Sultan Bahādur Shāh. The latest notable Sultan of Gujarāt was Mahmūd Bīgarhā's grandson, Bahādur Shāh, who reigned from the close of 1526 to February 1537, when his uneasy life was ended by a tragic death at the hands of the Portuguese. He earned a full share of military glory by his defeat of Mahmūd II Khiljī, involving the annexation of Mālwā in 1531–2, and by his storm of Chitōr in 1534, when the Rājpūts made their usual dreadful sacrifice.

In the following year, 1535, Bahādur was utterly defeated by Humāyūn Pādshāh, driven from his kingdom, and forced to take refuge in Mālwā. The fortress of Champānēr was gallantly taken by Humāyūn, who was himself among the earliest to escalade the walls. But the Mogul was soon recalled from the scene of his western triumphs by the necessity of meeting his Afghan rival, Shēr Khān (Shāh), and Bahādur was then able to return to his kingdom.

Ordinarily the relations between the Portuguese and the Government of Gujarāt were hostile, but the Mogul pressure forced Bahādur to buy the promise of Portuguese help by the surrender of Bassein, and to conclude a treaty of peace with the proud foreigners. Negotiations on the subject of the port and fortress of Diu, then of much importance as a trading station, induced Bahādur Shāh to visit Nuno da Cunha, the Portuguese governor, and go aboard his ship. No less than eight distinct accounts of what then happened—namely, four Portuguese and four Muhammadan—are on record, all differing in details. Colonel Watson, who examined them all critically, came to 'the conclusion . . . that on either side the leader hoped by some future treachery to seize the person of the other ; and that mutual suspicion turned into a fatal affray a meeting which both parties intended should pass peacefully and lull the other into a false and favourable security'.

[1] *Hudibras*, Part ii, Canto i, published in 1664.

It is certain that the Sultan of Gujarāt fell overboard, and while in the water was knocked on the head by a sailor. He was only thirty-one years of age. Manuel de Souza, captain of the port of Diu, also lost his life at the same time.

Bahādur Shāh's intemperance in the use of liquor and drugs clouded his brain and made him prone to acts of ill-considered impulse. He left no son.

Later history. The history of the province from the time of his death in 1537 to its annexation by Akbar after the lightning campaigns of 1572–3 is a record of anarchical confusion, into the details of which it is unnecessary to enter. Disturbances continued to be frequent even after the absorption of the kingdom into the Mogul empire.

Architecture. The exquisite architecture of Gujarāt, further beautified by wood-carving of supreme excellence, is the special distinction of the province. The Muhammadan conquerors adopted with certain modifications the charming designs of the old Hindu and Jain architects, filling Ahmadābād, Cambay, and many other towns with a multitude of buildings singularly pleasing to the eye, and enriched with most delicate stone lattices and other ornaments. The ancient Hindu monuments of both mainland Gujarāt and Kāthiāwār have been described by Dr. Burgess in two large, finely illustrated quarto volumes of the Archaeological Survey. The same author has described and illustrated with equal copiousness the Muhammadan architecture on the mainland in three other handsome volumes. The architects of the province still retain much of the skill of their ancestors. Ahmadābād is particularly rich in noble buildings, and during the time of its glory, extending from its foundation to the eighteenth century—a period of about three centuries—undoubtedly was one of the handsomest cities in the world. The population is said to have numbered 900,000, and millionaires were to be found among the merchants. Even now the city is wealthy and prosperous, the second largest in the Bombay Presidency, with a population approaching 200,000. According to a local saying the prosperity of Ahmadābād hangs on three threads—silk, gold, and cotton.

Kashmīr

The country. The dominions of the Mahārāja of Kashmīr—or, more accurately, of Kashmīr and Jamū (Jummoo), as defined by the treaty of 1846, made after the first Sikh war and still operative, include extensive mountainous regions unconnected with the Kashmīr of Hindu and Muhammadan history. In that history the name Kashmīr refers only to the beautiful valley on the upper course of the Jihlam (Jhelum), which is about eighty-five miles long and from twenty to twenty-five broad. The long and interesting story of the Hindu kingdom of the valley is painful reading on the whole, many of the Rājās having been atrocious tyrants.

The first Sultan. Early in the fourteenth century a Musalmān adventurer from Swat, named Shāh Mīrzā or Mīr, who had been minister to the Rājā, seized the throne and established a Muhammadan dynasty of Sultans which lasted until nearly the middle of the sixteenth century. The short-lived Chak dynasty overthrown by Akbar in 1586 did not obtain power until about 1560. Shāh Mīrzā, the first Sultan, took the title of Shamsu-d dīn.

PANEL, ADALAJ WAV, AHMADĀBĀD.

Sultan Sikandar. The sixth Sultan, Sikandar (about 1386–1410), who was ruling at the time of Tīmūr's invasion in 1398, managed to avoid meeting that formidable personage, and remained safely protected by his mountain walls. Sikandar was a gloomy, ferocious bigot, and his zeal in destroying temples and idols was so intense that he is remembered as the Idol-Breaker. He freely used the sword to propagate Islām and succeeded in forcing the bulk of the population to conform outwardly to the Muslim religion. Most of the Brahmans refused to apostatize, and many of them paid with their lives the penalty for their steadfastness. Many others were exiled, and only a few conformed.

Sultan Zainu-l 'Ābidīn. The eighth Sultan, Zainu-l 'Ābidīn, who had a long and prosperous reign of about half a century from 1417 to 1467, was a man of very different type. He adopted the policy of universal toleration, recalled the exiled Brahmans, repealed the *jizya* or poll-tax on Hindus, and even permitted new temples to be built. He abstained from eating flesh, prohibited the slaughter of kine, and was justly venerated as a saint. He encouraged literature, painting, and music, and caused many translations to be made of works composed in Sanskrit, Arabic, and other languages. In those respects he resembled Akbar, but he differed from that monarch in the continence which enabled him to practise strict fidelity to one wife.

Kashmīr coin of Zainu-l 'Ābidīn.

Later History. The reigns of the other Sultans are not of sufficient importance or interest to justify the insertion of their annals in this history. For eleven years (1541–52) a relative of Humāyūn, named Mīrzā Haidar, who had invaded the valley, ruled it, nominally as governor on behalf of Humāyūn, but in practice as an independent prince. Some years later the Chak dynasty seized the throne.

The details of the chronology of the Sultans of Kashmīr are uncertain, and any dates given must be regarded as being only approximate.

CHRONOLOGY

(Leading dates only)

Bengal

Independence of Fakhru-d dīn	about 1340
Husain Shāh	1493–1518
Nusrat Shāh	1518–32
Bengal annexed by Akbar	1576

Mālwā

Independence of Sultan Shihābu-d dīn Ghōrī	1401
Sultan Mahmūd Ghōrī	1432
Sultan Mahmūd Khiljī, founded Khiljī dynasty	1436
Mālwā annexed by Bahādur Shāh of Gujarāt	1531
Mālwā annexed by Akbar	1561–4

Gujarāt

Independence of Nāsiru-d dīn Muhammad Shāh	about 1401
Sultan Ahmad Shāh; foundation of Ahmadābād	1411–31
Sultan Mahmūd Bīgarhā	1459–1511
Naval battles with Portuguese	1507, 1509
Occupation of Goa by Portuguese	1510
Sultan Bahādur Shāh	1526–37

Mālwā annexed	1531
Chitōr stormed	1534
Bahādur defeated by Humāyūn	1535
Bahādur killed by Portuguese	1537
Gujarāt annexed by Akbar	1572–3

Kashmīr

Sultan Shamsu-d dīn	about 1334
Sultan Sikandar, the Idol-Breaker	about 1386–1410
Sultan Zainu-l 'Ābidīn	about 1417–67
Mīrzā Haidar	about 1541–52
Kashmīr annexed by Akbar	1586

Authorities

For my slight notice of the annals of Bengal I have used chiefly Firishta, and Stewart, *History of Bengal*, 1813.

Firishta gives the most convenient summary of Mālwā history.

The best and most authoritative abstract of Gujarāt Muhammadan history is that by Colonel Watson in the *Bombay Gazetteer* (1896), vol. i, part i. The same volume contains a good account of Māndū, the capital of Mālwā. I have also consulted Bayley, *History of Gujarāt* (1886); and Whiteway, *The Rise of Portuguese Power in India*, 1497–1550 (Constable, 1899).

Various articles in the *I. G.* (1908) are serviceable for all the kingdoms.

The Kashmīr history is given by Firishta and Abu-l Fazl (*Āīn*, vol. ii, transl. Jarrett), as well as in the *I. G.*, but many details remain obscure. The story of the Sultans was discussed by C. J. Rodgers at considerable length in *J. A. S. B.*, part i, 1885, in a paper on 'The Square Silver Coins of the Sultans of Kashmīr'.

The coins of the various kingdoms are described by H. N. Wright in the *Catalogue of the Coins in the Indian Museum, Calcutta*, vol. ii, Clarendon Press, 1907, with references to other publications.

The works by Burgess are the leading authority on the art of the province of Gujarāt, namely:

1. *Report on the Antiquities of Kāthiāwād and Kachh*, 1876 (ASWI, vol. ii = Imperial Series, vol. ii);
2. *Muhammadan Architecture in Gujarāt*, 1896 (ASWI, vi = Imp. Ser., xxiii);
3. *Muhammadan Architecture of Ahmadābād*, Part I, 1900 (ASWI, vii = Imp., Ser. xxiv);
4. *Ditto*, Part II. 1905 (ASWI, viii = Imp., Ser. xxxiii);
5. *Architectural Antiquities of Northern Gujarāt*, 1903 (ASWI, ix = Imp. Ser., xxxii).

BOOK V

CHAPTER I

The Bahmanī Dynasty of the Deecan, 1347–1526.

Bahmanī dynasty; Sultan Alāu-d dīn I. A series of rebellions between the years 1343 and 1351, caused by the mad tyranny of Muhammad bin Tughlak, left to the sovereign of Delhi only a small portion of the extensive empire which he had controlled for a few years.

Hasan, entitled Zafar Khān, an Afghan or Turkī officer of the Delhi Sultan, oeeupied Daulatābād in the Deccan in 1347, and proelaimed his independenee before the end of the year. He is known to history as Sultan Alāu-d dīn I, the founder of the Bahmanī dynasty of the Deeean, which played an important part in India for nearly two centuries, from 1347 to 1526. He assumed the name or title of Bahman, because he claimed descent from the early Persian king so-called, better known as Artaxerxes Longimanus, the Long-armed (Ardashīr Darāzdast), who is identified with Ahasuerus of the Book of Esther.[1]

Kulbargā, the capital. The new Sultan established his capital at Kulbargā, now in the Nizam's Dominions, to which he gave the Muhammadan name of Ahsanābād.[2] After the death of Muhammad bin Tughlak in 1351 Alāu-d dīn undertook the conquest of a large part of the Deeean, and when he passed away in 1358 was master of an extensive dominion, reaching to the sea on the west and including the ports of Goa and Dābhōl. The latter place, now a small town in the Ratnagiri District, Bombay, was the principal port of the Konkan from the fourteenth to the sixteenth century. The eastern frontier of the Bahmanī Sultanate was marked by Bhōnagīr or Bhōngīr (17° 31′ N.; 78° 53′ E.), now a considerable town in the Nizam's Dominions. The Pēn Gangā river formed the northern, and the Krishnā the southern boundary.

[1] The eurrent story derived from Firishta that the title Bahman or Bahmanī is a corruption of the word Brahman, because the first Sultan had been in the service of Gangū or Gāngū Brahman, is incredible and false. Hasan was a ficree, bigoted Muslim who would not have dubbed himself a Brahman for any consideration. The legend finds no support from coins or inscriptions and has been rightly rejected by King and Haig. The *Burhān-i Ma'āsir* eorreetly states that 'in consequence of his descent the King was known as Bahman'. It is immaterial whether the descent was claimed with good reason or not.

[2] Ahsanābād, or Hasanābād, with reference to the Sultan's name Hasan (see *E. & D.*, viii, p. 16 *n.*). Kulbargā is the Gulbarga of *I. G.* and Haig; *G* and *K* being often confounded in Persian writing. The Hyderabad officials use the erroneous form Gulbarga. The name may be correctly written as Kalburgā (कल्बुर्गा), or Kulbargā (कुल्बर्गा), or Kulburgā (कुल्बुर्गा). See King, p. 1 *n.* The second form has been adopted in the text.

Muhammad Shāh I; wars with Hindus. The reign of the second Sultan, Muhammad Shāh I (1358–73), was chiefly occupied by savage wars waged against the Hindu rulers of Vijayanagar and Talingāna or Warangal. Horrid cruelties were committed on both sides. The ferocious struggle continued until the Sultan was reputed to have slain half a million of Hindus. The population was so much reduced that the Kanarese country did not recover for ages. At last the butchery was stayed and the parties agreed to spare the lives of prisoners and non-combatants. Muhammad Shāh was as bloodthirsty when dealing with brigandage in his own dominions as he was against his external Hindu foes. Like the Mogul emperors later he sought to suppress robbery by indiscriminate massacres, and in the course of six or seven months sent nearly eight thousand heads of supposed robbers to be piled up near the city gates. He accumulated immense treasures and possessed three thousand elephants. Firishta, who did not disapprove of cruelty to unbelievers, gives him a good character, but the *Burhān-i Ma'āsir* states that his death was due to an 'irreligious manner of living', which probably means indulgence in strong drink. Saifu-d dīn Ghōrī, an eminent minister who had served the first Sultan faithfully, managed the internal affairs of the kingdom during the reign of the second, and continued his work until the accession of the sixth, when he died at an age exceeding a hundred years.

Fīrōz, 8th Sultan, 1397–1422. Passing over intermediate revolutions and short reigns, we come to the reign of Fīrōz, the eighth Sultan, who was a son of the youngest brother of Muhammad Shāh I.

> 'In 1396 the dreadful famine, distinguished from all others by the name of the Durgā Devī, commenced in Mahārāshtra. It lasted, according to Hindu legends, for twelve years. At the end of that time the periodical rains returned; but whole districts were entirely depopulated, and a very scanty revenue was obtained from the territory between the Godāvarī and Krishnā for upwards of thirty years afterwards.'[1]

Fīrōz was a fierce bigot, who spent most of his time in pitiless wars against his Hindu neighbours, 'being determined to use his best endeavours in the suppression of infidelity and the strengthening of the faith'. He went on an expedition almost every year, forcing the Rāya of Vijayanagar to pay tribute, and extending his conquests as far as Rājamahendri or Rājamundri at the apex of the Godāvarī delta. He so far violated the principles of his religion as to drink hard and enjoy music. He kept an enormous number of women from many countries, including Europe, and was reputed to be able to talk with each lady in her own tongue. He had facilities for importing European curiosities through Goa and Dābhōl. Fīrōz loved building, and constructed a fortified palace at Fīrozābād on the Bhīma to the south of the capital. He adorned Kulbargā with many edifices, the most notable being the principal mosque, alleged to have been planned in imitation of the mosque at Cordova in Spain. It is the only large

[1] Grant Duff, *History of the Mahrattas*, ed. 1826, vol. i, p. 59.

mosque in India which is completely roofed.[1] Fīrōz went on one expedition too many. About 1420, towards the close of his reign, he suffered a severe defeat at Pāngal, to the north of the Krishnā, and came home a broken-down old man. He spent the rest of his days in works of piety according to his lights and left affairs of state in the hands of two Turkī slaves. Notwithstanding his aversion to Hindus, he anticipated one measure of Akbar's policy by marrying two Hindu ladies, one being a princess of Vijayanagar. Although he gratified his curiosity by reading the Old and New Testament, it is not correct to affirm, as Meadows Taylor does, that 'in religion he was perfectly tolerant of all sects and creeds'. As a matter of fact, he was a particularly ferocious bigot.

Firishta was of opinion that the house of Bahman attained its greatest splendour in the days of Fīrōz.

Ahmad Shāh, 1422–35. The administration of the Turkī slaves being displeasing to the Sultan's brother Ahmad that prince, with the aid of a foreign merchant named Khalaf Hasan Basrī, deposed Fīrōz and murdered him with his son. Such tragedies were common in Bahmanī history and do not seem to have offended public opinion. The murderer ascended the throne without opposition, and resumed the war with the Hindus, burning to revenge the losses suffered by the 'army of Islām' in his brother's time. He attacked the Vijayanagar territory, with savagery even greater than that shown by his predecessors.

Coin of Fīrōz Bahmanī.

'Ahmad Shāh, without waiting to besiege the Hindu capital, overran the open country; and wherever he went, put to death men, women, and children without mercy, contrary to the compact made by his uncle and predecessor, Muhammad Shāh, and the Rāya of Vijayanagar. Whenever the number of slain amounted to twenty thousand, he halted three days, and made a festival in celebration of the bloody event. He broke down also the idolatrous temples and destroyed the colleges of the brahmans.'

Those atrocious proceedings enabled the Sultan to assume the title of Walī, or Saint. Ultimately peace was concluded with Vijayanagar. The operations against Warangal in 1424 or 1425 had finally destroyed the independence of that Hindu kingdom. About the year 1420 the Deccan again suffered from a severe famine.

Ahmad Shāh also engaged in wars with the Sultans of Mālwā and Gujarāt and with the Hindu chiefs of the Konkan. The war with

[1] Kulbargā decayed after the death of Fīrōz, when it ceased to be the capital, and then lay neglected for centuries. It has revived lately, being now a prosperous town of about 30,000 inhabitants with extensive trade. Haig denies that the mosque is copied from that at Cordova (*Historic Landmarks*, p. 94).

Gujarāt was ended by a treaty of alliance offensive and defensive, which subsisted for many years. Nizām Shāh benefited by it in 1462.

Change of capital to Bīdar. Ahmad Shāh, who had suffered from illness at Kulbargā, and regarded the place as unlucky, shifted his capital to Bīdar (Ahmadābād or Muhammadābād), distant about sixty miles to the north-east. The wisdom of the transfer is fully justified by the description of the new capital recorded by Meadows Taylor:

'There is no more healthy or beautiful site for a city in the Deccan than Bīdar. The fort had been already erected on the north-east angle of a tableland composed of laterite, at a point where the elevation, which is considerable, or about 2,500 feet above the level of the sea, trends southward and westward, and declines abruptly about 500 feet to the wide plain of the valley of the Manjera, which it overlooks. The fortifications, still perfect, are truly noble; built of blocks of laterite dug out of the ditch, which is very broad and has a peculiar mode of defence met with nowhere else, two walls of laterite, the height of the depth of the ditch, having been left at equal distances between the *faussebraye* and the counterscarp all round the western and southern faces of the fort.[1] . . . The city adjoined the fort, space being left for an esplanade, and stretched southwards along the crest of the eminence, being regularly laid out with broad streets. There was a plentiful supply of beautiful water, though the wells are deep; and in every respect, whether as regards climate, which is much cooler and healthier than that of Kulbargā, or situation, the new capital was far preferable to the old one. At the present time, though the city has diminished to a provincial town, and the noble monuments of the Bahmani kings have decayed, there is no city of the Deccan which better repays a visit from the traveller than Bīdar.'[2]

Alāu-d dīn II. Ahmad Shāh was succeeded quietly by his eldest son, Alāu-d dīn II (1435–57). Renewed war with Vijayanagar resulted ultimately in a peace favourable to the Sultan. Firishta notices the curious fact that during that war the Rāya (Deva Rāya II) engaged Muhammadan mercenaries to fight against the army of Islām, and even erected a mosque at his capital for the use of his Muslim soldiers. After the termination of the war the Sultan neglected his duties and abandoned himself to the fleshly delights of wine and women. The efficiency of the public service was much impaired by the quarrels between two factions—the one comprising the native or Deccanee Muhammadans allied with the Abyssinian (or Habshī) settlers, who were mostly Sunnīs; and the other the so-called 'foreigners', that is to say, the Arabs, Turks, Persians, and Moguls, who usually were Shīas. The enmity between the factions led to the commission of a horrid crime by permission of the drunken Sultan. When a force under one of his foreign officers had been defeated in the Konkan by the Hindus, the remnant took refuge in a fort named Chākan situated

[1] Scarp or escarp is the steep inner side of the ditch next to the rampart; counterscarp is the opposite slope of the ditch next to the besieger. *Faussebrayes* are defined as 'lower parapets outside the bastions' (Chambers, *Cyclop.*); or as 'a small mound of earth thrown up about a rampart' (Webster). Both the thing and name, I believe, are now obsolete.

[2] *Manual*, p. 169.

to the north of Poona. The Deccanee party, having trumped up false accusations of treasonable intent against the refugees, persuaded the Sultan to sanction the extermination of the Sayyids and Moguls in the fort. The Deccanee chiefs secured the confidence of their victims by a show of kindness, and then fell upon them treacherously, slaying every male, including 1,200 Sayyids of pure descent and about a thousand other foreigners. Khalaf Hasan, the man who had helped Ahmad Shāh to gain the throne, and had subsequently become prime minister, was among the slain. The women were treated 'with all the insult that lust or brutality could invoke'. The Sultan, when he found that he had been deceived, punished the authors of the massacre.

Humāyūn. Alāu-d dīn was followed by his eldest son Humāyūn (1457–61), who had already earned a terrible reputation for ferocious cruelty. An attempt to displace him in favour of a younger brother was easily defeated, and the new Sultan was free to indulge his maniacal passion for the infliction of pain. Men and women, suspected without reason of favouring rebellion, were stabbed with daggers, hewn in pieces with hatchets, or scalded to death by boiling water or hot oil.

> 'The fire of his rage blazed up in such a way that it burned up land and water; and the broker of his violence used to sell the guilty and innocent by one tariff. The nobles and generals when they went to salute the Sultan used to bid farewell to their wives and children and make their wills. Most of the nobles, ministers, princes, and heirs to the sovereignty were put to the sword.'

Humāyūn, who is remembered by the epithet Zālim, or the Tyrant, resembled his prototype Muhammad bin Tughlak of Delhi, in being 'learned, mad, merciless, and cruel'. Some authorities suggest that he died a natural death, but the more probable account avers that while intoxicated he was assassinated by his servants. A versifier ingeniously expressed the universal joy at the death of the monster by the chronogram:

> Humāyūn Shāh has passed away from the world.
> God Almighty, what a blessing was the death of Humāyūn!
> On the date of his death the world was full of delight,
> So 'delight of the world' gives the date of his death.[1]

Strange to say the tyrant was served by an excellent minister, Khwāja Mahmūd Gāwān, who apparently was unable to check his master's furious rage. The minister lived long enough to do good service under Humāyūn's successors, and to be murdered for his pains.

Muhammad Shāh III; conquests; famine. The next sultan of importance was Muhammad Shāh III, who reigned for nearly twenty years (1463–82), and enjoyed the services of Khwāja Mahmūd Gāwān, the capable minister who had served Humāyūn, and was equally competant as a general and as a civil administrator. The Khwāja took the strong fortress of Belgaum (1473), and

[1] The Persian words are ذوق جهان, *zauk-i jahān*. The numerical values of the letters total 865, the Hijrī year, corresponding to A.D. 1460–1; thus, z=700, *au* (w)=6, k=100, j=3, h=5, *ā* (*alif*)=1, and n=50.

recovered Goa, which had been lost by one of the earlier sultans to the Rāya of Vijayanagar, at a date not known exactly. The result of his operations was an increase of the Bahmanī dominions 'to an extent never achieved by former sovereigns'.

A disastrous famine, known as the 'famine of Bījāpur' because it began in that state, devastated the Deccan in 1473 or 1474 and caused many deaths. The rains failed for two years, and when they came at last, in the third year, 'scarcely any farmers remained in the country to cultivate the lands'.

The title of Ghāzī. When Kondapalli (Condapilly) was surrendered early in 1481, previous to the raid on Kānchī, to be described presently, an incident occurred which illustrates the ferocity of the spirit of fanaticism characteristic of the Bahmanī kings.

> 'The King,' Firishta relates, 'having gone to view the fort, broke down an idolatrous temple and killed some brahmans who officiated at it, with his own hands, as a point of religion. He then gave orders for a mosque to be erected on the foundations of the temple, and ascending the pulpit, repeated a few prayers, distributed alms, and commanded the *Khutba* to be read in his name. Khwāja Mahmūd Gāwān now represented that as his Majesty had slain some infidels with his own hands, he might fairly assume the title of Ghāzī, an appellation of which he was very proud. Muhammad Shāh was the first of his race who had slain a brahman; and it is the belief of the Deccanees that this act was inauspicious, and led to the troubles which soon after perplexed the affairs of himself and his family, and ended in the dissolution of the dynasty.'

The virtuous minister, it will be observed, was quite as fanatical and bloodthirsty as his master. Akbar in the following century earned the much desired title of Ghāzī in a similar way by smiting the helpless prisoner, Hēmū, his Hindu rival.[1]

Raid on Kānchī or Conjeeveram. The most remarkable military exploit of the reign was the successful raid made on Kānchī or Conjeeveram, one of the seven Hindu sacred cities, during the course of a campaign against Vijayanagar in 1481. The remote position of Kanchī, forty-two miles SSW. of Madras, had secured it from Muhammadan attacks, so that the inhabitants believed themselves to be perfectly safe. The Sultan was encamped at Kondapalli near Bezwāda, now in the Kistna (Krishnā) District of Madras, when glowing accounts of the rich booty to be obtained in the holy city induced him to plan a surprise. The story is best told in the words of Firishta, as follows:

> 'On his [Muhammad Shāh's] arrival at Kondapalli [Condapilly], he was informed by the country people that at the distance of ten days' journey was the temple of Kānchī, the walls and roof of which were covered with plates of gold and ornamented with precious stones, but that no Muhammadan monarch had as yet seen it or even heard of its name. Muhammad Shāh accordingly selected six thousand of his best cavalry, and leaving the rest of his army at Kondapalli, proceeded by forced marches to Kānchī. He moved so rapidly on the last day, according to the historians of the time, that only forty troopers kept up with him, among which number were Nizāmu-l Mulk Bahrī and Yūrish Khān Turk. On approaching the

[1] That is the true account of Akbar's action. See *post*, Book VI.

temple some Hindus came forth, one of whom, a man of gigantic stature, mounted on horseback, and brandishing a drawn sabre by way of defiance, rushed full speed towards the King, and aimed a blow which the latter parried, and with one stroke of his sword cleaved him in twain. Another infidel then attacked the King, whose little band was shortly engaged man to man with the enemy; but Muhammad Shāh had again the good fortune to slay his opponent, upon which the rest of the Hindus retired into the temple. Swarms of people, like bees, now issued from within and ranged themselves under its walls to defend it. At length, the rest of the King's force coming up, the temple was attacked and carried by storm with great slaughter. An immense booty fell to the share of the victors, who took away nothing but gold, jewels, and silver, which were abundant. The King then [March 12, 1481] sacked the city of Kānchī, and, after remaining there for a week, he returned to his army.'

The authorities differ considerably concerning the raid. The *Burhān-i Ma'āsir* certainly exaggerates when it asserts that the Muhammadans 'levelled the city and its temples with the ground and overthrew all the symbols of infidelity'. The force present was not capable of such laborious demolition, and as a matter of fact several fine ancient temples, built many centuries prior to the raid, are still standing. Mr. Sewell is too sceptical in rejecting the whole story of the Kānchī expedition as being 'exceedingly improbable'.

Murder of Mahmūd Gāwān. Muhammad Shāh, a confirmed drunkard, gave way to his besetting sin more and more as time went on. His intemperance was the direct cause of the crime which disgraced and deservedly embittered the last year of his life. Khwāja Mahmūd Gāwān, his great minister, being a Persian, necessarily was counted as a 'foreigner', and consequently was hated by the Deccanee faction, which unceasingly sought his ruin. At last, early in April 1481, the plotters managed to lay before their intoxicated sovereign a treasonable letter falsely attributed to the minister, although an obvious forgery. The besotted Sultan, without taking the slightest trouble to ascertain the facts, ordered the instant execution of his aged and faithful servant. When it was too late he found out the deceit practised on him and tried to drown his remorse in drink, until he killed himself by his excesses in March 1482.

Consequences of the crime. Meadows Taylor justly observes that the death of Mahmūd Gāwān was 'the beginning of the end', and that 'with him departed all the cohesion and power of the Bahmanī kingdom', a remark probably suggested by the epitaph of Colonel Palmer on Nānā Farnavīs that 'with him departed all the wisdom and moderation of the Mahratta government'. The minister was a devout and even fanatical Sunnī Musalmān, as ruthless as any one else in slaying and despoiling idolaters. Subject to that qualification, which counted as a virtue in the eyes of his co-religionists, his character seems to deserve the praise bestowed upon it by Firishta, which is echoed by Meadows Taylor in language still more emphatic, and deserving of quotation, even though it may seem tinged with exaggeration:

Character of Mahmūd Gāwān. 'The character of Mahmūd Gāwān', Taylor observes, 'stands out broadly and grandly, not only among all his contemporaries, but among all the ancient Muhammadans of India, as one unapproachably perfect and consistent . . . his noble and judicious reforms, his skill and bravery in war, his justice and public and private benevolence have, in the aggregate, no equals in the Muhammadan history of India. . . . Out of the public revenues of his ample estates, while he paid the public establishments attached to him, he built and endowed the magnificent college at Bīdar, which was practically destroyed by an explosion of gunpowder in the reign of Aurangzēb, and which, while he lived at the capital, was his daily resort ; and the grand fortresses of Ausā, Parēndā, Sholāpur, Dharūr [Dārūr], and many others attest alike his military skill and science.'[1]

Mahmūd Shāh, 1482–1518 ; end of the dynasty. Little more remains to be said about the annals of the Bahmanī dynasty. The successor of Muhammad III was his son Mahmūd, a boy of twelve years of age, who lived and in a manner reigned until 1518, but never possessed real power. The Sultan was a worthless creature, who, when he grew up, totally neglected the affairs of his government, spending his time with low-born favourites in vulgar debauchery. The provincial governors, one after the other, declared their independence, and only a small area round the capital, which became the separate Sultanate of Bīdar a few years later, remained under the nominal jurisdiction of Mahmūd. The actual government was in the hands of Kāsim Barīd, a crafty Turk, and after his death in those of his son, Amīr Barīd. It is unnecessary to relate the story of the murders, quarrels, and rebellions of Mahmūd's miserable reign. They may be read by the curious in the pages of Firishta and the *Burhān-i Ma'āsir*. After the death of Mahmūd four puppet Sultans in succession were placed on the throne, until in 1526 Amīr Barīd felt that the time had come for the assertion of his right to rule on his own account.

Character of the dynasty. Before we proceed to notice some of the more prominent events in the complicated history of the five separate Sultanates formed out of the fragments of the Bahmanī dominion, it will be well to pause for a moment in order to consider the nature of the achievement of the Bahmanī Sultans of the Deccan, and to estimate the position in history to which they are entitled.

The story of the dynasty as it appears in the books is not attractive reading. Between 1347 and 1518 the throne was occupied by fourteen Sultans, of whom four were murdered, and two others were deposed and blinded. With the exception of the fifth Sultan, a quiet peaceful man, all the sovereigns who attained maturity were bloodthirsty fanatics. The record of their wars with the neighbouring Hindu powers is a mass of sickening horrors. Humāyūn was a monster, comparable only with the most infamous tyrants named in history. Several of the Sultans were drunken debauchees, and little is recorded about any member of the family

[1] See map p. 43. Ausā (Owsah) is 70 miles NNW. of Kulbargā, Parēndā is 70 miles W. of Ausā, Sholāpur is 70 miles NW. of Kulbargā, and Dārūr is about 22 miles E. of Rāichūr. Burgess gives a photograph and plan of the ruined college (*A. S. W. I.*, vol. iii, plates xxviii, xxix). It is illustrated also in the *Ann. Rep. A. S. Nizam's Dominions* for 1914–15.

which is calculated to justify a favourable opinion of his character. The only person mentioned who deserves much praise is the minister Mahmūd Gāwān, and even he was fanatical and bloodthirsty. It would be difficult to specify any definite benefit conferred upon India by the dynasty. No doubt, as Meadows Taylor points out, the Bahmanīs gave a certain amount of encouragement to purely Muslim learning, and constructed irrigation works in the eastern provinces, which incidentally did good to the peasantry while primarily securing the crown revenue. But those items to their credit weigh lightly against the wholesale devastation wrought by their inhuman wars, massacres, and burnings.

Misery of the common people. Our estimate of the character of the Bahmanī Sultans and the effect of their rule upon the people committed to their charge need not be based merely upon inferences drawn from the story of their conspicuous doings. Observations on the conditions of life of the unregarded Hindu peasantry must not be looked for in the pages of Muhammadan historians, whether they deal with the north or the south. The scanty information recorded concerning the commonalty of India in ancient times is obtained almost wholly from the notes made by observant foreign visitors. Such a visitor, a Russian merchant named Athanasius Nikitin, happened to reside for a long time at Bīdar and to travel in the Bahmanī dominions between the years 1470 and 1474 in the reign of Muhammad Shāh III. By a lucky accident his notes were preserved, and have been made accessible in an English version.

The merchant tells us that:

'The Sultan is a little man, twenty years old,[1] in the power of the nobles. There is a Khorassanian Boyar [*scil.* Persian noble from Khurāsān], Melik Tuchar [*scil.* Maliku-t Tujjār, 'Lord of the merchants', or 'merchant-prince', a title of Khwāja Mahmūd Gāwān], who keeps an army of 200,000 men; Melik Khan keeps 100,000; Kharat Khan, 20,000; and many are the khans that keep 10,000 armed men. The Sultan goes out with 300,000 men of his own troops.

The land is overstocked with people; but those in the country are very miserable, whilst the nobles are extremely opulent and delight in luxury. They are wont to be carried on their silver beds, preceded by some twenty chargers caparisoned in gold, and followed by 300 men on horseback, and by 500 on foot, and by horn men, ten torchbearers, and ten musicians.

The Sultan goes out hunting with his mother and his lady, and a train of 10,000 men on horseback, 50,000 on foot; 200 elephants adorned in gilded armour, and in front 100 horsemen, 100 dancers, and 300 common horses in golden clothing; 100 monkeys, and 100 concubines, all foreign.'

The armies were armed mobs. It is obvious that such an overgrown establishment of armed men, women, and beasts, controlled by a selfish minority of luxurious nobles, must have sucked the country dry. There is no difficulty in believing the positive statement that the common people were 'very miserable'. The mass of the people in the Hindu Empire of Vijayanagar was equally oppressed and wretched. The huge armies maintained were little better than armed mobs, eager to murder tens of

[1] He was in his tenth year in 1463 (King, p. 98). The remark therefore applies to 1473 or 1474.

thousands of helpless peasants, but extremely inefficient in warfare. Similar unwieldy hosts were maintained by the neighbouring states, Muhammadan and Hindu. Various recorded incidents prove that such masses of undisciplined men had little military value, and often were routed by quite small forces of active assailants. But, on the whole, the armed mobs of the Muhammadan Sultans were a little more efficient than those of their Hindu opponents, and, in consequence, usually were victorious.

Fortresses and other buildings. It is characteristic of the nature of the rule of the Bahmanīs that Meadows Taylor, who judged the Sultans with excessive partiality, should declare that the fortresses built by them are ‘ perhaps their greatest and most indestructible monuments, and far exceed any of the same period in Europe ’. He mentions Gāwīlgarh and Narnāla, both in Berar, and especially the latter, as being choice specimens of the grandeur of design appropriate to mountain fortresses, and of work executed in good taste with munificent disregard of cost. The first gateway at Narnāla is decorated with elegant stone carving, which in Taylor's day was as perfect as it had ever been, and probably still is in the same condition. The works at Ausā and Parēndā are commended for the military science displayed in their trace. The fortresses were equipped with huge guns built up of bars welded and bound together, of which several specimens still exist.

The buildings at Kulbargā are described as being heavy, gloomy, and roughly constructed. Those at Bīdar, the capital from about 1430, which are much superior in both design and workmanship, seem deserving of more notice than they have yet received. The accounts given by Fergusson and Burgess offer few details. Enamelled tiles, a favourite Persian form of decoration, were applied to the Bīdar edifices.

The Muhammadan population of the Deccan. The Bahmanī Sultans failed in the atrocious attempt made more than once by members of the dynasty to exterminate the Hindu population of the Deccan, or in default of extermination to drive it by force into the fold of Islām. They succeeded in killing hundreds of thousands of men, women, and children, and in making considerable numbers of ‘ converts ’; but in spite of all their efforts the population continues to be Hindu in the main, the percentage of Musalmāns in the Nizam's Dominions and the Bījāpur District at present being only about eleven. The origin of that section of the inhabitants, as noted by Meadows Taylor, is mainly a consequence of the Bahmanī rule, under which large numbers of Persians, Turks, Arabs, and Moguls settled in the country and formed unions with native women. Many Hindu families also were forcibly converted, and the continuance of Muslim dynasties in large areas for centuries has kept up or even increased the proportion of the Musalmān minority, Muhammadans being usually more fertile than Hindus. The author cited was willing to credit the Bahmanī influence with ‘ a general amelioration of manners ’ in the Deccan, but that opinion might be disputed. The monuments of Hindu civilization certainly suffered severely.

SULTANS OF THE BAHMANĪ DYNASTY OF THE DECCAN

Name.	Accession.		Remarks.
	A. H.	A. D.	
1. Alāu-d dīn Hasan	748	1347	Full official title (according to the *Burhān-i Ma'āsir*) was Sultān Alāu-d dīn Hasan Shāh al-walī al Bahmanī. He had been known previously as Zafar Khān. Died a natural death.
2. Muhammad I	759	1358	Son of No. 1. Died from the effects of 'an irreligious manner of living', presumably meaning drink.
3. Mujāhid	775	1373	Son of No. 2. Drank hard: murdered by No. 4.
4. Dāūd	779 or 780	1377 or 1378	Son of brother of No. 2: murdered by a slave.
5. Muhammad II	779 or 780	1377 or 1378	Brother of No. 4. Died a natural death. No wars or rebellions. Erroneously called Mahmūd by Firishta.
6. Ghiyāsu-d dīn	799	1397	Son of No. 5, and a minor. Blinded and deposed.
7. Shamsu-d dīn	799	1397	Brother of No. 6. Deposed and imprisoned, or blinded, according to Firishta.
8. Fīrōz	800	1397	Son of younger brother of No. 2. Deposed and strangled by No. 9.
9. Ahmad	825	1422	Brother of No. 8: changed capital to Bīdar. Died a natural death.
10. Alāu-d dīn II	838	1435	Son of No. 9. Died a natural death.
11. Humāyūn	862	1457	Son of No. 10, probably assassinated.
12. Nizām	865	1461	Son of No. 11, a minor. Died suddenly.
13. Muhammad III	867	1463	Brother of No. 12. Died from effects of drink.
14. Mahmūd	887	1482	Son of No. 13. Died a natural death in Dec. 1518, when the dynasty practically ended.

NOTE.—The names, genealogy, and order of succession are in accordance with the *Burhān-i Ma'āsir* and other authorities, supported by the coins. Firishta, who differs in certain matters, is in error. The dates also are given variously in the books; the most serious discrepancy, amounting to four years, being that concerning the death of No. 10, and the accession of No. 11. Many discrepancies occur in the minute details of dates which are not shown in the table. Kalīmullāh, the last nominal Sultan, escaped to Bījāpur, and thence retired to Ahmadnagar, where he died.

Authorities

The Persian histories are the leading authorities, Firishta and others. The account of the dynasty in Meadows Taylor, *Manual of Indian History*[2] (Longmans, London, 1895), is based on Firishta, supplemented by local knowledge. Much additional material, completing the information from Persian books, has been printed by J. S. King in *The History of the Bahmani Dynasty*, founded on the *Burhān-i Ma'āsir* (Luzac, London, 1900); reprinted from *Ind. Ant.*, vol. xxviii (Bombay, 1899), with additions from other chroniclers. The history is further elucidated by T. W. Haig in 'Some Notes on the Bahmani Dynasty' (*J. A. S. B.*, part i, vol. lxxiii, 1904); and in *Historic Landmarks of the Deccan* (Pioneer Press, Allahabad, 1907).

Some interesting material is obtained from the notes of Athanasius Nikitin, a Russian merchant, as edited in *India in the Fifteenth Century*, by R. H. Major, Hakluyt Soc. (issued for 1858).

The inscriptions are treated by Haig, as above; and by Horowitz, *Epigraphia Moslemica* (Calcutta, 1909–10, 1912), *s. v.* Bīdar, Gāwīlgarh, Gulbarga, and Kolhāpur.

The coins are described and illustrated by O. Codrington in *Num. Chron.* 1898; and by H. N. Wright, *Catal. of Coins in I. M.*, vol. ii (Clarendon Press, 1907). Both writers give references to earlier papers.

The architecture has been discussed to some extent by Fergusson, and also by Burgess (*A. S. W. I.*, vol. iii, London, 1878). The subject is being further examined by the Archaeological Survey of the Nizam's Dominions, and by the Hyderabad Archaeological Society.

CHAPTER 2

The Five Sultanates of the Deccan, and Khāndēsh, from 1474 to the seventeenth century.

The five Sultanates. During the inglorious reign of Mahmūd Shāh Bahmanī (1482–1518), the provincial governors, as already mentioned, declared their independence one after the other, and set up five separate kingdoms or Sultanates, namely, the Imād Shāhī dynasty of Berar; the Nizām Shāhī of Ahmadnagar; the Ādil Shāhī of Bījāpur; the Barīd Shāhī of Bīdar; and the Kutb Shāhī of Golkonda.

Imād Shāhī dynasty of Berar (Birār). The earliest defection was that of the province of Berar (Birār), the most northern portion of the Bahmanī dominions, and more or less equivalent to the ancient Vidarbha, famous in Sanskrit literature. Berar was one of the four provinces into which the first Bahmanī Sultan of the Deccan had divided his dominions. Late in the fifteenth century the province comprised two districts, namely, Gāwīlgarh, the northern, and Māhūr, the southern. Early in the reign of Mahmūd Bahmanī, in the year 1484, according to most authorities, or 1490, according to others, the governor of Gāwīlgarh, a converted Hindu, named Fathullāh and entitled Imādu-l Mulk, proclaimed his independence, and made himself master of the whole province.

He thus founded a dynasty, the Imād Shāhī, which lasted for four generations, until about 1574, when the principality was absorbed by Ahmadnagar. The details of its separate history, so far as recorded, are not of interest. The province was ceded in 1596 to Sultan Murād, son of Akbar. The imperial governor resided at first at Bālāpur, and later at Īlichpur (Ellichpur).

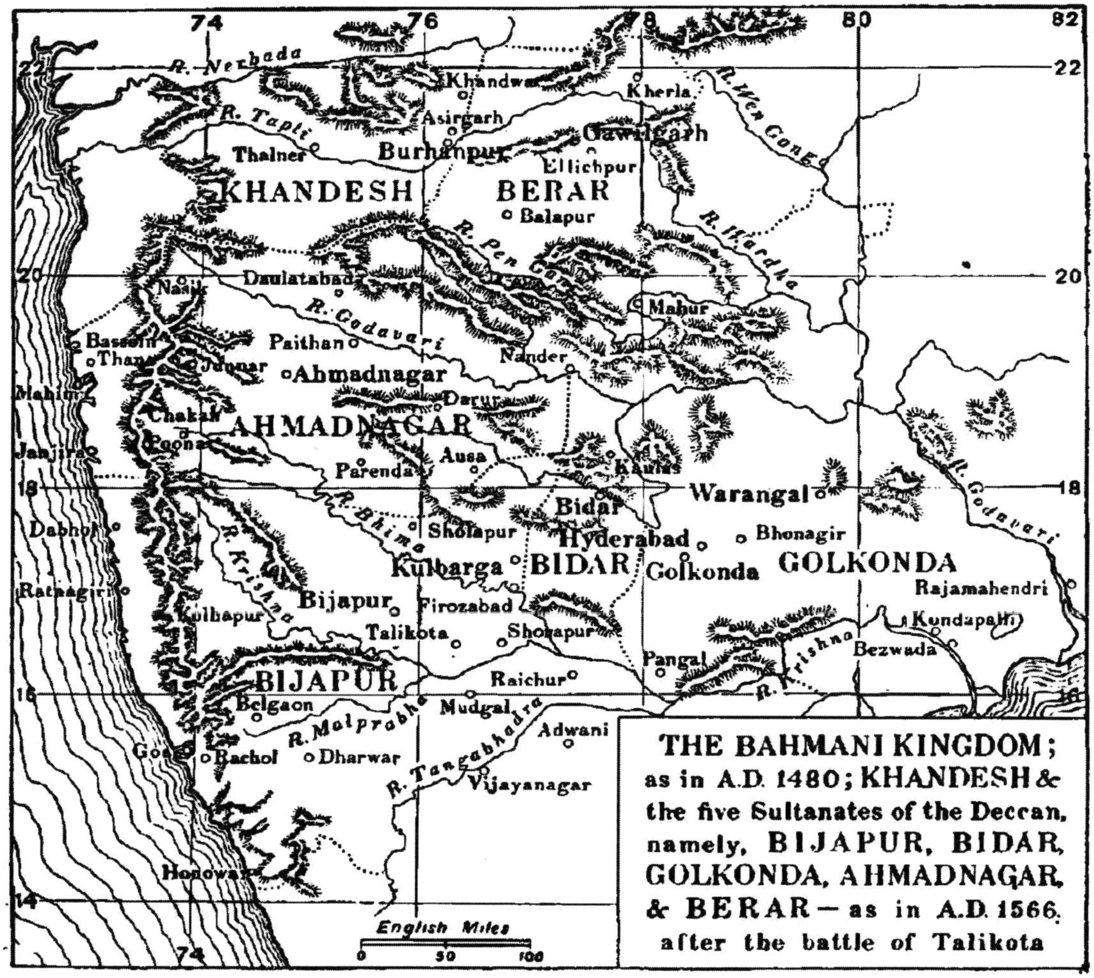

THE BAHMANI KINGDOM; as in A.D. 1480; KHANDESH & the five Sultanates of the Deccan, namely, BIJAPUR, BIDAR, GOLKONDA, AHMADNAGAR, & BERAR – as in A.D. 1566, after the battle of Talikota

Barīd Shāhī dynasty of Bīdar. The small principality governed by the Barīd Shāhī Sultans was simply the residuum of the Bahmanī Empire, consisting of the territory near the capital, left over after the more distant provinces had separated. Kāsim Barīd, minister of Mahmūd Shāh Bahmanī, was practically his own master from about the year 1492, which is given in some books as the date of the establishment of the dynasty. But he and his son Amīr long delayed to assume royal rank, and even after the death of Mahmūd in 1518 continued to set up and murder nominal

Bahmanī Sultans until 1526, when the formality was dispensed with, and Amīr openly assumed an independent position.[1] The dynasty lasted until about 1609 or a little later, when the territory was annexed by Bījāpur. The Barīd Sultans did little, if anything, deserving of remembrance; but some of their buildings are noteworthy.

DARGĀH OF AMĪR BARĪD SHĀH, BĪDAR.

Kutb Shāhī dynasty of Golkonda. The three considerable states formed out of the fragments of the Bahmanī empire were Ahmadnagar, Bījāpur, and Golkonda (Gulkandah). The Golkonda Sultanate, although founded the last of all, in 1512, and the

[1] According to Firishta, who depended on oral tradition for this dynasty, Amīr Barīd, who died in A. D. 1539 (A. H. 945), never called himself Sultan or by any equivalent title. His son, Alī Barīd, 'is the first of this dynasty who adopted the style of Shāh or King; for though his grandfather Kāsim Barīd assumed regalia, he did not take the royal title'. Compare the case of the so-called Sayyid dynasty of Delhi, the members of which never assumed the royal title or struck coins in their own names.

latest survivor, may be noticed first, because it remained in a comparatively detached position, taking only a minor part in the endless wars and quarrels, in which Ahmadnagar and Bījāpur intervened more freely. But there was much fighting with Bījāpur, and in 1565 Golkonda joined the transitory confederacy of the four Muhammadan kings which brought about the defeat and destruction of the Vijayanagar Rāj.

The territory of Golkonda. The new kingdom was the representative and successor of the ancient Hindu Kakatīya principality of Warangal,[1] which had been reduced by Ahmad Shāh Bahmanī early in his reign, about 1423. The territory was extensive, lying for the most part between the lower courses of the Godāvarī and Krishnā rivers, and extending to the coast of the Bay of Bengal, along the face of the deltas. The western frontier was mostly identical with the eastern boundary of the Bīdar principality. A northern extension was enclosed between the Godāvarī, Pen Gangā, and Wain Ganga rivers. The land was fertile, and the old irrigation works of Hindu times were maintained and extended by the Sultans.

The Sultans. The founder of the dynasty, a Turkī officer, who assumed the title of Sultan Kulī Kutb Shāh, had been appointed governor of the eastern province by Mahmūd Gāwān. He withdrew from the Bahmanī court after the wrongful execution of that minister, but continued to recognize the sovereignty of Mahmūd Shāh until 1512, when he refused to submit any longer to the Barīd ascendancy, and declared his independence.

The first Kutbī Sultan enjoyed a long life and prosperous reign, surviving until he had attained the age of ninety in 1543, when he was murdered at the instigation of his son Jamshīd. The parricide reigned for seven years. The crown was then (1550), after a short interval, offered to and accepted by a brother of Jamshīd named Ibrāhīm, who joined in the confederacy against Vijayanagar (1565), and died in 1580. His administration is reputed to have been good. In his time Hindus were freely employed in the service of the State and were permitted to attain high official rank. Ibrāhīm lived until 1611, after which date the dynasty almost ceased to have a separate history, its affairs becoming entangled with those of the Mogul emperors of Hindostan. The State was finally annexed by Aurangzēb in 1687.

The capital. The capital had been moved from Warangal to Golkonda by the first Sultan at the beginning of his reign. The new city was greatly developed in the reign of Ibrāhīm, but in 1589 it had become unhealthy. The court was then transferred to Bhāgnagar a few miles distant, which soon afterwards was called Hyderabad. The city thus created developed later as the capital

[1] Warangal is a corruption of Orukkal, meaning 'solitary rock', with reference to a prominent feature of the site of the old capital. Few of the numerous inscriptions at Warangal have been published, but they will be examined by the new Archaeological Department and the Archaeological Society of Hyderabad.

of the Nizams and now has a population of nearly half a million, taking rank as the fourth city in India. Golkonda, largely in ruins, is best known for the tombs of the Kutb Shāhī kings.

The Nizām Shāhī dynasty of Ahmadnagar. Nizāmu-l Mulk Bahrī, the head of the Deccanee party at Bīdar, who had contrived the death of Mahmūd Gāwān, came to a violent end himself not long after. His son Malik Ahmad, governor of Junnār (Joonair) to the north of Poona, then revolted. In 1490 he defeated decisively the army of Mahmūd Bahmanī, and established himself as an independent sovereign. After a time he moved his court to a more convenient and strategically better position further east, and so founded the city of Ahmadnagar. The new sovereign having assumed the title of Ahmad Nizām Shāh, the dynasty established by him is called the Nizām Shāhi. Ahmadnagar is still a considerable town and the head-quarters of a District in the Bombay Presidency.

The main efforts of Ahmad Nizām Shāh for years were directed to the acquisition of the powerful fortress of Dēogiri or Daulatābād, formerly the capital of the Yādava kingdom. Ultimately, he obtained the surrender of the place, in or about A. D. 1499, and thus consolidated his dominion.

The second and third Sultans. The second sovereign, Burhān Nizām Shāh, who reigned for forty-five years (1508–53), was engaged in many wars with the neighbouring States, and made a new departure about 1550 by allying himself with the Hindu Rāya of Vijayanagar against the Sultan of Bījāpur. Some years earlier (1537) Burhān had himself adopted the Shīa form of Islām. His successor, Husain Shāh, joined the confederacy which sacked Vijayanagar in 1565.

Later history. The subsequent history of the dynasty may be read in great detail in the pages of Firishta, who long resided at Ahmadnagar, but the incidents are not of much interest. Berar was absorbed in 1574. Chānd Bībī, the queen dowager of Bījāpur, who had returned to Ahmadnagar, made a gallant and successful resistance to Akbar's son, Prince Murād, in 1576, purchasing peace by the cession of Berar. But war soon broke out again, and in August 1600 the Mogul army stormed Ahmadnagar. Chānd Bībī then perished. According to some accounts she was murdered by a eunuch, according to others she took poison. Those events, which belong to the history of Akbar rather than to that of the minor kingdom, will be dealt with more fully when the story of his reign comes to be told. Akbar, although he formally gave Ahmadnagar the rank of a new Sūba or province, never obtained possession of more than a small portion of the kingdom. The remainder continued an obscure independent existence, and the State was not finally annexed until 1637 in the reign of Shāhjahān.

The Ādil Shāhī dynasty of Bījāpur ; the first Sultan. Bījāpur, the most important and interesting of the five sultanates or kingdoms, deserves more extended notice. The dynasty was known as the Ādil Shāhī, from the name of its founder, Yūsuf Ādil Khān, governor of Bījāpur, who declared his independence in 1489, almost simultaneously with his colleagues in Berar and Ahmadnagar.

Yūsuf Ādil, so far as public knowledge went, was simply a Georgian slave who had been purchased by Khwāja Mahmūd Gāwān, and by reason of his own abilities and the discerning patronage of the minister had risen to high office at the Bahmanī court, ultimately becoming governor of Bījāpur. But according to private information, accepted by Firishta on respectable authority, he was really a son of Sultan Murād II of Turkey, who annexed Salonica and died in 1451, leaving the succession to his son Muhammad, by whom Constantinople was taken two years later. If the romantic tale may be believed Yūsuf Ādil in his infancy had been saved by stratagem from the massacre of princes which usually occurred in Asiatic Turkey at the accession of a new sovereign, and had been brought up secretly in Persia, with the cognizance of his mother, who kept herself informed concerning his movements. When the disguised prince was seventeen years old he seems to have found continued residence in Persia to be unsafe, and therefore allowed himself to be disposed of as a slave and sold in Bīdar to the minister of the Bahmanī Sultan. The story obviously is open to critical doubt, but it is not absolutely incredible, and whoever cares to do so can believe it. Firishta apparently was satisfied as to its truth.

Firishta's history. Firishta's history, written in a spirit of remarkable independence, presents an agreeable contrast when compared with Abu-l Fazl's too courtly *Akbarnāma*. It is neither possible nor desirable to reproduce in this book Firishta's detailed account of the doings of 'the illustrious monarchs who have reigned over Beejapoor'. Most of the wars and intrigues which seemed so important to the historian at the beginning of the seventeenth century are now seen to have had little or no effect on the development of India as a whole, and to be of only provincial interest. Except for purposes of purely local study, it is not worth while to master or remember the details of the incessant fighting between the five kingdoms of the Deccan. But certain matters in the story of Bījāpur and its rulers still deserve a place in the pages of even a short history of India.

Preference of Yūsuf Ādil Shāh for the Shīa religion. Yūsuf Ādil Shāh waged wars against Vijayanagar and his Muhammadan neighbours with varying fortune. When residing in Persia in his youth he had learned to prefer the Shīa form of Islām, and subsequently made a vow to profess publicly that faith. In 1502 he carried out his purpose, making the Shīa creed the State religion, while giving free and untrammelled toleration to the Sunnīs. The change, although accepted by many of his subjects, aroused violent opposition, which resulted in a dangerous confederacy of the neighbouring princes against Bījāpur. The Sultan discreetly restored the Sunnī creed as the official religion and broke up the confederacy. When he had gained his purpose 'he renewed the public exercise of the Shīa religion'.

Capture of Goa by the Portuguese. In those days Goa was a favourite residence of Yūsuf Ādil Shāh, who at one time thought of making the port the seat of his government. It was the rendezvous of the Muhammadans of the Deccan who used to embark there for the pilgrimage to Mecca. In February 1510 (A.H. 915) the king's officers negligently permitted the Portuguese commander, Albuquerque, to surprise the city and occupy it without the loss of a man. The victor used his good fortune with moderation and forbade his soldiers under pain of death to do any injury to the inhabitants. But the Sultan, being determined to recover his much prized possession, prepared an overwhelming force and won back Goa in May of the same year 1510 (A.H. 916). Albuquerque's fleet, which was reduced to intense distress during the rainy season, received reinforcements in the autumn. The death of Yūsuf Ādil Shāh at the age of seventy-four, in October or November, weakened the defence, so that the Portuguese succeeded in storming the city after a hard fight. The resistance offered so incensed Albuquerque that he ordered a general massacre of the Muhammadan population without distinction of age or sex, and encouraged his soldiers to commit frightful cruelties. He treated the Hindus with kindness and established an effective government. The Portuguese thus finally won Goa in November 1510 (A.H. 916), and have retained it ever since.

Marriage with Marāthī lady. Instances of Muhammadan princes in the Deccan marrying Hindu wives have been mentioned. Yūsuf Ādil Shāh early in his reign defeated a Marāthā chieftain named Mukund Rāo, whose sister he espoused. She took the Musalmān name of Būbūjī Khānam, and became the mother of the second Sultan as well as of three princesses who were married to members of the royal families of the neighbouring Muhammadan States. Yūsuf Ādil Shāh freely admitted Hindus to offices of trust. The Marāthī language was ordinarily used for purposes of accounts and business.

Character of Yūsuf Ādil Shāh. The first Sultan or Shāh of Bījāpur is given a high character by Firishta, who testifies on good authority that he was 'a wise prince, intimately acquainted with human nature', handsome, eloquent, well read, and a skilled musician.

'Although he mingled pleasure with business, yet he never allowed the former to interfere with the latter. He always warned his ministers to act with justice and integrity, and in his own person showed them an example of attention to those virtues. He invited to his court many learned men and valiant officers from Persia, Turkistan, and Rūm, also several eminent artists, who lived happy under the shadow of his bounty. In his reign the citadel of Bījāpur was built of stone.'

He lies buried, not at Bījāpur, but at Gūgī or Gogī, farther to the east, near the grave of a saint whom he venerated.

'No mausoleum was built over him; and in the precincts of the holy burying-ground his open tomb is as simple as many others, and an endowment, which has been preserved, still provides a covering of cotton chintz for it, renewed from year to year. Thus, as the people of Gogī assert, with an honourable pride, there are not as yet faithful servants wanting to the noble king to light a lamp at night at his grave, and to say *fatihas* for his soul's peace, while the tombs of the great Bahmanī kings and of all his enemies in life are desecrated.' [1]

Ismaīl Shāh. The new king, Ismaīl, being a minor, the government was carried on by Kamāl Khān, an officer of the late ruler, as regent. He proved faithless, and conspired to seize the throne for himself, but lost his life in the attempt. Like other kings of the period Ismaīl was fated to spend most of his time in fighting his neighbours. He recovered from Vijayanagar the Rāichūr Doab, the much disputed country between the Krishnā and Tungabhadrā. Ismaīl was so much pleased at the arrival of an embassy from the Shāh of Persia, who recognized Bījāpur as an independent State, that he directed the officers of his army to wear the head-dress distinctive of the Shīa sect. He rests beside his father, whom he resembled in character and accomplishments. The son, Mallū, who succeeded him, proved to be incurably vicious and incompetent. Accordingly he was blinded and deposed, the sceptre passing into the hands of his brother Ibrāhīm after a few months.

Ibrāhīm Ādil Shāh I. The new ruler, who assumed the title of Ibrāhīm Ādil Shāh, rejected foreign practices, including the use of the Shīa head-dress, and reverted completely to Sunnī ritual. He favoured the Deccanees, with their allies the Abyssinians, as against the Persians and other foreigners. Many of the strangers entered the service of Rāma Rāya the *de facto* ruler of Vijayanagar. At this time revolutions occurred at Vijayanagar which will be noticed more particularly in the history of that kingdom. In 1535 the Bījāpur Sultan accepted the invitation of the chief of one of the Hindu factions and paid a visit to Vijayanagar lasting a week. He departed enriched by an enormous present of gold coin, in addition to valuable horses and elephants. Subsequently the Sultans of Bīdar, Ahmadnagar, and Golkonda combined against Bījāpur, which emerged victorious, thanks to the ability of the minister, Asad Khān, whose reputation is scarcely inferior to that of Mahmūd Gāwān. It is needless to follow in detail the wars and intrigues which lasted throughout the reign. The Sultan towards the end of his life abandoned himself to drink and debauchery, ruining his health and temper. The unlucky physicians who failed to cure him were beheaded or trampled under foot by elephants. Ibrāhīm came to a dishonoured death in 1557, and was buried at Gogī by the side of his father and grandfather.

Alī Ādil Shāh. Alī Ādil Shāh, having succeeded his father, Ibrāhīm, began his administration by publicly resuming the Shīa creed, professing it with a degree of intolerance which his ancestor had carefully avoided. In 1558, the Sultan having made a transitory alliance with Rāma Rāja, the combined Hindu and Muhammadan armies invaded the territory of Ahmadnagar, which they

[1] Meadows Taylor, *Manual*, p. 198.

ravaged mercilessly—the Hindus taking the opportunity to avenge without pity all the injuries which they had suffered from Muslim hands in the course of two centuries. The barbarous excesses committed by Rāma Rāja and the insolence shown by him to his Muhammadan allies alienated Alī Ādil Shāh, who was advised that no single Musalmān sovereign was capable of contending with success against the wealth and hosts of the arrogant Hindu prince. Ultimately all the four Sultans of Bījāpur, Bīdar, Ahmadnagar, and Golkonda were convinced that their interests required them to sacrifice their rivalries and combine in an irresistible league in order to effect the destruction of the infidel. With a view to draw closer the bonds of alliance, Alī Ādil Shāh married Chānd Bībī, daughter of Husain Nizām Shāh of Ahmadnagar, whose sister was given to the son of the Sultan of Bījāpur.

Alliance against Vijayanagar. In December 1564 the four allied sovereigns established their joint head-quarters at the small town of Tālikota, situated about twenty-five miles to the north of the Krishnā, in 16° 28′ N. lat. and 76° 19′ E. long. The town, now included in the Bījāpur District, Bombay, was then in the dominions of Alī Ādil Shāh, who received his allies as his guests.

The Vijayanagar Government, in full confidence of victory, prepared to meet the threatened invasion by the assemblage of enormous levies numbering several hundred thousand men. Two large armies were sent forward under the command of Rāma Rāja's brothers, Tirumala and Venkatādri, with orders to prevent the army of Islām from crossing the Krishnā. When the allied princes moved southwards to the bank of the river, twenty-five miles distant from Tālikota, they found that it was impassable, except at the ford of Ingaligi, which was protected by an immense host. They endeavoured to mislead the enemy by marching along the bank as if seeking for another crossing-place, and succeeded by this simple stratagem in outwitting their Hindu opponents and passing the river unopposed. The aged Rāma Rāja then moved up from Vijayanagar with the main army, and encamped somewhere near the fortress of Mudgal, so often the subject of dispute between the Hindus and the Musalmāns.

Battle of Tālikota. Battle was joined in the space between the Ingaligi ford and Mudgal, marked by a little village called Bāyapur or Bhōgapur. The forces on both sides being unusually numerous the fighting must have extended over a front of many miles. The conflict took place on Tuesday, January 23, 1565, equivalent to 20 Jum. II, A.H. 972.[1]

The Muslim centre was commanded by Husain Nizām Shāh of Ahmadnagar, who possessed a powerful park of artillery ; Alī Ādil Shāh of Bījāpur led the right wing ; and the left wing was entrusted to Alī Barīd Shāh of Golkonda.

'The artillery, fastened together by strong chains and ropes, was drawn

[1] Mr. Sewell correctly points out that the week-day was Tuesday, not Friday, as stated by Firishta.

up in front of the line, and the war elephants were placed in various positions, agreeable to custom. Each prince erected his particular standard in the centre of his own army, and the allies moved in close order against the enemy.'

Rāma Rāja, then an old man, although in full possession of his faculties, commanded the centre opposed to the king of Ahmadnagar. His brother Tirumala encountered Alī Ādil Shāh of Bījāpur, while his other brother, Venkatādri, fought against the princes of Bīdar and Golkonda. After much strenuous fighting the Bījāpur and Golkonda chiefs gave way and thought of retiring, but the Ahmadnagar Sultan stood firm in the centre. Just then a furious elephant rushed at the litter in which Rāma Rāja was seated, so that his frightened bearers let him drop. He was thus taken prisoner, and at once beheaded by Husain Nizām Shāh with his own hands. The head was placed on the point of a long spear so that it might be seen by the enemy. It was carefully preserved at Ahmadnagar and annually exhibited to pious Muslims up to 1829 when Briggs published his translation of Firishta.

'The Hindus, according to custom, when they saw their chief destroyed, fled in the utmost disorder from the field, and were pursued by the allies with such success that the river was dyed red with their blood. It is computed by the best authorities that above one hundred thousand infidels were slain during the action and the pursuit.'

Results of the battle. The victory, known to history as the battle of Tālikota, because the allies had assembled at that town, distant about thirty miles from the battle-field, was one of the most decisive of the conflicts recorded in the whole course of Indian history. The Hindus made no attempt to dispute the verdict of the sword. The great Hindu empire of the South, which had lasted for more than two centuries, was definitely ended, and the supremacy of Islām in the Deccan was assured. The noble city of Vijayanagar was blotted out of existence and remains desolate to this day. The details of the destruction wrought will be described more fully in the history of Vijayanagar. The dominions of both Bījāpur and Golkonda were enlarged considerably.

League against the Portuguese; death of the Sultan. In 1570 the sovereigns of Bījāpur and Ahmadnagar again joined their forces and attempted to capture the settlements of the Portuguese, then at the climax of their power. But even the help of the Zamorin of Calicut and the Rājā of Achīn did not suffice to enable them to win success. The envied and hated foreign infidels survived and prospered, until they had to yield the pride of place to other European powers. The siege of Goa by a huge army was raised after ten months, although the defence had been maintained by only seven hundred European soldiers, supported by three hundred friars and priests, a thousand slaves, and some ill-equipped boats. De Sousa records the curious fact that Alī Ādil Shāh sent to Archbishop Gaspar of Goa to fetch Fathers and books of the Law, but without any good result, because the request was made from mere curiosity.[1] Alī Ādil Shāh was killed in 1579 by a eunuch who had good reason for his act.

Ibrāhīm Ādil Shāh II. The heir to the throne, Ibrāhīm Ādil Shāh II, being a minor, was taken charge of by his mother, Chānd Bībī, while ministers ruled the kingdom. In 1584 the queen mother returned to her native city of Ahmadnagar, and never visited Bījāpur again. We shall hear presently of her gallant doings in the conflict with Akbar. In 1595 the last fight between Bījāpur and Ahmadnagar took place, and the Ahmadnagar monarch was killed. From that time the separate history of both States may be said to end, their annals becoming merged in those of the Mogul empire. Ibrāhīm Ādil Shāh II survived until 1626, when he died, leaving a great reputation as an able administrator. The testimony of Meadows Taylor, who was well acquainted with the country and local tradition, may be quoted:

> 'Ibrāhīm Ādil Shāh died in 1626, in the fifty-sixth year of his age. He was the greatest of all the Ādil Shāhī dynasty, and in most respects, except its founder, the most able and popular.
>
> Without the distraction of war, he applied himself to civil affairs with much care; and the land settlements of the provinces of his kingdom, many of which are still extant among district records, show an admirable and efficient system of registration of property and its valuation. In this respect the system of Todar Mull introduced by the Emperor Akbar seems to have been followed with the necessary local modifications.
>
> Although he changed the profession of the State religion immediately upon assuming the direction of State affairs from Shia to Sunnī, Ibrāhīm was yet extremely tolerant of all creeds and faiths. Hindus not only suffered no persecution at his hands, but many of his chief civil and military officers were Brahmans and Marāthās.[2] With the Portuguese of Goa he seems to have kept up a friendly intercourse. Portuguese painters decorated his palaces, and their merchants traded freely in his dominions. To their missionaries also he extended his protection; and there are many anecdotes current in the country that his tolerance of Christians equalled, if it did not exceed, that of his contemporary Akbar. He allowed the preaching of Christianity freely among his people, and there are still existent several Catholic churches, one at Chītapur, one at Mudgal, and one at Rāichūr, and others, endowed by the king with lands and other sources of revenue, which have survived the changes and revolutions of more than 300 years. Each of these churches now consists of several hundred members and remains under the spiritual jurisdiction of the Archbishop of Goa.'

Ibrāhīm's dominions extended to the borders of Mysore. At the time of his death he left to his successor a full treasury and a well-paid army of 80,000 horse.

[1] Transl. and quoted in Monserrate, *Commentarius*, p. 545, ed. Hosten (*Memoirs, A. S. B.*, 1914). Gaspar was archbishop from 1560 to 1567, and again from 1574 to 1576 (Fonseca, p. 71).

[2] Ibrāhīm's partiality for Hindus led his Muslim subjects to give him the mocking title of *Jagad-guru*, or 'World-Preceptor'. Akbar conferred that title in all seriousness on his own favourite Jain instructor, and received it himself informally from Hindu admirers.

The splendid architectural monuments of his reign will be noticed presently.

It is not necessary to pursue the local history further. The capital was taken and the country was annexed by Aurangzēb in 1686.

THE ĀDIL SHĀHĪ KINGS OR SULTANS OF BIJĀPUR

	Accession. A.D.	
1. Yūsuf	1490	Had been governor under the Bahmanī king.
2. Ismaīl	1510	Son of No. 1.
3. Mallū	1534	Son of No. 2; deposed and blinded after six months.
4. Ibrāhīm I	1535	Brother of No. 3.
5. Alī	1557	Son of No. 4; assassinated. Destruction of Vijayanagar in 1565.
6. Ibrāhīm II	1580	Nephew of No. 5; good civil administration; fine buildings.
7. Muhammad	1626	Son of No. 6; became tributary to Shāhjahān in 1636; Marāthā aggression began.
8. Alī II	1656	Son of No. 7; war with Sivājī.
9. Sikandar	1673	Made captive by Aurangzēb, and dynasty extinguished in 1686.

Fārūkī dynasty of Khāndēsh. Before quitting the subject of the Muhammadan kingdoms of the Deccan we may bestow a passing glance on the small kingdom of Khāndēsh in the valley of the Tāptī, whose rulers were known as the Fārūkī dynasty. The principality, which did not form part of the Bahmanī kingdom, was established in 1388 at the close of the reign of Sultan Fīrōz Tughlak of Delhi, and took a share in the innumerable local wars. It was sometimes a dependency of Gujarāt. The importance of the State resulted chiefly from its possession of the strong fortress of Asīrgarh. The seat of government was Burhānpur. The surrender of Asīrgarh to Akbar in January 1601 put an end to the dynasty and the independence of the State, which became the Sūba of Khāndēsh or Dāndēsh.

Art and Literature. The monuments of the Bahmanī dynasty at Kulbargā and Bīdar have been briefly noticed.

At Ahmadnagar the principal ancient building is the ruined Bhadr Palace in white stone, built by the founder of the city, which possesses few other architectural remains of importance. The chief mosque at Burhānpur, the capital of the Fārūkī kings of Khāndēsh, erected by Alī Khān in 1588, is described as a fine building adorned with stone carvings executed in perfect taste. But Fergusson formed the opinion that the edifices of the town have 'very little artistic value'.

At Golkonda and Bījāpur important schools of architecture developed, differing one from the other and from the styles of northern India. The precincts of the Golkonda fortress include a multitude of palaces, mosques, and other ancient buildings. The tombs of the Kutb Shāhī kings, which stand outside the fortress about half a mile to the north, are built of granite and characterized by narrow-necked domes of peculiar form.

The works executed to the orders of the Ādil Shāhī kings of Bījāpur are 'marked by a grandeur of conception and boldness in construction unequalled by any edifices erected in India'. The gigantic walls of the city, begun by Yūsuf, the first Sultan, and completed by Alī, the fifth sovereign, are six and a quarter miles in circumference, and still perfect for the most part.

TOMBS IN GOLKONDA STYLE, BĪJĀPUR.

The four leading builders at Bījāpur were the Kings Yūsuf (1490–1510), Alī (1558–80), Ibrāhīm II (1580–1626), and Muhammad Shāh (1626–56). The principal mosque, an admirably proportioned building, erected by Alī, is still perfect, and would accommodate five thousand worshippers. The same sovereign constructed aqueducts for the supply of water to all parts of the city, and also built the spacious audience-hall or Gagan Mahall (1561). The richly decorated tomb of Ibrāhīm II is an exquisite structure; and the mausoleum of his successor, Muhammad (1626–56), built at the same time as the Tāj, is a marvel of skilful construction. The dome is the second largest in the world. The names of the architects employed do not seem to be recorded, and it is impossible to say whether they were foreigners or of Indian birth. The style shows traces of both foreign and native ideas.

Fine libraries are known to have existed at Ahmadnagar and Bījāpur. One illuminated manuscript from the latter is in the British Museum. The excellent history of Muhammad Kāsim, surnamed Firishta, was written to the command of Ibrāhīm II of Bījāpur. The author mentions many earlier writers whose works are not now extant.

The town of Bījāpur, which long lay deserted and desolate, has revived in modern times, and is the prosperous head-quarters of a District in the Bombay Presidency, with considerable trade and a population of about 25,000 persons.

Authorities

The Five Sultanates and Khāndēsh

The principal authority is Firishta, whose narratives are supplemented by observations recorded by Sewell (*A Forgotten Empire*) and Meadows Taylor (*Manual of the History of India*). For relations with the Portuguese I have used Fonseca, *Sketch of the City of Goa* (Bombay, Thacker, 1878), a sound book based on the official records of the settlement.

The monuments are briefly described in Fergusson, *Hist. of Eastern and Ind. Archit.*², 1910, and other works there cited. The information about Bījāpur is tolerably full, and the principal buildings there are in good condition. See also V. A. Smith, *H. F. A.*, Oxford, 1911. A good detailed catalogue of the Bījāpur buildings (with plan of city) will be found in the *Revised Lists of Antiquarian Remains in the Bombay Presidency*, 2nd ed., 1897 (vol. xvi, *A. S. India*, New Imp. Ser.). All works on Bījāpur are superseded by the magnificent volume *Bījāpur and its Architectural Remains, with an Historical Outline of the 'Ādil Shāhi Dynasty*. By Henry Cousens, Bombay Government Central Press, 1916; pp. xii, 132; cxviii plates and 28 text illustrations; quarto, half-morocco. The coinage is described in the monograph by Mr. Cousens, pp. 127, 128, pl. cxv. The known specimens, issued by five of the Sultans, comprise three gold and two or three hundred copper coins, besides the curious *lārins*, made of stamped silver wire.

The newly formed Archaeological Society of Hyderabad has plenty of unpublished material of all kinds on which to work. The first number of the *Journal* contains an interesting article on Warangal.

CHAPTER 3

The Hindu empire of Vijayanagar, from A.D. 1336 to 1646.

Special interest of the history. Although the history of the Hindu empire of Vijayanagar is closely entwined with that of the Muslim Bahmanī empire and the later sultanates of the Deccan for more than two centuries, it is impracticable to combine the two histories in a single narrative. Separate treatment is inevitable, but a certain amount of repetition cannot be avoided. The story of the Hindu monarchy which set itself up as a barrier to check the onrush of the armies of Islām is one of singular interest, and might be narrated with a fullness of detail rarely possible in Indian history. The multitude of relevant inscriptions, numbering many hundreds, is extraordinary. Several European and Muslim travellers from the fourteenth to the sixteenth century have recorded the historical traditions of the empire with vivid descriptions of the system of government and the glories of the magnificent capital. The study of the polity, manners, customs, and religion of the Vijayanagar empire merits particular attention, because the State was the embodiment of the Telinga or Telugu and Kanarese forms of Hinduism which differed widely from the more familiar forms of the north. The sources of our knowledge are not confined to inscriptions and the notes of foreign observers. The Muhammadan historians who lived in the Deccan, headed by Firishta, give valuable information; and much may be learned from critical examination of the monuments and coins. A remarkable school of art was developed at Vijayanagar, and literature, both Sanskrit and Telugu, was cultivated with eminent success.

No complete history yet written. It is matter for regret that no history of the Vijayanagar empire in the form of a readable, continuous narrative, embodying the results of specialist studies after critical sifting, has yet been written. Mr. Robert Sewell's excellent book entitled *A Forgotten Empire, Vijayanagar*, published in 1900, which recalled attention to the long-neglected subject, and largely increased the store of historical material by making the Portuguese accounts accessible, is avowedly a pioneer work designed as 'a foundation upon which may hereafter be constructed a regular history of the Vijayanagar empire'. The profoundly learned essays by Mr. H. Krishna Sastri, which deal with the annals of the first, second, and third dynasties, as published in the *Annual Reports of the Archaeological Survey of India* for 1907–8, 1908–9, and 1911–12, add much to the information collected by Sewell, and go a long way towards removing the numerous difficulties which beset critical treatment of the subject. But those essays do not pretend to be more than a presentation of the data for a history, chiefly obtained from study of the inscriptions. The desired narrative in literary shape still is wanting, and much additional matter collected in the publications of other writers remains to be worked up.

My readers, therefore, will understand that it is not possible for me at present to offer a thoroughly satisfactory summary account of Vijayanagar history within the narrow limits of this chapter. Such an account cannot be prepared until the endless problems of detail and chronology presented by the original authorities have been disposed of by special studies and the net results incorporated in a well-digested narrative. I cannot attempt to go deeply into the difficulties. My account of the political history of the empire must be confined to a brief outline. The few pages available will be devoted chiefly to descriptions of the internal conditions of the State and of the havoc wrought by the Muhammadan victors in 1565.

Origin of the kingdom or empire. The traditionary accounts of the origin of the kingdom or empire vary widely. Sewell enumerates six or seven. There is, however, no doubt that the new power was the outcome of the efforts made by five brothers, sons of one Sangama, to stay the tide of Muslim invasion and to preserve Hindu *dharma* in the peninsula. Good authority exists for regarding the brothers as fugitives from the eastern Telinga or Telugu kingdom of Warangal, the capital of which was taken by the Muhammadans in 1323. Equally good, or perhaps better, authority views them as chieftains under the Kanarese dynasty of the Hoysala or Ballāla kings of the Mysore country, whose capital, Dhōra-Samudra, was sacked in 1327. It is certain that the activity of the five brothers was a reply to the Muhammadan attacks on both Warangal and Dhōra-Samudra. The mad tyranny of Muhammad bin Tughlak of Delhi prevented him from retaining control over his southern conquests. The Bahmanī kingdom founded by one of his revolted governors in 1347 upheld the standard of Islām independently of Delhi. When that kingdom broke up in the closing years of the fifteenth century, the five new sultanates formed from it, having inherited its traditions, were normally at war with Vijayanagar, and with the Telinga Rāj of Warangal, which reasserted itself at times, until 1425, when it was finally destroyed.

Foreign relations of Vijayanagar. The external history of the Vijayanagar empire, consequently, is mainly that of wars with the various Muhammadan dynasties of the Deccan, But from the middle of the fifteenth century both parties occasionally found it convenient to forget their principles and to enter into unholy temporary alliances. In the end the Muslims, who were more vigorous, better mounted, and better armed than the Hindus, won the long contest. Their destruction of the city of Vijayanagar in 1565, carried out with a completeness which no Prussian could surpass, effectually put an end to the Hindu empire of the south as such. But the victory did not immediately increase very largely the territory under Muslim rule. The peninsula to the south of the Tungabhadrā continued to be essentially Hindu, governed by a multitude of Hindu chiefs, uncontrolled by any paramount power. While the foreign relations of Vijayanagar were in the main concerned with the Musalmān sultanates, the Hindu empire also had important dealings with the Portuguese, who first arrived on the Malabar coast in 1498, and established themselves permanently at Goa late in 1510. The transactions with the Portuguese bring the affairs of Vijayanagar into touch with the outer world ; and we are indebted to Portuguese authors for the best accounts of the polity and manners of the great Hindu State.

Early chiefs ; Harihara I and Bukka. The two most prominent of the five brothers who led the Hindu opposition were named Hakka or Harihara (I) and Bukka. The traditional date for their foundation of Vijayanagar on the southern, or safe, bank of the Tungabhadrā,[1] facing the older fortress of Ānegundi on the

[1] The name of the city is sometimes written Vidyānagara or Vidyānagarī.

northern bank, is A.D. 1336. The building of it was finished in 1343. It is certain that ten years later the brothers were in a position to claim control over 'the whole country between the Eastern and the Western Oceans'. They never assumed royal rank. Bukka died in 1376. Two years before his decease he thought it advisable to send an embassy to Tai-tsu, the Ming emperor of China.[1] Most of his life was spent in waging ferocious wars against the Bahmanī kings. During the reign of Muhammad Shāh (1358–73) it is supposed that half a million of Hindus were destroyed.[2] His successor, Mujāhid Shāh (1373–7), on one occasion penetrated the outer defences of Vijayanagar and was able to damage an image of Hanumān the monkey-god by a blow from his steel mace.

Harihara II, independent king. Harihara II (acc. 1379) was the first really independent sovereign of Vijayanagar who assumed full royal state or titles. His reign coincided almost exactly with that of Muhammad Shāh I, the fifth of the Bahmanī sultans, and the only peaceable man of his family. Harihara consequently had a quiet time so far as the Muhammadans were concerned, and enjoyed leisure for the task of consolidating his dominion over the whole of southern India, including Trichinopoly and Conjeeveram (Kānchī). He was tolerant of various forms of religion, but gave his personal devotion to Siva-Virūpāksha. He died in August 1404, and, as usual, the succession was disputed.

Deva Rāya I. The next sovereign to secure a firm seat on the throne was Deva Rāya I (Nov. 1406 to about 1412). He and his successors had to engage in constant fighting with the Bahmanī Sultan Fīrōz, who took the field against the Hindus almost every year. Early in his reign (1406) Fīrōz invaded the Hindu territory in great force and actually entered some of the streets of the capital, although unable to take the place. He remained encamped to the south of the city for four months, ravaging the land and taking prisoners by tens of thousands. Deva Rāya was constrained to sue for peace and to submit to the humiliation of giving his daughter in marriage to the Muslim sovereign. The Sultan visited Vijayanagar during the marriage festivities, but took offence because, when he was leaving, the Rāya did not accompany him the whole way back to his camp. Thus the marriage bond failed to heal the hereditary enmity.

Right and left-hand castes. Nothing particular is recorded about the doings of Deva Rāya's successor, Vijaya (1412 to about 1419), but it is worth while to note that an inscription of the reign mentions the existence of the right-hand and left-hand groups of castes as an institution then not new. So much speculation has been devoted unsuccessfully to attempted explanations of that curious grouping of castes in the south that it is important to know that the distinction was already well established in A.D. 1400.

Deva Rāya II. Deva Rāya II (1421–48) had to meet the

[1] Bretschneider, *Mediaeval Researches*, ed. 1910, vol. ii, p. 222.

[2] We must remember that the far south remained immune from the Bahmanī attacks and continued to supply men and riches to Vijayanagar.

attacks of Fīrōz Shah's brother and successor, Ahmad Shāh (1422–35) a ferocious brute who held high festival for three days whenever on any one day the victims—men, women, and children—in a defenceless population, numbered twenty thousand. The Hindu kingdom of Warangal was finally overthrown by him in 1425.

The war with the Musalmāns continued during the reign of Alāu-d dīn Bahmanī (1435–57), and ended unfavourably for the Hindu cause. Deva Rāya, impressed with the facts that the Islamite armies owed their success largely to being better mounted than their opponents and supported by a large body of expert archers, tried the expedient of enlisting Muhammadans in his service and equipping them in the Bahmanī fashion. But the experiment was not a success, and the Rāya had to submit to the payment of tribute. The visit of the Italian Nicolo Conti, to Vijayanagar took place at the beginning of Deva Rāya's reign, and that of Abdu-r Razzāk in 1443, towards its close.

The story of Vijayanagar during the second half of the fifteenth century is obscure. The kings were of little personal merit, palace intrigues were rife, and the Government was feeble.

The first usurpation of Narasinga Sāluva. Narasinga Sāluva, the powerful and semi-independent governor of Chandragiri in 1486, was obliged to depose the weak nominal sovereign reigning at the time and take the cares of government on his own shoulders, an event known as the First Usurpation. In the course of a few years he effected extensive conquests in the Tamil country to the south and restored the credit of the Government. His administration made so deep an impression on the public mind that the Vijayanagar empire was often designated by Europeans as the 'kingdom of Narsingh'. He was constantly at war with the Muhammadans. The new sultanate of Bījāpur, which began its separate existence from 1489 or 1490, now took the leading position on the Muslim side, the last Bahmanī kings being restricted to a small principality close to Bīdar, their capital.

Second usurpation of Narasa Nāyaka. The power of Narasinga Sāluva was transmitted to his son Immadi Narasinga, who in 1505 was killed by his general, Narasa Nāyaka, a Tuluva That was the Second Usurpation. The details of the transactions connected with both usurpations are obscure and controverted.

Coin of Krishna deva Rāya.

Krishna Rāya. The third or Tuluva dynasty thus founded produced one really great ruler, Krishna deva Rāya, whose reign began in 1509 and lasted until 1529. He was, therefore, the contemporary of Henry VIII of England. After his coronation early in 1510 Krishna Rāya stayed at home in his capital for a year and a half, learning his kingly duties and forming plans for the aggrandizement of his realm. He set to work methodically on his scheme of conquest and at an early date reduced the fortress of Udayagiri in the Nellore District. Many other strong-

PORTRAIT IMAGE OF KRISHNA DEVA RĀYA.

holds surrendered to his arms. His most famous fight took place on May 19, 1520, and resulted in the recovery of the much disputed fortress of Rāichūr from Ismaīl Ādil Shāh of Bījāpur. The Hindus gained a glorious victory in a contest so deadly that they lost more than 16,000 killed. The story of the fight, vividly told by the contemporary Portuguese chronicler, Nuniz, is too long to be repeated here. The Rāya, a man of a generous and chivalrous temper, used his victory with humanity and moderation. In the course of subsequent operations he temporarily occupied Bījāpur, which was mostly destroyed by the soldiers tearing down buildings in order to get fuel for cooking; and he razed to the ground the fortress of Kulbargā, the early capital of the Bahmanīs.

In 1529 the noble Rāya 'fell sick of the same illness of which all his ancestors had died, with pains in the groin, of which die all the kings of Bisnaga'.

Description of the Rāya by Paes. Paes gives a good personal description of Krishna Rāya:

'This king is of medium height, and of fair complexion and good figure, rather fat than thin; he has on his face signs of small-pox. He is the most feared and perfect king that could possibly be, cheerful of disposition and very merry; he is one that seeks to honour foreigners, and receives them kindly, asking about all their affairs whatever their condition may be. He is a great ruler and a man of much justice, but subject to sudden fits of rage, and this is his title:

"Crisnarao Macação, king of kings, lord of the greater lords of India, lord of the three seas and of the land."

He has this title because he is by rank a greater lord than any, by reason of what he possesses in armies and territories, but it seems that he has in fact nothing compared to what a man like him ought to have, so gallant and perfect is he in all things.'

It is pleasant to read such unreserved praise in the writings of a foreigner.

Character of Krishna Rāya. The dark pages of the sanguinary story of the mediaeval kingdoms of the Deccan, whether Hindu or Muhammadan, are relieved by few names of men who claim respect on their personal merits. The figure of Krishna Rāya stands out pre-eminent. A mighty warrior, he

'was in no way less famous for his religious zeal and catholicity. He respected all sects of the Hindu religion alike, though his personal leanings were in favour of Vaishnavism. . . . Krishna Rāya's kindness to the fallen enemy, his acts of mercy and charity towards the residents of captured cities, his great military prowess which endeared him alike to his feudatory chiefs and to his subjects, the royal reception and kindness that he invariably bestowed upon foreign embassies, his imposing personal appearance, his genial look and polite conversation which distinguished a pure and dignified life, his love for literature and for religion, and his solicitude for the welfare of his people ; and, above all, the almost fabulous wealth that he conferred as endowments on temples and Brahmans, mark him out indeed as the greatest of the South Indian monarchs, who sheds a lustre on the pages of history.' [1]

In his time the Vijayanagar empire comprised substantially the same area as the modern Presidency of Madras, with the addition of Mysore and the other native States of the peninsula.

Achyuta Rāya. Krishna Rāya was succeeded by his brother, Achyuta, a man of weak and tyrannical character, lacking even in personal courage. He soon lost the fortresses of Mudgal and Rāichūr, situated between the Krishnā and the Tungabhadrā, which had been recovered by his able brother at a great price. Obscure intrigues led to an invitation to Ibrāhīm Ādil Shāh to visit Vijayanagar as the ally of one of the factions at court. He came, and was induced to retire by the payment of an immense subsidy in cash, amounting to something like two millions sterling, besides other valuable gifts.

Sadāsiva Rāya. When Achyuta died in 1542 his place was taken by his brother's son, Sadāsiva, who was a merely nominal king, the whole control of the government being in the hands of Rāma Rāja (or Rāya) Sāluva, son of Krishna Rāya's able minister, Sāluva Timma, and closely connected with the royal family by marriage. In 1543 Rāma Rāja made an alliance with Ahmadnagar and Golkonda in order to effect a combined attack on Bījāpur, which was saved from destruction by the abilities of Asad Khān, a clever and unscrupulous minister. Fifteen years later (1558) Bījāpur and Vijayanagar combined to attack Ahmadnagar. The territory of that State was so cruelly ravaged by the Hindus, and Rāma Rāja treated his Muslim allies with such open contempt, that the Sultans were convinced of the necessity for dropping their private quarrels and combining against the arrogant infidel.

Alliance of the four sultans. In 1564 the combination was duly effected, the parties to it being the four sultans or kings of Bījāpur, Ahmadnagar, Golkonda, and Bīdar. The ruler of Berar did not join. The allies began their southward march on Christmas

[1] Krishna Sastri in *Ann. Rep. A. S. India* for 1908–9, p. 186.

Day, 1564. In January, 1565, they assembled their combined forces at the small town of Tālikota in Bījāpur territory to the north of the Krishnā. That circumstance has given the current name to the ensuing battle, although it was fought on the south of the river at a distance of about thirty miles from Tālikota.

'At Vijayanagar there was the utmost confidence. Remembering how often the Moslems had vainly attempted to injure the great capital, and how for over two centuries they had never succeeded in penetrating to the south, the inhabitants pursued their daily avocations with no shadow of dread or sense of danger; the strings of pack-bullocks laden with all kinds of merchandise wended their dusty way to and from the several seaports as if no sword of Damocles was hanging over the doomed city; Sadāsiva, the king, lived his profitless life in inglorious seclusion, and Rāma Rāya, king *de facto*, never for a moment relaxed his haughty indifference to the movements of his enemies. "He treated their ambassadors", says Firishta, "with scornful language, and regarded their enmity as of little moment."'[1]

Battle of Tālikota, 1565. If mere numbers could have assured victory, the confidence of the rulers and people of Vijayanagar would have been justified. Estimates of the forces at the command of Rāma Rāja vary, but it seems certain that his vast host numbered between half a million and a million of men, besides a multitude of elephants and a considerable amount of artillery. On the other side, the Sultan of Ahmadnagar brought on the ground a park of no less than six hundred guns of various calibres. The total of the allies' army is supposed to have been about half that of the Vijayanagar host.

The battle was fought on January 23, 1565, on the plain between the Ingaligi ford and Mudgal. At first the Hindus had the advantage, but they suffered severely from a salvo of the Ahmadnagar guns shotted with bags of copper coin, and from a vigorous cavalry charge. Their complete rout followed on the capture of Rāma Rāja, who was promptly decapitated by the Sultan of Ahmadnagar with his own hand. No attempt was made to retrieve the disaster. About 100,000 Hindus were slain, and the great river ran red with blood. The princes fled from the city with countless treasures loaded upon more than five hundred elephants, and the proud capital lay at the mercy of the victors who occupied it almost immediately.

'The plunder was so great that every private man in the allied army became rich in gold, jewels, effects, tents, arms, horses, and slaves; as the sultans left every person in possession of what he had acquired, only taking elephants for their own use.'

Ruin of Vijayanagar. The ruin wrought on the magnificent city may be described in the words of Sewell, who is familiar with the scene of its desolation. When the princes fled with their treasures,

'then a panic seized the city. The truth became at last apparent. This was not a defeat merely, it was a cataclysm. All hope was gone.

[1] Sewell, p. 200.

The myriad dwellers in the city were left defenceless. No retreat, no flight was possible except to a few, for the pack-oxen and carts had almost all followed the forces to the war, and they had not returned. Nothing could be done but to bury all treasures, to arm the younger men, and to wait. Next day the place became a prey to the robber tribes and jungle people of the neighbourhood. Hordes of Brinjāris, Lambādis, Kurubas, and the like pounced down on the hapless city and looted the stores and shops, carrying off great quantities of riches. Couto states that there were six concerted attacks by these people during the day.

The third day saw the beginning of the end. The victorious Musalmans had halted on the field of battle for rest and refreshment, but now they had reached the capital, and from that time forward for a space of five months Vijayanagar knew no rest. The enemy had come to destroy, and they carried out their object relentlessly. They slaughtered the people without mercy; broke down the temples and palaces; and wreaked such savage vengeance on the abode of the kings, that with the exception of a few great stone-built temples and walls, nothing now remains but a heap of ruins to mark the spot where once the stately buildings stood. They demolished the statues, and even succeeded in breaking the limbs of the huge Narasimha monolith. Nothing seemed to escape them. They broke up the pavilions standing on the huge platform from which the kings used to watch the festivals, and overthrew all the carved work. They lit huge fires in the magnificently decorated buildings forming the temple of Vitthalaswāmi near the river, and smashed its exquisite stone sculptures. With fire and sword, with crowbars and axes, they carried on day after day their work of destruction. Never perhaps in the history of the world has such havoc been wrought, and wrought so suddenly, on so splendid a city; teeming with a wealthy and industrious population in the full plenitude of prosperity one day, and on the next seized, pillaged, and reduced to ruins, amid scenes of savage massacre and horrors beggaring description.'

The pathetic language of the Hebrew prophet lamenting the ruin of Jerusalem applies accurately to the Indian tragedy:

'How doth the city sit solitary, that was full of people! how is she become as a widow! she that was great among the nations, and a princess among the provinces, how is she become tributary! . . . The young and the old lie on the ground in the streets: my virgins and my young men are fallen by the sword. . . . How is the gold become dim! how is the most fine gold changed! the stones of the sanctuary are poured out in the top of every street.'[1]

Rāma Rāja's brother, Tirumala, who along with Sadāsiva the nominal king took refuge at Penugonda, himself usurped the royal seat some few years after the battle. This third usurpation, the beginning of the Fourth Dynasty, may be dated in or about 1570. The most remarkable king of the new dynasty was the third, by name Venkata I, who came to the throne about 1585. He seems to have moved his capital to Chandragiri, and was noted for his patronage of Telugu poets and Vaishnava authors. It is unnecessary to follow the history of his successors, who gradually degenerated into merely local chiefs. In March 1639–40 Venkata II granted the site of Madras to Mr. Day the English factor, and in 1645–6

[1] Lam. i. 1; ii. 21; iv. 1.

that transaction was confirmed by Ranga II, who was the last representative of the line with any pretensions to independence. Much of the Deccan was overrun by the Muhammadans and passed under the sovereignty of the Sultans of Bījāpur and Golkonda, who in their turn were overthrown by Aurangzēb in 1686 and 1687.

The most important of the principalities formed by Hindus in the far south out of the fragments of the Vijayanagar empire was that of the Nāyaks of Madura. Tirumala Nāyak is justly celebrated for his buildings, which exhibit much dignity of design and splendour in execution.

The Rāja of Ānegundi is now the representative of Rāma Rāja's dynasty.

The city in the fourteenth century. The grandeur of the city, the splendour of the buildings, the wealth of the bazaars, the volume of trade, and the density of the population are amply attested by a series of witnesses beginning in the fourteenth century, when Vijayanagar was only a few years old, down to the date of its irremediable ruin, and also by survey of the existing remains. No contemporary written account, except inscriptions, dating from the fourteenth century, has survived, but much traditional information relating to that time is embodied in the works of authors who wrote in the fifteenth and sixteenth centuries.

The city, after its foundation in or about 1336, 'speedily grew in importance and became the refuge of the outcasts, refugees, and fighting men of the Hindus, beaten and driven out of their old strongholds, by the advancing Muhammadans'. The historian Firishta admits that as early as 1378 the Rāyas of Vijayanagar were greatly superior in power, wealth, and extent of country to the Bahmanī kings. Goa was then temporarily in possession of the Rāya, and his capital drew much wealth from commerce passing through the ports of the western coast.

Bukka II (1399–1406) improved and enlarged the fortifications of Vijayanagar. His most notable work was the construction of a huge dam in the Tungabhadrā river, forming a reservoir from which water was conveyed to the city by an aqueduct fifteen miles in length, cut out of the solid rock for a distance of several miles. Firishta's account of the ceremonial at the marriage between Fīrōz Shāh Bahmanī and the daughter of Deva Rāya I gives some idea of the magnificence of the capital in 1406. We are told that the road for six miles was spread with cloth of gold, velvet, satin, and other rich stuffs, the sides of the way being lined with innumerable shops. The Rāya bestowed on his guest vast treasures in jewels and other precious things.

Nicolo Conti's description, 1420. The earliest foreign visitor whose notes have been preserved was an Italian named Nicolo Conti or dei Conti, who was at Vijayanagar about 1420, in the reign of Deva Rāya II. He estimated the circumference of the city to be sixty miles, and was much impressed by the strength of the fortifications, which were carried up the hills so as to enclose the valleys at their base. He considered the Rāya to be more powerful than any other monarch in India. The traveller observes that the king had 12,000 wives, of whom no less than 2,000 or 3,000 were required to burn themselves with him when he died.[1] The idol processions and three annual festivals were celebrated with exceeding splendour.

Abdu-r Razzāk in 1443. The next visitor was the learned Abdu-r Razzāk of Herat, who was sent by the Great Khān (Khākān Sa'īd) or Sultan Shāhrukh, son of Tīmūr, as ambassador to the Zamorin or Sāmurī of Calicut, a busy port on the Malabar coast. While the envoy was residing at Calicut a herald brought intelligence that the king of Vijayanagar required that he should be sent instantly to his court. The Zamorin, although at that time not directly subject to the authority of the Rāya, dared not disobey. Abdu-r Razzāk, accordingly, sailed to Mangalore, 'which is on the borders of the kingdom of Bījanagar', and thence travelled by land to his distant destination, through the country now known as Mysore. A few miles from Mangalore he saw a wonderful temple, a perfect square measuring about ten yards by ten, and five yards high, constructed wholly of 'molten brass'.

At Belūr he admired greatly a magnificent temple, which he dared not describe 'without fear of being charged with exaggeration'. Presumably he saw the fine structure erected in A. D. 1117 by the Hoysala King Bittiga, which still exists and has been surveyed by the archaeological department of Mysore.[2] In due course, towards the end of April 1443, the traveller arrived at Vijayanagar, where he was hospitably received and comfortably lodged. 'The city', he observes, 'is such that eye has not seen nor ear heard of any place resembling it upon the whole earth. It is so built that it has seven fortified walls, one within the other.' The writer goes on to illustrate his description by a comparison with the citadel of Herat.

'The seventh fortress is placed in the centre of the others, and occupies ground ten times greater than the chief market of Hirāt. In that is situated the palace of the king. From the northern gate of the outer fortress to the southern is a distance of two statute *parasangs* [about 7 or 8 miles], and the same with respect to the distance between the eastern and western gates. Between the first, second, and third walls there are cultivated fields, gardens, and houses. From the third to the seventh fortress, shops and bazaars are closely crowded together. By the palace of the king there are four bazaars, situated opposite one to another. On the north is the portico of the palace of the Rāi.[3] At the head of each bazaar there is a lofty arcade and magnificent gallery, but the palace of the king is loftier than all of them. The bazaars are very long and broad, so that the sellers of flowers, notwithstanding that they place high stands before their shops, are yet able to sell flowers from both

[1] Suttee (*satī*) was terribly common in the empire. The sacrifice was effected by burning in a pit, or, among the Telugus, by burial alive.

[2] There is no need to suppose that any place other than Belūr is meant. It is 80 or 90 miles by road from Mangalore.

[3] This sentence is from the version in Sewell. The rendering in *E. & D.* does not give sense. The rest of the quotation is from *E. & D.*

sides. Sweet scented flowers are always procurable fresh in that city, and they are considered as even necessary sustenance, seeing that without them they could not exist. The tradesmen of each separate guild or craft have their shops close to one another. The jewellers sell their rubies and pearls and diamonds and emeralds openly in the bazaar.

In this charming area, in which the palace of the king is contained, there are many rivulets and streams flowing through channels of cut stone, polished and even. . . . The country is so well populated that it is impossible in a reasonable space to convey an idea of it. In the king's treasury there are chambers, with excavations in them, filled with molten gold, forming one mass. All the inhabitants of the country, whether high or low, even down to the artificers of the bazaar, wear jewels and gilt ornaments in their ears and around their necks, arms, wrists, and fingers.'

Account by Paes in 1522. Passing by the accounts given by certain other travellers, we come to the detailed description recorded by Domingos Paes, a Portuguese, about 1522, in the reign of Krishna Rāya, just after the capitulation of Rāichūr, when the empire was at the height of its glory. The observations of Paes are far too long to copy, and it is not possible to find room for mention of more than a few particulars. His account, which is obviously truthful, may be accepted with confidence. It is well worth reading in full as translated by Sewell.

Size of the city ; the palace. Paes found a difficulty in estimating the size of the city, because the hills prevented him from seeing the whole at once. So far as he could judge, it was as large as Rome. The houses were said to exceed 100,000 in number. If that guess be near the truth, the population cannot have been less than half a million. The numerous lakes, water-courses, and orchards attracted his admiration. As to the people, he could only say that they were countless. He considered Vijayanagar to be 'the best provided city in the world . . . for the state of this city is not like that of other cities, which often fail of supplies and provisions, for in this one everything abounds'. Paes was shown round a large part of the palace enclosure, which contained thirty-four streets. He saw one room which was 'all of ivory, as well the chamber as the walls from top to bottom, and the pillars of the cross-timbers at the top had roses and flowers of lotuses all of ivory, and all well executed, so that there could not be better—it is so rich and beautiful that you would hardly find anywhere another such'.[1]

Space fails to tell of the other wonders of the palace, which the Muhammadans took special pains to destroy utterly. Nuniz, another Portuguese, who wrote some thirteen years later, in the reign of Achyuta Rāya, mentions that all the utensils used in the royal service were of gold or silver. Some of the golden vessels were of immense size.

The court. The ceremonial of the court was extremely elaborate, and everything was done with barbaric magnificence. The royal words, as at the Mogul court, were carefully noted down by

[1] Compare the 'ivory palaces' of Psalm xlv, 8.

secretaries, whose record was the sole evidence of the commands issued. Nuniz declares that

'no written orders are ever issued, nor any charters granted for the favours he (the King) bestows or the commands he gives; but when he confers a favour on any one it remains written in the registers of these secretaries. The King, however, gives to the recipient of a favour a seal impressed in wax from one of his rings, which his minister keeps, and these seals serve for letters patent.'

In that respect the practice differed widely from that followed in the northern courts, where regular office routine was observed. The king always dressed in white. On his head he wore 'a cap of brocade in fashion like a Galician helmet, covered with a piece of fine stuff, all of fine silk, and he was barefooted'. His jewels, of course, were the finest possible.

The army. The permanent army in the king's pay is said to have numbered 'a million fighting troops, in which are included 35,000 cavalry in armour'. On a special occasion the sovereign could raise a second million. Paes declares that in 1520 Krishna Rāya actually assembled for the operations against Rāichūr 703,000 foot, 32,600 horse, and 551 elephants, besides an uncounted host of camp-followers, dealers, and the rest. The statement of Megasthenes that Chandragupta Maurya in the fourth century B.C. kept and paid 600,000 foot, 30,000 horse, and 9,000 elephants, besides chariots, may be compared. Chariots had gone out of use before the time of the Rāyas. Nuniz gives many details in confirmation of his general statements on the subject, which agree substantially with those of Paes. The efficiency of the huge army described was not proportionate to the numbers of the force. The soldiers were in terror of the Muslims, and their action against a fortress like Rāichūr was ludicrously feeble. The men are described as being physically strong and individually brave. Sometimes they fought gallantly, but the army as an organized force was inefficient.

Administration. The empire was divided into about two hundred provinces or districts, each under a great noble, who was bound to furnish a certain amount of revenue and a fixed contingent of troops. The king also maintained a large force attached to his person. Each provincial governor could do much as he pleased within his territory, but was himself at the mercy of the king, who was an autocrat of the most absolute possible kind, unrestrained by any form of check. No mention is made of courts of justice. The Rāya kept a certain amount of lands in his own hands, like the *khālsa* of the Mogul empire. Whenever he wished he could deprive the nobles of their property, and he was regarded as the sole proprietor of the soil. The governors were expected to pay over to the treasury half of their gross revenue, and to defray all the expenses of their households, contingents, and government from the other half. While the great people were inordinately rich and luxurious, the common people suffered from grievous tyranny and were exposed to much hardship. Nevertheless, they multiplied freely, for all accounts agree that the empire was densely populated and well cultivated. The ordinary people were trained to show the utmost submissiveness to their superiors, and to work hard for their benefit.

Assessment. The assessment on the peasantry was crushingly heavy. Nuniz declares that they 'pay nine-tenths to their lord', but the exact meaning of that statement is not clear. They could not possibly have paid nine-tenths of the gross produce. The theoretical share of the State recognized by Hindu law all over India as a rule was one-sixth of the produce, but in practice the Government usually took much more. Wilks, who had access to sources of information not now available, states that in very ancient times the cultivators had the option of paying either in kind or in cash. In A.D. 1252 'Boote Pandi Roy' fixed money rates for Kanara on the basis of 30 seers of 'grain' for the rupee. In 1336 Harihara I of Vijayanagar fixed his cash demand on the basis of the rate of 33⅔ seers for the rupee, which was more favourable to the ryot. Payments in kind were absolutely forbidden. The existence of the rate stated as from 1336 is 'perfectly authenticated'. The money rent is said to have been equivalent at the Harihara price to the traditional one-sixth of the produce. When Wilks wrote at the beginning of the nineteenth century the current price was much the same as it had been in the fourteenth century, a remarkable fact. Harihara, while maintaining the traditional rate of assessment, secured a large increase of income by imposing a multitude of vexatious cesses, reckoned by Wilks as twenty. He thus pursued a policy directly the contrary of that adopted by Akbar, who boldly doubled the State proportion of the produce, raising it from one-sixth to one-third, while professing to relieve the cultivator by abolishing all cesses. There is good reason for believing that Akbar's orders for the abolition of cesses were not acted on, and that his assessment, as worked, was extremely severe. Harihara's measures probably had the same effect, and resulted in the extraction from the peasant of the last copper to be had. It is said that the ordinary practice in the south was to leave the cultivator only half of his crop.[1] The Sultans of Kashmīr in Akbar's time followed the same rule, which Akbar did not relax in that province.

Punishments. The extreme ferocity of the punishments inflicted for offences against property was well designed to protect the rich against the poor.

'The punishments that they inflict in this kingdom', Nuniz states, 'are these: for a thief, whatever theft he commits, howsoever little it be, they forthwith cut off a foot and a hand; and if his theft be a great one he is hanged with a hook under his chin. If a man outrages a respectable woman or a virgin he has the same punishment, and if he does any other such violence his punishment is of a like kind. Nobles who become traitors are sent to be impaled alive on a wooden stake thrust through the belly; and people of the lower orders, for whatever crime they commit, he forthwith commands to cut off their heads in the market-place, and the same

[1] *Ind. Ant.*, 1916, p. 36, quoting Caldwell.

for a murder unless the death was the result of a duel. . . . These are the more common kinds of punishments, but they have others more fanciful ; for when the King so desires, he commands a man to be thrown to the elephants, and they tear him to pieces. The people are so subject to him that if you told a man on the part of the King that he must stand still in a street holding a stone on his back all day till you released him, he would do it.'[1]

The narrative of Knox proves that similar horrors were constantly perpetrated under the kings of Ceylon. He gives horrible pictures of a man with a heavy stone on his back, and of execution by elephants and impalement. Indeed all, or almost all, ancient Hindu governments from very early times seem to have been equally cruel, as may be learned from many testimonies. The appalling torture involved in hanging an offender on a hook under his chin until he died seems to have been peculiar to Vijayanagar. When the severity of the penalties inflicted by the Vijayanagar kings is considered, it is not surprising to learn that there were 'very few thieves in the land'. Chandragupta Maurya attained the same result by similar drastic methods.

Duelling. The exceptional custom of duelling, which has been alluded to, deserves more particular notice. Nuniz states that 'great honour is done to those who fight in a duel, and they give the estate of the dead man to the survivor ; but no one fights a duel without first asking leave of the minister, who forthwith grants it'. The usage was not confined to Vijayanagar. Duels fought with swords were common among the Nāyars of Malabar until recent times, probably as late as the nineteenth century. The practice was imitated by the Musalmāns of the Deccan early in the sixteenth century, much to the horror of Firishta, who denounces 'this abominable habit', as being unknown in any other civilized country in the world. He attributed the introduction of the 'vile custom' into Ahmadnagar to Ahmad Nīzām Shāh, who was fond of the single-sword exercise and encouraged the young men to fight with swords in his presence. A general custom of duelling thus became fashionable in the Deccan, even among learned divines and philosophers, as well as among nobles and princes. The historian tells a story that in the streets of Bījāpur six men of good position, three on each side, lost their lives in the course of a trivial quarrel, within a few minutes.

I have not met with other references to the custom, which seems to have been unknown in northern India.

Legalized prostitution. Prostitution was a recognized institution and an acceptable source of revenue. The women attached to the temples, as Paes informs us,

'are of loose character, and live in the best streets that are in the city ; it is the same in all their cities, their streets have the best rows of houses.

[1] Knox, *An Historical Relation of the Island Ceylon, in the East Indies* (London, 1681), gives terribly realistic drawings of 'the execution by an eliphant' ; 'one impaled on a stake' ; and of 'the manner of extorting their fine'. The last-named plate shows a poor man crouching with a heavy stone on his back, while his rich creditor stands over him.

They are very much esteemed, and are classed among those honoured ones who are the mistresses of the captains ; any respectable man may go to their houses without any blame attaching thereto. These women (are allowed) even to enter the presence of the wives of the King, and they stay with them and eat betel with them, a thing which no other person may do, no matter what his rank may be. . . . Some of them eat flesh ; they eat all kinds except beef and pork, and yet, nevertheless, they cease not to eat this betel all day.'

Some such women were immensely rich ; one was reputed to possess 100,000 gold pieces.

Abdu-r Razzāk gives further details on the subject.

'Opposite the mint', he writes, 'is the office of the Prefect of the City, to which it is said 12,000 policemen are attached ; and their pay, which equals each day 12,000 *fanams*, is derived from the proceeds of the brothels. The splendour of these houses, the beauty of the heart-ravishers, their blandishments and ogles, are beyond all description. It is best to be brief on the matter.

One thing worth mentioning is this, behind the mint there is a sort of bazaar, which is more than 300 yards long and 20 broad. On two sides of it are houses (*khānahā*), and fore-courts (*safhahā*), and in front of the houses, instead of benches (*kursī*), lofty seats are built of excellent stone, and on each side of the avenue formed by the houses there are figures of lions, panthers, tigers, and other animals, so well painted as to seem alive. After the time of mid-day prayers, they place at the doors of these houses, which are beautifully decorated, chairs and settees on which the courtesans seat themselves. Every one is covered with pearls, precious stones, and costly garments. . . . Any man who passes through this place makes choice of whom he will. The servants of these brothels take care of whatever is taken into them, and if anything is lost they are dismissed. There are several brothels within these seven fortresses, and the revenues of them, which, as stated before, amount to 12,000 *fanams*, go to pay the wages of the policemen. The business of these men is to acquaint themselves with all the events and accidents that happen within the seven walls, and to recover everything that is lost, or that may be abstracted by theft ; otherwise they are fined.'

An interesting comparison might be made between the statements of the Persian envoy and the regulations in the *Arthasāstra* concerning the City Prefect and the courtesans in Maurya times. Then, as at Vijayanagar, the public women played an essential part in court ceremonial. The Maurya Government levied from each woman the earnings of two days in the month, that is to say, between six and seven per cent. of her income at least. Shāhjahān, also, was not ashamed to draw revenue from the same source.

Laxity in diet. The reader may have noticed the observation of Paes that some of the women used to eat flesh of all kinds except beef and pork. Although vegetarian Brahmans were numerous at Vijayanagar and greatly pampered by the authorities, the diet of the general population and of the kings departed widely from the Brahmanical standard. Animal food was very freely used. Paes dwells with pleasure on the variety of meat and birds procurable in the markets. The sheep killed daily were countless. Every street had sellers of mutton, so clean and fat that it looked like pork. Birds and game animals were abundant and cheap ;

those offered for sale included three kinds of partridges, quails, doves, pigeons, and others, 'the common birds of the country', besides poultry and hares. In the city fowls were purchaseable at about a halfpenny each, and in the country they were still cheaper. The same author mentions that pork also was sold and that pigs kept in certain streets of butchers' houses were 'so white and clean that you could never see better in any country'.

His statements are confirmed by Nuniz, who writes that:

'These Kings of Bisnaga eat all sorts of things, but not the flesh of oxen or cows, which they never kill in all the country of the heathen because they worship them. They eat mutton, pork, venison, partridges, hares, doves, quail, and all kinds of birds; even sparrows, and rats, and cats, and lizards, all of which are sold in the market of the city of Bisnaga.

Everything has to be sold alive so that each one may know what he buys—this at least so far as concerns game—and there are fish from the rivers in large quantities.'

That was a curious dietary for princes and people, who in the time of Krishna Rāya and Achyuta Rāya were zealous Hindus with a special devotion to certain forms of Vishnu. The kings of the first dynasty preferred to honour Siva.

Bloody sacrifices. The numerous bloody sacrifices, similar to those still performed in Nepāl, were equally inconsistent with the ordinary practice of Vaishnava religion. Paes mentions that all the sheep required for the market supply of mutton for Hindu consumption were slaughtered at the gate of one particular temple. The blood was offered in sacrifice to the idol, to whom also the heads were left. The same writer states that on a certain festival the king used to witness the slaughter of 24 buffaloes and 150 sheep, the animals being decapitated, as now in Nepāl, by a single blow from a 'large sickle' or *dāo*. On the last day of the 'nine days' festival' 250 buffaloes and 4,500 sheep were slaughtered.[1] Such practices prove clearly that the Hinduism of Vijayanagar included many non-Aryan elements. At the present day lizards and rats would not be eaten by anybody except members of certain debased castes or wild jungle tribes,[2] and such objects certainly are not now to be seen in the market anywhere in India, north, south, east, or west.

When and how did practices of the kind die out?

[1] Bishop Whitehead states that in the Telugu country as many as 1,000 sheep are sometimes sacrificed at once on the occasion of an epidemic (*Village Deities*, Madras, 1907, p. 136, as corrected in 2nd ed., Oxford University Press, 1916, p. 56). All the practices mentioned in the text seem to be Telugu or Kanarese. The modern Tamils usually are becoming averse to bloody sacrifices. The Kanarese still offer them freely.

[2] e. g. the Vaddas, who are numerous in Mysore, and said to come from Orissa, will eat any animal food, except beef or tortoise. 'Sheep, goats, pigs, squirrels, wild cats, lizards, and mice are equally welcome to them' (*Ethnogr. Survey of Mysore*, Prelim. Issue, No. XI, p. 10, Bangalore, Govt. Press, 1907). Sewell (p. 13) suggests that the kings may have belonged to the Kuruba tribe or caste, who are shepherds and blanket-weavers primarily. For the Kurubas see *Ethnogr. Survey*, No. I, 1906.

The government of Vijayanagar Telinga and foreign. Doubts may be felt as to whether the founders of Vijayanagar had been in the service of the Hoysala king or in that of the Rājā of Warangal, but it is certain that they were foreigners in the Kanarese country, the Carnatic, properly so called. Wilks, who was in a position to speak with authority on such matters, and believed that Bukka and his brethren were fugitives from Warangal, writes:

'This origin of the new government at once explains the ascendancy of the Telinga [Telugu] language and nation at this capital of Carnatic, and proves the state of anarchy and weakness which had succeeded the ruin of the former dynasty. The government founded by foreigners was also supported by foreigners; and in the centre of Canara a Telinga court was supported by a Telinga army, the descendants of whom, speaking the same language, are to be traced at this day nearly to Cape Comorin, in the remains of the numerous establishments, resembling the Roman colonies, which were sent forth from time to time for the purpose of confirming their distant conquests, and holding the natives in subjection. The centre and the west, probably the whole of the dominions of the late dynasty, including the greater part of the modern state of Mysoor, were subdued at an early period; but a branch of the family of Bellal [=Hoysala] was permitted to exercise a nominal authority at Tonoor until 1387, in which year we begin to find direct grants from the house of Vijeyanuggur as far south as Turkanamby beyond the Caveri. The last of thirteen rajas or rayeels of the house of Hurryhur [Harihara I], who were followers of Siva, was succeeded in 1490 by Narsing Raja, of the religious sect of Vishnoo, the founder of a new dynasty, whose empire appears to have been called by Europeans *Narsinga*, a name which, being no longer in use, has perplexed geographers with regard to its proper position.

Narsing Raja seems to have been the first king of Vijeyanuggur who extended his conquests into *Drauveda* [Drāvida, the Tamil country], and erected the strong forts of Chandragerry and Vellore; the latter for his occasional residence, and the former as a safe place for the deposit of treasure; but it was not until about 1509 to 1515 that Kistna Rayeel [Krishna Rāya] reduced the whole of Drauveda to real or nominal subjection.'

The fact that the kings and nobles of Vijayanagar were foreigners lording it over a subject native population would explain the abject servility of the commonalty and the severity of the government. It should be observed, however, that the Telugu or Telinga people themselves are noted for their submissiveness to official authority.[1]

Patronage of literature. The Rāyas of Vijayanagar, although their title was Kanarese in form, gave their patronage to Sanskrit and Telugu literature rather than to Kanarese. Sāyana, the celebrated commentator on the Vedas, who died in A.D. 1387, was minister in the early part of the reign of Harihara II, and his learned brother Mādhava served Bukka. The first dynasty had

[1] Wilks, reprint, vol. i, p. 9. See the good article 'Telugu' in Balfour, *Cyclopaedia*, based on Caldwell's works. The dates given by Wilks require some slight correction.

close associations with the great monastery of Sringēri. The achievements of Narasinga Sāluva, the founder of the second dynasty, were enthusiastically celebrated by Telugu poets. Krishna Rāya, himself a poet and author, was a liberal patron of writers in the Telugu language. His poet laureate, Alasāni-Peddana, is regarded as an author of the first rank. The tradition of the court was carried on by Rāma Rāja and the other Rāyas of the fourth or Aravīdu dynasty. Rāma Rāja and his brothers were themselves accomplished scholars, and under their protection a great revival of Vaishnava religion was accomplished.

Architecture and art. The kings of Vijayanagar from the beginning of their rule were distinguished as builders of strong fortresses, immense works for irrigation and water supply, gorgeous palaces, and temples decorated with all the resources of art, both sculpture and painting. It is impossible in this place to attempt description of their creations. They evolved a distinct school of architecture which used the most difficult material with success, and were served by a brilliant company of sculptors and painters. Enough of the sculpture survives to show its quality, but the paintings necessarily have disappeared. The descriptions recorded by the Portuguese authors and Abdu-r Razzāk permit of no doubt that the painters in the service of the kings of Vijayanagar attained a high degree of skill. The scenes from the Rāmāyana, sculptured in bas-relief on the walls of Krishna Rāya's Chapel Royal, the Hazāra Rāma-swāmī temple, built in 1513, are much admired. No adequate account of the buildings and sculptures at Vijayanagar has yet been prepared. Such a work, properly illustrated, would fill several large volumes.

THE RĀYAS OF VIJAYANAGAR

Name.	*Acc.* A. D.	*Remarks.*
Chiefs, not of royal rank		
HARIHARA I, his brother	1336	Traditionary date for foundation of Vijayanagar.
BUKKA (BHUKKA, or BUKKANA) I, and three other brothers, sons of Sangama; succession apparently disputed	1343	Bukka I died 1376.
Rāyas of royal rank		
First dynasty; descendants of Sangama		Worshippers of Siva Virūpāksha.
HARIHARA II, son of Bukka I	1379	
BUKKA II, son of Harihara II Disputed succession	?1404	A brother named Virūpāksha also a claimant.
DEVA RĀYA I	1406	
VĪRA VIJAYA	?1422	

THE RĀYAS OF VIJAYANAGAR (*continued*).

Name.	*Acc.* A.D.	*Remarks.*
Rāyas of royal rank		
First dynasty; descendants of Sangama		
DEVA RĀYA II (alias Immadi, Pratāpa, or Praudha); at first associated with Vīra Vijaya; became sole ruler	1424	Empire prosperous and extensive.
MALLIKĀRJUNA, son of Deva Rāya II	1447	Sāluva Narasingha minister in power from about 1455.
VIRŪPĀKSHA	1465	Decay of empire.
PRAUDHADEVA RĀYA (Padea Rao)	?	
Second or Sāluva dynasty		Worshippers of Vishnu.
NARASINGHA SĀLUVA	1486	
IMMADI NARASINGHA, alias Tammaya (Dharma) Rāya; son of Narasingha Sāluva	?1492	Power in hands of Narasa.
Third or Tuluva dynasty		
NARASA NĀYAKA	1505	Course of events open to doubt.
General revolt		
VĪRA NARASINGHA (Bhujabala)	?1506	
KRISHNA DEVA RĀYA	1509	
Battle of Rāichūr	1520	Climax of the empire.
ACHYUTA; brother of Krishna Rāya	1529	
SADĀSIVA, son of another brother of Achyuta	1542	Nominal king: Rāma Rāja in power.
Battle of Tālikota	1565	Break up of empire.
Death of Rāma Rāja; confusion	1565	
Fourth dynasty; Āravīdu or Karnāia		
TIRUMALA, brother of Rāmarāja	about 1570	Capital at Penugonda, now in Anantapur District.
RANGA, son of Tirumala	about 1573	
VENKATA I, brother of Ranga	1585	Capital removed to Chandragiri.
Other princes		
RANGA	1642	Local chief.
Practical end of dynasty	1646	Ranga's inscriptions continue to 1684.

NOTE.—Dates and many details, especially those relating to disputed successions, are often doubtful.

Vijayanagar.		*Bahmanī.*		*Bījāpur.*	
Harihara I, &c.	1336				
Bukka I	1343				
		Alāu-d dīn I	1347		
		Muhammad I	1358		
		Mujāhid	1373		
		Dāūd	1377		
Harihara II	1379	Muhammad II	1378		
		Ghiyāsu-d dīn	1397		
		Shamsu-d dīn	1397		
		Fīrōz	1397		
Bukka II	?1404				
Deva Rāya I	1406				
Vīra Vijaya	?1422	Ahmad	1422		
Deva Rāya II	1424				
		Alāu-d dīn II	1435		
Mallikārjuna	1447				
		Humāyūn	1457		
		Nizām	1461		
		Muhammad III	1463		
Virūpāksha	1465				
Praudha deva Rāya	?				
		Mahmūd	1482		
Narasingha Sāluva	1486				
				Yūsuf	1490
Immadi Narasingha	?1492				
Narasa Nāyaka	1505				
Vīra Narasingha	?1506				
Krishna deva Rāya	1509				
				Ismaīl	1510
Achyuta	1529				
				Mallū	1534
				Ibrāhīm I	1535
Sadāsiva	1542				
				Alī	1557
Tirumala	c. 1570				
Ranga	c. 1573				
				Ibrāhīm II	1580
Venkata I	1585				
Others	—			Muhammad	1626
Ranga	1642				

Authorities

The leading authorities used are Sewell, *A Forgotten Empire* (*Vijayanagar*), London, 1900, which alone gives the Portuguese narratives; and three articles, chiefly based on inscriptions and Telugu literature, by H. Krishna Sastri in *Annual Rep. A. S. India* for 1907–8, 1908–9, and 1911–12. Early discussions of the subject will be found in H. H. Wilson's *Introduction to the Descriptive Catalogue of the Mackenzie MSS.*, 1828, reprint 1882;

and in Wilks, *Historical Sketches . . . History of Mysoor*, 1810–14, reprint, 1869. The account in Meadows Taylor's *Manual*, good when written, is no longer up to date. I have also consulted S. Krishnaswami Aiyangar, *A Little Known Chapter of Vijayanagar History*, Madras, S.P.C.K. Press, 1916; Rice, *Mysore and Coorg from the Inscriptions*, London, 1909; the same author's *Mysore Gazetteer*, revised ed., London, 1897; and many articles in the *A. S. Progress Reports of the Southern Circle* (Madras); *Indian Antiquary*, &c.

The coins are described by Hultzsch, *Ind. Ant.*, xx (1891); and V. A. Smith, *Catal. Coins in I. M.*, vol. i, Oxford, 1906. The art of the dynasty is briefly noticed in *H. F. A.* New inscriptions are published continually. Many dates and other matters of detail remain unsettled, and cannot be disposed of until somebody takes the trouble to write a bulky monograph. The small book (144 pp. 8vo) by A. H. Longhurst, Superintendent, Archaeological Department, Southern Circle (Madras Government Press, 1917), entitled *Hampi Ruins described and illustrated*, has 69 illustrations, and is good as far as it goes. The price is 3 rupees or 4*s.* 6*d.*

BOOK VI

THE MOGUL EMPIRE

CHAPTER 1

The Beginnings of the Mogul Empire; Bābur, Humāyūn, and the Ṣūr Dynasty, A.D. 1526–56.

Bābur. Bābur, king of Kābul, whose aid Daulat Khān invoked against Sultan Ibrāhīm of Delhi, was the most brilliant Asiatic prince of his age, and worthy of a high place among the sovereigns of any age or country. His proper name was Zahīru-d dīn Muhammad, but the world knows him only by his Mongol nickname or cognomen of Bābur, which he adopted officially.[1] Fifth in descent from Tīmūr in the direct male line, and claiming kinship with Chingiz Khān through a female, he united in his person the blood of the two most dreaded Asiatic conquerors. He was cradled in war, and at the age of eleven was called to the throne of Samarkand. In the course of a stormy youth filled with romantic adventures he lost that throne twice. In 1504 he made himself master of Kābul, and so came into touch with India. The wealth of Ind naturally tempted his adventurous spirit and suggested more than one raid. In 1519, following in the footsteps of Alexander, he besieged and took Bājaur, slaying its infidel defenders without mercy. He then crossed the Indus and claimed the Panjāb as his inheritance in virtue of his descent from Tīmūr. But his operations at that time were only in the nature of a reconnaissance, as were those on two subsequent occasions. His entry into the Panjāb in 1524, on the invitation of Daulat Khān, the governor of that province, and Ālam Khān, an uncle of Sultan Ibrāhīm, was intended to be a serious invasion. The speedy defection of Daulat Khān, however, compelled Bābur to retire to Kābul for reinforcements, so that his final invasion was not begun until November 1525.

Coin of Bābur.

Invasion of India. Even then his total force, including camp-followers, did not exceed 12,000 men, a tiny army with which to attempt the conquest of Sultan Ibrāhīm's realm, comprising, as expressed in modern terms, the Panjāb, the United Provinces

[1] The name Bābur has no connexion with the Persian word *babar*, meaning 'lion' or 'tiger', but has the same meaning.

M 3

of Agra and Oudh, and parts of Rājputāna. Moreover, the vast mass of Hindu India lay behind the Afghan dominions. The enterprise, indeed, seemed to be rash, and Bābur candidly admitted that many of his troops were 'in great tremor and alarm'. Yet the bold attack succeeded.

Battle of Pānīpat, 1526. The hostile armies came to grips on April 21, 1526, on that plain of Pānīpat where the prize of India has been so often the reward of the victor. Bābur possessed a large park of artillery, the new-fangled weapon then coming into use in Turkey and Europe, but previously unknown in northern India. Its power had already made itself felt at the siege of Bājaur. Carts, 700 in number, drawn by bullocks, were lashed together by chains, so as to form a barrier in front of the enemy,[1] gaps being left sufficient for the cavalry to charge through. On the other side, Sultan Ibrāhīm brought into the field an immense host believed to number at least 100,000 men, supported by nearly 100 elephants. Although the exact numbers drawn up by Bābur in battle array are not stated, there is no doubt that they were immeasurably outnumbered by the enemy. But the Afghan Sultan, 'a young inexperienced man, careless in his movements, who marched without order, halted or retired without method, and engaged without foresight', was no match for Bābur, a born general, and a veteran in war although his years were few. The battle, which raged from half-past nine in the morning until evening, again demonstrated the inherent weakness of an ill-compacted Hindu host when attacked by an active small force under competent leadership, and making full use of bold cavalry charges. The decisive movement, the furious cavalry wheel round the flank of the enemy, delivering a charge in his rear, was exactly the same as that employed by Alexander against Pōros at the battle of the Hydaspes, and had the same result. When the sun set Sultan Ibrāhīm lay dead on the field, surrounded by 15,000 of his brave men, and the Hindu host had been scattered. 'By the grace and mercy of Almighty God', Bābur wrote, 'this difficult affair was made easy to me, and that mighty army, in the space of half a day, was laid in the dust.'

Occupation of Delhi and Agra. Delhi and Agra were promptly occupied, and the immense spoil was divided among all ranks of the victorious army with lavish generosity. The heat being terrible, the troops, who longed for the cool Kābul hills, began to murmur. Like Alexander, Bābur sought to rouse their pride by a stirring address, and, unlike his great predecessor, succeeded in persuading his men to follow the path of glory, and despise the dangers which beset them in a strange land.

Bābur secured the support of the Afghan chiefs by judicious management, and so was free to devote himself to the task of subduing Hindu India, a work more formidable even than the conflict with the army of the Sultan.

[1] Mrs. Beveridge rejects the earlier interpretation of '*arāba* as meaning guns; but the word may be rendered 'gun-carriages'.

Rānā Sanga. The leader of the Hindu confederacy was Rānā Sangrām Singh, commonly called Sanga, the head of the chivalry of the Mewār or Chitōr state, now usually designated as Udaipur, which was then, as it is to this day, the acknowledged premier kingdom of Rājasthān. The Rānā was worthy of his honoured position. He had already been the hero of a hundred fights, and could be truly described as 'the fragment of a warrior', lacking an eye and an arm, crippled by a broken leg, and scarred by eighty wounds from lance or sword.

He commanded an enormous host, composed of the contingents of 120 chiefs, and including 80,000 horse with 500 war elephants. The small army of Bābur was much dispirited at the prospect of the unequal fight. Its commander encamped twenty-three miles to the west of Agra at Sīkrī, where Akbar afterwards built his wondrous palace-city of Fathpur.

Bābur's vow. Bābur, conscious that the lives of himself and of every man under his command depended on victory, resolved to renounce his besetting sin. He broke his cups, poured out his stores of liquor on the ground, and vowed never again to touch strong drink. He kept his pledge.

Battle of Khānua. Battle was joined on March 16, 1527, at Khānua or Kanwāha, a village nearly due west from Agra and now in the Bharatpur State, just across the British border. The tactics which had won the victory at Pānīpat were repeated with the same result. The rout of the Hindu host was complete and final, although the gallant Rānā escaped from the field and survived for two years until 1529.[1]

Battle of the Ghāghra. Bābur followed up his victory by crossing the Jumna and storming the fortress of Chandēri, now in the Gwālior State. The Afghan chiefs of Bihār and Bengal were the next enemies to be attacked. They suffered defeat in 1529 on the banks of the Gogra (Ghāghra) near the junction of that river with the Ganges above Patna. The series of victories thus gained made Bābur master of a wide realm extending from the Oxus to the frontier of Bengal and from the Himalaya to Gwālior.

Death of Bābur. During 1530 Bābur was ailing. A well-known anecdote attributes his fatal illness to his parental devotion. His eldest son, Humāyūn, who was at Sambhal suffering from fever, was conveyed by boat to Agra where his father resided. Bābur entered the sick-room, and walked three times round the patient's bed, saying, 'On me be all that thou art suffering'. The son having recovered while his father died, people believed that the prayer of love had been answered. On December 26, 1530, Bābur breathed his last in his garden-house at Agra. His body was conveyed in accordance with his commands to Kābul, where it rests in the garden which he loved at the foot of one of the turreted hills guarding the city. A favourite consort sleeps by his side.

[1] He died in A.H. 935 and Samvat 1586. The time common to these two years extends from March 11 to September 4, 1529.

More than a century later, in 1646, his descendant Shāhjahān marked the spot by a pretty mosque and shrine of white marble.

Character of Bābur. 'Bābur', Mr. Lane-Poole observes, 'is the link between Central Asia and India, between predatory hordes and imperial government, between Tamerlane and Akbar. The blood of the two great Scourges of Asia, Chingiz and Tīmūr, mixed in his veins, and to the daring and restlessness of the nomad Tatar he joined the culture and urbanity of the Persian. He brought the energy of the Mongol, the courage and capacity of the Turk, to the listless Hindu; and himself a soldier of fortune and no architect of empire, he yet laid the first stone of the splendid fabric which his grandson Akbar achieved. . . .

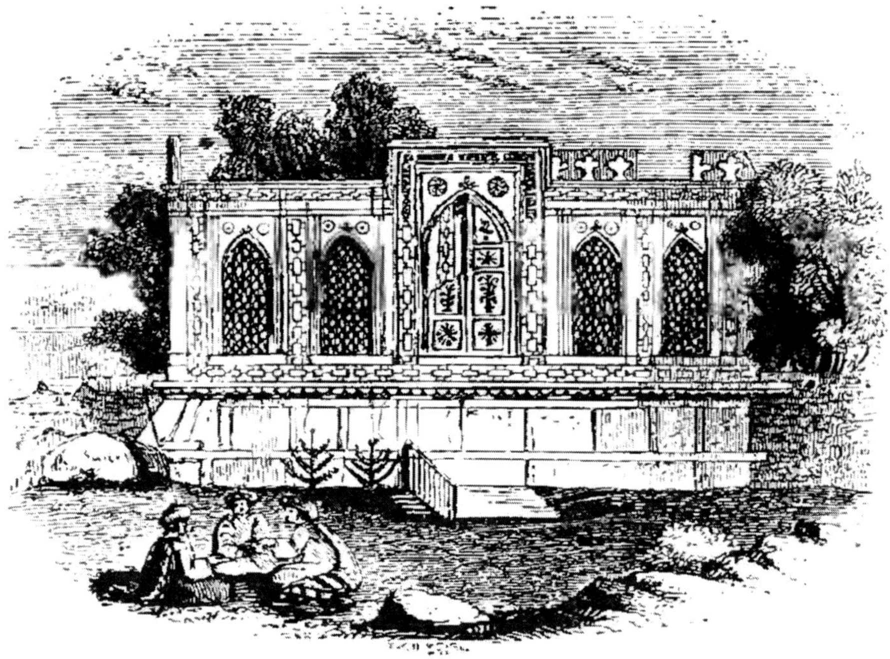

TOMB OF BĀBUR.

His permanent place in history rests upon his Indian conquests, which opened the way for an imperial line; but his place in biography and in literature is determined rather by his daring adventures and persevering efforts in his earlier days, and by the delightful *Memoirs* in which he related them. Soldier of fortune as he was, Bābur was not the less a man of fine literary taste and fastidious critical perception. In Persian, the language of culture, the Latin of Central Asia, as it is of India, he was an accomplished poet, and in his native Turkī he was master of a pure and unaffected style alike in prose and verse.'

His cousin, himself an excellent historian, records that Bābur 'excelled in music and other arts. Indeed, no one of his family before him ever possessed such talents, nor did any of his race perform such amazing exploits or experience such strange adventures.'

[1] Havelock, *The War in Affghanistan*, London, 1840, vol. ii, pp. 147, 149, 314–16; Masson, *Narrative*, vol. ii, p. 238.

Bābur's Memoirs. The *Memoirs* referred to, having been originally written in Turkī, were transcribed by his son Humāyūn with his own hand, and were translated into Persian with scrupulous accuracy by the Khān Khānān under the direction of Akbar. They were rendered into good English by Leyden and Erskine in 1826, and into French in 1871. A revised version by Mrs. Beveridge has been published.

Struggle for dominion in N. India, 1530–76. Bābur had neither time nor inclination for the work of consolidation or civil administration. All his energy was required to make good his military occupation of Upper India. When he died he had secured possession by force of arms of the Gangetic plain as far as the border of Bengal, which he did not attempt to conquer; but his position was extremely insecure, and could be maintained by his successors only through victorious fighting. The struggle of his descendants to establish a firmly seated dynasty with fairly complete control of northern India lasted from his death at the close of 1530 until 1576 when Akbar had been twenty years on the throne.

BĀBUR.

Accession and position of Humāyūn. Humāyūn, when he succeeded to his father's throne and his contested claim to the lordship of India, was nearly 23 years of age, and had served an apprenticeship in the arts of war and government. He had three brothers, Kāmrān, Hindāl, and Askarī. Kāmrān, the eldest, was already in possession of Kābul and Kandahār as governor, and Humāyūn found himself constrained to let him take the Panjāb also. Minor charges were assigned to the younger boys. The separation of Kāmrān's dominions left Humāyūn as king of Delhi in a difficult position, because he was threatened on one side by the strong kingdom of Gujarāt and on the other by the Afghan chiefs of Bihār and Bengal, while he was deprived of the resources in men and money which Afghanistan and the Panjāb could supply.

Character of Humāyūn. The personal adventures of Humāyūn and his rather ineffectual struggles against his manifold difficulties are narrated at length in Elphinstone's work. But they do not much concern the history of India, and a brief outline of the main facts will suffice for our purpose. Humāyūn, although a cultivated gentleman, not lacking in ability, was deficient in the energetic promptitude of his versatile father. His addiction to opium probably explains his failures to a considerable extent. When either he or Bābur is described as a cultivated gentleman, and there is much to justify the description, it must be understood that all these Tīmūrid princes were Asiatic despots, imbued with the sanguinary traditions of their family, class, and age. None of them—not even Akbar—had much regard for human life, and they were all capable of ordering ferocious massacres and inflicting cruel punishments.

Wars with Gujarāt and Shēr Khān. Humāyūn was under the necessity of continually fighting to retain his position in Upper India—the South never concerned him. In 1535 he made a brilliant raid into Gujarāt and exhibited his personal valour by forming one of the party which escaladed the strong fortress of Champanēr (about NE. of Baroda). He was unable to hold Gujarāt because of more pressing danger arising from the revolt of Shēr Khān, an Afghan chief in Bihār, who was established at Sahasrām, and had acquired the forts of Chunār and Rohtās. Humāyūn took Chunār and spent a long time during 1538 at Gaur in Bengal, where he thought more of pleasure than of business. He was forced to retreat westwards.

Shēr Shāh. Shēr Khān, who had assumed the title of king (Shāh or Sultan) and will henceforward be designated as Shēr Shāh, intercepted Humāyūn at Chausā on the Ganges (in the Shāhābād District), utterly defeated him, and compelled him to fly for his life in June, 1539. Nearly a year later, May 1540, Shēr Shāh again defeated Humāyūn still more decisively opposite Kanauj, now in the Farrukhabad District, U. P., and was recognized to be so strong that Kāmrān ceded the Panjāb to him.

The wanderings of Humāyūn. Humāyūn became a homeless wanderer, fleeing first to Sind and then to Mārwār (Jodhpur) in Rājputāna. The hunted ex-king, unable to obtain effective aid from any chief, was exposed to every kind of indignity and hardship, until he was forced to return to the deserts of Sind with a small band of dispirited followers. In the midst of his misery his son Akbar was born at Umarkōt on November 23, 1542.[1]

Humāyūn, after further adventures, retired to Persia in 1544 and claimed protection from Shāh Tahmāsp, who granted the request on condition that his suppliant should conform to the Shīa sect of Islām. Humāyūn, not being in a position to resist, was constrained to comply with the demand of his host and to promise that Kandahār when recovered should be handed over to Persia. The Shāh placed at his disposal a considerable force, with the aid of which Kandahār was taken in the autumn of 1545. Humāyūn after a short time broke faith with his protector and seized the city for himself. Kāmrān, his brother, was then expelled from Kābul, and Humāyūn recovered his little son Akbar, who had been detained by his uncle and exposed to many perils. Years

[1] The official date is October 15. See my work, *Akbar the Great Mogul*; and *Ind. Ant.*, 1915, pp. 233–4, with corrections of misprints in *Errata*.

of fighting followed with varying fortune. At last Kāmrān was taken prisoner and blinded.

Second reign and death of Humāyūn. Humāyūn, when relieved from his brother's opposition, was able to invade India. He occupied Delhi and Agra in June 1555, and so regained his father's capital cities. But he was not permitted to consolidate his conquest or to establish a regular civil government. He was still engaged in making the necessary arrangements when an accidental fall from the staircase of his library at Delhi ended his troubled life in January 1546. His second reign had lasted barely seven months. Although more than twenty-five years had elapsed since the death of Bābur in 1530, the effective reign of Humāyūn, including both his first and second periods of rule, had subsisted for only about ten years. During the remaining fifteen years members of the Sūr family had enjoyed a precarious sovereignty over Hindostan.

Reign of Shēr Shāh. It has been convenient to give a rough outline of Humāyūn's adventures as a continuous story. Attention must now be directed to the proceedings of his Afghan rivals. The family of Sultan Ibrāhīm Lodī did not seriously attempt to regain the kingdom lost at Pānīpat in 1526. Shēr Shāh, after the flight of Humāyūn in 1540, made vigorous efforts to subdue Rājputāna, Mālwā, and Bundēlkhand, which met with only partial success. He disgraced himself by ordering a treacherous massacre of the garrison of Rāisin in Central India, and was killed in 1545 while directing the siege of Kālanjar in Bundēlkhand.

Shēr Shāh's government. Shēr Shāh was something more than the capable leader of a horde of fierce, fanatical Afghans. He had a nice taste in architecture, manifested especially in the noble mausoleum at Sahasrām (Sasseram) in Bihār which he prepared for himself. He built a new city at Delhi and a second Rohtās in the Panjāb. He also displayed an aptitude for civil government and instituted reforms, which were based to some extent on the institutions of Alāu-d dīn Khiljī and were developed by Akbar.

He maintained his authority by means of a powerful army, said to have comprised 150,000 horse, 25,000 foot, and 5,000 elephants. His scheme for branding the horses in the government service in order to check the prevalent evil of fraudulent musters was copied by Akbar. He also anticipated that monarch in a system of land revenue assessment based on the measurement of the land, and if he had lived longer might have enjoyed a reputation equal to that of Rājā Todar Mall, Akbar's famous minister. Justice of a rough and ready kind was administered under his strict personal supervision, and the responsibility of village communities for crimes committed within their borders was enforced by tremendous penalties. No man could expect favour by reason of his rank or position, and no injury to cultivation was tolerated. Shēr Shāh, like Asoka and Harsha, accepted the maxim that 'it behoves the great to be always active'. His time was divided by

TOMB OF SHĒR SHĀH.

stringent rules between the duties of religion and those of government. He followed the example of the best Hindu sovereigns by laying out high roads, planting trees, and providing wells and sarāis for the accommodation of travellers. He reformed the coinage, issuing an abundance of silver money, excellent in both fineness and execution. That is a good record for a stormy reign of five years. If Shēr Shāh had been spared he would have established his dynasty, and the 'Great Moguls' would not have appeared on the stage of history. His right to the throne was quite as good as that of Humāyūn. Both princes were merely foreign military adventurers, seeking to carve out a kingdom by the sword, and Shēr Shāh was personally far abler than his rival.

Rupee of Shēr Shāh.

Islām Shāh ; Muhammad Ādil Shāh. When Shēr Shāh died the choice of the nobles fell on his second son, Jalāl Khān, who ascended the throne under the style of Islām Shāh, often corruptly written and pronounced as Salīm Shāh. His brief and disturbed reign ended in 1553. He issued many regulations, but did not share his father's ability. After an interval of disputed succession the throne was usurped by Muhammad Ādil Shāh, or Adalī, brother of a consort of Islām Shāh. He was inefficient, and left the control of his affairs in the hands of Hēmū, a clever Hindu tradesman. The right to the sovereignty was contested by two nephews of Shēr Shāh, whose fate will be related in a later chapter.

Rupee of Islām Shāh.

CHRONOLOGY

First battle of Pānīpat	April 21, 1526
Bābur proclaimed as Pādshāh	April 27, 1526
Battle of Khānua (Kanwāha), defeat of Rānā Sanga	March 1527
Battle of the Ghāghra (Gogra) river	1529
Death of Bābur ; accession of Humāyūn	Dec. 1530
Humāyūn in Bengal	1538
Defeat of Humāyūn at Chausā	June 1539
Final defeat of Humāyūn at Kanauj	May 1540
Enthronement of Shēr Shāh	Jan. 1542

Birth of Akbar at Umarkōt . . . . . Nov. 23, 1542
Death of Shēr Shāh; accession of Islām Shāh 1545
Death of Islām Shāh; Muhammad Ādil Shāh (Adalī) acc.; other claimants 1553–4
Restoration of Humāyūn . . . . June 1555
Death of Humāyūn . . . . Jan. 1556

AUTHORITIES

The main original authority for Bābur is his book of *Memoirs*, transl. by LEYDEN and ERSKINE, 1826, and by Mrs. A. BEVERIDGE, in progress. Contemporary accounts of Humāyūn are the *Memoirs* of JAUHAR, transl. by STEWART, 1832; *Life and Memoirs of Gulbadan Bēgam*, Akbar's aunt, transl. by Mrs. A. BEVERIDGE, R. A. S., 1902; and *Memoirs* of BĀYAZĪD BIYĀT, abstracted in *J. A. S. B.*, part i, for 1898, p. 296. Other leading Persian authorities for the period are the *Akbarnāma* of ABU-L FAZL, transl. by H. BEVERIDGE, and various authors in *E. & D.*, vols. iv, v; also FIRISHTA, transl. by BRIGGS. ERSKINE'S *History of India under Babar and Humāyūn*, 2 vols., 1854, is a valuable work on a large scale. LANE-POOLE'S *Bābar*, in Rulers of India, 1898, is an excellent and well-written little book, sufficient for most readers. The skeleton of the Sūr history is presented by E. THOMAS in *Chronicles of the Pathān Kings of Delhi* (1871). The story of the Sūr kings needs to be worked out critically in detail.

CHAPTER 2

The Early European Voyages to and Settlements in India; the East India Company from 1600 to 1708.

The foreigners and the Mogul Empire. Inasmuch as the influence of European settlers on the coasts made itself felt in Indian politics from the beginning of the sixteenth century, it is desirable to take a comprehensive, although summary view of the steps by which the western powers acquired a footing in India, before we enter upon the detailed history of the Mogul empire, as established by Akbar, and maintained for a century after his death. That empire was much concerned with Portuguese, and to a less extent with British affairs from the beginning of Jahāngīr's reign. Even as early as the days of Humāyūn the king of Gujarāt had found his advantage in engaging the aid of the foreigners. Akbar maintained frequent intercourse with Goa from the time of the conquest of Gujarāt in 1573, and it is impossible to understand fully the history of his reign without a certain amount of knowledge concerning the intruders from the west whom he was so anxious to expel from his borders. In this chapter the narrative, necessarily much condensed, will be carried down to 1708, the year in which the union of the rival English companies was completed, soon after the death of Aurangzēb, the last of the Great Moguls. The union of the companies, as Anderson observes, 'is an epoch which properly closes the Early History of the English in India'. It is convenient to give an outline of the whole story to that date in a single chapter, anticipating the narrative of the imperial history.

The Arab monopoly of Indian trade. We have seen how extensive was the trade, both overland and maritime, maintained between India and the Roman Empire during the first three centuries of the Christian Era, how that trade almost ceased in the fourth century, and revived to some extent in the fifth and sixth centuries. The Arab conquest of Egypt and Persia in the seventh century definitely closed the direct communication between Europe and India. Thenceforward all Indian wares which reached the West passed through Muhammadan hands, and so were transmitted from the markets of the Levant to Venice, which acquired enormous wealth and influence by its monopoly of Eastern commerce.

Portuguese exploration of African coast. The Portuguese kings of the fifteenth century looked with envy on the riches of Venice, and eagerly desired to obtain a share in her profitable trade. Prince Henry the Navigator devoted his life to the discovery of a direct sea route from Portugal to India, and, when he died in 1460, his adventurous captains had succeeded in passing the river Senegal on the west coast of Africa. But much further effort was needed before the circumnavigation of Africa could be accomplished. Ultimately the feat was performed by Bartholomeu Diaz de Novaes, who was driven by storms considerably to the south of the Cape, and made land half-way between the Cape of Good Hope and Port Elizabeth. He sailed up the eastern coast sufficiently far to satisfy himself of its north-easterly trend and to be convinced that the long-sought route had been opened. He returned to Lisbon in December 1488. The year in which he rounded the Cape should be stated as 1487, in preference to the traditional date, 1486.

Vasco da Gama's arrival at Calicut. The discovery was followed up ten years later by Vasco da Gama, who sailed in July 1497 with three tiny ships, none exceeding 120 tons, and, like his predecessor, worked round to the east coast of Africa. In April 1498 he reached Melinda, 200 miles north of Zanzibar, and there obtained pilots competent to guide him to India. On May 20, 1498, he anchored at Calicut, then governed by a Hindu prince known as the Zamorin, who ruled well a prosperous realm. The Zamorin was inclined to be friendly to the strangers, but the opposition of the Arab traders prevented da Gama from doing much business. After visiting Cannanore he went home and reached Lisbon at the end of August 1499.

Cabral's voyage. Next year (1500) the king of Portugal dispatched a larger fleet under Pedro Alvares Cabral, who established a factory or agency at Calicut, and obtained good cargoes at Cannanore and Cochin, which were under Hindu rulers. The Portuguese, who hated all Musalmāns and killed them without mercy, usually were on good terms with the Hindus. The king of Portugal, with papal sanction, assumed the lofty style of 'Lord of the Conquest, Navigation, and Commerce of Ethiopia, Arabia, Persia, and India'—a proceeding which shows that his ambition was not limited solely to commercial gain. The resistance of the Arab Māppilah (Moplah) merchants to the intrusion of their European rivals provoked horrid cruelties practised in retaliation by the Portuguese commanders.

de Almeida's 'blue water' policy. Two rival policies divided Portuguese opinion. Dom Francisco de Almeida, the first viceroy (1505-9), may be described as the leader of the 'blue water' school. He disbelieved in the policy of multiplying settlements on land, holding that Portugal did not possess men enough to occupy many forts, and that such factories as might be established should rely for protection on Portuguese fleets in command of the sea. He regarded as visionary any idea of establishing a Portuguese empire in the East, maintaining the doctrine that 'the greater the number of fortresses you hold, the weaker will be your power; let all our forces be on the sea. . . . Let it be known for certain that as long as you may be powerful at sea, you will hold India as yours; and if you do not possess this power, little will avail you a fortress on shore.'

Albuquerque's occupation policy. Affonso de Albuquerque, who succeeded de Almeida, with the rank of Governor, held different views. His purpose was to found a Portuguese empire in the East.

'His system', as Mr. Morse Stephens observes, 'rested on four main bases. He desired to occupy certain important points for trading purposes, and to rule them directly; he desired to colonize the selected districts by encouraging mixed marriages with the native inhabitants; where he could not conquer or colonize he desired to build fortresses; and when this was impracticable he desired to induce the native monarchs to recognize the supremacy of the king of Portugal and to pay him tribute.'

The ability and strong character of Albuquerque induced the Home Government to sanction his policy. But it failed, partly from its inherent defects, partly from the extraordinary folly of the attitude adopted by the Portuguese Government after he was gone.

Acquisition and government of Goa. In pursuit of his policy he effectively occupied the island of Goa—the principal port in the dominions of the Sultan of Bījāpur—in 1510, and worked out a system of administration for the small District acquired, the first bit of Indian territory directly governed by Europeans since the time of Alexander the Great. All Muhammadans were excluded from office. Portuguese officers were appointed as *Thānadārs*, each combining revenue and criminal jurisdiction, like an English District Officer, and assisted by Hindu clerks for whose education he established schools. He upheld the constitution of the ancient Hindu village communities, and enrolled native soldiers commanded by Hindu officers, the first 'sepoys'. An interesting innovation was the abolition of *suttee*, a measure not carried out in British India until 1829.

Albuquerque's designs. Albuquerque did not confine his attention to India. He aimed at depriving the Muhammadans, or Moors as he called them, of the whole trade between the East

J. C. Silva sculp. Olisip. in Typ. Reg. An. 1774.

ALBUQUERQUE.

and Europe, and concentrating it in European hands. One valuable section of that trade, which came from the Spice Islands or Moluccas, lying between Celébes and New Guinea, passed, along with the commerce of China and Japan, through the Straits of Malacca.

Importance of Malacca. In those days the town of Malacca on the west coast of the Malay Peninsula, which possessed a good though shallow harbour, was the principal emporium of the trade with the Spice Islands and the Far East. In these latter times it has been eclipsed by both Penang and Singapore, so that it became for some years a little town, rarely visited by ships. The rubber industry has revived it. In 1511 its possession carried with it the control of a vast commerce. Penang and Singapore did not become important until the nineteenth century. At the time of Albuquerque's attack Malacca was crowded by men of all the trading nations of the East, Arabs, Chinese, Javanese, Gujarātīs from the west, and Bengālīs from the east of India. Excepting the Muhammadans, whom he abhorred, Albuquerque showed favour to all those races. He indulged in the dream that the success of his enterprise would result in 'quenching the fire of this sect of Muhammad' and 'in the Moors resigning India altogether to our rule, for the greater part of them—or perhaps all of them—live upon the trade of this country, and are become great and rich, and lords of extensive treasures'. He held it to be 'very certain that if we take this trade of Malacca away out of their hands, Cairo and Mecca will be entirely ruined, and to Venice will no spices be conveyed, except what her merchants go and buy in Portugal'.

Exploration of the Spice Islands. When he had taken possession of the town in 1511 Albuquerque protected it by building a fortress held by a garrison, which secured Portuguese rule for a hundred and thirty years, after which time the place passed into the hands of the Dutch. It finally became British territory in 1824. From Malacca Albuquerque dispatched an expedition to explore the Spice Islands. Meantime, during the great commander's absence, Goa had been closely besieged by an army of the Sultan of Bījāpur, supported by Turkish and Egyptian contingents. After hard fighting Albuquerque effected its relief in 1512.

Attempt on Aden. One main object of Portuguese policy was the destruction of the trade carried on by Muhammadans in the Red Sea, and the Home Government strongly urged the effective prosecution of that purpose. Albuquerque attempted to take Aden but failed, and the Portuguese never succeeded in gaining a mastery over the navigation of the Red Sea.

Occupation of Ormuz. Albuquerque was more successful in the Persian Gulf. Shortly before his death in 1515 he occupied the island of Ormuz (Hormuz) and built a fortress there. At that time the port of Ormuz rivalled Malacca in importance, and like it was thronged by traders of all nationalities. The Portuguese retained possession until 1622, when they were ousted by an expedition of English ships sent from Bombay, and supported by a Persian contingent. From that date Ormuz declined, and its trade passed to the new port of Bandar Abbās, not far distant. The place is now of little consequence, but still exports a considerable quantity of excellent haematite, or iron ore.

Policy of mixed marriages. Albuquerque's policy of colonization by means of mixed marriages, which was peculiar to himself, deserves special notice. 'His aim', as Mr. Stephens observes, 'was to form a population which should be at once loyal to Portugal and satisfied to remain in India for life.' He did not expect to be able to retain many of the officers, and chiefly devoted his efforts to the willing detention of gunners and artisans. He married them off by the hundred to Muhammadan and Hindu women, especially the widows of the Muhammadans whom he had slaughtered. The brides had to submit to baptism, but on the other hand, if they asked for the houses which had been in possession of their deceased fathers or husbands, he ordered that those should be given to them.

He thus created the large class of Portuguese half-castes, often blacker in colour than ordinary Indians of full blood, who are now so numerous at Bombay and along the west coast. Most of these people have hardly a trace of the European about them, except high-sounding Portuguese names, and they devote themselves largely to domestic service. Their religion alone has prevented them from being absorbed into the mass of the population. Albuquerque did not foresee that his plan would produce a degenerate race absolutely destitute of the qualities to which Europeans owe their success in the world.

Indo-Portuguese coin.

Causes of decline and fall of Portuguese power. The strange story of the decline and fall of the Portuguese dominion in the East, which was rapid, and, I may add, fully deserved, cannot be told in this work. The cruelty of the Portuguese, especially to Muhammadans, was horrible, and Albuquerque himself did not hesitate to procure the poisoning of both the Zamorin of Calicut and a Persian official at Ormuz. After Albuquerque's death the Government of Portugal under the guidance of King John III, a bigoted fanatic, based its policy on a desire to make Christians by fair means or foul, rather than on political or commercial motives, and engaged in an insane attempt to force the natives of India to adopt Christianity. The Inquisition, which had been established at Goa in 1560, indulged from the beginning of the seventeenth century in an atrocious religious persecution, torturing and burning relapsed converts and unlucky wretches supposed to be witches. Those measures alone were enough to ruin the Portuguese design of creating an Indian dominion. The decay of the Portuguese empire in the East was hastened by other causes acting in a wider sphere. The local governments were utterly corrupt, the men were degraded by their marriages with native women, and the women were given up to debauchery. The temporary union of the crowns of Spain and Portugal in 1580 dragged the smaller country into the European quarrels of the larger, while Portugal, with its limited area and scanty population, lacked the resources to supply and control a distant empire. Thus the Portuguese rule on the coasts of the Eastern seas decayed as rapidly as it had grown, and the Portuguese settlements fell an easy prey to their Dutch and English rivals. Portuguese India now consists of three small settlements—Goa, 1,301 square miles; Damān, 100 miles N. of Bombay, 149 square miles; and the island of Diu, in the south of Kāthiāwār, 20 square miles. In Africa Portugal has Portuguese E. Africa on the Zambesi and Limpopo, with Portuguese Guinea on the Guinea coast; as well as Macao in China.

Dutch and English rivalry with the Portuguese. The Dutch and English almost simultaneously took measures to contest the claim of Portugal to the monopoly of Oriental commerce, and from the moment they appeared on the scene at the beginning of the seventeenth century the Portuguese were unable to resist them effectually. One after another most of the Indian settlements fell into their hands, and, in the first instance, passed into Dutch possession. The English then, in due course, took the place of the Dutch. Goa, it is true, escaped actual capture, although it was twice blockaded by Dutch fleets; but its importance had dwindled so steadily after the destruction of Vijayanagar in 1565 that in the seventeenth century it did not much matter who held it.

Indo-Dutch coin.

Dutch control of the Spice Islands and Far East trade. The United East India Company of the Netherlands, formed in 1602, promptly sent out large fleets. Batavia in Java, founded in 1619, became the head-quarters of the Company's operations. It is still the capital of the Dutch East Indies. The capture of Malacca from the Portuguese in 1641 gave the control of the commerce of the Spice Islands and the Far East to Holland, while during the twenty years between 1638 and 1658 Ceylon passed from Portuguese into Dutch hands.

Dutch settlements in India. The settlements of the Hollanders on the coasts of India, although numerous, were never individually considerable or important. Their first fort on the mainland of India was built at Pulicat, north of Madras, in 1609. From 1660 their principal station was Negapatam on the Madras coast. The attention of the Dutch Company was chiefly devoted to Java and the Spice Islands. The notorious massacre of Amboyna in 1623, when a number of Englishmen and Japanese were cruelly tortured to death, effectually checked British competition in that region. Cromwell, thirty-one years later, exacted an indemnity from Holland, and at the same time asserted by treaty with Portugal the British right to share in the trade. The Dutch, however, continued to be supreme in the Malay Archipelago. The Hollanders never acquired any formidable military power in India, so that the English in the course of the wars of the eighteenth century and the early years of the nineteenth found little difficulty in obtaining possession of the Dutch Indian settlements.

Indo-Danish coin.

Danish settlements. The Danish settlements demand a passing notice. A Danish East India Company was established in 1616, and four years later (1620) the factory at Tranquebar on the east coast was founded. The principal settlement of the Danes at Serampore near Calcutta dates from about 1676. The Danish factories, which were not important at any time, were sold to the British Government in 1845.

French settlements. The French appeared late on the scene, their official organization, 'La Compagnie des Indes', having been established in 1664. Their principal settlement, Pondicherry, founded ten years later, still is a moderately prosperous town. The French never succeeded in capturing a large share of the Indian trade, and their settlements never received sufficient steady support from home. The Republic still possesses Pondicherry, Chandernagore near Calcutta, and several smaller settlements of no political significance.

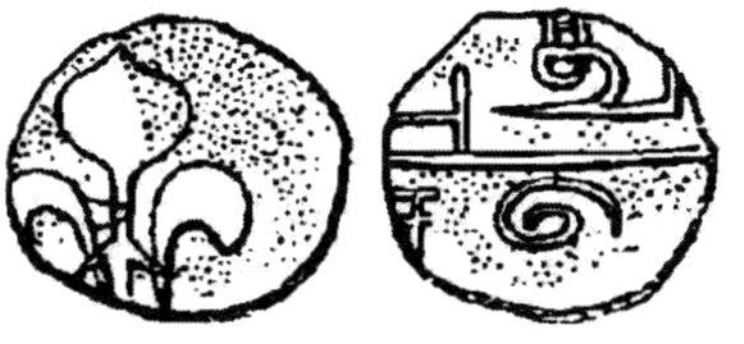

Indo-French coin.

The struggle between the English and French for supremacy in the peninsula during the second half of the eighteenth century will be narrated in due course as part of the general history of India.

First Charter of the East India Company. The glorious victory over the Spanish Armada in 1588 stimulated British maritime enterprise, and suggested plans for claiming a share in the lucrative commerce of the Eastern seas. Those plans assumed definite form on the last day of 1600 when Queen Elizabeth granted a charter with rights of exclusive trading to 'the Governor and Company of Merchants of *London* trading into the East Indies'.

Portcullis coin of Elizabeth, for India.

The Separate Voyages. The early 'Separate Voyages' organized by the Company were directed chiefly to the Spice Islands rather than to India. They were called Separate Voyages because each venture was arranged by a body of individual subscribers, who divided the profits among themselves. Joint stock enterprises began in 1612. A ship of the Third Separate Voyage in 1608 reached Surat and did some trade, but Portuguese opposition was strong; and it was not until 1612 that the English obtained by treaty with the Mogul governor of Gujarāt the right to trade at Surat, Cambay, and two other places.

After a fierce sea-fight in that year the British established their position in spite of the Portuguese, and founded a factory at Surat protected by an imperial *farmān*. Surat thus became the seat of a presidency of the East India Company, which in time developed into the Presidency of Bombay and the British empire in India. The Dutch also had a factory in Surat.

English capture of Ormuz. In 1615 the English again defeated the Portuguese at sea, and their capture of Ormuz in 1622, with the aid of a Persian military force, so weakened the Portuguese power that thenceforward they had little to fear from Portugal.

Embassy of Sir T. Roe. In 1615 James I sent Sir Thomas Roe as his ambassador to the Emperor Jahāngīr. During his stay of about three years in India, Sir Thomas, although he could not obtain all he asked for, succeeded in securing important privileges for his countrymen. From time to time British adventurers established many factories or trading stations at various points along the western coast, including one at Anjengo in Travancore. But their activity was not confined to that coast, the more easily accessible.

Settlements on Bay of Bengal. In the course of a few years they made their way into the Bay of Bengal, and founded factories. One of the earliest, built about 1625, was at Armagāon in the Nellore District, but the settlement at Masulipatam had been founded a few years before that date. The first fortification was at Armagāon, where the ruins of the Company's fort still exist.

Foundation of Madras. Business at Masulipatam and Armagāon was so hampered by the exactions of the local rulers that Mr. Francis Day, the Agent at Masulipatam, was directed to see if he could buy or rent a piece of land within the limits of which the Company's merchants might work without hindrance. The old Portuguese settlement at San Thomé near Madras was then in very low water, and the poverty-stricken Portuguese half-caste residents, who had lost most of their trade, were willing to welcome Mr. Day and his colleagues. The place possessed a fort, which Day probably could have rented if he pleased. But, on thinking the matter over, he preferred a site where he should be independent. Accordingly, with the help of the friendly local Portuguese, he arranged to rent a strip of land to the north of San Thomé, a mile broad and six miles long.

> 'It had nothing apparently to commend it. It was devoid of beauty of scenery, and had no harbour, although there was good anchorage in its roads. It was nothing but a dreary waste of sand, on which a monstrous sea broke in a double line of surf, giving it an inhospitable look, which it retains to the present day.'

The evil-smelling Cooum river protected it from unwelcome

visitors. On this unpromising spot Day resolved to build. He rented the land for a payment of about £600 a year. The agreement is said to have been drawn up and recorded on a gold plate, which was lost when the French took Madras in 1746. It was signed on March 1, 1639-40. Thus England acquired her first proprietary holding on Indian soil, and the foundation of the Presidency of Madras was laid. The lessor was the Rājā of Chandragiri, the representative of the old sovereigns of Vijayanagar. Day lost no time in starting the necessary buildings for the accommodation of his people and erecting a fort, to which latter step the Directors at home strongly objected. That fort, named after the patron saint of England, still gives its official designation to Madras as the Presidency of Fort St. George.

Foundation of Calcutta. Truculent and masterful Job Charnock, 'always a faithful man to the Company', founded Calcutta on an equally unpromising site in August 1690. He had been turned out of Bengal some two years earlier by the Mogul officers, as a consequence of Sir Josiah Child's foolish war with Aurangzēb, but being invited to return by the reigning Nawāb, Ibrāhīm Khān, accepted the invitation, and, landing with a guard of only thirty soldiers, doggedly set to work building and fortifying on the mud flat assigned to him. That was the beginning of Fort William—so called after William III—and also of the Presidency of Fort William or Bengal.

Acquisition of Bombay. Bombay was acquired by the Crown in 1661 as part of the dowry of Catharine of Braganza, queen of Charles II. The cession was made by the Portuguese in order to secure English support against the Dutch. A few years later the king, who had failed to appreciate the value of the acquisition, granted the island to the East India Company in return for the trifling sum of ten pounds a year.

Early Bombay coin.

Gerald Aungier. The real founder of the city was the early governor, Gerald Aungier (1669–77), who foresaw the future greatness of his charge, declaring that it was 'the city which by God's assistance is intended to be built'. Aungier, although rarely mentioned in the current general histories, was one of the noblest of the founders of the Indian empire. He is described as being 'a chivalric and intrepid man . . . a gentleman well qualified for governing', who made it his 'daily study to advance the Company's interest and the good and safety of the people under him'. He lies in a nameless grave at Surat, to which Bombay was subordinate in his time.

Keigwin's rebellion. The military revolt of Captain Keigwin at Bombay in 1683 was a curious incident. The gallant captain, who really was a loyal subject, was driven into rebellion by the tyranny of John Child, the President of Surat, who carried out the policy of his influential chief and namesake, Sir Josiah Child, in London. The rebels declared that 'we are therefore resolved not to suffer these abuses any longer, but revolt to His Majesty, taking all into our possession for his use'. Keigwin held Bombay for a year, governing it well and honestly. He then surrendered the island peacefully on honourable terms to a king's officer. Keigwin died in 1690 as an officer and a gentleman, bravely leading his men to an attack on one of the West India islands. The statement

BOMBAY FORT FROM THE SEA.

made in a multitude of books that the two Childs were brothers is erroneous. They do not appear to have been related in any way. After the rebellion Bombay became the head-quarters of the English in western India instead of Surat. The Bombay territory, however, did not attain much importance until the time of Warren Hastings. The noble harbour could not be fully utilized until the passage of the Western Ghāts had become practicable.

The United Company. Towards the close of the seventeenth century the East India Company encountered much opposition in England, which resulted in the formation of a rival body entitled 'The English Company trading to the East Indies'. The old company was brought to the brink of ruin. But its Directors were full of fight, and declared that 'two East India Companies in England could no more subsist without destroying one the other, than two kings, at the same time regnant in one kingdom'.

After much bitter and undignified quarrelling in both England and India an agreement was arranged in 1702. The difficult finaneial questions at issuc were finally sct at rest in 1708 by the award of Lord Godolphin, with the result that the rivals were combined in a single body styled 'The United Company of Merchants of *England* trading to the East Indies'. The United Company thus formed is the famous corporation which acquired the sovereignty of India during the century extending from 1757 to 1858.

Failure of Portuguese, Dutch, and French. The Portuguese, who had the advantage of the start in the race for the control of the Indian trade, deservedly lost everything from causes sufficiently obvious, which have been already indicated. The Dutch never seriously directed their attention to India proper, preferring to

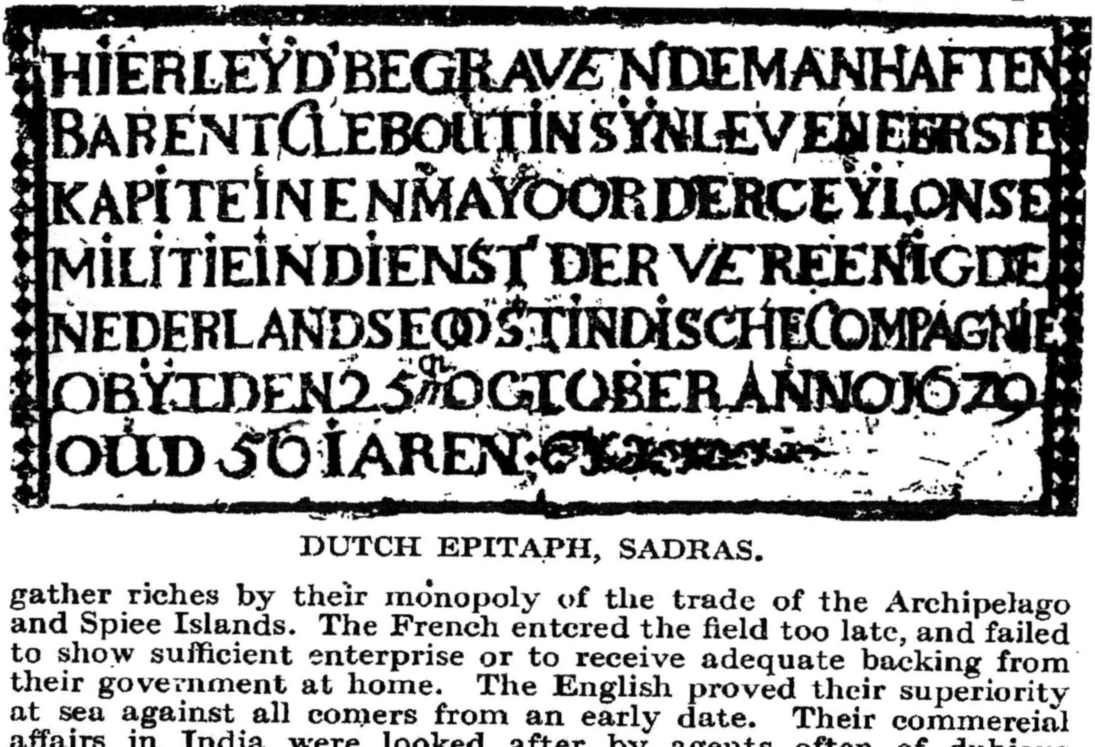

DUTCH EPITAPH, SADRAS.

gather riches by their monopoly of the trade of the Archipelago and Spiee Islands. The French entered the field too late, and failed to show sufficient enterprise or to receive adequate backing from their government at home. The English proved their superiority at sea against all comers from an early date. Their commereial affairs in India were looked after by agents often of dubious character, but always daring, persistent, and keen men of business. The trade was supported from the first by the efforts of the home government.

During the time of the Great Moguls the British territory in India was of negligible area, comprising only a few square miles in the island of Bombay, Madras eity, and three or four other localities. But even then the prowess of their sea captains had made their nation a power in Indian polities. Half a century after the death of Aurangzēb, when rich Bengal was acquired, nothing, not even an Act of Parliament, could stop the masters of the sea and the Gangetic valley from becoming the rulers of India.

CHRONOLOGY

Vasco da Gama arrived at Calicut	May 1498
Portuguese conquest of Goa	1510
Death of Albuquerque	1515
Trade of Goa injured by destruction of Vijayanagar	1565
Union of crowns of Spain and Portugal	1580
Defeat of the Spanish Armada	1588
Charter to E. I. Co. of merchants of *London*	Dec. 31, 1600
United E. I. Co. of the Netherlands	1602
Accession of Jahāngīr	1605
Third 'Separate Voyage'; Capt. Hawkins at Surat	1608
Joint stock voyages began; English factory established at Surat; Portuguese defeated at sea	1612
Embassy of Sir Thomas Roe	1615–18
Danish settlement at Tranquebar	1620
Capture of Ormuz by English and Persians	1622
Massacre of Amboyna	1623
Early English factories on Eastern coast	1625–34
Death of Jahāngīr; accession of Shāhjahān	1627–8
Grant of site of Madras	March 1, 1640
Accession of Aurangzēb	1658–9
Cession of Bombay; charter of Charles II	1661
French 'Compagnie des Indes' established	1664
Gerald Aungier at Bombay	1669–77
Pondicherry founded	1674
War of E. I. Co. with Aurangzēb	1685–7
Calcutta founded	1690
The new 'English Company trading to the East Indies'	1698
Union of the new and old companies	1702
Lord Godolphin's award; the 'United Company of Merchants of *England* trading to the East Indies'	1708

AUTHORITIES

Innumerable books might be cited. The slight sketch in this chapter is based chiefly on the summary in *I. G.* (1907), chap. ii; H. MORSE STEPHENS, *Albuquerque* (Rulers of India, 1892), an excellent book; FONSECA, *Sketch of the City of Goa* (Bombay, 1878), 'a most carefully compiled volume'; WHITEWAY, *The Rise of Portuguese Power in India* (Westminster, 1899); MALABARI, *Bombay in the Making* (London, 1910); ANDERSON, *The English in Western India* (Bombay and London, 1854); STRACHEY, *Keigwin's Rebellion* (Clarendon Press, 1916), a first-rate and most entertaining book; PENNY, *Fort St. George, Madras* (London, 1900); and BRUCE, *Annals of the E. I. Co.* (London, 1810).

Numerous references will be found in the works mentioned. An immense mass of unworked material is buried in the three series of volumes containing documents relating to the E. I. Co., published by the Clarendon Press at various dates, and mostly edited by Mr. William Foster and Miss Sainsbury.

CHAPTER 3

Akbar, 1555–1605.

Humāyūn's sons. When Humāyūn died he left two sons, Akbar, the elder, aged thirteen, and Muhammad Hakīm, the younger, who was more than two years junior to his half-brother. The Kābul provinee remained nominally in the charge of the younger prince, and, although regarded officially as a dependency of Hindostan, was ordinarily administered as an independent principality. Akbar, at the time of his father's death, was in camp with his guardian, Bairām Khān the Turkoman, engaged in the pursuit of Shēr Shāh's nephew, Sikandar Sūr, who had collected a force in the Panjāb and sought to win the crown for himself.

Enthronement of Akbar. Arrangements having been made to conceal Humāyūn's decease for a time sufficient to allow of the peaceful proclamation of Akbar's accession, the enthronement of the heir was duly effected at Kalānaur, in the Gurdāspur District, on February 14, 1556. The brick platform and seat used in the ceremony still exist and are now reverently preserved. But the enthronement ceremony merely registered the claim of Humāyūn's son to succeed to the throne of Hindostan. The deceased monarch never had had really assured possession of his kingdom, and during his brief second reign of a few months was in the position of an adventurer who had secured a momentary military success. He could not be regarded as an established legitimate sovereign. In fact, as already observed, the representatives of his great rival Shēr Shāh had claims quite as strong as those of Akbar to the lordship of Hindostan.

Two Sūr claimants. At that moment the effective claimants representing the Sūr dynasty were two nephews of Shēr Shāh. The first of the two, King Muhammad Shāh Ādil or Adalī, had actually succeeded for a time in establishing himself as the successor of Shēr Shāh's son, Islām Shāh, who had died in 1554. But at the time of Humāyūn's fatal accident he had retired to the eastern provinces and was residing at Chunār, near Mirzāpur. Shēr Shāh's other nephew, Sikandar, as already mentioned, was in the Panjāb engaged in operations on his own behalf.

Hēmū, a third claimant. King Adalī's interests in the north were in the charge of his capable Hindu minister and general, Hēmū, a trader or Baniyā by birth, who had already won many victories for his master. Hēmū, advancing through Gwālior, occupied both Agra and Delhi, thus gaining a very important advantage. Tardī Beg, who had been entrusted by the Protector, Bairām Khān, with the defence of Delhi, failed in his duty, and allowed the city to fall into the enemy's hands. For that offence he was executed by order of Bairām Khān. The punishment, although inflicted in an irregular fashion without trial, was necessary and substantially just.

Hēmū, after his occupation of Delhi, bethought himself that he was in possession of a powerful army, many elephants, and much treasure, while his sovereign was far away in Chunār. He came to the conclusion that he had better claim the throne for himself rather than on behalf of Adalī. Accordingly, he secured the support of the Afghan contingents by liberal donatives, and ventured to assume royal state under the style of Rājā Bikramajit or Vikramāditya, a title borne by several renowned Hindu kings in ancient times. He thus became Akbar's most formidable competitor, while both Adalī and Sikandar Sūr dropped into the background for the moment.

Second battle of Pānīpat. Bairām Khān, with Akbar, advanced through Thānēsar to the historic plain of Pānīpat, where, thirty years earlier, Bābur had routed and slain Sultan Ibrāhīm Lodī. Hēmū approached the same goal from the west. The Hindu general, although he had the misfortune to lose his park of artillery in a preliminary engagement, possessed a powerful host of 1,500 war elephants on which he relied, and was in command of troops far superior in number to those of his adversary.

The armies met in battle on November 5, 1556. At first Hēmū was successful on both wings. Probably he would have been the victor but for the accident that he was hit in the eye by an arrow and rendered unconscious. His army, when deprived of its leader, the sole reason for its existence, dispersed at once. Bairām Khān and Akbar, who had left the conduct of the battle to subordinate officers, rode up from the rear. Their helpless dying opponent was brought before them. The Protector desired his royal ward to earn the coveted title of Ghāzī by slaying the infidel with his own hand. The boy, naturally obeying the instruction of his guardian, smote the prisoner on the neck with his scimitar, and the bystanders finished off the victim. The commonly accepted story that young Akbar exhibited a chivalrous unwillingness to strike a wounded prisoner is a later, courtly invention. Hēmū's head was sent to Kābul and his trunk was gibbeted on one of the gates of Delhi. A tower was built with the heads of the slain, according to the ghastly custom of the times.

Famine, 1555–6. During the years 1555 and 1556 the upper provinces of India, and more especially the Agra and Delhi territories, suffered from an appalling famine due primarily to the failure of rain and much aggravated by the long continued operations of pitiless armies. Hēmū had displayed the most brutal indifference to the sufferings of the people, and had pampered his elephants with rice, sugar, and butter, while men and women ate one another. He deserved his fate.

End of the Sūr dynasty. The victors pressed the pursuit of the broken foe and promptly occupied both Agra and Delhi. During the year 1557 the pretensions of the Sūr family to the sovereignty of Hindostan came to an end. Sikandar Sūr, who surrendered, was generously treated and provided with a fief in the eastern provinces. King Adalī made no attempt to dispute the verdict of the sword at Pānīpat. He remained in the east, and was killed in a conflict with the King of Bengal. Akbar's position as the successor of Humāyūn was thus unchallenged, although he had still much fighting to do before he attained a position as good as that occupied by his father during his first reign.

Progress of reconquest. In the course of the years 1558–60 the recovery of the Mogul dominion in Hindostan progressed by the occupation of Gwālior, the strong fortress of Central India, Ajmēr, the key of northern Rājputāna, and the Jaunpur province in the east. An attempt on the Rājpūt castle of Ranthambhōr failed for the moment, to be renewed successfully a few years later. Preliminary arrangements for the conquest of Mālwā were interrupted by the events connected with Akbar's assumption of personal rule and the dismissal of Bairām Khān, his guardian and Protector.

Dismissal of Bairām Khān. Early in 1560 the young sovereign, then in his eighteenth year, began to feel galled by the tutelage of his guardian, who was a masterful man, prone to exert his authority without much regard for other people's feelings. Akbar's natural impatience was encouraged by Hamīda Bāno Bēgam, his mother; by Māham Anaga, chief of the nurses and ranking as a foster-mother of the sovereign; by her son, Adham Khān; and by Shihābu-d dīn, her relative, the governor of Delhi. All those personages, who had much influence over Akbar, disliked Bairām Khān for reasons of their own. In the spring of 1560 Akbar dismissed the Protector from office and announced his intention of taking the reins of government into his own hands. Bairām Khān, after some hesitation, submitted to the royal commands, and started for Mecca as ordered. But, on second thoughts, being angered because he was hustled on his way by an ungrateful upstart named Pīr Muhammad, he rebelled, although in a half-hearted fashion. He was defeated in the Panjāb and again compelled to submit. Akbar treated the ex-regent with generosity and allowed him to proceed on his journey towards Mecca with all ceremonial honour. Bairām Khān reached Pātan in Gujarāt, where he was murdered by a private enemy in January 1561. His little son, Abdurrahīm, was saved, and lived to become the principal nobleman in the empire. The intrigue against the Regent was engineered by a court clique who desired his destruction. Akbar at that time was under petticoat government and had little concern with state affairs. His personal conduct in the affair shows a generous temper, so far as appears. The faults of Bairām Khān certainly deserved indulgence from Akbar, who, like his father, was indebted for his throne to the loyalty of the Turkoman.

Petticoat government, 1560–2. The next two years are the most discreditable in Akbar's life. The young monarch, as his biographer repeatedly observes, 'remained behind the veil', and seemed to care for nothing but sport. He manifested no interest in the affairs of his kingdom, which he left to be mismanaged by unscrupulous women, aided by Adham Khān, Pīr Muhammad, and other men equally devoid of scruple. The conquest of Mālwā, entrusted to Adham Khān and Pīr Muhammad, was effected with savage cruelty to which Akbar made no objection. The fortress of Mīrthā (Merta) in Rājputāna was taken in 1562.

Emancipation of Akbar. The emancipation of Akbar from a degrading tutelage came in May 1562. His appointment in the previous November of Shamsu-d dīn as prime minister was extremely distasteful to Māham Anaga and her friends, who feared that their ill-used power might slip from their hands. Adham Khān one day swaggered into the palace where the prime minister was at work and stabbed him to death. Akbar, hearing the noise, came out from an inner apartment and narrowly escaped injury from the ruffian murderer. But a stunning blow from the heavy royal fist felled the traitor, who was then hurled from the battlements, thus suffering in a summary fashion the just penalty of his crime. From that time Akbar was a free man, although the final emancipation was deferred until two years later (1564), when he inflicted equally summary and just punishment on another murderer, his mother's brother, a half-insane monster named Khwāja Muazzam.

Political state of India. The political divisions of India as they existed in 1561 or 1562, when Akbar had reigned for five or six years, are exhibited in the map, and explained in the statement facing it.

Reforms. At a very early stage in his career he realized thoroughly that it was no longer possible for the Pādshāh of Hindostan to be the king of the Muslim minority only. His throne, if it was to be firmly established, must rest on the broad foundation of general loyalty, accorded willingly by Hindus and Musalmāns alike. That resolve, involving a policy the exact contrary of that pursued by Fīrōz Shāh Tughlak and most of the other Sultans, appears to have been the personal act of Akbar, the result of his own meditations, and not of outside suggestion. In pursuance of his new policy he made his first marriage with a Hindu princess early in 1562, some months before the execution of Adham Khān. The lady honoured was a daughter of Rājā Bihār Mall of Ambēr or Jaipur, and became the mother of the Emperor Jahāngīr. The marriage secured the loyalty and support of the powerful Jaipur family for several generations. Marriages with princesses of other Rājpūt states followed in later years. At this period (1562–4) Akbar effected several important reforms. He abolished the taxes on Hindu pilgrims ; forbade the enslavement of prisoners of war, thereby reversing the policy of Fīrōz Shāh Tughlak ; and also remitted the *jizya* or poll-tax on non-Muslims. It may be that the royal orders were not invariably acted on, and that local magnates at a distance from the capital often ignored the innovations ; but, however that may be, Akbar deserves immense credit for the originality and courage which prompted his orders. The reforms were his own doing, carried out many years before he came under the influence of Abu-l Fazl and the other persons whose names are associated with his later policy in matters of religion.

From March 1564, when Khwāja Muazzam suffered his well-earned punishment and Akbar was in his twenty-second year, he had become thoroughly emancipated from the control of the ladies of the household and the corrupt men through whom they acted. His policy for the forty-one remaining years of his reign was his own.

The ambition of Akbar. Akbar, one of the most ambitious of men, who loved power and wealth, brooking no rival near his throne, now set himself to effect the systematic subjugation of north-western and central India, to be followed later by the conquest of the west, east, and south. His designs were purely aggressive, his intention being to make himself the unquestioned lord paramount of India, and to suppress the independence of every kingdom within the reach of his arm. He carried out that policy with unflinching tenacity until January 1601, when the mighty fortress of Asīrgarh, his last acquisition, passed into his hands. Circumstances beyond his control prevented him from continuing his career of conquest until his death in October 1605.

He began by encouraging a great noble, Āsaf Khān (I), governor of Karā and the eastern provinces, to destroy the independence of Gondwāna, equivalent to the northern portion of the present Central Provinces, then governed by the Dowager Rānī Durgāvatī, an excellent princess, with whose administration no fault could be found. She was driven to her death, her country was overrun, and the wealth accumulated in the course of centuries was plundered without mercy. Her independence was her only fault. Injudicious flatterers of Akbar have printed much canting nonsense about his supposed desire to do good to the conquered peoples by his annexations. He never canted on the subject himself, or made any secret of the fact that he regarded as an offence the independence of a neighbour. 'A monarch', he said, 'should be ever intent on conquest, otherwise his neighbours rise in arms against him. The army should be exercised in warfare, lest from want of training they become self-indulgent.' Throughout his reign he acted consistently on those avowed principles.

Rebellions. The acquisition of the leading fortresses was an essential preliminary for securing the firm grasp of the imperial government on Hindostan or upper India. Gwālior, Chunār, and Mīrthā had been acquired early in the reign. The next object of attack was Chitōr in the territory of the Sīsōdia Rānā of Mewār in Rājputāna, now better known as the Udaipur State. Some delay in the execution of the Pādshāh's ambitious projects was caused by the outbreak of several rebellions headed by Uzbeg officers, who disliked Akbar's Persianized ways, and would have preferred Kāmrān's son, his cousin, to occupy the throne. In 1565 Akbar felt bound, as a matter of state necessity, to order the private execution of that cousin in order to prevent him from being used as a pretender. The act was the first of the long series

INDIA IN 1561

When Akbar ascended the throne in January 1556 he possessed no definite territory. Five years later he held firmly the Panjāb, with the Multān district; the basin of the Ganges and Jumna as far east as Prayāg (later known as Allahabad), and also Gwālior in Central India, and Ajmēr in Rājasthān. The Kābul territory (excluding Kandahār with its dependencies, then in Persian hands, see Raverty, *Notes on Afghanistan*, pp. 592, 600) was governed in practical independence by the guardians of Akbar's younger half-brother, Mīrzā Muhammad Hakīm. The various Himalayan States, including Kashmīr, were completely independent. Bengal, Bihār, and Orissa were under the government of an Afghān prince, Sulaimān Kararānī. Orissa then meant the modern Midnapore, Purī, Katak (Cuttack), and Balasore Districts. The numerous chiefs in Rājasthān or Rājputāna, Sind, and the extensive wild country now forming the Central Provinces, Chutiā Nāgpur, and Orissa Tributary States, recognized no man as master. Gujarāt, which had been occupied by Akbar's father, Humāyūn, was ruled by a Muhammadan dynasty, as was Mālwā. The five kingdoms of the Deccan plateau, namely, Ahmadnagar, Birār (Berar), Bīdar, Bījāpur, and Golkonda, constituted out of fragments of the Bahmanī Empire, were autonomous under Musalmān dynasties, constantly at war one with another or with Vijayanagar. The boundaries frequently changed. Bījāpur was the most powerful of the five States. The small Muhammadan principality of Khāndēsh in the valley of the Tāptī was practically independent. The whole peninsular area to the south of the Krishnā and Tungabhadrā rivers was under the lordship of the Hindu kings of Vijayanagar.

The Portuguese were strongly established on the western coast in fortified settlements taken from the Sultans of the Deccan, and situated at Goa, with a considerable territory attached; Chaul, Bombaim (Bombay) with neighbouring places; Bassein (see Malabari, *Bombay in the Making*, 1910, p. 21); Damān, and Diu. Their fleet controlled the mercantile and pilgrim traffic of the Arabian Sea and Persian Gulf. No other European power had gained any footing on the soil of India, and no Englishman had even landed in the country. All delineations of frontiers and boundaries necessarily are merely approximate. The boundaries of the Sultanates of the Deccan are taken from Sewell's map in *A Forgotten Empire* (1900).

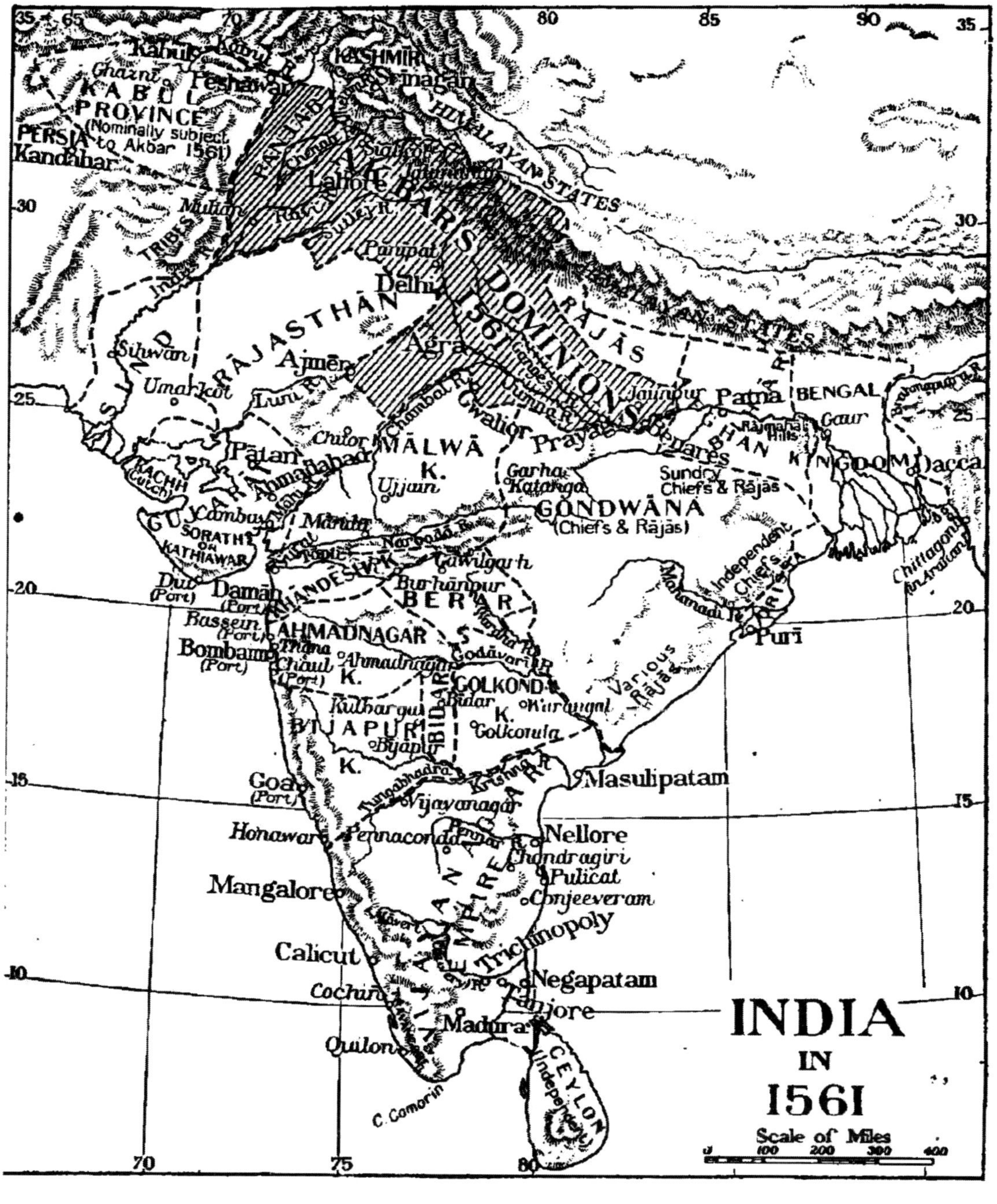
INDIA
IN
1561
Scale of Miles
Kabul
Ghazni
Peshawar
KABUL PROVINCE
(Nominally subject to Akbar 1561)
PERSIA
Kandahar
KASHMIR
Srinagar
HIMALAYAN STATES
Lahore
Multan
TRIBES
Panipat
Delhi
AKBAR'S DOMINIONS 1561
RAJASTHAN
RAJĀS
Agra
Ajmer
SIND
Sihwan
Umarkot
Jaunpur
Patna
BENGAL
Gaur
Chitor
MĀLWĀ K.
Gwalior
Prayag
Benares
Pātan
KACHH (Cutch)
Ahmadabad
Ujjain
Garha Katanga
Sundry Chiefs & Rājās
Dacca
Cambay
Mandu
GONDWĀNA
(Chiefs & Rājās)
SORATH OR KATHIAWAR
Gawilgarh
Independent Chiefs
Chittagong
Diu (Port)
Damān (Port)
KHANDESH
Burhānpur
BERAR
Bassein (Port)
AHMADNAGAR
Bombay (Port)
Thana
Chaul (Port)
Ahmadnagar
K.
Godāvari R.
Puri
Various Rājās
GOLKONDA
Kulbarga
Bidar
Warangal
K.
BIDAR
BIJAPUR
Golkonda
Bijapur
K.
Goa (Port)
Masulipatam
Vijayanagar
Honawar
Pennaconda
Nellore
Chandragiri
Pulicat
Mangalore
Conjeeveram
Trichinopoly
Calicut
Negapatam
Cochin
Tanjore
Madura
Quilon
C. Comorin
CEYLON (Independent)
70
75
80
85
90
35
30
25
20
15
10

of similar executions which have stained the annals of the Mogul dynasty. The rebellions of Khān Zamān and the other Uzbeg chiefs came to an end in 1567, leaving Akbar free to prepare for the siege of Chitōr. He deeply resented the independent position assumed by the Rānā, who was acknowledged universally to be the head of the Rājpūt clans. His family never allowed a daughter to enter the Mogul palace. Udai Singh, the reigning Rānā in 1567, unfortunately was a coward, unworthy of his noble ancestry, but his personal unworthiness did not prevent his brethren from organizing a gallant defence.

Siege of Chitōr. The siege of Chitōr, the most famous and dramatic military operation of the reign, lasted from October 20, 1567, to February 23, 1568, and would have lasted much longer had not Akbar by a lucky shot killed Jaimall, the chieftain who was the soul of the defence, having assumed the place which the recreant Rānā should have occupied. The garrison abandoned all hope when deprived of their leader. The women were immolated on funeral pyres to save them from dishonour, a dread rite known as *jauhar*, and usually practised by Rājpūts when hard pressed. The clansmen of the regular garrison threw themselves on the Mogul swords and perished fighting. Akbar was so enraged by the fierce resistance that he massacred 30,000 of the country people who had taken part in the defence.

The gates of the fortress were taken off their hinges and removed to Agra. The huge kettledrums which used to proclaim for miles around the exit and entrance of the princes, and the massive candelabra which lighted the shrine of the Great Mother also were carried away to adorn the halls of the victor. Chitōr was left desolate, so that in the eighteenth century it became the haunt of tigers and other wild beasts. In these latter days it has partially recovered, and the lower town is now a prosperous little place with a railway station.

Fate of Rājputāna. The fall of Chitōr, followed in the next year (1569) by that of Ranthambhōr, made Akbar master of Rājputāna, although not in full sovereignty. The clans of Mewār never submitted to him, and he had to fight them from time to time during the greater part of his reign. But no doubt remained that the Mogul had become the paramount power over his Rājpūt neighbours. Most of the princes were content to receive official appointments as salaried dignitaries of the empire, and several gave daughters in marriage to the emperor. Rājputāna or Rājasthān was reckoned as a province or Sūba with the headquarters at Ajmēr, and the chivalry of the clans for the most part became devoted soldiers of the Pādshāh.

The strong fortress of Kālanjar in Bundēlkhand to the south of the Jumna opened its gates in 1569, the year in which Ranthambhōr was taken.

Akbar was thus left at liberty to indulge his ambition in other directions, and to extend his conquests as far as the Arabian Sea on the west and the Bay of Bengal on the east.

Akbar's love of art. The activity of Akbar's versatile mind was never limited to the business of war and conquest. As early as his seventh regnal year he had taken pains to requisition the services of Tānsēn, the best singer in India, and he always retained an intelligent interest in music. Every form of art also attracted him, and as a boy he had learned the elements of drawing and painting under two renowned artists. He commemorated the gallantry of Jaimall and Pattā, the heroes of Chitōr, by causing their effigies to be carved and set on stone elephants placed at the gate of the Agra fort.

Buildings. He loved building and possessed excellent taste in architecture. The magnificent stone-faced walls of the Agra Fort were begun in 1565, and hundreds of buildings modelled on the designs of Bengal and Gujarāt architects were erected within the precincts. Most of them were pulled down by Shāhjahān, whose canons of taste differed. The palace-city of Fathpur-Sīkrī, twenty-three miles to the west of Agra, was begun in 1569, and finished about six or seven years later. It became the royal residence in 1570 or 1571.

Akbar's sons. Akbar, having had the misfortune to lose at least two infant children while living at Agra, came to regard that place as unlucky. A famous Muslim holy man, Shaikh Salīm Chishtī, who dwelt among the rocks at Sīkrī, promised the emperor three sons who should survive. The prophecy was fulfilled. The eldest, born in August 1569, and named Prince Salīm, in honour of the saint, became the Emperor Jahāngīr in due course. Murād, the second prince, born in 1570, died from the effects of intemperance, about six years prior to his father's decease. The third son, Dāniyāl, met the same fate, some four years later than his brother.

Fathpur-Sīkrī. The emperor, believing that the neighbourhood of Sīkrī, where the saint dwelt, would be lucky for himself, resolved to build a vast mosque there for the use of the Shaikh, and beside it a palace and royal residence, equipped with all the conveniences thought necessary in that age and adorned with all the resources of art.

After the conquest of Gujarāt in 1573 the new city was named Fathābād or Fathpur, 'Victory town'. In order to distinguish it from many other places of the same name it is usually known as Fathpur-Sīkrī. The great mosque is still perfect, and several of the more important palace buildings, now carefully conserved, are almost uninjured. They are constructed of the local red sandstone, a fine durable building material. Artists from all countries accessible to Akbar were collected to decorate the buildings with carving and frescoes. Most of the carving has escaped damage, but few fragments of painting survive.

Fathpur-Sīkrī was occupied as the capital of the empire for only about fifteen years from 1570 to 1585, when Akbar went north and quitted his fantastic city for ever, excepting a passing visit in 1601. The latest building of importance is the Buland Darwāza or Lofty Portal of the mosque, erected in 1575–6, probably as a triumphal arch to commemorate the conquest of Gujarāt.

Gujarāt. The rich province known as Gujarāt, lying between Mālwā and the Arabian Sea, had been held by Humāyūn for a short time, and long before had been subject to the Sultanate of Delhi in the days of the Khiljīs and Muhammad bin Tughlak. Akbar, therefore, could advance reasonable claims to the recovery of the province, which, in any case, invited aggression by its wealth. Just then, too, the government had fallen into disorder and the intervention of Akbar was actually asked for by a local chief.

Conquest of Gujarāt. The campaign began in July 1572. Surat was taken after a siege, and Akbar gave brilliant proof of his personal courage and prowess in a hard-fought skirmish at Sarnāl.[1] When the emperor, as he may now be called, started for home in the April following, he believed that the newly conquered province had been securely annexed and might be left safely in the charge of his officers. But he was hardly back in Fathpur-Sīkrī when he received reports of a formidable insurrection headed by certain disorderly cousins of his known as the Mīrzās, who already had given much trouble, and by a noble named Ikhtiyāru-l Mulk. Akbar, who was then in his thirty-first year and in the fullest enjoyment of his exceptional powers, bodily and mental, rose to the occasion. He prepared a fresh expeditionary force with extraordinary rapidity, looking after everything personally, and sparing no expense. He declared that nobody would be ready to start sooner than himself, and made good his promise. Having sent on a small advanced guard, he rode out of his capital on August 23 with a few attendants—all mounted on swift she-camels. The party, using what conveyance they could get, rushed across Rājputāna at hurricane speed and reached the outskirts of Ahmadābād, nearly six hundred miles distant, in eleven days all told —nine days of actual travelling—a marvellous feat of endurance. The emperor, with a tiny force of about three thousand horsemen, fought twenty thousand of the enemy near Ahmadābād on September 2, 1573, and gained a decisive victory. He was back again in his capital on October 4, Gujarāt having then become definitely part of the empire. The province was disturbed many times afterwards, but the imperial supremacy was never questioned until 1758 when the Marāthās occupied Ahmadābād.

The conquest of Gujarāt an epoch. The conquest of Gujarāt marks an important epoch in Akbar's history. The annexation gave his government free access to the sea with all the rich commerce passing through Surat, and the other western ports. The territory and income of the State were vastly extended, so that the viceroyalty of Gujarāt became one of the most important posts in the gift of the sovereign. Akbar now first saw the sea and came into direct contact with the Portuguese, thus opening up relations which seriously affected the history of India, and introduced new influences operating upon his mind. The province became the practising

[1] Near Thāsrā in the Kaira District, Bombay.

ground for Rājā Todar Mall, the able financier, who made his first revenue 'settlement' on improved principles in Gujarāt.[1]

Reforms. The conclusion of the conquest gave Akbar and his advisers an opportunity for introducing several administrative reforms.

The Government made a determined effort to check the extensive frauds continually practised by the officials and fief-holders who

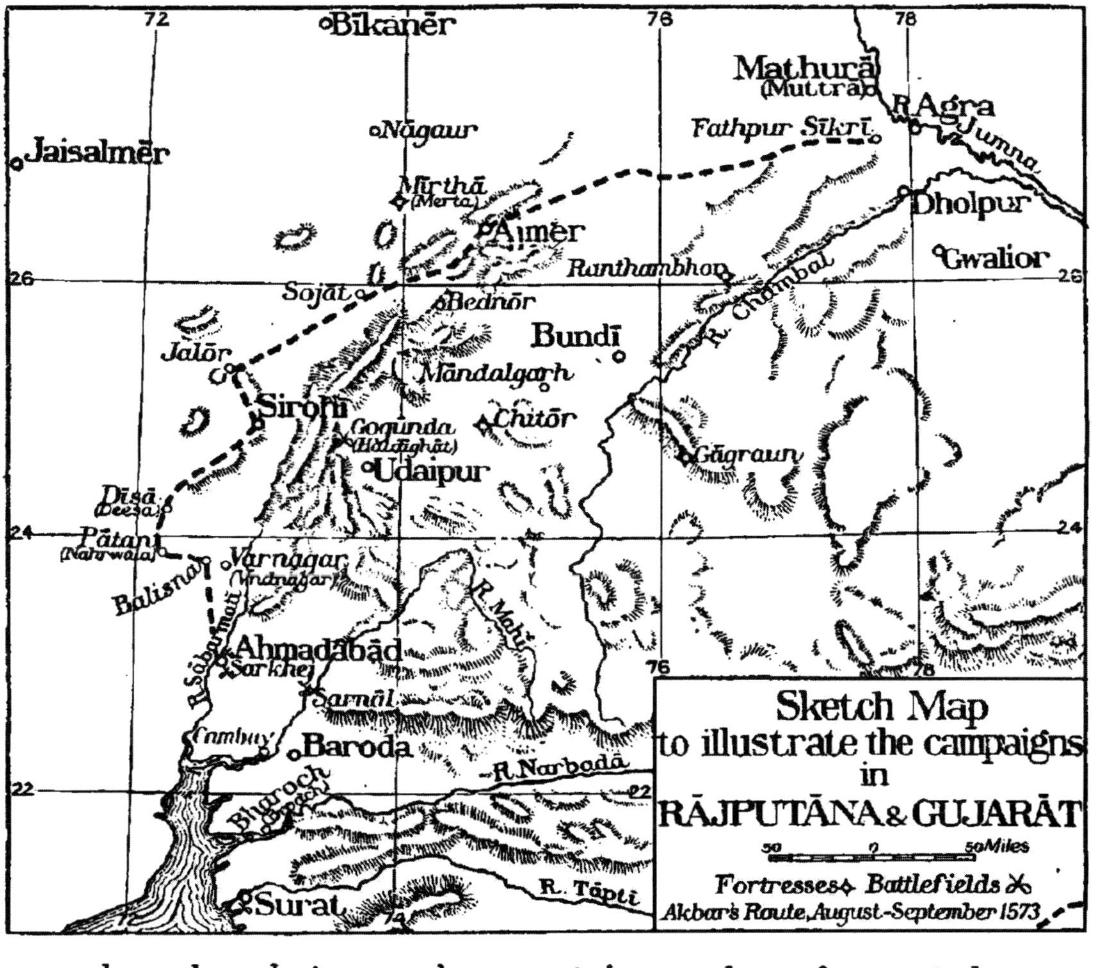

were bound each to supply a certain number of mounted men. The expedient principally relied on was known as the 'branding regulation', based on precedents set by Alāu-d dīn Khiljī and Shēr Shāh. Elaborate rules were laid down for branding every horse in the service of Government and thus making fraudulent

[1] The word 'settlement' in this technical sense is a translation of the Persian term *bandobast*. It includes all the processes necessary for the assessment of the 'land revenue' or crown rent, that is to say, the State's share of the produce of the cultivated land or its cash equivalent.

musters of cavalry more difficult. The measure met with so much covert opposition from influential persons whose interests were affected that the success attained was only partial.

Akbar sought to diminish the power of the fief-holders or *jāgīrdārs*, and to enhance the authority of the crown by 'converting *jāgīrs* into crown-lands (*khālsa*)', that is to say, by dividing the imperial territory into convenient jurisdictions under the direct administration of salaried officials. Fīrōz Shāh Tughlak had favoured the system of paying his officers by assigning to each a district, from which the assignee collected the land revenue and cesses which otherwise would have been paid to the State. Akbar perceived clearly that that system tended to increase the power of local magnates and predisposed them to rebellion, while being also injurious to the fiscal interest of the central Government. He was fond of money and always keen to increase his income. He therefore gave up the practice of assigning *jāgīrs* or fiefs, so far as possible, and preferred to appoint officials remunerated by definite salaries.

The consequent increase of officialdom, if it was to become an efficient instrument of government, involved the establishment of a bureaucracy or graded service of State officials. Akbar accordingly regularized the previously existing system of *mansabdārs*, or office-holders, and classified them in thirty-three grades. His arrangements will be described more particularly later. Here the fact is to be noted that all the above-mentioned measures of administrative and financial reform were worked out in the interval between the conquest of Gujarāt in 1573 and the invasion of Bengal in 1575. The regulations were further perfected in subsequent years.

Conquest of Bengal. Akbar needed no pretext to induce him to undertake the extension of his empire eastward and the subjugation of Bengal which long before had been subject to the Sultanate of Delhi. But even if he had been unwilling, the adventure was forced upon him by the rashness of Dāūd Khān, the young Afghan king of Bengal, who openly defied Akbar and believed himself to be more than a match for the imperial power. His father, Sulaimān Kararānī, had been careful to give formal recognition of the Pādshāh's suzerainty, while preserving his practical independence. In 1574 Akbar undertook the chastisement of the presumptuous prince. He voyaged down the rivers, and drove Dāūd from Patna and Hājīpur in the height of the rainy season, when Hindu custom forbade active operations. But Akbar cared for weather conditions as little as Alexander of Macedon had done, and insisted on the campaign being pressed, much against the inclination of his officers. He himself returned to Fathpur-Sīkrī. Dāūd was defeated early in 1575 at Tukarōī in the Balasore District. The battle would have been decisive and ended the war, but for the ill-judged lenity of old Munim Khān, the commander-in-chief, who granted easy terms and allowed Dāūd to recover strength. Another campaign thus became necessary, and Dāūd was not finally defeated and killed until July 1576, in a battle fought near Rājmahāl. From that date Bengal became an integral part of the empire.

Orissa was not annexed until 1592.

Defeat of Rānā Partāp Singh. In this year (1576), which saw the annexation of Bengal, Kunwar Mān Singh of Ambēr (Jaipur), whose sister by adoption was married to the emperor, inflicted a crushing defeat on the brave Rānā Partāp Singh of Mewār, the son of the craven Udai Singh. The battle was fought at the entrance of the Haldīghāt Pass, near the town of Gogūnda, and is spoken of indifferently by either name. The Rānā was driven to take refuge in remote fastnesses, and the strongholds of his kingdom passed into the hands of the imperialists. But before his death in 1597 he had recovered most of them. Ajmēr, Chitōr, and Māndalgarh always remained in possession of the Pādshāh's officers.

RĀNĀ PARTĀP SINGH.

The empire in 1576. The conquest of Bengal in 1576, twenty years after his accession, made Akbar master of all Hindostan, including the entire basins of the Indus and Ganges, excepting Sind on the lower course of the Indus, which did not come into his possession until many years later. He had thus become sovereign of the most valuable regions of India, extending from the Arabian Sea to the Bay of Bengal and from the Himālaya to the Narbadā; besides the semi-independent Kābul province. The territories under his rule, with their huge population, fertile soil, numerous manufactures, and vast commerce, both internal and sea-borne, constituted even then an empire richer probably than any other in the world. The subsequent additions to his dominions, comprising Kashmīr, Orissa, Sind, Kandahār, Khāndēsh, and a portion of the Deccan, with the complete absorption of the Kābul province, merely rounded off the compact empire which had been gradually acquired and consolidated in the first twenty years of his reign.

The 'House of Worship'. From 1575 Akbar ordinarily left the command of armies in the field to his trusted officers, Mān Singh, Todar Mall, Abdurrahīm, or others. Early in that year, when he returned from Patna, he busied himself with building in the gardens of the palace at Fathpur-Sīkrī near the mosque a handsome edifice called the House of Worship (*'Ibādat Khāna*) to be used as a debating-hall for the discussion of questions of religion and theology in which he was deeply interested. During the first three years, until 1578 or 1579, the discussions were limited to the various schools of Muslim theology. Even then they were sometimes embittered. From 1579 to 1582, when the debates came to an end, representatives of other religions were admitted and the disputants met in the private apartments of the palace. The site of the House of Worship has been utterly forgotten and no trace of the building, which was large and highly decorated, has been discovered. The probability is that Akbar pulled it down when he had no longer any use for it.

GOLD COINS OF AKBAR.

More reforms. The emperor during the years 1575 and 1576 also devoted much attention to the development of his administrative reforms, both those already mentioned and others. The record department was organized, and a record room was built at Fathpur-Sīkrī. The grading of the *mansabdārs* was made more systematic, and a plan was devised for dividing the older provinces into artificial districts each yielding a quarter of a million of rupees in land revenue. That plan was a failure and the Government soon reverted to the use of the recognized sub-districts called *parganas*.

The mint was reorganized in 1577–8, and placed in charge of the celebrated artist, Abdu-s Samad, who had been Akbar's drawing-master twenty years earlier. The mint was a well-managed department, and Akbar's coinage was both abundant in quantity and excellent in quality.

The First Jesuit Mission. Akbar became personally acquainted with European Christians for the first time in 1572, when he met certain Portuguese merchants at Cambay. In the next year, 1573, he extended his intercourse with the foreigners at Surat and adjusted terms of peace with Antonio Cabral, the envoy from the Viceroy at Goa. In 1576 and 1577 the emperor obtained some imperfect knowledge of the Christian religion from Father Julian Pereira, Vicar-General in Bengal, and from other sources, but only sufficient to make him eager to attain more accurate information. Antonio Cabral, who again visited him at the capital in 1578, not being qualified to answer all the imperial inquiries, Akbar resolved to obtain from Goa theological experts who should be able to resolve his doubt and satisfy his intense curiosity. In September 1579, accordingly, he dispatched to the authorities at Goa a letter begging them to send two learned priests capable of instructing him in the doctrines of the Gospels. He assured his expected guests of the most honourable reception and effectual protection.

The church authorities at Goa eagerly accepted the invitation, which seemed to open up a prospect of converting the emperor to Christianity, and with him his court and people.

The two principal missionaries selected, Father Ridolfo Aquaviva and Father Antonio Monserrate, both Jesuits or members of the Society of Jesus, were remarkable men, highly qualified for their task in different ways. Aquaviva won respect by a life of extreme asceticism. Monserrate, a person of much learning, was directed to prepare a history of the mission; and obeyed the command by writing an excellent Latin treatise, which ranks as one of the principal authorities for the reign of Akbar. The priests travelled from Damān and Surat through Khāndēsh, the wild Bhīl country, Mālwā, Narwar, Gwālior, and Dhōlpur to Fathpur-Sīkrī, where they arrived on February 28 (o.s.), 1580, and were received with extraordinary honour. The emperor's second son, Prince Murād, then about ten years of age, was made over to Father Monserrate for instruction in the Portuguese language and Christian morals.

The ' Infallibility Decree '. When Akbar returned triumphant from Gujarāt in 1573, a learned, although rather heretical, Muslim theologian named Shaikh Mubārak greeted him by expressing the hope that the Pādshāh might become the spiritual as well as the temporal head of his people—in fact, Pope as well as King. At the time Akbar could not take action on the suggestion, but he never lost sight of the idea. In 1579 he felt free to give practical effect to the theologian's hint. Shaikh Mubārak prepared a formal document, which may be conveniently called the Infallibility Decree, authorizing the emperor to decide with binding authority any question concerning the Muslim religion, provided that the ruling should be in accordance with some verse of the Koran. The measure professed to be ' for the glory of God and the propagation of the Islām '. It had no connexion with any other religion. The decree, which was forced upon the acceptance of the Ulamā, or Muhammadan doctors of divinity, obviously rendered superfluous the discussions in the House of Worship, which ceased accordingly. The building, as already observed, probably was then destroyed.

A little earlier in the same year (1579) Akbar had startled and offended religious people by displacing the regular preacher at the mosque, and himself mounting the pulpit, where he recited verses composed by Faizī, the elder son of Shaikh Mubārak. About the same time he began to show many indications that he had lost faith in the creed of the Prophet of Mecca. The Jesuits, when coming up from the coast at the beginning of 1580, were informed that the emperor had even forbidden the use of the name of Muhammad in the public prayers.

Muslim alarm and revolt. The excessive favour shown by the sovereign to his Jesuit visitors, his obvious lack of faith in Islām, and his partial compliance with the ritual of Parsees and Jains, who shared the royal condescension along with the Christian priests, grievously alarmed his Musalmān subjects and produced important political effects.

The Bengal rebellion. The Musalmān chiefs in Bengal and Bihār, mostly of Afghan origin, were specially alarmed by Akbar's conduct, which was interpreted, and not without reason, as an attack upon the Muhammadan religion. They were also irritated by his administrative measures as carried out with considerable harshness by his officers, and for those reasons determined on rebellion. The Kāzī of Jaunpur boldly issued a formal ruling, affirming the lawfulness of rebellion against Akbar as an apostate, an act of high treason for which he paid with his life.

The rebellion broke out in January 1580, and continued for several years. The rebels aimed at replacing Akbar by his orthodox half-brother Muhammad Hakīm of Kābul, who supported their movement by an invasion of the Panjāb. But the Bengal insurgents were separated from their ally by hundreds of miles, and the emperor rightly judged that they might be left to his officers, who would dispose of the trouble in time, as they did.

The expedition to Kābul. He resolved to meet in person the graver danger threatened from Kābul. He equipped an overwhelming force with the utmost care, and marched from the capital in February 1581. Muhammad Hakīm, a feeble, drunken creature, fled from the Panjāb, and offered little resistance to the advance of Akbar, who entered Kābul in August. His brother kept out of the way and never met him. The emperor was back safely in his capital on December 1. He permitted Muhammad Hakīm to remain as ruler of the Kābul territory until his death from drink in 1585, when his territories passed under the direct government of the Pādshāh.

A critical year. The year 1581 was the most critical in the reign of Akbar, if his early struggles be omitted from consideration. When he marched from Fathpur-Sīkrī in February, nearly all the influential Muhammadans were opposed to him, subtle traitors surrounded his person, and the eastern provinces were in the possession of rebels. Defeat by Muhammad Hakīm would have involved the loss of everything—life included. Akbar took no chances. He cowed the traitors by one terrible execution, the solemn and deserved hanging of Khwāja Shāh Mansūr, his Finance Minister, and overawed his brother by a display of irresistible force. We are fortunate enough to possess an accurate detailed narrative of the Kābul campaign, written by Father Monserrate, tutor of Prince Murād, who accompanied his pupil and the emperor.

When Akbar came home his demeanour showed that he had been freed from a great terror, and that he now felt himself thoroughly secure for the first time in his life. From the beginning of 1582 nobody dared to oppose him. He could do literally what he pleased. He enjoyed and used that liberty to the end of his life twenty-three years later.

The Dīn Ilāhī. He promptly took advantage of his freedom by publicly showing his contempt and dislike for the Muhammadan religion, and by formally promulgating a new political creed of his own, adherence to which involved the solemn renunciation of Islām. The new religion, dubbed the Divine Monotheism (*Tauhīd Ilāhī*) or Divine Religion (*Dīn Ilāhī*), rejected wholly the claims of Muhammad to be an inspired prophet, and practically replaced him by the emperor. Abu-l Fazl, Shaikh Mubārak's younger son, who had been introduced at court in 1574, became the high priest of the new creed, and the stage manager of the rather ridiculous initiation ceremonies. Many time-serving courtiers professed to become Akbar's disciples, surrendering to him life, property, honour, and religion, as the vows required, but the so-called religion never enlisted any considerable following, and it may well be doubted if a single person ever honestly believed in it. Abu-l Fazl, a man of immense learning and endowed with a singularly powerful intellect, certainly was far too intelligent to believe in his master's silly invention. But he was base enough to play the hypocrite's part and reap no small profit thereby, as the confidential secretary and adviser of the sovereign. Akbar's freak in professing to invent a new eclectic religion, compounded out of selections from several of the old religions, has received far more attention from most European historians than it deserves on its merits.

Akbar's rejection of Islām. From 1582, when the new religion was solemnly promulgated at a council, and indeed from a date considerably earlier, Akbar was not a Muhammadan, although on occasion he performed acts of conformity from motives of policy. He told Monserrate distinctly early in 1582 that he was not a Muslim, and that he paid no heed to the *kalima*, or Muhammadan formula of the faith. In that year and subsequent years he issued a stream of regulations openly hostile to Islām and inculcating practices learned from the Parsee, Hindu, and Jain teachers whom he received with marked favour and to whom he listened with profound attention. He appeared in public with

Hindu sectarian marks on his forehead,[1] while also showing reverence for the Virgin Mary, the Gospels, and the symbols of the Christian faith. His conduct at different times justified Christians, Hindus, Jains, and Parsees in severally claiming him as one of themselves. But his heart was never really touched by any doctrine, and he died as he had lived for many years, a man whose religion nobody could name. The authors who affirm that he formally professed Islām on his death-bed appear to be mistaken.

Fantastic ordinances. A few out of many fantastic ordinances may be mentioned. Regulations aimed at Islām, and amounting along with others to an irritating persecution of that religion, wholly inconsistent with the principle of universal toleration, included the following: No child was to be given the name of Muhammad, and if he had already received it the name must be changed. The erection of new and the repair of old mosques were prohibited. The *sijdah*, or prostration, hitherto reserved for divine worship, was declared to be the due of the sovereign. The study of Arabic, Muhammadan law, or commentaries on the Koran was discouraged, and even the use of the specially Arabic letters in the alphabet was forbidden.

Hindu prejudices were humoured by the prohibition of beef, garlic, and onions as food.

Stringent restrictions on the use of flesh meat imposed by a series of enactments seem to have been mainly due to Jain influence.

The worship of the sun, fire, and light, with sundry ritual observances enforced at court, were chiefly the result of Parsee teaching. Akbar's mode of life, on the whole, ceased to be that of a Muslim, and constantly approached the Hindu ideal of *dharma*, as modified by a Zoroastrian or Parsee tinge.

Akbar's audacity. The prestige resulting from the defeat of his brother in 1581, the suppression of the Bengal and Bihār rebellions, and the fate suffered by opponents of his policy enabled Akbar to do all the strange things mentioned above, besides many others equally startling, and yet to escape assassination or even any open display of disaffection.

If the British Government attempted such measures it could not last a week. Akbar must have possessed a wonderful personal magnetism to have ventured on legislation systematically outraging the sentiments and beliefs of the Muslim community, which had been the ruling class during all previous reigns since the Muhammadan conquest. The necessary backing of force, or the threat of force, which stood behind the audacious imperial policy, was supplied by the Rājpūt contingents under the command of the Rājās of Āmbēr (Jaipur), Mārwār (Jodhpur), and other states. But Akbar never was reduced to the necessity of relying wholly on Hindu support. Many Musalmān nobles continued to serve him to the end, whether they liked his proceedings or not.

Result of forty years' war. Whatever might be his religious

[1] The Jaipur portrait shows him wearing those marks.

vagaries Akbar never forgot his worldly ambitions. He secured the important strategical position at the confluence of the Ganges and Jumna by building the Allahabad fort in 1583. Three years later, in 1586, he made war on Kashmīr and annexed the country, simply because the local sultan desired to preserve his independence and presumed to withhold complete submission to the master of Hindostan. Southern Sind was similarly absorbed in 1591; Orissa was conquered by Mān Singh in 1592; Balōchistan, with the coast region of Makrān, was added to the empire in 1594; and Kandahār was surrendered by its Persian governor a year later.

Thus, in 1596, every part of India to the north of the Narbadā, besides the vast territories of Kābul, Ghaznī, and Kandahār, with their dependencies, acknowledged the might of Akbar. No man within that enormous area presumed to call himself independent, unless an exception be made in favour of certain tribes on the frontiers and in the hills. In 1586 the Yūsufzī and allied tribes of the north-western frontier succeeded in defeating one of Akbar's armies and killing Rājā Bīrbal, one of his dearest and most intimate friends. The emperor could afford to overlook such minor military mishaps, and might well feel proud of the results gained by forty years of war.

Ambitious projects. The soaring ambition of Akbar was not bounded by the Narbadā, or even by the limits of India and Afghanistan. He avowed his hopes both of regaining the ancient dominions of his ancestors in Central Asia beyond the Oxus, and of bringing under his control all the sultanates of the Deccan. Moreover, he ardently desired to expel the Portuguese from his province of Gujarāt, and vainly supposed that he could do so without the help of a fleet. But he never succeeded even in coming near to an attempt on Transoxiana, and his attacks on the Portuguese settlements were complete failures. His extremely restricted conquests in the Deccan fell far short of his expectation. Before the campaign in the Deccan is described it will be convenient to revert to Akbar's curious relations with Christianity and more especially with the Jesuit missionaries.

Akbar and the Jesuits. The first Jesuit mission of Aquaviva and Monserrate ended in 1583 with the withdrawal of Aquaviva. The hopes of Akbar's conversion which had been entertained at Goa were grievously disappointed. A second mission sent in 1590 at the emperor's urgent request was recalled in 1592, having effected nothing. The third mission, also dispatched in compliance with a pressing invitation, arrived in 1595 at Lahore where the court then resided, and became a more or less permanent institution, not without its effect on secular politics. The leading members were Fathers Jerome Xavier and Emmanuel Pinheiro. Their letters, of which many have been printed, are first-class authorities for the latter part of Akbar's reign. The missionaries, although they did not succeed in converting either the sovereign or his nobles, or indeed in making many converts of any kind won from

Akbar the right to make converts if they could, and obtained from him extraordinary privileges. Both he and his son Prince Salīm professed extravagant veneration for the Virgin Mary and for Christian images. It is clear that the excessive attention lavished on the priests was not the outcome of genuine religious fervour, but was dictated chiefly by the desire to secure Portuguese military help. Akbar in 1600 made special efforts to obtain the loan of the foreigners' superior ordnance for the siege of Asīrgarh, which he could not breach with his own guns ; while the prince, meditating rebellion, and in reality indifferent to religion, was equally eager to enlist their aid against his father. In 1601 Akbar sent a final embassy to Goa without any pretence of seeking religious instruction, but got no satisfaction from the wily Goanese authorities, who understood the game perfectly. The Jesuits on their part combined patriotic politics with missionary zeal and acted as unofficial agents of the Portuguese Government, or rather of the Government of Spain, with which Portugal was then united.[1]

An Englishman named John Mildenhall, who bore a letter from Queen Elizabeth, asking for trading facilities equal to those granted to the Portuguese, visited Akbar in the last year of his life, and did his best to oppose the Jesuits with their own weapons of intrigue and bribery.

Famine. A terrible famine, as bad as any recorded in the long list of Indian famines, desolated the whole of Hindostan or northern India and Kashmīr for three or four years from 1595 to 1598. The historians barely notice the calamity, the fullest description being that recorded by a minor author in these few words :

> 'A kind of plague also added to the horrors of this period, and depopulated whole houses and cities, to say nothing of hamlets and villages. In consequence of the dearth of grain and the necessities of ravenous hunger, men ate their own kind. The streets and roads were blocked up with dead bodies, and no assistance could be rendered for their removal.'

Some slight relief measures were adopted, but even the proverbial good fortune of Akbar could not either prevent or remedy the effects of long continued failure of rain.

The Deccan campaign. Akbar attempted by means of diplomatic missions to induce the rulers of Khāndēsh in the valley of the Taptī, and of the more distant sultanates of Ahmadnagar (including Berar), Golkonda, and Bījāpur, to formally recognize his suzerainty and consent to pay tribute. He did not trouble himself about the small principality of Bīdar, which continued to exist until some years after his death. The imperial envoys obtained no substantial success except in Khāndēsh, which promised obedience. The other states politely evaded Akbar's demands. He therefore determined on war, not to redress any injury or abate any grievance, but simply in order to enforce submission to his will.

[1] The union of the crowns of Portugal and Spain was effected in 1580, and lasted until December 1640.

Operations, which began in 1593, were impeded by internal dissensions on both sides. The imperialist generals, Prince Murād, and Abdurrahīm, the Khān Khānān, could not agree, while the states of the Deccan continued to quarrel among themselves.

A gallant princess, named Chānd Bībī, defended the city of Ahmadnagar with valour equal to that shown by Rānī Durgāvatī in Gondwānā thirty years earlier, but in 1596 was constrained to accept a treaty by which the province of Berar was ceded to the emperor. War soon broke out again, which was terminated in August 1600 by the death of Chānd Bībī and the fall of Ahmadnagar.

Akbar goes south. Meantime, the Sultán of Khāndēsh, Mīrān Bahādur Shāh, had repented of his submission and resolved to fight, relying on the strength of his fortress of Asīrgarh, which was defended by renegade Portuguese gunners.

Akbar, who had been detained in the Panjāb for thirteen years on account of his fear of an invasion by the Uzbegs, was relieved from that anxiety by the death early in 1598 of Abdullah Khān Uzbeg, the able ruler of Transoxiana. He perceived that the effective prosecution of the Deccan campaign was hopeless without his personal supervision. Accordingly, he marched from Lahore to Agra late in 1598, and in July of the following year was able to resume his advance southwards. He placed Prince Salīm in charge of the capital and Ajmēr with orders to complete the subjugation of the Rānā of Mewār. But the prince, who already meditated rebellion, ignored his father's commands, so that the Rānā was left in peace.

Meantime, in May 1599, Prince Murād had died of delirium tremens in the Deccan, and so had removed one competitor from Salīm's path. No rival now remained except Dāniyāl, a drunken sot.

About the middle of 1599 Akbar crossed the Narbadā, and occupied Burhānpur, the capital of Khāndēsh, without opposition. He then proceeded to make arrangements for the investment and siege of Asīrgarh, which was only a few miles distant from Burhānpur and could not be left in enemy hands. It was one of the strongest fortresses in the world at that date, and so amply furnished with water, provisions, guns, and munitions that its defenders might reasonably expect to hold out for years.

Siege of Asīrgarh. The emperor soon found that the task which he had set himself was beyond his military powers. His artillery was unable to breach the walls and he failed to obtain Portuguese guns. After the siege had gone on for about six months, from February to August 1600, he resolved to try treachery. He inveigled Bahādur Shāh into his camp for the purpose of negotiation, swearing by his own head that the king would be allowed to return in safety. But Akbar, who was pressed for time, shamelessly violated his oath and detained Bahādur Shāh, hoping that the garrison would surrender after the usual Indian fashion when deprived of their leader. He forgot the Portuguese gunners, who gallantly maintained the defence. The siege dragged on until January 17 (o.s.), 1601, when the gates were opened by golden keys, or, in other words, Akbar corrupted the Khāndēsh officers by heavy payments. That is the true story of the fall of Asīrgarh, which has been disgracefully falsified by Abu-l Fazl and the other official historians. The place was absolutely impregnable against Akbar's means of offence, and could not be reduced by investment. But he was unable to wait, because Prince Salīm had already begun his rebellion and it was indispensable that his father should return to the capital. Asīrgarh, thus shamefully won by perfidy and bribery, was the last conquest of Akbar, whose hitherto unbroken good fortune no longer attended him. The remaining years of his life were rendered miserable by the treachery of his eldest son, the child of so many prayers, by the scandalous death of Prince Dāniyāl, and other sorrows upon sorrows.

Three new provinces. The emperor made all possible haste in organizing the administration of the newly acquired territories, which were formally constituted as three Sūbas or provinces, namely, Ahmadnagar, Berar, and Khāndēsh. But the Ahmadnagar Sūba had little more than a formal existence, because the greater part of the kingdom remained in the hands of a member of the local royal family. Prince Dāniyāl was appointed Viceroy of southern and western India—that is to say, of the three new Sūbas, with Mālwā and Gujarāt. Akbar arrived at Agra in 1601, probably in May.

Submission of Prince Salīm. Prince Salīm continued in open rebellion, holding court as a king at Allahabad. In August 1602 he inflicted a terrible blow upon his father's feelings by hiring a robber chief named Bīr Singh Bundēla, to murder Akbar's trusted friend and counsellor, Abu-l Fazl, whom the prince hated and feared. A temporary and insincere reconciliation between father and son was patched up by Salīma Bēgam in 1603. But no real peace was possible until after the death of Prince Dāniyāl, which occurred in April 1604, when he died from the effects of drink, like his brother Murād. Salīm being then the only son left, Akbar became really anxious to arrange terms with him. The one other possible successor was Salīm's son, Prince Khusrū, a popular and amiable youth, whose claims were favoured by Rājā Mān Singh and Azīz Kokā.

In November 1604 Salīm was persuaded to come to court, probably under threats that, if he refused, Khusrū would be declared heir apparent. His father received him with seeming cordiality. He then drew him suddenly into an inner apartment, slapped him soundly in the face, and confined him in a bathroom under the charge of a physician and two servants, as if he were a lunatic requiring medical treatment. After a short time, the length of which is variously stated, Akbar released his son, restored him to favour, made him Viceroy of the provinces to which Dāniyāl had been appointed, and allowed him to reside at Agra as the acknowledged heir apparent.

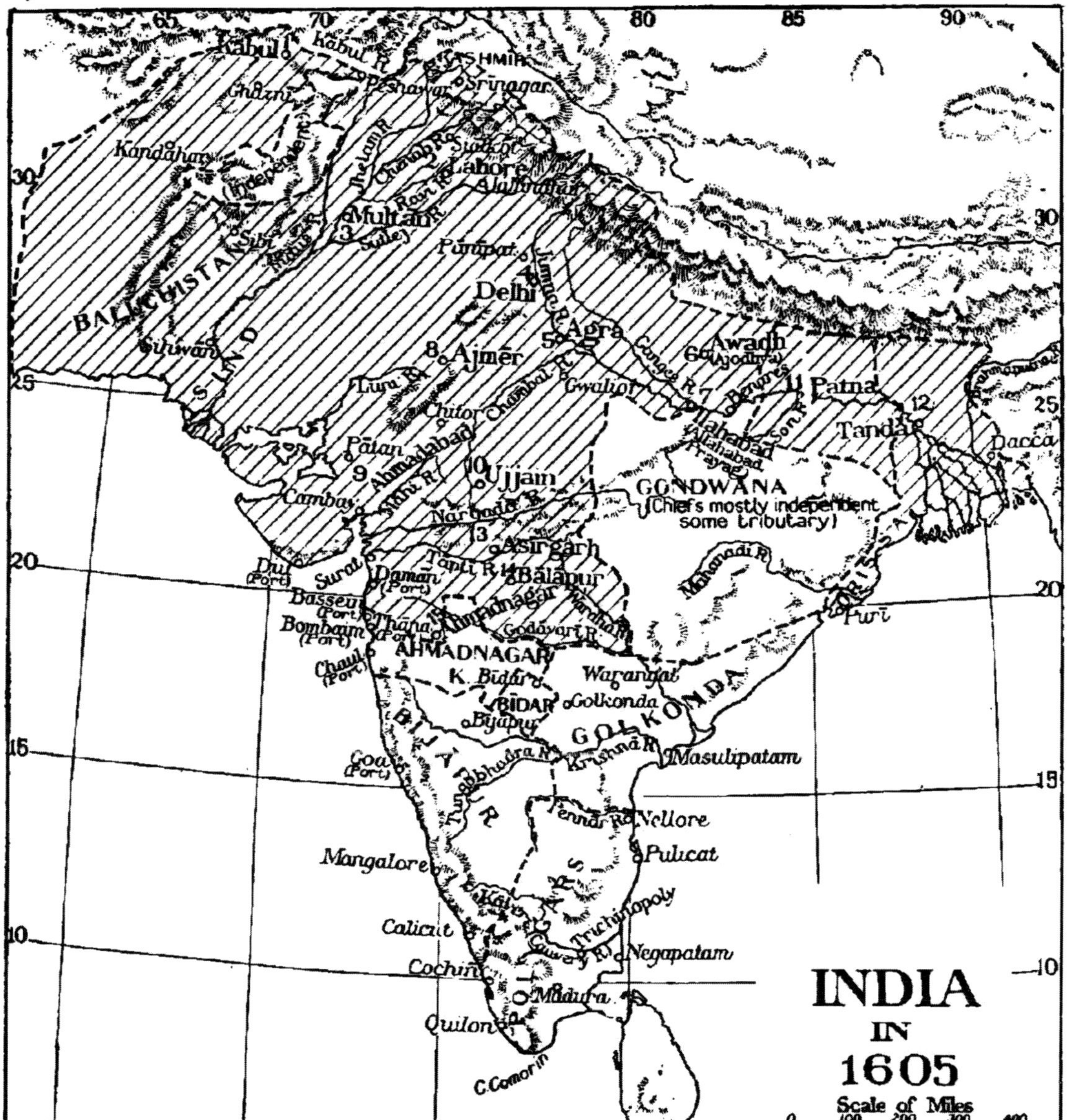

THE SŪBAS.

(1) Kābul ; (2) Lahore (Panjāb), including Kashmīr ; (3) Multān, including Sind ; (4) Delhi ; (5) Agra ; (6) Awadh (Oudh) ; (7) Allahabad ; (8) Ajmēr ; (9) Ahmadābād (Gujarāt) ; (10) Mālwā ; (11) Bihār ; (12) Bengal, including Orissa ; (13) Khāndēsh ; (14) Berar (Birār) ; (15) Ahmadnagar.

The prince was cowed by his father's rough handling and gave no further trouble.

Death of Akbar. In September 1605 Akbar became ill with severe diarrhoea or dysentery, which the physicians failed to cure. While on his death-bed and unable to speak he received Salīm and indicated by unmistakable gestures that he desired his succession. The emperor passed away in silence, after midnight, early on Thursday morning, January 17 (O.S.=27 N.S., and Wednesday night by Muhammadan reckoning). Even before his death rumours that he had been poisoned were current. Those rumours were repeated by many early authors after his decease. The symptoms of Akbar's fatal illness, so far as recorded, are consistent with the administration of a secret irritant poison, such as diamond dust, but the evidence is not sufficient to permit of a definite judgement on the question whether or not he died a natural death. He was buried at Sikandara near Agra in the mausoleum which he had begun, and which his successor rebuilt to a fresh design. His funeral was hurried and poorly attended. 'Thus', observes Du Jarric, the eminent Jesuit historian, 'does the world treat those from whom it expects no good and fears no evil. That was the end of the life and reign of King Akbar.'

Desecration of Akbar's grave. Unhappily, he was not allowed to rest in peace. The Jāts of the neighbourhood, whose revolt began in 1688 during the absence of Aurangzēb in the Deccan, attacked the mausoleum in 1691, breaking in the massive bronze gates, tearing away the costly ornaments, and destroying everything which they could not carry off. Their wrath against their Mogul oppressors led them to a still more shocking outrage. 'Dragging out the bones of Akbar, they threw them into the fire and burnt them.'

Succession of Salīm. The intrigues of Rājā Mān Singh and Azīz Kokā to set aside Prince Salīm and raise his son Prince Khusrū to the throne having failed, largely owing to Rājpūt resistance, Prince Salīm was allowed to take his father's place without further opposition.

Akbar's personal qualities. Akbar was of middle stature, probably about five feet seven inches in height, compactly built, and possessed of immense bodily strength, which he enjoyed using. His complexion was dark rather than fair, and his voice was loud. He looked every inch a king, and observers were specially impressed by his eyes, which have been vividly described by a Jesuit friend as 'vibrant like the sea in sunshine'. His naturally hot temper, usually kept under strict control, blazed out in wrath at times, as when he felled Adham Khān, or ordered an unlucky lamplighter to be thrown from the battlements because he had fallen asleep when on duty. His storms of passion subsided as suddenly as they arose, leaving no bitterness behind them. His manners were charming, and his sympathetic condescension to humble folk won all hearts. He was, as Bartoli neatly says, 'great with the great, and lowly with the lowly'. He honestly desired to do justice, and did it to the best of his ability in the stern fashion of his times, taking precautions against the too hasty execution of his sentences. Cruelty for its own sake gave him no pleasure, but he occasionally sanctioned barbarous punishments which shock the modern reader.

Intellectually, he was a man of boundless curiosity, and endowed with extraordinary versatility of mind. People said that there was nothing that he knew not how to do, and he loved doing mechanical work in wood or metal with his own hands. The founding of cannon and the manufacture of matchlocks specially interested him. His mechanical tastes and his habits of minute observation gave him a singular mastery over the details of departmental administration, which he combined happily with exceptional breadth of view. Every department, whether of his vast household or of the imperial government, came constantly under his watchful eye, and he spared himself no labour. He rarely slept more than three hours at a time and seemed to be almost incapable of fatigue.

AKBAR.

Formal illiteracy. Although when a boy he had steadily refused to learn his lessons, and was the despair of successive tutors, so that to the end of his days he could not decipher a written word or sign his own name, he was, nevertheless, well-read and well-informed in many subjects, after an unsystematic fashion. He loved to have books of history, theology, poetry, and other kinds read to him, and his prodigious memory enabled him to learn through the ear more than an ordinary man could learn through the eye. He was thus able to take an active part in the discussion of literary and abstruse subjects with such skill that the listener could hardly believe him to be illiterate in the formal sense. His special taste was for endless debates on the merits of rival religions, which he examined from a strangely detached point of view.

Religious history. Akbar was brought up as a Sunnī Musalmān, and, as he himself confessed, gladly persecuted heretics during the early years of his reign. Shaikh Mubārak, father of Faizī and Abu-l Fazl, then narrowly escaped execution. But it is probable that Akbar even in boyhood was never thoroughly orthodox. One of his tutors introduced him to the works of the Persian Sūfī mystics, and he evinced at an early age a strong liking for the society of Hindu holy men, whose speculations were much akin to those of the Sūfīs. Akbar was a mystic all his life, and on several occasions saw visions which seemed to bring

AKBAR ON THRONE.

him into direct communion with the Unknown God. He suffered from some form of epileptic disease, which may be regarded as the physical explanation of many of his peculiarities, including the melancholy which constantly oppressed him, and constrained him to seek relief in an unceasing round of diversions.

His religious history may be divided into three periods. Until 1575, or possibly until 1578, he was a convinced Musalmān of the Sunnī sect, regular in his observance of the prescribed ritual, a zealous builder of mosques, and a constant suppliant at the tombs of the saints. His last recorded mosque-building was the noble Buland Darwāza or Lofty Portal at Fathpur-Sīkrī erected in 1575–6. He continued to attend public worship regularly until 1578, and made his last pilgrimage to the shrine at Ajmēr in 1579. His substantial orthodoxy in the eyes of the world was not compromised by his leaning to Sūfī mysticism, which he shared with many learned doctors of the law.

From 1579, the year in which he ascended the pulpit and issued the Infallibility Decree, his belief in Islām was weak and shaky. By the beginning of 1582, after his victorious return from Kābul, that belief had wholly disappeared. He tried then the hopeless experiment of inventing a new religion to suit the whole empire, desiring that Hindus and Musalmāns should worship in unison the One God, recognizing the Pādshāh as His vicegerent on earth and the authorized exponent of His will.

The gradual changes in Akbar's religious views, largely brought about by his own thinking over the Sūfī studies of his boyhood and the diversity of creeds among his people, were furthered by the suggestions of Shaikh Mubārak, and the later confidential intercourse with the Shaikh's sons, Faizī and Abu-l Fazl, which began about 1575. Other influences co-operated with their teaching. Jains, Parsees, Hindus of various kinds, and Christians all took their share in modifying the opinions of the emperor and determining the lines of his policy.[1]

Toleration in theory and practice. The avowed principle of both Abu-l Fazl and Akbar was universal toleration (*sulh-i kul*). During the latter half of the reign that principle was fully applied in favour of Hindus, Christians, Jains, and Parsees, who enjoyed full liberty both of conscience and of public worship. But it was cynically violated in respect of Musalmāns, who were subjected to many acts of outrage of their feelings and of irritating persecution. Examples have been given above, and many more are on record. That failure of Akbar to act up to his own boasted principles is the principal blot on his public character to my mind.

Treatment of Hindus. Akbar's new policy in relation to his Hindu subjects was not determined mainly by his personal fancies or beliefs in matters of religion. At an early age he perceived

[1] Neither Akbar nor Abu-l Fazl ever enjoyed an opportunity of meeting learned Buddhists. The statements made in several books that Buddhists joined in the debates on religion are erroneous.

the political necessity that the Pādshāh should be the impartial sovereign of all his subjects, irrespective of creed. That sound political instinct determined his action as quite a young man in abolishing the *jizya* and pilgrim dues and in marrying Hindu princesses. Those measures were taken while he was still a sincere practising Muslim. Marriages between a Muhammadan king and the daughters of Hindu Rājās were not a novelty. Several of the Deccan Sultans had formed such alliances, which were not unknown at Delhi; but Akbar contracted his marriages in a different spirit, and accepted his Hindu male connexions as members of the royal family. No pressure was put on the princes of Ambēr, Mārwār, or Bīkanēr to adopt Islām, and they were freely entrusted with the highest military commands and the most responsible administrative offices. That was an entirely new departure, due to Akbar himself, not to Abu-l Fazl or another. The policy afforded the strongest support to the throne in the reigns of Akbar and his son, and continued to bear fruit even in the reigns of his grandson, Shāhjahān, and his great-grandson, Aurangzēb. But Aurangzēb's ill-judged policy of worrying Hindus gradually estranged the Rājpūt chieftains and largely contributed to the rapid dissolution of the empire which occurred after his death.

The Hindu queens, who were given Muslim titles and received Muslim burial, probably adopted Muhammadan modes of life to some extent, but contemporary pictures prove that they were allowed to practise their own religious rites inside the palace.[1] No doubt their society must have had some effect upon Akbar's religious opinions and practice.

Administration. The organization of the government undoubtedly was immensely improved by Akbar, who was the real founder of the Mogul empire. The autocracy or absolute power of the Pādshāh remained unshaken, whatever administrative arrangements might be made, and the merits of the government depended mainly on the character of the supreme ruler. Akbar's policy aimed at the enhancement of his personal authority and revenue. He therefore organized a tolerably efficient official service and developed an improved system for the assessment and collection of the revenue, with the help of Rājā Todar Mall, who, I think, was on the whole the ablest and most upright of the great imperial officers.

The administration was framed on military lines. The governor of a province, the Sūbadār, Nawāb Nāzim, &c., of later times, is called Sīpāhsālār, or commander-in-chief, in the *Āīn-i Akbarī*. He maintained a court modelled on that of his sovereign, and possessed practically full powers so long as he retained office. Subject to his liability to recall he was an absolute autocrat. The administrative officials, who exercised general powers in addition to their military duties, were called *manṣabdārs*, as in Persia, the word simply meaning 'office-holder'. The *mansabdārs* were divided into thirty-three classes, each member of each class

[1] *H. F. A.*, p. 332.

being supposed to furnish a certain number of cavalry to the imperial army. The three highest grades, 'commanders' of from 7,000 to 10,000, were ordinarily reserved for the princes. The other 'commands' or *mansabs* ranged from 10 to 5,000. But the numbers used for grading purposes did not agree with the actual facts. A 'commander of 5,000', for instance, might not be required to furnish more than 1,000 or 2,000 horsemen. The rules on those matters are too complicated for exposition in this place. The higher *mansabdārs* drew enormous salaries. Akbar, as already observed, preferred to pay his local officers by salaries rather than by assignments of territory and of the State revenue derivable from it. The permanent regular army was very small. The greater part of the imperial forces consisted of contingents furnished by the Rājās and *mansabdārs*, each under its own chief.

Every considerable official exercised general administrative and judicial powers, especially in criminal cases. Civil disputes ordinarily were left to the Kāzīs, to be settled under Koranic law. No regular judicial service existed, except in so far as the Kāzīs formed such, and each governor or other person in authority did what he pleased, subject to the risk of imperial displeasure. No code existed, and no written judgements were delivered. Officers were instructed to pay little heed to witnesses or oaths, and to rely rather on their own discernment and knowledge of human nature. Even capital punishment was inflicted at discretion, and might assume any form. No horror in the way of penalty could be considered illegal.

Revenue system. Rājā Todar Mall, following the precedent set by Shēr Shāh, carried out in many parts of the empire an improved system of 'settlement', or assessment of the land revenue, based on fairly accurate measurement and a classification of the kind of soil, whether newly broken waste, or old tillage, combined with consideration of the crop grown and the mean prevailing prices. He thus increased the imperial revenue and gave the peasant a certain amount of security. The revenue was collected directly from the individual cultivator, so far as possible. In modern technical language the 'settlement was ryotwar'. But the assessment was severe. Akbar, who preferred cash rents, took the equivalent of one-third of the gross produce instead of the one-sixth prescribed by the Hindu scriptures. The cultivators were supposed to be compensated by the abolition of a crowd of cesses. But we do not know how far the orders for such abolition were acted on, and have hardly any information concerning the actual working of Todar Mall's revenue system in the days of Akbar. The comparative peace which the imperial arms assured must have tended to create a considerable amount of agricultural prosperity. Trade certainly was brisk, and in ordinary years food was extraordinarily cheap.

Famines. Famines, however, occurred. We hear of several. The one of 1555–6 at the beginning of the reign was extremely severe; and that of 1595–8, when Akbar's career of conquest was almost completed, seems to have been one of the worst in the long list of Indian famines. It lasted for three or four years, and must have caused serious effects, of which there is no record.

Akbar's friends. Akbar, after his early years, chose his friends and great officers from among both Hindus and Muhammadans, with a leaning in favour of the former.

His most intimate Muslim friends were the brothers Faizī and Abu-l Fazl, sons of Shaikh Mubārak. Faizī, who cared little for wealth or office, devoted himself chiefly to literary pursuits. Abu-l Fazl, a man of profound learning, untiring industry, and commanding intellect, resembled Francis Bacon, his junior contemporary, in combining the parts of scholar, author, courtier, and man of affairs. He was a faithful servant of Akbar, 'the King's Jonathan', as the Jesuits called him, and was for many years his confidential secretary and adviser.

ABU-L FAZL.

Rājā Mān Singh, nephew and adopted son of Rājā Bhagwān Dās of Ambēr or Jaipur, was one of Akbar's best generals and governors. He is said to have ruled the eastern provinces with 'great prudence and justice'.

Rājā Todar Mall, who had no advantages of birth, made his way to the top of the imperial service by sheer merit and ability. He was a good commander in the field as well as an unrivalled revenue expert. He was free from avarice, and was, perhaps, the ablest man, excepting Abu-l Fazl, in the service.

Rājā Bīrbal, originally a poor Brahman versifier, obtained his promotion by making himself agreeable to Akbar in the capacity of companion and jester. In 1586 the emperor made a mistake in appointing him to command an army against the fierce Yūsufzī tribe on the north-western frontier. Naturally he failed, ran away, and was killed, much to the emperor's sorrow.

Many other notable personages adorn the annals of the reign. The Jesuit Fathers, especially Aquaviva, Monserrate, and Jerome Xavier, must be reckoned as among the intimate friends of Akbar, who had a genuine liking for them personally, quite apart from political motives.

Literature and art. A long, prosperous, and victorious reign encouraged literature and art, which were in brisk demand at a magnificent court, where they received intelligent patronage from Akbar. Important histories in Persian were composed by Abu-l Fazl, Nizāmu-d dīn, Badāonī, and other authors. The *Āīn-i Akbarī*, or *Institutes of Akbar*, compiled by Abu-l Fazl, as the result of seven years' labour, gives a wonderful survey of the empire. Among the poets or versifiers writing in Persian Faizī was considered the best. But the greatest author of the time, Tulsī Dās the Hindī poet, does not seem to have been known to Akbar personally. His noble work, the Hindī Rāmāyana, or *Rām-charitmānas*, is familiar to all Hindus in Upper India.

The ancient art of Indian painting, which had always continued to exist, although examples dating between the seventh and the sixteenth centuries are extremely rare, received a new direction from Akbar, who induced the Hindu artists to learn Persian technique and imitate Persian style. The works produced in a spirit of mere imitation were not altogether successful, but an Indo-Persian school developed gradually, and became rich in coloured drawings of high merit. The portraits of the Mogul period, which are especially deserving of commendation, attained their highest degree of perfection in the reign of Shāhjahān. The art of Akbar's time is cruder and more conventional. The frontispiece of my work *Akbar the Great Mogul* reproduces accurately the earliest known Indo-Persian painting, dating from about 1557 or 1558. The next earliest extant specimens are the fragments of fresco at Fathpur-Sīkrī, executed about 1570. Most of the ancient Hindu paintings appear to have been applied to walls in either fresco or tempera, or a combination of both processes, and necessarily were lost when the buildings fell to ruin or were destroyed.

RĀJĀ BĪRBAL.

The architecture of Akbar's reign is characterized by a happy blending of Hindu and Muhammadan styles, which is a reflex or expression in stone of his personal feelings and convictions. Abu-l Fazl truly remarks in an elegant phrase that 'His Majesty plans splendid edifices, and dresses the work of his mind and heart in the garment of stone and clay'. The best collection of his architectural achievements is to be seen at Fathpur-Sīkrī, but other notable buildings of Akbar's time exist elsewhere.

CHRONOLOGY

Leading Dates only.

Death of Humāyūn	Jan. 1556
Enthronement of Akbar	Feb. 1556
Second battle of Pānīpat; famine	Nov. 1556
Dismissal of Bairām Khān	1560
Execution of Adham Khān	1562
Uzbeg rebellions	1565–7
Fall of Chitōr	1568
Building of Fathpur-Sīkrī	1569–76
Conquest of Gujarāt	1572–3
Administrative reforms	1573–4
Conquest of Bengal; defeat of Rānā Partāp at Gogūnda or Haldīghāt	1576
'Infallibility decree'	1579
First Jesuit mission; Bengal rebellion	1580
Victorious expedition to Kābul	1581
Proclamation of *Dīn Ilāhī*	1582
Death of Muhammad Hakīm; absorption of Kābul	1585
Annexation of Kashmīr	1586
Second Jesuit mission	1590
Annexation of southern Sind	1591
Annexation of Orissa	1592
Annexation of Balōchistan and Makrān	1594
Annexation of Kandahār; third Jesuit mission	1595
Famine	1595–8
Annexation of Berar	1596
Fall of Ahmadnagar	1600
Surrender of Asīrgarh; embassy to Goa	1601
Prince Salīm in rebellion	1601–4
Arrest of Prince Salīm	Nov. 1604
Death of Akbar	Oct. 1605

AUTHORITIES

The principal contemporary authorities are of three kinds, namely, (i) the *Āīn-i Akbarī* by ABU-L FAZL, a survey of the empire and imperial system, as translated and annotated by Blochmann and Jarrett, Calcutta, 1873, 1891: (ii) three histories in Persian, namely, (1) the *Akbarnāma* by Abu-l Fazl, translated by H. Beveridge; vol. i, Calcutta, 1907, vol. ii, Calcutta, 1912, vol. iii, in proof; (2) the *Tabakāt-i Akbarī* by NIZĀMU-D DĪN, translated by Dowson in *E. & D.*, vol. v; and (3) the *Muntakhabu-t Tawārīkh* by ABDU-L KĀDIR AL BADĀONĪ, vol. ii, translated by Lowe, as corrected by Cowell, Calcutta, 1884: and (iii) accounts by various Jesuit writers, most of which are summarized by MACLAGAN in his article entitled 'Jesuit Missions to the Emperor Akbar' in *J. A. S. B.*, vol. lxv, part i, 1896. The Latin work, *Mongolicae Legationis Commentarius* by Father ANTONIO MONSERRATE, S.J. (1582), ed. by Rev. H. Hosten, S.J., Calcutta, 1914, which was not known to Maclagan, is of high importance.

Full details about those works and all minor authorities will be found in the author's book, *Akbar the Great Mogul*, A.D. 1542–1605, Clarendon Press, 1917. The essay entitled 'Akbar's Land-Revenue System as described in the *Āīn-i Akbarī* by Moreland and Yusuf Ali' (*J. R. A. S.*, 1918, pp. 1–42) is valuable and novel.

CHAPTER 4

Jahāngīr.

Accession of Jahāngīr. Jahāngīr's enthronement at Agra took place on October 24, 1605, a week after his father's death. He assumed the style of Nūru-d dīn Muhammad Jahāngīr Pādshāh Ghāzī, the first name meaning 'light of the faith' and the third 'world-seizer'. He had secured his succession by making two solemn promises, one that he would protect the Muhammadan religion, the other that he would not cause any harm to the persons who had supported Khusrū's claims. Both undertakings were honourably kept. The Muhammadans were gratified by his changed attitude to the Jesuit Fathers, whom he neglected as if he had never seen them, while the active adherents of Khusrū, including Rājā Mān Singh, received honours and dignities. He also issued various orders by way of reforms, the most important being the abolition of many transit and customs duties. But, as Sir Henry Elliot has shown, such orders had little practical effect. They need not be specified in detail. The provision of a golden bell-pull to be used by any importunate suppliant was a piece of silly make-believe.

Rebellion of Prince Khusrū. Prince Khusrū, who was extraordinarily popular, and had many well-wishers, could not bring himself to resign hopes of the crown which at one time had seemed to be within his grasp. According to one account he feared that his father might take the precaution of blinding him. Whether actuated by ambition or by fear or by both motives, he slipped out of the Agra Fort on April 6, 1606 (o.s.), and having collected a considerable force of troopers and obtained funds in various ways hastened to the Panjāb. His father pursued him with the utmost energy, dispensing with all the usual imperial hindrances to rapid movement. The governor of Lahore refused to open his gates to the prince, who, after some fighting, was captured while attempting to cross the Chināb on April 27, exactly three weeks after his escape from Agra. Jahāngīr, who never again displayed such energy, then pitched his camp in a garden near Lahore, and proceeded to take deliberate and fearful vengeance.

The rebel prince, loaded with chains, was brought before his father, who required the villagers to prepare a large number of sharp stakes. Two of Khusrū's principal followers were cruelly tortured by being enclosed in raw hides, one in that of an ox and the other in that of an ass; and in that fashion, seated on asses, were paraded through the city. One of the men died; the other, who barely escaped with his life, was afterwards pardoned. On Wednesday, May 7, two or three hundred of the prince's adherents were either hung from the trees or impaled on the prepared stakes set up along each side of the road. Jahāngīr, mounted on a splendidly caparisoned elephant, rode between the ranks, followed by his wretched son riding on a small unadorned elephant, with Mahābat Khān behind him, to point out the names of the writhing victims.[1]

Guru Arjun. When Khusrū was fleeing before his father, and in dire distress, he had asked the Sikh Guru, Arjun, at Tarn-Taran for assistance. The holy man, moved it is said, merely by compassion, gave the fugitive five thousand rupees. When the report came before the emperor Jahāngīr summoned the Guru, and after hearing his dignified reply fined him two hundred thousand rupees. The Guru, having refused to pay a single cowree, was savagely tortured for five days until he died (June 1606). The punishment, it will be observed, was inflicted as a penalty for high treason and contumacy, and was not primarily an act of religious persecution.[2] Khusrū was blinded, but not completely, and subsequently recovered the sight of one eye to some extent. Sultan Parvīz, the emperor's second son, was recognized as heir apparent.

Popular love of Khusrū. Sir Thomas Roe and his chaplain Terry sometimes met Khusrū when his captivity had been relaxed (about 1616) and he used to follow his father on the march under a strong guard. On one occasion Khusrū had some conversation with the ambassador, whom he questioned concerning his country and business. The prince blamed his father for not having bestowed on his guest any valuable gift, and promised Sir Thomas his prayers, all that he had to give.

> 'For that Prince,' Terry writes, 'he was a gentleman of a very lovely presence and fine carriage, so exceedingly beloved of the common people, that as Suetonius writes of Titus, he was *amor et deliciae, &c.*, the very love and delight of them; aged then about thirty-five years.[3] He was a man who contented himself with one wife, which with all love and care accompanied him in all his streights, and therefore he would never take any wife but herself, though the liberty of his religion did admit of plurality.'

After his death the beloved prince, as we learn from Mundy, was regarded as a martyred saint. On the way to his final resting-place in the Khusrū Garden near Allahabad, each spot where the bearers of his body halted was marked by a shrine, consisting of a cenotaph, surrounded by a little garden, watered and tended by a fakīr or two. His figure, shadowy though it be, is one of the most interesting and pathetic in Indian history.

Shērafgan. In 1607 an incident occurred which had important consequences as leading to the marriage of Jahāngīr with Nūrjahān,

[1] The date is that given by Mr. Beveridge. The detail about Mahābat Khān (Zamāna Beg) is from de Laet. Authors differ concerning the number of victims. The smallest number, namely 200, is given by Du Jarric.

[2] For the full story from the Sikh point of view see Macauliffe, *The Sikh Religion* (1909), vol. iii, pp, 84–100.

[3] He was younger than the chaplain supposed, having been born in August, A. D. 1587 (A. H. 995). Khāfī Khān dates his birth two years later, and may be right.

who became the power behind the throne and practically sovereign of Hindostan. The lady, whose personal name was Mihru-n nisā, was the daughter of a Persian refugee who had entered Akbar's service. She was given in marriage to Alī Kulī, surnamed Shērafgan, the 'tiger-thrower', who received from Jahāngīr after his accession the *jāgīr* of Bardwān in Bengal. For some reason or other Shērafgan fell under the suspicion of the emperor, who sent his own foster-brother, Kutbu-d dīn Koka, to remove Shērafgan and forward him to court. When Kutbu-d dīn attempted to carry out his orders an affray occurred, in the course of which both he and Shērafgan were killed. It is said that Jahāngīr had seen Mihru-n nisā when she resided in his father's harem before her marriage, and had then become enamoured of her. It is certain that he was deeply attached to his foster-brother. In his Memoirs, although he makes no allusion to the love-affair, he displays the most rancorous hostility to Shērafgan, remarking viciously that Kutbu-d dīn's men 'sent him to hell', and adding: 'It is to be hoped that the place of this black-faced scoundrel will always be there.' The lady was brought to court, and long resisted the ardent importunities of her imperial lover. At last, in **1611**, more than four years after her husband's death, she yielded and consented to become Jahāngīr's chief queen. She acquired at once unbounded influence over him, and freely made use of it to advance the interests of her family. Her father, who received the title of Itimādu-d daulah, and her brother, ennobled as Āsaf Khān, became the leading personages in the court, while all her other connexions were well looked after. It is said that at first she desired to unite her daughter by Shērafgan with Khusrū. When that could not be done she married the girl to Jahāngīr's youngest son, Shahryār. Her earlier title of Nūrmahall, 'Light of the Palace', was soon altered to Nūrjahān, 'Light of the World', with allusion to the imperial style of Nūru-d dīn Jahāngīr. For many years she wielded the imperial power. She even gave audiences at her palace, and her name was placed on the coinage.

Coin of Jahāngīr and Nūrjahān.

Favours to the Jesuits. The temporary apparent alienation of Jahāngīr from the Jesuit Fathers, arranged as a sop to Muslim opinion, ceased in 1606 when his favours to the priests were renewed. After some difficulty they were allowed to retain their elegant and commodious (*elegans et scitum*) church at Lahore, as well as the *collegium*, or priests' residence, a comfortable building equipped with verandahs and upper and lower rooms, suitable respectively for use in the cold and hot seasons. Each department of the mission work had its appropriate and convenient accommodation as in European colleges. At Agra about twenty baptisms took place in 1606, and when Jahāngīr was on his way to Kābul he accepted a Persian version of the Gospels and permitted the Fathers to act publicly with as much liberty as if they were in Europe. When the emperor returned to Agra he took two of the priests with him, leaving one at Lahore to look after the congregation there. Church processions with full Catholic ceremonial were allowed to parade the streets, and cash allowances were paid from the treasury for church expenses and the support of the converts. The zeal for Islām which Jahāngīr had displayed at the beginning of his reign gradually diminished, and he openly declared that he wished to follow in his father's footsteps.

Disputation. While Jahāngīr was at Agra a disputation was started by the emperor calling on the Fathers to explain certain scriptural pictures of David and other subjects. The arguments between the priests and their Muhammadan opponents lasted for more than a month with intervals, and the Jesuits were allowed to denounce Muhammad as a false prophet. When Nakīb Khan, the 'reader' and eminent historical student, who used to read histories to Akbar, grew angry at language which he regarded as blasphemous, Jahāngīr bade him keep quiet and laughed heartily. The emperor forced a Hindu courtier to express his agreement with the priests, and on hearing the declaration again burst out laughing (*ad quae effuse ridere rex*). The Jesuits naturally were delighted that the nobles were forced to do honour to Christ. But they recognized that much more effort would be needed before their purpose could be achieved. Their exertions were directed principally to the conversion of the emperor himself.

Christian pictures. Certainly his conduct gave them some reason to hope that he might be brought within the Christian fold. He showed an extraordinary fancy for pictures of religious subjects from the Old and New Testaments, the Apocrypha, and the Lives of the Saints. At Agra his throne was surrounded by paintings of John the Baptist, Saint Antony, and Saint Bernardin of Siena. On the right hand side of the window (*jharokhā*) from which he gave audience was an image of Christ the Saviour, holding a globe in his hand. On the left hand was a painting of the Virgin Mary, or the 'Mother of God' (*Deiparae*) in Roman Catholic phraseology, copied from the original believed to have been the work of St. Luke. Various halls, rooms, and courts in the palace were similarly decorated. Some of the designs Jahāngīr drew with his own hand (*quas sua ipse manu delineavit*), and he arranged them personally without suggestions from other people. He selected the pictures likely to be most pleasing, and used to send his artists with instructions to follow the Fathers' hints about the colours to be used and other matters. He possessed a large painting representing the scourging of the Redeemer, which was specially offensive to the Muhammadans. His gallery also included portraits of His Holiness the Pope, the King of Spain, and the Duke of Savoy. Jahāngīr personally explained to his court the meaning of a composition depicting the Adoration of the Magi, which had been brought from Rome to Goa by Father Joannes Alvarez, and gave directions that the picture should be handsomely framed.[1] The emperor frequently boasted to his friends, and not without justice, that he had acquired complete knowledge of the mysteries of the Christian faith. He carried a pair of golden scissors or tongs, with a large square emerald on each point, one gem being engraved with the likeness of Christ, and the other with that of His Mother. He used those signets to stamp the outside of all official missives and letters, whether addressed to Hindus, Muhammadans, or Christians. It is no wonder that Jahāngīr was popularly reputed to have become a Christian, and that the Jesuits entertained 'good hope of his conversion'. They recognized that the practice of polygamy was one of the principal obstacles to his acceptance of the Christian faith, and tried in vain to persuade him that it was his duty to repudiate all his wives save one.

Embassy to Goa. In 1607 Jahāngīr expressed a desire, as his father had done, to send a mission to the King of Spain and the Pope, but was persuaded to restrict the embassy to visiting the Viceroy of Goa. The ambassador selected was Mukarrab Khān, an intimate friend of the emperor, a keen sportsman and skilled surgeon. In accordance with Jahāngīr's special request Father Pinheiro accompanied the ambassador as a colleague. They started from Lahore, where the court then was, in September 1607, and reached Cambay in the April following, 1608. At that time the envoys could not present their credentials at Goa, because the viceroy designate had not arrived. As a matter of fact he never arrived, and the government of Portuguese India was carried on by Archbishop de Menezes until May 27, 1609, when Don Andreas Hurtados de Mendosa took charge and held office until September 5 of that year.

Captain W. Hawkins. Meantime, Captain William Hawkins, of the ship *Hector*, had arrived at Surat on August 24, 1608, bearing a letter from James I, King of Great Britain, to Jahāngīr, asking for the grant of trade facilities. Hawkins, in spite of strenuous opposition from Father Pinheiro and the Portuguese authorities, succeeded in reaching the court of Jahāngīr, who accepted his gifts, valued at 25,000 gold pieces, and gave him a most favourable reception. Hawkins was able to converse with the emperor in Turkī, without the aid of an interpreter. He was appointed to be a commander (*mansabdār*) of 400, with a salary of 30,000 rupees (which, it is said, was not paid), and was required to marry the daughter of an Armenian Christian named Mubārak Shāh (Mubarikesha). He lived on intimate terms with Jahāngīr, whose deep potations he shared. Jahāngīr granted all his demands.

Portuguese hostility. When Mendosa, the new viceroy at Goa, heard that Hawkins and other Englishmen had been granted privileges infringing on the commercial monopoly claimed by

[1] Although the wall paintings mentioned all perished long ago, many small drawings and paintings of scriptural and Christian subjects survive. See *H. F. A.*, p. 464, pl. cxv. Other records exist of Christian wall paintings in various localities.

the Portuguese, he treated the imperial concession as a hostile act and considered himself to be at war with Jahāngīr, whose ambassador he refused to receive. That hasty action greatly disturbed the merchants on the coast, and alarmed Jahāngīr, who revoked his concessions to the English. Father Pinheiro, who had gone on to Goa, was then employed by the viceroy as a plenipotentiary to negotiate with Mukarrab Khān, hostilities were stopped, and English ships were refused admission at Surat. Certain Englishmen who attempted to proceed to court were intercepted, several of them being killed.

Ruy Lourenço de Tavora, who succeeded Mendosa as viceroy in September 1609, invited the ambassador to come to Goa, but Mukarrab Khān having been recalled by Jahāngīr, Father Pinheiro took his place as the accredited envoy of the Great Mogul (*Pinnerus legati munus, quod a rege suo acceperat Proregi obtulit*), a strange position for a Catholic priest.

Hawkins quitted the court in 1611, baffled by the intrigues of the Portuguese and the instability of the imperial policy. He recorded interesting notes of his experience, which have been preserved by the diligence of Purchas, and will be quoted presently in part.

Bengal and the Deccan. In 1612 the rebellion of Usmān Khān in Bengal, which had begun in Akbar's time, was at last ended by the death of the rebel leader from wounds received in a stiff fight. From the beginning of the reign hostilities in the Deccan had never wholly ceased. A feebly conducted war against the forces of the Ahmadnagar Sultanate, then administered by an able Abyssinian, named Malik Ambar, went on continually without results worthy of notice. At this period the quarrels among the imperialist generals became so acute that the Khān Khānān (Abdurrahīm), who had been recalled, was again sent to see if he could do anything effectual. But Jahāngīr never succeeded in obtaining a firm control over any campaign in the Deccan or elsewhere.

English victory at sea. The same year, 1612, was marked by the entrance of British naval forces into Indian politics. At the end of November one English ship, the *Dragon*, commanded by Captain Best, 'assisted onely', as Purchas relates, 'with the *Osiander* a little ship (scarcely a ship, I had almost called her a little Pinnasse)', successfully fought a Portuguese fleet comprising four huge galleons, with five- or six-and-twenty frigates. Mr. Nathaniel Salmon commanded the tiny *Osiander* in that wonderful fight. It is not surprising to read that 'the great Mogoll, which before thought none comparable to the Portugall at Sea, much wondered at the English resolution, related to him by *Sardar Chan*'. The Mogul empire was then, as always, utterly powerless at sea; a fact which had much to do with its collapse.

War with Portuguese. About a year later (1613) the Portuguese abused their naval superiority as compared with the weakness of the Mogul government by seizing four of the imperial ships, imprisoning many Muslims, and plundering the cargoes. The outrage naturally was 'very disagreeable' to Jahāngīr, who ordered Mukarrab Khān, then in charge of Surat, to obtain compensation. From English sources we learn that the principal ship plundered was called the *Remewe*, and that it was said to have carried 'three millions of Treasure, and two women bought for the Great Mogol'. Jahāngīr's mother had a large interest in the cargo, and lost heavily.

The Portuguese acts of piracy resulted in war with the imperial government, whose officers attacked Damān. All accessible Portuguese residing in the Mogul dominions were seized, and even Father Jerome Xavier was sent in custody to Mukarrab Khān, 'to do with him as he shall see good'. The public exercise of the Christian religion was forbidden, and the churches were closed. The Portuguese were still 'in deep disgrace with the King and people' early in 1615, when William Edwards from Surat arrived at court bearing a letter from King James I. Although he was not formally accredited as an ambassador, he was very honourably received by Jahāngīr, who perceived that the English could now be used as a counterpoise to the Portuguese. Some years earlier the emperor had questioned Hawkins about the force needed to take Diu, and was told that the place could be reduced by fourteen British ships supported by a land force of twenty thousand men.

Submission of Mewār. The inglorious war with Mewār (Udaipur), which had gone on for so many years, was ended in 1614 by the submission of Rānā Amar Singh and his son Karan to Prince Khurram (Shāhjahān), who had pressed the brave Rājpūts until they were reduced to extremity. Jahāngīr was delighted by a success which Akbar had failed to achieve, and was willing to soften the humiliation of defeat by exceptionally courteous treatment of his gallant adversaries. After some time the emperor did special honour to them by directing artists at Ajmēr to fashion full-sized marble statues of the Rānā and his son. The commission having been executed with all speed, the statues were removed to Agra and erected in the garden below the audience-window (*jharokhā*). Unhappily those interesting works of art have disappeared. Mewār was required to contribute to the imperial army a contingent of one thousand horse, and Karan had to accept the dignity of a 'commander of 5,000'. The reigning Rānā was never compelled to attend court in person, and no Sīsōdia bride ever graced the imperial harem. With the exception of those concessions to the dignity of the premier chieftain of Rājasthān, the Rānā became as other Rājās, and officially was regarded as a mere zemindār or *jāgīrdār*.

In July of the same year, 1614, Rājā Mān Singh died in the Deccan. No less than sixty of his women committed *suttee* by fire.

Plague. Bubonic plague, a disease not previously recorded with certainty in India, appeared in the Panjāb early in 1616, at the close of Jahāngīr's tenth regnal year. The epidemic was marked by the symptoms unhappily familiar since the disease reappeared at Bombay in 1896. Rats and mice were first affected, and the mortality was severe, especially among Hindus. The pestilence, which spread to almost every locality in northern and western India, lasted for eight years. In 1619, while it was raging in Agra, Fathpur-Sīkrī, twenty-three miles distant, escaped. Historians have overlooked both this remarkable epidemic in Jahāngīr's reign and another outbreak, apparently of the same disease, which occurred in the Deccan in 1703 and 1704; erroneously supposing that 'the first trustworthy information of the occurrence of plague in India dates from the year 1812', when the disease broke out in Cutch and spread to Gujarāt and Sind.[1]

REV. EDW. TERRY.

Embassy of Sir Thomas Roe. The informal missions of Hawkins and Edwards, sent for the purposes of promoting the nascent trade between England and the East, and abating Portuguese pretensions, were quickly followed by the formal embassy of Sir Thomas Roe, the duly accredited ambassador from James I to Jahāngīr. The envoy, a gentleman of good education, a polished courtier, and trained diplomatist, was well qualified for the task assigned to him, which was the negotiation of a treaty giving security to English trade. Roe arrived at Surat, or rather Swally Road, in September 1615, and marched up country as soon as practicable to the court of Jahāngīr, then at Ajmēr. The chaplain whom he had brought out with him having died almost immediately, the ambassador summoned from Surat to take his place a young

[1] *I. G.* (1907), iv. 475. For the plague in the Deccan see *Storia do Mogor*, iv. 97.

English clergyman named Edward Terry, who happened to have come out on his own account as a curious traveller. The world is indebted to Terry for an account of his experiences, which is far superior to that of Roe as a description of the country and government. The chaplain was a good observer and extraordinarily sympathetic in his attitude towards the natives of India, whether Hindu or Muhammadan. He did not publish his narrative for more than thirty years after his return to England, and then unfortunately thought fit to pad it so thickly with moralizings that the modern reader becomes wearied and is apt to undervalue a really admirable book. Roe's *Journal* is chiefly useful as a faithful record of the manner in which business was done at a court saturated with intrigue, treachery, and corruption. Jahāngīr, half fuddled with strong drink and opium, had not the strength of will to resist the wiles of his designing queen, her equally unscrupulous brother, Āsaf Khān, and the deep villany of Prince Khurram (Shāhjahān). The ambassador's pen-picture of that prince is memorable.

JAHĀNGĪR.

'I never saw', he writes, 'so settled a countenance, nor any man keep so constant a gravity, never smiling, nor in face showing any respect or difference of men; but mingled with extreme pride and contempt of all, yet I found some inward trouble now and then assail him, and a kind of brokenness and distraction in his thoughts, unprovidedly and amazedly answering suitors, or not hearing.'

Roe proceeds to give a scandalous but not necessarily incredible explanation. At the Mogul court no suggestion of alleged wickedness can be summarily rejected as incredible.

'If I can judge anything,' the ambassador comments, 'he hath left his heart among his father's women, with whom he hath liberty of conversation. Nūrmahall in the English coach the day before visited him, and took leave, she gave him a cloak all embroidered with pearl, diamonds, and rubies, and carried away, if I err not, his attention to all other business.' [1]

Princes Khusrū and Khurram. Roe confirms his chaplain's testimony to the virtues and popularity of Prince Khusrū, whose life even then was unceasingly threatened by his brother, Prince Khurram, with the privity of Nūrjahān and Āsaf Khān. The

[1] The spelling has been modernized, but the old punctuation retained. Shāhjahān (Khurram) was then, in 1616, twenty-four years of age; and four years earlier, in 1612, had been married to Mumtāz Mahall, then aged nineteen, who was the daughter of Āsaf Khān, Nūrmahall's elder brother. Nūrmahall or Nūrjahān was born in Kandahār before her father came to India in 1591, and must have been about forty years of age in 1616. She died in 1645, aged about seventy. Roe had brought out an English coach, of which Jahāngīr's workmen made copies.

ambassador, who was in a good position for learning the facts, records that

'Sultan Khusrū, the eldest brother, is both extremely beloved, and honoured of all men (almost adored) and very justly for his noble parts'.

In another passage he amplifies his judgement by saying:

'If Sultan Khusrū prevail in his right, this kingdom will be a sanctuary for Christians, whom he loves and honours, favouring learning, valour, the discipline of war, and abhorring all covetousness, and discerning the base customs of taking, used by his ancestors and the nobility. If the other win, we shall be losers; for he is most earnest in his superstition, a hater of all Christians, proud, subtile, false, and barbarously tyrannous.'

The event proved the correctness of the shrewd ambassador's prediction, as well as the soundness of his estimate of Shāhjahān's character, which has been so grievously misunderstood by modern historians. Jahāngīr, unfortunately, considered Shāhjahān to be 'the first of his sons', until he rebelled. After that the emperor could not find language adequate to express his dislike for the former favourite.

Roe went home in 1618. Although he had failed to obtain the formal treaty desired, he secured considerable concessions to his countrymen and laid a solid foundation for the East India Company's trade.

The Deccan war. The aggressive war in the Deccan, where the principal opponent of the imperialists was Malik Ambar, the able Abyssinian minister at Ahmadnagar, dragged on throughout the reign. No decisive result ever was obtained, and good reason existed for believing that Abdurrahīm, the Khān Khānān, was in collusion with Malik Ambar. In 1616 the fort at Ahmadnagar was surrendered, and Prince Khurram was allowed to obtain a show of success. He was extravagantly rewarded with the title of Shāhjahān, and the enormous emoluments attached to the command (*mansab*) of '30,000 personal, with 20,000 horse'. Malik Ambar lived until 1626, when he died at an advanced age.

Surrender of Kāngra. The most notable military achievement of Jahāngīr's inglorious reign was the surrender to his authority in November 1620, of the strong fortress of Kāngra, which had defied even Akbar. Jahāngīr was extremely proud because an officer of his had been able to reduce a stronghold which had baffled his father. A little later the emperor visited the conquest, and gratified the sentiment of the Muhammadans, while outraging that of the Hindus, by erecting a mosque and slaughtering a bullock within the precincts of the fort. Jahāngīr, who was a sceptic without any personal hostility to Hinduism, at times found it expedient to prove by some overt act that he must be still deemed officially a follower of the Prophet.

Murder of Prince Khusrū. The 'tragical end' of the 'troublesome life' of Prince Khusrū came in January 1622. Nearly six years earlier, in 1616, Jahāngīr, for reasons not stated, had transferred his son from the custody of a faithful Hindu named Ani

Rāi to that of Āsaf Khān, the mortal enemy of the prince. Later, in or about 1620, the prisoner was made over to his brother, Prince Khurram, at the instigation of Āsaf Khān and Nūrjahān. The inevitable result followed in the beginning of 1622, when an assassin named Razā Bahādur strangled the captive by order of his brother. Jahāngīr records his son's death without comment or expression of regret, merely stating that 'a report came from Khurram that Khusrū, on the 8th (? 20th) of the month, had died of the disease of colic pains (*kūlanj*) and gone to the mercy of God'. There is no doubt that the prisoner was murdered. Details are given by Mundy from common report, but the most particular account is that given in de Laet's book, which in substance is as follows :

Shāhjahān, then residing at Burhānpur, sought to remove his brother without scandal. Having arranged a plan with the connivance of the Khān Khānān and other nobles, he went off on a hunting expedition so as to be out of the way. Razā, the slave appointed to the duty, knocked at the prince's door at an unseasonable hour of the night, pretending to have brought robes of honour and written orders for liberation from the emperor. When the prince refused to open his door it was forced, and he was strangled. The door was then closed and the body was left as it lay. His faithful and dearly loved wife, when she found him in the morning, raised a terrible outcry. Shāhjahān sent off a false report, carefully attested by the signatures of his courtiers, but Nūru-d dīn Kulī gave the emperor correct information. Jahāngīr professed to feel intense sorrow, although he must have known what would happen when he made over Khusrū to the charge of his avowed enemy who had sought for years to destroy him. Probably the emperor had yielded unwillingly to the advice of Nūrjahān, whose will was his law. His weakness, however, does not absolve him from responsibility.

Loss of Kandahār. In June of the same year, 1622, Shāh Abbās, the energetic King of Persia, retook Kandahār. He had tried without success to induce Jahāngīr to give up the place voluntarily. When diplomacy failed he took it by force without much trouble. Jahāngīr, who was grievously perturbed by the loss, planned a great expedition for the recovery of the town, and desired his son Shāhjahān to take the command. But at the time the emperor was in bad health, and Shāhjahān was determined not to imperil his succession to the throne by absence on the Persian frontier.

Rebellion of Shāhjahān. Instead of obeying his father's orders he went into open rebellion. Prince Shahryār was then appointed to take charge of the Kandahār expedition, but nothing came of the appointment, all the energies of the government being devoted to the suppression of the rebellion. A plan to bring from Agra to Lahore the whole of the immense treasure in gold and silver coin accumulated from the beginning of Akbar's reign was dropped when Shāhjahān gave indications that he intended to intercept the convoy. It is impossible to refuse some sympathy to the outraged father when he laments the ingratitude of the once best-beloved son, and moans :

> 'What shall I say of my own sufferings ? In pain and weakness, in a warm atmosphere that is extremely unsuited to my health, I must still ride and be active, and in this state must proceed against such an undutiful son.'

But he thanks 'God that has given me such capacity to bear my burdens'. He lamented more especially that the rebel had compelled the postponement of the recovery of Kandahār, and thus had 'struck with an axe the foot of his own dominion, and become a stumbling-block in the path of the enterprise'. Several nobles were executed for high treason, and Sultan Parvīz, Shāhjahān's elder brother, was summoned to take his proper place at his father's side as heir apparent. Jahāngīr was justly disgusted because Abdurrahīm, the Khān Khānān, an old man of seventy, and loaded with marks of imperial favour, had joined the traitors.

A battle fought at Balōchpur, to the south of Delhi, resulted in the death of the Brahman named Sundar, on whom Shāhjahān chiefly relied, and in the consequent defeat of the rebel army (1623). Shāhjahān was driven through Mālwā into the Deccan, and thence across Telingāna into Bengal, which province, with Bihār, he occupied. Another defeat sent the rebel back to the Deccan, where he tried to make friends with his old enemy Malik Ambar and the other rulers of the south. In 1625 a sort of peace was patched up between the prince and his father. Shāhjahān surrendered Rohtās and Asīrgarh, and sent his two elder sons, Dārā Shikoh and Aurangzēb, to court as hostages. But he never appeared there in person, remaining absent in Rājputāna or the Deccan.

Mahābat Khān. In the year following, 1626, strange events occurred. Mahābat Khān, who had become one of the principal personages in the empire, and had taken an active part in the pursuit of Shāhjahān, found himself in danger of destruction owing to the hostility of Nūrjahān. Jahāngīr and his consort were encamped on the Jhelum on their way to Kābul, and were about to cross the river with the rear-guard when Mahābat Khān surrounded the imperial tents with his Rājpūt horsemen, and captured the emperor. Nūrjahān was not detained, and was allowed to pass over the river. Her attempts to recover her husband by force having failed, she managed by stratagem to effect her purpose at Kābul. Mahābat Khān was then obliged to fly and join Shāhjahān, who was hard pressed, and thinking of escape to Persia. But he was encouraged by the death in October at Burhānpur of his brother, Parvīz, the only serious rival for the succession to the throne. Parvīz was officially supposed to have died from the effects of drink, but the general belief at the time that he was poisoned by his brother was well founded.[1] Hardly anything is on record

[1] Long afterwards Aurangzēb in a letter accused his father of the murder of both his brothers : 'How do you still regard the memory of [your brothers] Khusrau and Parvīz, whom you did to death before your accession and who had threatened no injury to you ?' (Sarkar, *Hist.*, vol. iii, p. 155).

concerning the personal qualities of Parvīz beyond the fact that he drank too much.

Death of Jahāngīr. Jahāngīr, who had been ailing for several years, died after a short illness while encamped at Chingiz Hatlī, a village near Bhimbhar at the foot of the hills on the road to Kashmīr, from which he was returning. His death occurred in October 1627, but his successor Shāhjahān was not able to take his seat on the throne until the following February, for the reasons which will be explained in the next chapter.

His personality. As appears from the foregoing narrative, the prominent public events of Jahāngīr's reign were few. The loss of Kandahār was not balanced by any substantial increase of territory elsewhere, and there can be no doubt that the empire was weaker as a military power in 1627 than it was when Akbar died in 1605. The administration generally was conducted on the lines laid down by Akbar, and the reign of Jahāngīr may be regarded as a continuation of that of his father, marked by a certain amount of deterioration due to Jahāngīr's personal inferiority when compared with his illustrious parent. His considerable natural abilities were marred by habitual and excessive intemperance, which added artificial ferocity to his innate violent temper. When angry, and especially if the security of his throne was threatened, he was capable of the most fiendish cruelty, taking a horrid delight in seeing men flayed alive, impaled, torn to pieces by elephants, or otherwise tortured to death. Hawkins and Roe were much disgusted by such savagery. Mere passionate caprice, even when no question of treason arose, sometimes induced him to commit shocking barbarities. For instance, he relates without shame the following anecdote :

> 'On the 22nd, when I had got within shot of a nilgaw, suddenly a groom and two bearers appeared, and the nilgaw escaped. In a great rage I ordered them to kill the groom on the spot, and to hamstring the bearers and mount them on asses and parade them through the camp, so that no one should again have the boldness to do such a thing.
>
> After this I mounted a horse and continued hunting with hawks and falcons, and came to the halting place.'

Many other sickening instances of his brutality will be found recorded in the pages of Roe, Terry, and other writers.

Jahāngīr's authentic *Memoirs*, either written by his own hand or dictated to a scribe, cover nineteen years of his reign and offer a wonderfully life-like picture of a typical Asiatic despot, a strange compound of tenderness and cruelty, justice and caprice, refinement and brutality, good sense and childishness. Terry truly observes :

> 'Now for the disposition of that King, it ever seemed unto me to be composed of extremes : for sometimes he was barbarously cruel, and at other times he would seem to be exceeding fair and gentle.'

He was capable of feeling the most poignant grief for the loss of a grandchild, and often showed pleasure in doing little acts of kindly charity. His writings are full of keen observations on natural objects. He went to Kashmīr nearly every hot season, and recorded a capital description of the country, carefully drawing up a list of the Indian birds and beasts not to be found in the Happy Valley. He loved fine scenery, and would go into ecstasies over a waterfall. He thought the scarlet blossom of the *dhāk* or *palās* tree 'so beautiful that one cannot take one's eyes off it', and was in raptures over the wild flowers of Kashmīr.

He was a skilled connoisseur in the arts of drawing and painting, and a generous patron of artists. He had himself some skill with the brush, and drew parts of the decorative designs on the walls of the palace at Agra. He appreciated music and song, and had nice taste in architecture. The unique design of Akbar's tomb was prepared in accordance with his ideas.

Jahāngīr prided himself especially on his love of justice, and his reputation for that quality still endures in India. When recording the capital sentence passed by himself on an influential murderer, he remarks:

'God forbid that in such affairs I should consider princes, and far less that I should consider Amīrs.'

The fearful penalties which he inflicted were imposed without respect of persons.

Religion. His religion is not easy to define. Grave Sir Thomas Roe roundly denounced him as an atheist, but he was not exactly that. He sincerely believed in God, although he did not frankly accept any particular revelation or subscribe to any definite creed. The mocking laughter with which he received denunciations of Muhammad as a false prophet is conclusive proof that he was not at heart a Muslim. The strange partiality which he showed for Christian images and ritual, and his intimacy with the Jesuit priests, did not induce him to accept the doctrines of the Church. Probably his favour to the priests was accorded chiefly from political motives, in order to secure Portuguese support and trade. The moment hostilities with Goa began the Christian churches were closed. He had not the slightest desire to persecute anybody on account of his religion. It is true that he passed severe orders against the Jains of Gujarāt, whom his father had so greatly admired, but that was because for some reason or other he considered them to be seditious.

While he loved talking to philosophical ascetics, whether Hindu or Muhammadan, he did not imitate his father in adopting Hindu practices, nor did he follow Zoroastrian rites. His personal religion seems to have been a vague deism, either that taught by heretical Muhammadan Sūfīs, or the very similar doctrine of certain Hindu sages. Ordinary Hinduism he spoke of as a 'worthless religion'. Jahāngīr, like his contemporaries, James I of England and Shāh Abbās of Persia, believed tobacco to be a noxious drug and forbade its use.

The material for discourse on Jahāngīr's interesting personality is so abundant that it would be easy to write at large on the subject. The reader perhaps will find what has been said more than enough.

The court. The court ceremonial was much the same as in the days of Akbar. Jahāngīr showed himself publicly three times a day. At sunrise he appeared on a balcony facing east, at noon on one facing south, and a little before sunset at a third facing west. On each occasion he received petitions and dispensed justice as he conceived it. Other state business was transacted

TOMB OF ITIMĀDU-D DAULA, AGRA.

chiefly between seven and nine o'clock in the evening in the private audience-hall, known as the *Ghusl-khāna* or 'bath-room', to which only privileged persons were admitted. Roe and Terry frequently attended such audiences. Before the evening had passed Jahāngīr often was dead drunk. Many anecdotes about his intemperance are on record.

The New Year festivities after the Persian manner, and the formal weighings of the sovereign against gold and other precious things on his birthday, calculated according to both the solar and the lunar calendars, were duly observed.

The selfish luxury and ostentation of the court and nobles had increased since Akbar's time, and constituted a terrible drain on the resources of the country. The pay of the higher officials was scandalously extravagant, even if allowance be made for certain deductions. Hawkins, who received the comparatively small post of a 'commander of 400', had a salary of 30,000 rupees a year, then worth more than 3,000 pounds sterling. Jahāngīr when pensioning an old servant of moderate rank gave him an allowance of 4,000 rupees a month or about £5,000 a year. The salary of a modern Viceroy is a mere pittance when compared with the sums paid to the greater nobles. No money to speak of was spent on useful public works or on education. All considerable expenditure was designed for the glory of the sovereign or his chief courtiers.

The administration was not good. Every governor could do much as he pleased, and ruthless severity was relied on for the repression of crime. Space fails to recount particulars.

Literature and art. Literature, chiefly in the Persian language, was encouraged. Jahāngīr himself could write sufficiently well. In addition to his *Memoirs* several historical works of some merit were composed, and he gave his patronage to the completion of a valuable dictionary entitled the *Farhang-i Jahāngīrī*. Art, as already mentioned, really interested Jahāngīr. His book is full of references to the subject, which it would be desirable to collect and discuss. The two most eminent painters of the reign were Abu-l Hasan, honoured with the title of Nādiru-z zamān, 'Wonder of the Age', and Ustād, or Master, Mansūr, who bore a synonymous title. The extant works of both those artists justify the enthusiastic praise bestowed upon them by their employer. The tomb of Itimādu-d daulah at Agra, the mausoleum of Akbar at Sikandara, and Jahāngīr's own sepulchre at Lahore testify to the good taste of the emperor and the skill of his architects.

CHRONOLOGY (O. S.)

Death of Akbar	Oct. 17, 1605
Enthronement of Jahāngīr	Oct. 24, 1605
Rebellion of Khusrū	Sunday, April 6, 1606
Capture of Khusrū	Sunday, April 27, 1606
Embassy to Goa	1607–9
Hawkins at court	1608–11
Marriage with Nūrjahān	May 1611
End of Usmān Khān's rebellion in Bengal	1612
Capture of four ships by Portuguese of Goa	1613
Submission of Rānā Amar Singh and Karan	1614
Sir Thomas Roe's embassy	1615–18
Bubonic plague begun (lasted eight years)	1616
Conquest of Kāngra	Nov. 1620
Death of Khusrū	Jan. 1622
Loss of Kandahār to the Persians	June 1622
Rebellion of Prince Khurram (Shāhjahān)	1622
Shāhjahān defeated and put to flight	1623, 1624
Submission of Shāhjahān	1625

Mahābat Khan seized Jahāngīr	1626
Death of Sultan Parvīz	Oct. 1626
Death of Jahāngīr	Oct. 28, 1627

AUTHORITIES

The leading authority is the annotated version of JAHĀNGĪR's authentic *Memoirs* (R.A.S. 1909, 1914), in two volumes, by ROGERS and BEVERIDGE, dealing with nineteen years of the reign. PRICE's translation of the interpolated text of the *Memoirs* (Or. Transl. Fund, 1832) should not be cited. The other principal Persian histories are discussed and partly translated in *E. & D.*, vol. vi. GLADWIN, *History of Hindostān, Reign of Jehāngīr* (vol. i, all published, Calcutta, 1788), a sound book, is chiefly valuable for the life of the emperor as Prince Salīm in Akbar's reign.

The European authorities are numerous and copious. One of the most important and least known is DU JARRIC, *Thesaurus Rerum Indicarum*, vol. iii, 1616 ; Book I, chaps. 16–23 incl., to the end of 1609. The observations of HAWKINS and many minor travellers will be found in PURCHAS, *Pilgrimes* (ed. Maclehose, 1905, or in other reprints). The best ed. of Sir THOMAS ROE's *Embassy* is that by FOSTER, Hakluyt Soc., 1899, 2 vols. His chaplain TERRY may be read in the reprint of *A Voyage to East India*, London, 1777. The *Travels* of PETER MUNDY (vol. ii, ed. Temple, Hakluyt Soc., 1914) give the history as current about 1630, shortly after Jahāngīr's death, and include numerous accurate personal observations on the state of the country. The narrative of President VAN DEN BROECKE (1629), translated from a chronicle and printed in DE LAET's book (1631), is full and seems to be generally accurate. Some additional facts may be collected from the works of BERNIER, TAVERNIER, MANUCCI, and other travellers, as well as from certain printed volumes of the records of the E. I. COMPANY. TOD gives the story of the Rājpūt campaigns from the Hindu point of view. The coins are described in the official catalogues of the B. M., I. M., and LAHORE MUSEUM. The art of the reign is noticed by FERGUSSON ; in *H. F. A.* (1911) ; in E. W. SMITH's *Akbar's Tomb* (Allahabad, 1909) ; and in various publications of the ARCHAEOLOGICAL SURVEY.

CHAPTER 5

Shāhjahān and the War of Succession ; Climax of the Mogul Empire.

Disputed succession ; executions. In October 1627, when Jahāngīr died on his way down from Kashmīr, two of his sons survived him. Prince Khurram or Shāhjahān, the elder, was then far away in the Deccan and could not arrive in Hindostan for many weeks. Prince Shahryār, the younger son, who was available at head-quarters, probably at Agra, thus possessed an advantage as against his rival. Both the princes claimed the throne, and neither had any thought of yielding to the other. Shahryār, who was married to the daughter of Nūrjahān by her first husband, Shērafgan, hurried off to Lahore to join his mother-in-law ; and assumed imperial rank. Shāhjahān was married to Mumtāz Mahall, daughter of Nūrjahān's brother, Āsaf Khān, who desired his son-in-law to succeed. In order to effect that purpose Āsaf Khān secured possession of Shāhjahān's young sons, and set up, much against his will, the unfortunate Prince Khusrū's son, Dāwar Baksh nicknamed Bulākī, as a stop-gap Pādshāh, until Shāhjahān could arrive. He was, in fact, as the chronicler observes, 'a mere sacrificial lamb'. Shahryār, whose lack of brains had earned for him the contemptuous sobriquet of Nā-shudanī, or 'Good-for-nothing', was incapable of contending against Asaf Khān, and was promptly blinded. Shāhjahān, a man of a different kind, able and ruthless, hurrying up from Junnār in the Deccan with all possible speed, sent orders for the execution of all his male collateral relatives. The atrocious instructions were carried out thoroughly, except that the titular emperor, Dāwar Baksh, was permitted to escape to Persia, where he lived as a pensioner of the Shāh. All the other male relatives were killed, one way or another. Authors differ concerning the names and number of the victims and the manner of their deaths, because the business was done secretly, and the exact truth was never disclosed. No doubt exists as to the wholesale character of the executions, which were carried out pitilessly, and, as Tavernier has justly remarked, have 'much tarnished' the memory of Shāhjahān, who does not deserve pity on account of the fate which overtook him with tardy steps.

Rebellions of Khān Jahān Lodī and Bundēlas. Early in February 1628 Shāhjahān solemnly took his seat on the throne at Agra, having previously been proclaimed at Lahore. The drastic removal of all possible claimants secured him undisputed authority for thirty years, during which period his right to reign was never seriously challenged. The rebellions which disturbed the early years of his rule did not imperil his position, and were suppressed without excessive difficulty. In the first year of the reign the turbulent Bundēla clan of Rājpūts occupying Bundēlkhand, the difficult hilly country to the south of the Jumna, revolted under the leadership of Jhujhār Singh, the son of Jahāngīr's criminal favourite, Rājā Bīr Singh. The rebel, who submitted for a time, broke out again later, and was killed by the Gonds in the eighth year of the reign, after enduring a long chase by the imperial forces.

In the second year of the reign a noble named Khān Jahān Lodī, carrying out the traditional hostility of the Afghan chiefs to the Mogul dynasty, allied himself with the Sultan of Ahmadnagar (Nizāmu-l Mulk), and went into rebellion. After an interval of submission Khān Jahān once more defied the imperial authority. In the fourth year he was defeated and killed..

The peacock throne. Shāhjahān, who had a passion for the collection of jewels, and took extraordinary pleasure in the display of costly magnificence at court, never lacked the funds needed to gratify his expensive fancies. The wealth of Akbar, the richest sovereign of his age, was far exceeded by the gigantic treasures of his grandson, who kept his principal hoard at Agra, in two great underground strong-rooms, one for gold and the other for silver, each seventy feet square and thirty feet high. Immediately after his formal enthronement in 1628 he determined to glorify himself by the construction of a throne more splendid and costly than that of any other monarch. The enormous stores of the imperial jewel-house were increased by extensive purchases of rare gems, and the combined accumulation was devoted to the decoration of the celebrated peacock throne, constructed under the superintendence of Bēbadal Khān in the course of seven years (1628–35). The throne was in the form of a cot bedstead on golden legs. The enamelled canopy was supported by twelve emerald pillars, each of which bore two peacocks encrusted with gems. A tree covered with diamonds, emeralds, rubies, and pearls stood between the birds of each pair. The gorgeous structure, which cost at least a hundred lakhs or ten millions of rupees, equivalent then to a million and a quarter of pounds sterling, continued in use until 1739, when it was carried off to Persia by Nādir Shāh. Some estimates put the cost at a very much higher figure. The work was a senseless exhibition of barbaric ostentation, and almost devoid of artistic merit. Six other thrones existed, one being an oval structure, like a bath-tub, seven feet long and five broad, without a canopy.[1]

Famine of 1630–2. The prodigal expenditure and unexampled splendour of the court, which occupy so prominent a place in most of the current descriptions of Shāhjahān's rule, had a dark background of suffering and misery seldom exposed to view. In the fourth and fifth years of the reign (1630–2), while the emperor usually was encamped at Burhānpur in Khāndēsh, intent on his aggressive schemes directed against the Sultans of the Deccan, an appalling famine of the utmost possible severity desolated the Deccan and Gujarāt. The official historian, Abdu-l Hamīd, contrary to the frequent practice of writers of his kind, makes no attempt to disguise the horror of the calamity, which he describes in a few phrases of painful vividness.

'The inhabitants of these two countries [the Deccan and Gujarāt] were reduced to the direst extremity. Life was offered for a loaf, but none would buy; rank was to be sold for a cake, but none cared for it. . . . For a long time dog's flesh was sold for goat's flesh, and the pounded bones of the dead were mixed with flour and sold. When this was discovered, the sellers were brought to justice. Destitution at last reached such a pitch that men began to devour each other, and the flesh of a son was preferred to his love. The numbers of the dying caused obstructions on the roads, and every man whose dire sufferings did not terminate in death and who retained the power to move wandered off to the towns and villages of other countries. Those lands which had been famous for their fertility and plenty now retained no trace of productiveness.'

[1] It is impossible to reconcile the measurement and cost of the peacock throne as stated by Tavernier (i. 381–4) with the figures of Abdu-l Hamīd Lāhorī (*E. & D.*, vii. 46). The descriptions by Tavernier, Bernier, and Abdu-l Hamīd all differ.

The details of the horrible picture are set out even more fully in the plain, unadorned notes kept by an English traveller, Peter Mundy, a merchant, who journeyed on business from Surat to Agra and Patna and back again while the famine and consequent pestilence were raging. At Surat the sickness was so deadly that out of twenty-one English traders seventeen died. For a large part of the way between Surat and Burhānpur the ground was strewn with corpses so thickly that Mundy could hardly find room to pitch a small tent. In towns the dead were dragged 'out by the heels, stark naked, of all ages and sexes, and there are left, so that the way is half barred up'. Meantime, the camp of Shāhjahān at Burhānpur was filled with provisions of all kinds.

So far as Mundy saw nothing to help the suffering people was done by the government, but the author of the *Bādshāh-nāmah* states that the emperor opened a few soup-kitchens, gave a lakh and a half of rupees in charity spread over a period of twenty weeks, and remitted one-eleventh of the assessment of land revenue. The remissions so made by 'the wise and generous Emperor' in the crown lands amounted to seventy lakhs. The holders of *jāgīrs* and official commands were expected to make similar reductions. The facts do not justify the historian's praise of the 'gracious kindness and bounty' of Shāhjahān. The remission of one-eleventh of the land revenue implies that attempts were made to collect ten-elevenths, a burden which could not be borne by a country reduced to 'the direst extremity', and retaining 'no trace of productiveness'. We are not told how far the efforts to collect the revenue succeeded; and as usual are left in the dark concerning the after effects of the famine. No statistics are on record. Even the nature of the consequent pestilence is not mentioned, but it is almost certain that cholera must have carried off myriads of victims. Sir Richard Temple, the editor of Mundy's work, has good reason for saying that 'it is worth while to read Mundy's unimpassioned, matter-of-fact observations on this famine' in order to realize the immensity of the difference in the conditions of life as existing under the rule of the Mogul dynasty when at the height of its glory and those prevailing under the modern British government.[1]

Life and death of Mumtāz Mahall. The marriage of Shāhjahān to the lady named Arjumand Bāno Bēgam, and entitled Nawāb Aliyā Bēgam, or alternatively Mumtāz Mahall, 'the ornament of the palace', has been mentioned as having been the main reason determining the adhesion of her father Āsaf Khān, the richest and most powerful noble in the empire, to the cause of Shāhjahān and his consequent opposition to his sister the dowager empress Nūrjahān, the widow of Jahāngīr and mother-in-law of Prince Shahryār. The marriage, which had taken place in the year 1612, when Prince Khurram (Shāhjahān) was twenty years of age, had been successful to a degree rare in polygamous households. The prince had had two children born to him by an

[1] The famine extended to Persia and many parts of India.

earlier consort. His remaining children, fourteen in number, eight sons and six daughters, were all borne to him by Mumtāz Mahall between the years 1613 and 1631. Husband and wife were devotedly attached to each other, and during her lifetime nothing is heard of the scandalous licentiousness which dishonoured Shāhjahān's later years. All the four sons who contested the throne in 1658 were her offspring, as were the two daughters, Jahānārā and Roshan Rāi (Roshanārā), who respectively supported the causes of Dārā Shikoh and Aurangzēb.

In June 1631 Mumtāz Mahall died in childbirth at Burhānpur, at the age of thirty-nine. Her body was interred there temporarily, and after six months, when her mourning husband quitted the Deccan, was transferred to Agra, where it was placed in a provisional sepulchre in the gardens of the Tāj, the unrivalled monument to her memory, which Shāhjahān began in 1632.

Little is known of the personal character of Mumtāz Mahall. She must have possessed uncommon charm to be able to secure for so many years her husband's errant affections, and to merit a memorial such as no other lady in the world has ever won. She appears to have been a devout Muslim, as most of the ladies of the imperial family were.

Her name is associated with the severe persecution of Christians which began in 1632, the year after her death, and lasted for about three years until 1635. The operations, which developed into a cruel anti-Christian persecution, began as a justifiable and legitimate war against the Portuguese settlers at Hūglī (Hooghly) in Bengal, who had committed many offences against the peace of the empire, and deserved chastisement for reasons unconcerned with religion.

The Portuguese at Hūglī. Portuguese traders, who had settled on the river bank a short distance above Sātgāon in Bengal in or about 1579, under the protection of an imperial *farmān*, had gradually strengthened their position by the erection of substantial buildings, so that the trade migrated from Sātgāon to the new port, which became known by the name of Hūglī (Hooghly).[1] If the intruders had confined their energies to the business of trade they might, perhaps, have remained undisturbed, in spite of the injury which they inflicted on the provincial customs revenue. They maintained a custom house of their own, and were specially strict in enforcing the levy of duty on tobacco, which had become an important article of trade since its introduction at the beginning of the seventeenth century. The Mogul officers were so little skilled either in sieges or in naval matters that they would have been disposed to submit to the loss of revenue rather than fight the foreigners, who were well armed and expert in the management of ships. But the arrogant Portuguese were not

[1] The name, which is spelt in old records as Ogolim, &c., probably is a corruption of *O golim* or *goli*, meaning 'the godown' or 'storehouse'. *O* is the Portuguese definite article (Hosten, in *Bengal Past and Present*, vol. x (1915), pp. 89–91).

content to make money quietly as merchants. They engaged in a cruel slave trade and habitually seized orphan children, whether Hindu or Muhammadan, whom they brought up as Christians. They were rash enough even to offend Mumtāz Mahall by detaining two slave girls whom she claimed.[1] The misdoings of the Portuguese had been brought to the notice of Shāhjahān before his accession. After the establishment of his throne he appointed Kāsim Khān as governor of Bengal, with instructions to exterminate the foreigners. The necessary preparations, which began in A.D. 1631 (A.H. 1040), were continued in the following year.

Siege and capture of Hūglī, 1632. The siege of Hūglī, begun on June 24, 1632, ended three months later in the capture of the place. The town, often described erroneously as a fortress,

> 'was situated on an open plain along the banks of the Ganges, and was exposed on all sides. It had neither wall nor rampart, but only an earthen embankment which they had thrown up, a thing of little value and still lesser strength.'

The governor of Bengal was so much afraid of European skill in gunnery and the management of ships that he collected a huge army, said to number 150,000, for the attack on the weak settlement. The Portuguese soldiers consisted of only 300 white men, with 600 or 700 native Christians. The tiny garrison held out for exactly three months until September 24, when the inhabitants embarked to go down the river. Most of the ships were lost, but a few reached Saugor Island, where a pestilence destroyed a large proportion of the survivors. In the opinion of the learned Jesuit historian, 'the defence of Calcutta in 1756 dwindles into insignificance before the feats of prowess achieved by the Portuguese of Hugli.' Multitudes were slain in the course of the siege. According to the *Bādshāh-nānah* :

> 'From the beginning of the siege to the conclusion, men and women, old and young, altogether nearly 10,000 of the enemy were killed, being either blown up with powder, drowned in water or burnt by fire.'

The imperialists had nearly a thousand fatal casualties. More than 4,000 prisoners were taken and brought to Agra, where they were offered the choice between conversion to Islām, and confinement or slavery under the most severe conditions. Comparatively few cared to save their bodies at the cost of their souls. The majority courageously faced torture and ill-treatment of every kind. 'So it came to pass', as the Muslim historian ferociously remarks, 'that many of them passed from prison to hell. Such of their idols as were likenesses of the prophets were thrown into the Jumna, the rest were broken to pieces.' 'The misery of these people', Bernier writes, 'is unparalleled in modern times.' The fierce persecution of Christians as such lasted until December 1635, after which date it gradually died down. Some of the Portuguese were allowed to reoccupy Hūglī, but the town never

[1] 'Filles', not 'daughters', as sometimes erroneously translated.

recovered its former prosperity. The misdoings of the piratical settlers met with a punishment so terrible that the feeling of compassion for their sufferings outweighs the righteous indignation directed against them for their abuse of power while they were strong.

The detailed story is best told by the Spanish friar, Manrique, whose text is not yet fully accessible in English.

The large numbers of killed and prisoners are explained by the Portuguese practice of forcing everybody under their control to adopt Christianity. The armed defenders, as already mentioned, seem to have been very few. The action of Shāhjahān quenched the hopes for the conversion of the royal family and Mogul India which had been encouraged by the proceedings of Akbar and Jahāngīr. Mumtāz Mahall's powerful brother, Āsaf Khān, did his best to shelter the Christians from the fury of the emperor.[1] Both Geronimo Veroneo, the reputed architect of the Tāj, and a wealthy Armenian who enjoyed high favour at court, spent large sums in ransoming miserable prisoners.

Destruction of Hindu temples. The excessive Muslim zeal which induced Shāhjahān to undertake a distinct persecution of Christians as such, in continuation of his legitimate warfare against the slave-raiders of Hūglī, prompted him in the same year (1632) to take severe action against his Hindu subjects, who, like the Christians, had ordinarily, although not invariably, experienced at the hands of Jahāngīr the same toleration which they had enjoyed in Akbar's reign. Jahāngīr had raised no objection to the erection of new temples, which is opposed to strict Muhammadan law. Shāhjahān now resolved to put a stop to the practice, and gave orders that

> 'at Benares, and throughout all his dominions in every place, all temples that had been begun should be cast down. It was now reported from the province of Allahabad that seventy-six temples had been destroyed in the district of Benares.'

No record of the destruction in other parts of the empire has been preserved, but it must have been considerable.

Shāhjahān's Deccan policy. Shāhjahān, as has been seen, was engaged in the prosecution of operations for the annexation of the Deccan sultanates of Ahmadnagar, Golkonda, and Bījāpur in the year 1631, when the famine occurred and his wife died. He then returned to Agra. It will be convenient to give in this place a connected summary view of the imperial plans and military operations in the Deccan during the earlier part of Shāhjahān's reign.

The policy of Akbar, who avowedly aimed at the subjugation of all the kingdoms of the Deccan, had so much success that the entire kingdom of Khāndēsh and a small portion of that of Ahmadnagar proper, as well as Berar, then a dependency of Ahmadnagar, were absorbed into the imperial dominions during the years 1600

[1] See Hosten, op. cit., especially pp. 43–5, 51, 81, 94, 99.

to 1605. The revolt of Prince Salīm, the deaths of his brothers, and the decease of the emperor himself in October 1605 prevented Akbar from pursuing his ambitious schemes any farther. Ahmadnagar, although formally constituted a separate *sūba* or province, actually came under the imperial rule only to a small extent. An able Abyssinian minister, Malik Ambar, succeeded in retaining or recovering the greater part of the kingdom, which was ruled in the name of a new sultan. Both Golkonda and Bījāpur continued to enjoy real independence, and had obtained large accessions of territory after the fall of the Hindu empire of Vijayanagar in 1565. Jahāngīr, while cherishing the same ideal as Akbar, made no considerable progress in the task of the subjugation of the Deccan. Shāhjahān, who was stationed there at the time of his father's death in 1627, resumed the family designs of conquest as soon as possible after his accession, and did a good deal to realize them.

Early operations. In A.D. 1630 the imperialists were compelled to raise the siege of Parēndā, a strong fortress belonging to Ahmadnagar. In the same year Fath Khān, the minister of Ahmadnagar, and son of Malik Ambar, who had died at an advanced age in 1626, entered into communication with the imperial government and informed Shāhjahān that in order to protect himself he had seized and confined his own sovereign, the Nizām Shāhī. The emperor replied by instructions to kill the captive. Fath Khān complied, and placed on the throne a boy of the royal family, named Husain Shāh. Shāhjahān, regarding Muhammad Ādil Khān, Sultan of Bījāpur, as contumacious because he desired to retain his independence, directed Āsaf Khān to require his submission, and, in the event of non-compliance, to conquer as much territory as possible and to lay the rest waste. In 1631 the imperial forces besieged Bījāpur, but were compelled to withdraw owing to want of supplies, the country-side having been laid waste, partly by the Bījāpurīs in self-defence, and partly by the invaders.

> 'On whatever road they went they killed and made prisoners, and ravaged and laid waste on both sides. From the time of their entering the territories to the time of their departure they kept up this devastation and plunder. The best part of the country was trodden under.'

That merciless warfare was not provoked by the government or people of Bījāpur. It was ordered deliberately with the sole purpose of gratifying the emperor's ambition and lust for riches.

End of the Ahmadnagar kingdom. Shāhjahān, on the completion of his savage operations, returned to Āgra, where he occupied himself with the planning and building of the Tāj. He appointed Mahābat Khān, Khān Khānān, to be viceroy of Khāndēsh and the Deccan.

Malik Ambar's son, Fath Khān, proved as faithless to Shāhjahān as he had been to his own sovereign. In 1631 he defended against the imperial forces the fortress of Daulatābād (Dēogiri), which his father had fortified. But the explosion of a mine, and the payment by the Khān Khānān of a bribe of ten and a half lakhs of rupees, were sufficient inducements to make him surrender. The fortress, which the besiegers were quite unable to take by fair fighting, was thus bought; as Asīrgarh had been bought by Akbar, and as many forts were ingloriously acquired by Aurangzēb some years later.

The shameless traitor Fath Khān was taken into the imperial service and granted a liberal salary. The young prince whom he had set on the throne of Ahmadnagar was consigned to Gwālior for lifelong imprisonment, and the kingdom of the Nizām Shāhīs was ended (A.D. 1632; A.H. 1042).

In the following year (1633) the emperor went to the Panjāb and Kashmīr. Prince Shujā failed to take Parēndā, and Mahābat Khān, Khān Khānān, died.

Campaign of 1635–6. In 1635 Shāhjahān resumed seriously his plans for the final reduction of the Deccan states, especially Bījāpur, where the independent attitude of the wealthy Ādil Shāhī dynasty was a standing offence in his eyes. A minor complication was introduced by the operations of the Marāthā chieftain, Shāhjī or Sāhū, who set up another Nizām Shāhī boy as the nominal Sultan of Ahmadnagar. Shāhjī will be heard of often again, especially as being the father of the more famous Sivājī. The appearance of the Marāthās on the stage of Mogul history may be dated from the early years of Shāhjahān's reign, or from about 1630 to 1635.

The emperor sent written commands to the Sultans of both Golkonda and Bījāpur requiring them to recognize his suzerainty, to pay tribute regularly, and to abstain from support of Shāhjī and his allies of Ahmadnagar. The ruler of Golkonda (Hyderābād), unable to resist the might of the Mogul, complied humbly with all demands, reading the *khutba* and striking coins in the name of Shāhjahān.

The Ādil Shāh of Bījāpur was less complaisant, and, although willing to make some show of compliance, was determined to resist the imperial aggression. Shāhjahān continued his ruthless policy, and 'the imperial order was given to kill and ravage as much as possible in the Bījāpur territories'. Three armies converged on the country of the hapless sultan, burning, robbing, enslaving, and slaying without mercy or distinction. For instance, in one village 2,000 men were killed; and in another place 2,000 prisoners, male and female, were sold as slaves. Akbar's prohibition of enslaving prisoners of war, even if it was obeyed in his reign, which may be doubted, had been long forgotten, and exercised no restraint over his pitiless grandson.

Treaty with Bījāpur, 1636. Although the capital city was saved by the desperate expedient of flooding the surrounding lands, effectual defence of the kingdom as a whole against the invading hosts was impracticable, and the Ādil Shāh was constrained to submit to terms only slightly less onerous than those imposed on Golkonda. The treaty, ratified by Shāhjahān on May 6, 1636, required the sultan to yield obedience to the emperor; to pay a peace-offering of twenty lakhs of rupees; to respect the frontier of Golkonda, now a tributary state of the empire ; and to abstain from aiding Shāhjī in hostile measures. The Ahmadnagar State was definitely blotted out of existence, its territories being divided between Shāhjahān and the Ādil Shāh, whose independence was in a manner recognized by the imperial abstention from the demand for a regular annual tribute. The concession was more formal than real.

Aurangzēb appointed viceroy of the Deccan. The settlement so effected lasted for about twenty years. The peace was followed immediately by the appointment (July 14, 1636) of the young Prince Aurangzēb, then nearly eighteen years of age, as Viceroy of the Deccan. His charge comprised four provinces, namely :

(1) Khāndēsh, in the valley of the Tāptī ; capital, Burhānpur ; fortress, Asīrgarh.

(2) Berar (Birār), lying to the south-east of Khāndēsh, and now attached to the Central Provinces ; capital, Ellichpur (Ilichpur) ; fortress, Gāwīlgarh.

(3) Telingāna, or the Telugu country ; a wild, ill-defined region of hills and forests, situated between Berar and the Golkonda State ; capital, Nāndēr ; fortress, Kandhār (Kandahār) ; both being now in the Nizam's Dominions.

(4) Daulatābād, including the imperial portion of the late Ahmadnagar kingdom ; capital, Aurangābād (formerly Khirkī), a few miles from Daulatābād, which was considered the principal of many important fortresses.

The four provinces together were reckoned to contain 64 forts, several of which were still in possession of Shāhjī or other hostile holders. The gross revenue was estimated at 5 'crores', or 50 millions of rupees, out of which Aurangzēb was expected to defray all expenses, civil and military.

Aurangzēb as viceroy, 1636–44. It is unnecessary to follow the young viceroy in all the fights and sieges which occupied much of his time. He annexed Baglānā, a small principality in the hills near Nāsik. Shāhjī submitted and surrendered certain forts. In 1637 Aurangzēb went to Agra for his marriage with Dilras Bāno Bēgam, daughter of Shāh Nawāz Khān, a nobleman belonging to a junior branch of the Persian royal family. She became the mother of three daughters and two sons, the princes Azam and Akbar.

The difficulties of Aurangzēb's first viceroyalty of the Deccan were many. The country could not pay its way, and the viceroy was continually embarrassed by the distrust shown by his father, who was completely under the influence of Dārā Shikoh, his eldest son, and the lifelong enemy of Aurangzēb. A famous accident was associated with the termination of Aurangzēb's first term of provincial government. On March 26, 1644, the Princess Jahānārā, Shāhjahān's favourite daughter, was dangerously burnt owing to her light skirt having caught fire from a candle in the palace at Agra. She hovered between life and death for four months, and was not finally cured until November.[1] In May Aurangzēb had visited Agra in order to see the patient. Three weeks after his arrival he was compelled to resign his official rank and allowances, retiring for the moment into private life. His temporary withdrawal from office has been usually misunderstood and represented as a hypocritical manifestation of religious fervour. It is now known that his action was forced by reasons purely political, having no concern with religious feelings. He had incurred his father's displeasure for some cause not recorded, and anticipated formal punishment by resignation. In one of his letters he states that his life was threatened, and it seems clear that his enforced retirement was due in some way or other to the machinations of his hostile brother, and his own resentment at his treatment.

After eight and a half months of unemployment Aurangzēb was appointed to the difficult government of the province of Gujarāt (February 16, 1645). He conducted the administration to the emperor's satisfaction, and in January 1647 was transferred to a dangerous post as Governor of Balkh and Badakhshān.

Kandahār. Kandahār, in virtue of its importance both as a strategical position and as the principal mart on the trade route between India and Persia, had been the subject of contention between the Persian Shāhs and the Indian Pādshāhs since the time of Humāyūn, who held the city for a few years. The Persians recovered it during Akbar's minority, but lost it in April 1545, owing to the treachery of the governor who betrayed it to an officer of Akbar. In 1622,[2] during Jahāngīr's reign, Shāh Abbās the Great regained possession of the place, and Persia held it until 1638, when Alī Mardān Khān betrayed it to a representative of Shāhjahān. The traitor was rewarded by the immediate gift of a lakh of rupees, and subsequent lucrative office under Shāhjahān, who attached high importance to the acquisition. He expended large sums on the fortification of the city and its dependencies. In the autumn of 1648 Shāhjahān heard of Persian preparations for the attack on Kandahār, but was persuaded to defer sending adequate reinforcements until the spring when they were too late.

Mogul Central Asian policy. Shāhjahān, like his father and grandfather, had always felt a strong desire to exercise complete control over the hilly region of Badakhshān, to the north of Kāfiristān, and the more distant province of Balkh, the ancient

[1] The familiar story made current by Orme and Stewart to the effect that Jahānārā was cured by an English surgeon named Gabriel Boughton (Bowden), who refused any reward other than a grant of trading privileges to the E. I. Co., cannot be true. The ship *Hopewell* did not arrive at Surat until September 1644. Jahānārā's accident occurred in March (o. s.) of that year, and her cure was completed in November. According to the Surat letter dated January 3, 1645, Boughton, 'late chirurgeon of the *Hopewell*', was nominated then for duty at Agra. It follows that he must have been at Surat all the latter part of 1644 and that he travelled to Agra in 1645 (Foster, *Ind. Ant.*, 1911, p. 254).

[2] Raverty gives the date as August 1622. Sarkar has 1623.

Bactria, lying between the Hindu Kush and the Oxus. The Mogul emperors at times dreamed even of extending their sway over all the countries connected with the early glories of their family, and of bringing Transoxiana, otherwise known as Bokhāra or Samarkand, under the sceptre of Hindostan. In 1645 (end of A. H. 1055), circumstances being favourable, Prince Murād Bakhsh and Alī Mardān Khān were able to occupy both Badakhshān and Balkh.

The prince, who hated such uncomfortable foreign service, fell into disgrace because he insisted on coming home. The prime minister, Sadullāh Khān, was then deputed to put things in order, and Murād Bakhsh after a short time was restored to favour. Shāhjahān, unwilling to abandon his long cherished ambition, now selected Aurangzēb to hold and consolidate the recent conquests. His efforts ended in disastrous failure. The imperial forces were compelled to evacuate Balkh. During the retreat (end of 1647) they lost about 5,000 men in the passes.

First siege of Kandahār, 1649. Aurangzēb, after his failure in Balkh, was transferred to the governorship of the Multān province. The emperor moved to Lahore and Kābul in order to guard against a threatened invasion by the Uzbegs, who had been emboldened by their success in defeating the ill-conceived Balkh expedition. The reader may remember that similar fears had detained Akbar near the north-western frontier for thirteen years from 1585 to 1598. Aurangzēb's stay at Multān was short. When news came in of the Persian designs on Kandahār the emperor determined to entrust Aurangzēb with the task of relieving the garrison. The prince made energetic preparations, but was sent too late, the city having been taken by the enemy long before he could arrive. The capitulation (February 11, 1649) was due to the inactivity and incapacity of Daulat Khān, the commandant. Aurangzēb was directed to recover Kandahār before the Persians should have time to consolidate their hold. He combined his forces with the army under the command of Sadullāh Khān, the prime minister, and attacked the city in May, without effect. The expeditionary force, equipped merely as a reinforcement, was useless for besieging purposes, being destitute of heavy ordnance, while the Persians were superior in military skill. The siege was raised on September 5, and Aurangzēb endured for the second time the humiliation of failure as a general. A victory gained over the Persians at Shāh Mīr on the Arghandab in August covered up the failure to retake Kandahār, and gave the Indian court an excuse for ceremonial rejoicing.

Second siege of Kandahār, 1652. Shāhjahān would not abandon his design of retaking Kandahār, to which he rightly attached high importance. The next three years were spent by him and Aurangzēb, who had returned to Multān, in organizing a powerful army with a siege-train and large supply of munitions for the investment of the city. Aurangzēb was nominally the commander-in-chief, but the conduct of operations actually was in the hands of Sadullāh Khān, the prime minister, acting under the orders of Shāhjahān at Kābul. Sadullāh Khān and Aurangzēb again combined their forces at the beginning of May 1652 near Kandahār and undertook the investment of the city. They had strict orders from the emperor not to attempt an assault until a practicable breach had been effected. All their efforts to effect such a breach failed, owing to the inefficiency of the Indian gunnery and the superior skill of the Persians. Early in July Shāhjahān was constrained to order the abandonment of the siege, and Aurangzēb once more tasted the bitterness of defeat. His failure, although more his misfortune than his personal fault, finally destroyed his father's confidence in his powers.

Third siege of Kandahār, 1653. Prince Dārā Shikoh, the emperor's favourite, who was shortly afterwards exalted by the title of *Shāh Buland Ikbāl*, or 'King of Lofty Fortune', bragged that he would soon redress his hated brother's failure. Immense exertions got together a fresh army and siege-train in the short space of about three months. But the elder prince's 'lofty fortune' did not help him. After operations lasting five months he too had to confess to failure, and raise the siege in September 1653.

The Mogul dynasty never again attempted to recover Kandahār, and the repeated defeats of the best armies which India could raise decisively established the military superiority of the Persians.

Cost of siege; imperial revenue. Trustworthy estimates place the cost of the three sieges of Kandahār (1649, 1652, 1653) at 12 'crores', or 120 millions of rupees, more than half of the annual income of the empire, which is stated to have been 22 'crores', or 220 millions of rupees, in 1648. During Shāhjahān's reign the ordinary rate of exchange with Europe was 2*s.* 3*d.* per rupee. The imperial revenue, therefore, may be reckoned as 24¾ millions of pounds sterling, or, in round figures, as about 25 millions.

Demolition of walls of Chitōr. Shāhjahān obtained some cheap compensation for his conspicuous defeats by the Persians in the destruction of the new fortifications of Chitōr, which Rānā Jagat Singh had ventured to construct, in defiance of a prohibition recorded by Jahāngīr. The submission of the reigning Rānā was secured by the cruel devastation of his territory, and a fortnight's work sufficed to demolish the walls of the fortress.

Aurangzēb again sent to the Deccan. Aurangzēb had not been a success as a general in the regions of the north-west, all his undertakings—the Balkh expedition, and the first and second sieges of Kandahār—having ended in disaster. He could not remain at court, where both his father and his elder brother were hostile, and it was necessary to place him somewhere at a distance. The emperor insisted on his resuming charge of the Deccan, to which he was reappointed immediately after his return from Kandahār. The prince crossed the Narbadā at the beginning of 1653, and lingered nine months at Burhānpur, where he had been captivated by the charms of a young singing woman named Hīrā Bāī, otherwise known as Zainābādī Mahall. Towards the end of the year he took up his residence at the official capital, either in the fort of Daulatābād or in the neighbouring town of Aurangābād.

The remaining events of importance in the reign of Shāhjahān, until the war of succession began in 1658, are chiefly concerned with Aurangzēb's proceedings in the Deccan.

Administrative difficulties. The financial and administrative difficulties which had beset Aurangzēb during his first term of office as viceroy of the Deccan were still more troublesome during his second term. The country had been ill governed by a succession of incompetent and frequently changed officers, who had allowed the cultivated area to decrease, villages to be abandoned, and the people to be cruelly oppressed. Nothing like the nominal assessment of the land revenue could be collected, and in consequence both the imperial treasury and the provincial income suffered, while the *jāgīrdārs*, to whom the land revenue of certain districts had been assigned for their personal support and for the maintenance of their military contingents, were unable to meet their obligations. Aurangzēb was obliged to draw heavily on his cash reserves, and his requests to his father for pecuniary assistance were either absolutely rejected or granted with extreme reluctance. The prince did his best to restore cultivation and improve the revenue, but the results of bad government for many years could not be quickly remedied. While much improvement was effected, much remained to be done when the war of succession broke out.

Murshīd Kulī Khān's 'settlement'. Aurangzēb was fortunate in commanding the services of an exceptionally skilled revenue officer named Murshīd Kulī Khān. For fiscal purposes the Deccan was divided into two sections, namely, the Pāīnghāt, or Lowlands, comprising Khāndēsh, or the Tāptī valley, with part of Berar, and the Bālāghāt, or Highlands, comprising the rest of the viceregal jurisdiction. Murshīd Kulī Khān, a Persian, originally in the suite of Alī Mardān Khān, came to the Deccan with Aurangzēb as Dīwān of the Highlands, and at the beginning of 1656 was promoted to be Dīwān of the whole Deccan. Before his time the management of revenue affairs had been marked by complete want of system. The assessment of the state demand was made in a rough-and-ready fashion by the imposition of a small charge on the land cultivated by each plough, without any attempt at survey or valuation. Murshīd Kulī Khān extended to the Deccan Todar Mall's system of survey and assessment, or 'settlement', so far as possible; but was wise enough to make many local exceptions, and to preserve the old practice of fixing a lump sum for each plough-land, whenever a more scientific arrangement would not work in practice. He also was willing to accept payment in kind, and to arrange for the division of the crop by various methods. Advances of cash to the peasantry for the restoration of cultivation were freely made with good results. A capable observer noted in 1658 that then there was no waste land near Aurangābād.

The hostility of Dārā Shikoh and the consequent estrangement of Shāhjahān greatly complicated the difficulties of administration. The emperor was so dissatisfied with Aurangzēb that he offered the Deccan to his son Shujā, who did not care to accept a transfer from Bengal.

Aurangzēb's aggressive policy. Aurangzēb did not confine his attention to the problems of internal administration. He was an ambitious, aggressive ruler, eager to carry on the traditional policy of his dynasty, and play the part of 'a great pike in a pond', as Chaplain Terry puts it. His main purpose was to destroy the independence of the sultanates of Golkonda and Bījāpur, and to transfer to himself and his supporters the immense riches and resources of both kingdoms. Mere ambition and greed always were motives sufficient to set any Mogul sovereign or prince in motion to wage a war of unprovoked aggression. But the emperor and his son, as bigoted Sunnī Musalmāns, took special pleasure in warring with the Sultans of Golkonda and Bījāpur, who adhered to the Shīa faith, and looked for alliance and protection to the Shāh of Persia rather than to the Pādshāh of Hindostan. The aggressive wars were waged with ruthless ferocity, and when ultimately the Sultans were dethroned they received no generous treatment from the victors. The defence of their independence by the two states is always described by the court historians in insulting language as villainous contumacy.

Pretexts for invasion never were lacking. Golkonda had become avowedly a tributary state since 1636, and arrears were always due. Although the sense of dignity (*'izzat*) of the Bījāpur sultan had been respected so far that he was not required to pay a fixed annual tribute, he was expected to make 'presents' every year, so that the distinction between his position and that of Golkonda was little more than a matter of form. Bījāpur never paid anything that it could avoid paying. Other reasons for displeasure against the sultans were easily found when wanted.

Mīr Jumla. Aurangzēb's chief helper in his designs on the Deccan kingdoms, and a little later on the throne of Hindostan, was the Persian adventurer, generally known as Mīr Jumla, a merchant from Ardistān. Following the example set by Mahmūd Gāwān under the Bahmanī dynasty in the fifteenth century, he began as a successful trader, and quickly went on to make himself virtual master of the Golkonda or Hyderabad kingdom as prime minister of Abdullah Kutb Shāh. Not content with his position as the chief of the Kutb Shāh's servants, he carved out for himself a domain virtually amounting to an independent kingdom, by conquering and annexing the Karnatik, or Kanarese country under the rule of the Rājā of Chandragiri, the representative of the Vijayanagar dynasty. Mīr Jumla's dominion, about 300 miles long by 50 broad, yielded a revenue of forty lakhs of rupees and supported a considerable army especially strong in its park of good artillery manned by European gunners.

The semi-independent position acquired by Mīr Jumla naturally aroused the jealousy of his nominal master, the Kutb Shāh, who attempted to bring his too powerful servant under his control. Mīr Jumla defended himself by intrigues with Bījāpur, Persia, Shāhjahān, and Aurangzēb. Ultimately he attached himself definitely to the Mogul service and accepted high office from Shāhjahān, thus becoming a traitor to the Kutb Shāh.

Aurangzēb's treacherous policy. Aurangzēb forced hostilities on that unhappy and incompetent monarch, whom he was determined to destroy. His purpose is frankly expressed in written instructions under his hand addressed to his eldest son, Prince Muhammad Sultan, which were :

'Qutb-ul-Mulk is a coward and will probably offer no resistance. Surround his palace with your artillery and also post a detachment to bar his flight to Golkonda. But before doing so, send a carefully chosen messenger to him, saying :

"I had been so long expecting that you would meet me and hospitably ask me to stay with you. But as you have not done so, I have myself come to you." Immediately on delivering this message, attack him impetuously, and if you can manage it, lighten his neck of the burden of his head. The best means of achieving this plan are cleverness, promptitude, and lightness of hand.' [1]

Such was the treachery which Aurangzēb and his father were not ashamed to employ against a Muhammadan king whose only offence was his independence.

Prince Muhammad Sultan presently entered Hyderabad, which was plundered by his soldiery, in spite of orders forbidding excesses. The prince and his father, Aurangzēb, who were not above taking advantage of the irregular action of their troops, appropriated many valuables, including a library of precious manuscripts. Hyderabad, however, was so rich that much wealth remained to tempt another attack. The king, meantime, had shut himself up in the fortress of Golkonda a few miles distant.

Siege of Golkonda ; peace. In February 1656 Aurangzēb began the siege of Golkonda, and progressed slowly, after the manner of Mogul generals when besieging strong places. Being resolved to annex the whole of the kingdom, the wealth of which he coveted, he rejected all proposals for peace. Shāhjahān, however, who had reasons of his own, was more accommodating, and accepted the Sultan's proposals for peace on certain terms, promising complete pardon. Aurangzēb held back that letter in order to extort more favourable terms, and the emperor, having been referred to, sanctioned his son's action. A little later Shāhjahān was induced by Prince Dārā Shikoh and Princess Jahānārā to put a summary stop to the war. Aurangzēb was compelled to raise the siege on March 30. The Kutb Shāh agreed to pay a considerable indemnity and to cede a district. By a secret agreement with Aurangzēb the Sultan also promised to make Prince Muhammad Sultan his heir.

Mīr Jumla prime minister. Mīr Jumla, who had joined Aurangzēb's camp with a powerful army, was now appointed

[1] *Adab*, 187 *b* ; in Sarkar, *History*, vol. i, p. 230.

prime minister of the empire in succession to Allāmī Sadullāh Khān who had recently died. The deceased minister, although unfortunate in his military adventures, was reputed one of the best Muhammadan administrators whom India has known.

The Rājā of Chandragiri, the representative of the great dynasty of Vijayanagar, tried to secure protection from the emperor, offering even to become a Muslim. But his efforts failed utterly and he was left to the tender mercies of Bījāpur, Golkonda, and Mīr Jumla.

Foundation of Madras. His grant in March 1639–40 of the site of Madras to an English factor, although unnoticed at the time, was one of the most important events in the reign of Shāhjahān, as being the beginning of British territorial acquisition in India.

War with Bījāpur. The Sultan or King of Bījāpur had taken advantage of the security afforded by the treaty of 1636 to extend his dominions to the east, south, and west. At the end of 1649 the powerful fortress of Jingī or Gingee, now in the South Arcot District, capitulated to him, and he also gained a certain amount of success against the Portuguese of Goa. The reigning Sultan, Muhammad Ādil Shāh (1626–56), ruled a realm extending across the peninsula from sea to sea, maintained a magnificent court, and had raised his kingdom to a degree of wealth and power previously unattained. That fortunate sovereign died on November 4, 1656. The succession of his only son, a youth eighteen years of age, naturally resulted in internal disturbances, which also offered an opportunity for the gratification of the ambition of the Mogul dynasty. Shāhjahān readily granted his viceroy power to act as he thought fit. Aurangzēb invaded the kingdom with the help of the traitor Mīr Jumla at the earliest possible moment. Bīdar fell at the end of March 1657, after a gallant defence ; Mahābat Khān and Aurangzēb cruelly ravaged the Bījāpur territory ; and on August 1 Kalyānī capitulated.

The complete conquest of the kingdom was in sight, when Shāhjahān intervened and ratified a treaty of peace, by which the Sultan agreed to surrender Bīdar, Kalyānī, and Parēndā, besides certain other places, and to pay a large indemnity. The final operations in the Deccan undertaken by Aurangzēb were directed to checking the daring raids of young Sivājī, the Marāthā leader, son of Shāhjī Bhonslā, who has been mentioned more than once. The dangerous illness of Shāhjahān, which began early in September 1657, and resulted in the war of succession, put a stop to all thoughts of further conquest in the Deccan. The sultanates obtained a respite for nearly thirty years.

Disputed succession. Although the preferential claim of the eldest son of a Chagatāi Mogul sovereign to succeed his father on the throne was generally acknowledged, his absolute right was not established sufficiently to secure his position without dispute. Humāyūn, Akbar, Jahāngīr, and Shāhjahān had all found themselves compelled to confront the rivalry of near relatives. Shāhjahān desired to be succeeded by his eldest son, Prince Dārā Shikoh, and took every practicable step to ensure the fulfilment of his desire. Unprecedented titles, honours, and wealth were lavished on the much loved senior prince, who was kept constantly near the imperial person, and, as Shāhjahān grew old, was allowed to exercise most of the imperial prerogatives. The emperor's three other sons observed with unconcealed jealousy the favour bestowed on the eldest-born, and all three were resolved to contest his succession. Each thought himself capable of reigning, and was prepared to stake life and everything else on the issue of the conflict which was regarded as inevitable whenever their father should die. The fact that all the four sons were children of one mother, Dilras Bāno Bēgam, was no check on their ambitions. They all accepted the Timūrid maxim that ' no one is a relation to a king ', and well knew that mere abstention from contest would not save the life of any of the brothers after one of their number had taken his seat on the throne definitely. The struggle for the succession had to be fought out to the bitter end—*takht yā takhta*, which may be loosely rendered as ' crown or coffin ', was the inevitable goal.

The long story of the war of succession has been vividly related by several contemporary authors in Persian, French, and English, whose narratives have been digested critically in Professor Sarkar's work, the second volume being wholly devoted to the subject. In this place it is not practicable to give more than a summary outline of the tragic happenings.

The sons of Shāhjahān. The four sons of Shāhjahān were Dārā Shikoh, Shujā, Aurangzēb, and Murād Bakhsh, all men of mature age in 1657, aged respectively 43, 41, 39, and about 33 years. All the four had had considerable experienee in military and civil affairs on a large scale. The eldest, who remained with his father, was viceroy of the Panjāb, and other provinces on the north-west, which he administered through deputies. Shujā ruled the great territories of Bengal and Orissa. Aurangzēb controlled the Deccan, while Murād Bakhsh governed Gujarāt and the west. Thus the four princes held the semi-independent government of regions, each of which had been a powerful kingdom, and could supply its ruler with abundant cash and many thousands of armed men. The gigantic hoard of treasure stored in the vaults of the Agra fort was to be at the disposal of the victor.

All the princes possessed the soldier's virtue of personal valour, which was displayed conspicuously by both Aurangzēb and Murād Bakhsh. Dārā Shikoh's considerable natural abilities were neutralized by the violence of his temper and the intolerable arrogance of manner, which gained him hosts of enemies. Shujā, an agreeable man, with some skill as a general, was rendered ineffective by his love of pleasure, and his unreadiness to take instant action at the decisive moment. Murād Bakhsh was a passionate, headstrong, tyrannical man, the bravest of the brave, but drunken, dissolute, and brainless. It is needless to draw a formal sketch of the character of Aurangzēb, whose consummmate ability as an unscrupulous intriguer and cool politician is apparent on the face of the narrative. Although his failures in Balkh and at Kandahār may be regarded as disparaging to his skill as a commander of armies, his imperturbable self-possession enabled him to emerge with success from most embarrassing tactical situations during the war of succession. His indomitable resolve to win the throne at any cost and by any means carried him through and gave him victory.

Religious hostility. The unorthodoxy of Dārā Shikoh was an important factor in the struggle. That prince, while continuing to conform to the Sunnī ritual and to be a professed Muslim of the Hanafī school, was deeply imbued with the heretical mysticism of the Sūfīs. He also associated gladly with Hindu philosophers and went so far as to take part in producing a Persian version of some of the Upanishads, which he declared to be a revelation earlier than the Korān.[1] He was so intimate with Father Buseo and other priests that he was believed by some persons to be within measurable distance of embracing Christianity. That attitude towards Islām infuriated Aurangzēb, who certainly was a devout Sunnī Muslim, whatever judgement may be formed of his moral character. He regarded his eldest brother as a pestilent infidel, deserving of worse than death. Shujā, who professed the Shīa faith, and Murād Bakhsh, who was reputed to be privately inclined to that form of religion, concurred with Aurangzēb in hostility to Dārā Shikoh's latitudinarian views, and were glad to help their own causes by appeals to religious fanaticism. The Rājpūts were the principal support of Dārā Shikoh, and if Jaswant Singh of Mārwār (Jodhpur) had not behaved with shameless treachery the eldest prince might have won.

Rebellion of Aurangzēb. During the autumn of 1657 endless plotting and counter-plotting went on. Shāhjahān, whose health was partly restored, sought to secure the succession of his first-born son, and to prevent civil war if possible. Aurangzēb continually temporized and endeavoured to shirk the responsibility of open rebellion. He was anxious to secure the fruits of his military successes in the Deccan, but failed in that design, and was constrained to give his whole attention to the contest with his father and brothers in the north. Both Shujā and Murād Bakhsh forced his hand by assuming the imperial style and striking coins, each in his own name. Shujā was the first to enthrone himself, doing so at Rājmahāl, then the capital of Bengal, in the autumn of 1657, immediately on receipt of the news of his father's dangerous illness. Murād Bakhsh took similar action at Ahmadābād, on December 5, in opposition to the advice of his ally, Aurangzēb, who preferred to move with extreme caution. At the end of October Aurangzēb took the prudent precaution of seizing all the

[1] For list of his works see 'Dara Shikoh as an Author' (*J. P. H. S.*, vol. ii, pp. 21–38); and Blochmann in *J. A. S. B.*, part 1, 1870, pp. 273–9. The spellings *Shikoh* and *Shukoh* are both legitimate.

ferries over the Narbadā, and so concealing the progress of events in the Deccan from his father and eldest brother, while securing his own passage into Hindostan. Late in December Shāhjahān sent peremptory orders recalling Mīr Jumla to court. Aurangzēb countered that step by arresting his confederate and attaching his property. The circumstances indicate that probably Mīr Jumla connived at his own arrest. Certainly he did not resent it, nor did he fail to continue to give his ally invaluable support when released. Aurangzēb had thus become a rebel, and could no longer continue his temporizing policy. Mīr Jumla's fine park of artillery proved to be extremely useful. At the beginning of February 1658 Aurangzēb began to exercise imperial prerogatives by granting titles and making appointments to high offices. He crossed the Narbadā on April 3 without opposition, and effected a junction with Murād's army in Mālwā, in the neighbourhood of Ujjain. At that time the agreement between Aurangzēb and Murād Bakhsh, as solemnly recorded in writing, was to the effect that the empire should be divided, Murād Bakhsh receiving the Panjāb, Kābul, Kashmīr, and Sind, while Aurangzēb should take the rest. No provision was made for Shujā. A little later Aurangzēb seems to have pretended that he desired Murād Bakhsh to become sole emperor, but at the beginning of the war the policy of partition had been accepted formally.

Rupee of Murād Bakhsh.

Battle of Dharmat, April 15, 1658. Shāhjahān experienced much difficulty in procuring generals to oppose princes of the blood-royal, especially inasmuch as he gave instructions that the lives of his rebel sons were to be spared if possible. The only prince available to lead an imperialist army at a distance was Dārā Shikoh's elder son, Sulaimān Shikoh, who was sent to fight Shujā. Rājā Jaswant Singh of Mārwār (Jodhpur) and Kāsim Khān were induced to undertake the duty of stopping Aurangzēb and Murād Bakhsh. The hostile armies, approximately equal in numbers, met at Dharmat, fourteen miles SSW. of Ujjain, on April 15 (o.s.), 1658, with the result that the imperialists were utterly defeated. Their disaster was due partly to the evils of divided command and jealousy between the Rājpūts and the Musalmāns, and partly to the bad choice of ground made and the erroneous tactics pursued by the Rājā. Kāsim Khān did little to help his master's cause, and the gallant Rājpūt clans suffered most of the casualties.

Battle of Samūgarh, May 29, 1658. The rebel princes pressed on, securing the passage of the Chambal over a neglected ford. Dārā Shikoh led out from Agra a superior and powerful force, which met the rebels at Samūgarh or Sambhūgarh, eight miles to the east of Agra Fort. The battle fought on May 29, in the terrible heat of summer, was vigorously contested, and the Rājpūts, although injudiciously handled, again did honour to the traditions of their race. Equal valour was displayed by Aurangzēb and Murād Bakhsh, who risked their lives without hesitation. The younger prince received three wounds in the face and the howdah of his elephant bristled with arrows. When the imperialists had suffered severely, and Dārā Shikoh's elephant had become the mark of the enemy's guns so that it was in imminent danger of destruction, the heir apparent was persuaded to come down and mount a horse. That action settled the fate of the battle. His remaining troops broke when they saw the empty howdah, and Dārā Shikoh fled to Agra with a few exhausted followers. His camp, guns, and all he possessed fell into the hands of the victors. Some accounts represent his defeat, and especially his descent from the elephant, as being due to the treacherous advice of Khalīlullah Khān, one of his generals, but the tactical errors committed by the imperialist commanders suffice to explain the disaster. The battle really decided the war of succession. All the subsequent efforts to retrieve the cause then lost, whether made by Dārā Shikoh himself, by his son, Sulaimān Shikoh, or by Shujā and Murād Bakhsh, were in vain. Aurangzēb proved himself to be by far the ablest of the princes in every phase of the contest, which was not ended until two years later, in May 1660, when Shujā met his miserable fate.

Fate of Shāhjahān and Murād Bakhsh. Aurangzēb lost no time. On June 8 he received the surrender of the Agra Fort with all its treasures, and made his father a prisoner for life. Father and son never met again. Murād Bakhsh rashly attempted open opposition and was silly enough to allow himself on June 25 to be inveigled into a manifest trap by his unscrupulous brother, while encamped at Rūpnagar near Mathurā. He was imprisoned first at Salīmgarh, Delhi, and then at Gwālior, where he was executed in December 1661. Aurangzēb, who, like Henry VIII of England, preferred to kill his victims with all the forms of law when possible, instigated a son of Alī Nakī, the dīwān whom Murād Bakhsh had murdered in Gujarāt in 1657, to claim the price of blood under Koranic law. The prince, after trial by a Kāzī, was duly declared deserving of death and beheaded in his prison.

Fate of Shujā and Prince Muhammad Sultan. Aurangzēb went through an informal ceremony of enthronement, equivalent to the coronation in European monarchies, on July 21, but refrained from inserting his name in the *khutba* or ' bidding prayer ', and from issuing coins. He devoted all his energies to the pursuit of Dārā Shikoh, who was hunted through Delhi and Lahore as far as Multān by Aurangzēb, who was then, in September, obliged to turn back in order to meet the danger threatening him by reason of Shujā's advance from Bengal, and the operations of Dārā Shikoh's son, Sulaimān Shikoh. The latter had defeated Shujā at Bahādurpur near Benares in February 1658, but was too far away to be able to help his father in time. Shujā, who was strong in artillery, and had a large fleet of boats, recovered from his defeat, and during the autumn entertained high hopes of success. But on January 5, 1659, his army was routed at Khajwah in the Fatehpore District, by a superior force under Aurangzēb in person, and he never again had any real prospect of vanquishing his enemy. Mīr Jumla pursued the prince unrelentingly with an army fivefold the strength of his; and drove him across Bengal to Dacca and thence over the Arakan frontier in May 1660. He and all his family were slaughtered by the Arakanese, but the exact details were never ascertained, and false reports that Shujā still lived continued to be current for some years.

Aurangzēb's eldest son, Prince Muhammad Sultan, having quarrelled with Mīr Jumla, had foolishly joined Shujā for a time and married his daughter. He paid the penalty by lifelong imprisonment and death by private execution in 1676 or 1677.

Fate of the sons of Dārā Shikoh. Sulaimān Shikoh, having been forced to take refuge in the hills of Garhwāl in August 1658, was received hospitably by the Rājā of Srīnagar in that principality, which must not be confounded with the town of the same name in Kashmīr. The Rājā honourably kept faith with his hunted guest, but his son yielded to the pressure applied by the emperor, and betrayed the prince in December 1660. The young man, who was singularly handsome, was brought in chains before his uncle, who solemnly promised that the prisoner would not be tortured by the slow poison of *postā*, or infusion of opium-poppy heads. The promise was shamelessly violated, and Sulaimān Shikoh's body and mind were gradually wrecked by the daily administration of the deadly draught in the state prison at Gwālior. His jailers finished him off in May 1662.

His younger brother, Sipihr Shikoh, was spared, and married a few years later to his cousin, the third daughter of Aurangzēb. The same treatment was accorded to the son of Murād Bakhsh, named Izid Bakhsh, who was married to the emperor's fifth daughter. Aurangzēb, while not shrinking from any severity deemed necessary to secure his throne, had no taste for indiscriminate, superfluous bloodshed; and, when he felt his power established beyond danger of dispute by the sons of his brothers, was willing to allow the youths to live. His subsequent dangers came from the side of his own sons.

Flight and defeat of Dārā Shikoh. The sad story of Dārā Shikoh remains to be completed. We left him at Multān in September 1657, when Aurangzēb turned back in order to dispose of Shujā, while his officers pursued Dārā Shikoh with untiring energy. The prince, who 'seemed doomed never to succeed in any enterprise', fled down the course of the Indus with an ever-diminishing force, and would not make a stand even at the strong fortress of Bhakkar, where a faithful eunuch guarded his treasure and some of his ladies. At this point, acting under the influence of unjust suspicions, he dismissed Dāūd Khān, one of his most faithful followers. Dāūd, astonished to hear such an order, took an awful step to prove his fidelity.

'He murdered the honourable ladies of his harem, in order to be free from anxiety about them; and then reported to Dārā how he had "composed his mind about certain objects which make men hesitate and shrink from desperate exertion and fighting at such times of danger".'

Even that horror did not eradicate suspicion from the mind of the prince. Dāūd Khān was constrained to quit his ungrateful master and enter the service of Aurangzēb, who welcomed him and raised him to high office.

Dārā Shikoh forced his way with difficulty through the Sihwān gorge, and so reached Tatta (Thathah). Driven thence he crossed the Indus delta and the terrible Rann, and so entered Cutch (Kachchh) where he was kindly received. But he dared not stay, and pressed on into Kāthiawār and Gujarāt. At Ahmadābād he found a friend in the governor Shāhnawāz Khān, who opened the gates of the city to him, and enabled him to occupy Surat. At that moment the unlucky prince, who had collected a considerable force, seemed to have a chance of success. If he had adopted the advice of the counsellors who recommended retirement to the Deccan, he might have become a dangerous rival of his brother. Unfortunately, delusive hopes of alliance with Shujā and Jaswant Singh, the treacherous Rājā of Mārwār, tempted him to advance to Ajmēr in reliance upon Rājpūt help. His programme was announced as being the release of Shāhjahān, not the assumption of royalty by himself. Jaswant Singh had promised to bring his Rāthōrs to the standard of the prince, but he yielded to the seductions and gold of Aurangzēb, and broke his plighted word.

Dārā Shikoh, when forced to fight, even without the expected Rāthōr contingent, made the best of his situation by entrenching himself in a strong, well-chosen position at the Pass of Deorāi, to the south of Ajmēr. The battle raged for three days, April 12–14, 1659, and ended in the rout of the prince, whose position had been turned by a body of hill-men in the imperialist service.

Betrayal of the prince. The hapless Dārā Shikoh now resumed his flight. Speeding across Rājputānā he again reached Cutch, once more traversed the waterless Rann, and entered Sind hoping to reach Kandahār, and so find an asylum in Persia. With extreme folly, and in opposition to urgent remonstrances, he placed himself in the power of a faithless Afghan named Jīwan Khān, chief of Dādar, a place nine miles to the east of the Bolan Pass. The treacherous host promptly betrayed his guest on June 9. It is some satisfaction to know that the traitor did not long enjoy the reward of his baseness. He and his retinue of about fourteen persons were stoned to death in a field near Sihrind by order of Aurangzēb. Manucci experienced 'great pleasure' at seeing the corpses, and notes that the Muhammadans with him 'uttered a thousand curses' over the body of Jīwan Khān. The same author points out that Aurangzēb was careful to destroy every person who had laid hands on any member of the imperial family.

Death of Nādira Bēgam. The only excuse for the obstinate folly of Dārā Shikoh on this occasion is to be found in the fact that he was not then in his right mind, by reason of the death of his cousin, Nādira Bēgam, the wife of his youth, and the mother of his sons. Throughout his dreadful journeyings, in heat, hunger, thirst, and every form of misery, that loving woman had borne her husband company. Her much tried strength failed as they approached Dādar, and when the prince threw himself on the hospitality of Jīwan Khān he cared little whether he lived or died. 'Death was painted in his eyes. . . . Everywhere he saw only destruction, and losing his senses became utterly heedless of his own affairs.'

The Timūrid princes, notwithstanding their polygamous habits and the freedom of their relations with women, often showed a capacity for feeling the passion of conjugal love in its utmost intensity. Akbar's strange nature does not seem to have been disturbed by any such deep passion. His attitude towards women was much like that of Napoleon. But Jahāngīr, Shāhjahān, Dārā Shikoh, and even Aurangzēb knew what it meant to love a wife. A beautiful album in the India Office Library is a pathetic memorial of Dārā Shikoh's love. It bears the inscription in his handwriting :

'This album was presented to his nearest and dearest friend, the Lady Nādirah Bēgam, by Prince Muhammad Dārā Shukoh, son of the Emperor Shāhjahān, in the year 1051' (= A. D. 1641–2).[1]

Betrayal of Dārā Shikoh. The rest of the tragic story is soon told. The captive prince, with two daughters and his second son, Sipihr Shikoh, a boy of fourteen, was made over to Bahādur Khān, who brought the party to Delhi. Aurangzēb indulged his spite by parading his brother, clad like a beggar-man, on the back of a small, dirty she-elephant through the streets of Delhi. The learned French physician, François Bernier, witnessed the sad procession.

'I took', he writes, 'my station in one of the most conspicuous parts of the city, in the midst of the largest bazaar ; was mounted on a good horse, and accompanied by two servants and two intimate friends. From every quarter I heard piercing and distressing shrieks, for the Indian people have a very tender heart ; men, women, and children wailing as if some mighty calamity had happened to themselves. *Gion-kan* (Jīwan Khān) rode near the wretched *Dara* ; and the abusive and indignant cries vociferated as the traitor moved along were absolutely deafening. I observed some *Fakires* and several poor people throw stones at the infamous *Patan* ; but not a single movement was made, no one offered to draw his sword with a view of delivering the beloved and compassionated *Dara*.'

His execution. A council was held to determine the prisoner's fate. His sister Roshan Rāi (Roshanārā) clamoured for his blood and was supported in her unnatural contention by most of the councillors. Bernier's patron, Dānishmand Khān, seems to have been the only person who opposed the capital sentence. The court

[1] *H. F. A.*, p. 458, plates cxix, cxx, cxxi.

theologians readily humoured Aurangzēb's liking for proceeding by legal forms, and passed sentence of death against Dārā Shikoh, as being a heretic. A popular riot on August 30, directed against Jīwan Khān, the traitor, determined Aurangzēb no longer to delay the execution. On the night of that day brutal murderers tore away Sipihr Shikoh from his father's embrace, and, after a violent struggle, beheaded Dārā Shikoh. The corpse was again paraded through the city and buried without ceremony in a vault under the dome of Humāyūn's tomb. The head certainly was shown to Aurangzēb for identification, but happily we need not believe the horrid stories concerning the emperor's conduct which are told by Manucci only, and are not in any way confirmed by other authorities. According to Bernier, Aurangzēb 'shed tears', and said, '*Ai bad-bakht!* Ah, wretched man! let this shocking sight no more offend my eyes, but take away the head, and let it be buried in *Houmayon's* tomb'. The tears are hardly credible.

Captivity and death of Shāhjahān. Shāhjahān, meanwhile, continued to be closely confined in the Agra Fort, under the special care of a tyrannical eunuch, who frequently gratified the malice of his perverted nature by inflicting galling petty indignities upon the captive monarch. Except for such torturing humiliations and the continuance of strict confinement to the fort the prisoner was not physically ill-treated. His lascivious tastes were gratified by the provision of female attendants, and his daughter Jahānārā was allowed to minister to her father. Shāhjahān lived until January 22 (o.s.), 1666, when he died a natural death at the age of seventy-four. Towards the close of his life he became extremely devout, detaching himself from worldly affairs, and occupying his time with religious exercises.

Character of Shāhjahān. Shāhjahān has received from most modern historians, and especially from Elphinstone, treatment unduly favourable. The magnificence of his court, the extent and wealth of his empire, the comparative peace which was preserved during his reign, and the unique beauty of his architectural masterpiece, the Tāj, have combined to dazzle the vision of his modern biographers, most of whom have slurred over his many crimes and exaggerated such virtues as he possessed. As a son he failed in his duty, remaining in rebellion for years. He mercilessly exterminated his collateral male relations, beginning with his elder brother, Khusrū, in order to clear his own path to the throne. As a father he displayed undue partiality for his first-born son, and showed little capacity for control over his family. The brightest feature in his character as a man is his intense love for Mumtāz Mahall, the mother of fourteen of his sixteen children. Probably he restrained his passions during her lifetime, but she died early in his reign (1631), and there is no doubt that during the remaining thirty-five years of his life he disgraced himself by gross licentiousness. In affairs of state he was cruel, treacherous, and unscrupulous, perhaps not worse than most other kings of his time, but certainly not better.[1] He had little skill as a military leader. The loss of Kandahār and the triple failure to recover that important position prove the inefficiency of the organization and command of his army.

The justice of Shāhjahān. Flatterers have recorded the most extravagant eulogies on his supposed justice, but examination of concrete facts does not warrant the panegyrics. Manucci, the Italian adventurer, who wrote an entertaining book of reminiscences, ventured to assert that Shāhjahān, in spite of his admitted lasciviousness, governed his kingdom 'most perfectly'. When the illustrations of the perfect government recorded by him are studied, it appears that Shāhjahān's 'justice' was merely the savage, unfeeling ferocity of the ordinary Asiatic despot, exercised without respect of persons and without the slightest tincture of compassion.

SHĀHJAHĀN.

Manucci witnessed the execution of Muhammad Saīd, the Kotwāl or Chief Police Officer of either Agra or Delhi, for alleged bribery. The description of the incident being short, may be quoted verbally:

> 'He kept his eye on his officials, punishing them rigorously when they fell short in their duty. This was the reason that he kept at his court an official with several baskets full of poisonous snakes. He would order that in his presence they should be made to bite any official who had failed to administer justice, leaving the culprit lying in his presence till the breath left him.
>
> Thus he did, as I saw, to the *cotual* (*Kotwāl*) called Mahomed Said (Muhammad Sa'īd), who is the magistrate. This man did not decide uprightly, and took bribes. Therefore an order was given that he should be bitten in one hand in his (Shāhjahān's) presence by a *cobra capello*, the most poisonous snake on earth. The official in charge of the snakes was asked how long the man could live. The official replied that he could not live more than an hour. The king remained seated until the *Kotwāl* expired. He then ordered that the body should lie two days in front of his court-house. Others who had deserved death were ordered to be thrown to mad elephants, who tore them to pieces' (i. 197).

On another occasion a favourite slave, who had been instructed not to give away betel to the courtiers, was seen to disobey the order. He was punished by being beaten to death in the emperor's presence. Shāhjahān, like his father, took a horrid pleasure in witnessing the shocking punishments inflicted at his caprice. Thieves, we are told, were never pardoned.

Administration. The stupid ferocity exhibited by the emperor

[1] Terry's vigorous, but just condemnation may be quoted: 'That murderer . . . all laws of honesty, of nature, being by him thrown down, trampled under foot, forgotten, and made void, to compass and gain his most unjust ends.' Roe's verdict has been quoted.

was imitated by his provincial governors, who never dreamed of studying the causes of crime, being content to attempt its repression by a policy of indiscriminate massacre. When Peter Mundy, one of the most prosaic and matter-of-fact observers conceivable, travelled to and from Patna in the years 1630 to 1633, early in the reign, he found the neighbourhood of Patna unsafe, because 'this country, as all the rest of India, swarms with rebels and thieves'. Multitudes of *chōr mīnārs*, or masonry pillars studded with the heads of alleged criminals, were found 'commonly near to great cities'. Each *mīnār* contained from thirty to forty heads set in plaster. At a place in the Cawnpore District the traveller counted 200 such pillars. When he returned some months later 60 more had been added. The 260 pillars in that small area recorded the massacre of at least 8,000 persons within a short time.

State of the country. Other travellers bear similar testimony to the misgovernment of the country. Bernier, who travelled and resided in the empire at the close of Shāhjahān's reign, and the earlier part of that of his successor, was a highly trained observer, in the service of a great noble of the court, who was reputed the most learned man of Asia. Bernier, while deeply interested as a student in what he saw, was free from personal bias for or against either Shāhjahān or Aurangzēb. While admitting the moral wickedness of Aurangzēb's measures taken to win the throne, the author adds with uncommon impartiality the remark:

> 'Yet even those who may maintain that the circumstances of country, birth, and education afford no palliation of the conduct pursued by *Aureng-Zebe*, must admit that this Prince is endowed with a versatile and rare genius, that he is a consummate statesman, and a great King.'

The testimony of the man who could write in that spirit cannot be brushed aside as an exaggeration recorded by a hostile European witness. He speaks of the actual state of the country at the most brilliant period of Mogul rule, when the dynasty was fully established, rich beyond compare, and undisturbed by foreign aggression. His pessimistic observations appear to apply specially to the upper provinces. The fertility and commerce of Bengal excited his enthusiastic admiration.

Bernier's gloomy impressions. The traveller's gloomy impressions are illustrated by the following passages. Having spoken of the despotic tyranny of local governors, he declares that it was

'often so excessive as to deprive the peasant and artisan of the necessaries of life, and leave them to die of misery and exhaustion—a tyranny owing to which those wretched people either have no children at all, or have them only to endure the agonies of starvation, and to die at a tender age—a tyranny, in fine, that drives the cultivator of the soil from his wretched home to some neighbouring state, in hopes of finding milder treatment, or to the army, where he becomes the servant of some trooper. As the ground is seldom tilled otherwise than by compulsion, and as no person is found willing and able to repair the ditches and canals for the conveyance of water, it happens that the whole country is badly cultivated, and a great part rendered unproductive from the want of irrigation. The houses, too, are left in a dilapidated condition, there being few people who will either build new ones, or repair those which are tumbling down' (p. 226).

'The country is ruined by the necessity of defraying the enormous charges required to maintain the splendour of a numerous court, and to pay a large army maintained for the purpose of keeping the people in subjection. No adequate idea can be conveyed of the sufferings of that people. The cudgel and the whip compel them to incessant labour for the benefit of others; and driven to despair by every kind of cruel treatment, their revolt or their flight is only prevented by the presence of a military force' (p. 230).

'Thus do ruin and desolation overspread the land' (p. 231).

'A *Persian*, in speaking of these greedy Governors, Timariots [=*jāgīrdārs*], and Farmers of Revenue, aptly describes them as men who extract oil out of sand. No income appears adequate to maintain them, with their crowds of harpies—women, children, and slaves' (p. 236).

Similar ruin and tyranny had been the fate of the Deccan during the years from 1644 to 1653, in the interval between the first and the second viceroyalty of Aurangzēb. When one pitiless governor of that time, Khān-i Daurān, died, his death was hailed as a divine deliverance.

Bernier praises Bengal. When the traveller visited Bengal, which had been long ruled almost as an independent kingdom by Prince Shujā, and did not need irrigation, his impressions were totally different. He found supplies plentiful and remarkably cheap. The trade of the country in rice, sugar, cotton fabrics, silks, saltpetre, opium, and many other commodities was astonishing in its extent. 'In a word,' he says, 'Bengal abounds with every necessary of life' (pp. 438 foll.). He quotes 'a proverb in common use among the Portuguese, English, and Dutch, that the Kingdom of Bengale has a hundred gates open for entrance, but not one for departure'.

Climax of the Mogul empire. Whatever be the view taken of the personal character of Shāhjahān or the efficiency of his administration, it can hardly be disputed that his reign marks the climax of the Mogul dynasty and empire. During the space of thirty years (1628–58) the authority of the emperor was not seriously challenged, and the realm was never invaded by any foreign foe. Although the loss of Kandahār and the failure of three attempts to retake it proved military inefficiency and encouraged Persian pride, those events had little effect on India, where the strength of the army amply sufficed to uphold the imperial system. It is true that Shāhjahān's son, Aurangzēb Ālamgīr, largely extended the southern frontier of the empire during the first thirty years of his reign; but it is also true that long before the annexation of the sultanates in the Deccan the Marāthās had searched out the weak places in the imperial armour, and the erroneous policy of the sovereign had undermined the foundations of his throne. The empire, which had suffered severely from the prolonged wars of succession, may be regarded as declining throughout the whole reign of Aurangzēb, notwithstanding his conquests in the south.

Art. In the realm of architecture and other forms of art it is unquestionable that the works of the highest quality in the Mogul period belonged to the reign of Shāhjahān. The puritan Aurangzēb cared for none of those things. His buildings are insignificant, with one or two exceptions, and the drawings and paintings of his time show deterioration on the whole. Many of Shāhjahān's artists survived into the reign of his son, and some of their productions executed during that reign are not distinguishable from earlier works; but, generally speaking, the atmosphere of Aurangzēb's court was unfavourable to the arts.

Indo-Persian architecture. The Indo-Persian architecture of Akbar and Jahāngīr, beginning with the noble mausoleum of Humāyūn, and including Fathpur-Sīkrī, Sikandara, the tomb of Itimādu-d daula (1628), and many dignified buildings at Lahore and other places, has great merits. It is generally more massive and virile than that of Shāhjahān, but the world is agreed in preferring the Tāj, with its feminine grace, to all its predecessors or successors.

It is impossible to give either descriptions or criticisms of particular buildings in this book. Generally speaking it may be said that the edifices of Shāhjahān are characterized by elegance rather than by strength, and by the lavish use of extraordinarily costly decoration. Marble was preferred to the red sandstone favoured by Akbar and Jahāngīr. The dainty *pietra dura* inlay, borrowed from Florence, and executed in semi-precious stones regardless of expense, was largely substituted for the simpler white marble mosaic or the sandstone carving of the earlier reigns.

The Hindu features so prominent in the buildings of Akbar and Jahāngīr were much diminished, although never wholly discarded.

The new city of Delhi called Shāhjahānābād, with its gorgeous palace, was occupied by the court in 1648 some ten years after the beginning of the works. The Tāj, begun in 1632, was completed with all its appurtenanees nearly twenty-two years later, in 1653; but the central mausoleum was ready in 1643. The lovely Pearl

FATHPURI MOSQUE AT TĀJ ENTRANCE.

Mosque (Motī Masjid) at Agra was finished in 1653, the year which saw the completion of the accessories of the Tāj. The middle of the seventeenth century, therefore, may be taken as the date at which Indo-Persian architecture attained the summit of excellence.

Drawing and painting. The arts of drawing and painting reached their highest point at the same time. The somewhat crude imitations of Persian work current in Akbar's days had gone out of fashion. The artists of Shāhjahān allowed themselves to be largely influenced both by the old Hindu tradition and by study of European pictures. A certain amount of shading was introduced, and a subdued scale of colour was preferred. Many of the artists were endowed with unsurpassed keenness of vision and steadiness of hand. Some were able to use with success a brush consisting of a single squirrel's hair. The portraits of Shāhjahān's time, which are free from the stiffness common in the preceding and succeeding ages, are wonderfully life-like and often perfectly charming.

Rupee of Shāhjahān.

Hindu architecture. The erection of new Hindu temples, frequently of immense size and cost, was freely permitted, or even encouraged, by both Akbar and Jahāngīr. For instance, Rājā Bīr Singh, the murderer of Abu-l Fazl, was allowed to spend 33 lakhs of rupees (=£371,250 at 2*s.* 3*d.*) on the Kēsava dēva temple at Mathurā, 'one of the most sumptuous edifices in all India'. Aurangzēb destroyed the building utterly in 1669, and replaced it by a mosque. In 1632 Shāhjahān had prohibited the erection of new temples. No important Hindu building, religious or secular, dates from his reign, so far as I am aware.

Literature. The most valuable part of the literature written in Persian continued to be the historical. Among the many works noticed by Elliot and Dowson or Sarkār the *Bādshāh-nāma* of Abdu-l Hamīd and the *Muntakhabu-l Lubāb* of Khāfī Khān (Muhammad Hāshim of Khwāf[1]) may be mentioned specially.

None of the numerous Hindī poets can compare with Tulsī Dās in influence or importance. The most eminent is Bihārī Lāl, the ingenious author of the *Satsāi*, completed in 1662.

[1] That is the real meaning of 'Khāfī'. Khwāf is in Khurāsān.

CHRONOLOGY (o.s.)

Reign of Shāhjahān

Death of Jahāngīr	Sunday, Oct. 28, 1627
Enthronement of Shāhjahān	Feb. 1628
Famine in Gujarāt and Deccan	1630–2
Destruction of Khān Jahān Lodī	1631
Death of Mumtāz Mahall	June 17, 1631
Siege of Hūglī, June 24–Sept. 24	1632
Destruction of new Hindu temples	1632
End of the kingdom of Ahmadnagar	1632
Treaties with Golkonda and Bījāpur	1636
Aurangzēb appointed viceroy of Deccan	July 1636
Marriages of Aurangzēb and Dārā Shikoh	1637
Acquisition of Kandahār	1638
Grant of site of Madras to Mr. Day	March 1639–40
Accident to Princess Jahānārā, and temporary disgrace of Aurangzēb	1644
Campaign in Badakhshān and Balkh	1645–7
Transfer of capital from Agra to Delhi (Shāhjahānābād)	1648
Kandahār taken by Persians; first siege by Aurangzēb	1649
Second siege of Kandahār by Aurangzēb	1652
Third siege of Kandahār by Dārā Shikoh	1653
Aurangzēb reappointed to Deccan	1653
Demolition of walls of Chitōr	1654
Murshīd Kulī Khān appointed Dīwān of the Deccan; siege of Golkonda by Aurangzēb; death of Sadullāh Khān and appointment of Mīr Jumla as prime minister; death of Muhammad Ādil Shāh of Bījāpur	1656
Invasion of Bījāpur	March 1657

War of Succession

Illness of Shāhjahān	September 1657
Battle of Bahādurpur, defeat of Shujā	February 1658
Battle of Dharmat, defeat of Jaswant Singh	April 15, 1658
Battle of Samūgarh, defeat of Dārā Shikoh	May 29, 1658
Captivity of Shāhjahān and Murād Bakhsh	June 1658
Informal enthronement of Aurangzēb	July 21, 1658
Battle of Khajwah, defeat of Shujā	January 5, 1659
Battle of Deorāi, defeat of Dārā Shikoh	April 12–14, 1659
Formal enthronement of Aurangzēb	June 1659
Execution of Dārā Shikoh	August 1659
Death of Shujā	May 1660
Betrayal of Sulaimān Shikoh	Dec. 1660

Authorities

The events, as viewed in relation to the biography of Aurangzēb, are discussed critically by Professor Jadunath Sarkar in *History of Aurangzēb*, vols. i, ii (Calcutta, 1912). For translations of the leading Persian authorities see *E. & D.*, vol. vii. The European authorities used include the travels of Bernier (transl. and ed. Constable and V. A. Smith, Oxford University Press, 1914); Olearius, transl. Davies (London, 1669); Manucci, transl. and ed. Irvine (London, Murray, 1907, 1908); Manrique, *Itinerario* (in Spanish, Roma, 1649); Mundy, ed. Temple, vol. ii (Hakluyt

Society, 1914); and TAVERNIER, transl. and ed. V. Ball (London, Macmillan, 1889).

The following works also have been consulted: DE LAET, *De Imperio Magni Mogolis, sive India Vera*, including the '*Fragmentum Historiae Indicae*' by President VAN DEN BROECKE (Elzevir, 1631, two impressions); GROWSE, Mathurā[3] (Allahabad, 1883); HOSTEN, 'A Week at the Bandel Convent, Huglī,' in *Bengal Past and Present*, vol. x (Calcutta); *Journal of the Panjāb Historical Society* (*J. P. H. S.*, Lahore and Calcutta); and Sir C. LYALL's article on 'Bihārī Lāl' in *Encycl. Brit.*[11]

The art of the reign is discussed in *H. F. A.* The coins are described in the official catalogues of the B. M., I. M., and Lahore (Panjāb) Museum, as well as in other publications.

The published inscriptions are listed in HOROWITZ, *Epigraphia Indo-Moslemica* (Calcutta, 1912).

CHAPTER 6

Aurangzēb Ālamgīr (1659–1707).

Second enthronement of Aurangzēb. The fate of Aurangzēb's father, brothers, and nephews has been related in the last preceding chapter, although some of the events took place in 1659 and 1660, after his formal assumption of the imperial dignity and titles. He re-entered Delhi in May 1659 and was enthroned for the second time in June with complete ceremonial. His name was then read in the *khutbah*, and coins were issued with his superscription (A.H. 1069). He assumed the title of Ālamgīr, by which he is usually designated in the writings of Muhammadan authors. His earlier title of Aurangzēb being more familiar to European readers has been retained in this work.

The new sovereign at once showed his respect for Muslim usage by discontinuing the Ilāhī era of Akbar, and reverting completely to the Muhammadan lunar calendar, notwithstanding its inconveniences in practice.

Nominal remission of taxes. Like many other newly installed rulers he sought the goodwill of his subjects by abolishing oppressive imposts, which were especially vexatious at the time by reason of a famine of intense severity.[1] He remitted nearly eighty taxes and cesses of various kinds, and issued strict orders prohibiting their collection. But the leading historian of the reign records distinctly that, with one or two exceptions, 'the royal prohibition had no effect', and the local officers continued to collect for their own benefit nearly all the prohibited taxes. In fact, when Khāfī Khān wrote in the reign of Muhammad Shāh, the local officers and landholders used to exact more than ever by way of transit duties, so that goods in transit often had to pay more than double their cost price.

Mīr Jumla's war with Assam, 1661–3. Aurangzēb's success

[1] See Tod, i. 310, for a vivid description of the horrors of the famine as experienced in Mewār in Samvat 1717 = A. D. 1660–1.

against his rivals had been due in large measure to his alliance with Mīr Jumla. After his accession that officer did further good service by hunting down Shujā and bringing him to his miserable end. The emperor was glad to keep Mīr Jumla in Bengal as governor at a distance from the capital. A raid by the Āhōms of Assam, who captured twenty guns from the commandant of Gauhātī, tempted the governor to plunge into the Assamese wilds and dream of an attack on China. He penetrated the difficult country as far as Ghargāon on the Brahmaputra, but was driven back by heavy rain and the lack of supplies. His experiences during the retreat were similar to those of his early predecessor, Muhammad Khiljī, son of Bakhtyār, in 1205, and resulted in the almost complete destruction of the invading army, although the invader secured a treaty on nominally favourable terms. Aurangzēb was not sorry when his too powerful subject died in 1663 from the effects of the hardships of the campaign. Mīr Jumla is highly praised for the humanity and justice which he displayed in the conduct of the operations.

SHĀYISTA KHĀN.

Shāyista Khān in Bengal. Mīr Jumla was succeeded in the government of Bengal by Aurangzēb's maternal uncle, Shāyista Khān, who was transferred from the Deccan in consequence of the events to be related presently. Shāyista Khān continued to govern Bengal for about thirty years (excepting an interval of less than three years, from 1677 to 1680), and died at Agra in 1694, when over ninety years of age. Early in his rule he cleared out the Portuguese pirates who infested the waterways of the Brahmaputra delta, and compelled the king of Arakan to cede the Chittagong (Chatgaon) district (1666).

Visit to Kashmīr. Aurangzēb became seriously ill in the summer of 1664 and went in the following cold weather to Kashmīr in order to restore his health, but he never revisited that country, which he disliked. Bernier, who was in the service of a learned noble with the title Dānishmand Khān, accompanied the emperor on the march, and arrived in the 'paradise of the Indies' early in 1665. He has recorded an admirable description of the incidents of the march and the objects of interest in the valley.[1] The journey was performed very slowly, the huge camp being detained for more than two months at Lahore in order to await the melting of the snow on the mountains of Kashmīr. The travelling was extremely uncomfortable, and the passage of the Chināb river in particular was a scene of confusion and danger. A horrid accident occurred in the Pīr Panjal Pass, when one of the elephants carrying the ladies stepped back and forced the animals behind him over the precipice, to the number of fifteen. Only three or four of the women were killed. Some of the elephants were observed to be still alive two days later.

Respite of the Deccan. In 1657, when the serious illness of Shāhjahān became known, Aurangzēb, who was then Viceroy of the Deccan, was within measurable distance of effecting the destruction of the sultanates of Bījāpur and Golkonda, which he ardently desired. The ensuing war of succession gave those much harried states a respite and enabled them to prolong their existence for nearly thirty years. But, meantime, Bījāpur suffered many losses from the operations of Sivājī, a young Marāthā chieftain, son of Shāhjī Bhonslē, originally an officer of the Ahmadnagar State, who had transferred his services to Bījāpur, a few years before the Nizām Shāhī kingdom was annexed to the empire.

Early life of Sivājī. Sivājī, who was born in 1627, began operations in a small way as a robber chief in Bījāpur territory, while still a boy, and took his own line, without consulting his father, in whose *jāgīr* the irregular proceedings took place. Shāhjī, however, who could not escape suspicion of having abetted his unruly son, suffered in consequence four years' confinement at Bījāpur, and was in imminent danger of losing his life. The young adventurer, when only nineteen years of age, made his first important advance by gaining possession of a hill-fort named Torna, about twenty miles to the south-west of Poona. He gathered round him the men of the hills in the Western Ghāts called Māwalis, who are described as an 'uncouth, backward, and stupid race'. But, however mentally defective they might be, they were well adapted to serve Sivājī's purposes, because they were hardy, brave, and intensely devoted to their new leader. They knew

[1] The dates are conclusively fixed in detail by Bernier in his letters to M. de Merveilles, the first being dated December 14, 1664, probably in N. S. He marched on the night of that day (ed. Constable and V. A. Smith, 1914, p. 350). Irvine (*Ind. Ant.*, 1911, p. 76) erroneously gives the date of Aurangzēb's illness as from May to August 1662, and that of the visit to Kashmīr as extending from December 1662 to October 1663. The error of two years committed by a writer so careful as Irvine is instructive, especially as it occurs in an essay designed to settle the obscure chronology of the reign. Lane-Poole gives the correct date. Sarkar (iii. 12) adopts the wrong date 1662, and makes no reference to Bernier.

every path and rock in their native wilds and could pit their knowledge of woodcraft against the military training of their Muslim enemies. Their ability to climb cliffs like monkeys specially fitted them for success in a war which was mainly devoted to the capture of the steeply scarped hill-forts so numerous in their country. Fort after fort yielded to the young chieftain, who built other strongholds on his own account. He next turned his attention to the Konkan, the rich strip of broken ground between the crest of the mountains and the sea. One of his officers gained possession of the important town of Kalyān in that region. In 1655 Sivājī committed an atrocious crime by directing the treacherous murder of the Rājā of Jāolī, who had refused to join him in rebellion.

SIVĀJĪ.

Murder and defeat of Afzal Khān. The Bījāpur authorities, being otherwise occupied, had not paid much attention so far to the operations of Sivājī. But, in 1659, while Aurangzēb was still busy securing his throne, they thought that the time had come to suppress the audacious rebel. An imposing army, numbering about ten thousand men and equipped with mountain guns, was organized and dispatched under the command of Afzal Khān, a brave and experienced officer. Sivājī, not being capable of meeting his foe in the field, opened negotiations, and a Brahman envoy was sent by the Musalman general to his adversary. The envoy played the traitor, permitting his sympathies as a Hindu to outweigh his duty to his master. The Brahman and Sivājī so arranged a plot to inveigle Afzal Khān into an interview at which he could be killed with little risk to the Marāthā. Afzal Khān fell into the trap readily, and, accompanied only by a single Sayyid officer, advanced close to Partābgarh and met Sivājī, who also had but one companion, Tānājī Mālusrē. The Marāthā professed the most abject submission and threw himself weeping at the general's feet. When Afzal Khān stooped to raise him and embrace him in the customary manner, Sivājī wounded him in the belly with a horrid weapon called 'tiger's claw', which he held hidden in his left hand, and followed up the blow by a stab from a dagger concealed in his sleeve. The treacherous attack succeeded perfectly, and the Marāthās ambushed in the surrounding jungles destroyed Afzal Khān's army. Among the immense amount of spoil taken four thousand good horses were specially welcome.[1]

[1] For the details I follow Mānkar, *The Life and Exploits of Sivājī*, 2nd

Shāyista Khān. Bījāpur never succeeded in retrieving the disaster, and Sivājī was left free to turn his arms against the more formidable Mogul power. In 1660 Aurangzēb, although still much occupied personally in the north, found it necessary to send Shāyista Khān, his maternal uncle, to the Deccan. The new commander did not know how to deal with his wily foe. Every day and on every march, we are told, the hill-men fell upon his baggage and carried off whatever they could secure. Shāyista Khān retired to Poona for the rainy season, taking precautions which he fondly imagined were sufficient to secure him from attack. But the cunning Marāthā was too much for him. Sivājī himself, attended by a few trusty followers, managed by means of clever stratagems to penetrate into the lodging of Shāyista Khān, who narrowly escaped death and was thankful to get off with the loss of three fingers and of his son. The humiliated general was obliged to ask for his recall. His request was granted, and he was posted to Bengal, as already stated.

Prince Muazzam and Rājā Jai Singh. Aurangzēb replaced him by his own son, Prince Muazzam, with whom was associated in the command Rājā Jai Singh of Jaipur, who was supposed to be a suitable person to deal with a Hindu enemy. But the new generals were as helpless as their predecessor had been, and were unable even to protect the rich port of Surat, which was plundered at the beginning of 1664 with ruthless cruelty. The Rājā, who had always maintained more or less friendly relations with Sivājī, persuaded him to surrender to the imperial authority in 1665. The Marāthā went to court under Jai Singh's protection and was received by Aurangzēb at Agra, but refused to comply with the rules of etiquette, and resented being treated merely as 'a commander (*mansabdār*) of 5,000', instead of as a sovereign prince. He was, consequently, kept under surveillance, from which he managed to escape with the connivance of Rām Singh, a son of Jai Singh, returning in safety to his own country in December 1666, after many adventures. His absence had lasted nine months.[1]

Rājā Jai Singh died in 1667, while still in the Deccan, having been poisoned by his son, Kīrat Singh, probably at the instigation of Aurangzēb, who publicly rejoiced at the news of the Rājā's death. He felt that the decease of his leading Hindu officer gave him greater liberty in his policy of persecution. He availed himself of the liberty so gained by destroying the gigantic temple at Mathurā.

ed., Bombay, 1886; a valuable little book, now almost unprocurable; and also Grant Duff.

[1] According to some authorities Aurangzēb received Sivājī at Delhi, but Agra certainly is correct. The *Tārīkh-i Marāthah* MS. in the I. O., as I learn from an unpublished essay by Mr. Zāhiru-d dīn Fārūkī, states that Sivājī displayed extreme conceit, refused to make obeisance, struck the chamberlain, and actually sat down in the imperial presence. Other accounts of the incident exist. Sivājī certainly considered himself to have been insulted at the audience.

Prince Muazzam and Rājā Jaswant Singh. The replacement of Jai Singh by Rājā Jaswant Singh of Mārwār (Jodhpur), who had served previously in the Deccan, did not effect any improvement in the situation of the imperialists. Both the Rājā and his colleague Prince Muazzam accepted large sums of money from Sivājī and deliberately abstained from effective operations. They even persuaded Aurangzēb to grant Sivājī the title of Rājā in 1667.[1] The Marāthā power continued to increase steadily, and the newly appointed Rājā was left at liberty to devote the years 1668 and 1669 chiefly to the organization of the internal arrangements of his Government. In 1670 active hostilities were resumed, and in December of that year Sivājī's officers exacted from the local authorities of certain places in Khāndēsh written promises to pay to Sivājī or his deputies one-fourth of the yearly revenue due to Government.

> 'Regular receipts were promised on the part of Sivājī, which should not only exempt them from pillage, but ensure them protection. Hence we may date the first imposition of Marāthā *chauth* on a province immediately subject to the Moguls.' [2]

That scandalous submission to blackmail is conclusive proof of the feebleness of Aurangzēb's Government even early in his reign. His administration, in truth, never was successful at any date during the half-century of his rule. In October of the same year Sivājī had again plundered the city of Surat for three days in a leisurely fashion, but was not able to damage the European factories.

Jāt rebellions. Grave disorders occurred close to the capital. Early in 1669 the Jāt peasantry of the Mathurā District rebelled under the leadership of a man named Gokulā, and killed the imperial *faujdār* or commandant, a zealous Musalmān, who had been in the service of Shāhjahān. A big battle ensued in which the rebels lost five thousand and the imperialists four thousand men. Severe measures restored quiet in the following year, but the trouble was renewed in 1681 and again in 1688, from which date it continued to the end of the reign.[3] We have seen how in 1691 the rebels inflicted the gravest possible affront on their enemy the emperor by plundering the sepulchre of his ancestor Akbar and burning his bones. When such scenes could occur close to Agra it is no wonder that the control of the Government over the Deccan provinces was feeble in the extreme.

Satnāmī insurrection. In this connexion mention may be made of an insurrection by the members of a Hindu sect called Satnāmī which occurred in the fifteenth year of the reign, A.D. 1672.[4] The sectarians are described by Khāfī Khān as 'a gang of bloody miserable rebels, goldsmiths, carpenters, sweepers,

[1] Grant Duff, ed. 1826, i. 220. [2] Grant Duff, ibid., p. 249.

[3] Professor J. Sarkar in *Modern Review*, April 1916, pp. 383–92.

[4] Elphinstone gives the name erroneously as Satnarāmī, and in the margin of ed. 5 the date is stated wrongly as 1676. The term *satnāmī* means 'devotees of the true Name', *scil.* God.

tanners, and other ignoble beings', who had their head-quarters at the town of Nārnaul, now in the Patiāla State. The insurgents, who numbered about 5,000, took possession of Nārnaul, and being persuaded that they were proof against human weapons fought with desperation. After some time they were defeated with great slaughter, few escaping the sword. The losses of the imperialist troops also were considerable, in spite of the charms consisting of extracts from the Korān which the emperor wrote out with his own hand and caused to be affixed to the standards of his officers.

Afghans and Sikhs. Nearly at the same time the imperial troops were engaged in difficult operations against the Afghan tribes, in the course of which the advantage usually lay with the tribes. Tegh Bahādur, the ninth Sikh guru, was executed in 1675 because he refused to accept Islām. The famous prophecy attributed to him will be quoted in the next chapter.

Coronation of Sivājī. Continued success emboldened Sivājī to claim for himself a dignity more exalted than the rank of a titular Rājā conferred at the pleasure of Aurangzēb. He aspired to the position of an independent king ruling in his own right, and not in virtue of delegation by a suzerain. In pursuance of his ambition he took his seat on the throne at his fortress of Rāigarh in June 1674, with all possible solemnity, and established a new era dating from his enthronement. Mr. Henry Oxinden, who had been sent from Bombay to negotiate a commercial treaty with the Marāthās, happened to be present at the festivities, of which he recorded an account.[1]

Southern conquests of Sivājī. In 1676 Sivājī planned and began to execute operations, described by Grant Duff as 'the most important expedition of his life'. His design was to recover the southern *jāgīrs* which had been held under the Bījāpur Government by his father and were still partly in the hands of Sivājī's younger brother, Vyankājī (Venkajee). Sivājī, at the head of a powerful force, visited Golkonda (Hyderabad), where he succeeded in inducing the Sultan to become his ally and lend him a train of artillery. Proceeding south he took the strong fortress of Jinjī (Gingee) in South Arcot, with Vellore and other important places, compelling his brother to surrender a half-share in the Tanjore principality. On his way home Sivājī captured Bellary, and a little later entered into alliance with his old enemy the Sultan of Bījāpur, thereby relieving the pressure exercised on the kingdom by the Mogul armies. The success of the Marāthā leader had been secured in large measure by Aurangzēb's entanglement in the hostilities with the Afghan tribes on the north-western frontier, which lasted until 1678, when peace was arranged.

Sarkar remarks with justice that

> 'ruinous as the Afghan war was to imperial finances, its political effect was even more harmful. It made the employment of Afghans in the

[1] Grant Duff, i. 263. Oxinden's narrative is inserted in Fryer's book, *A New Account*, &c., vol. i, pp. 198–210.

ensuing Rajput war impossible, though Afghans were just the class of soldiers who could have won victory for the imperialists in that rugged and barren country [Rājputāna]. Moreover, it relieved the pressure on Shivaji by draining the Deccan of the best Mughal troops for service on the N.W. frontier.'

Death of Sivājī. The victorious career of the Marāthā chieftain was ended by his death after a short illness at Rāigarh in the fifty-third year of his age. His decease, which was concealed for a time, probably occurred on April 5 (o. s.), 1680.[1] His countrymen believed that his passing was marked by the simultaneous appearance of a comet and a lunar rainbow, as well as by an earthquake ; but, as a matter of fact, Newton's comet, the one referred to, was not visible in India until November. Before proceeding with the narrative of the events of Aurangzēb's reign, it is desirable to give a short account of the institutions of Sivājī, and to attempt an appreciation of the qualities which enabled him to become the creator of a new nation and to take a commanding part in the history of his times.

The Marāthā country. Mahārāshtra, or the Marāthā country, in which the Marāthā language is the prevailing tongue, is most compendiously defined by Elphinstone as

> 'lying between the range of mountains which stretches along the south of the Narbadā [*scil.* the Sātpura], parallel to the Vindhya chain, and a line drawn from Goa, on the sea-coast, through Bīdar to Chānda on the Warda. That river is its boundary on the east, as the sea is on the west.'

The prominent feature of the country is the range of the Western Ghāts. The mountains are so formed that the flat summits are protected by walls of smooth rock, constituting natural fortresses, which various princes, throughout many centuries, had converted by elaborate fortification into strongholds almost impregnable against the means of assault available in ancient times. Most of the hill-tops are well provided with water.

The Marāthā people. The Marāthā people do not play a conspicuous part in early history.

The Brahmans of Mahārāshtra, especially the Chitpāwan section of the Konkan—the narrow strip of broken, rugged country between the crest of the Ghāts and the sea—are an extremely intelligent class, to which the Pēshwās belonged.

The bulk of the people would be classed according to the theory of Manu as Sūdras. Elphinstone's description is the best :

> 'Though the Marāthās had never appeared in history as a nation, they had as strongly marked a character as if they had always formed a united commonwealth. Though more like to the lower orders in Hindostan than to their southern neighbours in Kanara and Telingāna, they could never for a moment be confounded with either. They are small sturdy men, well made, though not handsome. They are all active,

[1] April 5 is the date according to Grant Duff and Orme. Fryer gives June 1 (iii. 167, with Crooke's note). Mānkar (p. 111) states the Hindu equivalent date as Sunday, Chait 15, 1602 Saka, in the Rudra year. But, according to chronological tables, April 5, 1680, was Monday.

laborious, hardy, and persevering. If they have none of the pride and dignity of the Rājpūts, they have none of their indolence or want of worldly wisdom. A Rājpūt warrior, as long as he does not dishonour his race, seems almost indifferent to the result of any contest he is engaged in. A Marāthā thinks of nothing *but* the result, and cares little for the means, if he can attain his object. For this purpose he will strain his wits, renounce his pleasures, and hazard his person ; but he has not a conception of sacrificing his life, or even his interest, for a point of honour. This difference of sentiment affects the outward appearance of the two nations ; there is something noble in the carriage even of an ordinary Rājpūt, and something vulgar in that of the most distinguished Marāthā. The Rājpūt is the most worthy antagonist—the Marāthā the most formidable enemy ; for he will not fail in boldness and enterprise when they are indispensable, and will always support them, or supply their place, by stratagem, activity, and perseverance. All this applies chiefly to the soldiery, to whom more bad qualities might fairly be ascribed. The mere husbandmen are sober, frugal, and industrious, and, though they have a dash of the national cunning, are neither turbulent nor insincere.

The chiefs, in those days, were men of families who had for generations filled the old Hindu offices of heads of villages or functionaries of districts, and had often been employed as partisans under the governments of Ahmadnagar and Bijāpur. They were all Sūdras, of the same cast with their people, though some tried to raise their consequence by claiming an infusion of Rājpūt blood.'

Sivājī's environment. Such was the country to which Sivājī belonged, and such were the people whose virtues and vices he shared. His father, Shāhjī, a member of the Bhonslē family or clan, was one of the class of chiefs mentioned by Elphinstone, and, as already noted, had passed from the service of Ahmadnagar to that of Bījāpur. Sivājī's mother, Jījī Baī, came from a family of higher social rank. She was an intensely devout Hindu, and by her example and teaching did much to stimulate the zeal of her famous son in defence of Brahmans, cows, and caste, the three principal objects of Hindu veneration. The devotion of the young chief was fostered by the Marāthī poets, Rāmdās and Tukārām, with whom he lived on terms of close communion. The former was his chosen guide, philosopher, and friend ; while the latter, who refused to come to his disciple's court, impressed on the mind of Sivājī the mystic doctrines which form the main subject of Hindu poetry.

'There is one Truth in the world : there is one Soul in all Being. Pin thy faith to This Soul, see thyself mirrored in Rāmdās : Do this, O Prince, and thou and the whole world shall be blest therein ; thy fame will pervade the Universe, saith Tukā.'

The more practical Rāmdās pointed out to his royal pupil the duties of kingship as he conceived them :

'Gods and Cows, Brahmans and the Faith, these are to be protected : therefore God has raised you up. . . .

In all the earth there is not another who can save the Faith ; a remnant of the Faith you have saved. . . .

When the Faith is dead, death is better than life ; why live when

Religion has perished? Gather the Marāthās together, make religion live again: our fathers laugh at us from Heaven!'[1]

The poet's pious opinion that

> Treachery should be blotted out

reads strangely when contrasted with his ode of congratulation on the treacherous murder of Afzal Khān. But Marāthā sentiment, which recked nothing of the means employed to attain a pious and patriotic end, had no censure to pass on the slayer of the impious Muslim, who, when on his way to the place appointed for him to die, was alleged to have foully defiled the most sacred shrines of the people whom he despised. The Marāthās, including Sivājī and the mother whom he adored, believed with one accord that their patron goddess sanctioned the execution of their oppressor even by treacherous means, which rightly shock the conscience of more scrupulous critics. The suggestion made in some of the Marāthā writings that Afzal Khān tempted fate by meditating the assassination of Sivājī is not in accordance with the ascertained facts. The troops of the Muhammadan general were kept out of the way, while the forest round the meeting-place swarmed with hidden Marāthās awaiting their chief's signal.

Sivājī, later in life when proceeding on his daring southern expedition in 1676, exhibited a marked access of religious fervour, and is reported to have even meditated the sacrifice of his own life in a temple, after the manner formerly common in the south.

The power of Sivājī over his people rested at least as much on his intense devotion to the cause of Hinduism as on his skill in the special kind of warfare which he affected, or on his capacity for organization. Indeed, it is safe to affirm that his religious zeal was the most potent factor in arousing the sentiment of nationality which inspired his lowly countrymen to defy the Mogul legions.

One of those countrymen proudly declares that

> 'the king was no doubt an incarnation of the Deity. . . . No such hero was ever born, nor will there be any in the days to come.'

Sivājī's special virtues. The foregoing observations go a long way towards explaining the personal influence wielded by Sivājī and his conspicuous success, both as a robber chief in the early part of his career and as the responsible ruler of a kingdom in his latter years. But they do not exhaust the subject. Sivājī possessed and practised certain special virtues which nobody would have expected to find in a man occupying his position in his time and surroundings.

It is a curious fact that the fullest account of those special virtues is to be found in the pages of the Muhammadan historian, Khāfī Khān, who ordinarily writes of Sivājī as 'the reprobate', 'a sharp son of the devil', 'a father of fraud', and so forth. An author who habitually applies such terms of abuse to his subject cannot be suspected of undue partiality towards him. Neverthe-

[1] Rawlinson, *Shivājī the Marāthā*, 1915, pp. 113–22.

less Khāfī Khān honours himself as well as Sivājī by the following passage:

'Ādil Khān of Bījāpur, on hearing of this [Afzal Khān's] defeat, sent another army against Sivājī, under the command of Rustam Khān, one of his best generals. An action was fought near the fort of Parnāla, and Rustam Khān was defeated.

In fine, Fortune so favoured this treacherous worthless man that his forces increased, and he grew more powerful every day. He erected new forts, and employed himself in settling his own territories, and in plundering those of Bījāpur. He attacked the caravans which came from distant ports, and appropriated to himself the goods and women. But he made it a rule that wherever his followers went plundering, they should do no harm to the mosques, the Book of God, or the women of any one. Whenever a copy of the sacred Kurān came into his hands, he treated it with respect, and gave it to some of his Musalmān followers. When the women of any Hindu or Muhammadan were taken prisoners by his men, and they had no friend to protect them, he watched over them until their relations came with a suitable ransom to buy their liberty. Whenever he found out that a woman was a slave-girl, he looked upon her as being the property of her master, and appropriated her to himself. He laid down the rule that whenever a place was plundered, the goods of poor people, copper money, and vessels of brass and copper, should belong to the man who found them; but other articles, gold and silver, coined or uncoined, gems, valuable stuffs and jewels, were not to belong to the finder, but were to be given up without the smallest deduction to the officers, and to be by them paid over to Sivājī's government.'

His army differed from all other Indian armies of the period, and even from the Anglo-Indian armies of Wellesley's time, in its complete freedom from the curse of female followers.

'No man in the army was to take with him wife, mistress, or prostitute; one who infringed this rule was to lose his head.'

Discipline was strictly maintained, and death was the penalty for either disobedience of orders or grave neglect of duty.

Organization of the army. The army, which originally consisted of infantry only, was organized in a sensible fashion with a due gradation of officers. The lowest rank of officer was that of *nāik*, or corporal, who commanded a squad of ten men. Above him were the *havīldār*, or sergeant, the *jumladār*, or captain of a company, the battalion commander, and the brigade commander, or brigadier. The brigade was reckoned as 5,000 men. The commander-in-chief was styled Sarnobat or Senāpati. When cavalry was introduced there was sometimes a separate chief for that arm. The troopers comprised *bārgīrs*, mounted by the state, and *silāhdārs* (*sillidars*), who provided their own horses. Sivājī disliked the *jāgīr* system, and preferred to pay his officers' salaries from the treasury. The garrisons of the forts were carefully constituted, and special precautions were taken against the risk of the commandants being corrupted. The forts played a very important part in Sivājī's kingdom, and required all possible care. Regular drill was not practised, but in that respect Sivājī's army was no worse than that of any rival power. The army retired into quarters for the rainy season, when military operations in Mahārāshtra are almost impossible.[1] The campaigning season began in accordance with Hindu practice by a grand review held at the Dasahra festival in October, and lasted until about April.

A considerable fleet was built and stationed at Kolāba, in order to check the power of the Sīdī or Abyssinian pirate chiefs of Janjīra and to plunder the rich Mogul ships.

Civil administration. Much of the revenue of the Marāthā state was derived from simple robbery, and another large portion came from payments in the nature of blackmail made by districts under the government of other powers which desired protection from plunder. The army was organized primarily for the purpose of plunder, and not so much for the extension of territory directly administered. The principal blackmail payment was called *chauth*, or 'the fourth', being one-quarter of the authorized land revenue assessment of the district claiming protection. We have seen how as early as 1670 a portion of Khāndēsh, although imperial territory, was compelled to submit to the payment of *chauth*. Sometimes an extra tenth, called *sardēsmukhī*, was extorted. The details were purposely made as intricate as possible, so that nobody except the professional Marāthā Brahman accountants could understand them. All clerical and account work was in Brahman hands. The fighting Marāthās, including Sivājī himself, ordinarily refused to learn the arts of reading, writing, and ciphering, which they considered unworthy of a soldier.

The kingdom or principality under the direct rule of Sivājī at the time of his death in 1680, although considerable, was not very extensive. The home territory consisted of a long narrow strip comprising chiefly the Western Ghāts and the Konkan between Kalyān, now in the Thāna District, and Goa, with some districts to the east of the mountains, the extreme breadth from east to west being about a hundred miles. The provinces or districts in the far south, and shared with Sivājī's brother, Vyankājī (Venkajee), were scattered in a fashion not easily definable. Sivājī's civil institutions applied only to the territories under his direct rule.

The government. The government of the kingdom was conducted by the Rājā, aided by a council of eight ministers, of whom the chief was the Pēshwā, or prime minister. The other members held departmental charges, such as finance, foreign affairs, and so forth. They included a Shāstrī, or officer whose duty it was to expound Hindu law, to deal with matters of religion, criminal jurisdiction, and astrology. The whole administration was based on the principles of the Hindu scriptures or *shāstras*. The eight ministers usually were actually employed on military business, the work of their offices at the capital being performed by deputies. Each district officer similarly had eight principal subordinate officials, to deal with correspondence, accounts, and the treasury.

[1] The older European writers call the rainy season in western India 'the winter'.

Civil disputes were settled in the immemorial Hindu fashion by a *panchāyat*, or jury of neighbours.

Revenue system. The revenue system was based on the practice of Dādājī Konadēo, Sivājī's early instructor. Farming of the revenues was stopped, and the assessment was made on the crop, the normal share of the state being two-fifths. But the Rājā's districts had suffered terribly from constant war, and Sivājī never had sufficient leisure to complete his revenue arrangements as a working system. The English traveller, Dr. Fryer (1673), paints an unpleasant picture of his government as in actual operation. Writing from Goa he speaks of Vengurla, now in the Ratnagiri District, as being under the 'tyrannical government of Sivājī'; and with reference to Kārwār, the important port in North Kanara, then recently occupied by the Marāthās, observes:

> 'It is a general calamity and much to be deplored to hear the complaints of the poor people that remain, or are rather compelled to endure the slavery of Sivājī. The Desāis [headmen of districts or petty chiefs] have land imposed upon them at double the former rates, and if they refuse to accept it on these hard conditions (if monied men) they are carried off to prison, there they are famished almost to death; racked and tortured most inhumanly till they confess where it is. They have now in limbo several Brahmans, whose flesh they tear with pincers heated red-hot, drub them on the shoulders to extreme anguish (though according to their law it is forbidden to strike a Brahman). This is the accustomed sauce all India over, the princes doing the same by the governors when removed from their offices, to squeeze their ill-gotten estates out of them; which when they have done, it may be they may be employed again. And after this fashion the Desāis deal with the Kunbīs [an agricultural caste]; so that the great fish prey on the little, as well by land as by sea, bringing not only them but their families into eternal bondage.
>
> However, under the King of Bījāpur the taxations were much milder, and they lived with far greater comfort.' [1]

The robber State. Similarly, when the first sack of Surat occurred in 1664, an Englishman named Smith saw Sivājī seated in a tent and employed in ordering the cutting off the heads and hands of those who concealed their wealth. No reason exists for branding that statement by an eyewitness as 'a gross exaggeration'.[2] Sivājī, when gathering plunder, behaved as Indian dacoits and banditti always have done, and still do, although his barbarities were mitigated by certain chivalrous practices already noted, which may be ascribed with probability to the teaching of Tukārām. Hindus are prone to worship power as such, and Sivājī's brilliant success alone would have sufficed to win popular veneration. When that success was combined with intense devotion to the gods, reverent liberality to Brahmans, and protection to cows the brave and victorious bandit was well qualified to be considered an incarnation of the deity. But the fact that Sivājī possessed

[1] *A New Account*, ed. Crooke, vol. ii, p. 3, but printed in modern fashion.

[2] Rawlinson, p. 98 note. The statement is quoted by Grant Duff (i. 199 note) from a most minute description in the records of the E. I. Company in London.

and practised certain unexpected virtues must not obscure the truth that he was primarily a fierce robber chieftain, who inflicted untold misery on hundreds of thousands of innocent people, Hindus and Muhammadans alike, merely for the sake of gain, using without scruple all kinds of cruelty and treachery to attain his wicked ends. The Marāthā state at any stage, whether during Sivājī's lifetime, or in its later developments under the Pēshwās and the chiefs who replaced them as leaders, never served any good purpose or conferred any benefit upon India, except in so far as it gratified Hindu sentiment in the particular ways above stated. The Marāthā independent rule in all its varieties until 1818 was the rule of professed robbers.

A change. It is hardly necessary to add that that description does not apply in any degree to the government of the Marāthā States as they now exist. A marvellous change has been wrought in the course of a century. Sindia, Holkar, and the Gaikwār of the present day differ from their predecessors of the seventeenth and eighteenth centuries as much as a great Scots noble in the service of King George V differs from his cattle-lifting ancestor. The Marāthā States are now sufficiently well administered, and their chiefs are pillars of the empire. The habits of the people, like those of their rulers, have been transformed, and the king's peace is never seriously broken.

Prohibition of histories. It is now time to quit the Deccan for a while and return to Aurangzēb in Hindostan. Some transactions in that region have been already noticed. A foolish order of the emperor in the eleventh year of the reign (A.D. 1668–9) put a stop to the compilation of the official annals maintained so carefully by his predecessors, and also forbade the publication of histories by private persons. The motive for the order seems to have been a morbid humility. Khāfī Khān, the principal authority for the reign, was seriously embarrassed in his pursuit of historical truth by the effects of the prohibition, experiencing much difficulty in determining the order of events during forty years. The period extending from the eleventh to the twenty-first regnal year in particular presented special difficulties.

The narratives of contemporary European travellers and the researches of modern scholars have done much to clear up the obscurity of which Khāfī Khān complained, but considerable uncertainty as to the precise order of events still remains. Readers should not assume that the dates adopted in this book are erroneous merely because they may differ from those given by Elphinstone or other historians of repute.

Aurangzēb a puritan. Aurangzēb was a Muslim puritan. He desired that his empire should be a land of orthodox Sunnī Islām, administered in accordance with the rules laid down by the early Khalīfs.[1] His conscience impelled him to take up that position, and he was willing to incur any political danger or loss of revenue rather than forgo his ideal. Authors who accuse Aurangzēb of

[1] See, for instance, letter xciv in Bilimoria's translation.

sanctimonious hypocrisy and feigning religious sentiments which he did not feel in his heart are mistaken, in my judgement. Although his religion did not hinder him from committing actions in the field of statecraft which are repugnant to the moral sense of mankind, his creed, as a creed, was held in all sincerity, and he did his best to live up to it. He resembled most other autocrats in assuming that the rules of morality do not apply to matters of state. There is no reason to suppose that he felt any remorse for his treatment of his father, and it is certain that his conscience was perfectly easy concerning the penalties which he inflicted on his brothers, sons, and other relatives. The safety of the state, as identified with the maintenance of his personal authority, was sufficient justification in his eyes for acts which we are disposed to call unfeeling crimes. Those acts in no way conflicted with his religious convictions.

Destruction of temples. In 1669, when he had been firmly seated on the throne for some ten years, and Rājā Jai Singh was dead, he felt himself at liberty to act on his theory of government more thoroughly than he had been able to do at first. We are informed by a credible author that on April 18, 1669 (Zulk'ada, 17, A.H. 1079) the emperor was shocked by the receipt of reports that in the provinces of Thathah, Multān, and Benares, but more especially in the last-named, Brahmans dared to give public lectures on their scriptures which even attracted Muhammadan students from distant places. Such open propaganda of Hindu idolatry seemed to Aurangzēb a scandal. Accordingly, commands were issued

> 'to all the governors of provinces to destroy with a willing hand the schools and temples of the infidels ; and they were strictly enjoined to put an entire stop to the teaching and practice of idolatrous forms of worship'.

Five months later the local officers reported that in accordance with the imperial command the temple of Bishannāth (*sic*) at Benares had been destroyed.

After a short interval (in Ramazān of the year A.H. 1080) Aurangzēb had the satisfaction of learning that the magnificent temple of Kēsava dēva at Mathurā had been levelled with the ground. It was one of the noblest buildings in India, and had been erected in the reign of Jahāngīr by Rājā Bīr Singh Bundēla, the murderer of Abu-l Fazl, at a cost of 33 lākhs of rupees, or £371,250. The foundation of a large and costly mosque was laid on the site.

> 'Glory be to God,' exclaims the historian, 'who has given us the faith of Islām, that in the reign of the destroyer of false gods, an undertaking so difficult of accomplishment has been brought to a successful termination! The vigorous support given to the true faith was a severe blow to the arrogance of the Rājās, and like idols they turned their faces awe-struck to the wall. The richly-jewelled idols taken from the pagan temples were transferred to Agra, and there placed beneath the steps leading to the Nawāb Bēgam Sāhib's mosque, in order that they might ever be pressed under foot by the true believers. Mathurā changed its name into Islāmābād, and was thus called in all official documents, as well as by the people.' [1]

[1] The dates for the demolition of temples are precisely fixed by the

Aurangzēb was far too intelligent to be blind to the political consequences of his action. He deliberately threw away the confidence and support of the Rājās in order to carry out his religious policy, thinking the spiritual gain to outweigh the material loss.

Beginning of the Rājpūt war. Rājā Jaswant Singh of Mārwār (Jodhpur), after his failure in the Deccan, had been sent in disgrace to the west of the Indus, a region abhorred by Hindus, and was appointed to the small post of commandant of Jamrūd at the mouth of the Khyber. Towards the close of 1678 he died, having been poisoned by order of Aurangzēb, if Tod and Manucci may be believed. The emperor thought that his disappearance offered a good opportunity for further progress in the policy of abasing the Rājās and Hindus generally. Two posthumous sons of Jaswant Singh having been born at Lahore, Aurangzēb made an attempt to seize the infants, which was frustrated by the gallantry of their Rājpūt guard, who sacrificed their lives to effect the escape of the children. The mother claimed the protection of Mewār (Udaipur), which was readily granted by the reigning Rānā, Rāj Singh. War then began between the imperialists and the clans of Mewār and Mārwār, but Ambēr (Jaipur) continued to support the imperial cause. Aurangzēb moved to Ajmēr early in 1679 and usually resided there for more than two years, until September 1681.[1]

Reimposition of the *jizya*. The death of Jaswant Singh emboldened the imperial bigot to reimpose the hated *jizya*, or poll-tax on non-Muslims, which Akbar had wisely abolished early in his reign. Aurangzēb's objects are defined by Khāfī Khān as the curbing of the infidels and the demonstration of the distinction between a land of Islām and a land of the unbelievers.

A nobly worded protest, too long to quote in full, but deserving of commemoration by extracts, was sent to the emperor about this time.

The writer, having recited the tolerant conduct of Akbar, Jahāngīr, and Shāhjahān, proceeds :

'Such were the benevolent intentions of your ancestors. Whilst they pursued these great and generous principles, wheresoever they directed their steps, conquest and prosperity went before them ; and then they reduced many countries and fortresses to their obedience. During your majesty's reign, many have been alienated from the empire, and further loss of territory must necessarily follow, since devastation and rapine now universally prevail without restraint. Your subjects are trampled under foot, and every province of your empire is impoverished, depopulation spreads, and difficulties accumulate. . . .

Ma'āsir-i Ālamgīrī in *E. & D.*, vii. 183. Aurangzēb's mosque, the Ālamgīrī Masjid, is the most prominent building in Benares, and occupies the site of the Saiva Visvesvara temple destroyed in 1669, erroneously called Bishannāth by the Muhammadan author. The name of Islāmābād has been long disused. For the temple of Kēsava dēva see Growse, *Mathurā*[3], Allahabad, 1883.

[1] The detailed chronology of the Rājpūt war is given by Sarkar, vol. iii, App. ix.

If Your Majesty places any faith in those books by distinction called divine, you will there be instructed that God is the God of all mankind, not the God of Muhammadans alone. The Pagan and the Musalmān are equally in His presence. Distinctions of colour are of his ordination. It is He who gives existence. In your temples, to His name the voice is raised in prayer; in a house of images, when the bell is shaken, still He is the object of adoration. To vilify the religion or customs of other men is to set at naught the pleasure of the Almighty. When we deface a picture we naturally incur the resentment of the painter; and justly has the poet said, "Presume not to arraign or scrutinize the various works of power divine."

In fine, the tribute you demand from the Hindus is repugnant to justice; it is equally foreign from good policy, as it must impoverish the country; moreover, it is an innovation and an infringement of the laws of Hindostan.'[1]

The testimony of the writer to the general misery caused by the misgovernment of Aurangzēb during the earlier years of his reign deserves particular notice. Rājputāna suffered all the horrors of war in their most extreme form; because the Rānā, who had retired to the western hills, devastated the plains in order to hamper the progress of the invader, while the Mogul armies destroyed the little that was left.

Temples were demolished wholesale with fanatical fury. For example, in May 1679, Khān Jahān Bahādur received warm praise from Aurangzēb for bringing from Jodhpur several cartloads of idols taken from temples which had been razed. The images were treated in the most insulting ways possible, 'until at last not a vestige of them was left'. During the campaign of 1679–80 enormous damage was wrought among the shrines of Rājputāna. At or near Udaipur 123, and at Chitōr in the same state 63 temples were overthrown. The friendly state of Ambēr (Jaipur) was treated with equal severity and suffered the loss of 66 temples. Thus, in two states, no less than 252 shrines were destroyed in one year. Many other figures will be found in Sarkar's *History*. Clearly it is no exaggeration to affirm that Aurangzēb in the course of his long reign caused the demolition of thousands of temples, inflicting irreparable injury on the monuments of ancient civilization and on

[1] The authorship of the letter seems to lie between Rānā Rāj Singh, to whom Tod ascribes it, and Sivājī, to whom Professor Sarkar attributes it, on the authority of R. A. S. MS. 71. If Sivājī endorsed it the actual composer must have been one of his Brahman advisers. The chief himself was illiterate and could not have dictated a composition so finished.

The rate of the *jizya* assessment in Bengal, according to Stewart (p. 308 *n.*) was 6½ per *thousand* on all property. Christians paid 1½ per *cent.* on their trading in addition. The sick, lame, and blind were excused. The following quotation explains Stewart's statement about the tax on Christians. 'As for the three European Companies, they flatly refused to pay it (the *jizya*), on which Aurangzebe, while exempting them from the impost, obtained its equivalent by raising the duties on Europe goods to 3½ per cent., instead of the 2 per cent. which had hitherto been allowed them by special charter' (Strachey, *Keigwin's Rebellion*, p. 45).

irreplaceable works of art. The testimony of books is amply confirmed by local traditions in all parts of the country, many of which I have heard on the spot. The ruin was not confined to new or recent structures. Temples of all ages were attacked indiscriminately.

Aurangzēb employed all his three adult sons, the Princes Muazzam, Azam, and Akbar, in the Rājpūt war, with poor success and several serious reverses. Mārwār (Jodhpur) was formally annexed to the empire late in 1679, but the conquest was far from complete, and fighting in that territory continued without interruption for nearly thirty years longer. If the traditions recorded by Tod may be accepted, the imperialists more than once owed their escape from overwhelming disaster to the unpractical chivalry of their opponents.

Revolt of Prince Akbar. Prince Akbar, although supposed to be his father's favourite son, dreamed of a throne for himself to be won by Rājpūt swords, and went over to the enemy on the first day of 1681. He addressed singularly outspoken remonstrances in reply to a letter from his father, written probably early in January 1681. Aurangzēb had endeavoured to win back his son by a combination of promises with threats, and in the course of his argument exposed his real sentiments concerning his gallant Rājpūt subjects by describing them as 'Satans in a human shape . . . beast-looking, beast-hearted, wicked Rājpūts'.

Akbar responded by urging his personal claims to consideration, and repelling his father's foul abuse of the clans.

> 'All sons have equal claims to the property of their father. . . . Verily, the guide and teacher of this path [*scil.* of rebellion against a father] is Your Majesty; others are merely following your footsteps. How can the path which Your Majesty himself chose to follow be called "the path of ill-luck"?'

The writer recalls how Akbar had conquered the realm of Hindostan with the help of the Rājpūts, and continues:

> 'Blessings be on this race's fidelity to salt, who without hesitation in giving up their lives for their master's sons, have done such deeds of heroism that for three years the Emperor of India, his mighty sons, famous ministers, and high grandees have been moving in distraction against them, although this is only the beginning of the contest.'

The Prince proceeds to expound the oppression of the government, the misery of the Deccan as well as of other provinces, and the universal official corruption.

> 'The clerks and officers of state have taken to the practice of traders, and are buying posts with gold and selling them for shameful considerations. "Every one who eats salt destroys the salt-cellar."'

Akbar continued with admonitions to his father to retire from the world, and 'make his soul', to use the Irish idiom. He added bitter personalities in verse:

> What good did you do to your father
> That you expect so much from your son?

O thou that art teaching wisdom to mankind
Administer to thine own self what thou art teaching to others!
Thou art not curing thyself,
Then, for once, give up counselling others.

A caustic pen was not enough to save the prince, who was no match for his wily father. Decisive action at the right moment would have overwhelmed Aurangzēb, who was almost destitute of troops for a short time. Akbar allowed the opportunity to slip, and spent his time in unseasonable pleasures. When he was ready to attack it was too late, reinforcements having reached the emperor. Aurangzēb, who always preferred guile to force, completed the discomfiture of his son by a trick. He forged a letter written in Akbar's name intimating the prince's intention to betray his allies, and arranged that it should fall into the hands of the Rājpūts. They were simple enough to take the bait, and in their wrath deserted in a body. When they discovered the deception the cause of the rebel was past mending, and he was forced to ride hard for the Deccan, escorted by a small retinue of faithful followers, and guided by Durgadās, the devoted servant of the Rāj. Sivājī having died in 1680, Akbar took refuge with his son Rājā Sambhājī, but ultimately was constrained to quit India and retire to Persia. His subsequent designs aimed against his father came to naught, and he died in exile in 1704.[1]

Hostilities with Mewār were ended in June 1681, by a treaty which provided for the cession of certain territory by the Rānā in lieu of the payment of the *jizya*, the demand for that odious impost being dropped. War in Mārwār, as already mentioned, continued for thirty years until 1709, when Aurangzēb's successor, Bahādur Shāh, formally and finally acknowledged the rights of Jaswant Singh's son, Ajit Singh, as Rājā and ruler of Mārwār.

Although Aurangzēb always commanded a certain amount of service from several of the Rājpūt clans, his unwise fanaticism alienated the two principal states, and deprived his throne of the loyal support gladly tendered to his wiser ancestors.

Aurangzēb goes to the Deccan. In 1681 Aurangzēb resolved to proceed to the Deccan in person, hoping that the presence of the sovereign might remove the danger threatening from Akbar's presence, secure the long-deferred conquest of the Sultanate, and curb the growing insolence of the Marāthās. The recent death of Sivājī seemed to offer a favourable opportunity. The Mogul generals, as Bernier observes, used to

'conduct every operation . . . with languor and avail themselves of any pretext for the prolongation of war which is alike the source of their emolument and dignity. It is become a proverbial saying that the Deccan is the bread and support of the soldiers of Hindostan.'

[1] For the correct date see *E. & D.*, vii. 196, and Sarkar, *History*. Beale and other writers wrongly give the year as 1706. The quotations from Akbar's letter are taken from Sarkar's article in *The Modern Review*, January 1915, pp. 44–8.

Fryer quotes the same saying, observing that the policy of Aurangzēb was

'frustrated chiefly by the means of the soldiery and great Amīrs (Ombrahs), who live lazily and in pay, whereupon they term the Deccan (Duccan) "the bread of the military men"'.

The emperor left Ajmēr in September, and arrived at Burhānpur in November 1681. In the year following he moved to Aurangābād; and in 1683 pitched his camp at Ahmadnagar, from which place he marched in 1685 to Sholāpur. Those years were spent in the unsuccessful attempt to capture Prince Akbar and in sundry operations against the Marāthās, disastrous for the most part.

The campaign against Golkonda in 1685 was entrusted to Prince Muazzam, who came to terms with the enemy, which were accepted officially but disapproved privately by the emperor.

Surrender of Bījāpur. The investment of Bījāpur ended in October 1686, by the surrender of the city and of the young king, Sikandar, who became a prisoner for life. The independence of the state and the existence of the Ādil Shāhī dynasty thus came to an end. Sikandar's death in prison fifteen years later was, as usual, attributed to poison. The noble city remained desolate for many years, but has now recovered some small measure of prosperity. The buildings of the kings rival and in some respects surpass the Mogul monuments of northern India.

Capture of Golkonda. Abu-l Hasan, King of Golkonda or Hyderabad, had incurred Aurangzēb's wrath in a special measure because he had employed Brahman ministers and had sent money to Sambhājī. The dissoluteness of his private life was alleged as another reason for treating him with the utmost severity. When the final attack on the fortress of Golkonda came in 1687 the king gave up his evil ways, and played a man's part by conducting a gallant defence, with the aid of a brave and faithful lieutenant named Abdu-r Razzāk. Aurangzēb and his generals tried every means known to them—mines, bombardment, and escalade—without success. The fortress, like Asīrgarh in Akbar's time, was so amply provided with food and munitions that it was prepared to hold out indefinitely. The emperor, therefore, following the precedent of his ancestor, had recourse to bribery, and gained admittance through the treachery of one of the officers of the garrison, who opened a gate. Abdu-r Razzāk, fighting to the last, fell covered with seventy wounds. Aurangzēb, admiring his courage and fidelity, placed him under the care of surgeons, who succeeded in effecting his cure. After about a year he accepted unwillingly a post in the imperial service.

Khāfī Khān states that Aurangzēb received the captive king 'very courteously' and provided him with a 'suitable allowance' for his maintenance in the fortress of Daulatābād. Manucci, on the contrary, tells a horrid and improbable story that Abu-l Hasan was beaten unmercifully in the presence of Aurangzēb in order to force him to account for his treasures.

The fall of Golkonda in October 1687 closed the story of the Kutb Shāhī dynasty.

Impolicy of the conquest. Aurangzēb had thus attained what he considered to be the main purpose of the campaign, and had won the prize which had seemed to be within his grasp thirty years earlier, but had then eluded him. All historians agree in pointing out the impolicy of the destruction of the Sultanates, which annihilated the only Muhammadan governments in the south, let loose a swarm of discharged soldiers to plunder the country, and freed the Marāthā chiefs from any fear of local rivalry. Aurangzēb did not yet fully understand the strength of his Marāthā enemies, whom he despised.

Execution of Rājā Sambhājī. In 1689 his troops captured Sivājī's successor, Sambhājī, with his Brahman minister Kalusha. The Rājā is said to have used abusive language to his captors. It is certain that he, his minister, and ten or twelve other persons were executed with horrid barbarity, their tongues being torn out and many other tortures inflicted. Aurangzēb personally ordered those atrocities, which stain his memory. Sambhājī's son, a boy of seven years of age, whose real name was Sivājī, but who is ordinarily known by the nickname of Sāhū or Shāhū, was spared, appointed a *mansabdār* of 700, and brought up in the imperial palace.

Farthest advance of Mogul power. The capture and execution of Sambhājī naturally aroused hopes that the Marāthā resistance would collapse. The imperialists actually did obtain a certain measure of success, and in 1691 were able to levy tribute even on Tanjore and Trichinopoly in the far south. That year, accordingly, may be taken as marking the most distant advance of the Mogul power.

Arrest of Prince Muazzam. Aurangzēb's eldest surviving son, Prince Muazzam or Shāh Ālam, had shown a sentiment of tenderness towards the Sultans of both Golkonda and Bījāpur, whose utter destruction he regarded as impolitic. He seems to have gone so far as to have entered into treasonable correspondence with his father's enemies and to have furnished supplies to Bījāpur during the investment of that city. His arrest for those alleged offences was effected in March 1687. He remained in confinement, at first of the severest kind, but later much relaxed, for more than seven years until April 1694, when he was released and appointed governor of Kābul. During the period of Prince Muazzam's imprisonment, his next brother, Prince Azam, believed himself to be the heir apparent and chosen successor of his father. He was much disappointed by the unexpected end of his brother's detention, which was arranged by the old emperor with his accustomed cunning. The immediate motive for the release of the eldest prince was an attempt of Prince Akbar to invade India with Persian help, and make a bid for the crown. He advanced with twelve thousand Persian horsemen to the neighbourhood of Mūltān, but was obliged to retire when confronted by a superior force under Shāh Ālam (Prince Muazzam).

A fatuous campaign. After the execution of Sambhājī the Marāthā government was carried on by his brother, Rājā Rām, who retired to Jinjī in the south. When he died a few years later (1700), his widow Tārā Bāī, an able and energetic woman, administered the affairs of the state as regent, and gave the Moguls no peace. Her capital was Sātārā. The natural expectation that the death of three Rājās within a few years should weaken the Marāthā resistance was completely falsified. From about 1698, if not earlier, Aurangzēb's prolonged campaign may be described as a complete failure. Although he seemed to be still physically strong, he had lost the capacity for controlling his subordinates, who wasted time and money in the most unblushing manner. Zulfikār Khān, son of Asad Khān, the prime minister, and supposed to be one of the best imperial generals, deliberately played with the siege of Jinjī for some seven years and purposely allowed Rājā Rām to escape. Prince Kāmbakhsh, the emperor's youngest and favourite son, entered into traitorous correspondence with the enemy, whom he even thought of joining, so that Zulfikār Khān was obliged to send him to his father under arrest, a liberty which Aurangzēb privately resented.[1] Plague and cholera desolated the Deccan for about eight years, floods more than once swept through the imperial camp, and hardly any pretence of fighting was maintained. Aurangzēb, with almost incredible fatuity, devoted his energies to the capture of individual forts, and, as a rule, was content to buy them from the commandants. Khāfī Khān gives a long list of forts so acquired, and mentions only one or two as having been honestly stormed. The story is an astonishing record of incompetence and folly. It seems clear that Aurangzēb towards the end of his unduly prolonged life was in his dotage and quite incapable of effective executive action, although still retaining his old cunning.[2] Khāfī Khān discreetly observes that Prince Azam had noticed 'the altered temper of his father, whose feelings were not always in their natural state'. Aurangzēb had never trusted anybody, and had tried to look after all the affairs of a great empire in person. Naturally he failed disastrously even while he was young. When he was approaching the age of ninety it was manifestly impossible for him to control even the war of the Deccan. The affairs of the rest of India slipped from his grasp almost completely, and the gigantic hoards of treasure amassed by his father were squandered without result.[3]

Thus the too cunning old autocrat wasted the last twenty-six

[1] See letter clxxiv in Bilimoria for the treason of Prince Kāmbakhsh. Gemelli-Careri calls the prince Sikandar, apparently in error, confounding him probably with the ex-Sultan of Bījāpur.

[2] 'One cannot rule without practising deception. . . . A government that is joined to cunning lasts and remains firm for ever, and the master of this [art] becomes a king for all time. . . . It is contrary to the Korān to consider stratagem as blameable' (Sarkar, *Anecdotes of Aurangzēb*, p. 96).

[3] In letter clxiii (Bilimoria) Aurangzēb expressly says that the expenses of the Deccan war were 'defrayed from the treasury of Northern India'.

years of his reign. The Deccan, from which he never returned, was the grave of his reputation as well as of his body.

Dr. Gemelli-Careri's description. One of the most interesting of the many narratives by European travellers who visited India during the reign of Aurangzēb is the account of the camp and court of the aged emperor in the Deccan early in the year 1695 as recorded by the learned Italian lawyer, Dr. Gemelli-Careri, who spent six years in going round the world, and undertook a troublesome and dangerous journey from Goa for the sole purpose of seeing the Great Mogul. Aurangzēb was then, in March and April, encamped at Galgala or Galgali, on the northern bank of the Krishni (Kistna), about fourteen miles distant from the town of Mudhol.[1]

The enclosure of the royal tents alone measured about three miles, and the whole camp, with a circumference of some thirty miles, had a population of half a million. The separate bazaars or markets numbered two hundred and fifty, and every class of goods, even the most costly, was on sale.

The traveller was accorded the honour of a private audience in the morning before the public reception, which began about ten o'clock. Aurangzēb received him courteously, questioning him about his travels and the war with the Turks in Hungary. The emperor, who was then approaching the age of eighty, was bowed by the weight of years, and leant on a crutched stick, but was able to write his orders on petitions without using spectacles. He was of small stature, with a large nose, and white rounded beard. His coat and turban were of white cotton, his sash or waistband of silk, all quite inexpensive, but his head-dress was adorned by a gold band and a great emerald surrounded by smaller stones. The traveller confirms the Muhammadan accounts of the extraordinary austerity of Aurangzēb's personal habits. He slept little, spent hours in devotion, confined himself to vegetable diet, and often fasted. His attendants marvelled how a man of his age could endure the hard conditions to which he subjected his body.

The public reception was conducted with the pomp customary at the Mogul court. Aurangzēb never either compelled other people to adopt his ascetic personal habits, or allowed any diminu-

[1] Gemelli-Careri details the stages of his journey (Tomo iii, pp. 87 foll.). The distance is about 125 miles on the map, or 150 for travelling. Galgala must be Galgali in the Bāgalkot Taluka of the Bījāpur District, Bombay, 7 *kōs* from Mudhol (16° 20′ N. and 75° 19′ E.). The position of the Galgala camp does not appear to have been defined until now. Lane-Poole, who quotes Gemelli-Careri, gives no indication of its situation. Later in the year 1695 Aurangzēb moved his camp to Brahmapuri or Islāmpuri in the Sholāpur District, miscalled Bairāmpur by Khāfī Khān and Lane-Poole. I have used the very rare Italian enlarged and revised second edition in nine volumes, Venezia, 1719. The traveller gives a curious woodcut of the emperor leaving his tent. The population of the camp was half a million (500,000), not 'five millions', as quoted by Lane-Poole. The correct number of infantry is 100,000, and that of camels 50,000 (Tomo iii, p. 103).

tion in the accustomed magnificence of his surroundings. His letters show that he was extremely jealous in his care of the royal prerogative and watchful to prevent the slightest infringements of etiquette.

Death of Aurangzēb. The last or almost the last petty success of the imperialists was won in 1705 by the capture of the fort of Wākinkera which had been evacuated by the enemy. About the same time the health of Aurangzēb broke down, and he was seized with fainting fits which rendered him temporarily unconscious. Whenever he grew a little better he gallantly fought his disorder and forced himself to make a public appearance. At last, 'slowly and with difficulty', he marched back to Ahmadnagar, where he had encamped twenty-four years earlier, filled with hopes of conquest and glory. Now, when he nerved himself to sit in the hall of audience, he was 'very weak and death was clearly stamped upon his face'. The fever increased, but he still attended scrupulously to the prescribed times of prayer. On the morning of Friday, February 21 (o.s.), 1707, when one watch of the day had gone, and the prayers and creed had been duly recited, his weary spirit was released. His viscera were buried where he died. His embalmed body was carried to the village of Rauza or Khuldābād near Daulatābād, and there laid to rest in holy ground beside the tombs of famous saints. He left written instructions that his obsequies were to be conducted with studied austerity. Four rupees, two annas (9*s.* 6*d.*), earned as the price of caps made by himself, were to be spent on his shroud. 305 rupees gained by copying Korāns were to be given to poor holy men. His body was to be buried bareheaded, and the top of the coffin was to be covered merely with a piece of white canvas. No canopy was to be raised over him.[1] His tomb is a perfectly plain block of plastered masonry on an open platform.[2]

Aurangzēb's ideal. Thus Aurangzēb died as he had lived, striving to attain the ideal of a strict Muslim ascetic of the school of Hanīfa. He endeavoured to follow the Law and Traditions in every detail of his personal conduct and habits. He learned the whole Korān by heart after his accession, and was well versed in the works of theologians, especially those of the Imām Muhammad Ghazzālī.[3] He was careful to educate his children, including his daughters, in sacred lore. He abstained scrupulously from the slightest indulgence in any prohibited food, drink, or dress; and, although well skilled in the theory of music, refused to enjoy the pleasures of that art from an early date in his reign. Every ritual prescription of prayer, fasting, and almsgiving was obeyed

[1] Sarkar, *Anecdotes*, p. 52.

[2] The tombs at Rauza ('the garden', *scil.* of Paradise) are described by Haig, *Historic Landmarks of the Deccan* (1907), pp. 56–8. *Khuld* means 'paradise', with allusion to Aurangzēb's posthumous title *Khuld-makān*, 'whose abode is in paradise'.

[3] Abū Hāmid Muhammad Zainu-d dīn of Tūs near Mashhad (A.D. 1058–1111), a renowned philosopher, mathematician, and astronomer.

exactly, even at the risk of his life. He desired all judicial proceedings to be conducted in precise accordance with Muslim law. He excluded Hindus from holding office so far as possible, cast down their temples, and harassed them by insulting regulations because he believed that he was bound to do so by the precedent of the early Khalīfs. For the same reason he enforced the levy of the *jizya*, and in his latest years refused to allow the least relaxation in the collection of the tax, even for the purpose of securing supplies for his own camp.[1] It is not to be wondered at that such conduct has won him the reverence of Muhammadans.

AURANGZĒB.

Failure as a sovereign. But when he is judged as a sovereign he must be pronounced a failure. The criticism of Khāfī Khān emphasizes equally his merits as an ascetic and his demerits in the practical government of an empire:

'Of all the sovereigns of the House of Tīmūr—nay, of all the sovereigns of Delhi—no one, since Sikandar Lodī, has ever been apparently so distinguished for devotion, austerity, and justice. In courage, long-suffering, and sound judgement he was unrivalled. But from reverence for the injunctions of the Law he did not make use of punishment, and without punishment the administration of a country cannot be maintained.[2] Dissensions had arisen among his nobles through rivalry. So every plan and project that he formed came to little good; and every enterprise which he undertook was long in execution and failed of its object. Although he lived for ninety [lunar] years, his five senses were not at all impaired, except his hearing, and that to only so slight an extent that it was not perceptible to others. He often passed his nights in vigils and devotion, and he denied himself many pleasures naturally belonging to humanity.'

The censures of the friendly Muhammadan critic do not exhaust the list of Aurangzēb's defects as a ruler. His intense suspiciousness,

[1] Sarkar, *Anecdotes*, p. 142.

[2] Confirmed by Gemelli-Careri. 'Il cessa d'être sanguinaire comme auparavant ; il devint même si bon (' good-natured ') que les Gouverneurs & les *Omrahs* ne lui obéïssoient pas régulièrement, se fiant à sa clemenee ' (French transl., iii. 227). See also Italian text, tomo iii, p. 105. His letters give further proof of the weakness of his rule.

already mentioned, poisoned his whole life. He never trusted anybody, and consequently was ill served. His cold, calculating temperament rarely permitted him to indulge in love for man or woman, and few indeed were the persons who loved him. His reliance on mere cunning as the principal instrument of statecraft testified to a certain smallness of mind, and, moreover, was ineffective in practice. Although he had many opportunities for winning military distinction, he failed to show ability as a general, whether before or after his accession. His proceedings in the Deccan during the latter part of his life were simply ridiculous as military operations. In fact, nothing in the history of Aurangzēb justifies posterity in classing him as a great king. His tricky cunning was mainly directed, first to winning, and then to keeping the throne. He did nothing for literature or art. Rather it should be said that he did less than nothing, because he discouraged both.

Aurangzēb's death-bed letters. The famous letters to his sons, written shortly before his death, must not be interpreted as implying that he felt remorse for the means by which he gained the throne, or for any acts of perfidy committed later in the supposed interest of the state. He regarded his treatment of his relatives as prompted and justified by self-defence; and it is true that his brothers, if they had not been executed by him, would have been delighted to take his life. Perfidy was the most essential element in policy to his thinking, and he did not hesitate to avow that belief, which has been and still is cherished by many kings and statesmen.

The death-bed letters simply express the weariness of an aged man who had lived too long, had failed in cherished plans, and was tormented by morbid fears about his fate in the next world—fears based upon his theological creed, and perfectly sincere.

The following collection of passages includes extracts from all the three letters, which are nearly identical:

'I know not who I am, where I shall go, or what will happen to this sinner full of sins. Now I will say good-bye to every one in this world and entrust every one to the care of God. My famous and auspicious sons should not quarrel among themselves and allow a general massacre of the people who are servants of God. . . . My years have gone by profitless. God has been in my heart, yet my darkened eyes have not recognized his light. . . . There is no hope for me in the future. The fever is gone, but only the skin is left. . . . The army is confounded, and without heart or help, even as I am; apart from God, with no rest for the heart. . . . When I have lost hope in myself, how can I hope in others? . . . You should accept my last will. It should not happen that Musalmāns be killed and the blame for their death rest upon this useless creature. . . . I have greatly sinned and know not what torment awaits me. . . . I commit you and your sons to the care of God and bid you farewell . . . May the peace of God be upon you.'

The sternest critic of the character and deeds of Aurangzēb can hardly refuse to recognize the pathos of those lamentations or to feel some sympathy for the old man on his lonely death-bed.

Transactions with European nations. The transactions in which European nations, chiefly the English, were prominently concerned lie so much apart from the general current of events in the reign that it is convenient to notice them separately, rather than in their chronological setting. But it is not possible to go into details of the incidents, which were numerous and complicated.

The Portuguese, in the days of Aurangzēb, were of so little account that the dealings between them and his government may be passed by. The struggle for the eastern maritime trade then lay between the English and the Dutch. But the Hollanders devoted their attention chiefly to the commerce with the Indian Archipelago and Spice Islands, keeping very quiet in their Indian factories. The small settlements on the coasts made by the French and Danes during the reign did not seriously concern the Mogul empire. The real trouble was with the English traders who began to assert themselves and to claim the right of fortifying their 'factories' or commercial stations.

The English factory at Surat was gallantly defended against Sivājī and his Marāthā robbers on two occasions, in 1664 and 1670. Sir George Oxinden's brave repulse of the marauders on the first occasion won approval and honours from Aurangzēb.

Rupee of Aurangzēb Ālamgīr.

Disputes concerning customs duties between the English traders on the Hūglī and Nawāb Shāyista Khān, the governor of Bengal, had the curious result of bringing about a semi-official war between England and the Mogul empire. The authorities of the East India Company in London ordinarily were averse to acquisition of territory or to fortifying their factories, but Sir Josiah Child, the masterful chairman or governor of the Company, who was ambitious, aimed at laying 'the foundation of a large, well-grounded, sure English dominion in India for all time to come'. In 1685 he persuaded King James II to sanction the dispatch of ten or twelve ships of war with instructions to seize and fortify Chittagong. The expedition, rashly planned and unfortunate in execution, was an utter failure. Subsequently, in 1688, the English found themselves obliged to abandon Bengal altogether.

Sir John Child, the President of Surat, acting under instructions from home, defied Aurangzēb's power on the western coast, with the result that the factory at Surat was seized, and orders were issued by the emperor to expel all Englishmen from his dominions. Ultimately terms were arranged on both sides of India. Ibrāhīm Khān, the successor of Shāyista Khān as governor of Bengal, invited Job Charnock, who had been chief of the settlement on the Hūglī, to return. The invitation was accepted. On August 24, 1690, Charnock hoisted the English flag on the banks of the Hūglī and laid the humble foundation of the small settlement destined to develop into the city of Calcutta.

The scandalous quarrels between the old East India Company of London and the New English Company, which lasted from 1698 to 1702 and to some extent later, were brought prominently to the notice of Aurangzēb, who could not make out which Company was the genuine one. His great officers profited largely by receiving heavy bribes from both associations, but the queer story is too long and intricate for brief narration.

After the ignominious failure of the warlike policy of the two Childs and the complete fusion of the rival companies in 1708 the English merchants kept clear of politics and fighting for almost half a century.[1]

Administration. In the latter years of Aurangzēb's reign the fifteen provinces (*sūbas*) of Akbar's time had increased to twenty-one. Thathah (Tatta), or Southern Sind, Kashmīr, and Orissa, formerly included respectively in Mūltān, Kābul, and Bengal, had been separated, and the provinces of the Deccan had become six instead of three.

The system of administration, while substantially the same as in Akbar's days, was worse in operation, because Aurangzēb failed to keep a firm hand over his subordinates, and when he grew old was unable to make his authority respected.

Several authors have taken much trouble to compare various statements of the revenue of the empire at different times, but their labours have been fruitless. The figures on record cannot be forced to yield trustworthy results. I therefore refrain from quoting or discussing them. The army, which made a brave show on paper or in camp, was of little military value. Manucci's estimate that 30,000 good European soldiers could sweep away the imperial authority and occupy the whole empire seems to be fully justified by the facts. The navy was utterly inefficient. The assertion of one of the Persian historians that Aurangzēb renounced the practice of confiscating the estates of deceased notables is contradicted decisively by the emperor's letters. The few letters translated by Bilimoria give three instances of such confiscation being ordered by Aurangzēb under his own hand. When Amīr Khān, governor of Kābul, died the authorities were instructed to seize everything belonging to him, so that 'even a piece of straw' should not be left (Letter XCIX). Similar orders were given concerning the estates of Shāyista Khān, the emperor's maternal uncle, and Mahābat Khān (Letters CXXVIII, CXLVI). The receipts from such confiscations were exceedingly large, and the treasury was not in a position justifying the surrender of revenue, 'because', as the emperor wrote, 'the royal treasury belongs to the public'.

[1] Mr. Strachey has proved that the two Childs, Sir Josiah and Sir John, were not brothers. They were not even related (*Keigwin's Rebellion*, Clarendon Press, 1916, App. A).

Leading Dates only

(For dates of war of succession see *ante*, p. 422.)

Formal enthronement of Aurangzēb; murder of Afzal Khān by Sivājī	1659
Cession of Bombay by Portuguese to English	1661
Mīr Jumla's expedition to Assam	1661–3
Aurangzēb's illness; first sack of Surat by Sivājī; foundation of French *Compagnie des Indes*	1664
Death of Shāhjahān; annexation of Chittagong by Shāyista Khān	1666
Prohibition of Hindu worship; demolition of temples; first Jāt rebellion	1669
First levy of *chauth* on Mogul territory; second sack of Surat by Sivājī	1670
Satnāmī insurrection	1672
Enthronement of Sivājī as independent Rājā	1674
Sivājī's expedition to the south	1676
Death of Rājā Jaswant Singh	1678
Reimposition of the *jizya*	1679
Death of Sivājī	1680
Rājpūt war; rebellion of Prince Akbar	1680–1
Second Jāt rebellion; Aurangzēb goes to the Deccan	1681
Sir Josiah Child's war	1685–6
Annexation of Bījāpur	1686
Annexation of Golkonda	1687
Total withdrawal of the English from Bengal	1688
Execution of Rājā Sambhājī	1689
Return of the English to Bengal and foundation of Calcutta	1690
Greatest southern extension of imperial authority	1691
Indecisive war in the Deccan	1692–1705
Union of the rival East India Companies	1702–8
Retreat of Aurangzēb to Ahmadnagar	January 1706
Death of Aurangzēb	February 21 (o.s.), 1707

AUTHORITIES

Copious extracts from KHĀFĪ KHĀN and other writers in Persian are translated in *E. & D.*, vol. vii. Professor JADUNATH SARKAR gives a summary history of the reign and many interesting details in *Anecdotes of Aurangzīb and Historical Essays* (Calcutta, 1912). Vol. iii of the same author's *History of Aurangzīb* comes down to A. D. 1681, excluding Deccan affairs. For a rather crude version of selected correspondence, BILIMORIA, *Letters of Aurangzebe* (London (Luzac) and Bombay, 1908), is useful. The leading authority for Marāthā affairs is GRANT DUFF, *History of the Mahrattas* (1826, and reprints). That work, being founded on personal knowledge and manuscripts now lost, ranks as an original source. The little book by MANKAR (2nd ed., Bombay, 1886), translated from a lost manuscript, is of considerable value. It is entitled *The Life and Exploits of Shivājī*, and has become very scarce. Professor RAWLINSON's sketch. *Shivājī the Marāthā* (Clarendon Press, 1915), is too slight and needs revision. Its special interest lies in the translations from Rāmdās and Tukārām.

ELPHINSTONE knew the Marāthā country and people so intimately that his narrative counts as a primary authority for some purposes. Many European travellers illustrate the story of the reign. The most serviceable works are those of BERNIER (ed. Constable and V. A. Smith, Oxford University Press, 1914); FRYER (ed. Crooke, Hakluyt Society, 1909, 1912, 1913); and GEMELLI-CARERI (French version[2], 1727). I have obtained from Rome a copy of the very rare Italian original, Venice, 1719, second edition, in nine volumes. The first edition appeared at Naples in 1699–1700 in 6 vols. TOD, *Annals of Rajasthan* (popular ed.); STEWART, *History of Bengal* (London, 1813); STRACHEY, *Keigwin's Rebellion* (Clarendon Press, 1916), and other books have been consulted. STANLEY LANE-POOLE'S *Aurangzīb* (R. I., 1896), the most readable account of the whole reign, requires considerable correction in certain details.

It may be well to note that the spelling Aurangzīb represents the Persian and Aurangzēb the Indian pronunciation.

CHAPTER 7

The Later Moguls; decline of the empire; the Sikhs and Marāthās.

War of succession: Bahādur Shāh. The practical certainty that his sons would fight for the throne of Hindostan as soon as he should die weighed heavily on the heart of Aurangzēb, who attempted to prevent the inevitable war of succession by admonitions which have been already quoted. He cannot possibly have believed in their efficacy. He also left behind him a memorandum suggesting a partition of the empire, but could not have had any real expectation that his heirs would accept that solution of the difficulty. The same reasons which had brought about the war of succession between Aurangzēb and his brothers forced his sons to fight. The eldest, Prince Muazzam, also called Shāh Ālam, was far away in Kābul, and so for the moment at a disadvantage. The second, Prince Azam, and the third, Prince Kāmbakhsh, who were both at hand in the Deccan, lost no time in asserting their claims. Each promptly proclaimed his accession, and struck coins in his own name. The immediate objective of all the three claimants was the seizure of Agra with its hoards of treasure. Whoever could first obtain possession of the cash in the Agra vaults would be able to buy unlimited support. Prince Muazzam, aided by an able officer named Munim Khān, moved down from Kābul with all speed, and met the army of his brother Azam at Jājau to the south of Agra on June 10, 1707. Kāmbakhsh, who had occupied Bījāpur and Golkonda or Hyderabad, was not able to leave the Deccan. The hotly contested battle at Jājau ended in the defeat and death of Prince Azam. Shāh Ālam secured the Agra treasure, which he distributed liberally among the nobles and soldiery. He assumed the style of Bahādur Shāh.

The new emperor then made arrangements to keep the Rājpūt chiefs quiet, and marched south to meet Kāmbakhsh, who was defeated near Hyderabad and died of wounds in January 1709.[1]

[1] No sympathy need be wasted on either Azam or Kāmbakhsh, who

Release of Shāhū. Bahādur Shāh, acting on the astute advice of Zulfikār Khān, released Shāhū (Sivājī II), the great Sivājī's grandson, who had been educated at court, and sent him back to his own country, then under the government of Tārā Bāī, the widow of the young prince's uncle, Rājā Rām. The expected civil war among the Marāthās which ensued prevented them from troubling the imperial government, thus justifying Zulfikār Khān's counsel.

News of Sikh rebellion. Bahādur Shāh, when returning from the Deccan, committed the government of the south to Zulfikār Khān, who passed on the duties of administration to Dāūd Khān, a ferocious Afghan ruffian, concerning whose barbarities Manucci relates many horrible stories.[1] When the emperor reached Ajmēr in 1710 he received reports that the town of Sihrind had been sacked by the Sikh sectaries under a leader known as Bandah ('the slave'), and sometimes described as the False Guru, who had committed innumerable atrocities. The news received was so serious that Bahādur Shāh resolved to proceed in person against the rebels. In order to render the situation intelligible it is necessary to narrate briefly the origin and early development of the Sikh movement.

The early Sikh gurus. The Sikhs, or 'disciples', originally were a pious sect of Hindus following the precepts of their first *guru* or prophet named Nānak, who lived from A.D. 1469 to 1539. He resembled Kabīr and many other sages in his teaching which laid stress on the unity of God, the futility of forms of worship, and the unreality of caste distinctions. The first four gurus were merely leaders of a peaceable reformed sect, with no thought of either military organization or political power. In 1577 Akbar, who liked the Sikh teaching so far as he knew it, granted to the fourth guru the site of the tank and Golden Temple at Amritsar, and so established that town as the head-quarters of the Sikh faith.

The fifth guru, Arjun, combined business with spiritual guidance, and acquired wealth from the offerings of the faithful. He was tortured and executed in 1606 by order of Jahāngīr because he refused to pay the fine imposed on him for having assisted Khusrū, not on account of his religious teaching. The Ādi Granth, or original Sikh Bible, was compiled in 1604 at the dictation of Arjun.

Hargobind. Hargobind, the sixth head of the sect (1606–45), when presented at his installation with the turban and necklace of his predecessors, refused to accept them, saying: 'My necklace

were both unfit to rule. The former is described as being 'very choleric, a debauchee, rough and discourteous to everybody, also avaricious' (Irvine, Manucci, iv. 462). The latter was a half-insane tyrant, who behaved with 'outrageous cruelty', doing acts to his servants, companions, and confidants, such 'as before eye never saw, nor ear heard'.

[1] Meadows Taylor describes the brute as 'an officer of great distinction, ability, and bravery'. Elphinstone, too, gives no indication of the man's real character.

shall be my sword-belt, and my turban shall be adorned with a royal aigrette.' He thus began the transformation of a sect of quiet mystics into a fierce military order or brotherhood. He was imprisoned for twelve years by Jahāngīr, and, after the death of that emperor, constantly fought the officers of Shāhjahān.

Tēgh Bahādur. Tēgh Bahādur, the ninth guru, rejected the demand of Aurangzēb that he should embrace Islām, and in consequence was executed (1675). According to a famous story he was accused while imprisoned at Delhi of turning his gaze in the forbidden direction of the imperial female apartments. He replied to the charge by saying :

'Emperor Aurangzēb, I was on the top story of my prison, but I was not looking at thy private apartments, or at thy queen's. I was looking in the direction of the Europeans who are coming from beyond the seas to tear down thy hangings (*pardas*) and destroy thy empire.'

The anecdote was firmly believed by the Sikhs, who used the prophecy as a battle-cry during the siege of Delhi in 1857. A somewhat similar prophecy is attributed to Guru Govind.

Govind Singh. The tenth and last guru, Govind Singh (1664–1708), was the real founder of the Sikh military power, which he organized to oppose the Muhammadans. He bound the Sikh fraternity together by instituting or adopting two sacraments, perhaps suggested by Christian example. The ceremony of *pāhul* or baptism consists essentially of drinking consecrated water stirred by a sword or dagger. The communion rite was specially designed to break caste. The communicants seated in a circle partake of a mixture of consecrated flour, butter, and sugar, and thus set themselves free from the restrictions of caste. The brotherhood so constituted was termed the Khālsa or Pure, and may be compared with the Templars and other military orders of mediaeval Europe. The Sikhs are not, and never have been, a nation in any intelligible sense. One member of a family may be a Sikh or Singh, while the others are orthodox Hindus. The members of the order are only a fraction of the population in the districts where they reside, and at the present day many Sikhs describe themselves as Hindus. In fact, the distinction between Hinduism and Sikhism is not well defined, the observance of the sacraments often being neglected by men who are recognized as Sikhs. Guru Govind required the members of the brotherhood to abjure tobacco, which he detested. 'Wine', he said, 'is bad; Indian hemp (*bhang*) destroyeth one generation; but tobacco destroyeth all generations.' The initiated members of the brotherhood were also commanded to wear the 'five *K*'s', meaning five things of which the Hindī or Panjābī names begin with that letter—namely, long hair, short drawers, an iron bangle or discus, a small steel dagger, and a comb. Those commands are not all fully observed now, and modern Sikhism owes its continued existence chiefly to the influence of the corporate spirit of the Sikh regiments. A supplementary *Granth* or Bible containing the compositions of Govind was compiled after his death.

He decided to support Bahādur Shāh (Shāh Ālam) in the war of succession, and consequently accepted service under that prince when he gained the throne. Govind, who was murdered at Nāndēr in the Deccan by an Afghan in 1708, was the last of the gurus. Since his decease the holy Granth has been regarded as the representative and successor of the Gurus.

Govind seems to have authorized a man of uncertain origin to take over the military command, but not the spiritual headship, of the Sikh Khālsa. The person so nominated is known as Bandah, 'the Slave', and sometimes is called the 'False Guru'. His special mission was the taking vengeance on Wazīr Khān, the commandant of Sihrind, who had cruelly executed the young sons of Guru Govind.

Bandah. Bandah accomplished his commission with appalling ferocity and completeness. Irvine draws a lively picture of his proceedings.

> 'The scavengers and leather-dressers and such-like persons, who were very numerous among the Sikhs, committed excesses of every description. For the space of four days the town [Sihrind] was given up to pillage, the mosques were defiled, the houses burnt, and the Muhammadans slaughtered; even their women and children were not spared . . .
>
> In all the parganahs occupied by the Sikhs, the reversal of previous customs was striking and complete. A low scavenger or leather-dresser, the lowest of the low in Indian estimation, had only to leave home and join the Guru, when in a short time he would return to his birthplace as its ruler, with his order of appointment in his hand. As soon as he set foot within the boundaries, the well-born and wealthy went out to greet him and escort him home. Arrived there, they stood before him with joined palms, awaiting his orders. A scavenger, from the nature of his duties, is intimately acquainted with the condition of every household. Thus the new ruler had no difficulty in exacting from every one their best and most valuable belongings, which were confiscated for the use of the Guru, or for his treasury. Not a soul dared to disobey an order, and men, who had often risked themselves in battle-fields, became so cowed, that they were afraid even to remonstrate. Hindus who had not joined the sect were not exempt from those oppressions.'

Bahādur Shāh and Munim Khān succeeded in defeating the Sikhs and driving them into the hills, but Bandah escaped.

Death of Bahādur Shāh. Bāhādur Shāh, then an old man in his sixty-ninth year, died in 1712. The prolonged repression which he endured under his father had destroyed his spirit. Although he had no vice in his character, and possessed a generous, forgiving disposition, he could not govern, and justly earned the nickname of *Shāh-i be khabar*, the 'Heedless King'.

War of succession: Jahāndār Shāh. His four sons engaged in the customary war of succession. Azīmu-sh shān, governor of Bengal, and the best of the four, was killed in battle with the other three, who then fell out among themselves. Jahāndār Shāh, the eldest and worst of them, a worthless profligate, became emperor.

Farrukhsiyar. After a disgraceful reign of eleven months he was killed in a barbarous fashion by order of Azīmu-sh shān's son, Farrukhsiyar, who ascended the degraded throne (1713). He executed many notable people, including Zulfikār Khān, and established a state of terror in the court by his savage fury. During the scandalous reign of Farrukhsiyar, who was a good-for-nothing and shameless debauchee, the power of the government was mostly in the hands of two brothers, Abdullah and Husain Ali, Bārha Sayyids, whose clan had been eminent in the imperial service since the days of Akbar. They deposed Farrukhsiyar in 1719, and put him to death in a horrible way.

The short reign of Farrukhsiyar was marked by a futile attempt to reimpose the *jizya*, and by the capture of Bandah, who was executed with fiendish tortures. About a thousand of his followers were killed in large batches (1715).

In the same year the East India Company, worried by the exactions of the Bengal provincial government, sent two factors to Delhi in order to seek redress. The envoys took with them £30,000 worth of gifts, and in the course of two years obtained valuable trade concessions and exemptions from customs duties. Their success was due partly to the fact that an English surgeon named William Hamilton cured the emperor of 'a malignant distemper', and partly to the fears of the Delhi government that the British fleet might hold up the Surat trade.

Muhammad Shāh. After the cruel murder of Farrukhsiyar the Sayyid king-makers placed on the throne several phantom emperors.[1] They quickly disappeared and were replaced by another worthless inmate of the palace, named Muhammad Shāh (1719), who, strange to say, retained his life and dignity until 1748. He got rid of Sayyid Husain Alī by assassination, and imprisoned Abdullah.

Break up of empire. In 1722 Āsaf Jāh (Chīn Kilich Khān) became Vizier. He found it impossible to bring the government into order, and in the year following retired to his province the Deccan, where he became independent and founded the existing dynasty of the Nizam, with effect from 1724.

In the same year Saādat Khān, the progenitor of the kings of Oudh, became ruler of that province, which he governed in practical independence. Similarly, Allahvardi Khān, the governor of Bengal (1740–56), ceased to pay tribute or to recognize in practice the sovereignty of the emperor. The Rohillas, an Afghan clan, made themselves masters of the rich tract to the north of the Ganges, which consequently became known as Rohilkhand. Thus, in the space of seventeen years after the death of Aurangzēb, the empire had broken up. The process of decay was continued in subsequent years. The capital was the scene of incessant intrigues and treasons, unworthy of record or remembrance.

[1] Their names are Rafīu-d darajāt, Rafīu-d daulat (Shāhjahān II), Nekūsiyar, and Ibrāhīm. The 'reigns' of the first three fall between February 18 and August 27, 1719. Ibrāhīm claimed the throne in 1720, from October 1 to November 8, and struck coins, now very rare. See the genealogy at the end of this chapter.

New system of Marāthā government. Meantime, momentous changes had been effected after long struggles in the Marāthā government, which resulted during Muhammad Shāh's lifetime in the Marāthās becoming the most considerable power in India. The excellent system of internal administration instituted by Sivājī had not survived that chief. It fell to pieces, as we have seen, in the hands of his son, Sambhājī. During the civil war between different parties of Marāthās which followed on the return of Shāhū to his native country, after his release by Bahādur Shāh, a new system of government was gradually evolved.

The first Pēshwā, Bālājī Visvanāth. Rājā Shāhū, who had to defend his position as Rājā against a rival claimant, leant for support chiefly on a Brahman from the Konkan, named Bālājī Visvanāth, who held from 1714 the office of Pēshwā, as the second minister was called in the early Marāthā administration.[1] By reason of his personal qualities Bālājī Visvanāth made the office to count in practice as the first, and not the second. When he died in 1720 his official position was inherited by his son, Bājī Rāo (I), a man still abler than himself. The appointment of Pēshwā thus became hereditary, and soon overshadowed the Rājā, who sank into a purely ornamental position, exactly as the Mahārājādhirāj of Nepāl has done in modern times. After Shāhū the descendants of Sivājī dropped out of sight so completely that all readers of history think of the Marāthā government in the eighteenth century as that of the Pēshwās. Their dynasty, as we may call it, comprised seven persons, and may be regarded as having lasted from 1714 to 1818, a little more than a century. Shāhū, who survived until 1748, granted his minister full powers in 1727.

Chauth and Sardesmukhi. Bālājī Visvanāth, as minister of Shāhū, had succeeded in introducing a certain amount of order into the Marāthā administration, and had made elaborate arrangements for collecting the assignments of revenue from provinces belonging to other powers on which his government chiefly lived. The Marāthās of those days administered only comparatively small districts directly, preferring to raise contributions from provinces governed, nominally at all events, by the emperor of Delhi or other potentates of that confused and anarchical time. In 1720 Muhammad Shāh, confirming arrangements made by Sayyid Husain Ali, recognized by treaty the authority of Rājā Shāhū, admitted his right to levy the *chauth*, or assessment of one-fourth of the land revenue over the whole Deccan, and permitted him to supplement that levy by an additional tenth of the land revenue called *sardesmukhi*.

Bālājī Visvanāth claimed that those levies should be calculated on the revenue as fixed either by Todar Mall in Akbar's, or by Malik Ambar in Shāhjahān's time, well knowing that no such amount of revenue could be raised from a ruined country. He thus secured

[1] In Sivājī's time the Pratinidhi did not exist, and the Pēshwā was the first minister.

the advantage of always keeping a bill for arrears in hand. He artfully arranged that several Marāthā chiefs should share the collections from a single district, in that way purposely introducing complications into the accounts and increasing the power of his Brahman caste-fellows, who alone had the knowledge and intelligence equal to dealing with such accounts. Nobody except the Brahmans rightly knew what was due, or to whom it was due.

The second Pēshwā, Bājī Rāo. Bājī Rāo (1720) inherited the instrument of extortion so cunningly devised by his father, and used it with supreme skill. He resolved to establish the power of his nascent nation by reorganizing the army, and directing it against the northern territories of Hindostan held by the nerveless hands of Muhammad Shāh. He also made arrangements by which he checked the growing power of Āsaf Jāh as ruler of the Hyderabad territories. The quarrels between Āsaf Jah and Bājī Rao ended in the rivals coming to terms (1731).

Origin of the Gaikwār, Sindia, and Holkar. We may take note that at the period in question the ancestors of the existing great Marāthā chiefs, namely, the Gaikwār of Baroda, Sindia of Gwālior, and Holkar of Indore, became prominent personages and laid the foundations of the fortune of their families, which by strange good luck survived at the final settlement in 1818 of the rivalry between the Marāthās and the British. The ancestor of the Gaikwār was an adherent of a defeated opponent of Bājī Rāo, whom the Pēshwā treated with politic generosity; the progenitors of Sindia and Holkar were men of humble origin who became officers of Bājī Rāo and rose gradually in his service.

Marāthā appearance before Delhi. The Marāthās, having made themselves masters of Gujarāt, Mālwā, and Bundēlkhand, made a startling demonstration of the weakness of the empire and of their own power by evading the imperial army and suddenly appearing in the suburbs of Delhi in 1737. They did not attempt to occupy the capital, and returned to the Deccan to meet Āsaf Jah, who had again taken the field against them. The Nizam, as we may now call him, was no match for his nimble enemy and was forced to make a formal cession of Mālwā to the Marāthās.

Weakness of the empire invited attack. Bājī Rāo, Elphinstone observes,

'took possession of his conquests; but before he could receive the promised confirmation from the emperor, the progress of the transaction was arrested by one of those tremendous visitations, which for a time render men insensible to all other considerations.

The empire was again reduced to the same state of decay which had on former occasions invited the invasions of Tamerlane and Bābar; and a train of events in Persia led to a similar attack from that country.'

Nādir Shāh; battle of Karnāl. Nādir (or Tahmāsp) Kulī Khān, 'the greatest warrior Persia has ever produced', had overthrown the Safavī dynasty in 1736, and been acclaimed king of that country under the style of Nādir Shāh. When established on his throne he easily found pretexts for the invasion and plunder of the rich and defenceless Indian plains. Advancing in 1739 through Ghaznī, Kābul, and Lahore, he met with no real obstruction until he had approached the Jumna, within 100 miles of Delhi, when he encountered the imperial army entrenched at Karnāl, not very far from the field of Pānīpat. After a fight lasting two hours the imperialists were routed, some 20,000 being slain, and immense booty falling into the hands of the conqueror. Muhammad Shāh made no attempt at further resistance, but attended Nādir Shāh in his camp, where he was received courteously. Both kings entered Delhi together, and good order was preserved until a false report of Nādir Shāh's death gave occasion to a rising of the inhabitants, in the course of which several hundreds of the invaders were killed. Nādir Shāh took terrible vengeance. Seated in the Golden Mosque of Roshanu-ddaula, situated in the main street of the city, he commanded and watched for nine hours the indiscriminate massacre of the people in uncounted thousands. At last he yielded to the prayers of Muhammad Shāh and stayed the carnage, which ceased instantly.

NĀDIR SHĀH.

Nādir Shāh then proceeded systematically and remorselessly to collect from all classes of the population the wealth of Delhi, the accumulation of nearly three centuries and a half. After a stay of fifty-eight days he departed for his own country laden with treasure of incalculable richness, including the world-famed peacock throne of Shāhjahān. He annexed all the territory to the west of the Indus and the now extinct Hakrā river (*nāla* of Sankrah) under the provisions of a treaty dated May 26, 1739. Afghanistan was thus severed from the Indian monarchy.

Anarchy ; Ahmad Shāh of Delhi. Nādir Shāh left the Mogul empire bleeding and prostrate. No central government worthy of the name existed, and if any province enjoyed for a short time the blessing of tolerably good administration, as was the case in Bengal, that was due to the personal character of the noble or adventurer who had secured control over it. Very few indeed of the prominent men of the time possessed any discernible virtues. It is not worth while to relate the intrigues which occupied the corrupt and powerless court of Delhi. Marāthā affairs will be noticed presently. Here it will suffice to note that in 1748 Muhammad Shāh was succeeded peaceably by his son Ahmad Shāh.

Ahmad Shāh Durrānī. A month before the death of Muhammad Shāh his army, under the command of the heir apparent, Prince Ahmad, and the vizier, Kamālu-d dīn, had repulsed at Sihrind on the Sutlaj Ahmad Shāh Durrānī, the Afghan chief who had succeeded Nādir Shāh in the eastern portion of that monarch's dominions. But, notwithstanding his repulse, the Durrānī was strong enough to exact tribute from the Panjāb.

After the accession of Ahmad Shāh to the throne of Delhi his Durrānī namesake came back and obtained the formal cession of the Panjāb from the helpless Indian government, which was distracted by civil war.

Āsaf Jāh, the founder of the Nizam's dynasty, having died at a great age in 1748, his grandson Ghāzīu-d dīn became Vizier at Delhi. That nobleman blinded and deposed Ahmad Shāh in 1754, replacing him by a relative who was styled Ālamgīr II.

Two years later Ahmad Shāh Durrānī invaded India for the third time, and captured Delhi, which again suffered from the horrors of massacre and pillage (1756). Mathurā, too, was once more the scene of dreadful slaughter. In the summer of 1757 the Durrānī returned to his own country.

We must now revert to Marāthā affairs.

Bālājī, third Pēshwā. Bājī Rāo, the second Pēshwā, who had become the ruler of the Marāthās with hardly any pretence of dependence on the nominal Rājā, engaged in war with the Nizam after his return from his Delhi raid in 1737. He died in 1740, leaving three sons, the eldest of whom, Bālājī Rāo, succeeded him as Pēshwā, although not without much opposition from other Marāthā chiefs. In 1750 Bālājī consolidated his authority, making Poona his capital, and becoming the head of a confederacy of chiefs. Raghujī, the most prominent rival chief, had meantime acquired possession of the province of Cuttack or Orissa.

Marāthā occupation of the Panjāb. In 1758, when Ragoba or Raghunāth, the brother of the Pēshwā, having taken possession of Lahore, had occupied the whole of the Panjāb, it seemed as if the Marāthās were destined to become the sovereigns of India. That prospect seriously alarmed the Muhammadan rulers. Shujāu-d daula, Nawāb of Oudh, accordingly combined with the Rohilla Afghans, who had settled in Rohilkhand a few years earlier, against the aggressive Hindus. Ahmad Shāh Durrānī, too, was not content that the Panjāb, which he had held for a time, should be in Marāthā hands. In 1759 he returned to India and reoccupied that province. Ālamgīr II, the nominal emperor of Delhi, was murdered at this time, and succeeded by Shāh Ālam, or Prince Gauhar Ali, then in Bengal. The new emperor was recognized later by Ahmad Shāh Durrānī.

Marāthā power at its zenith. The Marāthā power was now, as Elphinstone observes,

'at its zenith. Their frontier extended on the north to the Indus and Himalaya, and on the south nearly to the extremity of the peninsula; all the territory within those limits that was not their own paid tribute.

The whole of this great power was wielded by one hand . . . and all pretensions of every description were concentrated in the peshwa.'

Elphinstone's statement requires correction in so far that the 'one hand' which directed the Marāthā government was that of Sadāsheo (Sadāsiva) Bhāo, the Pēshwā's first cousin, and was not that of Bālājī himself, who was addicted to sensual indulgence and 'left the entire management of all the affairs of government' to his cousin, a man well trained in the conduct of business and accustomed to steady work.

Sadāsheo Bhāo, having organized a regular well-paid army, including a large train of artillery, and 10,000 infantry, disciplined more or less completely after the European manner and under the command of a Muhammadan general named Ibrāhīm Khān Gardī, believed himself qualified to dispute the sovereignty of India with the Durrānī. Muhammad Shāh, the nominal emperor of Delhi, was not taken into serious account.

Renewed invasion of Upper India. In 1760 the Marāthā government decided to renew the invasion of Upper India and to attempt the achievement of Marāthā supremacy. The command of the enterprise having been declined by the Pēshwā's brother, Raghunāth Rāo, the Pēshwā's son, Viswās Rāo, a lad of seventeen, was appointed titular generalissimo, 'according to the ancient custom of the Mahrattas', with Sadāsheo Bhāo as his adviser. The Bhāo, to use his ordinary designation, was actually in full control of the whole army. All the Marāthā contingents under their various chiefs were summoned to the standard, and the promise of the aid of the Jāts of Bhartpur under their leader, Sūraj Mall, was secured.[1] Both sides, that is to say, the Muhammadans, Ahmad Shāh Durrāni with his allies the Rohillas on one side, and the Marāthās on the other, negotiated for the adhesion of Shujāu-d daula, the young ruler of Oudh.

The Marāthā commander obtained possession of Delhi without difficulty and quartered his host there during the rainy season of 1760. The Durrānī encamped at Anūpshahr, on the Ganges, now in the Bulandshahr District. Shujāu-d daula mounted guard over his own frontier. When the rains had ended and the Dasahra festival had passed Ahmad Shāh Durrānī managed to bring his army across a dangerous ford of the Jumna on October 23 and 24. The Marāthā commander failed to take advantage of the opportunity thus offered to him.

The armies in contact. A few days later the advanced guards of the two armies came into contact, and at the end of October the Bhāo fixed his head-quarters at Pānīpat, enclosing his whole camp as well as the town with a ditch sixty feet wide and twelve feet deep. His guns were mounted on the rampart.

The Durrānī camped about eight miles from the Marāthā lines on a front of about seven and a half miles, defending his encampment by an *abattis* of felled trees. He pitched a small red tent for

[1] The Jāts took no part in the battle. They withdrew in disgust at the arrogance and folly of the Bhāo.

himself at some distance in front of his lines, and devoted incessant care to the inspection of his troops and defences. The Marāthās cut his communications, thereby causing severe distress in the Afghan camp. A bold and successful attack on the force of Gobind Pundit, which was operating on the lines of communication, opened up the sources of supply and delivered Ahmad Shāh from all danger of starvation.

The enormous crowd shut up in the Marāthā entrenchments then began to feel the pressure of hunger. Several engagements took place, but afforded no relief to the starving host. The Bhāo made desperate efforts to negotiate, going so far as to offer Ahmad Shāh peaceful possession of the Panjāb up to Sihrind. The Durrānī was inflexible. He agreed with the Rohilla leader that 'the Marāthās are the thorn of Hindostan', and that 'by one effort we get this thorn out of our sides for ever'.

Ahmad Shāh declared that the Hindostānī chiefs, all of whom desired to make terms, might negotiate or do what they pleased. He understood, he said, the business of war, and would settle the matter finally in his own way.

The Marāthās were thus reduced to the 'last extremity' and forced to fight. As the Bhāo said, 'The cup is now full to the brim and cannot hold another drop.'

Third battle of Pānīpat. He was constrained to take the offensive. At dawn on January 7, 1761, the Marāthā army advanced eastwards and battle was joined.[1] The fighting was fierce, and up to noon the balance of advantage rested with the Hindus. An hour later reinforcements pushed forward by the Shāh delivered a charge, which produced a terrible effect. Between two and three o'clock the Pēshwā's son, Viswās Rāo, was wounded and unhorsed. About three o'clock,

> 'all at once, as if by enchantment, the whole Mahratta army at once turned their backs and fled at full speed, leaving the field of battle covered with heaps of dead. The instant they gave way, the victors pursued them with the utmost fury; and as they gave no quarter, the slaughter is scarcely to be conceived, the pursuit continuing for ten or twelve *coss* [more than 20 miles] in every direction in which they fled.'

[1] The 'black mango-tree' which marked the battle-field is now replaced by a simple masonry memorial with railing (*Prog. Rep. A. S., N. Circle, 1910–11, Muhammadan and British Monuments*, pl. xv).

Explanation. The right side of the map faces nearly north-east. Eight miles separated the town from the Durrānī camp.

A. *Pānīpat town and Marāthā camp.* The contingents or 'divisions' are:—(1) Ibrāhīm Khān; (2) Āmājī Gaikwār; (3) Sheodēo Patēl; (4) the Bhāo and Viswās Rāo; (5) Jaswant Rāo; (6) Shamshēr Bahādur; (7) Malhar Rāo; (8) Jankājī Sindīa.

B. *The Durrānī camp, with* (C), *Ahmad Shāh's advanced tent.* The contingents or 'divisions' are:—(1) Barkhurdār Khān; (2) Amīr Beg, &c.; (3) Dhūndhī Khān; (4) Hāfiz Rahmat Khān; (5) Ahmad Khān Bangash; (6) Grand Vizier; (7) Shujāu-d daula; (8) Najību-d daula; (9) Shāh Pasand Khān; (10) Persian musketeers.

PLAN OF THE BATTLE OF PANIPUT.

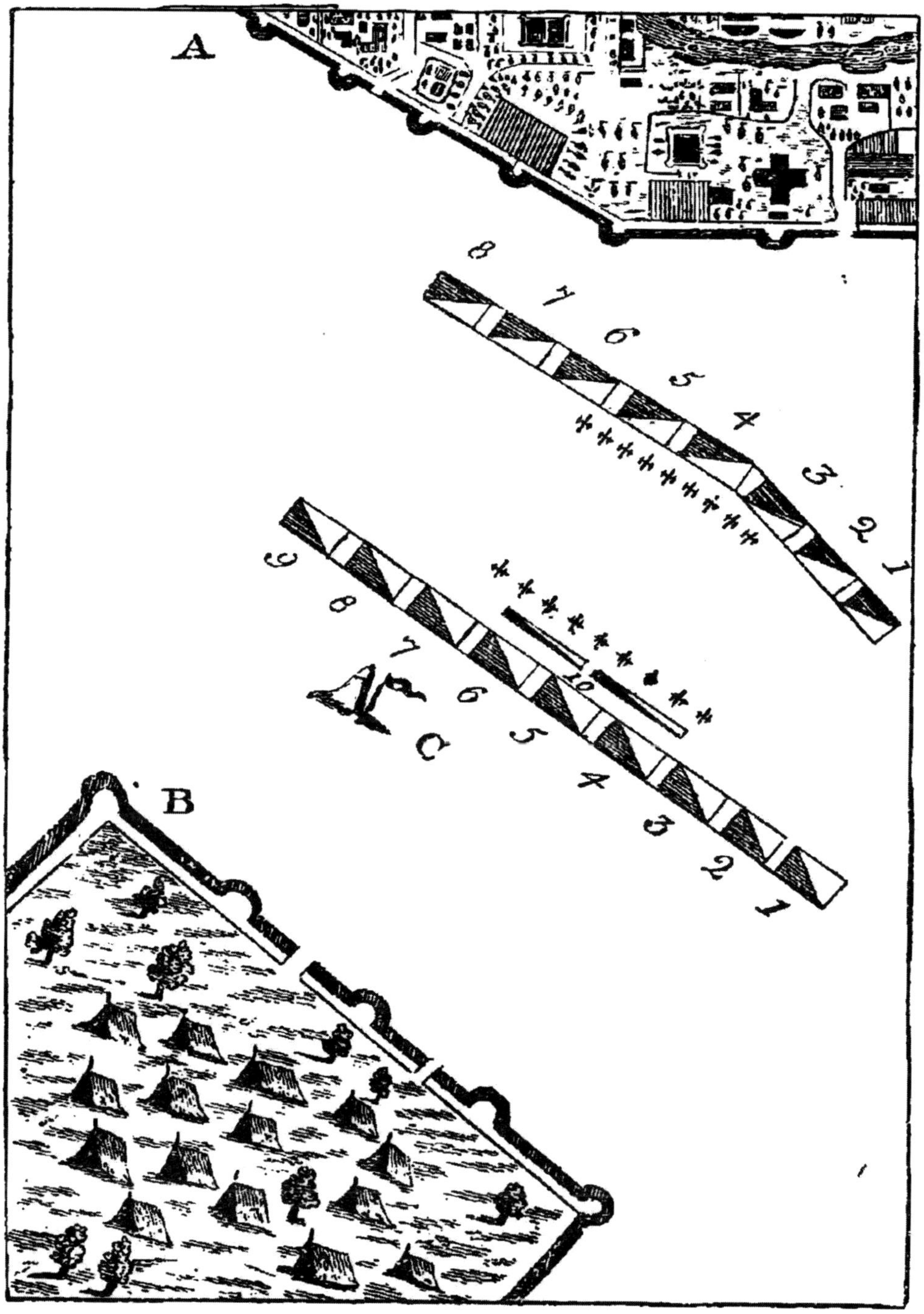

Such was the third battle of Pānīpat, a conflict far more determined and sanguinary than either of the battles fought on the same ground in the sixteenth century.[1]

Numbers engaged and killed. The forces engaged were large on both sides, but the Marāthās possessed a superiority. Kāsī Rājā Pundit, who was present at the battle and made exact inquiries based on the Shāh's muster rolls, states that Ahmad Shāh's army consisted of 41,800 cavalry, 38,000 infantry—say, in all, 80,000 in round numbers, supplemented by something like four times as many irregulars. That estimate evidently includes mere camp followers. He says that the Marāthās had 55,000 cavalry, besides 15,000 Pindāris, but reckons their infantry at only 15,000. They certainly were immensely superior in artillery. Elphinstone supposes that the total number of men within their lines may have been about 300,000. It is not known how many camp followers they had. The number of Hindus slaughtered was thought to approach 200,000. Thousands of prisoners were destroyed, 'so that in the Durrany camp (with an exception of the Shāh and his principal officers) every tent had heads piled up before the door of it.'

Nearly all the Hindu leaders of note were slain. The body of Viswās Rao was found and identified, but some slight doubt remained as to the correctness of the identification of the head and trunk said to be those of the Bhāo. Sindia and Holkar both escaped, as did the Brahman, famous in after years as Nānā Farnavīs. The losses were reported to the Pēshwā in enigmatical language easily interpreted :

'Two pearls have been dissolved, twenty-seven gold mohurs have been lost, and of the silver and copper the total cannot be cast up.'

The casualties on the side of the victors are not recorded.

Causes of the Marāthā defeat. Ahmad Shāh had won by patient, skilled generalship. The Bhāo had lost by reason of blind pride and obstinacy. He trusted in his guns and disciplined infantry, scornfully rejecting the wise words of the chiefs who counselled him to fight in the old and well-tried Marāthā fashion, and to free himself from the encumbrance of guns and followers. His fate was determined from the moment when he shut himself up in his lines with a multitude whom he could not feed.

The Shāh's ambition baulked. The Shāh had planned his ably conducted campaign with the purpose of seizing the empire of Hindostan. His ambition was baulked, as that of Alexander had been long before, by the mutiny of his soldiers. The Durrānīs mutinied in a body and passed completely out of his control, demanding payment of their arrears for two years past and immediate return to Kābul. Ahmad Shāh was powerless against such opposition and had to go home. Shujāu-d daula, the Nawāb of Oudh, who had taken no active part in the battle, although

[1] Battles of Pānīpat : (1) Bābur and Ibrāhīm Lodī, 1526 ; (2) Akbar and Hēmū, 1556 ; (3) Ahmad Shāh and Marāthās, 1761.

nominally on the side of the Shāh, also slipped away to his own dominions.

Effects of the battle in India. The effects of the battle on the political state of India are well summarized by Elphinstone, who observes that 'the history of the Mogul empire here closes of itself', and states that

'never was a defeat more complete, and never was there a calamity that diffused so much consternation. Grief and despondency spread over the whole Maratta people; most had to mourn relations, and all felt the destruction of the army as a death-blow to their national greatness. The pēshwā never recovered the shock. He slowly retreated from his frontier towards Pūna, and died in a temple which he had himself erected near that city. The wreck of the army retired beyond the Nerbadda, evacuating almost all their acquisitions in Hindostan. Dissensions soon broke out after the death of Bālājī, and the government of the pēshwā never recovered its vigour. Most of the Maratta conquests were recovered at a subsequent period; but it was by independent chiefs, with the aid of European officers and disciplined sepoys. The confederacy of the Maratta princes dissolved on the cessation of their common danger.'

Causes of decline of Mogul empire. The Mogul empire, like all Asiatic despotisms, had shallow roots. Its existence depended mainly on the personal character of the reigning autocrat and on the degree of his military power. It lacked popular support, the strength based upon patriotic feeling, and the stability founded upon ancient tradition; nor were there any permanent institutions to steady the top-heavy structure. Akbar, the real founder of the empire, was a man truly great, notwithstanding his frailties, and during his long personal reign of forty-five years (1560–1605) was able to build up an organization strong enough to survive twenty-two years of Jahāngīr's feebler rule. Shāhjahān, a stern, ruthless man, kept a firm hand on the reins for thirty years, and was followed by Aurangzēb, who maintained the system more or less in working order for almost fifty years longer. Thus, for a century and a half, from 1560 to 1707, the empire was preserved by a succession of four sovereigns, the length of whose reigns averaged thirty-four years, a very unusual combination. Even Jahāngīr, the weakest of the four, was no fool. The three others were men of unusual ability.

Akbar's exceptional gifts made him a most successful general as against Asiatic foes, and enabled him to construct a military machine much superior to anything of the kind possessed by other Indian states. That machine failed in the time of Shāhjahān when used against the Persians, but was still good enough to keep India fairly quiet during the first half of Aurangzēb's reign. The mechanism thenceforward steadily deteriorated. The last of the Great Moguls attained an age far beyond the limit of efficiency; his sons, benumbed by the crushing weight of parental control, lost all capacity for government; excessive luxury enervated the nobles, and gradually brought the army to the condition of a helpless mob. Then the hardy, frugal Marāthās pricked the bubble, and proved by experiment the worthlessness of the glittering imperial host. The long absence of Aurangzēb in the Deccan undermined the foundations of government, which degenerated in every department. Lack of control engendered oppression; and oppression begat poverty, entailing financial ruin, which was intensified by reckless spending and the lack of honest administration. The powerful Hindu support of the throne, won so cleverly by Akbar, was weakened by the erroneous policy of Shāhjahān and, in still greater degree, by the austere fanaticism of Aurangzēb. The prolonged anarchy involved in the repeated wars of succession was a potent influence in bringing about the ruin of the imperial fabric. Long before Aurangzēb's death the military power of the state had become contemptible, and the authority of the emperor could be defied with impunity. When the breath left his body no man remained in India who was fit to take the helm of the ship of state, which soon drifted on the rocks. The collapse of the empire came with a suddenness which at first sight may seem surprising. But the student who has acquired even a moderately sound knowledge of the history will be surprised that the empire lasted so long rather than because it collapsed suddenly.

It would be easy to expand such observations, and to indicate other causes, as, for example, the neglect of sea-power, which contributed to the ruin of the Mogul empire; but it is needless to work out the theme in further detail. Every attentive reader of the story can fill in the outline in his own fashion.

Revolution between 1756 and 1761. In 1715–17, when we last had occasion to notice the affairs of the East India Company, the mercantile representatives of the Company in Calcutta were content to devote their energies exclusively to trade and to avoid meddling with Indian politics or wars. They were then in no wise ashamed to send merchants bearing costly gifts in order to beg or buy commercial favours from the degraded wretch who polluted the throne of Aurangzēb. Until the catastrophe of 1756 they adhered to that humble policy. But during the short space of time which intervened between June 1756 and the tragedy of Pānīpat in January 1761 a marvellous change was wrought in the English position both in Bengal and in the peninsula. The conflicts in the south between the English and the French, in which each side was supported by Indian allies, began in 1746 with the loss of Madras and ended on January 6, 1761, the day before the battle of Pānīpat, with the unconditional surrender to British arms of Pondicherry, the chief French settlement. The events in Bengal were still more startling and fateful. The traders who fled in terror to Fulta in June 1756 were the masters of a rich kingdom exactly twelve months later.

The story of those memorable events and the connected happenings, which cannot be conveniently interwoven with the narrative of Mogul and Marāthā affairs, will be told in the chapters following.

The Later Moguls (principal names only)

AURANGZEB ĀLAMGĪR

- Muhammad Sultān (executed 1676)
- Muazzam, Bahādur Shāh I or Shāh Ālam I (acc. 1707, d. 1712)
  - Jahāndār Shāh (acc. 1712, murdered 1713)
    - Ālamgīr II (acc. 1754, murdered 1759)
      - Shāh Ālam II (acc. 1759, d. 1806)
        - Akbar II (acc. 1806, d. 1837)
          - Bahādur Shāh II (acc. 1837, deposed 1857)
  - Azīmu-sh shān (killed in battle)
    - Farrukhsiyar (acc. 1713, murdered 1719)
  - Rafīu-sh shān (killed in battle)
    - Rafīu-d Daulat (acc. and died 1719)
    - Rafīu-d Darajāt or Shāhjahān II (acc. and died 1719)
    - Muhammad Ibrāhīm (1720, for a month)
  - Jahānshāh (killed in battle)
    - Muhammad Shāh (acc. 1719, d. 1748)
      - Ahmad Shāh (acc. 1748, deposed 1754)
- Muhammad Azam (killed at Jājau, 1707)
  - Bedār Bakht (killed at Jājau)
- Akbar (d. in Persia, 1704)
  - Nekusiyar (acc. and d. 1719)
- Kāmbakhsh (killed at Hyderabad, 1709)

Leading Dates

Death of Aurangzēb	February 21 (o.s.), 1707
Battle of Jājau; defeat of Azam; accession of Bahādur Shāh	June 1707
Defeat and death of Kāmbakhsh	January 1709
Sikh rebellion	1710
Death of Bahādur Shāh; war of succession	1712
Accession of Farrukhsiyar	1713
Bālājī Visvanāth Pēshwā	1714
Execution of Bandah; mission from E. I. Co.	1715
Murder of Farrukhsiyar; accession of Muhammad Shāh . .	1719
Bājī Rāo I Pēshwā	1720
Independence of the Deccan and Oudh	1724
Marāthās appeared under Delhi	1737
Invasion of Nādir Shāh	1739
Bālājī Rāo Pēshwā; independence of Bengal	1740
Death of Muhammad Shāh; accession of Ahmad Shāh of Delhi .	1748
Ahmad Shāh deposed; accession of Ālamgīr II	1754
Sack of Delhi by Ahmad Shāh Durrānī	1756
Temporary occupation of Panjāb by the Marāthās	1758
Third battle of Pānīpat; Mādho Rāo Pēshwā	1761

Note.—The events connected with the French and English settlements are treated separately.

Authorities

Elphinstone enters into much detail. His narrative is based on the *Siyaru-l Mutākhirīn*; Khāfī Khān's history, now to be read in *E. & D.*, vol. vii; Grant Duff's *History of the Mahrattas*; and some few other books. A mass of minute and usually accurate information will be found in Irvine's articles in *J. A. S. B.*, part 1, for 1894, 1896, 1898, which are extracts from his unfinished book, designed to give the history in full from 1707 to 1803. He supplies references to all original authorities, printed and manuscript. The leading original authority for the battle of Pānīpat and connected events is the lucid narrative of Kāsi (Casi) Rājā Pundit, translated from the Persian and published in *Asiatic Researches*, vol. iii, 1799.[1] The plan of the battle is his. The history of the Sikhs may be studied in Cunningham, *History of the Sikhs* (1849 and 1853), or compendiously in Lepel Griffin, *Ranjīt Singh* (Rulers of India, 1898), an excellent little book. Several other works on the subject exist. The extensive treatise by Macauliffe, entitled *The Sikh Religion* (6 volumes. Oxford, 1909), is the only authoritative detailed account of the religion and scriptures of the sect. Among numerous secondary authorities for the period generally the works by H. G. Keene and Sidney Owen, both entitled *The Fall of the Mogul Empire*, may be mentioned. It is out of the question to give a list at all exhaustive.

[1] The translator and editor, as Grant Duff mentions (*Hist.*, ii. 149 *n.*, ed. 1826), was Mr. James Browne. He was Resident at Delhi from 1782 to 1785, and published a volume entitled *India Tracts* in 1788 (*Dict. Ind. Biogr.*, corrected). The book includes an account of the Sikhs, probably the earliest in English. Nānā Farnavīs gives a short description of the battle in the autobiographical fragment translated by Briggs in *Trans. R. A. S.*, 1829, vol. ii, part i. On the Marāthā side 'confusion prevailed in every direction'.

BOOK VII

THE RULE OF THE EAST INDIA COMPANY TO 1818

CHAPTER 1

The South; French and English; Haidar Ali and Mysore.

Period of transition, 1761–1818. Anglo-Indian history does not attain any semblance of unity until 1774, when, under the provisions of the Regulating Act of the preceding year, Warren Hastings was appointed the first Governor-General of Bengal and invested with a certain amount of ill-defined control over the other British settlements in India. The distinct recognition of the East India Company, representing the British Government, as the paramount authority in India was deferred until 1818.

The period between 1761 and 1818 which will be now discussed was one of transition. The Mogul emperor, whose acts had previously filled the pages of history, had shrunk into an insignificant phantom, almost powerless to influence the course of events. The traditional authority of the court of Delhi during the earlier years of the period merely served as the means of giving a colour of legality to the forcible and essentially lawless proceedings of the various parties who from time to time invoked the sanction of the imperial seal. After 1803 the ghost of imperial control was finally laid and the successor of Akbar became a purely titular sovereign, subsisting as a pensioner of the East India Company.

In the years following the disaster of Pānīpat, which had destroyed the first Marāthā confederacy and annihilated for the moment Hindu hopes of supremacy, the predatory armies of the Marāthās under the leadership of Sindia, Holkar, and other independent chiefs recovered strength with surprising rapidity, and soon acquired a position offering a reasonable prospect of renewed Hindu domination in both the Deccan and Hindostan. Two Muhammadan kingdoms in the south, ruled respectively by the Nizam and the upstart Haidar (Hyder) Ali, and also the Muslim Sūbadār of Bengal, disputed the Marāthā claims to levy systematic blackmail and so to exercise substantially sovereign authority over all the states within their reach.

Meantime the foreign settlers on the coast had begun to realize the practical value of European superiority in armament, the art of war, and general knowledge. They had learned, even before the close of the seventeenth century, that the 'country powers', to use the old phrase, were eager to compete for the help to be derived from small bodies of European gunners and disciplined soldiers.[1] The two principal European nations represented by the factories on the coast were drawn into conflict with each other and as allies of one or other of the warring neighbouring states. Within the brief space of fifteen years between 1746 and 1761 the European rivalry was decided once and for all in favour of the English, French influence both in the south and in Bengal being reduced almost to nothing. Subsequent French efforts did not affect the result of the conflict which had been decided nine days after the carnage of Pānīpat.

Treatment of the subject. The transactions of the transitional period thus summarily reviewed in outline are fully recorded in a multitude of documents and books written in French and English, not to mention Dutch or other tongues. The history, although crowded with incidents of a stirring and often heroic character, has lost much of its interest by reason of the lapse of time and the complete disappearance from the Indian scene of all the parties to the ancient quarrels, save the sole survivor. Few modern readers can brace themselves to the task of mastering in detail the copious narratives of Orme and other writers of the olden time, who seem to belong to a vanished world. People living in the twentieth century are more interested in studying the causes and effects of the events of the eighteenth century than in the particulars of the events themselves, which are apt to seem petty or trivial.[2] But an author whose fate it is to write while the whole world is convulsed in the agonies of the Great War, when an army of 100,000 men is regarded as a small force, must be on his guard against the illusion produced by mere bigness. The battles of the eighteenth century, fought upon a narrow stage where tens perished as compared with the thousands of to-day, were as significant as the gigantic struggles now (1917) in progress and were often more decisive. Clive won the rich prize of Bengal at the cost of twenty-two killed and forty-nine or fifty wounded. Even at Assaye (1803), where the number of wounded was considered to be 'fearfully large' and the enemy had at least a seven-fold superiority in numbers, the killed on the British side were less than four hundred, and the tale of wounded was estimated to be between fifteen and sixteen hundred. Yet the battle of Assaye had consequences far more definite and of more obvious political value

[1] In 1676 François Martin took by assault the fort of Valdūr for a local prince named Shēr Khān. 'Donc, pour la première fois avec F. Martin et dès l'époque de Louis XIV, longtemps avant Dumas, Dupleix ou Bussy, on voyait des Français entrer dans les querelles des souverains indigènes, commander et encadrer leurs troupes, espérant se faire payer de ces services en concessions territoriales ou commerciales' (Kaeppelin, p. 161).

[2] Wilks, when justifying himself for giving unusually detailed accounts of the Anglo-French fighting, gives as his excuse 'the extraordinary character of the war of Coromandel, in which the operations of a handful of troops assumed the political importance, and outstripped the military glory of the mightiest armies' (reprint, i. 207).

than many of the nameless wholesale massacres of these latter years.

The high importance of the period in question in the story of India's development demands attentive study of its essential features, although people no longer have leisure to acquire an intimate knowledge of local military operations or of the intrigues of forgotten potentates. In this book room cannot be found for more than a sketch of the period, and numberless deeds of heroism which it would be a pleasure to rescue from oblivion must be passed by in silence. It is convenient to begin with the transactions in the south.

The French possessions. It is needless to linger over the early feeble efforts of the French to secure a share of the Indian trade by setting up agencies (*loges* or *comptoirs*) at Surat and other ports.[1] The first serious effort to compete with the Dutch and English in common was marked by the establishment in 1664 of the French East India Company (La Compagnie des Indes Orientales), organized by Colbert, the correspondent of Bernier and finance minister of Louis XIV. Ten years later François Martin, accompanied by sixty other Frenchmen driven out of St. Thomé and Masulipatam by the Dutch, landed at the village of Pondicherry, eighty-five miles south of Madras, and by permission of the local authorities built a small commercial agency or factory, which was slightly fortified in subsequent years. The site of the village was purchased in 1683 and a town began to grow. The adventurers, equipped with extremely limited resources, were unable to resist the Dutch, who seized the settlement in 1693 and held it for six years, until they were constrained to restore it under the provisions of the treaty of Ryswick (1697).

During the following half-century Pondicherry was fortunate in its governors, who included F. Martin, Dumas, and Dupleix. Under their care the settlement prospered and its trade attained considerable dimensions. Dupleix assumed charge in 1742.

Chandernagore (Chandarnagar), the second in rank of the French settlements, was occupied first about 1673 and acquired permanently fifteen years later. Dupleix, who was in charge of the town before his transfer to Pondicherry, did much to improve the buildings and develop trade. Its situation on the Hooghly (Hūglī) above Calcutta prevented the settlement from ever possessing political importance. It is now a quiet country town with little external trade.

The other French settlements, Mahé on the Malabar coast, Kārikāl on the Coromandel coast, and Yanāon in the delta of the Godāvarī, acquired at various dates, are and always were insignificant.

The French possessions as a whole, notwithstanding the efforts of Dupleix and his predecessors, continued to be far inferior to the British in strength, wealth, and trade.

[1] For full details see H. Castonnet Des Fosses, *L'Inde Française avant Dupleix*, Paris (Challamel), 1887.

Madras taken by the French. The European war of the Austrian Succession extended to India in 1746. An English squadron which appeared on the Coromandel coast was weakly handled and retired without doing anything effectual. The way was thus opened for the French privateer captain, La Bourdonnais,[1] who attacked and captured Madras in September without the loss of a man. No serious resistance was offered and the town was held to ransom for eleven lakhs of pagodas, equal to about forty-four lakhs of rupees, payable in bills falling due at intervals. The attack had been arranged with the approval and aid of the Governor and Council of Pondicherry. La Bourdonnais argued that the commission which he held as admiral made him independent of the Pondicherry authorities, while Dupleix maintained that as head of the French settlements it was his business to settle the fate of the town. On that point he seems to have been in the right. La Bourdonnais, acting on his assumption of independence, had promised to restore the town in three months, but Dupleix repudiated the promise, and held possession until 1749, when he was compelled to relinquish it in accordance with the terms of the peace of Aix-la-Chapelle. The fleet of La Bourdonnais was disabled and almost destroyed by a storm in October 1746; and subsequently the commander was taken prisoner by the English, who released him and allowed him to return to France. On his arrival he was treated as a traitor and imprisoned in the Bastille. After three years' confinement he was liberated, but only to die. The circumstances of the surrender of Madras and the consequent quarrel between La Bourdonnais and Dupleix have been the subject of prolonged controversy, especially in the pages of French authors. The evidence, as now ascertained, establishes clearly that before the capitulation treaty was signed La Bourdonnais exacted an engagement to pay him personally 100,000 pagodas, of which 88,000 were actually paid over in cash, bullion, and jewels.[2] Dupleix carried his point

LA BOURDONNAIS.

[1] The name is written by several French authors as in the text, but the more accurate form is de la Bourdonnais.

[2] The proof is given by H. D. Love, *Vestiges of Old Madras* (Ind. Records Ser., Murray, 1913), vol. ii, pp. 369, 270, 584 *n*.

and kept the town until he was forced to give it up by the action of his superiors. He failed in an attempt on the other small English settlement on the Coromandel coast called Fort St. David, formerly known as Tegnapatam.

Defeat of the Nawāb. Anwaru-d dīn, the Nawāb of the Carnatic, whose capital was at Arcot, resented the pretensions of the French to dispose of Madras without his permission, and sent a considerable army under the command of his eldest son to capture the place. A tiny force of Frenchmen under Paradis won a complete victory over the Nawāb's host commanded by his son at Mailāpur (Mylapore) or St. Thomé close to Madras. All historians are careful to point out the importance of that fight as proving the helplessness of an old-fashioned Indian army against an extremely small body of disciplined Europeans.

NAWĀB MUHAMMAD ALI.

A naval attack on Pondicherry was repelled with heavy British losses in 1748 by Dupleix, whose reputation was justly enhanced by the success. His wider political ambitions may be dated from about that time. In his earlier days he had been concerned with bold commercial speculations rather than with high politics.

Disputed successions. The peace of Aix-la-Chapelle in 1748 ought to have definitely stopped all fighting between the French and English on Indian soil, but it did not; and the opposition between the local representatives of the two nations soon developed into an unofficial war waged without the sanction of the governments in Europe. At that time the English set the example of interfering in the tortuous politics of the principalities of the Far South by taking a side in a quarrel concerning the succession to the Rāj of Tanjore. The death of the old Nizam Āsaf Jāh, at an advanced age in 1748, gave rise to disputes among his sons and grandsons, which were complicated by somewhat similar contentions in the Carnatic, in all of which the local French and English authorities judged it expedient to intervene.[1]

[1] It is convenient to designate the ruler of the Deccan throughout as the Nizam. Āsaf Jāh held the title of Nizāmu-l Mulk, but is generally referred to by his contemporaries as the Sūbadār or Sūba of the Deccan. Macaulay calls Anwaru-d dīn 'Anaverdy Khan', and similar corruptions are found in other writers. So Muzaffar is disguised as 'Mirzapha', &c.

The succession to the Nizam's throne was not then claimed by the eldest of his six sons, who was employed in high office at the court of Delhi. Nāsir Jang, the second son, and Muzaffar Jang, a grandson, son of a daughter of Āsaf Jāh, fought for the vacant throne. A little later Anwaru-d dīn, whom Āsaf Jāh had appointed to be Nawāb of the Carnatic, was killed, and his heritage was claimed by his illegitimate son, Muhammad Ali, of the one part, and Chanda Sahib, the son-in-law of a former Nawāb, of the other part.

The French for reasons of their own backed Muzaffar Jang for the Nizāmat and Chanda Sahib for the Nawābī, while the English favoured Nāsir Jang and Muhammad Ali respectively. After the death of Anwaru-d dīn in 1749, Muhammad Ali took refuge in the fort of Trichinopoly supported by British troops, while Chanda Sahib with the aid of his French allies obtained possession of the rest of the Carnatic. Towards the close of 1750 Nāsir Jang was killed, and Muzaffar Jang, his rival, was solemnly installed at Pondicherry as Nizam. He paid the French well for their services and professed to recognize Dupleix as the titular sovereign of southern India from the Krishnā to Cape Comorin, or, in other words, of Mysore, Tanjore, and Madura. Soon afterwards, in 1751, Muzaffar Jang was killed and replaced by the old Nizam's third son, Salābat Jang, under French protection.

STRINGER LAWRENCE.

Temporary French success. So far the French seemed to have won the game. They had succeeded in raising two nominees of theirs in succession to the throne of the Deccan, and had secured the Carnatic, except Trichinopoly, for their friend Chanda Sahib. The local English authorities being unwilling to allow Muhammad Ali to be utterly crushed, sought to relieve Trichinopoly, a task for which the means at their disposal were inadequate.

Clive and Arcot. At this point Robert Clive entered upon the scene and turned the tables on the French. Clive, who had come out as a writer in the service of the East India Company, had been permitted to join the small military force of the Madras government under Major Stringer Lawrence, an officer of exceptional

TRICHINOPOLY FORT

capacity, and in 1751 held the rank of captain, being then twenty-six years of age. In order to relieve Trichinopoly he proposed to attack Arcot, Chanda Sahib's capital, and so divert the besiegers from Trichinopoly. The plan was approved.

'Fort St. David and Madras were left, the one with 100, the other with less than 50 men, in order to supply the greatest force that could be collected for this enterprise.'

After all was done the force consisted of only 200 Europeans and 300 sepoys, led by eight officers, four of whom were civil servants. The little band was allowed to occupy Arcot without opposition. The fort was ruinous and at first sight seemed incapable of defence, but Clive and his men worked wonders and threw up improvised fortifications. 'The acquisition of the fort of Arcot soon produced the effect which had been expected from it,' and attracted a large force of the enemy from under the walls of Trichinopoly. That force battered the tiny garrison of Arcot for fifty-three days (September 23 to November 14), and at last made one attempt at storm, which was repulsed with heavy loss to the assailants. That failure disheartened Chanda Sahib's army, which suddenly withdrew from before the town. The heroic garrison had lost 45 Europeans and 30 sepoys killed, besides a large number of wounded.

AUTOGRAPH OF CLIVE.

The gallantry of the defence, in which the sepoys had taken a most honourable part, made a deep impression throughout India. The British and their allies presently gained further successes at Kāveripāk east of Arcot and at other places, with the result that in 1752 the French resigned all claims to Trichinopoly. Chanda Sahib, having surrendered to the Rājā of Tanjore, was perfidiously executed, at the instigation of Muhammad Ali, by order of the Rājā, who desired apparently to get rid of an embarrassing prisoner.[1] Chanda Sahib is given a good character by Orme, who describes him as

'a brave, benevolent, humane and generous man, as princes go in Indostan. His military abilities were much greater than are commonly found in the generals of India, insomuch that if he had had an absolute command over the French troops, it is believed he would not have committed the mistakes which brought on his catastrophe, and the total reduction of his army.'

The military successes and the death of Chanda Sahib made Muhammad Ali undisputed Nawāb of the Carnatic. His worthless and discreditable life lasted until 1795.

Bussy. In 1751 Muzaffar Jang, having been made Nizam, was escorted to Aurangabad, then treated as the capital, by a distinguished French officer, usually known as Bussy.[2] On the death of

[1] See Wilks, reprint, i. 177.

[2] His full designation was Charles Joseph Patissier, Marquis de Bussy-Castelnau. In 1751 he was thirty-five years of age.

Muzaffar Jang and the accession of Salābat Jang in the same year, Bussy became the adviser and guide of the new Nizam, whose government he directed for seven years with eminent skill, until he was recalled by Lally. In 1753 Bussy obtained the assignment of the revenue of the 'Northern Circars' for the payment of his troops, but the country had been so devastated by long continued fighting that the revenue actually realizable was not large.[1] His temporary successful administration of the Deccan produced no lasting results and did not directly affect the course of the events in the Carnatic briefly summarized in the preceding pages, except that Bussy supplied Dupleix with funds to a certain extent. Incidentally, he amassed an immense fortune for himself, and 'in the course of a year passed from poverty to opulence'.

DUPLEIX.

Recall of Dupleix. In 1753 Dupleix became conscious of the failure of his plans, which had aimed at the complete expulsion of the English from India, including Bengal, and the establishment of France as the paramount power. He therefore opened negotiations with the Madras authorities, whom he attempted to deceive by producing a forged imperial grant purporting to appoint him Nawāb of the Carnatic. The negotiations came to nothing.

Meantime the Governments of both France and England were much disturbed by the advices received from India. The countries being officially at peace, the home authorities regarded it as intolerable that their servants should dare to wage unofficial wars in the Far East and enter into alliances with Indian princes on their own account without the slightest authorization. The whole scheme of ambitious policy pursued by Dupleix was directly opposed

[1] Wilks (reprint, i. 209) writes that Bussy obtained the 'absolute cession of the whole of those provinces, now denominated the northern Circars'. Mr. Roberts (*Historical Geography, India*, p. 111) denies that there was any unconditional grant of territory, asserting that merely an assignment of revenue was granted for the support of Bussy's troops 'as long as they were in the service of the Sūbadār'. While Bussy retained power the practical result was the same.

The Northern Sarkārs were equivalent to the modern Districts, Guntūr, Godāvarī, Kistna (Krishnā), Ganjām, and Vizagapatam, of the Madras Presidency.

to the standing orders of the French East India Company and of the king's Government. The official documents published by Cultru permit of no doubt on the subject. In 1752, for example, the Directors wrote that

'it is not compatible either with the Company's interest or with prudent onduct on your part to engage in wars in the interior of India . . . a solid and durable peace is the sole end at which you should aim . . . the object of the Company is not to become a land-power', and so on.

Accordingly the Governments of both countries agreed to stop the irregular proceedings in India. The French authorities deputed M. Godeheu, one of the Directors, to proceed to India with stringent orders requiring him to arrange terms of peace. Dupleix was recalled and Godeheu was authorized to arrest him if he should be disposed to resist. Dupleix, however, submitted to the royal orders without the slightest attempt at opposition and returned to France, where he lived until 1763. Godeheu has been abused most unfairly for his action. He simply did his unpleasant duty in carrying out the king's commands expressed in the most positive terms. He might, perhaps, have shown less harshness in his manner, but it is clear that he expected resistance and thought it necessary to be peremptory. Dupleix was not condemned to poverty by his superiors. On the contrary, he was given liberal passage money, and was allowed to retain a *jāgīr* assignment of revenue bringing in a large income, although the acceptance of the *jāgīr* had been a breach of French law. It was his misfortune that the almost immediate renewal of war between the two countries in 1756 stopped his Indian income. He had been granted the title of Marquis in 1752.

The Seven Years' War; Lally. The outbreak of the Seven Years' War in 1756 (May 17) again involved the French and English settlements in India in authorized hostilities. In those days communication between Europe and India was so slow that Count de Lally, the general selected by the French Government to drive the English into the sea, did not arrive at Pondicherry until April 1758.[1] By that time the relative positions of the two nations in India had changed radically, because the English were in firm possession of Bengal, and whatever might happen to Madras their footing in India was secure. At the time that fact, now obvious, was not so well understood, and Lally did not feel conscious of having been sent on a hopeless errand. He even cherished hopes of conquering Bengal. One of the first steps that he took was to recall Bussy and so to destroy French influence at the Nizam's court.

[1] His full personal style was Thomas Arthur, Comte de Lally, Baron de Tollendal. Two documents invested him with full powers, (1) as Lieutenant-General, commander-in-chief; and (2) as Commissary of the King, empowered to exercise complete control over all persons military and civil in the French settlements in India, as well as in Madagascar, the Ile de France or Mauritius, and Bourbon. The first bore date November 19, and the second December 31, 1756.

Failure of Lally. Lally, the son of an Irish exile and a French lady, was born in 1700, and from a very early age had taken an active part in the continental wars of the period, attaining high military distinction and marked favour at court. In 1756, when selected to represent his sovereign in the East, he was regarded as 'one of the wealthiest as well as one of the bravest men in the French army'. The Government which sent him out evidently believed him to be the best officer available for the purpose, and willingly furnished him with such men, ships, and money as could be spared. At that time France was deeply concerned for the defence of Canada, and was obliged to withdraw for that purpose certain forces originally intended for India. From the start Lally was pursued by ill luck. The admiral delayed on the voyage most unreasonably and never showed either a good fighting spirit or readiness to co-operate with the commander-in-chief of the land forces. The local authorities at Pondicherry, who knew that the royal commissary possessed full powers and carried strict orders enjoining him to suppress the numerous abuses in the administration, were deliberately negligent and almost openly hostile. They had made no preparations whatever for war, and had failed even to collect information, although they had been given full notice by ships which arrived long in advance of Lally.[1] He displayed the most feverish energy, and, in spite of want of supplies and every imaginable difficulty, quickly captured Fort St. David and other small places. His countrymen left his army to starve, so that the troops became mutinous. The attack which Lally launched against Madras in 1758 was hampered by the apathy of the Pondicherry Government, resisted by the able defence of Mr. Pigot and Stringer Lawrence, and finally stopped by the appearance of a British fleet. Lally, reduced to a condition of starvation and extreme distress, was constrained to give battle to a superior force commanded by Eyre Coote at Wandiwash in 1760, and was utterly defeated. He retired with difficulty to Pondicherry, which he defended gallantly from May 1760 to January 16, 1761, when he was forced by hunger to capitulate at discretion. It is said that towards the end food was so scarce that a dog sold for twenty-four rupees. Lally was sent to England as a prisoner of war. When he returned to France, at the close of hostilities in 1763, his enemies succeeded in having him arrested and confined in the Bastille. After two and a half years he was 'convicted of having betrayed the interests of the king, his dominions, and the Company of the Indies; of abuses of authority, &c.', and condemned to death. The sentence was executed with accompaniments of cruel insult a few days later.

Execution of Lally. Nobody now doubts that his condemnation was unjust and brought about by the malignity of his numerous

[1] The above accords with the narrative of Malleson and most authors. Wilks, who was very hostile to Lally, says, on the contrary, that 'no useful energy was omitted in seconding the impracticable orders of M. Lally' (reprint, i. 243). Lally certainly succeeded in 'putting everybody's back up' and had himself to thank for much grudging service.

enemies. It is also true that Lally was ill fitted for service in India. He neither knew nor cared anything about the customs of the country and made no effort to restrain his violent temper. An English writer notes that

'Monsieur Lally is arrived amongst us. Notwithstanding his fallen condition, he is now as proud and haughty as ever. A great share of wit, sense, and martial abilities, obscured by a savage ferocity, and an undistinguished contempt for every person that moves in a sphere below that of a General, characterizes this odd compound of a man. . . . He was so generally hated (if I may be allowed the expression) that the very dogs howled at him. It is a convincing proof of his abilities, the managing so long and vigorous a defence in a place where he was held in universal detestation.'

He was equally hated, and with good reason, by the natives of the country, whom he had outraged in various ways. After the revolution had begun the parliament of Paris reversed his condemnation and restored his estates to his son, in 1778.

Destruction of Pondicherry. The English victors felt bound to take stern measures for their own security. When Lally captured Fort St. David he had allowed the inhabitants only three days to evacuate the town, which he then destroyed. It was known that his orders directed him to 'demolish all the maritime places that he might take from the English, and to transport all the Europeans he should find in them to the Island of Bourbon'. Mr. Saunders, the able President of Madras, who took over Pondicherry, felt the necessity of making his own settlement safe. The fortifications and most of the buildings in the captured town were accordingly demolished, the inhabitants being allowed nearly three months in which to move. 'In a few months more', to quote Orme's words, 'not a roof was left standing in this once fair and flourishing city.'

Result of the operations. The result of the operations thus briefly sketched may be described in the words of Thornton:

'From the time when Pondicherry fell, the French power in the Carnatic was virtually at an end. Gingee [Jinjī] still remained in their possession, as did also Thiagur, which had been restored by the Mysoreans on their departure: but the former yielded to a force under Captain Stephen Smith; and the latter, after sustaining sixty-five days of blockade and bombardment, capitulated to Major Preston. Mahé, and its dependencies on the coast of Malabar, also surrendered; and early in the year 1761 the French had neither any regular force in any part of India,[1] nor any local possessions, except their factories of Calicut and Surat, which were merely trading establishments.'

Chandernagore had been captured by Clive and Watson in 1757.

The districts near the Godāvarī commonly known as the Northern Sarkārs ('Circars'), of which the revenues had been assigned by the Nizam to Bussy, were occupied (Guntūr excepted) in 1758–9 by a force dispatched from Bengal by Clive and landed at Vizaga-

[1] Parties of French gunners and other adventurers continued for many years to help Haidar Ali and other enemies of the British.

patam in October 1758.[1] Clive had responded to an appeal made by the Hindu Rāja of Rājamahendri, and, regardless of risk, had denuded Bengal of troops in order to make the expedition a success. The commander, Colonel Forde, a capable officer, completely defeated the army under French command at Kundūr (Condore), forty miles from Rājamahendri, stormed Masulipatam, and took possession of the districts. Subsequently he returned to Bengal and defeated the Dutch of Chinsura.

General defeat of France. Orme, when commenting on the results gained in India by the British forces, observes :

> 'For two years before, the fortune of France had been declining in every other part of the world ; they had lost their settlements on the coast of Africa, half their West India islands, the whole region of Canada; their naval force was utterly ruined, and their armies were struggling under defeats in Germany.' [2]

Capture of Manilla. The comprehensive policy of Pitt had aimed yet another blow at the enemy by means of an expeditionary force sent from Madras in 1762 to seize Manilla in the Philippine Islands, then belonging to Spain, an ally of France. The combined naval and military operations on the spot occupied only twelve days. The town was stormed with small loss to the assailants, and honourable terms were accorded to the garrison and inhabitants. The brilliant feat of arms had no permanent effect, and is now almost forgotten, because the colony was restored to Spain in the following year, 1763, when the general peace of Paris was signed. A Manilla trophy at Madras is the only visible memorial of the temporary British occupation of the Philippines, which have been annexed by the United States of America as the result of operations extending from 1898 to 1901.

Causes of French failure. The collapse of the French power which had seemed to occupy such a strong position from 1746 to 1751 demands explanation more explicit than that to be deduced from perusal of a summary narrative of the Anglo-French wars. Many causes contributed to the result.

The French East India Company was far inferior to its English rival in constitution, enterprise, and wealth. It was merely a minor department of the king's government and was usually administered badly in France. The shareholders, who were assured

[1] The Districts, excepting Guntūr, were ceded formally in 1765 ; Guntūr being reserved as the *jāgīr* of Basālat Jang, a son of the old Nizām. It came definitely into British possession in 1788, but the cession was not confirmed finally until 1823.

[2] In 1759 Wolfe captured Quebec in Canada ; the French were defeated at Minden in Germany, and several times at sea. In 1760 Canada submitted. Senegal in West Africa and several West Indian islands, which had been occupied during the war, were ceded to England at the peace in 1763. Although Pitt had resigned in October 1761, the Manilla expedition had been planned by him. The student should remember that in those days Prussia was the ally of England and was supported against her enemies by British efforts.

of a fixed dividend, took no active part in the management of the Company's affairs. The spirit of bold individual and corporate effort, so often exhibited in the doings of the English adventurers, was rarely imitated by the French, and few of their local officials were men of mark. Funds were always deficient. The home Government, entangled as it was in unceasing wars in Europe and America, could not furnish the money required for the successful working of ambitious schemes in India. Except Dupleix, and to some extent Bussy, the Company's representatives at the settlements rarely desired to meddle much with the politics of the adjoining states. They were content to hold only so much territory as sufficed to provide opportunities for unmolested trading on a modest scale. They were not prepared to support bold projects for acquiring sovereign power over extensive territories. Dupleix himself was a trader for the greater part of his career, somewhat daring in commercial speculations, and not always successful, but no politician. His plans of extended dominion are not traceable before 1748, when the possession of Madras and his justifiable elation at the successful defence of Pondicherry inclined him to entertain large ambitions. The compulsory restoration of Madras in 1749 was a severe blow to him. The loss of Arcot in 1751 and of Trichinopoly in 1752 ruined his prospects. His failure, however, did not depend merely on such local mishaps. His resources never were adequate for his purposes, and the British conquest of rich Bengal in 1757 rendered his dream of empire absolutely incapable of realization, no matter what happened in the course of fights near the extremity of the peninsula. The mastery of the sea, which usually, although not invariably, remained in British hands, gave the opponents of the French an advantage which no minor successes on land could balance. In April 1758, when Lally arrived, he was too late. The position of the French was then hopeless, and would have been equally past remedy if Dupleix had not been recalled in 1754. His continuance in office would not have made any difference. He was a ruined man before Godeheu's arrival. Bussy's influential position at the court of the Nizam afforded little support, beyond some financial assistance, to the grand projects of the governor of Pondicherry. Neither Bussy nor Dupleix singly, nor both combined, had a chance of success against the government which controlled the sea routes and the resources of the Gangetic valley. It is futile to lay stress upon the personal frailties of Dupleix, Lally, or lesser men in order to explain the French failure. Neither Alexander the Great nor Napoleon could have won the empire of India by starting from Pondicherry as a base and contending with the power which held Bengal and command of the sea. No southern potentate had ever either attained or seriously sought to attain the sovereignty of India. Even a local peninsular empire like that of Vijayanagar in the fifteenth and sixteenth centuries was unattainable in the conditions of the eighteenth century.

Character and merits of Dupleix. The character and achievements of Dupleix hardly merit the admiration which they have generally received. The hero worshipped by Malleson and Hamont loses much of his lustre under close inspection. Thornton's description of him as 'this man, in whose character, ambition, vanity, and duplicity reigned in a degree which makes it impossible to determine which predominated', although not exactly untrue, does not do Dupleix full justice. The ambition, vanity, and duplicity were all there, but ambition in a man who aspires to be a statesman cannot properly be counted as a vice. The vanity of Dupleix is undoubted and appears prominently in the intimate disclosures of Ānanda Ranga Pillai, now in course of publication. Vanity, however, is a weakness common to many great men. The Marquess Wellesley, who resembled Dupleix in ambition and contempt for his employers, was notoriously vain. The large plans of the French governor and the considerable success which he attained may be deemed sufficient cover for some personal frailties. The accusation of duplicity cannot be denied, although it is going too far to brand the repudiation of the treaty of La Bourdonnais as an act of 'atrocious perfidy'. Dupleix had a good case against the admiral, who rated his official powers too high. Putting that affair aside, there is no doubt that Dupleix was prone to tortuous intrigue and too ready to use the disreputable trickery practised by the decadent Indian princes of his time. He was content to be a Nawāb or Sūbadār, without much regard for veracity. His morality in money matters was of a low standard, and his wife, a Portuguese half-caste, was a shameless bribe-taker. Dupleix was not gifted with military talents, and was reputed to be somewhat lacking in personal courage. He was a capable administrator, but failed as a statesman mainly because he could not adjust the measure of his grand schemes to that of his limited resources. He deserves credit for the dignified fortitude with which he received his abrupt dismissal. The harshness displayed by Godeheu seems to have been due, not to malignity, but to a genuine fear that Dupleix might revolt.

Rise of Haidar Ali. While in the Peninsula the conflict between the French and English was in progress and in Bengal events of equal or greater importance were happening, which will be narrated presently, a new and formidable power under a Muhammadan prince was growing up in the south. The Mysore country, roughly equivalent to the mediaeval Hoysala kingdom, had been included in the empire of Vijayanagar. When that empire was broken up in 1565 the territory of Mysore gradually passed under the rule of the Hindu Wodeyar dynasty. That dynasty in the middle of the eighteenth century had lost its energy, and its weakness offered an opportunity to a bold adventurer.

Such an adventurer was Haidar (Hyder) Ali, born in 1722, the son of an officer of the Mysore Government. He secured the favour of Nanjarāj, the powerful minister, by organizing a small body of troops better equipped than the rest of the Rājā's army. His appointment in 1755, when he was thirty-three years of age, as

Faujdār or commandant of Dindigul may be regarded as the beginning of his successful career. At a later date he received the district of Bangalore as his *jāgīr* and became commander-in-chief of the Mysore army. In 1761, the year of Pānīpat and the fall of Pondicherry, he controlled directly more than half of the dominions of his nominal sovereign and actually was ruler of the whole kingdom. His fortunes then underwent a temporary eclipse, but two years later, in 1763, he emerged victorious.

Fate of Khandē Rāo. A cunning Brahman named Khandē Rāo who owed his advancement to Haidar Ali had presumed to join his patron's enemies. When the combination was defeated,

> 'Kundē Row was given up and confined; and his official servants as well as himself were of course plundered to the utmost extent of their means. Before it had been determined that Kundē Row should be surrendered, a joint message was sent to Hyder from the Raja and the ladies of the palace praying for mercy towards that unfortunate man as a preliminary to the adjustment of public affairs. Hyder replied that Kundē Row was his old servant, and that he would not only spare his life, but cherish him like a parroquet; a term of endearment common in conversing with women, from that bird being a favourite pet in the harems of the wealthy. When he was afterwards gently admonished of his severity to Kundē Row, he ironically replied that he had exactly kept his word; and that they were at liberty to inspect his *iron cage* and the rice and milk allotted for his food; for such was the fate to which he had doomed Kundē Row for the remainder of his miserable life.'

The unhappy captive survived for a year. In 1786, when Robson was writing, the cage containing the dead man's bones was still to be seen in the public bazaar of Bangalore.

Conquest and sack of Bednūr. In the same year, 1763, which saw the defeat of Khandē Rāo, Haidar Ali conquered Bednūr (Bednore), now represented by a petty country town or large village called Nagar in the western part of the Mysore State, but then a place of such importance that Wilks felt justified in describing it as 'the most opulent commercial town of the east; eight miles in circumference, and full of rich dwellings'. The same author affirms that the booty 'may, without risk of exaggeration, be estimated at twelve millions sterling'.

The huge figure suggests scepticism, but Wilks was in a good position to judge and no materials exist for forming a closer estimate.[1] Haidar Ali always spoke of the Bednūr windfall as 'the foundation of all his subsequent greatness'.

Career of Haidar Ali, 1766–9. The death of the Rājā of Mysore in April 1766 still further increased the power of the upstart, who ruthlessly plundered the palace, although he went through the form of recognizing a new Rājā.

The following three years were occupied by obscure complicated

[1] Mark Wilks, F.R.S., colonel and major-general, was born about 1760 and died in 1831. He quitted India in 1808, having been Resident in Mysore from 1803. Previously he had held various offices at Madras. The first volume of his great book was published in 1810.

intrigues and fights in which Muhammad Ali, the scoundrelly Nawāb of the Carnatic; the corrupt and weak government of Madras, his tools and abettors; the vacillating Nizam; the greedy Marāthās; and ambitious Haidar Ali were concerned in varying combinations. In 1767 the Nizam and Haidar Ali, who had joined forces for the moment, were severely defeated at Trinomalai by Colonel Joseph Smith. But the inefficient rogues at the Presidency so mismanaged the war that early in 1769 Haidar Ali appeared under the walls of Madras, and dictated a treaty providing for the mutual restitution of conquests, and binding each party to help the other if attacked. Thus ended the First Mysore War.

Double government. The 'double government' of the Madras Council and the Nawāb at that time was quite as bad as or worse than the similar arrangements in force in Bengal between 1757 and 1772. Corruption was rampant, and the country was horribly oppressed. Wilks, who had an intimate knowledge of all the persons concerned, observes that

> 'the strange combination of vicious arrangements, corrupt influence, and political incapacity which directed the general measures of the Government of Madras have been too constantly traced to demand recapitulation'.

CHRONOLOGY

The French Settlements

Establishment of the French East India Company (La Compagnie des Indes orientales)	1664
Foundation of Pondicherry	1674
Dutch occupation of Pondicherry	1693–9
Dupleix became Governor of Pondicherry	1742
Recall of Dupleix	1754

The First Anglo-French War

(War of the Austrian Succession)

Madras captured by the French	1746
British attack on Pondicherry repulsed; treaty of Aix-la-Chapelle; death of Āsaf Jāh, Nizam	1748
Restoration of Madras to the English; death of Anwaru-d din, Nawāb of the Carnatic	1749

The Second Anglo-French War

(unofficial)

Siege of Trichinopoly by Chanda Sahib and the French; defence of Arcot by Clive	1751
Trichinopoly given up by the French; death of Chanda Sahib	1752
Recall of Dupleix and end of the war	1754

The Third Anglo-French War
(The Seven Years' War)

War began 1756
Chandernagore taken by Clive and Watson; the Northern Sarkārs occupied by Bussy 1757
Lally arrived in India; captured Fort St. David, &c.; failed to take Madras; Col. Forde occupied the Northern Sarkārs . . 1758
Battle of Wandiwash 1760
Fall of Pondicherry 1761
Capture of Manilla by the British 1762
Peace of Paris; end of the Seven Years' War 1763
Execution of Lally 1766

Haidar Ali and the First Mysore War

Haidar Ali born 1722
Haidar Ali appointed Faujdār of Dindigul 1755
Haidar Ali became master of Mysore 1761
Defeat of Khandē Rāo by Haidar Ali; capture and sack of Bednūr 1763
Defeat of Haidar Ali and the Nizam by Col. Joseph Smith at Trinomalai 1767
Treaty of Madras; end of the war 1769

AUTHORITIES

It is unnecessary to describe the well-known general histories by MILL, THORNTON, MARSHMAN, &c. The small book by P. E. ROBERTS, *History of India to the End of the E. I. Co.* (in Historical Geography of the British Dependencies, Clarendon Press, 1916), is a generally sound and judicious summary of the history of the period treated in this chapter and of the whole Anglo-Indian history to 1858.

The story of the French Settlements is best told in P. KAEPPELIN, *La Compagnie des Indes Orientales* (Paris, Challamel, 1908); and H. WEBER, *La Compagnie Française des Indes* (Paris, Rousseau, 1904).

The leading authority on Dupleix is P. CULTRU, *Dupleix* (Paris, Hachette, 1901). G. B. MALLESON'S work, *History of the French in India* (1st ed., 1867; 2nd ed., Edinburgh, Grant, 1893), has much merit, but is more French than the French and spoiled by adulation of Dupleix. It was written with very imperfect knowledge of the documents in Paris. The same author's views are expressed on a smaller scale in *Dupleix* (Rulers of India, 1890), and reaffirmed by T. HAMONT, *Dupleix*, Paris, 1881.

Stringer Lawrence by Col. J. BIDDULPH (London, Murray, 1901) is a good little book, with an excellent portrait of Dupleix.

Copious details of the Anglo-French wars in the peninsula will be found in R. ORME, *A History of the Military Transactions*, &c. (London, 1763, 1778);[1] and in M. WILKS, *Sketches of the South of India*, &c. (London, 1810, 1817). Both those works rank as first-class original authorities. Wilks gives an excellent account of Haidar Ali.

The scarce *Life of Hyder Ally* by Captain FRANCIS ROBSON (London, Hooper, 1776); and the anonymous compilation, *Memoirs of Count Lally* (London, Kiernan, 1766), have been consulted, besides other works. *Haidar Ali and Tīpū Sultan* by LEWIN B. BOWRING (Rulers of India, 1893) is a valuable book, illuminated by accurate local knowledge.

[1] Orme was corrupt and extortionate; see *Vestiges of Old Madras*, vol. ii, especially p. 519.

CHAPTER 2

Bengal affairs; Sirāju-d daula; battles of Plassey and Buxar; the 'double government'; the famine of 1770.

Low standard of public life. In the eighteenth century, during the anarchical period which intervened between the death of Aurangzēb and the establishment of the British supremacy, the character of the princes and other public men of India had sunk to an extremely low level. Nearly all the notable men of that age lived vicious lives, stained by gross sensuality, ruthless cruelty, and insatiable greed.

Nawāb Shuj'āu-d dīn. One of the few good men of that evil time was Shuj'āu-d dīn, the Sūbadār or governor of the eastern provinces from 1725 to 1739, who is recorded to have been 'universally regretted as a man of strict veracity, general philanthropy, and unbounded liberality'. His administration of the provinces was marked by impartial justice, and he refrained from advancing pretensions to independence, being content to remit regularly the tribute due to his sovereign at Delhi.

Usurpation of Allahvardī Khān. Sarfarāz Khān, the son and successor of that admirable man, was scrupulous in performing all the ceremonies of his religion, but indifferent and incapable as a ruler. At the time of his accession the governor of Bihār was a brave, able, and unscrupulous officer, named Mīrzā Muhammad Ali, but better known by his title of Allahvardī (or Alīvardī) Khān, who had been raised from obscurity by Shuj'āu-d dīn, and had been appointed by him prime minister.

Allahvardī Khān, taking advantage of the troubles resulting from Nādir Shāh's invasion, and basely ignoring the debt of gratitude due to the son of his patron, revolted. Sarfarāz Khān having been killed in the ensuing battle, Allahvardī Khān took his seat upon the vacant provincial throne. He had previously bought from the corrupt court of Delhi letters patent appointing him governor of the eastern provinces. Having secured condonation of his rebellion and usurpation by further lavish presents to Muhammad Shāh and his courtiers, he never sent a rupee of tribute again, and ruled until the end of his life as an independent sovereign.

Allahvardī Khān as Nawāb. For eleven years Allahvardī Khān was mainly occupied in efforts to repel the plundering inroads of the Marāthās, who overran all Bengal to the west of the Ganges at one time or another. In 1742, Calcutta being threatened, the English inhabitants caused to be dug the imperfect fortification known as the Marāthā Ditch, which long formed the boundary of the settlement. Two years later the Nawāb secured a temporary respite by the treacherous massacre of Bhāskar Rāo Pundit, with nineteen of his retinue. More definite relief was attained in 1751 at the cost of the cession of Orissa (Cuttack) and the promise to pay twelve lakhs of rupees annually as the *chauth* of Bengal. Orissa remained under the heel of the banditti until 1803.[1] The Marāthās never attempted to establish any civil administration in the province, being content to allow the local chiefs to rule as they best could, subject to the necessity of satisfying so far as possible the boundless rapacity of the robber state.

Allahvardī Khān in his latter days, being then between seventy and eighty years of age, showed the weakness of an old man by bestowing doting affection on his grandson, Mīrzā Mahmūd (or Muhammad), infamous under his title of Sirāju-d daula. The young man, who was the son of the Nawāb's youngest daughter, a dissolute woman, was almost wholly evil.[2] In 1750, when he had dared to revolt against his grandfather, the dotard not only showed no resentment, but confirmed the youth's right of succession and allowed him to control the government. Allahvardī Khān to some extent atoned for his many political crimes by a strictly moral private life, and by carefully regulated administration much better than that of most of the contemporary princes. But he was in his eightieth lunar year when he died in April 1756, and for some time previously had become inefficient.

He had declined to act on advice to expel the English merchants from his dominions and is reported to have used this remarkable language :

> 'What have the English done against me that I should use them ill ? It is now difficult to extinguish fire on land, but should the sea be in flames, who can put them out ?'

Nawāb Sirāju-d daula. Sirāju-d daula, then nearly twenty-four years of age, succeeded to his grandfather's throne without much serious opposition, although his vices were notorious.[3] Disregarding the old man's sage counsels concerning the strangers who had come across the sea, the young Nawāb longed to seize the riches of the foreign merchants, which were magnified by report far beyond the reality. Grievances sufficient to give a plausible excuse for war were not wanting. The tiny English factory at Kāsimbāzār (Cossimbazar) near Murshīdābād, the capital of Bengal, was easily taken, and Sirāju-d daula moved on Calcutta with an army of about 50,000 men. The settlement was ill prepared for

[1] The Cuttack (Katak) province was distinct from the part of Orissa in British hands, comprising the Midnapur District and part of Hooghly (Hūglī).

[2] See the tract by S. C. Barman and B. N. Banerji entitled *Begams of Bengal*, Calcutta, Mitter & Co., 1915.

[3] The statement that Sirāju-d daula was only nineteen at the time of his death is found in Orme and most books, but Busteed (ed. 4, p. 7) makes him to be 'about 25 years old' at the time of his accession. That must be nearly correct, as he had rebelled six years earlier, and he could not have done so at the age of twelve or thirteen. Ives (p. 154) says : 'He had not quite compleated his 25th year, and but one of his reign, when he thus fell.' Law of Lauriston writes : 'Telle fut la fin de Souradjotdola, à la fleur de son âge, ayant à peine 25 ans' (*Mémoire*, ed. Martineau ; Paris, Larose, 1913).

resistance. The fortifications had been neglected and were commanded by private houses which had been allowed to grow up close to the walls. 'The garrison did not amount to two hundred; not more than a third of their number were Europeans, and few, if any, had ever been in action.' The militia was useless and deserted soon after the siege began. A determined enemy could have taken the place in an hour. The Nawāb appeared before the town on June 16, equivalent to the 17th of Ramazān, the month of the Muhammadan fast. On the 19th of that month the outposts were captured. The final capitulation took place in the afternoon of June 20, Ramazān 21. Mr. Drake, the governor, a peaceful merchant, who at the beginning of the operations, according to Stewart, 'had not betrayed any signs of personal fear, but exposed his person on the ramparts', did not maintain his courage to the end. He was afraid of being put to death if captured, yielded to disgraceful panic, and slipped away down the river in a ship, accompanied by the Commandant and all those who could get on board the vessels. Mr. Holwell, a member of the Council, was thus left behind with about 190 Europeans. He too, it was alleged, would have embarked if he could, but was unable to do so. He then made a gallant and determined defence for a short time, until he was forced to capitulate on the afternoon of June 20.

The 'Black Hole' tragedy. It is unnecessary to repeat in detail the oft-told story of the horrors of the Black Hole. But it is indispensable to observe that recent attempts to discredit the story as an invention are not well founded. The incident certainly occurred, although some uncertainty may exist concerning one or other detail. The Nawāb was not personally and directly responsible for the atrocity. He left the disposal of the prisoners to a subordinate who forced them all into a stifling guard-room, barely twenty feet square, and not large enough to hold a quarter of the crowd. Although the Nawāb did not personally order the barbarous treatment of his prisoners, he did not either reprove his officers for their cruelty or express any regret at the tragic result. It is generally stated that 146 were put in for the night, of whom only 23, including one lady, came out alive in the morning; but the exact number of the sufferers is not certain, and there is good reason for believing that the prisoners confined included several women of whom only one survived.

The fugitives at Faltā. The fugitives from Calcutta landed at Faltā, now in the Diamond Harbour subdivision, the site of an old Dutch factory on the Hooghly, a considerable distance below the capital, and there passed a miserable time until they were relieved in the following January. Many perished from a malignant fever. Mr. Drake dispatched a small vessel with news of the disaster to Madras, where the tidings caused much excitement and debate. It so happened that Admiral Watson with a small British squadron was then at Madras, and had Clive, now a colonel, with him. The squadron had sailed from England early in 1754.

The Gheria expedition. Clive, who had gone home in 1753 after his successes in the unofficial war in the south, returned in 1755 and landed at Bombay with three companies of the king's artillery intending to operate with the aid of the Marāthās against the French. The peace or truce negotiated by Godeheu and Saunders having rendered hostilities against the French impossible, the civil, naval, and military authorities agreed that the opportunity should be seized of rooting out the nest of troublesome pirates at Gheria or Vijayadurg, an excellent harbour on the coast,

GHERIA FORT.

170 miles south of Bombay. The expedition was entirely successful, and the important stronghold was captured at the expense of no more than twenty killed and wounded on the British side. About 250 'pieces of cannon' were taken with much other valuable booty.[1]

Bānkōt, with nine dependent villages, was ceded by the Marāthās, and thus

> 'became the first British possession on the mainland of western India. It was renamed Fort Victoria, and was highly valued as supplying Bombay

[1] Surgeon Ives gives a vivid account of the Gheria operations illustrated by good plates.

with provisions, and also as affording the inhabitants a change of air and scene.'

The fortress of Gheria was made over to the Marāthās.

Recapture of Calcutta. Watson and Clive sailed from Gheria to Madras, where they heard the bad news from Bengal. The local authorities, as early as July 20 (Orme), had sent a detachment of 230 or 240 men under Major Kilpatrick to Bengal, hoping that it would be in time to relieve Calcutta, the fall of which was not known until August 5. The climate and conditions at Faltā were so deadly that nearly all the men perished. According to Ives, only about thirty were alive and ten fit for duty when the larger relief force arrived in December. After two months' debate Clive was selected to command the land forces dispatched with Watson's ships. The squadron sailed from Madras on October 16. The voyage was difficult and dangerous owing to the season and the strength of the currents, so that the expedition did not reach Faltā until December 14. A series of successful operations brought the ships under the walls of Fort William on January 2, 1757. The enemy evacuated the fort without serious resistance, and Admiral Watson replaced the runaway Drake in his office as governor. The town of Hooghly (Hūglī) was then stormed. The admiral dispatched an officer to England with the news in a tiny sloop of only 60 tons. At the present time a steamer of 5,000 tons is considered to be rather small to carry the Calcutta mail.

Capture of Chandernagore. The commanders now had to consider the problem of meeting the Nawāb, who was marching from Murshīdābād with a large army. Complicated negotiations ensued, fully narrated and illustrated by documents in the vivid pages of Surgeon Ives. War with France having begun again, the fleet under Watson and the troops under Clive took the French settlement of Chandernagore in March, after a spirited resistance which caused many naval casualties. Clive described the place as being 'a large, rich, and thriving colony', of which the loss was 'an inexpressible blow to the French Company'. The French inhabitants mostly took refuge in the Dutch settlement of Chinsūra adjoining Hooghly. Later, in 1759, a stern decree commanded the utter demolition of the buildings, public and private. We have seen that the same policy was pursued at Pondicherry when it was taken in 1761. Both towns had to be rebuilt after the peace of 1763.

Plot with Mīr J'afar. The danger from the French having thus been removed, the admiral renewed his correspondence with the Nawāb, who, in February, had signed a treaty, which each party accused the other of violating.

In June, Clive, supported by Mr. Watts, resolved to depose Sirāju-d daula and replace him by Mīr J'afar, who had married Allahvardī Khān's sister, and was now engaged in a secret plot against his young master. Mīr J'afar accordingly executed a treaty, which was signed on the British side by Admiral Watson, Colonel Clive, and Counsellors Drake and Watts.

The forged treaty. This was the occasion on which Clive played the notorious trick on Amīnchand (Omichund), the rich Sikh banker, who was concerned in the plot, but had threatened to divulge it to the Nawāb, unless his silence was bought by a payment of thirty lakhs, or three millions of rupees, subsequently reduced to two millions. Clive deceived the banker by showing him a forged duplicate of the document, containing the promise of payment, which was omitted from the genuine original treaty. Admiral Watson honourably refused to sign his name to the forgery. His signature was then appended by Mr. Lushington under Clive's direction. It is impossible to justify Clive's action in this matter, and the special pleading of the authors who have attempted to defend the fraud is sophistical. Amīnchand at the time naturally was overwhelmed with disappointment, but the story that he lost his reason is untrue. Subsequently he resumed business with the English, and in his will bequeathed a considerable sum to the Foundling Hospital in London.[1] He also left money to the Sikh shrine of Guru Gobind.

The secret agreement with Mīr J'afar rendered a fight with the Nawāb inevitable. Accordingly, on June 13 Clive wrote a long letter reproaching him for various delinquencies, and ending with the intimation that as the rains were approaching and an answer could not be received in time, the writer found it necessary to 'wait upon' his correspondent immediately.

Battle of Plassey. The same day Clive marched northwards. His small force consisted of about 3,000 men in all, with eight six-pounder guns, and one howitzer, or two, according to Orme. The fort at Katwa (Cutwa) was yielded by the enemy without serious resistance, and a welcome addition to the supplies of the British force was obtained. The Nawāb's army, said to comprise 50,000 foot, 18,000 horse, and about fifty guns of heavy calibre. entrenched on the bank of the Bhāgīrathī river near the village of Plassey.[2] On June 23, Clive, after some hesitation whether he should fight at once or wait for the close of the rains, encamped in a mango grove which had partly disappeared in 1780 when Rennell drew his plan, and has now been wholly carried away by the river. The traitor Mīr J'afar was on the extreme left of the Nawāb's line. The enemy's intention was to envelop the small force under Clive's command, but the manœuvre was not successful. About three o'clock in the afternoon the Nawāb's host retreated to its entrenched camp, being considerably hampered by the cumbrous heavy guns, each of which was drawn by forty or fifty pairs of oxen, many of which were killed. A sudden attack by Eyre Coote caused a general

[1] 18,750 rupees in 1762, then equivalent to about £2,000 (Secretary's letter to author dated December 5, 1910). The banker, as Orme points out, owned the best houses in Calcutta and had many interests there which he could not afford to sacrifice.

[2] Clive assembled a council of war, and voted in the majority of thirteen for postponing action ; Eyre Coote led the minority of seven. In the course of an hour Clive changed his mind, and did the right thing.

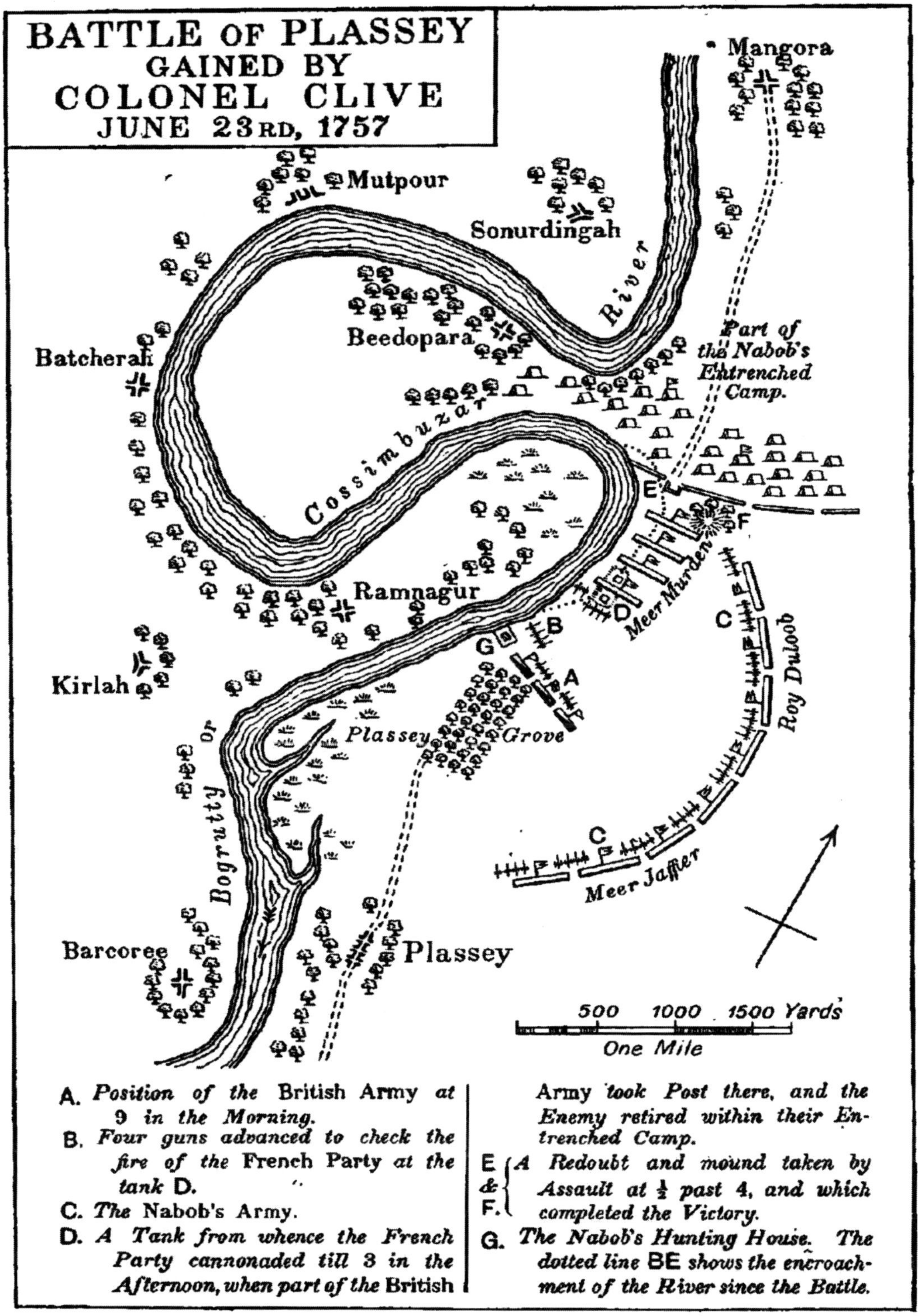

A. *Position of the* British Army *at 9 in the Morning.*

B. *Four guns advanced to check the fire of the* French Party *at the tank* D.

C. *The* Nabob's Army.

D. *A Tank from whence the French Party cannonaded till 3 in the Afternoon, when part of the* British Army *took Post there, and the Enemy retired within their Entrenched Camp.*

E & F. *A Redoubt and mound taken by Assault at ½ past 4, and which completed the Victory.*

G. *The Nabob's Hunting House. The dotted line* BE *shows the encroachment of the River since the Battle.*

rout, the only people on the Nawāb's side who fought at all steadily being a party of 'vagabond Frenchmen' under a leader named Sinfray or St. Frais. The rest of the host lacked confidence in their cause and failed to display courage or any other soldierly quality. The pursuit was continued for six miles. The Nawāb's whole camp with the guns, baggage, elephants, and horses fell into the hands of the victors, whose loss was extremely small, amounting to about 22 killed and 49 or 50 wounded. The enemy were supposed to have lost about five hundred killed, including their best general, Mīr Madan, whose death at an early stage of the contest much discouraged the Nawāb and his troops.[1] As a battle the fight at Plassey does not deserve critical examination. Mīr J'afar took care to do nothing but wait and see which side would win.

Results of the battle. However contemptible the battle might appear to a professional soldier, it was sufficient to decide the fate of Bengal, and, in a sense, of all India.

Sirāju-d daula fled starving and almost naked, but accompanied by Lutfu-n nisā, his wife or favourite concubine, whose fidelity casts a gleam of light on a dark and unpleasant story. Near Rājmahāl he was betrayed by a man in whose hut he had taken refuge, and was brought back to Murshīdābād, where Mīr J'afar's son Mīran caused him to be brutally hacked to death.

Mīr J'afar received the reward of his treason, and was formally installed as Nawāb by Clive, who exercised the real power. It is only fair to remember that Mīr J'afar had been grossly insulted by Sirāju-d daula, and that his treachery was not altogether unprovoked. The new ruler was made to pay well for his promotion. Clive and the other officials concerned obtained large sums for themselves, while the compensation due to the inhabitants of Calcutta for their losses was calculated on a liberal scale, beyond the immediate capacity of the provincial treasury, which contained far less than had been supposed. Clive received the gigantic sum of £234,000, and members of council from £50,000 to £80,000 each. A little later Clive also obtained from the Nawāb an assignment of revenue on the lands south of Calcutta, which was known as 'Clive's *jāgīr*', and brought in nearly £30,000 a year. Dupleix, it may be remembered, had enriched himself in similar fashion. Such transactions were not condemned by the public opinion of the age as they would be now, but discussion of their morality may be deferred until Clive's character as a whole comes under review. The exactions certainly imposed an excessive burden on the finances of Bengal and from that point of view were politically wrong and injurious.

The 'Twenty-four Parganas'. The somewhat complicated

[1] The figures concerning the strength of the armies, the details of the forces, and the number of casualties vary slightly in different contemporary authorities. The Nawāb certainly had numbers twenty-fold those of Clive, not to speak of his huge park of heavy artillery opposed to Clive's nine or ten little pieces.

transactions which gave the Company the rights of a zemīndār or landholder, not those of a sovereign, over a large tract near Calcutta and led to the grant of 'Clive's *jāgīr*' are best described in the precise language of a writer in the *Imperial Gazetteer* (*s.v.* 'Twenty-four Parganas'):

'After the battle of Plassey in 1757, the Nawāb Nāzim of Bengal, Mīr Jafar, ceded to the East India Company a tract of country which lay principally to the south of Calcutta and comprised about 882 square miles, known as the *zamīndārī* of Calcutta, or the Twenty-four Parganas *zamīndārī*. Under this grant the Company acquired the rights of a *zamīndār*;[1] and in the following year they obtained from the emperor's chief officer a *dīwānī sanad*, which particularized the lands held by them and fixed the assessment at Rs. 2,22,958, equivalent to nearly £28,000 at that time. In 1759 the emperor confirmed the grant by a *farmān* which gave the Company a perpetual heritable jurisdiction over the land. Meanwhile, by a deed of gift executed in 1759 Lord Clive had been presented, as a reward for services rendered by him to the Nawab Mīr Jafar, with the revenue of the District due from the Company; and this sum continued to be paid to him till his death in 1774, when, by a deed sanctioned by the Mughal emperor, the whole proprietary right in the land and revenues reverted to the Company.'

It is necessary to add that the Company, after some hesitation and controversy, had freely sanctioned the enjoyment of the *jāgīr* income by Clive until his death, and accepted the reversion when that event should occur.

Defeat of the Shāhzāda and the Dutch. During 1759 the Shāhzāda, or Prince, the Mogul emperor's son, who was in rebellion against his father, invaded Bihār, with the aid of the ruler of Oudh. Clive used effectually the Company's troops to repel the invasion, and to suppress certain rebellions.

The same year saw an unofficial war with the Dutch whose country was officially at peace with England. The endless intrigues of the period included secret negotiations between the Dutch of Chinsūra and Mīr J'afar, the Nawāb, who was uneasy under his new masters.[2] The Dutch settlement, it must be remembered, lay on the bank of the Hooghly close to the town of that name, and more than twenty miles above Calcutta. First one Dutch ship arrived. About two months later six more from Batavia, 'crammed with soldiers', appeared in the river, and Mīr J'afar held a formal reception of the Dutch authorities, who enlisted troops, and addressed a threatening remonstrance to the government at Calcutta complaining of various grievances. The danger to the British was obvious, but nerve was required to meet a risk.

[1] The text of art. 9 of the treaty with Mīr J'afar (1757) is: 'All the land lying to the south of Calcutta, as far as Kalpi, shall be under the Zamindari of the English Company; and all the Officers of those parts shall be under their jurisdiction. The revenues to be paid by them (the Company) in the same manner with other Zamindars' (Aitchison, ed. 4, vol. i, p. 185).

[2] Law of Lauriston, like earlier writers, notes that nothing at an Indian court was secret. 'A peine le nabab a-t-il formé un projet qu'il est aussitôt sçu du dernier de ses esclaves' (*Mémoire*, p. 107).

due to the hostile preparations of a technically friendly power. Clive took the responsibility on himself and made all arrangements to fight the Dutch both on the water and on the land. He conscripted all the European and half-European men in Calcutta, as well as the Armenians, and so put every person available into the field, to the number of 700 or 800. Colonel Forde, who had returned from the successful expedition to the Northern Sarkārs, was placed in command of the small military force, while Captain Wilson, with a squadron much inferior to the enemy in apparent strength, attacked the Hollanders' ships and captured them all. On the next day, November 25, Colonel Forde achieved an equal success. At a village called Biderra between Chandernagore and Chinsūra he utterly defeated the much larger Dutch force under the command of a French officer. The action, which was 'short, bloody, and decisive', resulted in the complete submission of the Dutch and their final withdrawal from the field of Indian politics. For that reason the battle of Biderra, the very name of which is seldom mentioned or remembered, has been reckoned by Colonel Malleson among the fifteen decisive battles of India. Chinsūra was left in the possession of Holland, which retained it until 1825, when it was ceded to the British Government in exchange for certain settlements in Sumatra. The place now forms part of the town of Hooghly.

Departure of Clive. In February 1760 Clive, who had been long desirous to quit India, sailed for England, making over charge to Mr. Holwell, pending the arrival from Madras of Mr. Vansittart, who had been appointed Governor of Bengal. The new Governor assumed office on July 27, 1760. Thus ended the memorable first administration of Clive, which may be reckoned as having lasted just three years from February 1757 to February 1760. During that time, whatever his official designation might be, his was the moving spirit. He was in his thirty-fifth year, 'in the midst of life's path', when he departed from the stage on which he had played so brilliant a part.

Tribute to the navy. While the conquest of Bengal and the suppression of Dutch hostility must always be credited mainly to Clive, the writers and readers of history often forget and ignore the large share in the operations taken by the navy. The transport of the relieving force from Madras to Faltā and up the river to Calcutta was a triumph of seamanship, the merit of which can be realized fully only by perusal of the details furnished by Surgeon Ives. The skill and gallantry displayed by the naval force in the attack on Chandernagore have never been surpassed, and the defeat of the Dutch ships was an equally brilliant achievement.

Admiral Watson, who had done so much to recover Calcutta, unfortunately died of a malignant fever two months after Plassey at the age of forty-three. The character of Charles Watson remained unstained during thirty years of honourable service. No action of his calls for either regret or apology. His friend was justified when he wrote that 'in a word, no man ever lived more esteemed, or died more regretted than Admiral Watson'. His merits received due recognition from his country. A monument to his memory was erected in Westminster Abbey at the cost of the East India Company, and his son was created a baronet.

A time of temptation. We now turn to the doings of men who were not deserving of much esteem when alive or much regret when dead. Their failings, which look so black on the page of history, were in large measure the outcome of the extraordinary circumstances in which they were placed by events wholly unexpected. The merchants and factors of the Company, trained solely with an eye to business conducted in a country where public opinion was wanting to check abuses, and accustomed to deal with corrupt, unscrupulous officials, whose favour they had been wont to court by intrigue and bribery, suddenly found themselves masters of an enormous territory and in a position to make and unmake kings. Riches were to be had for the asking, nay, without asking. The sudden affluence thrust upon the Calcutta community by the lavish compensation paid for the losses sustained at the time of the capture of the city and the huge 'presents' given by the new Nawāb as the price of his elevation turned the heads of all, and led to a scramble for riches which brought into painful prominence the evil features of human nature. Gentlemen, who in the ordinary course of nature would have been content to retire as successful traders and end their days in respectable obscurity, were tempted to sell their souls for gain and so condemned to leave for the scorn of posterity names tarnished by the stain of ignoble greed. The temptation was great and we must not be surprised that it was too much for the virtue of most of the persons exposed to its snares.

The unpleasant details of the period, and especially of the years during Clive's absence in England, which, unfortunately, have been recorded fully, may be passed over lightly in a book like this. The scandals which occurred were almost inevitable, and it is well to remember that they lasted only a short time. From 1772 a serious effort was made to reform the administration, and Warren Hastings, as Governor of Bengal from that year to 1774, did all that could then be done to lay the foundation of a better system.[1]

[1] Warren Hastings, when writing to the Directors on November 11, 1773, justly observed that 'whatever may have been the conduct of individuals or even of the collective members of your former administrations, the blame is not so much imputable to them as to the want of a principle of government adequate to its substance, and a coercive power to enforce it'. He then pointed out the absurdity of trying to govern a great kingdom by the organization of a trading company. 'Among your servants, who for a course of years have been left at large in possession of so tempting a deposit, it is not to be wondered at that many have applied it to the advancement of their own fortunes. . . . Few men are inspired with so large a share of public virtue as to sacrifice their interests, peace, and social feelings to it, and to begin the work of reformation on themselves.' In

Inherent difficulties. The inherent difficulties of the situation in which the officials of the Company found themselves placed were enormous, and could not have been wholly overcome if every Englishman in Bengal had been an angel of light. The Indian governments with which the British had to deal were thoroughly debased. Treachery and murder of the most atrocious kinds were almost universally recognized as ordinary methods of statecraft. English officials who had to transact business with the Indian public men of the eighteenth century could hardly help themselves from suffering a certain amount of moral deterioration or from yielding to the temptation of meeting guile by guile. The court of Delhi was hopelessly vicious and corrupt. Every one of the Pādshāhs or so-called emperors after the death of Bahādur Shāh in 1712 was absolutely worthless, and most of them were worse than worthless. The ministers were utterly unscrupulous, and nobody pretended to entertain patriotic sentiments. The minor courts, as a rule, were no better, and it would be difficult to name an honest man among the prominent Indian notables of the time, whether in the north or in the south.

The legal position of the personages claiming authority was confused and obscure. For instance, the ruler of Bengal whom the English overthrew at Plassey was supposed to be the subject and tributary of the Pādshāh of Delhi. As a matter of fact he was neither, and the theoretical suzerainty of the Great Mogul was valuable only as a saleable commodity. Everybody and everything was on sale. Those disagreeable facts must be realized before judgements of unrelenting severity are passed on the failings of the foreigners who had to work in such an atmosphere, and to deal with authorities who never actually were what they professed to be. The political position was further complicated by the existence of the predatory Marāthā power. The Marāthā government lived by and for plunder. It would be difficult to exaggerate the wickedness of the leaders of the Marāthā hordes and their allies the Pindārīs. The rapid introduction of good government into a country so disorganized was impossible. The Company could not possibly find competent rulers either in its own ranks or among the natives of the country. So we come back to the proposition that the disorders of the state in the years following the revolution caused by the battle of Plassey were unavoidable to a large extent. Grapes cannot be gathered from thistles, and thistles were an abundant crop in the India of those days.

Situation in 1760. In the beginning of 1760 both the Shāhzāda and the Marāthās again invaded the provinces which were reduced to a state of intense distress. Mīr J'afar was utterly incompetent to deal with his difficulties, and Clive's intention to leave to him all the responsibilities of government, while the English should

a later letter (December 18) he writes: 'God forbid that the government of this fine country should continue to be a mere chair for a triennial succession of indigent adventurers to sit and hatch private fortunes in' (Gleig, i. 368, 377).

'attend solely to commerce, which was our proper sphere and our whole aim in these parts', was frustrated. The situation when Mr. Vansittart took over charge in July 1760 is well described by Mill:

'The new governor found the treasury at Calcutta empty, the English troops at Patna on the very brink of mutiny, and deserting in multitudes for want of pay; the Presidencies of Madras and Bombay totally dependent upon Bengal for pecuniary resources; the provision of an investment actually suspended;[1] the income of the Company scarcely sufficient for the current expenses of Calcutta; the allowance paid by the Nabob for the troops several months in arrear; and the attainment of that, as well as of a large balance upon his first agreements, totally hopeless. Some change by which the revenue of the Company could be placed on a level with their expenditure was indispensable. . . . From the administration of Jaffier, resigned as he was to a set of unworthy favourites—old, indolent, voluptuous, estranged from the English, and without authority—no other consequences were to be expected than those which had already been experienced.'

Mīr Kāsim appointed Nawāb. The Calcutta authorities, being forced to make some change, resolved to transfer the control of the administration to the Nawāb's son-in-law, Mīr Kāsim, who appeared to be the most worthy member of the ruling family, and to leave Mīr J'afar on the throne as nominal Nawāb. Arrangements were made accordingly. Mīr J'afar's son, Mīran, a debauched and tyrannical man, having died suddenly, and perhaps been assassinated, Mīr J'afar retired, and Mīr Kāsim became Nawāb. The English promised military aid to their nominee, recouping themselves by securing the cession of the districts of Burdwan, Midnapur, and Chittagong for the payment of the troops—the first instance of the system of 'subsidiary alliances' adopted later on a large scale by Lord Wellesley'.[2]

The story of Mīr Kāsim. So far the arrangements made might be justified as offering a prospect of better government and the

[1] The 'investment' meant the supply of goods for export in the trade of the Company. Cash advances were made to the weavers and others who supplied the goods.

[2] Treaty dated September 27, 1760; articles 4 and 5 are: '(4) The Europeans and *Telingas* [Madras sepoys] of the English Army shall be ready to assist the Nawab, Mir Mahomed Kasim Khan Bahadur, in the management of all affairs; and in all affairs dependent on him they shall exert themselves to the utmost of their abilities. (5) For all charges of the Company and of the said Army, and provisions for the field, &c., the lands of Burdwan, Midnapur, and Chittagong shall be assigned, and *Sanads* [grants] for that purpose shall be written and granted. The Company is to stand to all losses and receive all the profits of these three countries, and we will demand no more than the three assignments aforesaid' (Aitchison, ed. 4, vol. i, p. 215). The current official story that Mīran was killed by lightning which fired his tent, was disbelieved by Jean Law of Lauriston, who was of opinion that Mīran was assassinated, the tent being set on fire during a thunderstorm to conceal the crime (*Mémoire*, ed. Martineau, Paris, 1913, p. 452).

restoration of financial solvency. They were spoiled and rendered suspect by the greed of the majority of the Company's officials, who exploited the change in the government to their personal profit. The new Nawāb was a man far more competent than his father-in-law, and might have done well if he had been given a fair chance. Vansittart and Warren Hastings, then a young man, who had been brought into the Council in 1761, were anxious to be just, but they were outvoted by their greedy colleagues, who wrongfully claimed a right to carry on the inland trade in country produce free of duties, while their Indian competitors should have to pay them.[1] The claim, which was utterly baseless, was enforced with much oppression and disregard of justice. The Nawāb sought an escape by moving his court to Monghyr (Mungir) much higher up the Ganges, where he occupied the ruinous fort then haunted by tigers, and evaded the demands of the Council by announcing that the trade of all parties alike should be free of duties. Watts and the other members of the majority of the Council disallowed the Nawāb's proposals, which Vansittart and Hastings had approved. A Mr. Ellis stationed at Patna was especially violent in his opposition to the Nawāb, who was driven into hostilities. Mīr Kāsim was 'rendered frantic', to use Vansittart's words, and in October 1763 retaliated in a barbarous fashion by the massacre of all the Europeans in his power, save one, Dr. Fullarton. Ellis was among the victims, who numbered about 200. The majority, about 150, were slaughtered at Patna by a brutal foreign adventurer named Walter Reinhard, commonly known by his nickname of Sombre, Sumroo, or Samrū, who survived until 1778. His widow, the famous Bēgam, had a long and adventurous career. Mīr Kāsim, defeated in several engagements, took refuge in Oudh, and old Mīr J'afar was brought back as Nawāb. He died in January 1765, and was succeeded as titular ruler by a son named Najmu-d daula. All these changes were utilized by the majority of the Council as opportunities for making fortunes by the exaction of huge 'presents' from each successive prince.[2] Even Vansittart, who had held out for a time, yielded to the temptation and took five lakhs of rupees in 1762. Warren Hastings did not soil his hands.

Battle of Buxar. The notice of Mīr Kāsim's fate in the preceding lines has anticipated the story of his final military defeat which was accomplished at the battle of Buxar, on October 23, 1764. Mīr Kāsim, whose army was more efficient than was usual in those times, had the half-hearted support of the titular emperor Shāh Ālam and the Nawāb-Vizier of Oudh. The British force was commanded by Major Munro, afterwards Sir Hector, a king's officer, who had come from Bombay with reinforcements,

[1] The Company was concerned only with the foreign trade. The claim to conduct the inland trade duty-free was based on a forced and inequitable interpretation of the *farmān* of Farrukhsiyar, which was loosely worded.

[2] For the details as disclosed to the House of Commons committee in 1773 see Mill, ed. 5 (1858), vol. iii, pp. 257–60. The student should note that the name of Warren Hastings is *not* in the list.

and had suppressed a sepoy mutiny with terrible but necessary severity. He led an army of 7,072 men, including 857 Europeans, and had a train of artillery comprising 20 field-pieces. The force of the allied enemies was variously estimated as numbering from 40,000 to 60,000 men. The fight, which was fiercely contested, lasted from nine in the morning until noon, when the enemy gave way. Pursuit was stopped by the destruction of a bridge of boats two miles distant from the battle-field. The enemy left 2,000 dead on the ground, in addition to about the same number drowned. The British lost 847 in killed and wounded, a large figure for an Indian battle. The victory, which was absolutely decisive, completed the work of Plassey. The emperor submitted, and came under British protection. In the following February the fortresses of Chunar and Allahabad were captured, so that the power of Shuj'āu-d daula, the Nawāb-Vizier of Oudh, was broken for ever.

Appointment of Clive. The Directors in London were aghast at the news of the misrule in India, and on April 26, 1764, avowed that they were 'at a loss how to prescribe means to restore order from this confusion'. They were obliged, under pressure from the proprietors, to invoke the aid of Clive, who had been created Baron Clive of Plassey in the peerage of Ireland as a reward for his earlier services.[1] A Select Committee was appointed to assist him, and the Directors could 'only say, that "we rely on the zeal and abilities of Lord Clive and the gentlemen of the Select Committee to remedy"' the evils of the state.

Clive arrived at Calcutta on May 3, 1765, armed with strict instructions and ample powers to reform abuses.

Contemporary events. Before proceeding to study the proceedings of Clive's second administration from May 1765 to February 1767, the reader should bear in mind the course of contemporary events outside of Bengal, and remember that in 1761 the Marāthā power had been temporarily shattered at Pānīpat, that in the same year French influence had been finally destroyed by the capitulation of Pondicherry, and that Haidar Ali had become supreme in Mysore. The battle of Buxar in 1764 had closed the story of the military conquest of Bengal and Bihār, which from that date were substantially British territory, however the fact might be obscured by confused legal fictions concerning the Pādshāh of Delhi, the Sūbadār of Bengal, and other personages whose real position differed widely from that officially ascribed to them. During the five years of Clive's absence from India (1760–5) the situation had changed radically, and strong measures were needed to check the gross abuses prevalent and to prepare the way for a decently ordered administration.

[1] Governments in the eighteenth century were slow to confer a peerage of the United Kingdom, or rather of Great Britain (England and Scotland), which carried with it a seat in the English House of Lords. An Irish peer ranked in England as a commoner and could become a member of the House of Commons, as Clive actually became.

Covenants and inland trade. Clive brought with him two members of the Select Committee nominated to assist him; the other two, General Carnac and Mr. Harry Verelst, being then employed in Bihār and at Chittagong respectively.[1] The orders of the Directors commanding the instant cessation of their servants' interference in the inland trade and the execution of covenants prohibiting the acceptance of 'presents' except within certain narrow limits, although received in January, had been laid aside by the Calcutta councillors, who simply ignored them. Clive insisted on the immediate execution of the new covenants; but, in accord with the Select Committee, disobeyed and tried to evade the perfectly clear orders from home concerning the participation of the Company's servants in the inland trade, which was forbidden absolutely by the Directors. Clive and his colleagues formed the opinion that in the circumstances then existing the limited amount of lawful trade open to the servants of the Company was insufficient to provide them with adequate remuneration. Their salaries, as is well known, were mostly of nominal amount. The Directors and proprietors of stock had always displayed a strong dislike to the appearance of a heavy charge for salaries on the face of the accounts. They took no heed of the enormous perquisites often amassed by individual officials, so long as there was no public scandal. Clive and his colleagues accordingly did not propose the obvious remedy of assigning adequate salaries to the officers and prohibiting them altogether from practising trade. That remedy had to come a little later, but at that time the Directors could not have been persuaded to sanction it.

The Society of Trade. Clive unfortunately was induced by his colleagues to accept and defend a fantastic scheme for enriching the senior servants of the Company, civil and military, by instituting a Society of Trade, for carrying on the forbidden inland trade in salt, betel-leaf, and opium. The operations of the Society in practice were almost confined to salt, in which a strict monopoly was created. The enormous profits were shared in certain proportions by the Company and the officers concerned. Clive himself held five shares, which he sold in 1767 to his colleagues, Messrs. Sumner, Verelst, and Sykes, for the considerable sum of £32,000.[2] The Directors rightly disallowed absolutely the monstrous scheme, but full effect was not given to their orders until September 1768. The proceedings relating to the business were too complicated for detailed exposition in this place. The reader who is curious about the particulars of an unpleasant affair will find everything concerning it in the pages of Bolts on one side and of Verelst on the other.

[1] The Select or Secret Committee took charge of all political and foreign affairs, thus becoming the parent of the Foreign Department of the Government of India. Ordinary administration remained in the hands of the Council.

[2] Bolts gives the text of the deed without date, which must have been in 1767.

Political arrangements. The victory of Buxar in 1764 had relieved Clive from the necessity of directing military operations and had left him free to devote his attention to political and administrative problems. The chief political questions, all closely connected one with the other, concerned the Nawāb or Sūbadār of Bengal, Shāh Ālam, the titular emperor or Pādshāh, and Shuj'āu-d daula, the Nawāb-Vizier of Oudh. The new Nawāb of Bengal was disposed of by converting him into a titled pensioner stripped of all power. Clive in one of his letters states that the young man was pleased with the arrangement and observed, 'Thank God, I shall now have as many dancing-girls as I please'. Nevertheless, Clive insisted on keeping up the fiction of the 'double government', and conducting the administration in the name of the Nawāb, whose authority was vested in two Nāibs or Deputies, Muhammad Razā Khān for Bengal, and a Hindu, Mahārājā Shitāb Rāi, for Bihār. The titular emperor, who was not in a position to have a will of his own and was thankful to get what he could, was provided for by the treaty of Allahabad. The districts of Allahabad and Korā, the latter being often described as Korā (Corah) and Karā (Kurrah),[1] were cut off from Oudh and assigned to Shāh Ālam, who was also granted an annuity of twenty-six lakhs of rupees (2,600,000) from the revenues of Bengal. The Mogul, in return, was required to resign all further claims on the revenue and to confirm formally the right of the Company to the territories in their possession.[2] He thus became in substance a dependant and pensioner of the Company.

Grant of the Dīwānī. Shāh Ālam was further directed to grant to the Company the Dīwānī of the whole of Bengal, Bihār, and Orissa. The province last named then included only Midnapur and part of the Hooghly District, the rest of Orissa or Cuttack (Katak) being in Marāthā hands since 1751. The Grant of the Dīwānī in 1765, as it is commonly called, meant that the emperor, so far as he could, conferred on the Company the appointment of Dīwān or coadjutor to the Nawāb in all matters connected with the revenue.[3] The general administration was still in the hands of the officers who posed as Deputies of the Nawāb. The Company did not take up the duties and responsibilities of Dīwān

[1] Korā is a town in the Fatehpur District, about 100 miles NW. of Allahabad. It was the capital of a *sarkār* or District in Akbar's time. Karā, about 40 miles NW. of Allahabad, is a small town in that district, which played a considerable historical part in earlier ages. Some of the early English documents speak of 'Corah' only, but the territory often is described as 'Corah and Kurrah' (Strachey, *Rohilla War*, p. 37 *n.*).

[2] Namely, the Twenty-four Parganas near Calcutta, the Districts of Burdwan, Midnapur, and Chittagong; and the Northern Sarkārs (Circars).

[3] Lord Mahon comically, although with all gravity, observes that 'Clive obtained from the fallen Emperor a Dewannee or public deed conferring on the English Company the sole right of administration throughout the provinces of Bengal, Orissa, and Bahar' (*The Rise of our Indian Empire*, ed. 1858, p. 85).

until seven years later. The so-called 'grant' was a paper transaction designed to give a show of legality to the Company's irregular position. English Supervisors appointed to superintend the operations of the Indian revenue officials were not a success.

Combination of officers. In 1766 a dangerous mutinous combination of the British officers of the Company's military forces, not quite amounting to open mutiny, took place, which needed Clive's strong nerve for its suppression, and seemed at one time to threaten a revolution. The Directors, eager for financial economies, insisted on the field allowance or *batta* to the officers being stopped. It had been doubled by Mīr J'afar, and the Company regarded the increased charge as a serious grievance. On the other hand, many of the junior officers could not live on their small pay without the allowance, and undoubtedly had substantial grounds of complaint when the extra pay was suddenly stopped. Many of the Company's civil servants sympathized with the officers and subscribed in support of their cause. The army had been organized by Clive in three brigades stationed respectively at Monghyr, Allahabad, and Bankipore near Patna. The officers of the third brigade at Bankipore remained loyal, but those of the other two brigades arranged to resist the orders for the stoppage of the allowance by throwing up their commissions simultaneously, hoping that the pressure thus exercised would compel Clive and the Select Committee to refrain from enforcing the Director's orders. The European privates and the Indian sepoys on the whole kept clear of the combination. Clive met the danger with unflinching firmness and within a fortnight had conquered it. Most of the officers submitted and were allowed to remain in the service, but a few were treated with vindictive severity and shipped to Europe with the accommodation provided for common sailors, a harsh measure of at least doubtful legality. Clive deserves full credit for the resolution which he displayed in a perilous emergency, but the details of the hard cases are not pleasant reading.

Departure and death of Clive. At the beginning of 1767 Clive felt himself free to return to England, which he had quitted unwillingly. While making no direct personal profit from the trip, he provided handsomely for his surgeon and two other members of his personal staff by dividing among them his large profits derived from the Society of Trade. He stated, and no doubt truly, that he himself was nearly six thousand pounds poorer than when he left England.

In February 1767 he left India for ever. The remaining seven years of his life, largely occupied by party conflicts at the India House and in Parliament, concern his biographer rather than the historian of India and need not be further noticed here. Those years were clouded by depression resulting from painful maladies and enhanced by the excessive use of opium taken to relieve the suffering. In 1774 he cut his throat at his London house in Berkeley Square.

Verelst and Cartier. He left the territories in his charge in a state of perfect outward tranquillity to his successor, Mr. Harry Verelst, an experienced man of considerable ability, and superior in character to many of his colleagues and contemporaries. Two years later Verelst handed on the government to Mr. John Cartier, who also enjoyed a good reputation and retired with a fortune deemed modest in those days.[1] Although Clive's exertions had done something to clear the air, grave abuses continued to exist, as will appear from the next chapter.

Policy and character of Clive. The acts commonly specified as those staining Clive's reputation are the deception practised on Amīnchand (Omichund) and the acquisition of an immense fortune by accepting from Mīr J'afar cash 'presents' on a vast scale to the amount of £234,000 besides the *jāgīr* worth about £28,000 a year. It is needless to discuss minutely the forged treaty business. Although Clive refused to repent of his action, which certain writers have tried to justify, the trick unquestionably was indefensible. both morally and politically. The matter of the 'presents' and the *jāgīr* is much more complicated when due consideration is given to the time and circumstances. Clive felt that as a conqueror he was entitled to help himself freely to prize-money, which in those days and long afterwards was claimed by victorious armies in a way which now would be deemed discreditable. Clive urged in his defence before Parliament that the Directors his masters had not merely approved his acts but had sent him out again to India, in order to retrieve their affairs by his 'zeal and abilities'. They had not only condoned the acceptance of the *jāgīr*. His enjoyment of the grant for a term of years was formally sanctioned and the reversion of it to the Company was secured. In 1773, Clive, when examined before the committee of the House of Commons. argued that

'at that time (1757) there were no covenants existing: the Company's servants were at liberty to receive presents: they always had received presents. . . . He never made the least secret of the presents he had received: he acquainted the Court of Directors with it: and they, who are his masters, and were the only persons who had a right to object to his receiving those presents, approved of it.'

The propositions thus stated are all true in fact, and the defence, so far as it went, was sound. The House of Commons, while expressing general disapproval of the practice current sixteen years earlier, refrained from formulating a personal condemnation of Clive and wisely recorded their judgement that 'Robert, Lord Clive, did at the same time render great and meritorious services to his country'.

Clive's proceedings respecting the Society for trade in salt, betel-leaf, and tobacco formed by him and the Select Committee in 1765 and continued in operation until September 1768, in defiance of the Directors' repeated positive orders and in violation of his

[1] Both Verelst and Cartier are given good characters by an anonymous writer in 1790, as quoted by Miss Monckton Jones (*Warren Hastings in Bengal*, 1772–4, p. 114 *n.*).

own express undertaking to abstain from trade, seem to me far more discreditable than his early acceptance of excessive 'presents'. It would be impossible to justify that judgement without entering upon a lengthy disquisition unsuitable for a book like this; and it must suffice to say that for once I agree with Mill in regarding the affair of the Society as being 'in its own nature shameful', and in rejecting as altogether unconvincing the elaborate arguments adduced in its defence by H. H. Wilson, Verelst, and other authors.[1]

CLIVE.

It appears to me impossible for the impartial historian to deny that Clive was too willing to meet Asiatic intrigues on their own ground; too greedy of riches, and too much disposed to ignore delicate scruples in their acquisition. That verdict undoubtedly tarnishes his memory and precludes the historian from according to him the unqualified admiration which his heroic qualities seem to exact. His most outstanding characteristic was an inflexible will which guided his conduct to success in affairs, whether military or civil. His military genius and his gift for leadership were

[1] For a full statement and an ample supply of documents see the work of Bolts on one side and that of Verelst on the other.

abundantly manifested both in the peninsula and in Bengal. His abilities as a statesman were exhibited chiefly in his second administration, when he confronted extraordinary difficulties with unflinching courage. The merits and demerits of that administration probably will continue to excite differences of opinion nearly as marked as those expressed in his lifetime. His affection for the dubious scheme of 'double government' was largely influenced by his desire to veil from rival European states the real position of the British masters of Bengal as 'the umpires of Hindostan'.[1] That policy is expressed with perfect clearness in a letter signed by Clive and his colleagues on January 24, 1767:

'We may, in our present circumstances, be regarded as the spring which, concealed under the shadow of the Nabob's name, secretly gives motion to this vast machine of government, without offering violence to the original constitution. The increase of our own, and diminution of his power, are effected without encroachment on his prerogative. The Nabob holds in his hands, as he always did, the whole civil administration, the distribution of justice, the disposal of offices, and all those sovereign rights which constitute the essence of his dignity, and form the most convenient barrier between us and the jealousy of the other European settlements.'[2]

The argument advanced in the last clause is an inadequate foundation for such a structure of make-believe. There is no reason to suppose that anybody was deceived by all the pretending. It is, however, proper to note that the French, although beaten and powerless on Indian soil, still retained a naval base at the islands of Bourbon and Mauritius in the Indian Ocean, and consequently were in a position to threaten trouble. From the Indian point of view Clive's second administration may be contemplated with some satisfaction as the beginning of the end of an evil time. From the British point of view the controversy concerning his qualities and defects is best closed by the resolution of the House of Commons quoted above.

Famine of 1770. The administration of Mr. Cartier, otherwise of little interest, was signalized by the famine of 1770, a disaster which, as Hunter truly observed, is 'the key to the history of Bengal for the succeeding forty years'. The famine was due to the early cessation of the rains in 1769, which caused the minor autumn crop of rice to wither and prevented the growth of the main crop due for cutting in December. The lack of roads and the other unfavourable circumstances of the time sufficed to produce a famine of unsurpassed intensity from that one failure of rain. Dacca and the south-eastern districts escaped nearly unhurt. The rest of Bengal and Bihār both north and south of the Ganges was rendered desolate, 'a silent and deserted province'. Yet the trouble was completely over, so far as the crops were concerned, in November 1770, and in the three following years the produce

1 The remarkable phrase used by Verelst on March 28, 1768 (*A View*, &c., App. p. 41). Nearly three years earlier Clive had written 'The Company are sovereigns in India' (ibid., p. 252).

2 Verelst, op. cit., App., p. 41.

was more than usually abundant. The worst suffering was endured between May and September. The best estimates indicate that one-third of the population perished. The effects of depopulation were long felt, so that even in 1789 Lord Cornwallis could describe Bengal to the extent of one-third as 'a jungle inhabited only by wild beasts'. The puny efforts of private charity, which seems to have been generous, could do little to alleviate the overwhelming distress. At Murshīdābād the Resident reported that the living were feeding on the dead and that the streets were choked with corpses. Such scenes were no novelty in India. They had been witnessed twice even in the reign of victorious Akbar, and many times throughout the centuries.

The obligation to relieve famine at any cost and to strain every nerve of the administration in order to save life, which was never acknowledged by any native government, Hindu or Muhammadan, was very imperfectly recognized even by the Anglo-Indian government before 1873. In 1770 such notions concerning the duty of a ruling power had not occurred to anybody, Indian or European, and if they had occurred, the means for putting them in practice did not exist. The East India Company's officers cannot be blamed for the failure to deal with the famine on modern lines. They did not then administer the country, of which the revenue affairs were solely in charge of Muhammad Razā Khān, who did not worry about the sufferings of the people. He collected the revenue almost in full and added 10 per cent. for 1771.

Warren Hastings, in his masterly review of the state of Bengal dated November 3, 1772, addressed to the Directors, tells the terrible truth about the methods of revenue administration under the 'double government' system.

> 'The effects of the dreadful Famine which visited these Provinces in the Year 1770, and raged during the whole course of that Year, have been regularly made known to you by our former advices, and to the public by laboured descriptions, in which every Circumstance of Fact, and every Art of Languages, have been accumulated to raise Compassion, and to excite Indignation against your Servants, whose unhappy lot it was to be the witnesses and spectators of the sufferings of their fellow-creatures.
>
> But its influence on the Revenue has been yet unnoticed, and even unfelt, but by those from whom it was collected; for, notwithstanding the loss of at least one-third of the inhabitants of the Province, and the consequent decrease of the Cultivation, the nett collections of the year 1771 exceeded even those of 1768, as will appear from the following Abstract of Accounts:'

which follow, but need not be quoted.

> 'It was naturally to be expected that the diminution of the Revenue should have kept an equal pace with the other Consequences of so great a Calamity. That it did not, was owing to its being violently kept up to its former Standard. To ascertain all the means by which this was effected will not be easy.'

Hastings proceeds to dilate on the difficulties of the investigation and to denounce specially an iniquitous tax called *najai*, which was ruthlessly levied.

'This Tax, though equally impolitic in its Institution and oppressive in the mode of exacting it, was authorised by the antient and general usage of the Country. It had not the sanction of Government, but took place as a matter of course.'

The consideration of the writer's further observations on the revenue system or lack of system in that age is reserved for the next chapter, which will deal with his memorable, although seldom mentioned administration of Bengal as governor for more than two years.

CHRONOLOGY

Shuj'āu-d dīn Sūbadār of Bengal	1725–39
Allahvardī Khān Sūbadār of Bengal	1740–56
Cession of Orissa (Cuttack) to the Marāthās	1751
Gheria expedition of Watson and Clive	1755
Sirāju-d daula Sūbadār or Nawāb of Bengal; capture of Calcutta	1756
Recapture of Calcutta; storm of Chandernagore; battle of Plassey; cession of Twenty-four Parganas; Mīr J'afar Sūbadār or Nawāb	1757
Defeat of the Dutch at Biderra	1759
Departure of Clive; Vansittart governor of Bengal; Mīr Kāsim appointed Nawāb or Sūbadar of Bengal	1760
Massacre of Europeans at Patna and elsewhere; restoration of Mīr J'afar as Sūbadār or Nawāb	1763
Battle of Buxar	1764
Death of Mīr J'afar; Clive governor of Bengal; Select Committee	1765
Mutinous combination of European officers	1766
Departure of Clive; Verelst governor of Bengal	1767
Cartier governor of Bengal	1769
Famine	1770

Authorities

The most useful of the general histories is that by THORNTON. The principal special works consulted are ORME; STEWART, *History of Bengal*, London, 1813; *Siyāru-l Mutākherīn*, vol. i, transl. BRIGGS (London, Or. Tr. Fund, 1832), and the rest by HAJI MUSTAPHA (Raymond), Calcutta, 1789. There is a reprint, 1902. IVES, E., *A Voyage from England to India, &c.*, London, 1773; HILL, S. C., *Three Frenchmen in Bengal*, London, Longmans, 1903; *Calendar of Persian Correspondence*, Imperial Record Dept., Calcutta, vol. i, 1759–67 (publ. 1911); vol. ii, 1767–9 (publ. 1914). HOLWELL'S *Narrative* is reprinted more or less fully in WHEELER, J. TALBOYS, *Early Records of British India*, Calcutta, Newman, 1878; BUSTEED, H. E., *Echoes from Old Calcutta*[4], London, Thacker, 1908, and in other works.

The long-promised *Life of Clive* by Sir G. FORREST has not yet appeared. The subject has been treated by Sir JOHN MALCOLM (Murray, 1836); GLEIG, G. R. (Murray, 1861); MALLESON (Rulers of India), and other authors. The *Life* bearing the name of CARACCIOLI, CHARLES (London, 1775, 1777), is a venomous libel written in the interest of the mutinous officers of 1766. The book, *Considerations on Indian Affairs* by BOLTS, W., is almost equally hostile and needs to be read with caution (London, 1772). In the same year VERELST, HARRY, replied by *A View of the Rise, Progress, and Present State of the English Government in Bengal.* VANSITTART, H., defended his administration in *A Narrative of the Transactions in Bengal, 1760–4* (3 vols., London, 1766). The four works last named include the texts of the treaties and numerous other documents.

All essential information about the famine is given in HUNTER, Sir W. W., *Annals of Rural Bengal*[7] (London, Smith, Elder, 1897).

CHAPTER 3

Warren Hastings as governor of Bengal, 1772–4; the Rohilla war; the Regulating Act.

Early life of Warren Hastings. The creditable conduct of Warren Hastings in the transactions of Mīr Kāsim's time has been briefly mentioned, but a more explicit statement of the leading facts of his early official career is needed to make his position fully intelligible. Unfortunately it is impossible to relate in this place the fascinating story of his life. The most material facts stated in the briefest possible manner are these.

Warren Hastings, a descendant of an ancient and honourable, although impoverished family, was born in December 1732, and came out to Calcutta as a writer in the East India Company's service before he had completed eighteen years of age. After an apprenticeship employed in office work he was posted to Kāsimbāzār (Cossimbazaar). When Sirāju-d daula captured that factory Hastings was made prisoner. He escaped, joined his countrymen at Faltā, and served under Clive, who recognized his merit. In 1761, being then in his twenty-ninth year, Hastings became a member of council at Calcutta. He went home in 1764, and returned to India in 1769 as second in council at Madras, where he was employed chiefly on commercial business. He did his work so well and honestly that the Directors selected him to succeed Mr. Cartier as governor of Bengal. He took charge of that office in April 1772 in the fortieth year of his age and the fullness of his intellectual powers.

Confidence of the Directors. It is important to note that Warren Hastings throughout the whole of his earlier service enjoyed the confidence of his superiors in an exceptional degree. The Directors, when sending him to Madras, bore testimony to his 'great ability and unblemished character'. In May 1771 the Secret Committee gave him still stronger marks of their esteem by writing confidentially to him that 'they could not have evidenced more clearly the confidence they repose in your abilities, zeal, and integrity than they have done by their appointment of you to preside in their council in Bengal'. Two years later they expressed their 'entire approbation' of his conduct, and their 'utmost satisfaction', offering at the same time their 'assurances of protection and support'.

The eulogy pronounced by the Prime Minister was still more emphatic and significant :

'On the passing of the Regulating Act in 1773, he [Lord North] stated in the House that as first Governor-General "he should propose a Person who, though flesh and blood, had resisted the greatest temptations—that tho' filling great Offices in Bengal during the various Revolutions that had been felt in that Country, never received a single Rupee at any one of them, and whose Abilities and intense application would be apparent to any gentleman who would consider what he had done during the first six months of his Administration".'[1]

The man who had earned such trust by twenty-three years of faithful service could not possibly have become in the next year the corrupt tyrant depicted in the outrageous libels which poisoned half of his life and still exercise an improper influence on current opinion. It was the misfortune of Hastings that from 1774 he became the object of the 'vile malevolence' of Philip Francis, who schemed incessantly to usurp his office, and spared no efforts in the attempt to ruin the man whom he envied and hated. The malignant spirit which had composed the venomous *Letters of Junius* found equally congenial occupation in organizing a conspiracy against Hastings,[2] contrived so artfully that even Pitt and Burke were beguiled.

Difficulties of Hastings. It is hardly possible to exaggerate the difficulties which confronted Hastings. The imperfect reforms begun by Clive had produced little real improvement, and a government worthy of the name did not exist. The task of Hastings was the creation rather than the amendment of a tolerable administration. Three months after taking charge he wrote that 'the new government of the Company consists of a confused heap of undigested materials, as wild as the chaos itself'. Various branches of business were 'all huddled together', no clear separation of departments being recognized. Arrears of work going back for years had to be cleared away, and honest men were extremely scarce. The small supply of competent officials had been so much diminished by the massacre of Patna in 1763 that mere youths had risen to positions far above their deserts or capacity. The young gentlemen who had been appointed to control the collection of the revenue, called Supervisors at first and Collectors later, monopolized the trade of the country, especially in grain, and were themselves the tools of their Bengālī 'banyans', or men of business, whom Hastings described as

[1] Quoted by Miss Monckton Jones in *Warren Hastings in Bengal, 1772–1774*, p. 104 (Oxford: Clarendon Press, 1917), from B.M. Add. MS. 29209, 9. The passage does not seem to have been published previously.

[2] The first series of the political pamphlets, 70 in number, entitled the *Letters of Junius*, appeared in the *Public Advertiser* between January 21, 1769, and January 21, 1772. The conclusive evidence that Francis was the author is cited by Busteed, *Echoes from Old Calcutta*[4] (1908), p. 59.

'devils'. The courts of justice were a byword; the country was ravaged by gangs of savage dacoits or brigands, and huge armies of marauders figuring as religious devotees (Sanyāsīs) ranged over the province in their thousands. The currency was in hopeless confusion, and coin was insufficient in quantity. The list of evils might be much prolonged, but it is sufficient to say in general terms that everything was wrong. Hastings, who had received stringent confidential instructions from the Directors to ferret out abuses regardless of persons, found it impossible to do all that was required of him, even though, as he said, his hand was against every man, and every man's hand against him. As it was, he confessed mournfully some years later that his loyal exertions had cost him 'a world of enemies'. He worked with untiring industry, and did all that man could do, but with necessarily imperfect success. He was forced sometimes to compromise and even to tolerate 'jobs'. His work laid the foundation on which Lord Cornwallis, more favourably situated. was able to build a coherent system. The actual achievement of Hastings will now be described in a summary fashion, omitting much.

WARREN HASTINGS
(as a young man).

The achievement of Hastings. The Company having resolved to 'stand forth as Dīwān', the task of collection of revenue was transferred from Murshīdābād to a Board of Revenue at Calcutta,[1] which thus became the official capital of British India from 1772, a distinction which it continued to enjoy until 1912, when royal command transferred the head-quarters of the Government of India to Delhi.

The allowance of the young Nawāb of Bengal, who had become merely a distinguished nobleman, was cut down by one-half, but economies in useless expenditure left him more money to spend

[1] The whole Council sat as the Board of Revenue. Strachey gives the number of councillors as nine; other books state it as twelve, and the latter number was advocated by Hastings. The number seems to have varied from time to time.

than he had had before. The appointment of Mannī Bēgam as guardian of the Nawāb was afterwards made the subject of foul and absurd charges preferred by Nandkumār and his base English associates. It is sufficient to say that the appointment was sanctioned unanimously by the Calcutta Council and warmly approved by the Directors. The titular emperor, eager to return to Delhi, had thrown himself into the hands of the Marāthās, who kept him practically a prisoner and used him as a tool.[1] He was constrained to make over to them the provinces of Allahabad and Karā which had been assigned to him for support. Hastings rightly withdrew the tribute or allowance of twenty-six lakhs which had been assigned to him as a dependant of the English. It would have been the height of absurdity to continue the payment for the benefit of the Marāthās, the most formidable enemies of the Company. Hastings kept on friendly terms with Shuj'āu-d daula, the ruler of Oudh, whose territories he regarded as a buffer state interposed between the British provinces and the Marāthās. His steady support of Shuj'āu-d daula involved him in the Rohilla war, the subject of so much lying declamation.

Hastings did what he could to improve the administration of justice, and constituted courts of appeal at Calcutta for both civil and criminal cases. The arrangements made were necessarily crude, and had to be so largely modified later that it would be useless to give details.

Some decision concerning the assessment of the land revenue, or 'settlement' in Anglo-Indian technical language, being urgently required, Hastings and his Council did the best thing then possible by granting farming leases for five years, which in 1777 were replaced by more objectionable annual contracts.[2] The system of farming leases, although far from ideal, was the only tolerable one practicable at the time.

The Council supported their President as a rule, with the exception of Sir Robert Barker, the Commander-in-Chief, who offered a factious opposition based on personal supposed grievances. Hastings uniformly displayed a conciliating, forbearing temper, and went a long way in his efforts to secure the willing support of his colleagues.

Trial of the Deputies. The Directors had insisted that Muhammad Razā Khān and Mahārājā Shitāb Rāi, nominally the deputies of the Nawāb, but in reality the governors of Bengal and Bihār respectively, should be put on their trial for alleged embezzlements on charges preferred by Nandkumār and other rascals. The necessary arrests were cleverly effected by Hastings, who entered on the business unwillingly, especially as regards Shitāb Rāi, a man of exceptionally high character. In him Hastings found 'no defect', observing that he had proved himself to be an 'able financier'. Some years earlier Shitāb Rāi had

[1] The reader should remember that Shāh Ālam had received no tribute from the Nawābs. The 26 lakhs were 'new money'.

[2] The change for the worse was due to Francis and his hostile colleagues.

earned from Captain Ranfurlie Knox, a brilliant officer, the high praise: 'This is a real Nawāb; I never saw such a Nawāb in my life.'[1]

Both the accused officers were honourably acquitted. Muhammad Razā Khān subsequently accepted office under the Company, but Shitāb Rāi died soon after his acquittal. The whole conduct of Hastings in the distasteful business forced upon him was highly creditable to his character.

Varied activity. Hastings, the greatest of Anglo-Indian rulers, resembled Akbar, the greatest of the earlier sovereigns, in possessing a genius for organization, and in combining a grasp of broad original principles with an extraordinary capacity for laborious attention to detail. When Hastings took over charge of Bengal he knew nothing about the complex revenue system of the provinces, and was obliged to learn, as he said, 'the whole science' from its rudiments. That was not an easy task in the days when no books of reference existed, and all details had to be got somehow out of cumbrous Persian files. Hastings was a master of Persian and Bengālī, had a good working knowledge of Urdū, and seems to have known some Arabic. His varied knowledge was essential to his masterly handling of every department. Although, as he remarked, 'we have not a lawyer among us', he understood the true principles of legal reform, and, if he had had his way, the absurd Supreme Court of the Regulating Act never would have been constituted. In his letter to Lord Mansfield dated March 21, 1774, when forwarding part of Halhed's work on Hindu law, he stated that he 'desired to found the authority of the British government in Bengal on its ancient laws', and that he hoped Halhed's book might 'serve to point out the way to rule this people with ease and moderation according to their own ideas, manners and prejudices'. It is no wonder that a man with such ideas was almost worshipped by the natives of the country. He held the balance even between Hindus and Muhammadans, and was as anxious to promote the accurate knowledge of Muslim law as he was to reveal the mysteries of Hindu jurisprudence. At that time no European knew Sanskrit, and Halhed was obliged to work on a Persian version of the abstract of Hindu law prepared in the sacred language by ten pundits. The famous Muhammadan college, the Calcutta Madrasah, was founded in 1781 by Hastings as Governor-General.

Like Akbar, he was full of eager, intelligent curiosity about subjects of all kinds. He was deeply interested in geography, and in the distribution of useful plants and animals. Major Rennell, the 'father of Indian geography', who had been appointed Surveyor-General of Bengal as early as 1764, was a valued friend of his. Rennell's wonderful *Bengal Atlas* bears the date of 1781.[2]

[1] *J. B. O. Res. Soc.*, iii. 127.

[2] For the progress of the survey to 1768 see Verelst, *A View*, App., p. 109.

A few years later Hastings supported Sir William Jones in founding the Asiatic Society of Bengal. Hastings sent two missions to Tibet. The first, under George Boyle, visited the Teshu Lama in 1774; the second, under Samuel Turner, saluted a new Teshu Lama nine years later. The instructions given to the envoys bear witness to the intellectual versatility of their chief. Hastings all through his life took a lively interest in literature and art, and always found time to read an immense number of books. It is sickening to think that the reputation of such a man should have been blackened first by the 'impish malignity' of Francis, and then, after it had been rehabilitated, destroyed a second time by Macaulay's false magazine article, which still holds the public ear in spite of endless annotation and refutation.[1]

SIR WILLIAM JONES.

In the time of Hastings the criminal law administered was still that of the Muhammadans, which included the infliction of the barbarous penalty of mutilation, 'too common a sentence of the Mahometan Courts'. Nobody knew precisely how far English law was in force within the limits of Calcutta, which had courts of its own, but it is certain that natives of the country had been sentenced to death for forgery in accordance with the stern law of England long before Nandkumār's case occurred. The dacoits or brigand gangs committed terrible depredations, and when convicted were punished with ruthless severity.

The Sanyāsīs. Even more formidable were the ravages of the Sanyāsīs, which are best described by quoting the language of Hastings from a letter dated March 9, 1773.

'The history of this people is curious. They inhabit, or rather possess the country lying south of the hills of Tibbet from Caubul to China. They go mostly naked. They have neither towns, houses, nor families, but rove continually from place to place, recruiting their numbers with the healthiest children they can steal in the countries through which they pass. Thus they are the stoutest and most active men in India. Many are merchants. They are all pilgrims, and held by all classes of Gentoos [Hindus] in great veneration. This infatuation prevents our obtaining any intelligence of their motions, or aid from the country against them, notwithstanding

[1] The concluding pages of Miss Monckton Jones's book contain a fine appreciation of the character and achievement of Hastings.

very rigid orders which have been published for these purposes, insomuch that they often appear in the heart of the province as if they dropped from heaven. They are hardy, bold, and enthusiastic to a degree surpassing credit. Such are the Senassies, the gipsies of Hindostan.'

The Sanyāsī bands often numbered several thousand men in each, and at one time no less than five sepoy regiments were engaged in hunting them down. Their incursions into Bengal ceased in the second year of the administration of Hastings, and history does not mention any further depredations by them in other provinces. The bands evidently melted away when the Bengal hunting-ground was closed by the vigilance of the governor. At the present day many queer criminal tribes and organizations still exist, little known except to the magistrates and police officers who have to deal with them, but nothing at all resembling the Sanyāsī hordes has been known for generations. I do not know what race supplied the nucleus of their bands, which, as Hastings tells us, were recruited by kidnapped children, who must have come from all classes.

Opium and salt. Hastings put the management of the manufacture and sale of both opium and salt on a sound financial basis. His regulations of 1773 formed the foundation of the modified system in force in our own time. The recent orders discouraging the cultivation of the poppy and the sale of opium have rendered the constitution of the opium department almost obsolete, but the licensed manufacture of salt continues.[1] Hastings also began the reform of the coinage and introduced the 'sicca rupee'.

The princes and the Crown. The views of Hastings concerning the desirable relations between the Crown and the rulers of the Native States were original and daring. When writing to Lord North, the Prime Minister of England, on February 26, 1775, he expressed himself in the following remarkable words:

'I am and always have been of opinion that whatever form it may be necessary to give to the British dominion in India, nothing can so effectually contribute to perpetuate its duration as to bind the powers and states with which this Government may be united, in ties of direct dependence [on] and communication with the Crown. This system has been adopted with respect to the Nabob of Arcot, and, I believe, has met with national approbation. I thought it might be adopted with the same success in regard to the powers on this side of India. Their confidence would be strengthened by such a relation, which would free them from the dread of annual changes and of the influence of individuals; and their submission, which is now the painful effort of a necessary policy, would be yielded with pride by men who glory in the external show of veneration to majesty, and even feel the respect which they profess where they entertain an idea of the power to command it. . . . I conceive that the late Act of Parliament [the Regulating Act], by admitting the King into a participation in the management of all the Company's affairs, and almost the sole control of their political concerns of course makes him the principal in them, and entitles him to those pledges of obedience and vassalage from the

[1] See *Imp. Gaz. of India* (1907), vol. iv, chap. viii.

dependents of the British empire in India, which the ideas of the people and immemorial usage have consecrated to royalty.'[1].

Hastings, when he wrote that passage, was thinking specially of Oudh, which no longer exists as a separate state. Things have changed so much since his time that his suggestion that each principal Indian state should have its accredited diplomatic representative in London, which seems to have been his meaning, is no longer suitable or practicable ; but he was right in recognizing the existence of the desire felt by the Indian princes to be in touch directly with their hereditary sovereign and not merely with the ever-changing officials of an administration. The reality of that desire was plainly manifested when Their Majesties personally received the loyal homage of the ruling chiefs in December 1911, and all legitimate means should be adopted to satisfy it.

The Rohilla war. The material facts of the much debated Rohilla war having been clearly established by study of the documents and embodied in books easily accessible, the matter may be disposed of in a few words, without the formal discussion and refutation of fairy tales. The country lying to the north-west of Oudh between the Ganges and the hills, comprising the ancient Hindu provinces of Katehar and Sambhal, was and is known as Rohilkhand, because during the 'great anarchy' Afghan tribesmen called Rohillas, being for the most part Yūsufzī from the neighbourhood of Peshāwar, had conquered the land. The bulk of the population consisted of Hindu peasants, but there were several considerable towns, including Bareilly and Pīlibhīt. No natural frontier separated Rohilkhand from Oudh, and the Nawāb-Vizier's dominions were most easily accessible to an enemy through the Rohilla territory. The Rohillas were not strong enough to keep out the Marāthās who raided their country several times. The Rohilla chiefs, who had temporized and intrigued with both the Marāthās and the Nawāb-Vizier, in June 1772 signed a treaty by which they promised to pay him forty lakhs, or four millions of rupees, if he would expel the Marāthās. Early in 1773 the freebooters returned, but were compelled to retire when threatened by the forces of Oudh and the Company. The Nawāb-Vizier, who had been put to much expense in equipping his army, demanded payment of the forty lakhs, but, as might be expected, got nothing.

In August of the same year Hastings, accompanied by two members of council, met Shuj'āu-d daula and concluded the treaty of Benares, which transferred Korā and Allahabad from the titular emperor, then a mere tool in Marāthā hands, to the Nawāb-Vizier in consideration of a payment of fifty lakhs. An agreement also was made that the Calcutta government should lend a brigade to the Nawāb-Vizier for the reduction of Rohilkhand at his demand on certain reasonable financial terms. The ruler of Oudh deferred action for various reasons, and the government of Bengal, which

[1] Note the phrase 'the British empire in India' used only eighteen years after the battle of Plassey. The quotation is from Gleig, i. 508.

doubted how far an apparently adventurous policy might be approved in England, welcomed the delay. In February 1774 the Council was surprised by receiving from Shuj'āu-d daula a demand for the promised brigade. It was sent accordingly under the command of Colonel Champion. The Rohillas were defeated on St. George's Day, April 17, at Mīran Katra in the Shāhjahānpur District, and their gallant leader, Hāfiz Rahmat Khān, was killed. Their province was annexed to Oudh, and some 18,000 or 20,000 Rohillas crossed the Ganges to the territory of their countryman, Zābita Khān. The Oudh troops burnt some villages and committed a certain amount of ravaging, but no extraordinary violence was used, and the peasantry resumed their daily life at once. One of the Rohilla chiefs was allowed to retain his rule in a portion of the territory, and is now represented by his descendant the loyal Nawāb of Rāmpur.

'Judged by its results,' Sir John Strachey observes, 'the policy of Hastings was eminently successful. . . . More than forty years elapsed before the power of the Marāthās was finally swept away, but during the whole of this time they never attacked or seriously threatened Rohilkhand. The occupation of that province gave to Oudh and to Bengal that permanent protection against the most dangerous of our enemies which it had been the aim of Hastings to secure.'

The proposition thus stated is absolutely correct. Hastings explained his policy to Colonel Champion in a letter dated June 4, 1774, as follows:

'The several propositions (made by Champion) . . . are diametrically opposite to the principle on which the Rohilla expedition was undertaken, which was not merely on account of the pecuniary acquisition of forty lacs of rupees to the Company—for, although this might be an accessory argument, it was by no means the chief object of the undertaking. We engaged to assist the Vizier in reducing the Rohilla country under his dominion that the boundary of his possessions might be completed, by the Ganges forming a barrier to cover them from the attacks and insults to which they were exposed by his enemies either possessing or having access to the Rohilla country. This our alliance with him, and the necessity for maintaining this alliance, so long as he or his successors shall deserve our protection, was rendered advantageous to the Company's interest, because the security of his possessions from invasion in that quarter is in fact the security of ours.'

There was nothing to be ashamed of in the policy of the Rohilla war. The House of Commons had the good sense to refuse to include the subject among the articles of impeachment.

Financial difficulties. Many committees of the House of Commons charged with the duty of investigating Indian affairs have sat from time to time. The earliest, appointed in 1766, resulted in the passing during 1767 of five Acts of Parliament, including one which required the Company to pay to the Treasury £400,000 annually for two years. At the moment everybody believed that the new Indian acquisitions were capable of yielding untold wealth. The Company soon discovered the baselessness of that pleasing belief. While the proprietors of the shares in the Company clamoured for high dividends, the expenses of governing immense territories swallowed up the expected profits, so that in 1773 the Company was almost insolvent and was forced to beg the ministry for the loan of a million sterling.

Need of legislation. The pressure of urgent financial difficulties and the obvious necessity of providing some form of legalized government for the Indian possessions of the Company forced Lord North's government to undertake legislation. It is unnecessary to relate in this work the course of the prolonged discussions in Parliament and at the India House which preceded the enactment of laws settling the disputes. Those discussions may be read at length in the works of Mill, Thornton, and many other authors. India is concerned only with the result, which was embodied in two Acts of Parliament. One disposed of the financial questions at issue, requiring among other things that the Company should submit half-yearly accounts to the Treasury.

Control of Parliament. The other (23 Geo. III, c. 63), commonly known as the Regulating Act of 1773, created a new form of government for India, and definitely subjected the Company to the control of the Crown, or, in practice, to the control of the ministry of the day, and ultimately of Parliament to which such ministry is always responsible.

The 'constitution' of India. The enactment of the Regulating Act may be regarded as the starting-point of the modern constitutional history of India. Although the idea of a 'constitution' is foreign to the traditional Indian modes of thought, which usually have been content to leave government in the hands of an autocrat or despot, the peculiar nature of the connexion of the Indian administration with a parliamentary monarchy in Great Britain has led to the gradual development of an extremely complicated Anglo-Indian constitution. By the term 'constitution' I mean the mixed body of positive law and established practice which regulates the form of the Indian government both in England and in India; determines the relations between the Home Government and the Government of India, sometimes called the Supreme Government; defines the power of the Supreme Government over the provincial administrations; delimits the functions of the legislature or law-making authority as distinct from the executive power; prescribes the powers of the judicial courts; lays down the principles of internal administration; and, last but not least, guides the adjustment of the delicate relations between the sovereign, the Government of India, and the rulers of the Native or Protected States.

Elements of the 'constitution'. That body of mixed law and custom rests primarily upon the statute law of Parliament, comprising about fifty enactments, more or less. Subsidiary, although by no means unimportant, elements in its composition are the prerogative power of the Crown as expressed sometimes by charters, sometimes by proclamations; orders issued by the Directors of the East

India Company, or by the Board of Control, or the Secretary of State; rulings of the Privy Council or House of Lords; laws or regulations passed or issued in India; survivals of ancient Indian institutions; and a long course of settled custom or practice.

The body thus constituted is a growing organism subject to incessant growth and development, which has proceeded at a rapid rate since the beginning of the twentieth century. No man can foresee the constitutional consequences of the Great War.

Analysis of the Regulating Act. The Regulating Act of 1773, which forms the basis of the Anglo-Indian constitution, dealt with several distinct subjects. My discussion of it and connected matters follows the competent guidance of Sir Courtenay Ilbert. Certain changes were made regulating the appointment of Directors of the Company and the voting by the proprietors of stock or shares which did not concern India closely and need not be further specified. It is, however, important to note that the Directors were required to submit to the king's ministers copies of all material correspondence concerning the affairs of the Company. A separate Act, as already mentioned, directed the submission of half-yearly accounts to the Treasury. The subjection of the Company to parliamentary control through the ministry was thus made complete.

Sovereignty. 'For the government of the Presidency of Fort William [Calcutta] in Bengal, a governor-general and four counsellors were appointed, and the Act declared that the whole civil and military government of this presidency, and also the ordinary management and government of all the territorial acquisitions and revenues in the kingdoms of Bengal, Behar, and Orissa, should, during such time as the territorial acquisitions and revenues remained in the possession of the Company, be vested in the governor-general and council of the Presidency of Fort William, in like manner as they were or at any time theretofore might have been exercised by the president and council or select committee in the said kingdoms.

The avoidance of any attempt to define, otherwise than by reference to existing facts, the nature or extent of the authority claimed or exercised by the Crown over the Company in the new territorial acquisitions is very noticeable, and is characteristic of English legislation.'

The clear assertion of the sovereignty of the king over India was deferred until 1858, and was further extended on January 1, 1877, by the Proclamation of Queen Victoria as Empress of India.

Persons appointed. The Governor-general and the four counsellors appointed to start the new government were named in the Act and secured in their positions for five years. That time limit thus fixed by statute in the first instance has been applied by custom to the subsequent appointments of lieutenant-governors and other high officials. Ample salaries were provided, namely, £25,000 a year for the governor-general, and £10,000 for each counsellor.[1] They were all forbidden to trade, receive presents, or otherwise add to their income by irregular means.

The persons appointed were: Governor-general, Warren

[1] The salaries have been much reduced.

Hastings, Esquire, recommended by Lord North in glowing language which has been quoted; members of council: (1) Lieutenant-General John Clavering, a distinguished officer, who was knighted two years later; (2) the Honourable George Monson, who had been in Parliament and had served in the army as second in command at the siege of Pondicherry in 1760; (3) Richard Barwell, Esquire, who had been in the Company's service since 1758; and (4) Philip Francis, Esquire, who had been employed as a secretary and in the War Office.

SIR PHILIP FRANCIS.

Supremacy of Bengal. 'The supremacy of the Bengal Presidency over the other presidencies was definitely declared. The governor-general and council were to have power of superintending and controlling the government and management of the presidencies of Madras, Bombay, and Bencoolen,[1] so far and in so much as that it should not be lawful for any Government of the minor presidencies to make any orders for commencing hostilities, or declaring or making war, against any Indian princes or powers, or for negotiating or concluding any treaty with any such prince or power without the previous consent of the governor-general and council, except in such cases of imminent necessity as would render it dangerous to postpone such hostilities or treaties until the arrival of their orders, and except also in cases where special orders had been received from the Company. A president and council offending against these provisions might be suspended by order of the governor-general and council. The governors of the minor presidencies were to obey the order of the governor-general and council, and constantly and dutifully to transmit to them advice and intelligence of all transactions and matters relating to the government, revenues, or interest of the Company.

The governor-general and council were to be bound by the votes of a majority of those present at their meetings, and in the case of an equal division the governor-general was to have a casting vote' [in addition to his ordinary vote].

The Supreme Court. The Act further empowered the Crown to establish by charter a Supreme Court of Judicature at Fort William, consisting of five barristers, namely, a Chief Justice, with a salary of £8,000 a year, and three judges, each with a salary

[1] In Sumatra, also called Fort Marlborough. The place was given up to the Dutch in 1824 in exchange for the town of Malacca and certain other stations.

of £6,000 a year.[1] Sir Elijah Impey, an old schoolfellow of Hastings at Westminster, was appointed Chief Justice; his colleagues being Robert Chambers, subsequently knighted, John Hyde, and Stephen Caesar Lemaistre. Impey and Chambers were men of considerable distinction, but their two junior colleagues had not earned any notable reputation prior to their appointment. The court was given civil, criminal, admiralty, and ecclesiastical jurisdiction.

'Its jurisdiction [subject to certain limitations] was declared to extend to all British subjects who should reside in the kingdoms or provinces of Bengal, Behar, and Orissa, or any of them, under the protection of the United Company. And it was to have "full power and authority to hear and determine all complaints against any of His Majesty's subjects for crimes, misdemeanours, or oppressions, and also to entertain, hear, and determine any suits or actions whatsoever against any of His Majesty's subjects in Bengal, Behar, and Orissa, and any suit, action, or complaint against any person employed by or in the service of the Company or of any of His Majesty's subjects".'

The Act contained many minor provisions concerning the judicial system and other matters which it would be tedious to enumerate.

Defects of the Act. Ilbert observes that

'the provisions of the Act of 1773 are obscure and defective as to the nature and extent of the authority exercisable by the governor-general and his council, as to the jurisdiction of the Supreme Court, and as to the relation between the Bengal Government and the court'.

The ambiguities and obscurities of the Act and the charter framed under it produced a plentiful crop of disputes, some of which will be noticed in the next chapter. Nobody could tell what law was to be administered by the court.

'The Act was silent. Apparently it was the unregenerate English law, insular, technical, formless, tempered in its application to English circumstances by the quibbles of judges and the obstinacy of juries, capable of being an instrument of the most monstrous injustice when administered in an atmosphere different from that in which it had been administered.'

Nobody knew how to define the classes of persons, European or Indian, who came under the jurisdiction of the court, or how far the court had power outside the limits of the European settlement. Endless problems arose out of the loose wording of the Act, and from the manifest absurdity of applying the English law of the eighteenth century to the natives of Bengal. Unfortunately, the statute had been drawn by persons who knew nothing about India and who failed to consult Hastings or anybody else who had some knowledge on the subject. The judges administering the law were equally ignorant of Indian conditions.

Another grave defect in the Act was the provision which allowed the Governor-general to be outvoted and overruled whenever three members of his council chose to combine against him. That foolish enactment wrought much mischief. Some of the most glaring faults of the Act were remedied after a few years' experience,

[1] The salaries are now lower.

but not until grave injustice had been done and the security of the state imperilled.

The rest of India. Marāthā affairs and the various happenings in Bombay, Madras, and other parts of India during the two and a half years of the rule of Hastings in Bengal as governor, before the arrival of the new members of council, will be more conveniently noticed in the next chapter in connexion with events slightly later in date.

CHRONOLOGY

Warren Hastings governor of Bengal	April 1772
Numerous reforms	1772–4
The Regulating Act	1773
The Rohilla war	1774

AUTHORITIES

The two special authorities, both based on an exhaustive study of original documents, are: STRACHEY, Sir JOHN, *Hastings and the Rohilla War* (Oxford: Clarendon Press, 1892); and M. E. MONCKTON JONES, *Warren Hastings in Bengal, 1772–1774* (Oxford: Clarendon Press, 1918). I have been favoured with the perusal of the proofs of the second book named, which is an excellent work, and should rank as the standard authority on the subject, excepting the Rohilla war, which has been disposed of in Sir John Strachey's conclusive monograph.

Other books on the Hastings period will be named at the end of the next chapter.

The Regulating Act is best studied in ILBERT, Sir COURTENAY, *The Government of India*[3] (Oxford: Clarendon Press, 1915).

CHAPTER 4

Warren Hastings as Governor-general; the policy and character of Hastings; Sir John Macpherson.

The new government. The Judges of the Supreme Court, who arrived in Calcutta on October 17, 1774, were followed two days later by the three Members of Council, General Clavering, Colonel Monson, and Mr. Francis, in another ship. The next day, before Mr. Barwell had taken his seat, the Council met to hear the Directors' instructions. By the orders from home a separate Board of Trade was established for the purpose of relieving the Council from a portion of the purely commercial business of the Company; strict economy in the military expenditure was enjoined; the land revenue system established by Hastings was approved; correspondence with the 'country powers'—or 'Political business' in modern official language—was to be conducted by the Governor-general, subject to the condition that every letter received or sent by him should be laid before the Council; inquiry was to be made into abuses; and, finally, all the members were enjoined to work together in harmony with a view to the preservation of peace, the safeguarding of the Company's possessions, and the due advancement of the Company's interest.

Hostility of Clavering, Monson, and Francis. The triumvirate from England at once fastened on the order to inquire into abuses, and displayed open hostility to Hastings. The meeting was adjourned until the 25th in order to allow Mr. Barwell to join, and from that date the Council was divided into two sections, Clavering, Monson, and Francis on one side, Hastings and Barwell on the other. The constitution of the body threw all real power into the hands of the majority and subjected Hastings to the mortification of seeing the officers of his choice dismissed and all his measures, so far as practicable, reversed. That state of affairs lasted for almost two years, until September 1776, when the death of Colonel Monson restored power to Hastings, who could do what he pleased with the help of his casting vote.

Disputes in council. The details of the unseemly wranglings in council during those two years need not be recounted at length. The members spent their time in firing off minutes against each other from day to day. They seem to have put everything in writing on the spot, and the unedifying recriminations may now be read in print in the ' consultations '. The biographer of Hastings must wade through the dreary mass in order to understand the personal position of his hero and to realize the astonishing endurance of the man, but the particulars of the disputes have little interest for the historian as distinguished from the biographer. In most respects the selfish spite of the triumvirate produced effects of only a temporary character, but a good deal of more or less lasting mischief was done, especially in relation to Oudh, which was compelled to cede the Benares province. The majority in council relied upon support from the Ministry in England, where Indian affairs were then closely intertwined with party politics. Both General Clavering and Mr. Francis aspired to the office of Governor-general, and were resolved to employ every means to drive Hastings into retirement before the expiration of the period of five years for which he had been appointed by Act of Parliament.[1] Happily they failed, and Hastings enjoyed eight and a half years of power from September 1776 to February 1785, which enabled him to save the nascent British empire in India from destruction and to establish it upon firm, well-laid foundations.

The case of Nandkumār. The most famous incident of the personal struggle between Hastings and his hostile colleagues is the case of Mahārājā Nandkumār (Nuncomar), the wealthy and influential Brahman who was executed for forgery on August 5, 1775. That case, like the other incidents of the struggle, has a biographical rather than historical interest, which means that the execution of Nandkumār in itself was a matter of no importance so far as the history of India is concerned. The immense bulk which the case assumes in English literature and in the eyes of

[1] His term of office was subsequently extended from year to year.

the general public is due to the malignant cunning of Philip Francis, who knew how to use the genius of Edmund Burke as his tool. The result of the joint labours of Francis and Burke, supplemented by the disingenuous partisanship of James Mill and the specious rhetoric of Macaulay, has been the growth of a legend almost wholly fictitious. The existence and acceptance of that legend have most unjustly besmirched the characters of Warren Hastings and Sir Elijah Impey, and have done much harm by producing in the public mind an unwarranted belief that the Indian empire rests upon foundations stained by the blood of the victim of a judicial murder, planned and executed by the Governor-general and Chief Justice. Nandkumār's case when looked at from that point of view is of historical interest and importance, and it is therefore necessary to set forth the essential facts.

The majority in council, eager to supplant Hastings, and professing to investigate abuses, invited charges against the Governor-general. Nandkumār, a thorough scoundrel, whose misdoings had been familiar to Hastings for many years, had ample reason to expect personal advantage from the overthrow of the Governor-general, who knew too much, and the victory of his enemies who knew nothing.

Nandkumār's false charges against Hastings. Accordingly, in March 1775 (11 and 13) Nandkumār responded to the manifest wishes of the majority of the council by submitting through Francis papers charging Hastings with gross corruption, and enclosing a letter purporting to be from Mannī Bēgam, the widow of Mīr J'afar, offering a bribe. The counsellors proceeded with indecent haste to assume the truth of all the charges, and to require the Governor-general, their President, practically to be tried by them. The letter purporting to come from the widow, a manifest forgery, was accepted without question. The papers having been sent home were submitted in 1776 to the law officers of the Company, who declared that the information of Nandkumār, even upon the *ex parte* case before them, could not possibly be true. Nothing more was heard about those accusations against Hastings until thirteen years later in 1789 when Burke founded a charge (No. III) upon them, and failed to convince the House of Lords, which unanimously acquitted Hastings in the matter. That fact is often forgotten.

Nandkumār prosecuted for conspiracy. To come back to Calcutta. After Nandkumār had made his accusations in March, Hastings and Barwell retorted in April by bringing a charge of conspiracy against him and others. The case came before all the Judges of the Supreme Court, who in their capacity of justices of the peace considered the evidence for a whole day (April 20) from 10 a.m. to 11 p.m., and allowed Nandkumār and the other accused persons to be on bail till the 23rd.[1] On the 21st Francis

[1] See Gleig and the extracts from Barwell's letters in Stephen; the *Story of Nuncomar*, chap. xvii, and sundry passages in Gleig, not to speak of the documents of the trial and the impeachment proceedings.

and his colleagues were shameless enough to pay an official call on Nandkumār. On the 23rd Hastings was bound over to prosecute at the next assizes. The trial took place in July, when all the defendants were acquitted of conspiring against Hastings, but Nandkumār and a Mr. Fowke were convicted of conspiracy against Mr. Barwell.

Nandkumār prosecuted for forgery. Before July came other things had happened. On May 6 Nandkumār had been arrested on a charge of forgery preferred by one Mohan Parshād, attorney for a party in a civil suit. On that date, after an investigation lasting from 9 a.m. to nearly 10 p.m., Judges Hyde and Le Maistre, acting in their capacity as Justices of the Peace, committed Nandkumār for trial on the charge of forgery and lodged him in jail. The proceedings for forgery arose naturally out of an old civil suit, and the complainant had decided to prosecute even before the Supreme Court was established. The delay which made the prosecution coincident in time with the conspiracy case was caused by the difficulty in getting hold of the document alleged to be forged. Marshman truly observes that the coincidence in time was 'purely accidental'.

Trial and execution of Nandkumār. The actual trial of Nandkumār for forgery began on June 9, and lasted until 4 a.m. on the 16th. The Court never adjourned, sitting in the hottest season of the year even on Sunday the 11th, from 8 a.m. until late at night, and on the last day until 4 a.m. All the four judges were present throughout, Hyde and Le Maistre asking more questions than Impey or Chambers. Nandkumār challenged eighteen persons on the panel whom he suspected of being unfavourable to him and was convicted by a unanimous jury of twelve Europeans. The rule prohibiting the appearance of counsel for the defence in felony cases was relaxed in his favour, and probably he would have been acquitted but for the evident perjuries committed in his defence, which made a deep impression on the jury. No man ever had a fairer or more laborious trial. The fairness of his trial is the only relevant issue. All the judges agreed as to the legality of the proceedings, and their law seems to have been correct. The only special share in the proceedings which fell to Impey was the summing up, a task performed by him fairly and impartially. After conviction legal objections were heard, so that sentence was not passed until June 24, and the execution was deferred until August 5. The Court could not recommend the home authorities under the provisions of the Charter to grant a reprieve, because all the judges were satisfied that the conviction was right, while the petition for respite disclosed no legal grounds for action. Clavering, Monson, and Francis refused positively to take any steps towards obtaining a reprieve.

Comment. Hastings had nothing to do with the case, and Impey simply did his duty, which he shared with three unanimous colleagues. The prisoner was convicted, not by the judges, but by an independent sworn jury, who alone had the task of passing a verdict on the facts. It is folly for critics now to retry the case. The attempt to impeach Impey many years later completely broke down. Macaulay's abuse of the Chief Justice is wholly undeserved. The above is a plain statement of the most material relevant facts, which are not open to serious dispute.[1] Hastings's oath that he had nothing to do with the forgery case is in exact accordance with the facts established by the record. The propriety of Impey's conduct in every stage of the proceedings is manifest to anybody who reads the papers with due attention. There is not the slightest foundation for Macaulay's denunciations of the conduct of either Hastings or Impey in connexion with the execution of Nandkumār. The critics of Warren Hastings may make out a case against him in regard to the Rohilla War, Rājā Chait Singh, or the Bēgams of Oudh. The facts of all those cases admit of divergence of opinion concerning his action, but nobody who has really understood the Nandkumār affair can believe it possible that a judicial murder was committed. The procedure was regular, legal, and deliberate, and the actual trial by jury was more laborious and exhausting, probably, than that of any other case on record. Everybody concerned, without regard to his health or convenience, toiled in the terrible heat of a Calcutta June for eight days from early morning until late at night to get at the truth, and no reason whatever exists for holding that any illegality or injustice was committed by either the four judges or the twelve jurymen.

That is enough, perhaps more than enough, about Nandkumār and the intrigues of Clavering, Monson, and Francis. We may now proceed with the history of India, stopping merely for a moment to note the final collapse of the opposition to Hastings in the council, and to discuss at some length the serious quarrel between the executive government and the Supreme Court.

Death of Monson and Clavering. The wearisome story of the incessant squabbling in council, of Hastings's action in empowering his agent in London to tender his resignation, and then cancelling the power, of the acceptance of the offer by the Directors and Ministry, of the complicated intrigues in London, and the final victory of Hastings need not be retold. Those matters concern the biographer rather than the historian. It may suffice to state that, as already mentioned, the death of Colonel Monson in September 1776 gave Hastings and Barwell the powers of the majority

[1] Many irrelevant matters have been introduced into the discussion by many writers. Questions of law were within the province of the judges who were much more likely to be right than their critics. Chambers had been Vinerian Professor at Oxford. So long as the judges decided honestly and in good faith, as they did, it is absurd to abuse them because other people might hold a different opinion on obscure points of law. 'Pitt, I think with perfect propriety, "treated the accusation of a conspiracy between Impey and Hastings for the purpose of destroying Nuncomar as destitute of any shadow of proof"' (Stephen, i. 88). The jury alone, it cannot be too often repeated, were responsible for the verdict on the facts. The rest followed in course of law.

by means of the Governor-general's casting vote, and that in June 1777 General (Sir John) Clavering made a rash attempt to seize on the office of Governor-general, in the belief that it had been vacated by the supposed resignation of Hastings. A dangerous crisis extending over four days was ended by the decision of the Supreme Court that Hastings had never actually resigned and that consequently no vacancy existed to be occupied by Sir John Clavering. A few months later, in November, Clavering also died. In August 1780 the Governor-general, in accordance with the code of honour observed at the time, fought a duel with Francis, who was wounded and went home after his recovery.[1] He had his revenge later.

The executive government and the Supreme Court. Before entering on the history of the relations between Hastings and the native states and the story of the Marāthā and Carnatic wars, it will be convenient to notice in some detail the violent conflict between the Supreme Court and the executive which came to a head in 1780, long after the recovery by the Governor-general of his power in council. For several years the executive and the Court had usually kept on good terms, in spite of the difficulties caused by the imperfect constitution of the government, the unsuitability of the Court and its law to the country, and the failure of the Regulating Act to determine the jurisdiction and powers of the Court, or to protect adequately the powers which every executive government must keep in its own hands. Hastings declared in December 1774 that

> 'the court of justice is a dreadful clog on the government, but I thank God the head of it is a man of sense and moderation. In all England a choice could not have been made of a man more disposed to do good and avoid mischief, which, however, is not wholly in his power, and I am sorry for it.'

In the following year, 1775, the Governor-general recorded his desire that the Chief Justice might be given either 'a fixed or occasional seat at the Council Board' for purposes of legislation and legal advice, thus foreshadowing the appointment of a Legal Member, which was not carried out until Macaulay was appointed in Lord William Bentinck's time. In 1777, as already noted, the Court unanimously supported Hastings against the violent usurpation attempted by Clavering, impartially condemning at the same time a foolish resolution passed by Hastings and Barwell that Clavering had forfeited his seat in council.

[1] 'My antagonists sickened, died, and fled. I maintained my ground unchanged, neither the health of my body, nor the vigour of my mind for a moment deserted me' (Confidential letter of W. H. to David Anderson, September 13, 1786, in Gleig, iii. 304). The extraordinary quarrel at Madras between Lord Pigot, the governor, and his council had some features in common with the case of Hastings. It occurred in 1776–7. The affair was too complicated and local to merit detailed description in this work. It could not be made intelligible without full exposition of the particulars.

But later, the temptations to assert the large powers apparently granted to the Court by the Regulating Act proved too much for the self-control of the judges, who allowed themselves to take action which threatened the very existence of the government. The fault lay more with the puisne judges than with Impey, the Chief Justice. The conflict was most marked in the conduct of two famous cases, the Cossijurah case and the Patna Cause, which must be briefly explained. Macaulay's account, largely based on Mill, is, as Stephens bluntly observes, 'false from end to end'. But, although we cannot accept the lurid picture painted by the essayist, the mischief actually done was serious and had to be stopped somehow.

The Patna Cause. To take the Patna Cause first. The litigation was between the widow and the nephew of a deceased rich Muhammadan, who left a large property in the Patna District of Bihār. The Court claimed jurisdiction over the nephew as being a farmer or contractor of the revenue, and so in the service of the Company, within the words of the Act. The Court further found that the proceedings of the local Company's officers, acting ostensibly as a court under the designation of a Provincial Council, were null and void, the Provincial Council having allowed its functions to be usurped by the Muhammadan muftis and *kāzīs*, whose proper duty was merely to advise as assessors on points of Muslim law and practice. Ultimately, the Court awarded heavy damages amounting to about £34,000. The Company allowed the time for appeal to the Privy Council to lapse, and, when granted an extension of time by a special statute in 1781, the Directors failed to prosecute the appeal which had been formally lodged. Thus the judgement of the Supreme Court held good, and the damages were paid by the Company.

The proceedings produced a good effect by drawing public attention to the impossible situation in Bengal. The powers claimed by the Supreme Court over people in the districts away from Calcutta, while justified by the language of the Regulating Act and the Charter of the Supreme Court, could not be exercised without fatal weakening of the authority of the executive. Accordingly, the Act 21, George III, c. 70, deprived the Supreme Court of jurisdiction in any matter concerning the revenue or its collection, and even went so far as to sanction customary 'severities' in the collection, which might mean a good deal in practice. It also legalized the Company's courts, and enabled the Indian government to make Regulations.

The Cossijurah case. The Cossijurah case may be more briefly dismissed. A creditor sued the zemindar of Cossijurah, a place about eighty miles distant from Calcutta, for debt in the Supreme Court, averring by affidavit that the defendant came within the jurisdiction of the Court as being a person 'employed' by the Company. Mr. Justice Hyde issued process. When it was resisted the Sheriff tried to enforce the orders of the Court by a posse or force of fifty or sixty sailors and other people collected for the purpose. The posse seized the zemindar's belongings in a rough fashion, regardless of Indian customs. Hastings, when he heard of it, sent an officer with a force of sepoys to arrest the sheriff's men, which they did. Impey never could persuade the government to submit the questions at issue to the king in council for decision, and apparently the legal aspect of the case was never settled. The violent action taken by the executive practically had the effect of confining the jurisdiction of the Supreme Court to Calcutta.

Sir James Fitzjames Stephen held that 'the Council acted haughtily, quite illegally, and violently, without any adequate reason for their conduct'. The illegality may be admitted, but the position was difficult, and the pretensions of the Court had to be resisted somehow, if the Government was to continue to exist. A ruler sometimes finds himself forced to transgress strict law.

SIR ELIJAH IMPEY.

Impey made head of the Company's courts. One other connected topic remains—the expedient by which Hastings and the council (Francis dissenting) patched up the quarrel. In October 1780 Impey was induced to accept the duty of supervising the Company's courts as president of the Chief Civil Court (*Sudder Dewanee Adalut*). After a short time the salary of Rs. 5,000 a month was attached to his new office in addition to the salary which he drew under the Act of Parliament as Chief Justice of the Supreme Court. The transaction, being obviously open to objection, was disapproved at home with the result that Impey was recalled and an unsuccessful attempt to impeach him on various grounds was made. He does not appear to have actually drawn any of the additional salary, or at any rate to have retained the money, if he ever drew any. The papers prove that both he and Hastings were actuated by creditable motives in making the arrangement, believing that in no other way could the prolonged conflict be adjusted. Macaulay's epigram that 'the Chief Justice was rich, quiet, and infamous' is wholly false. Impey stated the facts correctly when he wrote :

'I have undergone great fatigue, compiled a laborious code [Reg. vi of 1781], restored confidence to the suitors and justice and regularity to the courts of justice, and settled the internal quiet of a great empire, without any reward, and for my recompense shall have lost my office, reputation, and peace of mind for ever.'

Character of Impey. Impey afterwards entered Parliament and survived until 1809. He was a good judge and in no way deserving of the abuse showered upon him by Burke, Mill, Thornton, Macaulay, and a host of lesser detractors. Sir James Fitzjames Stephen observes :

'I have read everything I could find throwing light on Impey's character, and it appears to me that he was neither much blacker nor much whiter, in whole or in part, than his neighbours. He seems to me to have resembled closely many other judges whom I have known. . . . He seems to have had an excellent education both legal and general, to have been a man of remarkable energy and courage, and a great deal of rather commonplace ability. I have read through all his letters and private papers, and I can discern in them no trace of corruption.'

The same author closes the discussion of the subject by the observation that 'slightly to adapt the famous remark of De Quincey in his essay on *Murder as a Fine Art*, Impey has owed his moral ruin to a literary murder of which Macaulay probably thought but little when he committed it.'

Hastings's foreign policy. The period of about eight and a half years, from September 1776, when Monson died, to February 1785, when Hastings retired, during which he possessed the power as well as the rank of Governor-general, included the years of the most intense strain to which the kingdoms of Great Britain and Ireland have ever been subjected, save only in the darkest times of the Revolutionary War and the Great War. During those years of strain the British Government had to fight France, Spain, Holland, the revolted American colonies, besides the Marāthās, and Haidar Ali, and to appease formidable discontent in Ireland by the dangerous concession of an independent Parliament. It is impossible to pass a fair judgement on the policy of Hastings unless it is considered in relation to the events outside of India.

The overland route. He was a man of large ideas and wide vision who understood thoroughly that the part played by him in India was only one of many parts played by many various actors on the stage of the world. His prescience and breadth of view are well illustrated by the fact that in 1778 he had organized an overland service via Suez for rapid communication with Europe, through which he received timely accounts of the ill progress of the American war and of the peril arising from French intervention, which enabled him to take measures for defence in India with the necessary promptitude. The strenuous opposition of the Sublime Porte obliged the Directors to discontinue the service, which was not resumed until the time of Lord William Bentinck.[1]

Bombay intervention in Marāthā politics. Bombay has been rarely mentioned so far. The reason is that the settlement

[1] See *Bengal Past and Present*, vol. iv, July–December 1909, pp. 563–76, 586.

there had continued for more than a century after the cêssion to Charles II by the Portuguese to be a purely commercial station of no political importance. The territory of the presidency was confined to the narrow limits of the island of Bombay and Bānkōt or Fort Victoria, ceded in 1756 by the Marāthās in exchange for Gheria. But in 1775 the President in Council of Bombay, who was ambitious, sought to acquire the neighbouring island of Salsette, and the port of Bassein twenty-eight miles distant, which had been taken by the Marāthās from the Portuguese some years earlier. The Bombay government resolved to attain that object by intervening in domestic Marāthā politics and supporting one of the claimants to the office of Pēshwā, then in dispute. The government at Calcutta was not consulted in the first instance under the provisions of the Regulating Act because the Bombay authorities had not knowledge that the new government at Calcutta had been installed. That intervention of the Bombay government led to the First Marāthā War, which lasted until the treaty of Sālbāī in 1782.[1]

Origin of the First Marāthā War. The temptation to which the Bombay government succumbed arose in this way. Mādho Rāo, the fourth Pēshwā, an able man, and the last to exercise much personal authority, died in 1772, and was succeeded by the fifth Pēshwā, Nārāyan Rāo, who after nine months was murdered by the adherents of his uncle, Raghunāth Rāo, commonly called Ragoba. Civil war ensued between the partisans of the Regent, acting for an infant alleged, and probably with truth, to be a posthumous son of Nārāyan Rāo on the one side, and Raghunāth or Ragoba, who denied the child's claims, on the other. Ragoba invoked the aid of the Bombay government, promising the cession of Salsette and Bassein. When he failed to effect the cession, the Bombay people took possession of Salsette, and compelled Ragoba, who was in difficulties, to sign the treaty of Surat, acknowledging the rights of Bombay to both places. The local government was thus involved in a war with the Regency, in the course of which Colonel Keating won a battle at Arās (Adās, Arras) in the Kaira district of Gujarāt, at a heavy cost in casualties to his small force.

Treaties of Surat and Purandhar: convention of Wargāon. Meantime Francis and his colleagues had come into power. Disapproving strongly of the Bombay proceedings they sent peremptory orders to stop the war and recall Colonel Keating. They, with the concurrence of Hastings, dispatched an envoy (Col. Upton) who made with the Marāthās a disadvantageous compact, called the Treaty of Purandhar (1776). As it was never acted on,

[1] It is best to treat all the hostilities between 1775 and 1782 as a single war, the First Marāthā War. Some writers prefer to confine that name to the proceedings ending with the treaty of Surat. The Bombay government continued to display an insubordinate spirit even after it had acquired full knowledge of the new law, and strongly resented the autocratic attitude of the Governor-general and Council. Madras was equally averse to control, and often from less respectable motives.

its terms need not be recited. Four months later came a dispatch from the Directors approving of the treaty of Surat with Ragoba. In 1778 the Bombay government were emboldened by another dispatch from home to renew their alliance with Ragoba, who had gained successes, and to send an expedition towards Poona. It met with disaster, and was compelled to surrender. Colonel Camac, who was acting as the Civil Commissioner or political officer with the force, losing courage, concluded the disgraceful Convention of Wargāon (January 1779), which actually stipulated for giving British hostages as security for the restoration to the Marāthās of all acquisitions made since 1773, and for the surrender of Ragoba. He relieved the British from the disgrace of betraying him by taking refuge with Sindia and arranging terms with him. In due course the convention was repudiated by the Directors, and the officers concerned were dismissed. Hastings observed that the document 'almost made me sink with shame when I read it'.

Goddard's expedition. Hastings having recovered power, as explained above, felt bound to retrieve the disgrace and support the Bombay government to the best of his ability. He conceived the bold plan of dispatching a Bengal force right across India through hostile states and country then unknown, under the conduct at first of Colonel Leslie, and then of Colonel (General) Goddard. The expeditionary force of more than 6,000 sepoys under European officers, and encumbered, as was the fashion of those days, by a crowd of camp followers and traders numbering about 30,000,[1] being admirably led, reached Surat in safety. In February 1779 Goddard occupied Ahmadābād and made an alliance with the Gaikwār of Baroda, which continued unbroken through all subsequent troubles.

Capture of Gwālior. His brilliant operation was supported by another admirably conducted expedition sent by Hastings into Central India. In August 1780 Major Popham most cleverly escaladed the strong fortress of Gwālior at night and took it without losing a man. Colonel Camac succeeded in surprising Sindia's camp and frightening him.

Treaty of Sālbāī. Towards the close of 1779 the Nizam had organized a coalition embracing all the Marāthā princes, except the Gaikwār, and including Haidar Ali of Mysore, in the hopes of destroying the growing English power. The principal Marāthā army was defeated, and the Rājā of Nāgpur was bought off. Haidar Ali was threatened by the successful march of a Bengal force under Colonel Pearse by land through 700 miles of almost unexplored country, an exploit second only to Goddard's march to Surat. Ultimately, peace was arranged with the aid of Māhādajī Sindia, the ablest and most powerful of the Marāthā chiefs.[2]

[1] Rennell, *Memoir*[3], 1793, p. 236 *n.*

[2] The name (माहाद्जी in Nāgarī characters) should be spelt as in the text. Authors who call the chief Mādho or Mādhava are in error.

GWĀLIOR FORT.

The treaty, signed at Sālbāī in Sindia's territory, secured Salsette for the English, gave Ragoba a pension, and in other respects mostly restored the old condition of affairs. Although the terms of peace as thus concisely stated may seem to be of small moment, the treaty of Sālbāī (1782) should be remembered as one of the landmarks in the history of India because it assured peace with the formidable power of the Marāthās for twenty years, and marked the ascendancy of the English as the controlling, although not yet the paramount government in India. The enemies of Hastings sneered at his 'frantic military exploits'. We may applaud unreservedly the energy, boldness, tenacity, and resource which enabled him to grapple successfully with his hydra-headed enemies. He may be described with justice as the Indian Pitt, 'the Chatham of the East'.

1782, an 'annus mirabilis'. The year 1782, it may be noted, was remarkable for many other important events in various parts of the world, namely, the resignation of Lord North, who had been in power as Prime Minister of England since 1770; the repulse of the Franco-Spanish main attack on Gibraltar; a great naval victory gained by Rodney in the West Indies; the death of Haidar Ali; and the establishment of Grattan's Parliament in Ireland. It was truly an *annus mirabilis*, a year of wonders. In 1779 the French fleet had become for a short time superior to the British. Rodney's victory gave Britain again the command of the sea on which the retention of India depends.

Māhādajī Sindia. A few words must be devoted to Māhādajī Sindia, the chief through whom the treaty of Sālbāī was negotiated. He was the illegitimate son of Rānoji Patēl, a Marāthā of humble origin who had started life as slipper-bearer to the Pēshwā, but rose in the world, as happened in those times. Māhādajī was present at the battle of Panīpat and was one of the few Marāthās of note who escaped with his life, although permanently lamed by a severe wound. He succeeded to his father's *jāgīrs*, and soon became the most prominent of the Marāthā chiefs. In those days the glory of the Pēshwā had been obscured, and real power was shared mostly by four territorial chiefs, namely, Sindia of Gwālior, Holkar of Indore, the Gaikwār of Baroda, and the Rājā of Nāgpur. When Shāh Ālam, the titular emperor, quitted British protection in 1771 and attained his desire of re-entering Delhi, Sindia furnished his escort and in practice became his jailor. The military ability displayed in 1780 and 1781 by the commanders whom Hastings had selected convinced Māhādajī that it was safer to treat with the British than to fight them. Accordingly he came to an understanding with Hastings, who was in urgent need of peace with the Marāthās. Even without their hostility his enemies were almost more than he could manage, and his financial embarrassment was extreme. The result of the friendly understanding was the treaty of Sālbāī, signed at the village of that name in Sindia's territory. Māhādajī conducted the negotiations in two capacities, as plenipotentiary empowered by the Pēshwā and as guarantor for the due execution of the compact. The transaction greatly enhanced his influence, so that his power grew rapidly. He trained infantry in the European fashion under foreign officers and by their help became for a few years the arbiter of Hindostan. Hastings has been criticized for his indifference to the aggrandizement of Sindia, but the fact was that he could not afford to quarrel with the Marāthā chief.

Count de Boigne. The most celebrated of the foreign generals employed by Sindia was Count de Boigne, whose remarkable career may conveniently receive a passing notice in this place. Monsieur de Boigne, after service in the French and Russian armies, made his way to India in 1778 at the age of twenty-seven and obtained a commission as ensign in a Madras infantry regiment. While so employed he narrowly escaped from being involved in Baillie's disaster in 1780. Quitting the British army, he tried various ways of making his fortune, and finally settled down to Sindia's service. He served his master well and loyally, and was the principal instrument in establishing Māhādajī's temporary lordship over Hindostan. In 1796, after his principal's death, de Boigne left India, and retired to his native place, Chambéry in Savoy. In the course of his Indian adventures he had accumulated without dishonour immense wealth, much of which he expended on charitable institutions and municipal improvements in his birthplace. The rulers of France and Savoy loaded him with well-deserved titles and distinctions. In 1830 he died in his eightieth year. Count de Boigne was the worthiest of the many European free-lances or military adventurers who swarmed at Indian courts in the latter half of the eighteenth and the earlier years of the nineteenth century.

COUNT DE BOIGNE.

Two contested incidents. Before entering upon the history of the Second Mysore War and describing the heroic exertions of Hastings and Sir Eyre Coote to save the Carnatic from the fury of Haidar Ali and his son and to counteract the corrupt incompetence of the Madras local government, it will be advisable to discuss with some fullness of detail two hotly contested incidents in the career of Hastings. The incidents are his treatment of Rājā Chait Singh of Benares and his extraction of a large sum, supposed to have been about 76 lakhs of rupees, from the coffers of the Bēgams of Oudh. Both affairs were the outcome of the pressing difficulties, political and financial, which beset the Governor-general during the terrible years from 1778 to 1781. No fair judgement can be passed upon his actions unless the existence of those difficulties be constantly present to the mind of the reader of his story.

Rājā Chait Singh. The action of the Governor-general on which the 1st article of impeachment was based was as follows :

When the war with France broke out in 1778 and the British power was in imminent danger, the Governor-general-in-Council required from Rājā Chait Singh, the ruler of Benares and adjoining districts, a special war contribution of five lakhs of rupees (then more than £50,000). An equal sum was exacted in each of the two succeeding years, 1779 and 1780, being fifteen lakhs, or over £150,000 in all. The Rājā naturally disliked such demands, and in 1780 so delayed remittances that the government found difficulty in paying Colonel Camac's detachment. The Rājā also failed to place 1,000 horsemen at the disposal of the authorities for the defence of Bihār, a province adjoining his territory, as demanded by Sir Eyre Coote, the commander-in-chief. Hastings suspected that the Rājā was planning revolt, and was well assured that he had plenty of both men and money. He regarded Chait Singh's delay in making payment of the special contribution in 1780 and his neglect to furnish horsemen in the same year as acts of contumacy and disloyalty, holding that the Rājā, as a zemindar or large landholder, under the sovereignty of the Company, was bound to give ready support to his superior in time of stress, in accordance with well-established usage. In his *Narrative* Hastings frankly states that 'he considered Cheit Sing as culpable in a very high degree towards our state, and his punishment . . . as an example which justice and policy required. . . . In a word, I had determined to make him pay largely for his pardon, or to exact a severe vengeance for his past delinquency.' In pursuit of that resolve Hastings *intended* to levy a fine of 40 or 50 lakhs, and communicated his intention to his colleague, Mr. Wheler. No demand for such fine was ever actually made, and nobody except Mr. Wheler knew of the Governor-general's intention. Hastings went to Benares to execute his plans, repelled the humble advances made by the Rājā, and ordered his arrest, to which Chait Singh submitted quietly. A tumult arose, in the course of which a number of officers and sepoys were killed. Hastings was obliged to fly to the fortress of Chunar. After considerable fighting Chait Singh was defeated and compelled to take refuge among the Marāthās. He was deposed and a relative was installed in his place. The army seized the funds taken in his fort as prize-money, so that none of the money reached the Treasury. The new Rājā was assessed to land revenue at a sum nearly double that paid by Chait Singh, and was deprived of the power to coin money, as well as of civil and criminal jurisdiction over Benares city, and of criminal jurisdiction in the whole of his country.[1]

The main issue. For those proceedings Hastings was impeached on the allegation of Pitt that his conduct was 'cruel, unjust, and oppressive'. The main issue taken was the status of Rājā Chait Singh. Was he an independent sovereign prince or a mere zemindar? It was conclusively established that he was only a zemindar, not an independent prince, although allowed the exceptional privilege of coining money. His possession of civil and criminal jurisdiction proved nothing, because under the Muhammadan governments all large zemindars exercised such jurisdiction. The sovereignty of the Benares province undoubtedly had been vested in the Company from 1775. It is also certain that Chait Singh was an illegitimate son of his predecessor, and that his succession was due to the personal initiative of Hastings.

Criticism. Concerning the justice and propriety of the action taken by Hastings my opinion is that the grave necessities of the situation justified the demand of exceptional war subsidies from a subordinate ruler in the position of Rājā Chait Singh; that he could have afforded to pay them without undue strain; that he could have supplied and ought to have furnished the 1,000 horsemen finally demanded; and that Hastings was injudicious and imprudent in arresting the Rājā, whom he treated with improper harshness. The proposed fine of 40 or 50 lakhs was excessive. All legitimate objects apparently could have been attained without violence. No praise can be too great for the energy and resource shown by Hastings in dealing with the outbreak produced by the arrest of the Rājā. Probably the excessive severity practised and intended by Hastings was partly due to his personal resentment against the Rājā for having sought to curry favour with the hostile members of council while they were in power. The errors of Hastings in the business, whatever they may have been, did not deserve impeachment, and his acquittal on the Benares charge by a large majority of the Lords was right.

Affair of the Bēgams of Oudh. The next case for consideration is that of the exaction of about 76 lakhs of rupees from the Bēgams of Oudh, the mother and grandmother of the Nawāb-Vizier, Āsafu-d daula, and the employment of severities to compel the eunuchs in charge of the treasure to disgorge.

Abstract of the facts. The Company always had had a heavy bill pending against the Nawāb-Vizier for arrears of subsidy, due for the maintenance of the troops who secured his dominions against external aggression in the midst of wars. The Nawāb, Āsafu-d daula, was a wretched, worthless creature, wholly incapable of governing and surrounded by gangs of greedy adventurers, Indian and European. In 1781 the arrears were particularly

[1] Benares occupied a special position as the head-quarters of Hinduism and the resort of princes and people of all ranks from every part of India, so that the proper administration of the city was a matter of more than local concern.

heavy, and the requirements of the Marāthā, Benares, and Carnatic wars had exhausted the Company's treasury. After the suppression of Rājā Chait Singh, Hastings met the Nawāb at Chunar and concluded a treaty or arrangement by which it was hoped that the Nawāb's difficulties might be adjusted and the Company's necessities satisfied. Hastings undertook to clear the European adventurers out of Oudh and to relieve the Nawāb of a portion of the military charges. The Nawāb not only agreed but expressed a strong desire to resume the *jāgīrs*, or grants of lands made to the Bēgams and other persons, and to recover his father's treasure which the Bēgams had been allowed to retain in 1775, with the sanction of the majority in council hostile to Hastings. In 1781 the Governor-general held that the complicity of the Bēgams in Chait Singh's revolt was fully established and warranted the cancellation of the arrangement made in 1775 by which the ladies had been allowed to retain the treasure subject to a payment in satisfaction of all demands amounting to 30 lakhs (also stated as 50). When the Nawāb was required actually to resume the *jāgīrs* and recover the treasure he naturally hesitated to take proceedings against such near relatives, and the Resident, Mr. Middleton, failed to enforce compliance. Hastings, being determined to get the money from the 'old women' who, as he observed, 'had very nigh effected our destruction', wrote severe reproofs to Middleton for his remissness. The screw was then applied vigorously. The Bēgams' palace at Fyzabad was occupied by troops, and the ladies with their attendants, although not personally mishandled, were put to much inconvenience. Their two confidential eunuchs in charge of the treasure were placed on short commons, lightly ironed, and perhaps beaten. The Resident certainly handed them over to the Nawāb to do what he pleased with them. By those measures, which any Hindu or Muhammadan government would have regarded as normal, the money was obtained and the debt to the Company was cleared off. During the operations Hastings, who was in Calcutta, was not personally cognizant of the details of the severities employed. How far he would have sanctioned them if asked does not appear. It is beyond doubt that no grave personal injury was inflicted on the eunuchs, who lived rich and prosperous for years afterwards. During the impeachment the Bēgams were among the numerous persons who sent in unsolicited and obviously sincere testimonials in favour of Hastings while the trial was in progress.

Comment. If the urgent necessities of the time be remembered Hastings may be considered to have been justified in cancelling the arrangement sanctioned by his hostile colleagues in 1775, and in putting a certain amount of pressure on the Bēgams to make them disgorge. The severities used by his agents without his immediate personal knowledge, while not legitimate according to European standards of conduct, were thoroughly in accordance with Indian practice, and would have been regarded by Indian opinion as mild measures. The Bēgams themselves bore no malice for their rough treatment. Critics should remember that until quite recent days, and within my own experience, it was a point of honour in India not to pay money until coercion had been applied. Landholders with the cash tied up in their waistbands would submit to be beaten in order to satisfy the public opinion of their fellows before they would pay out the land revenue admittedly due. Hastings was familiar with such practices and must have had them at the back of his mind when he abstained from asking questions about the exact degree of coercion applied to the people at Fyzabad. The business, which formed the subject of the second charge at the impeachment, was ludicrously exaggerated by the prosecutors and made an excuse for much raving rhetoric. The Lords had the good sense to acquit Hastings on the charge by a majority of 23 to 6.

Second Mysore War. The way has now been cleared for the study of the last and most strenuous campaign conducted under the general direction of Hastings—the Second Mysore War, fought primarily for the defence of the Carnatic against Haidar Ali and his son Tippoo (Tipū), but involving various subsidiary military operations and political transactions. The war lasted from July 1780 to March 1784.

Capture of the French settlements. France having united her forces with those of the revolted American colonies, war between France and England was declared in 1778. Early intimation of the event was received by the Governor-general through the overland route, which had been opened for a short time, as already mentioned. The French settlements were promptly attacked, and Pondicherry fell after a gallant resistance. The little French station of Mahé on the Malabar coast was taken in the same month, and, after a short occupation, was dismantled. It was useful to Haidar Ali as a port through which he received supplies, so that the British attack upon the place annoyed him. Sir Thomas Rumbold, the governor of Madras, opposed the operation for that reason, but was overruled by Sir Eyre Coote, who felt bound to carry out the orders of the home government.

Hostile confederacy. The current histories generally state that the formation in 1779 of a confederacy against the English by the Nizam, including both the Marāthās and Mysore, was due to the Nizam's resentment at the annexation of the Guntūr District in the northern Sarkārs. That resentment was a factor in the Nizam's policy, but the Rumbold papers show that his displeasure had been aroused at an earlier date by the support given to his enemy Ragoba by the Bombay government, and by a project which Hastings had planned for an alliance with the Marāthā Rājā of Nāgpur. In 1780 Hastings, by giving up Guntūr, secured the neutrality of the Nizam, who was offended by Haidar Ali's intrigues at Delhi.[1]

[1] For the Rumbold papers see Marshman, *History of India*, vol. i (ed. 1869), Appendix; and Miss Rumbold's book, *A Vindication . . . of Sir*

The Madras government. The Madras government under Sir Thomas Rumbold in 1779 repeatedly sent warnings to Bengal that an attack by Haidar Ali was to be feared and that the local resources were insufficient to meet it. But in January 1780 Hastings wrote that 'I am convinced from Hyder's conduct and disposition that he will never molest us while we preserve a good understanding with him'. When Sir Thomas Rumbold was quitting India in bad health at the beginning of April 1780 he had come round to the same opinion and expressed a belief that peace would be maintained. Both Hastings and Rumbold were honestly mistaken. Although the Madras government was torn by internal dissensions and saturated with corruption, there is excellent reason for believing that the charges of personal corruption against Sir Thomas Rumbold were unfounded. The weakness and other defects of the local administration consequent on the rotten system of 'double government', which still recognized the worthless Nawāb as the sovereign of the Carnatic, poisoned the whole policy of Madras and prevented the elaboration of adequate measures for defence. Thornton observes that at that time the moral atmosphere of Madras 'was pestilential: corruption revelled unrestrained. . . . It is not wonderful that where public spirit and public decency were alike extinct, the government should have been neither wise nor strong.' The Nawāb was wholly in the hands of money-lenders, whose baneful influence dominated the Madras council.

Invasion by Haidar Ali. In June 1780 Haidar Ali moved from Seringapatam his capital, and descended on the Carnatic plain with a force of 70,000 or 80,000 men, including a body of four hundred Europeans under Lally junior. He plundered Porto Novo as well as Conjeeveram, distant less than fifty miles from the capital, and committed horrid cruelties on a systematic plan. The inhabitants, notwithstanding his savagery, seem to have preferred Haidar Ali to their own Nawāb, and furnished the invader with information which was refused to the British defenders of Muhammad Ali.

The country was stripped so bare that the most necessary supplies for even a small army were almost unprocurable. The force under the command of Sir Hector Munro, numbering only about 8,000 men, was continually hampered by lack of money, food, and transport. The commander-in-chief, then fifty-four years of age, was no longer the man he had been at Buxar. Indeed, his conduct amounted almost to imbecility, so that Marshman denounces him as 'the dastardly Munro'.

Fortunately, Haidar Ali was left to fight his battles alone. The Marāthās gave him no support. The Marāthā chiefs in Orissa were bought over by Hastings, who was clever enough to persuade them to allow the passage through their territory of a

Thomas Rumbold (London, Longmans, 1868). Rumbold went to Europe on urgent medical advice.

reinforcement under Colonel Pearse which marched from Bengal by land.

Disaster of Colonel Baillie. On September 10, 1780, an appalling and apparently wholly unnecessary disaster befell the British army. Colonel Baillie, who was marching with 2,813 men from Guntūr, subsequently raised to 3,720 by a reinforcement, in order to join Munro, who had 5,209, was overwhelmed by Haidar Ali's son Tippoo near Conjeeveram, although the commander-in-chief was only about two miles distant. Munro's excuses for his failure to succour Baillie were feeble and unconvincing, and Baillie's leadership was marred by errors. The detachment when surrounded fought so gallantly that out of eighty-six British officers engaged only sixteen surrendered unwounded. Baillie and all the survivors who were taken prisoners suffered unspeakable ill treatment. The painful details have been recorded by several of the victims.

Action of Hastings. A special dispatch vessel brought the ill news to Bengal. The spirit of Hastings rose nobly to the occasion. Forsaking all other plans he resolved to hasten peace with the Marāthās and to send every man and every rupee he could collect to save the Carnatic. Within three weeks Sir Eyre Coote was dispatched by sea with fifteen lakhs of rupees, about four hundred Europeans and some gunners, a thousand men in all, while the detachment under Pearse marched by land. The corrupt and incompetent governor of Madras, a person named Whitehill, was suspended, and every possible measure was taken to repair past mismanagement. Space fails to narrate in detail the incidents of the melancholy war which followed. Its unpleasant story is redeemed by acts of heroism which may be read in the pages of Wilks.

Battle of Porto Novo. After several months of ineffectual operations Haidar Ali was brought to bay at Porto Novo on July 1, 1781, and decisively defeated by Coote, with a loss estimated at 10,000 killed and wounded. The casualties on the British side were only 306. It is curious to find that on this occasion Sir Hector Munro, who served under Coote, was praised for 'conduct equally spirited and active', a strange contrast with his behaviour in the matter of Baillie's disaster. General Stuart, who afterwards displayed utter incompetence as commander-in-chief, also was commended for highly meritorious service.

Other less decisive successes were gained by Coote at Pollilore and Sholinghur.

Lord Macartney. Lord Macartney, a nobleman of considerable distinction, who had been sent out from England in the hope that he might reform Madras, took charge of the local government just before the battle of Porto Novo. He strongly disapproved of the Marāthā war, and was so eager for peace that he sent a most improper letter to the Marāthā chiefs, offering to guarantee any treaty that might be arranged by the Governor-general, and promising the restoration of Gujarāt, Salsette, and Bassein.[1] It is astounding that a subordinate administration should have dared to issue such a document. The blunder, which did not stand alone, necessarily produeed strained relations between the governments of Bengal and Madras, and the southern presidency continued to pay the penalty for official friction in high places.

Admiral de Suffren. In the course of 1782 the hopes of Haidar Ali were raised by the appearance of a powerful French squadron under the command of Admiral de Suffren (Suffrein), an able officer. Five actions were fought between him and Admiral Sir Edward Hughes, resulting in mueh damage to both combatants without decisive result. The interruption of sea-borne supplies caused a distressing famine at Madras and a large mortality. The French admiral was accompanied by Bussy, then 'gouty, worn out, and querulous', and eonsequently quite useless.

Failure and death of Haidar Ali. In December Haidar Ali died at the age of sixty.[2] Coote had been obliged by ill health to return to Caleutta, and General Stuart, his successor, lost the opportunity presented by the passing of the ruler of Mysore.

Haidar Ali knew before he died that he had failed. Whenever he had met Coote in the field he had been beaten; the hopes of French aid had come to naught; the Marāthās, according to their nature, had betrayed him, and even meditated an attack upon him from the north; while the Nāyars (Nairs) of Malabar were in revolt. 'Deeply refleeting on this unprosperous aspect of affairs,' he resolved to give up his attempt to hold the Carnatic, concentrating his attention on the western coast and the defence of Mysore. In August 1782 the Bombay government had dispatched Colonel Humberston (Mackenzie) to operate in Malabar. After the rains Haidar Ali sent Tippoo to defend his western provinces. While he was thus engaged his father died. Ingenious arrangements were made to conceal the fact of Haidar's decease until Tippoo had secured the succession.

Not long before his death Haidar Ali had a talk with his minister Pūrnia (Poornea), whom he addressed in this remarkable language:

> 'I have committed a great error; I have purchased a draught of spirits at the price of a lakh of pagodas;[3] I shall pay dearly for my arrogance:

[1] The fact is recorded without eomment by Mill (iv. 157), who seems to have been unconscious of the enormity of Lord Macartney's offence. On the other hand, the interference of Caleutta sometimes was practised in an irritating way.

[2] Wilks gives the date of his death as December 7 (reprint, ii. 33). Robson (p. 155) gives it as November 9. The concealment of the event for a time evidently caused doubts concerning the exact date. Thornton, Forrest, and a crowd of other authors state erroneously either that Haidar Ali died at the age of eighty or at a very advanced age. It is certain that he was only sixty, having been born in 1722.

[3] Wilks explains the meaning of the exact terms used. A lakh of pagodas was worth £40,000.

between the English and me there were perhaps mutual grounds of dissatisfaction, but not sufficient cause for war, and I might have made them my friends in spite of Muhammad Ali, the most treacherous of men. The defeat of many Braithwaites and Baillies will not destroy them. I can ruin their resources by land, but I cannot dry up the sea, and I must be first weary of a war in which I can gain nothing by fighting.'

He concluded by lamenting how he had been deceived by the Marāthās and disappointed by the French. Colonel Braithwaite, when encamped with about 2,000 men in the Tanjore territory, had been surrounded by a superior force under Tippoo and suffered the fate of Baillie, early in 1782.

HAIDAR ALI.

Sir Eyre Coote died in 1783, a few months after the decease of his antagonist.

Character of Haidar Ali. Haidar Ali in the south and Ranjit Singh in the north were the ablest of the fierce adventurers who rose to power during the turmoil of the eighteenth century. Both were illiterate and absolutely unscrupulous. Haidar Ali had no religion, no morals, and no compassion. He relied on savage terrorism and strict personal supervision of every act of government. 'No person of respectability', it was said, 'ever left his house with the expectation of returning safe to it,' and the highest officers in his service were liable to brutal floggings.[1] He spoke five languages fluently and ordered his affairs with regularity and

[1] On one occasion he flogged his son Tippoo severely in public. Compare Akbar's more private buffeting of Prince Salīm.

swift dispatch. Like Akbar, he remedied his lack of formal education by a memory of extraordinary power. He could go through complicated arithmetical calculations with accuracy equal and quickness superior to that of an expert accountant. He was skilled in the necessary art of appreciating character, and may be said to have justly earned his success in those wild times by the superiority of his personal endowments as compared with those of his equally wicked but less able rivals. No Indian politician in those days pretended to have any principles. Each one of them fought for his own hand with undisguised selfishness.

End of Carnatic war ; peace of Versailles. Before proceeding to glance for a moment at the subsidiary operations in Malabar, it will be well to dispose of the war in the Carnatic. Unhappy dissensions between Lord Macartney, the Company's governor of Madras, and General Stuart, a 'King's officer', holding a commission directly from the Crown, paralysed the operations in Madras territory and imperilled the safety of the army. A force besieging Cuddalore, where French and Mysorean troops had taken refuge, was even in danger of being lost when news arrived in June 1783 that peace between France and England had been signed at Versailles.[1] The combatants in India made no attempt to carry on unofficial hostilities. All military operations ceased on July 2, which, accordingly, is the date of the close of the Second Mysore War, so far as the Carnatic was concerned.

Defence of Mangalore. Tippoo not being a party to the Versailles compact, the war in Malabar continued. The Bombay authorities appointed General Matthews to the supreme command. The incidents of the contest included the taking of Bednūr (Bednore) by Colonel Macleod and its recapture by Tippoo, as well as many other interesting happenings deserving of notice if space permitted. The most notable event was Colonel Campbell's gallant defence of Mangalore, 'a common country fort of the fourth or fifth order', which held out until reduced by famine. General Macleod's failure to relieve the place may be reckoned as the most scandalous occurrence of the campaign, which was marked by more than one scandal. Campbell's defence, which was at least equal to Clive's famous performance at Arcot, had not the good fortune to receive equally brilliant literary applause and is rarely remembered or mentioned.

Treaty of Mangalore. Although Tippoo had gained considerable successes, his resources were much exhausted by long continued war,[2] and his capital was threatened by Colonel Fullarton, who

[1] Sometimes, as by Gardiner, called the Treaty of Paris.

[2] The exhaustion of the resources of Haidar Ali and Tippoo is explained by the general remarks of Mr. Verelst contained in a letter to the Directors dated March 28, 1768, which throw much light on the growth of British dominion in India. The writer dilates on 'the general indigence of the Mogul empire', and proceeds :

'The natural consequence of these circumstances has been, that the different powers find their finances narrow, and their treasures unequal to

had occupied Coimbatore with 13,000 men, and had devised a well-planned campaign. A strong, courageous government at Madras might have dictated an advantageous treaty. Unfortunately, Lord Macartney, who desired peace almost at any price, allowed himself to be manœuvred into the attitude of a suppliant. The advance of Colonel Fullarton was stopped, and envoys were sent to the camp of Tippoo, where they were treated with almost incredible insolence, to which they tamely submitted. At last, when Tippoo realized the danger of being attacked by both the British and Marāthās, and feared that the patience even of the long-suffering Lord Macartney might be exhausted, he graciously signed the treaty of Mangalore on March 11, 1784. The document provided for mutual restitution of conquests and the liberation of the surviving prisoners in the hands of the Sultan. Tippoo gave up 180 officers, 900 European soldiers, and 1,600 sepoys, 2,680 in all. But the abject governor of Madras had not spirit enough to insist on a complete jail delivery, and some miserable victims were left in the tyrant's hands to suffer a sad fate later.

Hastings, while loathing the disgraceful compact, and resenting the insults which attended its execution, lacked the cordial support of the ministry in England, and was not in a position to refuse ratification. 'What a man is this Lord Macartney!' he exclaimed; 'I yet believe that, in spite of the peace, he will effect the loss of the Carnatic.'[1]

Thus ended in dishonour the Second Mysore War, including the Carnatic War terminated in July 1783, and the Malabar operations closed in March 1784. Such a peace carried within it the seeds of a new war, which duly followed in the days of Lord Cornwallis. The Madras government, disobeying express instructions to negotiate on the basis of the treaty of Sālbāī, omitted to make any reference

the maintenance of a respectable army, or the prosecution of a war of any duration. Whenever, therefore, they are urged by ambition or necessity to enter on any expedition, they assemble new levies for the purpose with the most unreflecting precipitancy; they risk every thing on one campaign, because they seldom have resources for a second, and come to an engagement at all events, because the consequences of a defeat are less terrible than those which must ensue from the desertion, or sedition of an ill-paid and disaffected army. As their troops are chiefly raw men and aliens, they are without attachment to their general, or confidence in each other; a variety of subordinate commanders destroys all subordination and authority; and the certainty of beggary and starving, from the common accidents of war, throws a damp on the most ardent bravery.

These circumstances, I apprehend, gentlemen, have been very principal sources of our repeated victories over these immense Asiatic armies, which have fled before a handful of your troops. . . . A second, and no less powerful for the security of our situation, is the discordancy of the principles, views, and interests of the neighbouring powers. . . . The majority of the present princes of Hindostan have no natural right to the countries they possess' (*A View*, App., p. 101).

[1] Gleig, iii. 186.

to that document. Hastings had much trouble to persuade Sindia and the other Marāthā leaders that he was not responsible for the erroneous form given to the Mangalore compact by the perverse government of Madras.

Retirement of Hastings. The work of Hastings in India substantially closed when he gave unwilling assent to the humiliating treaty of Mangalore. The Court of Proprietors, or general meeting of the shareholders in the East India Company, gave him almost unanimous support, but Pitt, the Prime Minister, had become hostile, and towards the close of 1784 intimated his disapproval of several features in the policy of Hastings. The position of the Governor-general was much affected by the clash of parliamentary parties. In those days Indian affairs were the battle-ground of the party leaders to a degree never known before or since. It is impossible in this place to go into details of the parliamentary conflicts which ultimately led to the impeachment proceedings. Two India Bills prepared by Fox, the rival and opponent of Pitt, were defeated in 1783, much to the satisfaction of Hastings. But he equally disliked Pitt's bill, which became law in 1784, and clearly perceived that his resignation was desired. The general knowledge that his withdrawal from the Indian stage was imminent seriously weakened his authority both in the Calcutta council and at Madras. Under such conditions he could not desire to remain in office. He therefore resigned, and on February 1, 1785, made over charge to his colleague, Mr. John Macpherson, who was second in council.

Hastings in retirement. The life of Warren Hastings was prolonged after his retirement from India for thirty-three years until 1818, when he passed away at the age of eighty-five in peace with honour. He never again took an active part in public affairs, save as the victim of the long-drawn agony of the impeachment. When he went home he had every reason to believe that he would receive the rewards justly due for his eminent services to India and his country. The malice of Philip Francis, the frenzied zeal of Burke, and the cold hostility of Pitt not only robbed him of his reward, but consumed his moderate fortune, and subjected him to the fiercest ordeal of inquisition ever endured by any statesman.

Impeachment. The responsibility for his prosecution rests solely upon Pitt, whose decision still causes legitimate astonishment, even when viewed in the light of the words of his colleague Dundas contained in a letter dated March 21, 1787, addressed to Lord Cornwallis:

'The only unpleasant circumstance is the impeachment of Mr. Hastings. Mr. Pitt and I have got great credit from the undeviating fairness and candour with which we have proceeded in it, but the proceeding is not pleasant to many of our friends; and of course from that and other circumstances, not pleasing to us; but the truth is, when we examined the various articles of charges against him with his defences, they were so strong, and the defences so perfectly unsupported, it was impossible not to concur; and some of the charges will unquestionably go to the House of Lords.' [1]

That statement is open to much criticism, but the story of the impeachment belongs to the domain of biography and parliamentary polemics rather than to the history of India. It is sufficient to chronicle the bare facts that the trial began on February 13, 1788, and ended on April 23, 1795, with a verdict of acquittal; that sixteen questions were put to the twenty-nine lords who voted; that the acquittal was unanimous in two cases, including the principal charges of corruption; and that the minority in favour of conviction on the other charges ranged from two to six. The Court of Proprietors wished to give Hastings a pension of £5,000 and to pay his costs to the extent of £71,080, but Pitt and Dundas vetoed the proposed grants. The Directors managed to give him an allowance sufficient to permit of his living at Daylesford, an estate of 650 acres, as a benevolent country gentleman in decent comfort until the end. Throughout those long years he maintained an attitude of dignified serenity, and when his time came died like a gentleman. The Horatian motto, *Mens aequa in arduis*, inscribed under one of the best known of his many portraits, indicates exactly his bearing in the face of adversity.

Character of Warren Hastings. Probably no person equipped with tolerably accurate knowledge of the facts could now be found to deny that the impeachment of Hastings was undeserved. His few errors, so far as they were real, were those of a statesman exposed to imminent peril and beset by embarrassments so complex that fallible human judgement was bound to err occasionally. Can any statesman be named who never made a mistake, or perpetrated a job under pressure? If Hastings deserved impeachment, how many potentates and prime ministers would be entitled to impunity? Hastings should be judged by the standard applicable to sovereigns or prime ministers. It is impossible to contest the truth of the observation of Lord Cornwallis that he was 'unjustly and cruelly persecuted'. The foulness of the abuse heaped upon him by Burke and the other orators for the prosecution would be incredible were it not recorded to their everlasting shame.[2] The violence of Burke's language was so

[1] Ross, *Correspondence of Marquis Cornwallis*², vol. i, p. 293. The process of impeachment, which had many defects as a mode of trial, is obsolete and not likely to be revived. After the trial of Hastings it was used only once when Dundas (Lord Melville) was the accused person. He, too, was acquitted, in 1806. In an impeachment the House of Commons prosecutes through the agency of managers, and the House of Lords finds a verdict after the manner of a jury. Each peer votes separately, giving his finding on his honour. For criticism of the statement by Dundas and the reasons for the apparent weakness of the defences see Forrest, *Selections*, p. xv. Macaulay gives a brilliant description of the impressive scene at the opening of the trial.

[2] For an anthology of Burke's flowers of speech see *The History of the Trial of Warren Hastings, Esq.*, part v, pp. 151–4 (London, 1796).

disgusting that on one occasion it drew down the grave censure of the House of Commons.

James Mill, who had devoted many pages to unsparing criticism of the acts and policy of Hastings, felt himself constrained when quitting the subject to pen a partial recantation and bear emphatic testimony to the rare gifts of the man whom he had treated so ill. It is true that the praise is qualified by the absurdly false statement that Hastings 'had no genius, any more than Clive, for schemes of policy including large views of the past, and large anticipations of the future'. The exact contrary is the truth. Anybody who studies the letters and minutes written by Hastings cannot fail to recognize the largeness of his mind and the breadth of his views. The somewhat unwilling eulogy pronounced by Mill includes the following propositions which any of the rulers of India might be glad to have inscribed upon his tomb.

WARREN HASTINGS
(in old age).

'It is necessary, for the satisfaction of my own mind, and to save me from the fear of having given a more unfavourable conception than I intended of his character and conduct, to impress upon the reader the obligation of considering two things. The first is, that Mr. Hastings was placed in difficulties, and acted upon by temptations, such as few public men have been called upon to overcome: and of this the preceding history affords abundant evidence. The second is, that no man, probably, who ever had a great share in the government of the world, had his public conduct so completely explored and laid open to view. . . . It is my firm conviction, that if we had the same advantage with respect to other men, who have been as much engaged in the conduct of public affairs, and could view their conduct as completely naked, and stripped of all its disguises, few of them would be found, whose character would present a higher claim to indulgence than his. In point of ability, he is beyond all question the most eminent of the chief rulers whom the Company have ever employed, nor is there any one of them, who would not have succumbed under the difficulties, which, if he did not overcome, he at any rate sustained. . . . He was the first, or among the first, of the servants of the Company, who attempted to acquire any language of the natives, and who set on foot those liberal inquiries into the language and literature of the Hindus,[1] which have led to the satisfactory knowledge of the present day. He had the great art of a ruler, which consists in attaching to the Governor those who are governed; his administration assuredly was popular, both with his countrymen and the natives in Bengal.' [2]

It is not easy to recognize as the same man the tyrannical oppressor depicted in such lurid colours by Burke, Sheridan, and Macaulay. 'We may', as Wilson remarks in a note, 'look now with wonder, not unmixed with contempt, upon the almost insane virulence with which he was assailed, and think of him in no other character than that of the ablest of the able men who have given to Great Britain her Indian Empire.'

Warren Hastings should not be treated as a man lucky enough to escape conviction in court and qualified for the indulgence of superior persons. He is entitled to warm appreciation of his uncommon powers, and to the affectionate admiration of Europeans and Indians alike. As a young man he emerged unscathed from temptations to which his contemporaries succumbed. As a mature man of forty he took charge of Bengal with absolutely unsullied hands. Throughout his official life he laboured unceasingly for the public good. Whatever judgement modern critics may pass upon the propriety of certain acts of policy, nobody who knows the facts can deny that Hastings gave his best to the service both of England and of India.

His industry was almost superhuman, his resolution inflexible, his patience abounding, his courage imperturbable, and his dignity unfailing. Throughout the long years of the impeachment torture he bore with stoic equanimity the buffets inflicted by lesser men, and at last towards the close of his long life attained general recognition of his merits.

In private life, as a contemporary truly said, 'all who knew him loved him, and they who knew him most loved him best'.[3] His generosity was inexhaustible and often overstepped the bounds of prudence. It is impossible to read the letters to his 'beloved Marian' who shared his joys and sorrows for so many years, or those addressed to intimate friends without feeling the charm as well as admiring the ability of the writer.

Hastings in his old age was indeed the Happy Warrior,

> Who, if he rise to station of command,
> Rises by open means; and there will stand
> On honourable terms, or else retire,
> And in himself possess his own desire. . . .

[1] Add 'and Muhammadans'.

[2] The admitted popularity of Hastings among the 'natives of Bengal' is in itself a conclusive answer to the accusations of oppression. The oppressed do not love their tyrants.

[3] The extensive, although still very incomplete, publication of the private correspondence of Hastings produces the same effect on students of his life. 'Mr. Hastings's tastes were essentially domestic,' as a correspondent writes in Gleig, iii. 533.

Whose powers shed round him in the common strife,
Or mild concerns of ordinary life,
A constant influence, a peculiar grace. . . .
He who, though thus endued as with a sense
And faculty for storm and turbulence,
Is yet a Soul whose master bias leans
To home-felt pleasures and to gentle scenes. . . .
Whom neither shape of danger can dismay,
Nor thought of tender happiness betray. . . .
This is the Happy Warrior ; this is He
Whom every Man in arms should wish to be.

Pitt's India Act. The Bills prepared by Fox having been rejected by the Lords,

'like other ministers, Pitt found himself compelled to introduce and defend when in office measures which he had denounced when in opposition. The chief ground of attack on Fox's Bill was its wholesale transfer of patronage from the Company to nominees of the Crown. Pitt steered clear of this rock of offence. He also avoided the appearance of radically altering the constitution of the Company. But his measure was based on the same substantial principle as that of his predecessor and rival, the principle of placing the Company in direct and permanent subordination to a body representing the British Government.

The Act of 1784 begins by establishing a board of six commissioners, who were formally styled the "Commissioners for the Affairs of India", but were popularly known as the "Board of Control".'

The Board met for a time and Pitt took part in its deliberations, but it soon ceased to assemble, and its power was exercised by a single member, the President. In modern times a similar fate has befallen the Board of Trade.[1]

The Board was given power 'from time to time, to check. superintend, and control all acts, operations, and concerns which in any wise relate to the civil or military government or revenues of the territories and possessions of the said United Company in the East Indies'. At the same time a Committee of Secrecy was constituted, consisting of three Directors of the Company, through whom all important communications from the Board were to be sent. The remaining twenty-one Directors were excluded from any share of political power, and the Court of Proprietors, whose independence had offended ministers, was restricted from interfering with the decisions of the Board.

'The control of the Governor-general and Council over the minor presidencies was enlarged, and was declared to extend to "all such points as relate to any transactions with the country powers, or to war or peace,

[1] At first the Secretary in the Home Department was the President, *ex officio*, and without extra salary. Dundas was the third of such Presidents. 'The system was changed in 1793, when the presidentship was made a separate appointment with a salary.' Dundas continued to retain the office until 1801 (Malcolm). He was created Viscount Melville in 1802.

or to the application of the revenues or forces of such presidencies in time of war ".

An attempt to stay the inevitable development of British dominion in India was made by the emphatic declaration that 'to pursue schemes of conquest and extension of dominion in India are measures repugnant to the wish, the honour, and policy of this nation', and by the formal positive enactment that

'it should not be lawful for the Governor-general and his council, without the express authority and consent of the Court of Directors, or of the secret committee, to declare war, or commence hostilities, or enter into any treaty for making war, against any of the country princes or States in India, or any treaty for guaranteeing the possession of any country prince or State, except where hostilities had actually been commenced, or preparations actually made for the commencement of hostilities, against the British nation in India, or against some of the princes or States who were dependent thereon, or whose territories were guaranteed by any existing treaty.' [1]

WILLIAM PITT THE YOUNGER.

The Act contains many other provisions, but those cited are the most important. Nearly at the same time Acts passed at various dates remedied the worst defects of the Regulating Act of 1773, defining the jurisdiction of the Supreme Court, giving the Governor-general power to overrule his council, and introducing other administrative changes which need not be detailed.

Patronage remained in the hands of the Directors, who retained the power even of recalling a Governor-general. When they exercised that power in the case of Lord Ellenborough Queen Victoria was much annoyed.

The modern Secretary of State for India represents the President of the Board of Control, and his Council, which has a Secret Committee of its own, takes the place occupied by the secret committee of the Court of Directors. The 'double government'

[1] The quotations are partly from Mill and partly from Ilbert. The latter author notes that 'almost the whole' of Pitt's India Act (24 Geo. III. sess. 2, c. 25) 'has been repealed, but many of its provisions were re-enacted in the subsequent Acts of 1793, 1813, and 1833'.

of Crown and Company set up by Pitt's Act subsisted with little material change until 1858. The machinery was cumbrous and dilatory in working, but no government cared to undertake the task of eliminating the Company from the administrative mechanism until the shock of the Mutiny forced the hand of ministers.

Sir John Macpherson. Mr. (Sir John) Macpherson, the senior member of council, who took the place of Hastings pending the appointment of a permanent successor, had a bad record. Originally a ship's purser, he had been employed as a secret agent for the Nawāb of the Carnatic, whose affairs were a mass of corruption. He got into the service of the Company by backstairs influence, was deservedly, although irregularly, dismissed by Lord Pigot, governor of Madras; was reinstated by the Directors, and sent out to replace Barwell on the Bengal council. During his administration, which lasted for twenty months, Māhādajī Sindia, who had obtained the government of the provinces of Agra and Delhi with complete control of the titular emperor, and the imperial army,[1] had the audacity to demand payment of *chauth* for the British provinces. It need hardly be said that the impudent request met with a peremptory refusal. Macpherson does not seem to have been responsible for the scandalous action of Dundas, President of the Board of Control, who insisted on paying off the alleged debts of the Nawāb of the Carnatic amounting to about five millions sterling without examination. The action of the President, although not taken for the sake of personal gain, was essentially corrupt, being dictated by a desire to retain the parliamentary influence wielded by Mr. Paul Benfield and other dishonest usurers who had secured control of the Nawāb's finances. The same motive induced the minister to cancel the assignment of the Carnatic revenues to the Company, which had been arranged by Lord Macartney.[2] That nobleman resigned his office as governor of Madras when his principal measure was reversed. Negotiations for his appointment as Governor-general came to nothing, and Lord Cornwallis was appointed.

Sir John Macpherson effected some financial economies, chiefly by the reduction of salaries, but deserves no commendation. His successor, Lord Cornwallis, a thoroughly honest man, would neither believe a word he wrote, nor touch the corrupt jobs which he recommended. His government is described as 'a system of the dirtiest jobbing', and the man himself is justly held up to

[1] As a matter of form the Pēshwā was appointed *Vakīl-i mutlak*, or 'Vicegerent of the Empire', and Sindia was styled his deputy. The nominal emperor, of course, had to do as he was told. His name, however, still was respected to a certain extent, and his grants gave a pleasing appearance of legality to lawless proceedings. European writers of the period usually call the Pādshāh 'the King'.

[2] The alleged jobs of Hastings were trifles compared with the doings of Dundas, his accuser.

seorn as 'weak and false to a degree, and he eertainly was the most eontemptible and the most eontemned governor that ever pretended to govern '.[1]

Sir John Maleolm, while giving full credit to Hastings for his 'personal integrity' and the 'aetive energy of a great statesman' direeted to the saving of the interests of his country in India from ruin, is eonstrained to admit that 'the system of government over whieh he presided was eorrupt and full of abuses'.[2] Hastings did all that man eould do in the eireumstances to effect an improvement, and aetually sueeeeded to no small extent. But the system was too strong to be overthrown by a mere servant of the Company. The retirement of Sir John Maepherson, who belonged to the old unreformed sehool, marks the elose of an evil period in Bengal. The Carnatie had to endure even worse government for some years longer.

CHRONOLOGY

Hastings Governor-general; the Supreme Court	1774
Cession of Benares province to the Company; treaty of Surat; first Marāthā war began; execution of Nandkumār	1775
Treaty of Purandhar; death of Col. Monson	1776
War with France; occupation of French settlements	1778
Convention of Wargāon (Jan.); Nizam's confederaey	1779
Capture of Gwālior; invasion of Carnatic by Haidar Ali; Baillie's disaster	1780
Battle of Porto Novo; affair of Chait Singh	1781
Affair of the Bēgams of Oudh; Treaty of Sālbāī; Braithwaite's disaster; Admiral de Suffren; death of Haidar Ali; (*European events*—Resignation of Lord North, prime minister; relief of Gibraltar; Admiral Rodney's victory; Grattan's Parliament in Ireland)	1782
Surrender of Mangalore to Tippoo; peace of Versailles	1783
Ascendaney of Māhādajī Sindia; treaty of Mangalore; Pitt's India Act	1784
Resignation of Hastings; Sir J. Macpherson acting Governor-general	1785
Impeachment trial began	1788
Acquittal of Hastings	1795
Death of Hastings	1818

AUTHORITIES

FORREST, G. W. [Sir], *Selections from the State Papers of Governors-general, Warren Hastings*, 2 vols. (Oxford, Blackwell; and London, Constable, 1910) may be given the first place. Besides the general histories,

[1] *Cornwallis Correspondence*, (1859), ed. Ross², i. 383, 454. Thornton is much too favourable to Macpherson.

[2] *The Political History of India*, 1826, vol. i, p. 35. The author's explanation of the causes whieh brought about the abuses is too long to quote, but deserves study.

the following special works, among others, have been used. ANONYMOUS, *A History of the Trial of Warren Hastings, Esq.* (London, Debrett, 1796), gives an excellent and well-documented account of the impeachment and connected proceedings. The biographical works are numerous. The most accurate is GRIER, SYDNEY C., *The Letters of Warren Hastings to his Wife* (London and Edinburgh, Blackwood, 1905), a volume which contains much more than its title indicates. The leading *Life* still is that by GLEIG, G. R., 3 vols. (London, Bentley, 1841). Many smaller biographies exist, written by Sir ALFRED LYALL and other authors. I am inclined to think that the best is that by TROTTER, LIONEL, in *Everyman's Library* (Dent. 1910), which is superior to the volume by the same author in the Rulers of India series. All the biographies, except Sydney Grier's, contain mistakes. *A Vindication of Warren Hastings* by HASTINGS, G. W. (Frowde, 1909) ; and *The Private Life of Warren Hastings* by LAWSON, Sir CHARLES, (Swan, Sonnenschein, London, 1905), are useful, but not quite free from errors. V. A. SMITH, annotated edition of Macaulay's essay (Clarendon Press, 1911). Many other books and a multitude of pamphlets might be named. A huge quantity of unpublished MSS. about Hastings exists, and it is almost hopeless to look for a really satisfactory biography of him. The material is overwhelming in mass, and controversy is endless.

Everything about 'Nuncomar' will be found in STEPHEN, Sir JAMES, *The Story of Nuncomar and the Impeachment of Sir Elijah Impey*, 2 vols. (Macmillan, 1905), on one side ; and in BEVERIDGE, H., *Maharaja Nuncomar* (Calcutta, Thacker, Spink, 1886), on the other.

The latter work, a revised reprint of articles in the *Calcutta Review*, although learned and painstaking, seems to me to be thoroughly wrong-headed. It is based on the assumption that Hastings conspired with Impey to murder 'Nuncomar' because the death of the Mahārāja was of advantage to Hastings. It would be as reasonable to assume that the Governor-general poisoned Colonel Monson, whose death was still more opportune for him. When the *jury* convicted 'Nuncomar', the Chief Justice was bound to pass sentence. The proposition that Hastings and Impey joined in a conspiracy to murder, which was rejected by the law officers and by Parliament, is an atrocious calumny, inconsistent with the characters of both the men accused. The title 'Hastings' Confession' to chapter viii of Mr. Beveridge's big book is a most unfair *petitio principii*. No confession ever was made. Most of the points discussed in the book are irrelevant, and later works supply fuller information on some of them.

For all Marāthā affairs GRANT DUFF is the leading authority. I possess and have used two biographies of Nānā Farnavīs, one by MACDONALD, A., Captain, Bombay N.I., Bombay, 1851 ; and the other by BRIGGS, JOHN, *An Autobiographical Memoir, &c.*, reprinted from the *J. R. A. S.*, vol. ii, part i, London, 1829. Count de Boigne's life is narrated sufficiently by GRANT DUFF, and more fully by RAYMOND, G. M., *Mémoires*, *&c.* (Chambéry. 1830). WILKS, MARK, *Historical Sketches of the South of India, &c.*, is the principal guide for the Mysore war. Some other books are cited in the notes, and many more might be named.

CHAPTER 5

Lord Cornwallis; reforms; the third Mysore war; the 'permanent settlement'; Sir John Shore, a man of peace.

Lord Cornwallis. Charles, second Earl Cornwallis, was in his forty-eighth year when, in 1786, he accepted unwillingly and from a sense of duty the office of Governor-general. A soldier by profession, he had seen much active service. It was his misfortune that in October 1781 he was in command of the force which was compelled to surrender at Yorktown on the American coast, because the French fleet under de Grasse had secured for the moment command of the sea. Although the surrender ended the American war and assured the independence of the United States, the disaster, for which Cornwallis was not blamed personally, did not prevent his appointment to India. It was, as Marshman observes, 'the singular caprice of circumstances that the man who had lost America was sent out to govern India, and the man who had saved India was subjected to a prosecution for high crimes and misdemeanours'.[1]

It is refreshing for the historian to escape from the turbid politics of the time of Hastings and Macpherson and to pass into the more wholesome atmosphere of the Cornwallis régime. The new Governor-General, a member of the aristocratic oligarchy which then governed England, was raised by his peerage above the jealousies which must ever beset the path of a man promoted from the ranks of an official service and set to rule over his fellows. Hastings never could wholly overcome the disadvantages of his position, either as regards the Directors and ministry at home or his colleagues and subordinates in India. He was forced to make compromises

[1] '*An Historic Meeting.*

Yesterday members of the American Mission met the British War Cabinet and the Heads of the Departments most intimately concerned in the war at No. 10 Downing-street. The meeting was essentially a business meeting to consider how the United States could best work with us and with the other Allies for the single end we have in view. But the dullest imagination must be stirred by the gathering of the representatives of the two great English-speaking peoples for such a purpose upon such a scene. Until a century and a half ago they were one people with a common inheritance of blood and of language, of political and religious thought, of institutions, habits, character, and traditions coming down to them through countless generations. Then the claim of the colonists to self-government divided them from the Mother Country, and just because they were of the same family the kinsmen stubbornly fought their quarrel out. It was in the room and at the table where the decisions which made the severance inevitable were taken, and where the treaty of peace with the new Republic was signed, that their representatives took counsel together yesterday against the enemy of the polity and of the civilization they have developed' (*The Times*, November 21, 1917).

and opportunist arrangements, and even occasionally to perpetrate jobs, in order to secure his continuance in office and control over the instruments which he had to use. The personal rank and reputation of Cornwallis freed him from such necessities. He could afford to defy even the Prince Regent, when he sought to effect a scandalous job, and he enjoyed the full confidence of the ministry, so that his authority in every department of government was uncontested. He was invested with military control as commander-in-chief. He obtained powers to overrule for adequate reasons the majority of his council. The want of that authority had been the most serious embarrassment of Hastings. The other most glaring faults in the Regulating Act had been remedied by earlier legislation. Cornwallis was not a genius, but his lack of imagination and intellectual brilliancy was compensated by the strength of his character and his unflinching moral courage. No man ever presumed to question his integrity. His mistakes and failures do not affect the high respect due to his essentially noble nature and almost invariably straightforward conduct.

LORD CORNWALLIS.

Reform of civil service. The first three years of his lordship's term of office were mainly occupied in the reform of abuses, the eradication of corruption, and the provision of adequate salaries for the civil service. He was resolutely opposed to the old-fashioned commercial view of the Directors, who liked to see small salaries shown in the accounts, while they were indifferent to the largeness of the unofficial perquisites appropriated by their servants. Cornwallis, soon after his arrival, estimated the takings of the Resident of Benares at £40,000 a year. Such monstrous gains, of course, were stopped. The Resident was given the adequate but not then excessive salary of 5,000 rupees a month. Under the influence of the new system the Civil Service of India developed into the honourable body which it has continued to be ever since. Cornwallis was served by several admirable officials, among whom John Shore and Jonathan Duncan stand out pre-eminent. The administrative changes and reforms will be discussed more fully later.

Peace sought; war found. Lord Cornwallis came out to India as a man of peace, bound by Act of Parliament and his own convictions to refrain from conquests and alliances, except in defence of British possessions or those of an ally. Before he went home he had broken the power of the principal potentate in the far south and had taken half of his dominions. Like more than one of his successors he came seeking peace and found war. The self-denying ordinance enacted by Parliament could not be strictly observed; and even Cornwallis, who disliked trickery, was driven on at least one occasion to evade the Act by a subterfuge. The various Indian states, or 'country powers', as contemporary writers called them, were not stable kingdoms with settled boundaries, capable of entering into a permanent system of polity. Nearly all the kingdoms were of recent origin founded by adventurers, each of whom fought for his own hand, and schemed incessantly to outwit and subdue his neighbours. The policy of the Marāthās, in its essence predatory, could not be reconciled with general order. Nānā Farnavīs, the Pēshwā's powerful minister in those times, aimed at restoring the supremacy of his people. Tippoo in the far south, an arrogant fanatical tyrant, apparently not quite sane, and filled with bitter hatred of the English intruders, never relaxed his efforts to drive them out. No fixed authority could be found anywhere, and the British rulers of Bengal, as the strongest military and naval power, found themselves irresistibly constrained to acknowledge the duties imposed by the possession of strength, and to accept the position of 'umpires', not only in Hindostan or northern India, as in Verelst's time, but of the whole country, even down to Travancore and Coorg in the extremity of the peninsula. When the war with Tippoo began in 1790, only thirty-three years had elapsed since Plassey.

Causes of the Mysore war. In 1786 the Marāthās, meaning the Pēshwā acting under the advice of Nānā Farnavīs, Sindia, and Holkar, combined with the Nizam for the purpose of despoiling Tippoo, and in the following year forced him to cede a district and pay thirty lakhs of rupees. In 1788 Lord Cornwallis succeeded in obtaining Guntūr in the northern Sarkārs from the Nizam, who in return asked for troops under the provisions of the treaty of 1768. Lord Cornwallis, hampered by the Act of Parliament and anxious to avoid an open breach with Tippoo, adopted, as Grant Duff observes, 'a line of conduct more objectionable than an avowed defensive alliance'. He addressed a letter to the Nizam promising that if the English should at any future time obtain possession of the Carnatic Bālāghāt or uplands they would then fulfil their obligations to both the Nizam and the Marāthās. When the letter was written the territory in question was included in the Mysore state. The Governor-general further promised to send the battalions on demand, on condition that they should not be employed against the allies of the Company, including specifically the Marāthās. Tippoo's name was not included among the allies.

Cornwallis thus evaded the Act by framing a treaty in the form of a letter. Tippoo heard of the evasion, and his anger at it was one of the causes of the war which followed. In any case he had intended to fight the English, and if possible, destroy their power.

Invasion of Travancore. The immediate cause of the war was Tippoo's attack on Travancore, a state in alliance with and under the protection of the Company. It is needless to go into the special reasons which induced the Sultan to attack Travancore at that moment, as he proceeded to do. On December 29, 1789, he assailed the 'lines of Travancore', a rampart covering thirty miles of the northern frontier of the state, and suffered a repulse owing to a sudden panic among his troops. 'The plain country was a scene of merciless devastation, the inhabitants were hunted and sent in immense numbers to the usual fate of captivity and death.' Lord Cornwallis treated that attack as an act of war against the Company, and, ignoring the effects of his letter to the Nizam in July, wrote :

> 'That mad barbarian Tippoo has forced us into a war with him by attacking without any just provocation our ally the Raja of Travancore, whose territories it is not only our interest to defend, but we are specifically bound to do it by the late treaty of peace.'

Triple alliance. Orders were sent to the government of Madras to regard the invasion of Travancore as equivalent to a declaration of war against the Company, to collect military stores and transport, and to suspend all commercial expenditure. The provincial government, then under the control of two brothers named Hollond, of whom one, John, was governor, deliberately disobeyed the peremptory orders of the Governor-general in every particular. The rascals soon found that they had a master. John Hollond fled to Europe, and his brother, Edward John, who succeeded him as acting governor, was suspended from office. Subsequently, both of the Hollonds went to America and disappeared. The Governor-general, being now at war in defence of an ally, felt himself at liberty to conclude a 'tripartite treaty' or 'triple alliance' with the Nizam and the Marāthās against Tippoo.

The first two campaigns. General Medows, in command of the Company's forces, occupied Dindigul and other places, while troops from Bombay took possession of Malabar. Seasonal and transport difficulties prevented decisive operations.

In December 1790 Lord Cornwallis in person assumed command. After a siege he captured Bangalore, which he made his base. Hampered by appalling difficulties in the way of supplies and transport he struggled on and inflicted a severe defeat on the Sultan at Arikera (Arrakerry), only nine miles from Seringapatam, the capital. The victory proved fruitless. At the moment when success seemed assured Cornwallis was obliged by fear of starvation to destroy his siege train and retire on Bangalore.[1] Just then

[1] Full details of the sufferings of the army are given by Wilks. The Bombay force had to abandon a small hospital with 18 patients.

a Marāthā force arrived with ample supplies. If they had come a few days earlier the war might have been ended triumphantly. Lord Cornwallis bought the further aid or neutrality of the mercenary Marāthās with funds provided by seizing the Company's silver on its way to China. In those days modern financial facilities did not exist. There was no paper money, no funded debt, and no machinery of extensive credit. Each campaign had to be financed by chests full of coin, and the amazingly cumbrous arrangements for transport and supply were of a mediaeval character.[1]

Treaty of Seringapatam. Two campaigns having failed, Lord Cornwallis resolved to finish the business in 1792. With the help of an army from Bombay he approached Seringapatam in February, and convinced Tippoo that resistance was hopeless. Preliminary terms then arranged were converted on March 16 into the definite treaty of Seringapatam, which required the cession of half of the Sultan's dominions, the payment of 330 lakhs of rupees, the release of all prisoners, and the surrender of two of Tippoo's sons as hostages.

The Sultan was furious when he learned that the Governor-general insisted on the cession of Coorg, which did not come clearly within the precise language of the preliminary terms accepted. Lord Cornwallis could not possibly abandon to the rage of the Sultan the gallant little principality, which had already suffered unspeakable cruelties at Tippoo's hands ; but he should not have exposed himself by the use of loose language to even the suspicion of breaking faith. Tippoo had paid a large part of the indemnity and sent in his sons before he realized that he must lose Coorg.[2]

Territorial adjustments. The territorial adjustments, intended to give shares of equal value to the three allies, may be described in the words of Wilks :

> 'The selections of ceded territory brought the Mahrattas to the river Toombuddra [Tungabhadrā], their frontier in 1779 ; restored to Nizam Ali his possessions north of that river, and the province of Kurpa [Cuddapah] to the south, which had been lost about the same period. The English obtained Malabar and Coorg ; the province of Dindigul [now in the north of the Madura District], which had jutted inconveniently into their southern provinces, and Baramahal [now the NE. portion of the Salem District], an iron boundary for Coromandel, which placed her frontier fortress of Rayacota [Rāyakottai, now in Salem District] on the table-land of Mysoor to the east, as the undisputed cession of Coorg secured a similar advantage to the west.'

[1] The needs of Lord Cornwallis in 1792 were supplied by a huge supplementary army of Banjāras (' Brinjarics ', ' Lumbanies '), or professional nomad grain-carriers and dealers, numbering not less than 400,000. Wilks gives a curious account of them. Now that their ancient occupation has gone they have been mostly merged in the general population and become a mere caste. See Yule and Burnell, *Glossary, s. v.* Brinjarry.

[2] The dispute turned on the meaning of the word ' adjacent ' in the preliminary articles. See the full diary of the tedious negotiations in Malcolm, *Political History*.

The districts left to Tippoo were 'rugged and unproductive' in comparison with those of which he was deprived. Coorg was maintained as a protected state under its Rājā, and so remained until 1834, when the misconduct of its ruler made annexation necessary. The annexations under the treaty of Seringapatam largely extended the area of the Madras and Bombay presidencies.

Criticism. Lord Cornwallis is sometimes criticized for his failure to deal in a more drastic fashion with an implacable enemy. Subsequent events proved that the complete overthrow of Tippoo in 1792 would have saved another war;[1] but at the time the Governor-general believed that he had done enough to secure a lasting peace. Annexation of the whole of Mysore would have displeased both the Nizam and the Marāthās, offended public and official opinion at home, and contravened the policy of the Act of 1784. The partial annexation effected was approved by the ministry, and the Governor-general was promoted to the rank of Marquess. Tippoo compelled his subjects to pay most of the indemnity,[2] and at once began preparations for the next war.

Land policy. The most momentous and most hotly debated measure carried through by Lord Cornwallis was the Permanent Settlement of Bengal, Bihār, the Benares Province, and part of Orissa.[3] Comparatively few readers of this book can have had practical, inside knowledge of the nature and working of the Indian systems of land tenure and finance, which differ widely from those prevalent in Europe and other parts of the world. Explanation at some length of elementary facts familiar to experts is therefore indispensable for the majority of students who do not possess the experience gained by Collectors and Settlement Officers.

India always has been a country mainly agricultural, and for that reason the proper treatment of the problems connected with the land is the primary duty of an Indian government, so far as internal administration is concerned. Good policy concerning the land means contentment and peace; bad policy means discontent and disturbance. Indian finance always has depended on the land policy, because from time immemorial the right of the government, whatever its form might be, to a large share of the gross produce of the land has been admitted by everybody, and that share has been the principal source of the income of the state. Even now, when new sources of revenue have been developed by the action of modern conditions, the 'land revenue' constitutes about from 38 to 40 per cent. of the income of the government of

[1] General Medows would have preferred to dethrone Tippoo and restore the country to its Hindu rulers, the policy adopted later by Lord Wellesley (*Cornwallis Corr.*, ii. 78).

[2] Wilks tells of the 'horrible tortures' used to enforce the levy, which caused an extensive secret emigration into the Company's newly acquired territory.

[3] Attempts to introduce the permanent settlement into the northern Sarkārs (Circars) 'mostly failed' (*I. G.*, 1908, vol. xvi, p. 318, *s. v.* Madras Presidency).

India. In earlier days its percentage was considerably higher; amounting to 75 per cent. or more of the gross receipts.

The share of the state. The legitimate government share of the gross produce according to the best legal authorities was one-fourth, but Akbar demanded one-third generally, and one-half in Kashmīr. Theoretical limitations did not count for much. In practice, nearly every ruler, Hindu or Musalmān, took all he could get, and often the principle was avowed that the cultivating occupier, the 'ryot' (*raiyat*), should be left no more than a bare subsistence and seed grain, in order that he might not wax fat and kick. Very often so much was not left. Then the cultivators were forced to desert their lands, which lay waste, a prey to wild beasts. The temptation to kill the goose which laid the eggs proved irresistible in many cases. Even the early 'settlements' made by British officers frequently erred on the side of over-assessment, with disastrous results. The financial and economic benefits of moderate assessment are now universally recognized in British India, but the practical difficulties in the way of attaining the golden mean are immense. In Bengal of the eighteenth century the information accessible was so crude that a decently fair assessment was impossible. The Benares province was more fortunate, because it was a comparatively small area and was assessed by Jonathan Duncan, the best revenue officer of the period.

Modes of collection. The government share of the produce might be collected in kind, either by actual division and weighment of the crop, or by various methods of appraisement or estimating. It might also be valued and collected in cash, the system preferred by Akbar, and now universally adopted in British territory. The ancient tradition, it should be clearly understood, allowed no place for an economic, competitive landlord's rent. According to theory, the whole produce should be shared between the State (*sarkār*) and the peasant ('ryot'). Akbar encouraged direct payments by each peasant ('ryotwār settlement'), which, as Sir Thomas Munro rightly insisted, was 'the old system of the country'. But in practice that arrangement often proved to be unworkable, and the services of a middleman under one name or another, zemindar, or what not, had to be called in. His remuneration was in the nature of a commission on the collections. Akbar sanctioned the payment of such commission, where necessary, at the rate of 2½ per cent.[1] That allowance to middlemen easily passes into landlord's rent, and, as a matter of fact, is the origin of the landlord's rent now levied in Bengal and most parts of India. Ancient Indian law recognized no freeholders, except in Malabar, and certain other regions in the peninsula.[2] The prevailing

[1] The best definition of the position of an early Bengal zemindar is that in Harington's *Analysis*, reproduced in Seton-Karr, *Lord Cornwallis* (Rulers of India), p. 34. It deserves careful study. The Cornwallis zemindar is defined, ibid., p. 36.

[2] Munro found documentary evidence of private property in land in

opinion certainly was that the ultimate property in land vested in the State, and that opinion still is ordinarily held and acted on in the Native or Protected States of northern India. The corollary to that proposition is that the State or government could do what it pleased with tenures, subject only to vague customary rights, more or less recognized, but never defined, and never enforceable by law. Powerful people also needed to be careful, for fear of throwing land out of cultivation. Established 'ryots' were understood to have a prescriptive right to retain their fields so long as they paid at customary rates their 'land revenue', or government share of the produce, which in the old days was indistinguishable from rent. The British creation of 'proprietary right' in northern India has brought in a third party, the landlord or zemindar, who collects rents from the 'ryots' or peasants, and pays 'land revenue' as a share of the rent, not of the produce. The modern settlement officer values rents, not crops. If there is no actual rent, as in the case where a 'proprietor' cultivates his own land, a hypothetical rent is calculated, and 'rent-rates' are worked out for the whole cultivated area. In the eighteenth century no such refinements were possible. Rough assessments were usually made on the basis of previous collections, or, sometimes, as by Duncan in Benares, on estimates framed by hereditary skilled officers called *kānūngōs* ('canoongoes'). At other times the assessments were made in a still rougher fashion by putting up the 'land revenue' of a tract to auction. In that case the contractor was called a 'farmer', and the highest bidder got the contract. He then had to raise the sum agreed on as he best could from the middlemen and peasants under him. Warren Hastings was obliged to resort to the farming system as a makeshift for his hurried quinquennial 'settlement' of 1772–7. It is an evil system, intolerable except as a makeshift.

Questions of person and time. In the time of Lord Cornwallis everybody was agreed that the 'settlement' contract should be made with the established middlemen or zemindars, whose position had become hereditary, as usual in India.

The question of term remained open. Most native governments made rough 'annual settlements'. Akbar had preferred longer terms, and, actually, the Bengal 'settlement' made by his finance minister, Rājā Todar Mall, lasted for seventy-six years.

Chaos in Bengal. In the eighteenth century everything fell into confusion. In Bengal the village communities, which still held rural society together in Upper India, dissolved, and the *kānūngōs* ceased to maintain their records properly. Individual zemindars, originally mere collecting removable middlemen, developed into hereditary potentates, each controlling a huge extent of country. The Mogul government always had been in

N. Kanara going back for a thousand years (Gleig's *Life*[2], i. 347). The 'other regions' alluded to are—from Sunda [in Mysore] to the Wynaad [now included in the Malabar District], the Carnatic, Tanjore, and Madura (ibid., ii. 125).

the habit of allowing local landholders and middlemen, whatever their designation might be, to exercise practically despotic authority over the peasantry. The officials did not worry much about the details of administration, so long as the revenue came in sufficiently well to satisfy the persons in power, whoever or wherever they might be. Nobody's position or rights could be exactly defined in legal, precise terms. Lord Cornwallis suddenly introduced his 'permanent settlement' into the chaos thus sketched, and effected a revolution, without fully intending it. He was firmly persuaded that he had conferred a boon on the country which he did so much to ruin; and when he had departed his successors continued to pretend that all was well, being unwilling to admit failure. No official blundering could ruin altogether a fertile region like Bengal, filled with an industrious population.

Meaning of 'settlement'. The term 'settlement' so often used in the foregoing observations has in India a technical meaning, which needs definition. The term is a translation of the Persian word *bandobast*. In the time of Lord Cornwallis revenue records being written in Persian, the technical terms used mostly came from that language, which included many Arabic words. The vocabulary of official Persian differed little from that of modern 'High Urdū'. The comprehensive term *bandobast* or 'settlement' covered all the operations incidental to the assessment of the land revenue or government share of the produce. The survey which had been a necessary preliminary in Akbar's time, as it is now, had dropped out of use in all provinces. The main factors in a 'settlement' were the persons with whom the contract should be made, the amount of money demanded, the modes of collection, the penalties for default, and the term for which the arrangement should hold good.

Policy of the home authorities. The home authorities had been much disturbed by the reports concerning the vacillating policy pursued in Indian revenue matters, and were extremely anxious to secure a permanent revenue assessed on fixed principles. They were not keen about obtaining an increase of the annual amount. The farming system was condemned definitely, and all parties were agreed that the 'settlement' should be made with the recognized zemindars. Nobody advocated a survey or very detailed investigation of the assessable resources of the country, which settlement officers are accustomed to call the 'assets'.

Question of term. The term for which the settlement should be made was the principal topic debated. So far back as January 1776 Francis had written an able minute advocating a permanent, unchangeable assessment.[1] In a dispatch of 1786, the year in which Cornwallis came out, the Directors expressed their preference for a permanent settlement, never again to be revised. The Governor-general seems to have made up his mind from the first that such a measure must be passed. It is certain that in 1789 he had come to a fixed resolve on the matter, which could not be

[1] Ascoli, p. 34.

shaken by any argument. He succeeded in convincing the Prime Minister and the President of the Board of Control that he was right. The two statesmen shut themselves up in a country house for ten days to study the question and decided to support the opinion of the Governor-general. Accordingly the Permanent Settlement for Bengal, Bihār, and Orissa (i. e. Midnapur) was proclaimed in 1793, and for the Benares Province two years later. Shore urged with all his force the obvious common-sense view that the measure was premature and that an irrevocable step should not be taken on information which everybody knew to be extremely imperfect concerning a huge country largely waste and still suffering from the effects of the famine of 1770. He argued that ordinary prudence required that the agreements should be taken for ten years only, an arrangement which would allow time for inquiry and consideration.

Arguments of Cornwallis. Cornwallis replied to the effect that there had been plenty of inquiry, that the information was sufficient, that the government would be no wiser ten years hence, and that nothing save absolute permanence would stimulate the progress and improvement of the country. He cherished an idle dream that he would be able to create a class of landholders, like the best kind of English county magnates, who, under the magic influence of ownership and permanent assessment, would 'make the country flourish, and secure happiness to the body of inhabitants'. Being 'persuaded that nothing could be so ruinous to the public interest as that the land should be retained as the property of Government', he was further 'convinced that, failing the claim of right of the zemindars, it would be necessary for the public good to grant a right of property in the soil to them, or to persons of other descriptions.' He proceeds to say:

'I may safely assert that one-third of the Company's territory in Hindostan is now a jungle inhabited only by wild beasts. Will a ten years' lease induce any proprietor to clear away that jungle, and encourage the ryots to come and cultivate his lands, when at the end of that lease he must either submit to be taxed *ad libitum* for the newly cultivated lands, or lose all hope of deriving any benefit from his labour, for which perhaps by that time he will hardly be repaid?

I must own that it is clear to my mind that a much more advantageous tenure will be necessary to incite the inhabitants of this country to make those exertions which can alone effect any substantial improvement.

The habit which the zemindars have fallen into of subsisting by annual expedients has originated, not in any constitutional imperfection in the people themselves, but by the fluctuating measures of Government; and I cannot therefore admit that a period of ten years will be considered by the generality of people as a term nearly equal in estimate to perpetuity.

By the prudent landholders it will not, whatever it may be by proprietors of a contrary description. It would be unwise, therefore, to deny the former the benefit of a permanent system, because the mismanagement of the latter will not allow them to derive the same advantage from it.

It is for the interest of the State that the landed property should fall into the hands of the most frugal and thrifty class of people, who will improve their lands and protect the ryots, and thereby promote the general prosperity of the country.

If there are men who will not follow this line of conduct when an opportunity is afforded them by the enaction [sic] of good laws, it surely is not inconsistent with justice, policy, or humanity to say that the sooner their bad management obliges them to part with their property to the more industrious, the better for the State.

It is immaterial to Government what individual possesses the land, provided he cultivates it, protects the ryots, and pays the public revenue.

The short-sighted policy of having recourse to annual expedients can only be corrected by allowing those who adopt it to suffer the consequences of it, leaving to them at the same time the power of obviating them by pursuing the opposite line of conduct.'

Criticism. Such feeble reasoning, while plausible enough on paper to deceive able English ministers ignorant of Indian conditions, was so utterly unrelated to the realities that it hardly deserves the trouble of refutation. It may, however, be well to observe that the grant or declaration of a heritable, transferable right of property in the soil as a boon bestowed on the zemindars ignored the ancient rights of multitudes of under-proprietors of various kinds as well as the customary tenant-right or hold on the soil at fair customary rates enjoyed by the ryots; that no serious attempt was made to secure respect for such rights and customary possession; that the words 'his lands' applied to a vast zemindāri were false in fact and implied an agrarian revolution; that great zemindars were not in the habit of spending capital on land reclamation or improvement; that such operations actually were effected bit by bit on a small scale by individual ryots; that no shadow of reason existed for believing that the transferees of properties would 'improve the lands and protect the ryots' better than the old zemindars had done; that, as a matter of fact, the new men were much worse than the old; and that the policy avowed in the concluding paragraphs of the extract was heartless and cruel. Much more might be said, but so much is enough.[1]

Cruelty of the sale law. A tremendous change in usage and practice was introduced by the Permanent Settlement legislation through the enforcement of the sale of zemindāris by auction as the sole penalty for default. Previous rulers had been accustomed to imprison, flog, torture, or even kill defaulters; but whatever pain was inflicted fell upon individuals, without impairing the position of the defaulter's family, or inflicting loss of the vague rights recognized as existing. The notion that a big zemindar's interest in a whole barony or county was liable to be sold up and lost for ever because his agent had been a day late in paying the government revenue was wholly new to the Indian mind, which found extreme difficulty in grasping the terrible reality of the novel situation. Lord Cornwallis abhorred all forms of personal

[1] Mill's very much longer denunciation of the Cornwallis legislation is not open to hostile criticism to any material extent.

coercion, and in his anxiety to relieve landholders from corporal indignities subjected them to evils far worse. The rigid punctuality of payment required by the law could not be fully enforced. Large balances accrued in spite of the cruelty of the sale law, especially during the period of about fifteen years following the proclamation of the permanent settlement. Innumerable proofs of the mischief done might be cited, but it will suffice to quote the testimony of the Collector of Midnapur in 1802, who wrote that the zemindars

'all say that such a harsh and oppressive system was never before resorted to in this country; that the custom of imprisoning landholders for arrears of revenue was, in comparison, mild and indulgent to them; that, though it was no doubt the intention of government to confer an important benefit on them by abolishing the custom, it has been found by melancholy experience that the system of sales and attachments, which has been substituted for it, has in the course of a very few years reduced most of the great zemindars in Bengal to distress and beggary, and produced a greater change in the landed property of Bengal than has, perhaps, ever happened in the same space of time, in any age or country, by the mere effect of internal regulations.'

That indictment of the policy of Lord Cornwallis is literally true. The great landholders more or less completely ruined included the Rājās of Dīnājpur, Rājshāhi, Bishanpur, Nadiyā (Nuddea), Cossījurah, and many others.[1]

The auction purchasers. Nor were the persons substituted any better as landlords than their predecessors had been. On the contrary, as already stated, they were much worse, because the ill-understood foreign sale law afforded endless opportunities for trickery and chicanery to rogues who mastered the formalities of the collector's office, suborned the underlings, and often acquired valuable properties for a trifle. In many cases the purchasers were agents, attorneys, or bailiffs of the zemindars, and purchases were constantly effected in the names of persons other than the real buyers. The purchasers, far from showing an inclination to become 'prudent trustees of the public interests', were selfish, greedy speculators, indifferent to everything except their own immediate pecuniary interest, and bitterly hostile to the holders of all subordinate rights. Very often they resided in Calcutta or some other city, never going near the estates which they were expected to improve. In the years 1871–4, when I served as Assistant Collector in the permanently settled districts of the Benares province, I examined many old records and heard endless stories of the iniquities of the auction-purchasers, although in that province the evil never attained the magnitude which it reached in Bengal. The effect on the peace of the country-side was then disastrous and probably is still felt. A family which has lost its legal rights by an auction sale always regards the transaction as unjust, and usually becomes a centre of agrarian disturbance, frequently resulting in murder.

So far as the hoped for creation of a landed aristocracy of a

[1] *Fifth Report*, in Ascoli, pp. 214, 223.

progressive character from among either the old zemindars or the new men was concerned the permanent settlement was a ghastly failure. The pecuniary benefit was reaped chiefly by rogues.

Neglect of subordinate rights. In respect of the under-proprietors and peasants or 'ryots' of various classes, who possessed well-recognized, although ill-defined customary rights, while owing equally well-recognized and ill-defined duties, the result of the obstinate idealism of Lord Cornwallis was equally disastrous. The government contented itself with expressing pious aspirations in the wordy preambles to Regulations and in making fine promises of future legislation which were never fulfilled. The first serious attempt to grasp the problem of tenant-right was made by Act X of 1859, which unhappily proceeded on lines not in accordance with custom, and was on the whole a failure. Subsequent attempts to solve the problem do not seem to have met with much greater success, but I am not qualified by experience in the Lower Provinces to express a decided opinion on that point.

'No rent' combinations. Another evil result of the sentimental obstinacy of Lord Cornwallis was the demoralization of the tenantry, who often adopted a 'no rent' policy, and made it impossible for the landholder to fulfil his obligations. A man who could not collect his rents could not pay his land revenue. Lord Cornwallis was perversely wedded to the notion that all disputes concerning the land could be easily settled by referring the parties to the civil courts established by him. The break-down of those courts will be noticed presently.

Distraint ; the Fifth Report. In 1799 an attempt to relieve the embarrassment of the zemindars was made by giving them the power of distraint, as copied from English law. The newly acquired power, which was unsuitable to the country, was tyrannically abused. The famous *Fifth Report* of the Select Committee of the House of Commons, presented in 1812, and drafted by the Senior Clerk of the Board of Control, gives a comprehensive and distressing view of the evils wrought by the permanent settlement, coloured to a considerable extent by the desire of the committee to prove that the country, notwithstanding 'certain imperfections' in the 'system of internal government in the Bengal provinces', yet 'exhibited in every part of it, improvement on a general view, advancing with accelerated progress in latter times.'

Advantages of delay. If the settlement had been made for ten years only as Shore advised, or even for a longer term, the defects inevitable in a rough and ready measure designed and executed by officers very imperfectly informed concerning essential facts could have been noted and cured by suitable remedies. The rights of subordinate holders and ryots might have been properly secured, the old landholding families might have been preserved, the villanies attendant on auction sales could have been stopped, and grave financial loss would have been avoided.

Lack of local knowledge. The permanent settlement had yet one more injurious result. The land revenue being fixed for ever and its payment on the whole secured by a mechanical recourse to the process of sale, no motive remained to induce officials to study minutely rural tenures and conditions. The *kānūngōs* (canoongoes), the authorized hereditary custodians of knowledge concerning the land, were abolished, and the village accountants (*patwāris*) were declared to be merely private servants of the zemindars. No local collecting establishment was required. The extensive establishment of *tahsīldārs* and subordinate officials at the disposal of the Collector of a District in temporarily settled provinces does not exist in Bengal, where the Magistrate and Collector is, so to speak, deprived of eyes and ears. He is constrained to rely for local investigations almost entirely on the police, an unsatisfactory agency. Considerable tracts of Bengal had the good fortune to escape the wide net of the permanent settlement for various reasons which cannot be explained here. Such tracts have been surveyed, examined, and assessed by skilled settlement officers in modern times and the knowledge thus acquired has thrown much light on rustic economy. But in the province taken as a whole it is extremely difficult for officials to gain that accurate information concerning the land which is the ordinary equipment of a competent officer in other provinces. Under the Bengal Tenancy Act of 1885 power was taken to make a survey and prepare a record of rights even in permanently settled tracts. Such operations have taken place in north Bihār and certain other Districts. In so far as they have been completed they remove the reproach of official ignorance concerning those areas.

Financial loss. The financial loss caused by the permanent settlement is enormous, and cannot be less than 300 lakhs, or 30 millions of rupees a year, a burden which the rest of India has to bear.[1] Apologists for the measure may urge that the apparent loss has been made up by the increase of cultivation due to the permanency of the assessment. Several years ago when lecturing at Oxford I came to the conclusion and taught my pupils that the large increase in cultivation which has taken place cannot be justly ascribed to the Permanent Settlement legislation. Mr. Ascoli, an expert revenue officer serving in Bengal, independently has formed the same opinion.[2] Probably few disinterested and

[1] The figure is put considerably higher in *I. G.* (1908, vol. vii, p. 301, *s. v.* Bengal).

[2] 'There is little doubt that the extension of cultivation subsequent to 1793 was due entirely to natural causes, such as the normal increase of population. . . . There is nothing in the contemporary accounts, nor in the subsequent history of zemindāri management, to show that the extension of cultivation was in any way due to the efforts of the proprietors, or to suggest that similar results would not have been obtained under a different form of settlement. . . . The Permanent Settlement in itself had no immediate effect on the state of cultivation' (*Early Revenue History of Bengal*, 1917, p. 80). 'We have only to guard the Ryots from oppression, and they will create the revenue for us' (Sir T. Munro in Gleig's *Life*[3], i. 174).

well-informed persons outside of Bengal could now be found to applaud the wisdom of the Permanent Settlement. Right or wrong, it has become irrevocable. The author of this book has no doubt that it was wrong.

Districts. 'The division of the province into districts is the backbone of the whole system of reforms. The Supervisors, the Provincial Councils, and the earlier Collectors had exercised their doubtful authority over a series of fiscal divisions, *parganas*, zemindāries, &c. . . . The new districts were territorial units . . . reduced to twenty-three in number' in 1787. 'The process of rendering the districts more compact continued . . . but the system evolved by Shore . . . has formed the basis of all subsequent administration.'[1]

Judicial reforms. The judicial reforms, civil and criminal, were based on the district arrangement, and, although much modified in detail by later legislation, served as the foundation of the existing system, and were an improvement on the tentative institutions of Hastings. A civil court under a European judge was constituted for every district, and a gradation of appeal courts was established. Collectors were divested of judicial functions, and almost all disputes were referred to the civil courts. European judges were sent on circuit to perform the functions now performed by Sessions Judges, and the grosser faults of the Muhammadan criminal law were abolished, but that law, slightly modified, still supplied the place of a penal code, and supplied it very ill. The Judge of each district (*zillah*) had also the powers of a magistrate and the control of the police, who were officered by Indian *darogas*, each in charge of a police circle (*thāna*) about twenty miles square. The *daroga* received a salary of only twenty-five rupees a month, plus ten rupees for every dacoit or brigand convicted, and a commission on stolen property recovered. Murders, robberies, and other enormities were extremely numerous, and the *darogas* were a terror to the well-disposed rather than to the evil doers. The introduction of a more efficient police administration had to wait until the years 1859–62, when the High Courts were founded, the Penal Code and Code of Criminal Procedure enacted, and the police was organized on the model of the Royal Irish Constabulary.

Radical error of Lord Cornwallis. Lord Cornwallis had an extraordinary distrust of all 'native' or Indian officials.

[1] Ascoli, p. 39. 'The unit of administration in British India is the district, corresponding roughly with the Sarkār of the Mogul system. In British India 258 districts exist. . . . Many of the native or protected states, as for example the Nizam's dominions or Hyderabad state, follow the British system and make use of the district as the unit of administration.

Each such district is ordinarily a considerable area, as large as a good-sized English county, and supporting a population of 1,000,000 more or less. In the Madras presidency the districts are exceptionally large. . . . The average area of a district is about 4,430 square miles, and the average population is about 931,000' (*The Oxford Survey of the British Empire*, 1914, vol. ii, p. 249). The districts in the time of Lord Cornwallis were large and unwieldy.

'I conceive', he wrote, that all regulations for the reform of that [criminal] department would be useless and nugatory, whilst the execution of them depends upon any native whatever,'

and went on to insist that all judicial proceedings should be at least supervised by Europeans. His plan for paying liberal salaries applied only to the European service.[1] Such entire exclusion of all indigenous agency from any responsible position was, as Marshman justly observes,

'the great and radical error of Lord Cornwallis. . . . Under the impolitic system established in 1793, the prospects of legitimate and honourable ambition were altogether closed against the natives of the country.'

Space fails to enter into particulars of the working of the judicial system, but there can be no doubt that it broke down utterly on both the civil and criminal sides to such a degree that for many years justice was almost denied. The courts were far too few, were hampered by technicalities,[2] and clogged with arrears. In 1795 the Civil Court of Burdwan was more than 30,000 cases in arrear. Much information on the subject is contained in the *Fifth Report*. Magisterial powers were restored to Collectors in 1835. Cornwallis believed firmly, as many people now do, in the theoretical merits of the complete separation of executive from judicial functions. Practical men, who know the strength of the Indian tradition which looks to one officer, the Hākim, or person who can give orders (*hukm*), as the representative of the government, do not believe that the villagers are gainers by the multiplication of departments and the sub-division of authority. But the subject is too large for discussion in this place. The student, however, should note that the theories of Cornwallis failed to stand the test of practice.

The 'country powers'. Cornwallis did his best to avoid entanglements with the 'country powers'. He had, however, the spirit to tell Māhādajī Sindia in peremptory language that he must keep his hands off Oudh. Both that province and the Carnatic continued to be scandalously misgoverned. Neither Nawāb took the slightest practical notice of the abundant excellent advice tendered by the Governor-General.

[1] Sir Thomas Munro understood the subject far better and entertained the most liberal views on it.

[2] The Cornwallis Code drawn up by Mr. George Barlow, afterwards Governor-general, was an extended and spoiled edition of Impey's short code, which was much more practical and sensible. 'It would have been better to have curtailed nine-tenths of the regulations—to have confined appeals within narrower limits, and to have made the zillah [district] judges absolute' (Munro in Gleig's *Life*, i. 420). It is hardly necessary to point out that now the great majority of judicial officers on the civil side are of Indian birth, that thousands of their countrymen exercise criminal powers, and that some of the most efficient High Court judges are Indians. The general level of judicial integrity has been raised to an extent which would have seemed incredible to Lord Cornwallis, but not to Sir Thomas Munro, who fully understood the possibilities of improvement. Munro, perhaps, was the wisest of all Anglo-Indian statesmen.

Ghulām Kādir. Māhadajī was in a critical position in 1787 owing to attacks by Rohilla chiefs. In the year following (1788) a ruffian named Ghulām Kādir, son of Zābita Khān Rohilla, seized Delhi and plundered the palace. In the course of his proceedings he even flogged the princesses and brutally blinded the titular emperor, Shāh Ālam, in order to force the disclosure of supposed hidden treasure. When Sindia recovered Delhi Ghulām Kādir paid the penalty of his ill deeds by a death of torture.

Later career of Sindia. Sindia had established his power with the aid of M. de Boigne, the foreign officer already mentioned, who ultimately commanded three brigades of eight battalions each, with the needful complement of artillery and cavalry. The old Marāthā style of warfare was abandoned, and Sindia relied on regular troops, equipped much in the same way as those of the Company, and comprising both Rājputs and Musalmāns. M. de Boigne defeated Ismaīl Beg, a Muhammadan chief, at Pātan in Rājputāna in 1790; the Rājput allies of that chief at Mīrthā (Mairta, Merta) in the year following; and Holkar's army under a Frenchman named Dudrenec at Lakherī (Lukhairee) in 1792.[1]

Sindia then (1792) went down to Poona and took part in the solemn investiture of the Pēshwā as titular *Vakīl-i Mutlak*, or Vicegerent of the Empire, which dignity had been conferred by the Pādshāh some years earlier. Māhādajī died in 1794. Grant Duff describes him as

> 'a man of great political sagacity, and of considerable genius; of deep artifice, restless ambition, and of implacable revenge. . . . His countenance was expressive of good sense and good humour; but his complexion was dark, his person inclining to corpulency, and he limped from the effects of his wound at Paunipput. His habits were simple, his manners kind and frank, but sometimes blustering and coarse.'

He left no male issue, and was succeeded by his grand-nephew, Daulat Rāo, a boy of thirteen, whom he had intended to adopt.

The intrigues of the Marāthā courts during the time of Lord Cornwallis are too complex for narration in this work. The curious will find full details in Grant Duff's *History*.

Renewal of Charter. When the Regulating Act of 1773 was enacted the Charter of the East India Company had been confirmed for twenty years. As the time for renewal drew near a brisk discussion on the subject arose in England, and an agitation was started by merchants and manufacturers in favour of the opening of the trade. Lord Cornwallis was strongly opposed to substantial change, and saw dreadful visions of India filled by 'desperate speculators', if the Company's privileges should be abolished. The authorities also strongly objected to the importation of schoolmasters or missionaries. In short, all the old notions and prejudices still swayed official minds, and Parliament was easily persuaded to follow the guidance of the ministers, without examining

[1] For an account of these battles from the Rājpūt point of view see Tod, *Personal Narrative*, chap. xxviii, xxix (popular ed., vol. i).

their arguments too closely. In the end the charter was renewed for twenty years without material modification. The only concession made to the general public was the trivial allowance to private traders of 3,000 tons of cargo space yearly under conditions unacceptable to merchants.

MAHADAJI SINDIA.

The Revolutionary War. The execution of Louis XVI of France in January 1793 resulted in the beginning of the Revolutionary War between France and England, which lasted almost without interruption until the battle of Waterloo in 1815. Lord Cornwallis, who had determined to retire from India, went down to Madras in order to superintend the reduction of the French settlements, but found that the work had been done before his arrival. He sailed for home from Madras in October.

Character of Lord Cornwallis. The personal character of

Lord Cornwallis deservedly secured him universal respect during his lifetime, and his memory is still justly held in honour. The errors of policy which marked his Indian career were committed from the purest of motives and with the best intentions. The extent of those errors did not become apparent until long after he had disappeared from the scene, and both the government at home and the authorities in India were unwilling to admit the failure of much of his work. He continued to be employed in high office, and, as we shall see, was even sent out to India again. His incessant war against corruption and jobbery in every form was his especial glory. His reorganization of the Covenanted Civil Service and his establishment of the District or *zillah* as the unit of administration were enduring reforms for which he deserves full credit. He was a capable military commander, and knew how to control his subordinates. He was free from personal animosity, and always anxious to promote the most competent officials. His correspondence gives a pleasing picture of a thoroughly honest, hard-working, public-spirited ruler, exempt from avarice,[1] and actuated by an imperative sense of duty.

Sir John Shore. Lord Cornwallis maintained for sound reasons still valid the opinion that no servant of the Company ever should be appointed Governor-general. Unfortunately his esteem for his friend Sir John Shore induced him to make an exception to his rule and to recommend Sir John as his successor. The King and ministry concurring, Shore was appointed and took over charge in August 1793. Although his administration lasted for four and a half years, its history may be dismissed briefly. Sir John, notwithstanding his exemplary personal character and sincere piety, was one of the worst of the few really incompetent Governors-general. He had the candour to acknowledge his incompetence in a private letter dated March 9, 1796, when he wrote :

> 'The fact is this that the duties of my situation are too much, I fear, for my abilities. . . . Often have I wished that Lord Cornwallis were at the head of the Administration here, and that I were his coadjutor, as formerly ; all would then have been easy to him and to me' (*Life*, i. 363).

Like Galba, Shore might be described as *capax imperii, nisi imperasset*, 'fit to bear rule, had he never ruled' ; an admirable subordinate, but not big enough to stand the test of exercising supreme power.

Battle of Khardā. Shore, paralysed by a slavish obedience to the words of the Act of Parliament of 1784 and by unworthy fear of the Marāthās, broke faith with the Nizam, when that prince was threatened by the robber state. The Governor-general wrapped up his reasons for refusing to obey the call of honour in sophistical phrases, equivalent substantially to a declaration that it would not pay to keep faith.[2] He therefore allowed a powerful

[1] Both he and General Medows refused to take their shares of the Seringapatam prize-money.

[2] The words of the treaty did not definitely bind the government of

Marāthā combination, including the Pēshwā, Sindia, Holkar, and all the other leaders, to overwhelm the Nizam at the battle of Khardā in 1795.[1] The battle itself was nothing, the fighting being contemptible, but it was enough to reduce the Nizam to a state of vassalage and to exalt the dangerous Marāthā power to a pinnacle of arrogance. The war of 1795 was the last occasion on which 'the chiefs of the Mahratta nation assembled under the authority of their Pēshwā'. In all subsequent transactions each chief acted independently.

Marāthā troubles. The aggrandizement of the Marāthās was stayed by unexpected events, not by the foresight of the Governor-general. Mādho Rāo Nārāyan, the young Pēshwā, weary of the galling tutelage of Nānā Farnavīs, the 'Indian Machiavelli', committed suicide. That tragedy threw all Marāthā affairs into disorder and resulted in three years of obscure, confused intrigue. Nānā Farnavīs spent part of the time in prison. Towards the close of 1796 Bājī Rāo II, a son of Ragoba, and the bitter enemy of the minister, was recognized as Pēshwā, but trouble continued long afterwards.

The rebellion of the Nizam's son induced the ruler of the Deccan to recall the British battalions which he had dismissed. That recall checked the development of French influence which had threatened to become supreme. The Nizam was well served by a French officer named Raymond, who organized regular troops and fought against countrymen of his commanding similar forces on the Marāthā side at the battle of Khardā.

Mutinous combination of officers. Lord Cornwallis and the President of the Board of Control had discussed plans for amalgamating the king's troops with the Company's army, which came to nothing. The amalgamation, a most proper and necessary measure, was deferred until after the Mutiny. Cornwallis, however, had succeeded in reducing the excessive perquisites of officers in the military as well as in the civil departments, thereby causing deep discontent. Towards the close of 1795 the officers formed a dangerous mutinous combination, threatening even to seize both the Governor-general and the commander-in-chief and to take possession of the government. They demanded double *batta* or field allowances, promotion by strict seniority, and other personal privileges incompatible with good administration. Clive had suppressed a similar combination in a fortnight. Shore weakly gave in and granted even more than was demanded. When the news of his abject surrender reached England in December 1796

India to render the assistance asked for, but, as Wilson points out, the Nizam had been led to expect protection and had earned it by his cession of Guntūr.

[1] Khardā is now in the Ahmadnagar District, Bombay. For some reason not apparent all the history books call the place Kardla or Kurdla. Two battalions of female sepoys, each 1,000 strong, kept by the Nizam to guard his palace and ladies, took part in the battle, and behaved no worse than the rest of his army (Blacker, p. 213 *n.*).

the Directors at once decided to recall him. Dundas, the President of the Board of Control, made matters worse by yielding still more concessions, merely because the mutinous officers controlled an influential committee in London. Lord Cornwallis, who had been invited to return to India, refused to have anything to do with such cowardly transactions ; and in the end Lord Mornington was appointed Governor-general.

Oudh affairs. Once and once only did Sir John display any spirit. Āsafu-d daula, the debauched ruler of Oudh, died in 1797, after nominating as his successor a youth named Vizier (Vazīr) Ālī, also known as Mīrzā Alī, whom he recognized as his son. Shore somewhat hastily sanctioned the succession. Within four months he was satisfied that the young man was the offspring of a menial servant and totally unfit to rule as Nawāb-Vizier. The Governor-general went down to Lucknow, reversed his previous decision, and installed Sa'ādat Alī Khān, a brother of the late Nawāb. The new ruler paid the price of his elevation by signing a fresh treaty, which among other provisions ceded the important strategic position of Allahabad at the confluence of the Jumna with the Ganges. Some disturbance occurred which at one time threatened the life of Sir John Shore, who behaved with courage and discretion. His ordinary cowardice as Governor-general was political, not physical.

SIR JOHN SHORE.

In the following year (1799) Vizier Ali revenged his downfall by murdering Mr. Cherry, the Resident at Lucknow, and several other European gentlemen. The murderer fled, was surrendered by the Rājā of Jaipur, and ended his days at Calcutta in rigorous confinement.

Dr. Laurence, an intimate friend of Edmund Burke, who had died in 1797, threatened Shore with impeachment on account of his action, but did not proceed with the prosecution. Sir John Shore was created a peer as Baron Teignmouth. After his retirement he lost interest in India, and devoted his time chiefly to the concerns of the British and Foreign Bible Society and cognate institutions.

Ahalyā Bāī. Although it is impossible in this work to treat in detail the history of the various Marāthā states, I cannot refrain from commemorating the virtues of a lady who died in 1795, while Sir John Shore was Governor-general, after she had directed with success for thirty years the affairs of the Holkar dynasty and the administration of the Indore state. In 1765 Ahalyā Bāī, widow of Malhār Holkar and then in the thirtieth year of her age, was the sole representative of her late husband's dynasty. With the consent of the subordinate chiefs and the loyal co-operation of Tukajī Holkar, the commander-in-chief, who was not related to the reigning family, she ruled the state until her death in such a manner that she gained for herself unbounded veneration and for her subjects the blessings of righteous government. The historian, weary of the selfish wickedness of nearly all the Indian princes of the eighteenth century, finds agreeable relief in dwelling for a moment on the picture of Ahalyā Bāī as drawn by the skilful pen of Sir John Malcolm, who delineated her character after careful investigation of the facts. It would be a pleasure to transcribe the whole of his long and fascinating account, but room can be found only for a few extracts :

'The success of Ahalyā Bāī in the internal administration of her dominions was altogether wonderful. . . . The undisturbed internal tranquillity of the country was even more remarkable than its exemption from foreign attack. . . . Indore, which she had raised from a village to a wealthy city,[1] was always regarded by her with particular consideration. . . . The fond object of her life was to promote the prosperity of all around her. . . . She has become, by general suffrage, the model of good government in Malwa. . . . Her munificence was not limited to her own territories. . . . The beasts of the field, the birds of the air, and the fish of the river shared in her compassion. . . . She died at the age of sixty, worn out with care and fatigue. . . . She could read and understand the Purānas, or sacred books, which were her favourite study. . . . It is not common with the Hindus . . . to confine females, or to compel them to wear veils. The Mahrattas of rank (even the Brahmins) have, with few exceptions, rejected the custom [of seclusion], which is not prescribed by any of their religious institutions. Ahalyā Bāī therefore offended no prejudice, when she took upon herself the direct management of affairs, and sat every day for a considerable period, in open Durbar, transacting business. . . . The facts that have been stated of Ahalyā Bāī rest on grounds that admit of no scepticism. It is, however, an extraordinary picture—a female without vanity, a bigot without intolerance . . . her name is sainted, and she is styled an Avatar, or incarnation of the Divinity. In the most sober view that can be taken of her character, she certainly appears, within her limited sphere, to have been one of the purest and most exemplary rulers that ever existed.'[2]

Such a noble eulogy by a foreigner honours the writer as well as the lady.

[1] Indore city or Indūr is in 22° 43′ N. and 75° 54′ E. The original village was not founded until 1715. The city, which is growing steadily, covers an area of about five square miles, and in 1901 had a population of 86,886, excluding the people attached to the Residency. The place is now one of the largest trade centres in Central India, and the chief collecting and distributing centre for Southern Mālwā (*I. G.* (1908), *s. v.*).

[2] *A Memoir of Central India* (1832), vol. i, pp. 157–95.

CHRONOLOGY

Lord Cornwallis Governor-general	1786
Internal reforms	1786–90
Reverses of Māhādajī Sindia	1787
Ghulām Kādir; cession of Guntūr	1788
Third Mysore war began; battle of Pātan	1790
Battle of Mīrthā (Mairta, Merta)	1791
Treaty of Seringapatam: battle of Lakherī	1792
Revolutionary war began; permanent settlement of Bengal, &c.; renewal of charter of E. I. Co.	1793
Death of Māhādajī Sindia	1794
Sir John Shore Governor-general; battle of Khardā; suicide of Mādho Nārāyan Rāo, Pēshwā; permanent settlement of Benares; Cape of Good Hope taken from the Dutch; death of Ahalyā Bāī	1795
Bājī Rāo II, Pēshwā	1796
Sa'ādat Alī Khān, Nawāb of Oudh; departure of Sir John Shore (Lord Teignmouth)	1798

AUTHORITIES

The special works used include *Correspondence of Charles, First Marquis Cornwallis*, ed. Ross,[3] 3 vols. (Murray, 1859); SETON-KARR, W. S., *The Marquis Cornwallis* (Rulers of India, 1898); *Memoir of the Life and Correspondence of John, Lord Teignmouth*, by his son, SHORE, C. J., LORD TEIGNMOUTH, 2 vols. (London, 1843); MALCOLM, Sir J., *The Political History of India*, 2 vols. (Murray, 1826); ASCOLI, F. D., *Early Revenue History of Bengal and the Fifth Report, 1812* (Clarendon Press, 1917). The Bengal section of the text of the *Fifth Report* is most conveniently read in Mr. Ascoli's little book, which is excellent. The *Report* was officially published in full, with appendices and glossary, folio, 1812. It deals with Madras as well as Bengal. There is also an official 8vo edition of the whole text only, bearing the same date. Higginbotham, Madras, published a good edition of the complete work, arranged in two volumes, in 1883. An earlier reprint by the same firm appeared in 1866. Archdeacon Firminger has brought out an edition in one volume.

CHAPTER 6

Lord Wellesley; the fourth and last Mysore war; annexations; treaty of Bassein and the second Marāthā war; policy and achievement.

Lord Wellesley (Mornington). Richard, Baron Wellesley in the peerage of Great Britain and Earl of Mornington in the peerage of Ireland, took over charge of the office of Governor-general in May 1798. With the exception of Lord Curzon of Kedleston no Governor-general has come out so well informed concerning all the problems of Indian government as the Marquess Wellesley was. It is convenient to designate him from the first by his late and more familiar title. Wellesley, a ripe and accomplished scholar, had been for several years a member of the Board of Control and had devoted special attention to the acquisition of knowledge of Indian politics. When he took his seat at Calcutta he did not feel himself to be a novice surrounded by experts. His imperious temper and confidence in his own judgement were justified in no

SIR ARTHUR WELLESLEY.

small measure by the depth and accuracy of his knowledge. At the time of his accession to power he was almost thirty-eight years of age with his powerful faculties at their best. The Indian climate suited his constitution, so that he was able to perform an enormous amount of hard work without injury to his health. After leaving India he became Secretary of State for Foreign Affairs at a critical time in the course of the Peninsular War and twice served as Lord-Lieutenant of Ireland.

In almost everything he contrasted sharply with his predecessors, Lord Cornwallis and Sir John Shore, resembling them only in spotless integrity and unselfish public spirit. His temperament and ideas were closely akin to those of Warren Hastings. His views were large and comprehensive, imperialistic in modern phraseology; and, like Lord Dalhousie, he believed thoroughly in the superiority of British over any native Indian government. That conviction enabled him to make annexations right and left without any qualms of conscience. Every annexation appeared to him to be an undoubted and unqualified public benefit. The times and circumstances being such as they were, it is true that all the territories absorbed into British India benefited immediately by the change. If there were any countervailing disadvantages they were slow to appear. The Governor-general was fortunate in being well served by his brothers, Arthur, afterwards the Duke of Wellington, and Henry, who became Lord Cowley and ambassador in Paris. Many brilliant officers, Elphinstone, Malcolm, and others, who were trained under Wellesley, proved themselves well fitted to undertake at an early age the heavy responsibilities thrust upon them by the rapid growth of the British power in India.

Effects of Shore's policy. Malcolm justly observes that

'a period of six years' peace, instead of having added to the strength or improved the security of the British dominions in India, had placed them in a situation of comparative danger. Though the British strength was not lessened, the power and resources of the other states had increased. The confidence and attachment of our allies were much shaken, if not destroyed; and the presumption and hostile disposition of the principal native powers in India too clearly showed that it was to a principle of weakness or of selfish policy, and not of moderation, that they ascribed the course which had been pursued by the British government.'

It was proved from the events of Shore's administration

'that no ground of political advantage could be abandoned without being instantly occupied by an enemy; and that to resign influence, was not merely to resign power, but to allow that power to pass into hands hostile to the British government'.

The enemies alluded to were Tippoo and the Marāthās especially. The self-denying ordinance of the Act of 1784 and subsequent legislation which sought to tie the hands of the Governor-general, although honestly intended, was founded on a fundamental misunderstanding of the Indian situation. Instead of securing peace it ensured war. Nevertheless, in spite of the experience of the results of the brief period of pacificist inaction under the guidance of Shore, the experiment was tried once more by Lord Cornwallis in his second term of office, and by his successor, Sir George Barlow, with consequences far more disastrous than those which had followed Shore's desertion of the Nizam. We shall see presently what an amount of needless misery was caused to millions of innocent people by the pusillanimous policy of non-interference.

The action and inaction of Sir John Shore had given Tippoo time to regain his strength and mature his hostile designs ; had permitted a French party, supported by powerful contingents under French commanders, to become paramount at the courts of both Daulat Rāo Sindia and the Nizam ; had encouraged the Bhonsla Rājā of Berār to plan a scheme of resistance against British predominance ; had abandoned the Carnatic to anarchy and desolation ; and, after all, had left the finances of the Company in a state of exhaustion.

NAPOLEON.

The dominant fact. The newly arrived Governor-general, well qualified by previous study to understand the situation as a whole, took a comprehensive view of all the perils confronting his government and country. The modern reader when studying the records of Wellesley's imperious orders, of his wars and annexations, is apt to lose sight of the dominant fact that Great Britain was then engaged in the deadly struggle of the Revolutionary War, in which, as now (1917) in the Great War, everything was at stake. The political action of Warren Hastings had been dominated similarly by the dangerous position of his country between 1778 and 1783, while fighting France, America, and a host of other enemies. Wellesley, by reason of his rank, family connexions, official experience in Europe, and a mind trained to deal with matters of high politics, was in a position better than that of Hastings for grasping the relation between Indian politics and the wider issues of the Revolutionary War.[1] In 1798, when Wellesley assumed charge of the government of India, Napoleon, then known as General Bonaparte, had led an expedition into Egypt, and avowedly cherished designs for the conquest of India.

[1] Thorn gives a good exposition of the real, although not obvious connexion between Indian and European politics at the beginning of the nineteenth century. 'It had long been a maxim of French policy that the superiority of England could only be effectually reduced by the capture of her eastern possessions.' The Germans have pursued the policy of Napoleon by their attacks on Egypt, the 'neck of the British empire'.

Those designs were shattered by Nelson's splendid naval victory on August 1 at the battle of the Nile or Aboukir Bay; but the spectre of French ambition in the East long continued to trouble the repose of statesmen in London and Calcutta. Consequently, Wellesley's policy of subsidiary alliances and annexations, directed to the immediate purpose of making the British the supreme power in India, was largely determined by his resolve to exclude for ever all possibility of French competition. The policy pursued did not rest only upon the local Indian situation. India, whether she liked it or not, had been drawn into the vortex of European politics. Tippoo, the Nizam, and the Marāthās, each sought to gain French support, but all were too ignorant of European geography, history, and current affairs, to understand in the least degree what France could or could not do. The papers found after the death of Tippoo prove that that 'mad barbarian', as Cornwallis scornfully called him, was totally incapable of realizing the forces of the European world with which he blindly ventured to meddle. Bonaparte, who was equally ignorant of Indian conditions, seems really to have believed that valuable aid might be expected from Tippoo, and so contributed to the speedy ruin of that headstrong prince, to whom he had addressed a letter written in Cairo.

The Nizam disarmed. Wellesley, while recognizing the dangers of Tippoo's hostility, resolved to deal first with the Nizam, who had been estranged by Shore's desertion in 1795, and had endeavoured to strengthen himself by allowing M. J. Raymond to organize for him a powerful body of regular troops, similar to those commanded by M. de Boigne and his successors for Sindia. The Governor-general succeeded in persuading or compelling the Nizam to accept a revised form of subsidiary alliance, and to consent to the disbandment of the troops under French command. The accomplishment of Wellesley's plan was made easier by the death of Raymond, whose successor did not command equal influence. By means of clever diplomacy, combined with a skilfully planned military demonstration, the force organized by Raymond was disarmed and disbanded. Malcolm, who was one of the chief actors in the proceedings, relates how

> 'in a few hours, a corps, whose numbers amounted to fourteen thousand men, and who had in their possession a train of artillery, and an arsenal filled with every description of military stores, was completely disarmed, without one life having been lost'.

That bold stroke instantly reduced the Nizam to complete dependence on the Company, and removed him from the list of powers whose enmity should be feared, or whose amity should be sought. In those days the Sikh kingdom had not yet become formidable to India, and the only powers needing serious consideration were Tippoo and the Marāthās. The leading Marāthā chiefs were Sindia, Holkar, and the Bhonslā Rājā of Berār. The Pēshwā, Bājī Rāo, although nominally the head of all the Marāthās, enjoyed little substantial authority.

Declaration of war with Tippoo. Tippoo, after his defeat by Lord Cornwallis in 1792, had given many proofs of his inveterate hostility. The incident which immediately caused war was the publication in June 1798 of a proclamation by Monsieur Malartic, Governor-general of the Isle of France or Mauritius and Réunion, welcoming the proposals of Tippoo for an offensive and defensive alliance with France, and calling for volunteers to serve under the Sultan of Mysore for the purpose of expelling the English from India. The response to the call was insignificant, but the proceedings left no doubt as to the intentions of Tippoo. Wellesley, having carefully verified the authenticity of the document, called on him for explanations. His replies being evasive and contemptuous, the Governor-general, who had made effective preparations, declared war on February 22, 1799. The reasons for that action and for overruling the timid counsels of the government of Madras were recorded in an elaborate minute. At that time the second Lord Clive was governor of the southern presidency.

The war. The war was conducted with such lightning rapidity that few words are needed to describe its brief course. A Bombay force defeated a much larger body of the enemy on the Coorg frontier on March 6, 1799.[1] The main Carnatic army of about 37,000 men under General George Harris crossed the frontier on March 5; defeated Tippoo at Malavelli, twenty-eight miles east of the town of Mysore, on March 27; and stormed Seringapatam on May 4. The campaign was all over in two months. Tippoo, while fighting gallantly in a gateway, was shot through the head by a soldier. His body, extracted with difficulty from a heap of corpses, next day received honourable burial by the side of his father. The troops plundered the town. Their excesses were sternly repressed by the Governor-general's brother, Colonel Arthur Wellesley, who reported in his terribly laconic style:

> 'I came in to take the command on the morning of the 5th, and by the greatest exertion, by hanging, flogging, &c., &c., in the course of that day restored order among the troops, and I hope I have gained the confidence of the people.'

He gained it with absolute completeness. The prearranged plan of campaign had been carried out accurately in every particular, and the whole kingdom lay at the mercy of the conqueror.

Decay of Seringapatam. Bowring, writing in 1893, states that

> 'the old fortress of Seringapatan remains in much the same state as it was left in after the siege nearly a hundred years ago. The formidable fortifications have stoutly withstood the ravages of time, while the breach made in the curtain is still visible from the opposite bank of the river, where two cannons fixed in the ground denote the spot on which the English batteries were erected. Inside is shown the gateway on the northern face where Tipū fell in his death-struggle. The whole island is now insalubrious. A few wretched houses only remain where once was a great capital, and the ancient temple of Vishnu looks down, as if in mockery, on the ruins of the

[1] General Stuart's dispatch (*Wellesley Despatches*, pp. 115, 116). Lord Wellesley gives the date as the 8th (ibid., p. 107).

SERINGAPATAM IN 1792.

palace of the Muhammadan usurper. Part of this building has been demolished, and the rest turned into a sandal-wood store.'

The *Imperial Gazetteer* published in 1908 records some improvement in the decayed town.

Character of Tippoo. Tippoo, who was about fifty years of age at the time of his death, was a strange man, full of whims and caprices. He devised a new calendar, a new scale of weights and measures, a fantastic coinage, and so forth. He suffered from the delusion that he knew everything and was the wisest of men.[1] He worked hard at the business of administration and wrote instructions on all subjects, civil and military, with his own hand in Persian. He spoke fluently Persian, Kanarese, and Urdu. He left behind him two collections of letters, and possessed a valuable library, which was removed to Calcutta. His fierce Muslim bigotry did not prevent him from having recourse to Brahman prayers in time of danger, or even from making gifts to Hindu temples. He treated his enemies and prisoners with the most ferocious cruelty, of which innumerable painful details are on record, but was not more harsh than his neighbours to peaceful ryots in his own territories, which seem to have been well cultivated. He was personally brave, while too ignorant and conceited to merit praise as a general. His devotion to the faith induced the local Muhammadans to overlook his crimes and to regard him as a martyr of Islām. The tolerant British government permitted inscriptions in that sense to be inscribed on his tomb. The mausoleum, in which he and his father lie, is a handsome building, with ebony and ivory doors, the gift of Lord Dalhousie.

TIPPOO SULTAN.

Wellesley's Mysore policy. Lord Wellesley's intention had been to cripple permanently rather than to destroy utterly the power of Tippoo. The absolutely complete success of the operations of General Harris and the death of the Sultan were a surprise to

[1] 'A restless spirit of innovation, and a wish to have everything originate from himself, was the predominant feature of his character' (Sir T. Munro in Gleig's *Life*[2], i. 233).

the Governor-general, who was obliged to reconsider the problem of the disposal of Mysore. Wellesley explained in a dispatch addressed to the Directors that the Company and the allied Nizam enjoyed the 'free and uncontrouled right of conquest', while the Marāthās, having taken no share in the war, had 'forfeited every pretension to share in the advantages of the peace'. He therefore felt at liberty to secure the objects originally contemplated, namely, a reasonable indemnification for the expense incurred and adequate guarantees of safety for the future. The Governor-general was of opinion that the simple plan of dividing the conquests equally between the Company and the Nizam, who had given some help, would unduly aggrandize that Prince, while giving offence to other powers. He was convinced that no member of Haidar Ali's family possibly could prove an efficient and friendly ruler. After reviewing all conceivable alternatives, he came to the decision that the wisest course would be for the Company and the Nizam to take the districts which best suited each party and to make over the residue to a prince of the Hindu royal family which had been dispossessed by Haidar Ali. The prince selected for restoration as Rājā being a child five years of age, the whole of Mysore, except the districts assigned to the Nizam, practically became British territory. The exception was only temporary, because in the following year (1800) the Nizam surrendered his acquisitions in order to settle the Company's claims for the payment of the subsidiary force. A leading principle of Wellesley's policy was to secure territory the revenues of which should suffice to pay for the subsidiary force of each state concerned. He objected strongly to the old practice of having unpaid and unsecured bills for subsidiary payments continually the subject of negotiation. All the Indian states of that time were careless about finance, and almost always in arrear.

In pursuance of that policy the Company annexed Kanara, thereby obtaining the whole of the south-western coast, Malabar having been already annexed. Some other territory was also taken, and Seringapatam was retained in British control. The region assigned to the Nizam lay to the north-east. The State or Rāj of Mysore was thus reduced to the compact triangular inland block which it is still. The territory left to the Rājā, after the Nizam's surrender of his share, was completely surrounded by the British dominions and cut off from access to the sea.

Administration. The administration of the territory reserved for the child Rājā was entrusted to Pūrnia or Pūrnaiya (Poornea), the capable Brahman minister who had served Tippoo to the end. The arrangements were embodied in the supplementary treaty of Seringapatam, which included the usual articles providing for the payment of a subsidiary force, prohibiting political relations with other states, and excluding Europeans from employment. Articles 4 and 5 went far beyond the standard model by giving the Governor-general power to introduce regulations for the better internal government of the country, or even, if he should think proper, to bring the state under the direct management of the servants of the Company.

Although the independence of Mysore was avowedly destroyed by orders clothed in the form of a treaty, the mistake of introducing a British code of regulations was not committed. Pūrnia was allowed to manage his business in his own fashion. He had the good sense to employ irregular cavalry as his military force, an arrangement which suited the habits of the people. Every office, civil and military, was filled by natives of the country. The system thus started worked admirably while it was supervised in succession by Arthur Wellesley and Colonel Close. The precedent might have been followed with advantage in other cases.

Later history of Mysore. Pūrnia retained the executive power until December 1811, when the Rājā was allowed to undertake the administration. He lapsed into evil ways, so that in 1831 Lord William Bentinck was compelled unwillingly to act on the article of the treaty authorizing the assumption of the direct administration by the Company. For fifty years after that date Mysore was well governed by British Residents, working through native agency. Sir Mark Cubbon held the office for twenty-seven years. In 1881 Lord Ripon felt himself warranted in once more restoring the royal family to power. The experiment has been justified by success, and Mysore now ranks as one of the best administered of the Protected States. Indeed, it might, perhaps, claim with justice to be the best, but possibly such a claim, if made, would be disputed.[1]

The relatives and principal officers of Tippoo were treated by Lord Wellesley with humanity and liberality. The members of the Sultan's family were interned at Vellore, an arrangement which proved to be undesirable.

Subsidiary campaigns. The Governor-general's eminent brother, Colonel Arthur Wellesley, better known as the Duke of Wellington, enjoyed his first independent command when entrusted with the task of hunting down a Marāthā adventurer named Dhoondia Waugh (Dhūndia Wahag), who aspired to found a new dynasty.

A second series of supplementary operations took place in the difficult Malabar country, and was conducted by Colonel Wellesley with characteristic ability. The story of that forgotten minor campaign, while interesting to read in detail, is not susceptible of useful condensation.

Piracy in Malabar. Measures were taken to check piracy on the Malabar coast. Grant Duff, who gives the history of the pirate

[1] For details see Rice, *Mysore Gazetteer*[2] (1897). The author of this work can vouch for the excellent administration of the Archaeological Department established in 1908. The wise policy of employing natives of the country, as initiated in 1799, has secured a supply of capable officials. The position of the state in the midst of British territory leaves the local government free to attend solely to internal affairs. The chief now has the rank of Mahārāja. A representative assembly exists.

chiefs, observes that 'it is no slight stigma on the British Indian administration that this system of piracy was not finally suppressed until the year 1812'. In that year the Marāthā chief of Sāwantwārī, the pirate nest situated to the north of Goa, was compelled to give up all his vessels of war and to cede the port of Vengurla, now included in the Ratnagiri District.

The Mysore policy was approved by the ministry, and honours and rewards were conferred upon the principal personages concerned

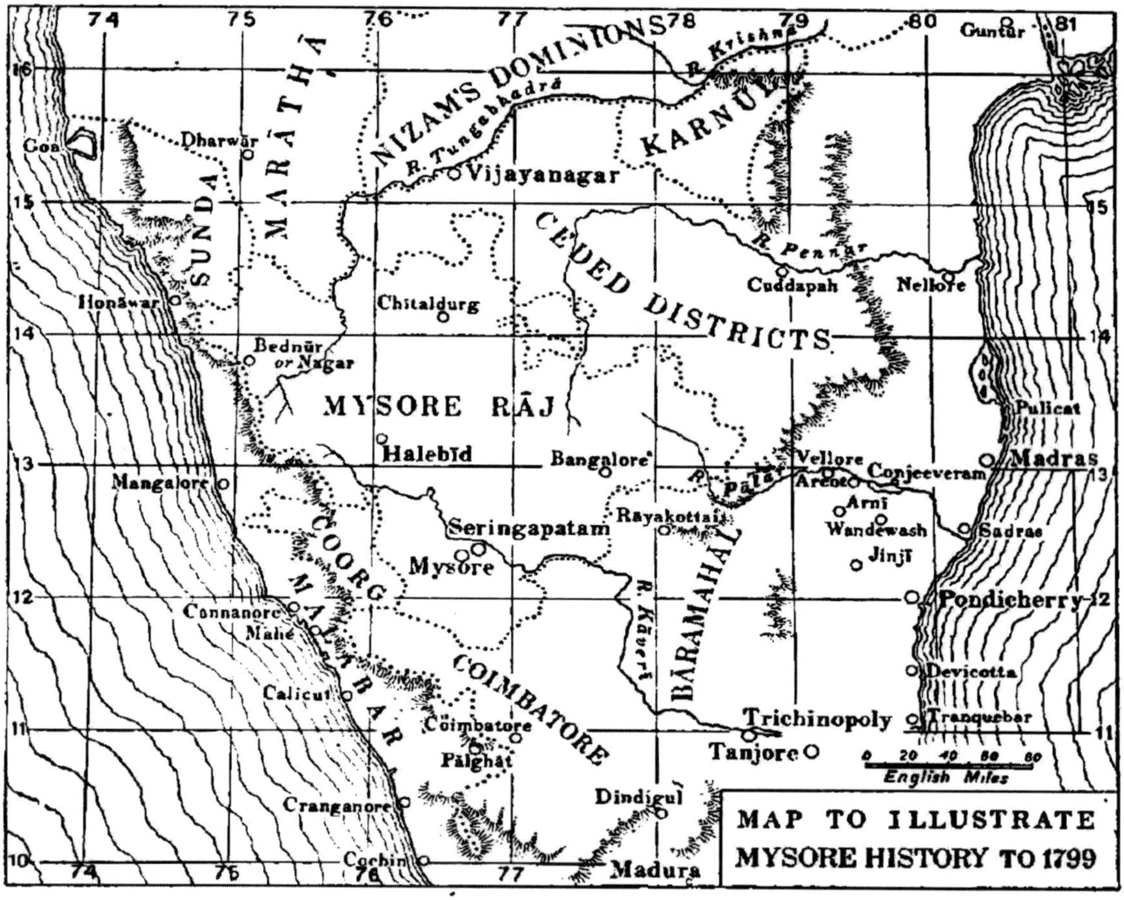

MAP TO ILLUSTRATE
MYSORE HISTORY TO 1799

in the conquest. The campaign was popular and applauded in Great Britain where many families had to deplore the cruelties inflicted by Tippoo on his prisoners.

Wellesley's 'forward policy'. Wellesley's 'forward policy' and his firm conviction that the extension of direct British rule was an unquestionable benefit to any region annexed led him to seize every opportunity for increasing the Company's dominions. His efforts to prove that his proceedings were in strict conformity with Pitt's India Act and subsequent legislation renewing the prohibition against ambitious designs are not convincing. In truth, he had unlimited relianee on his own judgement and little regard for the distant authority of his superiors in England. After the first enthusiasm over the eonquest of Mysore and the destruction of Tippoo had worn off the general tendeney of Wellesley's policy was distrusted by both the ministry and the Directors of the Company. The latter body espeeially displayed distinetly hostile sentiments and on several oeeasions passed irritating orders whieh gave the Governor-general just eause for complaint.

Annexations. He effeeted four annexations in addition to Mysore by taking over the administration of the Carnatie, the Tanjore Rāj, the Nawābī of Surat, and a large portion of Oudh. Those proceedings demand brief notiee. It is impossible to go into minute examination of the complicated facts of each ease.

A disputed sueeession gave an opportunity for the absorption of the small Marāthā prineipality of Tanjore founded by Sivājī's father, Shāhjī, a century and a half earlier. In Oetober 1799 the Rājā was persuaded to resign the administration to the Company and aeeept the position of a pensioned nobleman. The pension lapsed in 1855 owing to the failure of heirs. Tanjore is now an ordinary District of the Madras Presidency.

In the same year, 1799, similar arrangements were carried out coneerning Surat, on the occasion of the death of the loeal Nawāb. Subsequent cessions made under the provisions of treaties with the Marāthās, coupled with the absorption by lapse of the Māndoi state, resulted in the formation of the Surat District of the Bombay Presideney as now constituted.

The Carnatic. The reasons for the annexation of the Carnatic are set forth in the Governor-general's deelaration dated July 27, 1801. The papers seized at Seringapatam having proved that both Nawāb Muhammad Ali, who had died in 1795, and his son and suceessor, Umdatu-l Umrā, who died in July 1801, had corresponded secretly with Tippoo, Lord Wellesley announeed that they had 'placed themselves in the eondition of public enemies to the British Government in India'. He held accordingly that the family had forfeited its title to retain the rank of a ruling dynasty. After much negotiation he selected Prince Azamu-d daula,[1] a grandson of Muhammad Ali, as titular Nawāb, and took over the administration of the eountry. Whatever opinion may be formed concerning the validity of the reasoning based upon the Seringapatam papers, it was absolutely neeessary to terminate the disastrous system of 'double government', and to give the mueh oppressed inhabitants of the eountry a decent administration. The sufferings of the people in the Carnatic had been far more severe and much more prolonged than those of the Bengālis during the interval between the battle of Plassey and the appointment of Warren Hastings as governor. The aetion of the Governor-general was approved by the home authorities. The nobleman who

[1] Beale spells the name عظم, "'Azam,' not "'Azīm' (عظیم) as in most books.

now represents the Nawāb's family is known as the Prince of Arcot. The greater part of the existing Presidency of Madras consists of the annexations effected by Wellesley.

Oudh. Wellesley's action in depriving the Nawāb-Vizier of Oudh of a large part of his territory undoubtedly was high-handed and open to criticism both as regards the substance of the transaction and the manner of its execution. Wellesley explained his Oudh policy in a dispatch addressed to the Secret Committee of the Directors dated November 28, 1799. The gist of the matter is contained in the following passage :

> 'The affairs of Oude have occupied a considerable share of my attention. No probability existing that Zemann Shah [the Afghan chief] [1] will be able in the course of the present season to renew his hostile attempts against Hindostan, and a conjuncture so favourable coinciding with our successes in Mysore, the most eligible opportunity seemed to be opened for carrying into execution such a reform of the Nabob Vizier's military establishments as would secure us from all future danger on the frontier of Oude, and should enable me to introduce a variety of necessary improvements in the government of that country. With this view it was my intention to establish a considerable augmentation of our troops in Oude without delay, and to induce the Vizier to disband, under certain regulations, a proportional part of his own useless and dangerous force.'

That passage clearly shows that the Governor-general felt himself at liberty to do what he thought fit in Oudh, and to regard the formal consent of the Nawāb to the proposed measures as a mere matter of ceremony. The Nawāb tried to evade compulsion by offering or threatening to abdicate, but soon withdrew that proposal, on which he had no intention of acting. Negotiations proceeded until Wellesley lost patience, and in February 1800 administered a scathing rebuke expressed in language deliberately discourteous, to the Nawāb, whom he accused of threatening abdication 'with the sole view of defeating by delay the long meditated measure of a reform of your military establishment'. That, of course, actually was the motive of the Nawāb, who loathed all ideas of reform, and was simply writhing helplessly in the grasp of irresistible power. The Governor-general informed the Nawāb that his conduct was regarded as 'unequivocally hostile', and warned him that his perseverance in a 'fatal and imprudent' course would involve extremely disagreeable consequences.

In the end (January 1801) the Nawāb was forced to yield an unwilling assent to commands which he could not resist. He was required to go through the form of signing a treaty providing for the cession of the districts now constituting the Gorakhpur and Rohilkhand Divisions, besides certain territories between the Ganges and the Jumna, generally called the Doāb, in order

[1] Zamān Shāh, or Shāh Zamān, grandson of Ahmad Shāh Abdālī or Durrānī, had advanced as far as Lahore in 1796, but never came farther into India. He was blinded and imprisoned a few years later, and was still alive in 1842. Wellesley was inclined to make the most of the supposed danger of an invasion by Zamān Shāh.

to provide permanently for the cost of so many Company's troops as the Governor-general should be pleased to employ in Oudh or on the frontier of that province. The territories thus annexed, which comprise some of the most favoured regions in India, were long known as the Ceded Districts. They now form part of the Province of Agra.

Oudh thus became, like Mysore, a compact province of moderate size completely enclosed by British territory and absolutely impotent for military purposes. The Nawāb-Vizier, although he resented the transaction, gained considerable personal advantages. He was secured permanently from attack by the Marāthās or anybody else; was relieved from all pecuniary obligations to the Company; and was left free from any effective restraint on his vicious habits. The scandalous and shameless misgovernment of the country continued unabated without the slightest improvement until 1856 when the authorities in England insisted on annexation. Every Governor-general had lectured every ruler of Oudh to the same effect concerning the duty of reform without producing the slightest improvement. Sleeman's well-known book, *A Journey through the Kingdom of Oudh in 1849–1850*, gives an appalling and perfectly trustworthy picture of the horrors consequent on the selfish tyranny of debauched and negligent sovereigns.[1]

Subsidiary alliances. Oudh continued to afford a conspicuous illustration of the evils inherent in the system of subsidiary alliances, whether the troops provided for defence by the paramount powers were paid for by cash subsidies or by assignments of territory. Wellesley was right in preferring the system of payment by territorial cession, which eliminated many occasions for irritating discussions. But whatever mode of payment was adopted, the fundamental objection remained that

'the native Prince being guaranteed in the possession of his dominions, but deprived of so many of the essential attributes of sovereignty, sinks in his own esteem, and loses that stimulus to good government, which is supplied by the fear of rebellion and deposition. He becomes a *roi fainéant*, a sensualist, an extortionate miser, or a careless and lax ruler, which is equivalent in the East to an anarchist. The higher classes, coerced by external ascendancy, in turn lose their self-respect, and degenerate like their master; the people groan under a complicated oppression which is irremediable. Thus, in spite of the Resident's counsels and attempts to secure good government, the back of the State, so to speak, is broken; the spirit of indigenous political life has departed: the native community tends to dissolution; and annexation is eventually the inevitable remedy for its helplessness and chronic disorders.'

Subsidiary alliances. That description by Sidney Owen, echoing the opinions of Sir Thomas Munro, applies exactly to

[1] In 1819 the reigning Nawāb-Vizier offended Muslim opinion by assuming the style of king. Similar action by Tippoo, although disapproved, did not hinder him from attaining the reputation of a martyr, when he redeemed the error by a soldier's death. No ruler of Oudh ever aspired to the crown of martyrdom.

Oudh at any date until the annexation in 1856, and equally well to most of the states which were compelled to accept subsidiary alliances at the beginning of the nineteenth century. The conditions at present existing, when the rulers of the Protected States are bound to their king-emperor both by ties of genuine loyalty and by intelligent policy, are so radically different that an effort is needed to understand and appreciate the attitude of Wellesley on the one side or that of his critics on the other. The system of subsidiary alliances was a temporary expedient, serviceable in a transitional period, but long since obsolete. Substantial, although not formal annexation, as in the case of Mysore, accompanied by the rule of a capable indigenous minister, and unaccompanied by the uncongenial introduction of British law and courts too elaborate to serve their purpose, was an alternative by far preferable and infinitely more advantageous to the inhabitants.

But in Lord Wellesley's time the system of subsidiary alliances seemed to follow the line of least resistance. It was considered convenient to pretend that a country like Oudh still was an independent state, and to go through the farce of expressing the orders of the Governor-general in the form of a treaty between the 'high contracting parties'. Sir Arthur Wellesley never shared his brother's predilection for subsidiary alliances,[1] and it may be suspected that the wise arrangements effected in Mysore were sanctioned in pursuance of his advice.

The Regulations in the Ceded Districts. When the Ceded Districts were taken over in 1801 the Wellesleys arranged an informal system of administration, deviating where necessary from the Regulations of the Lower Provinces, so that the people might grow accustomed to British ideas and methods. In later years, as when the Panjāb was annexed in 1849, such a system, technically called 'non-regulation', was often applied with success. But when Wellesley resigned his arrangements were reversed, and in 1803 the country was subjected to the operation of the entire Bengal Regulations, except that the permanent settlement was not introduced (*J. U. P. H. S.*, 1918, pp. 91, 107). The establishment of civil courts after the Bengal pattern in territories taken over directly from the lawless government of Oudh gave occasion to much roguery, and largely neutralized the satisfaction given by the reign of peace and order.

Henry Wellesley. Lord Wellesley's appointment of his brother Henry as lieutenant-governor of the newly acquired Ceded Districts gave deep offence to the Directors, who held that the Civil Service had a right to the post and that their own patronage was infringed. Although Henry Wellesley was competent for the duties entrusted

[1] His reason, among others, for objecting to the system was that 'as soon as such an alliance has been formed, it has invariably been discovered that the whole strength of the tributary government consisted in the aid afforded by its powerful ally, or rather protector' (*Wellington Despatches*, p. 476). Munro held the same opinions, and in 1817 regarded the system as already obsolete (Gleig, *Life*[2], vol. ii, 6–10).

to him, his near relationship to the Governor-general naturally gave occasion for accusations of nepotism against Lord Wellesley who resented them fiercely. He could easily have found a suitable member of the Civil Service for the appointment, and his action produced much unnecessary friction with the Directors. Their subsequent action in recalling Lord Wellesley was largely influenced by their displeasure at the promotion given to his brother in an irregular manner. His habitually contemptuous attitude towards the Directors was a deplorable mistake.

Action in Egypt, &c. The measures taken by Lord Wellesley in co-operation with the British ministry to combat the world-wide ambition of Napoleon were not confined to Indian soil. An expedition planned by the Governor-general for the conquest of the Dutch settlements in Java was diverted by the Home Government to Egypt, where a sepoy force under General Baird, who had led the assault on Seringapatam, was landed early in 1801. The Indian contingent, which included some British troops, endured considerable hardships with credit, but had no fighting to do, in consequence of the previous defeat of the French. Indian troops did not again take part in European and Egyptian affairs until 1878, when Lord Beaconsfield summoned a force from India to Malta as a support to his anti-Russian diplomacy. The brilliant performances of the Indian contingent sent to France in 1914 at a critical time in the Great War are fresh in the memory of all readers. If Wellesley could have got his way both Ceylon and the French islands of Bourbon and Mauritius in the Indian Ocean would have been brought under the rule of the Company, but his designs to effect those objects were frustrated.[1] An embassy to Persia under Captain (afterwards Sir John) Malcolm in 1801 attained considerable political and commercial results, and was regarded by the Governor-general as a complete success. Since that time the government of India has always taken an active interest in maintaining control over the Persian Gulf. The necessities of the gigantic conflict still (1917) in progress have carried Indian arms far beyond Baghdad, and no man can predict the ultimate fate of Persia and Mesopotamia.

The French possessions. The peace of Amiens in 1802 having provided for the restoration of the French possessions in

[1] The ports of Ceylon, which had been occupied by the Dutch for 138 years, were taken from them by troops from Madras in 1796, and remained under the authority of the governor of Madras until 1798, when Ceylon was declared a colony under the Crown, and the Honourable Frederick North was appointed governor. For the disgraceful story of the war with Kandy in 1803–4 see chapter xix of Thornton's *History*. On March 2, 1815, the king of the inland kingdom of Kandy was dethroned for good reasons and the whole island passed under the sovereignty of King George III. The administration is controlled by the Secretary of State for the Colonies. The government of India is not concerned with the affairs of the island. The conquest of the French islands was deferred until the time of Lord Minto I in 1809 and 1810.

India, the government of France, which attached high importance to their recovery, dispatched a fleet to take possession. Wellesley, who foresaw that the truce could not last, boldly ordered Lord Clive, the governor of Madras, to withhold the surrender of Pondicherry and the other southern settlements pending further instructions. The French commander, not caring to attack, sailed back to Mauritius, and the prescience of the Governor-general was justified by the speedy renewal of the war. Wellesley showed equal promptness and resolution by his occupation of Portuguese Goa and Dutch Serampore. He never forgot the interdependence of India and the other parts of the British empire.

The Civil Service. The operation of Wellesley's capacious mind was not wholly confined to the direction of wars and high matters of foreign policy. He paid careful attention to the indispensable subject of finance, although his numerous wars did not permit of much economy. While he did not show any keen interest in education or other administrative departments devoted directly to the improvement of the condition of the natives of the country, he entertained the most comprehensive and statesmanlike views concerning the necessity for bestowing on the European administrators the best possible general and professional education. He seems to have believed that when the Company should be served by British officers of high character, and equipped with all the general and special knowledge required for the efficient performance of their duties, all desirable improvements in the country would follow. Present day conditions require much more, but Wellesley's stately sketch of the ideal training for members of the Indian Civil Service was drawn on sound lines and still merits respectful consideration. Some extracts from his long minute on the subject will repay the reader's attention.

'The civil servants of the East India Company . . . can no longer be considered as the agents of a commercial concern. They are, in fact, the ministers and officers of a powerful sovereign ; they must now be viewed in that capacity, with reference not to their nominal but to their real occupations. They are required to discharge the functions of magistrates, judges, ambassadors, and governors of provinces. . . . Their duties are those of statesmen in every other part of the world. . . . Their education should be founded in a general knowledge of those branches of literature and science which form the basis of the education of persons destined to similar occupations in Europe. To this foundation should be added an intimate acquaintance with the history, languages, customs, and manners of the people of India, with the Mahometan and Hindoo codes of law and religion, and with the political and commercial interests of Great Britain in Asia.'

The Governor-general goes on to recommend study of the Regulations of the Indian government and of the British constitution.

'The early discipline of the service should be calculated to counteract the defects of the climate and the vices of the people, and to form a natural barrier against habitual indolence, dissipation, and licentious indulgence.'

'To remedy the existing evils. the Governor-general proposed to establish a College in Calcutta, for the reception of writers for the three presidencies, who were there, for a limited period, to be subjected to the restraints of academic discipline, and trained in such studies as might fit them for their future duties. These were to be pursued under the superintendence of two clergymen, chaplains in the Company's service; for the native languages moonshees were to be provided.'

Wellesley was so eager to see his College at work that he started it without waiting for sanction, and was much mortified when the project was vetoed by the Directors, who substituted a much more modest scheme for teaching Indian languages at the head-quarters of each presidency.

A few years later, in 1809, the East India College at Haileybury near Hertford was founded. It continued for nearly half a century to give a training arranged approximately on the lines of Wellesley's plan, but carried out in England instead of at Calcutta.

Change in political relations with the Marāthās. The reduction of the Nizam to a condition of absolute dependence on the British power, resulting from the treaties of 1798 and 1800, with the simultaneous destruction of Tippoo, produced, as Malcolm observes, 'a complete alteration of our political relations with the Mahratta states'. When the government of India became bound to defend the territories of the Nizam as it would its own, and the Mysore state had practically become a British possession, the government of India virtually succeeded to all the local and political relations which had existed between the Marāthās on the one part and the Hyderabad and Mysore States on the other. The policy of non-interference in Marāthā affairs had ceased to be practicable, because the Marāthā chiefs always had claims outstanding against both Hyderabad and Mysore for the realization of *chauth* and on other accounts, while they could not subsist their own troops except by the plunder of neighbours. A predatory life was the essence of the existence of a Marāthā government. The only possible alternatives open to the Governor-general were either the abandonment of all conquests, or measures such as would induce the Marāthā governments to acquiesce in a state of general peace and tranquillity. The former alternative, although contemplated by the Directors, would have involved gross breaches of faith and would have consigned enormous territories to anarchy and misery. Lord Wellesley was not the man to entertain for a moment designs so pusillanimous and dishonourable. He was forced therefore to consider means by which he might hope to convert the Marāthās into peaceable neighbours, while leaving their domestic institutions unchanged.

Wellesley sought alliance with the Pēshwā. The prospect of success in that endeavour was not promising. Marāthā institutions and ideas were fundamentally incompatible with the *Pax Britannica* which Wellesley sought to impose on India. He probably realized that obvious fact, although he felt bound to make an effort in the hope of inducing the Marāthā chiefs to accept his postulate of a peaceful India. He proposed to effect his purpose through the Pēshwā, whom he desired and professed to treat as the actual ruler and head of all the Marāthās. His immediate aim, accordingly, was to persuade the Pēshwā, Bājī Rāo, to accept a treaty of subsidiary alliance on lines resembling those of the treaty with the Nizam. The Governor-general pursued that object with the utmost pertinacity, and apparently was not fully conscious that he was asking the Pēshwā and all the Marāthā chiefs to renounce their independence and sink into the position of mere dependants on the British power. Lord Wellesley was disposed to overrate the authority of the Pēshwā, and to give too little weight to the fact that Sindia and the other leading chiefs of that time paid little regard to the wishes or commands of their nominal head.

NĀNĀ FARNAVĪS.

Dominance of Mahādajī and Daulat Rāo Sindia. After the execution of the treaty of Sālbāī in 1782 the chiefs of the family of Sindia had been allowed to do as they pleased without interference from the Calcutta government. Warren Hastings had been too glad to obtain the help of Māhādajī in concluding the then indispensable peace to throw any obstacles in the way of his aggrandizement. Lord Cornwallis and Sir John Shore had pursued a policy of strict non-interference on principle. The result was that Mahādajī Sindia became the most powerful prince in India, and that when he died in February 1794 his power was transmitted to his successor, Daulat Rāo, with whom Lord Wellesley had to deal.

Marāthā anarchy. After Lord Wellesley had assumed charge in May 1798 Marāthā internal politics presented a scene of terrible confusion, vividly pictured in Grant Duff's pages. That author, writing of the year 1799, describes a state of absolute anarchy in the Pēshwā's territory, where the Pēshwā, Sindia, the Bāīs, or ladies of his family, the Rājā of Kolhāpur, and other parties, were all fighting one with the other. The flame spread into Hindostan, where Jaswant Rāo Holkar, a son of Tukājī, and a ferocious, drunken savage, now became prominent as a leader of banditti.

Death and character of Nānā Farnavīs. The death of Nānā

Farnavīs, who had been for thirty-eight years, since the death of Pēshwā Mādho Rāo in 1772, the leading Marāthā politician, occurred in March 1800. 'With him', the Resident observed, 'has departed all the wisdom and moderation of the Mahratta government.' His death, however, was welcome to the treacherous Pēshwā, Bājī Rāo II, who had long sought the ruin of the great minister. Grant Duff held that the Nānā 'was certainly a great statesman', notwithstanding a conspicuous lack of personal courage, and his rather unscrupulous ambition. In difficult times he tried to do his best for his master and country. He is described as having been in private life 'a man of strict veracity, humane, frugal, and charitable'. Most of his rivals were such scoundrels that the historian's praise of the Nānā's virtues is a pleasant surprise.

BĀJĪ RĀO PĒSHWĀ.

Shirzee Rao Ghatgay. The worst scoundrel of those evil days was Daulat Rāo Sindia's father-in-law and minister, the 'execrable' Sarji Rāo Ghātkē (Shirzee Rao Ghatgay), who took a fiendish pleasure in devising new and horrible modes of execution and in plundering defenceless citizens whom he subjected to atrocious tortures. He lived longer than he deserved until 1809, when a Marāthā chief 'transfixed him with his spear, and thus rid the world of a being, than whom few worse have ever disgraced humanity'.

Bājī Rāo II, Pēshwā. Bājī Rāo, the Pēshwā, vied with Sarjī Rāo in cruelty, and could sit on a balcony watching with delight the torture of an enemy dragged about at the foot of an elephant. One of his ruling passions, we are told, was 'implacable revenge', and he was so much the slave of that ignoble passion that he was incapable of taking broad and statesmanlike views of any political question. His main object always was to destroy and plunder somebody whom he disliked. He was the personification of treachery, and withal an arrant coward.

Battle of Poona, October 25, 1802. At last, on October 25, 1802, the turmoil in the Marāthā country was brought to a crisis by the battle of Poona, in which Jaswant Rāo Holkar inflicted a decisive defeat on the forces of Daulat Rāo Sindia and the Pēshwā.

Bājī Rāo fled with about 7,000 followers as soon as the result of the battle was known, and at once intimated his willingness to accept the subsidiary treaty pressed upon him by the Governor-general. The Pēshwā ultimately proceeded to Bassein, where he arrived early in December.

Amrit Rāo set up by Holkar. Jaswant Rāo Holkar, whose object was to persuade Bājī Rāo to return, at first pretended to use his victory with great moderation. But when he saw that the Pēshwā had no intention of coming back Holkar set up Amrit Rāo —brother by adoption of Bājī Rāo—as Pēshwā, and plundered Poona with the utmost cruelty. Several men died under the tortures they underwent.

Terms of the Treaty of Bassein. Colonel Close, the British Resident at Poona, proceeded to Bassein, where, on the last day of the year 1802, he concluded with Bājī Rāo the celebrated treaty known by the name of the place of signature. The compact purported to be a general defensive alliance, for the reciprocal protection of the territories of the Company, the Pēshwā, and their respective allies. The Pēshwā bound himself to pay 26 lakhs a year for a subsidiary force of not less than six battalions to be stationed within his dominions ; to exclude from his service all Europeans of a nation hostile to the English ; to relinquish all claims on Surat ; to recognize the engagements between the Gaikwār and the British ; to abstain from hostilities or negotiations with other states, unless in consultation with the British Government ; and to accept the arbitration of that government in disputes with the Nizam or the Gaikwār.

Restoration of Bājī Rāo. Thus 'the Pēshwā sacrificed his independence as the price of protection' ; no other course being open to him. He was wholly unable to stand alone, and had to choose between the Company, Holkar, or Sindia as his protector. The evil which at the moment seemed to him to be the least was chosen. He never intended to abide by the terms of the treaty, if by any means he could evade compliance.

The restoration of Bājī Rāo was accomplished by General Arthur Wellesley with his accustomed promptitude and ability. By making forced marches at extraordinary speed he saved Poona from destruction and installed the Pēshwā. Holkar's candidate, Amrit Rāo, who felt no desire to resist, was content to retire to Benares with a pension.

War. Meantime Sindia and the Rājā of Berār were concerting plans to defeat the Governor-general's policy. Neither prince could contemplate the voluntary acceptance of a subsidiary alliance involving the loss of independence. Holkar declined to join in the combination, preferring to retire to Mālwā in order to look after his own interests. Sindia and the Rājā declined to remove their troops from the Nizam's frontier, where they occupied a threatening position, and Sindia informed the Resident that the question of peace or war could not be decided until after consultation with the Rājā. The withdrawal of the Resident from the camp of the allies on August 3, 1803, served as a declaration of war.

Lord Wellesley too sanguine. Lord Wellesley undoubtedly was or professed to be too sanguine in hoping that he could induce all the Marāthā chiefs to surrender everything which made life worth living in their eyes, and to accept his invitations, which so closely resembled those of the spider to the fly. The critics of the Governor-general both in England and in India were not slow to perceive that his policy necessarily involved the outbreak of a general Marāthā war, which actullay began when the Resident withdrew from the camp of Sindia and the Rājā of Berār in August 1803. The truth is that a contest between the British and the Marāthās for the sovereignty of India had to be fought out, and that no treaty could long delay the inevitable trial of strength. Wellesley would have finished the business if he had been allowed to do so, but his recall postponed the final settlement until 1818.

Theatres of war. The war involved five sets of operations, namely, three major campaigns, that in the Deccan, a second against Sindia, and a third against Holkar, with two subsidiary campaigns in Bundēlkhand and Orissa. It is needless to describe in detail the minor operations, which were successful, and resulted in a notable improvement of the British military position. The conquest of Bundēlkhand secured the southern frontier of Hindostan or Upper India, while the annexation of Cuttack (Katak) joined the territories of Bengal and Madras.[1]

The Deccan campaign. The Deccan campaign was entrusted to the capable hands of Arthur Wellesley, who was armed with full powers, political as well as military. He began by occupying Ahmadnagar, and securing the most important strategical position in the country, the pass connecting the Nizam's dominions with the Marāthā territory of Khāndēsh, and traversing the range of mountains variously known by the names of Ajantā, Sahyādri, or Indrayādri. The army was divided into two corps, each of about 5,000 men, one under Colonel Stevenson, and the other under Arthur Wellesley. The arrangements for effecting a junction proved impracticable, and Wellesley was obliged, or believed himself obliged, to give battle while Stevenson was still about eight miles distant.[2]

Battle of Assaye. Wellesley, with less than 5,000 men, boldly attacked the Marāthā army, from seven to ten times superior in numbers, at Assaye, close to the north-western frontier of the Nizam's dominions. The fight, which was desperate, resulted in a complete victory for the Company's troops on September 23, 1803. After the battle Wellesley found it expedient to offer Sindia a suspension of hostilities in the Deccan, and proceeded to deal with the Bhonsla Rājā of Berār and Nāgpur.

Treaty of Dēogāon. The army of that chief, under the command of his brother, Venkājī, was decisively defeated at Argāon (Argaum) in the Akola District of Berār on November 29. The

[1] For full particulars see Thorn, chapters vii, viii.

[2] Munro, even after receiving General Wellesley's explanation, held that it would have been wiser to defer attack (Gleig, *Life*[2], i. 385).

strong fortress of Gāwīlgarh was stormed on December 15, and two days later the war with Berār was closed by the treaty of Dēogāon, drawn nearly on the same lines as the treaty of Bassein. The document also arranged for the cession of Cuttack.

Battle of Delhi. The hostilities with Sindia in northern India had equally brilliant results. General Lake, who was in command of about 10,000 men, operating in Hindostan, won a series of splendid victories. He began by an 'extraordinary feat', the capture by assault of Aligarh, a strong fortress situated between Agra and Delhi, and then proceeded to defeat Louis Bourquin, the French general who had succeeded Perron in the command of Sindia's regular troops, at a hard-fought battle near Delhi. The British force, outnumbered by four to one, had to face the fire of a hundred guns, many of large calibre. The losses of the victors necessarily were heavy.[1]

> 'I really do think', Lake wrote, 'the business was one of the most gallant actions possible; such a fire of cannon has seldom been seen, if ever, against which our men marched up within one hundred yards without taking a firelock from their shoulders, when they gave one volley, charged instantly, and drove the enemy. . . . I do not think there could have been a more glorious day.'

The poor old blind emperor, Shāh Ālam, was set on his throne again, and made as comfortable as he could be with suitable allowances. He counted no longer in politics. Agra, 'the key of Hindostan', was surrendered by the enemy.[2]

Treaty of Surjī Arjungāon. A little later Sindia's remaining forces were utterly defeated at Laswārī in the Alwar state. The battle was even more severe and bloody than that of Assaye. The war was ended by the treaty of Surjī Arjungāon on December 30. Sindia accepted a subsidiary alliance of the usual kind and surrendered much territory. Thus the power of both Sindia and Berar had been overthrown within less than five months. Lord Wellesley rejoiced especially over the destruction of Sindia's regular troops commanded by French officers, which had threatened to endanger the British supremacy in Hindostan.

[1] Sindia's strength lay chiefly in his artillery. The 'regular' infantry under French command lacked steadiness as a rule, but at Laswārī fought with extraordinary valour. "'Its discipline, its arms, and uniform clothing, I regard merely as the means of dressing it out for the sacrifice' (Munro in Gleig's *Life*[2], i. 392). Munro was right, as usual. Perron had retired from Sindia's service and passed through the British lines by permission. The only full account of Perron's career is in Compton's valuable work. For the true position of the Delhi battle-field see Jones, App. iii, and E. D. Maclagan in *J. P. H. S.*, vol. iii, pp. 127–41. The 76th Regiment (now 2nd Batt. Duke of Wellington's) did wonders at Delhi and elsewhere.

[2] A wonderful piece of ordnance, known as the 'great gun of Agra', was taken. It was a casting in brass or some similar alloy, 14 feet 2 inches long, with a calibre or bore 23 inches in diameter. It weighed 96,600 pounds and could fire a shot weighing 1,500 pounds. When General Lake tried to remove it to Calcutta, it sank in the Jumna. Subsequently, Lord William Bentinck caused it to be blown up and sold as old metal.

GATEWAY, GĀWĪLGARH.

War with Holkar. Holkar, who had remained aloof, now determined to fight on his own account, and deliberately preferred extravagant demands which forced Lord Wellesley to begin a fresh war. The British plan of campaign was skilfully designed to press the Marāthā chief from every direction, Lake operating in Hindostan, while Arthur Wellesley was to advance from the Deccan, and Colonel Murray from Gujarāt. Lake went into quarters at Cawnpore for the rainy reason, instructing Colonel William Monson to keep Holkar in check with three battalions of sepoys and a considerable body of cavalry. Murray was desired to advance from Gujarāt in support. Both commanders failed to carry out their instructions and mismanaged their business.[1] General Wellesley observed that they were afraid of Holkar and 'fled from him in different directions'. Monson, who according to the same caustic critic 'advanced without reason and retreated in the same manner', committed many military errors. His force suffered an overwhelming disaster in the Mukund Dara (Muckundra) Pass in Rājputāna, thirty miles to the south of Kotah. The remnants reached Agra in utter disorder on August 31.

Defence of Delhi. The destruction of Monson's detachment gave fresh courage to all the enemies of the Company and prompted the Jāt Rājā of Bhurtpore (Bharatpur) to renounce alliance with the British and to support Holkar in an attack on Delhi. Lieutenant-Colonel Ochterlony and Lieutenant-Colonel Burn, notwithstanding the dilapidation of the walls, maintained the defence for nine days, and compelled the assailants to retreat.

Battle of Deeg. On November 13, 1804, Holkar was defeated with heavy loss at the battle of Deeg (Dīg) and in the following month the formidable fortress of Deeg was captured with a hundred guns.

Siege of Bhurtpore. So far all had gone well in the war, except for the mishap due to Monson's and Murray's blundering, and a minor reverse in Bundēlkhand, but the tide of success was turned by Lake's failure before the walls of Bhurtpore (Bharatpur) early in 1805. General Lake, misled by his success at Aligarh and Deeg, disregarded prudent advice, and ignoring his lack of an adequate siege train and of the services of skilled engineers[2] insisted on making four assaults on the fortress, which was eight miles in circumference and defended by a strong garrison. All the assaults failed, the losses amounting to more than 3,000 men. The repeated failures disturbed the minds of people throughout India, but the Rājā of Bhurtpore had had enough of war and its exhausting

[1] Jones (p. 61) points out that the orders given by Wellesley to Murray were 'perplexing'. Monson's instructions from Lake also were not precise. It is right to add that Monson was an extremely gallant officer, who had led the storming party at Aligarh, and did good service even after his disaster.

[2] Blacker (p. 237) points out that at that time and for many years afterwards the Indian government did not attach sufficient importance to the engineering branch of the service.

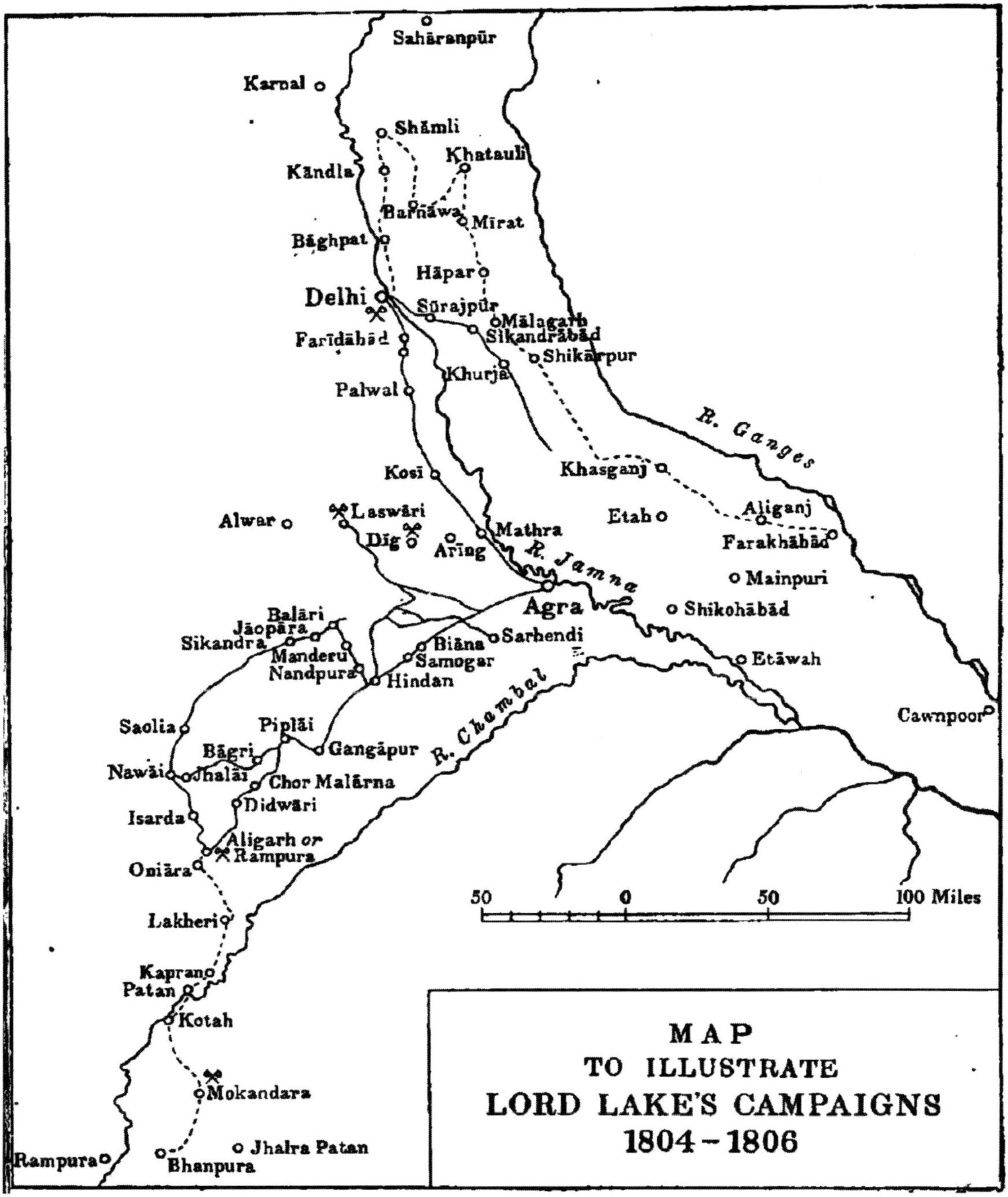

MAP TO ILLUSTRATE LORD LAKE'S CAMPAIGNS 1804–1806

expense. He returned to his allegiance and promised to pay an indemnity of twenty lakhs (2 millions) of rupees.

Recall of Lord Wellesley. The authorities in England, who had not at any time cordially supported the aggressive policy of Lord Wellesley, seized the opportunity presented by the receipt of the news of Monson's disaster and the outbreak of the fresh war with Holkar, and decided to recall their ambitious Governor-general, hoping 'to bring back things to the state the legislature had prescribed in 1793'. Attempts were made to impeach the Marquess, but were not pressed. Pitt, as usual, had recourse to

BHURTPORE FORT.

Lord Cornwallis, whom he regarded as an infallible cure for all Indian ills.

Policy and achievement of Wellesley. The Marquess Wellesley undoubtedly is entitled to a place in the front rank of the Governors-general by the side of Warren Hastings, the Marquess of Hastings, and Lord Dalhousie. Some authors would award him the first place, but in my judgement that honour belongs to Warren Hastings. Lord Weliesley, like Lords Lytton and Dufferin in later times, looked upon the affairs of India as seen by a British nobleman and politician from a Foreign Office point of view. He was a statesman, rather than an administrator, concerned chiefly with matters of high policy, and little inclined to examine closely the details of departmental administration. His policy was directed to two main objects. The first was the elevation of the British government to the position of paramount power in India; or to use his stately words, 'to establishing a comprehensive system of alliance and political relation over every region of Hindustan and the Deccan'. The second object was the full utilization of Indian strength so that it might play a proper part in resistance to the menace of Napoleon's world-wide ambition, which avowedly aimed at the overthrow of the British power in the whole of India. All the most important acts of Wellesley—such as the destruction of Tippoo, the treaty of Bassein, the Marāthā wars, and the series of annexations—were directed to the attainment of those two purposes, which were inseparably connected. The India of those days was bound to come under the domination of either France or England. It was impossible for her to withstand Napoleonic ambition unless when shielded by the might of England. Wellesley, as already observed, seized every opportunity for effecting annexations, because he believed sincerely that every such operation was a clear benefit to the people inhabiting the annexed territory. When replying to an address from the citizens of Calcutta, he formulated his policy distinctly in these words :

MARQUESS WELLESLEY.

> 'My public duty is discharged to the satisfaction of my conscience by the prosperous establishment of a system of policy which promises to improve the general condition of the people of India, and to unite the principal native states in the bond of peace, under the protection of the British power.' [1]

He did much to accomplish that grand design, and would have accomplished it wholly but for his recall.

His vision was clear and comprehensive. He saw what he wanted so distinctly, and showed resolution so inflexible in the execution of his well-laid plans, that he never failed in consequence of lack of personal foresight, although he was often baulked by the reluctance of the home authorities to accord their support,

[1] Marshman describes Lord Wellesley as 'the Akbar of the Company's dynasty'.

and occasionally, but not often, embarrassed by the failure of a trusted subordinate. He chose his agents, civil and military, with sagacity, and trusted them without reserve.

Calcutta owes to him many much needed improvements and the dignified Government House, modelled on the mansion of Lord Scarsdale, the ancestor of Lord Curzon of Kedleston. Lord Wellesley was familiar with the ancient literature of Greece and Rome, as well as with that of modern Europe. He possessed an intimate knowledge of Dante's noble poem. His style, whether in speech or writing, echoed the eloquence of Demosthenes and Cicero, with a tendency to excessive formality and magniloquence. He loved pomp and ceremony to such a degree that his taste for display sometimes invited ridicule and attracted hostile criticism. But his weaknesses as a public man were nothing when compared with his merits, which were fully recognized by a later generation of Directors, the year before his death. The Company then bestowed the rare honour of erecting his statue in his lifetime, and, knowing that his means were rather straitened, presented him with £20,000. When he was Governor-general he had spent with profusion and had scorned to take even sums of the nature of prize money to which he was entitled.

On September 26, 1842, Wellesley died at the age of eighty-two. In accordance with his express wish he was buried at Eton, close to the renowned school of which he retained a loving memory, and to which he had sent his two sons.

CHRONOLOGY

Lord Mornington (Wellesley) Governor-general (May); Ceylon declared a Crown colony	1798
Fourth and last Mysore war; capture of Seringapatam; annexation of Tanjore and Surat	1799
Death of Nānā Farnavīs; union of Ireland with Great Britain	1800
Annexation of the Carnatic and of the Ceded Districts of Oudh; expedition to Egypt	1801
Peace of Amiens; battle of Poona; treaty of Bassein	1802
Renewal of war with France; second Marāthā war; capture of Aligarh; battles of Delhi, Assaye, Laswārī, and Argāon; treaty of Dēogāon and cession of Cuttack; treaty of Surjī Arjungāon	1803
War with Holkar; defeat of Monson; battle and capture of Deeg	1804
Failure of siege of Bhurtpore; recall of Lord Wellesley	1805

(For exact details of the dates of Lord Lake's campaigns see Jones, App. ii.)

Mysore Wars

FIRST, 1767–9; ended by treaty dictated by Haidar Ali under the walls of Madras.

SECOND, 1780–4; Warren Hastings Governor-general; ended by treaty of Mangalore, based on mutual restoration of conquests.

THIRD, 1790–2; ended by peace dictated by Lord Cornwallis under the walls of Seringapatam; Tippoo being deprived of half of his kingdom.

FOURTH AND LAST, MARCH–MAY, 1799; Lord Wellesley Governor-general; ended by the death of Tippoo, partition of his dominions, and restoration of the Hindu Rājā in a portion of them.

The primary authorities are the *Selections of Despatches*, &c., ed. by SIDNEY J. OWEN, namely, those of the Marquess Wellesley, 1877; and those of the Duke of Wellington, 1880; both published at the Clarendon Press, Oxford, and skilfully edited. The earlier volume contains a good survey of Wellesley's administration. The *Political History* by Sir J. MALCOLM continues to be useful. WILKS deals fully with the Mysore war, and GRANT DUFF relates all Marāthā affairs in ample detail. The *Lectures* by Major H. HELSHAM JONES, R.E., delivered at the school of Military Engineering, Chatham, in 1881, which give an admirable professional account of the campaigns of Lord Lake against the Marāthās, 1804 [read '1803']–6, probably are difficult to procure. The *Memoir of the Life and Military Services of Viscount Lake* by Col. HUGH PEARSE (Blackwood, 1908) is more readable and accessible. The authoritative contemporary account is the *Memoir of the War in India conducted by General Lord Lake and Major-General Sir Arthur Wellesley*, &c., by Major W. THORN, quarto, London, 1818, with maps and battle-plans. The author shared in Lake's campaigns and kept a diary. The work gives full military details for each theatre of the war. The *Marquess Wellesley* by W. H. HUTTON (Rulers of India, 1897) is well written and based on special research. *Haidar Alī and Tipū Sultan* by L. B. BOWRING is good (same series, 1893). The revised edition of the *Mysore Gazetteer* (Westminster, Constable, 2 vols., 1897) is an excellent compilation, full of accurate information, the work of Mr. B. LEWIS RICE. G. B. MALLESON in *Final French Struggles in India* (new ed., London, Allen, 1884) gives a detailed account of the expedition to Egypt, and certain other matters of interest. H. COMPTON, in *A Particular Account of the European Military Adventurers of Hindustan, from 1784 to 1803* (Unwin, 1892), fulfils the promise of the title. It is a sound work on an ample scale.

CHAPTER 7

Reaction; peace at any price policy of Lord Cornwallis in his second administration and of Sir George Barlow; Lord Minto's strong foreign and cautious internal policy.

Reasons for recall of Wellesley. The dislike in England to Wellesley's policy was not confined to official circles. The body of the Court of Proprietors or shareholders in the East India Company was still more actively hostile. It is necessary to remember that in 1805 the Company continued to be a commercial organization, in almost exclusive possession of the overseas trade with India as well as China, and expected to make a good percentage of profit. The shareholders thought more of the 'investment', or provision of goods for export, than of empire. Although the extension of British dominion was certain to pay in the end, the immediate results of annexation were increase of debt, an empty treasury, diversion of funds from the 'investment', and consequent risks to the dividend. Such considerations induced a large majority of the stockholders to condemn Wellesley and clamour for his recall.

Lord Cornwallis a wreck. Malcolm observes that

'no one can be surprised that the choice of Lord Cornwallis as the successor to Lord Wellesley met with almost universal approbation in England at such a moment: and to those acquainted with that venerable nobleman's character, it will be a subject of still less surprise that his accumulated years and infirmities did not render him insensible to such a call'.

He was no longer the man who fifteen years earlier had sprung to arms in order to defend distant Travancore. He had come to regard almost the worst peace as better than the best war, and was willing to listen to the pleasant words of admirers who hailed him as the saviour of India. In truth, he was a wreck, unable to save anybody. He took over charge on July 30, went up country by river, and died at Ghāzīpur on October 5. He was insensible for some days before his decease, and had not been really fit for business from the time he landed. The state of his health forbids harsh judgement on the motives of his conduct, which in itself was both dishonourable and mischievous. Sindia had allowed the Resident's camp to be plundered, and had even dared to detain Mr. Jenkins the Resident. The Governor-general at first insisted on the release of his representative, but on reconsideration declared that the demand was 'a mere point of honour', not to be pressed if it should be the only obstacle to an arrangement with the Marāthā prince. To such disgraceful pusillanimity had the victor of Seringapatam sunk in his old age.

Reversal of policy. As long as he could hold a pen he busied himself reversing the whole of his predecessor's policy and renouncing so far as possible all his gains, for the sake of a peace that was no peace. He decided to abandon Gwālior and Gohud to Sindia, to make the Jumna the British frontier, to desert Jaipur and the other Rājpūt states, and to give the Marāthā bandits a free hand. He descended even to the baseness of anticipating with satisfaction that

'Sindia's endeavours to wrest those territories [in Rājputāna] from the hands of the Rajahs of Macherry and Bhurretpore may be expected to lay the foundation of interminable contests, which will afford ample and permanent employment to Sindia';

forgetting or refusing to see that the 'employment' of the plunderer would be paid for by the agonies of millions of helpless peasants. Lake's passionate remonstrances on the breach of faith, and the 'deep injury to the honour and reputation of the English nation', which such sentiments involved could not stay the drivelling infatuation of the Governor-general.

Sir George Barlow. When Cornwallis passed away his place was taken by the senior member of council, Sir George Barlow, who once again proved that a capable departmental official could make an exceedingly bad head of the Government. Sir George Barlow has been justly described as 'the meanest of the Governors-general'. His narrowness of view was made the more dangerous by the extreme personal dislike which he inspired. He showed himself even more zealous than the deceased Marquess had been in carrying out the behests of the ruling party at the India House so far as Hindostan or Upper India was concerned, and he broke faith so openly with Jaipur that the Directors felt constrained to regard his action as 'extremely questionable'. Sir George went so far as to bind the Government of British India not to make any engagement with the Rājpūt states for their protection against Marāthā oppression—a document described by Lord Hastings as 'the inexplicable treaty', which tied the hands of Lord Minto throughout his term of office, and hampered Lord Hastings until 1816. Lake's reiterated arguments produced no effect upon Barlow's obstinate mind. The commander-in-chief consequently resigned his political powers, and retired to Europe. He was created a Viscount and shortly afterwards died, in 1808.

Holkar. Before leaving India Lord Lake had pursued Jaswant Rāo Holkar by a series of wonderful forced marches, until that ferocious chief was driven to bay on the banks of the Biās. Lake was then in a position to impose any terms he chose; but Barlow insisted on giving back to Holkar power and provinces, while assuring him of full liberty to harry and ravage the Rājpūt states as much as he pleased. Even the Rājā of Bundī, who had helped Colonel Monson in his extremity, was abandoned to the cruelty of the Marāthā hordes. It is a sad and shameful story, still worse when read in detail than when presented in abstract.

The Nizam. Sir George Barlow, when not frightened by his terror of a Marāthā war, was ready to admit 'the utter impracticability of applying' extreme principles of non-interference to the case of the Nizam. When the Governor-general discovered that that incompetent prince had been led into a conspiracy to dismiss Mīr Ālam, his able minister, and to subvert the alliance with the British Government, Barlow decided that acquiescence in those proceedings was impossible, because 'by such an event the very foundations of our power and ascendancy in the political scale in India would be subverted', and so on. Consequently he applied the necessary pressure and stopped the intrigue.

Treaty of Bassein. He was equally firm in resisting suggestions from England to modify the treaty of Bassein, and in adopting that attitude was consistent, because he had recorded his deliberate approval of the compact when it was made. He held that the connexions with the Pēshwā must be either maintained as they stood or abandoned altogether. The latter course was rejected as being likely to result in

> 'the subversion of the British power—in the prosecution of which the Mahrattas would possess the means almost uncontrolled of efficient co-operation with a French force'.

The war with Napoleon had still to go on for nine years, and the worst phases of it had not yet appeared.

Financial surplus. Sir George Barlow's cringing before Sindia and Holkar had the great merit in the eyes of the shareholders in the Company that during his brief period of rule he was able to convert the financial deficit into a surplus, and to leave a full treasury to the credit of his unhonoured name. According to H. H. Wilson, 'the provision of the investment of goods for sale in England was, in fact, the mainspring of Sir G. Barlow's policy.'

Vellore mutiny. The only other event during Barlow's term of office which requires notice is the sepoy mutiny at Vellore in the Carnatic, wantonly produced by stupid orders of Sir John Cradock, the local commander-in-chief, issued with the sanction and approval of Lord William [Cavendish-]Bentinck, the governor.[1] The new regulations required the men to wear a novel pattern of turban, to train their beards in a particular way, and to abstain from putting sectarian marks on their foreheads. Anybody with a grain of sense could have foreseen that such folly would produce trouble. An outcry arose that the sepoys were all to be forcibly made Christians. Popular opinion in India, accustomed to violent 'conversions' to Islām under Muhammadan governments, is wont to regard Christianity rather as an impure mode of life, associated with the wearing of hats, the eating of beef and pork, the drinking of spirits, and the neglect of personal purity, than as a system of lofty theological doctrine. A man is a 'Kristān' who practises the objectionable habits thus indicated. The danger of the local situation was seriously inflamed by the presence at Vellore of Tippoo's family and some thousands of their dependants. At that place the sepoys suddenly broke out on July 10, 1806, seized the fort, and massacred two European companies, 113 strong, including 14 officers. Troops from Arcot took swift vengeance, and a series of courts martial followed. The whole business became the subject of acute controversy, some people thinking that the mutineers had been treated too harshly, while others clamoured for more executions. The complicity of Tippoo's sons was suspected rather than proved, but it is certain that the mutineers were in communication with the palace.[2] As a precaution the relatives of the late Sultan were removed to Calcutta. The childish regulations about the sepoys' dress and sectarian marks were more than enough to account for the tragedy, without seeking for any further explanation. The final orders were passed by Lord Minto, the new Governor-general, who halted at Madras on his way to Calcutta, and treated the cases in a spirit of sane moderation. After the expiry of some months the fears and distrust excited by the outbreak gradually died away. The Directors justly recalled both Lord William Bentinck and Sir John Cradock.

Lord Minto. When the news of the death of Lord Cornwallis

[1] Thornton, who had all the India Office records at hand, expressly states that 'the governor not only approved, but ordered the new turban to be adopted by a corps of fencibles under his own especial command'. Wilson agrees that both the governor and the commander-in-chief were blameable. 'Fencibles,' an obsolete term to denote troops raised only for home defence.

[2] Wilson observes that 'even with regard to the sons of Tippoo themselves, no proof could be elicited that they had been concerned in the conspiracy'.

reached London, Lord Minto, then President of the Board of Control, agreed with the Directors in supporting the confirmation of Sir George Barlow as Governor-general. The change of ministry consequent on Pitt's death upset those arrangements, and the new ministers suggested the Earl of Lauderdale as a candidate. The Directors strongly objected to his nomination. Lord Grenville, the Prime Minister, a warm admirer of Lord Wellesley, was equally opposed to the confirmation of Sir George Barlow. After much heated discussion all parties concurred in the nomination of Lord Minto, who accepted office with sincere reluctance.[1]

The Governor-general elect had enjoyed considerable parliamentary and official experience. His warm personal friendship for Burke had coloured his early views on Indian subjects, so that, before his elevation to the peerage, he had been as Sir Gilbert Elliot one of the managers of the prosecution of Warren Hastings, and had also been entrusted with the conduct of the projected impeachment of Sir Elijah Impey, which never matured. Those events belonged to a distant past. Time had so far ripened Lord Minto's character and judgement that the Prime Minister, notwithstanding his own attachment to Lord Wellesley's policy, could cordially approve the proposed appointment. The Directors, on the other hand, expected the new Governor-general to follow the guidance of Cornwallis and Barlow rather than that of Wellesley. Being a cautious, canny, and yet genial Scotsman, he steered a middle course with a degree of success which has not always been sufficiently appreciated.

Malcolm observes with his accustomed good sense that

'the administration of Lord Minto differs essentially from that of every Governor-general who preceded him. It was impossible for a man possessed of such clear intellect, and so well acquainted with the whole science of government, to be long in India without being satisfied that the system of neutral policy which had been adopted could not be persevered in without the hazard of great and increasing danger to the state. His calm mind saw, at the same time, the advantage of reconciling the authorities in England to the measure[s] which he contemplated.

Hence, he ever preferred delay, where he thought that it was unaccompanied with danger, and referred to the administration at home, whom he urged, by every argument he could use, to sanction the course he deemed best suited to the public interests. But the desire to conciliate, and carry his superiors along with him, did not result from any dread of responsibility; for wherever the exigency of the case required a departure from this general rule, he was prompt and decided. . . . The government of Lord Minto had no result more important, than the impression it conveyed to the authorities at home, of the utter impracticability of perseverance in that neutral policy they had desired to pursue. It was a progressive return to a course of action more suited to the extent, the character, and the condition of the British power ; but when compelled to depart from the line prescribed, the measures adopted by this nobleman were so moderate,

[1] 'I accepted . . . a situation which, so far from seeking, I thought a week before no human persuasion could have led me to undertake' (*Lord Minto in India*, p. 5).

and the sentiments he recorded so just, that it was impossible to refuse assent to their expediency and wisdom. A gradual change was thus effected in the minds of his superiors in England, and this change tended in no slight degree to facilitate the attainment of the advantages which have accrued from the more active and brilliant administration of his successor. . . . The marked feature in this nobleman's character was moderation; but that was combined with firmness and capacity.'

I concur heartily with the verdict of Thornton that Lord Minto 'well deserves to be held in remembrance as one of the eminent statesmen of India'.

Unappreciated merit. The appreciation of Lord Minto's personal character and policy has been placed at the beginning rather than at the end of the narrative of his administration for special reasons. One of those reasons is that the scale of this book does not permit the insertion of an adequate account of his achievements, especially of his admirably planned and executed expeditions overseas. The story of the conquest of Java, one of the most splendid feats of British arms, coupled with that of the reduction of the French islands, would suffice to fill a considerable volume. The restoration of Java to the Dutch at the general peace of 1815 has almost blotted out the memory of the conquest. A concise summary of Lord Minto's proceedings in connexion with the expeditions above mentioned cannot give the reader a just idea of the resolution, skill, and moderation with which the operations were conducted. Many circumstances contributed to dim Lord Minto's fame.[1] The six years of his administration coincided with the most critical period of the Napoleonic war, during which public attention was concentrated either on Wellington's glorious struggle in Spain and Portugal or on Napoleon's Russian adventure. Even the most brilliant successes in the eastern seas could not compete in interest with the events of the European drama. The distinction of Lord Minto's most masterly performance in the field of Indian politics—his defiance of Ranjit Singh, coupled with the extension of the British frontier to the Sutlaj—was obscured by the complete success of the policy enforced and by the Mahārājā's loyal observance of his engagements until his death thirty years later. Undue depreciation of Lord Minto's eminent merits sometimes seems to have been due to the belief that within the limits of India he merely carried on the policy of Sir George Barlow. The extracts from Malcolm quoted above should dispel that illusion. He could not have done much more than he did without antagonizing the authorities at home, and causing a Marāthā war, which he could not prosecute at the same time as the expeditions abroad. The moderate man always incurs the risk of censure from violent partisans. Lord Minto also had the misfortune to provoke the hostility of the powerful missionary societies and their numerous supporters, who roundly denounced the Governor-General as the enemy of Christianity because he had dared to restrain the exuberance of indiscreet theologians.

[1] 'Lord Minto's administration has never been sufficiently appreciated' (Marshman, *Abridgement* (1873), p. 306).

Lord Minto, who was then fifty-six years of age, took his seat in Calcutta on July 31, 1807. Sir George Barlow quietly resumed his place in council, which he continued to retain for several months until he was appointed governor of Madras, where, as will appear presently, he again failed as a ruler of men.

Foreign policy. 'The most brilliant chapter in Lord Minto's Indian government is that of his foreign policy. . . . Every fresh gain of France in Europe was followed by a corresponding loss in Asia. It was the glory of Lord Minto's administration that, whereas at its commencement dread of a French invasion of India haunted the imagination of statesmen, at its close France had lost all her acquisitions eastward of the Cape. The isles of Bourbon and of France, the Moluccas, and Java, had been added to the colonial possessions of Great Britain, the fleets of France were swept from the Indian seas, and England was without a rival in the Eastern hemisphere.' The Governor-general himself, when writing from Java in 1811, informed the Secretary of State for War that 'the British nation has neither an enemy nor a rival left from the Cape of Good Hope to Cape Horn'. Those results were attained by well devised naval and military operations.

LORD MINTO.

Diplomacy. Lord Minto also took much pains, but with less success, to curb by diplomacy the world-wide intrigues of Napoleon. It is unlikely that the autocrat of the French ever seriously contemplated an actual invasion of India, nor does such an operation appear to have been feasible. But he certainly did his best to stir up all the Asiatic nations within his reach against England. He sent a mission to Persia in 1808, which was countered by one dispatched from India by the Governor-general as well as by a royal embassy from England. An unseemly conflict arose between the rival British missions, and Lord Minto, so far as I can judge the merits of a tangled story, failed to display his usual discretion. It is not worth while to examine in detail forgotten quarrels. The royal ambassador obtained a treaty which the Governor-general was obliged to accept with a bad grace. Malcolm, who paid two visits to Persia under Lord Minto's direction, effected nothing except the collection of materials for his excellent *History of Persia*.

Elphinstone's embassy to Kābul in the same year never got farther than Peshāwar. Shāh Shuj'ā, to whom the mission was accredited, soon afterwards was expelled from his kingdom, so that no direct political results were obtained. The envoy devoted much of his time to investigation through agents and by all means at his command of the conditions existing in Afghanistan, then a completely unknown country. He embodied the results of his researches in a book of great value, entitled *An Account of the Kingdom of Caubul, &c.*, which was published in 1815, and still counts as an authority.

Ranjit Singh. Diplomacy, supported by the threatened advance of an army, effectually stayed the triumphant progress of Mahārājā Ranjit Singh, the able Sikh leader, whose ambition menaced the security of the British provinces of Upper India. Ranjit Singh, who was only twelve years old when his father died, was suspected of having murdered his mother, who certainly disappeared and was not heard of again. At the age of nineteen he acquired possession of Lahore with the title of Rājā from Shāh Zamān or Zamān Shāh, the Afghan ruler, in 1799. Three years later, in 1802, he made himself master of Amritsar, the Sikh holy city, and thus became a formidable chieftain. Continuing to extend his power in the Panjāb proper, he desired to annex the Sikh territories south of the Sutlaj, which had been 'a sort of no-man's land' between the Marāthās and the Sikhs, and had been reduced to a waste. Much of the country was inhabited only by wild beasts. In 1806 Ranjit Singh, at the invitation of his uncle, a notable of Jīnd, crossed the Sutlaj with a large force and occupied Lūdiāna.

Two years later the Cis-Sutlaj chiefs repented of having called in a person so powerful as the Mahārājā to take a side in their quarrels, and appealed to the Governor-general for protection.

Lord Minto dispatched as his envoy to the Sikh court Charles Metcalfe, then only twenty-four years of age. After much negotiation a treaty was signed at Amritsar on April 25, 1809, establishing 'perpetual amity' between the contracting parties.

The brief operative clauses were these :

'The British government will have no concern with the territories and subjects of the Raja to the northward of the river Sutlej.

The Raja will never maintain in the territory which he occupies on the left bank of the river Sutlej more troops than are necessary for the internal duties of that territory, nor commit or suffer any encroachments on the possessions or rights of the Chiefs in its vicinity.'

Thus the British frontier was advanced from the Jumna to the Sutlaj by a Governor-general who was supposed to refrain from all extensions of territory. Lūdiāna became the frontier cantonment.

Central India. Early in his administration Lord Minto had been obliged to secure peace in Bundēlkhand to the south of the Jumna by the capture from local chiefs of the fortresses of Ajaigarh and Kālanjar. He also made a military demonstration to warn off Amīr Khān, the Pathān leader of banditti, from invading Nāgpur, but drew back when confronted with the prospect of a Marāthā war. The Marāthās, with their Pathān and Pindāri associates, continued to oppress Central India and Rājputāna, which were in a state 'truly deplorable'.[1]

'People do not scruple to assert', as the Resident at Delhi reported, 'that they have a right to the protection of the British government. They say that . . . the British government now occupies the place of the great protecting power, and is the natural guardian of the peaceable and weak; but, owing to its refusal to use its influence for their protection, the peaceful and weak states are continually exposed to oppressions and cruelties of robbers and plunderers, the most licentious and abandoned of mankind.'

Lord Minto never felt himself at liberty to interfere effectually to stop those horrors. He could not have done so without committing himself to a general Marāthā war, and the strength of India was absorbed by the expeditions overseas. Jaswant Rāo Holkar became insane from the effects of intemperance and died in 1811. The British government had little intercourse with Indore for several years.

Travancore rebellion. The strangest event during Lord Minto's term of office was the mad rebellion in Travancore organized by the Dīwān or minister, Velu Tampi. The country had been shockingly misgoverned, and constant disputes had existed between the minister and the Resident concerning the administration and the arrears of payment for the subsidiary force. In December 1808 the minister, who felt much aggrieved at certain measures taken by the Resident, made a furious attack on the house of that officer, who barely escaped with his life. Velu Tampi then issued a violent proclamation calling on the inhabitants to defend caste and the Hindu religion, which elicited an eager response from the Nāyars. 'The whole country rose like one man. Their religious susceptibilities were touched, which in a conservative country like Travancore is like smoking in a powder magazine.' An officer and about thirty European soldiers of H.M. 12th Regiment were foully murdered, an incident which induced Thornton to echo an opinion that 'in turpitude and moral degradation' the people of the state 'transcend every nation upon the face of the earth'. That severe judgement is not justified by the later history of the state, which is now, and has been for many years, exceptionally well administered.[2] The rebellion, of course, never had any chance of success and was soon suppressed. The minister committed suicide and his brother was deservedly hanged for his active share in the murder of the soldiers.

Mutiny of Madras officers. An event much more dangerous was the mutiny of the officers of the Madras army, occasioned immediately by the stoppage of certain perquisites on tent contracts enforced by Sir George Barlow in compliance with peremptory orders of the Directors. The ill feeling was embittered by the

[1] For details see Tod.

[2] The country and people of Travancore are the most interesting in all India on many accounts.

injudicious action of the governor and other authorities. In 1809 the conspiracy, which had extended to many stations, collapsed, and most of the officers returned to their duty. 'Lord Minto, on learning the nature and extent of the disaffection, had proceeded without delay to Madras; but the crisis had passed before he arrived.' The punishments inflicted were few. Sir Samuel Auchmuty or Ahmuty, a competent officer, was appointed the local commander-in-chief. The affair destroyed Sir George Barlow's chances of again becoming Governor-general.

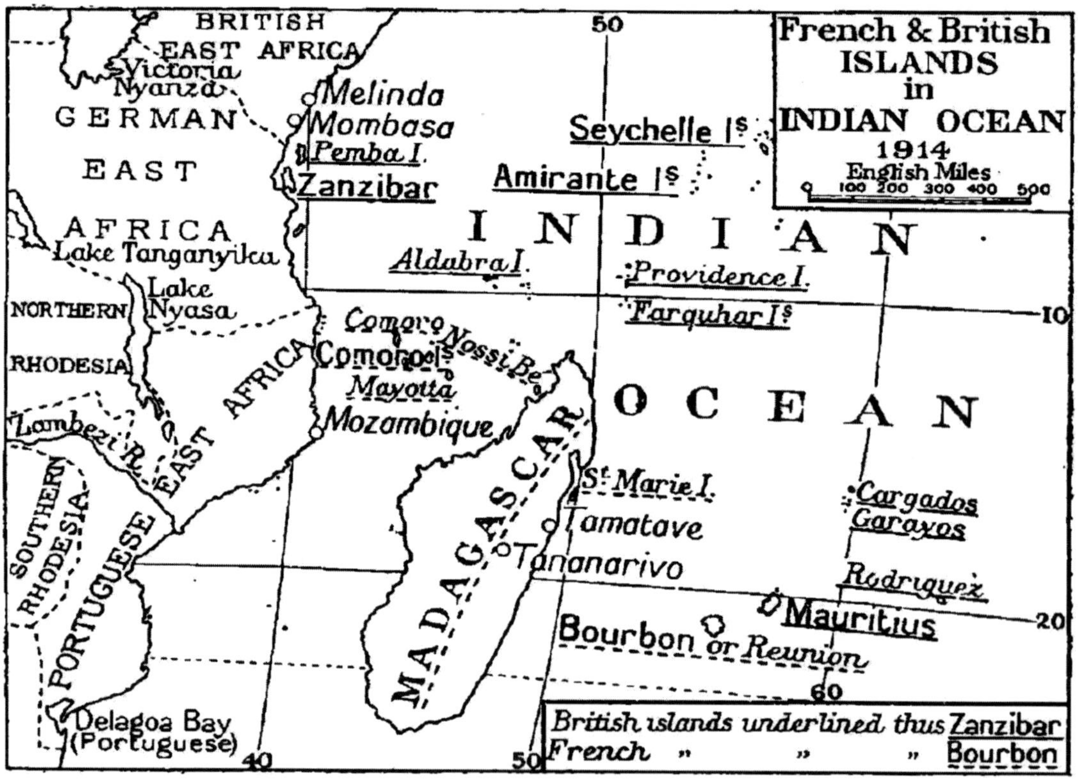

The French islands. The resolve of the British ministry to attempt the capture of the French islands in the Indian Ocean was prompted not only by the desire to inflict a heavy blow on the hostile power of France but by the necessity of stopping the devastations of the privateers which issued from the island harbours. The losses caused by privateering during Lord Wellesley's time were estimated at from two to three millions sterling; and in 1809, six 'Indiamen', or large vessels belonging to the Company, were captured. Lord Minto co-operated actively with the home authorities in planning and executing the difficult operations necessary, which proved thoroughly successful, in spite of some intermediate mishaps.

The island of Rodriguez was taken in 1809; Bourbon, or

Réunion, and Mauritius, or the Isle of France, after considerable fighting, capitulated in 1810. At the general peace Bourbon was restored to France; Mauritius being retained as a Crown colony, with Rodriguez and certain minor dependencies. The principal industry is sugar-planting, which has been developed by the aid of Indian coolies. The Indians resident number about a quarter of a million. The population is dense, the institutions and language being mainly French. The islands have suffered much from epidemics and hurricanes. A small garrison occupies Mauritius.[1]

Java expedition. The attack on the Dutch settlements in the Spice Islands or Moluccas, and in Java, then under French control, was a formidable business, which required careful organization, and hearty co-operation between the forces of the Crown and those of the Company. The Spice Islands, including Amboyna, notorious for the massacre of 1623, were occupied quickly in 1810, although not without some lively fighting. Batavia, the capital of Dutch Java, had been strongly fortified under French direction, because Napoleon attached high importance to its retention. Fort Cornelis, six miles from the town, was believed to be impregnable. But it had to yield. The storm may be described in the words of Lord Minto, who was present.

'August 28 [1811]. The enemy's impregnable works were stormed at daybreak on August 26, a new day in our military calendar. The place was most formidable in strength, and it really seems miraculous that mortal men could live in such a fire of round, grape, shells, and musketry long enough to pass deep trenches defended by pointed palissades inclining from the inner edge of the ditch outwards, force their way into redoubt after redoubt, till they were in possession of all the numerous works, which extend at least a mile. . . . The slaughter was dreadful, both during the attack and in the pursuit. . . . We have upwards of 5,000 prisoners, including all the Europeans left alive. . . . There never was such a rout.'

The storming troops were led by General (Colonel) Gillespie; the supreme direction was in the hands of Sir Samuel Auchmuty, commander-in-chief of the Madras army.

Lord Minto is sometimes alleged to have accompanied the expedition 'as a volunteer'. That is incorrect; he went as Governor-general in order that being on the spot he might be able to settle at once and with authority 'many important points regarding our future relations with the Dutch and with the native states in Java', and also secure harmonious working with the admirals. With the help of Mr. (Sir Stamford) Raffles admirable arrangements were made, and if the colony had been retained it would now be a possession of the highest value. But the general peace decreed its restoration to the Dutch, who still hold it, on a tenure which may be deemed rather precarious, considering the state of world politics as in 1917.

[1] The names of the islands have been changed repeatedly. In some of the older documents they are called collectively the Mascarene islands.

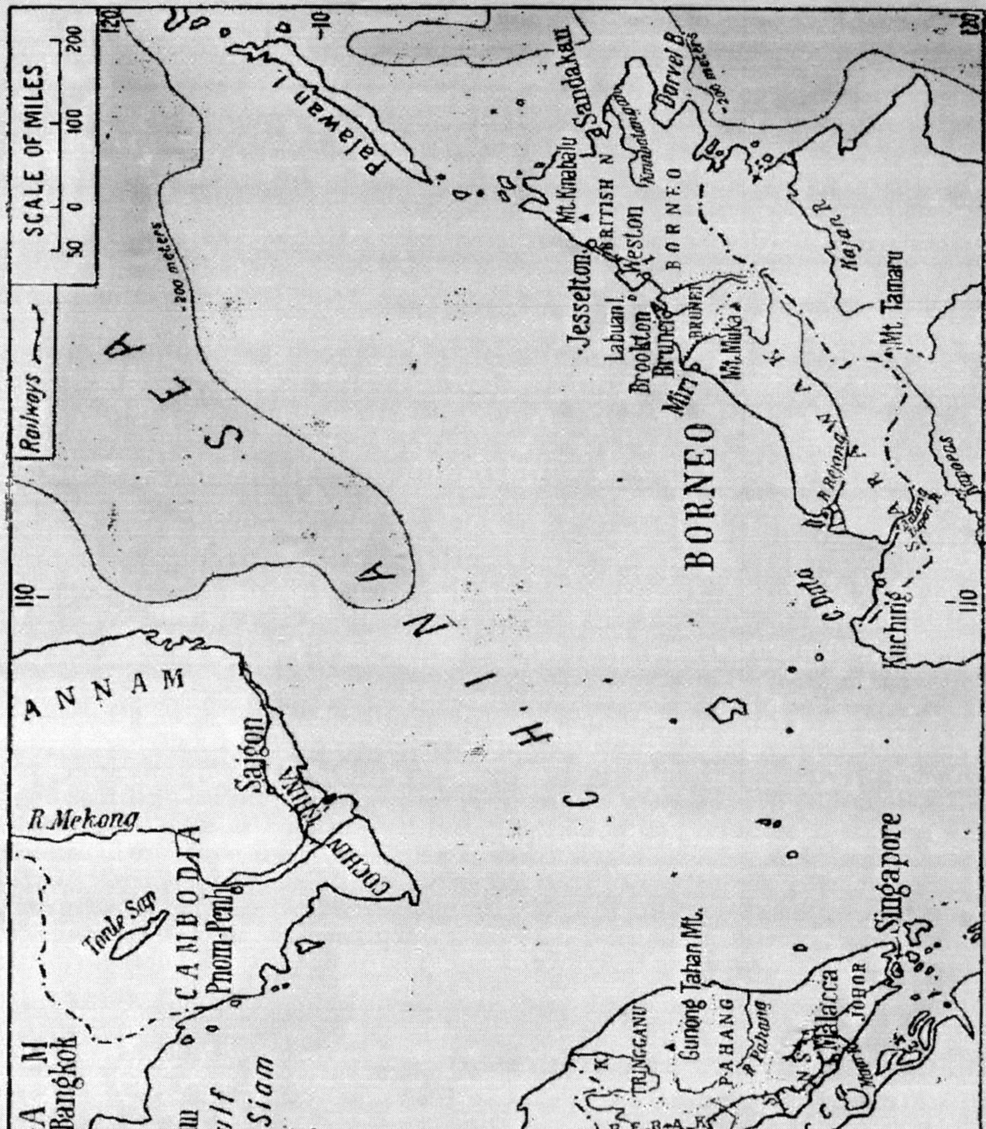

MALAY PENINSULA, ETC., 1914.

Charter legislation, 1813. The legislation of 1813 for the renewal of the Company's charter was preceded by the exhaustive inquiries of a Select Committee of the House of Commons, culminating in the *Fifth Report*, sufficiently noticed in an earlier chapter. The debates in Parliament were prolonged and interesting. Napoleon having closed the continental ports, British merchants insisted on the opening of the Indian trade. The concession was granted, subject to certain limitations. The Company still retained an interest in Indian commerce, but only as one competitor among many, and made little or no profit, although the captains of the magnificent 'Indiamen' acquired ample fortunes. For the purposes of government the Company continued until 1858 to be merely a 'fifth wheel in the coach' of the administrative machinery. Parliament, being unwilling to raise the thorny question of patronage of Indian appointments, declined to adopt Lord Grenville's suggestions that the Crown should assume the direct administration and that the Civil Service should be recruited by a limited competition between nominees of the public schools. The Company preserved for twenty years longer its exclusive rights in the China trade, of which tea was the principal item.

The question of the admission of missionaries was hotly debated. Their admission under licence was allowed. Provision was made for the spiritual needs of the European population by the appointment of a bishop of Calcutta and three archdeacons paid from Indian revenues. A grant for public education was made for the first time, a lakh of rupees, then worth more than £10,000, being

> 'set apart and applied to the revival and improvement of literature and the encouragement of the learned natives of India, and for the introduction and promotion of a knowledge of the sciences among the inhabitants of the British territories in India'.

Improved arrangements for the training of the civil and military servants of the Company were sanctioned. Subject to the above provisions and many others, the charter was renewed for twenty years.

CHRONOLOGY

Lord Cornwallis Governor-general for second time (July 31–Oct. 5)	1805
Sir G. Barlow Governor-general	1805
Vellore mutiny	1806
Lord Minto Governor-general	1807
Missions to Persia and Kābul	1808
Travancore rebellion	1808–9
Treaty of Amritsar with Ranjit Singh; mutiny of Madras officers	1809
Capture of French islands	1809–10
Conquest of the Moluccas	1810
Conquest of Java	1811
Pindārī raid on Mirzāpur; *Fifth Report*	1812
Renewal of charter of E. I. Co.; retirement of Lord Minto	1813

Authorities

MALCOLM'S *Political History*, THORNTON, and H. H. WILSON'S continuation of Mill are useful for the whole period. Vol. iii of *Cornwallis Correspondence*, ed. Ross, gives some documents.

The leading authorities for Lord Minto are his *Life and Letters*, 1751–1806, 3 vols., 1874; and *Lord Minto in India*, 1880, both well edited by his grand-niece the COUNTESS OF MINTO. *Ranjit Singh*, by LEPEL GRIFFIN (1898, in 'Rulers of India'), is excellent. The separate work on the Java expedition is the *Memoir of the Conquest of Java* by Major W. THORN, 4to, London, 1815, with maps, plans, and plates. A full account of the local rebellion will be found in AIYA, *Travancore State Manual*, Trivandrum, 1906, vol. i.

For the charter legislation see ILBERT, *The Government of India*, and App. x of vol. vii of H. H. WILSON (continuation of Mill—vol. i of Wilson's *History of British India*, ed. 1858).

CHAPTER 8

The Marquess of Hastings; Nepalese, Pindārī, and Marāthā wars; establishment of British supremacy in 1818.

The Marquess of Hastings. Francis Rawdon-Hastings, Baron Rawdon in the peerage of Great Britain, and Earl of Moira in the peerage of Ireland, represented two of the most ancient noble families in England, those of Rawdon and Hastings. The Rawdons settled in Ireland in the seventeenth century and became Earls of Moira. Francis Lord Moira in early life had spent nearly eight years in America as an officer during the War of Independence, and afterwards had seen some military service in Europe, but for the greater part of his life had attained little distinction. He was notorious for profuse, generous extravagance, resulting in dissipation of a noble fortune, and was on terms of the closest and most expensive intimacy with the Prince Regent, afterwards King George IV, whose friendship was not an honour. Lord Moira having rendered the prince certain special political services in 1812, was nominated by him in 1813 as successor to Lord Minto, and was accepted by the Directors. He was then nearly fifty-nine years of age, and apparently much too old for a term of arduous Indian exile. His record gave no indication that he would prove himself worthy to be ranked with the greatest of the Governors-general, and that, notwithstanding his advanced age, he would be strong enough to bear the heavy burden of civil government combined with supreme military command for nine and a quarter years. The length of his administration was surpassed only by that of Warren Hastings. He never went to the hills, and never failed to be at his desk at four o'clock in the morning. Early in 1817, as a reward for his conduct of the Nepalese war, he was created Marquess of Hastings in the peerage of Great Britain.

It will be convenient to designate him from the beginning by that title.

Seven quarrels pending. The seeds of the wars which were the main business of the early years of the administration of Lord Hastings had been sown by the enforcement of the timid non-intervention policy prescribed by the home authorities, carried out whole-heartedly by Lord Cornwallis and Sir George Barlow, and only slightly modified by Lord Minto. During the government of that nobleman the seeds had began to germinate, so that his successor, on assuming office, found 'seven different quarrels likely to demand the decision of arms' awaiting his orders.

MARQUESS OF HASTINGS.

Nepalese aggressions. The most urgent of the seven quarrels was that with the hillmen called Gūrkhas, who had overthrown the ancient dynastics of the Nepāl Valley in 1768, and had subsequently created a large state possessing considerable military force, which extended over the whole hill region of the lower Himalayas from the Sutlaj on the west to the frontier of Bhutan on the east. The cession of the Gorakhpur territory by the Nawāb-Vizier of Oudh in 1801 had brought the British districts into contact with the Gūrkha possessions in the Tarāi or strip of lowland lying under the hills. The Gūrkhas displayed an aggressive, hostile spirit and constantly made inroads across the ill-defined frontier. Lord Minto was obliged to take notice of daring invasions in the Būtwal region to the north of what is now the Bastī District and in another region called Sheorāj farther to the east. The tracts wrongfully seized by the Nepalese were reoccupied by Company's troops without open opposition. A fresh aggression in May 1814, when the Nepalese without provocation attacked three police stations in Būtwal, killing eighteen policemen, brought on war.

War with Nepāl, 1814–16. Lord Hastings, who from the beginning was his own commander-in-chief, at once proved his strategical genius. He devised an admirable plan of campaign designed to attack the enemy at four distinct points on a frontier of about six hundred miles, and supplemented his military dispositions by negotiations with various hill chiefs. If the Governor-general's instructions had been obeyed prompt success certainly would have attended the army, which was amply sufficient in numbers and equipment. But, unfortunately, four out of five generals employed displayed extraordinary incompetence in different fashions, so that the early operations failed, and all India was excited by news of defeats suffered by the Company's forces. General Gillespie, who had won a high reputation by the storm of Fort Cornelis in Java, lost his own life and uselessly

A NEPALESE STOCKADE.

sacrificed many men by making a rash frontal attack on a strong wooden stockade, in direct violation of the commander-in-chief's orders. Gillespie, unaccustomed to mountain warfare, followed the tactics customary in the Indian plains, and paid the penalty. During the progress of the operations the Company's troops gained experience of the novel conditions, and learned how to make stockades for their own protection. Three other commanders wasted their efforts from sheer imbecility. The failures were partly compensated for by successes in Kumāon and on the upper Sutlaj. Colonels Nicholls and Gardner occupied Almora in Kumāon, thus driving a wedge into the Gūrkha territory, and General (Sir David) Ochterlony, who had defended Delhi against Holkar, operated from Lūdiāna with such skill that in May 1815 he compelled the brave Gūrkha leader, Amar Singh, to surrender the fort of Malāon.

Treaty of Sagauli. A treaty was then signed, but at the last moment the government of Nepāl refused ratification, and hostilities were resumed. Sir David Ochterlony, advancing in February 1816 in strong force and with reasonable precautions, was soon in a position to threaten the capital, so that the enemy consented to ratify the treaty in its original form. That document, the treaty of Sagauli (Segowlee), signed in March 1816, provided for the cession by the Nepalese of Garhwāl and Kumāon to the west of the Kālī river, the surrender of most of the Tarāi,[1] withdrawal from Sikkim, and the acceptance of a British Resident at Kathmāndu, the capital. The clause requiring the admission of a Resident was more distasteful to the enemy than the loss of territory.

Advantages gained. The terms, although by no means harsh to the Nepalese, secured extremely important advantages to the British government and the people of India. The Kumaun (Kumāon) province, now organized as the Kumaun Division, comprising the Nainī Tāl, Almora, and Garhwāl Districts, has proved to be an acquisition of the highest value. The temperate climate, being suitable to European constitutions, has favoured the growth of large ‘ hill-stations ’, where a considerable population of pure Europeans and persons of mixed descent can settle permanently and rear families. Nainī Tāl, the summer capital of the government of the United Provinces, and Almora, are the principal of such settlements in Kumaun. The prosperity of the country has increased enormously since the annexation, which was warmly welcomed by the inhabitants. The Gūrkha rule had been oppressive. The rapid growth of the revenue has materially helped the finances of India and the informal ‘ non-regulation ’ system of administration, which was wisely adopted, suits the peculiarities of the hillmen.

The Dehra Dūn District, including the hill station of Mussoorie subsequently formed, was also annexed.

The existing Simla District is made up of sundry patches of territory, some of which were obtained in 1815–16, and some at various later dates by amicable arrangements with hill chiefs. The first residence, a thatched wooden cottage, erected in 1819, was gradually followed by others. In 1827 Lord Amherst, then Governor-general, spent the summer at Simla, which in course of time developed into what it now is, the official capital of India for a large part of the year. A considerable tract ceded by the Nepalese was made over to the Rājā of Sikkim.

Peace unbroken. The peace concluded more than a century ago with Nepāl has never been broken. The kingdom, indeed,

[1] The Tarāi boundary was modified more than once later, and the frontier was defined by masonry pillars.

far from being hostile, may be regarded justly as one of the pillars of the Indian empire. During the Mutiny of 1857–9 Sir Jung Bahādur, then the Minister responsible for the government, rendered valuable assistance, which was suitably recognized by territorial concessions and in other ways. Almost immediately after the Nepalese war Gūrkha soldiers began to enter the Company's army. An elaborate system of recruiting was developed subsequently by friendly agreement between the two governments, under which the Gūrkha regiments have become one of the most efficient and trustworthy elements in the Indian army. Their services in many fields, and notably in France and elsewhere during the Great War, are more or less familiar to everybody. Gūrkhas also enlist as military police and are highly esteemed in that capacity.

Internal independence of Nepāl. The government of the kingdom, while unswerving in its friendly attitude, is jealous of its independence, which it has managed to retain intact. The Resident does not attempt to interfere in the internal administration, and has to submit to considerable restriction on his movements. Most of the hill territory has not been visited by any European, and British subjects even of Indian birth are rarely admitted to the interior.

'The political status of Nepāl is somewhat difficult to define. It may be said to stand intermediate between Afghānistān and the Native States of India. The point of resemblance to Afghānistān is in the complete freedom which Nepāl enjoys in the management of its internal affairs, while in both countries foreign relations are controlled by the Indian Government. The analogy to the Native States is that, by treaty, Nepāl is obliged to receive a British Resident at Kātmāndu, and cannot take Europeans into service without the sanction of the Indian Government' (*I. G.*, 1908).

The situation is further complicated by the fact that Nepāl recognizes the nominal suzerainty of China as the result of ancient events. The acknowledgement takes, or recently took, the form of the dispatch every five years of a mission carrying presents to the Chinese Court. Possibly the establishment of the Chinese Republic may modify the practice.

Interest of Nepāl. The country is of exceptional interest for many reasons, and exploration would yield many valuable results to science, historical and physical; but the increase of knowledge gained by insisting on free access to the interior could not be purchased save at an excessive price. The existence of Nepalese Buddhism and an enormous Buddhist literature of a peculiar character was revealed by Mr. Brian H. Hodgson, who resided at Kathmāndu from 1820 to 1844, and conducted extensive researches which have placed a vast mass of material at the disposal of the learned. Nepāl offers special advantages for the study of the interaction of Buddhism and Brahmanical Hinduism as living religions and social systems.

Anarchy and robbers. The awful anarchy in Rājputāna

and Central India resulting from the refusal of the British government to assert itself as the paramount power raged unchecked, or almost unchecked, from 1805 to the close of Lord Minto's administration. Lord Minto undoubtedly would have been compelled to take strong action if he had remained in office. The outrages were the work of three distinct though closely related organizations —the Marāthās, the Pathāns, and the Pindārīs.[1] The Marāthā chiefs, of whom Sindia, Holkar, and the Bhonsla of Nāgpur and Berār were the most prominent, each possessed considerable territories more or less defined in extent, which they used as a base from which to make predatory raids. Sir George Barlow gave them his licence to harry Rājputāna as much as they pleased, and they did not fail to make full use of their opportunities. The Marāthā armies were no longer recruited mainly from the Deccan, but included Muhammadans and Hindus of various classes and from diverse countries. The Pathān bands of Musalmān freebooters had at first no definite territory, and were content to plunder wherever they could find an opening, and to lend their swords to any chief who would provide pay and booty.

'The Pindarries, who had arisen, like masses of putrefaction in animal matter, out of the corruption of weak and expiring states, had fortunately none of those bonds of union which unite men in adversity. They had neither the tie of religious nor of national feeling. They were men of all lands and all religions. They had been brought together less by despair than by deeming the life of a plunderer, in the actual state of India, as one of small hazard, but great indulgence. . . . The Pindarries, when they came to a rich country, had neither the means nor inclination, like the Tartars, to whom also they have been compared, to settle and repose. Like swarms of locusts, acting from instinct, they destroyed and wasted whatever province they visited. Their chiefs had, from grants or usurpation, obtained small territorial possessions ; but the revenues of their land were never equal to the maintenance of one-tenth part of their numbers, and they could, therefore, only be supported by plunder.'

They are supposed to have numbered 20,000 or 30,000 about the beginning of the nineteenth century ; but all calculation of their numerical strength is fallacious, and, as Munro pointed out, contemporary reports showed a strong tendency to exaggerate their numbers. They were 'so amalgamated with the whole of the loose part of the military population of India, that it had become a system, not a particular force, that was to be subdued'.

They made their forays in bodies often numbering each two or three thousand horsemen under the command of a chosen leader, carrying neither tents nor baggage. They rode forty or fifty miles a day straight for their destination.

'They then divided, and made a clean sweep of all the cattle and property they could find : committing at the same time the most horrid atrocities, and destroying what they could not carry away. . . . The Pindarries who first settled in Central India may be said to have been introduced by the

[1] The word Pindārī or Pindāra seems to be Marāthī and to mean 'consumers of *pinda*', a fermented drink.

Mahrattas. Ghazee u Deen, a person who served under the first Bajerow [Bājī Rāo I, A. D. 1720–40], died when employed with a detachment at Oojein.'

Subsequently the Pindārīs usually were loosely attached to the armies of either Sindia or Holkar.

'Condemned from their origin to be the very scavengers of Mahrattas, their habits and character took, from the first, a shape suited to the work they had to perform. . . . All appear to have shared in the ignorance, the meanness, the rapacity, and unfeeling cruelty, by which they were, as a body, distinguished.'[1]

In the time of Lord Hastings the three chief leaders were Chītū (Cheetoo), Wāsil Muhammad, and Karīm Khān. Chītū was a Mewātī, and professed allegiance to Daulat Rāo Sindia.

Pindārī atrocities. It is impossible to find space for a full description of the devastation wrought and the cruelties practised by the various classes of plunderers, but a few brief quotations from contemporary authors are indispensable in order to enable the reader to realize in an imperfect degree the horrors of those terrible years.

James Tod during his memorable term of service in Rājputāna from 1812 to 1823 enjoyed and used ample opportunities of witnessing the havoc wrought by the banditti of all classes and of watching the rapid reparation effected largely by his own exertions after the destruction of the robber hordes.

Describing Mewār as it was about A. D. 1817, he writes :

'Expression might be racked for phrases which could adequately delineate the miseries all classes had endured. . . . The capital will serve as a specimen of the country. Oodipoor [Udaipur], which formerly reckoned fifty thousand houses within the walls, had not now three thousand houses occupied, the rest were in ruin, the rafters being taken for firewood. The realization of the spring harvest of 1818, from the entire fiscal land, was about £4,000 ! . . . Such was the chaos from which order was to be evoked . . . On the same day, and within eight months subsequent to the signature of the treaty, above three hundred towns and villages were *simultaneously* re-inhabited, and the land, which for many years had been a stranger to the plough-share, was broken up. . . . The chief commercial mart, Bhilwara, which showed not a vestige of humanity, rapidly rose from ruin, and in a few months contained twelve hundred houses, half of which were occupied by foreign merchants.'

A Marāthā chief named Ambājī extracted two millions sterling from Mewār in the course of eight years.[2]

'The cruelties they [the Pindārīs] perpetrated were beyond belief . . . every one whose appearance indicated the probability of his possessing money was immediately put to the most horrid torture, till he either pointed out his hoard, or died under the infliction. Nothing was safe from the pursuit of Pindaree lust or avarice ; it was their common practice to burn and destroy what could not be carried away ; and, in the wantonness

[1] The quotations are from chap. x of Malcolm, *A Memoir of Central India*[2], 1832.

[2] *Annals of Mewār*, chap. xvii.

of barbarity, to ravish and murder women and children, under the eyes of their husbands and parents . . .

A favourite mode of compulsion with them was to put hot ashes into a bag, which they tied over the mouth and nostrils of their victim, whom they then thumped on the back till he inhaled the ashes. The effect on the lungs of the sufferer was such that few long survived the operation. Another common mode was to throw the victim on his back, and place a plank or beam across his chest, on which two people pressed with their whole weight.' [1]

Malcolm observes that

'the women of almost all the Mahomedan Pindarries dressed like Hindus, and worshipped Hindu deities. From accompanying their husbands in most of their excursions they became hardy and masculine: they were usually mounted on small horses or camels, and were more dreaded by the villagers than the men, whom they exceeded in cruelty and rapacity.' [2]

Raids on British territory. The Pindārīs began to raid the Company's territory in 1812, when they harried Mirzapur and South Bihār. But for a long time both the home authorities and the members of council in Calcutta hesitated to take the necessary measures for the extermination of the plague. A fierce incursion early in 1816 into the northern Sarkārs settled the question. That region had enjoyed unbroken peace for half a century. In twelve days the brigands plundered 339 villages, 182 persons were cruelly killed, 505 severely wounded, and 3,603 subjected to different kinds of torture. Many women destroyed themselves in order to escape dishonour. But it is needless to pursue farther the tale of horror. Even the Directors were roused by the news, and in September they authorized the necessary measures of repression. Before that dispatch had been received, Lord Hastings, with his usual fearlessness, had made up his mind to act, sanction or no sanction, and to act effectively.

Diplomacy. The Governor-general understood fully the intimate nature of the relations between the powerful Marāthā chiefs and the plundering hordes of Pathāns and Pindārīs. He laid his plans with a distinct consciousness that the operations directed primarily against the Pindārī lairs in the Narbadā Valley might develop, as they actually did, into a general Marāthā war; and resolved that his preparations should be on a scale adequate for the final settlement of the problem. He supplemented his military arrangements by diplomacy, and succeeded in negotiating a subsidiary treaty with the regent of the Bhonsla's territory, known as Āpā Sāhib. The Rājā of Jaipur asked for protection, and Lord Hastings was willing to execute a treaty, but the Rājā drew back, and in the end was the last of the Rājpūt princes to come to terms with the British government. The Muhammadan Nawāb of Bhopāl signed a treaty, and proved to be a staunch and faithful ally. Since 1844 the state usually has been ruled by ladies. Sikandar Bēgam rendered signal services to the government of India in 1857. During the course of 1817 alliances were

[1] H. T. Prinsep, *History*, i. 39. [2] *Central India*[2], ii. 177.

arranged with Udaipur (Mewār), Jodhpur (Mārwār), and Zālim Singh, the Regent of Kotah.[1] Bājī Rāo continued his usual game of perfidious intrigue, but had to sign a compact supplementary to the treaty of Bassein. Besides consenting to the outlawry of his guilty favourite Trimbakjī, who had foully murdered the Gaikwār's Brahman envoy, with the privity of the Pēshwā, Bājī Rāo was obliged to renounce his headship of the Marāthā confederacy, and to cede the Konkan province on the Bombay coast, with certain other territory and strongholds. Both the Pēshwā and Apā Sahib, who had become the Bhonsla ruler of Nāgpur by the murder of a rival, conspired incessantly to defeat the plans of the Governor-general. Negotiations with Sindia, Holkar, and Amīr Khān, the leader of the Pathān banditti, also were undertaken.

The army. Lord Hastings, while neglecting no diplomatic precaution, relied chiefly on his military preparations, conceived on a comprehensive scale and designed with true strategical genius. With a view to an energetic campaign during the cold season of 1817–18 he mobilized a great army of about 120,000 men with 300 guns. The European troops included in that total numbered about 13,000, namely 8,500 infantry, more than 2,000 cavalry, and the rest gunners. The entire force was divided into two armies, namely the Northern or Army of Hindostan, under the personal command of the Governor-general and commander-in-chief; and the Southern or Deccan Army, commanded by Sir Thomas Hislop, whose principal lieutenant was Sir John Malcolm. Both Sir Thomas Hislop and Sir John Malcolm were invested with extensive political powers.

Strategy. The plan of the operations, the most extensive ever conducted in India before or since, may be described as a vast encircling movement.

> 'The Pindāris were to be rooted out of their haunts which lay in Mālwā, somewhat to the east of Ujjain, north of the Narbadā and between Bhopāl and the dominions of Sindia and Holkar; to accomplish this it had been decided to surround them on all sides—on the north and east from Bengal, on the south from the Deccan, and on the west from Gujarāt—and to keep the native states in check. An extended movement, therefore, was about to be made inwards, from the circumference of a great circle, whose centre was somewhere near Handiā [in the Allahabad District], and whose diameter was nearly 700 miles in length; the enormous distances which separated the different bases of operations, the absence of rapid means of intercommunication, and the necessity of simultaneous action, all contributed to render the task which had been undertaken an exceedingly difficult one.'

Sindia isolated. Lord Hastings reached Cawnpore by the river route in September 1817, and at the end of October advanced to the Sind river in Bundēlkhand.[2] Sir Thomas Hislop took up his

[1] The strange story of that 'consummate politician', Zālim Singh, the blind Regent, who ruled Kotah for sixty years, should be read in Tod's lively narrative.

[2] The Sind river rises in the Tonk state, flows through Central India and Bundēlkhand, and falls into the Jumna.

central position near Handiā in November. It is hardly necessary to state explicitly that the Pēshwā, Sindia, and all other Marāthā chiefs were hostile, and prepared to violate any engagements into which they had been constrained to enter. Sindia was isolated by clever strategical movements and effectually neutralized during the war, much against his inclination.

Cholera. The operations suffered a check in November from a violent outbreak of cholera in the camp of Lord Hastings, which lasted in a virulent form for ten days, causing much mortality and many desertions. The epidemic, first observed in the delta of the Ganges at the beginning of the rainy season of 1817, killed two hundred people a day in Calcutta for some time in September, and gradually crept up country, attacking the crowded camp of Lord Hastings with exceptional severity. The whole encampment was a hospital, and about one-tenth of its occupants perished, including many personal servants of the Governor-general and his historian. The disease abated when the camp moved to healthier ground, but the epidemic spread over a large part of the world, and, with fluctuations, lasted for twenty years.

Popular belief sometimes erroneously represents the epidemic of 1817 as the first appearance of cholera in India. The disease, however, had been observed as early as the seventeenth century, and had been extremely fatal to Colonel Pearse's detachment when marching to Madras in 1781.

End of the Pindārīs. By the end of 1817 the primary object of the campaign had been almost accomplished, the Pindārīs having been driven out of Mālwā and across the Chambal. A month later, towards the close of January 1818, all the organized bands of Pindārīs had been annihilated, and the time had come for inducing the remnants to settle down to a quiet life. Karīm Khān surrendered and was granted the estate of Ganēshpur, then in the Gorakhpur, and now in the Bastī District, where his descendants still reside. Wāsil Muhammad, who had taken refuge with Sindia, and was surrendered by that prince, committed suicide while in captivity. Chītū (Cheetoo), the most formidable of the three conspicuous leaders, was hunted with unremitting vigour until he was driven into a jungle near Asīrgarh, where a tiger devoured him. Thus the Pindārīs were finally disposed of. Amīr Khān, the Pathān chief, was made happy by the grant of the principality or Nawābī of Tonk.

Battle of Kirkee. The Pēshwā, who, as already observed, had been hostile throughout, assembled a large force near Poona. Mr. Elphinstone, the Resident, and Colonel Burr, commanding the troops, found it necessary to retire to Kirkee (Khadkī), four miles to the north-west of the city. Bājī Rāo then burnt the Residency, and on November 5, 1817, attacked with about 26,000 men the force under Colonel Burr, which did not exceed 2,800. The attack lasted from four in the afternoon until dark, when the Pēshwā retired after suffering heavy losses. Reinforcements arrived and the British reoccupied Poona.

Battles of Sītābaldī and Nāgpur. Āpā Sahib Bhonsla presently followed the Pēshwā's example by assailing Mr. Jenkins, the Resident at Nāgpur, who had only about 1,400 men at his disposal, comprised in two weak regiments of Madras infantry, three squadrons of Bengal cavalry, and the European gunners of four six-pounders. That small force took up its position on the ridge known as Sītābaldī, consisting of two eminences connected by a narrow neck. Āpā Sahib's army of about 18,000 men, including 4,000 Arabs, and supported by thirty-six guns, attacked on the night of November 26. The fight continued the next day. The assailants were on the point of overwhelming the weary garrison, when Captain Fitzgerald made two brilliant charges with his tiny force of cavalry and converted defeat into victory. The gallant defenders had more than a quarter of their number killed or wounded during the action which lasted for eighteen hours. A few days later reinforcements arrived and Āpā Sahib surrendered. His troops, refusing to acknowledge defeat, fought another battle close to the city of Nāgpur on December 16, which resulted in their total rout with the loss of their camp, elephants, and guns.

Deposition of the Bhonsla. The Governor-general rightly decided on the deposition of the faithless Āpā Sahib, and the annexation of his dominions lying to the north of the Narbadā, which became known as the Sāgar (Saugor) and Narbadā Territories.

Battle of Mahīdpur. The operations against Holkar were conducted by Sir Thomas Hislop with the aid of Sir John Malcolm. Attempts at negotiations failed, and the murder of Tulsī Bāī, the Regent, by the soldiers under the command of a Pathān named Ghafūr Khān on the morning of December 20, made a fight inevitable. On the same day the British commander forded the Sīprā river, to the north of Ujjain, and carried the enemy's position at the point of the bayonet. Holkar's guns, which were well served, inflicted heavy losses, 174 killed and 606 wounded, on the victorious army. The loss of the enemy was estimated at 3,000. The battle is described by the military historian as having been 'the only general action of primary order in India since 1804'. Holkar attempted no further resistance and signed the required treaty on January 6, 1818.

Battle of Ashtī. The Pēshwā's army, which had been hotly pursued and was under the command of Bāpū Gokhale (Gokla), a brave officer, was forced to give battle on February 20, 1818, at Ashtī or Ashta, now in the Sholāpur District, Bombay. The action, fought solely by cavalry on both sides, resulted in a complete victory for the Company's troops gained with extremely slight loss. The Marāthā general was killed, the Pēshwā became a fugitive, and the titular Rājā of Sātārā, the representative of Sivājī, was captured.

End of the war; Koregāon. The fights above described in outline—at Kirkee, Sītābaldī, Nāgpur, Mahīdpur, and Ashtī—decided the war, but considerable subsidiary operations remained, which were accomplished in due course. The fortress of Asīrgarh did not capitulate until April 1819, after standing a short siege. The wonderful defence of Koregāon (Koregaum) for eleven hours on January 1, 1818, by Captain Staunton, with 500 Bombay native infantry, 250 irregular cavalry, and two six-pounders served by twenty-four European gunners from Madras, against the whole army of the Pēshwā, numbering more than 20,000, merits a passing notice. The little garrison suffered 276 casualties. The action, called the 'Indian Thermopylae' by Tod, is commemorated by a stone obelisk at the village. Except at Mahīdpur, where the European element in the army of the commander-in-chief was considerable, the actions in the fourth Marāthā war were won almost exclusively by native Indian troops under the command of trusted British officers. No soldiers could have done better than the men who defended Kirkee, Sītābaldī, and Koregāon.

Surrender of the Pēshwā. Bājī Rāo, finding resistance or even escape hopeless, had surrendered on June 3, 1818, to Sir John Malcolm, who entered into wholly unnecessary negotiations, and granted him the excessive annuity of eight lakhs (800,000) of rupees a year. The Governor-general, knowing that the fugitive must have surrendered at discretion and that he was not in a position to argue about terms, disapproved of Malcolm's action, but felt bound to confirm it officially. The question concerning the propriety of Malcolm's proceedings evoked much difference of opinion. Personally I agree with Grant Duff and Lord Hastings in holding that Sir John allowed his feelings of compassion for fallen greatness to overbear his judgement. Bājī Rāo, a perjured, vicious coward, possessed no personal claim whatever to the absurdly generous treatment which be received. The office of Pēshwā having been extinguished, Bājī Rāo was allowed to reside at Bithūr, a sacred place near Cawnpore, where he lived for many years. His adopted son, known as Nānā Sahib, gained an infamous immortality in the Mutiny.

Political settlement. The political settlement resulting from the war was planned by Lord Hastings on broad lines, as his strategy had been, and in a comprehensive spirit which took count of all the conditions of the complex problem. He desired a permanent, not merely a temporary settlement, which should secure general peace under the avowed paramount control of the British government, with the minimum of interference in the internal affairs of states allowed to retain their autonomy. No native state within India proper could any longer claim absolute independence.

Paramount power established. Prinsep, writing in 1824 or 1825, observes

'that the universal extension of the British influence has been attended with advantage to the people of India is a proposition not likely to be combated at the present day. The different state of Malwa, and of all provinces recently brought within its range, as viewed now that the system has had five years trial, compared with the condition of the same countries in 1817–18, establishes the fact incontestably. . . . But we may be allowed to observe, that such a result could not have been produced by the simple extirpation of the Pindarees, and suppression of the predatory system;

without the general controlling government established at the same time, the relief must have been temporary, and the effect would before this have disappeared.'

Rājpūt states and Mālwā. The same judicious and well-informed author shows the necessity for a certain amount of control over the Rājpūt states and of interference in their affairs.

COLONEL TOD AND HIS JAIN PUNDT.

'Independently of quarrels and wars prosecuted from motives of ambition or avariec, there were hereditary feuds and jealousies between the different tribes of Rajpoots, the Kychuhas [Kachchhwāhas], for instance, and the Rhatōrs, both these again, and the Chouhans, which must for ever have prevented their living together in harmony without a general sense of the necessity of submitting to the behest of a controlling power.'

The same reasoning applied to Mālwā. The problem of each state was separately examined, discussed, and decided with the aid of a group of exceptionally able officers, including Metcalfe,

Malcolm, Elphinstone, Tod, and many others. The sympathetic labours of Tod in Rājputāna are recorded for all time in his immortal *Annals*. The decisions were embodied in a long series of treaties, beginning with Kotah and ending with Jaipur or Ambēr. Full details will be found in the special treatises cited at the end of this chapter.

Marāthā states. Among the greater Marāthā chiefs, Sindia and Holkar were fortunate enough to retain considerable kingdoms and to be allowed a large measure of independence. Holkar was further lucky in securing the services of a competent minister named Tantia Jōg. The foundations put down by Lord Hastings were well and truly laid. The present representatives of all the dynasties embraced in the comprehensive system devised by the Governor-general are faithful supporters of the paramount power, yielding willing homage to the person of their King-Emperor, and, as a rule, administering their dominions, whether small or large, with sufficient regard to equity.

Abolition of the Pēshwā. The Governor-general, after very mature consideration of the question, decided

'in favour of the total expulsion of Bajee Rao from the Dukhun, the perpetual exclusion of his family from any share of influence or dominion, and the annihilation of the Pēshwa's name and authority for ever'.

He felt that those stern measures were warranted by the uniformly insidious conduct of Bājī Rāo, who had violated all engagements and placed himself at the head of the confederation against the British power, choosing the moment for treacherous defection which seemed to him the most critical. No less penalty would have sufficed as 'a warning example to the sovereigns of India, and an awful lesson on the consequences of incurring the full measure of our just indignation'. The measure adopted was unexpected, and the intended lesson was learnt by all concerned.

Sātārā. A concession was made to Marāthā opinion by the reservation of a small area around Sātārā in the Western Ghāts as a separate semi-independent principality for the descendant of Sivājī captured at Ashtī. The experiment was not a success. The principality was suppressed in 1848 by Lord Dalhousie and now forms a District of the Bombay Presidency. Grant Duff, who was placed by Lord Hastings in charge of the Rājā, collected the materials for his invaluable *History of the Mahrattas* while employed at Sātārā.

The Bhonsla. The perfidy and crimes of Āpā Sahib Bhonsla fully justified his deposition and the annexation of the Sāgar and Narbadā Territories. A new Rājā was set up in the regions south of the river under British control. In 1853 Lord Dalhousie applied the doctrine of lapse and annexed the whole of the Bhonsla dominions, which, with certain additions, now constitute the Central Provinces, Nāgpur being the official capital. Care should be taken not to confound the Central Provinces with Central India, a group of Native or Protected States, roughly corresponding with the ancient Mālwā, and including the dominions of Sindia and

Holkar.[1] The Agent to the Governor-general resides at Indore, Holkar's capital.

An elastic 'non-regulation' system of administration was judiciously applied to the Sāgar and Narbadā Territories, which are familiar to all readers of Sleeman's fascinating *Rambles and Recollections*.

Conclusion. This chapter may be fitly closed by quoting the passage with which Prinsep concludes his 'Political Review', published in 1825:

'The struggle which has thus ended in the universal establishment of the British influence is particularly important and worthy of attention, as it promises to be the last we shall ever have to maintain with the native powers of India. Henceforward this epoch will be referred to as that whence each of the existing states will date the commencement of its peaceable settlement, and the consolidation of its relations with the controlling power. The dark age of trouble and violence, which so long spread its malign influence over the fertile regions of Central India, has thus ceased from this time; and a new era has commenced, we trust, with brighter prospects—an era of peace, prosperity, and wealth at least, if not of political liberty and high moral improvement.'

The validity of the prediction that no further struggle with the native powers of India need occur is not affected by Lord Ellenborough's momentary and probably unnecessary fights with Sindia's army in 1843; nor by the annexations of Sind and the Panjāb, provinces lying outside the limits of India proper and in 1825 really independent.

Since Prinsep wrote, some progress in the evolution of 'political liberty' has been effected, and not a few signs of 'high moral improvement' may be noted by a sympathetic observer.

CHRONOLOGY

Lord Hastings (Earl of Moira) Governor-general	(Oct.) 1813
War with Nepāl	1814–16
Treaty of Sagaulī (Segowlee)	1816
Pindāri and Marāthā war	1817–19
Battles of Kirkee, Sītābaldi, Nāgpur, and Mahidpur	1817
Defence of Koregāon; battle of Ashtī; political settlement	1818
Capitulation of Asīrgarh	1819

The three Marāthā Wars

First, 1775–82: Warren Hastings Governor-general; Convention of Wargāon, 1778; capture of Gwālior, 1780; treaty of Sālbāī, 1782.

Second, 1803–5: Lord Wellesley Governor-general; capture of Aligarh; battles of Delhi, Assaye, Laswārī, Argāon, and Deeg; treaties of Deogāon and Surjī Arjungāon; siege of Bhurtpore.

Third, 1817–19: Lord Hastings Governor-general; battles of Kirkee, Sītābaldī, Nāgpur, Mahīdpur, and Ashtī; defence of Koregāon; capitulation of Asīrgarh; abolition of the Pēshwā; ended by general political settlement and about twenty treaties.

(The brief conflict with Sindia's army in 1843 is not counted as a Marāthā war.)

[1] The term Central India was officially applied at first to Mālwā alone, but is now used so as to include the states in the Bundēlkhand and Baghēlkhand Political Agencies.

THE FAMILY OF THE SEVEN PESHWĀS

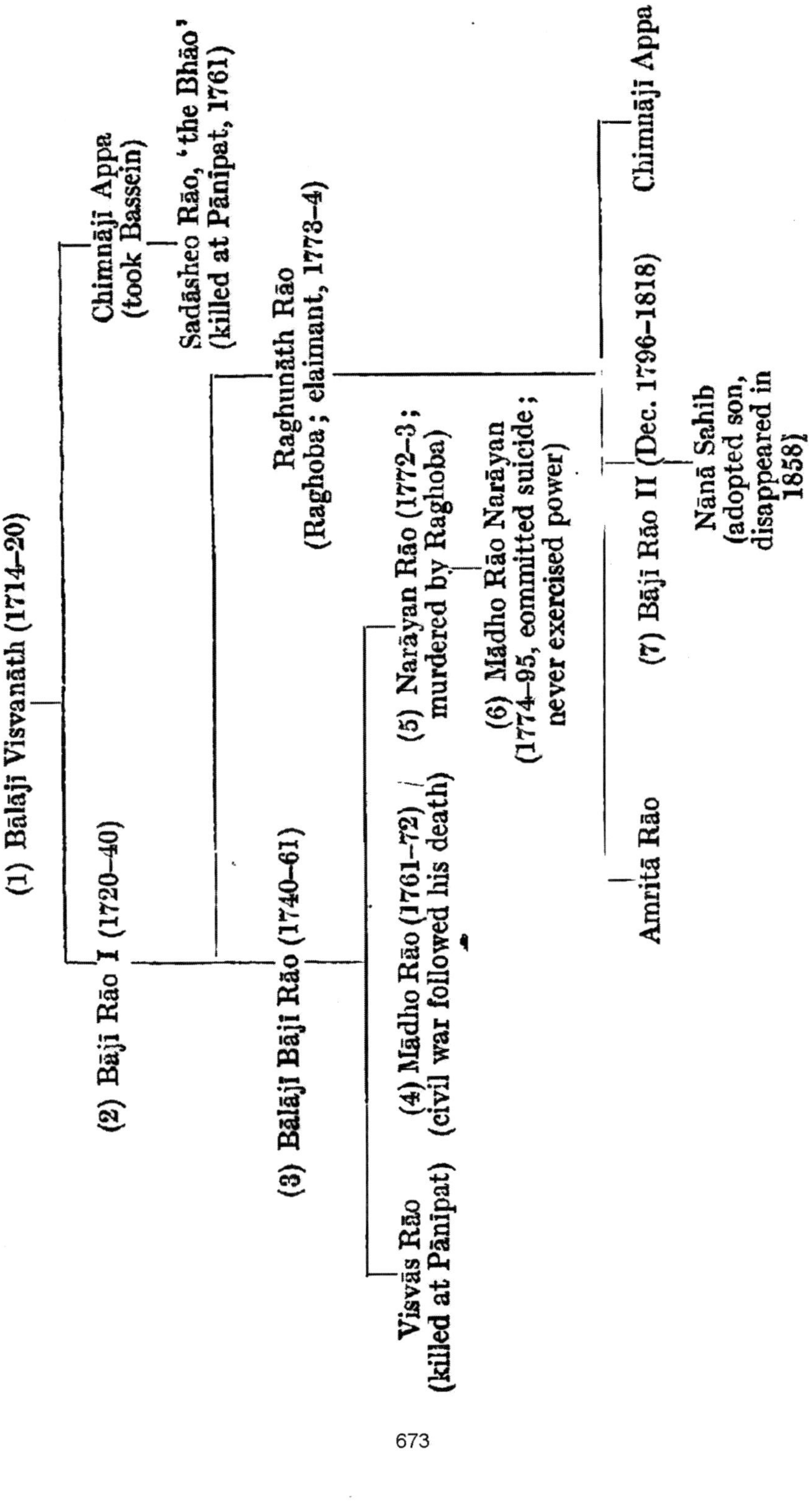

Authorities

The two leading contemporary printed authoritative works on the wars of the Marquess of Hastings are (1) *Memoir of the Operations of the British Army in India during the Mahratta War of 1817, 1818, and 1819*, by Lt.-Col. Valentine Blacker, Q.M.G. of the army of the Deccan, quarto, London, 1821, which gives full professional details; and (2) *History of the Political and Military Transactions in India during the Administration of the Marquess of Hastings, 1813–1823*, by Henry T. Prinsep, B.C.S., Assistant Secretary to the Governor-general, 2 vols., 8vo, London, 1825; based on an earlier quarto work published in 1820. The book ends with a political and financial review.

The Marquess of Hastings, K.G., by Major Ross-of-Bladensburg (Rulers of India, 1893), is a well-written and lucid summary of the whole history. Wilson devotes the entire third volume of his *History* (vol. 8 of Mill and continuation) to the administration of the Marquess, which is treated at considerable length in several histories by other authors, Malcolm, Marshman, Thornton, &c. The *Private Journal* of the Marquess, edited by his daughter, the Marchioness of Bute, 2 vols., London, 1858, and a *Summary* published by the Marquess himself in 1824 give further particulars.

BOOK VIII

THE RULE OF THE EAST INDIA COMPANY FROM 1819 TO 1858

CHAPTER 1

The Marquess of Hastings continued; reconstruction and internal reforms; Mr. Adam and the press; Lord Amherst; the first Burmese War.

Abominable Marāthā system. The admiration felt and expressed by many Hindus for Sivājī may be explained easily and justified partially by many reasons, notwithstanding his glaring crimes of violence and treachery. Bājī Rāo and the other Marāthā chiefs at the close of the eighteenth and the beginning of the nineteenth century are not entitled to either respect or esteem. With the solitary exception of one woman, Ahalyā Bāī, they rarely possessed any discernible virtues, while they were all stained by perfidy, cruelty, rapacity, and most of the other vices. The abominable system of government which they administered was incapable of effecting any benefit to or improvement of mankind in any direction.

'The contempt of all morality, in their political arrangements, was with the Mahrattas avowed and shameless.'

The constitution of their government and army was

'more calculated to destroy, than to create an empire. . . . The Mahrattas, from their feeling and policy as well as from those habits of predatory warfare on which the whole construction of their government was founded, were the natural enemies of the British power. There could be no lasting peace between states whose object and principles of government were always in collision.'[1]

In short, the Marāthās were robbers by profession, whose activities could not be endured by decent neighbours. They were openly leagued with all the ruffians who came to the front in a time of disorder, and the suppression of their lawless rule was the first duty of that government which, in spite of itself, had become the controlling power in India.

The complete and final overthrow of the Marāthā domination in 1818 should not excite the slightest feeling of regret or sympathy in the breast of any person, Indian or European. Nobody who possesses even a slight acquaintance with the facts of history can doubt that the utter destruction of the Marāthā capacity for evil

[1] The proposition applies to the case of the Central Empires against the world in 1918.

and the substitution of orderly government were necessary and of incalculable benefit to India.[1]

The merit of Lord Hastings. It is the peculiar merit of Lord Hastings that he realized both the necessity and the benefit. His comprehensive mind provided with ample sufficiency the means needed to ensure the indispensable preliminary destruction of a wholly evil system,[2] and worked out with equal grasp of realities the measures best calculated for the construction of a new and lasting fabric. His work lives after him. The existing pleasant relations between the surviving Marāthā states and the government of India stand on the foundations well and truly laid by the Marquess of Hastings. The ill faith of the Pēshwā and the Bhonsla met its just reward. Sindia and Holkar, who could not reasonably have complained if they too had been condemned to heavy penalties, were wisely left in a position where they were able to reap immense advantages immediately. Holkar's revenue rose in a few years from a pitiful sum of barely four lakhs to thirty-five lakhs a year. Sindia soon found himself the master of a profitable kingdom. He ceded Ajmēr, the strategical key to Rājputāna, receiving other districts in exchange, so that on the whole he did not lose territory, and had every reason to be satisfied with the treatment he received. Everywhere towns and villages sprang up from their ashes, and the returning ryot soon created revenue for the prince in amounts immeasurably exceeding the precarious gains of predatory raids.

Variety of transactions. Even during the progress of the wars which chiefly occupied the earlier years of his administration, Lord Hastings engaged, to use Wilson's words, in

> a variety of transactions . . ., which, although of minor moment, involved objects of considerable magnitude, arising from the determination to preserve the tranquillity of India undisturbed; from the necessity still existing of shielding maritime commerce from piratical depredations;

[1] It may be well to support the propositions in the text as based on Malcolm's writings by the equally competent testimony of Sir Thomas Munro:

'The Mahratta Government, from its foundation, has been one of the most destructive that ever existed in India. It never relinquished the predatory spirit of its founder, Sewajee. That spirit grew with its power; and when its empire extended from the Ganges to the Cavery, this nation was little better than a horde of imperial thieves. All other Hindoo states took a pride in the improvement of the country, and in the construction of pagodas, tanks, canals, and other public works. The Mahrattas have done nothing of this kind; their work has been chiefly desolation. They did not seek their revenue in the improvement of the country, but in the exactions of the established *chout* from their neighbours, and in predatory incursions to levy more' (Gleig, *Life*[2], ii. 14).

Those propositions are absolutely true without qualification.

[2] 'Nothing is so expensive as war carried on with inadequate means. It entails all the expense without the advantages of war' (Sir Thomas Munro in Gleig, *Life*[2], ii. 371).

from the duty of providing for British as well as Indian interests in the eastern seas ;'

and from treaty relations with the Native States.

Suppression of piracy. The annexation of the Pēshwā's territory involved the adjustment of relations with the Konkan districts lying between the Western Ghāts and the sea. The pirate chiefs, who had been incompletely chastised in 1812, were thoroughly subjected in 1820, and required to cede the remainder of the coast between Kolhāpur and Goa. The measures adopted 'extinguished all vestiges of the piratical practices for which this part of the coast of India had been infamous, since the days of Roman commerce'.

Effective operations against the pirates of the Red Sea and Persian Gulf were also carried out.

Affairs of Cutch. The Rāo of Cutch (Kacchh), the peninsula lying to the north of Kāthiawār, and separated from the mainland by the 'Runn' (Ran), formerly an arm of the sea, had been caught in the wide sweep of the net of treaties. He soon grew tired of control, and early in 1819 began hostilities. A small force of Company's troops, aided by the nobles of the state, who were opposed to the Rāo, captured Bhūj, the capital. The Rāo surrendered, and was deposed by Lord Hastings. An infant prince was appointed in his place, and the administration was conducted by a regency under the control of the Resident until 1834. The proceedings alarmed the Ameers of Sind, and war with them was averted only by the forbearance of the Governor-general under provocation.

Earthquakes. Although the country of Cutch has suffered much from famine, pestilence, and earthquakes, it is now tolerably prosperous, and is governed on modern lines. The practice of female infanticide, once terribly prevalent, has been materially checked, if not suppressed. Shortly after the capture of Bhūj the principality endured a series of earthquake shocks, about a hundred in number, which lasted from June 16 to November 23, 1819. A large portion of the Western Runn subsided, including the small town of Sindrī, which disappeared under the waters. In some places the land appears to have risen. The changes of level due to earth movements in Cutch, the Runn, and the neighbouring Indian desert have transformed the face of the country during historical times.

Sir Bartle Frere observes :

'From the frontiers of Sirhind to Jeysulmere, the Thurr [Thar, or Indian Desert] contains frequent traces of ancient watercourses which once flowed where no stream now flows even in the heaviest rains ; and ruins of ancient towns and villages, which have for ages been utterly deserted, prove that the country in former days was more populous, and contained more water and cultivation than at present.

Further south similar indications are very frequent, though owing to the want of permanent buildings in the Thurr itself they are more frequently met with in the plain country east and west of it. Thus the plain between Hyderabad and Oomercote ['Umarkōt, Amercote] presents everywhere indications of having been thickly populated as far back as the Bhuddist period, and well irrigated by canals from the Indus, which no longer carry water in consequence of a slight change in the relative levels of the Indus and the plain to be irrigated.' [1]

Students of the movements of Alexander the Great and other events in ancient story must bear such facts in mind.

Singapore. The ministers in London had never taken much interest in the conquest of Java, or cordially supported the far-seeing policy of Lord Minto and Sir Stamford Raffles. When the final defeat of Napoleon at Waterloo in 1815 freed Holland from French domination and restored the independence of the country, the Cabinet was glad to get rid of Java and hand it back to the Dutch unconditionally. No pains were taken either to maintain the engagements made by the British with the Javanese chiefs or to secure the interests of British commerce in the Archipelago. The Dutch were thus tempted to allow themselves to be

'actuated by a spirit of ambition, by views of boundless aggrandizement and rapacity, and by a desire to obtain the power of monopolizing the commerce of the eastern archipelago'.

They resumed, in short, their traditional exclusive policy, which had led to the massacre of Amboyna two centuries earlier.

Lord Hastings, wiser than his masters in Europe, saw the necessity of securing a safe trade route with China and the Far East. He approved the proposition of Raffles to acquire the island of Singapore at the extremity of the Malay Peninsula, which was occupied accordingly in 1819, much to the annoyance of the Dutch. The foresight of the Governor-general and his enthusiastic lieutenant has been justified abundantly. The island wilderness of 1819, tenanted by a handful of poor Malay fisher-folk, is now the noble colony of Singapore, with a population of 309,185 in 1911. The city, with its capacious harbour situated in a position dominating the Straits of Malacca, the principal gate to the Far East, and strongly fortified, is 'the port of call for practically all the shipping of the eastern world'. Before the Great War, 11,000 vessels, with a tonnage of about fifteen million tons, passed in and out of the port each year. 'A stupendous revenue' is raised from tin mining and opium, and the population includes an astonishing variety of races and nationalities, among whom eight different classes of industrious Chinese are the most prominent.

The occupation of Singapore by Lord Hastings was a service to the empire hardly second to his unification of India and the consolidation of the British authority in that country. Now that Japan and the United States are in alliance with Great Britain (1918) it is needless to dilate upon the strategical importance and commercial value of Singapore.

[1] 'Notes on the Runn of Cutch and neighbouring region,' p. 193 of reprint dated 1870 from ? *Geographical Journal*. See also Raverty, 'The Mihrān of Sind' (*J. A. S. B.*, 1892, vol. lxi, part i, pp. 456–66).

A few years after the occupation of the port the difficulties with the Dutch were settled by friendly agreement—the British government giving up its settlements in Sumatra in exchange for the Dutch settlements in India.

Singapore is the leading element in the Straits Settlement Colony, which has received many extensions since the time of Lord Hastings. A competent writer affirms that

'a complete history of that extension and growth, and the devious ways by which they have been brought about, would make a fascinating tale and a long one'.

The ancient port of Malacca, which seemed to have closed its honourable career, has been revived by the development of the rubber industry. Penang, too, which had superseded Malacca for a time, is now prosperous, although far inferior to Singapore. The whole colony is extraordinarily progressive, with infinite possibilities. But it is now administered, like Ceylon, under the control of the Colonial Office, and its development does not directly concern the history of India.[1]

Various occurrences. The dealings of the Governor-general with the protected states other than those of Rājputāna and Mālwā were ordinarily marked by discretion and forbearance. But his encouraging the Nawāb-Vizier of Oudh to assume the royal title in defiance of the shadowy authority of the Pādshāh of Delhi was generally regarded as a mistake. The Nizam refused to take the same liberty. In 1816 the people of Cuttack (Katak) in Orissa were driven to rebellion by over-assessment, undue enhancement of the salt tax, and the chicanery of Bengālī underlings, who defrauded the ignorant inhabitants. When the necessary military operations took place, the insurgents submitted promptly in reliance on a promise that their grievances would be remedied. The promise was faithfully redeemed by the reduction of the excessive taxation and the establishment of a sympathetic administration under a special commissioner. The province has never been disturbed again.

Murshidābād half-rupee.

The titular emperor. Lord Hastings stopped the presentation of *nazars* (*nuzzurs*), or formal presents offered to a superior, which it had been the practice for the head of the government to tender to the titular emperor. He rightly held 'such a public testimony of dependence and subservience' to be irreconcilable with any rational system of policy when the paramount authority of the British government had been openly proclaimed and established. With strange incon-

[1] The island was finally taken over from India and the Crown Colony organized in 1867.

sistency the Company's coinage was allowed to bear the name and titles of Shāh Ālam until 1835, when Act XVII prescribed a new coinage with European devices.[1]

Bareilly outbreak. Nearly at the same time as the Cuttack insurrection a dangerous outbreak occurred at Bareilly in Rohilkhand, the immediate provocation being the imposition of a small municipal tax. Other grievances also came into play, and a Muhammadan Mufti having taken the lead the usual cry of 'religion in danger' was raised. An inoffensive young English gentleman was murdered, and the insurgents fought the troops with such fury that they lost more than three hundred killed. The casualties among the troops were twenty-one killed and sixty-two wounded. The incident deserves notice because it is a good illustration of the way in which the unexpected happens in India, and of the facility with which an ordinary complaint against the administration can be used to excite a fanatical outburst of religious enthusiasm. The reader may remember that in Lord Minto's time the differences between the Hindu minister and the British Resident in Travancore were similarly utilized as the foundation for a war of religion.

The lesson of Hathrās. In the next year (1817) Dayarām, a zemindar in the Aligarh District, who had shown a contumacious spirit, refused to dismantle his fortress at Hathrās. Lord Hastings, who was then preparing for the Pindārī war, took measures which left nothing to chance and soon rendered the fort untenable by means of an incessant shower of bombs from forty-two mortars. The Governor-general, who was his own commander-in-chief, had satisfied himself at an early date that considerations of false economy had unduly limited the use of artillery, and had caused failures at Bhurtpore and elsewhere. He was resolved not to repeat the error. The lesson taught by the speedy fall of Hathrās did not need repetition.

Public works, education, and finance. The Marquess resumed the much-needed improvements in Calcutta, which had been suspended since the departure of Lord Wellesley. He also repaired an ancient canal, and thus secured a good water supply for Delhi. Generally, throughout the country, he paid attention to roads and bridges, a subject neglected by previous administrations. He was steadfastly opposed to the ignoble policy of keeping the natives of the country in ignorance, which had strenuous supporters at the India House.

> 'This Government', he boldly declared, 'never will be influenced by the erroneous position that to spread information among men is to render them less tractable and less submissive to authority. . . . It would be treason to British sentiment to imagine that it ever could be the principle of this

[1] See Thurston, *History of the Coinage of the E. I. Co.* (Madras, 1890); and J. M. C. Johnston, 'Coinage of the East India Company' (*Num. Chron.*, 1903, p. 71, Pl. III). In 1827 Lord Amherst permitted the gentlemen of his suite to present 'nuzzurs', but did not himself tender any.

Government to perpetuate ignorance in order to secure paltry and dishonest advantages over the blindness of the multitude.'

Those liberal sentiments, far in advance of the ideas current at the time, were translated into action. Both the Marquess and Lady Hastings established schools, to which they made generous contributions from their own purse, and the Governor-general accepted the office of patron of a college founded by Bengālī gentlemen. His action in regard to the press will be noticed more conveniently in connexion with the administration of Mr. Adam.

Finance, notwithstanding the long-continued wars on a large scale, was managed so well that government bonds, which stood at 12 per cent. discount in 1813, rose to 14 per cent. premium ten years later.

Reforms begun. The publication in 1812 of the *Fifth Report,* discussed in an earlier chapter of this work, and the elaborate debates on the renewal of the charter in 1813 reopened all the problems of Indian administration, which demanded still further reconsideration in consequence of the upheaval caused by the destruction of the Marāthā power in 1818. Efforts were made in all the older British possessions to reform the abuses in the judicial system, civil and criminal; and some progress was made in reversing the mistaken policy of Lord Cornwallis, which excluded men of Indian birth from all responsible or decently paid office. Lord Hastings was keenly alive to the necessity of reform; and several of his lieutenants entertained the most sensible and enlightened opinions.

In Bengal official opinion opposed extensive change in the judicial arrangements, but something was done to remedy abuses by increasing the number of courts and enhancing the powers of Indian officials. At the instance of the directors a determined attempt was made in Madras to revive the old system of *panchāyats,* or native juries of neighbours, for the settlement of disputes, which produced little result owing to the unwillingness of the people to serve.

The rigorous separation between the judicial and revenue services on which Lord Cornwallis had laid so much stress was abolished, and the offices of collector and district magistrate were combined in every presidency at various dates, in some cases after the departure of Lord Hastings. Generally speaking the employment of natives of the country in positions of considerable authority was slowly extended. As new territory was acquired the absurdity of introducing a complicated code of English laws among communities wholly unprepared to receive it began to be recognized, and the necessity for a simpler, more elastic form of administration was acknowledged. The 'non-regulation' system for the government of newly acquired or backward territory was developed in the time of Lord Amherst, but its application had begun during the term of office of Lord Hastings. We have seen how Cuttack was quieted at once the moment that a reasonable system for the management of rude people was introduced by a special commissioner.

Settlement problems. The complex problem of land 'settlement' in every province came under review. In the territories now known as the Province of Agra an extremely elaborate system of survey and assessment was enacted by Regulation VII of 1822, which failed because it was too elaborate to work in practice. Ten years after the departure of Lord Hastings, Regulation IX of 1833 laid the foundation of the modern system of 'settlement' in Upper India.

The proposal to make 'permanent settlements' the general rule in all provinces was often mooted, and at times was on the point of being decreed. It was not finally negatived until 1883. 'Settlements' are now most commonly sanctioned for periods of either thirty or twenty years.

Munro's 'ryotwar settlement'. The name of Sir Thomas Munro—a man equally distinguished as a soldier and an administrator—who was perhaps the wisest of the many brilliant officers who served Lord Hastings,[1] is specially associated with the 'ryotwar settlement' of the greater part of the Madras Presidency, which he is often alleged erroneously to have 'introduced' during his service in various capacities before 1820 and as Governor of Madras from 1820 to 1827.

Writing in 1825 he warmly repudiated the charge of having invented or introduced 'the Rayetwar system, which, though the old system of the country, is by some strange misapprehension regarded in England as a new one'. He proceeded to explain that official opinion had been unduly biased by familiarity with the Bengal zemindārī system, which was unknown in Madras, except in the Northern Sarkārs (Circars).

> 'The greater part of our [Madras] territories have been acquired from Native Princes who did not employ Zemindars, and who collected the revenue, as we now do, from the Rayets, by means of Tishildars, receiving a monthly salary, and appointed and dismissed at pleasure. Most of our provinces have in ancient times been surveyed and assessed; but as the accounts have in general been altered or lost, we make a new survey and assessment, in order that we may know the resources of the country; and in order that every Rayet may know the exact amount of his assessment, and thus be protected against any extra demand. . . . It is our business to let the distribution of property remain as we find it, and not attempt to force it into larger masses upon any theoretical notion of convenience or improvement. There are many Rayets who have not more than four or five acres; there are some who have four or five thousand. Between these extremes, there are great numbers who have from one [hundred] to five hundred.'[2]

[1] Canning declared that 'Europe never produced a more accomplished statesman, nor India, fertile as it was in heroes, a more skilful soldier'. In 1824 Munro stated that 'I have introduced no new system either in the revenue or the judicial department. . . . I have never wished to introduce any new system of revenue, but I wish in all cases to have no renters, but to collect directly from the occupants or owners, whether they are small or great. Renters are no necessary part of any revenue system' (Gleig, op. cit., ii. 205).

[2] Gleig, *Life*[2], ii. 268.

The system. 'The basis of this system is the division of the whole area into fields by a cadastral survey, each field being valued at a fixed rate per acre and the assessment settled thereon. A holding is one or more of such fields or of their recognized subdivisions. The registered occupant of each field deals directly with Government, and so long as he pays the assessment he is entitled to hold the land for ever and cannot be ejected by Government, though he himself may, in any year, increase or diminish his holding or entirely abandon it; should the land be required for a public purpose, it must be bought at 15 per cent. above its market value. Inheritance, transfer, mortgage, sale, and lease are without restriction; private improvements involve no addition, either present or future, to the assessment. Waste land may be taken up by any person, under the rules laid down, and once granted to a ryot it is his as long as he pleases.'[1]

SIR THOMAS MUNRO.

Munro, who laid down the general principle so contrary to the views of Lord Cornwallis, that 'no theoretical improvement should make us abandon what is supported by experience', was right in maintaining the *ryotwar* system of 'settlement'. But the assessments made in his time and for long afterwards were far too high, and the Madras practice of collection was disfigured by cruel severities, which he did something to modify. The modern system dates only from 1855, and differs from that of Munro's time in several important particulars, notably in the ryot's absolute freedom to relinquish his land, and in the full protection given to private improvements. The assessments have been largely reduced, and the penalty of imprisonment for default is no longer enforced. The Madras system as now worked seems to be excellent, but I have not any personal experience of its operation.

Bombay system. The Bombay system has a general resemblance to that of Madras,

'but the actual holdings are to a large extent grouped into small "survey numbers" with practically immutable boundaries, which are solidly and carefully marked out upon the ground; and in Bombay this fact constitutes so characteristic a feature of the revenue system that the occupant who holds a survey number on the condition of paying the revenue assessed on it is said to hold on the "survey tenure".'[2]

[1] *I. G.* (1908), xvi. 318. [2] *I. G.* (1907), iv. 209.

The early assessments in Bombay, as in Madras and most other provinces, were too heavy and caused much distress. The reformed system dates from 1847.[1]

In the Agra Province, comprising the Ceded and Conquered Districts, with certain other territory, the 'settlement' contract ordinarily was made with groups of zemindars forming a brotherhood or community in each village, through their headmen, the lands of a 'village' being the unit of assessment. The system, as already mentioned, rests upon Regulations VII of 1822 and IX of 1833, as largely modified by subsequent legislation and orders.

Resignation of Lord Hastings. The closing years of the brilliant administration of Lord Hastings were darkened for him personally by the censure passed by the home authorities on his indiscreet indulgence to the banking house of Palmer and Co., which had acquired an undue and corrupt control over the Nizam's government, similar to that exercised by Paul Benfield over the Nawāb of the Carnatic in an earlier generation. The Governor-general permitted himself to be influenced by the fact that one of the partners was married to a ward of his, a young lady whom Lord Hastings regarded as a daughter. The Governor-general, who left India poorer than when he came out, was absolutely cleared of any corrupt motive, but was so distressed by the strictures on his indiscretion that he sent home his resignation in 1821. He made over charge on January 1, 1823, to Mr. John Adam, the senior member of council,[2] after nine and a quarter years of unremitting labour. The directors passed cordial votes of thanks, and granted him at different times sums amounting to £80,000 In 1824 he became Governor of Malta, and on November 28, 1826, he died at sea off Naples.

Mr. Adam. The administration of Mr. Adam for seven months until he was relieved by Lord Amherst in August 1823, is remembered only for his expulsion from India of Mr. James Silk Buckingham, the able editor of the *Calcutta Journal*, who offended the authorities by the freedom of his criticisms on official persons and doings. The incident offers a convenient opportunity for reviewing briefly the history of journalism in India from the days of Warren Hastings to the present time.[3]

History of the Indian press. The first Indian newspaper printed in English was Hickey's *Bengal Gazette*, which began its stormy course in January 1780 and was suppressed early in 1782. The editor spent a long time in jail on account of the libels he published on Mrs. Hastings and various people. Hickey's paper was succeeded by the *Indian Gazette* and several other journals.

[1] *I. G.* (1908), viii. 294.

[2] Thornton calls him 'second member'.

[3] The principal, although not the sole authority, is Malcolm's essay entitled 'Free Press' in *Political History*, vol. ii, 1826. Heber observes that Mr. Adam was 'one of the most popular men in India', both with his countrymen and with Indians. Hickey's name is sometimes spelt Hicky.

Lord Cornwallis found it necessary in 1791 to order the deportation of another editor. The right of the Governor-general to inflict that penalty having been affirmed after a long discussion by the unanimous judgement of the Supreme Court, the editor in question was actually deported in 1794.

Five years later, in 1799, a censorship was instituted and approved by the directors. In Lord Wellesley's time, when French privateers were active and the free publication of shipping news was observed to guide them in their depredations, severe restrictions on the newspapers were enforced as being necessary for the public safety. Lord Minto, influenced by the same reasons, maintained a vigilant control over the press, and formulated a revised code of regulations for the censorship in 1813.

Lord Hastings, in 1817, while recognizing the necessity for supervision, preferred to exercise it through rules prohibiting the discussion of certain matters; and therefore abolished the censorship. The Marquess had no objection to fair, honest criticism, believing, as he said, that

> 'it is salutary for supreme authority, even when its intentions are most pure, to look to the control of public scrutiny: while conscious of rectitude, that authority can lose nothing of its strength by its exposure to general comment'.

His rules were directed against the abuse of liberty.

Mr. James Silk Buckingham, the editor of the *Calcutta Journal*, founded by him in 1818, took full advantage of the liberal opinions of Lord Hastings, and commented boldly on public measures. He also indulged in sarcastic comments on high officials. Mr. Adam, who did not agree with Lord Hastings on the subject, and was irritated by Buckingham's articles, required every printer of a newspaper to take out a licence. When that measure failed to muzzle the editor of the *Calcutta Journal*, Mr. Adam deported him. That proceeding gave rise to acute controversy. Buckingham, on arrival in London, was compensated for his losses by a liberal subscription raised among his friends. Some years later he entered parliament as member for Sheffield, and afterwards obtained a pension of £200 a year from the East India Company. His adventurous life ended in 1855.[1] Lord William Bentinck (1828–35), while avowing the conviction that it is 'necessary for the public safety that the press in India should be kept under the most rigid control', allowed great freedom in practice.

His successor, Sir Charles Metcalfe, in September 1835, removed all restrictions, incurring thereby the wrath of the directors. From that date until 1878, when Lord Lytton's government imposed restrictions on *vernacular* papers, the Indian press continued to be free, unless for offences against the ordinary law. Lord Lytton's

[1] For the strange career of Buckingham, who was a voluminous author, see Higginbotham, *Men Whom India has Known*[2], 1874. His *Autobiography* (1855) unfortunately remained unfinished, and does not deal with the most interesting part of his life.

measure was repealed by his successor, Lord Ripon. The outbreak of atrocious political crime, much of which was traced directly to the instigation of newspaper articles, constrained the government of India to pass a restrictive Press Act in 1908 and a more stringent one in 1910.

During the agony of the nations in the Great War since 1914, paramount regard for the public safety has forced even the free democracies of England and America to endure restrictions on newspaper publication which would have been regarded as intolerable at any other time. No theories about natural liberty can be allowed to override the requirements of the defence of the realm.

Vernacular press. No independent Hindu or Muhammadan government in India ever made any use of the printing-press. Excluding the excessively rare publications issued by the early Jesuit presses on the western coast, and at a later date by missionaries in the south, the first vernacular work printed in India was Halhed's Bengālī grammar, issued in 1778. The earliest Bengālī weekly newspaper, the *Samachar Darpan*, appeared in 1818 at Serampore under the editorship of the famous missionary and historian, John Clark Marshman, with the cordial approval of the Marquess of Hastings. It is needless to dilate on the rapid modern development of the Indian newspaper press both in English and in various vernacular languages. The early papers written in English circulated only among the small European population. Their modern successors have access to a large Indian public.

Burmese war. The war with Burma, which lasted for almost two years, from March 1824 to February 1826, was the principal event of Lord Amherst's short administration. The operations were originally purely defensive on the British side, the Governor-general's declaration of war having been forced by deliberate Burmese acts of aggression, and the avowal by the Burmese court of its intention to take both Chittagong and Calcutta.

Origin of the war. Bodoahprā, the ferocious king of Burma, who had a long and generally victorious reign of thirty-seven years, died in 1819, and was succeeded by his grandson Hpagyīdoa. The Burmese having conquered Arakan in 1784, multitudes of Arakanese refugees crossed into British territory, and constantly stirred up trouble by conflicts with the Burmese.

In 1813 the Burman troops occupied Manipur, and in 1821–2 Assam was annexed to the Burmese Empire. An incursion into Kāchār (Cachar) at the beginning of 1824 actually brought on a fight with the Company's troops. Some months earlier the Burmese had forcibly occupied an island (Shuparu, or Shapārī) on the Chittagong frontier well within British territory, and had killed some sepoys. In January 1824 the best Burmese general, known by his title of Mahā Bandūla, was sent in command of a considerable army with orders to expel the British from Bengal. The court of Ava, intoxicated by its numerous military successes against neighbours, believed its army to be invincible, and, in profound ignorance of all the facts, regarded the white foreigners with ineffable contempt. Mahā Bandūla felt no doubts about the success of his proposed invasion of Bengal, and was provided with golden fetters for the Governor-general.

Missions to Burma. The Calcutta government had made persistent efforts to establish friendly relations with the Burmese court. Lt.-Col. Symes had been sent on a mission by Sir John Shore as early as 1795. He was sent again in 1802.[1] Captain Canning followed him in 1803 and once more in 1811–12. All the missions were unsuccessful, and the envoys were invariably subjected to studied insult. The king intrigued with the Pēshwā in 1817. Lord Hastings ignored the provocations offered by the government of Ava, having his hands more than full with the affairs of India. But the attack on British territory and the projected invasion of Bengal early in 1824 could not be ignored, and necessarily led to war.

Lord Amherst's policy. Lord Amherst's government aimed primarily at turning the Burmese out of Assam, Manipur, and Kāchār. The Governor-general at first did not intend to invade Arakan or Burma through the difficult mountain country—his purpose was to secure the Bengal frontier. Without going into the details of the operations by land, which included some failures, it may suffice to say that all the primary objectives of the war had been attained by June 1825, when Manipur was occupied by the Company's troops. The Burmese had evacuated Kāchār and been driven from Assam earlier in that year. Those successes were brought about indirectly by the British attack on Rangoon and the Irrawaddy (Irāwadī) valley, which became the principal theatre of the war. Mahā Bandūla was recalled to meet the invasion from the sea, and the Company's forces had thus a comparatively easy task in clearing the enemy out of Assam and the other hill states on the north-eastern frontier of Bengal.

An attempted invasion of Arakan by land failed, owing to terrible sickness among the troops.

Barrackpore mutiny. The preparations for that unlucky expedition in October 1824 led to a painful incident, the mutiny of the 47th Native Infantry and a few other troops stationed at Barrackpore, the Governor-general's country seat on the Hooghly fifteen miles above Calcutta. The sepoys, who dreaded the loss of caste if they should be sent by sea, also had a real material grievance owing to the impossibility of obtaining land transport, which had to be provided by the men themselves under the rules then in force. As usual the genuine grievance was made the occasion for raising the cry of religion in danger. The 47th, when paraded, refused to obey the orders to either march or ground arms and remained sullenly, although passively, defiant. A battery of European artillery, supported by two British regiments, then opened fire and killed many. Others were subsequently tried and

[1] Lt.-Col. Michael Symes, *Embassy to the Kingdom of Ava,* published in 1800, and reprinted with additions in Constable's Miscellany, 2 vols. duod., Edinburgh, 1831.

hanged, and the number of the regiment was removed from the Army List. The business was not well managed by the military authorities. The tragedy apparently might have been averted by judicious handling of the men, without sacrifice of indispensable discipline.

Origin of the Rangoon expedition. The expedition to Rangoon was undertaken on the advice of Captain Canning, who had been one of the envoys to Burma and was supposed to know the country. Lord Amherst was induced to believe that the occupation of the port would frighten the king into submission. The disappointment of that ill-founded expectation led to a costly war, involving much sacrifice of life and treasure. The expedition originally was not designed to advance into the interior, and in consequence no arrangements had been made for transport, which was supposed to be available locally if it should be needed. As a matter of fact, none was to be had.

The campaign. The fleet assembled at Port Cornwallis in the Andaman Islands carrying troops to the number of about 11,500 under the command of Sir Archibald Campbell; and Rangoon was occupied in May 1824 without serious resistance. The trouble began in the following month, when the rains broke; and the army of occupation suffered terribly from disease and putrid food. The town had been evacuated of its inhabitants, and, as the military secretary to the commander writes,

'the plains, for many miles around us, were swept of their herds; the rivers were unprovided with one friendly canoe; the towns and villages were deserted, and every man beyond our posts [was] in arms against us'.

The weakened force of the invaders endured bravely the miseries of its situation, and fought many actions against the encircling multitudes of Burmese. The end of October, when the rains ceased, brought some relief in comfort, but the sudden change of temperature aggravated the sickness and mortality, which were greater in October than in any previous month. In November the health of the troops improved; reinforcements were received, and a fleet of boats was being built. Tenasserim and Pegu were occupied by detachments.

At the beginning of December the whole army from Arakan under the command of Mahā Bandūla was entrenched in its positions opposite the British force. On the 6th of that month he was defeated and compelled to retire to Donabew (Danabyu), about sixty miles above Rangoon. The Burmese general entrenched himself in his new position with remarkable skill, constructing a formidable stockade more than a mile long, and composed of huge teak beams 'from fifteen to seventeen feet high, driven firmly into the earth, and placed as closely as possible to each other', supported in the rear by brick ramparts and provided with many guns of poor quality.

The first attack on the stockade was repulsed. On April 2, 1825, a lucky accident gave the British force possession of the place. A rocket having killed Mahā Bandūla, the whole garrison fled or dispersed during the night, abandoning everything, including a welcome store of grain. The enemy also evacuated the important town of Prome which was occupied on April 4, and used as a comfortable and healthy cantonment for the expeditionary force during the rainy season.

When operations were resumed early in December, the British troops, after fighting several actions with success, quickly reached

BANDŪLA'S ARMED OBSERVATION POST.

Yandabo, only four marches from the capital, on February 22, 1826. Two days later the Burmese government accepted the terms imposed by the victors.

Treaty of Yandabo. The treaty of Yandabo provided for the payment of a crore of rupees, or one million pounds sterling; as well as for the cession of Assam, Arakan, and the coast of Tenasserim, including the portion of the province of Martaban lying east of the Salween river. The king of Burma further agreed to abstain from all interference in Kāchār (Cachar), Jaintia, and Manipur. A quarter of the indemnity was paid at once, and a second quarter towards the end of the year, whereupon the British evacuated Rangoon. The Burmese retained Pegu, including Rangoon, until the next war. A commercial treaty of an unsatisfactory kind was arranged subsequently, and the appointment of a resident British envoy was accepted. But until 1830 no such officer was appointed. From that date Colonel Burney held the appointment for seven years, discharging his difficult duties with tact and success.[1] King Hpagyīdoa sank into a state of melancholy, and had to be kept in strict seclusion. He was deposed quietly by his brother in 1837, and allowed to end his days in peace as a prisoner, well treated.

The Burmese version. The Burmese official account of the war, as recorded in the *Royal Chronicle*, deserves quotation :

'In the years 1186 and 1187 [of the Burmese era], the *Kula pyu*, or white strangers of the west, fastened a quarrel upon the Lord of the Golden Palace. They landed at Rangoon, took that place and Prome, and were permitted to advance as far as Yandaboo ; for the King, from motives of piety and regard to life, made no preparation whatever to oppose them. The strangers had spent vast sums of money in their enterprise, so that by the time they reached Yandaboo their resources were exhausted, and they were in great distress. They then petitioned the King, who in his clemency and generosity, sent them large sums of money to pay their expenses back, and ordered them out of the country.'[2]

Criticism. The errors in the planning and execution of the operations against the Burmese caused much needless waste of life and treasure.[3] The actual fighting was nearly all done by the European troops, the commander of the expedition, Sir Archibald Campbell, having little confidence in the native army. The Madras regiments showed fortitude under privation, but, according to Lord William Bentinck, 'entirely failed' in attacks when employed without European support. Notwithstanding the valour of the soldiers, the Rangoon expedition probably would have been a failure but for the help sent by Sir Thomas Munro, the competent Governor of Madras. Lord Amherst was not qualified either by natural ability or by training to direct a war and Sir Archibald Campbell's strategy was open to criticism.

The Burmese soldier fought well, considering that, as Phayre observes, he 'fought under conditions which rendered victory impossible'. The army was composed mainly of untrained

[1] Burney, a Malay and Pālī scholar, published works on his special subjects.

[2] Lawrie, p. 60. The passage is of interest as indicating the value of official documents in many cases when the means of checking their statements do not exist.

[3] Munro wrote in April 1826 :

'There has been no want of energy or decision at any time in attacking the enemy ; but there has certainly been a great want of many of the arrangements and combinations by which the movements of an army are facilitated, and its success rendered more certain.' Munro proceeds to recognize the difficulties, and to give Lord Amherst credit for persevering (Gleig, op. cit., ii. 279).

peasants, badly armed. The home-made gunpowder was defective, and the artillery consisted of 'mostly old ship-guns of diverse calibre, and some of them two hundred or more years old'. The expeditionary force, if it had been properly directed and equipped, should have made short work of the resistance. The Burmese displayed extraordinary skill in the construction of stockades, superior even to those of the Nepalese. A competent writer declares that 'the position and defences at Donoobew, as a field-work, would have done credit to the most scientific engineer'.

Fall of Bhurtpore. The mishaps during the earlier stages of the Burmese war excited feelings of unrest throughout India, as similar failures in the first Nepalese campaign had done in the time of Lord Hastings. Durjan Sāl, cousin of the child Rājā of Bhurtpore, who had been enthroned with the approval of Sir David Ochterlony, the Resident at Delhi, ventured to dispute the succession to the principality and proclaimed himself as Rājā. The Resident at once moved troops to enforce the decision of the agent of the supreme government; but Lord Amherst, then anxious about the ill success in Burma, denounced his action as premature, and passed censorious comments which provoked the resignation of the veteran, who was replaced by Sir Charles Metcalfe. Sir David Ochterlony, who was old and in bad health, died a few months later. Sir Charles Metcalfe soon succeeded in persuading the Governor-general that the paramount power could not allow itself to be flouted by a petty princeling. The fortress was besieged by Lord Combermere, the commander-in-chief, with an adequate force and a suitable train of heavy artillery. The fortifications were breached in January 1806 by the explosion of a huge mine, and the failures of Lord Lake twenty years earlier were amply avenged. The glory of the achievement was dimmed by the excessive rapacity for prize-money displayed by Lord Combermere.[1]

Resignation of Lord Amherst. No other political event during the administration of Lord Amherst calls for notice. The Governor-general resigned owing to domestic reasons, and quitted India in March 1828, making over charge to Mr. Bayley, the senior member of council. Lord Amherst was not intellectually fit for his high office, and ought not to have been appointed. Parliament, with its accustomed generosity, pardoned his errors, and awarded him cordial thanks for the final success of the operations against Burma and Bhurtpore.

Steamships. The Burmese war offered the first opportunity for the employment of steamships in war in the Indian seas. A small vessel named the *Diana* rendered valuable service at Rangoon.[2] A little later, in April 1827, Sir Thomas Munro and

[1] Wilson gives full particulars of the siege, with a reference to Capt. Creighton's *Narrative of the Siege and Capture of Bhurtpore* (4to London, 1830), which is in the India Office Library. For the rapacity see Metcalfe's opinion in Marshman, ii. 409.

[2] Lord William Bentinck observed that 'if five powerful steamers had

a vast crowd of all classes assembled on the Madras beach 'to see the *Enterprize* steam-vessel manœuvre for the gratification of the public'. The incident serves as a reminder of the extreme rapidity with which scientific invention had advanced within the space of a hundred years. The moralist, unhappily, cannot discern a corresponding advance in human nature.

CHRONOLOGY

First Bengālī newspaper	1818
Deposition of Rāo of Cutch; earthquakes; occupation of Singapore; Nawāb-Vizier of Oudh takes the title of king	1819
Sir Thomas Munro Governor of Madras	1820–7
Regulation VII	1822
Departure of Lord Hastings; Mr. Adam acting Governor-general; deportation of Mr. Buckingham; Lord Amherst Governor-general	1823
War with Burma	1824–6
Barrackpore mutiny	1824
Fall of Bhurtpore; treaty of Yandabo	1826
Resignation of Lord Amherst; Mr. Bayley acting Governor-general	1828

AUTHORITIES

The books cited are additional to those named in the foot-notes and in the last preceding chapter.

For Singapore: Oxford Survey of the British Empire (Oxford, 1914), vol. ii; A. T. RITCHIE and R. EVANS, *Lord Amherst* (R. I., 1894); a rather unsatisfactory book.

For the Burmese War: PHAYRE, *History of Burma* (1883), chap. 21, the clearest chronicle; Major SNODGRASS, *Narrative of the Burmese War* (London, Murray, 1827), a short and unpretentious contemporary military account; Colonel W. E. B. LAURIE, *Our Burmese Wars* (London, Allen, 1880), Part I, a diffuse work; and correspondence of Sir T. MUNRO in GLEIG, *Life* ², vol. ii. The life of Sir Thomas Munro has been also written by Bradshaw (R. I., 1894), and by Arbuthnot, 1881. I have used Gleig. No critical military history of the war seems to exist.[1] *The Narrative of a Journey*, &c., by REGINALD HEBER, Bishop of Calcutta from 1823 to 1826, was published soon after his death in the latter year, and has gone through several editions. It contains many interesting observations on the India of Lord Amherst's time.

then been at our command to bring up in quick succession all necessary reinforcements and supplies, the war would probably have terminated in a few months, and many millions of treasure, many thousands of lives, and extraordinary misery and sickness would have been spared' (Boulger, *Lord William Bentinck* (in R. I.), p. 199).

[1] Professor Ramsay Muir observes that 'there is probably no part of the history of British India upon which less material is easily available than the first Burmese war. No documented life of Lord Amherst has been published, and the printed documents on the war are very inadequate.'

CHAPTER 2

Lord William Cavendish-Bentinck; reforms; relations with native states; abolition of suttee; suppression of thuggee; renewal of charter; Sir Charles Metcalfe.

Lord William Cavendish-Bentinck. The second son of the third Duke of Portland was William, known by the courtesy title of Lord William Cavendish-Bentinck, and commonly called Lord William Bentinck. He had been Governor of Madras at an unusually early age, and, having been recalled on account of the Vellore mutiny, had been variously employed since that event. He never admitted the justice of his recall, and made no secret of his intense desire for compensation by appointment as Governor-general. He even went so far as to violate propriety by applying for the office when the Marquess of Hastings resigned. On that occasion Lord Amherst was preferred, but in 1827 the directors consented to gratify Lord William Bentinck's ambition and appointed him. He did not actually take over charge until July 1828; Mr. Butterworth Bayley having acted meantime as Governor-general. Nothing specially worthy of record occurred during his tenure of power, but some of the reforms which distinguished the term of office of Lord William Bentinck were prepared by the Bayley administration. The new Governor-general was almost fifty-four years of age when he entered upon his duties as ruler of India.

LORD WILLIAM CAVENDISH-BENTINCK.

After his return from India in 1835 he declined the offer of a peerage, preferring to share in active political life as a member of the House of Commons.[1] In 1837 he was elected as a Liberal

[1] The younger sons of a British peer are commoners in law and eligible to sit in the House of Commons. The eldest son of a peer is accorded by courtesy the use of the second territorial title held by his father. The younger sons of a Duke are called Lord without any territorial title.

member for the city of Glasgow. He died on June 17, 1839, in the sixty-fifth year of his age.

Diverse opinions. While the dictum of the poet that

> 'peace hath her victories
> No less than those of war'

may pass unchallenged as a statement of fact, it is unquestionable that the glories of the successful warrior arouse interest to a degree with which the legislation of the domestic reformer cannot pretend to compete. The administration of Lord William Bentinck for almost seven years from July 1828 to March 1835, with nothing to show which can be described as a victory of war, has to its credit many achievements justly entitled to be called victories of peace, and important enough to earn for their author a high place among the rulers of India. Two of those achievements—the abolition of suttee and the suppression of thuggee—may even be styled 'renowned', and so justify the revised and more familiar reading of Milton's lines. The almost exclusively peaceful career of Lord William Bentinck in India has given occasion for strangely divergent appreciations of the merits and demerits of his work; ranging from the vitriolic denunciation of Thornton, through the guarded commendation of Wilson, and the almost unqualified praise of Marshman, to the exuberant eulogy of Macaulay, his colleague and brother Whig. Thornton, constrained to admit that one act of the Governor-general, the abolition of suttee, will be 'held in eternal honour', can find nothing else deserving of approval in the history of seven years, and concludes his inadequate record of the facts by the surprising observations:

> 'The best and brightest of his deeds has been reserved to close the history of Lord William Bentinck's administration. It remains only to state that he quitted India in May 1835, having held the office of Governor-general somewhat longer than the ordinary period; but having done less for the interest of India and for his own reputation than any who had occupied his place since the commencement of the nineteenth century, with the single exception of Sir George Barlow.'

A few lines above that passage we find the remarkable allegation that

> 'but for the indulgence of similar extravagance in a variety of ways, the administration of Lord William Bentinck would appear almost a blank, and were all record of it obliterated posterity would scarcely observe the deficiency, while it is certain they would have little reason to regret it'.

Wilson held that

> 'a dispassionate retrospect of the results of his government will assign to Lord William Bentinck an honourable place amongst the statesmen who have been intrusted with the delegated sovereignty over the British Empire in the East'.

Marshman, with greater warmth, affirms that

> 'his administration marks the most memorable period of improvement between the days of Lord Cornwallis and Lord Dalhousie, and forms a salient point in the history of Indian reform . . . with the intuition of

a great mind, he discovered the weak points of our system of administration, which was becoming effete under the withering influence of routine, and the remedies he applied went to the root of the disease. He infused new blood into our institutions, and started them upon a new career of vigour and efficiency . . . the impulse of his genius, which became the mainspring of a long succession of improvements.'

The climax of eulogy is attained in the inscription composed by Macaulay :

'This statue is erected to William Cavendish-Bentinck, who during seven years ruled India with eminent prudence, integrity, and benevolence; who, placed at the head of a great empire, never laid aside the simplicity and moderation of a private citizen ; who infused into Oriental despotism the spirit of British freedom ; who never forgot that the end of government is the welfare of the governed ; who abolished cruel rites, who effaced humiliating distinctions ; who allowed liberty to the expression of public opinion ; whose constant study it was to elevate the moral and intellectual character of the Government committed to his charge ;—this monument was erected by men who, differing from each other in race, in manners, in language, and in religion, cherish, with equal veneration and gratitude, the memory of his wise, upright, and paternal administration.'

The doings of a man whose character could evoke judgements so contradictory as those cited merit narration and consideration.

Financial economies. The undoubted unpopularity of Lord William Bentinck with the members of the European services, civil and military, was primarily due to the strictness with which he enforced financial economies at the beginning of his administration. The directors, frightened by the heavy cost of the Burmese War, insisted on retrenchment, and issued peremptory orders to withdraw the 'half-batta', or field allowances still enjoyed by officers of their army. Lord William Bentinck, who simply carried out the orders from home, was not in any way responsible for them, although the angry sufferers vented their indignation upon him. The allowances of the Civil Service, which could better bear pruning, were also diminished.

Confidential reports. The Governor-general further irritated that service by his suspicious attitude and inquisitorial proceedings, described by Thornton in these bitter words :

'Under pretence of improving the character of the civil service and providing for the advancement of merit, he sought to establish a system of universal espionage, better suited to the bureau of the holy office of the Inquisition than to the closet of a statesman anxious to be regarded as the representative of all that was liberal. Every superior officer, court, and board, was required to make periodical reports on the character and conduct of every covenanted servant employed in a subordinate capacity. Like most of his lordship's projects, this plan met neither with approbation nor success, and it was soon abolished.'

Flogging in native army. In 1833 Lord William Bentinck followed the example of Lord Cornwallis and the Marquess of Hastings by taking on himself the office of commander-in-chief. In that capacity he issued two important orders affecting the native army—one giving the sepoys enhanced rates of pay after long service, and the other abolishing the punishment of flogging. Both measures were good in themselves, but the fatal objection to the second one was that flogging was retained as a penalty for the European king's troops. Thus an 'odious distinction', as Sleeman observes, was created, subjecting the white man, the member and support of the ruling race, to a grave personal indignity from which his dark-skinned comrade in arms was exempt. No consideration could justify such a distinction, and the order on the subject must be counted as one of the errors of Lord William Bentinck, which in large measure explains and justifies his unpopularity with the European services.[1] Subsequently, early in the administration of Sir Henry Hardinge, courts-martial were again empowered to inflict corporal punishment not exceeding fifty lashes on soldiers of the native army, but the power has been exercised very rarely.

In the whole British army the penalty of flogging in time of peace was prohibited in April 1868, by an amendment of the Mutiny Act. It was completely abolished by the Army Act of 1881.

Relations with Native States. The action of Lord William Bentinck's government in its dealings with the Native or Protected States and with tribal chiefs cannot be unreservedly commended, although the blame for the vacillating and contradictory policy pursued may be held to rest upon the authorities in England more than upon the Governor-general. The directors, under the delusion that everything had been settled by Lord Hastings, quickly relapsed into their old timidity, and repeatedly forbade any sort of interference with Rājās and chiefs. Lord William Bentinck, who set great store upon obedience to his instructions, came out steeped in the notion that the paramount power could afford to allow disorder in the Native States. Hard facts convinced him in course of time and against his will that a certain amount of interference was unavoidable, and constrained him in the end to interpose with more force than would have been needed at an earlier stage of the troubles induced by the dereliction of duty on the part of the paramount power.

An admirable review of the situation in each state, filled with copious details, may be found in Book III, chapter viii of Wilson's *History*, which proves conclusively the wide extent of the evil wrought by a timorous, selfish policy aiming at a return to the ignoble ideal of Sir George Barlow. In Oudh the reforming minister, Hakīm Mehdi, was deserted by the British government, and driven from the kingdom.[2] The Nizam's dominions were permitted to fall into disorder; support to the infant Holkar was refused, with a like result; and dangerous quarrels were allowed to develop in

[1] An interesting discussion of the subject will be found in Sleeman, *Rambles and Recollections*, chap. 76, ed. V. A. Smith, Oxford University Press, 1915. That book, published in 1844, was written some years earlier. The remarks on flogging were printed in a pamphlet dated 1841.

[2] See article on 'Hakīm Mehdi' by Prof. S. B. Smith in *J. U. P. H. S.*, i. 168–84.

Gwālior. The Gaikwār assumed an attitude of open hostility. The Rājpūt States were almost encouraged to engage in civil war; the improvements in Udaipur were checked, and the prosperity of the state created by Tod and his fellow labourers rapidly declined; at Jaipur, the policy of the Governor-general,

'after exhibiting the extremes of interference and of abstinence from interfercnee, terminated in a catastrophe which was wholly unprecedented, and which was followed by a still closer and more authoritative connexion'.

The 'catastrophe' alluded to was the furious attaek made on the British officers stationed at the local court in June 1835, shortly after the departure of Lord William Bentinck, but due to his vacillating policy. The Resident was severely wounded, and Mr. Blake, his assistant, was killed.[1] The crime was traced to Jota Rām, the ex-minister, and a knot of Jain bankers, who supported his cause in the tortuous politics of the state.

The subject might be developed at length, but what has been said suffices to show that the policy of Lord William Bentinck is not entitled to indiscriminate eulogy, and that his failure to act upon the principles of Wellesley and the Marquess of Hastings produced its inevitable effects.[2]

Mysore. At times his action in regard to the Protected States was vigorous enough. In 1831 the misgovernment of the Rājā of Mysore provoked a rebellion, which induced the Governor-general to proceed under a clause in the treaty of 1799, and to place the state under British administration. That arrangement lasted for fifty years until 1881, when Lord Ripon felt justified in effecting the 'rendition of Mysore' to a young Mahārājā, who had been carefully trained. Happily the experiment proved successful; the Mahārājā did his duty, and the state is still admirably administered.

Small annexations. Three small annexations were effected, two on the north-eastern frontier, and one in the extreme south. The Jaintiā Parganas to the north-east of Sylhet were annexed in 1835, because the Rājā refused to surrender men who had kidnapped British subjects and sacrificed them to the goddess Kālī.

When the Rājā of the neighbouring territory of Kāchār (Cachar) died in 1830, his dominions lapsed to the British government under the provisions of a treaty made a few years before, and without opposition from the inhabitants. The country is now prosperous and well cultivated, producing valuable crops of rice and tea.

Coorg. The annexation of Coorg (Kodagu) in 1834 was forced

[1] See Sleeman, *Rambles*, ed. V. A. Smith, 1915, pp. 503, 504.

[2] Sir Henry Durand '"often said—and it was an opinion shared by many thinking natives—that the surest way of extinguishing native states was to abstain from all interference in their affairs. I see that a late writer in the *Quarterly Review* quotes a remark to the same effect made by the well-known Minister, Sir Madava Rao; "If left to themselves they will wipe themselves out"' (editor's note in Durand, *The First Afghan War* (1879), p. xxii).

on the government by the outrageous conduct of Vīra Rājā, who practised the most bloodthirsty tyranny. He cherished intense animosity against the English, in spite of the fact that they had rescued his country from the savage cruelty of Haidar Ali and Tippoo ; he closed his frontiers, permitting nobody to leave, and admitting nobody who declined to declare himself an enemy of the English ; he murdered all his male relatives and many of the female, often with his own hands. After his surrender seventeen bodies, dug up from a pit in the jungle, comprised the remains of the Rājā's aunt, the child of his sister, and the brother of her husband, with others. His adherents contrived a plot to seize Bangalore and overthrow the Company's government. All endeavours to bring the furious chief to reason having failed, troops in four columns were sent into his country. After a few days, and some considerable fighting, they occupied Mercāra the capital,[1] and the Rājā surrendered. No male relative having survived, and it being obviously useless to set up a stranger as Rājā, the country was annexed and administered in subordination to Mysore. The little province is now governed by a commissioner, under the supervision of the resident at Bangalore (Mysore), and the government of India. For some years after 1865 coffee-planting was profitable, but the industry has since declined. Rice is the main ordinary crop.

Coorg is a strange land, inhabited by queer tribes. Their religion is the worship of ancestors and demons, slightly tinged with a Hindu colouring introduced by domiciled Brahmans. The absence of true Hindu feeling is shown by the fact that the brown monkey is eaten and regarded as a great delicacy.

The Rājā and his family. The criminal Rājā was treated with excessive lenity. He was deported first to Vellore and then to Benares, and in 1852 was granted by Lord Dalhousie leave to visit England with his favourite daughter, then ten years old. He died in London about 1863. The curious and tragic sequel to the family history is told briefly in the foot-note.[2] It is often asserted that Vīra Rājā must have been insane, but that explanation of his ferocity does not seem to be tenable. His father, Linga Rājā, was nearly as bad, and governed on the

[1] Madhukaira of Wilson. The correct form is said to be Medukeri, meaning 'clean town' (*I. G.*).

[2] The princess having been brought up as a Christian by her father's desire, was baptized by the name of Victoria in 1852, the Queen being her godmother. The royal favour encouraged the Rājā to claim seven lakhs of rupees from the East India Company, but he lost his suit after litigation lasting several years. His daughter married Colonel C. and had a child by him. The union was unhappy, and she died in 1864. Some time later visitors in a cab called at the Oriental Club, Hanover Square, for Colonel C., who drove off with them, saying he would return shortly. He was never seen again. The child also disappeared. Both must have been secretly murdered and buried somewhere in London. The story of the disappearance of Colonel C. was related by his son to the author. The Rājā died before his daughter, and was buried in Kensal Green cemetery.

same principles. Vīra Rājendra, the elder brother of Linga, who was equally ferocious, appears to have been really a maniac at times.

Anti-Russian policy. The ill-coneeived policy, which brought about the first Afghan war and the annexation of Sind a few years later, was initiated by the Home Government in Lord William Bentinck's time. It was founded on an excessive fear of a Russian advance towards India by way of Herat and Kandahār. Negotiations with the Ameers of Sind were opened, nominally to secure commercial privileges on the waters of the Indus, then unexplored by Europeans, but in reality mainly directed to political objects. The Ameers, much against their will, were constrained to sign commercial treaties, stipulating among other things that the parties would 'never look with a covetous eye on the possessions of each other'. In 1830–1 Lieutenant Alexander Burnes, acting under the instructions of Lord Ellenborough, then President of the Board of Control, was sent up the Indus with a present of English horses for Mahārājā Ranjit Singh, who reeeived his visitor with marked distinction. Later in the same year the Governor-general paid a highly ceremonial visit to the Mahārājā at Rūpar (Roopur) on the Sutlaj. The meeting resulted in 'a treaty of perpetual friendship with the great Sikh ruler, who agreed in his turn to encourage trade along the Sutlej and upper Indus, and to respect the territories of the Sind Amīrs'.[1] Shāh Shujā, the Afghan prince who lived in exile at Lūdiānā, the British frontier station, then made an attempt to recover the throne of Afghanistan from Dōst Muhammad, his rival in possession. Shāh Shujā, notwithstanding the help given by Ranjit Singh and the benevolent neutrality of the government of India, suffered a total defeat, and was obliged to return to Lūdiānā.

Malay peninsula. Lord William Bentinck took much pains to make himself personally acquainted with the local conditions of the immense territories under his government, and travelled almost continually. In 1829 he visited Malacca and the neighbouring settlements, where he effected certain administrative changes. The connexion of the settlements with Bengal lasted, as already noted, until 1867. The Governor-general appreciated the importance of Singapore, which was made the capital, instead of Penang, in 1830.

Steam navigation. He was a man of his age, with a mind open to the ideas of reform then in the air, and was ready to recognize the developments of applied science. The subject of communication by means of steamships especially interested him. The earliest steamship plying regularly in Great Britain had appeared on the Clyde in 1812; and, as has been seen, a small vessel of the kind did valuable service at Rangoon in 1824. Lord William Bentinck quickly saw the importance of utilizing the novel form of navigation both on the Indian rivers and for the abridgement of

[1] Trotter, *Lord Auckland*, p. 41; but the text is not quoted.

the voyage between England and India. The Court of Directors willingly supported his arrangements for the creation of a steam fleet on the Ganges, but his efforts to improve the communications with England by a steam service to Suez did not command equal enthusiasm at the India House, and the new service was allowed to drop. The regular communication between Europe and India via Suez was deferred until 1843, when it was undertaken by the then newly formed Peninsular and Oriental Company, which still flourishes.[1] Lord William Bentinck did not attempt to introduce railways into India. That innovation was left for Lord Dalhousie in 1848. The earliest railway in Great Britain had been opened in 1825 on a small scale.

Finance. The all-important subject of finance received its due share of attention from Lord William Bentinck, who took well-considered steps to increase the revenue, especially that from the opium monopoly, as well as to reduce the expenditure. The reductions in the military budget were, perhaps, excessive; but on the whole the financial administration was successful, and transformed the deficit into a surplus.

N. W. P. 'settlements'. The 'settlements' in the North-Western Provinces, now called the Province of Agra, made under Regulation IX of 1833, already mentioned, increased the revenue at the same time as they provided a record of rights and an assessment generally fair, although sometimes rather heavy. The largest share of the credit for the successful working of the Regulation is due to Mr. Robert Merttins Bird, who was appointed in 1832 member of the newly constituted Board of Revenue at Allahabad. He was aided by a staff of highly qualified settlement officers, whose reports are still a mine of information.[2]

'Resumption'. A considerable increase in the land revenue of the permanently settled provinces was obtained by the 'resumption' and assessment of a large number of estates which had been alleged to be revenue free. The process, which continued after Lord William Bentinck's time to 1850, is the main explanation of the increase in the land revenue of Bengal from 286 lakhs in 1790–1 to 323 lakhs in 1903–4.

Extension of employment of Indians. The financial reforms and economies effected by Lord William Bentinck were intimately connected with his personal policy concerning the larger employment of the cheaper Indian element in the judicial and executive administration of the country. He had the courage to reverse boldly the erroneous policy of Lord Cornwallis and to act decisively on the principles laid down by Sir Thomas Munro and Sir Charles

[1] The Company, originally established for the service of the ports in the 'Peninsula', meaning Spain and Portugal, obtained the right to extend its operations to India under royal charter granted in 1840.

[2] Probably the author is now (1918) the only person living who has read all those old *Reports*. He had to go through them when preparing the *Settlement Officer's Manual for the N. W. P.*, published at Allahabad in 1881.

Metcalfe. He followed generally the lines prescribed by Metcalfe in the following passage:

'Native functionaries in the first instance in all departments. European superintendents, uniting the local powers of judicature, police, and revenue in all their branches through the districts over which they preside. Commissioners over them, and a Board over them, communicating with and subject to the immediate control of the Government.'

In pursuance of the new policy a Board of Revenue was constituted at Allahabad; Commissioners of Revenue and Circuit were appointed; certain classes of judicial work were entrusted to collectors; the office of district magistrate was combined with that of collector; the cumbrous and useless provincial courts were abolished; Indian officers were entrusted with responsible judicial and executive duties, decently paid; in especial, the functionaries now known as subordinate judges were appointed; and, in short, the administration was organized very much in the form which it still (1918) retains. Madras, however, never adopted the institution of commissioners. Lord William Bentinck, filled with the spirit which carried the British Parliamentary Reform Act of 1832, was the first of the modern Governors-general; and, in spite of the errors noted in the early part of this chapter, deserves credit for the clear vision which enabled him to construct for the first time a really workable, efficient framework of administration, offering to the natives of the country reasonable opportunities for the exercise of their abilities, and capable of the expansion still in progress.

Indian army. Lord William Bentinck held sensible views about the Native or Indian Army, which had deteriorated rapidly in value after 1818. The Madras sepoys, who had done such splendid service in earlier days, were inefficient in Burma and Coorg, while the Bengal Army was being slowly ruined by the excessive indulgence of caste prejudices, the retention of worn-out officers, European and Indian, and general slackness of discipline. The Governor-general in a minute recorded on March 13, 1835, and first published by Mr. Boulger, rightly declared 'the Indian army to be the least efficient and the most expensive in the world'. The general soundness of his opinions on army matters was proved by the events of 1857, and by many incidents which occurred prior to the outbreak of the mutiny in that year.

Abolition of suttee. The most famous of Lord William's actions, the abolition of suttee, was the result of a resolve certainly formed very early in his term of office, and probably almost decided on before he quitted England. The proposal 'to wash out this foul stain upon British rule' had been often discussed by his predecessors and private persons in a half-hearted fashion without result, because the government dreaded the reproach of interference with Hindu religion and was nervous about possible resentment among the sepoys of the native army. Lord William Bentinck displayed no undue haste in his preparations for the overdue reform. He secured the unanimous approval of the judges of the highest criminal court, and a decided preponderance of opinion in his favour from army officers, high police officials, important civil administrators, and many notable private individuals, among whom Rāmmohan Rāi is the best known to fame. The Governor-general's inquiries satisfied him that no substantial danger of popular excitement or of disaffection in the army was to be feared. He then carried Regulation XVII of 1829, which settled the controversy for ever. The Regulation applied directly to the Bengal presidency only, that is to say, to all British India except the Madras and Bombay presidencies; but was quickly followed by similar enactments in those territories; the Bombay law taking a different form for special reasons. The burning or burying alive of widows was declared illegal and punishable by the criminal courts as 'culpable homicide', equivalent to 'manslaughter' in English law. When violence or compulsion should be used, or the freewill of the victim should be interfered with by the administration of drugs, the offence might be treated as murder and punished with death. The Regulation was upheld by the Privy Council in 1832, when the appeal of certain influential Bengālīs was dismissed. No popular excitement was aroused, nor was the loyalty of the native army affected by the measure. The reasoning of the Governor-general's minute was justified in all points by experience, and his action, as Thornton candidly allows, deserves 'eternal honour'.

The principle. The decision of Lord William Bentinck affirmed the important principle that a civilized legislature might lawfully and rightly forbid acts which violate the universal rules of morality and the ordinary feelings of humanity, even when such acts have, as suttee had, the sanction of immemorial custom, Brahmanical tradition, and, to a certain extent, of ancient scriptures deemed sacred. Although it may be, and presumably is true that no section of Hindu opinion would now venture openly to demand the repeal of the legislation of 1829 and the authorization of suttee, the feeling in favour of the rite probably is not extinct. A case occurred in Bihār as late as 1905, and sporadic cases during the nineteenth century in various localities are on record. We may, however, believe that the sentiment which favoured the atrocity is no longer general, and is dying out. If that belief be correct, the legislation of Lord William Bentinck may claim credit for having effected a definite improvement in Hinduism. Other cases might be cited to show that contact with a foreign civilization and a different code of ethics has been instrumental in developing a neo-Hinduism more humane than the old.[1]

[1] 'The term Suttee, or Satī, is strictly applicable to the person, not the rite; meaning "a pure and virtuous woman"; and designates the wife who completes a life of uninterrupted conjugal devotedness by the act of *Saha-gamana*, accompanying her husband's corpse. It has come in common usage to denote the act' (H. H. Wilson). For details of the horrors of the practice see J. Peggs, *India's Cries to British Humanity*, &c., 2nd ed., London, Seely, 1830; 3rd ed. 1832. That book, based mainly on official documents, deals also with infanticide, slavery, the cruelties connected

History of suttee. It is almost certain that the practice of voluntary self-immolation by a widow is a refinement on the earlier and more savage custom of sacrificing widows and slave girls at the master's sepulchre without asking their consent. That custom was prevalent among many of the tribes in Central and Western Asia, and even in Eastern Europe, who may be called Scythians in a general way, and there can be little doubt that the suttee rite was brought into India by early immigrants over the north-western passes. The Greek authors state that it was practised in the half-foreign city of Taxila along with other startling customs, and that it also prevailed among the Kathaioi, who dwelt on the banks of the Rāvī. A custom that was notorious and well established in the Panjāb in the fourth century B. C. must have been introduced much earlier. The high antiquity of suttee, therefore, must be admitted, and it is also true that the practice is commended in some ancient scriptures of recognized authority. The rite was never universal, either in all parts of India, or among all castes and classes, nor was it ever regarded as obligatory on all widows. The voluntary self-immolation of a widow was ordinarily treated as a special act of devotion and an exceptional honour to her family. But the sacrifice was often, and especially in the case of princes, compulsory, so that scores or hundreds of women might be, and actually were, burnt at the funeral of a single Rājā, with or without their consent. The most wholesale burnings on record were those perpetrated from the fourteenth to the sixteenth century at the obsequies of the Telugu Rāyas of Vijayanagar.[1]

Between the years 1815 and 1828 suttees were extremely numerous in Bengal, and especially in the districts around Calcutta. The worst year was 1818, when 839 burnings were recorded for the whole of the Bengal presidency, including Rohilkhand, of which 544 occurred in the Calcutta division. In 1828 the corresponding numbers were 463 and 309. The evil, therefore, existed on a large scale, and called urgently for remedy.[2]

The practice had been often locally prohibited both by Hindu princes and by European officers. It was forbidden in the Pēshwā's personal domains and in the Tanjore Marāthā principality. Early

with the pilgrimage to Jagannāth, the scandals of the pilgrim tax, and other evils of unreformed Hinduism previous to 1830.

[1] Nuniz states that 'when a captain dies, however many wives he has, they all burn themselves; and when the king dies, they do the same'. Sometimes the sacrifice was accomplished by burial alive. The same author credits the King or Rāya with 500 wives, 'and all of these burn themselves at his death'. The earlier traveller, Nicolo Conti, was informed that the King had 12,000 wives, of whom 2,000 or 3,000 were selected 'on condition that at his death they should voluntarily burn themselves with him, which is considered to be a great honour for them' (Sewell, *A Forgotten Empire* (1900), pp. 84, 370, 391). A cinder mound near Nimbāpuram, north-east of Vijayanagar, marks the scene of those appalling holocausts (Longhurst, *Hampi Ruins*, Madras, 1917, p. 41).

[2] The figures give the suttees officially reported. Many unreported cases must have occurred.

in the sixteenth century Albuquerque forbade it at Goa; and at different times individual British officers had ventured to prohibit it in their respective jurisdictions. But a general law was needed in order to effect appreciable reform.

The Regulation, as confirmed by later enactments, has been generally effective, and its provisions have been adopted substantially by many of the Protected States. Modern cases of suttee in British provinces are rare.

Thuggee. The government of Lord William Bentinck has to its credit the suppression of a second semi-religious atrocity, the organized secret system of murder called Thuggee, which was practised by both Muhammadans and Hindus with the supposed sanction of the Hindu goddess, variously named Kālī, Dēvī, Durgā, or Bhawānī. The initiated regarded their victims as sacrifices pleasing to that deity, on whose protection they relied with unquestioning faith. They never felt the slightest compunction or remorse for their crimes, however horrible, believing themselves to be predestined to their mode of gaining a living, as their victims were to death. The system probably attained its highest development in the early years of the nineteenth century, during which thousands of travellers must have been slaughtered annually. One man confessed to having been concerned in the murder of 719 persons.

The Thugs, or cheats, as the word means,[1] formed a secret society, extending over the whole of India, except the Konkan on the western coast. They used among themselves a secret code of words and signs intelligible to initiated Thugs everywhere. Initiation was effected by an impressive ceremonial, including the consumption of *gur* or raw sugar in a sacramental manner. The organization was complete, each man having his special duty, whether as strangler, gravedigger, scout, or other. The gangs varied greatly in strength, the largest recorded having numbered 360 men. In every part of the country they enjoyed protection and aid from many chiefs, landholders, and merchants, ostensibly respectable. Such persons were sometimes actually members of the secret society. Thugs occasionally obtained employment in the service of European gentlemen, and performed their duties to the satisfaction of their employers, taking leave now and then to go secretly on an expedition.

The Thugs, favoured by the insecure state of the roads and the lack of efficient police, travelled in gangs large or small, usually unarmed, and appearing to be pilgrims, ascetics, or other harmless wayfarers. By means of ingenious tricks and false pretences they secured the confidence of their intended victims, who were murdered at a place appointed where the graves had been dug in advance. Such burying places were extremely numerous. Sleeman published a map showing 274 of them in the small province of Oudh, about half the size of Ireland, and was horrified to learn that one such

[1] The Hindī word is *ṭhag*, pronounced with a hard aspirated *t*. The verb *ṭhag-lānā* or *ṭhag-lenā* means 'to cheat'. *Ṭhak* is the Marāthi form.

cemetery was within a march of his court house at Narsinghpur in the Sāgar and Narbadā territories, now included in the Central Provinces. Murder was usually, but not invariably, effected by strangulation with a handkerchief or scarf used as a noose, which experience showed to be the safest method. The gangs, although on rare occasions detected and broken up in some particular locality by the action of a chief or magistrate, had little to fear, and enjoyed almost complete impunity. The ordinary peasants and watchmen frequently were in league with them and shared their bloodstained gains; while, as noted above, they always had the support of powerful protectors. The moral feeling of the people had sunk so low that there were no signs of general reprehension of the cold-blooded crimes committed by the Thugs. They were accepted as part of the established order of things; and, until the secrets of the organization were given away by approvers, it was usually impossible to obtain evidence against even the most notorious Thugs.

History of Thuggee. The secret society of Thugs undoubtedly was extremely ancient. The members believed that its operations are represented in the sculptures at Ellora, executed in the eighth century, and they may have been right. They also believed that the so called 'saint' Nizāmu-d dīn Auliya of Delhi in the fourteenth century was a member of their order, and that he thus obtained the wealth at his disposal, and not otherwise satisfactorily accounted for. The earliest definite mention of the Thugs in literature is in the chronicle of Jalālu-d dīn Fīrōz Khiljī, Sultan of Delhi, at the close of the thirteenth century, when a thousand were brought before him. He refused to execute them, merely deporting them to Bengal, where probably they introduced the practice of river thuggee, common in that province until lately, and possibly not wholly extinct. Tradition credits Akbar with having executed 500 Thugs in the Etāwah District (now in U.P.); and the French traveller, de Thevenot, has recorded an accurate description of their proceedings in the days of Shāhjahān. Fryer describes the execution of fifteen stranglers at Surat by order of Aurangzēb.[1] English magistrates in the south became aware of the crimes of the Thugs after the capture of Seringapatam in 1799, when many sepoys mysteriously disappeared. The earliest accounts of the system in the English language were printed in 1816 and 1820. Individual officers occasionally succeeded in arresting and punishing a few of the murderers; but the system remained unbroken until 1829, when Feringhia, the approver, saved his life by betraying all the secrets of the society to Sleeman and his colleagues. Systematic inquiries based on the testimony of numerous approvers, and conclusively confirmed by the exhumation of bodies and in a hundred other ways, enabled the officers placed on special duty to hunt down the gangs, and break up the society. Probably the chain of Thug tradition has been severed, and the crime in its old form may be regarded as extinct. But in India it is never safe to

[1] *A New Account*, ed. Crooke (Hakluyt Soc.), i. 244.

assume that an institution many centuries old is absolutely dead. Cognate crimes, especially the poisoning of travellers by *datūra*, are still common, and I have tried or investigated many cases of the kind.[1] Some of the *datūra* poisoners appear to be descendants of Thug families. The murder trade, like everything else in India, was hereditary. 'Thuggee Sleeman,' otherwise known as Sir William Sleeman, K.C.B., took the most prominent part in destroying the Thug organization. He was aided by many competent colleagues, and supported cordially by Lord William Bentinck, who passed a series of special Acts to regulate the proceedings of the officers selected to crush the gangs. During the years 1831–7, 3,266 Thugs were disposed of in one way or another; 412 out of that number being hanged, and 483 admitted as approvers. The approvers and their descendants were detained for many years in a special institution at Jubbulpore (Jabalpur).

SIR WILLIAM SLEEMAN.

Renewal of the Charter, 1833. As the time for the renewal of the charter of the East India Company in 1833 approached, all parties concerned made preparations for the inevitable discussion and contest. The directors, when they appointed Lord William Bentinck to be a reforming Governor-general, were thinking of the advantage they would gain in the coming debates by their ability to produce a good budget of reforms. A parliamentary select committee, appointed in 1829, submitted in 1832 a voluminous report on things Indian; and outside of official circles, merchants and manufacturers agitated for the abolition of the monopoly of the China trade, for the legalization of land-owning by Europeans in India, and other changes desired.

Neither the ministry nor Parliament was yet prepared to take over the direct administration, so that little serious opposition was offered to the renewal of the charter for the customary period of twenty years. The Company was unable to resist the demand for the opening of the China trade. Thus the Company of merchants founded in the days of Queen Elizabeth lost the last vestige of

[1] The *Datūra* genus of plants is common in India. The white and purple species are alike used by thieves to stupefy victims, but the white is considered the most efficient (Balfour).

its commercial character and became merely an agency, performing its duties, as declared by the Charter Act, 'in trust for His Majesty, his heirs and successors, for the service of the Government of India.' The fleet of 'Indiamen' was dispersed. Complicated financial arrangements provided for the liquidation of the Company's commercial assets and the payment of a fixed dividend for forty years. The directors succeeded in retaining the right to recall governors and military commanders, a prerogative on which they set a high value.

Changes in India. The government of India was empowered to legislate by passing formal Acts, not merely informal Regulations, for the whole of India. The title of the head of the government was changed from 'Governor-general of Bengal in Council' to 'Governor-general of India in Council'. The power of legislation was withdrawn from Madras and Bombay, but had to be restored later. Europeans were allowed to acquire and hold land in India, practically without restriction. That enactment was specially designed to benefit the growing industry of indigo planting, but it also permitted the formation by enterprising speculators of admirably managed estates in undeveloped regions. In the Gorakhpur and Bastī districts of the United Provinces, being part of the territory ceded by Oudh in 1801, many such estates were created by the clearance of forest on a large scale. Those properties, with which I am familiar in detail, are models of estate administration. The new liberty did not produce such good results in the indigo planting regions, where grave abuses grew up, which resulted in serious trouble in 1859 and 1860.[1]

The Council of the Governor-general was reinforced by a fourth member, the Law or Legal Member, empowered to act as member of council only at meetings for the purpose of making laws and regulations. Macaulay was the first law member. The investigations initiated by him resulted many years later in the Penal Code and the Codes of Criminal and Civil Procedure.

A new presidency at Agra was sanctioned, but that provision never came into operation, because the Upper Provinces were almost immediately placed under a Lieutenant-governor instead of a Governor-in-Council by an amending Act.

Bar of race, &c., removed. Probably the most important provision in the Act was sec. 87, which laid down the principle that

> 'no native of the said territories, nor any natural-born subject of His Majesty resident therein, shall, by reason only of his religion, place of birth, descent, colour, or any of them, be disabled from holding any place, office, or employment under the Company'.

The language then used is even more emphatic than that of the similar paragraph in Queen Victoria's proclamation of 1858, which is :

[1] See the drama, 'Nil Darpan', or the 'Indigo Planting Mirror', of which an English translation was published in Calcutta in 1861. It is not pleasant reading.

'And it is our further will that, so far as may be, our subjects, of whatever race or creed, be freely and impartially admitted to office in our service, the duties of which they may be qualified by their education, ability, and integrity duly to discharge.'

The promises implied in those solemn declarations by the Sovereign and Parliament have been redeemed gradually and cautiously; too slowly to satisfy impatient reformers. At the moment of writing (1918) gentlemen of Indian birth share in all the highest executive and judicial offices, excepting only the posts of Governor-general, lieutenant-governor, chief commissioner, or ruler of a province under any other designation. Further extension of the application of the principle is under consideration (1918).

Higher education. The subject of education was connected intimately with the reforms prescribed by the Charter Act. The provisions for the employment of natives of India in high offices could not be carried into effect until Indians possessed of adequate educational equipment should be available in sufficient numbers. The work of administration in a British government must necessarily be conducted in the English language, and the old-fashioned Hindu and Muslim modes of instruction clearly could not provide candidates suitable for responsible appointments. That consideration alone was enough to determine that the higher education must be imparted chiefly through the English language.

Macaulay, who was appointed President of the Board or General Committee of Education, at once became the leader of the Anglicists, in opposition to the Orientalist conservatives, who championed the claims of Arabic and Sanskrit. His able although somewhat one-sided minutes induced the Governor-general in Council, just before the retirement of Lord William Bentinck on March 20, to issue the Resolution dated March 7, 1835, stating that

'the great object of the British Government ought to be the promotion of European literature and science among the natives of India, and that the funds appropriated to education would be best employed in English education alone'.

The word 'alone' went too far; and subsequent legislation and orders redressed the error by providing due encouragement for the vernacular tongues and classical languages of the East.

The controversy of 1835 is dead, and nothing would be gained by rekindling its ashes. Everybody may accept the judgement of Mr. Boulger that

'the momentous decision to make the English language the official and literary language of the Peninsula represents the salient feature of his [Lord William Bentinck's] administration, and makes his Governor-generalship stand out as a landmark in Indian history'.

The missionaries, under the guidance of the Rev. Dr. Alexander Duff, gave the government of India valuable aid in promoting the cause of sound education.

Lord William Bentinck, in the same month of March 1835, which saw the issue of the Resolution on education, crowned his work by the foundation of the Calcutta Medical College, which proved an eminent success in spite of the croakings of wiseacres who confidently predicted its failure.

'Contact with a dead body', they argued, 'had for twenty centuries been considered a mortal pollution by the Hindoos, and it was traditionally affirmed that native prejudices were invincible. But these anticipations, when brought to the test of actual practice, proved, as usual, to be the phantasms of a morbid imagination. Natives of high caste were found to resort freely to the dissecting room, and to handle the scalpel with as much indifference as European students. In the first year they assisted in dissecting sixty subjects, and the feeling of ardour with which they entered on these studies, and the aptitude for acquiring knowledge which they exhibited created a universal feeling of surprise.'

Those observations, recorded by Marshman in 1867, now seem strangely out of date. It is needless to dilate on the eminent scientific attainments of modern physicians and surgeons of Indian birth.[1]

Sir Charles Metcalfe. Sir Charles Metcalfe, who had accepted the office of Lieutenant-governor of the North-Western Provinces, and had also been nominated provisional Governor-general, had hardly taken charge of his up-country appointment when he was summoned to Calcutta in order to relieve Lord William Bentinck, who wished to go home. Sir Charles Metcalfe continued to be head of the government for almost twelve months, and would have been confirmed had he not given mortal offence to the directors by his abolition of the restrictions on the press. His action in that business has been sufficiently discussed in connexion with the administration of Mr. Adam. Metcalfe, smarting under the censure of the India House, resigned the service and retired to England. Subsequently he was appointed Governor of Jamaica, and then Governor-general of Canada, being raised to the peerage. He died in 1846. He may be justly reckoned as the most eminent of the many illustrious Anglo-Indian officials, whose names fill so large a place in history from the time of Lord Wellesley to that of Lord William Bentinck.

CHRONOLOGY

Lord William Cavendish-Bentinck Governor-general (July); financial economies	1828
Abolition of suttee by Regulation XVII	1829
Suppression of thuggee	1829–37
Annexation of Kāchār (Cachar); Singapore made capital of Malay Peninsula Settlements	1830
Deposition of Rājā of Mysore; journey of Burnes up the Indus; meeting at Rūpar with Ranjit Singh	1831
British Reform Act	1832
Regulation IX (N. W. P. 'settlements'); renewal of charter; numerous reforms; abolition of flogging in the native army	1833
Annexation of Coorg	1834

[1] In 1908 twenty-two medical schools existed in India (*I. G.*).

Annexation of Jaintiā Parganas ; education Resolution ; foundation of Medical College, Calcutta ; retirement (March 20) of Lord William Bentinck; Sir Charles Metcalfe Governor-general; attack (June) on Resident of Jaipur 1835
Death of Lord William Bentinck 1839

AUTHORITIES

The only separate Life of Lord William Bentinck is that by D. BOULGER (R. I., 1897) ; a good little book, containing important documents not previously published. The most useful of the general histories are those by H. H. WILSON and MARSHMAN. The works of Sir W. H. SLEEMAN are the primary authority on thuggee ; especially *Ramaseeana* (Calcutta, 1836), a roughly compiled collection of documents, now rare, but accessible in several libraries ; and *Rambles and Recollections* (London, 1844 ; ed. 3 by V. A. SMITH (Oxford University Press, 1915). MEADOWS TAYLOR gives a fascinating account of the organization in *Confessions of a Thug* (1839 ; ed. C. W. STEWART, Oxford University Press, 1916), with a small but harmless admixture of fiction. R. V. RUSSELL and HĪRA LĀL present a lucid summary of Sleeman's works in *The Tribes and Castes of the Central Provinces of India*, vol. iv (Macmillan, 1916).

The Charter Act of 1833 may be best studied in ILBERT. RAMSAY MUIR also supplies a careful abstract. The most essential passages of MACAULAY'S *Minutes* are quoted by Boulger. His Minutes on education from 1835 to 1837 were collected by WOODROW (Calcutta, 1862). A copy is in the I. O. Library.

CHAPTER 3

Lord Auckland and Lord Ellenborough ; the First Afghan War ; annexation of Sind ; affairs of Gwālior ; abolition of slavery.

Lord Auckland. The directors' nomination of Lord Heytesbury, formerly ambassador to Russia, as successor to Lord William Bentinck was accepted by the Tory government of Sir Robert Peel, and the new Governor-general was actually sworn in. When Lord Melbourne's Whig government came into power, the ministry, declaring that Lord Heytesbury did not possess their confidence, revoked his appointment, and substituted Lord Auckland, a member of their own party. The precedent thus set was a bad one, as tending to engulf Indian affairs in the muddy waters of party politics. Lord Auckland, a respectable official peer, with hosts of personal friends, was regarded as a safe man, likely to conduct the administration of India on lines much the same as those of his peaceful predecessor. When appointed he was fifty-one years of age, and up to that time nobody seems to have suspected that he, being 'unstable as water', could not excel, or to have supposed it possible that he would drag the honour of England in the dirt and expose India to the most grievous military disaster and the most shameful humiliation she had ever suffered. When he had actually done those things, unscrupulous ministerial support and disciplined party spirit conspired to hush up his misdoings, and even permitted him to become once more First Lord of the Admiralty. The 'dismal story' of the First Afghan War and the connected transactions with the Ameers, including the equally painful sequel of the unprincipled annexation of Sind by Lord Ellenborough and Sir Charles Napier, will be told as briefly as possible. Before that story is dealt with certain other transactions of less moment demand notice.

Early domestic reforms. Lord Auckland's early proceedings justified the hopes of those who had recommended his appointment. He developed his predecessor's plans for the promotion of education and the cultivation of medical science, with the proper amendment that government scholarships should not be confined to the pupils of colleges where English was taught. He also gave effect to the neglected instructions of the directors requiring the abolition of the pilgrims' tax, the cessation of all official control of temple endowments, and the prohibition of the complimentary attendance on duty of the Company's troops or civil officers at popular religious ceremonials. Preliminary steps were taken towards the creation of great works of irrigation. So far so good; and Lord Auckland, if he had not been drawn by scheming ministers in England and evil advisers in India into political intrigues and military adventures for which he had no capacity, might have spent his five years of office in the business of useful, quiet administration, and then retired with unsullied reputation. His deplorable weakness of character, which prevented him from devising any fixed policy of his own, and made him the tool of other men's ambition and craft, led him to commit a series of dishonourable actions foreign to his kindly nature, and to sanction a policy truly described as 'baleful, lawless, and blundering'.

Famine of 1837–8. In 1837–8, while the Governor-general was on tour, Northern India suffered from a severe famine, which is estimated to have caused the death of at least 800,000 people. Relief works were undertaken by the State, the succour of the infirm and helpless being left to private charity for the most part. The expenditure was considerable, amounting to 38 lakhs of rupees in 1838, but the results were unsatisfactory.

Native States. The death in 1837 of the King of Oudh, a worthless debauchee named Nasīru-d dīn Haidar, resulted in a ridiculous attempt at rebellion, made by the Pādshāh Bēgam, or principal Queen-Dowager, which was promptly suppressed. The misgovernment of the kingdom continued as usual.[1]

[1] Lord Auckland tried to force on the new king a revised treaty providing for an additional subsidiary force at heavy cost. The whole treaty was disallowed by the Directors, but the Governor-general, with lamentable lack of candour, failed to communicate that fact to the king, informing him only that the additional subsidiary force would not be demanded. The curious book, *The Private Life of an Eastern King*, by William Knighton, which passed through three editions in 1855 and 1856, gives many details of the disreputable court of Nasīru-d dīn Haidar. The Oxford University

The Rājā of Sātāra in the Western Ghāts, who had been set up by Lord Hastings in 1819, engaged in a long-continued series of foolish treasonable intrigues with the Portuguese and other people. The Bombay government made every effort to convince the Rājā of his folly, and gave him opportunities for repentance; but he refused to listen, and was necessarily deposed, his brother taking his place (1839).

The Nawāb of Karnūl (Kurnool) in the Madras presidency, a descendant of Aurangzēb's officer, Dāūd Khān, made an equally insane attempt to levy war, which resulted in his deposition and the annexation of his territory (1842); which subsequently, with certain additions, was formed into the existing Karnūl district.

A warning to Holkar was sufficient to bring about desirable reforms at Indore.

Palmerston's anti-Russian policy. The troubles of Lord Auckland originated in the anti-Russian policy of Lord Palmerston, the Secretary of State for Foreign Affairs in London, who took alarm at dispatches from St. Petersburg giving information of alleged negotiations between the rival chiefs in Afghanistan and the Shah of Persia. The Foreign Secretary regarded with excessive anxiety the prospect of Persia acquiring Herat, and holding that city in dependence on Russia. Lord Palmerston seems to have neglected the sound advice to use large maps, afterwards given by Lord Salisbury, and to have made the assumptions, as Sir Henry Durand puts the matter,

> 'that Afghanistan was at the time our frontier; that the capture of Herat by Persia involved imminent peril to the security and internal tranquillity of our Indian Empire; and that Persia, in prosecuting the siege of that place had, acting in concert with Russia, entered upon a course of proceeding avowedly unfriendly, if not hostile to British interests, and at variance with the spirit and intent of the definitive [Persian] treaty.'

In reality Afghanistan was then separated from British India by the Panjāb, Bahāwalpur, Sind, and the Rājputāna desert, which, as the author quoted truly observes, constituted 'no bad frontier'. The exaggerated fears of diplomatists

> 'invested Herat with a fictitious importance wholly incommensurate with the strength of the place and its position in regard to Candahar and the Indus'.

Or, to express the facts in the simplest language, it did not matter to India whether Persia held Herat or not. But Lord Auckland had not the sense to see that truth, and was led away by ill-chosen and unwise advisers to break treaties only six years old; to bully the weak; to pursue a fantastic policy; to persist in that policy when the reasons for it, such as they were, had ceased

Press is bringing out a new edition along with the companion work, *The Private Life of an Eastern Queen*. Mrs. Meer Hassan Ali, author of the valuable *Observations on the Mussulmauns of India* (ed. Crooke, Oxford University Press, 1917), also lived at Lucknow in the reign of Nasīru-d dīn Haidar. Her book appeared in 1832.

to exist ; to violate the principles of strategy ; to throw away thousands of lives by entrusting them to incapable commanders ; and finally, at least to acquiesce silently in the garbling of the documents submitted for the information of Parliament.

The truth of all those propositions will now be established by a summary narrative. The proceedings of the Governor-general undoubtedly were prompted by Lord Palmerston and his colleague, Sir John Hobhouse, President of the Board of Control, who publicly assumed full responsibility for the war. The ministry was so deeply committed to the policy of which the war was the outcome that even the most objectionable acts of Lord Auckland escaped official censure. Advantage was taken of the storm of Ghaznī and certain other favourable events in the earlier stages of the operations to divert public attention, and to veil the tricks of a tortuous diplomacy behind a shining cloud of military glory. Outside of the Foreign Office and the Board of Control the policy of the Governor-general was condemned by the Duke of Wellington and everybody qualified to give a valuable opinion. The judgement of Anglo-Indian historians, too, seems to be substantially unanimous ; and it is unlikely that now anybody could be found who would be prepared to justify either the First Afghan War or the treatment of the Ameers of Sind by Lords Auckland and Ellenborough.

Government of Sind. In those days Sind was governed by various Balōchī chiefs belonging to the Tālpur family, and known consequently as the Tālpur Ameers (Amīrs or Mīrs). The family had split into three branches ; one of which, and the most important, had its capital at Hyderabad in Middle Sind. Another branch was established at Mīrpur Khās on the western edge of the desert ; and the third branch administered Northern Sind from the town of Khairpur, east of the Indus. The Khairpur territory included the important commercial town of Shikārpur and the island fortress of Bukkur (Bakhar).

Government of Afghanistan. It is not necessary to plunge deeply into the tangled history of the various regions now grouped together by European writers under the name of Afghanistan. It may be sufficient to note that Ahmad Shāh Durrānī's grandson, Shāh Shujā, who had become King of Kābul for some years, was driven out of the country in 1809, and that after a time he settled at the British cantonment of Lūdiāna as a pensioned refugee. The Kābul territory had no established government for some years. In 1826 Dōst Muhammad Khān, an able member of the Bārakzai clan, made himself lord of Kābul and Ghaznī. The English called him the King of Kābul, and he was the actual ruler with whom Lord Auckland had to deal. He had assumed the title of Amīr in 1835, after defeating an attempt of Shāh Shujā to recover the throne lost many years before. Shāh Shujā then returned to his residence at Lūdiāna.

Political relations with Sind. British political relations with the Ameers of Sind began in 1809, when Lord Minto negotiated a treaty with three chiefs establishing ' eternal friendship between the contracting parties ', providing for the exchange of envoys, and prohibiting ' the establishment of the tribe of the French in Sinde '.

That treaty was confirmed in 1820, when Americans, in addition to the French, were excluded.

The expedition of Burnes up the Indus, arranged in the time of Lord William Bentinck (1830–1) by Lord Ellenborough, then

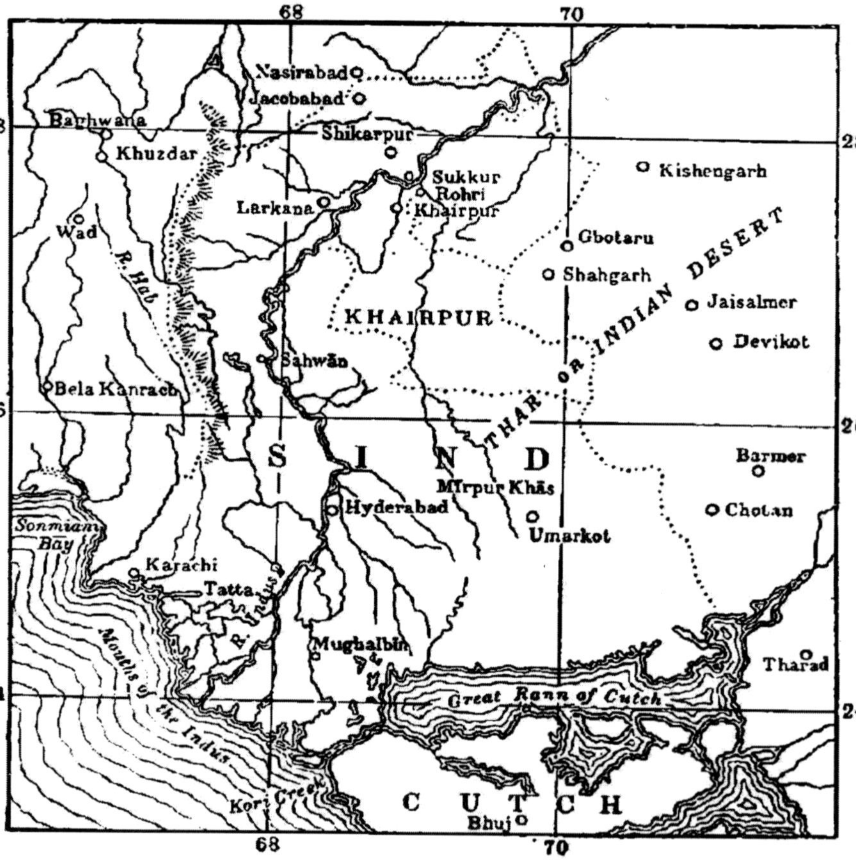

MAP OF SIND.

President of the Board of Control, resulted in the treaties of 1832. The engagement then made with the Hyderabad Ameers stipulated, among other things, that ' the two Contracting Powers bind themselves never to look with the eye of covetousness on the possessions of each other ' ; that Indian merchants and traders might travel on business over the rivers and roads of Sind, on three conditions, namely :

' (1) that no person shall bring any description of military stores by the above river or roads :

(2) that no armed vessels or boats shall come by the said river :

(3) that no English merchants shall be allowed to settle in Sinde, but shall come as occasion requires, and having stopped to transact their business, shall return to India.'

The shorter treaty with the Khairpur Ameers was to the same effect.

Those treaties were in full force at the beginning of the Afghan War.

Political relations with Kābul. Lord Auckland entered upon the duties of his office in March 1836. Later in that year he received from the Secret Committee of the Directors a dispatch dated June 25, which recited the anxiety felt by the British Foreign Office concerning Russian advances towards Herat, and instructed the Governor-general to

'judge as to what steps it may be proper and desirable for you to take to watch more closely, than has hitherto been attempted, the progress of events in Afghanistan, and to counteract the progress of Russian influence in a quarter which, from its proximity to our Indian possessions, could not fail, if it were once established, to act injuriously on the system of our Indian alliances, and possibly to interfere even with the tranquillity of our own territory.

The mode of dealing with this very important question, whether by dispatching a confidential agent to Dost Muhammad of Kābul merely to watch the progress of events, or to enter into relations with this chief, either of a political, or merely, in the first instance, of a commercial character, we confide to your discretion, as well as the adoption of any other measures that may appear to you desirable in order to counteract Russian advances in that quarter, should you be satisfied from the information received from your own agents on the frontier, or hereafter from Mr. McNeill, on his arrival in Persia, that the time has arrived at which it would be right for you to interfere decidedly in the affairs of Afghanistan.

Such an interference would doubtless be requisite, either to prevent the extension of Persian dominion in that quarter, or to raise a timely barrier against the impending encroachments of Russian influence.'[1]

That unhappy dispatch, the product of Lord Palmerston's fantastic fears, was the foundation of Lord Auckland's discreditable proceedings. It also bound the British ministry to support him in the exercise of his discretion, and to see him through the consequences of his acts.

Burnes was sent to Kābul, on pretence of negotiating a commercial treaty, but in reality to talk politics. Dōst Muhammad wanted Peshāwar, which Ranjit Singh had annexed. Lord Auckland, who was much afraid of the Mahārājā, would not hear of putting any pressure on him. Burnes consequently had nothing to offer to the Ameer, who then turned towards Russia, and showed civilities to an informal Russian agent who had come to his court. Burnes left Kābul in April 1838.

Tripartite treaty. In July the Governor-general executed a tripartite treaty with Ranjit Singh and 'His Majesty', the refugee Shāh Shujā. The instrument was directed to the restoration

[1] Not in Kaye. Quoted from Colvin, p. 87.

to the throne of Kābul of Shāh Shujā, who was expected to become a pliant instrument of Palmerstonian diplomacy; and was alleged to be popular in his own country, an allegation hardly borne out by his history.[1]

Army of the Indus. Lord Auckland at first did not intend to send an army, hoping that the Sikhs and Shāh Shujā's levies would effect his crooked purpose. But the Governor-general soon allowed himself to be drawn by his private advisers, John Colvin, Macnaghten, and others, into more ambitious schemes. He issued a verbose declaration on October 1, and gave orders to assemble the Army of the Indus for the invasion of the dominions of Dōst Muhammad, who had never injured the British government. The Persians had been obliged to withdraw from the siege of Herat in September, and the news of that event, received during October, deprived Lord Auckland's warlike preparations of their sole justification. But he was not to be stopped by such a trifle, and went on with his plan to dethrone Dōst Muhammad. The Bengal section of the army, 14,000 strong, assembled at Fīrōzpur in November. The Bombay contingent, under Sir John Keane, was landed in Sind. The two forces were to unite at Kandahār. In order not to offend Ranjit Singh the Bengal army was sent round through the Bolān Pass, and so had to traverse a distance of more than a thousand miles between Fīrōzpur and Kābul. The plan violated all the conditions of sound strategy, and was that of a lunatic rather than of a sane statesman.

Military operations. The operations of the Bombay contingent involved an open breach of the treaties of 1832. Lord Auckland, through his secretary, W. H. Macnaghten, cynically directed the resident at Hyderabad that

> 'while the present exigency lasts, you may apprise the Ameers, that the Article of the Treaty with them, prohibitory of using the Indus for the conveyance of military stores, must necessarily be suspended during the course of operations undertaken for the permanent establishment of security to all those who are parties to that Treaty'.

Shikārpur, Bukkur (Bakhar),[2] and other places in Sind were occupied with equal disregard of solemn engagements. Frivolous charges of breach of treaty and accusations of hostility were advanced against the Ameers, who were forced in February 1839 to sign a treaty, so-called, which destroyed their independence. A subsidiary force was imposed on them; they were compelled to pay three lakhs of rupees a year for it; and to admit the Company's rupees as legal currency. In many other respects the

[1] Masson, however, denied that the Shāh was 'unpopular with his Afghans'; who resented the presence of the British Army, not that of the Shāh (*Narrative*, 1842, p. viii). Durand held that 'the irascible vanity of Burnes . . . impelled him to a line of conduct hasty and injudicious, and which, wanting in truth, composure, and dignity, exasperated the Ameer' (p. 46).

[2] Bukkur (Bakhar) is the island fortress in the Indus lying between Sukkur (Sakhar) and Rohri (Rūrhī).

chiefs were fleeced and treated unfairly, but it is needless to pursue further the unpleasant subject.

Both the Bengal and the Bombay forces managed to reach Kandahār after undergoing intense suffering from want of water and supplies. The miseries of the march through the sixty miles of the Bolān Pass were especially severe, and about 20,000 camels were lost. Shāh Shujā's public entry into Kandahār in April 1839 was a failure, as the public declined to attend.

Sir John Keane, who was now in supreme command, started for Kābul by the Ghaznī road. He had been told that Ghaznī would not resist, and in consequence had left behind his few heavy guns. He found, on the contrary, a formidable fortress, inaccessible by storm. His troops, with only two days' rations in hand, were in imminent danger of starvation, when the situation was saved by the daring of certain junior engineer officers, who undertook to blow open the Kābul gate of the stronghold.[1] The 'gambler's throw' succeeded, the fuse being fired by Lieutenant Henry Durand, of the Bengal Engineers, who afterwards became Sir Henry, and lieutenant-governor of the Panjāb. In the storm which followed the explosion the loss of the Afghans was heavy while that on the British side was small. The ministry in London, delighted at the undeserved success thus gained by their rash policy, showered honours and rewards upon Lord Auckland, Sir John Keane, and the political officers. The engineers received scant attention.

Occupation of Kābul. The unexpected fall of Ghaznī compelled Dōst Muhammad to quit his capital and escape northwards. The invaders occupied Kābul in August without opposition. It is said that Shāh Shujā's solemn entry was more like a 'funeral procession' than a triumph. Lord Auckland left 10,000 troops under General Cotton as an army of occupation, and General Nott was called up from Quetta to command at Kandahār. The other troops were sent back to India. The government was thenceforward conducted really by Sir William Macnaghten, the political officer, the Shāh being allowed little substantial power. His royalty was maintained solely by the British force. Lord Auckland, having placed his protégé on the throne, should have left him to keep it if he could. Dōst Muhammad surrendered in November 1840, and was sent down to Calcutta where he was well treated, and assigned a liberal allowance. Shortly afterwards General Cotton returned to India. Lord Auckland insisted on replacing him by General Elphinstone, who had been a good officer in his time, but was now growing old, and was an invalid. He was assured by his predecessor that he would 'have nothing to do here; all is peace'. Macnaghten, who was in charge of the political department, declared the general tranquillity to be 'perfectly miraculous', and officers were allowed to bring up their wives and families from India. In fact, all reasonable precautions were neglected, and many foolish things were done.

[1] Havelock (ii. 122) praises the tactical dispositions of Sir John Keane. His work includes good descriptions and many military documents.

Towards the close of 1840 the directors became alarmed at the dangerous military situation and the excessive cost of the prolonged occupation. They suggested 'the entire abandonment of the country, and a frank confession of complete failure'; but Lord Auckland insisted on going on with his mad scheme.

Disasters. I do not propose to repeat in its miserable details the remainder of the story, which may be read in a multitude of books. Revolts broke out in all directions. The presence of the infidel foreigners was detested by the Afghans, who had just cause of complaint by reason of the licentious conduct of Burnes and many of the soldiers. General Elphinstone proved to be imbecile, and everybody in a responsible position behaved with unexampled folly. The troops were withdrawn from the Bālā Hissār, or citadel, and encamped in an indefensible position on the plain, separated from their stores. The higher officials, civil and military, quarrelled. The rank and file, practically leaderless, lost discipline, and would not fight when called on. A few brilliant subordinates, Durand, Broadfoot, and others, types of the best class of British officers, were powerless to avert the ruin to which the madness of their seniors irresistibly dragged the whole force. In December 1841 the necessity for retirement to Jalālābād, where Sale occupied the fort with a small detachment, was obvious. By that time the isolated stores dépôt had been destroyed, and starvation could be avoided only by a decisive retreat, as recommended by Durand. But

'Elphinstone and his advisers thought otherwise. There was an unearthly faintness upon their hearts; and it was as though some great crime had caused the wrath of God to settle down upon the host, withering the hearts of its leaders, unnerving the right arms of England's soldiery, and leaving them no power to stand before their enemies.'

Macnaghten, who had himself incurred suspicion of bad faith, was entrapped on December 23 into an interview with Dōst Muhammad's son, Muhammad Akbar, and treacherously slain. His three companions, Trevor, Mackenzie, and Lawrence, were overpowered, disarmed, and taken prisoners.

'The escort, instead of charging to the rescue, fled to the cantonments, and left the envoy and his brave companions to their fate.

In the cantonments all was apathy, and indecision. Although within sight of the scene, no attempt was made to avenge the slaughtered envoy and to recover his body from a cowardly mob who bore off in triumph his mangled remains, to parade them in the city of Cabul.'

The final catastrophe. The general, disregarding the advice of Pottinger, renewed negotiations. A treaty was signed on January 1, 1842; the guns, muskets, and ordnance stores having been previously given up. Snow fell, and the Shāh offered the English ladies an asylum in his citadel. Pottinger once more urged the occupation of the Bālā Hissār. Elphinstone again refused, sending in merely the sick and wounded.

On January 6 the dispirited army, still numbering about 4,500 troops and 12,000 followers, encumbered by a train of doolies or

BĀLĀ HISSAR, KĀBUL.

litters bearing the women and children, started for Jalālābād. On the 8th only about 800 men of all arms emerged from the Khurd Kābul defiles. The women and children, the married men, and wounded officers on that day 'were transferred into Akbar's keeping'.

On the 11th only 200 were left.

'On January 13, Dr. Brydon, sorely wounded, and barely able from exhaustion to sit upon the emaciated beast that bore him, reached Jellalabad, and told that Elphinstone's army, guns, standards, honour, all being lost, was itself completely annihilated. Such was the consummation of a line of policy which from first to last held truth in derision, trod right under foot, and, acting on a remote scene, was enabled for a time unscrupulously to mislead the public mind.'

Having written the epitaph of the victims in those scathing words, Durand proceeds to give Macnaghten credit for high courage, which, however, 'cannot palliate moral delinquency'.

'Macnaghten was not single in his high courage. The bones of many a chivalrous soldier long bleached upon the barren mountains and deep defiles between Cabul and Jellalabad. But if any called for the avenging swords of their countrymen with peculiar emphasis it was those of the European horse artillery, who, calm and stern to the last in their discipline and daring valour, fought and fell heroically, the admiration of all who witnessed their conduct and survived to tell the tale.'

It is well to close the sad story on that heroic note.

Defence of Jalālābād. The steps taken by Lord Auckland to retrieve the disaster during the few weeks of power left to him were not effective. His nerves broke down, and he feared to sanction measures which would tie the hands of his successor, who was on the way out from England. The interest of this intermediate period of the war lies chiefly at Jalālābād, where Sale's garrison held out, awaiting the long delayed relief. The credit for the successful defence of the place rests with Captain George Broadfoot, the garrison engineer, rather than with Sir Robert Sale, who had accepted the advice of a council of war to surrender. After a prolonged debate Broadfoot's honourable and passionate pleading won over a majority of the senior officers to do their plain duty and hold out to the last. Once that question was settled in the right way, every man in the garrison worked and fought with a will; so that, even when a violent earthquake on February 19 shattered the defences, the damage was instantly repaired.[1]

Meantime General Nott maintained his grip on Kandahār, and Captain Halkett Craigie at Khelāt-i-Ghilzai defied a host of enemies; but Colonel Palmer at Ghaznī was forced to surrender.

Lord Ellenborough's arrival and action. At the close of February the new Governor-general, Lord Ellenborough, who came out to relieve Lord Auckland in the ordinary course, took charge. General Pollock, a capable commander, effected the relief of

[1] Both Sale and Broadfoot were killed in the first Sikh War. The story of the debate, discreditable to both Sale and Macgregor, is narrated at length by Durand, and in Kaye's third edition.

Jalālābād on April 16, finding on his arrival that the garrison had already virtually raised the siege by means of a vigorous sortie.

Lord Ellenborough's first instructions had been sensible and well considered, although erring perhaps on the side of caution. But the news of the fall of Ghaznī and of a small reverse near Quetta shook his resolution, so that he issued orders for the immediate evacuation of all posts held in Afghanistan, showing little concern for the recovery of the prisoners, about a hundred and twenty in number, or for the vindication of the British name. Meantime Shāh Shujā had been murdered, and strong remonstrances from all quarters, both in England and in India, forced Lord Ellenborough to reconsider his decision. At last, on July 4, he wrote letters to Pollock and Nott, professing to maintain the orders for withdrawal, but permitting the two generals to act in concert, if Nott should 'decide upon adopting the line of retirement by Ghaznī and Kābul'. Thus the Governor-general shifted his own responsibility upon the military commanders, who accepted it eagerly, and promptly concerted the needful measures.

General Nott's advance. Nott, who had crushed armed resistance in the neighbourhood of Kandahār during May, started for Kābul on August 7, with 8,000 fine soldiers in high spirits and confident of victory. He found Ghaznī abandoned, and, before passing on, reduced the town and fortifications to ruins. After some fighting on the road he came into touch with Pollock on September 17.

General Pollock's advance. Pollock, taking all proper military precautions, had successfully forced the passes, and reached Kābul on September 15. A few of the English prisoners were then rescued. Some days later the judicious promise of liberal reward brought in the rest, who had been moved about from place to place during their captivity, and were in danger of being sold into Central Asia as slaves. They do not appear to have been subjected to personal violence or outrage, and might be considered fortunate to have been as well treated as they were. General Elphinstone had died while in the hands of the Afghans.

No difference of opinion was expressed as to the propriety of punishing in some way the guilty city of Kābul. Some officers recommended the destruction of the Bālā Hissār, but Pollock preferred to blow up the great covered bazaar, where Macnaghten's body had been exposed. Eight years later it was rebuilt by Dōst Muhammad. The city also suffered much from unauthorized burning and plundering.

Evacuation. Lord Ellenborough having rightly adhered to the policy of complete withdrawal from the Afghan 'hornets' nest', the army returned to India, and early in November encamped at Peshāwar. Another army of observation protected it from the possible hostility of the Sikhs, who could not be relied on since Ranjit Singh's death.

Proclamations. The Governor-general's proclamation, misdated October 1, but really written later, announced a complete change of policy, and denounced the 'errors' of the previous administration in language which, however true, was unbecoming. That manifesto was followed in a few days by a ludicrous proclamation celebrating the recovery of the gates of Somnāth, said to have been carried off by Mahmūd of Ghaznī and afterwards preserved at his tomb. Lord Ellenborough had given stringent instructions to General Nott to be sure and bring back those 'sandalwood gates'.[1]

The proclamation, a silly imitation of Napoleon's Pyramids manifesto, celebrated the return of the gates, 'which had so long been the memorial of the humiliation of the people of India, and had now become the proudest record of their national glory'.

Nobody cared a straw about the gates, which were conducted in solemn procession, amidst universal ridicule, as far as Agra, where they were stowed away in a lumber room of the fort. When examined by experts they proved to be made of pine, not sandalwood, and to bear an Arabic inscription of Sabuktigīn. They are clearly local Muhammadan work, executed at Ghaznī, and may or may not have been made to replace the sandalwood originals carried off by Sultan Mahmūd from Somnāth. The proclamations were followed by splendid reviews and other spectacles at Fīrōzpur a form of display which Lord Ellenborough loved too well.

Restoration of Dōst Muhammad. Dōst Muhammad was allowed to return to Afghanistan unconditionally, and to resume the throne from which he had been so needlessly displaced. He retained it for the remainder of his long life, dying in 1863 when nearly 80 years of age. The Governor-general was made an earl, and the various commanders who had carried out the measures of retribution were liberally honoured and rewarded. The vote of thanks to Lord Ellenborough was opposed in Parliament and not without reason. But the war had been a Whig war, instigated by Sir John Hobhouse and Lord Palmerston, and the party politicians were keen to hide away the disgrace, while making the most of the retribution. The crime of the first Afghan War was covered over by the ministry as far as possible, and has not always met with the stern reprobation from the historians of England which its enormity deserves.

Designs on Sind. The Afghan difficulty having been thus disposed of, and Lord Auckland's policy killed with the men who had tried to put it into effect, Lord Ellenborough turned his attention to Sind. He was eager to find a pretext for the annexation of that country, and it was not long before his search was rewarded. Lord Auckland had broken treaties with the Ameers of Sind in the most cynical fashion. Lord Ellenborough went farther, and deliberately provoked a war in order that he might annex the province.[2] So long as it remained independent the navigation of

[1] According to Burnes (*Travels*[2], ii. 150), Ranjit Singh, when negotiating with Shāh Shujā, had required him to obtain the gates.

[2] It is not worth while to examine the flimsy pretexts. 'Certainly', Thornton observes, 'the rights of princes were never assailed on such slender ground as these charges afforded.'

the Indus was liable to be blocked by hostile tribes. The desire to obtain control of the great waterway seems to have been the leading motive of the annexationists in the time of Lord Auckland as well as in that of Lord Ellenborough.

The Ameers, who were not strong enough to resist the exactions imposed upon them, had abstained from open hostility during the Afghan War, even when the army of occupation was destroyed.

Sir Charles Napier. In 1842 Lord Ellenborough removed Outram and the other officers of the Political Department which he hated and sent Sir Charles Napier to Sind vested with sole authority, civil and military, as representative of the Governor-general in all the territory on the lower Indus. Napier, who was bent on annexing the province, pursued a bullying policy, always assuming that the government of India was at liberty to do what it pleased, without the slightest regard to treaties.

At last his proceedings goaded the Balōchīs into making a tumultuous attack on the residence of Colonel Outram, who had been recalled to Sind as the British Commissioner (February 15, 1843). That outbreak gave the excuse which Napier desired, and of course made formal war inevitable.

The conquest. Two days later (February 17) Napier, with only about 2,800 men and 12 guns, routed an army of 22,000 at Miānī (Meeanee), a few miles from Hyderabad. The British loss, although considerable in proportion to the numbers engaged, was small in amount; that of the Sindians was believed to exceed 5,000, killed and wounded. In the following month another fight at Dabo on a similar scale had the same result. A proclamation was then issued announcing the conquest and annexation of the country, and, after some desultory fighting, the inevitable was accepted, and the Ameers were exiled. Sir Charles Napier felt no scruple in accepting £70,000 as his share of the prize-money; but the chivalrous Outram, although a man of small means, disapproving of his chief's policy, refused to accept the £3,000 which formed his share, and distributed the money among charitable institutions. Outram, a warm personal friend of Sir Charles, could not profess to think his conduct right. He wrote to him:

> 'I am sick of *policy*; I will not say yours is the *best*, but it is undoubtedly the shortest—that *of the sword*. Oh, how I wish you had drawn it in a better cause!'

Outram. Outram, 'the Bayard of India, *sans peur et sans reproche*',[1] went home and exerted himself manfully to plead the cause of the despoiled and exiled Ameers of Sind, urging that they 'never contemplated opposing our power, and were only driven to do so from desperation'. But it was too late. As Mr. Gladstone observed many years afterwards, 'the mischief of retaining was less than the mischief of abandoning' the new conquest.

[1] The compliment was paid by Sir Charles Napier at an earlier date, and is inscribed on Outram's tomb in Westminster Abbey (Trotter, *The Bayard of India*, 1909, in Everyman's Library).

Napier as governor. The province was retained, and Napier was appointed its first governor.[1] The directors, while formally condemning the policy which had resulted in annexation, took no steps to undo the transaction. Napier ruled his conquest well until 1847, as a strong, masterful, military despot, and when he returned to England was received with enthusiasm. Annexation has resulted in a great increase of material prosperity, and an elaborate irrigation system has been developed. The recall of Lord Ellenborough in 1844 by the directors was based, not on the injustice of the conquest of Sind, but on other reasons, which will be explained presently. In 1844 several regiments of Madras and Bengal troops, who were unwilling to serve in Sind without extra allowances, mutinied. The mutinies were dealt with by the military authorities in a feeble manner.

Gwālior affairs. Yet another fierce conflict marked the brief and stormy period of Lord Ellenborough's rule. The death early in 1843 of Jankajī Sindia, the adopted son of Daulat Rāo, threw the politics of Gwālior into confusion. The danger of the situation to British interests consisted in the fact that, while court factions were quarrelling, all real power had passed into the hands of the army, which was more than 40,000 strong, possessed of 200 guns, and thoroughly insubordinate. Such a force was a real peril to its neighbours, especially when, as the Governor-general observed, there was within three marches of the Sutlaj 'an army of 70,000 men [Sikhs], confident in its own strength, proud of its various successes against its neighbours, desirous of war and of plunder, and under no discipline or control '. Lord Ellenborough assembled a force under the command of Sir Hugh Gough, the commander-in-chief; and at Christmas time, 1843, crossed the river Chambal. That act was taken by the Gwālior troops as a declaration of war. The Governor-general and commander-in-chief, although partially prepared for battle, came so suddenly on the enemy that Lord Ellenborough was accompanied by ladies and was intending to breakfast quietly under the trees, when he was greeted by artillery fire. The hard-fought battle which ensued took place at Mahārājpur near Gwālior, with the usual result, but at the cost of heavy loss to the victorious British. Another victory was gained on the same day by a distinct corps under General Grey at a place called Paniār. Those two battles broke down all opposition. The Gwālior State lay at the disposal of Lord Ellenborough to do what he pleased with it. He wisely refrained from annexation, contenting himself with disbanding the dangerous army, and making reasonable arrangements for the better government of the State. Although the conflict might have been postponed, it is unlikely that it could have been avoided ultimately; and it was fortunate that, when the deadly struggle with the Sikhs began in 1846, the forces of

[1] Alī Murād of Khairpur, having supported the British, was allowed to retain territory, which is now the Khairpur State. The area is 6,050 square miles, and the State seems to be fairly prosperous. Sind is now attached to the Presidency of Bombay.

the Company had not to guard against the threat of the Gwālior army on their flank. The suppression of that army should not, I think, be reckoned among the sins of Lord Ellenborough. During the Mutiny the Gwālior Contingent, as the reorganized forces of the State were then called, mutinied, retook Cawnpore from General Windham, and exposed the British power to no small danger. The princes of the Sindia family have continued to be uniformly loyal ; and the reigning Mahārāja has done notable service in the cause of civilization during the Great War.

Abolition of slavery. The most important measure of internal reform carried out in the time of Lord Ellenborough was the passing of a law (Act V, 1843) prohibiting the legal recognition of slavery in India. The law of India was thus brought into agreement with that of England. The enactment was the work of Lord Ellenborough's colleagues. The Indian legislature avoided all the difficulties about emancipation or compensation, which had attended the enfranchisement of the West Indian negroes, by simply refusing to recognize slavery as a legal status. The law on the subject is now included in the Penal Code.

Although Megasthenes, in the fourth century B.C., was led to believe that no slave existed in India, he was certainly misinformed. It is clear that in most parts of the country slavery in various forms existed from time immemorial. Even now the institution can hardly be said to be wholly extinct, although it has no legal sanction. Before 1843 there were many millions of slaves in India. Up to 1819 the revenue authorities in the Malabar District of Madras were accustomed to sell the slaves of a revenue defaulter in the same way as his other property. If space permitted innumerable proofs of the prevalence of slavery and the abuses inseparable from the institution might be adduced.[1] The public conscience, however, chiefly among Europeans, gradually began to feel qualms about the maintenance of slavery, and the Act of 1843 does not seem to have aroused opposition or caused any excitement.

Lotteries and police. The state lotteries in the presidency towns, the proceeds of which had been devoted to local improvements, were also suppressed ; and the Bengal police administration was made somewhat more efficient by the appointment of deputy magistrates, and by improvements in the pay and promotion of police *dārōgas*.

Reasons for recall of Lord Ellenborough. The published correspondence of Queen Victoria throws light upon the reasons for the appointment and recall of Lord Ellenborough. The Queen, Sir Robert Peel, and the Duke of Wellington concurred in the opinion that Lord Ellenborough, in spite of his 'tendency to hasty decisions', was 'better qualified than any man in England

[1] Much painfully interesting information on the subject, derived chiefly from official documents, is collected in the work by Peggs, already cited, entitled *India's Cries to British Humanity*, Book V, 2nd ed., 1830 ; or 3rd ed., 1832. The Indian slave trade at various times and in many provinces was extensive.

for the office of Governor-general '. The directors, however, never liked him, and during his term of office he frequently complained of their constant hostility. That hostility was not without justification. The directors were offended and disgusted by the arrogant tone of his correspondence ; by his gasconading proclamations ; by his open contempt for the Civil Service ; by his love of theatrical display ; and by the aggressive bent of his policy.

The Queen, who always gave him her personal support, resented his recall ; but, in my judgement, the directors acted wisely and in the interest of India by exercising the power which had been reserved to them at the last renewal of the charter.

CHRONOLOGY

Lord Melbourne (Whig) Prime Minister : Dōst Muhammad Ameer of Kābul	1835
Lord Auckland Governor-general (March) ; Dispatch from Secret Committee about Afghan affairs and Herat (June 25) . .	1836
Accession of Queen Victoria (June) ; mission of Burnes to Kābul	1837
Famine in northern India	1837–8
Tripartite treaty (June) ; Lord Auckland's Declaration (Oct. 1) .	1838
New treaty forced on Ameers of Sind (Feb.) ; death of Ranjit Singh (June) ; capture of Ghazni (July) ; occupation of Kābul (Aug.) ; deposition of Rājā of Sātārā	1839
Risings of Afghan tribes ; surrender of Dōst Muhammad . .	1840
Murder of Burnes (Nov.) ; murder of Macnaghten (Dec.) . .	1841
General Elphinstone's treaty with Akbar Khān (Jan. 1) ; retirement began (Jan. 6) ; Dr. Brydon reached Jalālābād alone (Jan. 13) ; Lord Ellenborough Governor-general (Feb.) ; relief of Jalālābād ; reoccupation of Kābul ; restoration of Dōst Muhammad ; annexation of Karnūl	1842
Battles of Miānī and Dabo ; annexation of Sind ; defeats of Gwālior army at Mahārājpur and Paniār ; suppression of slavery (Act V) and of state lotteries	1843
Mutinies of Bengal and Madras regiments in Sind ; recall of Lord Ellenborough ; Sir Henry Hardinge Governor-general (July) .	1844

AUTHORITIES

The leading authority is the *History of the War in Afghanistan*, by J. W. KAYE (publ. in 1851 ; 4th ed., 3 vols., Allen, 1878) ; it is so carefully documented that little material change was made in the later editions. Next in importance is *The First Afghan War and its Causes*, the unfinished work by Sir HENRY MARION DURAND (Longmans, 1879). Of the many books written by other persons who took part in the campaign, I have used chiefly [Sir] H. HAVELOCK, *Narrative of the War in Affghanistan* (2 vols., Colburn, 1840).[1] *The Earl of Auckland* (R. I., 1905) by L. J. TROTTER is an excellent summary. *John Russell Colvin* by Sir A. COLVIN (R. I., 1911), although not convincing as an *apologia*, gives certain additional facts. The controversy between Sir Charles Napier and Sir James Outram elicited many books and pamphlets. I have consulted OUTRAM,

[1] Havelock then approved of Lord Auckland's policy.

Rough Notes on the Campaign in Sinde and Afghanistan in 1838–9 (Richardson, 1840), a publication regretted by the author; *The Conquest of Scinde* (Boone, 1845); and *History of General Sir Charles Napier's Administration* of Scinde (Chapman & Hall, 1851), both by Major-General Sir WILLIAM NAPIER. *The History of the Indian Administration of Lord Ellenborough* by Lord COLCHESTER (London, 1874) gives the Governor-general's letters to the Queen and Duke of Wellington without comment. THORNTON alone narrates fully the dealings with Native States. MARSHMAN lays stress on internal reforms. The blue book, *Correspondence relative to Sinde, 1838–43* (London, 1843), 516 pp., supplies the text of 475 documents. The first Afghan blue book of 1839 was garbled by the omission of important passages in the letters of Burnes. KAYE exposed the facts in 1851, and a revised blue book was issued in 1859. See Kaye, ed. 4, vol. i, pp. 202–4.

CHAPTER 4

Sir Henry (Lord) Hardinge; first Sikh War; treaties of Lahore; Lord Dalhousie; second Sikh War; second Burmese War; annexations; reforms.

Sir Henry (Lord) Hardinge. The British government, in sending Sir Henry Hardinge to rule India, sent one of England's noblest sons. At Vimiera, Albuera, Ligny, and countless other battles of the Peninsular and Waterloo campaigns he had proved his prowess as a soldier and his capacity as a general. He had been wounded four times, losing his left hand at Ligny, and had had five horses shot under him. In civil life he had served as a member of parliament for twenty years, and had held office as secretary for war and chief secretary for Ireland. Although, like Lord Hastings, he was fifty-nine years of age when he came out to India, the advance of years had not quenched the fire of his youth or impaired his capacity for high command. In July 1844 he relieved his flighty predecessor, who assured him that India was in a state of 'universal peace, the result of two years of victories'. In December 1845 the Sikhs crossed the Sutlaj, and so falsified the shortsighted optimism of Lord Ellenborough.

Internal administration. The new Governor-general, although obliged from the first to take precautions against the Sikh peril, was able for a year and a half to devote much of his attention to improvements in internal administration and to the suppression of cruel customs. He took preliminary steps towards planning the Indian railway system of the future; made progress in the designs for the Ganges Canal; supported education; and took measures for suppressing suttee and infanticide in the Native States.[1]

[1] Among the Sikhs in the Panjāb the suttee murders were atrocious. Four ladies burned with Ranjit Singh; one, against her will, with Kharak Singh; two with Nao Nihāl Singh; 310 (10 wives and 300 unmarried ladies of his zenana) were sacrificed at the obsequies of Rājā Suchet Singh; in September 1845 four wives of Jawāhir Singh were forced on the pyre

Human sacrifices. He also sanctioned systematic arrangements for the extinction of the horrible practices of human sacrifice prevalent in the Hill Tracts of Orissa. The results obtained at first in the Orissan operations during Sir Henry Hardinge's time were poor, owing to defects in the agency employed, but in the years from 1847 to 1854 Lieut.-Col. (Major-General) John Campbell and other officers specially appointed succeeded in stamping out the atrocious customs. The purpose of the sacrifices usually was to increase the fertility of the soil by burying bits of the flesh of the victims in the fields. The cruel rites varied in different localities. Campbell describes one which may be taken as a sample :

> 'One of the most common ways of offering the sacrifice in Chinna Kimedy is to the effigy of an elephant rudely carved in wood, fixed on the top of a stout post, on which it is made to revolve. After the performance of the usual ceremonies, the wretched Meriah [consecrated victim] is fastened to the proboscis of the elephant, and amidst the shouts and yells of the excited Khonds, is rapidly whirled round, when, at a given signal by the officiating " Zani ", or priest, the crowd rush in, seize the Meriah, and with their knives cut the flesh off the shrieking victim as long as life remains. He is then cut down, the skeleton burnt, and the horrid orgies are over. In several villages, I counted as many as fourteen effigies of elephants which had been used in former sacrifices.'

Between 1837 and 1854 no less than 1,506 Meriah victims were rescued.

The Khond people gradually became convinced that their fields produced crops as good as formerly, and that sickness was not more prevalent. Animals were substituted for human victims, and it is believed that the Meriah horrors have been finally suppressed.[1]

Origin of the Sikh War. The main business, however, of Sir Henry, or to call him by his later title, Lord Hardinge, was the Sikh War, forced upon him by the arrogance of the army of the Khālsa.

Mahārāja Ranjit Singh, when stopped by Lord Minto in 1809 from pursuing his intended conquests to the south of the Sutlaj, was left free to do as he pleased to the north of the river.[2] 'By the year 1820 his power may be said to have been consolidated and absolute throughout the whole Panjāb proper from the Sutlej to the Indus.' The city and province of Peshāwar, wrested from the Afghans, became tributary to him in 1823 ; but the Sikhs never reduced the frontier to obedience, or extended their influence beyond the range of their forts. The possessions of the Mahārāja

by the soldiery ; and, after Sobrāon, the widow of Sardār Shān Singh burnt voluntarily. Sir Lepel Griffin in 1898 described that as being the last case in the Panjāb.

Infanticide was practised extensively in the Panjāb, Rājputāna, Mālwā, Cutch, Kāthiāwār, and elsewhere.

[1] But Sir W. Lee-Warner, writing in 1904 (*Life of Dalhousie*, p. 211), says : 'nor have cases of Meriah passed entirely out of the calendars of Indian crime.'

[2] He was allowed to retain certain lands south of the river which he had acquired earlier.

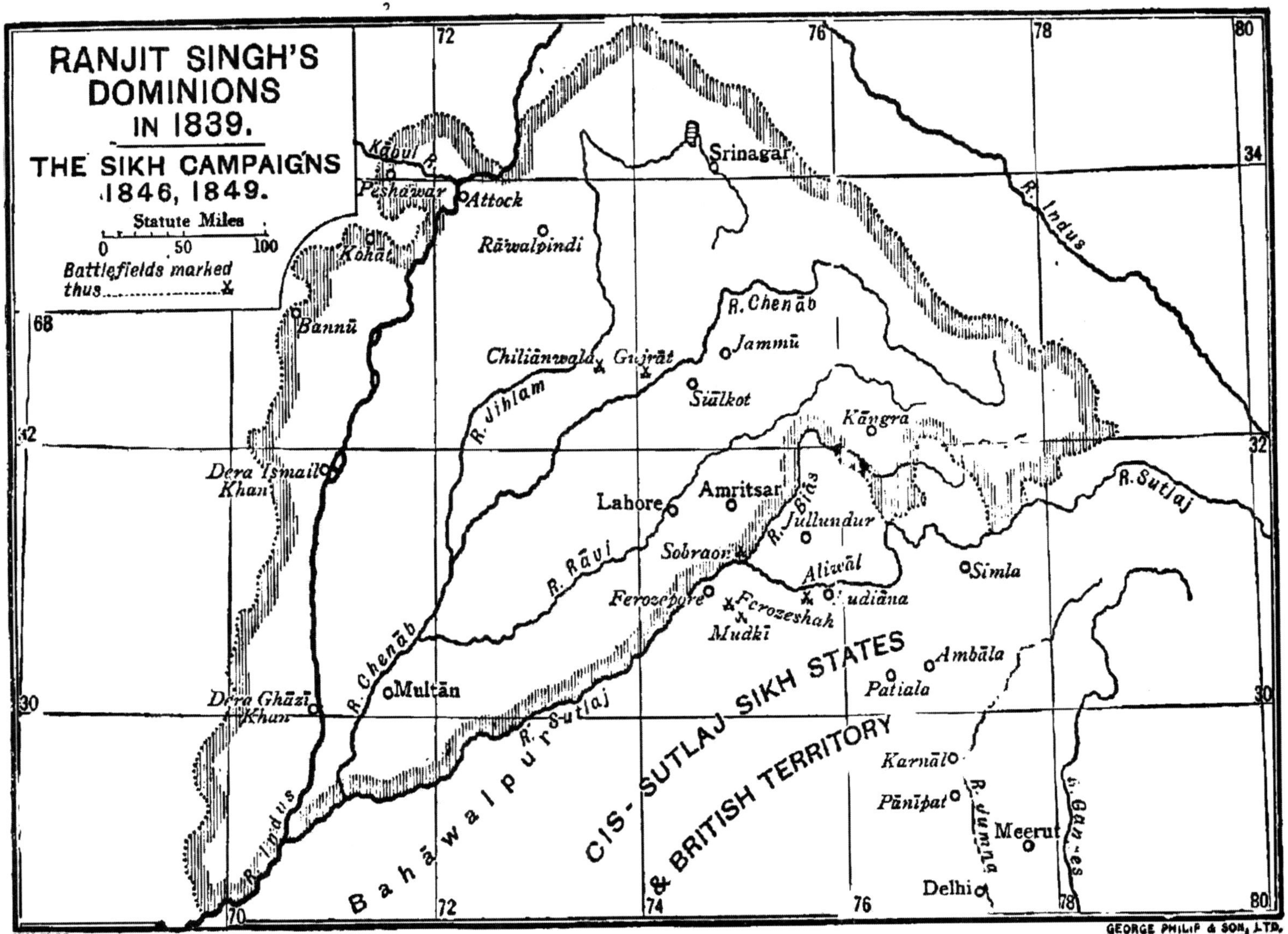
RANJIT SINGH'S DOMINIONS IN 1839.
THE SIKH CAMPAIGNS 1846, 1849.
Statute Miles
0 50 100
Battlefields marked thus
Kābul R.
Peshāwar
Attock
Rāwalpindi
Kohāt
Bannū
Srinagar
R. Indus
R. Chenāb
Jammū
Chiliānwala
Gujrāt
Siālkot
R. Jihlam
Kāngra
Dera Ismail Khan
Lahore
Amritsar
R. Biās
Jullundur
R. Sutlaj
Sobraon
Aliwāl
R. Rāvi
Ferozepore
Ferozeshah
udiāna
Simla
Mudkī
Ambāla
Patiala
Multān
R. Chenāb
Dera Ghāzi Khan
R. Sutlaj
CIS-SUTLAJ SIKH STATES & BRITISH TERRITORY
Karnāl
Pānīpat
R. Jumna
Meerut
Delhi
R. Indus
Bahāwalpur
68
70
72
74
76
78
80
30
32
34
WAXTYPE
GEORGE PHILIP & SON, LTD.

at the time of his death in 1839 at the age of fifty-nine included Kāngra and Kashmīr, as shown in the map.

Ranjit Singh, who had ruined his health by drink and debauchery, was struck with paralysis in 1834, and again in 1838, the year in which he met Lord Auckland. The general knowledge that his death must soon occur, and that he had no heir fit to succeed him, weakened his authority in his latter days, and prepared the way for the six years of misrule which ensued upon his decease. It is

MAHĀRĀJA RANJIT SINGH.

needless to detail the crimes which stained the Panjāb during that evil time. The nature of the events is indicated sufficiently in Sir Lepel Griffin's summary :

'The six years which followed were a period of storm and anarchy, in which assassination was the rule, and the weak were ruthlessly trampled under foot. The legitimate line—Kharak Singh, the imbecile [and only son of Ranjit]; and his handsome, reckless, vicious son, Nao Nihāl Singh [a youth of eighteen]—was soon extinguished in blood. Then came the turn of the impostors : Mahārāja Sher Singh, a drunken debauchee [and pretended son of Ranjit], murdered together with his son by the fierce

Sindhanwalias; and Dhulip [Dilīp] Singh, the son of the dancing girl, whose end would have been as swift and bloody as the others, had not a propitious fortune and the collapse of the Sikh army allowed him a secure refuge in the unrequited generosity of the British Government.

As Ranjit Singh had sown, so was the harvest. The fathers had eaten sour grapes, and the children's teeth were set on edge. The kingdom founded in violence, treachery, and blood did not long survive its founder. Created by the military and administrative genius of one man, it crumbled into powder when the spirit which gave it life was withdrawn; and the inheritance of the Khālsa passed into the hands of the English, who will hold it against all comers, if only they rule with the justice, beneficence, and strength which alone make empires enduring.'

The early Śikh plundering bands had consisted almost wholly of irregular cavalry. Foot-soldiers were of little account, and artillery did not exist. Ranjit Singh transformed the army of the Sikh Khālsa, or military order, into an essentially infantry force, supported by powerful artillery, and moderately good cavalry. His principal officers were foreigners, mostly French or Italian, including Generals Ventura and Allard, who had served under Napoleon, and the ferocious Neapolitan, Avitabile. In 1845 the Sikh army comprised 88,662 men, of whom 53,756 were regular infantry. The guns of all sorts amounted to 484, besides 308 camel swivels.

In December 1845 the Khālsa, which had accepted as its nominal sovereign a child five years of age named Dhuleep (properly, Dilīp) Singh, falsely alleged to be a son of Ranjit, compelled the Rānī, mother of the child, and her counsellors, Lāl Singh and Tēj Singh, to authorize the invasion of British territory by crossing the Sutlaj. The soldiers hoped to take the authorities unawares and to secure the plunder of Delhi. They numbered about 50,000 or 60,000.[1]

Declaration of war. No ruler of India could refuse to accept such a challenge. The Governor-general issued his declaration of war on December 13, 1845, stating that

'the Sikh army has now, without a shadow of provocation, invaded the British territories.

The Governor-general must therefore take measures for effectually protecting the British provinces, for vindicating the authority of the British Government, and for punishing the violators of treaties and the disturbers of the public peace.

The Governor-general hereby declares the possessions of Maharaja Dhuleep Singh, on the left or British bank of the Sutlej, confiscated and annexed to the British territories.'

The war. The Governor-general in his anxiety to avoid war had incurred serious risk, against the advice of the commander-in-chief, by refraining from pushing large forces forward. The first action at Mudkī (Moodkee) between Lūdiāna and Fīrōzpur

[1] Cunningham notes a tendency to overrate the numbers of the Sikh enemy. He also proves the reality of the erroneous belief held by the Khālsa soldiery that the English meditated an invasion of Sikh territory.

consequently was fought at a disadvantage and on the defensive, but resulted in the defeat of the Sikhs. Three days later the British army, having received reinforcements, attacked the invaders in their entrenchments at a village commonly called Ferozeshāh, about twelve miles from the Sutlaj.[1] The battle lasted for two days; and, after a desperate struggle, in which the British army lost 2,415 killed and wounded, the Sikhs were driven from their entrenchments and compelled to retire. Five aides-de-camp of the Governor-general were killed, and four wounded. The situation of the British force was extremely critical on the night of December 21, when the troops had to bivouac on the ground won. Fighting was renewed at dawn, and ended in the retirement of the Sikhs. It is impossible within the limits of this work to discuss the interesting military details, which may be read in the excellent account recorded by the Governor-general's eldest son, who attended his father as an aide-de-camp.

The third battle, fought close to the Sutlaj at Aliwāl to the west of Lūdiāna, on January 28, 1846, ended in the driving of the Sikhs across the river, in which many were drowned. Every enemy gun, to the number of fifty-two, fell into the hands of the victors.[2]

Battle of Sobrāon. The final battle of the brief campaign was fought on February 10, 1846, in the Ferozepore (Fīrōzpur) District on the eastern bank of the river, facing the village of Sobrāon,[3] on the opposite or Lahore bank. The Sikhs, numbering about 30,000, with seventy guns, occupied strong entrenchments, connected by a good bridge with the opposite bank, where their reserve was posted. The position involved obvious risk. The British force carried the works with the bayonet alone, and forced the Sikhs to retire on the bridge. The concluding act of the drama is vividly described by the Governor-general's son and heir, who was present:

'Compelled to retire, they gave way in such admirable order as to excite the admiration of the British soldiers. At last the fire slackened, and then ensued a scene which defies description. Pressed on all sides by our advancing infantry, the enemy were hemmed in in one confused mass at the head of the bridge, there to be shot down or hurled into the river below. Happening to be an eye-witness of what then occurred, I saw the bridge at that moment overcrowded with guns, horses, and soldiers of all arms, swaying to and fro, till at last with a crash it disappeared in the running waters, carrying with it those who had vainly hoped to reach the opposite shore. The river seemed alive with a struggling mass of men.

[1] The name really is Phīrūshahr (Pheerooshuhur), or 'Phirū's town' (Cunningham, *Hist. of the Sikhs*², p. 301 *n.*). The *I. G.* spells Pharūshahr.

[2] Gough (p. 119) notes a curious incident after Aliwāl: 'By order of the Governor-general a royal salute was fired from the British camp, the bands raised the National Anthem. The Sikhs on the opposite bank, not to be outdone, followed suit with both; and their bands were heard playing "God save the Queen".' Gough puts the number of guns captured as 67; the number in the text is as stated by Viscount Hardinge in his book.

[3] Properly Subrāhān, the plural of Subrah, the name of a tribe inhabiting the village (ibid., p. 320 *n.*).

The artillery, now brought down to the water's edge, completed the slaughter. Few escaped, none, it may be said, surrendered. The Sikhs met their fate with that resignation which distinguishes their race.'

On the side of the conquerors

'the total number of killed amounted to 300, of wounded to 2,063. The lowest official estimate of the Sikh loss is 8,000.[1] The trophies of the victory comprised 67 pieces of artillery and 200 camel-swivels. Prince Waldemar [of Prussia] and his aides-de-camp were again present in the field. As true soldiers, they were not satisfied with being distant spectators, but were continually under fire.'

Rewards. Great anxiety had been felt in England when the news of the battles of Mudkī and Aliwāl arrived. The accounts of the tactics pursued seemed to indicate a certain amount of rashness on the part of Sir Hugh Gough, the gallant commander-in-chief; so that plans for placing the Governor-general in supreme military command had been considered. The announcement of the final victory at Sobrāon, which closed the Sutlaj campaign by the destruction of the Sikh field army, dispelled all fears, and gave just cause for rejoicing. The war on the British side having been purely defensive, no regrets tempered the joy of victory. Peerages and other rewards were conferred on the Governor-general and commander-in-chief; and all ranks shared in the honours and bounties which were distributed freely, as was right, considering the critical nature of the contest with the bravest and steadiest enemy ever encountered in India by a British army.

Treaties of Lahore. The victory opened the way to Lahore, which was promptly occupied by the Governor-general. The Sikhs were not in a position to contest the terms imposed, which required the cession of all lands on the British side of the Sutlaj, as well as of the Jullundur (Jālandhar) Doāb, between that river and the Biās, the payment of half a million sterling, the cession of Kashmīr and Hazāra as the equivalent of a million, the surrender of many guns, and the limitation of the Sikh army to 20,000 infantry and 12,000 cavalry.

The government was to continue in the hands of the young Mahārāja, with Lāl Singh as his minister, under the supervision of Sir Henry Lawrence, who was appointed Resident. A British force was to remain in occupation of Lahore until the close of the year, but not longer. The arrangement did not work, and before long the more friendly Sikh leaders requested that the occupation might be prolonged for eight years until the Mahārāja should come of age. An amended treaty accordingly was executed in December 1846. Sir Henry Lawrence remained as the real ruler, but nominally as the president of a council of regency. He gathered round him a cluster of brilliant colleagues as assistants, including his brother John, Herbert Edwardes, and many others well known to fame in later years. Sir Henry Lawrence's attempt to conduct the administration on more or less civilized lines was much disliked by the chiefs, and especially by the Queen Mother, who had to be

[1] Cunningham, as usual, was inclined to reduce the number.

deported. Meantime the Sikhs, who had managed to retain many guns, and still could muster a formidable force of fighting men, were preparing for a fresh conflict. It did not break out until after Lord Hardinge's departure.

Makeshift arrangements. Lord Hardinge's arrangements for the administration of the Panjāb obviously were open to criticism, and lacking in prospects of permanence. But at the time annexation was hardly possible, and the Governor-general rightly was determined to avoid a subsidiary alliance of the old, obsolete kind. Annexation was dangerous, because the small European force had been much weakened by the casualties of the campaign, and certain incidents had proved that full confidence could not be reposed in the sepoy army. Lord Hardinge hoped rather than believed that peace might be preserved because the Sikh military power had been so much weakened by the territorial cessions enforced and by the losses suffered by the Khālsa.[1] The valley of Kashmīr, with the neighbouring dominions of several petty hill chiefs, was made over to Rājā Gulāb Singh, an upstart Dogra chieftain of Jummoo (Jumū), on payment of three-quarters of a million sterling. The modern Kashmīr State was thus established. The British retained the Hazāra District, now (1918) included in the North-West Frontier Province.

A Muhammadan leader tried to prevent Gulāb Singh from taking possession of his new acquisitions, but was easily suppressed. The British force engaged in the operation was actually supported by a contingent of 17,000 Sikhs who had been fighting in the campaign just concluded.

All the political arrangements were made by Lord Hardinge on his own responsibility, without the advice of the council in Calcutta. He enjoyed the full confidence of the Home Government, which warmly supported him in all his acts.

Close of Lord Hardinge's administration. Lord Hardinge, in his anxiety to secure financial economy, somewhat hastily made considerable reductions in the army, which seriously embarrassed his successor. The old Duke of Wellington's blunt comment, 'I never could understand why he was in such a damned hurry,' was a just, if unconventional criticism.

In January 1848 Lord Hardinge made over charge to his successor, Lord Dalhousie, to whom he expressed the rash assurance that, so far as human foresight could predict, 'it would not be necessary to fire a gun in India for seven years to come.' The prediction, like many others of its kind, was quickly falsified.

Subsequent career of Lord Hardinge. Viscount Hardinge, after quitting India, continued to serve his queen and country to the end of his unsullied life, first as Master of the Ordnance, and then as commander-in-chief. The military strength of the United Kingdom had been allowed to sink to a dangerously low

[1] He wrote to Henry Lawrence: 'I confess I think the probability is against the continuance of a Sikh government' (*Life of Sir H. Lawrence*, p. 385).

level during the long peace between the battle of Waterloo in 1815 and the beginning of the Crimean War in 1854. No one man could remedy the neglect of two generations which resulted in the deplorable scandals of the campaign in the Crimea. Lord Hardinge, who did his best, has to his credit several valuable reforms, including an absolutely necessary increase of the artillery, the introduction of the Enfield rifle, the foundation of the School of Musketry at Hythe, and the purchase of the site for the camp and manœuvre ground at Aldershot. In 1855 he was promoted to the rank of Field-Marshal, and on September 13, 1856, he died in his seventy-first year. The regrets of his grateful sovereign are inscribed on his tomb.

LORD DALHOUSIE.

The Earl of Dalhousie. The chosen successor of the veteran Viscount Hardinge was a young Scots nobleman, the Earl of Dalhousie, only thirty-five years of age. He had made a reputation as an industrious and able official while in the ministry as President of the Board of Trade, at a time when the duties of the post were exceptionally arduous owing to the rapid development of the railway system, then a novelty. His appointment was received with general approval, but he had good reason for doubting his ability to stand the strain of governing India. In the year following he wrote: 'I was broken down in health when I started and had no business to come. I landed in Calcutta an invalid, almost a cripple.' During the whole eight years of his term of office he was never really well, and usually was suffering from acute pain. The day he quitted India he crawled on board the ship with the aid of crutches. Notwithstanding his physical disability and almost incessant suffering, the marvellous strength of his will enabled him to perform an amount of work of the highest quality which exceeded the powers of most statesmen, even when blessed with perfect health.

The first four years of his government were largely occupied by the second Sikh and the second Burmese war. It will be convenient to narrate in outline the history and results of those campaigns before discussing Lord Dalhousie's manifold activities in other fields.

Revolt of Mūlrāj. Dīwān Mūlrāj, who occupied a semi-independent position as Governor of Mūltān, combining the business of trade on a large scale with that of administration, was called upon by the government at Lahore to render accounts. After some delay he intimated that he preferred to resign. Two young officers, Vans Agnew of the Civil Service and Lieutenant Anderson, were then sent by the Resident to take over charge of the fortress of Mūltān and install the Sikh Governor who had been appointed to succeed Mūlrāj. In April 1848 both these officers were suddenly attacked and hacked to death. Mūlrāj, who rewarded the murderers for their deed, regained possession of Mūltān, which was far too strong to be taken from him except after a regular siege. Lord Gough, the commander-in-chief, with whom Lord Dalhousie reluctantly but resolutely concurred, decided that it would be unwise to attempt the siege of Mūltān during the hot weather and without adequate force or a suitable siege train. He therefore, in spite of all entreaty, deferred operations until the cold weather. He has been much blamed for that decision, but so far as I understand the matter he was right. The correctness of his judgement is not impugned by the fact that during the hot season Lieutenant Herbert Edwardes pressed Mūlrāj hard with a small force locally raised, and compelled the chieftain to remain within the walls of his fortress.

The siege of Mūltān began in September 1848 ; but, after a few days, had to be raised, because the apparent success of Mūlrāj had tempted the Sikh troops to revolt, so that the besiegers soon found themselves in danger of being cut off by a hostile host.

Anticipating a little the order of time, it may be stated that the citadel of Mūltān, after a gallant defence, capitulated on January 22, 1849. Mūlrāj was tried, convicted, and transported.

War. Lord Dalhousie immediately recognized that the outrage at Mūltān necessitated a final war with the Sikhs. His decision was announced in the famous phrase : ‘ Unwarned by precedent, uninfluenced by example, the Sikh nation has called for war, and, on my word, sirs, they shall have it with a vengeance.’ [1]

Extensive preparations were made. The Governor-general moved up to the frontier, and Lord Gough, the commander-in-chief, crossed the Panjāb with 20,000 men and nearly 100 guns. Another large force was brought up from Bombay.

Chiliānwālā. Before Mūltān fell the battle of Chiliānwālā had been fought by Lord Gough on January 13, 1846. The Sikhs entrenched themselves with their backs to the Jhelum river, as they had done with their backs to the Sutlaj at the battle of Sobrāon in the first Sikh war. Lord Gough reached Chiliānwālā about noon, with the intention of reconnoitring the position, encamping for the night, and fighting the next day. But when the enemy's guns suddenly opened fire, and the Sikhs in full force advanced from their entrenchments, all possibility of encamping

[1] The idiom ‘ with a vengeance ’ has been sometimes misunderstood. It simply means ‘ to extremity ’, or in French, *à outrance*, and has nothing to do with ‘ vengeance ’ in the sense of revenge.

vanished, and Lord Gough was forced to fight at once. The firing began about one o'clock in the afternoon, and consequently the daylight hours available at that season were few. The result of the fight was that the enemy was driven back to Tupai on the river bank, and if daylight had lasted would have been forced into the water. But the coming on of darkness, combined with certain errors committed by subordinate commanders, especially the faulty handling of the cavalry on the British right, prevented the attainment of complete success. The Sikhs were even able to recover some of their guns during the night. The British force suffered severely, losing 2,338 men killed and wounded. Lord Gough also lost four guns and the colours of three regiments. On the other hand, twelve or thirteen guns were taken from the enemy.

The news of the battle produced a painful impression in both India and England, the Sikh strength having been much underrated by public opinion, which had expected an easy triumph. The home authorities hastily ordered the recall of Lord Gough and his supersession by Sir Charles Napier, the conqueror of Sind.

March to Gujarāt. The battle of Chiliānwālā had been necessarily fought by Lord Gough with inadequate force. The fall of Mūltān a few days later released a large body of troops, who made their way northwards by forced marches, and more than replaced the heavy casualties of the battle. The British now became for the first time superior to the enemy in artillery. Want of supplies prevented the Sikh general from retaining his strong entrenched position at Rasūl near Chiliānwālā. When he moved eastwards to Gujarāt, a town near the Chināb, Lord Gough perceived that the right time for the final conflict had come. Refusing to be tempted into premature action by the enemy's provocations, he marched slowly in February towards his chosen battle-ground, where he intended to deliver the decisive blow with concentrated forces adequately supplied with guns.[1]

Battle of Gujarāt, February 21, 1849. The Sikh position was established to the south of the town of Gujarāt, with the Chināb on their left. The battle began about 9 a.m. on February 21 by a vigorous artillery duel which greatly weakened the Sikh defence. The general advance of the British began at 11.30, and an hour later the whole Sikh army was in full flight. By one o'clock the town, camp, and baggage of the enemy, with most of their guns, were in the hands of the victors.

The decisive victory was gained at the comparatively small cost of 96 killed and 670 wounded. The fugitive army was hotly pursued as far as the Afghan frontier by an active force of 12,000 men, and the conquest was completed by the occupation of Peshāwar.

Lord Gough observed in his farewell orders that 'the tide of

[1] Lord Dalhousie's advice is entitled to some of the credit due for the adequate use of artillery preparation at the 'battle of the guns', as Gujarāt has been called.

conquest, which heretofore rolled on the Punjaub from the west, has at length reached it and overcome it from the east; and that which Alexander attempted, the British Indian army has accomplished.' The fierce controversy which has raged round Chiliānwālā and certain less important actions fought by Lord Gough found no fuel for its fires in the story of the battle of Gujarāt. The preparations for the final struggle were carefully thought out and successfully matured, while the conduct of the battle itself left no opening for hostile criticism. The news was received with intense pleasure at home, and fresh honours and rewards were gladly bestowed on everybody concerned, from the Governor-general and the commander-in-chief down to the rank and file.

Annexation. The Panjāb having twice become the prize of war, and two attempts at maintaining a Sikh administration having failed disastrously, Lord Dalhousie rightly decided on avowed annexation. The decision was his alone, taken without reference either to the council in Calcutta or to superior authority in England. The Governor-general explained that

> 'there was no government in the Panjāb, and if I had not proclaimed a distinct policy of one kind or another, I should have had the country in one month in riot and utter anarchy, and harm would have been done which years and years could not have made good. What I have done I have done as an act of necessity.'[1]

SIR HENRY LAWRENCE.

The boy Mahārāja Dhuleep Singh was required to resign for himself, his heirs and his successors, all right, title, and claim to the sovereignty of the Panjāb, or to any sovereign power whatever.

Form of government. Lord Dalhousie, who did not see eye to eye with Sir Henry Lawrence the late resident, was unable either to dispense with the services of that able officer, or to entrust him with the control of the civil administration, a task for which his romantic temperament and unmethodical habits were thought to render him unsuitable.

As a temporary arrangement the provincial government was

[1] Lord Dalhousie, in acting thus promptly, followed the advice of John Lawrence. Henry thought annexation inexpedient.

placed in the hands of a board, consisting of Sir Henry Lawrence, his brother John, and a civilian colleague from Bengal. As soon as opportunity offered Henry Lawrence was transferred to Rājputāna, the board was abolished, and John Lawrence was appointed chief commissioner. Whoever might be in local charge, the government was directed by the Governor-general, who insisted that his policy, not that of anybody else, must be carried out.

Organization of a new administration. The new government had everything to do. The administration of Ranjit Singh, even when he was at his best, had been of the rough-and-ready kind. He did not concern himself for a moment with the welfare of the people; concentrating his attention on the army, and the extraction of every rupee from the cultivators on which he could lay hands. No civilized rulers could possibly continue to govern on such principles. Lord Dalhousie selected the best men in the Indian services, civil and military, in order to construct a reasonably regular, though flexible and informal, machinery of government, and was rewarded by seeing that prosperity and contentment in the Panjāb resulted from his efforts. The Lawrences, Herbert Edwardes, John Nicholson, Richard Temple, and many other officers whose names are more or less familiar, contributed to the organization of the model province; but they always worked under the eye of their indefatigable master, who, perhaps, deserves, even more than his brilliant subordinates, the credit for the results obtained.

Reforms in all departments. External security was provided for by a chain of forts and cantonments and the constitution of the mobile Frontier Force, including the Corps of Guides; while internal order was assured by general disarmament and the enrolment of civil and military police. Ranjit Singh had been accustomed to take as land revenue in kind half of the gross crop produce. The new government was content with a moderate cash assessment. Communications, which had been wholly neglected, were rapidly improved, and all possible steps were taken to encourage the people to settle down to peaceable occupations. Village schools were founded, and an informal judicial system was brought into operation. The province was divided into convenient districts, administered by picked officers, of whom about half were military and half civil servants. Care was taken not to crush the newly conquered people under the weight of the Bengal Regulations, the administration being organized on the more elastic non-Regulation pattern. By those measures and many others equally beneficent the Panjāb quickly became not only prosperous but generally contented, and the men who had fought the British so bravely in 1849 willingly stood shoulder to shoulder with them in 1857. The old ruling classes, however, for whom Henry Lawrence felt warm sympathy, had some reason to complain of the heavy hand of his brother John.[1]

[1] The fundamental differences of temperament and opinion between the Lawrence brothers are expounded at length in the *Life of Sir Henry*

Second Burmese War. The war with Burma, although involving consequences not much inferior in importance to those of the Sikh War, was of less military interest, and may be described sufficiently in few words. The humiliations inflicted on and the losses endured by Burma in 1826 had not lowered the pride of the court of Ava, which never missed an opportunity of expressing its contempt for Europeans or for insulting the representative of the Governor-general, who had to be withdrawn in 1840. Certain acts of oppression on British merchants in 1851 were brought to the notice of Lord Dalhousie, who required reparation and the payment of a trifling sum as damages. No satisfaction having been obtained, Commodore Lambert was sent to Rangoon to demand redress. That officer, contrary to his orders, seized one of the king's ships. The Burmese then fired, the Commodore returned the fire, and so hostilities began, more by accident than by design.[1] But, even if the naval officer had been less hasty, war could not have been long postponed, because the Burmese Government declined to abate its arrogance, or to deal on friendly terms with the Government of India. The operations were brief and successful. The great pagoda of Rangoon was gallantly stormed on April 14, 1852; Prome was occupied by General Godwin in October, and the whole of the Pegu province in November. Dalhousie declined to obey instructions from England to advance to Ava, contenting himself with the annexation of Pegu, the inland boundary on the river being fixed at Meaday, above Prome. The king having resolutely refused to sign a formal treaty, the new province was annexed by proclamation. The brilliant success of the second Burmese War was mainly due to the Governor-general himself, who avoided all the errors of Lord Amherst, and saw personally to every detail of the equipment of the troops. He also visited the country, and organized the administration, as he had done in the Panjāb.

Results. The Government of India thus acquired control, direct or indirect, of the entire eastern coast of the Bay of Bengal from Chittagong to Singapore, while the Burmese kingdom was absolutely shut out from access to the sea except through British territory. Such a condition could not last indefinitely, and the third Burmese War in the time of Lord Dufferin was the natural and inevitable consequence of the second. Pegu, for the most part an alluvial plain of extraordinary fertility, now constitutes the Pegu Division, comprising five Districts. The population increases rapidly, and British administration has brought an

Lawrence, by Sir Herbert Edwardes and Herman Merivale (Smith Elder, 3rd ed., 1873).

[1] 'There is no doubt that Lambert was the *immediate* cause of the war by seizing the King's ship, in direct disobedience of his orders from me. I accepted the responsibility of his act, but disapproved and censured it. He replied officially that he had written home, and he was sure Palmerston would have approved!' (*Private Letters*, July 23, 1853, p. 260). Lambert was promoted.

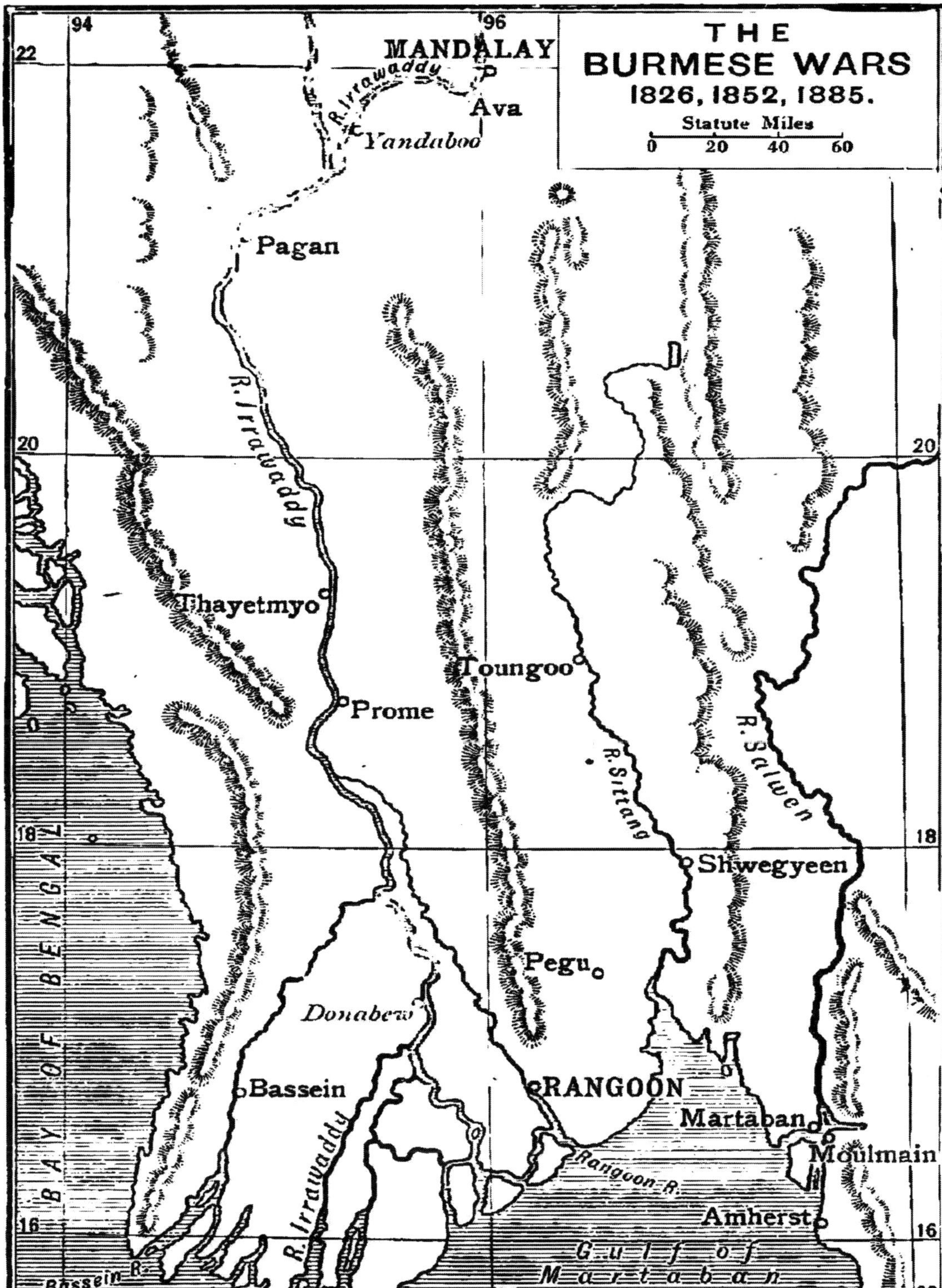
THE
BURMESE WARS
1826, 1852, 1885.
Statute Miles
0 20 40 60
MANDALAY
Ava
Yandaboo
R. Irrawaddy
Pagan
Thayetmyo
Toungoo
Prome
R. Sittang
R. Salwen
Shwegyeen
Pegu
Donabew
Bassein
RANGOON
Martaban
Moulmain
Rangoon R.
Amherst
Gulf of Martaban
Bassein R.
BAY OF BENGAL
WAXTYPE
GEORGE PHILIP & SON, LTD.

enormous growth of material prosperity. Prome is connected with Rangoon by railway.

Until 1862, when Sir Arthur Phayre became the first chief commissioner, British Burma was administered under the Government of India by two commissioners, one of Pegu (Sir Arthur Phayre), and the other of Tenasserim.

Sikkim. A third annexation of foreign territory on a very small scale had been effected in 1850, when a portion of the Sikkim State situated between Nepāl and Bhutān was taken from the Rājā as a penalty for his treacherous seizure in the previous year of Dr. Campbell, the frontier political officer, and Dr. (Sir John) Hooker, the eminent botanist.

Annexation by lapse. We now turn to the much debated question of Lord Dalhousie's action in relation to the Native States, and the numerous cases in which the doctrine of lapse to the paramount power on failure of heirs was enforced. The doctrine was no new thing, and in every case the annexations actually effected were approved by the Home Government.

The test case is that of Sātārā, the little Marāthā principality in the Western Ghāts created by Lord Hastings in 1819. The Rājā appointed by the Marquess having been deposed in 1839 for treasonable practices, his brother was substituted, and ruled well until his death without heirs in 1848. The Rājā, immediately before his death, had adopted a son without the consent of the paramount power. Everybody was agreed that the son so adopted should inherit the private estate of the deceased. The question whether or not he should succeed to the Rāj was quite a different matter. As far back as 1834 the directors had laid down that the recognition of an adoption as securing a political succession was an indulgence, and that such an 'indulgence should be the exception, not the rule, and should never be granted but as a special mark of favour and approbation'. The principle thus enunciated was extended in 1841 by the decision of the court 'to persevere in the one clear and direct course of abandoning no just and honourable accession of territory or revenue, while all existing claims of right are at the same time scrupulously respected'. The case of Sātārā obviously came within those rules, and the only issue was whether or not it was expedient to apply them.

Lord Dalhousie and almost all the leading officials in India who were consulted concurred in holding that no sufficient reason existed for treating Sātārā as an exception to the rule. The Court of Directors confirmed the action of the Governor-general, saying:

> 'We are fully satisfied that by the general law and custom of India, a dependent principality like that of Sātārā, cannot pass to an adopted heir without the consent of the Paramount Power; that we are under no pledge, direct or constructive, to give such consent; and that the general interests committed to our charge are best consulted by withholding it.'

That clear ruling places on the shoulders of the Home Government the full responsibility for all the cases of annexation by reason of lapse effected by Lord Dalhousie. In one instance only, that of

Karauli in Rājputāna, was his recommendation disallowed; the reason being that Karauli was an ancient Rājpūt principality. Lord Dalhousie, although personally in favour of annexation, did not press his opinion, and expected it to be overruled. He declared that he was 'very well content' with the final decision in the matter'.[1]

Pension of the ex-Pēshwā. The two other principal cases of annexation by lapse, namely those of Nāgpur and Jhānsī, as well as several minor instances, like Jaitpur in Bundēlkhand and Sambalpur in Orissa (now in Central Provinces), were all covered in principle by the Sātārā ruling. The annexation of Oudh in 1856 and the stoppage of the pension of the ex-Pēshwā, after his death in 1852, had nothing whatever to do with the doctrine of lapse. Dhondhū Pant, the adopted son of Bājī Rāo, and afterwards infamous as the Nānā Sahib, was allowed to inherit without question the enormous treasure accumulated by the ex-Pēshwā, and was given a *jāgīr* besides. The extravagant pension of eight lakhs of rupees a year secured by Sir John Malcolm to Bājī Rāo unquestionably was merely a personal allowance for his lifetime. His adopted son's claim to continuance of it was baseless and unreasonable.

Annexation of Oudh. The annexation of Oudh was ordered directly and peremptorily by the Home Government in a mode more drastic than that recommended by Lord Dalhousie, who was then on the eve of departure. He had not time to take all the precautions needed to ensure the safety of the transaction. The refusal of Lord Canning, his successor, to enforce disarmament in Oudh had serious consequences. Dalhousie, who had not been afraid to disarm the Panjāb, would not have shrunk from a similar operation in Oudh, on which he had actually resolved.[2]

Sleeman's opinions. Sir William Sleeman, resident at Lucknow from 1849 to 1856, while convinced that the persistent misgovernment of Oudh should not be allowed to continue, held strong opinions adverse to direct annexation. His words are:

'If our Government interpose, it must not be by negotiation or treaty, but authoritatively on the ground of existing treaties and obligations to the people of Oudh. The treaty of 1837 gives our Government ample authority to take the whole administration on ourselves, in order to secure what we have so often pledged ourselves to secure to the people; but if we do this we must, in order to stand well with the rest of India, honestly and distinctly disclaim all interested motives, and appropriate the whole of the revenues for the benefit of the people and royal family of Oude. . . . Were we to take advantage of the occasion to *annex* or *confiscate* Oude, or any part of it, our good name in India would undoubtedly suffer; and that good name is more valuable to us than a dozen Oudes. . . . We suffered from our conduct in Scinde; but that was a country distant and little known, and linked to the rest of India by few ties of sympathy. . . . It will be otherwise with Oude. Here the giant's strength is manifest, and we cannot

[1] Lee Warner, ii. 173.

[2] *Private Letters*, February 12, 1858, p. 401.

"use it like a giant" without suffering in the estimation of all India. Annexation or confiscation are [*sic*] not compatible with our relations with this little dependent state. . . . I shall recommend that all establishments, military, civil, and fiscal, be kept entirely separate from those of our own Government, that there may be no mistake about the disinterestedness of our intentions towards Oude. . . . By adopting a simple system of administration, to meet the wishes of a simple people, we should secure the goodwill of all classes of society in Oude, and no class would be more pleased with the change than the members of the royal family themselves, who depend upon their stipends for their subsistence, and despair of ever again receiving them under the present Sovereign and system. . . . We have only the right to interpose to secure for the suffering people that better Government which their Sovereign pledged himself to secure for them, but has failed to secure. . . . The native States I consider to be breakwaters, and when they are all swept away we shall be left to the mercy of our native army, which may not always be sufficiently under our control.'

Sleeman appears to have desired that the Government of India should arrange to manage the country by European agency in perpetuity, leaving the surplus revenue to the royal family. He suggested as an alternative that the European management might last only during the minority of the heir apparent, then about eleven years of age, who should be bound on coming of age to govern in accordance with the advice of the resident.[1]

Dalhousie's action. The annexation was actually effected by Sir James Outram, who had succeeded Sleeman as resident early in 1856. Lord Dalhousie, being anxious to secure the appearance of the king's consent, availed himself of the discretion as to the method of procedure allowed by the directors' orders, to offer a treaty, with the intimation that, if it should not be accepted within three days, the resident would assume the government of Oudh. The treaty propounded vested the government of the country in the Company for ever ; guaranteed the royal title to the king and his lawful heirs, with allowances amounting in all to fifteen lakhs of rupees (then 1,500,000 pounds sterling) ; and a limited jurisdiction in the palace and royal parks. On February 7 the king definitely refused to sign the treaty. The annexation was then effected by proclamation without opposition. The trouble which ensued was of later date.

Space fails to justify the decision of the British Government by adducing proofs of the frightful and increasing misrule in Oudh. The ghastly picture is faithfully exhibited in Sleeman's famous book describing his tour in 1849–50. Outram's reports fully confirmed the statements of his predecessor. Nobody who knows the facts can deny the necessity for taking over the administration, but it would have been wiser to follow Sleeman's advice without modification as to the method of effecting the necessary change. Lord Dalhousie certainly made a mistake in trying to extort an ostensible consent from the king, who was right in refusing to set his signature to a sham 'treaty'. The Governor-general

[1] *A Journey*, Private Correspondence, vol. ii, pp. 377–93.

should have proceeded, 'not by negotiation or treaty', but 'authoritatively', as Sleeman rightly advised him.

Berār and the Carnatic. Two other transactions in connexion with the Native States require passing mention. Incessant troubles about the Nizam's payments for the support of the Hyderabad Contingent were settled for a time by an arrangement made in 1853, which assigned Berār with certain adjoining districts, all estimated to pay a revenue of fifty lakhs, in order to provide for the maintenance of the force. The arrangement did not work as smoothly as was expected, and required modification some years later. Difficulties continued to be experienced, and in 1902 the Nizam agreed with Lord Curzon to assign Berār to the Government of India under a perpetual lease, so that it is now, all but in name, part of British India, and is attached to the Central Provinces.

The death of the titular Nawāb of the Carnatic in 1855 gave an opportunity for the revision of the rank and allowances of his family. Careful investigation in England and India satisfied the responsible authorities that the rank of Nawāb, which carried with it a semi-sovereign position, had been held since 1801 by each Nawāb as a purely personal honour, and that Government was not bound to continue it after the death of the holder. Lord Dalhousie, concurring with the Government of Madras, therefore decided on the abolition of the rank of Nawāb, and the abatement of many attendant evils. The present representative of the family is known as Prince of Arcot, and is officially recognized as the premier nobleman in the presidency.

Administration. A large volume would be needed to describe with particulars Lord Dalhousie's incessant, almost feverish activity in supervising every department of the state, and introducing innovations or improvements. He made the machinery of the Supreme Government more workable by getting rid of antiquated survivals in procedure and by arranging the work on a sensible departmental basis. The absurd arrangement by which the Governor-general in person, or in his absence the next senior member of council, administered the provincial government of Bengal, was terminated, and a lieutenant-governor was appointed (1854). A particularly inefficient body called the Military Board, which was supposed to look after public works, was suppressed, and the Department of Public Works (P.W.D.) was constituted nearly in its existing form. The expenditure on public works, which had been on the most niggardly scale, was enormously increased, and works of great magnitude, such as the Grand Trunk Road, were undertaken. Due attention was paid to irrigation canals, especially the Ganges Canal. Lord Dalhousie utilized his English experience as president of the Board of Trade to sketch a well-considered plan of trunk and branch railways, which forms the basis of the existing railway system. The earliest line, a short one from Bombay to Thāna, was opened in 1853. A year later Calcutta was connected with the Rānīganj coal-fields, and a few miles of rails were laid in the Madras presidency. Various difficulties prevented Lord Dalhousie from seeing any more lines open, but preliminary operations on a large scale were proceeding when he retired.

The Governor-general also founded the electric telegraph system, with the help of a clever medical professor of chemistry, named O'Shaughnessy, for whom he obtained a knighthood with much difficulty, because the gentleman was not a member of either the army or the covenanted civil service. The expedients to which O'Shaughnessy was reduced in order to circumvent the innumerable obstacles in his path were very strange. The utterly inefficient postal arrangements which had satisfied 'John Company' were boldly swept away, and the uniform half-anna postal rate was introduced. Before Dalhousie's reforms it cost a rupee to send a letter from Calcutta to Bombay. During several years of Lord Dalhousie's administration the North-Western Provinces, now the Agra Province, were well governed by Mr. James Thomason, who was lieutenant-governor from 1843 to 1853. Thomason warmly supported and in part anticipated the Governor-general in the policy of extensive public works, the promotion of education, the reform of the jail administration, and every other form of activity proper to a government claiming to be civilized. The famous education dispatch sent out by Sir Charles Wood (Lord Halifax) in 1854, which laid the foundation of the existing system of vernacular schools, was thoroughly in accordance with the ideas of both Dalhousie and Thomason. The Governor-general lost no time in giving the fullest possible effect to the instructions sent from England, which had been prepared with the help of Macaulay, Marshman, and other capable advisers.

Last, but not least, the subject of army organization must be mentioned. Lord Dalhousie prepared nine elaborate minutes on the question, which were put on one side at the India House, and scarcely noticed. In fact, two of them were mislaid and could not be traced. Hunter was of opinion that if the advice recorded in those masterly documents had been heeded, it is possible that the Mutiny might not have occurred. But the validity of that opinion is extremely doubtful.

Renewal of Charter, 1853. In 1853 the charter of the East India Company was renewed for the last time, not for any definite period, but during the pleasure of Parliament. The constitution of the Court of Directors was improved, the covenanted civil service was thrown open to competition, and power was taken to appoint a separate provincial government for Bengal.

Lord Dalhousie's achievement. No summary confined to a reasonable space can do justice to the manifold activity of Lord Dalhousie, who never allowed ill health and pain to hinder him from giving all his boundless energy to the service of the state. Many of his actions aroused hostile criticism, often drawing down on his head unmerited abuse. He felt painfully the wounds inflicted by the darts of unfair calumny, but was not moved by the smart to swerve from the path which he had marked out for himself. A saying of his quoted by Hunter has, as that author observes, 'the ring of a great soul'.

'"I circulate these papers;" he wrote hastily on one case in which he had successfully insisted on justice being done at the risk of a tumult, "they are an instance of the principle that we should do what is right without fear of consequences. To fear God and to have no other fear is a maxim of religion, but the truth of it and the wisdom of it are proved day by day in politics."'

Undoubtedly Dalhousie always sought to do what he considered right from his point of view, which did not always command the whole field as seen by others, who were not affected by his limitations. He was a masterful man, and had some of the defects inseparable from his type of character. When it was suggested that he should take office in the ministry at home after leaving India, he explained to his confidential correspondent that various reasons prevented him from accepting any official position, and added: 'Moreover, you have hit another reason. I should never act with other men. It is not (I hope and believe) that I arrogantly insist on my own opinion, but I can't take the same views as other fellows seem to do—in fact, I suppose I am crotchety.' The writer of the last clause did not do himself justice. It is, however, true that he was ill-fitted to work smoothly with colleagues, and a man with temperament so autocratic was bound to make enemies and develop heat in official business. His intellectual power is undeniable; but he worshipped efficiency a little too zealously, and sometimes forgot that even inefficient people have sentiments which need consideration. An unmethodical sentimental person like Sir Henry Lawrence irritated his practical mind intensely. No criticism can alter the fact that Lord Dalhousie must always be allowed a place in the front rank of the Governors-general, by the side of Warren Hastings, Wellesley, and the Marquess of Hastings.

The examination of the question as to how far his policy provoked the Mutiny will be undertaken more conveniently in the next chapter.

CHRONOLOGY

Sir Henry (Lord) Hardinge Governor-general (July)	1844
First Sikh War began; battles of Mudkī and 'Ferozeshah' (December)	1845
Battles of Aliwāl (January) and Sobrāon (February); treaties of Lahore	1846
Successful operations in Hill Tracts of Orissa	1847–54
Lord Dalhousie Governor-general (January); revolt of Mūlrāj; second Sikh War; annexation of Sātārā by lapse	1848
Battles of Chiliānwālā and Gujarāt; annexation of the Panjāb	1849
Penal annexation of part of Sikkim	1850
Second Burmese War; annexation of Pegu	1852
First Indian railway opened; renewal of charter	1853
Sir Charles Wood's education dispatch	1854
Crimean War; many reforms	1854-6
Departure of Lord Dalhousie; Lord Canning Governor-general; annexation of Oudh; death of Lord Hardinge	1856

Authorities

Viscount Hardinge (R. I., 1900) by the second Viscount HARDINGE, who was on his father's staff, contains much matter previously unpublished, and ranks as a primary authority. The standard work on the Sikhs generally is *A History of the Sikhs* by J. D. CUNNINGHAM (1st ed., 1849, suppressed ; 2nd ed., 1853, written largely from the Sikh point of view). It should be read with *Ranjit Singh* by Sir LEPEL GRIFFIN (R. I., 1898), a brilliant and wise little book, which gives the best account of the Mahārāja. Further light is thrown on both the Sikh Wars in *The Sikhs and the Sikh Wars* by General Sir CHARLES GOUGH and A. D. INNES (Innes & Co., 1897) ; and in the *Life and Campaigns of Hugh Gough, Field Marshal, first Viscount*, by R. S. RAIT (1903). The story of the suppression of the Khond horrors is told by Major-General JOHN CAMPBELL in the *Narrative of his Operations in the Hill Tracts of Orissa for the Suppression of Human Sacrifices and Female Infanticide* (London, Hurst & Blackett ; printed for private circulation, 1861).

MARSHMAN devotes much space to the time of Lord Dalhousie. Special books dealing with the subject are : *The Marquess of Dalhousie* (R. I., 1905) by Sir W.W. HUNTER ; the large *Life* by Sir W. LEE WARNER (1904); *Private Letters of the Marquess of Dalhousie*, ed. by J. A. BAIRD (Blackwood, 1910) ; and *The Marquis of Dalhousie's Administration of British India*, by EDWIN ARNOLD (2 vols., Saunders & Otley, 1861). The second Burmese War is treated by Colonel W. F. B. LAURIE in *Our Burmese Wars and Relations with Burma* (Allen, 1880).

Biographical works dealing with the doings of individual officers are too numerous to specify. Two little books on Thomason may be mentioned, namely, *James Thomason*, by Sir W. MUIR (Edinburgh, Clark, 1897); and another with the same title by Sir R. TEMPLE (R. I., 1893).

CHAPTER 5

Lord Canning ; the Mutiny ; the Queen's Proclamation and the passing of the East India Company.

Viscount Canning. Viscount Canning, son of Mr. George Canning who had been Prime Minister in 1827, was in his forty-fourth year when he relieved Lord Dalhousie on the last day of February 1856, and had had considerable political experience as a member of Parliament and a minister, his last office being that of postmaster-general. Lord Dalhousie, although rather more guarded in his farewell utterances than some of his predecessors had been, was disposed to believe that all was well in India, and that his successor would enjoy a peaceful time. Even the dangerous annexation of Oudh had been effected quietly without any serious opposition.

No prevision of the Mutiny. The outgoing Governor-general certainly had not the slightest prevision of the storm that was to break in May, and naturally had not made any arrangements to meet it. Although Lord Dalhousie had displayed anxious forethought in the preparations for the Burmese War, and had organized admirably the supply and transport services, he was not a military genius. His minutes on army organization, which have been mentioned, were mainly directed to the purpose of maintaining in India an adequate proportion of European troops. He deplored and resisted as far as he could the orders from home which required him to send a considerable portion of his small European garrison to China and Persia. So far his views were perfectly sound, but he must share with his predecessors the censure due for permitting the continuance of a most dangerous military situation in India. He had not taken any precautions to protect the enormous store of munitions at Delhi, which was left in the hands of the native army, or to secure the essential strategical position of Allahabad. Whatever thought was devoted to military preparation in India was directed to the Panjāb. Everywhere else the old haphazard distribution of the troops continued, and nobody, military or civil, seems to have realized the obvious perils incurred.

LORD CANNING.

Crimean, Persian, and Chinese Wars. Those perils were much aggravated by the wars in which Great Britain was involved in 1856. The Crimean War came to an end in March, but in the closing months of that year India was drawn by Palmerstonian policy into a connexion with two wars which did not properly concern her, and both of which were unnecessary. Under orders from the Home Government, which had taken alarm at the occupation of Herat by Persia, an expedition under Sir James Outram was sent from Bombay to the Persian Gulf in October, and did not return until March 1857. The high-handed action of the representatives of Great Britain in China brought on hostilities over a trifling incident in November, which lasted with certain interruptions until 1860. British troops proceeding to India were then ordered to go round by China, and help in the operations at Canton. The knowledge that the English were engaged in so many wars, and that the proportion of European troops in India was dangerously low, while the most important strategical points in the interior were in sepoy hands,[1] fostered

[1] The Delhi arsenal contained not less than 300 guns and mortars, 20,000 stands of arms, 200,000 shot and shell, and an enormous quantity

the unrest which then prevailed in the native army, and to a considerable extent among the general population. The circumstances of the time were favourable to designs of rebellion against the foreigners, who seemed to be weaker than usual.

Discontent in native army. Long before 1856 Lord William Bentinck had denounced the sepoy army as being the most expensive and inefficient in the world. Many incidents proved its deterioration, and the constant extension of frontiers involved the service of the men in strange countries which they disliked. While serving in such places they expected extra allowances, and whenever difficulty was experienced in satisfying their claims mutinies occurred. At least four mutinies are recorded during the thirteen years preceding the great explosion; the regiments concerned being the 34th N.I. in 1844, the 22nd N.I. in 1849, the 66th N.I. in 1850, and the 38th N.I. in 1852. Lord Canning in his first year of office directed that all recruits for the Bengal army should be attested, like the Madras sepoys, with an obligation to serve wherever required. Although the change did not directly affect the men already in the ranks it was unpopular, because the service was to a large extent hereditary and movements by sea endangered caste.

Strength of army. On May 10, 1857, the strength of the Company's army in India, including Pegu, was 238,002 of all ranks, of whom 38,000, or 19 per cent. (including officers of the native army), were Europeans, the remainder 200,002 being natives of the country. The strength of the Bengal Army, which alone revolted to a serious extent, was 151,361, comprising 22,698 Europeans and 128,663 Indians. About 40,000 troops were in the Panjāb beyond the Sutlaj, including 8,631 Europeans, besides 11,049 in the Cis-Sutlaj districts, including 4,790 Europeans. Thus 13,421 Europeans were concentrated in the Panjāb and Cis-Sutlaj territories.[1]

The proportion of British troops in the region now called the United Provinces of Agra and Oudh was extremely small, while the strategical points and most of the guns were left in the hands of the native army. No European force existed in Bengal and Bihār, except at Calcutta and at Dinapore near Patna. It is astonishing that successive Governors-general and commanders-in-chief should have been content to allow the continuance of such a dangerous distribution.

Lax army discipline. The state of discipline in the native, and especially in the Bengal army, had sunk very low, largely owing to the inveterate Bengal practice of promoting both British and Indian officers by strict seniority and retaining them long

of other material. The only Europeans employed were a few officers and non-commissioned officers of the Ordnance Department. The palace enclosure was inhabited by about 12,000 discontented dependants of the titular emperor. The key position of Allahabad was treated with similar carelessness.

[1] The figures are given by G. D. (see Authorities *post*), p. 731.

after they had become useless.[1] General Godwin, for instance, who commanded in the second Burmese War, was seventy years of age, and Sūbadārs of forty or even fifty years' service were not uncommon. About 40,000 of the men came from Oudh, and with the native officers formed close family parties subversive of discipline. The large percentage of Brahmans recruited fostered the caste spirit to a mischievous extent. Other causes contributed to the laxity of discipline, which it would be tedious to expound. The fact of the laxity is certain.

Unrest of civil population. It is equally certain that the minds of the civil population of all classes and ranks, Hindus and Muhammadans, princes and people, were agitated and disturbed by feelings of uneasiness and vague apprehension. The disturbance of sentiment was not manifested by insurrections, as the discontent of the army had been signalled by mutinies, but events showed clearly that men's minds had been long unsettled. The ruling classes were rendered uneasy by the numerous escheats and annexations. They knew nothing about subtle distinctions of 'dependent' or 'subordinate' states, and the like, which filled so large a space in the correspondence between the Government of India and the Home authorities. They simply saw that principality after principality was escheated and annexed for one reason or another, so that no ruler of a native state felt safe. Every one of the escheats, lapses, and annexations which marked the eight years of Lord Dalhousie's rule could be justified by sound arguments and the general principles enunciated by the Government in England; but the pace was too fast, and the cumulative effect of the transactions was profoundly unsettling. The introduction of British law and the revenue settlements with village zemindars diminished everywhere the authority of the classes accustomed to rule their estates and chieftainships as petty autocrats; and the establishment of general internal peace threw multitudes out of employment. The annexation of Oudh, in particular, let loose swarms of unemployed men in various ranks. When Outram was obliged to take leave the chief commissionership at Lucknow unfortunately was given by Lord Canning to Mr. Coverley Jackson, a man of violent and overbearing disposition, who quarrelled incessantly with his colleagues, especially with Mr. Gubbins, the equally hot-tempered judicial commissioner. The administration took too little heed of the susceptibilities of the great landholders, and Lord Canning's refusal to disarm Oudh left abundance of weapons in every village.

Both the army and the civil population were pervaded by fear that the Government intended to make everybody Christians, as the old Muhammadan governments had often manufactured 'converts' wholesale.[2] The Indian people, as a rule, do not

[1] In Madras and Bombay the native officers were promoted by selection.

[2] 'Never were the natives more grievously mistaken than they have been in adopting the notion foisted on them by designing and ambitious men—that their religion was at stake; for that notion I believe to have

bother about doctrines. They recognize as a Muhammadan any circumcised person, who is willing to repeat the short Muslim formula and to submit to the external conditions of Muslim life. Hinduism, of which caste is the essential institution, does not trouble about any man's beliefs, but public opinion insists that every man should follow the *dharma*, or Law of Duty, of his caste. Christians had no caste, and no regard for the rules of ceremonial purity and diet, whether Muslim or Hindu. Popular opinion regarded as a *Kristān* (Christian) anybody who was prepared to eat beef or pork indifferently, and consume strong drink without scruple, while disregarding all the conventions about ablutions and ceremonial which Hindus and Muhammadans, each in their own way, hold dear. Many circumstances conduced to the widespread apprehension that the people were to be made Christians. Missionary activity was largely increased and openly favoured by powerful officials, especially in the Panjāb. The introduction of European improvements, railways, telegraphs, and the like, which now are accepted as part of the natural order of things, was a shock to the people of the middle of the nineteenth century, and seemed to portend a general Europeanization, which was considered to be much the same thing as general Christianization. It would be easy to elaborate the subject at much greater length, and to adduce other causes which contributed to fill the powder magazine in which the sepoy mutiny of May 1857 exploded.

Greased cartridges. The introduction of the Enfield rifle, one of the necessary reforms effected by Lord Hardinge, while commander-in-chief in England, led directly to the explosion. An ill-considered regulation directed the sepoys to bite the end of the cartridge, and in January 1857 reports were made that the sepoys believed the cartridges to be greased with cows' and pigs' fat for the express purpose of destroying their caste and making them all Christians. At first the alarm was believed by the Indian authorities to be wholly unfounded, but subsequent inquiry proved that the fat of cows or oxen really had been used at Woolwich, and that in consequence the men would have lost caste by biting cartridges so greased.[1] The regulation demanding that the end of the cartridge should be bitten was rescinded, directions were given that ready greased cartridges should not be issued, liberty being allowed to the men to make their own arrangements, and elaborate explanations and assurances were freely promulgated. But it was all of no use. The terror had seized the minds of the whole army, and the men would not believe the assurances of their officers or the Government.

Chupatties and lotus-flowers. The general unrest was indicated by the mysterious *chupatties*, or griddle-cakes, which began to circulate from village to village about the middle of 1856,

been at the root of the late rebellion' (Baboo Ramgopal Ghose, quoted by G. D., p. 612).

[1] 'On this inflammable material, the too true story of the cartridges fell as a spark on dry tinder' (Sir C. Aitchison, *Lord Lawrence*, p. 76).

and the similar circulation of lotus-flowers which went on at the same time, but among the regiments only.

'A messenger would come to a village, seek out the headman or village elder, give him six chupatties and say: "These six cakes are sent to you; you will make six others, and send them on to the next village." The headman accepted the six cakes, and punctually sent forward other six as he had been directed.'

Nobody could say where the transmission of the *chupatties* began. Some witnesses opined that it started near Delhi; others, perhaps with greater probability, thought the arrangement originated in Oudh. The process continued for many months.

'It was a common occurrence for a man to come to a cantonment with a lotus-flower, and give it to the chief native officer of a regiment; the flower was circulated from hand to hand in the regiment; each man took it, looked at it, and passed it on, saying nothing. When the lotus came to the last man in the regiment, he disappeared for a time, and took it to the next military station. This strange process occurred throughout nearly all the military stations where regiments of the Bengal native army were cantoned.'[1]

The exact meaning of the symbols used for such cryptic messages was never divined. The Indian Government of those days had no organized secret service or intelligence department; but even if such an institution had existed probably it would have been baffled. All the resources of modern detective agencies were unable to explain the 'tree-daubing' mystery which accompanied the cow-killing agitation in the eastern districts of the United Provinces in my own time. I often tried to obtain a reasonable explanation, without success.

Beginning of the Mutiny. On January 23, 1857, the troops at Dumdum near Calcutta openly displayed their aversion to the cartridges. On March 29, at Barrackpore, the adjutant of the 34th N.I. was cut down on the parade-ground by a Brahman sepoy, his comrades looking on without stirring, except one, a Muhammadan named Shaikh Paltū, who gallantly ran to defend his officer. The necessary punishments followed. Meantime the growing excitement among the sepoys was marked by numerous incendiary fires at Barrackpore. During March and April twenty-five similar fires occurred at distant Umballa, on the border of the Panjāb. At Meerut the men of the 3rd Cavalry refused the cartridges, and on May 3 the 7th Oudh Infantry mutinied at Lucknow. Eighty-five of the cavalry mutineers at Meerut having been sentenced to long terms of imprisonment, their sentences were promulgated at a special parade on Saturday, May 9. Next day, Sunday, while evening service was being held, the cavalry and two infantry regiments broke open the jail, released their comrades, burnt the officers' houses, murdered every European on whom they could lay hands, and hurried off to Delhi. The beginning of the Mutiny is usually counted from that day, May 10.

[1] G. D., pp. 35, 36.

General Hewitt, the imbecile officer commanding at Meerut, did nothing, although he had 2,200 European soldiers at his disposal. He made no attempt to pursue the mutineers, who reached Delhi early on Monday morning, and soon made themselves masters of the city and palace. All Europeans whom the rebels could find—men, women, and children—were ruthlessly massacred. Happily a gallant telegraph operator was just in time to telegraph the news to Lahore, and so warn the authorities in the Panjāb. Lieutenant Willoughby, the officer in charge of the magazine, supported by eight brave comrades, defended the position against a raging mob for several hours, and, when it was impossible to hold out longer, blew up the place. The tremendous explosion killed large numbers of the assailants, and destroyed a considerable part of the munitions, but unfortunately much remained. The mutineers, who were quickly joined by other regiments and by all the disorderly elements in the city and neighbourhood, proclaimed the restoration of the Mogul Empire, and placed the aged titular emperor, Bahādur Shāh, on his throne. They showed him little respect, and such government as existed appears to have been administered by the military leaders. The disorders rapidly spread over the Agra Province, then known as the North-Western Provinces, which soon became 'a sea of anarchy', from which all control had vanished. Murder, burning, and plundering raged unchecked in almost every district. The presence of six hundred European troops enabled the lieutenant-governor, Mr. John Colvin, who had succeeded Mr. Thomason, to retain possession of the fort at Agra, the capital.

On June 8 a few thousand troops from Umballa, reinforced from Meerut, took up a position to the north of Delhi on the Ridge, a low and narrow eminence of sandstone rock which is the northernmost spur of the Āravalli Range, running along the western side of the city, and beyond it in a direction slightly east of north until it reaches the bank of the Jumna. Lack of numbers and of heavy artillery rendered the capture of Delhi impossible until the arrival of additional troops and a siege train from the Panjāb, collected by the skill and energy of Sir John Lawrence and his colleagues, gave reasonable hopes of success. On September 14 the Kashmīr gate was blown in. In the course of a few days the whole city was occupied and the rebels were driven forth in headlong flight. The joy of the victors was marred by the death of John Nicholson, the most renowned of the many heroes of the siege and storm. All India had watched breathlessly for the fate of the ancient capital. Its fall was the turning-point of the Mutiny. From that date the ultimate success of the British Government was no longer in doubt, and the waverers, who had held back while the issue was doubtful, hastened to render aid to the Government. Much hard fighting had to be done and much suffering endured before peace and order could be fully restored. That end was not attained until late in 1859. The Cis-Sutlaj Sikh chiefs and their retainers gave gallant and loyal help in the retaking of Delhi and afterwards.

Five areas of operations. The military operations during the Mutiny years, 1857–9, which took place in several distinct areas, do not admit of brief relation in a continuous narrative. The serious fighting was mostly confined to the North-Western Provinces, in which Delhi was then included, and to Central India with Bundēlkhand. Within those limits five areas may be distinguished, namely : (1) Delhi, where the capture of the city was the end of operations on a large scale ; (2) Lucknow ; (3) Cawnpore : (4) Rohilkhand ; and (5) Central India with Bundēlkhand.

Lucknow. At Lucknow, Sir Henry Lawrence, who had replaced Mr. Jackson as chief commissioner, was obliged to retire at the beginning of July into the residency with all the European and Christian population, and a small force of loyal sepoys. Sir Henry Lawrence having been killed early in the siege, the command was taken over by Brigadier Inglis. The defence was maintained with extraordinary courage and resource against swarms of assailants until September 25, when Outram and Havelock forced their way in after desperate fighting, bringing a much needed reinforcement and rendering possible an extension of the position. The final relief was deferred until November 15–17, when Sir Colin Campbell, who had been sent out from England, as commander-in-chief, succeeded in overcoming fierce opposition, and in entering the city. On November 23 the British evacuated Lucknow, which could not be held by the small numbers available. In March 1858 three weeks of incessant conflict made Sir Colin Campbell master of the city. The back of the Oudh rebellion was thus broken. The remnants of the rebel regiments in the province were gradually surrounded by Lord Clyde (Sir Colin Campbell) during the autumn of 1858, and driven across the frontier into Nepāl, where most of them perished miserably.

Cawnpore. At Cawnpore, General Sir Hugh Wheeler commanding the station, who was seventy-five years of age, made a grievous mistake by refusing to occupy the strong magazine, which was easily capable of effective defence.[1] He relied with astounding folly on a weak entrenchment about two hundred yards square, constructed in an open parade-ground, and enclosing two barracks, one of which was thatched. The rampart, 'a fence not high enough to keep out an active cow', as Trevelyan observes, was a mere field dike four or five feet in height made of loose earth, which had not been consolidated. Behind such a mockery of defences the gallant garrison, consisting of about four hundred men capable of bearing arms, and a multitude of women, children, and helpless people, in all nearly a thousand, held out with astonishing endurance for twenty days from June 7 to 27, when a capitulation was arranged. Bājī Rāo's adopted son, Dhondhū Pant, commonly called the Nānā Sahib, who resided in a palace at Bithūr, near Cawnpore, and had always pretended to be on the most friendly terms with his European neighbours, had assumed the

[1] Trevelyan, p. 115. The magazine was blown up by the rebels when evacuating Cawnpore (ibid., p. 354).

THE RESIDENCY, LUCKNOW.
(Before the Mutiny.)

command of the rebels. He promised solemnly to convey the garrison safely to Allahabad, but shamelessly and pitilessly massacred the whole, save a very few who escaped in various ways. Most of them were shot down at the river side, where boats had been collected on pretence of conveying the victims to Allahabad. About two hundred women and children were confined in a small building known as the Bībīghar, and hacked to death on the night of July 15 by express orders of the Nānā and his colleague Tantia Topi. The relieving force under Havelock, which entered Cawnpore on the 17th and drove the Nānā out, was just too late to prevent one of the most atrocious crimes on record. The justly

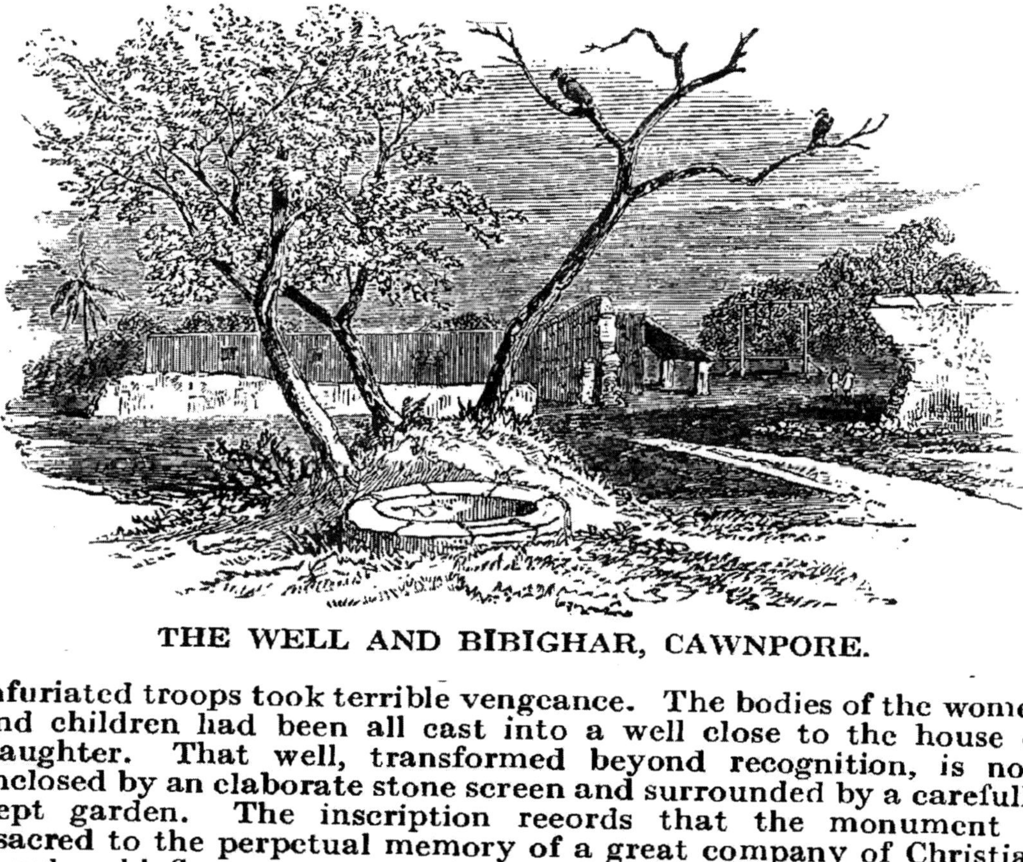

THE WELL AND BĪBĪGHAR, CAWNPORE.

infuriated troops took terrible vengeance. The bodies of the women and children had been all cast into a well close to the house of slaughter. That well, transformed beyond recognition, is now enclosed by an elaborate stone screen and surrounded by a carefully kept garden. The inscription records that the monument is 'sacred to the perpetual memory of a great company of Christian people, chiefly women and children'. The exact number of the 'great company' never can be known.[1]

The Nānā, who had proclaimed himself as Pēshwā, deliberately aimed at the extermination of all Europeans and Christians, with their friends and associates. His savage slaughter of women

[1] Trevelyan states the number confined in the Bībighar as 206, including five men. The *I. G.* (ii. 512) gives the tale of women and children butchered as 125. Shepherd provides incomplete lists of names. One lady was carried off alive. The five men were killed separately.

and children was an essential feature of his policy. During his few days of rule at Cawnpore numerous other murders were committed besides the two massacres on a large scale above mentioned. The horrors of Cawnpore, a 'memory of fruitless valour and unutterable woe', surpass by far those which occurred at any other station.

The military operations at and about Cawnpore, which were closely associated with the movements for the relief and capture of Lucknow, were too complicated to admit of summary description. The Gwālior Contingent, which had rebelled, defeated General Windham and occupied Cawnpore on November 27 and 28. Sir Colin Campbell recovered the town on December 6.

Rohilkhand. At Bareilly, the capital of Rohilkhand, the sepoys mutinied on the last day of May 1857. Khān Bahādur Khān, a grandson of Hāfiz Rahmat Khān, slain in the Rohilla War of Warren Hastings, was proclaimed governor under the title of Nawāb Nāzim. He retained power for nearly a year until the city was reoccupied by the British under the command of Sir Colin Campbell (Lord Clyde) in May 1858. During the interval several rebel chiefs, including for a time the Nānā, had taken refuge in Bareilly. The Nawāb of Rāmpur, notwithstanding his kinship with Khān Bahādur, and the purely Muhammadan character of the local rebellion, maintained throughout unswerving loyalty to the British Government. His services received due recognition after the suppression of the disturbances.

Central India and Bundēlkhand. The operations in Central India and Bundēlkhand were protracted and difficult, executed throughout in country which presented obstacles of every kind. The task of clearing the enemy out of that region was entrusted to Sir Hugh Rose (Lord Strathnairn), a general of division in the Bombay army, supported by a distinct force from Madras under Brigadier Whitlock. The brilliant operations of the small army under Sir Hugh Rose, only about 4,500 strong in all, including four sepoy regiments, were summarized by Lord Derby in these words :

> 'In five months the Central India Field Force traversed 1,085 miles, crossed numerous large rivers, took upwards of 150 pieces of artillery, one entrenched camp, two fortified cities, and two fortresses all strongly defended, fought sixteen actions, captured twenty forts; and never sustained a check against the most warlike and determined enemy, led by the most capable commanders then to be found in any part of India.'

The merit of that wonderful record is enhanced when it is remembered that most of the operations were conducted in extreme heat, deadly to the European soldier, and distressing to men of any race. Sir Hugh Rose himself experienced sunstroke five times. Although the fighting on several occasions was desperate, the sun probably caused losses to the Field Force greater than those inflicted by the enemy.

The Rānī of Jhānsī. At the beginning of June 1857 the native troops had mutinied at Jhānsī. On the 7th of that month they committed a perfidious massacre of the Europeans, men, women, and children, comparable in wickedness with the slaughter at Cawnpore, but on a smaller scale. Three days later Rānī Lakshmī Bāī, a young woman twenty years of age, principal widow of the late Rājā Gangādhar Rāo, was proclaimed ruler of the state which Lord Dalhousie had annexed as a lapse. The Rānī was supported by Gangā Bāī, another consort of the deceased prince. It is uncertain whether or not Lakshmī Bāī was privy to the massacre which preceded her assumption of authority. When she had been installed, she certainly proved herself to be a resolute and bitter enemy of the British Government, earning from Sir Hugh Rose the compliment that she was the 'best and bravest' of the rebel leaders. She showed courage far superior to that of Tantia Topi, the Nānā's general, with whom she co-operated. She was left undisturbed until 1858, when Sir Hugh Rose advanced to attack her.

Tantia Topi. Leaving Indore at the beginning of 1858 he advanced northwards, fighting his way, and early in February relieved the garrison of Sāgar (Saugor), which had held out for more than seven months. After a siege lasting a fortnight Jhānsī was taken in April; a large force under Tantia Topi which attempted to relieve the fortress having been beaten off. Kālpi, the principal arsenal of the rebels, fell in May. The Rānī and her ally then retired on Gwālior. By a bold stroke they occupied that important stronghold, and compelled Sindia, who had remained loyal, to take refuge at Agra. In June the Rānī, wearing male attire and fighting bravely, was killed by a Hussar, and Gwālior was recovered by a specially gallant feat of arms. Tantia Topi became a hunted fugitive, until, in April 1859, his career was ended on the gallows. Although he stoutly denied that either he himself or his chief the Nānā was responsible for the Cawnpore massacres, the guilt of both was established by a mass of testimony. During the year 1859 order was gradually restored.

The leading military events of the Mutiny campaigns have been indicated in the foregoing pages, but many subsidiary operations took place in Rājputāna and elsewhere. A rising in Bihār is remembered for the glorious defence of a small house at Arrah by a few Englishmen and loyal Sikhs against a host of rebels. The Bombay presidency, under the competent rule of Lord Elphinstone, kept quiet on the whole; although in the Marāthā country the excitement was dangerous, and at Kolhāpur (Kolapore) developed into open mutiny, which was quickly suppressed. In the Madras presidency no serious disturbance occurred.

The Native or Protected and friendly States. The rulers of all the larger native or protected states remained faithful, even when their troops showed signs of disaffection or revolted. Intelligent ministers able to read the signs of the times and to appreciate the reserves of strength at the disposal of the Government preserved from ruin the states under their administration. The services of Sir Dinkur Rāo at Gwālior and Sir Sālār Jang at Hyderabad were particularly memorable. Jung Bahādur, the powerful minister and real ruler of independent Nepāl, declared openly for the British, and sent troops who gave effective help in the restoration of order. The inestimable aid given by the Sikh chiefs has been already mentioned. Dōst Muhammad, the Amīr of Kābul, adhered to his treaty obligations, and resisted the temptation to regain Peshāwar.

SIR JUNG BAHĀDUR.

Reserves of British strength. The Home Government showed no remissness in sending out reinforcements, which were collected from every quarter, including China. Some came by the overland route across Egypt, but many had to come round the Cape. The close of the foolish little war with Persia fortunately enabled the Government of India to utilize the troops set free from the Persian adventure. The defence of the empire was materially simplified by the long lines of telegraph constructed under Lord Dalhousie's orders. The few miles of railway in existence at the beginning of the disturbances were not of much military use ; but, before the troubles came to an end, important lines had been constructed up-country which facilitated the extinction of the smouldering embers of rebellion. The sepoys, and even the Nānā and some other people who should have known better, were silly enough to imagine that they could destroy the British Empire in India by massacring all Europeans or Christians within their reach. They wholly failed to understand the latent strength of a great European nation holding command of the sea, and in their ignorance rushed blindly upon destruction. The rebel proclamations conclusively prove the intensity of the delusions cherished by the insurgents.

Partial popular rebellion. The rising, although primarily a military mutiny of the Bengal army, immediately provoked by the greased cartridges, was not confined to the troops. Discontent and unrest, as has been explained, were widely prevalent among the civil population, and in several places, as, for instance, at Sahāranpur and Muzaffarnagar, the populace rose before the sepoys at those stations mutinied. The vague fear that the

Government meditated the forcible conversion of the people to Christianity, as they understood the term, had penetrated into the villages and disposed men's minds to rebellion. The disorderly elements in the population naturally took advantage of the disturbances caused by the dread of interference with religion, and utilized the opportunity for mere pillage. In a large part of the North-Western Provinces, in the districts where Muhammadans are numerous and the influence of the Delhi court was strongly felt, the revolt took a Muslim colour, and assumed to some extent, especially at Bareilly, the character of a holy war against the infidel. Persons whose experience was confined to that region often erroneously assumed that the rebellion was the result of a Muhammadan conspiracy. But elsewhere the revolt was more Hindu than Muhammadan. The Nānā, who had no desire to become a subject of the Pādshāh, proclaimed himself Pēshwā, and sought to restore the Hindu Marāthā empire. During the first few days of his brief rule at Cawnpore he even ventured to cut off the hands of a Muhammadan butcher who had slaughtered a cow in the course of his business, and by that act forfeited all hopes of cordial Muhammadan support. The Rānī of Jhānsī seems to have fought as a strict Hindu for her own hand. The special circumstances of Oudh caused a general rebellion in that province, without distinction of creed. Very few of the large landholders remained loyal. The jealousy between Hindus and Muhammadans, the political rivalry between Pēshwā and Pādshāh, and innumerable animosities of various kinds so divided the rebels everywhere that they never were able to combine effectually for the execution of a well-considered plan. The campaigns degenerated into a bewildering maze of local risings, massacres, sieges, attacks, and reprisals, indescribable except by means of interminable detail. No leader of considerable capacity arose among the rebels, who never had the remotest chance of ultimate success against the forces of an organized government.

Good and evil. The two years of disturbance were marked by many deeds of horror, by infinite suffering, and not a few acts on both sides which it is painful to recall. On the other page of the account may be reckoned uncounted deeds of heroism, and numerous instances of loyalty, kindness, and unselfish devotion which do honour to human nature.

The last of the Moguls. Bahādur Shāh, the aged titular emperor, was throughout only a tool in the hands of his sons and the leaders of the rebel soldiery, powerless for good or evil, and not fully responsible for the acts of the men who professed to be his subjects—the mere shadow of a king. On September 21, after the fall of Delhi, he was arrested by Lieutenant Hodson, head of the Intelligence Department, with the promise that his life would be spared. In January 1858 he was brought to trial, and after two months' investigation was condemned to exile.

The old man was sent down to Calcutta, and thence to Rangoon, where he died in 1862, at the age of eighty-seven. On the day after the surrender of the emperor, his two sons and a grandson were arrested at the same place, Humāyūn's mausoleum. No promise to spare their lives was given. Hodson, who had only a small force with him, carried them off in the face of an excited mob, and on the way shot them dead with his own hand. His act has been the occasion of much bitter controversy. The evidence seems to point to the conclusion that in all probability it would

BAHĀDUR SHĀH II.
(The last of the Moguls.)

have been feasible to prevent a rescue and to carry the princes safely to Delhi for formal trial. If that view be correct, and it is open to dispute, Hodson's passionate action was at the best unnecessary and unseemly. His victims undoubtedly had been concerned in the massacre of Europeans, and if they had been arraigned certainly would have forfeited their lives.

Thus ended the dynasty of Akbar.

The slayer of the princes was killed at Lucknow in March 1858.

The Delhi territory. The recovery of Delhi having been mainly due to the unremitting exertions of John Lawrence and his brilliant officers, the Governor-general deemed it fitting that the imperial city with the surrounding territory should be placed under the government of the man who had reclaimed it from the grasp of the rebels. The Delhi territory accordingly was transferred, in February 1858, from the control of the government of the North-Western Provinces to that of the Panjāb. Since the beginning of 1912, when the official capital of India was moved from Calcutta to Delhi, the group of ancient cities, enlarged by the addition of a new imperial city, and associated with a small adjacent district, has been committed to the charge of a chief commissioner directly subordinate to the Government of India.

The Mutiny a fortunate occurrence. Sir Lepel Griffin ventured to affirm that 'Perhaps a more fortunate occurrence than the Mutiny of 1857 never occurred in India'. The saying, which may seem to be a hard one, suggests so much that it might be made the text on which to build a treatise. If we can place ourselves, so far as may be, in the attitude of a general who knowingly sends thousands of men to their death, counting their lives well bestowed to serve a worthy cause, and can close our eyes to the horrors of Cawnpore and a hundred other scenes, the hard saying may be understood and accepted as true. The ultimate explanation of the Mutiny and partial rebellion of the people, expressed in general terms without regard to specific grievances, is that the movement was a revolt of the old against the new, of Indian conservatism against aggressive European innovation. The conflict between the old ideas and the new had to be fought out somehow; and the inevitable fight, if it had not been begun in 1857 on the issue of the greased cartridges, was bound to have been started a year or two later on some other pretext. A conflict so momentous could not be decided without infinite suffering and copious shedding of blood.

The Mutiny, to continue the quotation,

'swept the Indian sky clear of many clouds. It disbanded a lazy, pampered army, which, though in its hundred years of life it had done splendid service, had become impossible; it replaced an unprogressive, selfish, and commercial system of administration[1] by one liberal and enlightened; and it attached the Sikh people to their rulers, and made them what they are to-day (1898), the surest support of the Government. Lastly, it taught India and the world that the English possessed a courage and national spirit which made light of disaster, which never counted whether the odds against them were two or ten to one; and which marched confident to victory, although the conditions of success appeared all but hopeless.'

The death of the Company. The shock of the news of the revolt, which brought sorrow and mourning into so many homes, roused the Government and people of England to a sense of their responsibility for British rule in India, and gave the deathblow

[1] Rather a harsh description of the Company's administration after 1833.

to the antiquated system which interposed the mechanism of the East India Company between the Crown and the Indian Empire. The day for that mechanism, which had done good work in its appointed time, was past. In January 1858 the Company put the case for their administration before Parliament and the nation by means of a petition expressed in stately, dignified language, which produced little appreciable effect upon public opinion. Another equally able document followed in April, and a third in June, without result. The directors put their claims to favourable consideration on high ground, boldly averring

'that your petitioners . . . do not seek to vindicate themselves at the expense of any other authority; they claim their full share of the responsi-

EAST INDIA HOUSE, 1858.

bility of the manner in which India has practically been governed. That responsibility is to them not a subject of humiliation, but of pride. They are conscious that their advice and initiative have been, and have deserved to be, a great and potent element in the conduct of affairs in India. And they feel complete assurance that the more attention is bestowed, and the more light is thrown upon India and its administration, the more evident it will become that the government in which they have borne a part, has been not only one of the purest in intention, but one of the most beneficent in act, ever known among mankind; that during the last and present generations in particular, it has been, in all departments, one of the most rapidly improving governments in the world; and that, at the time when this change is proposed, a greater number of important improvements are in a state of rapid progress than at any former period. And they are satisfied that whatever further improvements may be hereafter effected in India, can only consist in the development of germs already planted, and in building on foundations already laid, under their authority, and in a great measure by their express instructions.'

The well-phrased periods fell on deaf ears. The Bill finally approved by the Conservative Cabinet easily passed through both Houses, in spite of the opposition of Lord Ellenborough, and on August 2 received the royal assent as 'An Act for the Better Government of India' (21st and 22nd of Victoria, cap. 106). On the first day of September the Court of Directors held 'its last solemn assembly', and the East India Company issued 'its last instructions to its servants in the East'; and offered to its Sovereign an empire in these touching words, worthy of a great occasion:

'Let Her Majesty appreciate the gift—let her take the vast country and the teeming millions of India under her direct control; but let her not forget the great corporation from which she has received them, nor the lessons to be learned from its success.'[1]

Compliment to the services. The generous language in which the ancient Company took leave of its servants deserves quotation:

'The Company has the great privilege of transferring to the service of Her Majesty such a body of civil and military officers as the world has never seen before. A government cannot be base, cannot be feeble, cannot be wanting in wisdom, that has reared two such services as the civil and military services of the Company. To those services the Company has always been just, has always been generous. In those services lowly merit has never been neglected. The best men have risen to the highest place. They may have come from obscure farmhouses or dingy places of business; they may have been roughly nurtured and rudely schooled; they may have landed in the country without sixpence or a single letter of recommendation in their trunks; but if they have had the right stuff in them, they have made their way to eminence, and have distanced men of the highest connections and most flattering antecedents.'[2]

The Act established the Government of India in its still existing form (1918). The President of the Board of Control was replaced by the Secretary of State for India, and the expert advice formerly obtained from the directors was provided for by the establishment of the council of India, a body consisting largely of retired high officials.

The East India Company continued as the shadow of a great name to retain a formal existence until 1874 for the purpose of financial liquidation in accordance with the Charter Act of 1833.

The Queen's proclamation. The transfer of the government to the Crown was announced on November 1, 1858, to the princes and peoples of India by a proclamation read at Allahabad and other principal stations. The manifesto, which was admirably drafted, owed some of its merits to suggestions made by Her Majesty. The text is as follows:

Victoria, by the Grace of God of the United Kingdom of Great Britain and Ireland, and of the Colonies and Dependencies thereof

[1] The full text of the documents is printed by G. D. in his Appendix, with a careful abstract of the provisions of the Act.

[2] G. D., p. 575.

in Europe, Asia, Africa, America, and Australasia, Queen, Defender of the Faith.

Whereas, for divers weighty reasons, we have resolved, by and with the advice and consent of the Lords Spiritual and Temporal, and Commons, in Parliament assembled, to take upon ourselves the government of the territories in India, heretofore administered in trust for us by the Honourable East India Company.

Now, therefore, we do by these presents notify and declare that, by the advice and consent aforesaid, we have taken upon ourselves the said government; and we hereby call upon all our subjects within the said territories to be faithful, and to bear true allegiance to us, our heirs and successors, and to submit themselves to the authority of those whom we may hereafter, from time to time, see fit to appoint to administer the government of our said territories, in our name and on our behalf.

And we, reposing especial trust and confidence in the loyalty, ability, and judgement of our right trusty and well-beloved cousin Charles John, Viscount Canning, do hereby constitute and appoint him, the said Viscount Canning, to be our first Viceroy and Governor-General in and over our said territories, and to administer the government thereof in our name, and generally to act in our name and on our behalf, subject to such orders and regulations as he shall, from time to time, receive through one of our Principal Secretaries of State.

And we do hereby confirm in their several offices, civil and military, all persons now employed in the service of the Honourable East India Company, subject to our future pleasure, and to such laws and regulations as may hereafter be enacted.

We hereby announce to the native princes of India, that all treaties and engagements made with them by or under the authority of the East India Company are by us accepted, and will be scrupulously maintained, and we look for the like observance on their part.

We desire no extension of our present territorial possessions; and, while we will permit no aggression upon our dominions or our rights to be attempted with impunity, we shall sanction no encroachment on those of others.

We shall respect the rights, dignity, and honour of native princes as our own; and we desire that they, as well as our own subjects, should enjoy that prosperity and that social advancement which can only be secured by internal peace and good government.

We hold ourselves bound to the natives of our Indian territories by the same obligations of duty which bind us to all our other subjects, and those obligations, by the blessing of Almighty God, we shall faithfully and conscientiously fill.

Firmly relying ourselves on the truth of Christianity, and acknowledging with gratitude the solace of religion, we disclaim alike the right and the desire to impose our convictions on any of our subjects. We declare it to be our royal will and pleasure that none be in any wise favoured, none molested or disquieted, by reason of their religious faith or observances, but that all shall alike enjoy the equal and impartial protection of the law ; and we do strictly charge and enjoin all those who may be in authority under us that they abstain from all interference with the religious belief or worship of any of our subjects on pain of our highest displeasure.

And it is our further will that, so far as may be, our subjects, of whatever race or creed, be freely and impartially admitted to office in our service, the duties of which they may be qualified by their education, ability, and integrity duly to discharge.

We know, and respect, the feelings of attachment with which the natives of India regard the lands inherited by them from their ancestors, and we desire to protect them in all rights connected therewith, subject to the equitable demands of the State ; and we will that generally, in framing and administering the law, due regard be paid to the ancient rights, usages, and customs of India.

We deeply lament the evils and misery which have been brought upon India by the acts of ambitious men, who have deceived their countrymen by false reports, and led them into open rebellion. Our power has been shown by the suppression of that rebellion in the field ; we desire to show our mercy by pardoning the offences of those who have been misled, but who desire to return to the path of duty.

Already, in one province, with a desire to stop the further effusion of blood, and to hasten the pacification of our Indian dominions, our Viceroy and Governor-General has held out the expectation of pardon, on certain terms, to the great majority of those who, in the late unhappy disturbances, have been guilty of offences against our Government, and has declared the punishment which will be inflicted on those whose crimes place them beyond the reach of forgiveness. We approve and confirm the said act of our Viceroy and Governor General, and do further announce and proclaim as follows :

Our clemency will be extended to all offenders, save and except those who have been, or shall be, convicted of having directly taken part in the murder of British subjects. With regard to such the demands of justice forbid the exercise of mercy.

To those who have willingly given asylum to murderers, knowing them to be such, or who may have acted as leaders or instigators of revolt, their lives alone can be guaranteed ; but in apportioning the penalty due to such persons, full consideration will be given to the circumstances under which they have been induced to throw off their allegiance ; and large indulgence will be shown to those whose crimes may appear to have originated in too credulous acceptance of the false reports circulated by designing men.

To all others in arms against the Government we hereby promise unconditional pardon, amnesty, and oblivion of all offences against ourselves, our crown and dignity, on their return to their homes and peaceful pursuits.

It is our royal pleasure that these terms of grace and amnesty should be extended to all those who comply with these conditions before the 1st day of January next.

When, by the blessing of Providence, internal tranquillity shall be restored, it is our earnest desire to stimulate the peaceful industry of India, to promote works of public utility and improvement, and to administer the government for the benefit of all our subjects resident therein. In their prosperity will be our strength, in their contentment our security, and in their gratitude our best reward. And may the God of all power grant to us, and to those in authority under us, strength to carry out these our wishes for the good of our people.

VISCOUNT CANNING'S PROCLAMATION

Issued at Allahabad, November 1, 1858

Her Majesty the Queen having declared that it is her gracious pleasure to take upon herself the government of the British territories in India, the Viceroy and Governor-General hereby notifies that from this day all acts of the government of India will be done in the name of the Queen alone.

From this day, all men of every race and class who, under the administration of the Honourable East India Company, have joined to uphold the honour and power of England, will be the servants of the Queen alone.

The Governor-General summons them, one and all, each in his degree, and according to his opportunity, and with his whole heart and strength, to aid in fulfilling the gracious will and pleasure of the Queen, as set forth in her royal proclamation.

From the many millions of her Majesty's native subjects in India, the Governor-General will now, and at all times, exact a loyal obedience to the call which, in words full of benevolence and mercy, their Sovereign has made upon their allegiance and faithfulness.

LEADING DATES OF MUTINY PERIOD

Viscount Canning Governor-general (Feb.); end of Crimean War (March); general service order; circulation of symbols	1856
Persian War	1856–7
War in China	1856–60
Local mutinies and incendiary fires (Jan.–April); outbreaks of mutinies at Lucknow, Meerut, and Bareilly (May); massacre at Jhānsī; occupation of the Ridge (June); massacres at Cawnpore (July); recapture of Delhi, and slaughter of the princes (Sept.); reinforcement of Lucknow garrison (Sept.); final relief of Lucknow; and defeat of Windham at Cawnpore (Nov.); recovery of Cawnpore by Sir Colin Campbell (Dec.)	1857
Relief of Sāgar (Saugor); trial of the titular emperor (Jan.–March); recovery of Lucknow (March); recovery of Jhānsī (April); recovery of Bareilly and Kālpī (May); Rānī of Jhānsī killed; Gwālior reoccupied, and Sindia restored (June); Act for the Better Government of India (August); Queen's Proclamation (Nov.)	1858
Execution of Tantia Topi (April); gradual restoration of order	1859
Death of Bahādur Shāh, titular emperor	1862

Four volumes in the R. I. series deal with the Mutiny, namely, *Earl Canning* (1903) by Sir H. S. CUNNINGHAM, moderately good; *Lord Lawrence* (1905), excellent, by Sir C. U. AITCHISON; *Clyde and Strathnairn* (1895), a lucid military narrative with little biographical matter, by Sir OWEN T. BURNE; and *John Russell Colvin* (1912), by Sir AUCKLAND COLVIN, describing affairs at Agra. *The History of the Indian Revolt, &c.*, by G. D., is a valuable illustrated chronicle, coming down to November 1858, and published by Chambers in December of that year. The book includes many dates, details, statistics, and documents not to be found easily elsewhere. It seems to be accurate. The best book on the subject for most readers is the compact one-volume *History of the Indian Mutiny*, by T. R. E. HOLMES (publ. Allen, 1883; 4th ed., 1891). The huge work by Kaye and Malleson, 6 large vols., is too big and detailed for most people. Its bibliography is complicated. The whole was published by Allen. Vols. i–iii, entitled *A History of the Sepoy War, 1857–8*, are by J. W. KAYE, who died in 1876. The remaining vols. are by G. B. MALLESON. But his first vol. deals with the same period as Kaye's third, seen from a different point of view. Malleson's other two vols. finish the story. Details are: vol. i, 9th ed., 1880; ii, 5th ed., 1881; iii, 4th ed., 1880. Vol. iv (=vol. i of Malleson's *History of the Indian Mutiny*, 2nd ed., 1878= vol. iii of Kaye); vol. v, 1st and 2nd ed., 1879. Malleson's 3rd vol., completing the work, is dated 1880. In the same year F. PINCOTT added an *Analytical Index* to the whole, in a separate volume. The large *History of the Indian Mutiny* by Sir G. W. FORREST (vols. i, ii, 1904; vol. iii, 1912) corrects certain errors in earlier writers; but lacks unity, a large part consisting of reprints of essays previously published. For Cawnpore, the rare book, *A Personal Narrative, &c.*, by W. J. SHEPHERD, 2nd ed., Lucknow, 1879, is a valuable original authority. I have also used G. O. TREVELYAN, *Cawnpore* (Macmillan, 1865). The multitude of publications on the Mutiny is legion. I have looked into many of them. Numerous incidents are the subject of controversy, and the evidence often is conflicting.

BOOK IX

INDIA UNDER THE CROWN; THE VICEROYS FROM 1858 TO 1911

CHAPTER 1

Lord Canning continued; reconstruction; Lord Elgin I; Lord Lawrence; Lord Mayo; and Lord Northbrook; from 1858 to 1876, a period of almost unbroken peace.

Policy of Lord Canning. The policy of Lord Canning during the trying times of the Mutiny period was exposed naturally and legitimately to keen criticism, which too often degenerated into coarse abuse. The European business community of Calcutta, especially, pursued him with rabid hostility until near the close of his career. A petition was sent to the Queen praying for his recall, and averring that the calamities of the country were 'directly attributable to the blindness, weakness, and incapacity of the Government'. The Governor-general desired to temper stern punishment with mercy, and to restrain within reasonable limits the bloodthirsty proposals of panic-stricken people, who felt that their lawful business was interrupted by the long-continued disturbances. Queen Victoria rightly refused to act on the hostile petition, and subsequently expressed the warmest opinion of her Viceroy's 'admirable administration'.[1] Even Calcutta opinion veered round towards the end, and probably everybody would now accept the view of his Finance Minister that Lord Canning was 'a nobleman who never, in the midst of the greatest peril, allowed his judgement to be swayed by passion, or his fine sense of honour and justice to be tarnished by even a passing feeling of revenge'. That just appreciation is not weakened by the admission that the Viceroy was human and made some mistakes. In 1861 he went home, worn out by his public labours and domestic sorrow, to die a few weeks after his arrival in England.

The Oudh proclamation. One of the Viceroy's errors was the preparation of a draft dispatch and proclamation confiscating, with a few exceptions, the whole land of Oudh, as a penalty for the almost universal rebellion of the landholders and people of that province. Lord Ellenborough, then President of the Board of Control, disapproving strongly of the terms of the document, most improperly published it in substance with his censure, before his communication could reach India. His action almost

[1] *Letters*, cr. 8vo ed., iii. 453. The title of Viceroy conferred by the Queen's Proclamation of 1858 has not yet been recognized by statute.

caused a Cabinet crisis, which was avoided by his resignation. He never held office again. The proclamation, although not officially published in its original too drastic form, was not cancelled or withdrawn. The application of the principles of general confiscation and regrants to suitable persons were wisely left to the discretion of Mr. Montgomery, the Chief Commissioner of Oudh. The province was 'settled' on terms sufficiently satisfactory to the great landlords, but adequate arrangements for the protection of under-proprietors and tenants were left to a later time. The Oudh tenures differ materially from those of the Agra Province. During the course of 1860 Oudh was thoroughly pacified. Since that time the province has enjoyed unbroken peace.[1]

Army reorganization. The Bengal army was almost completely destroyed during the two years of disturbances, about 120,000 out of 128,000 men having mutinied. Probably most of the mutineers were killed in battle, executed, or done to death in the pestiferous jungles of the Nēpāl border. The annihilation of the principal Native army was reason enough for a radical military reorganization, which was necessary also on other grounds. The problem naturally divided itself into two main branches concerning respectively the Native or Indian army, and the European forces, which again comprised Queen's regiments and Company's regiments. The abolition of the Company necessarily involved the dissolution of the Company's army. All troops, whatever administrative arrangements might be adopted, became soldiers of the Queen. The experience of the Mutiny led to the decision that in the Bengal Presidency, including the Panjāb, the proportion of British to native troops should normally be one-half. In the Madras and Bombay armies the proportion of one-third Europeans was considered sufficient. Nearly all the artillery was made over to the charge of Europeans. The British officers of the whole Native army were organized as three presidential Staff Corps. That arrangement has been cancelled, and the Native army is now designated as the Indian Army. The fine services rendered by that army in France, Mesopotamia, Egypt, Palestine, and East Africa are fresh in the memory of all readers, and will not be forgotten quickly. Many experienced persons, including Lord Canning, wished to retain a local European army. The Home Government overruled that recommendation and decided on complete amalgamation of the Queen's and the Company's forces. About 10,000 out of 16,000 men in the Company's army took their discharge rather than continue to serve under the changed conditions. Some of the men displayed a mutinous spirit. So far as I can judge the policy of amalgamation was right. It is useless to go into details of the reformed army organization. Innumerable changes have since been effected from time to time, and no man can tell what further developments may follow the Great War and its endless surprises.

[1] The author served for a considerable time in Oudh both as Deputy Commissioner and as Commissioner.

Indigo disputes. In 1859 and 1860 disputes between the European indigo planters and the Bengal peasantry became acute; and in some districts, especially in Nuddea (Nadiyā), serious disturbances occurred. The planters endeavoured to enforce the cultivation of indigo against the will and interests of the tenantry. A commission which was appointed to investigate the complaints of the ryots found them to be substantiated. The Secretary of State rightly refused to sanction a proposal that a tenant should be liable to criminal prosecution for refusal to fulfil a civil contract to grow indigo. The Bengālī drama by Dīna Bandhu Mitra, entitled *Nīl Darpan*, or *The Indigo-planting Mirror* published in 1860, gives, as already mentioned, a painfully realistic picture of the oppression practised by some of the planters and their agents. The play aroused angry passions, and the translator of it into English was fined and imprisoned for libel.[1]

Legal changes. The useful work of codification, for which preparations had been made many years before by eminent legal experts, actually assumed definite shape in Lord Canning's time. The Penal Code, enacted in 1860, has required wonderfully little substantial change since. The first edition of the Criminal Procedure Code appeared in 1861, and in the same year the old Supreme Courts and the *Adālats* of the Company were replaced by Chartered High Courts.[2] The appointments reserved ordinarily for members of the Civil Service of India were scheduled about the same time, but power has been taken by the Secretary of State to depart from the schedule for adequate reason. Changes were made in the constitution of the Executive and Legislative Councils of the Governor-general, which have been much developed in later years, and are still (1918) in progress.

The Rent Act X, of 1859, applicable to Bengal, Bihār, the Agra Province, and the Central Provinces, but not to the Panjāb or Oudh, attempted to protect the tenantry against tyrannical eviction by enacting the arbitrary rule that twelve years' continuous occupation of a particular field, not of an entire holding, should confer tenant-right or 'a right of occupancy' in that field. The hard and fast rule thus laid down did not accord with the ancient vague customs of the country. The Act, since replaced by later provincial legislation, did some good, but at the cost of an enormous mass of litigation, to which no end is in sight. The problem of 'tenant-right' is one of immense difficulty.

Famine of 1861. A grievous famine, the result partly of two seasons of deficient rainfall and partly of the Mutiny disturbances, desolated portions of the Agra Province, the Panjāb, Rājputāna, and Cutch in the year 1861. The distress was worst in the tract

[1] Grierson, *I. G.* (1908), ii. 433.

[2] 'The Indian High Courts Act of 1861 closed the series of constitutional statutes consequent on the transfer of the government of India to the Crown. Such Acts of Parliament as have since then been passed for India have done little more than amend, with reference to minor points, the Acts of 1858 and 1861' (Ilbert).

between Agra and Delhi. The mortality was estimated at 8½ per cent. of the population in the districts most affected. The Government expended considerable sums on relief measures, and the administrative arrangements for the emergency showed an advance on the methods used in dealing with earlier famines.

Finance. The Mutiny had not only destroyed the Bengal army, it had shaken the old system of government to its foundations and utterly discredited the crude methods of finance which had come down from early times. The long-continued military operations had necessarily produced an enormous deficit. Lord Canning accordingly applied for and obtained the services as Finance Minister of Mr. James Wilson, an experienced English official who had been Financial Secretary to the Treasury. When he died in 1860, after only nine months' work in India, he was succeeded by Mr. Samuel Laing. Those two ministers filled up the deficit by introducing an income tax and other new imposts, and by enforcing large economies in military expenditure. The system of financial administration also was much improved. Mr. Laing came to the conclusion that 'the revenue of India is really buoyant and elastic in an extraordinary degree', an opinion confirmed by more recent experience. In railways, canals, and other public works India possesses assets of enormous capital value, and there is no reason to be uneasy about the financial stability of the country. Unfortunately the Indian Government is prone to panic on the subject, and far too ready to resolve on short-sighted petty economies whenever it finds itself slightly embarrassed. Such an official panic occurred in 1911, without any substantial justification.

Education. The comprehensive dispatch on education sent out by Sir Charles Wood (Lord Halifax) in 1854, and warmly welcomed by Lord Dalhousie, had borne fruit at once by the rapid development of vernacular schools in the villages. The application of the principles of the dispatch to the higher branches of education had to be deferred for a short time. The revolt of the Bengal army and the resultant disturbances were not allowed to interfere with the evolution of educational policy. In 1857, the first year of the Mutiny, the three universities of Calcutta, Bombay, and Madras had been founded, their constitution being modelled on that of the University of London, at that time a purely examining institution. At a later date additional universities were established at Lahore and Allahabad. It is impossible to foretell how many universities ultimately may be needed to satisfy the wants of the Indian Empire. The formation of new administrative areas, such as the Province of Bihār and Orissa, separated in 1912; the growing desire for provincial autonomy, so that each of the larger governments may be equipped completely with its own High Court, university, and all the other departments of a fully organized administration; the marvellous development of education and administrative skill in the more advanced Native or Protected States, are factors which render inevitable a large increase in the number of Indian universities.

The Nizam, the ruler of the premier Protected State, has resolved on the establishment of a Hyderabad University, in which Urdu will be the primary language of instruction, although a knowledge of English will be compulsory on the students. A special and well-paid staff of translators is now (1918) engaged in preparing the necessary Urdu text-books. The Urdu language, which resembles English in the simplicity and flexibility of its syntax, and in the extraordinary wealth of its vocabulary, drawn from Western Hindī, Sanskrit, Persian, Arabic, English, and other sources, should be capable of expressing ideas on any subject, literary, philosophical, or scientific. The Hyderabad experiment, which is being conducted by capable hands, may be expected to result in a marked improvement in the Urdu language, and the formation of a recognized authoritative literary form of the tongue.

Even the small Hindu State of Travancore, in the extremity of the peninsula, desires to be independent of Madras leading strings and to possess a university of its own.

Each of the larger provinces and sub-provinces, such as Burma, eastern Bengal, and Bihār with Orissa, has either obtained a provincial university, or will obtain such an institution in the course of a few years.

There is no necessity that Indian universities should be modelled on one type. Plenty of room exists for diversity of type and function, while all may be fitted to supply the necessary stream of educated officials and members of the learned professions. England finds its advantage in the differentiation between the ancient universities of the south, with their store of venerable traditions, and the vigorous, practical, yet truly educational modern institutions of the north. The Indian Empire requires variety of education still more.

Effect of the universities. It is impossible to measure or estimate the effect of the foundation of the three original Indian universities. Whatever hostile criticisms might be justly directed against their constitution or administration, the absurdity of the early choice of books for study, and the comical results of imperfect acquaintance with the English language exhibited in the utterances oral or written of the first generations of graduates, there can be no question that the new institutions acted as a powerful stimulus both to thought and to the acquisition of knowledge. Notwithstanding the mistakes made, the universities served as a bridge between East and West which could not have been provided in any other way. Many of the defects which disfigured the administration of the universities in their earlier days have been removed, although much remains to be done, and room for improvement will always exist.

The Government of India before the Mutiny was little more than a continuation of the old Mogul administration, somewhat more orderly and systematic, but deeply saturated with old-world prejudices and habits. A shock of no ordinary violence was needed to wake up the sleepy hollows both at the India House and at the

Council Chamber in Calcutta. The Mutiny administered that wholesome and indispensable shock. The foundation of the three universities in the very year of the Cawnpore massacres and the siege of Delhi symbolized the birth of a new India. The old fogies, many of them men of renown, but still old fogies so far as all questions of reform were concerned, could not have conceived the idea of the establishment of institutions where all the wisdom of the West would be offered to and eagerly accepted by the East. Nor could they have believed that in a few years the possession by Indian-born graduates of an absolutely perfect command over the English language, and familiar intimacy with the best European works on literature and science would become accomplishments so widely diffused as no longer to attract special notice. Both the Indian Government and large sections of the population are now in touch with the outer world so closely that they have become acutely sensitive to every breath of western thought and feeling, in the political, social, intellectual, and ethical provinces. On the other hand, the influence exercised by India on Europe and the United States of America is no longer negligible. East and West have met for good or evil, and cannot remain apart. The meeting is largely the work of the Indian universities.

Lord Elgin I. Lord Canning's successor, the Earl of Elgin and Kincardine, commonly called Lord Elgin, took over charge in March 1862. Previous service as Governor-general of Canada and Special Envoy to China seemed to mark him as a person well qualified to conduct the government of India. But in November 1863 he died of heart disease, and was buried at Dharmsāla in the Panjāb. The only noticeable event of his brief term of office was the 'Umbeyla campaign' on the north-western frontier, rendered necessary by an outburst of Muhammadan fanaticism to the west of the Indus. The expeditionary force met with strenuous resistance, and at one time was in danger of destruction, but vigorous action brought the campaign to a tolerably satisfactory conclusion before the close of 1863. The government was carried on by two acting officers until the appointment of a permanent successor could be arranged.

Sir John Lawrence. The justifiable dissatisfaction of the Home Government with the conduct of the Umbeyla campaign had much to do with the selection as Governor-general of Sir John Lawrence, the saviour of the Panjāb. His special services and his intimate acquaintance with frontier politics were considered to outweigh the familiar and sound objections to the appointment of a member of the Civil Service as Governor-general. He was not raised to the peerage until after he had left India. Ministers would have been well advised if they had conferred the higher rank upon him at the beginning of his term of office, and so elevated him above his fellows.

Peaceful administration. The heaviest part of the task of reconstruction necessitated by the mutiny storm had been accomplished by the government of Lord Canning. The process was continued by Sir John Lawrence, who made it his business, in the words of the Queen's Proclamation, 'to stimulate the peaceful industry of India, to promote works of public utility and improvement, and to administer the government for the benefit' of all Her Majesty's subjects. The story of the government of Sir John Lawrence consequently is almost wholly concerned with matters of internal administration.

SIR JOHN LAWRENCE.

War with Bhūtān. A little war with Bhūtān, a small and backward state on the hill frontier of Bengal, and more or less dependent on Tibet, was occasioned by the misconduct of the Rājā in kidnapping Mr. Ashley Eden, who had been sent to negotiate on the subject of frontier raids. The business, which had been mismanaged by the Government of Bengal, was patched up in 1865 by a treaty which enforced the cession of a strip of territory about a hundred and eighty miles long and twenty or thirty broad.

Withdrawal of doctrine of lapse. Sir John Lawrence, who had been at one time a disciple of Lord Dalhousie's annexation policy, changed his attitude in consequence of the events of the Mutiny, which had proved the inestimable value of loyal Native States. In 1859 Lord Canning, with the full approval of Sir John Lawrence, announced the withdrawal of the doctrine of lapse, and informed all concerned that in future the adopted son of a chief would be allowed to succeed to the state as well as to the private property of his adoptive father.

Relations between the Crown and the Protected States. The assumption by the Queen of the direct government of British India, previously administered by the East India Company in trust for the Crown, did not effect any formal legal change in the relations between the Sovereign and the Protected States. The Proclamation of 1858, on the contrary, sharply distinguishes between the people of the States and Her Majesty's subjects. The relevant passages are :

'We hereby announce to the native princes of India, that all treaties and engagements made with them by or under the authority of the East

India Company are by us accepted, and will be scrupulously maintained, and we look for the like observance on their part.

We desire no extension of our present territorial possessions; and while we will permit no aggression upon our dominions or our rights to be attempted with impunity, we shall sanction no encroachment on those of others.

We shall respect the rights, dignity, and honour of native princes as our own; and we desire that they, as well as our own subjects, should enjoy that prosperity and social advancement which can only be secured by internal peace and good government.'

That language clearly maintains the position of the chiefs of the Protected States as allies of the Paramount Power. It does not convert either them or their people into subjects of the Crown. The Act of 1876, in virtue of which the Queen assumed the title of Empress of India with effect from January 1, 1877, undoubtedly changed the legal relation, and brought the Protected States inside the boundary of the Indian Empire. The practical difference between the position in 1858 and that brought about in 1877 is not great. From the earlier date every ruling chief had become conscious of a definite personal subordination to the Queen of England, not dependent on formal treaties made between his ancestors and the East India Company. The formulae of international law, although still embodied in state documents and officially recognized to some extent, obviously had ceased to be applicable to the new state of facts. The Supreme Government no longer felt any scruple about interfering in the internal affairs of a Protected State for adequate reason, or even in changing the ruler, if such a drastic course should be necessary. Nobody, however, desired to make a change of ruler the pretext for the annexation of the principality and its absorption into British India. The conviction so strongly held by Lord Dalhousie and the Home Government of his day that the administration of any ordinary British District must necessarily be superior to that of any Native State, so that absorption or annexation could not fail to be beneficial to the population concerned, was no longer prevalent. The grounds for that conviction were disappearing daily; and during the half-century following the Mutiny they ceased to exist. At the present day (1918) the administrative machinery of the best governed Protected States, adapted from the British model, is all that can be reasonably desired; and the actual administration, it is believed, gives little cause for complaint. A sentiment of strong personal loyalty, supported in many cases by close personal friendship, now binds the leading chiefs to their Sovereign, who on his part esteems and trusts them as supporters of his throne and pillars of the Empire.[1]

[1] Ilbert, after enumerating the restrictions on the full sovereignty of the Protected States, observes that 'the result of all these limitations on the powers of the Native Indian States is that, for purposes of international law, they occupy a very special and exceptional position. "The principles of international law", declared a resolution of the Government of India in 1891 (*Gazette of India*, No. 1700 E., August 21, 1891), "have no bearing

Afghan policy. Sir John Lawrence rigorously acted on his decision to abstain from interference in any degree with the internal affairs of Afghanistan. When the Amīr Dōst Muhammad died in 1863 at an advanced age, the Governor-general deliberately allowed his relatives to fight out their claims to the succession among themselves for years, and openly proclaimed his readiness to recognize any competitor who should emerge victorious from the strife. After much contest, Shēr Ali, a younger son of the late Amīr, won the prize in 1868 and became ruler of the whole territory. The Government of India then recognized him as Amīr without hesitation, as it had recognized one of his rivals at an earlier stage of the struggle. That policy, sometimes described by its admirers as 'masterly inactivity', had the advantage of being cheap and cautious. On the other hand, it seemed to the Afghan chiefs rather cold-blooded and selfish, and made it difficult to establish really friendly relations between the Governor-general and the Amīr.

In those days the Russian power was making rapid advances across the Khanates of Central Asia, and ambitious Muscovite generals sometimes permitted themselves to dream dreams of the conquest of India. Neither the Home Government nor the Government at Calcutta could regard with indifference movements which seemed at the time really to threaten the safety of the empire. Sir John Lawrence, while willing to safeguard the independence of the actual ruler of Afghanistan, whoever he might be, against foreign aggression, whether Russian or Persian, refused to enter into a binding alliance with the Amīr, preferring to retain in his own hands perfect freedom of decision as to the methods by which aggression should be repelled. When Shēr Ali had finally established his power, the Governor-general helped him to maintain it by a modest gift of arms and cash.

The Orissa famine. The famine resulting from the early failure of the rains in 1865 and the consequent destruction of the main rice crop due to be harvested in December is commonly mentioned as the Orissa famine of 1866. But in reality famine conditions extended along the whole of the eastern coast from Calcutta to Madras, and penetrated far inland. The Districts of Mānbhūm and Singhbhūm in Chutiā Nāgpur, as well as the Ganjām Division of Madras, suffered severely. The Madras Government of Lord Harris dealt effectively with the districts under its jurisdiction. The Bengal administration and the Government of India failed disastrously. The isolated province of Orissa was affected so terribly that probably nearly a million of persons

upon the relations between the Government of India as representing the Queen-Empress on the one hand, and the Native States under the sovereignty of Her Majesty on the other. The paramount supremacy of the former presupposes and implies the subordination of the latter."' Roughly speaking it may be affirmed that the inhabitants of a Native State are aliens as regards British India, and are British subjects as regards foreign powers.

died within its limits. The failure of the rains in that region was immensely aggravated in September 1865 by floods from the rivers which overwhelmed a thousand square miles of low-lying country, and submerged for many days the homes and fields of a million and a quarter of people.

Famine policy. In the great majority of cases, where the distressed region is connected by passable means of communication with more favoured countries, sound famine policy dictates absolute non-interference with private trade in grain. The Government should abstain from prohibition of export, from commandeering stocks, from fixing prices, and from importing food through its own agents. Provided that communication with better supplied districts is physically possible and that considerable reserve stocks exist in the grain-pits of the stricken region, that policy is absolutely sound, although it will always be unpopular. Sleeman, disregarding loud clamour, civil and military, acted on those principles in the Sāgar and Narbadā territories during the famine of 1833 with complete success.[1]

But when stocks have been depleted, practicable communications are lacking, and private enterprise is unable to work at a profit, the policy of non-interference is no longer applicable. The Bengal Government, forgetting that obvious distinction, failed to realize the fact that in Orissa 'the people, shut up in a narrow province between pathless jungles, and an impracticable sea, were in the condition of passengers in a ship without provisions'.

Sir John Lawrence, who had seen the necessity of importing rice as early as November 1865, permitted himself to be talked over by the members of his council and the Bengal Government, who blindly relied upon private enterprise. He should have used his powers as Governor-general and overruled his council. When the attempt to import food was made it was too late. Inadequate measures to prevent suffering in 1865 and 1866 were followed by extravagant expenditure in 1867 and 1868. The record of the famine administration, taken as a whole, has been rightly characterized as having 'left a deep stain on the reputation of the Bengal authorities'; nor can Sir John Lawrence be acquitted of failure to exercise timely and effective control.

Competent expert opinion offers the assurance that 'so far as human foresight can judge, it is not possible for such a spectacle to recur. . . . There is now no difficulty in respect to communications', by means of railways, roads, and navigable canals; while irrigation, not needed in ordinary years, has been provided for by costly works, which, although they do not pay directly, are effectual as insurance.[2]

The failure to meet the emergency in Orissa stimulated the Government of Sir John Lawrence to increased exertion in the construction of public works of various kinds in other provinces.

[1] *Rambles and Recollections*, ed. V. A. Smith, 1915, pp. 149–60 (Oxford University Press).

[2] C. W. Odling, *Orissa*, a paper read before the Victoria Institute, 1907.

The Governor-general established the sound financial principle that reproductive public works, that is to say, those which earn the interest on their cost, should be paid for by loan.

Commercial failures. The civil war in the United States of America produced an abnormal demand for Indian cotton, and consequent extravagant speculation. The management of the Bank of Bombay unfortunately lent itself to the support of wild schemes, which in 1865 resulted in a commercial crash involving the suspension of payments by the Bank. Many people who had believed themselves to be wealthy were ruined in a moment.

Tenancy legislation. Sir John Lawrence, throughout his career, took a deep interest in the fortunes of the peasantry, and always was inclined to support their cause as against that of the greater landholders. He succeeded in passing a measure (Act XXVI of 1866) for the protection of under-proprietors and tenants in Oudh; but was warned by the Secretary of State 'to take especial care, without sacrificing the just rights of others, to maintain the talookdars of Oude in that position of consideration and dignity which Lord Canning's Government contemplated conferring on them'.

The talookdars, who are combined in a powerful association, have been able to take good care of their interests, while the country as a whole is densely populated and prosperous.[1]

The Panjāb Tenancy Act, passed at a later date, was drafted in the time of Sir John Lawrence.

Sir John Lawrence as Viceroy. The validity of the arguments against the appointment of a member of the Civil Service of India to the office of Governor-general was confirmed rather than discredited by the history of the viceroyalty of Sir John Lawrence. He was never able to shake off the habits of the Panjāb official of old days, and admittedly was too indifferent to the ordinary daily maintenance of the dignity of his great office. His reputation rests upon his administration of the Panjāb after the annexation and on the invaluable services rendered by him at the time of the Mutiny, not on his work as Viceroy, which could have been done as well or better by a worse man.

He was created a Baron on his retirement. He then filled up his time by accepting the office of Chairman of the London School Board and by much active work in connexion with the Church Missionary Society and kindred institutions. In June 1879, when he had become almost blind and wholly worn out, he died at the age of sixty-eight. His memory was fitly honoured by burial in Westminster Abbey and the erection of statues in Calcutta and London.

Lord Mayo. In January 1869 Sir John Lawrence made over charge to a man of a very different type, Richard Bourke, Earl of Mayo, an Irish nobleman, then almost forty-seven years of age,

[1] The term *talukdār* in Oudh has a meaning quite different from that which it has in Bengal. For a summary history of revenue and rent legislation in Oudh see *I. G.*, 1908, vol. xix.

who had served his native country as Chief Secretary with distinction. His selection as Viceroy by Mr. Disraeli, although sharply criticized, was not disturbed by the Radical Government which came into power in 1868 under the leadership of Mr. Gladstone. Lord Mayo during his three years of office justified the hopes of the statesman who had appointed him, and proved himself to be a thoroughly efficient Governor-general and Viceroy. His exceptional personal charm endeared him especially to the rulers of the Protected States, who regarded him as the ideal representative of the Sovereign. He worked hard at all the problems of administration, and lost his life owing to his zealous efforts to improve the defective system of government in the convict settlement of the Andaman Islands.

LORD MAYO.

Afghanistan and Russia. A personal interview between Lord Mayo and the Amīr Shēr Ali at Umballa (Ambāla), in March 1869, removed the unpleasant impression left on the mind of the Afghan ruler by Sir John Lawrence's cynical declarations and secured the personal friendship of the Amīr, although his specific requests were not granted. Lord Mayo increased his cash subsidy and supplied him with arms. Informal negotiations conducted in Russia by Sir Douglas Forsyth with the sanction of the Home Government induced the Tsar to recognize the Oxus as the northern boundary of Afghanistan, and also, after some delay, to admit the justice of the Amīr's claim to Badakhshān.

Protected States. A serious case of misgovernment in the Alwar State, Rājputāna, was disposed of by transferring the powers of the vicious young Mahārāja to a council. Difficult problems arising in the turbulent little states of the Kāthiāwār peninsula were dealt with judiciously. Lord Mayo founded the Mayo College at Ajmēr for the education of the sons of chiefs and nobles, but the institution was not actually opened until 1885. Similar colleges have been established at Lahore and at Rājkōt in Kāthiāwār. The obstacles to complete success in the working of institutions of the kind are so great that too much must not be expected from them.

Visit of H.R.H. the Duke of Edinburgh. The visit in 1869 of H.R.H. the Duke of Edinburgh, Queen Victoria's second son, was an event of high significance as marking the beginning of close personal relations between the Sovereign and her Indian peoples. The policy thus initiated was continued in later years by the tour of H.R.H. the Prince of Wales, afterwards King Edward VII, by the Indian service of H.R.H. the Duke of Connaught, and by the visit of the late Prince Edward. It was crowned by the memorable solemnity at the close of 1911, when the King-Emperor George V and his gracious consort received in person the fervent homage of all India.

Finance. Lord Mayo was firmly resolved to adjust the finances of the Indian Empire so that the expenditure in normal years should be within the income. He succeeded in his purpose by imposing certain additional taxes and enforcing rigid economy. He reorganized the Public Works Department, and paid the closest personal attention to the working of every department in order to secure efficiency without waste. He introduced the system of state railways.

His most memorable financial reform was a measure of decentralization which made every Provincial Government responsible for its own finance within certain defined limits. Previously every local government had engaged in a scramble for grants from the Supreme Government, so that the provincial administrations had no interest in economy, while the Government of India was unable either to make accurate estimates or to exercise effective control over imperial finance.

Murder of Lord Mayo. The administration of jails and the penal settlement at the Andaman Islands was one of the many subjects which engaged Lord Mayo's untiring energy. When inspecting the convict settlement at the Andamans he unfortunately prolonged his visit until after dark. Just as he was stepping into the boat a Muhammadan frontier tribesman, who had been transported for a blood-feud murder, sprang out of the bushes upon the Viceroy's back and stabbed him to death, on January 24, 1872. The murderer had determined to kill some high European official and was proud of his success in slaying the Viceroy. Lord Mayo was dead when brought on board the frigate. The crime excited universal horror in India and Europe.

Lord Northbrook. The duties of the head of the Government having been carried on by two officiating incumbents, the newly appointed permanent Governor-general, Lord Northbrook, assumed charge of his office in May 1872. He was a member of the wealthy banking house of Baring, and brought to the discharge of his novel functions excellent business capacity and varied official experience. His period of office presents few incidents worthy of special notice.

Afghan policy. Lord Northbrook lacked the personal charm of his predecessor. In his relations with the Amīr of Afghanistan, acting under instructions from the Duke of Argyll, then Secretary of State, he resumed the cold, repellent attitude of Sir John Lawrence, with the result that Shēr Ali developed feelings of hostility to the English and turned to Russia for the support which India refused. When the Conservative Government came into power in 1874 the Viceroy was unable to concur in the policy suggested by Lord Salisbury, who desired to send a special mission to Kābul.

The Gaikwār. The strange case of Malhār Rāo, Gaikwār of Baroda, was the only remarkable incident marking the relations between Lord Northbrook and the Protected States. Malhār Rāo, who had become Mahārājā in 1870, grossly misgoverned his dominions, behaving with folly, extravagance, and cruelty. Colonel Phayre, the Resident appointed by the Government of Bombay, devoted all his energy to the exposure of abuses, with the result that the Government of India ordered an inquiry, which resulted unfavourably to the Gaikwār. Sir Lewis Pelly was then appointed Special Commissioner and Agent to the Governor-general. He arrived at Baroda in December 1874. Meantime, in November, an attempt had been made to poison Colonel Phayre by the administration of diamond dust in his food. Grave suspicion resting on the Gaikwār, he was arrested in January 1875 under the orders of the Government of India, which arranged for the constitution of a commission to try his case and report. The commission was composed of six members under the presidency of the Chief Justice of Bengal. The three Indian members, namely, the Mahārājās of Gwālior and Jaipur, with Sir Dinkur Rāo, the eminent minister, found a verdict of 'not proven'; while the three English members were fully satisfied as to the Mahārājā's guilt. The Government of India, with the sanction of the Secretary of State, although declining to formally convict Malhār Rāo of attempted murder, deposed him as the penalty for 'his notorious misconduct, his gross misgovernment of the State, and his evident incapacity to carry into effect necessary reforms'. The deposed prince ended his days at Madras in 1893. A boy named Sayājī Rāo, a distant relative of the family, was placed on the throne and carefully educated. During his minority the state was ably administered by Sir T. Mādhava Rāo. The Baroda Government continues to be of a progressive and enlightened character (1918).

Bihār famine. The authorities had been so frightened by the censure passed on the mismanagement of the Orissa famine in 1866, that in 1873–4, when a calamity of the same kind, but on a much smaller scale, occurred in Bihār and part of Bengal, relief operations under the direction of Sir Richard Temple were conducted regardless of expense with unnecessary extravagance. Nearly seven millions sterling were spent.

Tour of Prince of Wales. The Prince of Wales, afterwards King Edward VII, made an interesting tour through the Indian Empire in 1875–6, and received many proofs of cordial loyalty.

Retirement of Lord Northbrook. Lord Northbrook had the misfortune to differ from the Home Government, not only with regard to Afghan policy, but on the question of taxing Manchester cotton goods. His retirement in 1876, ascribed officially to domestic reasons, must have been influenced by the discomfort of his relations with the ministry in London.

CHRONOLOGY

Withdrawal of doctrine of lapse; army amalgamation; Rent Act X of 1859	1859
Indigo disputes and riots in Bengal	1859–60
Enactment of Indian Penal Code	1860
Establishment of High Courts; enactment of Code of Criminal Procedure; Indian Civil Service Act; famine in N.W. India	1861
Lord Elgin I Governor-general	1862
Umbeyla or Black Mountain campaign	1862–3
Death of Amīr Dōst Muhammad	1863
Sir John Lawrence Governor-general	1864
Failure of Bank of Bombay	1865
Famine in Orissa and on eastern coast	1865–7
Shēr Ali established as Amīr of Afghanistan	1868
Lord Mayo Governor-general; meeting with Shēr Ali at Umballa; visit to India of H.R.H. the Duke of Edinburgh	1869
Murder of Lord Mayo (January 24); Lord Northbrook Governor-general (May)	1872
Bihār famine	1873–4
Deposition of Malhār Rāo Gaikwār	1875
Tour of Prince of Wales	1875–6
Retirement of Lord Northbrook	1876

Authorities

In addition to the books cited in the notes and in the last preceding chapter, reference for the most authoritative account of the legal changes in the time of Lord Canning may be made to Ilbert, *The Government of India*, Clarendon Press, Oxford, 2nd ed., 1907; 3rd ed., 1914. Famines, relations with the Native or Protected States, and other administrative subjects are well discussed in *I. G.* (*Indian Empire*), 1907, vols. iii, iv. For Lord Mayo, Sir W. W. Hunter, *The Earl of Mayo* (R. I., 1892) suffices. The larger *Life* by the same author in two vols. was published in 1875. I have looked into *Thomas George, Earl of Northbrook, a Memoir*, by Bernard Mallet (large 8vo, Longmans, 1908).

CHAPTER 2

Lord Lytton; Royal Titles Act; famine; finance; Vernacular Press Act; second Afghan War; Lord Ripon; reversal of Afghan policy; internal administration; Lord Dufferin; Panjdeh incident; third Burmese War; Tenancy Acts.

Lord Lytton. Mr. Disraeli (Lord Beaconsfield) selected as Lord Northbrook's successor, Edward Robert, second Baron Lytton, son of the first Baron, the well-known novelist, dramatist, and politician. The appointment in 1875 of the second Lord Lytton to the government of India was a surprise to everybody, because the Viceroy designate, then forty-four years of age, was a diplomatist by profession, wholly lacking in administrative experience, and known outside of the Foreign Office chiefly as a man of letters under the name of 'Owen Meredith'. In a private letter the Prime Minister explained his choice by observing that 'the critical state of affairs in Central Asia demands a statesman', adding that his nominee by accepting the post would have an opportunity not only of serving his country, but of winning enduring fame. Lord Lytton, who had already refused the Governorship of Madras on account of his delicate health, was unable to resist the pressure put upon him by Mr. Disraeli, and felt constrained to accept the offer of the Viceroyalty as 'a high and glorious command, which it would be a dereliction of duty to disobey'. He assumed charge at Calcutta in April 1876, and retained office for a little more than four years until June 1880. After spending some years quietly in England he became Ambassador at Paris, where he died in 1891 at the age of sixty.

LORD LYTTON.

The administrative inexperience of Lord Lytton did not hinder him from dealing brilliantly with one of the worst famines on record; from carrying into effect indispensable measures of financial reform; or, generally speaking, from maintaining a high standard of executive efficiency. His state papers and speeches are models of clear thinking expressed in an admirable style.

His reputation has been obscured by the lack of an adequate biography; by certain foreign peculiarities of manner and habits which offended conventional opinion; and, above all, by reason of the bitter partisan controversies aroused by his Afghan policy, executed by him under the instructions of Lords Beaconsfield and Salisbury. The equally venomous criticism of the Vernacular Press Act further discredited him in popular opinion. Those causes have prevented Lord Lytton from attaining the 'enduring fame' promised by the Prime Minister, and perhaps may be said to have left a general impression that he was a failure as a ruler of India. If such an opinion exists it is based upon insufficient grounds. The best parts of his internal policy were of permanent value, and served as the basis of developments effected by his successors; while the most essential measures of his Afghan policy, by which I mean the occupation of Quetta and the securing of the Kurram valley, either remained undisturbed, or, if reversed for a time, had to be reaffirmed a few years later.

The Royal Titles Act. The necessity for official recognition of the patent fact that Queen Victoria since 1858 had become the paramount sovereign of all India, including the Native or Protected States, had been emphasized by incidents during the tour of the Prince of Wales in 1875–6. Lord Northbrook's Government recommended that Her Majesty should be designated as Sovereign. The Prime Minister took up the idea, and intimated in the speech from the throne in 1876 that a measure would be introduced for making the desired change in the royal titles. Unfortunately the proposal met with considerable opposition in Parliament, and came to be regarded from a party point of view. The Bill, however, passed, and the duty of giving effect to the Act devolved upon Lord Lytton. He regarded the enactment as the beginning of 'a new policy by virtue of which the Crown of England should henceforth be identified with the hopes, the aspirations, the sympathies and interests of a powerful native aristocracy'. He believed strongly in the appeal to the loyal sentiment of the princes and nobles, and was right. The form of title chosen, 'Kaisar-i Hind', 'the Caesar of India', on the analogy of 'Kaisar-i Rūm', the well-known designation of the Byzantine emperors, was generally approved as being the best that could be devised.

The proclamation of Her Majesty's assumption of the new dignity was made with due solemnity in an Imperial Assemblage at Delhi on January 1, 1877; the 'Most Eminent Order of the Indian Empire' was founded; and the occasion was marked by the release of prisoners and other acts of grace. Lord Lytton, however, was not able to carry out all his intentions. General agreement has been attained that the formal acknowledgement of the already existing suzerainty of the British Crown may be described correctly as 'an act of political wisdom and foresight'.

Famine of 1876–8. The rejoicings of the solemn assembly were marred by the development of an exceptionally severe famine due to the failure of the rains of 1876 in Mysore, the Deccan, and large areas of the Madras and Bombay presidencies. Short-sighted critics grumbled at the expense of the ceremonial, but Lord Lytton rightly decided against suggestions for postponement. The meeting with the Governors of Madras and Bombay and with the princes whose dominions were involved in the famine proved to be of high administrative value. The Viceroy observed in a private letter that 'as regards the famine difficulties the Imperial Assemblage has been a godsend'. The opportunity for personal conference was especially fruitful with reference to the Madras presidency, where the Governor, the Duke of Buckingham and Chandos, although animated by the best intentions, insisted with perverse obstinacy in pursuing an erroneous and ruinous policy. Even after the conversations at the Assemblage the Duke persisted in his opposition to the instructions of the Supreme Government, so that the Viceroy was constrained to make a toilsome and perilous journey to the south in order to enforce his decisions.[1] He succeeded by the display of much tact and forbearance, but not until immense mischief had been done. In the Bombay Presidency the business was so well managed that the cost was about four millions sterling as against ten millions spent in Madras with less effect in the saving of human life.

The famine lasted for two years, from 1876 to 1878, extending in the second year to parts of the Central Provinces and the United Provinces (then the N.W.P.), with a small area of the Panjāb. The total area affected was estimated at 257,000 square miles, with a population of more than fifty-eight millions. The excess mortality in British India alone was supposed to exceed five millions, exclusive of the immense number of deaths in the Native States.

The Madras errors. The Madras administration erred by strangling private trade from the first, and attempting the impossible task of providing all supplies through Government agency. Lord Lytton insisted on applying the principles of Turgot, which, as we have seen, had been successfully applied on a small scale by Sleeman to the Sāgar and Narbadā Territories in 1833. The Madras authorities, overwhelmed by the magnitude of the disaster, failed completely in organization. The Viceroy found that 'the whole action of the Calcutta grain trade was on the point of being paralysed by the conduct of the Madras Government'; that the mortality in Madras was terrible, and 'not a little attributable to the defective management and unsound principles of the local government'; that the population on the relief works was a 'mere mob'; that there was no organized system of village relief; that the relief camps in and around Madras were 'simply huge popular picnics'; and that the whole system was 'rotten to the core'.

Lord Lytton's achievement. The drastic reforms introduced checked the abuses, but nothing could prevent an exceptionally heavy mortality. Large regions were bare of food of any kind. The injudicious early interference with private trade no doubt had much to do with the failure of supplies. Lord Lytton explained the sound principles of famine relief in an elaborate address to the Legislative Council in December 1877, and obtained sanction to the appointment in the following year of the first Famine Commission, which submitted its Report in 1880. That document is the foundation of the existing elaborate provincial Famine Codes. The Viceroy, who desired to spend freely on railways and irrigation works as preventives of famine, was checked by orders from England restricting expenditure within narrow limits.

Few people ever think of Lord Lytton except either as the man whose policy resulted in the Afghan War and the murder of Cavagnari; or as the author of the much abused Vernacular Press Act. Whatever may be thought about those matters, he deserves

[1] Lord Lytton was obliged to undergo an operation before he could start.

high credit for sound views on famine policy, thoroughly thought out and expressed with forceful lucidity. The whole existing system of famine administration rests on the foundations well and truly laid by him. Lord Lytton's singularly logical mind was constituted on a French rather than an English model. The foreignness of his mental constitution as well as of his manners made him more or less unintelligible to many of his countrymen.

Finance. Lord Lytton's intelligent appreciation of finance was not confined to the formation and enunciation of sound views upon famine problems. He also paid much attention to the complicated question of the cotton duties, and desired if possible to dispense altogether with sea customs revenue. He extended the decentralization scheme initiated by Lord Mayo. The inequalities of the salt tax were remedied in a large measure ; and he succeeded in abolishing the barbarous salt customs hedge, described by Sir John Strachey, the Finance Minister, in the following words:

'A Customs line is maintained extending from a point north of Attock to near the Berar frontier, a distance of more than 1,500 miles. Similar lines some hundreds of miles in length are established in the Bombay Presidency, to prevent untaxed salt from Native States entering British territory. Along the greater part of this enormous system of inland Customs lines, which, if they were put down in Europe, would stretch from London to Constantinople, a physical barrier has been created comparable to nothing that I can think of except the Great Wall of China. It consists chiefly of an impenetrable hedge of thorny trees and bushes, supplemented by stone walls and ditches, across which no human being or beast of burden or vehicle can pass without being subjected to detention and search. It is guarded by an army of some 8,000 men, the mass of whom receive as wages 6 or 7 rupees a month. The bare statement of these facts is sufficient to show the magnitude of the evil.' [1]

Vernacular Press Act. Nearly the whole period of Lord Lytton's administration was overshadowed by the strained relations between Russia and England, arising out of the events which led to the Russo-Turkish War of 1877, the treaty of San Stefano in March 1878, and the congress at Berlin in June of that year, from which Lord Beaconsfield claimed to have brought back 'peace with honour'. At that time all parties in England were opposed to the passing of Constantinople under Russian dominion ; and when the British Prime Minister was successful at the last moment, in defeating Muscovite ambition, his action was almost universally applauded. The successes of Russia had excited the minor journalists in India and led to the publication in vernacular newspapers of many seditious articles, extolling Russia, depreciating England, suggesting the assassination of British officers,

[1] I cannot find any record of the date of the construction of the hedge, which replaced innumerable inland customs posts scattered throughout the interior of the country. 'The whole customs line was abandoned in 1879, with the exception of a portion along the Indus, maintained to prevent the still lightly-taxed Kohāt salt being smuggled across the river' (*I. G.*, 1907, iv. 251). The same authority states the strength of the former salt 'army' as being 'nearly 13,000 officers and men'.

and advocating combination for the purpose of overthrowing the British Rāj. The Government of India came to the conclusion that the safety of the state required immediate preventive legislation to curb the excessive license of the papers not printed in English. The Bill was strongly supported by all the members of the Legislative Council who spoke, as well as by all the provincial governments consulted, except that of Madras, where the vernacular press was insignificant. Accordingly, in 1878, the Vernacular Press Act was passed.

The object of the Act, prevention not punishment, was to be attained chiefly by the requisition of security bonds under strictly regulated conditions. During the four years of its currency the Act was put in force only once. It was repealed under Lord Ripon's Government in 1882, reliance being then placed on an amended section (124 A) of the Penal Code, which provided penalties for seditious writing. Later emergencies, and especially the necessities of the Great War, have rendered more stringent legislation unavoidable.

Lord Beaconsfield and Lord Lytton. Having thus dealt with the more prominent features of Lord Lytton's internal administration, we now proceed to discuss briefly his relations with Afghanistan. The general outlines of his policy were laid down by Lord Beaconsfield, the Prime Minister, and Lord Salisbury, the Foreign Secretary. The Viceroy cordially concurred with the policy of the ministry, and, when quitting office, addressed Lord Beaconsfield as his 'dear and honoured chief', to whom the writer owned 'unreserved allegiance', and felt bound 'by every tie of personal gratitude, political sympathy, and public duty'. The outgoing Prime Minister marked his sense of the Viceroy's services by raising Lord Lytton to an earldom.

Hostility of Amīr Shēr Ali. In 1873 the refusal of Lord Northbrook, acting under instructions from the Gladstone ministry, to give Shēr Ali definite assurances of protection, had determined the Amīr to take the side of Russia, which then seemed to him to be the more formidable power. In 1876, when Lord Lytton became Viceroy, the hostility of the Amīr to England was manifest. The ministry and the Viceroy were agreed on the policy of forcing the ruler of Afghanistan to declare himself to be either a friend or an enemy, of preventing his country from falling under the control of Russia, and, if necessary, of taking effective steps for destroying the Amīr's capacity for mischief to British and Indian interests.

Occupation of Quetta. An important preliminary step was taken in 1876 by the occupation of Quetta (also called Kwatah or Shāl) in Balōchistan, which was effected by amicable arrangement with the Khān of Khelat (Kalāt). The strategical position thus secured dominated the road to Kandahār and gave the Government of India full control over the Bolān Pass. The occupation, which was not disturbed by Mr. Gladstone's Government in 1880, is the most important permanent result of the Beaconsfield and Lytton policy. The Afghan flank was turned, and the direct routes to Kābul became matters of secondary importance. Quetta, with the surrounding territory, now forms a prosperous British district, with much trade. The large cantonment is connected with India by a railway.

Second Afghan War. In 1878 the crisis was brought on by the Amīr's public and honourable reception of a Russian envoy, and his refusal to receive a representative of the Viceroy. When Sir Neville Chamberlain, under instructions from Lord Lytton, presented himself at Ali Musjid, and demanded passage through the Khyber Pass in order to communicate the views of the Government of India to the Amīr at Kābul, he was turned back. The deliberate affront necessarily led to war, which began on November 21, 1878.[1] The military operations, admirably planned and brilliantly executed, involved the simultaneous advance of General Browne through the Khyber, of General (Lord) Roberts from the Kurram Valley, and of General Biddulph from Quetta. The combination was so completely successful that Amīr Shēr Ali fled into Russian territory, from which he never returned. He died at Mazār-i Sharīf in February 1879, having failed to obtain the expected Russian help.

Difficulties. So far all had gone well with the British plans. Hostile criticism could find little scope, and the military success attained was beyond expectation. Difficulties then began to be felt owing to the non-existence of any responsible Afghan authority. The late Amīr's declared heir apparent had died just before the war, and Shēr Ali had been obliged unwillingly to release from confinement his other son, Yākūb Khān, whom he acknowledged as his successor.

Treaty of Gandamuk. Lord Lytton was disposed to separate Kandahār as a distinct principality and to reduce Kābul to such comparative insignificance that it could not be formidable, whoever might be its chief. When Yākūb Khān was accepted by the Afghans, the Viceroy recognized him in May 1879 as Amīr of Kābul, and, as a concession, promised to restore both Jalālābād and Kandahār. The treaty of Gandamuk, negotiated by Major (Sir Louis) Cavagnari with Yākūb Khān, provided for the control of Afghanistan foreign affairs exclusively by the Government of India, for British occupation of the passes, and for the posting of a British minister or envoy resident at Kābul.[2] Lord Lytton would have preferred that the envoy should be stationed elsewhere, but when Yākūb Khān insisted on his residing at Kābul the Viceroy accepted the obvious risk.

Massacre. Sir Louis Cavagnari, the envoy, arrived in Kābul on July 24, with a small escort, and was assigned quarters in the Bālā Hissar. On September 3 he and all his men were massacred by two or three regiments described as being mutinous. The

[1] The text of the Viceroy's declaration of war, dated at Lahore, November 21, 1878, is given in App. II of the *Official Account*.

[2] The text of the treaty is given in App. V of the *Official Account* of the war.

residency was burnt. Yākūb Khān certainly did nothing to save his guests, and probably was cognizant of the intended attack. Credible information showed that he had incited his troops to a religious war, but the exact extent of his personal share in the crime necessarily remained obscure.

Retribution. Measures of retribution were taken with commendable promptitude and skill. General Stewart at once re-occupied Kandahār, General Roberts led a force of 5,000 men to the Peiwār Kotal on the Kurram route, and the troops on the Khyber line were rapidly reinforced. On September 27 Yākūb Khān, the Amīr, took refuge in the British camp. General Roberts arrived before Kābul on October 8, and entered the city four days later. After a time he was obliged to withdraw to the entrenched camp at Shērpur, which was defended successfully against vigorous attacks. Kābul was then reoccupied.

Resignation of Lord Lytton. On April 28, 1880, the Conservative ministry of Lord Beaconsfield was replaced by a Radical cabinet under Mr. Gladstone, pledged to reverse the policy of its predecessors. Lord Lytton resigned, and the Marquess of Ripon was appointed his successor. The Marquess, who was fifty-three years of age, had become a Roman Catholic. The appointment for the first time of a member of the Roman Church to be Governor-general and Viceroy of India aroused a storm of opposition in England.

Ayūb Khān and Maiwand. Complications were caused by the action of a son of Shēr Ali, named Ayūb Khān, who had made himself Governor of Herat after the flight of his father. On July 27, 1880, Ayūb Khān, who had assembled a large force, defeated General Burrows at Maiwand and drove the remnant of the vanquished brigade to take shelter within the walls of Kandahār.[1] The garrison was relieved by General Roberts, who made his celebrated march from Kābul with a force of 2,800 Europeans, 7,000 Indian soldiers, and 8,000 followers. The distance of 318 miles was covered in twenty-three days.

Amīr Abdurrahmān. In the end a nephew of Shēr Ali named Abdurrahmān, who had long lived in Russian territory as a pensioner, received sufficient support from his countrymen to be recognized as Amīr of Afghanistan, including Kandahār, which was definitely evacuated by the British forces. The Government of India undertook to support and defend the Amīr against foreign enemies. Ayūb Khān, after recovering possession of Kandahār for a time, was finally defeated by Abdurrahmān, who proved himself to be a strong ruler. Lord Lytton's policy of breaking up Afghanistan into separate states was disallowed and has not been revived.

Results of the Lytton policy. But, as already observed, tangible and valuable results of his action remained. Khelat

[1] The strength of the brigade was 2,476. The casualties amounted to almost half of the force, being: killed and missing, 971 ; wounded, 168. Ayūb Khān's army numbered about 20,000, including irregulars.

(Kalāt) had passed permanently under British control; the occupation of the strong strategical position at Quetta secured the uninterrupted use of the Bolān Pass, and commanded the road to Kandahār so effectively that the evacuation of that city became a matter of slight importance. The decision to restore it to the Amīr probably was right. Although the Kurram valley also was given up in 1880, it was reoccupied in 1892 at the request of the Tūri tribe, and is now administered by an agency of the North-West Frontier Province. The cantonment is at Pārachinār. The Afghan policy of Lord Lytton, looked at broadly, cannot be justly described as a failure, notwithstanding its partial reversal by Lord Ripon under the direction of Mr. Gladstone's Government. Subsequent developments in the time of later Viceroys, effected by the construction of strategical railways and other methods, were rendered feasible by the action of Lord Lytton. A moderate exertion of military power would now suffice at any time for the occupation of Kābul, Kandahār, Ghaznī, or any other important point in Afghanistan on the Indian side of the Hindu Kush. The events of 1917 and 1918, by which Russia has been extinguished as a political and military force for many years, to say the least, have altered the situation so radically that it is difficult for the younger generation now living to realize the reasonableness and intensity of the apprehensions concerning Russia's approach to India which led to the second Afghan War. It should be remembered that all parties, Lord Lawrence as well as Lord Lytton, were agreed that Russia should be excluded from exercising political control over Afghanistan, or from advancing towards the Indian frontier beyond certain limits to be defined. The differences of opinion concerned the methods to be pursued for the attainment of the objects concerning which everybody agreed.

Lord Lytton's error. Lord Lytton at times permitted his imagination to play with visionary schemes for the extension of British influence in Central Asia and for the advancement of the Indian frontier to a dangerous extent. But he did not attempt to realize such dreams. The logical policy actually pursued was carefully thought out and skilfully executed, with one lamentable exception. Nothing should have induced him to yield to Yākūb Khān's request for the stationing of a permanent British envoy at Kābul, a step practically certain to result in disaster. It is impossible to ascertain the Amīr's motive in making the request. He may have made it with the deliberate intention of provoking a massacre, or he may not. However that may be, an attack on the envoy was almost a certainty, and Cavagnari ought not to have been sent to Kābul. With that important reservation Lord Lytton's Afghan policy does not seem to me deserving of censure, when the circumstances of the time are realized and duly considered.

The 'twin gates of Hindostan'. The proposed separation of Kandahār as a principality under British protection did not involve any violation of national feeling or ancient sovereignty.

The tribes of the Kābul province are totally distinct from those of Kandahār, and the political connexion of the two regions under Bārakzai princes was quite recent. With reference to the ' forward policy ' generally and the question of a ' scientific frontier ', it is well to remember that the close connexion of Kābul, Ghaznī, and Kandahār with India Proper dated from ancient times, and had endured for many centuries with interruptions. The Mauryas in the third century B. C., whose capital was at Patna, held the whole country now called Afghanistan as far as the Hindu Kush. Bābur was lord of Kābul when he gained the throne of Hindostan in 1526, and the Kābul province continued to be ruled by his descendants as an integral and important part of the Indian Empire until 1739. Akbar was appointed Governor of Ghaznī in his boyhood, and Kandahār, regained by him in 1595, had been in his father's possession. It would be easy to illustrate at great length the intimate relations which existed for ages between India and the region extending to the Hindu Kush, but it will suffice to quote the explicit statement of Abu-l Fazl, Akbar's learned Secretary of State and historian.

'The wise of ancient times', he justly observes, 'considered Kābul and Kandahār as the twin gates of Hindostan, the one leading to Turkistān and the other to Persia. The custody of those highways secured India from foreign invaders, and they are likewise the appropriate portals to foreign travel.'[1]

When the modern advocates of a forward policy thought of drawing a line of ' scientific frontier ' so as to include the ' twin gates of Hindostan ' they had ample historical justification for their ideas. The expediency of an advance at any given moment must be judged according to the circumstances of the occasion. Questions of international law or abstract justice rarely arise out of dealings with the many diverse tribes of Afghanistan or the military adventurers who have acquired dominion over the country from time to time. Even now, in 1918, we may accept as true the remark of Lord Lytton's daughter that ' impartial observers can only conclude that after many vicissitudes of policy, and a large expenditure of men and money by the Indian Government, the problem of our permanent relations with Afghanistan is still awaiting a durable and satisfactory solution '.

Rendition of Mysore. In 1867 during the viceroyalty of Sir John Lawrence the Secretary of State and the Government of India had decided to restore the Mahārājā of Mysore to power when he should come of age. That event took place in 1881, when the promise made fourteen years earlier was duly fulfilled. The young Mahārājā, an adopted son, who had been carefully trained, succeeded in governing his dominions creditably, with the aid of capable ministers, until his much lamented death in 1894. Another minority followed, which came to an end in 1902, when the present Mahārājā assumed power. Mysore, as already observed, is

[1] *Āīn*, tr. Jarrett, ii. 404.

administered admirably, the half-century of direct British management from 1831 to 1881 having given opportunities for the development of a succession of efficient, well-educated officials.[1]

General census. In the same year (1881) the first general census of all India, except Nepāl and Kashmīr, was taken. The statistics then collected disclosed an enormous mass of important and novel information. Since that date a fresh enumeration has been effected every ten years. The Reports of the various census Commissioners are storehouses of facts and observations concerning the social conditions of the infinitely diverse peoples of India.

Local self-government. The action of Lord Ripon's government concerning Afghanistan and the Vernacular Press Act has been noticed sufficiently. The name of the Marquess is chiefly remembered for a series of Acts passed in 1883–5 introducing the so-called scheme of local self-government, based on the creation of District Boards and subordinate bodies, modelled more or less closely on the English system of County Councils and Rural District Boards. At the same time the powers of Municipal Boards were extended, and the Government of India intimated that the chairman of a municipality should be a non-official, whenever possible. The Supreme Government recognized the fact that one general system could not be imposed upon all provinces. A large discretion necessarily was left to local governments and administrations concerning the manner in which the new institutions should be constituted and operated. The degree to which the elective principle has been introduced varies greatly in different parts of India. The practice of appointing to office by popular election, which is not in accordance with the general sentiment, is difficult to work in a country where caste is the predominant institution, and the electors are sharply divided by differences in race, religion, traditions, and other respects.

The District Boards are concerned primarily with local roads, but are expected to take an interest in education, sanitation, famine relief, and several other departments.

The actual working of the Boards has hardly justified the hopes of Lord Ripon. He avowed that 'it is not primarily with a view to improvement in administration that this measure is put forward and supported. It is chiefly desirable as a measure of political and popular education. His Excellency in Council has himself no doubt that, in the course of time, as local knowledge and local interest are brought to bear more freely on local administration, improved efficiency will, in fact, follow.'

Perhaps.

The Ilbert Bill. A great turmoil was caused in the year 1883 by the introduction of a measure commonly known as the Ilbert Bill, because it was introduced by the Legal Member of Council,

[1] For everything concerning Mysore see the revised ed. of the *Mysore Gazetteer*, an excellent work by B. Lewis Rice, C.I.E., in two thick vols. (Constable, Westminster, 1897).

Mr. (afterwards Sir Courtenay) Ilbert. Up to that time no persons other than Europeans, or in more technical language, 'European British subjects', could be appointed justices of the peace with jurisdiction over persons of the same category, in districts outside the limits of the Presidency towns.[1] The bill proposed to remove from the Code of Criminal Procedure 'at once and completely every judicial disqualification based merely on race distinctions', and consequently to confer on many native or Indian-born magistrates authority to deal with Europeans, as with anybody else. The proposal, although in appearance reasonable and fair, roused the most violent opposition among the planters in the indigo and tea districts and among other classes of the non-official European population in all parts of India. They feared, and not altogether without reason, that their safety in up-country places might be endangered in certain contingencies. A strong counter-agitation was started among the educated Indians, the result being an outbreak of bitter racial feeling such as had not been experienced since the days of the Mutiny. The excitement of the public mind became so threatening that the Government was obliged to withdraw the Bill, and to be content with a much less drastic amendment of the Code, which reserved to European alleged offenders the right to claim trial by jury. The ill-feeling roused by the unlucky Bill did not die down for a long time.

Resignation of Lord Ripon. Lord Ripon resigned office in December 1884. Although he was in reality a commonplace man of moderate abilities, who had never attained in his own country a reputation higher than that of a steady, experienced official, with hereditary rather than personal claims to cabinet rank, the occasion of his departure aroused the most extraordinary demonstrations of enthusiasm for his person among his Indian admirers who lamented his resignation. Hundreds of addresses were presented to him, and his journey from Simla to Bombay resembled a triumphal procession. It is hardly necessary to add that the attitude of his countrymen was different.

The chosen successor of Lord Ripon, Frederick Blackwood, Earl of Dufferin, was a person of a totally diverse type, who may be justly described as a man of genius. He was then fifty-eight years of age, and was specially fitted by reason of his exceptional tact to heal the soreness caused by his predecessor's proceedings.

Qualifications of Lord Dufferin. Sir Alfred Lyall, who was well qualified to judge, believed that

> 'no Governor-general ever came to India so well equipped by antecedent experience for the work as Lord Dufferin. The appointments previously held by Lord Dufferin had been of such a kind that if they had been purposely undertaken as a course of preparatory training for the Indian Viceroyalty, a more appropriate selection could hardly have been made. In Syria, and long afterwards in Turkey, he had learnt the difficult art

[1] The terms 'British subject' and 'European British subject' as used in Indian legislation have technical meanings open to much diversity of interpretation. See Ilbert, *The Government of India.*

of dealing with Asiatic rulers and officials ; he had studied their weakness and their strength. At St. Petersburg and Constantinople he had represented the interests of England on the Eastern Question, and all the issues connected with the wider field of Central Asia were familiar to him. Lastly, in Egypt he had been entrusted with a task that has been continually imposed upon the English Government in India—the task of reforming and reconstructing under European superintendence the dilapidated fabric of an Oriental State.'

Those observations, which demonstrate that Lord Dufferin was unusually well qualified to deal with foreign policy, must be subjected to the reservation that he did not possess any specialized knowledge of Indian affairs, such as that possessed by some of his predecessors who had served on the Board of Control, and that he had little aptitude or taste for the problems of internal administration, which he usually left for the disposal of his colleagues and secretaries.

LORD DUFFERIN.

Lord Dufferin's success. Lord Dufferin, after he had been at the head of the Government of India for some time, became keenly sensible of the unknown dangers which beset the ruler of the Indian Empire. 'I have now', he wrote, 'been two years and a half in this country, that is to say, one-half of my term, and I feel now, and have always felt, like a man engaged in a very dangerous steeplechase over a course interspersed with horribly stiff fences and exceedingly wide brooks. . . . One feels that there can be neither rest nor peace nor breathing time until one has got safe past the winning-post at the end of one's five years.'

He rode his fences so skilfully that he never had occasion to lament a fall. When about to retire he was able to offer the customary congratulations on the peaceful state of the country ; and had the good fortune to find that his hopeful language was not falsified by the event, as had happened to so many of his predecessors.

Mr. Lecky's well-phrased appreciation of Lord Dufferin's character deserves quotation. 'He was a great diplomatist and a great statesman ; a man who possessed to a degree that was hardly equalled by any of his contemporaries, the qualities of brilliancy and the qualities of charm ; a man of unequalled tact and versatility, and who combined with these gifts a rare sagacity of judgement and a singularly firm and tenacious will.' His 'rare gift of carrying out great works with the minimum of friction was perhaps the most distinctive feature of his great Indian career'.

The Panjdeh incident. After the conclusion of Lord Lytton's Afghan War, the advance of the Tsar's armies in Central Asia continued rapidly and without serious check until the beginning of 1885, when a Russian force came into contact with the Afghan outposts at Panjdeh. On March 29 the Russian commander sent an ultimatum to the Afghans requiring them to withdraw from their position. The Afghans, claiming to be within their own boundary, refused. A sharp action ensued. The Russians, who were victorious, then proclaimed the annexation of Panjdeh, which lies between Herat and Merv. This incident aroused a storm of warlike passion in both India and the United Kingdom, before which even Mr. Gladstone's pacific Government had to bend. Active preparations for a war with Russia began, and the Muscovite authorities, seeing that England was in earnest, withdrew some of their pretensions, so that the affair was adjusted by negotiation.

Immediately after taking over charge Lord Dufferin had occasion to apply the personal qualifications which have been described to the troubled waters of Afghan politics, and especially to securing the goodwill of the Amīr, Abdurrahmān. The Viceroy arranged an interview at Rāwalpindi with the Amīr, who crossed the frontier on the very day on which the Russians attacked his troops at Panjdeh.

The Amīr, taking the sensible view that the affair at Panjdeh should be treated merely as a frontier skirmish, did not much care whether or not the Russians secured the disputed bit of territory. The thing he really cared about was 'the exclusion at all hazards of British troops and officers from Afghanistan'. Being equally resolved to keep out the Russians, he wished to be allowed to defend himself with English aid in the shape of arms and money only, not men. That resolve of the Amīr's was a relief to Lord Dufferin, who much disliked the prospect of being compelled by existing engagements to risk an army on the Russo-Afghan frontier. He remarked that 'we have undertaken to defend the inviolability of a frontier nearly a thousand miles from our own borders'; and felt that it was much more satisfactory not to be obliged to stake anything beyond so many lakhs of rupees. He recognized that the obligations undertaken by Lord Ripon to defend Abdurrahmān were 'very absolute and specific'—not to be evaded, whatever the cost might be.

The Amīr went home pleased. The immediate difficulty was ultimately settled by diplomacy and the appointment of a boundary commission, which gave the disputed tract at Panjdeh to Russia. In business of this kind the personal gifts and special experience of Lord Dufferin were invaluable.

Burmese intrigues with France. Early in the same year, 1885, the Governor-general learned that Theebaw, the King of Burma, had concluded a treaty with the French Government, under which France obtained certain peculiar consular and commercial privileges of a threatening character. A trained diplomatist like Lord Dufferin could not allow the intrusion of France into the affairs of Burma, which the Government of India regarded as its own exclusive concern. About the same time King Theebaw showed his dislike and contempt for the British by imposing an enormous fine of twenty-three lakhs of rupees upon the Bombay and Burma Trading Company and ordering the arrest of the employés of the Company. His action is believed to have been suggested by Monsieur Haas, the over-zealous French agent.[1]

Third Burmese War. Lord Dufferin then, with the sanction of the Home Government, dispatched an ultimatum to the Burmese court demanding the immediate settlement of all matters in dispute. The king, who, like his predecessors, was disposed to overrate the strength at his command, sent an evasive reply, and ordered his troops to resist the British advance. On November 14 the Indian army crossed the frontier. The lessons of previous campaigns had been so well learned that no serious opposition was encountered. On the 27th of the same month King Theebaw agreed to surrender, and on the following day, Mandalay, then the capital, was occupied. The war, which had been of a merely nominal character, was thus ended in a fortnight. King Theebaw and his family were deported at once to India, and ultimately settled at Ratnagiri in the Bombay Presidency, where the deposed monarch lived for many years. His personal fate need not excite sympathy or regret. His accession had been marked by the ruthless massacre of about eighty of his relations, and during his short reign he had shown himself to be an intemperate and cruel tyrant.

Annexation of Upper Burma. Lord Dufferin, from the first, had made up his mind to annex the country. Before the war he had written to the Chief Commissioner of Lower Burma: 'If, however, the French proceedings should eventuate in any serious attempt to forestall us in Upper Burmah, I should not hesitate to annex the country; and, as at present advised, I think that this mode of procedure would be preferable to setting up a doubtful prince.'

The Viceroy's action seems to have been determined chiefly as a matter of high politics in order to exclude the threatened French interference from the side of Siam. The grievances of the Trading Company, although real and serious, evidently occupied a secondary place in his thoughts.

[1] For a good account of the intolerable provocations offered by Theebaw, who had come to the throne in 1878, see pp. 33–43 of *Burma* by J. G. Scott, 'Shway Yoe' (London, Redway, 1886), a little book of permanent interest, long out of print. Theebaw was encouraged by knowledge of the British difficulties in Afghanistan and South Africa in 1879 and 1880. The British Resident at Mandalay was withdrawn in 1879.

A formal proclamation of annexation was issued on January 1, 1886. The absorption of the whole Burmese Empire had thus been effected in sixty years, beginning with the annexation of Arakan and Tenasserim in 1826. Pegu had followed in 1852.

The easy conquest of Upper Burma completed the tale of annexations on a considerable scale open to a Governor-general of India. Nothing more remained to be taken.

India and Burma. The natural bonds connecting the Indian Empire with Burma are slight. The Burmese, although they had obtained Buddhism and various elements of civilization from India in ancient times, had little in common with the peoples of India. Caste, the distinctive Indian institution, is unknown in Burma, which is more akin to China than to India. Those facts make it difficult for the Supreme Government of India to do full justice to the claims of its great dependency to the east of the Bay of Bengal. It is not improbable that Burma would be better administered and would enjoy improved opportunities for progress if it were detached from India, as the Straits Settlements are. Those settlements might be treated as a dependency of Burma.

Guerilla warfare. The deposition of King Theebaw and the formal annexation of his dominions were accomplished with facility which proved deceptive. The real trouble began when the formal war was finished. The robber bands, which had long infested the country and were regarded by spirited young men as affording suitable outlets for their love of adventure, were now reinforced by swarms of disbanded soldiery led by sundry pretenders to the throne. The irregular resistance of such bands lasted for five years, and became so formidable that at one time 30,000 regular troops were employed against them. Civil government was gradually introduced during that long period of disturbance, and in the end the country settled down. In 1897 Upper and Lower Burma were united so as to form a single immense province administered by a Lieutenant-governor. In due time he will develop into a Governor with all the trappings of the ruler of a Presidency. The country possesses infinite material possibilities, and the people have many virtues, as well as some faults.[1]

Restoration of Gwālior Fort. A graceful concession to sentiment was made in 1886 when Lord Dufferin handed over to the Mahārājā Sindia the famous fort of Gwālior, 'the pearl in the necklace of the castles of Hind'. Morār was given up at the same time, the town of Jhānsi being taken in exchange. The arrangements pleased all parties, and the military strength of the empire was not impaired, changes in the art of war having destroyed the strategical value of the ancient fortresses.

Queen Victoria's jubilee. The 'jubilee' of Queen Victoria, marking her completion of fifty years of sovereignty, was celebrated

[1] 'The potential wealth in Upper Burma, not to speak of Western China, the Shan States, and Karennee, is simply incalculable. . . . Upper Burma is, undoubtedly, more fertile and promising than our older provinces' (Scott, op. cit., p. 162).

COUNCIL CHAMBER, MANDALAY.
(Since demolished.)

in 1887 at every station and town throughout India with appropriate ceremonial and genuine enthusiasm. The character of Her late Majesty commanded the spontaneous veneration of all classes.

Rent or Tenancy Acts. Lord Dufferin's Government passed three important Rent or Tenancy Acts regulating the rural economy of large provinces. The Bengal Tenancy Act of 1885, designed as an improvement on Act X of 1859, was based on the principles of fixity of tenure and judicial rents. The objeetion that it violated the terms of the Permanent Settlement was rightly disallowed. The Governor-general had no diffieulty in showing that the Act aimed at putting into practice the unfulfilled intentions of Lord Cornwallis.

The conditions in Oudh being different, and tenant-right or 'right of occupaney' being enjoyed by only a small minority of the peasantry, the legislature sought to strengthen the position of the numerous tenants-at-will by granting them a statutory holding for seven years, with a right to compensation for improvements (1886).

In the Panjāb, where the land is largely cultivated by the owners, the question of 'right of oecupancy' is less urgent than it is in Bengal and the United Provinces. The Act of 1887 gave the protécted tenants a limited guarantee against eviction and enhancement of rent. The relations between landlord and tenant everywhere present problems of such extreme eomplexity and difficulty that legislation on the subject never can attain more than an imperfect and moderate degree of suceess.

Retirement of Lord Dufferin. In 1888 Lord Dufferin, who felt the burden of advancing years and was influenced by domestic anxieties, expressed a desire to retire from India and resume diplomatic employment. Lord Salisbury, who had returned to power in 1886, willingly complied with the wishes of the Viceroy and kept the embassy at Rome open for him until he should be ready to assume eharge. At the close of the year Lord Dufferin was relieved by the Marquess of Lansdowne, another brilliant Irish nobleman, and was rewarded for his services by a step in the peerage as Marquess of Dufferin and Ava.

If Lord Dufferin may not be given a place in the front rank of the Governors-general, he certainly merits recognition as one of the most successful. His premature retirement was generally regretted.

CHRONOLOGY

Lord Lytton Viceroy; Royal Titles Act; occupation of Quetta	1876
Famine in Deccan and south	1876–8
Imperial Assemblage (January 1)	1877
Vernacular Press Act	1878
Second Afghan War	1878–80
Abolition of customs hedge	1879

Resignation of Lord Lytton; Lord Ripon Viceroy (April); battle of Maiwand (July 27); march of Roberts to Kandahār (August); reversal of Afghan policy	1880
Rendition of Mysore; first general census of India	1881
Repeal of Vernacular Press Act	1882
Education Committee's report	1883
Ilbert Bill controversy	1883–4
Lord Dufferin Viceroy	1884
Panjdeh incident; third Burmese War	1885
Tenancy Acts (Bengal, Oudh, Panjāb)	1885–7
Annexation of Upper Burma (January 1); restoration of Gwālior Fort	1886
Queen Victoria's 'jubilee'	1887
Resignation of Lord Dufferin; Lord Lansdowne Viceroy	1888

Authorities

The R. I. series ends with Lord Mayo. No large scale biography of the first Earl of Lytton, the Viceroy, exists. The leading authority is *The History of Lord Lytton's Indian Administration, 1876 to 1880; compiled from Letters and Official Papers by* Lady Betty Balfour, his daughter (Longmans, 1899). That volume (551 pp.), prepared with the help of Sir J. Strachey and Sir A. Lyall, contains many documents not accessible elsewhere. All military details are stated authoritatively in *The Second Afghan War 1878–80; Official Account produced in the Intelligence Branch, Army H.Q., India* (734 pp., Murray, 1908); originally 'secret', but revised in 1907 for publication and sale.

The Second Afghan War, 1878–79–80; its Causes, its Conduct, and its Consequences, by Col. H. B. Hanna (3 vols., Constable, 1899–1910), is virtually a huge Radical pamphlet, bitterly hostile to Lords Beaconsfield, Salisbury, and Lytton, and their advisers, and avowedly designed to 'deal a deadly blow to the Forward Policy'. Sir Alfred Lyall, *Life of the Marquis of Dufferin and Ava*, 2 vols., 1905.

The following secondary authorities may be consulted: R. C. Dutt, *India in the Victorian Age*, 1904, written from the National Congress point of view; L. J. Trotter, *History of India under Queen Victoria, 1836–1880* (1886); and Marshman and E. M. D., *Abridgment* (Blackwood, 1901).

CHAPTER 3

Lord Lansdowne; frontier defence; Manipur; exchange and currency; Lord Elgin II; Chitrāl and Tirāh campaigns; plague and famine; Lord Curzon; famine; foreign affairs and frontier arrangements; internal administration; Lord Minto II; constitutional changes; anarchist crime; Lord Hardinge of Penshurst; visit of Their Majesties.

Lord Lansdowne. The Marquess of Lansdowne, who succeeded Lord Dufferin, had gained official experience in his earlier days as Under-Secretary for War and also for India. Later he had served, like his predecessor, as Governor-general of Canada. He remained in office as Viceroy a little longer than the customary period of five years, and enjoyed a generally quiet time, notwithstanding two small frontier expeditions. The third Burmese War had closed the paths of conquest, and the alarms about Russian aggression had gradually faded away.

Frontier defence. The Viceroy devoted special attention to questions of frontier defence, and adopted measures well calculated to prevent future panics. He established friendly relations with the Amīr of Kābul by sending Sir H. Mortimer Durand as a special envoy on a temporary mission. The envoy travelled without any escort, trusting himself unreservedly to the honour and hospitality of his host. The result was eminently satisfactory. Various frontier difficulties were then settled in a friendly spirit, and arrangements were made to demarcate the southern and eastern frontiers of Afghanistan by a boundary since known as 'the Durand line'. The subsidy to the Amīr was raised from twelve to eighteen lakhs. Efficient arrangements had been made at an earlier date for guaranteeing the security of Quetta, and in 1889 the Viceroy, when visiting that station, was able to announce that the once dreaded Bolān Pass had become 'a safe and peaceable highway'. The pass proper is fifty-four miles in length. The North-Western Railway now extends to Chaman, about fifty miles beyond Quetta. An extension to Kandahār could be constructed without much difficulty. All political arrangements in the Balōchistan region were effected through Sir Robert Sandeman, an officer of extraordinary ability, endowed with a singular faculty for exercising personal influence. He died in 1892. Critics in the Indian National Congress party, who were incapable of appreciating the value of an insurance policy, and could not see anything beyond the immediate expense, rashly accused Lord Lansdowne of 'silly imperialism' and 'wasteful expenditure'. The value of the Viceroy's foresight has been tested and proved by the prolonged crisis of the Great War. The strength of the frontier defences has justified the Government of India in denuding the country of troops to an extent which would have been madness if Lord Lansdowne, building upon the foundations laid by Lord Lytton, had not provided the means for guarding against attack and for sending up reinforcements as required.

Hunza and Nagar. In 1891 and 1892 a gap in the defences of the north-western frontier was closed by the occupation of Hunza and Nagar in the Gilgit Valley, two strongholds commanding the road to Chitrāl and certain passes over the Hindu Kush. The capture of the almost inaccessible forts was effected by Indian troops with extraordinary gallantry.[1]

Manipur. The small hill principality of Manipur, situated on the borders of Assam to the east of Kāchār (Cachar), was the scene of an unexampled and audacious crime in 1891. Troubles having arisen owing to a disputed succession, the Government of India decided to exile the Sēnapati, or commander-in-chief of the local

[1] The little campaign is vividly described in one of the best books of travel ever written, *Where Three Empires Meet*, by E. F. Knight (1893). The three empires mean India, Russia, and China.

forces, who was a brother of the Rājā lately deposed. Mr. Quinton, the Chief Commissioner of Assam, with an escort of five hundred men, was ordered up to Manipur to make the necessary arrangements. The Sēnapati not only refused to obey the summons of the Viceroy's representative, but offered armed resistance. Fighting went on until sunset on March 24. An interview between the Chief Commissioner and the Sēnapati having been arranged, the British officers were treacherously attacked. Mr. Quinton and certain members of his staff were captured and deliberately beheaded by the public executioner. The escort retired towards Kāchār. During the retirement strange incidents happened, some of a highly creditable, and others of a painful nature. At the end of April the outrage was avenged, the Sēnapati and some of his accomplices being hanged. A boy was appointed Rājā. During his minority the state was administered by the Political Agent, who introduced many reforms. The young Rājā, who had been educated at the Mayo College, Ajmēr, was invested with powers in 1907.

Khelat (Kalāt) and Kashmīr. After the death of Sir Robert Sandeman in 1892 the Khān of Khelat (Kalāt) committed so many acts of violence, including the murder of a bedridden cripple aged ninety-four, that he was required to abdicate in favour of his son. The Mahārājā of Kashmīr, who had found the difficulties of government too much for him, surrendered his powers for a time to a council of regency. Reforms having been effected, the Mahārājā subsequently resumed his functions.

Exchange. In India the standard of value for several centuries had been silver, that is to say, all debts, public or private, had to be paid in silver rupees. Early in the nineteenth century the rupee had been worth sometimes as much as one-eighth of an English gold sovereign, or, as expressed in British silver currency, two shillings and sixpence. About 1870 the rupee was commonly reckoned as being worth the tenth part of a sovereign or two shillings in silver, and it was customary to convert rupees into pounds sterling or sovereigns at the rate of ten to one, a thousand rupees being taken as equivalent to a hundred pounds. About 1873–4 the value of silver in relation to gold was disturbed by various causes, with the result that in 1878 a thousand rupees were worth little more than fifty pounds. The Government of India being obliged to make large payments in England for diverse purposes, the heavy and fluctuating fall in exchange threw Indian finance into confusion, while European officials and other persons who could not avoid remitting family charges and savings to England in order to make payments there in gold under English law were gravely embarrassed, and injured by the loss of a large percentage of their income. Proposals to remedy the intolerable state of affairs were discussed for many years without result. At last, in 1893, the Government of India and the Home Government decided to close the mints against the free coinage of silver, and subsequently resolved to admit gold as a legal tender, so that debts, whether public or private, might be lawfully paid in either silver or gold. The result of Lord Lansdowne's legislation, as modified some years later in Lord Curzon's time, has been to steady the rate of exchange, which now is approximately 1*s*. 4*d*. to the rupee. In other words, a sovereign is valued at fifteen rupees, and a thousand rupees are worth about sixty-six sovereigns. The limitation of coinage has given the rupee an artificial value as money, usually far exceeding its intrinsic value as silver bullion. The disadvantages of the arrangement are two, namely, that a premium is placed on the counterfeiting of rupees even in good silver, and that the value of the large hoards of silver bullion in the hands of the Indian population is depreciated. But, notwithstanding those disadvantages, and the necessary loss of income to European residents in India, nobody has been able to devise a better plan. The subject is too intricate and technical to admit conveniently of further exposition. The currency measures initiated by Lord Lansdowne's government secured financial prosperity, and provided the yearly surplus of revenue which enabled Lord Curzon to effect his numerous reforms.

Lord Elgin II; frontiers. In 1894 Lord Lansdowne was relieved by Lord Elgin, son of the nobleman who had been at the head of the Government for a short time in 1862–3. The new Viceroy had never held any important office and could not be credited with the possession of any conspicuous personal distinction. His administration lasted for four years. Relations with Russia were improved by a treaty settling the frontier of the two empires in the lofty mountains of the Pāmīrs; the demarcation of the Afghan boundary was completed; and the frontier line between Burma on one side and China and Siam on the other was marked out.

Chitrāl. A disputed succession in the little state of Chitrāl, lying among the mountains to the west of Gilgit and south of the Hindu Kush, led to a small war in 1895, during which the Political Agent underwent a siege and a detachment of a hundred Sikhs was destroyed. In due course the fort was relieved and the leaders of the opposition were deported. Since then Chitrāl has been quiet.

Tirāh. Two years later a more serious frontier operation was rendered necessary by the rising of the strong Afrīdī clans, who closed the Khyber Pass. The valleys south of the pass, until then unexplored, were penetrated, and the active resistance of the clans was broken. The campaign was on an unusually large scale, 40,000 troops or more being employed. The thorough subjugation of the tribes seems to be as far off as ever.

Plague and famine. The latter part of Lord Elgin's term of office was clouded by the calamities of pestilence and famine. Bubonic plague, the same dread disease which had ravaged London and other parts of England in 1663–5, was known to be endemic or locally indigenous in certain places in India, especially on the slopes of the Himalayas, where it had existed without attracting much notice. An epidemic spread over a considerable region in Cutch and Sind in 1812, where it lasted for ten years. In 1836 the disease extended over a large area in Rājputānā. But no very widely diffused outbreak in India seems to be recorded after 1616, in the reign of Jahāngīr, when the pestilence wrought havoc in almost every locality of northern and western India, lasting for eight years. Jahāngīr, an acute observer, described the symptoms accurately, and noted how the disease affected rats and mice. The Deccan was smitten in 1703 and 1704.

The great modern epidemic, which has not yet disappeared (1918), began at Bombay in 1896, having been introduced apparently from China. It spread by degrees into nearly every province. Up to the end of 1903 more than two million deaths had been reported, and the actual mortality must have been much greater. While the disease was a novelty and confined to a comparatively small area the various provincial authorities tried to combat it by strict quarantine regulations and other measures which offended the sentiment of the population, especially that of the Hindus. Violent opposition was aroused. At Poona two young British officers employed on plague duty were murdered deliberately, while sanguinary riots occurred at Bombay and other places. Experience having proved that it was impossible to prevent the disease from spreading the early regulations were modified, and everybody was forced to recognize that the pestilence had come to stay. A method of inoculation with a serum has been efficacious when given a fair trial. It is impossible to predict when the plague will disappear, as it disappeared long ago from Europe as an epidemic disease. The stray cases which have reached Europe of late years have not developed any general pestilence.

The famine of 1896–7, believed to have been the most severe ever known, was estimated to have affected a population of nearly seventy millions. It was especially intense in the United Provinces, the Central Provinces, Bihār, and the Hissār District of the Panjāb. All the statistics of the visitation are on a gigantic scale. The calamity was fought as effectively as possible by Sir Antony MacDonnell, the Lieutenant-governor of the United Provinces and Oudh. The administration of the Central Provinces, where special difficulties were encountered, was far less successful. A Commission under Sir James Lyall reported in 1898 on the results, and again discussed the principles of famine relief, a subject on which general agreement is not easily attained. No system can do more than mitigate the horrors of an intense and extended famine due to failure of rain in an enormous area.

Lord Curzon. At the beginning of 1899 Lord Elgin was succeeded by Lord Curzon of Kedleston, then not quite forty years of age, the youngest of the Governors-general, excepting Lord Dalhousie. Although the new Viceroy had not enjoyed the exceptional experience of Lord Dufferin in offices of the highest rank, no ruler of India before or since took up the task of governing the Indian Empire with an equipment of special, laboriously acquired knowledge so vast as that possessed by Lord Curzon of Kedleston. He had spent a large part of the ten years preceding his assumption of the Viceroyalty in travels of extraordinary range, chiefly in Asia. His immense book on Persia is a lasting monument commemorating the zeal and intelligence with which he accumulated exact knowledge concerning the strange countries which he explored.

'He had spent nearly one year at the India Office and three years at the Foreign Office. He had visited India four times and had travelled widely within its borders. He knew at first hand the North-west Frontier, always an object of deep anxiety. He had a close personal acquaintance with the other countries of Asia, and had studied and pondered the problems they presented. He had met a singular variety of Asiatic rulers, including such diverse potentates as the Shah of Persia, the Amir of Afghanistan, the King of Korea, the King of Siam (with whom he frequently corresponded), the Emperor of Annam, and the King of Cambodia. Among administrators of lesser rank may be mentioned Li Hung Chang, with whom he was on terms of considerable intimacy. This preliminary experience of intercourse with Asiatics of exalted position was of great value in his new office, which brought him into contact with the princes and chiefs of India.' [1]

LORD CURZON OF KEDLESTON.

In addition to those peculiar qualifications for office in India, Lord Curzon was endowed with gifts fitted to win eminence in any field of human activity, gifts which included eloquence, style, industry, imagination, sympathy, a faculty for

[1] Lovat Fraser, 3rd ed., p. 16.

organization, and other merits rarely combined in one man. Such manifold capacity naturally tempted the possessor to exercise his powers, and to embark on a course of reform, which led him to deal with every department of the administration, and to leave his personal mark on each. Most critics are agreed that Lord Curzon, like Lord Dalhousie, whom he resembled in some respects, went too fast. India does not like to be 'hustled', and unrestrained activity in reform is certain to produce a reaction. The feverish energy of Lord Dalhousie undoubtedly was one of the elements in the great reaction of the Mutiny ; and it is not unjust to affirm that the outbreak of unrest and grave political crime which ensued after Lord Curzon's resignation was in some measure stimulated by feelings of irritation induced by the cumulative effect of incessant change. Lord Curzon, like everybody else, of course, made mistakes from time to time ; but it may be said with truth that almost every one of the innumerable administrative changes effected by him was in itself an improvement. Yet, the pace was too fast, and the improvements were too many.

The calm judgement of history cannot now be passed upon the achievements of a ruler of India who happily is still (1918) engaged in important public duties at a time of unexampled difficulty. The administration of India by Lord Curzon is too near to be viewed in true perspective, and impartial consideration of his more disputable acts is hindered by the passions of contemporary party politics. Moreover, the inner history of events so recent has not been, and cannot at present be disclosed. That difficulty, the lack of authentic documents with the consequent paucity of information, hampers the historian more or less throughout the period since the Mutiny. The books dealing with the administration of the Viceroys, even when of considerable bulk, have been so discreetly edited as to leave much untold. After the time of Lord Lansdowne authentic accessible records are particularly scanty.

A slight outline sketch of a few of the more outstanding features of Lord Curzon's brilliant administration is all that can be attempted in this work.

Famine of 1900. At the very beginning of his term of office he was confronted by a formidable famine, which became intense in 1900 and smote with especial severity the favoured province of Gujarāt, usually exempt from such distress. The calamity was encountered with untiring energy by the Viceroy and multitudes of brave men and women working under him, who often sacrificed their lives in the cause of the suffering millions. A Famine Commission under the presidency of Sir Antony Macdonell, which reported in 1901, was disposed to think that relief, especially in the Central Provinces, had been distributed with too lavish a hand. Excessive liberality results, not only in financial embarrassment, but in the demoralization of the people. The exact line between excess and defect is not easily drawn.

Afghan affairs. In 1901 Abdurrahmān, Amīr of Afghanistan, was succeeded by his son Habībullah. Lord Curzon managed to keep on friendly terms with the new Amīr, although not without difficulty. The Amīr claimed the title of King, and was conceded the style of 'His Majesty' in official correspondence. The allowances promised by Lord Lansdowne continued to be paid. The Great War has seriously affected the political position of Afghanistan, as of almost every country in the world, to such an extent that the policy of previous times has little applicability to the present. The future is incalculable.

Persian Gulf. All British statesmen have been and are agreed that foreign powers should be excluded from political control over the Persian Gulf, where British naval power should be supreme. In Lord Curzon's time Turks, French, Russians, and Germans all tried to secure a footing on the shores or islands of the Gulf. The Viceroy himself visited the region and took effective steps to protect the interests of his country. In the course of the world conflict the utter impotence of Persia has been revealed, and new prospects have been opened by the operations in Mesopotamia.

Tibetan expedition. The most notable and most debatable incident in Lord Curzon's foreign policy was the Tibetan expedition of 1903–4. The friendly relations between the governments of the Grand Lama and of India which existed in the time of Warren Hastings had come to an end long before Lord Curzon entered upon his office. The Tibetans showed a resolve to keep their country sealed against all intercourse with India, and disregarded conventions laboriously arranged. When Lord Curzon assumed charge the relations of India with Tibet were at an 'absolute deadlock'. A Russian agent having been received at Lhasa, and the attitude of the Tibetans having become unmistakably hostile, the Viceroy thought that the time for action had arrived, his letters to the Grand Lama's government not having been accorded any reply. In November 1903 he persuaded the Home Government to sanction a limited advance to Gyantse, about half-way to Lhasa, in order to obtain reparation. Strict instructions were given by the Secretary of State that the operations should be temporary, and that the mission should be withdrawn as soon as its object was attained. The Tibetans having offered armed resistance, the further advance to Lhasa was sanctioned in July 1904. In August the mysterious city was 'unveiled', and temporarily occupied. The expedition, which had crossed a pass 19,000 feet above the sea, returned safely during the autumn. Differences of opinion between the home and viceregal governments developed, so that little was gained by the operations beyond an extension of geographical knowledge, and the satisfaction of reaching Lhasa, which had been so long inaccessible. Tibet had to pay a small indemnity, and the suzerainty of China over the country was confirmed by the diplomacy of the British Foreign Office. Since the establishment of the Chinese Republic, Tibet seems to have become independent again. So far as I can judge the expedition was unnecessary and all but fruitless.

North-West Frontier Province. Lord Curzon is entitled to the credit of eminent success in his management of the tribal frontier. Previously the dealings with the tribes to the north of Sind had been in the hands of the provincial government of the Panjāb, which had the Frontier Force and Guides at its disposal. The results had been unsatisfactory and scores of raids or punitive expeditions had failed to produce any permanent effect. Lord Curzon, adopting and modifying an idea of Lord Lytton, created in 1901 the North-West Frontier Province, administered by a Chief Commissioner with head-quarters at Peshāwar, and responsible directly to the Government of India. The reform was carried out in a manner needlessly irritating to the Panjāb Government, which lost all the territory to the west of the Indus, except the Dēra Ghāzī Khān District. The new province also received the Hazāra District and was thus provided with charming sites for hill stations. The measure, although it might have been brought into operation with less friction, deserves unreserved commendation on its merits. The province as at present constituted has a ragged appearance on the map, and is so constructed that its administration must be difficult. Means to make it more compact and manageable may be found at some future time. The large area formerly known as the North-Western Provinces (N.W.P.) was rechristened in order to avoid confusion, and was styled the Agra Province. The whole region, including Oudh, under the jurisdiction of the Lieutenant-governor, whose head-quarters are at Allahabad and Naini Tāl, is now called the United Provinces of Agra and Oudh (U.P.). The designation is not convenient, the capital being Allahabad, not Agra. Oudh was mentioned in the name in order to gratify local sentiment, which objected to the complete merger of the small kingdom in its large neighbour. The local government spends some time each year at Lucknow, the capital of Oudh.

Frontier tribes. In his transactions with the frontier tribes on the Panjāb border the Viceroy sought to apply, so far as differences of conditions would permit, the system of peaceful influence worked so successfully by Sir Robert Sandeman in Balōchistan. He based his arrangements on the principles of 'withdrawal of British forces from advanced positions, employment of tribal forces in the defence of tribal country, concentration of British forces behind them as a safeguard and a support, and improvement of communications in the rear'.

The policy, which involved the organization of a considerable force of Frontier Militia, has been justified by success. Only one little frontier war, that against the Mahsūds, occurred during Lord Curzon's time. It was called a 'blockade', for the sake of appearances.

Native States and Berār. The Viceroy, who took the most lively interest in the Native or Protected States, forty of which he visited, has been criticized, and apparently with justice, for showing too much readiness to interfere in their affairs. His successor, Lord Minto, was more restrained in his action. The most important transaction with a Native State was the settlement in 1902 of the long-standing Berār difficulty by means of a confidential personal discussion with the Nizam, at which no one else was present. The little province was made over to the Government of India under the fiction of a perpetual lease, so as to preserve the nominal sovereignty of Hyderabad. Berār ceased to exist as a separate province and was attached as a Division to the Central Provinces. The financial terms arranged were favourable to the Nizam, who is said to have been satisfied. The opportunity was taken to get rid of the Hyderabad Contingent as a distinct force, and to merge it in the Indian army. So far as is known the arrangements work well.

Viceregal energy. The inexhaustible energy of Lord Curzon, which ill health could not quench, attacked the problems of internal administration on every side. He explored minutely the details of every department and overstrained his strength by doing too much himself. The marked tendency to draw all business up to head-quarters had a pernicious effect upon the more independent members of the services, who felt that their power of action was unduly restricted and that the exercise of responsible discretion was discouraged.

Land revenue. The land revenue administration having been made the subject of much hostile criticism, the Viceroy replied in January 1902 by an exhaustive 'Resolution', written by himself. He demonstrated that famines were due to drought, not to over-assessment, and laid down principles designed to ensure greater elasticity both in assessment and in collection.

Land Alienation Act. All observers are agreed that the almost universal indebtedness of the peasantry and the numerous transfers of ownership or tenant-right to members of the trading and money-lending classes are evils to be deplored. But they are evils more easily deplored than remedied. It is extremely difficult to prevent a willing seller from concluding with an eager buyer a transaction in no way immoral, although deemed by authority to be contrary to the public interest. The mischievous effects of the alienation of land were felt with especial severity in the Panjāb, where agitators have not been slow to take advantage of the discontent of dispossessed landholders. The Government of Lord Curzon attempted a remedy by passing the Land Alienation Act (XIII of 1900) applicable to that province. The broad effect is described as being that 'money-lenders, shopkeepers, and professional men cannot buy land from hereditary cultivators, or hold such land on mortgage for more than twenty years without the consent of the State'. The sale of land to the excluded classes under decree of court is also forbidden. The difficulty of working such an arbitrary prohibition and the facility of evasion are obvious. The principle of the Act has been extended to certain other territories. Co-operative rural banks, modelled on a German system, have been established in the hope of lessening the burden of debt on the peasantry.

Higher education. The Viceroy bestowed intense study on

the education problem, even to the injury of his health. His labours, aided by those of a preliminary committee and a commission, resulted in the enactment of the Universities Act, 1904. The Act reduced the excessive numbers of members of the Senates, reformed the constitution of the Syndicates or executive bodies, placed in the hands of the Government of India the final decision concerning the affiliation or disaffiliation of colleges, and provided for the official inspection of affiliated colleges.

Grave abuses loudly calling for reform undoubtedly existed, especially in Bengal. It is equally certain that Lord Curzon's motive was the improvement, not the destruction of higher education. Vested interests were hit hard by the Act. For that reason, combined with certain others, based on objections to the stringency of official control, a most unjust accusation that the Viceroy entertained feelings of hostility to the educated classes was loudly proclaimed and widely credited. The unpopularity of Lord Curzon among those classes during the latter part of his term of office was mainly, or at least, largely due to the action taken by his Government concerning the universities and colleges. Much of the fuel for the flaming excitement aroused by the so-called 'partition of Bengal' was supplied by the defenders of university and college abuses, and the honest advocates of educational independence as they understood that term. The appointment of a Minister of Education was arranged after Lord Curzon's resignation.

The 'partition of Bengal'. The so-called partition of Bengal was not originally planned by the Viceroy. The discussion about the rearrangement of certain provincial boundaries had begun among his subordinates in 1901, but no definite proposal was made until two years later, in 1903, when the Lieutenant-governor of Bengal propounded a certain plan for lightening the intolerable burden resting upon his shoulders. At that time he was supposed to administer a territory comprising 189,000 square miles with a population of seventy-eight millions. The task could not be performed with any approach to success. Eastern Bengal especially was utterly neglected, financially starved, and allowed to present 'the most astounding record of modern crime in existence'.

Lord Curzon, after paying a visit to Eastern Bengal, recognized the absolute necessity of reducing the jurisdiction of the Lieutenant-governor. Various possible arrangements were considered and publicly discussed. In 1905 the proposals of the Government of India took definite shape. Their main features, as modified by the Secretary of State in Council, were the separation from the Calcutta Government of the Divisions of Dacca, Chittagong, and Rājshāhi, the suppression of the Chief Commissionership of Assam, and the formation of a new province called 'Eastern Bengal and Assam' under a Lieutenant-governor with his capital at Dacca. The scheme was sanctioned, and different Secretaries of State repeatedly declared that the decision was irrevocable. The arrangement, contrary to expectation, provoked intense and passionate hostility in Calcutta and throughout Bengal, where a cry was raised that the Bengālī nation was being maliciously torn asunder. Serious crimes were committed in support of the agitation, but by the end of 1910 the excitement had died down, and Eastern Bengal had begun to experience the benefits of a government on the spot which cared for its interests. Unfortunately, as I think, the ministry in power in 1911 thought fit to reverse the decision so often affirmed. H.M. the King-Emperor was advised to announce at the Coronation Durbar the adoption of the plan now in force which restored the Chief Commissionership of Assam, and created the new province of Bihār and Orissa, including Chutiā Nagpur, with its capital at Patna-Bankipore. Bengal proper thus remained undivided under the Calcutta Government. The sufferer was Eastern Bengal, with its preponderance of Muhammadan population, which was again made over to the tender mercies of Calcutta. Perhaps the most neglected part of India will now be given better treatment than it ever received in the past. The withdrawal of the Bihār and Orissa province has given material relief to the over-worked Government of Bengal, which can now spare some time and money for the eastern districts.

The relics of the past. Although some of Lord Curzon's predecessors, notably Lord Lytton, and now and then a provincial governor, had displayed some sense of the duty incumbent on a civilized government to cherish the crumbling relics of the past and to explore the treasures of ancient art buried in the soil of innumerable forgotten cities, high authorities were, as a rule, too much immersed in the current business of war, policy, or administration to pay serious attention to the less obvious claims of science upon their attention.

The official efforts made from time to time to preserve the monuments of former ages and to investigate the hidden remains of antiquity were spasmodic, desultory, unscientific, and planned on a penurious scale. Lord Curzon stands alone as the reverent liberal guardian of the heritage of the present from the past, and as the earnest advocate of adequate, instructed exploration. He justly claimed credit for initiating a 'scientific and stedfast policy' in the matter.

> 'I hope', he said, when addressing the Asiatic Society of Bengal in 1900, 'to assert more definitely during my time the Imperial responsibility of Government in respect of Indian antiquities, to inaugurate or to persuade a more liberal attitude on the part of those with whom it rests to provide the means, and to be a faithful guardian of the priceless treasure-house of art and learning that has, for a few years at any rate, been committed to my charge.'

The promise then made has been nobly redeemed.

Lord Curzon's achievement. Every important building or group of monuments known to exist in any province or state has been examined, and in the great majority of cases decay has been arrested by processes of conservation, usually executed with discretion. Research has not been neglected. The exploration of buried remains and the study of inscriptions have been prosecuted vigorously in conjunction with the urgent work of a comprehensive scheme of conservation. The Government of India has at present no reason for self-reproach with regard to its care for the extant memorials of the past, and in most provinces research and exploration of many kinds have been active. The Protected States have become deeply interested in the process of recovering the ancient history of India. Several states, notably Mysore, Travancore, and Hyderabad, maintain admirable archaeological departments of their own, directed by competent Indian experts. The enormous development of historical and archaeological study in India since the beginning of the twentieth century owes much to the example set by Lord Curzon and to the fascinating Reports published by Sir John Marshall, the Director-General of Archaeology, and his colleagues since 1902. Other influences have contributed to the advance made, but none has been more potent than the encouragement liberally given by the Government of India.

Utilitarian economists. The congratulations of a historian on the brilliant success attained need to be balanced by some words of caution. The Indian Government, saturated with traditions of cheeseparing economy, is exceptionally liable to unreasonable financial panic and usually is disposed to be severely utilitarian, grudging every rupee not devoted to the ordinary purposes of commonplace administration. When control happens to be in the hands of officials destitute of imagination and the historic sense, as is too often the case, expenditure on the conservation of ancient monuments or on the prosecution of scientific research is apt to be regarded as an extravagance to be pruned away whenever the slightest financial stringency is felt. Such a combination of unfavourable conditions occurred in 1911, when the Government of India committed itself to the absurd assertion that the work of the Archaeological Department was substantially complete, and that the administrative structure so carefully built up by Lord Curzon might be shattered. Energetic efforts were needed to save the organization, and happily were successful on that occasion. But the attack is not unlikely to be renewed. All persons who care to preserve the links uniting the present with the past or are able to appreciate the grandeur and beauty of the work done by the men of the olden time should be on their guard against the narrow-minded prejudices of utilitarian economists. The notion that the survey and study of the monuments and hidden remains of ancient India have been substantially completed to such an extent that little more remains to be done is so ludicrously false that formal refutation is hardly necessary. In reality the field for investigation is practically infinite, and centuries hence a Director-General of Archaeology may still find plenty of work to do.

Resignation of Lord Curzon. Lord Curzon went to England in 1904 for six months on the understanding that he should return to India for a further term of office. An acute controversy between him and Lord Kitchener, then Commander-in-Chief, concerning army organization and especially the position of the Military Member of Council, ended in the acceptance of Lord Kitchener's views by the Secretary of State. The offices of Commander-in-Chief and Military Member were combined, so that the head of the army alone became responsible for military advice to the Government. Lord Curzon, who held that the change involved the undue supersession of the civil power, resigned in 1905. During his six months of absence the government had been conducted by Lord Ampthill, previously Governor of Madras.

Lord Minto II ; opium trade. The permanent successor selected was Lord Minto, great-grandson of the Governor-general who had conquered Java and Mauritius almost a century earlier. The government of Lord Minto (1905–10) was mainly occupied with two subjects, constitutional changes and an outbreak of violent anarchist crime. Before briefly noticing those topics an important measure affecting the Indian revenue may be mentioned. The export trade in opium, which brought a large profit to the Indian treasury, had long been under diplomatic discussion between the Governments of Great Britain and China. In 1907 the arrangements for putting an end to the traffic had been so far advanced that the Anti-Opium Society announced its own dissolution, because it had accomplished the purpose for which it had been founded, namely, the advocacy of the 'act of national righteousness' now sanctioned. Many reasons make it difficult to foretell the ultimate effects of the change on the manners and morals of the Chinese, whose virtuous regulations have been modified. India certainly loses an annual revenue of eight to ten crores of rupees.

Indian Councils Act, 1909. The constitutional changes effected under authority of the Indian Councils Act of Parliament of 1909 were the result of long discussions carried on for nearly three years between the Government of India under Lord Minto and the India Office, presided over by Viscount Morley, then Secretary of State. The reforms, which concerned both the Executive and the Legislative Councils of the Governor-general and the provincial governments, were designed as a continuation of the Charter Act of 1853, and the Councils Acts of 1861 and 1892.

The Act of 1909 empowered an increase in the number of members of each of the Madras and Bombay Executive Councils from two to four. The Secretary of State took the opportunity of exercising the power he already possessed to appoint an Indian member to a seat on the Governor-general's Executive Council. Thus, for the first time, a native of India was admitted to share in the innermost secrets of the Supreme Government. Similar appointments to the provincial Executive Councils have been made, and Indians have been given seats in the Council of India which advises the Secretary of State.

The membership of the Imperial Legislative Council has been raised from twenty-one to a maximum of sixty. Similarly the provincial Legislative Councils, which are no longer confined to Madras and Bombay, have been more than doubled in membership.

A large proportion of the councillors is elected by Chambers of Commerce and other bodies.

Class representation. Elaborate arrangements, varying in each province, have been made for the representation of minorities and special interests, such as the Muhammadan population, the tea and jute industries, and the communities of European planters.

'The object aimed at', Sir Courtenay Ilbert observes, 'was to obtain, as far as possible, a fair representation of the different classes and interests in the country, and the regulations and rules were framed for this purpose in accordance with local advice and with reference to the local conditions of each province. The consequent variety of the rules makes it impossible to generalize their provisions or to summarize their contents. All of them may be regarded as experimental; some of them are avowedly temporary and provisional.'

The principle of sectional and class representation, which was opposed by several prominent Indian politicians in closely argued papers, has obvious disadvantages, and was accepted reluctantly by Lord Morley. Opponents of the representation of particular religions and interests urge that 'the principle of class representation is always objectionable, on the ground that it makes a distinction between the different classes of the community and makes the fusion of their interests impossible'; that other communities, especially the Sikhs, have as good a claim as Muhammadans; that the best men should be elected or appointed without regard to their creed; that, as a matter of fact, Hindu electors often choose a Muhammadan representative; and that, generally speaking, the idea of class representation is unnecessary and retrograde.

Such objections have much force, but on the whole the advantages of a class system of representation in India, where the different sections of the population are sharply divided, seem to outweigh the disadvantages.

The future. Liberty for the discussion of the annual budget and other matters of public interest has been accorded to the Legislative Councils. No approach to finality in the development of the Councils, whether executive or legislative, has been attained in 1918. The certainty that further extensive changes in the constitution of the Indian Governments must follow the close of the Great War renders superfluous more detailed discussion of the essentially transitory arrangements based on the Act of 1909.

Political machinery. Political reformers are prone to pay undue attention to the mere machinery of government and to attach excessive importance to reforms such as those effected by Lords Morley and Minto. The warning language of Lord Curzon merits consideration.

'I wonder', his Lordship said in the House of Lords, 'how these changes will, in the last resort, affect the great mass of the people of India—the people who have no vote and who have scarcely a voice. Remember that to these people, who form the bulk of the population of India, representative government and electoral institutions are nothing whatever. . . . The good government which appeals to them is the government which protects them from the rapacious money-lender and landlord, from the local *vakīl* [attorney], and all the other sharks in human disguise which prey upon these unhappy people. I have a misgiving that this class will not fare much better under these changes than they do now. At any rate I see no place for them in these enlarged Councils which are to be created, and I am under the strong opinion that as government in India becomes more and more Parliamentary—as will be the inevitable result—so it will become less paternal and less beneficent to the poorer classes of the population.'

India and Parliament. The profound change in the relations between the Home Government and the Government of the Viceroy and Governor-general in Council which has taken place since Queen Victoria assumed the direct sovereignty of the Indian Empire is far more important than the repairs of constitutional mechanism. Although the formal, legal position of the Government of India with regard to the Home Government is much the same as it was in 1858, and the powers of the Governor-general in Council seem on paper to be unchanged, the practical difference between the conditions of 1918, to take that year, and 1858 is enormous. When an Under-Secretary of State in Lord Morley's time ventured to describe the Viceroy as the 'agent' of the Secretary of State the blunt phrase jarred on the ears of many. But it gave expression in a form too emphatic to the truth that the old semi-independent authority of the Governor-general in Council has gone for ever. The main lines of the policy of the Government of India and the action of that Government in all grave matters now are and will continue to be either prescribed or sanctioned in advance from Whitehall, while the control exercised by Parliament tends to become more and more stringent. The task of governing India so as to reconcile the paternal despotism still necessary on the spot for many purposes with the ideas of a democratic Parliament at Westminster becomes daily more difficult, and will become impossible unless Parliament is content to wield its supreme authority with restraint. The problem may possibly be solved by Parliament giving its sanction to the development in India of self-government to an extent hitherto regarded as beyond the vision of practical politics. Nearly the same, but not quite the same idea is expressed by Sir Valentine Chirol in the following passage:

'The future of India lies in the greatest possible decentralization in India, subject to the general, but unmeddlesome control of the Governor-general in Council, and in the greatest possible freedom of the Government of India from all interference from home, except in regard to those broad principles of policy which it must always rest with the Imperial Government, represented by the Secretary of State in Council, to determine.'

Stress must be laid on the words 'in Council', because, ever since the resignation of Lord Curzon, both the Secretary of State and the Viceroy have shown a strong and mischievous tendency to ignore the existence of their Councils. The authorities recognized by law for the ordinary conduct of the Government, apart from exceptional emergencies, are the Secretary of State in Council and the Governor-general in Council, not the Secretary of State and the Viceroy as autocrats settling the affairs of the empire by private, 'demi-official' correspondence between themselves. Long ago Sir Philip Francis and his colleagues pressed their claim as of right to see the so-called 'private' correspondence between Warren Hastings, then Governor-general, and the Resident in Oudh. If the copious 'private' correspondence between different Secretaries of State and Viceroys since 1905 should be published the extent of the existing abuse would become manifest and might be abated.

Anarchist conspiracy. The termination in August 1905 of the Russo-Japanese war in favour of Japan produced a wave of intense excitement throughout Asia. The significance of the defeat of an apparently mighty European empire by a comparatively small Asiatic state could not be mistaken, and India did not fail to note it. The outbreak of atrocious political crime, which marked Lord Minto's term of office and was at its height in 1909, undoubtedly was stimulated by the meditations of discontented young men upon the Japanese success. The agitation concerning the Universities Act of 1904, the partition of Bengal in 1905, and other local grievances arising from Indian administrative measures became merged in a dangerous revolutionary and anarchist conspiracy, directed in India from Bengal and Poona, and supported by foreign organizations in Europe and America. That conspiracy, which could not be regarded as extinct even in 1918, was partially countered in 1910. Constant incitement to crime having been offered by many newspapers and other publications, restrictions on the licence of the press and other emergency measures were necessarily enacted. Many Bengālī and other officers who displayed the highest courage in the execution of their duties sacrificed their lives in the cause of social order and in the service of their sovereign lord the King. The nature of the dangers to which the State was exposed in February 1910 is indicated sufficiently by the following extract from Sir Herbert Risley's speech in the Legislative Council :

'We are at the present moment confronted with a murderous conspiracy, whose aim it is to subvert the Government of the country and to make British rule impossible by establishing general terrorism. Their organization is effective and far-reaching; their numbers are believed to be considerable; the leaders work in secret and are blindly obeyed by their youthful followers. The method they favour at present is political assassination; the method of Mazzini in his worst moods. Already they have a long score of murders or attempted murders to their account. There were two attempts to blow up Sir Andrew Fraser's train, and one of the type with which we are now unhappily familiar, to shoot him on a public occasion. Two attempts were made to shoot Mr. Kingsford, one of which caused the death of two English ladies. Inspector Nanda Lal Banerji, Babu Ashutosh Biswas, the Public Prosecutor at Alipore, Sir William Curzon-Wyllie, Mr. Jackson, and only the other day Deputy-Superintendent Shams-ul Alum have been shot in the most deliberate and cold-blooded fashion. Of three informers two have been killed, and on the third vengeance has been taken by the murder of his brother in the sight of his mother and sisters. Mr. Allen, the magistrate of Dacca, was shot through the lungs and narrowly escaped with his life. Two picric acid bombs were thrown at His Excellency the Viceroy at Ahmedabad, and only failed to explode by reason of their faulty construction. Not long afterwards an attempt was made with a bomb on the Deputy Commissioner of Umballa.

These things are the natural and necessary consequences of the teachings of certain journals. They have prepared the soil in which anarchy flourishes; they have sown the seed and are answerable for the crop. This is no mere general statement; the chain of causation is clear. Not only does the campaign of violence date from the change in the tone of the Press, but specific outbursts of incitement have been followed by specific outrages.'[1]

The case for the restraint of criminal writing in the press was unanswerable. The development and long-continued existence of a formidable murderous conspiracy of the nature as outlined in the extract quoted is a disagreeable fact needing to be steadily remembered. It suggests many reflections and cautions. The plot in its later developments spread to the Panjāb and received support from German intrigues and money. Serious attempts to undermine the loyalty of the Indian army have been made, and the execution of a considerable number of the leading conspirators has been absolutely necessary.

Lord Hardinge of Penshurst. The anarchist crimes continued in the time of Lord Hardinge of Penshurst, who succeeded Lord Minto in 1910. Lord Hardinge, whose previous service had been in the Foreign Office, is grandson of the Governor-general who conducted the first Sikh war. A bomb attack made on the Viceroy at Delhi wounded him and killed an attendant who was immediately behind Lord Hardinge on the elephant. The criminals escaped.

Census of 1911. The census of 1911 disclosed the population of the Indian Empire as being more than 315 millions, an increase of 7·1 per cent. since 1901.

	1901.	1911.
Population of Indian Empire . .	294,361,056	315,156,396
Population of Calcutta and suburbs .	1,106,738	1,222,313
Population of Bombay city . .	776,006	979,445
Population of Delhi city . . .	208,575	232,837

Visit of Their Majesties. The Viceroyalty of Lord Hardinge of Penshurst will be for ever memorable by reason of the visit of Their Majesties the King-Emperor and his consort at the close of 1911,[2] and for the beginning of the Great War in 1914. I do not

[1] Sir Andrew Fraser was Lieutenant-governor of Bengal; Mr. Kingsford was magistrate of Muzaffarpur; Mr. A. M. T. Jackson, magistrate and collector of Nāsik, was a learned Sanskrit scholar, and a special friend of Hindus. Yet he was shot by a young Hindu fanatic. Sir William Curzon-Wyllie, Political Secretary to the Secretary of State, was killed at the India Office by a student.

[2] Their Majesties left London, November 11, 1911; arrived at Bombay, December 2; made state entry into Delhi, December 7; held Coronation Durbar, December 12; left Delhi, December 16; arrived at Calcutta, December 30; left Calcutta, January 8, 1912; arrived in London, February 5, 1912.

attempt to describe the events subsequent to the momentous visit of Their Majesties, or to give details of the splendid ceremonies arranged by the Viceroy and his colleagues for the fitting reception of the Sovereign. The programme was thoughtfully devised and well executed with due regard to the requirements of the occasion.

His Majesty, speaking under the advice of his responsible ministers, made two unexpected announcements. That concerning the reversal, described officially as the 'modification', of the partition of Bengal has been sufficiently discussed on an earlier page. The other, informing an astonished world that the official capital of the Indian Empire would be transferred forthwith from Calcutta to Delhi, where a new city would be built for the accommodation of the Supreme Government, is open to criticism at least as damaging as that invited by the sudden change of policy on the Bengal question. The arguments adduced by the Government of India in support of the transfer of the capital to Delhi are so unconvincing and so liable to easy refutation that it is impossible to avoid the suspicion that the Secretary of State was influenced by unavowed motives. However that may be, the unconstitutional manner in which the policy of the ministry was proclaimed secured the act against reversal or modification, and no useful purpose would now be served by dissecting the assertions put forward by Lord Hardinge's government.

Results of the visit. The happy results of the visit of Their Majesties are not in any way dependent on the opinion which may be held concerning the merits of the two chief announcements made by the King-Emperor on the advice of his ministers, with whom alone the responsibility for policy rested. The intense and profound emotion which greeted the Sovereign and his gracious consort was the spontaneous, heartfelt offering of India to their royal persons. An eyewitness writes :

> 'That incomparable moment when the Monarchs seated themselves upon their high thrones, beneath a shining golden dome, in the midst of a hundred thousand of their acclaiming subjects, will assuredly remain in the minds of those present as the most vivid memory of their lives. It was a majestic and a moving rite, fraught with deep emotion, compelling thought into unwonted channels. The greetings of the multitude set the final seal upon the validity of the British Empire in the East.'

The writer of those words felt that the solemn assembly was 'the ultimate expression of the potent force of kingship, which in that resplendent scene reached a height we may never see again'.

Since that auspicious day the devouring lust of Germany for riches and dominion has plunged the whole world into misery beyond the power of words to express, and has constrained almost every other nation under heaven to join in the fight for right and all that makes life worth living against the demoniac armed might of the nation which lives by and for war, which knows no pity, and jeers at any arbitrament save that of the sword. In that noble fight, still, at the moment of writing (April 1918), in one of its most critical stages, India has borne and is bearing her part.

The brotherhood in arms sanetified by the blood of myriads of gallant men shed on the battle-fields of Asia, Afriea, and Europe will, we trust, develop into a still more eomprehensive eommunity of sentiment between Englishmen and Indians and between all the seetions of the vast population of Hind, so infinitely diverse on the surfaee, and yet so subtly bound together by hidden eords woven on the looms of immemorial antiquity.

The momentary apparition of Their Majesties to reeeive the eager homage of their Indian lieges will not be forgotten when these present horrors are overpast, and a bleeding, but purified world resumes its normal eourse.

CHRONOLOGY

Lord Lansdowne Vieeroy	1888
Manipur massaere	1891
Oeeupation of Hunza and Nagar	1891–2
Lord Elgin II Vieeroy	1894
Chitrāl expedition	1895
Plague epidemic began	1896
Famine	1896–7
Tirāh expedition	1897
Lord Curzon Vieeroy	1899
Famine; Land Alienation Aet	1900
Death of Queen Vietoria; Habībullah, Amīr (King) of Afghanistan; ereation of North-West Frontier Provinee	1901
Tibetan expedition	1903–4
Universities Aet; Lord Curzon in England; Lord Ampthill temporary Viceroy	1904
Partition of Bengal; Lord Minto II Vieeroy	1905
Indian Couneils Aet; anarehist erimes	1909
Lord Hardinge of Penshurst Viecroy	1910
Visit of Their Majesties; announeement of ehange of eapital and reversal of partition of Bengal	1911

AUTHORITIES

[Sir] G. FORREST, *The Administration of the Marquis of Lansdowne, 1888–94* (Caleutta, Supert. of Govt. Printing, 1894); LOVAT FRASER, *India under Curzon and After*[2] (Heinemann, 1912), a very useful book; *Lord Curzon in India*, being *A Selection from his Speeches*, &c., ed. by Sir T. RALEIGH (Maemillan, 1906); *Speeches of Lord Curzon of Kedleston* (Caleutta, Thacker, Spink & Co., 1901); W. H. HUTTON, chap. vii in TROTTER, *History of India* (S.P.C.K., 1917); ILBERT, in *The Government of India*[3], 1914 (or Suppl. to ed. 2), diseusses the Indian Councils Aet of 1909. I have also used the blue books on the subjeet. Sir VALENTINE CHIROL, in *Indian Unrest* (Macmillan, 1910), with Introduetion by Sir A. LYALL, deseribes the earlier stages of the eriminal eonspiraeies. The Royal and Imperial visit is fully deseribed and illustrated in *The Historical Record of the Imperial Visit to India, eompiled from the Official Records* (Murray, London, 1914, publ. for Government of India; 4to, illd.). The author's Indian serviee extended from 1871 to 1900, so that parts of the narrative for that period may be eoloured by his personal reeollections.

APPENDIX A

Some events from 1912 *to October* 1918 *specially concerning India and the Indian Army.*

1912

Jan. 8.	Departure of Their Majesties from Calcutta.
Feb. 5.	Arrival of Their Majesties in London.
April 1.	Province of Bihār and Orissa constituted; Lord Carmichael Governor of Bengal.
Oct. 1.	Chief Commissionership of Delhi constituted.
Dec. 22.	Lord Hardinge wounded by a bomb.

1913

Conference of British, Chinese, and Tibetan representatives at Simla; decisions not ratified by China.
Trade, both import and export, exceptionally active.

1914

Aug. 4.	Declaration of war by Great Britain against Germany.
Sept. 26.	Indian Corps began to land in France.
Nov. 5.	Declaration of war by Great Britain against Turkey.
Dec. 18.	Prince Kāmil Husain Pasha appointed Sultan of Egypt.

1915

Mar. 10.	Battle of Neuve Chapelle.
Nov. 22.	Battle of Ctesiphon near Baghdad.
Nov. 29.	Retreat of British force in Mesopotamia.
Dec. 3.	General Townshend enters Kut-el Amara.

1916

Mar.	Failure of Indian Government to supply Mesopotamian force.
April 4.	Lord Chelmsford Viceroy.
April 29.	Kut-el Amara taken by the Turks.
July	The Sharif of Mecca declared his independence as King of the Hedjaz.
Dec. 7.	Mr. Lloyd George Prime Minister.

1917

Feb. 24.	Kut-el Amara retaken by the British.
Mar. 11.	Capture of Baghdad by the British.
Mar. 12.	Revolution in Russia.
Mar. 15.	Abdication of the Tsar.
April 5.	Declaration of war on Germany by the United States.
June 27.	Report of Mesopotamian Commission published.
July 19.	Wholesale retreat of Russian army.
Aug. 27.	Pronouncement of Secretary of State intimating that the policy of H.M. Government aims at 'gradual development of self-governing institutions' and 'progressive realization of responsible government'.
Oct.	British successes on the Euphrates; Mr. Montagu arrived in India.

Dec. 3. Germans driven out of East Africa.
Dec. 9. Surrender of Jerusalem to the British.
Dec. 11. Entry of General Allenby into Jerusalem.

1918

Feb. 22. Jericho occupied.
Feb.–Mar. Collapse of Russian power.
Mar. 21. Beginning of renewed German offensive in France; retreat of 3rd and 5th British armies.
April Long advance of British force in Mesopotamia.
July 16. Execution of the ex-Tsar by the Bolshevists.
July-Oct. Continued defeats and retreat of the Germans in France and Belgium.
Aug. 6. Debate in Parliament on Montagu-Chelmsford *Report*.
Sept. 30. Surrender of Bulgaria.
Oct. 1. Damascus taken by British, Indian, and Arab troops.
Oct. 24. Debate and division in House of Lords on reform question.

APPENDIX B

EAST INDIA COMPANY

1600 (December 31). Queen Elizabeth's charter.
1661. Charter of Charles II.
1708. Final fusion of rival Companies.
1773. Regulating Act (Governor-general of Bengal).
1784. Pitt's India Act (' Board of Control ').
1793. Charter renewed.
1813. ,, ,, (India trade thrown open.)
1833. ,, ,, (Company's trading functions abolished; China trade thrown open.)
1853. ,, ,, (Competition for Civil Service.)
1858. Government of India Act (Direct government by Crown: Queen's Proclamation).
1874. Formal dissolution of the Company.

APPENDIX C

GOVERNORS-GENERAL

I. *Governors-general of Bengal or of Fort William (Regulating Act of* 1773).

(*Temporary and officiating in italics.*)

1774 (October). Warren Hastings, Esq. (Right Honourable).
1785 (February 1). *Sir John Macpherson.*
1786 (September). Earl (Marquess) Cornwallis.

1793 (August). Sir John Shore (Lord Teignmouth).
1798 (March). *Sir Alured Clarke.*
1798 (May). Earl of Mornington (Marquess Wellesley).
1805 (July 30). Marquess Cornwallis (for second time).
1805 (October 5). *Sir George Barlow.*
1807. Baron (Earl of) Minto I.
1813 (October 4). Earl of Moira (Marquess of Hastings).
1823 (January 1). *John Adam, Esq.*
1823 (August 1). Baron (Earl) Amherst.
1828 (March 8). *William Butterworth Bayley, Esq.*
1828 (July). Lord William Cavendish-Bentinck.

II. *Governors-general of India* (*Charter Act of* 1833).

1833. Lord William Cavendish-Bentinck.
1835 (March 20). *Sir Charles (Lord) Metcalfe.*
1836 (March 1). Baron (Earl of) Auckland.
1842. Baron (Earl of) Ellenborough.
1844. Sir Henry (Viscount) Hardinge.
1848. Earl (Marquess) of Dalhousie.
1856. Viscount (Earl) Canning.

III. *Governors-general and Viceroys* (*Queen's Proclamation*).

1858 (November 1). Earl Canning.
1862. Earl of Elgin I.
1863. *Sir Robert Napier (Lord Napier of Magdala).*
1863. *Sir William Denison.*
1864. Sir John (Lord) Lawrence.
1869. Earl of Mayo.
1872. *Sir John Strachey.*
1872. *Lord Napier of Merchistoun.*
1872. Baron (Earl of) Northbrook.
1876. Baron (Earl of) Lytton.
1880. Marquess of Ripon.
1884. Earl of Dufferin (Marquess of Dufferin and Ava).
1888. Marquess of Lansdowne.
1894. Earl of Elgin II.
1899 (Jan. 6). Baron (Earl) Curzon of Kedleston.
1904. *Lord Ampthill.*
1904. Baron (Earl) Curzon of Kedleston (reappointed).
1905. Earl of Minto II.
1910. Baron Hardinge of Penshurst.
1916. Baron Chelmsford.

Note.—India in Transition by H.H. the Aga Khan (Lee Warner, 1918) is an important work containing many valuable observations and ideas. The remarks of H.H. concerning Indian universities in chap. xxiii coincide with those recorded independently on p. 736 *ante*.

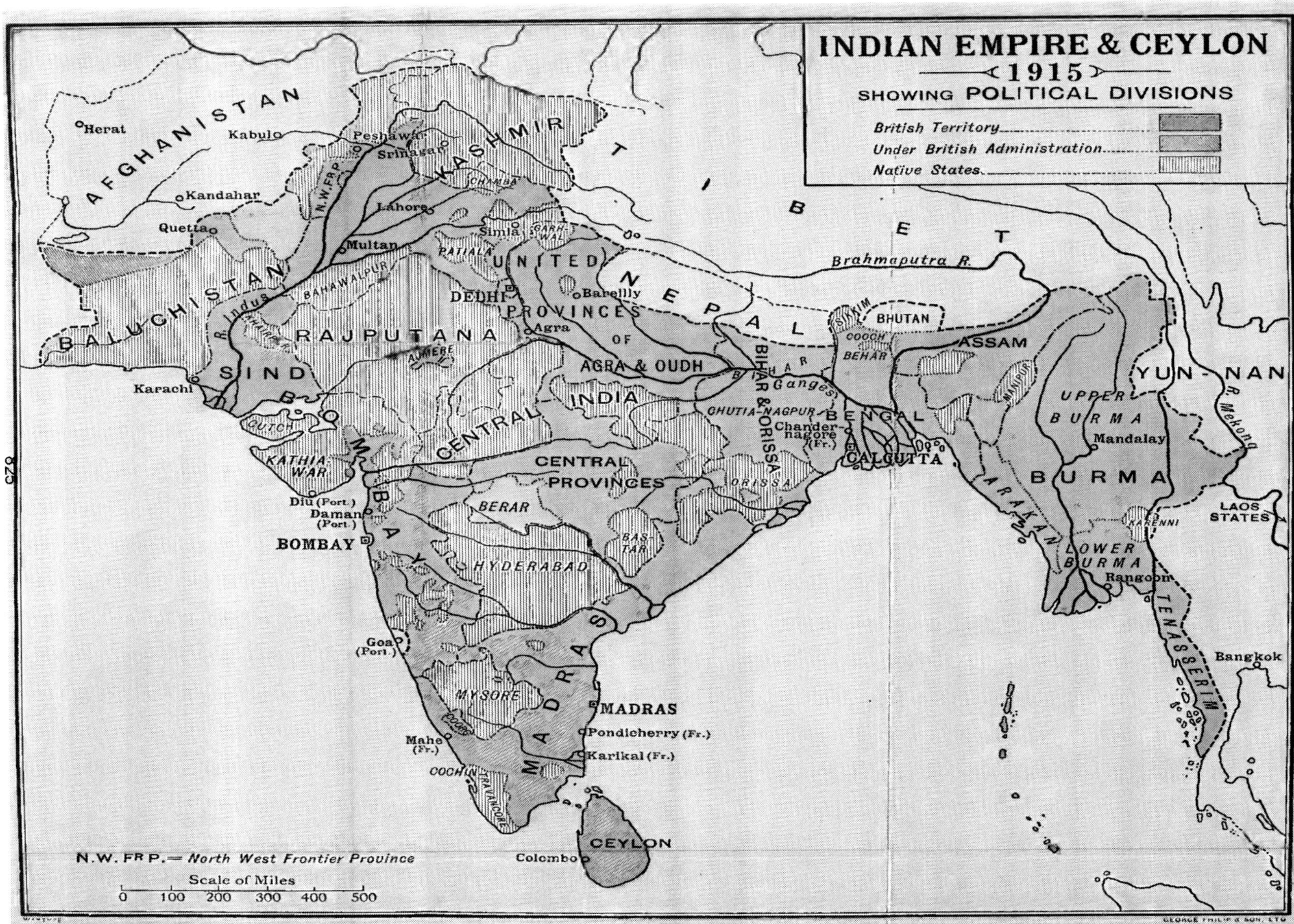
INDIAN EMPIRE & CEYLON
1915
SHOWING POLITICAL DIVISIONS
British Territory
Under British Administration
Native States
AFGHANISTAN
Herat
Kabul
Kandahar
Quetta
Peshawar
Srinagar
KASHMIR
CHAMBA
N.W.FR P.
Lahore
Multan
Simla
GARHWAL
PATIALA
TIBET
Brahmaputra R.
BALUCHISTAN
R. Indus
BAHAWALPUR
KHAIRPUR
RAJPUTANA
AJMERE
DEHLI
UNITED PROVINCES OF AGRA & OUDH
Bareilly
Agra
NEPAL
SIKKIM
BHUTAN
COOCH BEHAR
ASSAM
MANIPUR
YUN-NAN
R. Mekong
Karachi
SIND
BOMBAY
CUTCH
KATHIA-WAR
CENTRAL INDIA
BIHAR & ORISSA
BIHAR
Ganges
CHUTIA-NAGPUR
Chandernagore (Fr.)
BENGAL
CALCUTTA
ORISSA
UPPER BURMA
Mandalay
BURMA
ARAKAN
LAOS STATES
KARENNI
LOWER BURMA
Rangoon
TENASSERIM
Bangkok
Diu (Port.)
Daman (Port.)
CENTRAL PROVINCES
BERAR
BASTAR
HYDERABAD
Goa (Port.)
MADRAS
MYSORE
COORG
Mahe (Fr.)
Pondicherry (Fr.)
Karikal (Fr.)
COCHIN
TRAVANCORE
CEYLON
Colombo
N.W. FR P. = North West Frontier Province
Scale of Miles
0 100 200 300 400 500

INDEX

ABBREVIATIONS

Ci., city; *co.*, country; *k.*, king; *km.*, kingdom; *r.*, river; *t.*, town; *vi.*, village.